WORLD REGIONAL GEOGRAPHY

WORLD REGIONAL GEOGRAPHY

Lydia Mihelič Pulsipher
University of Tennessee at Knoxville

with the assistance of
Conrad "Mac" Goodwin
and
Alex Pulsipher

W. H. Freeman and Company
NEW YORK

Acquisitions Editor: Melissa Wallerstein

Development Editor: Susan Moran

Project Editor: Mary Louise Byrd

Cover and Text Design: Blake Logan

Illustration and Map Coordinators: Bill Page, Shawn Churchman

Maps: University of Tennessee,
Cartographic Services Laboratory,
Will Fontanez, Director

Illustrations: Fine Line Illustrations

Photo Researcher: Inge King

Production Coordinator: Paul W. Rohloff

New Media and Supplements Editors: Bridget O'Lavin, Matthew Fitzpatrick

Composition: Progressive Information Technologies

Manufacturing: Von Hoffman Press

Executive Marketing Manager: John Britch

Library of Congress Cataloging-in-Publication Data

Pulsipher, Lydia M. (Lydia Mihelič)
World regional geography / Lydia Mihelič Pulsipher; with the
assistance of Conrad "Mac" Goodwin, Alex Pulsipher.
p.   cm.
Includes bibliographical references (p.   ) and index.
ISBN 0-7167-3092-8
1. Geography.   I. Goodwin, Conrad M., 1940–   II. Pulsipher, Alex.
III. Title.
G128.P85   1999   99-28227
910—dc21   CIP

Printed in the United States of America

Second printing, 2000

To five colleagues who shaped my development as a geographer:

Hildegard B. Johnson
Edwin B. Doran Jr.
Campbell W. Pennington
Clarissa T. Kimber
Janice Monk

BRIEF CONTENTS

PREFACE **xix**

ABOUT THE AUTHOR **xxvii**

ONE   GEOGRAPHY: AN EXPLORATION OF CONNECTIONS **3**

TWO   NORTH AMERICA **51**

THREE   MIDDLE AND SOUTH AMERICA **105**

FOUR   EUROPE **169**

FIVE   THE RUSSIAN FEDERATION, BELARUS, CAUCASIA, AND CENTRAL ASIA **225**

SIX   NORTH AFRICA AND SOUTHWEST ASIA **267**

SEVEN   SUB-SAHARAN AFRICA **313**

EIGHT   SOUTH ASIA **363**

NINE   EAST ASIA **411**

TEN   SOUTHEAST ASIA **471**

ELEVEN   OCEANIA: AUSTRALIA, NEW ZEALAND, AND THE PACIFIC **518**

APPENDIX A: READING MAPS **App A-1**

APPENDIX B: POPULATION DATA BY COUNTRY **App B-1**

GLOSSARY **G-1**

PRONUNCIATION GUIDE **PG-1**

BIBLIOGRAPHY **B-1**

INDEX **I-1**

CONTENTS

PREFACE   XIX
ABOUT THE AUTHOR   XXVII

ONE

GEOGRAPHY: AN EXPLORATION OF CONNECTIONS   3

WHERE IS IT? WHY IS IT THERE?   4
What Is Geography?   5
The Region as a Concept   5

GEOGRAPHIC PERSPECTIVES ON HISTORY AND PREHISTORY   8
Human Origins   8

AT THE GLOBAL SCALE   The Adaptive Role of Menopause   10

The Origins of Agriculture and Animal Husbandry   10

MODERN CULTURAL AND SOCIAL GEOGRAPHIC ISSUES   12
Culture Groups   12

Values and Ways of Knowing   13
Religion   14
Language   15
Material Culture and Technology   16

Issues of Gender   17

AT THE GLOBAL SCALE   Gender   18

The Issue of Race   19

PHYSICAL GEOGRAPHY: PERSPECTIVES ON THE EARTH   20
Landforms: The Sculpting of the Earth   20

Plate Tectonics   21
Landscape Processes   21

Climate   23

Temperature and Air Pressure   23
Precipitation   23
Climate Regions   25

THE ENVIRONMENT   26
Sustainable Development   26

Sustainable Agriculture   27
Sustainability and Urbanization   27
Population and Sustainability   31

Global Warming   31

POPULATION PATTERNS   32
Global Patterns of Population Growth   33
Local Variation in Density and Growth   33
Age and Gender Structures   36

AT THE GLOBAL SCALE   Missing Females in Population Statistics   37

Growth Rates and Wealth   38
Is the World Overpopulated?   39

ECONOMIC ISSUES IN GEOGRAPHY   39
Workers in the Global Economy   39
What Is the Economy?   41
What Is the Global Economy?   42
Measures of Well-Being   44

POLITICAL ISSUES IN GEOGRAPHY   46
Geopolitics   46
Nations and Borders   46
International Cooperation   47
A Note on Chapter Organization   48
Selected Themes and Concepts   48
Selected Readings   49

TWO

NORTH AMERICA   51

INTRODUCTION   52
Themes to Look For   52
Terms to Be Aware Of   53

PHYSICAL PATTERNS   53
Landforms   54
Landform Processes   54
Climate   54

Contents

HUMAN PATTERNS   56

The Peopling of North America   56
The European Transformation   56
The Expansion of European Settlement   56

The Economic Core   58
Expansion West of the Mississippi   58
European Settlement and Native Americans   59
The Changing Social Composition of North America   60
Population Patterns   60

CURRENT GEOGRAPHIC ISSUES   62

Sociocultural Issues   64

Immigration   64

AT THE LOCAL SCALE Ethnicity in Toronto   66

Religion   67
Race   68
Gender and Family Structure   69
Aging   70

Political and Economic Issues   71

Agriculture   72
The Industrial Economy   73

AT THE LOCAL SCALE Megalopolis   75

Government and Globalization   77
Systems of Government   78
Gender on the National Political Scene   78

Environmental Issues   78

Loss of Environmental Quality   79
Loss of Habitat for Plants and Animals   80
Resource Depletion   80

Measures of Human Well-Being   80

SUBREGIONS   82

New England and Canada's Atlantic Provinces   84
Québec   85
The Economic Core   86

AT THE LOCAL SCALE Urban Sprawl   89
The American South (the Southeast)   90
The Great Plains Breadbasket   93
The Continental Interior   94

AT THE LOCAL SCALE Meat Packing in the Great Plains   95
The Pacific Northwest   97
The Southwest   99

REFLECTIONS   102

Selected Themes and Concepts   102
Selected Readings   103

THREE

MIDDLE AND SOUTH AMERICA   105

INTRODUCTION   106

Themes to Look For   107
Terms to Be Aware Of   107

PHYSICAL PATTERNS   107

Landforms   107
River Systems   108
Climate   110

HUMAN PATTERNS   113

The Peopling of Middle and South America   113
The Conquest   113

A Global Exchange of Crops and Animals   115

The Legacy of Underdevelopment   117
Population Patterns   118

Population Numbers and Distributions   118
Migration and Urbanization   120

CURRENT GEOGRAPHIC ISSUES   123

Sociocultural Issues   123

Cultural Diversity   123
Race and the Social Significance of Skin Color   124
The Family and Gender Roles   124
Children in Poverty   125
Religion in Contemporary Life   125

Contents

Economic and Political Issues   127

    Phases of Economic Development   127

AT THE COUNTRY SCALE The Mexican Debt Crisis and the Painful SAP Cure   132

    New Trajectories in Economic Development   132
    Agriculture and Rural Resistance   133
    The Informal Economy   134

AT THE LOCAL SCALE The Informal Economy in Peru   135

    Is Democracy Rising?   136

Environmental Issues   137

    The Vanishing Forests of the Amazon Basin   138
    Environment and Development   140

Measures of Human Well-Being   141

SUBREGIONS   144

The Caribbean   144

    Cuba and Puerto Rico Compared   146
    Haiti and Barbados Compared   147

Mexico   147

    The Maquiladora *Phenomenon*   148
    Foreign Trade   150
    Population   150
    Migration   150

Central America: 151

    Guatemala, Honduras, and El Salvador   153
    Nicaragua   154
    Costa Rica and Belize   154
    Panama   155

The Northern Andes and Caribbean Coast: 155
Guyana, French Guiana, and Suriname   155
Venezuela and Colombia   156
The Central Andes: Ecuador, Peru, Bolivia   157

AT THE LOCAL SCALE Learning from the Incas: Agricultural Restoration in the Peruvian Highlands   159

The Southern Cone: Chile, Argentina, Paraguay, Uruguay   159
Brazil   161

    Urbanization   163
    Brasília   164
    Curitiba   164

REFLECTIONS   165

Selected Themes and Concepts   166
Selected Readings   167

FOUR

EUROPE   169

INTRODUCTION   170

    Themes to Look For   170
    Terms to Be Aware Of   170

PHYSICAL PATTERNS   171

Landforms   171
Climate   172

HUMAN PATTERNS   173

Sources of European Culture   174
Growth and Expansion of Continental Europe   174
An Age of Revolutions   175
Decline and Rebirth   177
Population Patterns   178

    Population Density and Access to Resources   179
    Urbanization in Europe   180
    Population Growth Patterns   180

CURRENT GEOGRAPHIC ISSUES   181

Sociocultural Issues   182

    Immigrants and European Ideas Toward Outsiders   182
    European Ideas About Gender   184
    Variability of Social Welfare Concepts Across Europe   186

Economic and Political Issues   188

    The European Union   188

*Trends in European Economic
     Sectors* 191
*Political Challenges to the European
     Union* 193
Women and Political Power in Europe 195

Environmental Issues 195

The Seas 196
The Rivers 197
The Air 197

Measures of Human Well-Being 198

SUBREGIONS 200

West Europe: The United Kingdom,
     Republic of Ireland, France, Germany,
     the Netherlands, Belgium, Luxembourg,
     Austria, Switzerland 200

Benelux 200
France 203
Germany 204
The British Isles 205

South Europe: Portugal, Spain, Italy,
     Greece 206

Spain 208

AT THE LOCAL SCALE The Moorish Legacy
in Southern Spain (Andalucía) 209

Italy 209

North Europe: Norway, Sweden, Finland,
     Denmark, Iceland, Estonia, Latvia,
     Lithuania 210

Scandinavia 211
The Baltic States 213

East and Central Europe: Slovenia, Croatia,
     Bosnia, Yugoslavia (Serbia and Macedonia),
     Albania, Poland, Czech Republic, Slovakia,
     Hungary, Romania, Bulgaria, Ukraine,
     Moldova 214

*Soviet Legacies in Agriculture
     and Industry* 215
*The Balkans: Understanding an Armed
     Conflict* 219

REFLECTIONS 221

Selected Themes and Concepts 221
Selected Readings 222

FIVE

THE RUSSIAN FEDERATION, BELARUS, CAUCASIA, AND CENTRAL ASIA 225

INTRODUCTION 226

Themes to Look For 227
Terms to Be Aware Of 227

PHYSICAL PATTERNS 227

Landforms 227
Climate 229

HUMAN PATTERNS 229

The Rise of the Russian Empire 229
Soviet Russia 230
Population Patterns 231

CURRENT GEOGRAPHIC ISSUES 235

Economic and Political Issues 235

The Command Economy 235
Economic Reform 237
Political Reforms 239
*Geopolitical and Geoeconomic Legacies
     of the USSR* 239

Measures of Human Well-Being 241
Sociocultural Issues 242

Cultural Dominance of Russia 243
*Cultural Revival in the
     Post-Soviet Era* 243
Religion 243
*Gender and Opportunities
     in Free Market Russia* 244
*Unemployment and Loss of
     Safety Net* 245

AT THE LOCAL SCALE Norilsk 246

*Crime and Corruption as Sources
     of Social Instability* 246

Environmental Issues 247

Resources: Distribution and Use 247

Industrial and Nuclear Pollution 248
Irrigation and the Aral Sea 249

SUBREGIONS 251

The Russian Federation and Belarus 251

European (Western) Russia 251
Belarus and Kaliningrad 254
The Internal Republics 255
Russia East of the Urals 255

AT THE LOCAL SCALE An Ethnic Republic
Reasserts Itself 256

Caucasia: Georgia, Armenia,
Azerbaijan 259
The Central Asian Republics: Kazakhstan,
Kirghizstan, Tajikistan, Turkmenistan,
Uzbekistan 260

REFLECTIONS 263

Selected Themes and Concepts 264
Selected Readings 264

SIX

NORTH AFRICA
AND SOUTHWEST ASIA 267

INTRODUCTION 268

Themes to Look For 268
Terms to Be Aware Of 269

PHYSICAL PATTERNS 269

Climate 269
Landforms and Vegetation 270

HUMAN PATTERNS 271

Agricultural Beginnings 271
The Coming of Islam 272
Western Domination 273
Population Patterns 275

*Gender Roles and Population
Growth* 277
Migration and Urbanization 277
Refugees 279

CURRENT GEOGRAPHIC ISSUES 280

Sociocultural Issues 280

Religion in Daily Life 280

CULTURAL INSIGHT The Five Pillars of Islamic
Practice 281

Family and Group Values 281
Gendered Roles, Gendered Spaces 281

The Lives of Children 284
Minorities and Language 284

Economic and Political Issues 285

The Oil Economy 285
Agriculture 286
Attempts at Diversification 286
A Tangle of Hostilities 287
Islamism and Democracy 288

Measures of Human Well-Being 288
Environmental Issues 290

Water Issues 290

AT THE LOCAL SCALE Turkey's Anatolian River
Basin Project 292

Sustainable Development 293

SUBREGIONS 294

The Maghreb (Northwest Africa):
Morocco, Western Sahara, Algeria, Tunisia,
Libya 294

Violence in Algeria 296

CULTURAL INSIGHT Algeria's Dangerous
Political Music 296

The Nile: Sudan and Egypt 297

Sudan 297
Egypt 298

The Arabian Peninsula: Saudi Arabia, Yemen,
Oman, UAE, Qatar, Bahrain, Kuwait 299

Saudi Arabia 300
Yemen 301

The Eastern Mediterranean: Israel, Lebanon,
Syria, Jordan 302

The Emergence of Israel 302

Contents

AT THE LOCAL SCALE Palestinians in
Israel   303

Religious Fundamentalism in Israel   305

The Northeast: Turkey, Iran, and Iraq   305

Turkey   305
Iran   306

CULTURAL INSIGHT The Turkish Narghile   307
Iraq   307

AT THE LOCAL SCALE The Bandar
Express   308

AT THE REGIONAL SCALE The Iran-Iraq War
1980–1988   309

REFLECTIONS   309

Selected Themes and Concepts   310
Selected Readings   310

SEVEN

SUB-SAHARAN AFRICA   313

INTRODUCTION   314

Themes to Look For   315
Terms and Attitudes to Be Aware Of   315

PHYSICAL PATTERNS   315

Landforms   315
Climate   315

HUMAN PATTERNS   317

The Peopling of Africa   318
The Coming of the Europeans   319
The Scramble to Colonize Africa   319
The Aftermath of Independence   321
Population Patterns   321

Defining Density   322
Population Growth   323
*Settlement Patterns, Rural
  and Urban*   324
Public Health Issues   325

CURRENT GEOGRAPHIC ISSUES   327

Sociocultural Issues   327

Religion   328

AT THE REGIONAL SCALE The Gospel
of Success   329

*Gender Relationships in Work
  and Reproduction*   329
Female Genital Excision   332
Ethnicity and Language   332

Economic and Political Issues   333

Botswana: A Case Study   334
*Independence: The Difficulties
  of Change*   335

The Current Economic Crisis   335
Agriculture   336
Industry   337
The Informal Economy   337
*Alternative Paths to Economic
  Development*   338
*Political Problems: Colonial Legacies
  and African Adaptations*   339
Shifts in African Geopolitics   340

AT THE REGIONAL SCALE African Women
in Politics   341

Measures of Human Well-Being   344
Environmental Issues   344

Desertification   344
Forest Resources   345
Tropical Disease   346
Wildlife   346
Water   346

SUBREGIONS   347

West Africa: Cape Verde Islands, Senegal,
Gambia, Mauritania, Mali, Niger, Burkina
Faso, Guinea-Bissau, Guinea, Liberia, Sierra
Leone, Côte d'Ivoire, Ghana, Togo, Benin,
Nigeria   347

Nigeria   348
*Water Management in Mali
  and Nigeria*   350

Central Africa: Cameroon, Central African
Republic, Chad, Gabon, Congo, São Tomé y
Príncipe, Zaire/Congo   350

Zaire/Congo: A Case Study   351

The Horn of Africa: Ethiopia, Somalia, Djibouti,
Eritrea   352

East Africa: Kenya, Uganda, Rwanda, Burundi,
Tanzania   354

The Islands   356

Southern Africa: Angola, Zambia, Malawi,
Mozambique, Namibia, Botswana,
Zimbabwe, South Africa, Lesotho,
Swaziland   356

*Majority Rule Comes to
  South Africa*   356

CULTURAL INSIGHT The Thumb Piano   359

REFLECTIONS   359

Selected Themes and Concepts   360
Selected Readings   361

EIGHT

SOUTH ASIA   363

Contents

INTRODUCTION   364

> *Themes to Look For*   365

PHYSICAL PATTERNS   365

Landforms   365
Climate   365

HUMAN PATTERNS   367

A Series of Invasions   368
The Legacies of Colonial Rule   369
Since Independence   371
Population Patterns   372

AT THE REGIONAL SCALE Should Children
Work?   375

CURRENT GEOGRAPHIC ISSUES   376

Sociocultural Issues   376

> *Language and Ethnicity*   376
> *Religion*   377
> *Caste*   379

CULTURAL INSIGHT Food Customs
in South Asia   380

> *Geographic Patterns in the Status
> of Women*   380

CULTURAL INSIGHT The Founder of Nonviolent
Protest   381

*The Cultural Context of Bride Burning
and Female Infanticide*   383

Economic Issues   383

> *Agriculture*   384
> *Industry over Agriculture*   385
> *Economic Reform*   386

Innovative Help for the Poor   386
Political Issues   386

> *Patrons and Clients*   387
> *Religious Nationalism*   387
> *Regional Political Conflicts*   387

AT THE REGIONAL SCALE Babar's
Mosque—The Geography of Religious
Nationalism   388

> *The Future of Democracy*   389

Measures of Human Well-Being   389
Environmental Issues   390

> *Deforestation*   391
> *Water Issues*   391

SUBREGIONS   392

Afghanistan and Pakistan   392
Afghanistan   393
Pakistan   394
Himalayan Country: Nepal, Bhutan,
Himalayan India   394

AT THE LOCAL SCALE Salt for Grain and
Beans   396

Northwest India   396

> *Delhi*   398

Northeastern South Asia   399

> *West Benegal and Bihar*   400
> *Eastern India*   401
> *Bangladesh*   401

Central India   402

> *Bombay*   403

Southern South Asia   404

> *A New Silicon Valley*   404
> *The Special Case of Kerala*   405
> *Sri Lanka*   405

AT THE LOCAL SCALE Kerala's Fishing
Industry   406

REFLECTIONS   407

Selected Themes and Concepts   408
Selected Readings   409

NINE

EAST ASIA   411

INTRODUCTION   412

> *Themes to Look For*   412
> *Terms to Be Aware Of*   413

Contents

PHYSICAL PATTERNS 413

Landforms 413
Climate 414

The Dry Continental Western Zone 414
The Monsoon East 414

HUMAN PATTERNS 416

The Beginnings of Chinese Civilization 416
Confucianism 417
Rising European Influence 417
Revolution Comes to China 419
Population Patterns 420

Population Density 420

CURRENT GEOGRAPHIC ISSUES 420

Political and Economic Issues 421

Contrasting Bureaucracies 421
Economic Transitions and Crises 422
China's Policies for Regional Development 424
Market Reforms 424

Sociocultural Issues 429

Cultural Adaptation to Capitalism: Doing Business with Strangers 429
Population Policies, Gender Attitudes, and the East Asian Family 430
Family, Work, and Gender Relationships in Industrialized East Asia 432

AT THE LOCAL SCALE Chinese Marriage Customs in Cities and Villages 432

Minorities in China, Taiwan, and Japan 432

Measures of Human Well-Being 435
Environmental Issues: China 436

Air Quality 437
Water: Too Much and Too Little 437

AT THE LOCAL SCALE The Three Gorges Dam 439

Environmental Issues Elsewhere in East Asia 440

SUBREGIONS 441

China's Northeast 442
Central China: The Sichuan and Chang Jiang Basins 445

AT THE LOCAL SCALE Silk and Sericulture 447

AT THE LOCAL SCALE Shanghai's Urban Environment 448

China's Northwest 449

Southern China 452
Taiwan 454

AT THE LOCAL SCALE Leisure Time in Taiwan 455

Japan 456

Landforms, Climate, and Vegetation 456
Japan's Rise to Economic Power 458
The Many Faces of Japan 460

Korea, North and South 461

The Creation of Two Koreas 461
Gender Roles 463
Contrasting Economies 463

Mongolia 464

Physical Geography 465
History 465
Gender Roles 466
Economic and Gender Issues 466

REFLECTIONS 467

Selected Themes and Concepts 468
Selected Readings 468

TEN

SOUTHEAST ASIA 471

INTRODUCTION 472

Themes to Look For 472
Terms to Be Aware Of 473

PHYSICAL PATTERNS 473

Landforms 473
Climate 474

HUMAN PATTERNS 475

The Peopling of Southeast Asia 476
Further Cultural Influences 476
Colonialism 477
Struggles for Independence 478
Population Patterns 479

Population Dynamics 479
Southeast Asia's AIDS Tragedy 480
Migration 481

CURRENT GEOGRAPHIC ISSUES 484

Sociocultural Issues 484

Cultural Pluralism 484
Religious Pluralism 485
Family, Work, and Gender 487
Work Patterns 488

Contents

Economic and Political Issues   488

    The Dance of the Tigers   488
    Agriculture   488
    Industrialization   490
    The Association of Southeast Asian
      Nations   490
    Economic Crisis: The Perils of Globalization
      and Rapid Growth   491
    Resentment Toward the Overseas
      Chinese   491

AT THE REGIONAL SCALE Building Cars
  in Asia   492

    Pressures for Democracy   493

AT THE LOCAL SCALE *Pancasila*, Indonesia's
  National Ideology   493

Measures of Human Well-Being   494

Environmental Issues   495

    Deforestation   495
    Mining   496
    Air Pollution   497
    Energy Production   497
    Urbanization and Industrialization   498

SUBREGIONS   499

Mainland Southeast Asia: Thailand
  and Burma   499

    Is Thailand an Economic Tiger?   501

AT THE LOCAL SCALE The Yadana Project:
  A Natural Gas Joint Venture   502

Mainland Southeast Asia: Vietnam, Laos,
  Cambodia   503

    Vietnam   505

Island and Peninsula Southeast Asia: Malaysia
  and Singapore   506

    Malaysia   506
    Singapore   507

Island Southeast Asia: Indonesia   508

    Harvesting the Rain Forest   509
    Urban Factories   510

Island Southeast Asia: The Philippines   511

REFLECTIONS   513

Selected Themes and Concepts   514
Selected Readings   515

ELEVEN

**OCEANIA: AUSTRALIA, NEW
ZEALAND, AND THE PACIFIC   518**

INTRODUCTION   518
    Themes to Look For   518

PHYSICAL PATTERNS   518

  Island Formation   519
  Continent Formation   519
  Climate   520
  Flora and Fauna   522

HUMAN PATTERNS   524

  The Peopling of Oceania   524
  Arrival of the Europeans   524
  The Colonization of Australia
    and New Zealand   526
  Oceania's Growing Ties with Asia   526
  Population Patterns   527

CURRENT GEOGRAPHIC ISSUES   527

Sociocultural Issues   528

    European Roots Reexamined   528
    Forging Unity in Oceania   531
    Gender Roles   532
    Being a Man: Persistence
      and Change   533

CULTURAL INSIGHT Waltzing Matilda   534

Economic and Political Issues   534

    Export Economies   534

Contents

New Orientations 535
Tourism in Oceania: The Hawaiian Case 535
The Stresses of Reorientation to Asia 537
The Future: Mixed Asian and European Orientation? 537
Measures of Human Well-Being 538

Environmental Issues 540

Australia: Human Settlement in an Arid Land 541
New Zealand: Loss of Forest and Wildlife 542
The Pacific Islands: At the Mercy of Global Trends 543

REFLECTIONS 544

Selected Themes and Concepts 545
Selected Readings 546

APPENDIX A: READING MAPS App A-1

APPENDIX B: POPULATION DATA BY COUNTRY App B-1

GLOSSARY G-1

PRONUNCIATION GUIDE PG-1

BIBLIOGRAPHY B-1

INDEX I-1

PREFACE

Like most professors, I see research and teaching as complementary activities, and I frequently use my fieldwork experiences and observations in the classroom. For the most part, the Eastern Caribbean has been the site of my studies. There, I have done a variety of projects in historical and cultural geography, in historical archaeology, and in cross-disciplinary gender studies. It is in the Caribbean that I gained a finely tuned education in how people seemingly remote from the great centers of power and currents of exchange nonetheless have felt the effects of these forces in their daily lives and on the landscapes around them. For example, while doing archaeology on colonial sites, my students and I found evidence of the ever-widening global economy that has engulfed the Caribbean over the last 500 years: English ceramic mugs, Chinese porcelain, European cutlasses and gun parts, and African board game pieces were commonplace on seventeenth- and eighteenth-century sites. In West Indian markets and solid waste dumps, we encountered more recent artifacts of trade like New Zealand butter and cheese tins, Russian Lada cars, African fish tins, and American pharmaceuticals. My studies of present-day West Indian domestic sites also revealed the impact of emigration and return migration on family organization, especially gender roles. As I watched elderly West Indian women deal with the loneliness that comes when all one's children have migrated to distant industrial centers, I was prompted to find out more about how the migrants and their hosts were getting along in London or New York or Miami. Through all these studies I became increasingly aware of the impact of the global tourism economy on the cultures and environments of remote and beautiful places.

GOALS OF THE TEXT

The motivation to write this text came out of nearly two decades of teaching and research. When teaching at the introductory level, I found myself longing for a text that conveyed to students more of the current insights from geographic research. I wanted a text that was less centered on the Western economic perspective, and one that better conveyed the diversity of human culture and covered the lives of women and children as well as men. And I wanted a book that made global patterns of trade and consumption come alive for students by showing the effects of these systems on the daily lives of ordinary people in a wide variety of places.

Experience has taught that one task of a world geography course is to give students a solid grounding in regional characteristics. Abstract cultural or economic ideas become far more meaningful to students when they have place knowledge on which to hang those ideas. The goal of this text, then, is to give students a framework on which to build their own knowledge of world places —a framework that can work for a lifetime at all scales from international to local. The intent is to encourage students to ask questions about the physical, cultural, and political circumstances in a place. It should entice them to follow current events anywhere on earth and help them acquire the analytical skills that come from studying issues specific to a place.

LEVELS OF SCALE

The text is structured to explore human geography at varying levels of scale—global, regional, subregional, and local. The value of using different scales in geography is that one is led to see connections between what is happening in one's own place of residence to what is happening on a regional or global scale or in someone else's place of residence half a world away.

The Global Scale: This largest scale is explored most explicitly in Chapter 1. This chapter functions as an introduction to concepts of physical geography (plate tectonics, climate), social geography (culture groups, gender, and race), and political and economic geography (the global economy, geopolitics). The student will encounter these concepts again and again in the regional chapters.

An advantage of presenting basic concepts in Chapter 1 is that the instructor is then free to cover the regions in any order. No regional chapter depends on any other to explain needed concepts. Occasionally the reader is referred to another chapter for related material.

The Regional Scale: The text divides the world into ten major regions, each covered in a single chapter. I wanted the text to flow logically and the order to be predictable so that one could ask students to compare social or environmental or gender issues across regions. To facilitate comparisons, I have given the regional chapters a similar framework. Thus, instructors and students always know approximately where to look in a chapter for information on physical geography, population, family structure, economic and political circumstances, the environment, and so forth. Thus, while redundancy of content has been avoided, all the regional chapters contain the same components in more or less the same order.

■ An **Introduction** presents key trends and themes.

■ Sections on **physical geography**, **history**, and **population patterns** present basic factors that contribute to a region's present-day geography.

■ The core of each chapter is the **issues** section. This section combines a portrait of the region's basic sociocultural, economic, and political geography with in-depth exploration of contemporary issues.

1. A section on **sociocultural issues** addresses such topics as family structure, gender roles, the lives of children, and religion in contemporary life.

2. A section on **economic and political issues** emphasizes the connection of the region to large-scale or global trends and looks at the distribution of power within a region.

3. A section on **environmental issues** shows how economic and political trends and societal values affect the use of resources and are changing the environment.

4. A special section evaluates **human well-being** in a region using a variety of measurements, including gross national product (GNP) and the United Nations Human Development Index (HDI), and Gender Empowerment Measure (GEM). The cornerstone of the section is a table that presents these indices, plus male and female literacy figures in most cases, so that students and the instructor may compare levels of well-being within and across regions.

■ A brief final section called "**Reflections**" offers a perspective on the region's future.

Population Patterns

A look at the population density map of the continent of Africa (Figure 7.4) will surprise many American readers, who may have the erroneous impression that Africa is particularly densely populated. In fact, people are very unevenly, but generally sparsely, distributed across the continent. Only a few places exhibit the densities that are widespread in Europe, India, and China. Nonetheless, there are serious population issues in Africa. Some countries like Rwanda, Burundi, and Nigeria have pockets of very high density but few resources to support these people; this is sometimes because the resources have been diverted to serve the needs of others outside the region. And in a number of countries, population growth rates are so high that they sap the power of the society to develop adequate educational and health infrastructures. The result is that living standards actually sink rather than rise.

Defining Density

To some extent, whether population is dense or sparse depends on a region's carrying capacity. **Carrying capacity** refers to the maximum number of people a given territory can support sustainably with food, water, and other essential resources. There are several environmental factors that affect the carrying capacities of African lands. In some persistently arid places, the shortage of water limits the possibilities for cultivation or grazing. In some persistently wet places, the leached soils cannot sustain long-term cultivation. Some places with alternat-

---

Sociocultural Issues

Part of the delightful challenge of learning about South Asia is to spot the connections between cultural aspects of life: religion, food, caste, gender. These links exist in all societies, but here, perhaps because of the venerable age and overlapping of cultural features, when connections are revealed they can be particularly illuminating.

Language and Ethnicity

In South Asia everyone is a minority. The Indian writer and diplomat Shashi Tharoor observes that his own country illustrates this point eloquently:

A Hindi-speaking male from the Gangetic plain state of Uttar Pradesh might cherish the illusion that he represents the "majority community," . . . but he does not. As a

---

TABLE 9.2

Human well-being rankings of East Asian countries

Country	GNP per capita (in U.S. dollars), 1996	Human Development Index (HDI) global rankings, 1998[a]	Gender Empowerment Measure (GEM) global rankings, 1996	Female literacy (percentage), 1995	Male literacy (percentage), 1995	Life expectancy, 1998
Selected countries for comparison						
United States	28,020	4	11	99	99	76
Kuwait	19,040 (1995)	54	75	75	82	72
East Asia						
China	750	106	33	73	90	71
Hong Kong[b]	24,290	25		88	96	79
Japan	40,940	8 (high)	38	99	99	80
Korea, North	Not av.[c]	75	Not av.	95	95	66
Korea, South	10,610	30 (high)	83	97	99	74
Macao[b]	Not av.	Not av.				80
Mongolia	360	101	Not av.	75.6	87.8	57
Taiwan[b]	Not av.	Not av.				75

[a]The high designations in column 3 (HDI) indicate where the country ranks among the 174 countries classified into three categories (high, medium, low) by the United Nations.
[b]Data constructed from several sources.
[c]Not av. = not available.
Source: *Human Development Report 1998*, United Nations Development Programme; *1998 World Population Data Sheet*, Population Reference Bureau.

The Subregional Scale: The final third of each regional chapter provides a more detailed level of analysis. Each region is divided into five to eight subregions, covered in turn in separate sections that point out the distinctive human and physical geographic features. Often there is an opportunity to revisit issues explored on the regional scale earlier in the chapter to see the effects on particular subregions.

EXPLORING THE LOCAL SCALE

In writing the text, I have paid special attention to local scales, whether a town, a village, or a single household. My hope is, first, that stories of individuals and families will make geography interesting and real to students and, second, that seeing the effects of abstract processes and trends on ordinary lives will make the processes clearer to students. For this reason I have integrated examples illustrating real people and their activities into the text. In addition, I have included several special features that discuss life on the local scale.

The Continental Interior

Among the most striking features of the continental interior (Figure 2.23) are its huge size, its physical diversity, and its very low population density. This is a land of extreme physical environments; rugged terrain, frigid temperatures, or lack of water are not unusual. These physical features hamper many economic activities and explain the low population density. Most parts of the region have under two persons per square mile.

Today, increasing numbers are migrating to the region, some to take advantage of its open spaces and often dramatic scenery, others to exploit its considerable natural resources. The two groups often find themselves in conflict with each other and with the indigenous people of the continental interior. In fact, this region is one of the most intense battlegrounds in North America between environmentalists and resource developers.

Physically, the continental interior may be divided into four distinct zones: the Canadian Shield; the frigid, rugged lands of Alaska; the Rocky Mountains; and the Great Basin. The Canadian Shield is a vast glaciated territory lying north of the Great Plains and characterized by thin or nonexistent soils, innumerable lakes, and large meandering rivers. Along the southern portion, needle-leafed boreal forests, taiga, stretch from Labrador in the east to Alaska in the west. Farther north, the forest gives way to the tundra, a region of winters so long and cold that several feet below the surface the ground is permanently frozen. Shallow-

---

VIGNETTE — The Parvanov family lives in a small apartment outside Sofia, Bulgaria. The family appears to have the material wealth of the middle class: adequate food, a nice home, a car in the garage. But looks are deceiving; there is trouble. Because of recent high rates of inflation, Mr. Parvanov's salary is now worth only U.S. $30 a month, so he moonlights on a construction job. Mrs. Parvanov holds three part-time jobs: she works as a clerk, as an assistant in a building company, and at night machine-knits clothes she sells in the local market. Theodora, the 19-year-old daughter, attends university by day and helps her mother knit at night. Yet with all this effort (six jobs in all), the family earns only about U.S. $100 a month. With this tiny amount they must also support two grandparents whose pensions will no longer cover food, let alone medicine. The car hasn't been driven in months because gasoline is too expensive. They are able to survive only because the Bulgarian government heavily subsidizes the costs of food, rent, and other basic services, a situation that will not last much longer. [Adapted from Robert Frank, Price of isolation: Impoverished Bulgaria is ready for reform, *Wall Street Journal*, February 28, 1997, p. 1.]

■ **Personal vignettes** are true stories of real individuals (names disguised) that illustrate major themes.

■ Boxes titled **"At the Local Scale"** explore more detail as appropriate.

■ Boxes titled **"Cultural Insight"** explore the cuisine, music, and occasionally architecture of a region or locality.

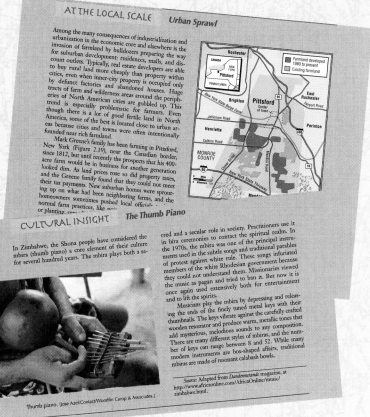

AT THE LOCAL SCALE   *Urban Sprawl*

Among the many consequences of industrialization and urbanization in the economic core and elsewhere is the invasion of farmland by bulldozers preparing the way for suburban development: residences, malls, and discount outlets. Typically, real estate developers are able to buy rural land more cheaply than property within cities, even when inner-city property is occupied only by defunct factories and abandoned houses. Huge tracts of farm and wilderness areas around the peripheries of North American cities are gobbled up. This trend is especially problematic for farmers. Even though there is a lot of good fertile land in North America, some of the best is located close to urban areas because cities and towns were often intentionally founded near rich farmland.

Mark Greene's family has been farming in Pittsford, New York (Figure 2.19), near the Canadian border, since 1812, but until recently the prospects that his 400-acre farm would be in business for another generation looked dim. As land prices rose so did property taxes, and the Greene family found that they could not meet their tax payments. New suburban homes were sprouting up on what had been neighboring farms, and the homeowners sometimes pushed local officials [...] normal farm practices, like [...] or planting, [...]

CULTURAL INSIGHT   *The Thumb Piano*

In Zimbabwe, the Shona people have considered the mbira (thumb piano) a core element of their culture for several hundred years. The mbira plays both a sacred and a secular role in society. Practitioners use it in bira ceremonies to contact the spiritual realm. In the 1970s, the mbira was one of the principal instruments used in the subtle songs and traditional parables of protest against white rule. These songs infuriated members of the white Rhodesian government because they could not understand them. Missionaries viewed the music as pagan and tried to ban it. But now it is once again used extensively both for entertainment and to lift the spirits.

Musicians play the mbira by depressing and releasing the ends of the finely tuned metal keys with their thumbnails. The keys vibrate against the carefully crafted wooden resonator and produce warm, metallic tones that add mysterious, melodious sounds to any composition. There are many different styles of mbiras, and the number of keys can range between 8 and 52. While many modern instruments are box-shaped affairs, traditional mbiras are made of resonant calabash bowls.

Source: Adapted from *Dandemutande* magazine, at http://www.africaonline.com/AfricaOnline/music/zimbabwe.html.

Thumb piano. [Jose Azel/Contact/Woodfin Camp & Associates.]

MAPS AND GRAPHICS

I wanted the maps to be pedagogically important. Thus I have been fortunate to be able to work closely with Will Fontanez and his capable staff at the University of Tennessee Cartographic Services Laboratory in their planning and design.

For each major section of the regional chapter, there is a special type of illustration, usually a map, to help students visualize the spatial distribution of geographic features.

■ Each chapter begins with a large map of the entire region, showing landforms and bodies of water, as well as political divisions and cities. This map functions as a reference map for the entire region.

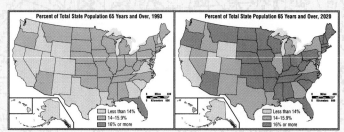

■ Every chapter contains a climate map and a population density map, and is liberally illustrated with thematic maps.

■ Each subregion has its own map highlighting political divisions, transportation networks, and cities, with populations indicated. Occasionally a theme is also highlighted in a subregion map. A small "locator" map orients the subregion within the broader region.

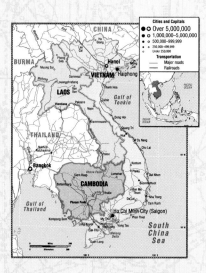

STUDENT AIDS

I have added several features to help students get the most from their reading.

■ "Themes to Look For" alerts students to some broad trends in a region that are particularly important in the chapter.

■ "Terms to Be Aware Of" points out some of the biases and unconscious assumptions in our use of particular descriptors and place names.

■ Important terms and concepts are set in boldface type the first time they appear in the chapter.

■ "Selected Themes and Concepts" at the end of the chapter summarizes some of the region's most important geographic features, often using boldfaced terms in a context that makes clear their significance.

■ Selected Readings at the end of each chapter provides ideas for student research.

■ At the back of the text are a number of useful sections: A section on **map reading** guides students in interpreting maps. A **glossary** defines all boldface and foreign terms in an easily accessible location. A **pronunciation guide** is included for all but the most familiar place names and foreign terms. A **citation bibliography** provides an extensive list of the sources of information used in writing the text.

Themes to Look For

You may notice several themes appearing repeatedly as you read this chapter. Among them are the following:

1. The dominance of Islamic culture: a major source of debate in the region is the degree to which Islamic beliefs should influence government, law, gender roles, and behavior in general.

2. The impact of oil, particularly in the oil-rich countries of the Persian Gulf: oil has provided wealth for a few, but the economy remains undiversified, dependent on oil or a few other resources only.

3. The attempt to make a desert region inhabitable for an increasing population: how to obtain water and expand agriculture are two burning and interrelated issues.

Terms to Be Aware Of

The term **Middle East** is not used in this chapter because of the Eurocentric bias it carries; the term is symptomatic of the tendency to lump the whole of Asia together, differentiating it only by its distance from Europe (near, middle, far). Furthermore, the term does not normally include the western sections of North Africa or eastern portions of Southwest Asia—Iran, for example. On the other hand, the reader should know that some people who live in the region do use the term themselves. The term **Islamist** is now being used for those Muslims who favor a religiously based state that incorporates strictly enforced Islamic principles as part of the legal system.

Chapter 3 Middle and South America / *The Peopling of Middle and South America*

Selected Themes and Concepts

1. Mountains and volcanoes often form at **subduction zones**, where the edge of one tectonic plate plunges below the edge of another. A long spine of mountains runs down the western edge of Middle and South America, produced by the subduction of three eastward-moving plates—the Pacific, Nazca, and Cocos—under the three westward-moving American plates.

2. There are four main **temperature-altitude zones** commonly used to describe climates in Middle and South America. They are, in order of rising altitude, *tierra caliente* (the "hot lands"), *tierra templada* (the "temperate lands"), *tierra fría* (the "cool lands"), and *tierra helada* (the "frozen lands").

3. The conquest of Middle and South America by the Spanish and Portuguese transformed life in the region. Much of the Native American population died of disease, and new populations were introduced from Europe, Africa, and Asia. During the colonial period, a minority of European descent controlled wealth and power in the region.

4. As a result of conquest and colonization, the region of Middle and South America is now one of cultural complexity. Native American culture remains particularly strong in the highlands of Middle and South America and in the Amazon and Central American lowlands. Many different European cultures, but especially those of Spain and Portugal, have blended with strong cultural strains imported from Africa and with Native American cultures to create a mosaic of **Creole** cultures. South Asian indentured labor brought new influences in the nineteenth and twentieth centuries, and recently East Asian investors and industrialists have joined the cultural mix.

5. **Rural-to-urban migration** has fed the rapid growth of cities in the twentieth century. There are "push" and "pull" reasons for migration. **Push** factors—like loss of agricultural jobs, lack of educational facilities, and rising poverty—impel people to leave the countryside. **Pull** factors—like new opportunities in industry or domestic work or the chance for an education—attract people to the cities.

6. In developing countries, often one city becomes the focus of industrial development and migration. As a result, it grows rapidly to a size much larger than all other cities in the country and becomes the seat of wealth and power. Such cities, called **primate cities**, draw investment, government services, and talented people away from other cities in the country.

7. Cities are concentrated along coastal zones, with only a few in lowland interiors. Some cities are in upland and highland regions in Mexico and in Central and South America.

8. Disparity in the distribution of income and wealth is more severe in this region than elsewhere on earth, even though this region is not the poorest region overall. Native Americans and other people of color tend to be the poorest.

9. The **extended family** is the basic social institution of Middle and South America. In this region, family members have distinct roles defined by gender. *Marianismo* is a set of values that dictates the behavior of women, who are expected to remain mostly in the home to serve the needs of husband and family. Men measure themselves by the model of *machismo*, which recognizes manliness in the ability to father children, to be master of one's household, and to be an engaging raconteur in the male community.

10. **Liberation theology**, a movement within the Roman Catholic Church, encourages the poor to organize to change their own lives and promotes social and economic reform. **Evangelical Protestantism** is the fastest-growing religious movement in the region. The movement preaches the "gospel of success" to the poor: a life dedicated to Christ will result in prosperity of the body and soul.

11. Since early colonial times, the economies of Middle and South American have been **extractive**, that is, based on the export of unprocessed agricultural and mineral materials.

12. The countries of the region have experimented with different strategies for encouraging economic development. To encourage industrialization, some countries adopted **import substitution** policies. State-owned industries, protected by tariffs on competing imports, tried to fulfill consumer demands. In the 1970s, countries borrowed billions of dollars to fund development projects, such as hydroelectric dams, roads, and mechanized agriculture. When development failed to produce income, countries defaulted on their debts, leading to a **debt crisis**. Major lending institutions imposed **structural adjustment programs (SAPs)** that required debtor countries to lay off government employees, cut back on social spending, and privatize national industries.

13. During the colonial period, intraregional trade was discouraged, which inhibited economic development. Now regional trade agreements, such as **Mercosur**, are breaking down trade barriers among member countries, offering hope for expanded, regionally integrated economic growth.

14. After a history of authoritarian and military rule, all countries in Middle and South America except Cuba now have democratically elected governments. Democracy remains fragile, and corruption continues to be a problem.

15. The region of Middle and South America was one of the first to alert the world to the dangers of environmental deterioration. Deforestation, erosion, loss of species diversity, and urban air pollution are among the environmental issues raised in this region.

Selected Readings

Anderson, Arthur J. O., and Charles E. Dibble, eds. *The War of Conquest—As It Was Waged Here in Mexico: The Aztecs' Own Story as Given to Fr. Bernardino de Sahagun*. Salt Lake City: University of Utah Press, 1978.

Blouet, Brian W., and Olwyn M. Blouet. *Latin America and the Caribbean—A Systematic and Regional Survey*, 3rd ed. New York: Wiley, 1997.

Butzer, Karl W. The Americas before and after 1492: An introduction of current geographical research. In *Annals of the AAG* 82 (1992): 345–368.

Chaney, Elsa M., and Mary Garcia Castro, eds. *Muchachas No More—Household Workers in Latin America and the Caribbean*. Philadelphia: Temple University Press, 1989.

Chant, Sylvia, ed. *Gender and Migration in Developing Countries*. London: Belhaven Press, 1992.

Clawson, David L. *Latin America and the Caribbean Lands and People*. Dubuque, IA: Wm. C. Brown, 1997.

Denevan, William M. The pristine myth: The landscape of the Americas in 1492. *Annals of the AAG* 82 (1992): 369–385.

Harsis, Randall. *The Latin Americans: Understanding Their Legacy*. New York: McGraw-Hill, 1997.

Hays-Mitchell, Maureen. Street vending in Peruvian cities: The spatio-temporal behavior of ambulantes. *Professional Geographer* 46 (1994): 425–438.

Keeling, David J. *Buenos Aires: Global Dreams, Local Crises*. New York: Wiley, 1996.

Klak, Thomas. Globalization, neo-liberalism and economic change in Central America and the Caribbean. In *Latin America 2000: Globalization and Modernity*. Robert A. Gwynne and Cristóbal Kay, eds. London: Edward Arnold, 1999.

MacDonald, Gordon J., Daniel L. Nielson, and Marc A. Stern, eds. *Latin American Environmental Policy in International Perspective*. Boulder, CO: Westview Press, 1997.

Meyerson, Julia. *Tambo: Life in an Andean Village*. Austin: University of Texas Press, 1990.

Olmos, Margarite Fernandez, and Lizabeth Paravisini-Gebert, eds. *Sacred Possessions: Vodou, Santeria, Obeah, and the Caribbean*. New Brunswick, NJ: Rutgers University Press, 1997.

Parker, Christian. *Popular Religion and Modernization in Latin America: A Different Logic*. Maryknoll, NY: Orbis Books, 1996.

Patai, Daphne. *Brazilian Women Speak: Contemporary Life Stories*. New Brunswick, NJ: Rutgers University Press, 1988.

Rabinovitch, Jonas, and Josef Leitman. Urban planning in Curitiba. *Scientific American*, March 1996, pp. 46–53.

Rengert, George. *The Geography of Illegal Drugs*. Boulder, CO: Westview Press, 1996.

Richardson, Bonham C. *The Caribbean in the Wider World 1492–1992*. Cambridge: Cambridge University Press, 1992.

Sauer, Carl Ortwin. *The Early Spanish Main*. Berkeley: University of California Press, 1966.

Stewart, Douglas Ian. *After the Trees: Living on the Transamazon Highway*. Austin: University of Texas Press, 1994.

Turpin, Jennifer, and Lois Ann Lorentzen. *The Gendered New World Order*. London: Routledge, 1996.

Watts, David. *The West Indies Patterns of Development, Culture and Environmental Change Since 1492*. Cambridge: Cambridge University Press, 1987.

Weatherford, Jack. *Indian Givers: How the Indians of the Americas Transformed the World*. New York: Crown, 1988.

THE SUPPLEMENTS

A wealth of ancillaries are available for students and instructors, all designed under the author's supervision to closely reflect the content and philosophy of the main text.

Instructor's Preparation and Class Management Aids

Instructor's Resource Manual: Abundant suggestions for making the best use of the text in the classroom, prepared by Tom Bell and Jennifer Rogalsky, University of Tennessee at Knoxville. The manual includes suggested lecture outlines, points to ponder for class discussion, and ideas for exercises and class projects.

Instructor's CD-ROM: The instructor's CD-ROM contains all the illustrations and captions from the book, 500 images from the National Geographic Society, and all animations and images from the student CD-ROM, along with W. H. Freeman's popular presentation manager PRO software.

Web site: The Web site is a general resource with updated information and exercises, useful for enrichment and review, with links to current information sites arranged by regions and topics. The site may be accessed at **www.whfreeman.com/geography.**

Test Bank: The Test Bank, prepared by Andy Walter of Florida State University, is carefully designed to match the pedagogical intent of the text. More than 2000 test questions (multiple choice, short answer, matching, true/false, and essay) are available in print form and as an electronic file, in both IBM and Macintosh formats. These questions can be easily and quickly modified to correlate with the needs of individual instructors.

Slide Set with Captions: A set of more than 100 slides of *National Geographic* images, available to adopters, provides additional photographs not in the text, along with contextual lecture notes. Additional extension sets are available to continuing adopters.

Overhead Transparency Set: 100 overhead transparencies showing maps from the text are available to adopters. All labels have been resized for easy readability.

Student Learning Aids

Student CD-ROM: A student CD-ROM is included with every copy of the text. The CD is designed to provide a sense of place through numerous *National Geographic* images and recipes/cuisines from around the world. Interactive map exercises and quizzes enable the student to brush up on place location and sharpen her or his ability to analyze geographic material.

Study Guide/Mapping Workbook: Working with World Regional Geography—prepared by Tom Bell and Jennifer Rogalsky, University of Tennessee, Knoxville—is a study guide and book of mapping exercises designed to hone student skills in geographic analysis. The content has been carefully composed to complement the text.

Atlas: Students may purchase the text packaged with Hammond's *The New Comparative World Atlas* at the instructor's discretion.

ACKNOWLEDGMENTS

I have a special place in my heart for all the many colleagues who have reviewed and commented on various drafts of individual chapters. Many invested days, even weeks, in reading and crafting comprehensive suggestions. Not only have they greatly improved the quality of the book, many have offered words of encouragement that were especially needed during this long process. The following list cites the names of reviewers who commented on at least one chapter:

Helen Ruth Aspaas
Virginia Commonwealth University

Brad Bays
Oklahoma State University

Stanley Brunn
University of Kentucky

Altha Cravey
University of North Carolina, Chapel Hill

David Daniels
Central Missouri State University

Dydia DeLyser
Louisiana State University

Sam Dennis
Penn State University

James Doerner
University of Northern Colorado

Bryan Dorsey
Weber State University

Lorraine Dowler
Penn State University

Hari Garbharran
Middle Tennessee State University

Baher Ghosheh
Edinboro University

Janet Halpin
Chicago State University

Peter Halvorson
University of Connecticut

Michael Handley
Emporia State University

Robert Hoffpauir
California State University, Northridge

Glenn G. Hyman
International Center for Tropical Agriculture

David Keeling
Western Kentucky University

Thomas Klak
Miami University, Ohio

Darrell Kruger
Northeast Louisiana University

David Lanegran
Macalester College

David Lee
Florida Atlantic University

Calvin Masilela
West Virginia University

Janice Monk
University of Arizona

Heidi Nast
DePaul University

Katherine Nashleanas
University of Nebraska

Tim Oakes
University of Colorado, Boulder

Darren Purcell
Florida State University

Susan Roberts
University of Kentucky

Dennis Satterlee
Northeast Louisiana University

Kathleen Schroeder
Appalachian State University

Dona Stewart
Georgia State University

Karen Till
University of Minnesota

Ingolf Vogeler
University of Wisconsin, Eau Claire

Susan Walcott
Georgia State University

My immigrant father, Joe Mihelič, started his five-year-old daughter on a life of geographic observation when he put a world map on the wall of our kitchen and began to explain the lay of the land near our home in the Mississippi Valley of eastern Iowa. Years later, my brother John Mihelič insisted that I should write a book like this one. He has been a loyal cheerleader during the process. My friends Carol and Cedric Osborne in Montserrat, West Indies, and Joann and George Rothery and Gloria and Kyle Testerman in Knoxville listened to my writer's gripes and were patient sounding boards for ideas. My dear colleagues in the Geography Department at the University of Tennessee, both graduate students and faculty, allowed me time off from teaching duties during the busiest writing times and applauded my progress. Will Fontanez and the cartography shop staff unfailingly and cheerfully pursued the goal of beautiful informative maps. Special thanks are owing to Tom Wallin, Hilary Burns, Jennifer Barnes, Katherine Becksvoort, Charles Lafon, Russell Peeler, and Susan Carney for their work in preparing the maps.

Sara Tenney and Liz Widdicombe at W. H. Freeman were the first to persuade me that together we could develop a new direction for World Regional Geography, one that included the latest thinking in geography presented in an accessible writing style. I am indebted to my development editor, Susan Moran, and to the staff for all they have done to ensure that this book is beautifully designed, well written, and well presented to the public. Susan was unfailingly insightful and probing, yet kind and patient. She was always a loyal advocate for the reader. I would also like to gratefully acknowledge the efforts of the following people on the staff of W. H. Freeman: Melissa Wallerstein and Susan Brennan, acquisitions editors; Mary Louise Byrd, project editor; Blake Logan, designer; Bill Page and Shawn Churchman, illustration coordinators; Paul W. Rohloff, production coordinator; Inge King, photo researcher; Robert P. Christie, Matthew Fitzpatrick, and Bridget O'Lavin, supplements editors; and John Britch, marketing manager.

Most of the text grew out of conversations with my son Alex, who is in his mid-twenties and headed for a career as a geographer. Alex worked full time at research and writing, helping me to prepare the physical, historical, political, and economic parts of the text. He has also served as the student's advocate, especially in writing style, and he has overseen the content for the supplements package. Also fully active in the process was my husband, Mac Goodwin, an anthropologist and archaeologist who specializes in European colonial sites in the United States, the Caribbean, and the Pacific. He took time away from archaeology to manage the bibliographic research, choice of graphic content, documentation, and production of the manuscript. He also researched and wrote first drafts for some subregions, vignettes, and special features. And he patiently supported me through this rewarding but difficult process of thinking and writing about the world.

ABOUT THE AUTHOR

Lydia Mihelič Pulsipher has been a professor of geography at the University of Tennessee since 1980. Her research interests are in human adaptations to life in the American tropics since 1500, in culture change, and in agricultural origins and dispersals. She also writes and teaches about gender issues in geography. She has taught at Hunter College in New York City and Dartmouth College in New Hampshire, and her West Indian research has been presented in several geography-related exhibits at the Smithsonian Museum of Natural History in Washington, D.C. She received her B.A. from Macalester College, her M.A. from Tulane University, and her Ph.D. from Southern Illinois University.

While writing WORLD REGIONAL GEOGRAPHY, Lydia Pulsipher was assisted by her husband and son. Her husband, Conrad "Mac" Goodwin, is a historical archaeologist who specializes in sites created during the European colonial era in North America, the Caribbean, and the Pacific. He has particular expertise in the archaeology of agricultural systems, formal gardens, domestic landscapes, and urban spaces. He holds a research appointment in the Department of Anthropology at the University of Tennessee.

Alex Pulsipher grew up helping his mother and stepfather do historical geography and archaeology research on the Caribbean island of Montserrat. Research and daily life among the people of Montserrat helped him develop a strong interest in cultures and their interactions. While a student at Wesleyan University in Connecticut, Alex spent a year in South Asia, where he was drawn to the history and geography of the region. He went on to complete his degree in Indian history.

WORLD REGIONAL GEOGRAPHY

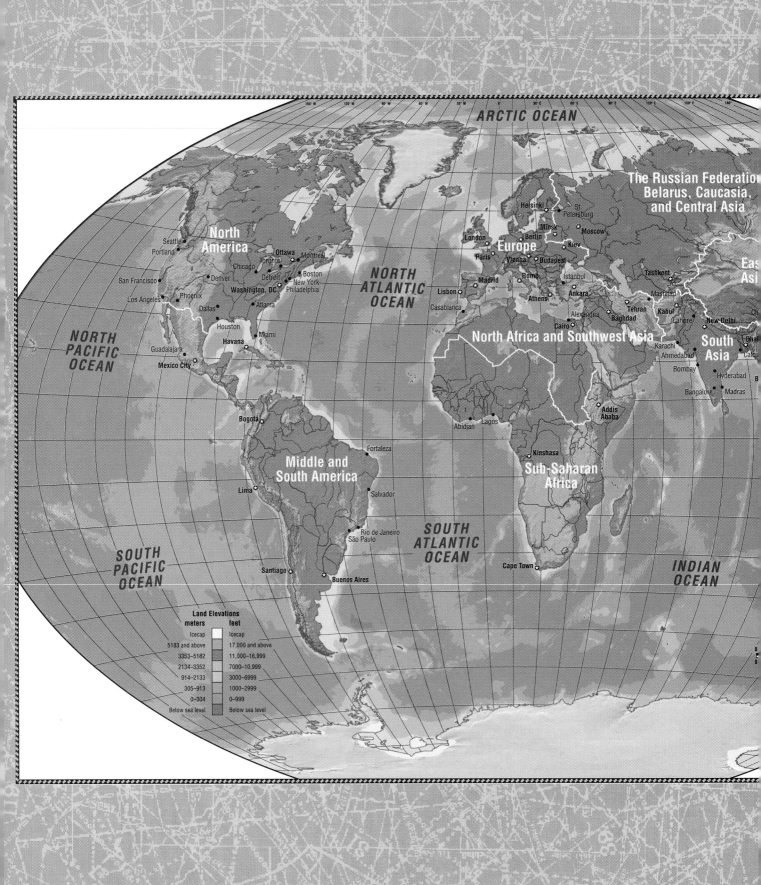

ARCTIC OCEAN

The Russian Federation
Belarus, Caucasia,
and Central Asia

Helsinki
St. Petersburg
London
Minsk
Moscow
Berlin
Paris
Kiev
Europe
Vienna Budapest
Madrid
Rome
Istanbul
Tashkent
Lisbon
Athens
Ankara
Mashhad
Casablanca
Alexandria
Tehran
Kabul
Baghdad
Lahore
New Delhi
Cairo
Karachi
Ahmedabad
Bombay
Hyderabad
Bangalore
Madras

North
America

Seattle
Portland
Ottawa
Montreal
Chicago
Toronto
San Francisco
Denver
Detroit
Boston
Washington, DC
New York
Philadelphia
Los Angeles
Phoenix
Dallas
Atlanta
Houston
Miami
Guadalajara
Havana
Mexico City
Bogotá

NORTH
ATLANTIC
OCEAN

NORTH
PACIFIC
OCEAN

North Africa and Southwest Asia

Abidjan Lagos

South
Asia

Addis
Ababa

Middle and
South America

Fortaleza

Kinshasa

Sub-Saharan
Africa

Lima

Salvador

Rio de Janeiro
São Paulo

SOUTH
ATLANTIC
OCEAN

SOUTH
PACIFIC
OCEAN

Santiago

Buenos Aires

Cape Town

INDIAN
OCEAN

Land Elevations

meters	feet
Icecap	Icecap
5183 and above	17,000 and above
3353–5182	11,000–16,999
2134–3352	7000–10,999
914–2133	3000–6999
305–913	1000–2999
0–304	0–999
Below sea level	Below sea level

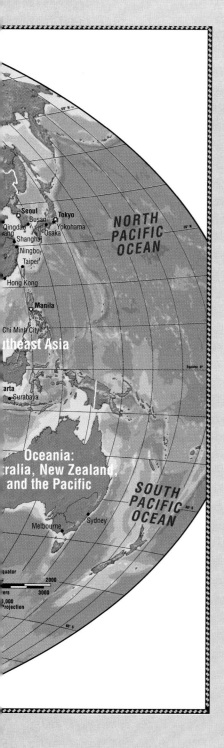

CHAPTER

ONE

GEOGRAPHY:

AN EXPLORATION OF
CONNECTIONS

WHERE IS IT?
WHY IS IT THERE?

Where are you? Why are you there? You may be in a house or a library, or sitting under a tree on a fine fall afternoon. You are also probably in a community, perhaps a college campus, and you are in a country, a region of the world, perhaps North America or South Asia or the Pacific. But why are you where you are? There are some immediate answers, like "I have an assignment to read." Then there are the larger explanations that have to do with belief in the value of an education, career plans, willingness on the part of someone (perhaps you) to sacrifice to pay your tuition, even past social movements in Europe and America that opened up higher education to more than just a minority. Perhaps even your specific desire to learn more about world geography has brought you to the location you are in now.

The familiar questions of where and why are central to geography. Like all of us who have to find the site of a party on Saturday night, or the location of the best grocery store, or the fastest and safest route home, geographers are interested in location and spatial relationships. Different places look different, sound different, and smell different, and that difference is significant. Understanding all that has contributed to the look and feel of a place, to the standard of living and customs of its people, is the special endeavor of geographers.

To make it easier to relate to the many interests of a geographer, please try this exercise. On a piece of blank paper draw a map of your favorite childhood landscape. Relax, and let your mind recall the things that were most important to you in this place. If this was a landscape in which you lived, you might want to start by drawing and labeling your home, and then filling in other places you encountered regularly as you went about your life, like your backyard and the objects in it, the home of your best friend, your school. Don't worry about creating a work of art or drawing things correctly. Just make a map that reflects your experience as you remember it.

When you are finished, think about how the map reveals the ways your life was structured by space. Were there places you were not supposed to go, but

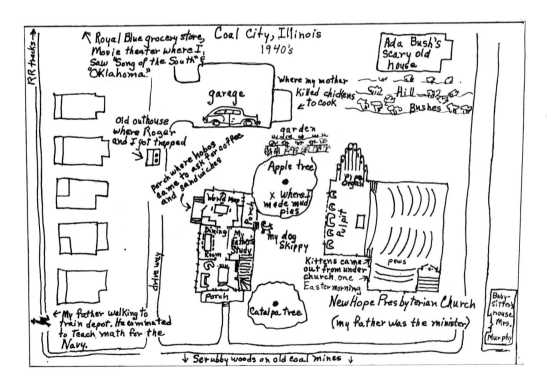

Lydia Pulsipher's childhood map.

did anyway? Does your map in any, even very subtle, way reveal emotions like fear, pleasure, or longing? Does it indicate your sex, your ethnicity, or the makeup of your family? Are some places drawn in greater detail than others? What scale did you choose? Did you draw just a house and yard, or a neighborhood, or a square mile or more? The amount of space you covered with your map may represent the degree of freedom you had at that age to go about on your own, or it may represent something entirely different.

In making your map and analyzing it you are learning several skills central to geography: landscape observation; description of the earth's surface; historical reconstruction of bygone places; **spatial analysis,** the study of how people or things or ideas are, or are not, related to each other across space; and **cartography,** the making of maps. As you progress through this book you will have the chance to learn other geographic skills. Whether you are planning a road trip, looking at the photograph of an intriguing landscape, thinking about investing in East Asian stocks, searching for a good place to market an idea, or trying to understand current events, geographic skills will make the task easier and more engaging.

What Is Geography?

A brief formal definition of **geography** might be that it is the study of our planet's surface and the processes that shape it. But such a succinct statement does not begin to convey the fascinating interactions of physical and human forces that have given our planet its diversity of landscapes. Geography, as an academic discipline, links the physical sciences, such as geology, physics, chemistry, biology, and botany, with the social sciences, such as anthropology, sociology, history, economics, and political science. This wide-ranging discipline embraces remarkable variety, yet is unified by a common interest in understanding the world in spatial terms. Just as historians are interested in change over time, geographers are interested in variation over space and, most of all, in the explanations for that variation. Among geographers' most important tools are maps, which they use to record and analyze spatial relationships.

Geographers usually specialize in one or more fields of study, or "subdisciplines." Table 1.1 gives some examples of the different kinds of geographers who might be found in any college or university geography department.

Many of these different kinds of geographers also specialize in a particular place or region of the world, which they may study from a variety of perspectives. **Regional geography** is the analysis of the geographic

characteristics of a particular place (the size of that place can vary radically). The study of a particular place from a geographic perspective can reveal heretofore unacknowledged connections between physical features and ways of life that are key to understanding the present (and past) and are essential in planning for the future.

I have chosen a "world-regional" approach for this book because experience has taught that what people new to geography crave most is general knowledge about places. That knowledge is produced by the subfields described in Table 1.1, and in this book we will use all of them to provide a holistic perspective on each of the world's regions.

The Region as a Concept

A **region** may be thought of as a unit of the earth's surface that contains distinct patterns of physical features or of human development. We could speak of a limestone region, or a region that produces table wine, or one that is characterized by a particular vegetation type. This sounds simple enough but, in fact, the concept of "region" is one that geographers argue about a good bit. Many people use the idea of region as a way of dividing up the world into manageable parts (see the map at the beginning of this chapter), yet a precise definition of particular regions is elusive. For one thing, it is rare for any two regions to be defined by the same set of indicators. One assemblage of places may be thought of as a region because of its distinctive landscape and cultural features, like food, music, and dress. Another may be defined primarily by its dominant economic activity and its wealth, or lack thereof. Still another group of places might be considered a region primarily because of its particular political system. Furthermore, as we shall see, the boundaries between regions are nearly always blurred and debatable.

One might think that there would be clear boundaries between the world regions, but the more closely one looks at the border zones, the fuzzier the divisions appear. Take the case of the boundary between North America and Middle America (Mexico and the countries of Central America). Just where is the true regional border? What criteria shall we use to establish this border? Although the Rio Grande is the official international division between the United States and Mexico, it is not really a marker of separation between cultures or even economies. On both sides of the river today there extends a wide band containing a blend of Native American, Spanish colonial, Mexican, and Anglo-American cultural features: language, food customs, music, family organization, to name but a few

TABLE 1.1

Geography subdisciplines

Geomorphologists further our understanding of how landforms such as mountains, plains, river valleys, and the ocean floor developed in the past and continue to change. Geomorphologists in academic geography departments (as opposed to geology departments) are often particularly interested in how humans alter landforms through deforestation, cultivation, and the manipulation of watersheds and other environments.

Climatologists look at long-term weather patterns (climates), studying the interaction of climate, vegetation, and landforms. Recently, climatologists have begun studying the possibility that humans are altering climate on a worldwide scale by releasing carbon dioxide and other gases into the atmosphere. This happens, in particular, through the burning of wood and fossil fuels (oil, gas, and coal).

Biogeographers study the geography of life on earth—where plants, animals, and other living organisms are found today and were found in the past. They also examine how the distribution of ecosystems is shaped by human activity, climate change, plate tectonics, and other environmental and evolutionary processes.

Cultural geographers describe and explain the spatial patterns and ecological relationships of culturally distinct groups of people. A cultural geographer might study how the religious or philosophical beliefs of a particular cultural group influence the ways they practice agriculture, or see themselves in relation to nature, or organize their settlements, or set down behavior rules for males and females from childhood through old age.

Human (or cultural) ecology specialists combine the interests of biogeographers and cultural geographers. They examine the specific ways in which humans and physical environments (including all types of life-forms) interact.

Historical geographers study long-term spatial processes, such as change over time in human habitats or migrations, or the spread of technology, ideas, and other aspects of culture.

Economic geographers look at the spatial aspects of economic activity, such as how resources are allocated and exchanged from place to place. They also examine how people interact with their environment as they go about earning a living. For example, an economic geographer might focus on where in a city women tend to work and how they get there, or on the amount and type of space occupied by particular economic enterprises like popcorn vending, shopping malls, or the international cocaine trade.

Political geographers are interested in the spatial expressions of power and the institutions humans have devised to channel that power—such as representative democracy or authoritarian religious states. Often, political power struggles have a graphic landscape component like the Great Wall of China, the Berlin Wall, or the burned villages of Bosnia.

Urban geographers study spatial patterns and processes within cities, and the ways urban areas interact with surrounding suburban and rural areas.

Gender geographers offer a new perspective in viewing the world by examining gender relations and the roles and status of men and women in society. They also explore how activities that are in some way linked to a person's sex are expressed spatially; and they analyze the meaning of these spatial patterns.

Cartographers specialize in depicting geographic knowledge graphically in maps. They are interested in both the science and the esthetics of portraying visual information to the map reader. Though maps are often still drawn by hand, computers are increasingly the cartographer's chief tool.

Remote sensing analysts discern patterns on the earth's surface by examining high-altitude photographs and other images collected from space by military and space programs.

Geographic Information Systems (GIS) analysts use computers to analyze large bodies of statistical information about spatial relationships. An example of their work would be the analysis of changing patterns of agricultural crops needing transport, and the location and capacity of the trucks, trains, and ships needed to do the job.

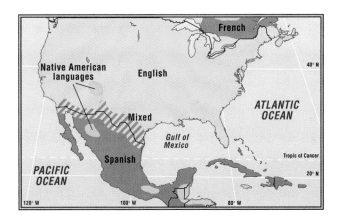

FIGURE 1.1 The striped band shows the area along the border of the United States and Mexico where English and Spanish are both commonly spoken languages. [Adapted from *The World Book Atlas* (Chicago: World Book, 1996), p. 89.]

(Figure 1.1). And the economy (agriculture, manufacturing, trade, tourism) is likewise based on interactions across a wide band of territory. In fact, the Mexican economy is much more closely connected to the economy of the United States than to that of Central America.

Why, then, does this book place Mexico with Middle America? Because Mexico, on the whole, has more in common with Central and South America than with North America. The use of Spanish as the official language is particularly important. The dominant language of Middle and South America is Spanish and in Brazil it is Portuguese, whereas the dominant language of the United States and Canada is English, except in Québec, where French is primary and English secondary. These language patterns are symbolic of the larger cultural and historical differences between the two regions, which will be discussed in Chapters 2 and 3. Even though Mexico does have a lot in common with parts of the southwestern United States, on the whole the similarities do not override the differences. It is important to note, however, that this situation may change over time, as economic connections between North America and Mexico strengthen and as more Mexican emigrants enter the United States. Indeed, in the not too distant future it might make sense to include Mexico as part of the world region of North America.

If regions are so difficult to define and describe and so changeable, why do geographers use them? The obvious reason is that it is impossible to discuss the whole world at once, so one seeks ways to divide it up into manageable parts based on some rational criteria. There is nothing sacred about the criteria or about the boundaries arrived at; they need to be practical. In defining the world regions for this book, I have considered multiple factors, such as political boundaries, cultural characteristics, and physical features. Geographers find that by using multiple factors they can arrive at regional definitions with which more people can agree.

In this book I have organized the material into regions at three levels, or scales: global regions, world regions, and subregions (Figure 1.2). At the **global** scale, explored in this chapter, the entire world is treated as a single area, a unity that is still new to all of us on earth but more and more relevant as we become used to thinking of our earth as a global system. I use the term **world region** for the largest divisions of the globe, such as East Asia, Southeast Asia, North America, and so forth. There are 10 world regions, each of which is covered in a separate chapter. The world regions are then divided into **subregions,** which may be independent countries or groups of countries, or even part of a single country. For example, the world region of North America contains several subregions. In Canada, the province of Québec is considered a subregion because of its distinct French heritage. In the United States, no one state stands out so distinctively. Here, subregions tend to be groups of states, like the Southwest or the Northeast. And in some cases, subregions include territory on both sides of the international border.

The regions and subregions in this book vary dramatically in size and complexity. A subregion can be as big as a continent, like Australia, which is part of the world region of Oceania and is nearly 3 million square miles (7.8 million square kilometers) in area. Or a subregion can be as small as the group of tiny islands known as Micronesia, also in Oceania, which all together cover only 270 square miles (919 square kilometers).

The remainder of this first chapter provides basic explanations of human and physical geography concepts emphasized in this book. Humans are central to geography. As social animals, humans shape the earth's surface through their efforts to support themselves in a particular environment, and they are themselves shaped by their experiences within environments. In this first chapter, I will cover background material from the several subfields of human geography (historical, cultural/social, economic, political, and environmental geography) to help the reader understand how people in the various regions of the world have worked out their relationships with the local physical environment, with each other, and with the wider world. The material on physical geography is intended to give the reader some background on the physical processes that shape the earth's surface and create its patterns of weather and climate.

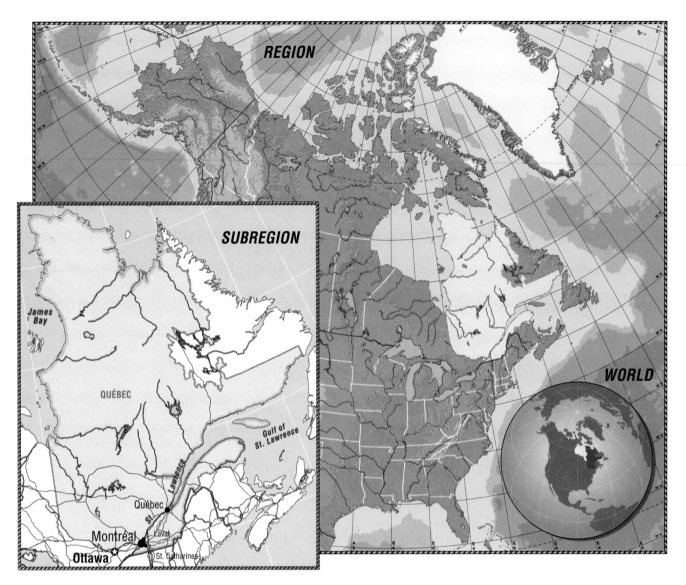

FIGURE 1.2 Here, the three regional scales are depicted: the entire globe, a region (North America), and a subregion of North America (Québec).

GEOGRAPHIC PERSPECTIVES ON PREHISTORY AND HISTORY

In this book we are concerned primarily with present-day issues in the various world regions and with the processes that are bringing all parts of the world into closer association—processes that, taken together, are often called "globalization." But to understand the modern world it is helpful to reflect briefly on how the human relationship with the earth has evolved over time.

Human Origins

Humans are relatively new forms of life on earth. If we compress the roughly 3.8 billion years of life on earth into a 24-hour time scale (Figure 1.3), our species *(Homo sapiens sapiens)* appeared only about two seconds ago. Agriculture began only one-quarter of a second ago and the industrial revolution seven-thousandths of a second ago. In other words, measured by the actual age of the earth, we humans have been here only a very short time, a fact that is all the more amazing when one considers how pervasive our impact on the earth has become.

One set of questions pertinent to understanding the role of humans on earth today has to do with how the human species spread across the landmasses of earth and adapted to different environments. Eventually, hu-

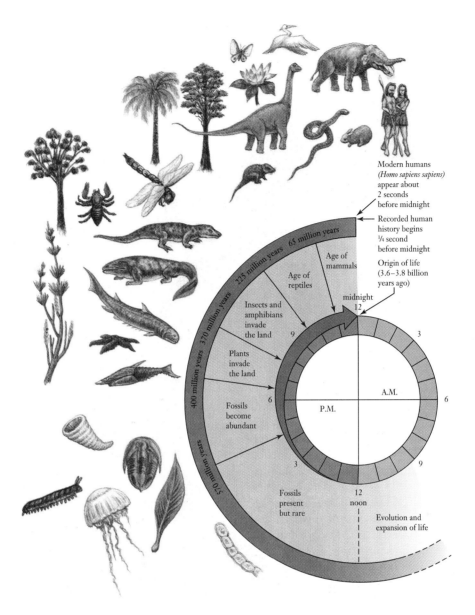

FIGURE 1.3 This simplified representation of biological evolution on earth from the first living organisms to modern humans *(Homo sapiens sapiens)* emphasizes how recently, relatively speaking, humans appeared on earth. [Adapted from G. Tyler Miller, Jr., *Living in the Environment, Eighth Edition* (Belmont, CA: Wadsworth, 1994), p. 158.]

mans occupied all continents and developed related, but distinctive, strategies for using and modifying the earth's resources in their efforts to sustain life.

The prevailing opinion among a variety of experts is that the human species had its start in Africa. Human ancestors with the ability to walk upright existed there at least 3.2 million years ago. The debate continues as to why and when hominids began to walk upright; but with this ability, called **bipedalism,** hominids could travel faster and thus gain access to a much wider range of resources. Moreover, because bipedalism left the arms and hands free, it encouraged the use of tools.

Bipedalism is only one of four (or more) characteristics that separate humans from the apes. The other three are a larger brain, smaller canine teeth, and most important, a reliance on culture as a mechanism for ordering life and passing on knowledge to descendants. All four, and perhaps others (see the box "Adaptive Role of Menopause"), apparently contributed to the ability of our early ancestors to live successfully in a wide variety of environments. By about 400,000 years ago, the close ancestors of humans *(Homo erectus)* had moved out of Africa and across Eurasia. Modern humans *(Homo sapiens sapiens)* apparently emerged from *Homo erectus* within the last 200,000 years, a time of particularly rapid and

9

AT THE GLOBAL SCALE   *The Adaptive Role of Menopause*

Recently, increased scientific interest in gender as a factor in the early stages of human evolution has inspired a number of insights. Some suggest that bipedalism emerged because walking upright, which would have freed the hands for carrying food and children, aided successful hominid reproduction by making it possible for males and females to cooperate (perhaps, but not necessarily, monogamously) in raising more than one youngster at a time. This ability would allow for an increased survival rate of the young and, hence, greater success of the species. Another interesting idea has to do with the possible adaptive advantage of menopause. Most mammals remain fertile until they die. But the human female experiences decreasing fertility after age 40; usually by age 50 she can no longer conceive.

Jered Diamond, an evolutionary biologist and biogeographer, suggests that menopause in the middle-aged human female is actually adaptive to the survival of her larger kin group. Because a woman stops bearing young while she is still vigorous, she can finish raising her half-grown children and then help her own offspring with the care of her grandchildren. Thus menopause furthers the persistence of a woman's genes much more effectively than if she simply continued to reproduce until death. Diamond thinks menopause is such a distinctive characteristic of humans that he ranks it with bipedalism, large brains, small incisors, and culture as features that make us distinctly human.

repeated climate change. Succeeding generations of modern humans had to adjust to many different climatic regimes, and to changing vegetation and varying food resources. This need to adapt to environmental variety is thought to have stimulated cultural innovation. And the lower sea levels during glaciations helped people migrate over land bridges to places like the islands of Indonesia and the continents of Australia and the Americas. By 30,000 years ago, modern humans occupied many places throughout Africa, Europe, Asia, Australia, and perhaps even North and South America. All previous versions of hominids were apparently by then extinct.

The Origins of Agriculture and Animal Husbandry

The emergence of agriculture and animal husbandry represents a monumental change in the ways that humans interacted with the earth's resources: the rate at which the earth's surface was modified and rates of human population growth. Hence, the story is of interest to anyone who worries about the long-term effects of modern increases in population and in human use of the earth's resources. The development of agriculture was accompanied by fundamental changes in the organization of human society that are at the root of several phenomena explored in this text: disparities in wealth, hierarchies of power, urbanization, trade.

Phrases like "plant and animal domestication" or "the invention of agriculture" create the impression that humans made the transition to cultivating plants and tending animals rather abruptly, maybe with a flash of insight. Most scholars don't think so. It seems more likely that even very early ancestors of humans used and manipulated wild plants and animals for many hundreds of thousands of years. The transition to gardens, fields, and pastures was probably gradual, the natural outgrowth of a long familiarity with the environmental requirements, growth cycles, and reproductive mechanisms of whatever plants and animals humans liked to eat, chew, smoke, ride, or wear.

For years, scholars argued that the practices of cultivation and animal husbandry were invented in one or two locations on earth and then diffused from those centers of innovation. Genetic studies are now showing that many different groups of people in many different places around the globe learned independently to create especially useful plants and animals through selective breeding. Some of the more well-known centers of domestication are shown on the map in Figure 1.4. Probably both independent invention and diffusion played a role in agricultural innovation. Sometimes the ideas of domestication and cultivation were relayed to new places; in other cases the farmers or herders themselves moved into new zones, taking agriculture or improvements such as new tools or new methods or new plants and animals with them.

Scholars used to assume that people turned to cultivating instead of gathering their food either because they had to in order to feed burgeoning populations, or because agriculture provided such obviously better

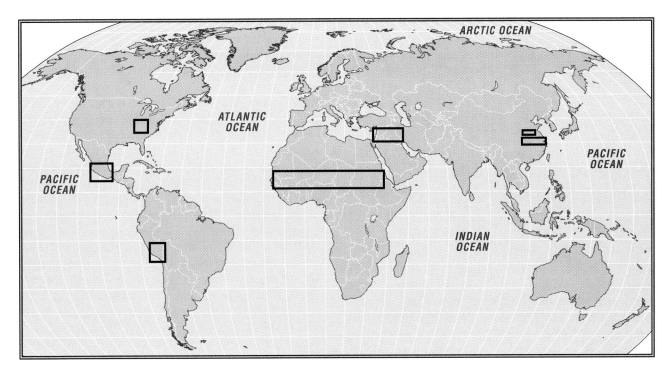

FIGURE 1.4 There are seven main areas in the world where agriculture emerged from independent development of plant and animal domestication. [Adapted from Bruce D. Smith, *The Emergence of Agriculture* (New York: Scientific American Library, 1995), p. 12.]

nutrition. It now seems that neither of these explanations is valid. First of all, the risk attached to exploring new food sources when there were already too many mouths to feed would be too great. Second, agriculture did not necessarily improve nutrition or supplies of food. A varied diet based on gathered (and occasionally hunted) food probably provided a wider, more secure range of nutrients than an early agriculturally based diet of only one or two cultivated crops. More likely, populations expanded after agricultural successes, and not before.

Richard MacNeish, an archaeologist who has studied plant domestication in Mexico and Central America, suggests that the chance to trade was at the heart of agricultural origins worldwide. Many of the known locations of agricultural innovation lie near early trade centers. People in such places would have had at least two reasons to pursue cultivation and animal raising: they would have had access to new information and new plants and animals brought in by traders; and they would have had a need for something to trade with the people passing through. Perhaps, then, agriculture was at first just a profitable hobby for hunters and gatherers that eventually, because of market demand, grew into a "day job"—the primary source of sustenance. Trade in agricultural products may also have been a hobby that led to trouble.

E. N. Anderson, writing about the beginnings of agriculture in China, suggests that agricultural production for trade may have been the impetus for several global situations now regarded as problems: rapid population growth, social inequalities, environmental degradation, and famine. Briefly explained, his theory suggests that groups turned to raising animals and plants in order to reap the profits of trading them. As more labor was needed to supply the trade, humans produced more children. As population expanded, more resources were put into producing food for subsistence and for trade. Gradually, hunting and gathering technology was abandoned as populations, with their demands for space, destroyed natural habitats. Meanwhile, a minority elite emerged when the wealth provided by trade did not accrue equally to everyone. Yet another problem was that a drought or other natural disaster could wipe out an entire harvest; thus, as ever larger populations depended solely on agriculture, famine became more common.

Although this scenario is undoubtedly oversimplified, Anderson's theory illustrates some points important for understanding modern geographic issues. With the emergence of agriculture and animal husbandry, the potential for human impact on the world's environments increased markedly as fields of cultivated plants and pastures for cattle, sheep, and goats replaced forests and grasslands. This trend has become even more pronounced in recent decades as we have become more dependent on the application of chemicals (hormones, fertilizers, pesticides) and on large amounts of irrigation water.

MODERN CULTURAL AND SOCIAL GEOGRAPHIC ISSUES

We have already noted that **culture** is an important distinguishing characteristic of humans. It consists of all that we use to carry on our life on earth that is not directly part of our biological inheritance. Culture is represented by the ideas and materials and institutions that humans have invented and passed on to subsequent generations. Culture includes language, music, belief systems, and moral codes and gender roles (as, for example, those prescribed in Confucianism or Islam or Christianity). **Material culture** includes all the things, living and inert, that humans use: clothing, houses and office buildings, axes, guns, computers, earthmoving equipment from hoes to work animals to bulldozers, books, musical instruments, domesticated plants and animals, agricultural technology, food ways, and much more. **Institutions** may be thought of as all those associations, formal and informal, that help us get along together. The family in its many different forms is an informal institution. So is a community, which can consist of the people who share a physical space (a neighborhood) or those who share a belief system. A society's preferred way of transacting business, whether through personal relationships or through highly organized bureaucracies, could be another type of informal institution. Formal institutions include religious organizations like the Presbyterian Church (U.S.A.); local, state, and national governments and their agencies; nongovernmental organizations that provide philanthropic services; and businesses and corporations.

Culture Groups

A group of people who share a set of beliefs, a way of life, a technology, and usually a place are said to be a **culture group**: for example, the Tarahumara of northern Mexico or the Hui people of the Loess Plateau in China. The term "culture group" in this book and elsewhere is often used interchangeably with "ethnic group." But both these terms can quickly become problematic, because, like the concept of region or race, the concepts of culture and ethnicity are fuzzy

around the edges. In the modern era, for instance, many people are moving beyond their customary cultural or ethnic boundaries, migrating to cities or to distant rural areas. In these new places they are taking on new ways of life, even new beliefs, yet still identifying with their origins. To take one example, we hear that the formerly nomadic Kurds in Southwest Asia are asserting their right to create a nation state in the territory in which they once lived but that is now claimed by Syria, Iraq, Iran, and Turkey. We may picture a typical Kurd as a woman living in a type of tent and processing and weaving the wool from her family's herd of sheep; but then we learn that many Kurds who actively support the cause of the herders are now urban dwellers in Turkey or Iraq, far from the pastures. They live in apartments and work as clerks or housekeepers or rug dealers. Although these people think of themselves as ethnic Kurds and are so regarded in the larger society, they do not follow the traditional Kurdish way of life. Hence, it could be argued that these urban Kurds both are and are not part of the Kurdish culture or ethnic group.

Another problem with the concept of culture is that it is often applied to a very large group that shares only the most general of characteristics. For example, one often hears the terms "American culture," "Western culture," "modern culture," "African-American culture," or "Asian culture." In these cases, the group referred to is too enormous to share more than a few broad characteristics. It might be fairly said, for example, that U.S. culture is characterized by beliefs that promote the rights, autonomy, and responsibility of the individual; by high levels of consumption (people in the United States tend to own more things than people of comparable lifestyles in Europe); and by technological dependence (on television sets, radios, automobiles, computers), as well as by a market economy based on credit and widely accessible middle and higher education.

We quickly run into serious disagreements if we try to be more specific about U.S. culture—if we try to name a common religious heritage, for example, or food preferences, or precise tastes in television programming. And though we might all agree that we value individualism, people in the United States constantly debate just how independent the individual should be, at what stages in life, and at whose expense. Think for a moment about current discussions regarding whether we should have public school uniforms, or if the terminally ill have the right to choose "managed death," or how much control women should have over their reproductive systems. In fact, U.S. culture encompasses many subcultures that share some of the core set of beliefs with the majority but disagree over parts of the core and over a host of other matters. The same is true of all other regions of the world.

Values and Ways of Knowing

All cultures have ways of establishing, preserving, and passing on notions and knowledge about how things are. All knowledge systems are grounded on a set of values. For example, knowledge based on scientific rules of observation, experimentation, and proof is now widely accepted in many parts of the world. But while many of us living a technological way of life—whether in Asia, Africa, Europe, or the Americas—may think that science-based knowledge is all that is valid, many others would disagree; and it is wise to be aware of this when embarking on the study of places around the world. Many people, including the most eminent of scientists, who grew up in cultures with beliefs based on folk knowledge are convinced that there are multiple ways of knowing and that humans can gain valuable insights from spiritual as well as scientific experience. Even in highly technological societies, medical researchers are now investigating biofeedback, the power of mental processes to influence the physical condition of the human body, a phenomenon long recognized by traditional healers around the world. In some parts of Latin America and Asia, folk healers and practitioners of modern scientific medicine are cooperating in treating patients. As you read about different cultures you will undoubtedly encounter some perspectives that are alien to your way of thinking.

Occasionally one will hear the saying, "After all is said and done, people are all just alike" or "People ultimately all want the same thing." It is a heartwarming sentiment, but it is often wrong. We would be wise, when studying our fellow humans, not to expect, or even want, them to be like us. The fact that people are not all alike is in large part what makes the study of geography interesting. Rather than searching hungrily for similarities with others, it is more fruitful to look for the reasons behind the differences. **Cultural diversity** is one of the mechanisms that make humans so successful and so adaptable. The various cultures serve as a bank of possible strategies for dealing with the continuous social and physical challenges faced by the human species. The reasons for differences in behavior from one culture to the next are usually complex, but they are often related to differences in values. I have chosen an illustrative example that highlights differences in values between modern urban individualistic culture and rural community-oriented culture.

Take the case of clothing for women. In urban places today in many parts of the world, it is often acceptable, even desirable, for a woman to choose clothing that will make her stand out in a crowd, clothing that allows her to make a strong statement about who she is as an individual and how well off she is. On a rainy afternoon recently, I saw a beautiful middle-aged Asian woman walking alone down a fashionable street in Honolulu, Hawaii. She wore a white suit, with white high heels, a matching hat and bag, and over it all an elegant, clear raincoat. Everyone noticed and admired her because she exemplified an ideal Honolulu woman: beautiful, self-assured, with the wherewithall to keep herself outstandingly well dressed. My guess is that she was a businesswoman.

But in the village of her grandmother, whether it be in Japan or Korea or Taiwan or rural Hawaii, people would regard such dress as outrageously immodest and dangerously antisocial and anticommunity. In a rural Asian community her clothes would breach a widespread traditional ethic that no individual should stand out from the group. Furthermore, her costume exposed her body to open assessment and admiration by strangers of both sexes. To villagers, that would be a sign that she lacked modesty. Her style of dress and the fact that she walked alone down a public street unaccompanied by her father or husband might have signaled, in a village context, that she was not a respectable woman, something that seemed not at all the case to those of us who saw her in Honolulu.

So there you are! A particular behavior may be admired when evaluated by one set of values, yet considered despicable when evaluated by another.

If groups have different sets of values and standards, does that mean that there are no overarching human values? No standards? This question increasingly

According to an ancient Hindu verse, one who kills, eats, or permits the slaughter of a cow will "rot in hell for as many years as there are hairs on the body of the cow so slain." [Michele Burgess/Stock, Boston.]

worries geographers, who try to be sensitive both to the particularities of place and to larger issues of human rights. Persons who lean too far in the direction of appreciating difference could be led to the tacit acceptance of inhumane behavior, such as the oppression of minorities and women, or the sexual exploitation (sex tourism) or mutilation (clitorectomy) of female children, or even torture and genocide. Acceptance of difference, and of different ways of knowing, does not mean that in extreme situations we cannot make judgments about the value of certain customs or points of view. Many geographers and others interested in human rights have observed that, while it is important to take a stand against cruelty, deciding when and where to take that stand is rarely easy.

Religion

The religions of the world are formal and informal institutions that embody value systems. Most have roots deep in history and many include a spiritual belief in a higher power (God, Yahweh, Allah) as the underpinning

for the espoused values. These days, religions often focus on reinterpreting age-old values for the modern world. Some, like Islam, Buddhism, and Christianity, proselytize; that is, they try to extend their influence by seeking converts. Others, like Judaism or Hinduism, accept converts only reluctantly.

Religious beliefs are often reflected in the landscape. For example, Hindu religious traditions venerate cows as sacred. Cattle can walk through city streets in India with virtual impunity. In other places, village buildings may be grouped around a mosque or synagogue, and an urban neighborhood organized around a Catholic church. Such settlement patterns demonstrate the central role of religion in community life. In some places, religious rivalry is a major feature of the landscape: spaces may be clearly delineated for the use of one group or another. Northern Ireland serves as one example, with its Protestant and Catholic neighborhoods; Bosnia and Serbia are other examples, with their Muslim and Christian villages.

Religion has also been used as an instrument of colonization, a way to impose a quick change of atti-

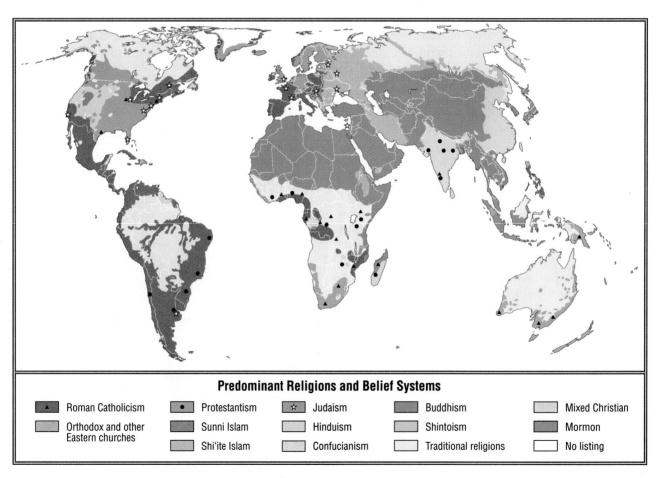

Predominant Religions and Belief Systems

▲ Roman Catholicism	• Protestantism	☆ Judaism	Buddhism	Mixed Christian
Orthodox and other Eastern churches	Sunni Islam	Hinduism	Shintoism	Mormon
Shi'ite Islam	Confucianism	Traditional religions	No listing	

FIGURE 1.5 Major religions around the world. [Adapted from *Oxford Atlas of the World* (New York: Oxford University Press, 1996), p. 27.]

tude on conquered people. Figure 1.5 shows the distribution of the major religious traditions on earth today. Note the distribution of Catholicism in the parts of the Americas colonized by France, Spain, and Portugal. In the seventh and eighth centuries, Islamic peoples spread their religion via trade and conquest across North Africa and throughout Central Asia and eventually into what are now South and Southeast Asia. The distribution of major religions has changed many times over history; and a world map is too small in scale to convey their complexity or their intricacy where two or more religious traditions intersect at the local level. As the world's cultural traditions become more and more mixed and urban life spreads, **secularism,** a way of life informed by values that do not derive from any one religious tradition, is spreading.

Language

Language is one of the most important means for delineating culture regions. The modern global pattern of languages (Figure 1.6) reflects the complexities of

Predominant Languages

Indo-European Family
- Celtic group
- Germanic group (incl. English, German)
- Balto-Slavic group (incl. Russian, Ukrainian)
- Greek
- Albanian
- Iranian group
- Armenian
- Romance group (incl. Spanish, Portuguese, French, Italian)

- Indo-Aryan group (incl. Hindi, Bengali, Urdu, Punjabi, Marathi)

Caucasian Family

Afro-Asiatic Family
- Semitic group (incl. Arabic)
- Kushitic group
- Berber group

Khoisan Family

Niger-Congo Family

Nilo-Saharan Family

Uralic Family

Altaic Family
- Turkic group
- Mongolian group
- Tungus-Manchu group
- Japanese and Korean

Sino-Tibetan Family
- Sinitic (Chinese) languages
- Tibetic-Burmic languages

Tai Family

Austro-Asiatic Family
- Mon-Khmer group
- Munda group
- Vietnamese

Dravidian Family (incl. Telugu, Tamil)

Austronesian Family (incl. Malay, Indonesian)

Indigenous Languages

No Listing

FIGURE 1.6 This map shows the spatial distribution of the world's major language families. Distinct languages (Spanish and Portuguese, for example) are part of a larger language family (Romance languages). [Adapted from *Oxford Atlas of the World* (New York: Oxford University Press, 1996), p. 27.]

both human diffusion and isolation over several hundred thousand years. In reality, the map does not begin to depict the actual complexity of the distribution; there are somewhere between 2500 and 3500 languages spoken on earth today.

Although the pattern of languages has continually shifted over time as people interacted through trade and migration, that pattern was most dramatically changed after the age of exploration and colonization began around 1500. From then on, the languages of European colonists often replaced the languages of the colonized. Hence, we find large patches of English, Spanish, Portuguese, and French in the Americas and English in Australia and New Zealand. Pockets of these and several other European languages are found in Africa, and in Asia as well. In the Americas, the European languages largely replaced Native American languages; but in Africa and Asia, the European tongues coexist with native tongues. Many people became bilingual or trilingual.

Today, with increasing trade and instantaneous global communication, a few languages are coming to dominate, and some languages are becoming extinct because children no longer learn them. The most important languages of international trade (called "lingua francas") are English, Spanish, and French. Of these, English is the dominant, largely because the British colonial empire introduced English as a second language to many culture groups across the globe. Now the need for a common world language in the computer age is pushing the world community toward accepting English as the primary lingua franca.

Special efforts may be required to preserve the language diversity that still exists today. For many people, a particular language serves as a marker of a cultural and geographic affiliation they wish to preserve. For example, the newly independent country of Slovenia (once part of Yugoslavia) jealously guards its language, Slovenian. Slovenia is a small country of just 2 million people, surrounded by more populous countries (Austria, Hungary, Italy, and Croatia), each using another language. It is already so influenced by the neighboring cultures that the Slovenian language is one of only a few distinctive **cultural markers** left. The worry is that Slovenian will be used less and less as the country becomes integrated into Europe, where French, German, and English are the lingua francas. As a result, Slovenians invest a great deal of energy in preserving their language. They have one of the highest rates of book publishing on earth and republish many English and German texts in Slovenian. They even attempt to extend its use beyond the borders of Slovenia by inviting the children and grandchildren of emigrants to return from North America and Western Europe for heavily subsidized summer language courses.

Material Culture and Technology

Each culture group uses particular materials and technology that help to define that culture, its resource base, standard of living, trading patterns, and belief systems. Archaeologists use the link between material artifacts and culture when they discern from an excavated assemblage of potsherds (bits of broken pottery) and other material remains what was going on long ago in a particular place. If you think for a moment about any tangible item within your view, you will probably be able to construct a short essay describing how that item actually and symbolically represents much more about your culture than just its obvious usage would suggest.

Housing provides an example of how material culture relates intimately to a particular culture. The common American suburban ranch house (living room, dining room, kitchen, two baths, three bedrooms, laundry, two-car garage, front lawn and backyard), with its distinctive architecture and landscape, silently reveals a great deal about American family values. It assumes a nuclear family structure (mother, father, children), a type that remains an ideal in American society but now constitutes less than 30 percent of American families. This sort of house is less suited to extended families that include aunts, uncles, and grandparents or to single-parent families; it often has to be modified to accommodate these types of families. The ranch house assumes certain ideas about privacy (separate bedrooms) and gender roles (Mom's special spaces may be the kitchen and laundry). This house speaks of a certain level of affluence and leisure, set apart as it is on a green lawn requiring constant maintenance; and it also symbolizes American ideas about private property and polite neighborliness and mobility. Because we move so often in our quest for a better job and standard of living, yet insist on privately owned homes, a vast system of interchangeable dwellings has evolved across America, supported by an institution: the American domestic real estate market. Families moving across the country can find similar houses with nearly the same floor plan and yard in just about any community.

An astute foreign observer, therefore, could learn a great deal about Americans by simply "reading" the domestic material culture of their homes and surrounding landscapes. The same observer could look at housing in Japan or Mongolia or London or the West Indies and also learn much about the particular culture's notions of proper family structure and gender roles, intimacy rules, aesthetic values, property rights, use of resources, and trading patterns. Such an observer might even learn how modifications of existing housing are reflecting social change.

Issues of Gender

Recently, geographers have begun to pay more attention to gender as a phenomenon in everyday life. In virtually all parts of the world, and beginning at least tens of thousands of years ago, the biological fact of maleness and femaleness has been translated into specific roles for each sex. While the activities assigned to men and women can vary greatly from culture to culture and from era to era, nonetheless there are some rather startling consistencies across the globe and over time. For example, the historian Carol Jones points out that when British colonial officials (all men) encountered Chinese elites (also men), they immediately had much in common regarding their attitudes toward women. Both groups came from societies that trained everyone to see women as inferior to, and destined to serve, men. With rare exceptions this attitude still prevails throughout the globe. Men are usually expected to fulfill public roles. That is, they work outside the home, they are the traveling executives or animal herders or hunters, they fill positions in government and the professions. Women are usually expected to fulfill private roles. They keep house, bear and care for the children and tend the elderly, plant the gardens, prepare the meals, fetch the water and firewood, and in some cultures run the errands. In nearly all cultures women are defined as dependent on men, either their fathers, husbands, or adult sons. Because their activities are focused on the home, women typically have less access to education and paid employment, and hence have less access to wealth and political power. When they do work outside the home, women tend to fill lower paid positions, whether as laborers, service workers, or professionals. Throughout, this book examines how these gender differences are played out in different geographic settings.

Gender is both a biological and a cultural phenomenon (Figure 1.7). There are clear differences between men and women in their reproductive roles; and there are certain physical differences as well. In some physical exercises, average women have more endurance and are capable of more precise movements than average men; and in populations that enjoy overall good health, women tend to outlive men an average of three to five years. On the other hand, on average, men have larger

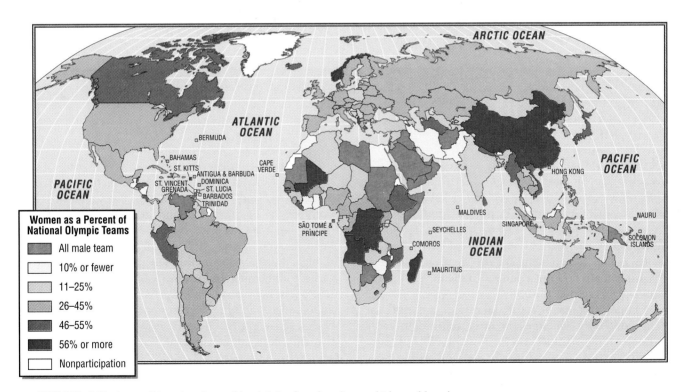

FIGURE 1.7 The traditional notions of femininity, female roles, and ideas of female strength, speed, and endurance are being seriously challenged by Olympic athletes. In the first modern Olympic games in 1896, women were barred from participating. In 1996, women made up one-third of the Olympic competitors, and in some countries, like China, more than half of the athletes were women. [Adapted from Joni Seager, *The State of Women in the World Atlas* (New York: Penguin, 1997), pp. 48–49.]

AT THE GLOBAL SCALE   *Gender*

A well-traveled friend, who has had the chance to observe ideas about women in a variety of places, is fond of saying that despite modernization, in nearly all cultures there are still only three recognized roles for a respectable woman. She may be a daughter in her father's house, a wife in her husband's house, or, if widowed, a mother in the home of her married children. If she occupies other kinds of spaces away from supervision by a male family member, she risks the shame of being identified as a woman of ill repute—a sex worker.

At first, this may seem an outrageously extreme statement because, for women in North America and Europe and perhaps Australia and New Zealand, there seem to be so many other options. Yet further reflection reveals a great deal of truth in the statement even for these women. Even the most liberated women are constantly aware of the negative assessments leveled at them for overstepping the spatial boundaries: for working outside the home; for living alone; for taking up formerly male occupations such as veterinarian, professor, engineer, construction worker, or archaeologist; for choosing not to get married; or for buying a house.

Furthermore, all women have experienced how easy it is to become defined (often by the catcalls of strange males) as a not-quite-respectable woman, or one who is asking for trouble (violence) simply by placing her body in the wrong place at the wrong time, alone on a deserted street corner at midnight, for example.

The limitations imposed on women in most societies are brought into relief by examining what is acceptable for men. Men may go to a variety of locations and live in a variety of places without bringing the weight of social sanction down on them. Furthermore, in most cultures, men are privileged in ways that work directly to the disadvantage of women. For example, male sexuality is accepted, nurtured, and promoted. Males are even thought to need frequent, easily available physical sexual release. And since men are thought superior, the sexual needs of males are expected to be met by females. Most societies thereby prepare the ground for the entry of some females into commercial sex work. Devalued since birth, surplus females in some societies are actually placed by their families in sex work where they are consigned to the lowest and most despised societal rank.

muscles, can lift heavier weights, and can run faster (but not necessarily for longer periods). Women also are somewhat handicapped in physical capacities during pregnancy, gestation, and nursing, and, for some, during menstruation, but their susceptibility to pregnancy is limited to about 30 years. Beyond about age 45, women are no longer subject to the physical limits imposed by reproduction.

These average physical differences are real but they have been amplified in most cultures to carry greater social significance than the biological facts would warrant. The **culturally defined differences** between the sexes have enormous impact on the everyday lives of males and females. Customary ideas about masculinity and femininity, proper gender roles, and sexual orientation are perpetuated from generation to generation within a particular culture group. Perhaps more than any other culturally defined characteristic of humans, there is significant agreement from place to place and over time that gender is important.

The historical and modern global picture is not a pleasant one for women. In nearly every culture, in every region of the world, and seemingly for a great deal of recorded history, women have been and are defined as second class. It is hard to find exceptions, though the intensity of this second-class designation varies considerably. In Europe, Asia, the Americas, and Africa, on tiny islands in the Pacific and the Caribbean, in cold places and hot, in cities and villages, people of both sexes accept the idea that males are more productive and more intelligent than females, despite strong evidence to the contrary. In nearly all cultures, boys are more desired as children because as adults they have greater earning capacity (due in large part to built-in discrimination against females) and will perpetuate the family name (because of patrilineal naming customs). Across the globe, women are more likely to die in infancy, to start work earlier in their young lives than men, to be compensated less for their work, to work longer hours, and to eat less well. Females have less access to medical care and wield less political power in the larger society. When domestic violence occurs, statistics show that females are the victims 96 percent of the time. The actual conditions of women vary, of course, and there are notable exceptions to their low social position. Yet, region to region, the evidence is overwhelming that women have an inferior status.

The obvious question is, "How and why did women become subordinate to men?" Researchers are now pursuing the answers to this question, but serious inquiry began only recently because, oddly enough, the prejudice against women was so pervasive that very few thought the question significant. (See the box "Gender.")

And yet, looking only at women's woes misses half the story. Men also are put at a disadvantage by strict gender expectations that may ride roughshod over personal preferences. Probably for most of human history, young men have borne the lion's share of onerous physical tasks and dangerous undertakings. It is they who have had to leave home at a young age as migrants to distant, low-paying jobs. But note that in recent times young women are migrating at about the same rate as men. It is overwhelmingly young men who have died alone in faraway wars and who have been told to repress feelings and emotions. Men who grow up with negative attitudes toward women have been taught those attitudes by their families (often female kin) and the larger society. This book will repeatedly return to the question of gender in an effort to puzzle out the meaning of this most perplexing cross-cultural phenomenon.

The Issue of Race

Just as ideas about gender affect life in all world regions, people's ideas about race affect human relationships everywhere on earth. As is probably well understood by all readers, all people alive now on earth are members of one species, *Homo sapiens sapiens*. While the physical variety that we see in humans across the globe today may seem to mark obvious and deep differences between groups of people, in fact the popular markers of race (skin color, hair texture, face and body shapes) are not recognized as significant by biologists. There are wide variations within supposed discrete categories, such as a certain skin color or nose type. In addition, many more numerous but invisible biological characteristics, such as blood type and DNA patterns, actually cut across skin color distributions and are shared by what are popularly viewed as different races. In fact, over the last several thousand years there has been such massive gene flow among human populations that no modern group presents a discrete set of characteristics. Biologically speaking, we are all cousins.

In all major cities worldwide, one will encounter a great diversity of people. Here, in Detroit, Michigan, a group of people from several places around the world are being sworn in as U.S. citizens. [Jim West/Impact Visuals.]

19

It is likely that some of the easily visible features of particular human groups evolved to meet an environmental situation, but precise explanations of just how this might work are hard to come by. For example, it appears that darker skin evolved in places close to the equator, where sunlight is most intense. Some think that dark skin may have evolved as a protection against skin cancer. An argument against this idea is that the shades of skin in equatorial zones vary widely from very dark to light brown. More important, skin cancer tends to strike in old age, long after the reproductive years, so light skin would not have inhibited reproduction. Another possible explanation is that sunlight striking the skin helps the body absorb the important nutrient vitamin D; but too much vitamin D can result in improper kidney functioning. Perhaps dark skin protects against too much vitamin D absorption in equatorial zones, while in high latitude zones, where the sun's rays are more dispersed, light skin allows for the absorption of sufficient vitamin D.

While some human body features may have come into being because they helped the bearers survive better, many characteristics do not serve any apparent adaptive purpose. They are probably the accidental result of random chance and ancient inbreeding within isolated groups.

Although it may be comforting to learn that, biologically speaking, race is meaningless, we cannot overlook the fact that in some parts of the world, race (often paired with culture or ethnicity) carries significant political and social import. Race seems to have taken on unprecedented significance over the last 500 years, since the beginning of the so-called age of exploration, which resulted in the colonization of much of the globe by Europeans. Some have suggested that European colonizers adopted **racism**—the negative assessment of unfamiliar, often darker skinned people—to make it easier to justify taking land and resources away from supposedly inferior beings. Still, it would be wrong to suggest that disparaging appraisals and exploitation of others are recent cultural innovations, or exclusively European traits, or necessarily connected to race or ethnicity. Such inhumane behavior has existed a long time in all parts of the globe. For a thousand years and more, the Huns and like-minded Central Asian nomad warriors swept back and forth between Europe in the west and China in the east, killing thousands from horseback. The Mongols raided China, Manchurians raided Mongolia and China, the Japanese raided Korea, Muslims sacked parts of Central Africa. The Moors from North Africa conquered and colonized Spain, Spain conquered Native Americans, the Turks conquered southeastern Europeans, and the ancient Mexicans harassed the Mayans. As will become clear repeatedly in this book, for at least tens of thousands of years, the human animal has committed some

atrocious acts against its own kind, often in the name of race.

We should not infer, however, that human history has been primarily marked by conflict and exploitation. Actually, the opposite is probably true. The human species has been so successful on earth because of a strong inclination toward altruism, willingness to sacrifice one's own well-being for the sake of others. Writ small, this altruism can be found in the sacrifices individuals make to help family, neighbors, and community. Writ large, it includes charitable giving to help anonymous, distant people in need. Interestingly, it is precisely our tendency to altruism that probably causes such deep consternation within us over the relatively infrequent occurrences of inhumane behavior.

PHYSICAL GEOGRAPHY: PERSPECTIVES ON THE EARTH

One of the best ways to improve one's understanding of the world is to view it from new perspectives. Just as one might rotate a puzzle piece to see where it best fits or walk around a sculpture several times to fully appreciate its form, physical geographers use a range of analytical perspectives to assist them in understanding the complexity of earth's physical processes. Here, we will first look at the study of landforms, also known as **geomorphology;** then we examine the long-term study of weather patterns, known as **climatology.**

Landforms: The Sculpting of the Earth

Probably all humans have stopped now and then to marvel at the landforms they see around them and to wonder what awesome forces produced them. The processes that created mountain ranges, continents, or the deep ocean floor are some of the most powerful and slow moving that we are aware of. Originating deep beneath the earth's surface, these forces are capable of moving entire continents, and often take hundreds of millions or even billions of years to do their work. However, many of the features that we notice on a daily basis, such as a beautiful waterfall or dramatic rock formation, are formed by more delicate and, by comparison, more rapid processes that take place on the surface of the earth. All of these forces are studied by geomorphologists, geographers who focus on the processes that constantly shape and reshape the earth's surface.

Plate Tectonics

One of the most all-encompassing theories within physical geography is the theory of **plate tectonics,** which proposes that the earth's surface is composed of large plates that float on top of an underlying layer of molten rock. The plates are of two types. Oceanic plates are dense and relatively thin, and form the floor lying beneath the world's oceans. Continental plates are thicker and less dense, with surfaces that rise above the oceans, forming the earth's continents. Despite their massive size, these plates are slowly moving, driven by forces that are not completely understood.

The movement of the plates creates several important processes at plate boundaries. Plates rubbing together create the catastrophic shaking of the landscape we know as an **earthquake.** Mountain ranges arise mostly from the folding and warping of plates as they press into each other. Volcanoes may arise at certain plate boundaries or at weak points in the middle of a plate, where gases and molten rock, called **magma,** can come to the earth's surface through fissures and holes in the plate. Volcanoes and earthquakes are particularly common around the edges of the Pacific Ocean, an area known as the **Ring of Fire.** In the Philippines, for example, the Mount Pinatubo volcano had a major eruption in 1991 that killed 550 people, ruined the livelihoods of 650,000, and may have influenced global climatic patterns.

Many geomorphologists agree with the **Pangaea hypothesis,** first suggested by the early twentieth-century geophysicist Alfred Wegener. He proposed that all the continents were once joined in a single vast continent about two hundred million years ago. Eventually Pangaea fragmented, the continents drifted apart, and, after millions of years they reached their present positions. The continents are believed to have been separated by the creeping movement of tectonic plates. As shown in Figure 1.8, the continents piled up huge mountains on their leading edges as the plates carrying them collided with other plates. Hence, the theory of plate tectonics accounts for the long linear mountain ranges that run across a number of continents, for example from Alaska to Chile in the Western Hemisphere, and from Southeast Asia to the European Alps in the Eastern Hemisphere. The highest mountain range in the world, the Himalayas of South Asia, was created when what is now India, at the northern end of the Indian-Australian Plate, ground into Eurasia, pushing up huge sections of thick continental crust. The only continent that is without these long, linear mountain ranges is Africa. Often called the plateau continent, Africa is believed to have been at the center of Pangaea and to have moved relatively little since the breakup of that continent.

Landscape Processes

The processes of plate tectonics are **internal processes,** driven by forces that originate deep beneath the

In the United States, people living along the Mississippi River floodplain are at risk nearly every year. When winter snows and early summer rains are particularly heavy, floodwaters rise over the banks and drown fields of soybeans and corn, destroy houses, and damage farm buildings—as happened at Wapello, Iowa, in 1993. People who live along the Yangtze and Yellow rivers in China and the Brahmaputra delta in Bangladesh are at even greater risk; in some years, thousands die as a result of summer floods. [Chris Stewart/Black Star.]

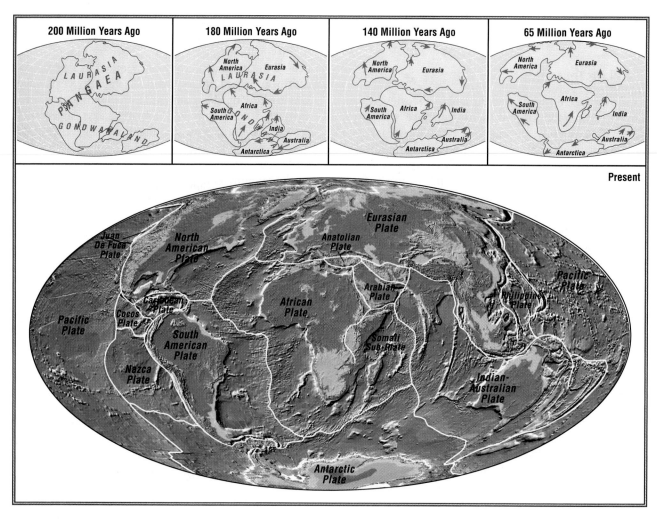

FIGURE 1.8 The breakup of Pangaea and continental drift (top) and the modern boundaries of the major tectonic plates (bottom). [Adapted from (top) *Goode's World Atlas,* 19th ed. (Rand McNally, 1995), p. 8; and (bottom) Frank Press and Raymond Siever, *Understanding Earth, Second Edition* (New York: W. H. Freeman, 1998), p. 509.]

surface of the earth; but the landforms thus created have been further shaped by more familiar **external processes.** No exposed part of the earth's crust is able to withstand the unceasing onslaught of sun, wind, rain, snow, and ice, much less the effects of earth's innumerable life-forms. Rock may be broken down into smaller pieces through the process of **weathering.** Freezing water or plant roots may get into cracks and expand, driving the rock pieces apart; iron or other minerals may dissolve in water or break down due to exposure to oxygen in the air. **Mass wasting** is the movement of loosened rock and soil down a slope due to gravity, in the form of rockfalls, landslides, and mud flows. In the process of **erosion,** fragmented rock and soil are moved over distance by the action of wind and moving water;

when the velocity of the wind or water slows, particles settle out in the process called **deposition.**

In the case of rivers, deposition can raise the riverbed, causing the water to overflow the banks and washing huge quantities of silt onto the surrounding land. With this happening repeatedly over time, the land around a river will rise and become flatter as small valleys between hills are filled in by silt, creating what is called a **floodplain.** Where rivers meet the sea, floodplains often fan out roughly in the shape of a triangle, creating a **delta.** Because deltas are by nature on flat land and are continually built up with more sediment, the course of the water through the delta may change from year to year, making it a difficult and unpredictable place to inhabit or use.

Climate

The processes associated with climate are much more rapid than the excruciatingly slow processes that shape landforms. Indeed weather, which is the short-term expression of climate, can change in a matter of minutes. Climate is the more long term balance of temperature and precipitation that keeps weather patterns fairly consistent year after year. By this definition, the last major global change of climate took place 15,000 years ago when the glaciers of the last ice age began to melt.

Energy from the sun gives the earth a temperature range hospitable to life. The atmosphere and oceans absorb huge amounts of solar energy, insulating the earth from the deep cold of space. Solar energy is also the engine of climate, as differences in the amount of energy absorbed at different points on the earth's surface are responsible for the wide range in temperatures that we experience when traveling north or south from the equator. The most intense, direct sunlight falls in a broad band stretching about 30° north and south of the equator. Within this band occur the highest average temperatures on earth. Moving away from the equator, sunlight becomes less intense, and average temperatures drop.

Temperature and Air Pressure

Temperature and air pressure interact continuously in complex patterns that produce the wind and weather patterns we all experience daily. **Air pressure** can best be understood by thinking of air as existing in a particular unit of space, for example a cubic foot. Air pressure refers to the amount of force exerted by the molecules in that square foot on the air outside it. To understand the relationship between temperature and air pressure, we need to know two things:

1. Warm temperatures are associated with low air pressure.

2. Cool temperatures are associated with higher air pressure.

If you have ever been to the beach on a hot day, you may have noticed a cool breeze blowing in off the water. The breeze is explained by the fact that air tends to move from areas of high pressure to areas of low pressure. On a hot day, the air over land heats up, expands, and rises, creating an area of low air pressure. Water takes much longer to heat up than land does, so air over an adjacent body of water will be cooler and higher in pressure than air over land. Air in the high pressure area over the water will move toward the low pressure area over the land, thus creating the cool sea breeze. Often at night the breeze reverses its direction, blowing from the now cooling land onto the water. The shift happens because water also takes a lot longer to cool down than does land, so at night the air over land quickly becomes the cooler of the air masses. The now cooler, denser air over the land will flow toward the warmer, less dense air over the water.

This kind of air movement has a continuous and important influence on global weather patterns. Over the course of a year, continents will heat up and cool off much more rapidly than will the oceans that surround them. Hence, wind tends to blow in to the land from the oceans during the summer, and to the ocean from the land during the winter. It is almost as if the continents were breathing once a year, inhaling in summer and exhaling in winter. These yearly shifts in pressure can be seen in maps of air pressure (Figure 1.9) that compare the months of January and July. The huge size of the Eurasian continent gives it the earth's most extreme yearly change in temperature and air pressure.

Precipitation

Perhaps the most tangible way we experience changes in temperature, air pressure, and wind direction is through the falling of rain or snow. Although the precise workings of precipitation are not fully understood, it happens primarily because warm air holds more moisture than does cool air. When air is warm, water vapor is dissolved in it in the form of tiny, invisible droplets. When air that has absorbed water vapor is pushed up to a higher altitude, the lower temperatures reduce the air's ability to hold moisture. The water vapor condenses into larger, visible droplets, and clouds form. Precipitation comes when the cooling droplets condense into drops large enough to fall as rain or snow.

Several conditions that encourage cloud-laden air to rise in altitude influence the pattern of precipitation observed around the globe (see Figure 1.11). A rain belt around the equator is primarily the result of warm tropical air rising and pushing clouds up to the point where they will release moisture. This belt of damp equatorial air becomes the source of moisture for the huge downpours of the Asian summer **monsoon.** During the northern summer, the Eurasian continental landmass heats up, and the "inhaling" effect of this heating draws the warm, moist air around the equator north onto the land. In the higher temperatures over land, the moisture-laden clouds continue to rise until they reach cooler zones where water vapor condenses and the clouds release their burden of moisture. The tremendous downpours that result affect much of coastal and interior East Asia, and virtually all of Southeast and South Asia (see Figure 8.3).

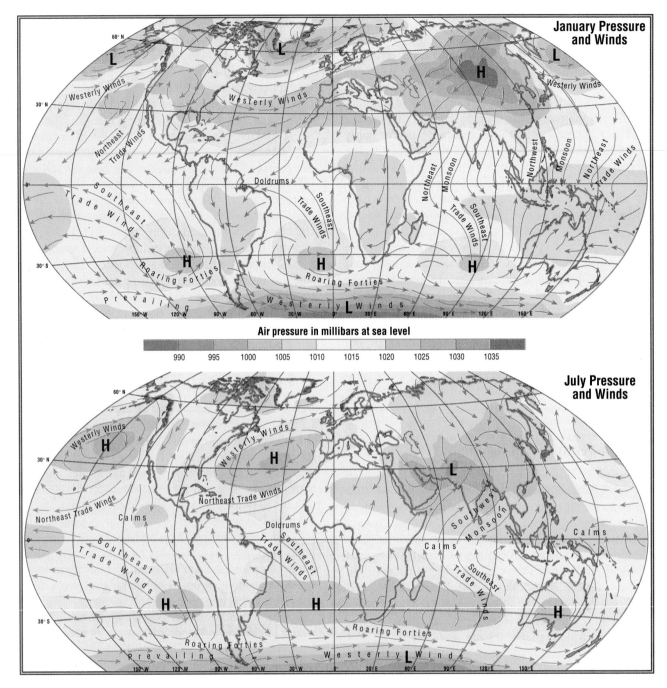

FIGURE 1.9 Mean surface pressure, January and July. [Adapted from *Goode's World Atlas,* 19th ed. (Rand McNally, 1995), pp. 14–15.]

Precipitation also occurs when moisture bearing air is forced to rise over mountain ranges, where the air cools and the moisture condenses into rainfall. This process, known as **orographic rainfall,** is most common where wind blows moist air from over the ocean onto the land and up the side of a coastal mountain range (Figure 1.10). The climate of the slopes on the side facing the wind is wet, while the climate on the other side of the range may be quite dry. The dry side is called the **rain shadow,** and it may extend for hundreds of miles across the interiors of continents. North America's northern Pacific coast, South America's far southern Pacific coast, the mountains of western India, the Himalayas of Eurasia, and the mountains of eastern Australia are among many examples.

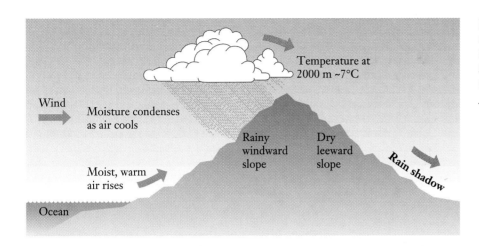

FIGURE 1.10 Orographic rainfall. [Adapted from Frank Press and Raymond Siever, *Understanding Earth, Second Edition* (New York: W. H. Freeman, 1998), p. 291.]

Much of the moisture that falls on North America and Eurasia is **frontal precipitation,** caused by the interaction of large air masses of different temperatures. These air masses develop when air stays over a particular area long enough for a large portion to take on the temperature of the land or sea underneath it. Often when we listen to a weather forecast we hear about warm fronts or cold fronts (Figure 1.12). A front is the area where warm and cold air masses come in contact, and it is always named after the air mass whose leading edge is moving into an area. At a front, the warm air tends to rise up over the cold air, carrying its clouds to a higher altitude, and rain or snow may follow. This kind of precipitation is common across North America and northern Eurasia, and also in the Antarctic Ocean (see Figure 1.12).

Climate Regions

Geographers have several systems for classifying the world's climates that are based largely on the patterns of temperature and precipitation just examined. This

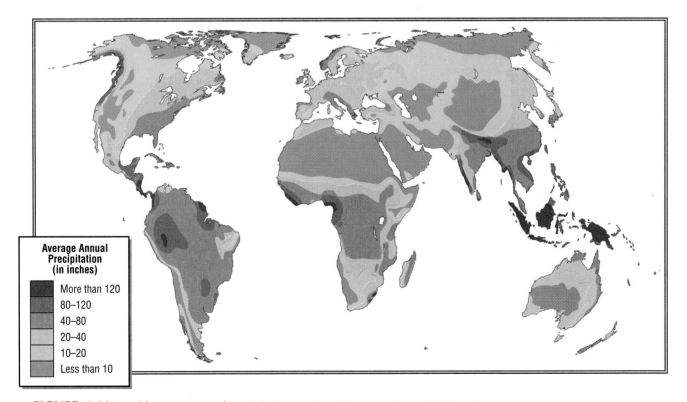

FIGURE 1.11 World average annual precipitation. [Adapted from *Goode's World Atlas,* 19th ed. (Rand McNally, 1995), pp. 16–17.]

FIGURE 1.12 Cold fronts and warm fronts. Since warm air usually overlies colder air along fronts, a cold front (a) slopes backward and a warm front (b) slopes forward.

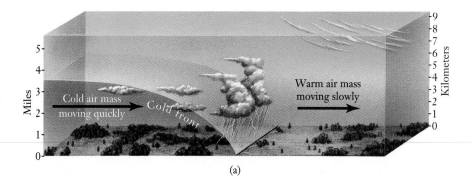

(a)

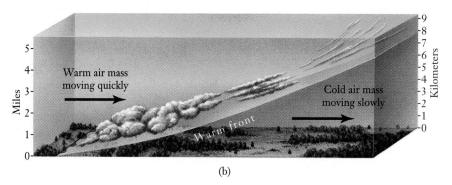

(b)

book uses a modification of the widely known Koppen classification system, which divides the world into several types of climate regions labeled A, B, C, D, and E (Figure 1.13; see pages 28–29). As we look at each of the regions and read the climate descriptions, the importance of climate to vegetation becomes evident. Keep in mind that the sharp boundaries on the map are in reality much more gradual transitions.

THE ENVIRONMENT

The litany of contemporary environmental horrors is now familiar even to grade-school children: ozone depletion, global warming, acid rain, chemical pollution of groundwater, the startling and escalating extinction of animal and plant species, tropical deforestation, oil and chemical spills, and nuclear accidents. In daily newspapers we read how many acres of tropical trees are felled between the time of our morning coffee and our evening meal (over 1500 acres on an average day). We are told how many of us will be likely to develop skin cancer in the coming decades as a result of the depletion of the ozone layer, and how many of us will die from it (more than 6500 a year in the United States alone).

Addressing these and other environmental problems may be the greatest challenge our species has yet faced. Certainly, there are many strategies worth trying, but all of them, even those based on high technology, will require us to change our ways and especially our habits of mass consumption of resources.

Sustainable Development

The depletion of the ozone layer and environmental damage in general are often the unwanted side effects of industrialization, mechanized agriculture, urbanization, and other forms of **economic development.** A concern is that by destroying resources (as in deforestation) or poisoning them (as in pollution of water and air supplies) we may be depriving future generations of the resources they need. Many look to the concept of sustainable development for a solution.

Sustainable development is often defined as the effort to improve present standards of living in ways that will not jeopardize those of future generations. Many think there is great promise in repairing environmental damage already done while at the same time allowing development to continue, especially for the vast majority of earth's people who have been left behind in poverty. Nevertheless, sustainable development is still a somewhat controversial concept that no country has yet translated into policy. A clearer picture of what practices are and are not sustainable is emerging, however. This section gives a broad overview of sustainability as it relates to agriculture, urbanization, water, energy use, and gender.

Sustainable Agriculture

Sustainable agriculture is farming that meets the demand for food and fiber (cotton, jute) without poisoning the environment or using up water and soil resources. Just how sustainable the world's agricultural systems are is unclear, but there is a global pattern of soil degradation (Figure 1.14). Some of the most productive fields on earth, those in the American Midwest, are losing tons of soil, mostly due to mechanized plowing and mass production cultivation methods. In many fields, streams, rivers, and other areas, the overapplication of fertilizers, pesticides, and herbicides is causing massive die-offs of birds, insect pollinators, fish, and other life-forms. The cheapest and most popular methods used to irrigate dry areas have turned the soil salty and made it less fertile. Irrigation diverts water from rivers and streams, often causing them to shrink or even dry up completely. In addition, the common practice of pumping water from natural underground reservoirs removes the water faster than it is replaced.

Some think that we are about to reach the limit of our productive capacity as populations boom and environmental problems proliferate. Others say that technology promises to make present lands more productive and unused lands useful. So far, our record of developing and applying new agricultural technologies is mixed (Figure 1.15). Certain areas have experienced spectacular increases in production. But as farming expands into fragile lands in order to feed growing populations, cultivation poses environmental risks leading to deforestation, erosion, drought, or soil infertility.

The definition of sustainable agriculture recognizes that food production must meet the needs of the planet's billions of inhabitants. Today, about one-fifth of humanity subsists on a diet too low in total calories and vital nutrients to sustain adequate health and normal physical and mental development. The problem, so far, is not that the world's agricultural systems cannot produce enough, but rather that food often does not get to hungry people. In the wealthy countries of the world, where surpluses in basic foods such as grain have been regular for years, land has been purposely taken out of production to encourage a rise in prices. When rich countries do produce beyond their needs, and send free food to areas suffering famine, local farmers are often forced out of business because the markets where they previously sold their produce are flooded with free food. Many experts now agree that

This starving family is from the Sudan, where civil war in the 1990s has caused the breakdown of food production and distribution systems. Some people have been forced out of their homelands and are now refugees. Food historian E. N. Anderson, geographer Carl Sauer, and anthropologist Marshall Sahlins have all observed that famine and desperate poverty are usually the result of political not natural disasters. [Chris Cox/FSP/Gamma-Liaison.]

the most promising solution to hunger seems to be for individual countries to develop their own sustainable plans for agricultural development. The successes and failures that different countries have encountered will be examined further in the regional chapters. In general, it is safe to say that truly sustainable agricultural solutions have been few and far between.

Sustainability and Urbanization

The world is fast becoming urbanized. In 1700, less than 10 percent of the world's total population, about 7 million people, lived in cities. Only five of those cities had populations as high as several hundred thousand people. By 1900, 43 cities had populations of more than 500,000; several of these had more than 1 million. In 1995, there were more than 400 cities of over 1 million and more than 10 cities with 10 million. By 1998, according to the Population Reference Bureau, 43 percent of the world's population lived in cities.

Timothy Weiskel, of Harvard University's Pacific Rim Research Center, points out that cities, with their dense populations and increasingly extensive modification of the earth's surface, represent a major biogeophysical transformation of the earth. Archaeological evidence has shown that even in prehistoric

Types of Climate Regions

Tropical Humid Climates (A). These climates occupy a wide band within 15° to 20° on either side of the equator. Here we have simplified the variations to just two distinct **A** climates: tropical wet and wet/dry.

In the **tropical wet climate,** rain falls predictably every afternoon and usually just before dawn. The natural vegetation is the tropical rain forest, a broad-leafed evergreen forest consisting of hundreds of species of trees that form a several-layered canopy above the soil.

The **wet/dry tropical** climate, also called **tropical monsoon,** experiences a wider range of temperatures than the tropical wet climate, and may actually receive more total rainfall, but rain comes seasonally and in great downpours, during the heat of the summer. The tropical forest in these regions is less vigorous and may show signs of having to survive long dry periods that occur unpredictably.

Arid (Desert) and Semiarid (Steppe) Climates (B). Arid and semiarid climates (**B** climates) may be either desert or steppe. **Deserts** generally receive very little rainfall, and most of that comes in downpours that are extremely rare and unreliable, but are capable of bringing a brief, beautiful flourishing of desert life. Usually, deserts have little vegetation and have almost no cloud cover, which leads to huge swings in temperature between day and night. Life is a battle for both plants and animals, since they must be able to survive heat exhaustion during the day and freezing at night. **Steppes** are similar to deserts in climate, but more moderate, usually receiving about 10 inches more rain a year and being covered with grass.

Arid and semiarid climates are found in two major locations: the subtropics (meaning slightly poleward from the tropics) and the midlatitudes. Subtropical deserts and steppes are found between 20° and 30° north and south latitude, where high-pressure air descends in a belt around the planet. They are generally much warmer than the midlatitudinal deserts and steppes, which are found further toward the poles in the interiors of continents, often in the rain shadows of high mountains. While soils are generally thin and unproductive in most deserts and steppes, the midlatitude steppes can have some of the thickest and richest soil in the world. The slightly colder temperatures in these steppes keep rates of decay down and hence encourage the accumulation of organic matter in the soil over time. The Great Plains of North America are an example of steppe lands with rich soils.

Temperate Climates (C). In this book we distinguish between just three **temperate climates.**

Midlatitude C climates, like those in the southeast United States and China, are moist all year and have short, mild winters and long, hot summers. A variant of the midlatitude C climate is the **marine west coast climate,** like that of western Europe, noted for monotonous, drizzling rain.

Subtropical C climates differ from midlatitude C climates in that winters are dry.

Mediterranean C climates have moderate temperatures but are dry in summer and wet in winter. Plants do not get moisture when temperature and evaporation rates are highest, so the plant species that live in this zone tend to be **xerophytic,** that is, adapted to dry conditions: scrubby, shiny leaves, capable of storing moisture. California, Portugal,

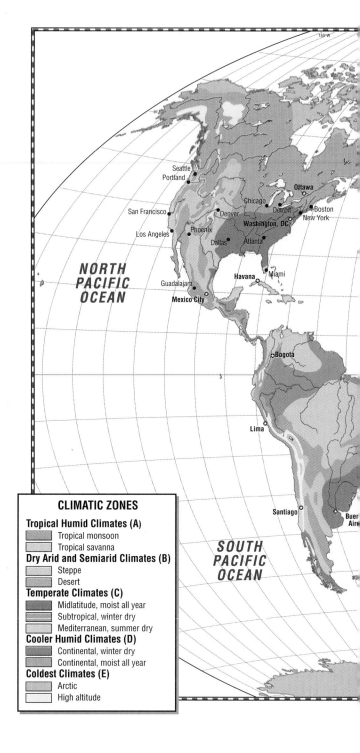

CLIMATIC ZONES

Tropical Humid Climates (A)
- Tropical monsoon
- Tropical savanna

Dry Arid and Semiarid Climates (B)
- Steppe
- Desert

Temperate Climates (C)
- Midlatitude, moist all year
- Subtropical, winter dry
- Mediterranean, summer dry

Cooler Humid Climates (D)
- Continental, winter dry
- Continental, moist all year

Coldest Climates (E)
- Arctic
- High altitude

northwest Africa, southern Italy, Greece, and Turkey are examples of places with this climate type.

Cool Humid Climates (D). Stretching across the broad interiors of Eurasia and North America, cool humid climates experience extreme continental heating and cooling. One type of cool humid climate experiences a short, hot summer; and the other, a cool summer. As one moves north, these climates have increasingly short and mild summers and long and cold winters. In the more southern reaches of cool humid climates, where midsummer can be very hot, the natural vegetation is

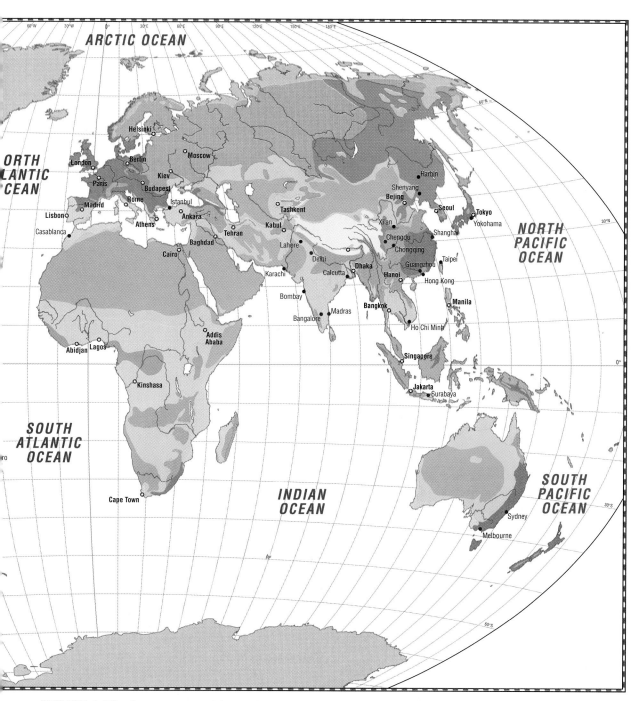

FIGURE 1.13 Climate regions of the world.

broad-leafed deciduous and evergreen forests. Here the soil is deep and rich, due to lower temperatures that inhibit decay, as in the midlatitude steppe. In the more northern areas during at least six months of the year, vast needle-leafed evergreen forests called taiga stretch across the cold interior. Soils here can be deep, but not quite as rich as they are further south; growing seasons are so short that cultivation is minimal.

Arctic and High-Altitude Climates (E). These climates **(E)** are by far the coldest and also some of the driest.

Though moisture is present, there is little evaporation because of low temperatures. The climate is often called tundra, after the low-lying vegetation that covers the ground; the dwarfed vegetation is a response to the 11 to 7 months of below freezing temperatures. What little precipitation there is usually comes during the warmer months, and even this may fall as snow. The high-altitude version of the E climate is found in the Rocky and Himalaya mountains and in a thin strip down the high Andes in South America.

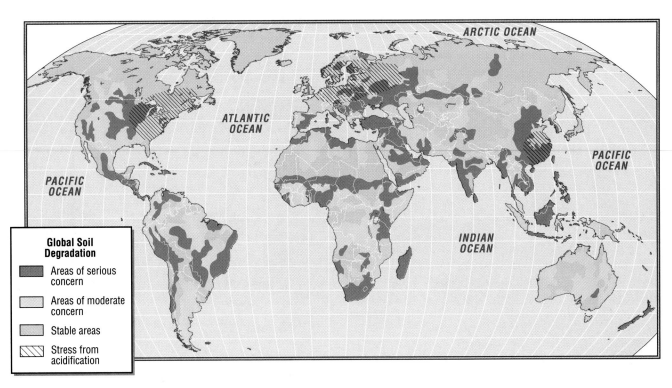

FIGURE 1.14 Global soil degradation. [Adapted from John L. Allen, *Student Atlas of Environmental Issues* (Dushkin/McGraw-Hill, 1997), p. 109.]

times, urban settlement was associated with overcrowding, water contamination, outbreaks of disease, and malnutrition. In supplying building materials, food, and fuel to the cities, the surrounding areas, or **hinterland,** experienced deforestation, soil erosion, water depletion, and loss of natural habitat for both plants and animals.

The archaeological record of urban life echoes the environmental record of many of today's cities.

Although many of us enjoy city life, it is the relatively idyllic urban existence of a modern wealthy city that we cherish. Yet most urban dwellers today cope with far more difficult realities. Many cities have been built with insufficient attention to providing pure water for human use and to the sanitary processing of wastewater. In rapidly growing cities in Asia, Africa, and Latin America, a majority of the population does not have access to working toilets, and desperate citizens

FIGURE 1.15 Change in food production between 1965 and 1990, by region. [Adapted from John Bongaarts, Can the growing human population feed Itself? in *Global Issues, 1995–96* (Guilford, CT: Dushkin/Brown & Benchmark, 1995), p. 119.]

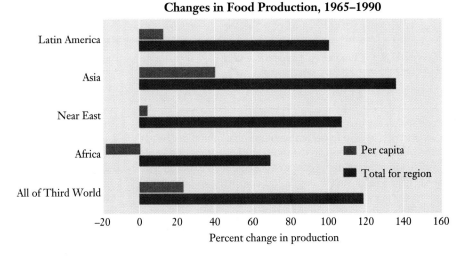

relieve themselves on city streets. Sewage and other wastewater is often simply pumped into a nearby river, swamp, or ocean, even from modern high-rise structures and luxury hotels. Increasingly, people must boil all the water they use, even for bathing, or must buy drinking water that has been purified. The poorest urban inhabitants (often a majority) lack money to buy water or the fuel to boil it. They simply get sick, and one result is that many babies and young children die before the age of five. Retrofitting cities of several million inhabitants with adequate wastewater collection and purifying systems is so costly that few can consider it, yet there are no new affordable sources of clean water for these cities.

Many cities also have inadequate electricity service, forcing households to cook with highly polluting fuels such as wood, coal, or animal dung. These fuels also increase the risk of fire, especially in the massive self-built shantytowns surrounding the urban core, where most urban residents in Africa, Asia, and Middle and South America live. Technological and other advances will no doubt help alleviate the problems, but for the time being, in the world's cities, we are falling far short of the sustainable development ideal of meeting the needs of the present without compromising the ability of future generations to meet their own needs.

Resource Consumption

One of the most interesting revelations that comes from geographic analysis of patterns of population and use of resources is that as people move from agricultural work to industry or service sector jobs, they begin to use more resources and to use them more rapidly. Moreover, they draw the resources they use from a wider and wider area. Water once fetched from wells may now be piped in from hundreds of miles away. Clothing once made laboriously by hand at home is now purchased from manufacturers half a world away. Consumers have access to a variety of products at lower prices than they would pay for locally produced items. But there is a downside. When water is piped into the house or yard, the very convenience encourages waste. When clothes can be purchased at low prices, closets become crowded. There is a tendency to overconsume. In fact, resource use has become so skewed toward the affluent with cash to pay that in any given year the relatively rich minority on earth (as little as 20 percent of the world's population) consumes more than 80 percent of the resources. Hence, the poorest 80 percent of the population use only the remaining 20 percent of the resources.

The United States and other developed countries, together accounting for just 22 percent of the world's

In sections of Calcutta, India, the only available public water comes from small pipes located at curbsides. Here a woman (left center) fills buckets for washing dishes and clothes from a public spigot (under her left hand). [Dilip Mehta, Contact/The Stock Market.]

population, produce 90 percent of the hazardous waste. They also consume well over 50 percent of the world's fossil fuel, metal, and paper resources. The economist E. F. Schumacher, in his book *Small Is Beautiful* (1973), has commented that "the problem passengers on spaceship Earth are the first class passengers." Schumacher's point is an important one, but it does not recognize the complexity of the situation. Population pressure and rising expectations among the poor in places like India, China, and Southeast Asia also result in serious environmental damage. Governments across the globe can and do make startlingly unwise environmental decisions.

Global Warming

One subject seemingly on everyone's mind these days is the theory of **global warming**, which proposes that the earth's climate is becoming warmer as atmospheric levels of carbon dioxide and other gases drastically increase. These gases are collectively known as "greenhouse gases" because their presence allows large amounts of heat to be trapped in the earth's

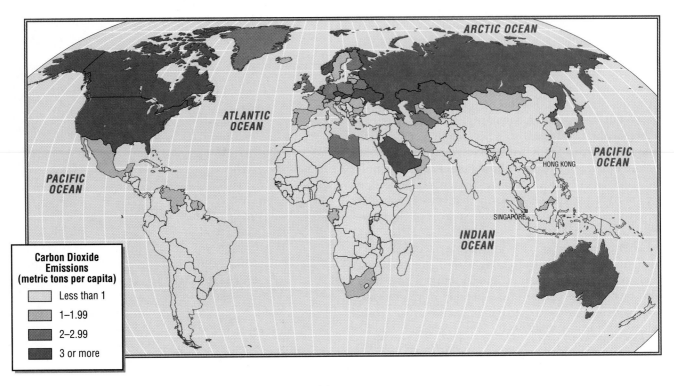

FIGURE 1.16 Carbon dioxide emissions around the world. [Adapted from *Scientific American,* May 1996, p. 24.]

atmosphere in much the same way that heat is trapped in a greenhouse. Greenhouse gases are released in the burning of coal, oil, and other fossil fuels; they have been on the increase in the last several hundred years since large amounts of fossil fuels began to be burnt following the industrial revolution.

Climatologists and other scientists have already started to document the reality of global warming, but the specific ways in which it will affect the planet are unclear. Some scientists forecast the melting of the polar icecaps. This process could displace hundreds of millions of people residing in coastal areas that would be submerged by rising sea levels. Other scientists forecast a shift of warmer climate zones north in the Northern Hemisphere and south in the Southern Hemisphere. Such a shift might displace huge numbers of people, as the zones where crops can grow would change dramatically. Plant and animal species that could not adapt to the change rapidly enough might disappear in a mass extinction. Another effect of global warming could be more chaotic and severe weather.

Most of the responsibility for present levels of greenhouse gas emissions rests on the shoulders of the industrialized nations, as Figure 1.16 shows. While industrialized countries have tentatively agreed to reduce their emissions slightly below 1990 levels before the first decade of the twenty-first century, there are few provisions for enforcement. Furthermore, many industries, especially oil and gas, have resisted the reductions, arguing that global warming is unproved. Meanwhile, many environmentalists see the currently agreed upon reductions as far too low. They see a need for stepped-up energy conservation and for more research into alternatives such as solar, wind, and geothermal energy. The problem is compounded by the fact that as industrialization and urbanization spread in countries like India and China, the potential is great for much higher levels of greenhouse emissions. In these countries, the benefits of industrialization have so far taken precedence over environmental concerns.

POPULATION PATTERNS

Demography, the study of population patterns and changes, is an important part of geographic analysis. Since geographers are concerned with the interaction between people and their environments, it is essential to know how many people there are on earth, how fast their numbers are growing, where they are located, and what their patterns of migration and consumption are.

Global Patterns of Population Growth

The pattern of human population growth has been exponential. Exponential growth starts out slowly, but after a few doublings quickly rises to enormous numbers. It took roughly 1 million years, or 10,000 generations, for human population to reach 2 billion, which happened in about 1945. By 1995, in just 50 years, the world's population more than doubled to 5.5 billion. Even if all growth stopped and all couples agreed to have only two children, population would continue to grow to 8 billion before zero growth set in. Growth would continue for a while because so many of the earth's people are now so young, on average, that a majority are just approaching the reproductive years. Often the exponential pattern of human population growth is depicted with what is called the **J curve** (Figure 1.17), even though the pattern of recent rapid growth only vaguely resembles the stem of a J.

The explanation for why human growth remained slow for so long and then rapidly increased lies not only in exponential mathematics but also in changing relationships between humans and the environment. For a million years or more, the perils of fluctuating food availability, natural hazards, and disease kept human death rates high. The young were especially likely to die, and thus many did not live to reproduce. The most dramatic change in growth rates came with the technological, industrial, and scientific revolutions, beginning in different parts of the world at different times over the last thousand years or so. These revolutions aided humans to exploit land and resources and advanced their ability to treat disease. Human life expectancy increased dramatically, and more and more people lived long enough to reproduce successfully, often many times over. Not surprisingly, the statistics show that the astonishing upsurge in human population began about A.D. 1500.

Today, human population is growing in virtually all parts of the world, more rapidly in some than others, and the general upward trend of the J curve persists. Nevertheless, there are indications that the rate of growth is slowing globally. In 1993, the world growth rate was 1.7 percent, meaning that there were 17 births per 1000 people. In 1998, the world growth rate had decreased to 1.5 percent, or 15 births per 1000, but even this decreased rate still results in a doubling time of just 46 years. If present trends continue, world population may level off at somewhat less than 11 billion before 2050. Eleven billion people will tax the earth's resources beyond imagining, especially if most have lifestyles based on mass consumption, as is increasingly the case.

Local Variation in Density and Growth

There are more than 6 billion people on earth today. If evenly distributed across the land surface, they would produce an **average population density** of about 95 people per square mile (38 per square kilometer). As you can see from the population density map (Figure 1.18), people are not evenly distributed across the face of the earth. Certain general statements can be made

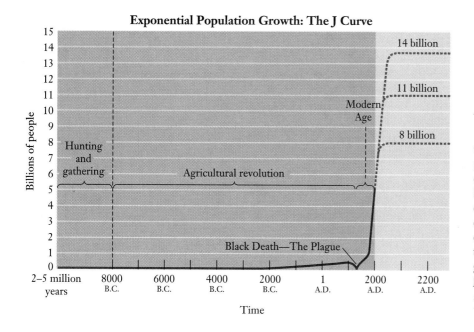

FIGURE 1.17 The J curve depicts the exponential growth of human population. Based on the doubling effect, the curve is deceptive because it starts out slowly, but after only a few doublings rises to enormous numbers. This is because each doubling amounts to more than the total of all previous growth. [Adapted from G. Tyler Miller, Jr., *Living in the Environment, Eighth Edition* (Belmont, CA: Wadsworth, 1994), p. 4.]

33

about the distribution. First, nearly 90 percent of all people live north of the equator and most of them live between 20° and 60° north latitude. Even within that limited territory people are concentrated on about 20 percent of the available land. For the most part, people choose to live in lowland regions (nearly 80 percent live below 1650 feet [500 meters]), in zones that have climates warm and wet enough to support agriculture. Many people live along rivers and most people live fairly close to the sea, within about 300 miles (500 kilometers); but mountainous or dry coastal zones are avoided, as are wetlands. In a very general way, people are located where resources are available; they are thinly settled where resources are in short supply. Few people live in places that are very dry or wet, or very cold or hot, or have high mountains, because there are insufficient means to sustain life.

Beyond these extremes, the wealth of the physical environment is not a sufficient explanation for population density. Many places with meager resources contain a great many people because the resources to support them can be garnered from far and near. If people have the means to pay for them, food, water, and clothing, raw materials for building and manufacturing and for producing electricity, and other material support can all be imported. An extreme example is Macao, the Portuguese trading enclave in South China. The population density in Macao is the highest on earth: 57,400 per square mile (22,000 per square kilometer). Life there is sustained not by local physical resources but by trading connections enhanced by Macao's location on the edge of the huge and populous Chinese mainland. For many centuries, cities around the world have relied on distant resources, and this is increasingly true for more and more of the world's people no matter where they live.

Just as there is no easy correlation between population density and richness of resources, there is also no easy correlation between density and poverty or wealth. Some rather densely occupied places, like parts of Europe or Japan, are very wealthy. Other densely populated places, like parts of India or Bangladesh, are desperately poor. To explain density patterns today, we must look to cultural, social, and economic factors; such events as past experiences with colonialism; and present circumstances that attract migrants to some places and cause them to flee others.

Usually, the figure most important to understanding population growth in a region is the **rate of natural increase,** the relationship between the numbers being born (birth rates) and the numbers dying (death rates) in a given population, without regard for the effects of migration. Generally speaking, a young population will grow more rapidly than an older population because a larger proportion of the population is in their reproductive years. The rate of natural increase is

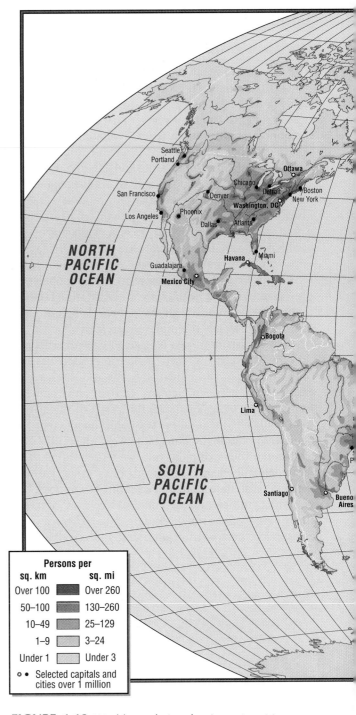

FIGURE 1.18 World population density. [Adapted from *Hammond Citation World Atlas,* 1966.]

usually expressed as a percentage. Take the example of Austria in Europe, which has 8,100,000 people. The birth rate is 11 per 1000 people and the death rate is 10 per 1000 people. The rate of natural increase is 1 per 1000 (11 − 10 = 1), or 0.1 percent per year. Just 17

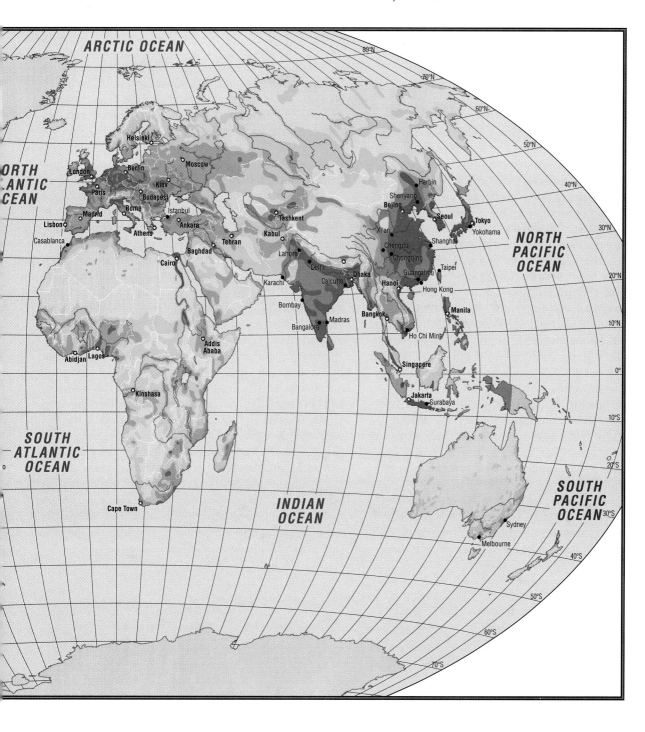

percent of Austrians are under 15 years of age and 15 percent are over 65 years of age. Austria is growing very slowly and at its current rate will take 866 years to double its population. For the sake of comparison, consider Côte d'Ivoire in West Africa, which has 14,700,000 people. The birth rate is 50 per 1000 and the death rate is 15 per 1000. The growth rate is thus 35 per 1000 (50 − 15 = 35), or 3.5 percent. At this rate, Côte d'Ivoire will double its population in just 20 years. As you might expect, the population of Côte d'Ivoire is very young: 47 percent are under 15 years of age and just 2 percent are over 65.

Age and Gender Structures

The **age distribution,** also known as **age structure,** of a population is the proportion of the total population in each age group; the **gender structure** is the proportion of males and females in each age group. The age and gender structures point to social conditions of the past and present, and knowing these structures helps us predict population trends of the future.

The population pyramid is a useful device for depicting and comparing the age and gender structures. Careful study of the pyramids of places like Austria and Côte d'Ivoire (Figure 1.19) reveals the age distribution of the population. As we have noted, most people in Côte d'Ivoire are very young, so they are clustered at the bottom of the pyramid, in the age categories 0 through 15. The pyramid tapers off quickly as it rises upward in age, reflecting the fact that in Côte d'Ivoire most people die before they reach old age.

On the other hand, Austria's "pyramid" is not really a pyramid in form, but has an irregular shape indicating periods when birth rates were lower than at other times. The narrow base indicates that there are now fewer people in the youngest category than in young adulthood or middle age. And the youngest (0–4) are decidedly outnumbered by those in the categories over 70! This diagram illustrates that over the last 80 years, Austria has undergone a number of experiences that have alternately encouraged and discouraged births:

deaths among young adults (especially men) during World War II account for the underrepresentation of men in the 65 and older group. Higher birth rates after the end of World War II account for the bulge in the 30 to 49 range. Recently, Austrians have been choosing to have one child or none, and the low birth rate accounts for the small number in the 0–4 range.

Population pyramids also reveal subtle gender differences within populations. Look closely at the right (female) and left (male) halves of the pyramids in Figure 1.19. Notice that the sexes are not evenly balanced on either side of the line. In the Austrian pyramid, near the top, there are more women than men, reflecting the deaths among male soldiers in World War II and the fact that in wealthy countries women tend to live about five years longer than men. The gender imbalances in the Côte d'Ivoire pyramid occur at much younger ages and are less easy to explain. Because gender-based research is so new, explanations for the imbalances are only now being developed.

One possible explanation is that throughout life males and females may be treated differently (see the box "Missing Females in Population Figures" and Figure 1.20). In societies afflicted by poverty, female babies are sometimes fed less than boys and may die in early childhood more often than male babies. Poor women frequently do not receive needed nutrition and medical care during pregnancy, and hence more tend to die as a result of childbirth. In some places, rules requiring female seclusion from males make professional health care less accessible. All of these factors are probably affecting the survival rates of women and girls in Côte d'Ivoire.

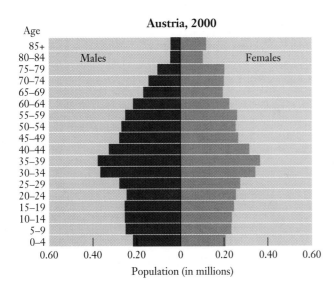

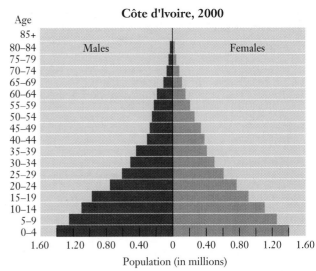

FIGURE 1.19 Population pyramids for Austria and Côte d'Ivoire. [Adapted from U.S. Census Bureau, International Data Base, at http://www.census.gov/cgi-bin/ipc/idbpyrs.pl.]

AT THE GLOBAL SCALE   *Missing Females in Population Statistics*

There is now considerable evidence that between 60 million and 100 million females are missing from the world population. The normal ratio of females to males at birth is about 100 to 105. Boy babies are somewhat weaker than girls, so within the first five years of life the ratio evens out naturally. However, since 1900, the ratio of females to males has been declining; in 1990, it was about 97.6 to 105. Just why the ratio of females to males appears to have started to decline around 1900 is not yet satisfactorily explained; however, the likely explanation is the nearly global preference, especially overt in some developing countries, for male children over female. Some of the missing females were conceived but were never born because their parents chose to abort female fetuses. Others died at a young age because their parents committed female infanticide, or because they received inadequate health care and poor nutrition compared to males.

Even surviving females may be invisible in statistics. Much data is collected without distinguishing between the sexes, thus obscuring important statistical differences. For example, research has shown that across the world, in every country from Sweden to Swaziland, females benefit less from development than do males. But development statistics do not show gender differences, so the lower well-being of females is not apparent. Another aspect of the "missing female" problem is found in global statistics related to work. Almost universally, women's work has been so undervalued that it is virtually missing from national work statistics. Women's contributions as subsistence farmers, as homemakers, as domestic servants, as child-care providers, as volunteers, and as workers elsewhere in the informal sector of economies have not been considered labor. Nor have women's earnings been calculated into national income statistics. Even though the oversight has been documented for more than 20 years, the customs of statistics gathering have not changed, and the missing female phenomenon continues.

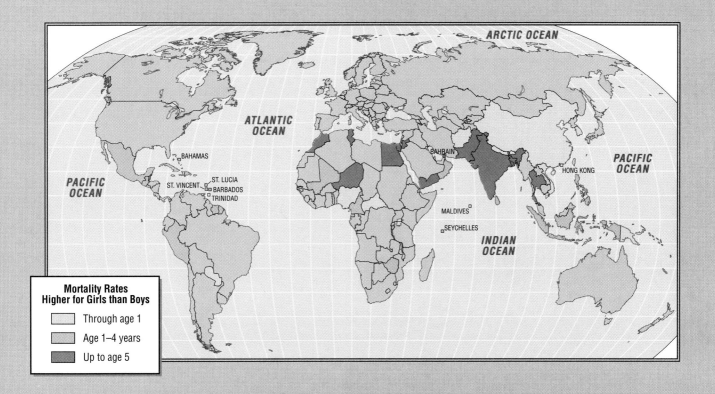

FIGURE 1.20 In the shaded countries, the mortality rate for girls is abnormally high. The darker the color, the longer the risk to girls lasts. [Adapted from Joni Seager, *The State of Women in the World Atlas* (New York: Penguin, 1997), p. 35.]

Growth Rates and Wealth

Although there is a wide range of variation, places with slow population growth rates usually tend to be affluent and places with fast growth rates tend to have widespread poverty. The reasons that poor people tend to have more children than the rich are complicated. Again, the cases of Austria and Côte d'Ivoire can serve as examples. Austria has a gross national product (GNP) per capita of $26,890, roughly similar to that of the United States. (GNP per capita is a measure of each person's average share in the wealth produced annually in a country.) Austria's highly educated population is 100 percent literate and is employed in high-tech industry, research, teaching and writing, manufacturing, and upscale tourism. The costs of preparing a child to compete in this economy are high in terms of time, effort, and money invested, and many couples choose not to have children. Côte d'Ivoire, on the other hand, has a GNP per capita of $510. Most people live in rural villages and practice subsistence agriculture (producing mostly for family consumption). Most work is done by hand. More children mean more labor, so each new child is seen as a potential contributor to the family well-being and income, and as an eventual caregiver when the parents are aged. Not producing sufficient children who will live to adulthood is a bigger worry than producing too many, because 120 children per 1000 die before they are five years old (in

Austria 8 per 1000 die before they are five). It is not surprising then that only 8 to 13 percent of the women in Côte d'Ivoire use birth control (more than 80 percent do in Austria), because they wish to have as many children as possible.

As agricultural production is mechanized, there is less need for agricultural labor and, instead, there is a demand for fewer, well-trained specialists. Furthermore, subsistence lifestyles based on family production are losing their appeal because cash is needed to buy new things like television sets, bicycles, blue jeans, caps, T-shirts, meat, sugar, canned goods, sneakers, and the like. In cash economies, those numerous children become a drain on the family economy. Each child must be educated in order to qualify for a good cash-paying job; and children in school all day and doing their lessons in the evening are not able to produce an income until they are 18 or 20 years old.

Those societies going through the transition from subsistence to cash economies must learn all these consequences firsthand. It often takes one full generation or more to see the benefit of having fewer children and to successfully choose to do so. When this happens, reproduction rates drop, and demographers say that the region has gone through the **demographic transition.** That is, a period of high reproductive rates has given way to a period of much lower reproductive rates, at the same time that major social and economic changes are taking place within the society (Figure 1.21).

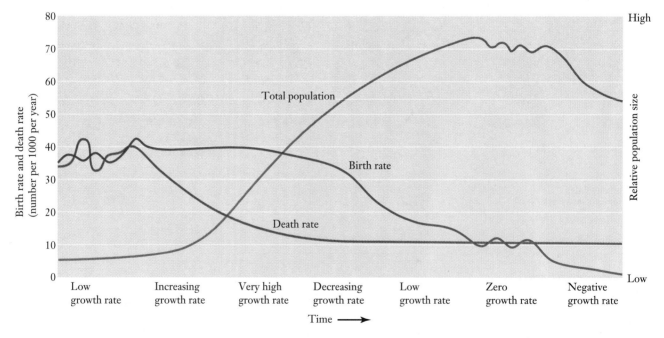

FIGURE 1.21 The demographic transition. [From G. Tyler Miller, Jr., *Living in the Environment, Eighth Edition* (Belmont, CA: Wadsworth, 1994), p. 218.]

Is the World Overpopulated?

At the end of the twentieth century, there is general agreement that human population growth worldwide is in need of curtailment; but the explanations for why this is necessary vary. Some social scientists worry about the societal effects of overcrowding and poverty. Others believe that if poor countries can grow more slowly in population they can develop economically and thereby achieve higher standards of living. Some environmentalists think that overpopulation is leading to the general deterioration of environments and quality of life. Many biologists, biogeographers, and botanists focus their concerns on the thousands of plant and animal species threatened by human population expansion.

There is no unanimity on the subject of slowing population growth. Some think that technology will provide new ways to use the earth's resources more frugally. A few national leaders openly resent being told by countries that have already had the chance to become wealthy that their nations cannot pursue a course they see as necessary for overcoming poverty. Occasionally, as has happened in Eastern Europe and Southeast Asia, leaders even avow policies to encourage births in order to revive aging populations or to offset population booms in neighboring lands. Some religious leaders (among them are Catholic and Protestant, Islamic, Hindu, and Jewish leaders) see human reproduction as a religious mission never to be tampered with. Also, many women from different regions are concerned that too often population control policies are enforced upon their sex much more assiduously than on men. However, the trend today is for family-planning campaigns to be aimed at both sexes.

ECONOMIC ISSUES IN GEOGRAPHY

Geographers have long been interested in the ways in which economies in different parts of the world interact with each other. These interactions affect the ways in which people arrange themselves across the land in cities and towns, and on farms, and which resources they use. In recent decades, people are in general becoming more interested in economic geography, as they find their lives increasingly influenced by what is often called the **global economy**, meaning the worldwide system in which goods and services are exchanged.

Here are a few examples of people whose day-to-day lives are strongly affected by the global economy.

Workers in the Global Economy

VIGNETTES

Olivia lives in Soufriere on St. Lucia, an island in the Caribbean. Soufriere was once a quiet fishing village but now hosts cruise ship passengers several times a week. Olivia is 60. She, her daughter, Anna, and three grandchildren live in a wooden house surrounded by a leafy green garden dotted with fruit and banana trees. A few chickens peck at food scraps and fruit that drops off the trees. Anna has a tiny shop at the side of the house, from which she sells matches, cigarettes, toilet paper, sugar, flour, tinned food, soft drinks, locally grown spices, and preserves she makes from the garden fruits. On the days when the cruise ships dock, Olivia strolls down to the market shed on the beach with a basket of papaya, rolls of cocoa paste made from cocoa beans picked in a neighbor's yard, nutmeg, cinnamon, ginger, and roasted peanuts packed up in tiny paper bags. She calls out to the passengers as they are rowed to shore, offering her spices and snacks for sale. In a good week she makes U.S. $40, and her daughter usually makes about U.S. $100 in the shop. Most days, Olivia tends the garden and her daughter constantly looks for other little ways to make a few dollars, stringing beads or taking in washing, so usually the family of five makes do with about U.S. $160 a week (U.S. $8000 per year). From this they pay rent on the house, the electric bill, and school fees for the granddaughter who will go to high school in the capital next year, and they buy clothes for the children and whatever food they can't grow themselves.

Henry works in the galley on a German cruise ship that plies the Caribbean in the winter months. Every November he leaves his home in a rural Philippine village where he has a wife and two daughters and a son. He won't return until June. He rides a crowded bus to Manila and there buys the cheapest ticket he can find on a freighter to Panama, where he meets the cruise ship on December 1. All winter he works a 12-hour shift in the galley preparing food for the chefs and then cleaning up after the three sumptuous meals served every day to the 60 passengers. He receives U.S. $40 a day, or U.S. $3.33 an hour, plus meals, medical care if he needs it, and a hammock to sleep in, in the crew cabin. (Crew in the

From a distance, cruise ship passengers still see the village of Soufriere, St. Lucia, as a quaint place; when carried ashore by lighter they encounter a small but vibrant entrepreneurial community. [Lydia Pulsipher.]

world's merchant marine are paid according to the pay scale of their home country.) He gets one day off every two weeks. He has little chance to spend his money, so by June he will have sent home U.S. $6000 to his wife. While he is gone, she tends their garden and takes care of the children and her elderly parents, who live downstairs in the new concrete home they finished building themselves (and paying for) two years ago. Occasionally she clerks in the local general store where they buy food, kerosene, and most of their needs, except clothes. Their total family income is U.S. $7700 a year, which makes them exceptionally well off for their village. There is money in the bank; and all the children plan to attend technical college for at least two years.

At 4:30 A.M. six days a week, Vondana walks five miles to catch the bus to Madras in South India, where she works in a shirt factory owned by a man from Malaysia who markets the shirts to the United States. She works from 7:00 A.M. to 5:00 P.M. Her family, which consists of several elderly aunts, her father's parents, her parents, and her three younger brothers, lives in a mud brick house next to the two acres the family sharecrops for the village headman. They usually grow cotton until the soil refuses to produce, and then they grow beans for a year. The headman takes two-thirds of the crop as his rent.

Vondana, who attended school for two years, began learning to sew when she was 12 and obtained the factory job when she was 14. She is now 21 and makes the equivalent of U.S. $12 a week, or $624 a year. She gives all but one dollar to her father every pay day. Vondana pays a few cents for her bus rides and lunch (in India, transport and food are subsidized by the government) and saves the rest for shoes. Her father uses the money to buy sugar, flour, rice, and cloth for the family clothes, and to pay the school fees for his three sons, who are expected to finish middle school.

Tanya is a 50-year-old grandmother who works at a fast-food store in North Carolina in the United States; she makes less than $6 an hour. She had been working at Goodner Mills, sewing shirts, until it closed and moved abroad. There just aren't any other jobs around that pay that well ($8 an hour, with experience) and Tanya may not be able to pay the college tuition for her son, Daniel. He wants to be an engineer and would be the first in the family to go past high school. For now, he is working at the gas station. His sister quit school after 11th grade and married. Tanya's husband is a delivery truck driver for a snack-food company and has made enough over the years to slowly build and improve a small home for them along a ridge outside Greenville. Her daughter lives with her

Vondana works in a factory similar to this shirt factory in Bangalore, India. [Dilip Mehta, Contact/The Stock Market.]

husband and baby in the old mobile home Tanya and her family used to live in. Between them, Tanya and her husband make $25,000 a year; but from this they must pay their mortgage and car loan, regular monthly expenses for food and utilities, and help their daughter, whose husband is out of work and can't afford a car to look for a job. And of course there is that hoped-for college tuition for Daniel looming.

These four families, living worlds apart, have at least one thing in common. They are all part of what is now called the global economy. The wage workers are paid at startlingly different rates for jobs that require about the same skill level. But the different costs of living they experience are what make the difference between the relative affluence of Henry's family and the near poverty (at least by local standards) and threatened hopes of Tanya's family, which actually has the highest income by far.

Most people want to achieve a better life than their parents had, but some have a better chance at succeeding than others. Henry's children may have the best chance because their parents actually have some savings and their father's experience traveling around the world has given him many connections and the foresight to know where and how to push his children into the best opportunities. Vondana, clearly the poorest, seems trapped by her status as a female wage earner on whom many people, both old and young, depend.

Her lack of education means that she has little chance for advancing.

Olivia and her family, though not well off, do not think of themselves as poor, because they have what they need and others around them live in similar circumstances. They are still on the fringes of the global economy, but already the tourist trade is promising increased income. Yet the global economy will also make them more dependent on circumstances beyond their control: the tourist trade is notoriously fickle—in an instant the tour companies can choose another port of call. Olivia's granddaughter has her eye on a tourism job; but to get one in management she will need to go to the University of the West Indies in Barbados to earn the required college degree. How will her family pay for that? If she does not get a degree, she will be left competing with many other undertrained young people for waitress, kitchen, and maid jobs in resort hotels.

What Is the Economy?

At the beginning of this chapter we observed that economic geography is the study of how people interact with their environment as they go about earning a living. The **economy** is the forum where people make their living. To geographers, the economy includes the spatial, social, and political aspects of how resources are first recognized as useful, then extracted, exchanged, transformed into new items or commodities or bodies of knowledge (e.g., computer software), perhaps traded again, and relocated to wherever they are used. By **resources,** we mean anything that is recognized as useful, including material resources like mineral ores and timber and nonmaterial resources like skills and brainpower. **Extraction** refers to the ways a material resource is acquired: mined, grown, logged, or otherwise produced. **Exchange** refers to all kinds of barter and trade for money, goods, or services.

The **formal economy** includes all aspects of this activity that take place in official channels. To take examples from the opening vignettes, Olivia's daughter in her shopkeeper's role, Henry, Henry's wife when she clerks in the store, Vondana, and Tanya and her husband and son are all employed in the formal economy. They are all registered workers who earn recorded wages and presumably pay taxes to their governments. One important way in which the activity of formal economies is measured is by their gross national product, a number that gives in monetary terms the total value of all goods and services officially recognized as produced in a country during a given year.

Many goods and services are produced in circumstances that are not officially recognized, that is, in the **informal economy.** Work in the informal economy is often done for no cash payment, or if cash is earned, it is not reported as income. Only recently have economists begun paying serious attention to informal economies, but estimates are that one-third or more of the world's work falls into this category. Those in the vignettes on pages 39–41 who work in the informal economy include: Olivia, when she sells fruit to the tourists; Olivia's daughter, when she works around the house or makes things to sell (very likely when she sells her own produce she does not count the income as taxable); Vondana's kinfolk, when they hunt for fuelwood, fetch water, or produce and prepare food; Henry's wife, when she does anything around the house or cares for the elderly and her children; and any of the children in any of the four families, when they do housework or make a little money doing odd jobs. Indeed, all who contribute to their own or someone else's well-being in daily unpaid service could be said to be operating in the informal economy.

We usually talk of economies as having sectors, meaning that there are distinguishable categories of economic activities. The **primary, or extractive, sector** includes agriculture, mining, forestry, or any other economic activity that extracts resources from the earth. The **secondary, or industrial, sector** is that in which raw materials are transformed into manufactured goods. The **tertiary, or service, sector** includes all those activities that amount to doing services for others. The service sector includes transportation, banking, clerking, washing dishes, repairing, child care, care of the elderly, cleaning, some types of teaching, and routine management. We used to include librarians, professors, researchers, physicians, lawyers, and those engaged in other occupations, like computer engineering, that require postgraduate training, in the service sector; but now another category has been created, the **quaternary sector,** to cover those who are highly trained in the collection, processing, and manipulation of information.

What Is the Global Economy?

Those parts of a country's economy that are in some way involved in international trade could be said to be involved in the global economy. The economic processes that created the paper these words are printed on might be an example. The paper may have been made from trees that were cut down in Siberia or Southeast Asia and shipped across the Pacific to a paper mill in Oregon. Most of us participate in the global economy on a daily basis, consuming resources that have traveled enormous distances as they were transformed from raw materials into finished products. This type of activity has grown tremendously in the past 200 years, but it existed at least 2000 years ago when silk fabrics and other goods were produced and then traded along land routes across Central Asia connecting Rome with China, or along sea routes connecting Arabia with East Africa and what we now call East and Southeast Asia.

Starting in about A.D. 1500, long-distance trade entered a period of expansion and change, as many more places and peoples became involved. During the era of European exploration, Europeans began to take over distant lands and peoples for economic exploitation. These acquired lands became known as **colonies.** In the sixteenth and seventeenth centuries, in the Americas and Asia (and later in Africa), Europeans began extracting resources and organizing systems that processed the resources into higher value goods to be traded back in Europe or wherever there was a market. For example, sugarcane was grown on Caribbean, Brazilian, and Asian plantations, made into sugar and rum, and sold in Europe and North America. In a real sense, this colonial system of production and trade was the beginning of the modern global economy. Local places, rather than being drawn upon primarily to support local people, were producing a few key products for export (usually to Europe) and became themselves dependent on imports to meet basic needs, like food and clothing, and the means of production like machinery and draft animals.

Colonialism began to wane in the nineteenth century because the costs of controlling huge empires exceeded the profits they produced. But private investors continued exporting resources and manufactured goods from former colonies. A key institution in the development of the modern global economy is the **multinational corporation.** These are organizations that operate as highly integrated international systems, extracting resources from several places, producing products in factories carefully located to take advantage of cheap labor and transport facilities, and marketing their products wherever the profits will be highest. One of the key characteristics of multinationals is their ability to influence the economic and political affairs of the countries they operate in.

While multinational corporations began as producers of a particular product or set of products, today many are banks or **conglomerate companies** that have purchased interests in dozens of loosely related enterprises across the globe. They are now primarily the conduits for the flow of investment funds, or **capital.** For example, what was once a family-owned Mexico City cement company I'll call Mexcem recently borrowed heavily from international banks to acquire controlling interests in cement industries in Texas, Mexico, and the Philippines and several other Southeast Asian countries. Now the focus of the company is no longer just the profitable production of cement in and for Mexico. Its focus is on gaining monopoly control over cement production in all its markets. It hopes to outmaneuver its rivals by using borrowed

Old North Sound was one of hundreds of eighteenth-century sugar plantations in the British West Indies that provided huge sums of money to England from the labor of enslaved Africans and helped fund the industrial revolution. [St. Johns Antiqua Museum.]

money to locate new cement-dispensing sites strategically and to introduce cutting-edge technology in its various plants.

Such international investment has a number of benefits. In this case, high-quality cement may be more efficiently and cheaply delivered in all the markets served. Competition may spur technological advancement, perhaps even environmentally friendly innovations. Jobs will be created in Asia and Mexico and Texas. And for the Mexican company, location in diverse markets may open up opportunities for profit that far exceed the company's previous situation. These profits, if then invested in Mexico, can break the cycle of the flight of capital. This cycle has persisted since colonial times, when investors took their profits back to Europe instead of reinvesting them locally.

But there is another side to the story. In their quest for huge profits, Mexcem officials may ignore the human costs or undesirable environmental impacts of corporate actions, especially in distant branches. Already a number of small cement providers in Southeast Asia have failed because they could not meet Mexcem's low prices and fast delivery. And by taking the profits home to Mexico, Mexcem will contribute to capital flight from Asia. Moreover, Mexcem itself is now in a precarious position. To acquire its new subsidiaries it went deeply in debt and must regularly meet huge payments. If it misses installments, its creditors could quickly foreclose. Now thousands of jobs from Texas to Southeast Asia rest on financial maneuvering in Mexcem headquarters in Mexico City.

An old question that continues to be debated today is whether there should be free movement of goods and capital without restrictions, or **free trade.** Traditionally, most countries have sought both to protect their economies from fluctuations in the global economy and their industries from foreign competition. To this end, governments use **tariffs,** essentially taxes imposed on imported goods, and **import quotas,** fixed limits on the amount of a given good that may be imported over a period of time. Virtually every industrialized country in the world has at some time used these and other mechanisms to nurture industries that have subsequently provided the backbone of national prosperity. Critics of free trade argue that tariffs and import quotas help developing countries be less dependent on the global economy, protecting them from the periodic ups and downs of global markets that can wreak havoc on smaller national economies. However, such protections are currently losing favor. Proponents of free trade argue that unrestricted movement of goods and services across international borders encourages efficiency and high quality and gives consumers choices of products at lower prices. It allows companies to sell to larger markets and therefore to take advantage of economies of scale. Local economies grow faster, thereby providing people with jobs and opportunities to raise their standard of living.

Restrictions on trade imposed by individual countries are now being reduced through regional **trade blocs.** These are associations of neighboring countries with free trade agreements. Arrangements such as the North American Free Trade Agreement (NAFTA), the European Union (EU), the Southern Common Market (Mercosur) in South America, and the Association of Southeast Asian Nations (ASEAN) are removing tariffs

The air that envelops Cairo, Egypt, is by some measures the most polluted in any urban area in the world. Environmental regulations are either nonexistent or unenforced. Here, smoke and dust from cement factories cover newly cleaned surfaces within seconds. Much of the funding for Cairo's factories has come from international loans or from internationally controlled companies. The factories provide needed jobs for desperately poor local residents. [Mohamed El-Dakhakhny/AP/Wide World Photos.]

and quotas between many countries. Such arrangements are thought by some to be a step in the direction of eventual global free trade. There are already a number of international trade agreements that limit the extent to which any signatory government can protect its economy from international regulations.

Resistance to this trend toward globalization of trade is coming from a variety of sources. Labor unions and other workers' organizations argue that local economies in both wealthy and poor countries are being wrecked as corporations relocate factories to take advantage of cheaper labor. Multinationals often view countries with strong unions and laws that protect workers' rights and working conditions as less attractive. Some fear that a "race to the bottom" in wages and working conditions will ensue as countries compete for the attention of potential investors. Environmentalists argue that multinational corporations are

plundering the natural resources of newly industrializing countries.

Foreign investment and free trade are important because they affect a country's **development.** Usually the term "development" is used to describe economic changes that lead to an improvement in standards of living. These changes often accompany the greater productivity in agriculture and industry that comes from technological advances like mechanization and computerization. Increasingly, experts are advocating a broader definition of development that will include measures of human well-being and measures of environmental quality.

Measures of Well-Being

There are many ideas on how best to measure development. Countries are usually compared on economic grounds alone, most often on **gross national product (GNP) per capita.** The GNP per capita is a figure giving the total value of all goods and services produced in a country in a given year, divided by the number of people in the country. This figure is used as a crude indicator of how well people are living in a given country (see column 1 of Table 1.2). There are several problems with this measure. First, GNP per capita is an average figure, meaning it can hide the fact that there are a few fabulously rich people in a country and a mass of the abjectly poor. A GNP per capita of U.S. $20,000 would be meaningless if a few lived on millions per year and most lived on $500 per year. Second, the purchasing power of currency varies widely across the globe, so a GNP of U.S. $5000 per capita in Jamaica might represent a middle-class standard of living, while that same amount in New York City could not support a healthy standard of living.

A third problem with GNP per capita is that it measures only what goes on in the formal economy, when the informal economy may actually account for more activity. Researchers looking at all types of societies and cultures have recently shown that women perform about 60 percent of the work done on a daily basis. Nonetheless, only their paid work performed in the formal economy makes it into the statistics. Statistics also neglect the contributions of millions of men and children who work in the informal economy as subsistence farmers or as seasonal laborers. A recent worldwide study conducted by the United Nations uncovered the fact that 250 million children under the age of 14 are employed in the informal economy, half of them full time! Most live in Asia.

Perhaps the most important failing of GNP per capita as a measure for comparing countries is that it is a strictly economic index; all other aspects of development are ignored. There is no way to tell, for example,

TABLE 1.2

Sample human well-being table

Country	GNP per capita (in U.S. dollars), 1996	Human Development Index (HDI) global rankings, 1998[a]	Gender Empowerment Measure (GEM) global rankings, 1998[b]
Japan	40,940	8 (high)	38
United States	28,020	4 (high)	11
Kuwait	19,040 (1995)	54 (high)	75
Barbados	6,560	24 (high)	18

[a] The high, medium, and low designations indicate how the country ranks if the 174 countries are classified into just three categories.
[b] Total ranked in the world = 104.
Sources: 1998 World Population Data Sheet, Population Reference Bureau; and *Human Development Report 1998*, United Nations Development Programme.

whether or not a country is spending down its natural resources at a rapid rate in pursuit of quick riches, or how well it is educating its young, or treating women, or caring for the sick, or maintaining its environment. There are a number of movements to refine the definition of development to include these factors and more. I have chosen two to use in this book, along with the traditional GNP per capita figure: the United Nations Human Development Index (HDI) and the United Nations Gender Empowerment Measure (GEM). Together, they get at some of the subtleties and nuances of well-being and make comparisons between countries somewhat more valid. Because these more sensitive indexes are also more complex than the purely economic index, all are still in the process of refinement.

The United Nations Human Development Index (HDI). The newly devised HDI is still grounded in data on income, but purchasing power is factored in and so is numerical data on health and education. The index considers adjusted real income, which takes into account what people can buy with what they earn. Countries are ranked according to their measure on the HDI factors. The rank orders of countries are quite different from those based solely on GNP per capita (see Table 1.2); but there is no way in the HDI to score a country directly on how equal its distribution of income or purchasing power is. This is only indirectly indicated by the information on health and educational empowerment. Hence, it is assumed that a country that is providing widely available health and education services has a more equitable distribution of wealth than a country providing low levels of access to health care and education.

The United Nations Gender Empowerment Measure (GEM). In recognition of the fact that in most countries women lag behind men in opportunity and income, the United Nations has devised the GEM, which scores and ranks countries according to how well they make possible female participation in the political and economic life of the country. The indicators used are things like percent of women holding parliamentary seats, percent of income that is earned by women, and percent of administrators and managers who are women. While the GEM helps us to infer something of the relative power of men and women in a society, the indicators now available for use are unsatisfactory. In most countries, very little data is collected separately on men and women, and in many cases data on women is ignored altogether, making comparisons impossible. Most important, a high rank does not indicate that a country is treating women and men equally, but only that the high-ranked country is doing better than those ranked lower. For example, although women are half of the world's population, nowhere on earth do women hold 50 percent of the parliamentary seats.

The Human Well-Being Table. Table 1.2 shows all three of the previously described rankings for four countries: Japan, the United States, Kuwait, and

Barbados. Notice how the rankings change in the four columns. Kuwait's rank drops significantly from the GNP per capita column to the HDI column; Japan and Kuwait fall drastically in the GEM ranking; Barbados rises steadily from one to the other. More information than given here is required to understand these changes in rank on the different indexes. Perhaps you can already suggest some explanations. Each chapter in this book is designed to provide historical, demographic, cultural, social, economic, and political information that will help the reader to interpret the rankings for the countries in that region. A human well-being table like this, with a short discussion explaining the rankings, will be included in each world region chapter.

POLITICAL ISSUES IN GEOGRAPHY

One can think of political issues in geography as being primarily about power: the exercise of it, the allocation of it to different segments of society, and the spatial distribution of it within world regions and between them. The political issues that are most commonly discussed in geography have to do with geopolitics, or the power plays between countries as they jockey for territory, resources, or influence. Other political topics include types of government, changing borders between countries, and international service organizations.

Geopolitics

The term **geopolitics** is not often used in these post–cold war days, but the activity it describes is hardly out of fashion. It refers to the use of strategies by countries to ensure that their best interests are served in relations with other countries. For example, sometimes the people of a state perceive a threat to a border from a neighboring state. They may then move settlers and perhaps even military forces into that zone to make a show of power. In the 1970s, Brazil applied this strategy in its northwest when its leaders thought that Venezuela or Colombia was contemplating a move into Amazonia. The years of the **cold war,** from 1946 to the early 1990s, provide an example of geopolitics operating over the long term. The United States and its allies in Western Europe faced off against the Union of Soviet Socialist Republics (USSR) and its allies in

Eastern Europe (and for a while China) in a contest of ideologies that included a number of skirmishes and the constant threat of nuclear war. The West espoused a version of free market capitalism and democracy and the East a centrally planned economy and socialist state. The cold war was also a contest to control other parts of the world, and it eventually influenced (at least in subtle ways) internal and external policy in virtually every country on earth.

These days, geopolitics, defined broadly, could refer to much of what is in the international news. In the new and unstable post–cold war climate, literally every country is jockeying for a good position in what most are hoping will be a new era of trade and prosperity, not war.

Nations and Borders

In this text you will often see regions defined by the countries within them; countries are a common unit of geographic analysis, and their boundaries are a major feature of the maps you see in this text. Why a country has its particular boundaries is a complex subject, but the following discussion gives a sense of some of the issues.

The eighteenth-century French writer Jean-Jacques Rousseau believed that humans realized their true potential by joining together to create a **nation state** anchored to a particular territory. According to this view, a **nation** is not a country but a group of people who share language, culture, and political philosophy. A nation state is thus a political unit (a country) formed by people from a single nation. Japan is an example of a nation state because its people, with only minor exceptions, share a common cultural heritage and a common political unit. France, although it is often cited as a classic nation state, is not one in the purest sense, for there are minorities like the Basque, North African, Turkish, and Caribbean peoples, some of whom are French citizens.

The concept of the nation state and ideas of self-government spread from France to the Americas, and nearly all European colonies in the Americas achieved independence in the nineteenth century (the United States earlier, in 1776). In Africa, India, and Asia, most colonies did not become independent states until the second half of the twentieth century.

Few of these newly independent states, or even older European states, were true nation states. Often when a state was organized in a former colony, a nation state based on ethnicity was not feasible. In rare cases, a former colony became a **pluralistic state,** in which power was shared between ethnic groups. More typically, power accrued to an elite or to only one of several ethnic groups that had gained certain advantages during the colonial period. Others were left out.

Some 200,000 Serbs, expelled from the Krajina region of Croatia, cross through Bosnia to reach Serbia during one of the many "ethnic cleansing" episodes of the conflict in former Yugoslavia. [Peter Turnley/Corbis.]

In extreme cases, some groups found that the territory they had customarily occupied was claimed by several new states and they no longer had a homeland. For example, the once nomadic Kurds, who ranged through parts of Turkey, Iraq, and Iran, still do not have a recognized territory and are unlikely to get one soon. Here and in many other places, ethnic groups are warring with national governments over rights to territory. The idea of the nation state can be a powerful way to bond a large group of people to work together, but a substantial territory is rarely occupied by only a single culture group. With no clear way to divide territory among groups, the idea has often led to conflict.

The emergence of the idea of the sovereign nation state increased the importance of precise legal boundaries in human society. The borders of coun-tries are demarcations of power and control. When we look at a map, we are looking at a spatial representation of the outcomes of power struggles over territory. Some such struggles have only recently been resolved or are still under way. In the 1990s, the map of Eastern Europe changed markedly at the end of the cold war, and the map of Africa also underwent change as former colonies fractured into smaller units. In the future it may be the map of Canada that changes, if the province of Québec is successful in seceding and becoming an independent nation state. In all these examples it is conflict over cultural or ethnic difference that instigated the new or changed boundaries, but control of resources is often a strong secondary issue.

International Cooperation

While the aspirations of culture groups to have their own states continues to be an important trend in the world today, other factors are at work to lessen the importance of individual countries. Economic cooperation, in particular, is lessening the emphasis on borders. For example, most countries of Europe have joined in an economic union to abolish tariffs and other restrictions on the movements of goods and people between countries. As a consequence, the borders between what were once very sensitive nation states are now melting away.

There is also some evidence that the role of the individual state may eventually decline as international organizations play an increasing role in world affairs. The prime example of government-to-government cooperation is the United Nations, an assembly of 185 member states that sponsors more than 40 programs and agencies focusing on science research, humanitarian aid, planning for development, fostering of general health, and peacekeeping assistance in hot spots around the world—such as Bosnia-Herzegovina, Lebanon, Israel, Rwanda, and Haiti. The United Nations has very little legal power and can only enforce its rulings through the power of persuasion. Even in its peacekeeping mission there are no true UN forces. All peacekeeping forces consist of troops from the member states, who wear UN designations on their uniforms.

The World Bank (officially named the International Bank for Reconstruction and Development) and the International Monetary Fund (IMF) are financial institutions funded by the developed nations to help developing countries reorganize and formalize their economies. These two institutions wield enormous power in international development through their lending activities.

Nongovernmental organizations (NGOs) and

newer transnational social movement organizations (TSMOs) are an increasingly important embodiment of globalization. Many are associations of individuals from around the world who share views on a political issue, such as saving endangered species. They range from groups like the World Wildlife Association and the World Conservation Union to Médecins Sans Frontières (Doctors Without Borders) and Parliamentarians for Global Action. Often the education efforts of these organizations succeed in raising awareness among the general public and have prepared the way for formal agreements in the United Nations. These organizations, operating on a global scale, are the embodiment of community-level social groups considered by political scientists to be essential to participatory democracy.

A Note on Chapter Organization

This chapter has reviewed the main features of the discipline of geography and discussed the major geographic issues that will guide the description and discussion of each world region. Each chapter is organized along the same lines and covers the same general topics. The order of the topics changes somewhat from chapter to chapter, simply because circumstances in a particular region may lend themselves to a particular arrangement of topics; but the reader who wishes to compare general economic or demographic conditions in two or more world regions will be able to do so. Statistical comparisons of regions are encouraged by the human well-being tables discussed in every chapter.

Selected Themes and Concepts

1. Geography may be defined as the study of the earth's surface and the processes that shape it, both physical and human.

2. A **region** is a unit of the earth's surface that contains distinct patterns of physical features or of human development.

3. Culture is represented by the ideas and materials and institutions that humans have invented and passed on to subsequent generations. A **culture group** is a group of people who share a set of beliefs, a way of life, a technology, and usually a place. Language and religion are two examples of **cultural markers,** characteristics that help define a culture group.

4. According to the theory of **plate tectonics,** the earth's surface is composed of large, slow-moving plates that float on top of an underlying layer of rock. The movement and interaction of the plates create many of the large features of the earth's surface, particularly mountains.

5. Sustainable development is often defined as the effort to improve present standards of living in ways that will not jeopardize those of future generations. Sustainability is an issue in agriculture, use of re-

sources, the emission of greenhouse gases that might lead to global warming, and other areas as well.

6. Demography is the study of population patterns and changes. The **rate of natural increase** is the relationship between the numbers being born (birth rates) and the numbers dying (death rates) in a given population. The **age distribution,** or **age structure,** is the proportion of the total population in each age group. When the age structure of a population is weighted toward the young, the population will grow more rapidly.

7. The **global economy** is the worldwide system in which goods and services are exchanged. Key institutions in the global economy are **multinational corporations,** which operate extraction and production facilities in multiple countries, and **conglomerate companies,** which purchase interests in loosely related enterprises across the globe.

8. The term **geopolitics** refers to the use of strategies by countries to ensure that their best interests are served. Much political contention today centers around the striving of culture groups to establish **nation-states,** political units, or countries, formed by people who share a language, culture, and political philosophy.

Selected Readings

Blumberg, Rae Lesser, Cathy A. Rakowski, Irene Tinker, and Michael Monteon, eds. *EnGENDERing Wealth and Well-Being—Empowerment for Global Change.* Boulder, CO: Westview Press, 1995.

Bowers, C. A. *Educating for an Ecologically Sustainable Culture—Rethinking Moral Education, Creativity, Intelligence, and Other Modern Orthodoxies.* Albany: State University of New York Press, 1995.

Boyd, Andrew. *An Atlas of World Affairs*, 10th ed. London and New York: Routledge, 1998.

Braidotti, Rosi, Ewa Charkiewicz, Sabine Hausler, and Saskia Wieringa, eds. *Women, the Environment and Sustainable Development—Towards a Theoretical Synthesis.* London: Zed Books in association with INSTRAW, 1994.

Brandt, Barbara. *Whole Life Economics: Revaluing Daily Life.* Philadelphia: New Society Publishers, 1995.

Chatterjee, Pratap, and Matthias Finger. *The Earth Brokers—Power, Politics and World Development.* New York: Routledge, 1994.

Cohen, Joel E. *How Many People Can the Earth Support?* New York: W. W. Norton, 1995.

Crush, Jonathan, ed. *Power of Development.* London: Routledge, 1995.

Day, Lincoln H. *The Future of Low-Birthrate Populations.* London: Routledge, 1992.

Einhorn, Barbara, and Eileen Janes Yeo, eds. *Women and Market Societies: Crisis and Opportunity.* Aldershot, UK: Edward Elgar, 1995.

Ellen, Roy, and Katsuyoshi Fukui. *Redefining Nature—Ecology, Culture and Domestication.* Oxford and Washington, DC: Berg (Oxford International Publishers), 1996.

Fitzgerald, Stephen. *China and the Overseas Chinese: A Study of Peking's Changing Policy 1949–1970.* Cambridge: Cambridge University Press, 1972.

Grove, Richard H. *Green Imperialism—Colonial Expansion, Tropical Island Edens and the Origins of Environmentalism, 1600–1860.* Cambridge: Cambridge University Press, 1995.

Jackson, Peter. *Maps of Meaning—An Introduction to Cultural Geography.* London: Unwin Hyman, 1989.

Kobayashi, Audrey, and Suzanne Mackensie, eds. *Remaking Human Geography.* Boston: Unwin Hyman, 1989.

Mazur, Laurie Ann, ed. *Beyond the Numbers—A Reader on Population, Consumption, and the Environment.* Washington, DC: Island Press, 1994.

McAfee, Kathy. *Storm Signals: Structural Adjustment and Development Alternatives in the Caribbean.* Boston: Oxfam America, 1991.

Merchant, Carolyn. *Earthcare—Women and the Environment.* New York: Routledge, 1995.

Milton, Kay, ed. *Environmentalism—The View from Anthropology.* London: Routledge, 1993.

Nelson, Barbara J., and Najma Chowdhury, eds. *Women and Politics Worldwide.* New Haven, CT: Yale University Press, 1994.

Nussbaum, Martha C., and Glover Jonathan, eds. *Women, Culture, and Development: A Study in Human Capabilities.* Oxford: Clarendon Press, 1995.

United Nations Development Programme at *http://www.undp.org.* The Human Development Reports cited throughout the text are on the Web at *http://www.undp.org/undp/hdro.*

Waring, Marilyn. *If Women Counted—A New Feminist Economics.* San Francisco: Harper & Row, 1988.

World Bank at http://www.worldbank.org/html/welcome.html.

World Resources Institute at http://www.wri.org.

CHAPTER

TWO

NORTH AMERICA

INTRODUCTION TO NORTH AMERICA

Good morning America, how are you?
Say, don't you know me, I'm your native son.
I'm the train they call The City of New Orleans.
I'll be gone five hundred miles when the day is done.

Riding on The City of New Orleans
Illinois Central Monday morning rail
Fifteen cars and fifteen restless riders
Three conductors and twenty-five sacks of mail
All along the south-bound odyssey, the train pulls
    out of Kankakee
Rolls along past houses, farms and fields
Passing trains that have no name, freight yards of
    old black men
And graveyards of rusted automobiles.

Dealing card games with the old men in the club car
Penny a point ain't no one keeping score
Pass the paper bag but hold the bottle
Feel the wheels rumbling 'neath the floor
And the sons of Pullman porters and the sons
    of engineers
Ride their fathers' magic carpets made of steel
Mother with her babes asleep rocking to the gentle beat
And the rhythm of the rails is all they feel.

Nighttime on The City of New Orleans
Changing cars in Memphis, Tennessee
Halfway home we'll be there by morning
Through the Mississippi darkness rolling down to the sea.
But all the towns and people seem to fade into a
    dark dream
And the steel rail still ain't heard the news
The conductor sings his song again, the passengers will
    please refrain,
This train got the disappearing railroad blues.

Chorus:
Good night America, how are you?
Say, don't you know me, I'm your native son.
I'm the train they call The City of New Orleans
I'll be gone five hundred miles when the day is done.
                    —*Words and music by Steve Goodman,*
                        as performed by Arlo Guthrie

When I reflect on the contrasting regional patterns of North America, I often think of Arlo Guthrie singing "The City of New Orleans." It is a sad song in a minor key, commemorating one of the last passenger trains in the United States. The sleek silver train named *The City of New Orleans* made a 16-hour journey from Chicago southwest through Illinois toward St. Louis, and then along the Mississippi River all the way to New Orleans on the Gulf of Mexico. The song alludes not only to the different landscapes and lifeways along the line, but also reminds one of the migration of poor southerners, many of them black, who left the fields of the South and rode the northbound trains to new homes in the factory ghettos of the North. Sometimes *The City of New Orleans* whisked them home again to visit dying grandparents and dilapidated hometowns. There are many such pieces of music in North America's heritage, melodies and verse that evoke the physical and cultural variety of the continent.

Most readers of this book will be residents of North America; and each reader, whatever her or his experiences, will already have some impressions of this land. I encourage you to bring your own experience to the project of defining the geographic character of North America. I invite you to think of this chapter as a guide that will assist you to enhance what you already know and to construct, over a lifetime, an evermore complex and evolving understanding of the geography of North America.

You might want to pull out the map of your childhood landscape that you constructed at the beginning of Chapter 1. Now, as you read this chapter, you can

Many North American suburbs contain dozens of houses built according to just two or three plans, like this one in Maryland. Paint color, trim, position of house on the lot, and landscaping detail are used to give some variety to the neighborhood. [Frank Fisher/Gamma-Liaison.]

set that map in its wider context. You may even be able to see how features of your map—things you noticed as a young child—are actually related to larger patterns, both physical and cultural, across the continent.

Themes to Look For

Some central themes in North American life emerge in this chapter.

1. North Americans seem to favor a transient quality of life, the ability to move on, to check out a new part of their continent. This tendency is linked to the strong strain of individualism that characterizes the way people design their lives. Links to family and community are important; but individual success, often defined by achieving notoriety and prosperity, is in the plans of most young people. Changing one's geographic location is accepted as part and parcel of achieving success.

2. To facilitate this mobility, Americans have provided themselves with duplicated landscapes across the continent. One can find the same or similar suburbs, homes, lawns, office towers, strip malls, ethnic restaurants, home improvement centers, and huge shopping and entertainment malls in virtually every major city in Canada and the United States.

3. Despite this sameness, there are real differences between regions, and often stark cultural disparities within regions. North Americans are right now becoming more, rather than less, culturally and economically diverse.

4. Although Americans as a whole are prospering more than ever, the gap between rich and poor is actually widening. The number of millionaires is soaring, while the number of people who cannot afford basics is also growing.

Terms to Be Aware Of

The region discussed in this chapter consists of Canada and the United States. The term **North America** is used when referring to both countries. Even though it is common on both sides of the border to call the people of Canada "Canadians" and people in the United States "Americans," this text will use the term **United States** rather than *America* for the United States. The term *American*, then, refers to citizens of, or patterns in, both countries, not just the United States. In the discussions of physical and economic geography I point out that Mexico also might logically be included in North America.

Diversity is reflected in this group of children as they enjoy a birthday party in the Bunker Hill development, Boston's largest public housing facility. [Joel Sartore/National Geographic.]

Other terms relate to the growing cultural diversity on the continent. For example, the text uses both the terms **Hispanic** and **Latino.** "Hispanic" is a loose ethnic (not racial) term that refers to all Spanish-speaking people from Latin America and Spain. Hispanics may be black, white, Asian, or Native American. "Latino" is an alternative term for the same group. In Canada, the people of an ethnic group that is becoming assertively distinct from the rest of Canada are the **Québecois,** or French Canadians. They are the largest of an increasingly complex range of minorities in that country, the rest of whom are as yet content to be called simply Canadians.

PHYSICAL PATTERNS

The continent of North America begins near the Arctic Circle and stretches all the way south to the Isthmus of Tehuantepec in what is today southern Mexico. The physical geography of a place as large as North America is enormously complex. It can be helpful to break such a large territory into just a few smaller segments, learn a bit about them, and then store that information in your head as a sort of template on which you can later sketch greater detail, both physical and cultural.

Landforms

With that plan in mind, have a look at the opening map to this chapter. The most dramatic and complex North American landform is the wide mountainous mass in the west that sweeps down from the Bering Strait in the far north, next to Alaska, all the way down through Mexico. The Rocky Mountain zone of Canada and the United States and the Sierra Madre of Mexico are major parts of this broad swath of mountains and basins. Another, more modest and rounded, mountain formation stretches along the eastern edge of the continent. These are the Appalachians. In between lies a great, irregularly shaped central lowland of flat or undulating plains. This vast lowland encompasses virtually all the territory between the Rocky and Appalachian mountains, stretching through the middle of the continent from the Arctic to the Gulf of Mexico.

East of the Appalachians, there is only a narrow coastal zone in the north. Toward the south, this zone widens into a broad band fringing the Atlantic down through Florida. Then it sweeps to the west, where it joins the southern reaches of the interior lowland along the Gulf of Mexico. Along most of this Atlantic and Gulf seaboard, the slope is so nearly flat that the edge of the continent actually lies well under water; hence, there is a transition zone between land and sea characterized by swamps, lagoons, and sandbars.

Landform Processes

Like all the landmasses on earth, the broad features of the North American continent are the product of the tectonic movement of the earth's crust. Some 500 million years ago, the core of North America was formed when pieces of yet older continents collided. These collisions were part of the process that eventually created the ancient supercontinent of Pangaea. The collisions that formed Pangaea caused the buckling of the land that is still visible in the Appalachians and other old belts of mountains.

Some 200 million years ago, Pangaea began to pull apart (as shown in Figure 1.8) and the shapes of the continents as we know them today emerged. In North America, the broad band of mountains along the western edge is the result of the Pacific Plate pushing against the North American Plate. The Pacific Plate is also slipping in a northerly direction, while the North American Plate is moving in a southerly direction. The two plates are presently moving past each other at the rate of several centimeters a year. This movement creates the constant threat of earthquakes.

During periodic ice ages, over the last 2 million years, glaciers have covered the northern portion of the lowlands (as well as adjoining mountain ranges to the west and east) and extended south well into what is now the central United States. They were instrumental in creating the flat and undulating landscapes of the central lowlands. The most recent ice age ended between 15,000 and 10,000 years ago; the ice, sometimes as much as two miles thick, scoured the surface of the Canadian Shield in the far north and lands to the south, and then dumped the sediment as it melted. The Great Lakes are situated in the low places left by glacial scour; so are the smaller lakes, ponds, and wetlands that dot Minnesota, Wisconsin, Michigan, and much of central Canada.

Wind and water have carried away dust from the sediment dumped by the melting glaciers and have redeposited it elsewhere. In the upper Mississippi Valley, the surface of the land is covered, often yards deep, with such windblown particles, called **loess.** This deep layer of soil has proved particularly adaptable to large-scale mechanized agriculture.

Climate

Every major type of climate found on earth is found in North America, except for the truly tropical. This wide range of climates is primarily a result of the fact that the continent is a large landmass, stretching from close to the Arctic Circle in the far north all the way down to within 25° of the equator at the tip of Florida. This huge stretch of land experiences very different temperatures north to south and from the interior of the continent to the marine fringes. The climatic variety of North America is also affected by the various landforms, which exert an influence on the movement and interaction of air masses. Finally, the different parts of the continent have access to differing amounts of moisture, depending on their proximity to large bodies of water, the lay of the land, and the movement of air.

Look at the climate map (Figure 2.1) and observe the broad band of cooler humid climate across the northern part of the continent, reaching south of the latitude of the Great Lakes. You can see that adjacent to this band, along the Pacific coast, there is a thin band of wet climates cool in the north, warmer in the south. The moisture comes from wet air that passes onto land from the Pacific Ocean. When the wet air encounters the coastal ranges, it rises, cools, and dumps frequent rain along the windward (western) slopes. To the east of the coastal highlands, the climates are much drier. For the most part, the air masses tend to hold what moisture they have left as they move east across the Great Basin and Rocky Mountains.

FIGURE 2.1 Regional climate.

On the eastern side of the Rocky Mountains, in the Great Plains region, the moisture patterns begin to change. Here the main source of moisture is the Gulf of Mexico. When the continent is warming in the spring and summer, the rising air pulls in moisture from the Gulf. This warm, wet Gulf air interacts with cooler, drier air masses moving from the north, creating often violent rainstorms. Generally, the Great Plains are wettest in the east and south and driest in the north and west.

East of the Great Plains, the climates are generally more humid, with deficient rainfall only rarely a problem. In eastern North America, toward the north, climates are cool and moist; in the south, they are warm and usually quite wet. The Gulf of Mexico supplies most of the moisture in the east; but along the Atlantic coast, some moisture is supplied by the Gulf Stream, a warm ocean current that flows up the eastern seaboard from the tropics. It brings a supply of warm, wet air that frequently creates high humidity and rain, and sometimes hurricanes.

Temperatures are affected by the huge size of the North American continent as well as by location relative to the North Pole or to the equator. Land tends to heat up and cool off more rapidly than water; thus, temperatures in the North American continental interior are hot in summer and cold in winter. But since proximity to water generally modifies temperature extremes, and since oceans nearly surround North America, wide fringes of the continent experience temperatures moderated by the adjacent oceans.

HUMAN PATTERNS

The history of North America can be viewed as successive movements of people across the vast continent, beginning with the original peopling of the continent from Eurasia, down to the waves of European immigrants who settled across the country in the nineteenth century. The patterns of these movements have helped to establish a set of distinct subregions. Today, movement continues to be a defining characteristic of North American life. Americans are among the most mobile people in the world.

The Peopling of North America

The story of how humans first came into North America began in Siberia, with small bands of hunters from eastern Siberia crossing the Bering land bridge. This bridge was a huge, low landmass, over 1000 miles wide, that linked Siberia and Alaska between 25,000 and 14,000 years ago; this was the last ice age, when the polar ice caps were considerably thicker and sea levels lower. Temperatures rose again about 10,000 years ago, and the land bridge sank below the rising sea. By this time, hunter-gatherers had fanned out across the North American continent, south throughout Central America, and well into South America, occupying virtually every climate region.

Over thousands of years, those peoples settling in the Americas developed distinctive regional cultural traditions. They domesticated plants, built permanent shelters, and at times created elaborate social systems. Many of the developments in North America were made possible by the domestication of corn, which was introduced into the southwest desert about 3000 years ago from Mexico, where people had been cultivating it for perhaps 5000 years. Other Mexican domesticates, particularly squash and beans, were also brought north. These foods provided the early people in what are now Canada and the United States with a relatively wide range of cultivated food plants whose impressive harvests made possible large, urbanlike regional settlements—like that at Cahokia in Illinois.

The European Transformation

North America today bears little resemblance to the land that the Native Americans knew for hundreds of generations. The landforms and climate are roughly the same, but virtually every other aspect of the continent's geography has been transformed, from the vegetation to the overall cultural orientation of the population. The major factor in this transformation was the sweeping occupation of North America by Europeans, beginning in the seventeenth century.

The rapid expansion of European settlement was made possible largely by the long biological and technological isolation of Native American populations from the rest of the world. Diseases brought by the new settlers from Europe, Africa, and Asia sometimes wiped out entire Native American cultures; on average, they killed 90 percent of any given group within 100 years of contact. European violence toward Native Americans also took a large toll. Those Native Americans living in the eastern part of the continent who survived were forcibly relocated westward onto relatively small reservations with few resources. Simple numbers tell much of the story. There were roughly 18 million Native Americans throughout the continent in 1492, 9 million in 1542, and just over 400,000 in 1907. During this time, Euro-American settlement rolled over North America like an unstoppable tide, fed by masses of immigrants from Europe and smaller numbers from Africa and Asia.

The unifying tendencies of the European transformation of the continent have been continually countered by tendencies toward regional variation. Hence, although North America's human geography is in many ways more unified than in most other parts of the world, there are still many distinct regions. Understanding what these regions are and how they have emerged over time is an important part of appreciating the human geography of North America.

The Expansion of European Settlement

Europeans were present in North America as early as A.D. 1000, when Nordic peoples settled for a time in Newfoundland. They had little known lasting influence. Christopher Columbus arrived in the Caribbean in 1492, and numerous French and Spanish explorers roamed the continental interior during the sixteenth century. Nonetheless, the European transformation did not really begin in North America until the early seventeenth century, when the English established colonies along the Atlantic coast in modern-day Massachusetts and Virginia. During the next nearly 200 years, English-speaking colonists built cities, towns, villages, and plantations up and down the east coast of North America, taking over most Native American lands well into the Appalachian Mountains. However, from the very beginning there were distinct regional differences between colonies.

The southern colonies of Virginia, the Carolinas, and Georgia were dependent on the cultivation of cash crops such as tobacco or cotton, much of it grown on large plantations. Because land was readily available to potential laborers, plantation owners had a hard time securing the stable labor force necessary for their huge operations. The unfortunate solution was the enslavement of Africans, who were first brought to North America at Jamestown, Virginia, in 1619. Although slavery was not widely accepted at first, within 50 years enslaved Africans were becoming the dominant labor force on some of the larger southern plantations. By the start of the Civil War in 1861,

slaves made up a large proportion (about one-third) of the population throughout the southern states.

In many ways, the plantation system was detrimental to the economic development of the South. Plantations generated few of the "spin-off" enterprises that could have invigorated the South's regional economy and little money that could have been invested in businesses or education. Much of the South's wealth was concentrated in the hands of a small class of plantation owners, who invested their money in Europe and the northern colonies instead of at home. Many white Southerners were subsistence farmers, meaning that they consumed most of what they produced. They farmed the less fertile land and had little money to invest. The technology required for plantation agriculture was relatively simple. Most slaves, like the poor whites, were forced to live so simply that their consumption needs did not provide a market for goods. The plantation economy declined after the Civil War (1861–1865), and the South sank deeper into poverty, remaining economically underdeveloped well into the twentieth century. As Figure 2.2 shows, the largest concentrations of African Americans, descendants of the slaves, continue to reside in the southern states.

In the northern colonies of New England and southeastern Canada, relatively poor subsistence

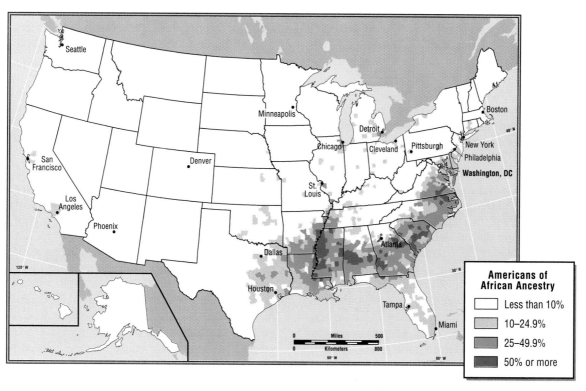

FIGURE 2.2 Distribution of the African-American population in 1990. [Adapted from Roger Doyle, *1994 Atlas of Contemporary America* (New York: Facts on File, 1994), p. 58.]

farmers dominated in agriculture. In contrast to the southern colonies, there were no plantations and not many cash crops were exported. Instead, income was often augmented by exports of timber and animal pelts. Some communities were completely dependent on the rich fishing grounds, called the Grand Banks, located off the shores of Newfoundland and Maine. In southern New England, port cities like Boston, Massachusetts, and Providence, Rhode Island, traded the resources of the interior to the then-emerging global market, and early manufacturing industries were established.

The Economic Core

New England and southeastern Canada were eventually surpassed in numbers of people and in wealth by the mid-Atlantic colonies of New York, New Jersey, and Pennsylvania. These states benefited from more fertile soils, a slightly warmer climate, multiple deepwater harbors, and better access to the resources of the interior. By the end of the Revolutionary War (in 1783), the mid-Atlantic region had become the **economic core,** or dominant economic region, of North America.

Agriculture and manufacturing boomed in the early nineteenth century, drawing immigrants from much of northwestern Europe at first. Their farms were capable of producing grain in such vast quantities that the region was often called the "bread colonies." Cities such as New York, Philadelphia, and Baltimore also prospered from the spread of industrialization and trade with the vast interior of the country. This relatively small, early core region yielded almost a third of U.S. output on the eve of the Civil War.

Throughout the nineteenth century, the borders of the economic core expanded as connections with interior areas deepened. Rivers, canals, railways, and roads provided cheap transportation that connected the big cities of the mid-Atlantic coast with the entire Great Lakes area, as well as with the area that became the states of Ohio, Michigan, Indiana, Illinois, and Wisconsin. The early settlers in those states were farmers who catered to the needs of growing urban populations, but by the mid-nineteenth century much of the economy was based on the steel industry. That industry stimulated the mining of coal and iron ore, as well as the manufacture of a wide range of goods.

By the late nineteenth century, a large industrializing region stretched from the Atlantic to Chicago and from Toronto to Cincinnati. This industrializing economic core, sometimes referred to as "the foundry," dominated the other regions of North America economically and politically well into the twentieth century. Most other areas produced food and raw materials for the industrial core's markets and depended on its

factories for a wide array of manufactured goods—ranging from hand tools to locomotives. A detailed discussion of the rise and decline of this region is given on pages 86–90.

Expansion West of the Mississippi

As the eastern parts of the continent became more densely occupied, many prospective immigrant farmers turned their attention west. Much of the land immediately west of the Mississippi was dry grassland, or prairie, which seemed desolate and strange to people whose roots were in the well-watered fields and forests of northwestern Europe and the eastern United States. Nevertheless, in the later nineteenth century many settlers interested in crop farming founded homesteads on the Great Plains and adapted to the lack of trees and shortage of water. After a few difficult years, the soil usually proved amazingly fertile. Settlement of the vast grasslands of the United States and Canada proceeded into the early twentieth century, as there was a steady demand for the grain and other crops that could be grown here. Then a series of dry years, coupled with years of deep plowing, led to dust storms in the 1930s; these destroyed the plains, forcing many settlers to set their hopes, instead, on California and the heavily forested lands of the Pacific Northwest.

While there were some good agricultural lands along the Pacific, the tremendous distance from the markets of the economic core meant that little produce could be exported. In the Northwest, settlers turned their attention to the abundance of trees able to fill the rising demand for building materials. Soon logging became the dominant industry in the Pacific Northwest, as vast stands of enormous redwoods, Douglas firs, spruce, and many other species were clear cut throughout the region.

By the mid-nineteenth century, the Southwest was also being populated by people from the eastern half of North America and from Europe. Most of this land had formerly belonged to Mexico, and farmers and ranchers from Mexico were already settling in some parts in the 1700s and throughout the 1800s. By the twentieth century, a vibrant agricultural economy was developing in California. Here, the mild Mediterranean climate made it possible to grow vegetables almost year-round; and with the advent of refrigerated railroad cars in the early twentieth century, these vegetables could be sent to the major population centers of the East. Massive government-sponsored irrigation schemes greatly increased the amount of cultivable land. These schemes totally transformed the natural course of water drainage in southern California and much of the West, as whole rivers were diverted to fields and urban developments hundreds of miles away.

European Settlement and Native Americans

As Euro-Americans expanded throughout North America in the nineteenth century, many Native American groups who had occupied the eastern half of the continent were forced to relocate on arid western lands that Euro-Americans found less useful. Some groups, such as the Cherokee, had been willing to participate in Euro-American society. They often traded cattle, owned farms, ran ferries and flour and saw mills, and imparted some of their own ideas on democratic institutions to the European settlers. But even these groups were persecuted. In the mid-nineteenth century, the Cherokee were forced to march from their green, hilly homelands in the southeastern United States to the dry, flat plains of Oklahoma. As Euro-Americans occupied the Great Plains and prairies, many of the reservations set aside for these Native Americans were further shrunk or relocated on less desirable land (Figure 2.3).

Native American populations are now expanding, after plunging from perhaps 18 million to less than 400,000 by 1900. In 1998, there were about 2.3 million Native Americans in North America, and they consti-tuted just 1 percent of the total population. Only about half a million live in Canada, one-fifth in Ontario Province, and one-fifth in British Columbia. Ironically, today, Americans often identify with the Native peoples rather than against them. Many Americans now claim some Indian blood (in Canada, those who are a mixture of European and Indian call themselves métis). This makes it difficult to determine who should be called a Native American, and just how many there are.

Today, reservations cover 52 million acres in the United States and 6 million acres in Canada. Nearly every reservation is insufficient in resources to support its population at a standard of living enjoyed by other North Americans. After centuries of mistreatment, many Native Americans are more familiar with poverty than with true Native ways. Many have become severely demoralized, often turning to alcohol, and many live as impoverished "wards of the state," totally dependent on meager welfare money. For many years, Native young people faced a hard choice: they could remain in poverty with family and community on the reservation, or they could seek a more affluent way of life far from home and kin in situations where they would lose touch with traditional ways and might encounter considerable prejudice.

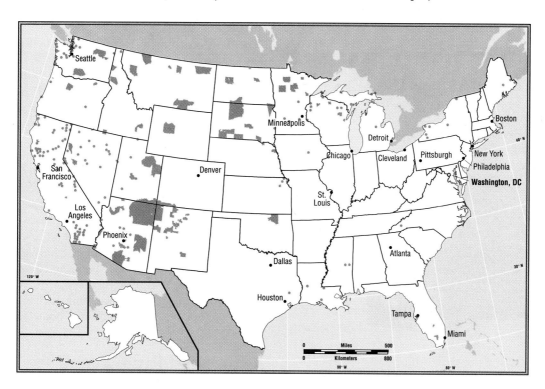

FIGURE 2.3 The colored areas and dots represent federal reservations set aside for Native Americans. Two hundred years ago, Native Americans "owned" about 75 percent of what became U.S. territory. Today, they have been pushed to the west and exert control on slightly over 2 percent of U.S. lands. [Adapted from *Native American Heritage Map* (Washington, DC: National Geographic Society, 1991).]

Recently, several avenues to greater affluence on the reservations have opened up. Some tribes have sought and received substantial monetary compensation from the government for past losses. Others find themselves on reservations that have sprouted oil and gas wells or coal and uranium mines. Still other tribes have opened gambling casinos designed to lure non-Native gamblers. Loopholes in the old treaties have let tribes establish casinos in places where local law would otherwise forbid them. While these few roads to prosperity can produce enormous income in some cases, the stress on weakened tribal structure can be intense. In some cases, graft has diverted funds to a few elite. In other cases, access to cash has often meant an increase in alcohol consumption, which then leads to family violence. After long years of little access to mainstream American life, young people have little idea of how to

In the early 1990s, Canadian Mohawks, viewing gambling as cultural pollution, strongly opposed the operation of a Mohawk casino across the border in New York. The protesting Mohawks destroyed some of the U.S. machines, causing a bitter dispute in the Mohawk Nation. [Sarah Leen/Matrix.]

construct a life beyond poverty; as a result, suicide rates are high among young Native Americans.

Some tribes have been enormously successful in taking creative approaches to development. The Choctaw in Mississippi have developed factories that produce plastic utensils for McDonald's restaurants, electrical wiring for automobiles, and greeting cards. They employ not only their own people but 1000 non-Indians who come onto the reservation to work. The Salish and Kootenai tribes of Montana have reduced their unemployment level to below that in the vicinity by creating jobs for themselves in farming, tourism, and recreation. In Canada, Native Americans have a higher standard of living than do their U.S. counterparts, and the government spends much more per capita on them. But Canadian tribes have less access to land and far less autonomy in deciding their own futures. Nonetheless, for groups that reject the norms of Euro-American society, the risk of forced relocation is still very real, as the Dineh people can attest. The Dineh are currently being forced off their ancestral homeland on a reservation in New Mexico to make way for a large coal mining operation.

The Changing Social Composition of North America

The transformation of North America by European-led settlement delineated a series of regions that still remain today, though the boundaries and distinctive characteristics of these regions are increasingly blurred. The economic core no longer dominates, as industry spreads to many parts of the country. Those regions that were once dominated by agriculture, logging, or mineral extraction now have industries as well. In cultural terms, distinctive ethnic groups are becoming blended as succeeding generations marry outside their ethnic groups and move to new locations. In Los Angeles, for example, one-third of all U.S.-born middle-class Latinos and more than one-quarter of all U.S.-born middle-class Asians marry someone of another ethnic group. Non-European immigrants from Middle and South America, India, Southeast Asia, East Asia, and Africa are finding a wide variety of social and economic niches as they add to the cultural diversity of their new homeland.

Population Patterns

The population map of North America (Figure 2.4) reveals that the nearly 300 million people who live in this region are very unevenly distributed across the continent. Canadians, who make up approximately one-tenth of the population of North America, live primarily along the southeastern border with the United States. Sixty percent of Canadians live in southern

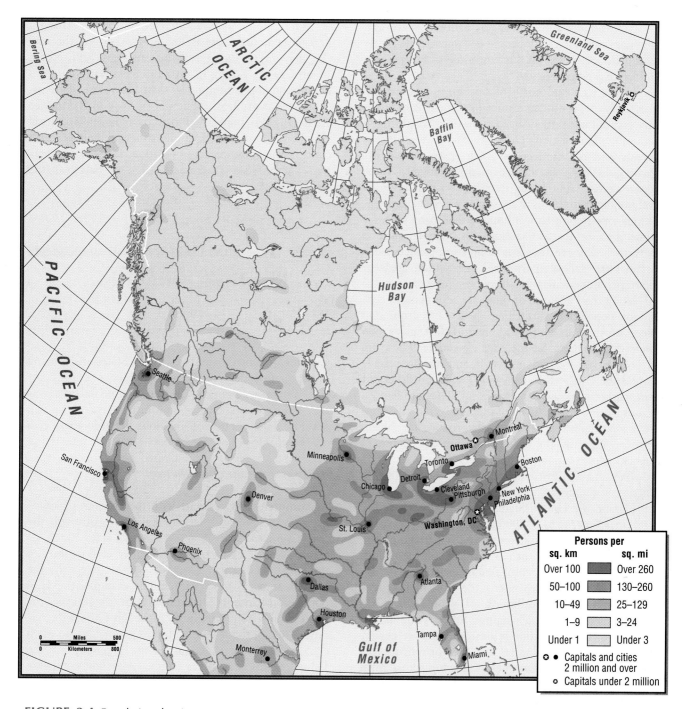

FIGURE 2.4 Population density. [Adapted from *Hammond Citation World Atlas,* 1996.]

Ontario in the Great Lakes region, and in Québec along the St. Lawrence River. The greatest concentration of people in the United States is not far south of the border with Canada, in the northeastern part of the United States. Seven of the twelve most populous states in the United States and several of the largest cities lie in a quadrant marked by Boston and Washington, D.C., along the Atlantic seaboard, St. Louis on the Mississippi River, and Milwaukee/Chicago on Lake

Michigan. Population is concentrated in this part of North America because this is also the economic core, referred to previously. Densities average from 25 to more than 260 people per square mile (10 to over 100 per square kilometer), with urban areas having significantly higher densities.

This population core is flanked to the south and west by a zone of less dense settlement on rich agricultural land that is dotted with many medium-sized cities, most under 2 million in population. On average, rural densities are 3–129 people per square mile (1–49 per square kilometer) in this landscape of large fields, woodlands, and grasslands.

To the west and north of this zone, in what this book calls the continental interior, North America is only very lightly settled. In fact, a good two-thirds of this subregion, including the territory in northern Canada and Alaska, has less than three people per square mile (less than one per square kilometer). Much of the western continental interior also remains relatively unpopulated; this is mostly as a result of mountainous topography, lack of rain, and, in many places, a growing season that is too short to sustain agriculture. Nevertheless, there are some population clusters, such as the Utah valley, in irrigated agricultural areas or where rich mineral deposits have been located.

Along the Pacific coast there are several more centers of population, stretching in a band from San Diego north, with concentrations in Los Angeles, San Francisco, Portland, Seattle, and Vancouver. These are all port cities, focused on water and airborne trade around the Pacific Rim and with the American continent, partially via the Panama Canal. They are flanked by agricultural zones, many of them irrigated, that supply a major portion of the fresh produce for North America. Recently, these cities have become centers of innovation in computer technology.

The vast majority of North Americans live in cities; only about one-quarter of the population in both Canada and the United States lives in areas classed as rural (meaning towns of 2000 or less, and farms). Even these rural residents are for the most part employed in urban areas. Less than 3 percent of the North American population is employed in agriculture.

Since Americans are among the most mobile people on earth, the distribution of people in North America is constantly changing. Every year, almost one-fifth of the population relocates. Some are changing jobs, others are going off to school or retiring to a warmer climate, some are merely moving across town or out to the suburbs to a more amenable residence. Still others are moving into the region from outside: immigrants arrive in North America at the rate of about 3000 per day. Those regions that are perceived as offering advantages change over time, so the movement of migrants and immigrants ebbs and flows. Individual communities, states, and provinces measure their success by how well they do at attracting new residents. New residents usually contribute to the local economy by finding work, buying or renting homes, becoming taxpayers and consumers, and by increasing the number of representatives in state, provincial, and federal legislatures. Hence, the success or failure of public officials is judged in part by whether a region is gaining or losing population.

The rate of natural increase in North America (0.6 percent per year) is low, just one-third the rate (1.8 percent) of the rest of the Americas. Still, North Americans are adding to their numbers fast enough to double the population in less than 120 years. Many social issues central to public debate in North America are related to population patterns—issues like legal and illegal immigration, family structure, gender, birth control, the aging of the population, and ethnic diversity. These issues are discussed at some length in the following section.

CURRENT GEOGRAPHIC ISSUES

Citizens of Canada and the United States share many of the same concerns. We will examine a series of social, economic, political, and environmental issues as they affect both countries, and in the process we will develop a perspective on relations between these two countries. Three key words characterize the interaction between Canada and the United States: *asymmetries*, *similarities*, and *interdependencies*.

Asymmetries. Let's start with the concept of asymmetry, which means "lack of balance." Although the two countries are about the same size, much of Canada's territory is sparsely inhabited cold country to the north and west. In about every other way, the United States is much larger. For example, the U.S. population (close to 270 million) is nearly 10 times the size of Canada's (30 million). Although Canada's economy is one of the largest and most productive on earth (U.S. $300 billion annually), the economy of the United States is 10 times larger ($4 trillion annually).

On the international scene there is also asymmetry. The United States is a superpower in economic, military, and political terms. It has a world leadership role that preoccupies it. The foreign policy of the United States is chiefly concerned these days with post–cold war politics, relations with Russia, Europe, China, Japan, Southeast and Southwest Asia, and a host of other problematic places. Canada is only an afterthought in U.S. foreign policy debates, in part because the country is so close and so secure an ally. But, for Canada, managing its relationship with the United States is the foreign policy priority. As a result, Canadians focus more on what is going on in the United States and how they should react to it than Americans focus on Canada.

Similarities. Despite the asymmetries, the two countries have much in common. Both are former British colonies and from this experience have developed comparable political traditions. Both are federations (of states or provinces) and are representative democracies; and their legal systems are also alike. Not the least of the features they share is the longest undefended border in the world. There are official checkpoints on highways; but for thousands of miles there is not even a fence, and in places the international line runs through bedrooms and backyards with no notice taken. Thousands of residents pass out of one country and into the other many times in the course of a single day by simply going about their usual farming, hunting, or housekeeping.

Well beyond the border country, Canada and the United States share many other landscape similarities. Their cities and suburbs look pretty much the same. Billboards line highways and freeways advertising the same brand names. Shopping malls have followed suburbia into the countryside, drawing millions of affluent buyers away from old urban centers. The same fast-food franchises dispense the same questionable nutrition. And the two countries share similar patterns of ethnic diversity that developed, as we shall see shortly, in nearly identical stages of immigration from abroad.

Interdependencies. Canada and the United States are perhaps most intimately connected by their long-standing economic relationship (Figure 2.5). By 1996, that relationship had evolved into a two-way trade flow of U.S. $272 billion annually. Each is the other's largest trading partner. Canada sells 80 percent of its exports to the United States and buys 70 percent of its imports from the United States. The United States, in turn, sells 22 percent of its exports to Canada and buys 19 percent of its imports from Canada. Notice that asymmetry emerges even in the realm of interdependencies: Canada's smaller economy is much more dependent on the United States than the reverse. Nonetheless, if Canada were to disappear tomorrow, as many as a million American jobs would be threatened. The lopsided quality of the relationships will probably persist; because of its size, large population, and giant economy,

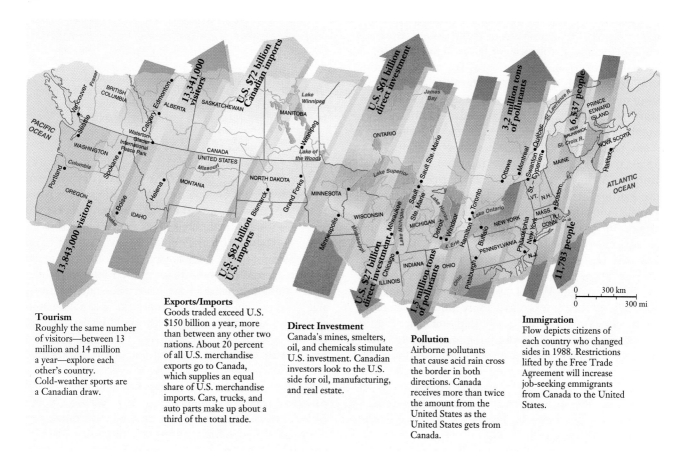

Tourism
Roughly the same number of visitors—between 13 million and 14 million a year—explore each other's country. Cold-weather sports are a Canadian draw.

Exports/Imports
Goods traded exceed U.S. $150 billion a year, more than between any other two nations. About 20 percent of all U.S. merchandise exports go to Canada, which supplies an equal share of U.S. merchandise imports. Cars, trucks, and auto parts make up about a third of the total trade.

Direct Investment
Canada's mines, smelters, oil, and chemicals stimulate U.S. investment. Canadian investors look to the U.S. side for oil, manufacturing, and real estate.

Pollution
Airborne pollutants that cause acid rain cross the border in both directions. Canada receives more than twice the amount from the United States as the United States gets from Canada.

Immigration
Flow depicts citizens of each country who changed sides in 1988. Restrictions lifted by the Free Trade Agreement will increase job-seeking emmigrants from Canada to the United States.

FIGURE 2.5 Transfers of tourists, goods, investment, pollution, and immigrants between the United States and Canada. [Adapted from *National Geographic*, February 1990, pp. 106–107.]

the United States is likely to remain the dominant partner. As former Canadian Prime Minister Pierre Trudeau once told the U.S. Congress, "Living next to you is in some ways like sleeping with an elephant: No matter how friendly and even-tempered the beast, one is affected by every twitch and grunt."

Sociocultural Issues

Many sociocultural issues in North America have geographic aspects. Only a few can be covered here, so I have chosen issues that seem to be especially widespread and likely to persist into the future. First are some issues—immigration, religion, and minorities—related to the fact that North America now contains people from many other parts of the world who struggle to find common ground. Then this chapter discusses three issues—gender, family, and aging—related to social organization in these two large, complex, and prosperous countries.

Immigration

Most Americans have roots in some other part of the globe. The earliest forebears of many of them entered the North American continent (already fully inhabited by Native Americans) along the eastern seaboard in the seventeenth and eighteenth centuries, most coming from the British Isles and France. Those who settled in what became the United States also came in large numbers from Germany, Italy, Spain, and also from many parts of central Africa via the slave trade. After 1880, more and more people migrated from central Europe (Austria-Hungary, Poland, Russia) and southern Europe (Italy, Yugoslavia, Greece). Some went to Canada; most went to the United States. In the nineteenth and early twentieth centuries, a few thousand Asians came to the Pacific coast of North America as low-paid laborers on farms and in mines, and to build the new western railroads.

After World War I, while immigration from Europe continued, more and more immigrants came from Latin America, the Caribbean, and Asia. Figure 2.6 shows the proportion of immigrants to the United States from different areas of the world, and how the distribution changed over time. Be aware that the data lump all Asian immigrants together so that there is no way to tell how many came from specific Asian countries—like India, Pakistan, Indonesia, Vietnam, or the Philippines, and so forth.

Once in North America, the different immigrant groups tended to settle in particular parts of the continent. Early newcomers were particularly attracted to rural agricultural locations; and because immigrants from the British Isles and France already occupied

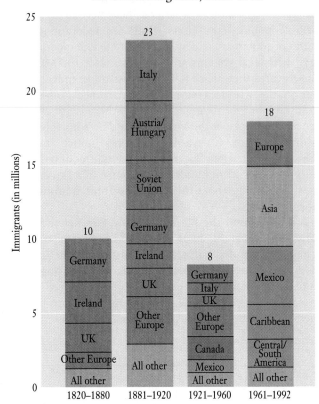

Regions and Countries of Origin for U.S. Immigrants, 1820–1992

FIGURE 2.6 National origins of U.S. immigrants, 1820–1992. [Adapted from Philip Martin and Elizabeth Midgley, Immigration to the United States: Journey to an uncertain destination, *Population Bulletin* 49 (September 1994): 25.]

eastern Canada and the U.S. Northeast, later waves of immigrants from Europe tended to settle farther west. Scandinavians went to the U.S. upper Midwest, to Minnesota and surrounding states. Many Germans settled in a band across the central Midwest, from Ohio to Missouri; other Germans went to southern Appalachia and to south Texas. Early immigrants who found suitable territory sent for friends and relatives, and word of an attractive American location would spread to adjacent villages in Europe. For example, in the late 1800s, villagers from the Dolensko valley of Slovenia in central Europe settled in the iron range country of northern Minnesota, where they tended to work in forest industries just as they had in Slovenia. As industrial development spread across North America, many immigrants chose urban locations; and again, particular ethnic groups gravitated to particular neighborhoods, drawn by shared culture and language. By the 1920s, Dolensko valley Slovenes were getting jobs in the steel mills and settling in Lorain, Ohio.

While Canada shared the same general immigration pattern as the United States, by far the greatest proportion of its early settlers came from the British Isles and France, and there has long been a steady stream immigrating to Canada from the United States. In recent years, an even larger number is moving from Canada to the United States. The English, Irish, and Scots tended to settle in the Maritime Provinces or around the Great Lakes and on farms in the prairie provinces. The French settled primarily along the lower St. Lawrence River and remain concentrated in and near Québec. Canada never had a slave-based economy, so African Canadians have their roots primarily among those who escaped to Canada from the United States or who later came voluntarily from the Caribbean or Africa. They tend to live in the cities of Ontario and Québec. During most of the twentieth century, Canada has encouraged immigration to fill up its empty lands. Early on, the push was to settle the prairies; and many farmers arrived initially from the British Isles and then from eastern Europe, including Russia and the Ukraine. In the late twentieth century, as in the United States, the origin of the immigrants has switched away from Europe to Latin America, the Caribbean, and Asia. In the 1990s, 55 percent of Canada's new immigrants came from Asia.

Issues of Diversity Related to Immigration. For both Canada and the United States, the relatively recent influx of large numbers of immigrants from areas other than Europe has challenged long-held assumptions that the dominant culture of North America would forever be derived from Europe, with but a few small minorities of Native Americans, African Americans, Hispanics, and Asians. Of the two countries, Canada seems to be more receptive to the change. In the United States, attitudes toward new immigrants are sometimes testy, and the sentiment is growing that future immigration should be controlled.

Recently, Canadians have accepted with equanimity many refugees from Asia and Africa, and they display a benign attitude toward the issue of assimilation. In Canada, immigrants are allowed, even encouraged, to retain their culture, use their native languages in schools, and maintain fairly strict (and usually voluntary) residential segregation. Québec stands out as an example of ethnicity so strong that the province threatens to secede from Canada. Its features are discussed at some length in the subregional section, following. Toronto, Ontario, on the other hand, provides a somewhat different model of how Canadians accommodate to ethnicity (see the box "Ethnicity in Toronto").

In the United States, immigration and cultural diversity are topics of considerable public debate. Immigrants from every part of the world have made the country what it is, yet some new questions regarding the role of immigration in U.S. society are being raised.

Do New Immigrants Cost U.S. Citizens Too Much Money? An often heard view is that immigrants cost taxpayers money by using public services like food stamps and welfare. Several studies have shown that in the long run, immigrants contribute more to the economy than they cost. Most immigrants start to work soon after arrival. They pay taxes and many tend to use fewer public services than they pay for. Even immigrants who draw on public services tend to do so only in the very first few years after they arrive; and they are often refugees who have been forced from their homes abroad by some debilitating tragedy. Once they have jobs, payback begins in the form of taxes.

A problem can arise, however, if most of their tax money is paid to the federal government, because the costs of services to immigrants tend to come out of local coffers. For example, in Los Angeles County, new immigrants make up 25 percent of the population (most are from Mexico and various parts of Asia). These 2.3 million people paid $4.3 billion in taxes in 1991–1992. They received $947 million in county services (less than one-quarter of the taxes they paid), but more than half their taxes went to the federal, not local, government. The state took another 37 percent, and Los Angeles County received just 3 percent; hence, it was left holding an $808 million "immigrant deficit." In this case, the real problem is not that immigrants are not paying taxes sufficient to cover their cost to society, but rather that the tax moneys are going to the wrong level of government.

Do Immigrants Take Jobs Away from U.S. Citizens? Some people in the United States, particularly professional people, are in competition with highly trained immigrants for positions, but often there are not enough trained native-born people to fill these positions. The computer technology industry, for example, regularly recruits abroad in places like Bangalore, India, where there are many high-tech firms. In the last several decades, however, many immigrants have tended to be semiskilled laborers. These less skilled immigrants compete with the least educated citizens, and in some parts of the country they do tend to drive down the wages of this latter group by increasing the pool of labor. Often, however, these less educated immigrants fill low-paying service and agricultural jobs that U.S. workers have already rejected. Although such immigrants are often willing workers, the wages they earn are too low to support a decent way of life. Some argue that it is wrong to let in immigrants who will be consigned by lack of skills to a state of poverty in their new home.

Are Too Many Immigrants Being Admitted to the United States? It is certainly controversial for a nation created by immigrants to begin to question the

AT THE LOCAL SCALE   *Ethnicity in Toronto*

The lines dividing Toronto's ethnic neighborhoods aren't strict or exclusionary, but when a city bus moves through town, Italians get off at particular stops, Chinese at others, and Greeks at yet others. Many of the neighborhoods have been rehabilitated and upgraded, or **gentrified,** to attract the middle-class children and grandchildren of much poorer laborers who arrived earlier in the twentieth century. There are about 400,000 Torontonians of Italian descent, many of whom live in Corso Italia (the Little Italy of Toronto), an area of shops, sidewalk cafés, and elegant homes and apartments. The Chinese community of 350,000 is the fastest growing. Many recent arrivals are prosperous Chinese businesspeople from Hong Kong, who feared the consequences of China's reassumption of control of Hong Kong in June 1997. There is Koreatown, with herb shops and import emporiums. Koreans own many of the fresh produce and grocery stores throughout the city. The Greek community is assembled around the National Bank of Greece and the Greek Orthodox Church. Jews and Caribbean people are sprinkled in small enclaves throughout the city, while Polish people often settle together and specialize in owning bakeries and butcher shops. All in all, there are said to be at least 80 different ethnic neighborhoods in the city.

Throughout Toronto, city street signs are written in English, the lingua franca, as well as in the predominant language of the neighborhoods—in this case, Vietnamese. [David R. Frazier/Tony Stone Images.]

very idea of immigration. Several circumstances have caused some to call for curtailing immigration into the United States. First, after a lull at midcentury, the immigration stream has picked up again; by the 1990s (with estimated illegal immigration included), it exceeded the previous high of 1906. At these high rates, by the year 2050, the United States population will be close to 400 million, nearly one-quarter larger than it would be if all immigration stopped now. Second, illegal immigration reached unprecedented levels during the 1980s and 1990s, lending some credibility to the argument that immigration has become a threat. Illegal immigrants are not screened for criminal background, tend to have low skills, and their numbers are uncontrolled. On the other hand, because they must hide from the authorities, they do not partake of public programs, so their drain on the economy is probably not great. Finally, for some, the fact that so many of the new immigrants are from Latin America and Asia is an added worry (Figure 2.7). Will Euro-Americans and African Americans lose their sense of home in a United States of America where the largest minority is

U.S. Population by Race and Ethnicity, 1996 and 2050

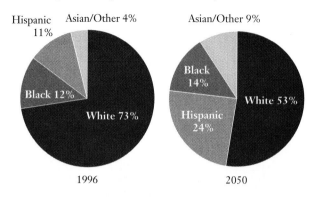

FIGURE 2.7 The changing U.S. ethnic composition. [Adapted from Jorge del Pinal and Audrey Singer, Generations of diversity: Latinos in the United States, *Population Bulletin* 52 (October 1997): 14.]

Hispanic, where Spanish is a prominent second language, and where another large minority is from Asia? Will the U.S. national identity be diluted by so many newcomers from totally different backgrounds? Others see the new immigrants from non-European places as adding important talents and creativity to the U.S. cultural mix. They point out that ethnic diversity has already contributed significantly to U.S. leadership in international affairs.

VIGNETTE On a recent night at the Madison, a [New York] midtown club, South Asians jammed the dance floor. It was Bombay Bizar night; most of the crowd were students and young professionals who had traveled over bridges and through tunnels to meet and possibly date their own kind. The men were clean-cut and buttoned-down, except for a few Punjabi homeboys from Queens sporting goatees and baggy jeans. A striking number of women wore short black skirts and Sanskrit "om" pendants. Ancil Chachra, a burly accountant, said earnestly: "My parents won't let me live if I don't get an M.B.A. And you know what? I agree with them."

As the evening wore on, the open bar got heavy traffic and the crowd loosened up. A sophomore from N.Y.U. said he goes to the Madison, in part, to meet Indian girls. "I don't mind dating other girls, but I want to marry an Indian. Of course," he added, "I wouldn't necessarily want to marry a girl I met in a club."

At about 2 A.M., D. J. Karma cued a remix of the Hindi hit "Jaanu Meri Jaan." Everybody seemed to know the words. At each chorus, Karma lifted the needle and

the crowd shouted, "Sara Hindustan!" ("All over India!"). As "Jaanu Meri Jaan" modulated into Michael Jackson's "Billie Jean," a turbaned Sikh in a gold lamé jacket smiled and spread his arms in a Punjabi wedding dance. [From Richard McGill Murphy, Seinfeld Masala, *New York Times Magazine*, October 19, 1997, p. 72.]

Religion

Because so many immigrants were Christian in their home countries, Christianity is the predominant religious affiliation claimed by North Americans. Nonetheless, one is free to accept whatever creed one likes, or none at all; and virtually every medium-sized city has at least one synagogue and one mosque and one Buddhist temple. In some particular localities, adherents of Islam, Judaism, or Buddhism are numerous enough to constitute a dominant cultural influence. Religion in North America has some interesting and unusual geographic dimensions (Figure 2.8). Two of these are the distribution of particular faiths and the regional differences in the role of religion in daily life.

There are many versions of Christianity in North America, and their distributions are closely linked to the settlement pattern of the immigrants who brought them. The map in Figure 2.8 shows the dominance of Roman Catholicism, especially in places where Hispanic and French people have settled—in the United States, in southern Louisiana, the Southwest, and the far Northeast; and in Québec and other parts of Canada. Lutheranism is dominant where Scandinavian people have settled, primarily in Minnesota and the eastern Dakotas. The Baptists dominate the religious landscapes of the South. This faith was introduced by early European immigrants seeking religious freedom. The Baptist denomination did not become dominant until after the Civil War, when those who became known as Southern Baptists became spokespeople for what they called "southern culture," a concept that was never particularly well defined but which for a while included racial segregation. Generally speaking, Southern Baptists tend to take the teachings of the Bible more literally than many other Christian denominations, so this part of the United States has come to be called "the Bible Belt." Christianity, and especially the Baptist version thereof, is such an important part of community life in the South that new settlers in the region are asked almost daily what church they go to. This is a question that is rarely asked in most other parts of the continent. Those who reply "none" or something other than "Baptist" may be left with the feeling that they have disappointed the questioner.

The issue of religion and politics in the United States has long been a ticklish one, in large part

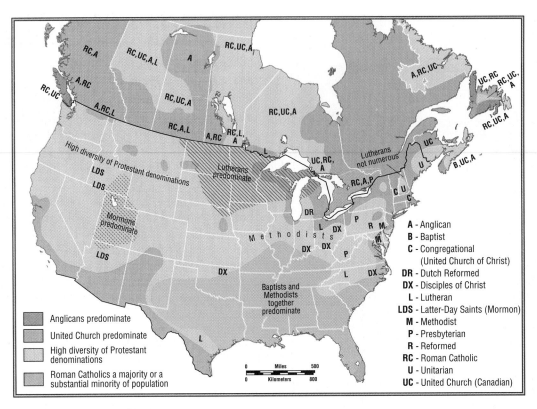

FIGURE 2.8 Religious affiliation across North America. [Adapted from Jerome Fellmann, Arthur Getis, and Judith Getis, *Human Geography* (Dubuque, IA: Brown & Benchmark, 1997), p. 164.]

because the framers of the Constitution supported the idea that church and state should remain separate. Even now, most people try to avoid mixing the two in daily life and conversation. In the last decade or two, however, some of the more conservative Protestants (known sometimes as the "Christian Coalition") have banded together to further their agenda within the political arena. In line with their strict interpretation of the Bible, they have pushed for prayer in the public schools, the teaching of the biblical version of creation rather than evolution as an explanation of the development of life-forms on earth, and the banning of abortion as a method of birth control. Although the Christian Coalition has met with the most success in the South, its goals are shared by people scattered across the country. The long-term outcome of this interesting development in American religious and political life is not yet apparent, but recent national surveys indicate that a majority of Americans favor the continued separation of church and state and think abortion should be kept as a legal alternative.

Race in North America

Although ethnic and racial diversity is abundant in North America, as previously discussed, the term *race* in this region usually refers in some way to the situation and life experience of those who trace their ancestry in whole or in part to Africa. Discrimination and lack of opportunity have clearly hampered the ability of African Americans to reach social and economic parity with Americans of other races and ethnic groups, despite many of the formal barriers having been officially and legally removed. Statistical differences in levels of well-being and prosperity remain between African Americans and Euro-Americans and Asian Americans. African Americans as a group experience lower life expectancies, higher infant mortality rates, lower levels of academic achievement, higher poverty rates, and greater unemployment than do other Americans (though some data shows that Hispanics of all racial backgrounds fare even worse).

There is considerable public debate over the causes and significance of these differences. Certainly, over the last few decades, many African Americans have joined the middle class and achieved success in the highest ranks of government and business. In particular, African-Caribbean immigrants to North America are outstandingly successful, yet their roots in slavery and past discrimination are very similar to those of African Americans. Furthermore, numerous surveys show that Americans of whatever background favor equal opportunities for groups that have experienced past discrimination. Nonetheless, most middle-class African Americans report experiencing both overt and covert prejudice.

What holds back so many young African Americans from moving up the social and economic ladder? The experts differ, but there is consensus that poverty and low social status breed the perception among the victims that there is no hope for them, hence no point in trying to succeed. Furthermore, the basic skills for success are not being imparted at home or in school to the poorest of Americans, of whatever background. The increasing numbers of poor, single-parent families is also thought to play a role. Fifty years ago, African-American families were primarily two-parent units, and fathers played a central role. Now, nearly 75 percent of African-American children are born to single mothers, and often the fathers of these children do not play a major role in their support and upbringing. The causes of this change are complex and not yet well understood. They are undoubtedly partly related to a welfare system that requires that a single-parent situation exist in a home before funds can be allotted, as well as to employment discrimination against African Americans. The absence of the fathers leaves enormous responsibilities of both child rearing and breadwinning in the hands of often undereducated, poor young mothers.

Certainly, African Americans are now overrepresented among the poor; in large part, this is because of the residual effects of slavery and the vicious racism of the recent past. But there is growing evidence that the pattern of poverty, underachievement, and poor health among African Americans is part of a larger class problem rather than simply a race problem. For example, there are many poor white Americans in the same predicament. They also experience proliferating single-parent families, absent fathers, low achievement, and poor health. The crux of the problem may well be the growing economic disparity between poor and rich Americans. The middle class has fled to the suburbs, so rich and poor rarely even encounter each other in daily life. Thus, it is difficult for the affluent of whatever race to see how they might help individuals move out of poverty; and it is difficult for the poor to witness models of success. Cited as support for this class-based explanation is the fact that there seems to be room in the middle and upper classes for African Americans with education and skills. Privileged Americans of whatever racial background are sharing neighborhoods, workplaces, places of worship, and marriages with markedly decreasing attention to matters of skin color.

Gender and Family Structure

The family has repeatedly been identified as the institution most in need of shoring up in today's fast-chang-ing and ever more impersonal world. Earlier in this century, most people lived with members of several generations in extended families. Family members pooled their income and shared chores. Aunts, uncles, cousins, siblings, and grandparents were almost as likely to provide daily care for a child as its mother and father. Humans have long preferred to reside in communities of kinfolk, but today it is the **nuclear family** that is held up as a model. This version of the family consists of a married father and mother and their children. It is actually a rather recent invention of the industrial age.

Beginning after World War I and especially after World War II, many young people migrated from the farms to distant cities. Away from their larger kin groups, they established new families composed of just the basic reproductive unit. Soon suburbia, with its interchangeable single-family homes, provided the perfect domestic space for the emerging nuclear family. This small, compact family suited industry and business, too, because it had no firm ties to other relatives and hence was portable. An industry could draw on a large labor pool willing and able to move. Many North Americans born since 1950 or so moved as often as five to ten times before reaching adulthood. The grandparents and aunts and uncles left behind missed helping to raise the younger generation, and they had no one to look after them in old age. Institutional care for the elderly proliferated.

In the 1970s, the whole system began to fall apart. It was hard to move so often. Suburban sprawl meant onerous commutes to jobs for men and long lonely days at home for women. Women began to want their own careers; but having careers, they no longer could leave for a new location with an upwardly mobile husband. Many workers of both sexes found that their social life increasingly revolved around work; family life receded in importance. With kinfolk no longer around to shore up the marital bond, divorce rates rose drastically. One in three U.S. marriages now ends in divorce. In Canada, the rate is even higher, at about two in five.

By the late 1980s, the nuclear family was an endangered species. As Figure 2.9 shows, the percentage of nuclear families continually shrank. By 1994, only about 26 percent of American households were nuclear, while the fastest growing family unit was headed by a single parent. More Americans of both sexes are now living alone than ever before. The majority of these people are over the age of 45; many were once part of a nuclear family and have chosen to leave it or were widowed. Ken Bryson, of the U.S. Census Bureau, says there is no longer a typical American household but only an increasing diversity of forms.

Some of these new forms do not necessarily represent an improvement over the nuclear family. One-quarter of U.S. children of all races are now born to

Household Composition, 1970–1994 (percent)

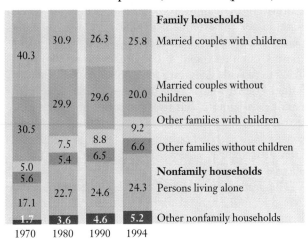

Family households

30.9 26.3 25.8 Married couples with children
40.3

29.9 29.6 20.0 Married couples without children

30.5 9.2 Other families with children

7.5 8.8
5.4 6.5 6.6 Other families without children
5.0

Nonfamily households

5.6
17.1 22.7 24.6 24.3 Persons living alone

1.7 3.6 4.6 5.2 Other nonfamily households

1970 1980 1990 1994

FIGURE 2.9 Changing U.S. family composition, 1970–1994. [Adapted from Steve W. Rawlings, *U.S. Census Briefs: Households and Families* (Washington, DC: U.S. Bureau of the Census, 1995), p. 22.]

In 1996, the U.S. Census Bureau reported that children are more likely than adults to be poor: 20 percent of American children live in poverty, whereas just 11.4 percent of people aged 18 to 64 do.

There are many social consequences of the change in family structure, especially the rise in single-parent families and the movement of women into the workplace. One frequently overlooked consequence is that volunteerism in America is declining. Housewives had formerly provided important services to hospitals, schools, and individuals such as elderly neighbors. These services must now be paid for by government and by individuals, or done without. Over the past 30 years, participation in voluntary activities has declined as much as 50 percent, as reported by parent-teacher associations, the League of Women Voters, and the American Red Cross.

Aging

In most societies, those between youth and old age (15 and 65) must support those who are younger or older. The age structure of a population tells us how great the burden is likely to be. Wealthier, developed societies tend to have lower birth rates, and their members have longer life spans. Over time, the proportion of those younger than 15 becomes smaller, while the proportion of those over 65 becomes larger. During the twentieth century, the number of Americans over the age of 65 has grown rapidly. In 1900, 1 in 25 individuals was over the age of 65; by 1994, 1 in 8 was. By 2050, when most of the current readers of this book will be over 65, 1 in 5 Americans will be elderly.

unmarried women. The single-parent family is the fastest growing type, and already 27 percent of U.S. children live in this type of household. While most single parents do a good job of raising their children, the responsibilities can be overwhelming, especially because such families tend to be hampered by poverty and lack of education. The vast majority of single-parent households are headed by women, and female-headed households have incomes that are on average 33 percent lower than incomes in families headed by single males.

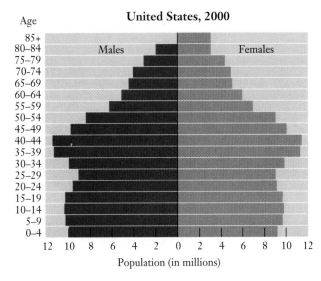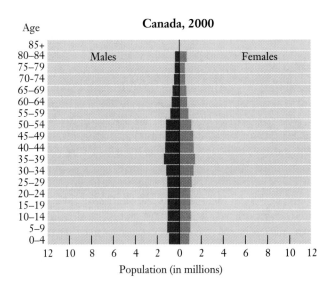

FIGURE 2.10 Population pyramids for the United States and Canada. [Adapted from U.S. Census Bureau, *International Data Base,* at http://www.census.gov/cgi-bin/ipc/idbpyry.pl.]

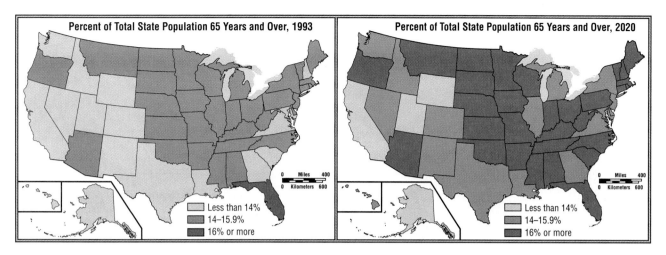

FIGURE 2.11 The highest percentages proportionally of people 65 and older are found in the Sunbelt and in a north-to-south belt from North Dakota to Texas. [Adapted from Frank B. Hobbs, with Bonnie L. Damon, 65+ in the United States, U.S. Bureau of the Census, *Current Population Reports, Special Studies P23-190* (Washington, DC: U.S. Government Printing Office,1996), pp. 5–10.]

In North America, the number of elderly will shoot up with particular rapidity between the years 2010 and 2030. This future spurt is the result of a marked jump in birth rate that took place in the years after World War II, from 1947 to 1964. The so-called baby boomers born in those years are the largest age group in North America, as indicated by the wide band through the middle of the population pyramids in Figure 2.10. In the years from 2010 to 2030, this group will reach age 65 and retire. During this period, payments from social security and private pensions will be high, and medical costs will leap upward. The boomers had fewer children than their parents had, so there will be fewer people of working age to pay the taxes and pension fund contributions necessary to meet these costs. Moreover, people in this smaller population will have fewer brothers and sisters with whom to share the daily personal care and companionship needed by their elderly kin. Most families will not be able to afford assisted living and residential care, which by the year 2000 will cost from $30,000 to $60,000 per year for one person. We might expect that once the boomers begin to retire in large numbers, the makeup of many households and the spaces in which they live will reflect people's efforts to find humane and economical means to care for elderly family members at home.

One way to lessen the strain on the younger generation would be for healthy people to keep working as long as possible. The working elderly could support themselves and save more private funds for later retirement, and they could also help their adult children meet daily expenses. However, an older generation that works longer may deprive younger adults, in their 40s and 50s, of timely promotions to better-paying jobs. Members of this next generation might consequently find themselves less able to save for their own retirement.

The map in Figure 2.11 shows where the elderly were concentrated in the 1990s. In some states (the Dakotas, Nebraska, Alabama, and Maine, for example), the elderly are dominant because the young have left in large numbers for other parts of the country. In other states (Florida, Texas, New Mexico, Arkansas, Arizona, and California), the elderly are new residents, attracted by the warm, pleasant climate of the Sunbelt. (California has the largest number of the elderly, as well as many young.) In many places across North America, local economies depend on spending by retirees. These places will lose income and jobs if people retire later and if fewer wealthy retirees migrate to the Sunbelt. And, since retirees often volunteer, agencies that now depend on elderly volunteers will have to pay for labor.

Political and Economic Issues

North America is today the wealthiest region in the world and politically one of the most influential. The United States has the world's largest economy, one of its most stable systems of government, and the most powerful armed force. Hence, it is not surprising that on the world stage the United States is constantly looked to for leadership in matters such as international security and global trade. Canada, despite its smaller population and resource base, is more than just a sidekick of the United States in these matters. It has secured a high standard of living for its population, using economic and political models that differ somewhat from those of the United States. Moreover,

The Manske cousins, who own adjoining farms in Wisconsin, employ contour furrows to check erosion. They grow alternating rows of corn (the cash crop) and alfalfa (providing hay for the dairy cows) to further help control runoff. [Jim Richardson/Richardson Photography.]

Canada is increasingly playing a central role in the international community, giving generous foreign aid and participating vigorously in a variety of United Nations peacekeeping missions.

The economic and political systems of Canada and the United States have much in common. Both evolved from societies based primarily on agriculture; and after an era of industrialization, both are now increasingly service-based economies with computer processing of information becoming ever more important. Also, although Canada and the United States have traditionally thought of themselves as free marketplaces, both governments have nonetheless intervened extensively to support and mold the development of their economies. The two countries have similar political systems and face similar issues, issues that are often in some way related to ethnic diversity, large size, regional differences, and international roles.

Agriculture

Agriculture was once the backbone of the North American economy. It employed 90 percent of the work force in 1790 and 50 percent in 1880. Over the course of the nineteenth and early twentieth centuries, European immigrants set up tens of thousands of highly productive, family-owned farms, spreading over most of the United States and southern Canada. These farms provided the majority of America's exports up until 1910. Over the years, the U.S. federal government has provided support to farmers in the form of loans, crop insurance, price supports for certain farm products, and—in times of low demand for farm goods—programs that even pay farmers not to plant

all of their land. Though most Americans live in cities, they have willingly paid taxes to help maintain the agricultural infrastructure. They have been rewarded with a bountiful system, which not only supplies them with cheap food but also exports crucial surplus commodities to much of the world. Figure 2.12 shows the distribution of agricultural activity in North America.

In recent decades, farming has become a much smaller source of employment—now less than 3 per-

This market garden farm in Santa Barbara, California, caters to suburban buyers who pay a seasonal fee for a weekly supply of organically grown fresh vegetables. They come to the farm to pick up their share. [Jim Richardson/Richardson Photography.]

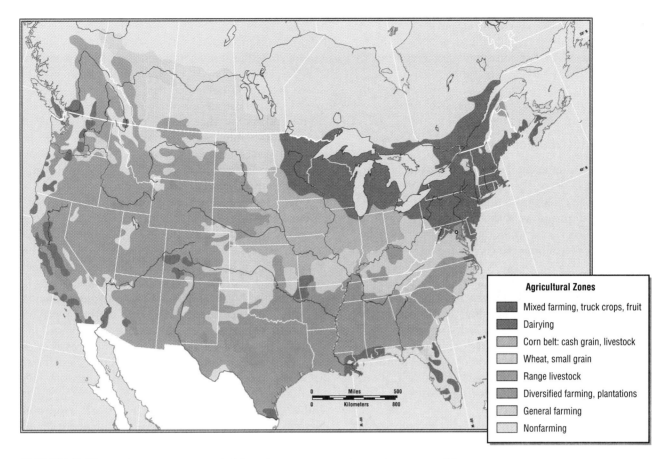

Agricultural Zones

- Mixed farming, truck crops, fruit
- Dairying
- Corn belt: cash grain, livestock
- Wheat, small grain
- Range livestock
- Diversified farming, plantations
- General farming
- Nonfarming

FIGURE 2.12 North America is remarkable in that some type of agriculture is possible throughout much of the continent. The major exceptions are the northern reaches of Canada and Alaska, and the dry mountain and basin region (the continental interior) lying between the Great Plains and the Pacific coastal zone. Even in the latter, however, peripheral areas like southern California, southern Arizona, and the Utah valley are cultivated with the help of irrigation. [Adapted from Arthur Getis and Judith Getis, eds., *The United States and Canada: The Land and the People* (Dubuque, IA: Wm. C. Brown, 1995), p. 165.]

cent of the North American work force. Today's highly mechanized and highly productive farms need far fewer workers than in the past. Many small farmers are being forced off their land by falling prices for farm produce as well as by the cost of increasingly sophisticated agricultural equipment; an investment of half a million dollars per farm for equipment is not unusual. It now takes so much investment money and so much land to make a living as a farmer that many people are predicting the death of the family farm.

Already, most of the food North Americans eat and export is grown on large, corporate-owned factory farms, which also earn the bulk of agricultural profits in North America. Corporate agriculture provides a variety of food products at low prices. On the other hand, in many rural areas the rise of corporate agriculture has depressed local economies and created social problems. Communities in places like rural Iowa and Nebraska were once composed of farming families with similar

incomes and social standing and a commitment to the locale. Many have now become highly stratified settlements, composed of a few wealthy farmer-managers and a majority of low-income, often migrant, laborers who are employed in food-processing plants. The result is increasing class disparity, low levels of education for many, less functional local government, and little promise for the future. The U.S. federal government is increasing its efforts to protect family farms, and some states have joined the effort. The state of Nebraska, for example, has a law on the books that actually bans corporate agriculture completely.

The movement toward mechanized corporate agriculture is being moderated, but certainly not halted, by the increasing number of small, often family-owned and operated, farms that produce specialty foods for urban markets. Though these farms produce only a tiny amount of the food in North America, they are far ahead of larger farms in achieving a sustainable relationship with the environment; small farmers are more likely to use only naturally occurring fertilizers and pesticides. Many scientists and agricultural practitioners believe that natural (sometimes called "organic") rather than chemical aids to cultivation are less likely to remain in the food and to pollute the environment.

The Industrial Economy

In the late twentieth century, the industrial economy of North America went through several changes. It became more dispersed across the continent, and, like the role of agriculture in an earlier era, industry's role in the economy declined while the service and information sectors grew in importance.

The Decline of the Old Industrial Core. As the unions won higher pay and better working conditions for most workers in the industrial Northeast, or the economic core, these benefits added to the costs of production. The region began to lose its advantageous position. By the 1960s, many industries were moving elsewhere to take advantage of cheaper labor that was less union organized. At first, the southeastern United States was a major destination for these industries, since wages and energy costs were significantly lower than elsewhere in the country. However, by the 1980s and especially after the passage of the North American Free Trade Agreement (NAFTA) in 1994, certain industries were moving farther south to Mexico or overseas; labor in these places was vastly cheaper, and laws

mandating environmental protection and safe and healthy workplaces were missing or much less regularly enforced. As this trend continues, the leading sectors of the U.S. economy are increasingly high-tech industries based largely on computers and information processing. These industries are often located near major research institutions that can supply a steady stream of ideas and highly skilled thinkers and technicians. Favored places are, for example, California's Silicon Valley, near Stanford University, or Raleigh-Durham, near the University of North Carolina.

Yet another factor in the shift away from the economic core was the dramatic growth of trade between North America and Asia. In the 1990s, trade with Asia actually surpassed trade with Europe, placing the Pacific coast in a better position than the traditional heart of the economic core on the Atlantic coast. It seems unlikely that in the future a single economic core will again emerge, because the currently leading sectors, mainly high-tech and trade/finance-related industries, are not as restricted by local resources as were the older manufacturing and heavy industries. They are thus free to locate in a wide variety of places.

Industrial Change and the Interstate Highway System. Facilitating the dispersion of industry across the continent has been the North American transportation infrastructure. The transportation industry has received substantial federal funds, called **subsidies,** given to promote economic development in outlying regions and to encourage their inclusion in the two

The Saturn plant in Springhill, Tennessee, was laid down over the rural landscape south of Nashville. Even within the confines of the Saturn plant, old field patterns are still clearly visible in this recent air photo. [Saturn Corporation.]

AT THE LOCAL SCALE   *Megalopolis*

A giant, highly urbanized area stretches in a 500-mile-long band along the eastern seaboard part of the economic core. "Megalopolis" is the name for this band of urbanization, applied by the French geographer Jean Gottman. It begins with Boston, Massachusetts, on the New England coast and stretches south and west across portions of 10 states, through New York City, Philadelphia, and Baltimore, terminating south of Washington, D.C. Megalopolis encompasses not only these five cities but many other adjacent smaller places—places like Manchester, New Hampshire, and Wilmington, Delaware. It covers less than 2 percent of the area of the United States, yet contains nearly 20 percent of the U.S. population.

Gottman's first great insight was that this vast urban area was not a supercity. Rather, Megalopolis is composed of multiple independent urban nodes whose outer fringes have coalesced. There is no center, no centralized network of services, no shared governmental institutions. In fact, the region crosses literally tens of thousands of administrative units, large and small: federal, state, county, township, municipal, and neighborhood. The one common experience shared by its residents is urbanness—including high overall population densities that intensify toward city interiors. Its residents must accept crowding, traffic congestion, and high costs of living (especially for housing), but they enjoy lots of choices in occupations, housing, neighborhoods, social activities, restaurants, shopping, entertainment, education, and employment. Yet Megalopolis also contains rural landscapes where farmers may produce high-quality specialty foods for the cities.

In the absence of unifying government, Megalopolis is tied together mainly by its transportation system. Thirty percent of the U.S. export trade passes through its six main ports, while its residents rely on a network of interstate highways, railways, and airways superimposed on a complex web of local streets and roads.

Gottman's second great insight was that this urban region was, at the time of writing (in the 1960s), a unique phenomenon in human history, but one that was likely to appear elsewhere in the world. His prediction has come to pass—there are by now several such areas around the globe: Tokyo-Kobe-Osaka in Japan, Rio and its satellite cities in Brazil, Mexico City-Puebla in Mexico.

Why did Megalopolis develop where it did? The answer lies both in its site (its absolute location on the eastern seaboard of the United States) and situation (its location relative to other features). First of all, the northeastern seaboard has a particularly convoluted coastline, with many protective peninsulas and deepwater inlets that are now useful seaports. The topography inland is also a key to modern use. Many of the biggest U.S. cities developed along rivers just where the foothills (the piedmont) of the Appalachian mountains meet the rather narrow coastal plain. The abrupt change in elevation created unnavigable falls and rapids, the fall line. Oceangoing shipping could go no farther west, so goods had to be off-loaded to other means of transportation; this led to a demand for warehouses and labor to shift cargo. The fall line also created a natural waterpower source where grain could be milled and lumber sawed.

The situation of Megalopolis relative to other places also contributed to its long and complex pattern of growth. The farms and settlements in the vast interior of the continent created a market for all manner of manufactured products shipped through Megalopolis, first from Europe and later from other points in the Americas. Agricultural products from the interior farms found their way into the world market through the coastal cities. Meanwhile, the cities of Megalopolis produced their own products and ideas for global exchange. Thus, the location of these cities on the edge of a massive and rapidly developing continent provided an unusually rich milieu for long-term growth.

Today, Megalopolis has to contend both with the results of its own incredible long-term success and with changing patterns of world production and trade. Because it developed early, much of its built environment is now in decline, including its **infrastructure** of industrial plants, power and other utilities, waste treatment plants, port facilities, and interurban rail and interstate highway transport systems. Because industrial competition is increasing globally, the cities of Megalopolis have to deal with shrinking earnings just when they need to levy taxes to rebuild and update the infrastructure that will keep them competitive.

national economies. Perhaps the most important such investment has been the **interstate highway system,** which in the United States is funded 90 percent by the federal government, 10 percent by the states. This system of 45,000 miles (72,000 kilometers) was completed in 1990. Canada has one main east-west artery that connects with the U.S. system in several places. The interstate highway system has not only vastly improved cross-country travel, it also has become the primary circulatory system of the continent. Though rail and air transport are still essential, much of the continent's fast-transport needs are now served by large trucks plying the interstate highway system. Such trucks facilitate "just-in-time" delivery of parts and materials for the increasingly dispersed industrial sector. For example, a large truck can exit Interstate 75 in the rural South, visit a small automotive parts factory in a nearby town to pick up finished car door handles, and in half an hour be back on the Interstate on its way to an auto assembly plant in Kentucky or Tennessee. A firm that makes fancy bathroom wall panels for consumers in New York penthouses can locate in rural west Tennessee and deliver orders in less than 24 hours.

The interstate highway system has changed the way Americans live. Industrial workers in dispersed industries now often live in rural areas, raising gardens and small cash crops to supplement their wages. The possibility of rapid travel has encouraged urban sprawl and suburban development. These, in turn, have led to the proliferation of large shopping malls on the edges of old urban centers. In the beginning of suburban development, workers used to travel from their homes to the inner city to work; but increasingly, factories and firms have followed their workers to the suburbs. Now, most commutes take place around the periphery of cities, and the inner cities have been nearly abandoned.

The Changing Job Picture.   Both Canada and the United States are grappling with a complex set of problems created by technological advances. In both countries, more and more workers of all types are being replaced by machines and computers. Since World War II, a huge number of agricultural and manufacturing jobs have been lost as increasingly sophisticated technologies made it possible to employ fewer people to produce the same amount of goods. As a consequence, most North Americans now work in the service sector. This sector includes a wide range of occupations in transportation, health care, child care, education, banking, and research and development. The better-paying, longer-term service sector jobs generally require a degree from a technical school, college, or university. At present, only 25 to 30 percent of U.S. adults and 40 percent of Canadian adults have these qualifications. Although there are signs that these

numbers are increasing, it is likely that a majority of North Americans will remain without the needed education for some years to come. In the meantime, the jobs requiring only a high school diploma are increasingly low-paid positions that offer little security—work as cooks, custodians, cash register operators, health care and office workers, for example. Because this type of employment pays significantly less than did the manufacturing jobs of the past, many families that once did well on one income are now struggling for solvency even with two family members working.

The U.S. and Canadian governments have responded differently to the changing employment situation. For many decades, Canada has more strongly protected its working population from job loss or declines in income by enacting strict labor laws; and it has spent more on social programs that lessen the financial burdens of working people in times of crisis. While these policies have made the financial lives of working people more secure, they have also made Canada slightly less attractive than the United States to new businesses. Because employers must pay slightly higher taxes and sometimes higher wages in Canada, and must be more restrained in firing workers, new jobs cannot be created as easily as in the United States. Hence, Canada's unemployment rate is usually several percentage points higher than that of the United States.

Although finding a good job is tough for low-skilled workers in both countries, life for these workers is more stressful in the United States because there is little job protection and government unemployment assistance. Perhaps that is one reason poor rural and urban areas in the United States that have lost agricultural and manufacturing jobs have experienced rises in violent crime, drug abuse, and family disintegration—all social problems usually connected to declining incomes.

Canada's record of protecting workers' jobs, incomes, and health care may turn out to be a more efficient economic strategy. In recent years, Canada's rate of economic growth has been around 4 percent, roughly double the U.S. growth rate. Some social scientists speculate that this is due to a greater proportion of the Canadian population being well enough off to boost the economy with their consumption of goods and services. Similarly, the Canadian health care system, which is heavily subsidized by the government, may actually aid the economy. It is less expensive per capita and more effective in preventing illness than the largely private health care system in the United States. While the United States spends 13 percent of its gross domestic product (GDP refers to production that takes place entirely within the country) on health care, Canada spends only 10 percent. Moreover, Canada does slightly better than the United States on most indicators of overall health, such as infant mortality and

TABLE 2.1

Health-related indexes for Canada and the United States

Country	Health care costs as percent of GDP, 1995	Deaths per 1000	Infant mortality per 1000 live births	Maternal mortality per 100,000 live births	Life expectancy at birth
Canada: publicly funded health care	9.6	7	6.3	4	78
United States: privately funded health care	14.2	9	7.0	8	76

Sources: 1998 World Population Data Sheet and *Statistical Abstract of the United States 1997*, Population Reference Bureau; from http://www.census.gov/prod/www/abs/cc97stab.html.

life expectancy (Table 2.1). While there are some signs of growing sensitivity to these issues, in the United States, spending on social programs in recent years has actually been reduced.

Government and Globalization

One of the most hotly debated issues in North America today is **globalization:** the process of economic integration on a worldwide scale. One way that economies may become integrated is by breaking down barriers to trade. Since the end of British colonial status for the United States and Canada, tariffs and subsidies have protected a wide range of manufacturing industries in both countries. A number of tariffs remain against low-priced manufactured goods (such as textiles and shoes) of developing countries out of concern that these goods could drive Canadian and U.S. companies out of business. In recent years, the two countries have adopted free trade with each other on an increasing scale—that is, they have allowed trade to proceed relatively uninhibited by international barriers such as tariffs. The process began with the United States–Canada free trade agreement of 1989 and continued with the creation in 1994 of NAFTA. This agreement invited Mexico into the trade pact with Canada and the United States. Today, NAFTA is the world's largest trading bloc in size of population included and in dollar value of trade. By the time of its full implementation in 2009, NAFTA will have integrated the economies of the United States, Canada, and Mexico through reduction or removal of most tariffs and other trade barriers.

While NAFTA is bringing tremendous opportunities for economic advancement, it also poses challenges. On the one hand, it is strengthening an already deep relationship between Canada and the United States. Moreover, NAFTA may reduce the prices that U.S. and Canadian consumers pay for the many goods that can be produced more cheaply in Mexico, where workers receive lower wages. On the other hand, NAFTA is often criticized for hurting low-income people in North America because of jobs lost when U.S. and Canadian employers relocate to Mexico. Some corporations may relocate in order to avoid the cost of complying with U.S. and Canadian laws that set comparatively higher standards for workers' health and safety, and environmental protection. For example, a zone of U.S.-owned factories along the U.S.-Mexican border creates air and water pollution that is a nuisance on both sides of the border.

There is vigorous debate today over the best strategies for operating in the global economy. The U.S. "leaner and meaner" approach of low government involvement in the economy, it is argued, allows the U.S. economy to be more dynamic in its response to new opportunities. However, as was pointed out earlier, lower incomes for a majority of people may limit the pace of economic growth. Moreover, Canada appears to be ahead of the United States in maintaining the health and increasing the educational level of a majority of its citizens. Finally, the massive size of the U.S. economy may make it a less useful example than Canada for other countries to follow into the global era. The size and diversity of the U.S. economy means that the country is less likely than most to suffer serious instability as a result of shifts in the global economy. It may be that there is no single best strategy for responding to globalization.

Systems of Government

Both Canada and the United States have democratic systems of government, yet there are significant differences in these systems. Canada follows the British **parliamentary system.** It has an executive branch, consisting of the prime minister and cabinet, and a legislature (the Canadian parliament). The executive branch is more closely bound to the legislature, and the Canadian federal government has more and stronger powers (at least constitutionally) than does the U.S. federal government. The U.S. system is founded on the idea of curtailing the strength of the federal government. The system is set up to maintain a balance of power among the three branches of the U.S. federal government (the executive, legislative, and judicial) and to safeguard the right of individual states to govern themselves. Over the years, both the Canadian and U.S. federal governments have moved away from the original intentions of their constitutions. While Canada's originally strong federal government has become weaker, the initially more limited federal government in the United States has extended its powers.

Expanding on its power to regulate trade between states, the U.S. federal government has occasionally guided the economic development of whole regions. In the Southeast in the 1930s, the federal government established and funded the Tennessee Valley Authority (TVA) to promote social and economic development through a many-faceted river basin management system. The TVA emphasized building a network of hydroelectric dams and, later, a heavily subsidized nuclear power industry. The U.S. federal government has also expanded its power by offering money to states in return for their compliance with newly enacted or newly enforced laws. While this practice has made many poorer states increasingly dependent on the federal government, it has also led some state and local governments to enact policies they would not have enacted on their own. In the 1960s, several such federally funded programs gave considerable support to the U.S. civil rights movement. Such programs provided education enhancement—Head Start for preschoolers, employment training and job opportunities, and community development agencies such as Volunteers in Service to America (VISTA). A number of U.S. Supreme Court decisions have promoted racial integration in the schools and the workplace.

Gender on the National Political Scene

There are some powerful contradictions on the political front in North America as far as gender is concerned. On the one hand, women apparently decided the U.S. presidential election of 1996, voting overwhelmingly for Bill Clinton; and women's issues like family leave, equal pay, day care, and reproductive rights have been forced into the national debates. On the other hand, women are apparently making slow progress toward economic equality with men; they are still consistently behind by a wide margin. Although women are now about half the labor force, they still earned only 72 percent of what men earned in 1994 (this is up from 59 percent in 1970); and at least some of the gain results from the fact that women tend to work more hours than men. Although women own more businesses than ever before, they still represent only a small percentage of total business owners; and their businesses tend to be smaller and more precarious, because they are underfinanced. In the realm of education, North America sends a significantly larger percentage of its women to college than any other developed economy, and Canada does even better on this score than the United States. Canadian women have attained virtually the same level of education as men in most categories. In the United States, women are still behind. By 1993, 24.8 percent of U.S. men but only 19.2 percent of women had a bachelor's degree.

Men still hold 70 percent of the top executive positions in business and government, and they earn about 30 percent more, on average, than women in those positions. Whereas North American women might be expected to influence future national policy the most as elected officials, they remain a tiny minority in these positions. As of September 1998, in the U.S. Congress, just 11.2 percent were women. In the Canadian Houses of Parliament, women members made up 21.2 percent. Both the United States and Canada are well behind other countries in percentages of women in national legislatures: Cuba (22.8), South Africa (23.7), Mozambique (25), Norway (36.4), and Sweden (40).

Environmental Issues

The typical North American engages in a number of lifestyle habits that have environmental consequences. Most of those consequences fall into three categories: loss of environmental quality, loss of natural habitat for plants and animals, and resource depletion. The divisions between these categories are often blurred. For example, consider the consequences of building the typical suburban home and then tending its lawn and disposing of the waste produced by those living inside. Habitat for wild creatures and plants is lost on the site of the home and on the site of the landfill where the solid waste is disposed of. Fertilizer runoff may pollute nearby streams. Resources for building and maintaining the home and lawn, such as wood and petroleum products, may be drawn from very distant sources outside North America; and their extraction may have caused environmental damage in these areas.

Loss of Environmental Quality

The creation and disposal of waste is responsible for most loss in environmental quality, and Canada and the United States are among the leading global producers of waste. With roughly only 5 percent of the world's population, together they produce 26 percent of the greenhouse gases released globally by human activity; carbon dioxide is primary among them. The United States leads in such production, and Canada is not far behind.

Hazardous Waste. Although all waste is potentially harmful, there is an official U.S. government category called **hazardous waste.** This is waste produced by nuclear power generation and weapons manufacture, by mineral mining and drilling, by waste incinerators (which produce dust and ash), and by industry (which produces 80 percent of all liquid hazardous waste). Many other harmful wastes are not defined or regulated by law, such as chemical wastes from small businesses and private homes. The more than 1855 military bases across the continent are thought to generate more wastes than the top five U.S. chemical companies combined. In addition numerous toxic substances are used and disposed of in the average North American household, including oven cleaners; drain, toilet, and window cleaners; weed killers; and gasoline.

VIGNETTE Lisa Crawford was a self-described average person working in Fernald, a rural community in southern Ohio. In the mid-1980s she and her family lived in a rented farmhouse across the road from a "Feed Materials Production Center." Lisa assumed it was an animal feed factory and thought the rural environment would be a great place to raise her son—fresh well water, fresh air, clean living. This bucolic prospect was changed when Lisa learned that she lived across the road from a U.S. Department of Energy (DoE) military nuclear facility producing nuclear materials for weapons. One day her landlord called to say that the well water was contaminated, and soon Lisa and her family learned that Fernald was also one of the major storage facilities for "hot" nuclear waste. For a while at a loss about how to respond, Lisa eventually joined with a nurse friend to found a community action group called Fernald Residents for Environmental Safety and Health (FRESH). FRESH is now one of the country's first effective grassroots groups that brought to public scrutiny environmental conditions at military facilities.

After years of pressing for truthfulness and accountability, it was eventually disclosed that the "Fernald facility had released 394,000 pounds of uranium and 14,3000 pounds of thorium into the air. Another 167,000 pounds of uranium were discharged into the Great Miami River," from where it entered the Great Miami aquifer. Six waste pits on the site hold 892,000 cubic yards of radioactive waste. In 1989 the DoE closed the facility. It is now waiting for cleanup under a special program called "Superfund." The DoE estimates it will take 50 years and $50 billion dollars to clean up the Fernald site. [Adapted from Joni Seager, *Hysterical housewives and other mad women,* in *Feminist Political Ecology,* ed. Dianne Rocheleau, Barbara Thomas-Slayter, and Esther Wangari (London: Routledge Press, 1996).]

The United States generates much more hazardous waste per capita than does Canada. Canada, with a population about one-tenth that of the United States, generates less than one-fortieth of the world's known hazardous waste. Meanwhile, with a population of 268 million, the United States generates five times the amount of hazardous waste of the entire European Union (population 300+ million). Within the United States, the disposal of hazardous waste has a definite geographic pattern. The country tends to bury its hazardous waste in pits, ponds, landfills, or deep wells, posing risks for future generations. The sociologist Robert D. Bullard has shown that a disproportionate amount of hazardous waste is disposed of in the South, and within that region in locations inhabited by poor Native American, African American, and Hispanic people. Bullard writes that "nationally, 60 percent of African Americans and 50 percent of Hispanics live in communities with at least one uncontrolled toxic-waste site."

Acid Rain. The burning of fossil fuels emits sulfur dioxide and nitrogen oxides into the air. These gases may combine with moisture in the air or may fall as particles on the landscape, where they are later dissolved in rainwater. The result is acidic water called **acid rain.** Acid rain can kill certain forest trees and, when concentrated in lakes and streams, can kill fish and wildlife. The acids become especially concentrated in snow cover. As acidic snows melt in the spring, water acidity peaks just when plants and animals are beginning a growth spurt or reproduction. The distribution of acid rain in North America also displays a distinctive geographic pattern. The acidic content in rainwater is higher than normal in eastern North America, from East Texas to Ontario to Newfoundland, and including the entire eastern seaboard. Acid rain intensity is greatest along the

U.S.-Canadian border. The United States, with much the larger population and large industrial infrastructure near the border, produces acid rain. Fisheries and forests in both countries have been damaged.

Loss of Habitat for Plants and Animals

The British biogeographer I. G. Simmons has observed that there is an inherent conflict between nature's best interests and those of modern society. Many species of plants or animals are in danger of becoming extinct because human activity is destroying the environments in which they live. Earlier in North American history, millions of acres of forests and grasslands were cleared to make way for farms. Now the last bits of natural land near cities are disappearing to make way for residential developments, freeways, golf courses, office complexes, and shopping centers. The destruction of wetlands is especially significant. Wastelands, swamps, bogs, and riverine environments are important reproductive zones for many bird and aquatic species.

Some animal species have successfully adapted to living close to humans. Raccoons and opossums raid the garbage cans of single-family homes in suburban neighborhoods, where there is often enough vegetative cover to provide them with breeding spaces. Certain strains of deer have made a place for themselves on the edges of suburbia, where large areas of lawn and stable paddocks provide grass for grazing. Even foxes and coyotes have been known to remain on land suddenly strewn with new houses; sometimes they prey on family pets.

Cities often try to provide new habitat for wildlife by creating greenways through and around the urban settlement. These can be pleasant spaces for humans, but such greenways are usually far too small to support most of the plants and animals that once lived in the vicinity. Only a few species of animals (especially scavengers) and weedlike plants can endure in these places.

Resource Depletion

Among domestic resources in danger of depletion, water is one of the most important. In the humid eastern part of the United States, water has been in short supply only rarely, during relatively mild droughts of several months. Even here, though, cities have to look farther and farther afield for sufficient water resources, as populations have grown and water usage, particularly for industry, has increased. New York City, for example, gets most of its water from the distant Adirondack Mountains in upstate New York.

Landscapes are less and less well watered the farther west one goes. Taxpayers across the United States have subsidized the building of thousands of stock tanks in the Great Plains to ensure water for cattle dur-

ing dry times. In the far Southwest, rainfall is too sparse to support agriculture. To make farming possible, both the federal and California state governments have built costly dams and hundreds of miles of canals to bring water from the Sacramento River and other northern rivers to the state's Central Valley and water from the Colorado River to southern California's Imperial Valley. Irrigated California fields now supply most of the country's fresh fruit and vegetables, but at a high hidden cost to the U.S. taxpayer. Some of the diverted water also goes to urban areas—so much so that cities like Los Angeles and San Diego could not survive without it. Increasingly, it is recognized that in California, New Mexico, and Arizona, many of the uses to which the federally supplied water is put (for agriculture or lawn watering) are uneconomical. But subsidized water supplies are so accepted that the diseconomies are not questioned.

In many parts of the country, irrigated agriculture is now much more common than in the past. Farmers on the Great Plains used to practice special dry farming techniques to conserve moisture in the soil; now they have turned to irrigation instead. They are using fossil water, water that has been stored over the millennia in natural underground reservoirs called aquifers. The Ogallala (Figure 2.13) is the largest such aquifer underlying the Great Plains. Scientists say that water is being withdrawn from this ancient reservoir at rates that far exceed replenishment. Now the land is beginning to sink above the depleted resource, especially along the Gulf coast. Even in well-watered parts of the eastern United States, farmers are using irrigation to take the risk out of farming. Between the wide rivers of tidewater Virginia, where water shortages are only an occasional problem, it is not uncommon to see elaborate mechanical irrigation systems.

In the years to come, Americans would be wise to expect limitations on the amount of water used for irrigation in the West and Southwest and hence changes in agricultural production that is presently dependent on irrigation. There will probably be more conflict over moving water from one part of the country to another. Big water users will no longer be rewarded with lower rates, as they are now. In the years to come, people across the United States can expect pressure to conserve water and to change their attitudes toward water use.

Measures of Human Well-Being

Both Canada and the United States consistently rank high on global scales of well-being, yet a comparison of these two wealthy countries makes it clear why old ways of making such comparisons are misleading. If we looked only at gross national product (GNP) per capita for the two countries, we would see Canada's GNP is

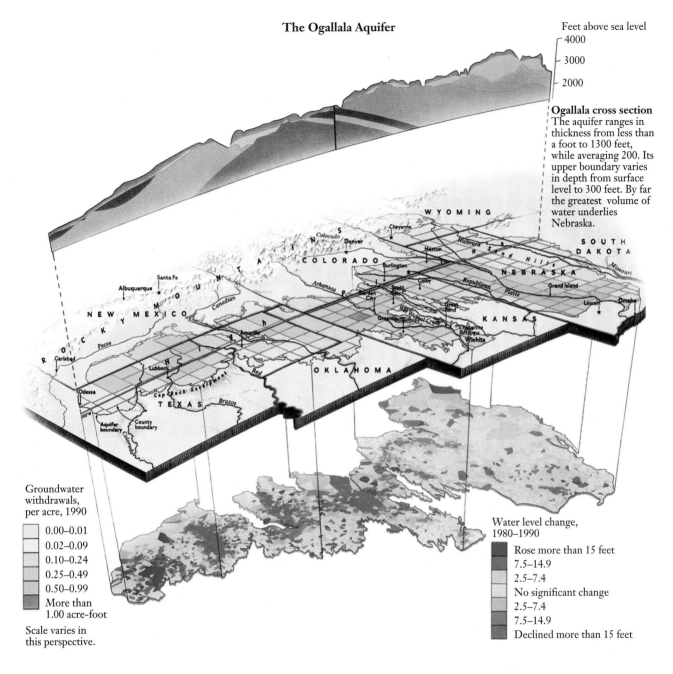

The Ogallala Aquifer

Feet above sea level
4000
3000
2000

Ogallala cross section
The aquifer ranges in thickness from less than a foot to 1300 feet, while averaging 200. Its upper boundary varies in depth from surface level to 300 feet. By far the greatest volume of water underlies Nebraska.

Groundwater withdrawals, per acre, 1990

0.00–0.01
0.02–0.09
0.10–0.24
0.25–0.49
0.50–0.99
More than 1.00 acre-foot

Scale varies in this perspective.

Water level change, 1980–1990

Rose more than 15 feet
7.5–14.9
2.5–7.4
No significant change
2.5–7.4
7.5–14.9
Declined more than 15 feet

FIGURE 2.13 The Ogallala aquifer. From the 1940s to 1980, the aquifer lost an average of 10 feet of water overall, and more than 100 feet of water in some parts of Texas. During the 1980s, the decline was less. Thanks to abundant rain and snow, water management, and new technologies, the water level declined only a foot. [Adapted from *National Geographic,* March 1993, pp. 84–85.]

U.S. $19,020 and that of the United States is $28,020. Based on these numbers, we might conclude that Canadians are not doing nearly as well as people in the United States. But remember that GNP per capita ignores all aspects of well-being other than income and is only an average for the entire country.

Table 2.2 reveals that when education and health are also considered, Canadians are doing better than U.S. citizens. For making wider comparisons, the table includes several other highly developed countries and the world figure for GNP per capita. The United Nations Human Development Index (HDI), column 3 in the table, combines three components—life expectancy at birth, educational attainment, and adjusted real income—to rank 174 countries on how well their citizens achieve basic human capabilities. On this scale,

TABLE 2.2

Human well-being rankings of Canada, the United States, and selected countries

Country	GNP per capita (in U.S. dollars), 1996	Human Development Index (HDI) global rankings, 1998	Gender Empowerment Measure (GEM) global rankings, 1998
Japan	40,940	8	38
United States	28,020	4	11
Germany	28,870	19	8
Sweden	25,710	10	1
France	26,270	2	31
Canada	19,020	1	7
Kuwait	19,390 (1995)	54	75
Australia	20,090	13	12
World	5,180	Not av.[a]	Not av.[a]

[a] Not available.

Sources: 1998 World Population Data Sheet, Population Reference Bureau; and *Human Development Report 1998*, United Nations Development Programme.

Canada ranks first and the United States fourth. When the country's record on enabling women to participate as equals with men is measured, Sweden is first and Canada drops to seventh, and the United States drops to eleventh place. Despite the overall high ranking, women in the United States are not doing as well as men in ways that affect their ability to participate in society. In Canada the same is true, but the disparity is somewhat less. Many statistics illustrate that in both the United States and Canada, women are, on average, poorer than men, are paid less for the same work, are less the focus of medical research, and occupy fewer supervisory positions. They are also drastically underrepresented in elected positions.

Canada and the United States share privileged and influential positions in the global community. Both have high rates of personal consumption, and through the mass media they affect the tastes and desires of the entire globe. They also share a number of other enviable economic features, but Table 2.2 does not tell the full story. Both countries also show signs that inequalities are growing within their borders (though the situation in the United States is worse). The wealthiest are growing ever richer and the poorest are losing ground. A recent United Nations report noted that between 1975 and 1990, the wealthiest 1 percent of the U.S. population increased its share of total assets from 20 percent to 36 percent. The annual per capita income of the poorest 20 percent ($6485) sank to less than one-fourth that of the U.S. average annual income per capita ($25,860 at the time of the study). By contrast, Japan's poorest 20 percent make one-half the average annual income per capita ($34,630), or $18,657. The report also notes a lack of job security in the United States, a deterioration in job quality (many new jobs are temporary, without benefits or a future), and coming problems in health care financing. In the United States, 56 percent of health costs are paid for by the individual, the highest ratio by far in the industrial world—double that of Canada and Japan.

SUBREGIONS OF NORTH AMERICA

A good way to appreciate the diversity of regional patterns in North America is to juxtapose places arbitrarily. Take, for example, the gold and green grainfields and isolated farmsteads of the Great Plains and compare them with the much smaller farms and mining towns tucked in the hills and hollows of the layered, blue gray Appalachian Mountains. Or think how warm and dusty Hispanic border towns along the Rio Grande differ from ramshackle, foggy New England fishing villages. Or how sleek, tall, efficient, and culturally diverse Toronto, Ontario, contrasts with another beautiful port city, Charleston, South Carolina, with its southern lowlands culture that focuses increasingly on its African-American heritage.

The standard way to grasp the cultural geography of a place as big and varied as North America is to impose some sort of regional order on the whole. You divide the region into subregions—the Northeast, the Southwest, the Midwest—and then sketch in the features that give each subregion "character of place." Defining regions is a ticklish business, and geographers often have trouble reaching consensus on just where regional boundaries should be drawn. Joel Garreau, a

Washington Post editor, had a great deal of fun designing what he calls "an emotional map" of North America. Garreau paid special attention to the ways in which the continent is changing, especially along cultural or ethnic lines. He noted that state and province boundaries are particularly useless for sketching the regional characteristics of the continent. In his successful book, *The Nine Nations of North America* (1981), he proposed a set of regions that not only cut across state boundaries but also ignore national boundaries (Figure 2.14). Because Garreau's scheme offers many creative insights, I have decided to use a modified version in the discussion of the subregions of North America. However, whereas Garreau included northern Mexico in one region and created another that linked Miami with the islands of the Caribbean, I treat the Caribbean and Mexico separately in Chapter 3, "Middle and

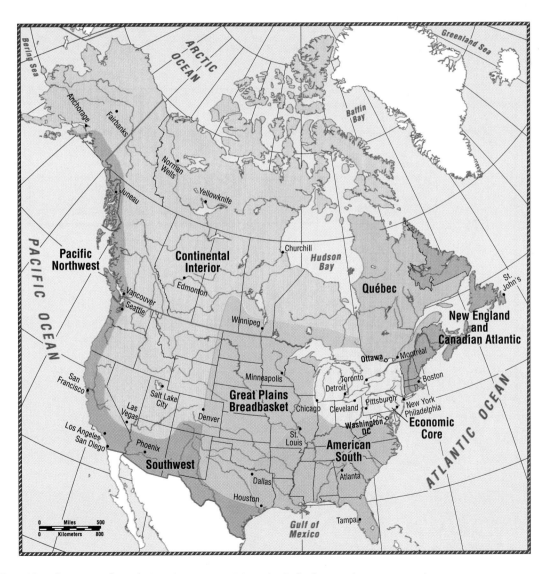

FIGURE 2.14 Subregions of North America. [This and the individual subregional maps are adapted from Joel Garreau, *The Nine Nations of North America* (Boston: Houghton Mifflin, 1981).]

South America." The state of Hawaii, lying in the Pacific Ocean more than 2000 miles west of the North American continent, is included in Chapter 11, "Oceania: Australia, New Zealand, and the Pacific."

New England and Canada's Atlantic Provinces

Among the earliest parts of North America to be settled were New England and Canada's Atlantic Provinces (Figure 2.15). Of all the regions of North America, these maintain perhaps the strongest connection with the past and hold a certain cultural prestige and reputation as North America's **cultural hearth.** They are especially noted as the source of early American house styles (Cape Cod and Georgian colonial, for example) and interior furnishings. (Copies of New England–designed furniture are found in all classes of American homes.)

Economically, the Atlantic Provinces of Canada and northern New England remain relatively poor. They still depend on a seriously depressed fishing sector and on timber, vegetable crops, dairying, and other extractive industries. Southern New England is using its celebrated "Yankee ingenuity" to reinvent itself as a high-tech center reliant on the intellectual skills of those attracted by its many universities. As New England shifts its economic focus, it is also becoming both more urban and much more ethnically diverse.

A Harsh but Productive Land

Many of the continuities of New England and the Atlantic Provinces with the past derive from the region's geography. During the last ice age, glaciers scraped away much of the topsoil, leaving behind picturesque mountains with rounded, bare summits, the source of some of the finest building stone in North America. But, without much topsoil, the land is only

FIGURE 2.15 The New England and Atlantic Provinces subregion.

marginally productive. Although many farmers settled here, they struggled merely to survive. Today, while much of the landscape is rural, farming is not particularly productive, and many areas try to capitalize on their rural and village ambiance and historic heritage by enticing tourists as well as retirees who will build homes and stay for a decade or more.

After being cleared in the days of early settlement, New England's evergreen and hardwood deciduous forests have slowly filled in the fields abandoned by struggling farmers. But now these second-growth forests are threatened. Logging companies are clear-cutting larger areas, driven in part by the fear that huge numbers of trees may be lost to the recent severe infestation of the northeast budworm. In rural areas, paper milling from wood remains an important industry, supplying jobs when other blue-collar activities are dying out.

Abundant fish were the major attraction that drew the first wave of Europeans to New England in modern times. Throughout the 1500s, hundreds of fishermen from Europe's Atlantic coast came to the Grand Banks, off the shores of Newfoundland and Maine, where they took in huge catches of cod and other fish. The Grand Banks have recently been badly depleted by modern fishing vessels (some from outside North America), which use enormous mechanized nets. These nets, while bringing in some valuable species, damage the fragile sea bottom and kill many unmarketable sea creatures that are nonetheless essential to the marine ecosystem. Fishing in this region has also been affected by competition from fish farming.

Today, many parts of southern New England thrive on industries that demand its skilled and educated workers. New England's considerable human resources derive in large part from the strong emphasis put on education and hard work by the earliest Puritan settlers, who established many high-quality schools, colleges, and universities. The city of Boston has some of the nation's foremost institutions of higher learning (Harvard, the Massachusetts Institute of Technology, Boston University, Boston College, Northeastern University). Boston has capitalized on its supply of university graduates to become North America's second most important high-technology center after California's Silicon Valley.

An Increasingly Urban, Diverse Land

At present, New England finds itself confronted by some startling discontinuities with its past. As the remaining agricultural enterprises and rural industries become increasingly mechanized and larger in scale, many New Englanders are flocking to the cities for work. Once in the city, they become aware of the fact that New England is no longer the Anglo-Saxon stronghold it used to be. Today, in places like Middletown, Connecticut, corner groceries are owned by Koreans and Mexicans; Jamaicans sell meat patties and hot-wings; restaurants serve food from Thailand; schoolteachers are Filipino, Brazilian, and West Indian; and a recent mayor was not English, Irish, or even German in descent, but full-blooded Sicilian.

Québec

Québec is the most culturally distinctive region in Canada or the United States (Figure 2.16). For more than 300 years, a substantial portion of the population has been French speaking. The French Canadians are now in the majority and struggling to resolve Québec's relationship with the rest of Canada.

In the seventeenth century, France made a concerted effort to gain a hold in what is now Canada. Settlers, who maintained high birth rates, were encouraged; by 1760, there were 65,000 French in Canada. Most lived on long, narrow strips of land along the St. Lawrence River; and the imprint of this system is still visible today in the long-lot field pattern. Settlers were given a narrow strip of riverfront from which the property stretched back for a considerable distance. The resulting long and narrow farms gave access to fishing and riverborne trade, the fertile soil of the river's floodplain, and the interior forest where the settlers could hunt. Houses were located along the river, with the narrow fields stretching behind them. Early French colonists commented that one could travel along the St. Lawrence and see every house in Canada. Later, the long-lot system was repeated inland so that today narrow farms also stretch back from roads that parallel the river, forming a second tier of long lots.

Compared to most other regions in Canada and the United States, Québec remained relatively poor through the first half of the twentieth century. Most farms along the St. Lawrence grew only enough food to feed the family. Much of the industrial growth of the province was in the hands of a small number of Anglo-Canadian residents (those of British heritage). The Roman Catholic Church's emphasis on traditional values subtly discouraged cultural change or birth control, and played a role in keeping Québec largely poor, agricultural, and increasingly overpopulated.

After World War II, Québec's economy grew steadily, propelled by increasing demand for the natural resources from the north of Québec, such as timber, iron ore, and hydroelectric power. Many of the cities of the St. Lawrence River valley prospered from the processing and transport of these resources, although most of the profits often stayed in the hands of Anglo-Canadians. Québec's new prosperity was most visible in the rapid growth of Montréal. This city's

FIGURE 2.16 The Québec subregion.

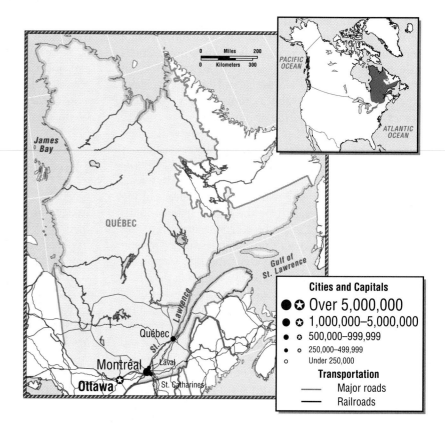

interior location, near the confluence of several rivers, had always made it an attractive site for British entrepreneurs interested in exploiting and exporting the natural resources of Québec.

As many French Canadians moved into the cities, the so-called Quiet Revolution occurred. With increasingly better access to education and training, the Québecois were for the first time able to challenge English speakers for higher paying jobs and power. Gradually, the conservative Catholic agricultural society gave way to a more cosmopolitan one that was increasingly resentful of discrimination at the hands of English speakers. In the 1970s, support for increased autonomy and outright national independence grew. At that time, Québec passed laws that heavily favored the French language in education, government, and business. In response, many English-speaking Québecois relocated to Ontario and elsewhere. Québecois themselves began to fear for Québec's economic survival if the province left Canada. Nevertheless, a referendum on independence failed only narrowly in 1996.

Québec's northern portions extend into rich timber and mineral deposits (iron ore, copper, and oil) around Hudson Bay. These resources are hard to reach due to the remoteness and difficult terrain of the Canadian Shield, a vast expanse of undulating coniferous forests and tablelands, dotted with small lakes and wetlands. Québec is interested in developing hydroelectric power in the vicinity of James Bay (part of Hudson Bay) in order to run mineral-processing plants, sawmills, and paper mills. Protests from the Cree and other Native peoples that the enormous shallow lakes created by the dams were flooding sacred ancestral hunting and burial grounds have caused further hydroprojects to be put on hold.

The Economic Core

The word "foundry" is used to designate a place where metals are melted and poured into molds. The word evokes images of smokestacks, red-hot forges, coal dust, and tired workers hurrying through the dusk to identical frame houses set close together along colorless urban streets. The economic core of the north central part of the United States and southern Ontario (Figure 2.17) is sometimes called "the foundry" because this region was once the heart of North American iron- and steel-based heavy industry. This region is still industrial, but it no longer dominates economically as it once did; many communities are struggling to redefine themselves in the aftermath of plant closings.

For our purposes, the southern boundary of the economic core runs along the Ohio River south of Cincinnati and Indianapolis. It then curves to the northwest, taking in Chicago and the western shores of Lake Michigan; it extends to Sault Ste. Marie, Ontario,

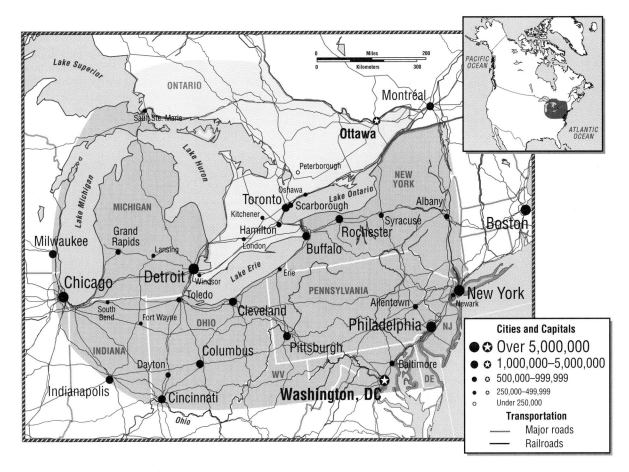

FIGURE 2.17 The economic core subregion.

and on to the southern border of Québec, encompassing Ottawa, Toronto, and Windsor, Ontario. Keep in mind that regional boundaries are often indeterminate. One could extend this industrial region south to Louisville, Kentucky, and west to St. Louis, Missouri, and Davenport/Rock Island and even Dubuque, Iowa, because these are cities that have had large manufacturing sectors.

The economic core is less than 5 percent of the total land area of the United States and Canada; yet at the beginning of the last quarter of the twentieth century, its industries produced more than 70 percent of the continent's steel and a similar percentage of its motor vehicles and parts. This concentrated output was possible because the great steel mills and automotive plants could be supplied with energy and mineral resources available either from within the region or from just beyond its borders. Coal came from Appalachia and southern Illinois; oil and gas came from Pennsylvania; and iron ore came from the great Mesabi Range in Minnesota and the Steep Rock deposit in Ontario.

Today, much of the region is in decline or undergoing reorganization. As the map in Figure 2.18 shows, industrial jobs and manufacturing jobs are now to be found in the South, Middle West, and Northwest, well beyond the old industrial heartland. Brand-new state-of-the-art automobile factories built by Japanese (Honda) and American (Saturn) firms are situated in rolling, green, rural landscapes in Kentucky and Tennessee. Industrial resources are also coming from different places. Much of the U.S. coal now comes from Wyoming, and Canada's coal comes from British Columbia and Alberta, although Appalachian production has remained steady. Steel, the mainstay of the automotive and construction industries, can be more cheaply derived from scrap metal or purchased abroad from Brazil, Japan, or Europe. Hence, huge outdated factories sit empty or underused throughout much of the economic core, and thousands of factory workers have retrained or have entered an early, impoverished retirement. In recent times, some have taken to calling this obsolete industrialized region the "Rust Belt."

It would be wrong to think of the economic core, even during its heyday, as solely a region of factories and mines. In between the great industrial cities of this region are thousands of acres of some of the best farmland in North America. In fact, the tremendous success of agriculture laid the groundwork for industrial

A working class neighborhood of Youngstown, Ohio, as viewed from the Republic Steel plant. Early twentieth- century frame houses surround a large Roman Catholic church. [Richard Kalvar/Magnum Photos.]

development. As farmers prospered, they bought more and more mechanized equipment, appliances, and consumer goods, much of it made in nearby cities. The richest farmers put up money themselves to build the factories. Food-processing industries packaged meat and turned grain into cereal, flour, and bread. Even the trains, trucks, and barges that moved the grain and manufactured products were built in the region. Today, some of the appliance and food-related industries remain in the old economic core; but many, like the meat-packing industry, have consolidated or moved to the South, where labor unions hardly exist and safety regulations are more lax (see the box "Urban Sprawl").

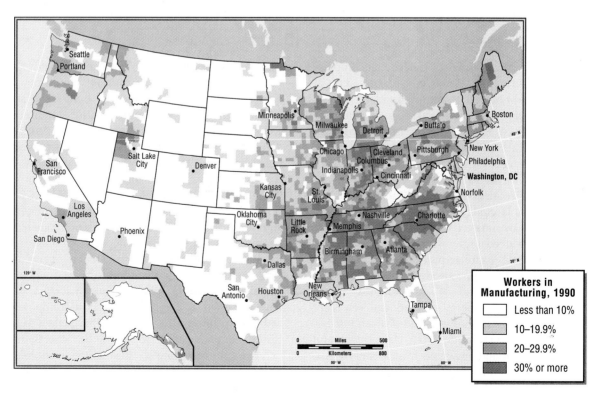

FIGURE 2.18 Percentage of people in the manufacturing sector. [Adapted from Roger Doyle, *1994 Atlas of Contemporary America* (New York: Facts on File, 1994), p. 131.]

AT THE LOCAL SCALE   *Urban Sprawl*

Among the many consequences of industrialization and urbanization in the economic core and elsewhere is the invasion of farmland by bulldozers preparing the way for suburban development: residences, malls, and discount outlets. Typically, real estate developers are able to buy rural land more cheaply than property within cities, even when inner-city property is occupied only by defunct factories and abandoned houses. Huge tracts of farm and wilderness areas around the peripheries of North American cities are gobbled up. This trend is especially problematic for farmers. Even though there is a lot of good fertile land in North America, some of the best is located close to urban areas because cities and towns were often intentionally founded near rich farmland.

Mark Greene's family has been farming in Pittsford, New York (Figure 2.19), near the Canadian border, since 1812, but until recently the prospects that his 400-acre farm would be in business for another generation looked dim. As land prices rose so did property taxes, and the Greene family found that they could not meet their tax payments. New suburban homes were sprouting up on what had been neighboring farms, and the homeowners sometimes pushed local officials to halt normal farm practices, like noisy nighttime harvesting or planting, spreading smelly manure, or importing bees to pollinate fruit trees.

Last year, though, Pittsford issued $410 million in bonds so that it could pay Greene and six other farmers for promises that they would not sell their 1200 acres to developers, but would continue to farm. Advocates of farmland preservation argue that farms provide more than food and fiber. They provide environmental benefits, soul-soothing scenery, economic diversity, and, especially, tax savings. Saving prime

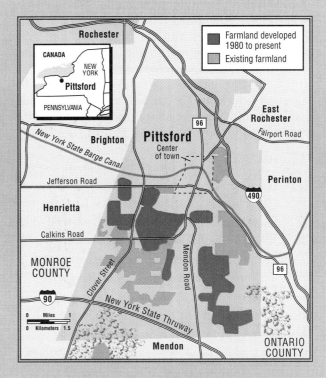

FIGURE 2.19 The Pittsford, New York, area. [Adapted from the *New York Times*, March 20, 1997, p. D-19.]

farmland from suburban development helps the nation by keeping down the demand for imported food and by protecting against volatility in food prices. The facts are that urban sprawl eats up two acres a minute, a million acres a year, including 400,000 acres of land that is especially suited for high-quality specialty crops.

The loss of millions of manufacturing jobs in the old industrial core has had some regrettable consequences. The sociologist William Julius Wilson, in his book *When Work Disappears: The World of the New Urban Poor* (1996), takes special note of the demoralizing effect of plant closings on working-class families in the old industrial cities. "Neighborhoods that are poor and jobless are entirely different from neighborhoods that are poor and working," he says. "Work is not simply a way to make a living and support a family. It also

constitutes a framework for daily behavior because it imposes discipline."

Industrial jobs drew millions of rural black and white men and women from the South to the industrial core after World War II. It is their sons and daughters who are now without work and without funds to retrain and relocate. Consider the case of one inner-city black neighborhood on the west side of Chicago, called North Lawndale. In 1960, two large factories employed 57,000 workers, and a large retail chain employed thousands of secretarial staff in its corporate headquarters nearby. One factory closed in the late 1960s, removing 14,000 jobs; by 1974, the retail headquarters had moved downtown; and by 1984 the other large factory had closed, eliminating a breathtaking 43,000 jobs. North Lawndale began to disintegrate with the first loss. Because no one had money to spend anymore, thousands of service jobs disappeared and with them many middle-class families. Then the housing stock deteriorated as families and businesses left, landlords abandoned buildings, and financial institutions refused to support any reinvestment.

VIGNETTE

At the eastern limit of the economic core, Nancy DeWent, 47, fears that a similar fate is in store for her New York City neighborhood. In 1997, she lost her job at the Swingline factory, where for 19 years she had assembled staplers, working up to a wage of $11.58 an hour. The corporate owner of Swingline says moving to Mexico, where workers like Nancy will be paid a reported 50¢ an hour, will save $12 million annually. Nancy has a nine-year-old son to support, and she worries that she is too old to start over and too young to retire. According to Kevin M. Murphy, an economist who analyzes wages and labor force participation, the best bet for Nancy and her neighbors is to return to school for technological training. The demand for skilled labor, especially computer-related labor, is increasing and likely to continue to do so for years to come. [Adapted from Martin Crutsinger, Conflicting views cloud true impact of NAFTA, *Knoxville News Sentinel*, July 8, 1997, Sec. C, p. 1.]

The American South (the Southeast)

The regional boundaries of the American South are perhaps fuzzier and based more on a perceived state of mind and way of life than is the case for most other U.S. regions. This region, in fact, covers only the southeastern part of the country rather than the whole of the southern United States (Figure 2.20). Somewhere in Texas, the American South grades into the Southwest, a region with noticeably different environmental and cultural features. But what characteristics best define the South? And where shall its borders be drawn?

As this text defines the South, the region extends as far north as the southern edge of Washington, D.C., and includes the southern reaches of Indiana and Illinois. It extends as far west as eastern Oklahoma and

Dallas, Texas. Within the borders of this region there is a complex of features that many would identify as southern: the food, the music, the open friendliness of the people, the dialects, the country Baptist churches, the rolling hills and crooked roads, the early onset of spring, the field patterns and crops like tobacco and cotton, and the rural settlement patterns. Southern cultural features are hard to measure; there are few clear distributions, the patterns are not contiguous, nor are all these characteristics ever present in one place. Furthermore, arguments ensue if one tries to actually define just which accents, or what recipes, or which styles of music, and so forth, are "southern." Some places located in the South have few recognizable southern qualities. Miami, on the far tip of Florida, seems to have lost all vestiges of the Old South. With its cosmopolitan Latino culture and trade and immigration ties to the Caribbean and South America, Miami is redefining what it means to be southern.

When the subject of the American South came up at a dinner party in Slovenia in the fall of 1993, the author, from Tennessee, was more than a little intrigued to hear what her dinner partners had to say. Slovenia is a small country of 2 million people just to the south of Austria, in southeastern Europe. None of the people had ever actually been to the American South, but they had vivid impressions of the region nonetheless. They cited country music, jazz, the blues, plantations, cotton, tobacco, black people, the Civil War, poverty, the fight for civil rights, hard-to-understand dialects of English, Bible-thumping preachers, the use of handguns and lots of murders, and especially Jack Daniel's whiskey. For whatever reason, the American South has a global reputation.

Some of the least attractive of these perceptions have a basis in statistics. For example, while overall violent crime has decreased in the United States since 1980 (Figure 2.21), there is a concentration of violent crime and property crime in the South. Despite the fact that high rates of violent crime also show up in California, Arizona, Maryland, Michigan, and New York, the South has the highest murder rate, the highest rate of violent crime, and the highest rate of murders with a gun in the United States. Tougher sentencing for these violent crimes means that the South has the highest per capita prison population in the country.

Many images of the South, even those held by Americans themselves, are outdated. The South today is a different place from the South during the civil rights efforts of the 1960s, let alone the Civil War. It is true that the region is still home to a large concentration of black Americans. And significant segregation still persists by custom in that, generally, black and white people tend to live and worship separately. But the workplace is now integrated, and many African Americans are in supervisory and administrative positions, especially in government and educational institu-

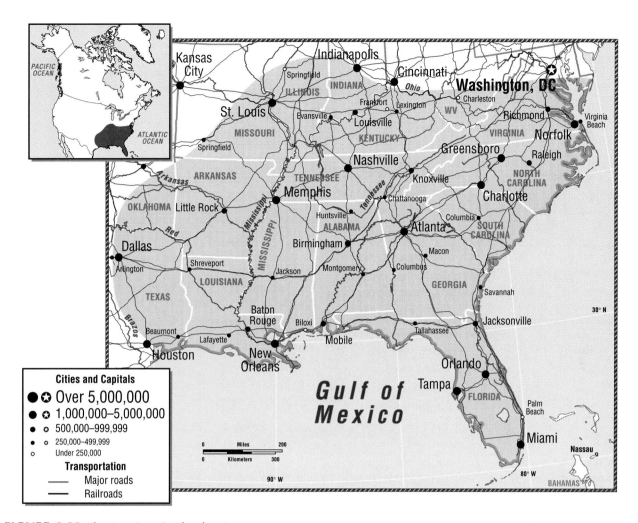

FIGURE 2.20 The American South subregion.

tions. Whites vote for black officials; many schools in both rural and urban settings are integrated; and many more whites and blacks share neighborhoods in the South than in the North.

Poverty is still a problem for too many, although it is much less prevalent than it once was. The South has the nation's highest concentration of black families living below the poverty line. On the other hand, most southerners, black or white, now earn a relatively affluent living in manufacturing and services, compared with their parents. That older generation may have toiled as illiterate laborers on plantations or on poor, eroded, hilly farms in Appalachia. For years, the poor fled the South for jobs in the industrial North; but today these now elderly migrants, both white and black, and their adult children, are being attracted back to the region by well-paying jobs, business opportunities, lower taxes, lower costs of living, a milder climate, and safer, more spacious, and friendlier neighborhoods.

The South is steadily improving its position as a growth region. The federally funded interstate highway

system opened the region to auto and truck transport. Inexpensive industrial locations, close to arterial highways, have drawn many businesses to the South, such as auto and modular home manufacturing, food processing, forest-based building products, light-metals processing, high-tech electronic assembly, furniture manufacturing, and high-end crafts production. More recently, tourists by the hundreds of thousands have been driving south on the interstate highway system, many attracted by bucolic rural landscapes, the scenery of national parks, and recreational theme parks.

Agriculture is now mechanized, and at once diversified and specialized. Many cash crops other than tobacco, cotton, and rice are now grown in the South. Strawberries, blueberries, and vegetables are often produced on small holdings by part-time farmers who may also have jobs in nearby factories. Specialty items like mushrooms and herbs are produced for urban consumers. Most of the country's broiler chickens are now produced on huge operations throughout the South. Interestingly, the laborers on these factorylike chicken

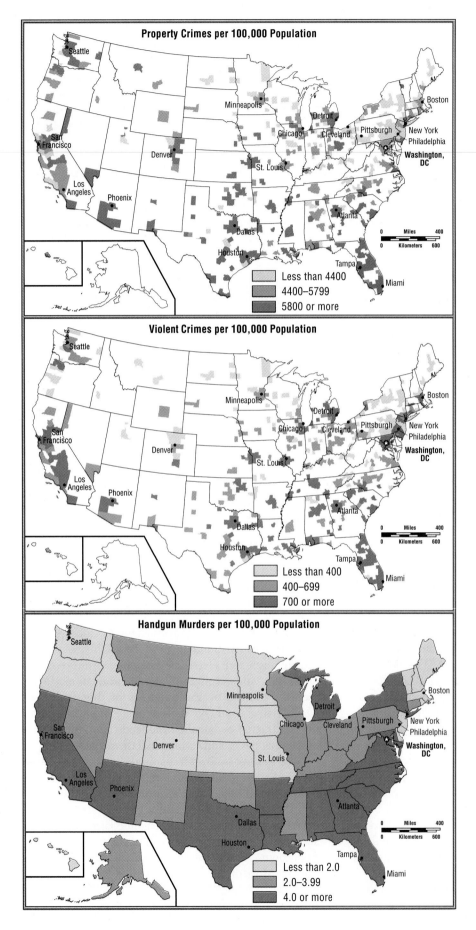

FIGURE 2.21 Concentrations of selected crimes in the United States. [Adapted from Roger Doyle, *1994 Atlas of Contemporary America* (New York: Facts on File, 1994), pp. 166–168.]

farms are not local; rather, they are refugee immigrants from Russia, Vietnam, Haiti, Honduras, the Philippines, and Ukraine, who are willing to take the low-wage jobs, at least for a while. They live in communities of prefab homes, another major product of the South.

The Great Plains Breadbasket

The Great Plains (Figure 2.22) gets its nickname, "the breadbasket," from the fact that this huge area produces immense quantities of grain: wheat, corn, sorghum, barley, and oats, much of it exported to Europe and other parts of the world. The gently undulating prairies give the region a certain visual regularity, while its weather and climate, in contrast, can be unpredictable in the extreme, making life at times precarious.

European settlers did not begin to stake claims on the Great Plains until the 1860s. Many of these settlers were from the cool, wet lowlands of northern Europe. They soon learned that little of what they knew about farming in Europe or eastern North America would be of use. Summers in the middle of the continent, even as far north as the Dakotas, can be oppressively hot and humid; winters can be alternately terribly cold and dry or so abounding in snow that tunnels have to be dug to get from the house to the barns. The summer rains in some years are plentiful; but in other years, hardly a

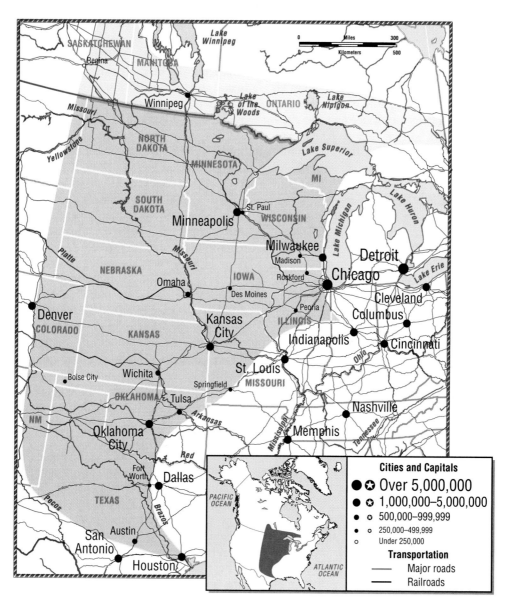

FIGURE 2.22 The Great Plains "breadbasket" subregion.

drop falls and a year's labor may come to naught as the crops wither.

The incessant wind was also unfamiliar to the Europeans. During late spring and summer, the wind often blows continuously for days. Particularly strong wind gusts can make it difficult to breathe out of doors or even to walk upright. The stress can produce psychological reactions ranging from anxiety to panic. The winds also cause stress in crop plants: wind may flatten the fields or increase the rate of evaporation to the point that precious rainfall is sucked back up into the atmosphere in a matter of hours. Tornadoes are an especially great hazard in the south central plains, but most of the plains region south of the Canadian border is subject to these storms, which can wipe out whole towns in a matter of moments.

The women and men who settled on the plains have eventually learned to adapt to high wind and unpredictable rainfall. They plant windbreaks, shelter belts of several rows of dense evergreens, around their farmsteads to temper the force of the wind and conserve moisture. They harness the wind to pump groundwater for stock tanks and domestic use. Farmers have taken to irrigating their crops regularly with water pumped electrically from deep aquifers so that they won't have to worry about the unpredictability of rain. The photograph on page 97 shows the giant green circles made by the central pivot irrigators, used on prairies or in the semiarid conditions of eastern New Mexico.

The crops now grown on the Great Plains were chosen because they suit the environment and world market conditions. The land and climate do not support the root and vegetable crops favored in the East or in Europe. In order to succeed, farmers have had to choose crops—wheat, corn, oats, barley—that mimic the original plains grasses in their environmental requirements. In recent years, sorghum, sugar beets, sunflowers, and many other crops have been added to the Great Plains repertoire; but wheat, much of it genetically engineered to resist frost damage, remains the primary crop. Winter wheat, sown in the fall and reaped in the early summer, is grown on the southern and central plains. Fast-growing summer wheat is grown in the north, where the winters are too severe for young wheat plants to survive. Most wheat is now harvested by traveling teams of combines that start harvesting in the south in June and move north over the course of the summer.

Women have done much of the farm work on the Great Plains since the first settlers arrived. For generations they cared for farm stock and milked cows; grew, preserved, and cooked most of the food; managed the bookkeeping; and drove farm equipment and fixed motors. They also bore and raised large families. Many taught in the country schools and organized the church-related social functions that drew widely dispersed farm families together once or twice a week. By the middle of the twentieth century, the more successful Great Plains farmers educated their children of both sexes at large state universities. It is not unusual now to find farm families where several members have college degrees. Increasingly, female members of farm families manage farms or work at professions in nearby towns.

Cattle raising is another important activity on the Great Plains. These days, cattle are raised on pastures and then shipped to feedlots where they are fattened for market on a diet rich in sorghum and corn. Cattle (and other livestock like hogs and turkeys) are slaughtered and processed for market in small plants across the plains, rather than in the great meat-packing plants of Chicago or Kansas City, as once was the case (see the box "Meat Packing in the Great Plains"). Erosion remains a serious problem on the plains—soil is disappearing more than 16 times faster than it can form. Grain fields and pasture grasses do not hold the soil as the original dense prairie grasses once did, and the sharp hooves of the cattle loosen the soil leading to wind and water erosion. Experts estimate that each pound of steak produced in a feedlot results in 35 pounds of eroded soil.

Population patterns on the Great Plains are changing. The few cities around the periphery of the region are growing as young people leave the small towns on the prairies. Mechanization has reduced the number of jobs in agriculture and encouraged the consolidation of ownership. Now the men and women who farm may own several large farms in different locales. They often choose to live in cities, traveling to their farms seasonally. Hence, they are called "suitcase" or "sidewalk" farmers. As a result of this depopulation, thousands of small prairie towns are literally dying out. Those people left are struggling to continue to provide schools and opportunities for their own young and, in some towns, for the thousands of children of poor immigrants attracted by low-paying jobs. The town of Lefors, in the Texas panhandle, recently tried to give land away to anyone who would come to live there; but there are no jobs in Lefors. No one accepted the offer.

The Continental Interior

Among the most striking features of the continental interior (Figure 2.23) are its huge size, its physical diversity, and its very low population density. This is a land of extreme physical environments; rugged terrain, frigid temperatures, or lack of water are not unusual. These physical features hamper many economic activities and explain the low population density. Most parts of the region have under two persons per square mile.

Today, increasing numbers are migrating to the region, some to take advantage of its open spaces and of-

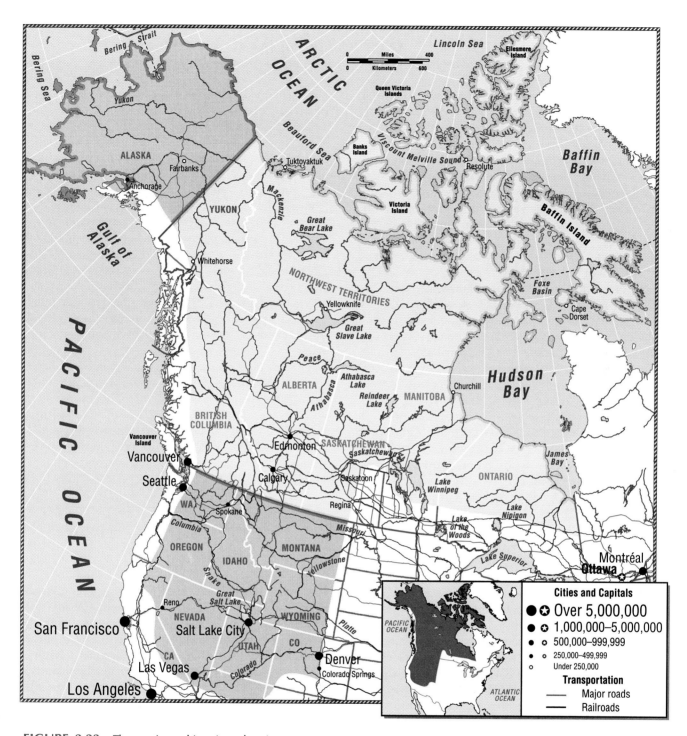

FIGURE 2.23   The continental interior subregion.

ten dramatic scenery, others to exploit its considerable natural resources. The two groups often find themselves in conflict with each other and with the indigenous people of the continental interior. In fact, this region is one of the most intense battlegrounds in North America between environmentalists and resource developers.

Physically, the continental interior may be divided into four distinct zones: the Canadian Shield; the

frigid, rugged lands of Alaska; the Rocky Mountains; and the Great Basin. The Canadian Shield is a vast glaciated territory lying north of the Great Plains and characterized by thin or nonexistent soils, innumerable lakes, and large meandering rivers. Along the southern portion, needle-leafed boreal forests and taiga stretch from Labrador in the east to Alaska in the west. Farther north, the forest gives way to the tundra, a

AT THE LOCAL SCALE   *Meat Packing in the Great Plains*

A meat-packing job in the Great Plains used to provide a stable income of $30,000 or more a year back in the 1970s. Up to the 1980s, the work force was unionized and virtually all workers were native to the region—of German, Slavic, or Scandinavian background. But in the 1980s, a number of meat-packing companies that were highly unionized simply closed their doors. Others have opened up under nonunion rules, often in small towns in Iowa or Nebraska or Minnesota. The labor is supplied not by local residents but by immigrants from Mexico and Central America and from Laos and Vietnam. Now the companies pay $6.00 an hour, which yields an income, after taxes, of less than $12,000 a year. And union-won work rules are no more. The hours are long or short at the convenience of the packing house manager, and those who protest may be summarily fired.

Many of the Latinos and Asians are refugees from war in their home countries, and most of the Asians have spent a decade or more in refugee camps in Southeast Asia before coming to the United States. These immigrant workers have trouble affording housing on their wages, and Middle Westerners are reluctant to rent to them. Hence, many live in makeshift housing, like the Laotian families in Storm Lake, Iowa, who occupy a series of old railroad cars and shanties.

Down the road, Latino workers live in two dilapidated trailer parks.

A few hours away from Storm Lake by car, in Marshall, Minnesota, Roberto Trevino is the personnel director at the Heartland Company, a turkey-processing plant. He supervises 500 workers, 70 percent of whom are from Latin America and Asia, and a few from Somalia (also war refugees). All wear white smocks and caps and labor with dangerous machinery in icy temperatures. They slaughter, carve, trim, and package 32,000 turkeys a day and ship them under more than 60 different brand names. Trevino is himself the college-educated son of Hispanic farm workers and feels his company is providing a stepping stone to the immigrants. "If you are new in this country, . . . you take the jobs Americans don't want and you may not get ahead. But you do it for your kids," he says. Yet even he admits that these jobs are far from stable and don't begin to provide income sufficient to raise a family. The Reverend Tom Lo Van, a Laotian Lutheran pastor, sees little chance that the Laotian youth will prosper from their parents' toil. "This new generation is worse off," he says. "Our kids have no self-identity, no sense of belonging . . . no role models. Eighty percent of [them] drop out of high school."

region of winters so long and cold that several feet below the surface the ground is permanently frozen. Shallow-rooted, ground-hugging plants like mosses, lichens, dwarf trees, and some grasses are the only vegetation. Northern parts of Québec and Labrador are also part of the Canadian Shield. The rugged lands of Alaska lie to the northwest of the shield. Southern Alaska and lowland fingers reaching into the north country are covered with needle-leafed forests, while glaciers are found in some of the highlands. Tundra lies farther north. The Rocky Mountains stretch in a wide belt from southeastern Alaska to New Mexico. The highest areas are generally treeless, with glaciers or tundra-like vegetation, while forests line the slopes on the lower elevations. Between the Rockies and the Pacific coastal zone is the Great Basin, a dry region of widely spaced mountains covered mainly by desert scrub and a few woodlands. In some places irrigated agriculture is possible.

The continental interior has the greatest concentration of Native Americans in the United States (see Figure 2.3) and Canada. Most of them live on reservations in the United States and southern Canada that are not part of their native lands. But many of those who live in the vast tundra and northern forests of the Canadian Shield still occupy their original territory. They are able to hunt and fish and generally maintain the ways of their ancestors, although most now use snowmobiles and modern rifles.

Though much of the continental interior remains sparsely inhabited, nonindigenous people have settled in considerable density in a few places. Where irrigation is possible, agriculture has been expanding—as in the Utah valley; lowlands along the Snake and Columbia rivers of Idaho, Oregon, and Washington; and as far north as the Peace River district in the Canadian province of Alberta. Cattle and sheep ranching are activities throughout much of the Great Basin. Overgrazing and erosion are a problem; more serious is groundwater pollution from chemical fertilizers or the malodorous effluent from huge feedlots where large numbers of beef cattle are fattened for market.

In the semiarid environment near Tuscarora, Nevada, central pivot irrigators bring forth crops that otherwise would not grow. Often the water comes from a well at the center of each circle that taps an underground aquifer, depleting it at an unsustainable rate. [Alex S. MacLean/Landslides.]

Efforts by the U.S. government to curtail abuses on federal land, which is often leased in extensive holdings to ranchers, have not been very successful. Although timber harvesting is common in the more accessible forests of the Canadian Shield and the Rockies, by far the largest industries in the continental interior are mining and oil drilling. Since the mid-nineteenth century, the region's wide range of minerals has supported most major permanent settlements in the region. Life in these towns, however, has never been stable because the economy is either "booming," when mineral prices are high on the world market, or "busting," when prices are low. Many ghost towns dot the landscape. In recent times, the most stable mineral enterprises have been oil-drilling operations along the north coast of Alaska. Although drilling in an arctic environment is expensive, transporting the oil through the Trans-Alaska Pipeline is relatively cheap. The pipeline runs southward for thousands of miles through mountains and tundra, often above ground to avoid shifting as the earth above the permafrost freezes and thaws. It terminates at the port of Valdez in southern Alaska. The pipeline constitutes a major ecological disruption, interfering with caribou migrations and always posing the threat of oil spills. A giant spill from the ship *Exxon Valdez* in 1989 devastated 1100 miles of Alaskan shoreline, killed wildlife, and ruined Native livelihoods and commercial fishing.

Ever more immigrants and vacationers are flocking to the region for its natural beauty. The large number of national parks attract millions of North American tourists; there are more than 350 million visits to U.S. national parks per year—1.5 visits per capita! Many towns in particularly attractive locations have swelled with both seasonal and permanent residents. In the United States, pressure has been put on the federal government to set aside more land for parks and wilderness preserves and to limit or eliminate activities like mining and logging. More than half the land in this subregion is federally owned; in Utah, Arizona, and Nevada, 75 percent of the land is held by the federal or state government. Much of this land is leased to mining or logging operations. A switch to more recreational and preservation-oriented uses would force a major shift in employment throughout the region.

The Pacific Northwest

Once a fairly isolated region, the Pacific Northwest (Figure 2.24) is now at the forefront of forces transforming much of North America. In particular, the economy is shifting from logging, fishing, and farming to high-tech industries. As this happens, people's attitudes about their environment are also changing. Forests that were once valued for their timber are now valued for their natural beauty and wildlife.

The physical geography of this long coastal strip is made up of mountains and valleys. Most of the agriculture, as well as the largest cities, is located in the southern part, in a series of valleys and lowlands lying between two long, rugged mountain zones extending north and south. Moving into Alaska, these mountains become increasingly high and rugged, reaching their climax at Mount McKinley, the highest peak in North America. Throughout the region, the climate is extremely wet. Winds blowing in from the Pacific bring large amounts of moist and relatively warm air inland, where it is pushed up over the mountains, resulting in copious orographic rain- and snowfall. The close proximity of the ocean gives this region a milder climate than is found at similar latitudes farther inland. The balmy climate,

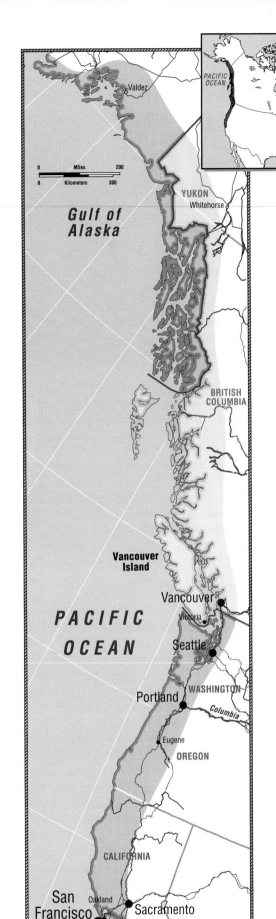

FIGURE 2.24 The Pacific Northwest subregion.

Cities and Capitals

● ✪ Over 5,000,000
● ✪ 1,000,000–5,000,000
● ✪ 500,000–999,999
• ✪ 250,000–499,999
○ Under 250,000

Transportation
——— Major roads
——— Railroads

along with the spectacular scenery, attracts many vacationing or relocating Canadians and U.S. citizens.

In this rainy, temperate zone, enormous trees and vast forests have flourished for eons, and in the last two centuries they provided the major source of employment for immigrants. Pacific Northwest logging still provides most of the construction lumber and an increasing amount of the paper used in the United States and Canada.

As the forests have shrunk, environmentalists have harshly criticized the logging industry for its wasteful and destructive practices, such as clear-cutting. This method involves cutting down all the trees on a given plot of land, regardless of age, health, or species. It is the cheapest and most widely used method of harvesting timber. However, clear-cutting destroys habitats and leaves the land susceptible to erosion and the adjacent forest susceptible to pests. The trees that grow back after clear-cutting tend to be of a single species, allowing harmful insects and infections to spread from tree to tree more easily.

Several large hydroelectric dams have attracted industries in need of cheap electricity: aluminum smelting and associated manufacturing industries in aerospace and defense. These industries are major employers, but their demand for labor is erratic and periodic layoffs are common. In addition, the hydrodams have been criticized by another major employer in the region, the fishing industry. The dams block off the seasonal migrations of salmon to and from their spawning grounds, so some of the region's most valuable fish cannot produce young.

Given the problems associated with these industries, it is not surprising that many people are enthusiastic about the increasing role of high-tech districts within the urban areas of the Pacific Northwest: San Francisco, Portland, Seattle, and Vancouver. High-tech companies are clean and efficient, and they produce high-priced finished goods that are easy to transport. With the Silicon Valley just outside San Francisco and with the growing number of companies around Seattle, the Pacific Northwest is the world leader in high-tech enterprise.

A leadership role is not new to the Pacific Northwest, since controversial trends often start here and then sweep eastward over the rest of the United States and Canada. Universities in the Pacific Northwest led both countries in protesting the

A logging site in British Columbia. [Natalie Fobes/ National Geographic.]

Vietnam War, in developing environmentalism, in raising dietary consciousness (specifically through the vegetarian movement), and, most recently, in raising national consciousness regarding the human rights of gay and lesbian people. San Francisco, at the extreme southern fringe of the Pacific Northwest—some would argue it fits better in the Southwest—has been the center of many such movements. Similarly, integration with the growing economies of Asia has been well under way here for many years, as has the adjustment of a predominantly white society to large numbers of Asian immigrants. Hence, the Pacific Northwest often leads in adjusting to realities that the rest of the United States and Canada may still be resisting.

The Southwest

The Southwest (Figure 2.25) continues, as it has in the past, to grapple with the complexities of its deep ties to both Mexico and the United States. The region was first colonized by Spaniards, who at the end of the sixteenth century established sheep ranches and missions in the area that today forms central and southern California, southern Arizona, New Mexico, and Texas. Settlements were few and poorly connected; therefore, as the United States expanded into the region, Mexico found it increasingly difficult to hold on to its claimed territory. By 1850, nearly all of the Southwest was under U.S. control, although part of the area maintained a distinctive Hispanic culture, the Spanish language, and other connections with Mexico. Today, Hispanic culture is intensifying in the Southwest and even spreading as large numbers of immigrants flow across the border and as the economies of the United States and Mexico become increasingly interdependent under the North American Free Trade Agreement.

The varied landscapes of the Southwest include the coastal hills and interior valleys of California, the widely spaced mountains and dramatic mesas and canyons of southern Arizona and New Mexico, and the gentle coastal plain of south Texas. But the common physical themes throughout are warm average annual temperatures and arid climate. Most areas receive less than 20 inches of rainfall a year, and the dominant vegetation is scrub and widely spaced trees. Because of the aridity, ranching is the most common form of land use. Where irrigation is possible, however, it is much more profitable to grow fruits and vegetables as there is a nearly year-round growing season.

California's Central Valley is the leading agricultural district in the United States, and one of the most valuable in the world. Most of this land is devoted to high-value crops such as grapes, tomatoes, lettuce, or other vegetables that are grown year-round and shipped throughout the United States and Canada. Many of these crops are produced on vast, plantation-like farms. Migrant Mexican workers supply most of the labor, and many of them come illegally to work at very low pay. These workers actually lower the cost of North American food by working for such low wages, and too often they are mere children.

Although agriculture is important, the bulk of the region's economy is nonagricultural. Minerals are the basis of important economic activity, with copper mining prominent in southern Arizona and New Mexico. Oil drilling and refining, and associated chemical industries are important along the coasts of southern California and Texas. Both these coastal zones nurture a number of other processing and manufacturing industries that need the cheap transport provided by the ocean. Manufacturing is also important along the U.S.-Mexican border. Foreign-owned factories, or *maquiladoras,* are often located in Mexican towns just across the border from American towns. In places like El Paso/Ciudad Juárez, Laredo/Nuevo Laredo, Nogales/Nogales, and San Diego/Tijuana, U.S. companies have set up *maquiladoras* to produce manufactured goods for sale in the United States, taking advantage of cheaper Mexican wages, lower taxes, and more lax environmental regulations. These factories are a key part of a larger transborder economy. In fact, the U.S.-Mexican border is one of the world's most **permeable national borders,** with as many as 200 million legal border crossings a year. Increasingly, the towns on the U.S. side of the border are losing their manufacturing and other labor-intensive jobs to their Mexican twins.

These depressed U.S. border towns provide a striking contrast to other prosperous cities and towns of the region. The Southwest's mild climate, sunny

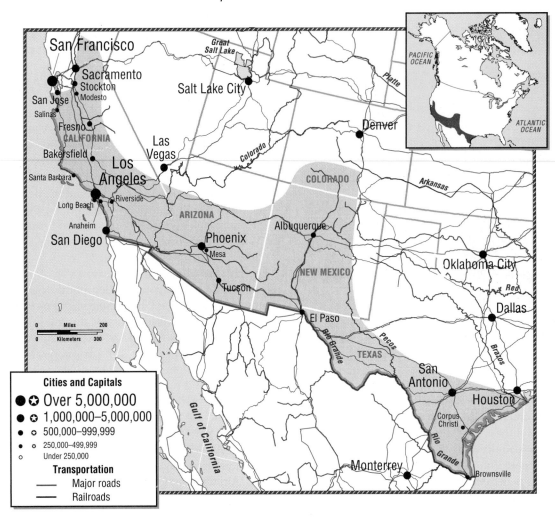

FIGURE 2.25 The Southwest subregion.

weather, and spectacular scenery have made the region a popular destination for several important industries. For many years, the U.S. film industry, located in southern California, has drawn people from all over the world. The warm water ports of San Diego and Los Angeles also provide strategic locations for military installations and access to the markets of Latin America and Asia via the trade routes of the Pacific. Los Angeles—with major trade, transport, media, and finance industries, as well as important research facilities—recently surpassed New York as the largest city in the United States. Cities such as Austin, Texas, have attracted high-tech industries lured by the warm climate and what is perceived as a more laid-back lifestyle. The climate also draws large numbers of vacationers and retirees to the Southwest. Many small towns have been swamped by migrants, and entire semiplanned communities of 10,000 or 20,000 people have grown up in the desert in the space of a few years.

The incredible influx of migrants from the rest of North America, Mexico, and, more recently, Asia is choking the major cities of the Southwest with so many people, houses, and cars that the area is losing much of its attractiveness. This is perhaps most evident in Los Angeles's infamous **smog**, a combination of industrial air pollution and car exhaust that frequently hovers over the city, causing a variety of health problems for its inhabitants. The intensity of Los Angeles's smog is due in large part to the city's warm land temperatures and west coast seaside location; this often results in **thermal inversion:** a warm mass of stagnant air is trapped beneath cooler air that blows in off the ocean. This inversion is held in place, often for days, by the mountains that surround the city. People fleeing pollution and congestion in Los Angeles often head for the cities of southern Arizona and New Mexico.

Meanwhile, a whole range of contentious issues surround the estimated 2.4 million illegal aliens currently residing in the United States, most of whom are Mexicans. Many of these people remain in the Southwest, where in addition to contributing to the local economy they keep down the wages of low-skilled

Reflections

October 1997: Jose Madrid, 11, picks green chilies in New Mexico. "I'm not good at math, but I'm good at money," he says. Like many child migrant workers in the United States, he goes to school only intermittently. [Eric Draper/AP/Wide World Photos.]

workers. Inadvertently, they have also increased tension over the status of the English language in the United States. Although English speakers in the Southwest far outnumber Spanish speakers, many fear that English could be challenged in much the same way that it has been challenged by French in Québec. Accordingly, Arizona and California recently became the first states in the Southwest to make English the official language of government. Bilingual programs,

installed in the 1970s to aid children make the transition from Spanish to English, are being abolished.

REFLECTIONS ON NORTH AMERICA

It is not hard to rhapsodize about North America: the sheer size of the continent, its incredible wealth in natural and human resources, its superior productive capacities, and its powerful political position in the world are features enjoyed by no other world region. North America enjoys such prosperity, privilege, and power as a result of both fortunate circumstances and the hard work of its inhabitants. Perhaps the most important factor in North America's success has been its democratic governments and supporting institutions, which allow for flexibility as times and circumstances change.

Yet life has not been good to all in North America. Many people of both sexes—Native Americans, enslaved Africans and their descendants, and ethnic minorities—suffered as Canada and the United States were being created out of what had been lands long occupied by indigenous people. The environmental impact of European settlement was, and continues to be, significant; and the standard of living expected by subsequent immigrants from all parts of the world and their descendants promises to increase steadily the strain on North American environments. Furthermore, as Canada and the United States developed into wealthy world powers, the impact of North America on

Los Angeles keeps expanding farther and farther into dry, desertlike foothills. Such development destroys the natural vegetation that holds the soil in place, so large landslides and mud slides may occur when the snowcap melts in the spring or during the occasional heavy rains coming in off the Pacific. Here, the lots have been graded to control runoff. [Alex S. MacLean/Landslides.]

distant environments and people, through trade and cultural diffusion, must be acknowledged.

It is not a foregone conclusion that North America will continue in its leadership role far into the future. North American models for development are being challenged as inappropriate for much of the rest of the world. As we shall see, societies elsewhere are beginning to prosper without following North American examples, and often without first installing democratic institutions. Environmental concerns, now so much a part of the North American consciousness, are not central in many developing countries. Material prosperity is often the chief goal, just as it still is in North America. Many around the world are eager to bring the North American miracle to their lands, regardless of negative environmental impacts.

Although the outcome is far from clear, the closer formal economic association with Mexico through NAFTA may turn out to be just the beginning of new alignments between North America and the nations of Middle and South America. As we shall see in Chapter 3, over the last few centuries Middle and South America have had very different experiences from those of North America, yet recent social and economic changes have been dramatic. It is not inconceivable that the Americas eventually will be a much more economically, and possibly socially and politically, integrated part of the world.

Selected Themes and Concepts

1. North America, as a result of its great size and its location relative to the poles and the equator, contains all climate types except the truly tropical.

2. Settlement in North America has been characterized by successive movements of people across the vast continent from ancient times to the present. Predominantly European settlement over the last nearly 500 years, coupled with the physical diversity of the continent, has established a distinct pattern of subregions.

3. The pattern of economic and social dominance by particular subregions has changed over time.

4. Native Americans experienced enormous losses of people and territory and suffered a decline in their standard of living during European settlement. They are now slowly increasing in numbers, and some groups are finding innovative ways out of pervasive poverty.

5. Although Canada and the United States are approximately the same size, Canada has a population only one-tenth that of the United States. Population distribution in both countries is very uneven, with the greatest concentration falling within several hundred miles of the eastern boundary between the two countries—in southeastern Canada and the northeastern United States.

6. Only one-quarter of the population in both countries lives in rural areas. The urban majority is especially mobile, with approximately one-fifth of the population moving every year.

7. Although the two countries are each other's main trading partner and enjoy many similarities in standard of living and general culture, their relationship is asymmetrical, primarily because Canada's population and economy are about 10 percent that of the United States.

8. Both countries were settled by immigrants and people from Africa and their descendants, and both continue to accept hundreds of thousands of immigrants yearly. Now the source of the immigrant stream is shifting away from Europe and Africa and toward Middle and South America and Asia. As a result, the cultural diversity of both countries is increasing.

9. The **nuclear family** has long been the norm but is now decreasing in importance as the single-person household grows in importance, especially among middle-aged and elderly people.

10. Canada and the United States are both economically and politically powerful and are looked to for leadership in international matters. Both countries are also facing changes: jobs in agriculture and industry are being lost to mechanization and overseas locations and their own economies are becoming service and information based, with jobs requiring more education.

11. Both Canada and the United States are still striving for gender equality in pay, political representation, and opportunities for jobs and advancement.

12. North America's high standard of living and growing populations are impinging on the natural habitat of both plants and animals. The environmental consequences, such as **acid rain** and **hazardous wastes,** are causing a deterioration in environmental quality for humans as well.

Selected Readings

Blouet, Brian W., and Frederick C. Luebke, eds. *The Great Plains—Environment and Culture.* Lincoln: University of Nebraska Press, 1977.

Bullard, Robert D. *Dumping in Dixie: Race, Class and Environmental Quality.* Boulder, CO: Westview Press, 1994.

Butzer, Karl W., ed. The Americas before and after 1492: An introduction to current geographical research. *Annals of the Association of American Geographers* 82 (September 1992): 345–368.

Corner, James, and Alex S. MacLean. *Taking Measures Across the American Landscape.* New Haven, CT: Yale University Press, 1996.

Doyle, Roger. *1994 Atlas of Contemporary America.* New York: Facts on File, 1994.

Dubeck, Paula J., and Kathryn Borman. *Women and Work— A Handbook.* New York: Garland, 1996.

Einhorn, Barbara, and Eileen Janes Yeo, eds. *Women and Market Societies: Crisis and Opportunity.* Aldershot, UK: Edward Elgar, 1995.

Faux, Jeff. Is the American economic model the answer? *The American Prospect* 19 (Fall 1994): 74–81. http://epn.org/prospect/19/19faux.html.

Garreau, Joel. *The Nine Nations of North America.* Boston: Houghton Mifflin, 1981.

Grant, Richard, and Jan Nijman. Historical changes in U.S. and Japanese foreign aid to the Asia-Pacific region. *Annals of the American Association of Geographers* 87, no. 1 (1997): 32–51.

Hanson, Susan, and G. Pratt. *Gender, Work, and Space.* New York: Routledge, 1995.

Hudson, John. *Making the Corn Belt—A Geographic History of Middle-Western Agriculture.* Bloomington: Indiana University Press, 1994.

Janelle, Donald G. *Geographical Snapshots of North America.* New York: Guilford Press, 1992.

Kaplan, David. Two nations in search of a state: Canada's ambivalent spatial identities. *Annals of the American Association of Geographers* 84, no. 4 (1994): 585–606.

Krugman, Paul R. *Peddling Prosperity: Economic Sense and Nonsense in an Age of Diminished Expectations.* New York: W. W. Norton, 1995.

Leckie, Gloria J. Female farmers in Canada, 1971–1986. *Professional Geographer* (May 1993): 180–193.

Ley, David. *The New Middle Class and the Remaking of the Central City.* New York: Oxford University Press, 1997.

Lippard, Lucie. *The Lure of the Local: Senses of Place in a Multi-Centered Society.* New York: New Press, 1997.

Martin, Philip, and Elizabeth Midgley. Immigration to the United States: Journey to an uncertain destination. *Population Bulletin* 49 (September 1994).

Morris, Willie. *Yazoo: Integration in a Deep-Southern Town.* New York: Harper's Magazine Press, 1971.

Pinal, Jorge del, and Audrey Singer. Generations of diversity: Latinos in the United States. *Population Bulletin* 52 (October 1997).

Scheuerman, Richard, and John Clement. *Palouse Country: A Land and Its People.* College Place, WA: Color Press, 1993.

Spencer, Jon Michael. *The New Colored People—The Mixed-Race Movement in America.* New York: New York University Press, 1997.

Wilson, Deborah S., and Christine Moneera Laennec, eds. *Bodily Discursions—Genders, Representations, Technologies.* Albany: State University of New York Press, 1997.

Zelinsky, Wilbur. *The Cultural Geography of the United States—A Revised Edition.* Englewood Cliffs, NJ: Prentice Hall, 1992.

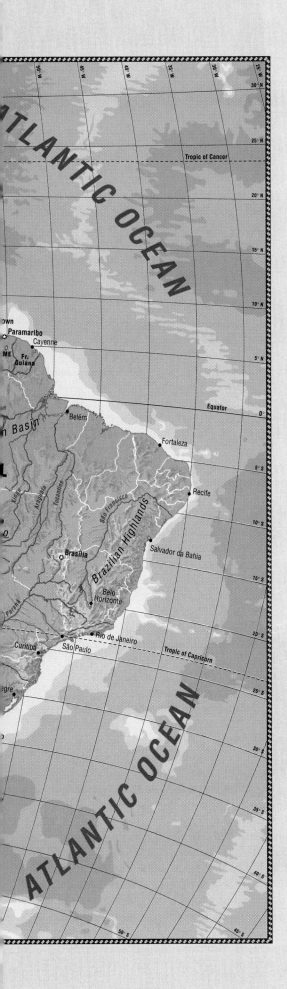

CHAPTER

THREE

MIDDLE
AND
SOUTH
AMERICA

INTRODUCTION TO MIDDLE AND SOUTH AMERICA

Far from the Americas, in a small, bustling marketplace in central Europe, a young man tidies up his vegetable stand piled high with vegetables and fruits from around the world. Among them are green beans, huge bell peppers, long, slim, hot paprika peppers, red- and yellow- and white-skinned potatoes, tomatoes in a variety of shapes and colors, large green avocados, hard-shelled yellow squashes, and pineapples. He, like the shoppers around him on this early Saturday morning in Ljubljana, Slovenia, is little aware that he is participating in a global exchange that began more than 500 years ago. These particular vegetables and fruits originated in ancient times in the gardens of people in Middle and South America, people mistakenly labeled "Indians" by a confused Columbus in 1492. Before the late 1500s, no Europeans had even tasted these New World vegetables and fruits now so essential to European diets. Since then, cultures around the world have adopted foods from the Americas. The so-called ethnic cuisines of Europe, Africa, Asia, and the Pacific all contain major ingredients that originated in the Americas and were unknown elsewhere before 1500.

Tomatoes, pineapples, and green peppers are among the many plants domesticated in the Americas that rest beside many Old World foods (oranges, grapes, bananas, and eggplant) in this central European vegetables stand. [Lydia Pulsipher.]

Middle and South America were the first parts of the New World that Europeans encountered after the initial landfall in the Bahamas in 1492. Very soon thereafter, the Americas were contributing priceless treasures to the world at large. Their gold and silver eventually financed much of the industrial revolution in Europe. Their crop plants drastically changed standards of living and the economies of far-flung places. For example, the potato was first brought under cultivation thousands of years ago in the Andes. By 1750, it had so improved the diet of the poor majority in Europe that it helped make possible a population explosion. Manioc, although less nutritious, played a similar role in West Africa. And American cotton became the primary fiber of the new textile industries in the British Isles and the British colony of India.

In the 1980s, when Ronald Reagan, then president of the United States, visited Middle and South America, he reported that he was surprised to find that the countries were all so different. In fact, Middle and South America are in many ways more complex than North America. Physically, the region spans a wider stretch of the earth's surface and exhibits a more varied mosaic of environments. Culturally, also, it is richer than the continent to the north. Large Native American populations influence daily life through their very presence, but also through their legacies of plants, languages, religious beliefs, material culture, and customs. Immigrant groups from Europe, Asia, and Africa have also left distinctive marks, often because circumstances and isolation encouraged a certain cultural conservatism on the part of many of them. And the ethnic variety is made yet more complex by highly stratified social systems based on class, sex, and race. Politically, too, the region is more complex; it includes over three dozen independent countries implementing somewhat different models of self-government with different degrees of success. Economically, also, there is greater variety than in North America and a wider difference in levels of well-being within and between countries.

Despite the distinctive features of the many parts of Middle and South America, there are commonalities throughout the region. Most of these hark back to their shared experience as colonies of Spain and Portugal (and of Britain, France, and the Netherlands in the Caribbean). Colonialism introduced a version of capitalism to the region that did not provide a way for the region to develop itself, but instead made it a producer of raw materials for development elsewhere, chiefly Europe. This focus on production for export greatly altered local landscapes: complex mosaics of land devoted to multiple uses were transformed into monotonous stretches of a single crop like sugar or cotton or were even stripped away for the mining of silver, copper, or gold. Colonialism also toppled Native Americans from power in their own homelands and instituted a highly stratified class system that placed them at the bottom. This system still prevails and has produced the nearly universal pattern of a huge, poor, mostly brown-skinned, majority; a tiny, rich, often white, minority; and a small, relatively powerless, often racially mixed, middle class.

Today, in every country of the region there are efforts to reverse the patterns of the colonial era, and successes are not hard to spot. Self-help projects and efforts to democratize everyday life are evident in countless villages and city neighborhoods. The military, which in the past was often called on to maintain order (for good or evil), is now much less evident. Economic modernization is not only proceeding but is increasingly linked to the idea that development is not just a matter of sleek skyscrapers and massive dam projects. To be judged successful, development must first and foremost change for the better the lives of the majority.

Themes to Look For

The preceding discussion points out a few major themes that you will be encountering repeatedly in this chapter:

1. The cultural variety and richness of the region.

2. The colonial influence on the economy: the economies in much, but not all, of the region continue to depend primarily on agriculture and the extraction of mineral resources.

3. The highly stratified social system: a small, rich, often white minority has political and economic power over a large, poor, and mostly brown majority.

4. As a result of economic and political inequalities, there is a huge disparity of income.

In addition, there are a few other important themes that appear consistently throughout the chapter:

5. The migration of huge numbers of people from the countryside to the city is transforming traditional patterns of life in the region.

6. The extended family, with defined roles for men and women, continues to shape personal lives in the region.

Terms to Be Aware Of

In this book **Middle America** refers to Mexico, the narrow ribbon of land containing Central America, and the islands of the Caribbean. **South America** refers to the vast landmass south of Central America. **Latin America,** the term most often used for what we here call Middle and South America, is used only occasionally in this book, for several reasons. *Latin* actually re-

fers to the culture of ancient Rome and to the languages (Italian, Spanish, French, Portuguese) that developed from the Latin language. *Latin America* is so called only because it was colonized, for the most part, by Spain and Portugal, which are thought of as having Latin origins. (Actually, the cultures of Spain and Portugal are the products of many non-Latin influences as well.) Used to refer to the Americas, the term *Latin* tends to freeze a huge area in a sort of permanent colonial status. The designation ignores the other cultures present in the region, most notably the different Native American groups, but also people who arrived during and after the colonial period—Africans, Dutch, Germans, British, Chinese, Japanese, and others from elsewhere in Asia. Nor does the term acknowledge the new, distinctly American culture, often called **Creole** culture, that has been created from these many strands.

The terms *New World* and *Old World* are problematic. Is the New World so designated because it is actually newer, in some way, than the Old World or only because it was new to Europeans in 1492? Despite some misgivings, in this book we still occasionally use the New World/Old World designations, because they are convenient. When we say **New World,** we mean all of the Americas; when we say **Old World,** we mean an entity that includes virtually the entire rest of the world, because the whole of Eurasia, Africa, and Oceania has interacted in some way over the last 20,000 years, exchanging cultural attributes.

PHYSICAL PATTERNS

Landforms

You can see from the map opening this chapter that the region of Middle and South America stretches south and east across a wide expanse of the earth's surface. It extends from the midlatitudes of the Northern Hemisphere all the way across the equator to Tierra del Fuego, near Antarctica in the Southern Hemisphere. The primary landforms of this huge territory may be divided into just two types: highlands and lowlands.

The landforms of Middle and South America have been shaped by tectonic forces and the erosion and deposition that follow tectonic uplifting. On the eastern side of the region, the small Caribbean Plate is caught between the large North American and South American plates, and the two larger plates are pushing along the eastern edge of the Caribbean Plate beneath the arc of the Leeward and Windward islands (see Figure 1.8). The Caribbean Plate is not moving fast enough, so the

Ash clouds obscure the top of Montserrat's volcano during a visit by the author in June 1997. Ash from earlier pyroclastic flows blanket much of the landscape like snow and is several meters thick in many places. Earth tremors and ash falls were nearly continuous for three years. By mid-1998, the volcano had quieted down (with no more magma rising), but an international team of vulcanologists studying the situation says the southern two-thirds of the island will remain uninhabitable for years to come. A similar volcano on the nearby island of Martinique exploded in 1902, killing more than 30,000 people. All the homes in this picture had to be abandoned, and yet 4000 of Montserrat's 11,000 inhabitants remain on the island. They have moved to the arid but safer north, where they are creating a new community for themselves. If you are wondering why people stay in volcanic zones, despite the danger, the fact is that these zones have many attractive features: rich soils, plenty of orographic rainful, lush vegetation, moderate temperatures, and beautiful, dramatic landscapes that tug at the heartstrings. [Lydia Pulsipher.]

two large American plates are sliding under it, a process called **subduction.** Subduction can create mountain chains by crumpling and uplifting the edge of the overriding plate. In addition, molten rock may ascend to the surface through fissures in the overriding plate and erupt as volcanoes. Enough material may accumulate from such eruptions to form a mountain.

Most of the islands of the Caribbean are volcanic in origin, and volcanic eruptions are still building mountains there today. The people of Montserrat, for example, have had to cope with a series of volcanic eruptions since July 1995. In June 1996 the Soufriere Hills volcano let loose a violent **pyroclastic flow**—a blast of super-heated rocks, ash, and gas that moves at great speed,

often out of the side of a mountain. The eruption killed 20 people; subsequent eruptions destroyed the capital, Plymouth, and about 20 settlements in the southern two-thirds of the island.

Along the western edges of the three American plates (North American, Caribbean, and South American), mountain building is much further along than in the Caribbean. Here the three plates have encountered the massive eastward-moving Pacific Plate and its two appendage plates, the Nazca and the Cocos (see Figure 1.8). The eastward-moving plates plunge beneath the three American plates in another zone of subduction. The sustained pressure has raised some significant wrinkles in the earth's surface and sprouted many volcanoes. All along the western edge, from Alaska in the northwest to Tierra del Fuego, the American continents sport a grandly curving and nearly continuous complex mountain chain, more than 10,000 miles long (Figure 3.1). This mountain chain is known as the Sierra Madre in Mexico, by various local names in Central America, and as the Andes in South America.

The lowlands stretch to the east of these mountains. In the north, a narrow coastal plain borders the Gulf of Mexico; in Central America, wide aprons of sloping land descend to the Caribbean coast. Much of the Caribbean Basin lies below the sea, and only a few dozen islands rise above its surface. In South America, a huge wedge of variable lowlands, widest in the north, stretches from the Andes east to the Atlantic Ocean. These lowlands are interrupted in the northeast and the southeast by two modest highland zones known as the Guiana Highlands and the Brazilian Highlands (see Figure 3.1).

River Systems

The lowlands of South America can be divided, despite their great expanse, into just three main river systems, all of which flow into the Atlantic Ocean. The three river systems (see Figure 3.1) are the Orinoco, the Amazon, and the Paraná; the lower reaches of the latter are called the Río de la Plata. The Orinoco River begins in southeastern Venezuela, circles around the Guiana Highlands, is fed by several Colombian tributaries from the northeastern slopes of the Andes, and extends northeast through Venezuela, flowing into the Atlantic just south of the Caribbean island of Trinidad.

The largest feature in the South American lowlands is the Amazon Basin (see Figure 3.14). Most of the basin lies within Brazil, but as the map at the beginning of the chapter shows, the northern and western upland perimeters are shared with the Guianas, Venezuela, Colombia, Ecuador, Peru, and Bolivia. The Amazon Basin is itself of global significance: it contains the earth's largest expanse of tropical rain forest, 20 percent of the earth's fresh water, and more than 100,000 species

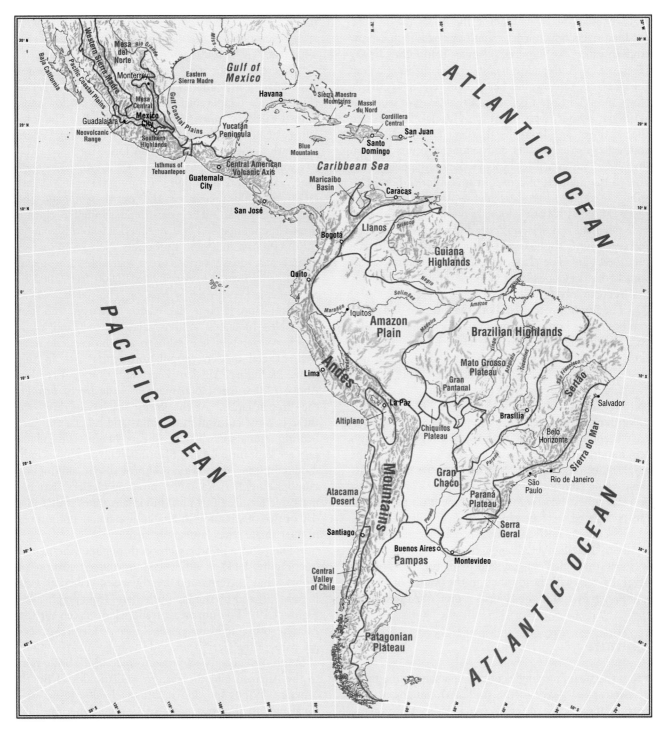

FIGURE 3.1 Principal landforms and rivers. [Adapted from David Clawson, *Latin America and the Caribbean* (Dubuque, IA: Wm. C. Brown, 1997), pp. 17, 18, and 34.]

of plants and animals. The river basin has more than 14,000 miles of navigable waterways; and the channels are so deep that ocean liners can steam 2300 miles up-river, all the way to Iquitos, jokingly referred to as Peru's "Atlantic seaport."

The vast Amazon River system has a west-to-east momentum: its main branches flow from the foot of the Andes Mountains across the central lowlands of South America toward the Atlantic. Many of the streams that eventually link up to form the main course of the

109

Amazon River begin life high in the Andes to the west. Rushing rivers flow north or south through high, narrow Andean valleys for hundreds of miles before they finally reach the lowlands and turn eastward for the long trip to the Atlantic. On the flat land, their velocity suddenly slows and the heaviest particles of their load of sediment settle out. Other rivers, from the Guiana Highlands to the northeast and from the Brazilian Highlands to the southeast, also feed water and sediment to the Amazon lowlands. The annual renewal of sediment supplies nutrients to the millions of acres of tropical forest here. Despite the relative sameness of the Amazon landscape, there is a good bit of ecological diversity within the region—rainfall varies, cloud cover and wind patterns vary, soil types vary—so the whole area is not favorable to true rain forest. In some places the natural vegetation is seasonally dry deciduous tropical forest or, where rainfall is less frequent, even grassland.

The interior reaches of both the Orinoco and Amazon basins are home to some of the last remaining relatively undisturbed Native American cultures found in the New World, such as the Yanomamo. When Europeans first came to these river basins there were perhaps 2 million people living from hunting and gathering and shifting cultivation. In 1900, there were 230 known ethnic groups, often referred to as "tribes." Since then, 87 have become extinct; and in some isolated groups, only a few hundred members survive. Many have died as the result of introduced diseases, others because of mistreatment while laboring on rubber plantations or in mines, and still others because of encroachment on their habitats by logging, new settlements, and agriculture.

The Paraná River system has its origins in the southern Brazilian Highlands, but as it travels southwesterly through Paraguay and Argentina, it is fed by several rivers with headwaters in the Andes of Bolivia and Paraguay and in the pampas region of Argentina.

Climate

From the steaming jungles of the Amazon, to the high, glacier-capped peaks of the Andes Mountains, to the parched moonscape of the Atacama Desert, the climatic variety of Middle and South America is remarkable (Figure 3.2). This climatic diversity results from several factors. The wide range of temperatures reflects the great distance spanned by the landmass on either side of the equator; Mexico lies 33° north of the equator, and Tierra del Fuego, the southern tip of South America, lies 55° south of the equator. Also there are the tremendous changes in altitude created by the region's long mountainous spine, and the variable precipitation that results from global patterns of wind and ocean currents. Of these factors, it is mainly altitude that most people in the region use to conceptualize the variety of climates

they encounter. Temperatures generally decrease with rising elevation, at the rate of about 3.5°F for every 1000 feet (6.4°C/1000 meters) increase in elevation.

There are four main **temperature-altitude zones** descriptive of the climates of Middle and South America (Figure 3.3). Temperatures are warmest in the lowlands, known as *tierra caliente,* or the "hot lands." The lowlands extend up to about 3000 feet (1000 meters). Where moisture is adequate, tropical rain forest thrives, as well as a wide range of tropical crops, such as bananas, sugarcane, cacao, and pineapples. From 3000 to 6500 feet (1000 to 2000 meters) is the *tierra templada,* the "temperate lands." The year-round springlike climate drew large numbers of Native Americans to this zone in the distant past and, later, Europeans. Here crops such as corn, beans, squash, various green vegetables, wheat, and coffee are grown. From 6500 to 12,000 feet (2000 to 3600 meters) is the *tierra fría,* or "cool lands," where many midlatitude crops like wheat, fruit trees, and root vegetables (potatoes, onions, and carrots) and cool-weather vegetables like cabbage and broccoli do very well. Several modern population centers are in this zone, including Mexico City and Quito, Ecuador. Above 12,000 feet (3600 meters) is the *tierra helada,* the "frozen lands." At the lowest reaches of this zone there is some cultivation of grains and tubers; and fur-bearing animals like llamas, sheep, vicuna, and guinea pigs are kept for food and fiber. High up on cold, windy mountain faces, vegetation is almost absent, and mountaintops emerge from under snow and glaciers. The remarkable feature of tropical mountain zones is that in a day or two of strenuous hiking, one can encounter most of the climate types known on earth.

The pattern of precipitation throughout the region (see Figure 1.11) is influenced by the circulation of global wind patterns and nearby ocean currents (see Figure 1.9) and by the lay of the land (topography; see Figure 1.10). The northeast trade winds sweep off the Atlantic, bringing heavy seasonal rains to Central America, parts of the Caribbean, and the huge Amazon Basin of South America. The southeast trade winds bring rain to the Amazon and the eastern midlatitudes of South America. Winds blowing in off the Pacific bring seasonal rain to the west coast of Central America. The combination of heavy rain and high year-round temperatures gives many of these areas a dense cover of tropical rain forest. Similarly, the winds that sweep north of Antarctica from the west, the subpolar westerlies, bring steady cold rains to the southern coast of Chile, where the forest and climate are similar to those of the Pacific Northwest of North America.

Topography has a major influence on precipitation. The southern Andes block rains from the subpolar westerlies, thus creating an extensive rain shadow along the southeastern coast of Argentina. The central Andes create another rain shadow in northern Chile and Peru,

FIGURE 3.2 Regional climate.

but this time on the western side of the mountains. Here the Andes block moist air borne by the northeast and southeast trade winds off the Atlantic.

Finally, the pattern of precipitation is also influenced by the adjacent oceans and their currents. Along the west coast of Peru and Chile, the cold surface waters of the Peru Current bring cold air that is unable to carry much moisture. The combination of the Peru Current and the central Andes rain shadow has created possibly the world's driest desert, the Atacama of northern Chile.

An interesting and as yet only partly understood aspect of the Peru Current is its tendency to change

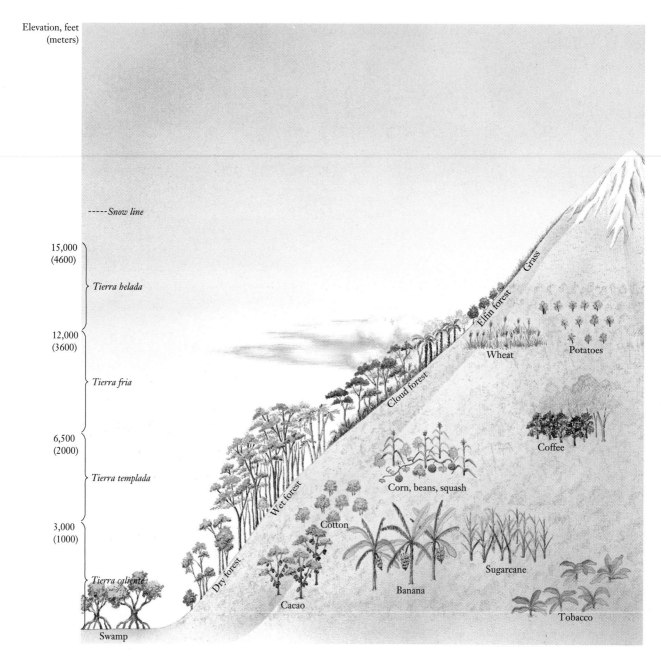

FIGURE 3.3 Temperature-altitude zones of the region. Each zone is suited for growing different crops, and the natural vegetation changes with altitude as well. As altitude increases, temperatures usually decrease and cloud cover may increase. The rain forest that flourishes at lower elevations may give way in higher elevations to vegetation adapted to the somewhat lower temperatures and less direct sunlight: tree ferns, ground ferns, herbaceous plants like heliconia, philodendron, grasses, and trees of moderate, or even stunted, height. [Illustration by Tomo Narashima.]

significantly every few years. Instead of bringing cold water and drought, it brings warm water and rain to parts of the west coast of South America. This mysterious change in the current is called "El Niño" by Peruvian fishermen, who have long noticed that their catches of fish fall drastically every so often as nutrient-poor warm water replaces the nutrient-rich cold water of the Peru Current. (El Niño, which signifies "the Christ Child," is so called because it often reaches its peak sometime in December.) El Niño (see Figure 11.3) is now understood to have a worldwide impact, periodically changing expected weather patterns. El Niño brings cold air and drought to normally warm and humid western Oceania, torrential rains to the dry Peruvian coast, unpredictable weather patterns to Mexico, droughts to the Amazon, and perhaps fewer hurricanes to the Caribbean.

HUMAN PATTERNS

Ways of life in Middle and South America today are greatly affected by a series of changes that resulted from the conquest of the Americas by Europe. That conquest wiped out much of Native American civilization and set up colonial regimes in its place. It introduced many new cultural influences to the Americas and resulted in the lopsided distribution of power and wealth to a few and poverty to the majority.

The Peopling of Middle and South America

Between 13,000 and 19,000 years ago, groups of hunters and gatherers from Asia were spreading throughout North America after crossing the Bering land bridge. Many were also venturing south through Mexico and Central America. Anthropologists now think that in a period of only several thousand years these people managed to adapt to a wide range of ecosystems: the dry mountains and valleys of northern Mexico, the tropical rain forests and upland zones of Central America, the vast Amazon Basin, the Andes Mountains, and the cold, windy grasslands near the tip of South America.

By 1492, the North American population numbered at least 18 million; but in Middle and South America there were at least 50 million people, and in some places even rural population densities were high enough to threaten sustainability. These people altered the landscape in many ways. They modified drainage to irrigate crops, constructed raised fields in lowlands, terraced hillsides, built paved walkways across swamps and even mountains, constructed cities with sewer systems and freshwater aqueducts, and raised up huge earthen and stone ceremonial structures that rivaled the pyramids of Egypt. The trauma of the conquest and of the ensuing 500 years of European dominance has obliterated many remarkable accomplishments of Native American cultures, some of which are only now coming to light through archaeological research.

The Conquest

The European conquest of Middle and South America was one of the most horrendous and significant events in human history, rapidly altering landscapes and, in many cases, ending the lives of millions of people. Europeans instigated the conquest after learning of the Americas from Christopher Columbus following his first voyage in 1492. Most early colonizers came from Spain and Portugal on Europe's Iberian Peninsula. By the 1530s, a mere 40 years after Columbus's arrival, all major population centers in the Americas had been conquered and were rapidly being transformed by Iberian colonial policies (Figure 3.4). The superior military technology of the Iberians speeded the process considerably, but the major factor that explains the speed of the conquest was the vulnerability of Native Americans to diseases brought by the Europeans. In about 150 years, a total New World population estimated at 70 million to 100 million was reduced by more than 90 percent to just 5.6 million. Epidemics of diseases like smallpox and measles killed nine out of ten people in one of the most massive annihilations in human history. These were nonfatal childhood illnesses for most Europeans but deadly plagues to the more biologically isolated and therefore less immune Native American populations. The only documented Native American disease that afflicted Europeans was syphilis, but strains of similar diseases already existed in the Old World.

The Caribbean was the region first contacted by Europeans. Columbus established the first Spanish colony in 1492 on the island of Hispaniola, now occupied by Haiti and the Dominican Republic. This initial seat of empire expanded to include the rest of the Greater Antilles—Cuba, Puerto Rico, and Jamaica. It later served as the staging ground for the conquest of the mainland and remained important as guardian of the Caribbean trade routes back to Europe. At first, Native Americans were enslaved to work on plantations and in mines. However, their populations soon plummeted in response to disease, malnutrition, and brutality. This prompted the Spanish in the early 1500s to initiate the first shipments to the Americas of enslaved Africans.

The first part of the mainland to be conquered was Mexico, home to several advanced Native American civilizations, most notably the Aztecs in the central valley of Mexico. Although they lacked the wheel and gunpowder, the Aztecs had some technologies (like urban water and sewage systems) and levels of social organization (like highly organized marketing systems) that rivaled or surpassed civilizations of the time in Asia or Europe. Recent historians have concluded that, on the whole, all social classes of Aztecs lived better and more comfortably than did their contemporaries in Europe. On the eve of conquest, central Mexico was divided into many small states, and most of them had recently suffered military defeats at the hands of the Aztecs. Thus, when the Spanish conquistador Hernando Cortez landed on the coast in 1519 near present-day Veracruz, Mexico, with several hundred armored soldiers, 16 horses, and a large herd of pigs, many native peoples allied with him against the Aztecs. Cortez was also

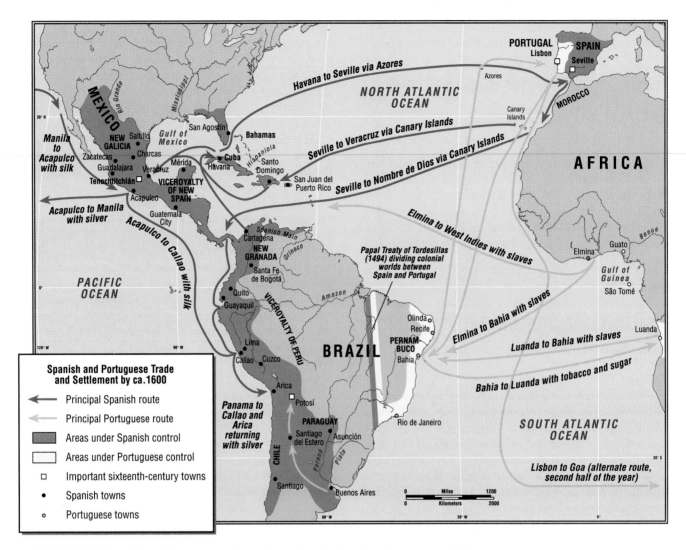

FIGURE 3.4 Spanish and Portuguese trade routes and territories in the Americas ca. 1600. The two major trade routes from Spain to its colonies led to the two major centers of its empire, Mexico and Peru. Whereas the Spanish colonies could trade only with Spain, there were direct trade routes from Portuguese colonies in Brazil to Portuguese outposts in Africa. Many millions of Africans were enslaved and traded to Brazilian plantations and mines. [*Adapted from Hammond Times Concise Atlas of World History*, 1994, pp. 66–67.]

aided in his conquest by the legend of the god Quetzalcoatl, who was said to have had fair skin and a beard and to have arrived from the east. Many Native Americans believed that Cortez was Quetzalcoatl fulfilling his promise to return one day.

Unsuccessful in their first attempt to capture the Aztec capital of Tenochtitlán, the Spanish succeeded a few months later when a smallpox epidemic, inadvertently brought in by them, was in full sway. They demolished the capital in 1521, including its grand temples, public spaces, causeways, residences, and aqueducts. Mexico City was built on its ruins, to become the seat of part of the Spanish Empire in the Americas. Called the Viceroyalty of New Spain, this part of the empire ex-

tended from Panama in the south all the way to what is now San Francisco on the northern California coast. Wealth from the gold and silver mines of Mexico flowed through the port of Veracruz on the Caribbean, from where it was taken to Spain.

Around 1500, South America was home to the vast Inca Empire, the largest pre-Columbian state in the Americas, stretching from southern Colombia to northern Chile and Argentina. The main population clusters were in the Andean highlands, where there was sufficient water and where the high altitude made the climate cool enough to eliminate the diseases of the tropical lowlands. Proximity to the equator meant the absence of severe winters, and growing seasons were long. Inca highland agriculture was advanced, particularly in the development of staple crops like the numerous varieties of potatoes that were grown in different upland environments.

The conquest of the Incas bore a remarkable similarity to that of the Aztecs. A tiny band of Spaniards, this time led by Francisco Pizarro, trekked inland from the coast, also aided along the way by legends of a white-skinned, bearded god. Pizarro himself admitted that his campaign received its greatest assistance from a smallpox epidemic (brought by earlier Spanish scouts) that preceded his arrival.

Out of the ruins of the Inca Empire the Spanish created the Viceroyalty of Peru, which originally encompassed all of South America except Portuguese Brazil. The newly constructed capital city of Lima flourished on the trade of the huge silver mines established in the highlands of Bolivia at Potosí.

Spain and Portugal could easily have gone to war over the lands of the Americas. That they did not is largely due to Roman Catholic diplomacy that produced the Treaty of Tordesillas of 1494. This treaty divided the Americas at approximately 46° west longitude. Portugal took all lands to the east, which gave it much of what is today Brazil; Spain took all lands to the west.

The conquest of coastal Brazil by the Portuguese was similar to the Spanish conquest of other areas, in that land was seized and people were killed or enslaved; and yet it differed in some key respects. Brazil was apparently only lightly populated, with people who lived in small villages that were not permanent. There were no highly organized urban cultures as in parts of Middle America or the Andes. Most Atlantic coastal cultures were annihilated early on, and the populations of the huge Amazon Basin declined sharply as contagious diseases spread through trading. However, it proved difficult to extract quick wealth from tropical rain forest environments, so most of the Amazon was left alone for several centuries. Instead, the Portuguese focused on extracting mineral wealth from Minas Gerais in the Brazilian Highlands (see Figure 3.23), especially gold and precious gems, and on establishing plantations along the Atlantic coast. Only in the nineteenth and twentieth centuries did commercial interest in the Amazon increase to the point that serious colonization took place. Today, indigenous Amazonians are some of the last Native Americans still struggling to preserve their own ways of life.

A Global Exchange of Crops and Animals

A number of plants and animals were exchanged among the Americas, Europe, Africa, and Asia. These plants and animals exerted a strong geographic influence wherever they found a new home. Many plants from the Old

The Franciscan priest Bernardino de Sahagún interviewed Aztecs who had survived the conquest of 1519–1521. They reported thinking at the time that the armored Spanish soldiers on horseback were actually single, huge, otherworldly creatures. This is one of the pictures they drew for Sahagún to illustrate their recollections. [Arthur J. O. Anderson and Charles E. Dibble, *The War of the Conquest* (Salt Lake City: University of Utah Press, 1978), p. 31.]

World are today essential to agriculture in Middle and South America: rice, sugarcane, bananas, citrus, melons, onions, apples, wheat, barley, and oats—to name just a few. When disease decimated the native population of the New World, the colonists turned the abandoned land into pasture for herd animals imported from Europe, including sheep, oxen, cattle, donkeys, horses, and mules. European draft animals helped fill in Native American irrigation canals, drain lakes, and plow the relics of complex Indian gardens into huge one-crop fields of sugarcane or wheat. Surviving Native Americans living on the plains of Mexico and Argentina adopted horses, using them to hunt large game. Others learned to herd sheep, and used the fleece in ancient spinning and weaving technology.

Plants first domesticated by Native Americans have not only changed diets globally, they have become essential components of agricultural economies across the globe. In Africa, for example, corn is a widely grown garden crop, and peanuts and cacao (chocolate) are essential cash crops. Peppers are a cash crop in China, and pineapples in the Pacific. Table 3.1 lists some of the more common globally used plants from Middle and South America and their sites of probable domestication in the Americas.

TABLE 3.1

Major domesticated plants originating in the Americas and now used commercially around the world

Type	Common name	Scientific name	Place of origin
Seeds	Amaranth	*Amarantus cruentus*	Southern Mexico, Guatemala
	Beans	*Phaeseolus* (4 species)	Southern Mexico, Guatemala
	Maize (corn)	*Zea mays*	Valley of Mexico
	Peanut	*Arachis hypogeae*	Central lowlands of South America
	Quinoa	*Chenopodium quinoa*	Andes of Chile and Peru
	Sunflower	*Helianthus annuus*	Southwestern and southeastern North America
Tubers	Manioc (cassava)	*Manihot exculenta*	Lowlands of Middle and South America
	Potato (numerous varieties)	*Solanum tuberosum*	Lake Titicaca region of Andes
	Sweet potato	*Ipomoea batatas*	South America
	Tannia	*Xanthosoma sagittifolium*	Lowland tropical America
Vegetables	Chayote (christophene)	*Sechium edule*	Southern Mexico, Guatemala
	Peppers (sweet and hot)	*Capsicum* (various species)	Many parts of Middle and South America
	Squash (includes pumpkin)	*Cucurbita* (4 species)	Tropical and subtropical America
	Tomatillo (husk tomato)	*Physalis ixocarpa*	Southern Mexico, Guatemala
	Tomato (numerous varieties)	*Lycopersicon esculentum*	Highland South America and Mexico
Fruits	Avocado	*Persia americana*	Southern Mexico, Guatemala
	Cacao (chocolate)	*Theobroma cacao*	Southern Mexico, Guatemala
	Papaya	*Carica papaya*	Southern Mexico, Guatemala
	Passion fruit	*Passiflora edulis*	Central South America
	Pineapple	*Ananas comosus*	Central South America
	Prickly pear cactus (tuna)	*Opuntia* (several species)	Tropical and subtropical America
	Strawberry (commercial berry)	*Fragaria* (various species)	Genetic cross of Chile berry + wild berry from North America
	Vanilla	*Vanilla planifolia*	Southern Mexico, Guatemala, perhaps Caribbean
Ceremonial and drug plants	Coca (cocaine)	*Erythroxylon coca*	Eastern Andes of Ecuador, Peru Bolivia
	Tobacco	*Nicotiana tabacum*	Tropical America

Source: B. Kermath and L. Pulsipher, *Guide to Food Plants Now Used in the Americas* (Washington, DC: Smithsonian Press, forthcoming).

The Legacy of Underdevelopment

Today, despite Middle and South America's fairly rich resources, most of the people are poor and the region as a whole operates at a disadvantage in the global economy. The business environment is often unstable. Many countries depend on the export of raw materials, and the prices of these materials can rise and fall dramatically in response to varying supply and demand. Furthermore, most of the profits from the region's industries do not stay in the region. Most industries are owned by foreigners or a few politically powerful elites who tend to invest or spend their profits abroad. Both characteristics are legacies of the postconquest era, when the colonizers established an economic system that mainly benefited the mother country and a small population of on-site colonial officials. Local economic development was stifled as a result.

The first colonial enterprises to be established were based on the extraction of raw materials, such as gold, silver, and other minerals; timber; and various agricultural products. What potential these industries may have had for generating other kinds of local development was inhibited by Spanish and Portuguese attempts to maintain tight control over trade. Trade with countries other than Spain was forbidden, and even trade between the Spanish colonies had to pass through a Spanish port. If a port in Peru wanted to trade legally with a port in Mexico, the goods first had to cross the Atlantic to be taxed in Spain and then be reshipped back to Mexico. These restrictions were so cumbersome that they nurtured a huge underground economy and institutionalized dishonesty. They also led to considerable resentment toward the Spanish authorities.

In the early nineteenth century, wars of independence transformed the region. The leaders of these revolutions were primarily discontented people of mixed European and Native American descent (mestizos) who had been shut out of the colonial system by elites. Soon the modern countries of Middle and South America emerged, and Spain was left with only a few colonies in the Caribbean (Figure 3.5). For the most part, the revolutionaries simply took over from their colonial predecessors: they became a new elite that controlled

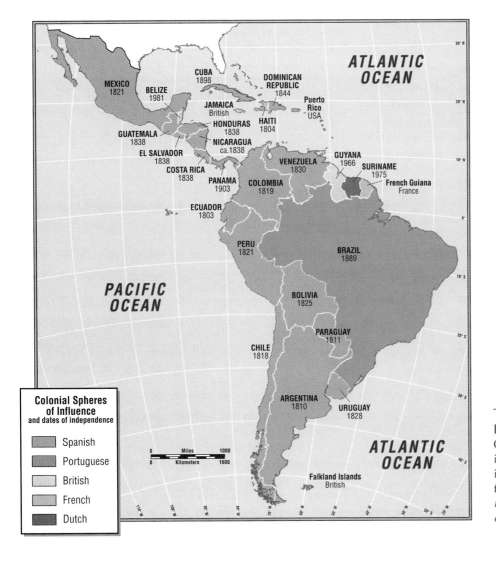

FIGURE 3.5 Except in the Caribbean, all of Spain's colonies in the New World achieved independence in the 30-year span from 1810 to 1840. [Adapted from *Hammond Times Concise Atlas of World History*, 1994, p. 69.]

the state and monopolized economic opportunity. They did little to expand economic development or the public's access to political power. Existing extractive, export-based industries were maintained, while the technologically advanced manufacturing industries that were transforming Europe and North America were neglected. By the late nineteenth and early twentieth centuries, wealthy European and North American investors were able to buy up many extractive industries in Middle and South America; profits continued to be invested or spent in Europe or North America, not in the region. Hence there was little investment capital for local development, and a larger and larger percentage of the population became impoverished.

During the twentieth century, some countries in the region have experimented with radical ways of fostering development, as we shall see in the section on economics and politics. Today, the economies of Middle and South America are much more complex and technologically sophisticated than they once were. Nevertheless, the colonial pattern of elite dominance and dependence on extractive industries remains, contributing to a persistent pattern of underdevelopment and unequal distribution of wealth.

Population Patterns

The events of the last 500 years have much affected the present distribution and character of human settlement in Middle and South America. Conquest and colonization brought the swift demise of Native Americans; but soon they were more than replaced by millions of people from Europe, Africa, and Asia. It would be hard to find a situation elsewhere in human history that rivaled this massive shift in human population. Today, the patterns of human settlement continue to change, but these changes are being generated from within the region rather than coming from without. Population continues to climb, but now more because of high birth rates than migration. At present, the major migration trend is internal: rural-to-urban migration is taking place everywhere in the region and transforming traditional ways of life.

Population Numbers and Distributions

As of 1996, 486,000,000 people were living in Middle and South America, close to 10 times the population of the region in 1492. And this is about 90 million more than presently live in North America.

The population density map (Figure 3.6) reveals a very unequal distribution of people in Middle and South America, just as in most places on earth. It is often thought that people concentrate where the physical environment is favorable, but that is only partly the case. If you compare the population density map with the map at the beginning of this chapter, you will see that there is no obvious consistency to how the density patterns relate to general landforms and environments. Some of the highest densities, like those around Mexico City and in Colombia and Ecuador, are in highland areas. But elsewhere, high concentrations are found in lowland zones along the Pacific coast of Central America and especially along the Atlantic coast of South America. In tropical and subtropical zones, the uplands, known as *tierra templada*, are particularly pleasant and healthful and were comparatively densely occupied even before the conquest began 500 years ago. Most of the coastal lowland concentrations, in what is known as *tierra caliente*, are near important seaports. People are attracted to port cities by the possibility of jobs in the vibrant and varied economy and by the interesting social life. Living near the sea is also attractive because the water modifies the hot, humid climate, making it relatively cooler and breezier compared to lowlands in the interior.

The map also reveals the relatively empty lands in the region, especially in South America. Cold and windy Patagonia is nearly unoccupied, and so are the desert regions of Chile and Peru along the Pacific coast. The vast Amazon River basin is also only lightly settled. Despite recent efforts to develop and populate this wet tropical zone, it seems able to sustain only hunting and gathering, dispersed, shifting agriculture, and light forestry. Some, though, think that advancing technology will make it possible to use and settle the Amazon environments more intensively in the future.

Twentieth-century rates of natural population increase have been high in Middle and South America. Recall from Chapter 1 that the rate of natural increase is population growth from births alone, not counting growth from immigration. Although these rates are now declining, the time needed for the region's population to double is still just 38 years (in North America it is 117 years). Such quick population doubling is a disturbing prospect for a region in which the majority of people already suffer from a low standard of living. Any gains that might have gone toward improving life for them will be checked by the costs of supporting more and more new people. In just 38 years twice as many schools will be needed, twice as many hospitals, and so forth, merely to maintain the present level of inadequate service.

There are a number of reasons why rates of natural increase remain high when compared with those of North America, Europe, and East Asia, or even with world averages. One reason is that until recently, most Latin Americans lived in agricultural areas. Children

FIGURE 3.6 Population density. [Adapted from *Hammond Citation World Atlas, 1996.*]

were seen as sources of wealth because they could do useful work at a young age and eventually would care for their aging elders. Also, high infant death rates encouraged parents to have many children to be sure of raising at least a few to adulthood. The Catholic Church has discouraged systematic family planning. Further, as will be discussed later, the cultural mores of *machismo* and *marianismo* have reinforced the idea that both men and women ought to validate themselves as adults by reproducing prolifically. Finally, when medical care improved modestly beginning in the 1930s, death rates began to decline rapidly. By 1975, death rates were

119

about one-third of what they had been in 1900. Because birth rates did not decrease as quickly as death rates, population growth was especially rapid between 1940 and 1975.

By the 1980s, Latin Americans were beginning to use contraception and population growth rates started to fall. Now the region is beginning to go through the demographic transition. Between 1963 and 1997, the rate of natural increase for the entire region fell from about 2.5 to 1.8 percent, still a high rate of growth compared with North America, Europe, and East Asia (all at 1.0 or less in 1997). The bar graph in Figure 3.7 compares the record of selected countries during the same period.

A population with a 1 percent growth rate will double every 70 years. A population with a 2 percent growth rate will double every 35 years. The Caribbean as a whole has the lowest growth rate (1.4 percent), with Cuba (0.6 percent) and Barbados (0.5) having the very lowest rates in this region, about the same as North America (0.6 percent). Some factors explaining these low rates are that both Cuba and Barbados do well at providing women with education and meaningful work, and both provide good health care. Infant mortality rates are exceedingly low, so people can expect to see their one or two children grow to adulthood. Barbados prospers from manufacturing, tourism, and agriculture; and Cuba has made a strong effort to improve social welfare over the last 35 years. Meanwhile, in Middle America, people are poor and women have little access to education and employment, so that area has the highest rate of natural increase (2.3 percent). South America, also afflicted with high rates of poverty, has an overall rate of 1.7 percent. Within South America, however, there is considerable variation: Bolivia 2.4, Brazil 1.6, and Uruguay 0.6 percent in the period from 1993 to 2000. Again, this variability can be explained by considering the differing standards of living and access to education and jobs, especially for women.

Migration and Urbanization

Perhaps the most important social force at work in the world today is **migration.** Why? Because it is happening at unprecedented rates and because the phenomenon abruptly introduces large numbers of people from rural areas into new, often crowded urban situations. This new place of residence may or may not provide more opportunity, but it will surely expose the immigrants to values and ways of life that contrast sharply with those they have known. Since the early 1970s, the region of Middle and South America has been a leader in migration rates.

Geographers recognize that there are both "push" and "pull" reasons for migration. **Push** factors are those that convince someone to leave a place because what the person wants in life—a job, education, or a suitable mate—is not available. **Pull** factors draw a person to new areas that offer attractive opportunities, like a higher paying job, adventure, a chance to go to school. These two types of factors induce many people in Middle and South America to leave rural villages for towns and cities. As a result of this rural-to-urban migration, cities throughout the region have grown remarkably quickly. More than 70 percent of the people in the region now live in towns of at least 2000; but increasingly,

FIGURE 3.7 Rates of natural increase have declined in a number of Middle and South American countries. [Adapted from *Human Development Report 1998,* United Nations Development Programme.}

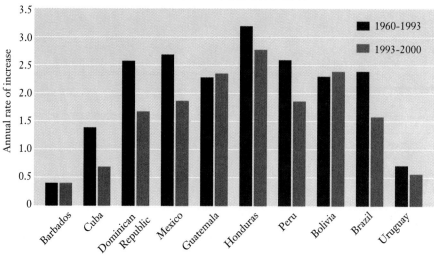

Trends in Average Natural Population Increase, 1960–1993 and 1993–2000

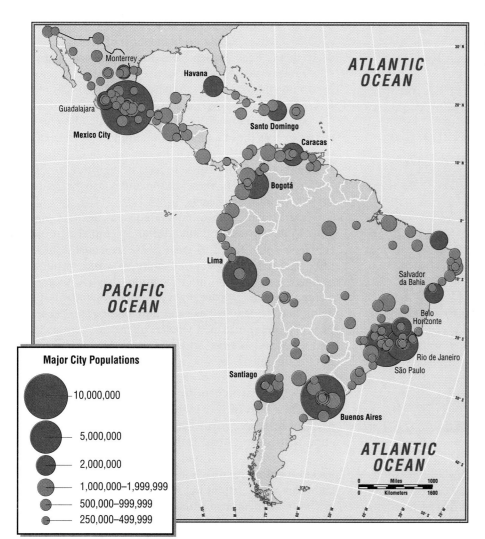

FIGURE 3.8 Urban concentrations in the region.

Major City Populations
- 10,000,000
- 5,000,000
- 2,000,000
- 1,000,000–1,999,999
- 500,000–999,999
- 250,000–499,999

one city in a given country, often the capital, draws most of the migrants. It is now common in developing countries in Middle and South America and elsewhere for one city to be vastly larger than all others, sometimes accounting for one-quarter or more of the country's total population. Such cities are called **primate cities.** Figure 3.8 shows the pattern of urban development, and Table 3.2 shows that four of the world's ten largest cities are now in Middle and South America.

This converging of people into just one or two cities in a country leads to lopsided **spatial development.** Wealth and power are concentrated in one place. Other towns and cities have a hard time competing for talent and investment funds and government services; many provincial cities languish, also losing people to migration. Investors and government services tend to ignore distant rural areas, while rural areas surrounding the primate city are too heavily impacted. The new migrants are usually poor and unskilled; searching for cheap places to live, they often squat on nearby rural land that is not

theirs. Primate cities are usually in underindustrialized countries. They attract people even though they do not provide enough jobs, housing, or services for the flood of hopeful migrants.

Because this rush to the cities has not been accompanied by a rise in general prosperity, no city in the region is prepared. Spending on urban infrastructure, such as roads and sanitation, and on social services has failed to keep pace with the inflow of people, and the signs of urban decay are everywhere. While there are pockets of wealth in the cities where the powerful live and work, these spaces are often heavily guarded against the slums that ring the edges and are sprinkled through the interior of almost every city. The most recent urban migrants can't afford to buy or lease land, so they organize themselves into swarms of "squatters" who invade a piece of property after dark and set up simple dwellings by morning. Once established, these communities are extremely hard to dislodge: the impoverished are such a huge portion of the urban population that most

TABLE 3.2

Estimated population of world's 10 largest cities (including adjacent suburbs) in the year 2000

City	Population (in millions)
Tokyo	30.0
Mexico City	27.9
São Paulo	25.4
Seoul	22.0
Bombay	15.4
New York City	14.6
Osaka	14.3
Rio de Janeiro	14.2
Calcutta	14.1
Buenos Aires	12.9

Source: Randall Hansis, *The Latin Americans* (New York: McGraw-Hill, 1997), p. 24.

The squatters can be enterprising and admirable people who have simply made the most of the bad hand dealt them. Such settlers sometimes organize themselves to pressure for social services: schools, day care, part-time jobs for young mothers, sewer systems. Some foresighted urban governments, like that in Fortaleza (Ceará), in northeastern Brazil, contribute building materials so that the squatters can build more permanent structures with at least crude indoor plumbing. Moreover, although crime rates are usually high due to the level of desperation, these communities can be quite supportive for the residents.

Interestingly, rural women are just as likely to migrate to the city as rural men. Rural development projects have often failed to treat the sexes equally: they offer men training in new technologies while, through oversight or conscious discrimination, they fail to give women chances to participate. Women's standards of living may actually fall as rural development proceeds. In urban areas, unskilled women migrants can usually find work as domestic servants; nonetheless, they have a difficult time. Low wages force them to live in the household where they work. There they are often subject to sexual harassment by men in the family, yet are themselves blamed if they fail to adhere to rigid standards of behavior. Furthermore, their chances for creating their own normal family life are extremely low. Opportunities to meet and marry men of their own background are limited, while the chances of having a child as a single parent are very high. Male urban migrants tend to depend on short-term day work, most often in low-skill jobs in construction, maintenance, small-scale manufacturing, and petty commerce. They must compete with a large throng of eager workers, and most often therefore are underemployed. Many make

other people, even those in positions of power, will not directly challenge them. The result is that many of the once grand parks and thoroughfares of Middle and South American cities, as well as beaches and any accessible privately held open urban land, are now strewn with thousands of shanty communities.

Squatter communities, like this one in Fortaleza, Brazil, sometimes become permanently established with the help of government funding for cinder blocks, roofing tiles, and plumbing. [Lydia Pulsipher.]

some cash in the informal economy (that which is not officially recognized and not taxed), doing work like street vending, running errands, cleaning, washing cars, recycling trash, or engaging in crime.

It is important to recognize that migration represents the flight of human talent from one place to another and that it always takes some resources to move. Hence, it is usually those who already have some advantages of education and unusual ambition who migrate to cities (where their talents may, however, go to waste). Thus, the sending communities are deprived of young adults in whom they have invested years of nurturing and educating. This loss, often referred to as "brain drain," happens at several levels or scales in Middle and South America. There is migration from villages to regional towns, from towns to the main cities, and from the entire region to North America and Europe. The benefit of immigration to the receiving societies, whether cities like Rio de Janeiro or Mexico City, or countries like the United States, is too little recognized. For example, in 1950, one-fifth of medical doctors in the United States were immigrants; by 1970, one-half were. The United States saves money when other nations supply the early education for these physicians, sometimes even providing government scholarships for higher education. Then these physicians spend their most productive years practicing in the United States. And so it is with immigrants generally: most who migrate are people with some education above the average and with the initiative and creativity to take a long journey into unfamiliar territory.

CURRENT GEOGRAPHIC ISSUES

Historically, power and wealth in Middle and South America have been concentrated in the hands of a few, and the last century of economic reform hasn't changed that reality. In fact, disparities are increasing under the latest phase of reform that calls for cutbacks in social programs for the poor. On the other hand, there are signs that democracy is growing in everyday life and in the form of free elections. Most governments are now popularly elected, and grassroots movements are developing in squatter settlements and in communities facing environmental threats. Even forms of religious practice are changing to encourage community and individual action. The discussion of these contemporary trends in Middle and South America should help readers compare and contrast this region with other world regions.

Sociocultural Issues

Under colonialism there evolved a series of **social structures** that guided daily life—standard ways of organizing the family, rules for gender roles, rules for race relations, and ways of religious observance. These social structures are still widely in place, but they are changing in response to urbanization, economic development, and the diffusion of ideas from outside the region. The results are varied. In the worst case, change is leading to the breakdown of family life and the abandonment of children; in the best case, to a new sense of initiative on the part of women and the poor.

Cultural Diversity

The region of Middle and South America is one of the most culturally complex on earth. This diversity springs from the different indigenous groups present when the Europeans came and from the many different cultures that were introduced during the colonial period. In the Caribbean, the Guianas, and Brazil, the European newcomers annihilated indigenous cultures, and these regions became populated almost entirely by people from the Old World. From 1500 to the early 1800s, some 10 million Africans were brought to plantations on the islands and coastal zones of Middle and South America. Far fewer settlers came from England, Ireland, France, Spain, and Portugal. After abolition freed African slaves in the Caribbean in the 1830s, more than half a million Asian indentured servants were brought from India, Pakistan, and China as agricultural workers. Their cultural impact remains most visible in Trinidad, Jamaica, and the Guianas. In some parts of Mexico, and in Guatemala, Ecuador, and other Andean zones, indigenous people have remained dominant, and to the unpracticed eye they may appear somewhat unaffected by colonization.

Mestizos are those who are racially and culturally a blend of Native American and European roots. They are now the majority in Mexico, Central America, and much of South America. In some places, such as Argentina, Chile, and southern Brazil, Euro-Americans are now so numerous that they dominate the landscapes and ways of life. The Japanese, though a tiny minority everywhere in the region, are increasingly influential in innovative agriculture and industry in Brazil, the Caribbean, and Peru. In some ways, diversity is increasing as the media and trade introduce new influences into the region. On the other hand, in urban areas, where different groups of people live in close proximity, increasing contact between people of widely different backgrounds is accelerating the rate of **acculturation** (cultural borrowing) and **assimilation** (loss of old ways and adoption of new ones). In the big cities, like

Mexico City, Lima, and Rio de Janeiro, there is a blend of many different strains, so that no one cultural component remains unaffected by the others.

Race and the Social Significance of Skin Color

People from Latin America, and especially those from Brazil, often proudly make the public claim that race and color are of less consequence than in North America; and they are right in certain ways. It is possible to, in effect, "erase" the color of one's skin through acculturation. For example, a Native American or a dark-skinned person of any background may, by acquiring an education, a good job, a substantial income, the right accent, and the right mate, become recognized as not being any particular color at all. This feature of Middle and South American society may seem surprising to readers from North America, who will recognize that rarely in their experience is skin color totally disregarded.

In North America, the offspring of a white father and a dark-skinned mother received the racial designation of the mother, but in Middle and South America they acquired their social status depending on how much European, Native American, or African blood they were thought to have and who, precisely, the father was. The social ranking of mixed-race females, in particular, was negotiable. If born into an elite family and recognized as the offspring of a high-status male, such mixed-race females might be groomed for a proper marriage to another high-status male and hence would produce high-status, but nonwhite, children. In this way it was possible for part–Native American or part-African people to be of the elite class. If not recognized by a high-status father, a mixed-race female child would probably not be educated or protected like an upper-class child. She would not be a candidate for a high-status marriage and might have to resort to a street occupation to make a living for herself and any offspring. Hence, over the generations racial designations became more and more complex, and social class was not assigned on the basis of race alone. By the nineteenth century, the fine distinctions of race according to precise skin color were less important. Today, the terms *clear-skinned* for "light" and *black*, *mulatto*, or *pardo* for "brown" tend to have descriptive rather than racial meaning. The dark skin of an upper-class person would not be thought of as racially significant; but family, wealth, education, and occupation would be very significant.

Nevertheless, being able to erase the significance of skin color through accomplishments is not quite the same as color having no significance at all. Although there are poor light-skinned people throughout the region (often the descendants of relatively recent migrants from central Europe), overall, those who are poor, less well educated, and of lower social standing tend to have darker skins than those who are educated and well-off. This fact seems to indicate that race and color have not yet disappeared as social factors in Middle and South America.

The Family and Gender Roles

The **extended family** is the basic social institution in all the societies of Middle and South America. Throughout this region, it is generally accepted that the individual should subvert his or her interests to those of the family and local community and that, in so doing, individual well-being is best secured.

Today, the spatial arrangement of domestic life illustrates the strong family ties. Families of adult siblings, their mates and children, and elderly grandparents frequently live together in domestic compounds of several houses surrounded by walls. Such compounds are rare in North America, where the single-family home is the norm. In Middle and South America, social groups out together in public are most likely to be family members of several generations rather than unrelated groups of single young adults or of married couples, as would be the case in Europe or North America. A woman's best friends are likely to be her female relatives. A man's busi-

The Paco Burgos family in the Peten work together on their milpa, a cleared cultivation plot in the forest that serves as the main source of food. Corn, beans, and squash are the primary crops. [Miguel Luis Fairbanks/National Geographic.]

ness or social circle will almost certainly include male family members or long-standing family friends.

Gender roles have their roots in the extended family, as well. During the early colonial period, a model of womanhood based on Spanish and Portuguese moral attitudes became entrenched. Women, it was taught, were the vehicle whereby the family was perpetuated and kept pure; hence the spatial freedom of women was limited. They were to be secluded within the home and protected from harm (especially from impregnation by a man unacceptable to the family). When in public, decent women were to be well covered with protective layers of skirts, mantillas, and capes, and they were to be well chaperoned, too, not only to shield them from the eyes of lecherous males but also to ensure that the women would withstand temptation, should it arise. It was assumed that women would become sexually promiscuous given the least chance, because they lacked willpower and moral fortitude. Some of these traditions derived from the long influence of Islam on Spain and Portugal. But the influence of the medieval Catholic Church is also very apparent.

Throughout Middle and South America, the Virgin Mary is held up as the model for women to follow. Through their adoration of the Virgin, they absorb a set of values, known as *marianismo,* that also seek to control their activities and movements through space. The ideal young woman, a strictly protected virgin, is submissive and long-suffering. She is delivered to her husband chaste and prepared to serve his needs and those of their future children. She is the day-to-day manager of the house and of the family's well-being, training her sons to enter the wider world and her daughters to serve within the home. Her husband, the titular head, is expected to provide some of his income to his family; but he is normally absent, braving the outside world to work and/or tend to his social network, which is deemed just as essential to the family's prosperity and status in the community as his work. Over the course of her life, a woman's power increases as her skills and sacrifices for the good of all are recognized and enshrined in family lore.

The rules for how men are to contribute to family stability and well-being are less clearly spelled out than are the rules for women. In fact, men have a good bit more spatial autonomy and freedom to shape their lives than do women, simply because they have the right to move about the community and establish relationships, both economic and personal. In addition, there is an overt double sexual standard for males and females. While demanding from his wife strict faithfulness in mind and body, a man is free to associate with the opposite sex. Males measure themselves by the model of *machismo,* which recognizes manliness as consisting of the ability to father children, seduce pretty women, be an engaging raconteur in social situations, and also be ap-

parent master of one's own household. Under the old rules of *machismo,* the ability to acquire money was secondary to more obvious proofs of "maleness." Now a new market-oriented culture prizes visible affluence as a desirable male attribute.

Many factors are transforming the family and gender roles. For one thing, couples are now having two or three children, instead of five or more. As discussed earlier, with infant mortality declining steeply, it is no longer necessary to have many children simply to see a few survive to adulthood. Because people still marry early, most parents are free of child-raising responsibilities by the time they are 40. For men, the change may require simply an adjustment of the *machismo* idea that manliness is defined by high fertility. But for women, there is the empty nest syndrome: 30 or more years of active life loom, to be filled in some way. As it happens, economic change throughout the region has provided a solution. Increasingly, women, despite little formal education, have been able to find factory jobs or other employment that puts to use the skills they perfected while supervising a family: time and people management, maintenance of equipment, organizational skills, the ability to anticipate problems, and long-range planning. Increasingly, for middle-aged and even for young women, employment outside the home (often in a distant city) is a way to gain a measure of independence and also contribute to the family's needs. Many families simply bend to accommodate these new situations, others lose whole segments to migration, and some disintegrate.

Children in Poverty

In societies that traditionally place such high value on the family and children, it is difficult to understand recent news stories about homeless children in such countries as Mexico, Guatemala, Colombia, and Brazil. Many of these children have been pushed out of the home space by overburdened parents. Now they must not only fend for themselves on the street but endure official abuse at the hands of police. Travelers to the region may experience the extreme distress of eating in an outdoor restaurant ringed with sturdy iron fences through which stretch the skinny arms of children begging for food. Unfortunately, abandoned children are to be found in all parts of the world, and the explanations are numerous. But it is no coincidence that many of these stories emanate from urban locations in Middle and South America.

In recent years, with little work available in rural areas, young people, and especially young women, have left their protective families and villages to migrate to cities, where they usually end up in crowded shantytowns. Often overly naïve, these women are equipped for only the most menial jobs and rarely earn a living

A Nicaraguan boy sniffs glue from a baby-food jar in the Oriental Market in Managua while his friend pulls his own jar out of his shirt. [Richard Sennott/*Minneapolis/St. Paul Star Tribune.*]

wage. They soon see that they must ally themselves with a man to gain some measure of security or even just a place to live. Soon, children result. The man may already have several informal mating relationships, so his resources are stretched too thin to adequately support more. Their extended families are not around to aid the young mothers, who must keep working. There are no older, solid role models to help with child care and enforce traditional values like chastity, sobriety, and good parenting. Children grow up neglected, malnourished, and unruly, with lonely, dysfunctional mothers who may turn to drugs or alcohol for solace. Recent reports tell of children who turn to brain-damaging glue sniffing as a way to ease their despair.

In these stories of abandoned and abused children, we are seeing social alienation that results not only from severe economic inequity but also from gender inequity and the spatial dislocation of migration. Although *marianismo* idealizes women and their roles, it does not equip women to take control of their own lives and bodies. Essentially a medieval institution, *marianismo* encourages passivity and subservience to men. But in the anonymity of the modern urban environment, away from family disapproval, often men no longer feel responsible for their actions or a need to protect the mothers of their children. Despite these very real problems, however, it is important to remember that the vast majority of parents in Middle and South America, even those in the worst of urban slums, heap loving care on their children, providing all that they possibly can and sacrificing so that their children might have a better life.

Religion in Contemporary Life

From the outset, the Roman Catholic Church was the major partner of the Spanish and Portuguese colonial governments. It received extensive lands and resources, and sent many missionary priests to convert Native Americans. For many centuries, the Catholic Church encouraged working people to accept their low status, obedience to authority, and postponement of rewards until heaven. Thus, while serving to unify the region and spread European culture, the church also reinforced class differences. For example, until recently the church did not ordain non-European clergy, thus missing a chance to connect deeply with the masses of Native American, African, and mixed-race poor. Furthermore, the church ignored those teachings of Christ that admonish the privileged elite to share their wealth and attend to the needs of the poor. Nevertheless, poor people throughout Spanish and Portuguese America embraced the faith and still make up the majority of church members. They have, however, put their own ethnic spin on Catholicism, creating multiple folk versions of the religion, with music, liturgy, and interpretations of Scripture that vary greatly from the European.

The Catholic Church began to see its power erode in the nineteenth century in places like Mexico. Populist movements seeking relief for the poor seized and redistributed church lands and canceled the high fees that the clergy had been charging for simple rites of passage like baptisms, weddings, and funerals. Over the years, the church became less obviously connected to the elite and more attentive to the needs of the poor. Common people gained the right to read the Bible in their own languages and to replace Gregorian chants with ethnic music. After Vatican II in the 1960s, women were allowed to perform certain rites during Mass.

Just as the Catholic Church began to change its stance vis-à-vis the common people, a more radical movement known as **liberation theology,** which promised to reform the church from the ground up, emerged in the 1970s. A small group of priests and activists mixed teachings of Christ about social responsibility with Marxist social theory advocating the more equitable distribution of wealth. The movement portrays Jesus Christ as a revolutionary who symbolically spoke out for redistribution of wealth when he divided the loaves and fishes among the multitude. Poverty is viewed as a problem of an entire society rather than as personal failing. The priests teach literacy and self-help community organization skills in order to empower the poor to change their own situation. In the 1980s, when repressive authoritarian regimes were prominent in places like Brazil, Chile, Guatemala, and El Salvador, liberation theology clergy endorsed the idea that perpetuating gross inequality and political repression was sinful. Social and economic reform was promoted as liberation from evil.

At its height, the liberation theology movement had more than 3 million adherents in Brazil alone and was the most articulate movement yet for region-wide social change. Today, the movement is somewhat reduced in strength. On the one hand, some of its positions have been adopted by the Vatican, and on the other, in places like Guatemala and El Salvador it has become the target of state-sponsored terrorism that vilifies participants as communist conspirators. Also, this movement has had to compete with newly emerging evangelical Protestant movements that have many attractions for the poor.

Evangelical Protestantism has diffused into Middle and South America from North America. It is now the fastest-growing religious movement in the region, and already about 10 percent of the population, or more than 40 million people, are adherents. Like liberation theology, it appeals to the rural and urban poor, that segment of society most in need of hope for a better future. However, evangelical Protestants do not tempt their converts with the idea of social revolution but with the personal "gospel of success." Their teaching stresses that those who are true believers and give themselves to Christ and to a new life of hard work and clean living will experience prosperity of the body as well as of the soul. The movement is charismatic, meaning it focuses on personal salvation and empowerment of the individual through miraculous healing and transformation. People are thought to become "reborn." The movement has no central authority but consists rather of a host of small, independent congregations. The leadership is passed around so that both males and females in the congregations develop organizational and public speaking skills. A number of studies have shown a real change in the lives of individuals formerly beset with dejection, lethargy, and vice. After a few years of active church membership, many individuals seize educational and entrepreneurial opportunities and do indeed achieve success through their belief in the gospel of Christ. There is considerable evidence that the gospel of success may be an important impetus to the emergence of a middle class.

The geographer David Clawson has provided a map showing the percentages of people throughout the region who are Protestant (Figure 3.9). The extent to which these geographic patterns reflect the spread of the evangelical version of Protestantism is not yet well understood. Evangelical Protestantism is known to have caught on in formerly Catholic countries like Brazil and Chile. Brazil now has 34 million Protestants (75 percent of the total for the region), and in Chile nearly a third of the more wealthy and literate people are Protestants. The evangelical movement is also strong in the Carib-

bean, Mexico, and Middle America, among both the poor and middle classes. The revival tents of North American evangelical pastors are a common site in the urban fringe of cities throughout the region.

Economic and Political Issues

The greatest challenge facing leaders throughout the region is a widening gap between those who have money and power and those who don't. Although this region is not as poor on average as sub-Saharan Africa, South Asia, or Southeast Asia, it does have the widest spread between rich and poor. The richest 20 percent of the population is roughly 80 times richer than the poorest 20 percent, and region-wide roughly 40 percent of the population is living in severe poverty.

High levels of income disparity are troubling in many ways. From a moral standpoint, many argue that it is wrong to let a tiny number of people hoard wealth and resources while so many people have so little. From an economic perspective, wherever large numbers of people sink into poverty the potential for a nation's growth diminishes, as poor people are less able to contribute to economies with their own purchasing power or with their skills, which tend to remain at a low level. The danger of political instability also increases; high levels of income disparity increase the possibility of violent rebellion by the impoverished masses and equally violent repression by wealthy elites. In Bolivia, Peru, Chile, Brazil, Argentina, Colombia, Guatemala, Honduras, El Salvador, Mexico, and Haiti, hundreds of thousands have died in repeated waves of state repression, revolution, counterrevolution, and coups d'état.

Recent years have seen improvements on a range of issues. Some countries are trying to enact economic policies that create greater economic stability and greater opportunity for poor people. Most countries are also recognizing that democratic political institutions offer the best promise to defuse conflicts and social tensions before they turn violent.

Phases of Economic Development

The countries of Middle and South America have gone through three major phases of economic development: an early extractive phase, a socialist reformist phase, and the current free market reformist phase. Though these phases are distinct, patterns set in place during each of them still strongly influence the present.

Early Extractive Phase. Beginning with the conquest and lasting until the early twentieth century, the early extractive phase was based on the extraction of crops,

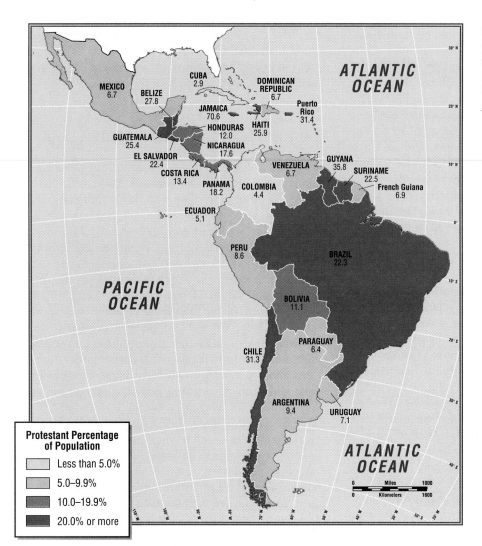

FIGURE 3.9 Protestants in the population by percentage. [Adapted from David Clawson, *Latin America and the Caribbean* (Dubuque, IA: Wm. C. Brown, 1997), p. 210.]

animal products, forest products, and mineral resources. Early agricultural development was centered on the main Iberian agricultural institution, the **hacienda.** This is a large rural estate, of the type granted to conquistadors such as Hernando Cortez as a reward for conquering the indigenous American civilizations. Haciendas were based on similar Roman institutions once used to colonize Iberia itself, and they persisted for centuries in the Americas. Laborers on the haciendas were virtually bound to the land like slaves or feudal serfs, while the owner lived in luxury, often in a distant city, collecting tribute. Haciendas were inefficient, often using only a fraction of their potential agricultural land and utilizing inexpensive but outdated cultivation techniques. Their lack of specialization also made them less able to produce goods at a lower cost.

As transport connections with ports improved, providing greater access to global markets, many ha-

ciendas shifted over to more efficient styles of production. Some became **plantations,** which are like large "factory farms." Owners make huge investments in equipment and labor in order to maximize production of a single crop, such as sugar, coffee, or various tropical fruits. Unlike haciendas, which were often established in the interior in a variety of climates, plantations are for the most part situated in tropical coastal areas with year-round growing seasons (Figure 3.10). Their coastal location also gives easier access to global markets via ocean transport. Another increasingly important institution was the livestock **ranch.** As markets for meat, hides, and wool grew in Europe and North America, many haciendas specialized in raising cattle and sheep. Today ranches are found in the drier grasslands and savannas of South America, Central America, and northern Mexico and even in the wet tropics on formerly forested land. On both plantations and

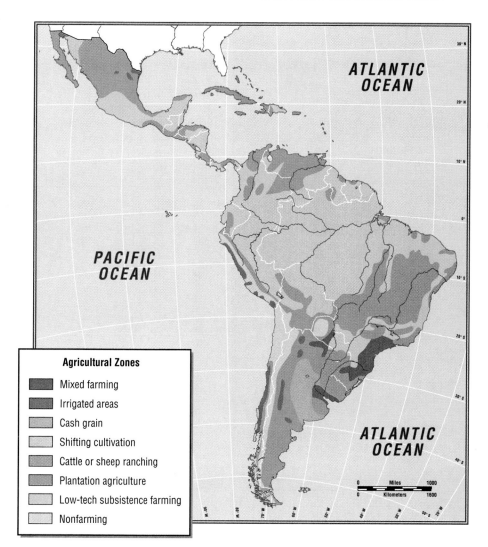

FIGURE 3.10 Agricultural zones. [Adapted from Edward F. Bergman, *Human Geography—Cultures, Connections, and Landscapes* (Englewood Cliffs, NJ: Prentice Hall, 1995), p. 194.]

Agricultural Zones
- Mixed farming
- Irrigated areas
- Cash grain
- Shifting cultivation
- Cattle or sheep ranching
- Plantation agriculture
- Low-tech subsistence farming
- Nonfarming

ranches, as with haciendas, the vast majority of the profits continue to go to the owner, who does not live on the premises.

The other main industry of the early extractive period was mining. Today there remain rich mines throughout the region, producing gold, silver, copper, tin, precious gems, titanium, bauxite, and tungsten (Figure 3.11). Most of these products are exported in a raw, unprocessed state, rather than being made into more valuable materials. Thus there are few linkages with local economies that could provide the basis for industry and broader prosperity.

Socialist Reformist Phase. Major changes occurred during this phase of the early twentieth century. In response to waves of popular political protest against elite dominance of the economy and society, a number of

governments proclaimed themselves socialist democracies. Mexico and Argentina were the most prominent among them. Many countries came under the leadership of charismatic popular leaders—Juan Perón in Argentina is the most famous—who promised to redistribute their nations' wealth to the masses of poor people. A major strategy proposed by the reformers of this era was to do away with the extractive system, whereby raw materials were exported cheaply to Europe and North America in return for expensive manufactured goods. Accordingly, some countries embarked on a course of government-funded **import substitution industrialization.** These countries used public funds to set up factories to manufacture goods that previously had been imported. They then placed high tariffs on competing imported goods to force up their prices and make locally produced goods more attractive. The idea was that import

129

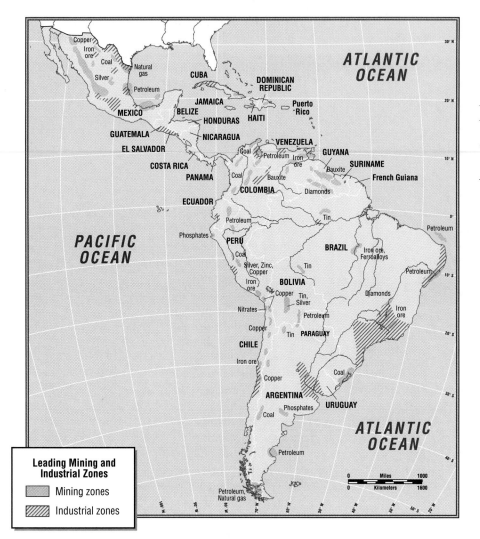

FIGURE 3.11 Mining and industrial zones. [Adapted from David Clawson, *Latin America and the Caribbean* (Dubuque, IA: Wm. C. Brown, 1997), p. 274; and Jerome Fellman, Arthur Getis, and Judith Getis, *Human Geography— Landscapes of Human Activities* (Dubuque, IA: Brown & Benchmark, 1997), p. 312.]

substitution would create jobs, lower the prices of consumer products, and help to keep the consumers' money within the country. Public funds were used because private investors could not be attracted.

This strategy did create jobs in the short run, but many other parts of the system did not work. The quality of goods produced by state-owned factories that faced no local competition fell below that of imported goods. Imported goods remained in demand but were now available only through the black markets. The conditions for corruption had thus been created. Furthermore, the local markets for manufactured goods were too small and the consumers too poor for companies to make a profit. The region as a whole might have sustained manufacturing industries, but at this point the old colonial trade barriers still stood between countries. Moreover, there was no useful international transport system to carry goods between countries. Consider how

trade and prosperity in the United States would be constrained if each state had trade barriers against all others, and interstate transport consisted only of rudimentary dirt roads and a few railroads that did not easily connect at the borders.

The result was that most economies in the region remained highly dependent on the export of raw materials, which were sure to earn at least some money on the global market. For the most part, extractive industries remained in the hands of local elites and foreign investors who continued to take most of the profits abroad rather than reinvest in the country. Thus, by the late 1960s and early 1970s, it had become clear that governments were not going to be able to deliver on their past promises to redistribute wealth. In response, more radical socialist and communist movements began to take shape. Feeling their dominance threatened, military and civilian elites cracked down on the popular movements, often with the encouragement of the United States, which feared the spread of communism and the cold war to Middle and South America. Throughout the region, elite-led governments came to power, many of them military dictatorships.

Current Free Market Reformist Phase. The new leaders sought to legitimize their rule by creating new economic growth. However, there was a lack of investment capital within Middle and South America, so loans had to be obtained from outside the region. During the 1970s and the early 1980s, Latin American countries borrowed billions of dollars from the major international banks for development projects. Only some of these projects resulted in real growth. Many of the projects were ill conceived: there were no markets for the new products, or raw materials were more expensive than anticipated, or labor was insufficiently educated to handle the tasks, or technical faults went uncorrected because expertise was not at hand. In other cases, development money was pocketed by corrupt officials and businesspeople within the region and in Europe and North America. By the early 1980s, it appeared that many countries that had borrowed funds had failed to achieve the planned economic growth and spread of wealth to the poorest. And because of the failure to develop, they were unable to pay back their loans. The damage was made worse by the fact that the biggest borrowers had been the largest economies in the region, such as Mexico, Brazil, and Argentina. Hence, huge debts now burdened the countries that had been the most likely to grow.

The result was the **debt crisis** of the mid-1980s, which ushered in the current free market reformist phase. The banks resolved that they would no longer lend to the debtor nations of Middle and South America and elsewhere unless they first submitted to a series of known as **structural adjustment programs** (**SAPs**). SAPs are belt-tightening measures meant to free up money for loan repayment. They were developed and implemented by the International Monetary Fund (IMF), mainly at the request of the major international banks. The IMF sees SAPs as helping countries by reducing unnecessary state interference in economies and by increasing the level of integration with the global economy. Governments are required to fire many of their own employees, to sell state-owned import substitution industries to private owners, and to remove tariffs, subsidies, or other measures protecting the local economies from foreign competition. SAPs also remove regulations that prevent main industries from being bought up by foreigners; the object is to increase the availability of investment capital. Finally, SAPs cut funds going to social services or programs aimed at redistributing the wealth to the poor. The idea is that such programs in-

hibit entrepreneurialism and ambition. The money is used instead for debt repayment. SAPs, therefore, in one way or another, have affected the daily lives of most people throughout the region.

The record of SAPs is mixed. They have promoted some kinds of economic growth, especially in extractive industries that attract foreign investors. In some countries, such as Chile and Peru, foreign investment has led to higher rates of economic growth. In a few cases, foreign involvement has also led to greater publicity regarding the exploitation of labor; the international media are more attentive to abuses by well-known global companies than by obscure local firms. For example, media attention to Kathie Lee Gifford apparel, which has used sweatshops within the region to produce clothes for the North American market, was enough to prompt the company to improve its treatment of workers. But SAPs have also facilitated the export of profits outside the region. Perhaps most problematic is the fact that SAPs have not reduced the debt burden, which increased from $354 billion to $470 billion between 1982 and 1991.

SAPs have failed to deal with the problem of income disparity. Since SAPs were introduced, the number of people living in poverty has increased from roughly 35 percent in 1980 to 39 percent in 1994 (see the box "Mexican Debt Crisis"). For example, Chile's reforms have produced growth rates as high as 7 percent in recent years, but also some of the highest rates of income disparity in the world. Between 1994 and 1996, the average yearly income for the 40 percent of the Chilean population classified as poor was $1440, while the top 10 percent of the population had incomes of $48,000 a year. In part, the increase in the number of poor is due to the fact that in most countries minimum wages are now half, or less than half, of what they were in 1980. Meanwhile, public funding for education and health care has declined, and many argue that the cuts make the region poorly equipped to move into the technological age. Today, only 45 percent of those eligible for education are enrolled in high school.

Industrialization has always had great potential in Middle and South America; but while some areas developed industries, very few have seen the wider prosperity that industrialization brought to Europe, Japan, or North America. In part this is because many industries have continued the pattern established in the early extractive period of using large amounts of resources and labor while generating few linkages with local economies. Linkages occur, for example, when a factory's need for component parts nurtures a network of other factories that supply its needs. However, in the new manufacturing industries that are coming to the region to take advantage of cheap labor, such as the *maquiladora* industries of Mexico and Central America, there are few local linkages because most materials to be assembled are

131

AT THE COUNTRY SCALE

The Mexican Debt Crisis and the Painful SAP Cure

One vivid example of an SAP-type policy gone awry was the removal of barriers to the flow of investment money between Mexico and the United States and Canada, which resulted in the Mexican economic crisis of 1995–1997. This policy was actually a part of the North American Free Trade Agreement, but similar policies have been promoted as parts of SAP packages throughout the region. Mexico, like the rest of Middle and South America, is a riskier place to invest than the United States or Canada. To compensate, Mexican banks and businesses offer higher rates of return on investments than do their U.S. or Canadian counterparts. In 1994, NAFTA, in the eyes of many U.S. and Canadian investors, seemed to reduce the risk of investment in Mexico, as huge sums rushed into the Mexican economy. However, the investors did not thoroughly look into the quality of the investments made, and money often went into ineffective or corrupt businesses. By 1995, it became clear that banks and businesses would be unable to fully pay back investors. As a result, U.S. and Canadian investors stampeded out of the Mexican economy, which was then crippled by the sudden need to pay back billions of dollars that it did not have.

Responses to the Mexican crisis were problematic. The International Monetary Fund initiated a massive $48 billion bailout package financed by taxpayers from the United States and other wealthy countries. Most of this money went to compensate for their losses the people who had created the crisis, mainly the big U.S. investment houses and the wealthy Mexican bankers and entrepreneurs who were their business partners. The IMF argued that this was the only way to prevent total collapse of the Mexican economy. However, many observers have pointed out that the people who created the crisis have been given little incentive not to do so again in the future. Meanwhile the Mexican people, most of whom did nothing to create the crisis, have suffered considerably. In return for the bailout package, Mexico had to submit to an SAP-type package that slashed government spending, increased taxes, and limited wage increases. Particularly hard hit were the masses of lower income Mexicans, many of whom were already living at or near the poverty level. For example, in Mexico City before the crisis, to purchase a minimum basket of goods necessary to support a four-person family, three minimum-wage salaries were required. To repay the bailout package, the government limited planned increases in the minimum wage. Taking inflation into account, the limits amount to an 18 percent yearly decline in the buying power of minimum-wage earners.

Among the geographic effects of the economic crisis are increased poverty within Mexico, increased migration into the United States by people who are desperate to send money home to impoverished families, a plentiful supply of cheap labor in the *maquiladoras* (factories) along the U.S. border, and a rush of U.S. tourists to Mexico, where vacation prices are now lower.

---

imported and the finished products are immediately exported. Many hope that a new wave of economic integration in the region via free trade blocs may solve this problem.

New Trajectories in Economic Development

In some parts of the region, alternatives to SAP-type policies are emerging. These could result in a fourth phase of economic development, characterized by greater economic stability and a reduction in income disparity. A number of countries in South America have joined together in regional free trade associations that many believe have tremendous potential to fuel economic growth. The most successful thus far is the Southern Common Market (**Mercosur**), a group that includes two of South America's economic powerhouses, Argentina and Brazil, and their two smaller neighbors Uruguay and Paraguay (Figure 3.12). Chile has a free trade agreement with Mercosur and is thus considered an associate member. Mercosur is focused on overcoming the difficulty of small national markets by combining national economies into a much larger common market. Together, these countries have 200 million potential consumers and an economy worth over $1 trillion a year. With such a large combined economy, the Mercosur countries hope to be able to afford some protections for industries and more generous government wealth redistribution policies—all while still remaining competitive on a global scale.

Agriculture and Rural Resistance

VIGNETTE Every day except Sunday, Aguilar Busto Rosalino rises well before dawn and goes to work on a banana plantation. From 5:00 A.M. to 6:00 P.M., stopping only for a half-hour lunch break, he spends his entire day putting plastic bags containing pesticide around bunches of young bananas. He prefers this to his old job of applying a more powerful pesticide, work that left him and 10,000 other plantation workers sterile. He works very hard because he is paid according to how much work he gets done. Usually he earns between $5 and $14.50 a day. Right now he is working for a plantation in Costa Rica that supplies bananas to Del Monte, but he thinks that in a few months he will be working for another plantation nearby. It is a common practice for these operations to fire their workers every three months so that they can avoid having to pay the employee benefits that Costa Rican law mandates. Although Aguilar makes barely enough to live on, he has no intention of protesting for higher wages, as he knows that this will only get him put on a blacklist of people that the plantations agree they will not hire. [Adapted from Andrew Wheat, Toxic bananas, *Mutinational Monitor* 17, no. 9 (September 1996): 6–7. http://www.essential.org/monitor/hyper/mm 0996.04.html.]

Throughout Middle and South America, more and more rural people are finding themselves in situations not unlike that of Aguilar Busto Rosalino. For centuries, while many people labored on large farms, or haciendas, the owner would allow them a bit of land to grow a small garden or some cash crops. However, in recent years governments have encouraged a shift to large-scale, absentee-owned, export-oriented farms and plantations like the one where Aguilar works. Export agriculture is favored because it has the potential to

FIGURE 3.12 Mercosur trade group.
[Adapted from *The Economist,* October 12–18, 1996, p. 186.]

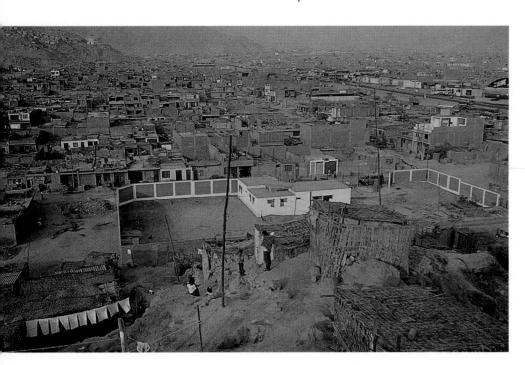

More than two and a half million people live in the shantytowns that ring Lima. Many, perhaps most, are people from rural agricultural areas who migrated here to find work. [William Albert Allard, *National Geographic.*]

earn large amounts of the foreign currency needed to pay off debts. SAPs have also encouraged governments to relax their restrictions on foreign ownership, so it is easier for foreign multinationals like Del Monte and others to dominate the most profitable agro-industries. These companies are usually highly efficient, state-of-the-art operations. No longer are garden or sharecropping parcels available for seasonal laborers. Meanwhile, smaller scale farmers who cannot afford the latest production techniques are squeezed out. Governments subject to SAPs have cut supports for local agriculture and have gone back on a host of other promises of aid they once made to small farmers. Increasingly, the only new land available to farmers of limited income is in rain forest areas where soil fertility lasts only a few years. If they cannot find new land, farmers migrate to cities or work as wage laborers on plantations under conditions similar to those experienced by Aguilar Busto Rosalino.

These trends in rural agriculture have sparked resistance in a number of locations. In Brazil, 65 percent of the land is owned by wealthy farmers who make up just 2 percent of the population. Since 1985, more than 2 million small-scale farmers have been pressed to sell their land to larger farms specializing in the production of cattle and other agricultural products for export. These larger farms, whether state or privately owned, earn money that helps pay off the country's debt; but the now landless farmers have been forced to migrate. To help these farmers, organizations like the National Movement of Landless Rural Workers began taking over unused portions of some larger farms, saying in effect that it is wrong for some people to have more agricultural land than they can use while others live at the brink of starvation. Since the mid-1980s, the landless movements have coordinated the occupation of more than 21 million hectares of land (an area about the size of Kansas) by 151,427 families. Public opinion polls show that 77 percent of Brazilians support the movement. Nevertheless, rural landowners have used private armies or local military police to remove and, in some cases, massacre landless families. The national government has intervened to avert more violence, and has started its own program to settle landless families on farms.

In the southern Mexican state of Chiapas, agricultural activists have been less successful. There a rebellion by Native American agricultural workers began on the day the North American Free Trade Agreement took effect in 1994. Most land in Chiapas is held by a wealthy elite who grow cash crops for export. Meanwhile about three-quarters of the rural population is malnourished, and one-third of the children do not attend school. NAFTA is seen as a threat because it has diverted the government from land reform to the support of large-scale export agriculture. Unlike Brazil, the Mexican government has, for the most part, chosen to repress the rebellion rather than to seek a peaceful solution.

The Informal Economy

The measures taken to streamline the economies of Middle and South America—the belt tightening, the canceling of subsidies for housing, food, health care, and industries, the reduction of government jobs—all

AT THE LOCAL SCALE   *The Informal Economy in Peru*

Street vending is the most visible part of the informal economy in most cities of Middle and South America. The vendors sell useful items like vegetables, spices, cooked snack foods, sunglasses, and umbrellas. Some sell luxury goods at prices lower than those in shops—products like perfume, cosmetics, and handwoven rugs. Street vendors use public streets and sell to the public, so governments in most countries try to formalize and control this activity in order to protect public health, ensure orderly urban spaces, and collect taxes.

The informal economy is a lifesaver in Peru, which has been hit by unprecedented economic recession, losses in real wages, and underemployment for as much as 70 percent of urban workers. It is thought to employ a majority of the working urban population. By the year 2000, perhaps as many as 68 percent of urban workers were in the informal sector, and they generate an estimated 42 percent of the country's total gross domestic product. Most work as street vendors; up to one-quarter of the working population are so employed.

The geographer Maureen Hays-Mitchell, who studies street vending in Peruvian cities, found a vibrant, highly organized system in which the vendors assess the market and risks entailed in this semi-illegal activity. She found street vending in Peru to be a highly rational sector of the informal economy, fraught with intense competition for particular urban spaces and requiring continuous strategizing for market advantages. She also found that not only was street vending an important source of sustenance for the vendors, but it improved the overall quality of urban life by making goods available in convenient places and at affordable prices, something the inefficient formal retailing system seemed unable to do.

Street vendors specialize in particular products and carefully place their stands where they can attract the most customers for the products they sell. Vendors sell food and small gifts in front of hospitals during visiting hours; candy, games, and toys in front of schools; shoeshines and newspapers near hotels and restaurants; lotion, hats, and bikinis near beaches. Few opportunities are left unexploited: movie patrons can buy comics and magazines while waiting in line; outside jails, visitors, guards, and even prisoners can buy food, souvenirs, and handicrafts produced by inmates. The most popular locations, though, are along the edges of streets surrounding a city's central retailing district, the entrances to specific buildings and stores, and the intersections of major streets. A single city block may contain, on average, from 15 to 30 street vendors.

A desirable location has itself become a commodity for sale, though the vendors have no legal right to any particular space. Hays-Mitchell observed vendors painting the outlines of their stands on the street itself. The operators have sometimes sold the rights to use such spaces to new vendors for several hundred dollars.

Source: Maureen Hays-Mitchell, Street vending in Peruvian cities: The spatio-temporal behavior of ambulantes, *Professional Geographer,* 46, no. 4 (1994): 425–438.

---

have forced the ordinary worker into new modes of making a living (see the box "The Informal Economy in Peru"). Throughout this region many, perhaps a majority of those who lost their jobs and benefits are now operating in the **informal economy.** Randall Hansis, in his book *The Latin Americans: Understanding Their Legacy* (1997), tells the story of such a worker, paraphrased as follows:

VIGNETTE **Maria del Rosario Valdez lost her government job as an elevator operator in Mexico City in the 1980s. Unable to find formal employment, she created her own "informal" business: selling secondhand clothing to poor people. Every Thursday evening she boards a bus for Texas that is filled with people doing similar things—buying and selling toys, auto parts, cosmetics, kitchenware. All along the way, wherever the bus stops, the passengers themselves interact with others in the informal economy—people selling tacos, pastries, cassettes, ice cream. For centuries, such underground businesspeople have operated outside the law throughout the Americas, paying no taxes but supporting their families.**

By early morning the bus reaches the border. Maria takes a cab to a huge warehouse where she chooses things she knows will sell from the towers of clothing collected from all over the United States. Some clothes are new—unsalable overstock. She fills boxes and suitcases with about 500 pounds of clothing, for which she pays about

135

$150. Later she will pay another $150 in bribes to Mexican customs officials. Once back in Mexico City, early Saturday, Maria heads immediately to her stall in the market. There she bundles leftover unsold clothing (to be hawked door-to-door in the poor barrios by another woman) and lays out her new purchases. She will sell for 10 or more hours each day until Thursday, when she leaves for the border once again. [Adapted from Randall Hansis, *The Latin Americans: Understanding Their Legacy* (New York: McGraw-Hill, 1997), pp. 178–179.]

This story raises a number of important issues. The informal economy, which often entails recycling used items, contributes to the conservation of resources and can in some cases serve as an incubator for businesses that might eventually provide legitimate jobs for more than one person. However, many argue that informal workers are just treading water, making too little to ever expand, and paying only bribes, no taxes. It is troubling that so many industrious people are being pushed by SAPs out of stable legal employment and into a world of bribery and cross-border smuggling, where there is no protection of health and safety. In many ways, the growth of the informal economy is a symptom of the increasing disparity in this region between those with tremendous access to wealth and power and those with practically none.

Is Democracy Rising?

For the first time in a long while, all countries except Cuba have openly elected governments. However, democracy is as yet fragile and superficial. Officials often remain in power not because they have broad public support but because they are backed by elite-based alliances that include the military, rural landowners, wealthy urban entrepreneurs, foreign corporations, and even foreign governments like the United States. The international drug trade remains a major hurdle to be overcome before the region can reach political stability.

Democracy has often been compromised by foreign involvement in the region's politics. For years, the Soviet Union dominated the economy and politics of Cuba, while Cuba, in turn, manipulated politics in places like Bolivia and Grenada. The United States has repeatedly intervened in many countries, buying influence, propping up dictators (for example, Batista in Cuba, Somoza in Nicaragua, Duvalier in Haiti, Balaguer in the Dominican Republic, Pinochet in Chile), toppling elected officials (Allende in Chile), or supporting insurgency against elected officials (the Contras against the Sandinistas in Nicaragua), even staging

an invasion in 1989 in Panama to oust its then president. Usually the United States has intervened for the stated purpose of preventing a communist takeover or squelching the drug trade. However, the result has often been neglect of the democratic process.

Government corruption is common in the region and undermines democratic institutions. When corruption reaches the highest levels of government, it sets a damaging example for the rest of society. Virtually every country in the region has had a serious scandal in the past few years involving high-level officials performing million-dollar favors for friends and families or simply stealing money from taxpayers. For years, in Mexico, banks regularly and openly recorded massive transfers of money into foreign bank accounts at the end of every six-year presidential term. The last president, Carlos Salinas, fled the country at the end of his term in 1996 with more than $300 million.

The international drug trade is a major factor contributing to corruption, violence, and the subversion of the democratic process throughout Middle and South America. Middle America and northwestern South America are the primary sources for the raw materials of the drug trade—coca for cocaine, poppies for heroin, and marijuana. Figure 3.13 shows the flow of cocaine to North America from Middle and South America. Many growers are small-scale farmers of Native American or mestizo origin, who can make a better income for their families from these plants than from other cash crops. The money that fuels the drug trade comes from North America and, to a lesser extent, from Europe, and the enormous profits are often laundered in offshore banks in the Caribbean. Although drugs are illegal in all of Middle and South America, in countries like Colombia, Bolivia, and Mexico, public figures from the local police on up to the highest officials are paid not just to turn a blind eye to the industry but also, as in the case of former Colombian president Ernesto Samper, to govern in ways that allow the drug trade to flourish. Because law enforcement is intentionally lax in drug-producing areas, drug lords can fund their own private armies to protect drug transport routes and force the compliance of local citizens.

Many who study the drug trade in Middle and South America are critical of the U.S. "war on drugs," which they argue has encouraged tendencies toward a violent, undemocratic political culture. While these countries are trying to turn away from long-standing tendencies toward military rule, the United States is giving massive support to military establishments in the form of weapons and training. Antidrug efforts by the United States have led to the largest U.S. military presence in the region in history. This encourages the military within specific countries to maintain too high a political profile. Increasingly, many are arguing that the United States and Europe could most effectively combat the region's

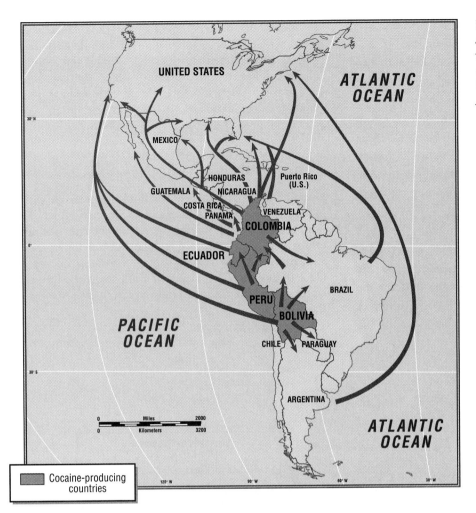

FIGURE 3.13 Cocaine sources and traffic in the Americas. [Adapted from George F. Rengert, *The Geography of Illegal Drugs* (Boulder, CO: Westview Press, 1996), p. 16.]

drug trade by focusing on reducing the demand for drugs within the U.S. and European populations.

Democratic institutions, though widespread, are fragile enough that a return to military rule or some other form of authoritarian administration is not out of the question. Democracy is strongest where people are educated, healthy, and economically secure. Thus the process of deepening democracy goes hand in hand with efforts to create more socially and economically equal societies.

Environmental Issues

VIGNETTE   The Ecotour travel bureau in Manaus, Brazil, was bustling with activity the morning we went to arrange our visit to see untouched rain forest and the legendary wetlands associated with the Río Negro branch of the Amazon on which Manaus is situated. The agent reassured us that we were surrounded by hundreds of thousands of acres of forest, but on the wall a hazy wide-angle photo of the territory he was describing clearly showed that this was no untouched forest. Only a narrow band of forest several hundred feet deep stretched along the river's edge. Beyond that, the photo showed huge expanses of the telltale scars of red-brown eroded soil that indicate logging for the export market is probably under way.

Over the next three days, we learned that even the patch of forest along the river was anything but untouched. It had been regrowing for perhaps 20 years; the trees were mostly shiny-leaved ficus trees, not the multispecies assemblage typical of untouched forest. And walking was difficult through the dense undergrowth of shrubs and vines; in a fully grown forest the forest floor would have been too dark to support such growth. After just a few minutes of struggling through the brush, we were suddenly out of the forest and into a badly eroded field of cassava and corn along a tributary to the Río Negro. The cassava field provided a good illustration of the damage that results when tropical rain forest is destroyed. Without the continuous "rain" of decaying detritus (dead leaves,

137

bark, twigs, insect bodies), and now exposed to bright sun and hard, pounding rainfall, the soil in the cassava field had lost its most fertile particles to erosion and then baked hard into a sort of lumpy, dusty red concrete called laterite.

Several families of extraordinarily poor cassava growers and processors were settled on the banks of the tributary. Their children had the distended bellies caused by nutritional deficiencies. Cassava is a popular garnish and side dish in Brazilian haute cuisine; but, for those who eat little else, it is a pseudo food, high in hunger-quelling calories, very low in nutrition. However, it will grow prolifically in the worst of soils and hence has become famine food for the poorest people across the world. In this case, cassava was the main food for the families that grew and processed it for use as a garnish in the upscale Manaus homes and restaurants across the river. [Lydia Pulsipher, personal observation, 1988.]

This short description of a few days along the Amazon touches on a number of themes that are related to environmental issues in Middle and South America: deforestation, problems with ecotourism, and ways in which disparity of wealth can be linked to environmental degradation.

The Vanishing Forests of the Amazon Basin

During the 1980s and early 1990s, forests were cleared in Middle and South America at the rate of 12.3 million hectares (30.3 million acres—about the size of Ohio) per year. About 75 percent of the forest lost annually from this region—about 9 million hectares (22.2 million acres)—is cleared from the huge forestlands of Brazil. These lie mostly within the Amazon Basin (Figure 3.14).

Amazon environments, though vast, are subject to multiple threats: multinational corporations are logging trees for the global market in fine tropical

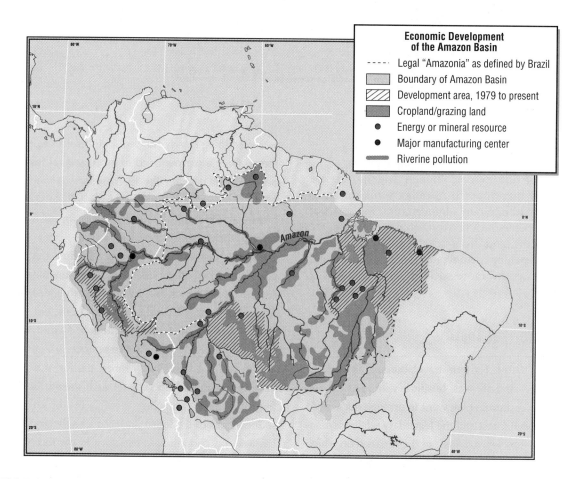

FIGURE 3.14 Amazon Basin. [Adapted from *Student Atlas of Environmental Issues*, 1997, p. 82.]

Fires in Brazilian rain forest leave a moonlike landscape in their wake. During unusually dry cycles, both forests and grasslands are threatened by fires, many set to clear land for subsistence cultivation, others by foreign-owned lumber companies. During a drought in February and March 1998, millions of acres of northern Brazilian grasslands and forest were burned over. [John Maier, Jr.,/NYT Pictures.]

woods, and the land is being cleared for commercial cattle ranching and for settlements for the landless poor from southern and eastern Brazil. Most new settlers have little knowledge of how to farm the poor soils sustainably. After a few years of farming, they must abandon the land, now eroded and depleted of nutrients. Pastures created on former tropical forestlands can be equally short-lived.

Much of the logging in the Amazon is presently carried out by Asian multinational companies, which have already logged up to 50 percent of the tropical forests in Southeast Asia. Firms from Burma, Indonesia, Malaysia, the Philippines, and Korea are purchasing forestlands in Brazil after already securing the rights to forests in those parts of the Amazon Basin that are in Ecuador, Peru, Venezuela, Suriname, and French Guiana. In all these countries, environmental regulations are only just being developed, while the logging companies are already hard at work. Environmental groups such as Friends of the Earth, Brazil, are using satellite data to monitor the extent of deforestation in the Amazon. Official estimates of deforestation in Brazil are that 5 percent of the forest is lost every decade; but Friends of the Earth say these estimates are low and that environmental regulations are much too weak. They add that the new laws unfairly discriminate against some experienced small farmers who log selectively on their land. Other Brazilians worry that in the face of international environmental lobbying, Brazil is losing sovereign control over its own resources.

If this massive portion of earth's rain forest were largely destroyed, scientists think many of the earth's ecosystems would be affected. The absorption of carbon dioxide and release of free oxygen, one of the main physical functions of the forest, would be curtailed, thus contributing to global warming through the greenhouse effect. Planting fast-growing trees in forest plantations is one method of maintaining the exchange of carbon dioxide and oxygen and offers the possibility of saving some natural forests from cutting in the future, but forest plantations do not replicate the destroyed natural forest.

The forests in other parts of Middle and South America are also at risk. About 65 percent of the forest clearing in this region has been intended to create pastures for beef cattle grown primarily for export. The U.S. fast-food industry is a major consumer, and the forests of Central America (Costa Rica, El Salvador, Nicaragua, and Panama) and the Caribbean (Cuba, the Dominican Republic, and Jamaica) have been among the main targets for clearing. If deforestation continues in these areas at present rates, the natural forest cover will be entirely gone in 20 years.

The term **ecotourism** has no firm definition, but increasingly it has come to refer to nature-oriented vacations in endangered landscapes taken by travelers from industrialized nations. The purpose is twofold, and perhaps even contradictory. First, countries promoting this type of tourism hope it will make them money and provide jobs. Second, it is thought that ecotourism will have lower social and environmental costs than does resort-oriented tourism. In fact, ecotourism is turning out to be not very lucrative. The experience in itself engenders in the tourist frugality and the enjoyment of simple pleasures—a reflective frame of mind. Moreover, it is difficult to design ecotourism experiences that are authentic and that don't themselves do environmental damage.

139

Finally, the story of the encounter with the cassava growers illustrates the environmental effects that so often ensue from widespread poverty. The cassava growers must make do with very few of the necessities for well-being; meanwhile, they themselves, due to ignorance and lack of choice, can be among the worst perpetrators of environmental disaster. Yet appealing to them to change is folly in view of their limited alternatives. In any case, they are only a tiny part of the huge and long-term system of environmental exploitation.

By now, the Amazon is an example of what geographers have lately been calling **contested space**. Everybody, most of all the original inhabitants, wants a piece of the place to use as they see fit. Deep in the interior, a few savvy Native American leaders learn litigation skills to fend off wily oil-developing conglomerates trying to take their lands. Governments lure surplus urban populations with the offer of cheap land along newly built roads. Unemployed factory workers, unskilled at agriculture, barely eke out a living on small homesteads they carve out of the forests. Displaced Indians work as gold miners. Ranchers buy up worn-out once-forested land for cattle pastures. Ecotourism entrepreneurs take their clients to bogus landscapes or, worse, to pristine forests where they further degrade the environment. In Manaus, a well-financed government research agency promotes the use of forest products, while another government agency, less well-financed, tries to undo the resulting damage and protect the indigenous tribes from the relentless encroachment of development.

Environment and Development

The region of Middle and South America was one of the first to alert people to the link between environmental deterioration and economic development. In the 1980s and 1990s, media stories told how road building, resettlement, rampant forest clearing, mining, dam building, and commercial agriculture were causing the loss of forest cover, the demise of precious plant and animal species, disastrous erosion, and the ruin of indigenous cultures. For a while, governments within the region argued that development was so desperately needed that environmental regulations were an unaffordable luxury.

Now Middle and South Americans appear to be choosing a middle ground: embracing development as necessary to raise standards of living, yet hoping to mitigate the negative environmental and social effects of this development. There are many grassroots environmental movements throughout the region, from the neighborhood on up to the national level. Most such organizations monitor, evaluate, and often challenge development projects—sometimes via public protest, sometimes via political negotiating, sometimes via public education. They may work with international nongovernmental organizations. Two cases are discussed here; and in the section on the subregions of Middle and South America the text describes two locally designed projects sensitive to environmental concerns—one fostering urban quality of life in Curitiba, Brazil (see page 164), and one reviving ancient cultivation systems in the Peruvian Andes (see box on page 159).

Case 1. Hydroelectric dams provide energy that can be used for industrialization and to electrify urban areas. Such dams are increasingly constructed by private firms and must turn a profit. In the swampy central Paraná River basin in Argentina, the Paraná-Medio hydroelectric dam project is to be privately funded by a Metairie, Louisiana, firm which will get a 50-year concession for electricity sales to Buenos Aires. The dam reservoir would turn a large wetlands ecosystem into the world's second-largest man-made lake. A U.S.–based assessment firm has said the environmental effects would be negligible, but Brazilian and Argentine scientists say that the lake would inundate the habitat of more than 1100 animal species. This disruption could harm 300 species of fish, fishing tourism, and the livelihood of fisherpeople. Upstream flooding would eliminate seasonal grazing and rice farming and kill many valuable trees.

The public debate has persuaded the government to reevaluate the project, but energy is crucial to most kinds of development, and is presently in short supply in much of Latin America. Figure 3.15 compares commercial energy use per capita for several world regions. South America uses less energy than even Central America, and only about one-tenth that used per capita in North America. Hydropower is favored because it does not produce air pollution like coal or gas does. The Paraná dam is only one of a score of privately funded hydrodam projects being proposed for South America's major river systems.

Case 2. The Machiguenga people, who have hunted and fished for 5000 years in Peru's central Urubamba region, oppose Shell Oil's plan to extract enough natural gas from their land to power the city of Lima for 100 years. Shell has a bad reputation in the area for environmental and human rights abuses committed in connection with oil drilling several years ago. Now the company promises to address past grievances. Shell has hired scientists to map and inventory the local environment and a social anthropologist to prepare detailed guidelines for workers so that local customs are not violated. But the company's helicopters, power saws, and bulldozers disrupt the environment: the noise disturbs wildlife; rivers are polluted by erosion and fuel spills; and when Shell reseeds cleared lands, the company plants only the cetico tree where once hundreds of dif-

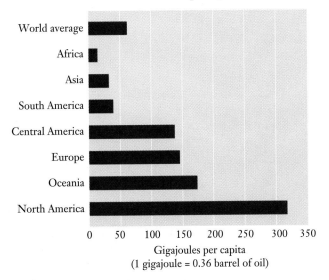

Per Capita Commercial Energy Consumption, 1995

Gigajoules per capita
(1 gigajoule = 0.36 barrel of oil)

FIGURE 3.15 Commercial energy consumption per capita by world region in 1995. [*1997 United Nations Energy Statistics Yearbook.*]

ferent species grew. By-products of gas production will include arsenic, cadmium, lead, and mercury, yet the land-use agreement does not include any compensation in case of accidental environmental damage.

These two cases illustrate how people in Middle and South America are learning to be their own environmental advocates in the tension-filled process of development. Although for now the balance of power still seems to lie with those who do not put the environment first, even remote Native American groups are beginning to work with local and international conservation groups in pressuring for stronger legislation and in negotiating with multinational firms and international lending agencies.

Measures of Human Well-Being

VIGNETTE Miss Eliza arises at six in the morning, prepares tea, bread, and fruit for her two daughters and her elderly Aunt Hettie, whose two-room wooden house she shares. Auntie helps ready the children for school, and Miss Eliza rushes off with a "head-load" of vegetables and spices to catch the jitney to Montego Bay, Jamaica.

There, in the central market, she hustles all day, finding just the right breadfruit for a good customer, putting together a basket of spices and condiments (nutmeg, pimento, cinnamon, fiery hot sauce) for some tourists off a cruise ship, negotiating with a fellow higgler for some special cuttings of dasheen to plant in her home garden. During all this time she doesn't think once about the fact that her yearly income for herself, Aunt Hettie, and the two children is just $4000. Rather, every single moment of her life is spent dealing with the realities of having very little. [Lydia Pulsipher, fieldwork, 1992.]

As geographers, we need ways to compare the well-being of people like Miss Eliza with that of others, in other places. Table 3.3 provides you the opportunity to do just that, according to several different indices.

You will remember from the explanation in Chapter 1 that gross national product (GNP) per capita figures (here listed in column 2 of Table 3.3) are often used as a crude indicator of well-being. These figures are often misleading, however, because they are averages that mask a very wide disparity of wealth in Middle and South America and they ignore aspects of well-being other than income. In column 2, the countries in Middle and South America are compared with Japan, the United States, and Kuwait in per capita GNP. You can see immediately that they all lag far behind the first three. From this we can learn that purchasing power is very likely limited throughout the region. But purchasing power is not the best measure of well-being.

In column 3, the United Nations Human Development Index (HDI) combines three components—life expectancy at birth, educational attainment, and adjusted real income—to arrive at a ranking of 174 countries that is more sensitive to factors other than just income. You can see that some countries in the Americas rank higher than Kuwait (54) on the HDI index despite their relatively low GNP figures: Argentina, Barbados, the Bahamas, Chile, Colombia, Costa Rica, Mexico, Trinidad and Tobago, and others. Their rankings are higher partly because education is somewhat more available across gender and class in Middle and South America than in Southwest Asia, where Kuwait is located and where women are secluded. Nonetheless, investment in basic and secondary education in Middle and South America is not sufficient to prepare people for skilled jobs, and poor health care is holding down life expectancy. The HDI data also indicates that poverty is especially deep in Haiti, Guatemala, Honduras, Nicaragua, and Bolivia, and low incomes are not ameliorated by government

TABLE 3.3

Human well-being rankings of selected countries

Country	GNP per capita (in U.S. dollars), 1996	Human Development Index (HDI) global rankings, 1998[a]	Gender Empowerment Measure (GEM) global rankings, 1998[b]	Female literacy (percentage), 1995	Male literacy (percentage), 1995
Selected countries for comparison					
Japan	$40,940	8 (high)	38	99	99
United States	28,020	4 (high)	11	99	99
Kuwait	19,040 (1995)	54 (high)	75	75	82
Caribbean					
Antigua and Barbuda	7,330	29 (high)	Not av.[c]	Not av.	Not av.
Bahamas	11,940 (1995)	32 (high)	15	98	98
Barbados	6,560 (1995)	24 (high)	18	97	98
Cuba	1,260 (GDP 1998)[d]	85 (medium)	25	95	96
Dominica	3,090	41 (high)	Not av.	Not av.	Not av.
Dominican Republic	1,600	88 (medium)	58	82	82
Grenada	2,880	51 (high)	Not av.	Not av.	Not av.
Guadeloupe	Not av.	Not av.	Not av.	Not av.	Not av.
Haiti	310	159 (low)	71	42	48
Jamaica	1,600	84 (medium)	Not av.	95	96
Martinique	Not av.	Not av.	Not av.	Not av.	Not av.
Netherlands Antilles	Not av.	Not av.	Not av.	Not av.	Not av.
Puerto Rico	Not av.	Not av.	Not av.	Not av.	Not av.
St. Kitts and Nevis	5,870	50 (high)	Not av.	Not av.	Not av.
St. Lucia	3,500	58 (high)	Not av.	Not av.	Not av.
St. Vincent and the Grenadines	2,370	55 (high)	Not av.	Not av.	Not av.
Trinidad and Tobago	3,870	40 (high)	17	97	99

[a] The high and medium designations indicate where the country ranks among the 174 countries classified into three categories (high, medium, low) by the United Nations. Total ranked in the world = 174. The only country in the Western Hemisphere to rank low is Haiti.

[b] Total ranked in world = 104 (no data for many).

[c] Not av. = Not available.

[d] From Paul Goodwin, Jr., *Global Studies Latin America*, 8th ed. (Guilford, CT: Dushkin Publishing Group/Brown & Benchmark, 1998).

TABLE 3.3 (CONTINUED)

Country	GNP per capita (in U.S. dollars), 1996	Human Development Index (HDI) global rankings, 1998[a]	Gender Empowerment Measure (GEM) global rankings, 1998[b]	Female literacy (percentage), 1995	Male literacy (percentage), 1995
Central America					
Belize	2,700	63 (high)	40	70	70
Costa Rica	2,640	34 (high)	28	95	95
El Salvador	1,700	114 (medium)	34	70	73
Guatemala	1,470	111 (medium)	35	57	73
Honduras	660	119 (medium)	Not av.	73	73
Mexico	3,670	49 (high)	37	87	92
Nicaragua	380	126 (medium)	Not av.	67	65
Panama	3,080	45 (high)	44	90	91
South America					
Argentina	8,380	36 (high)	Not av.	96	96
Bolivia	830	116 (medium)	65	76	91
Brazil	4,400	62 (high)	68	83	83
Chile	4,860	31 (high)	61	95	95
Colombia	2,140	53 (high)	41	91	91
Ecuador	1,500	73 (medium)	69	88	92
French Guiana	Not av.	Not av.	Not av.	Not av.	Not av.
Guyana	690	100 (medium)	39	97	99
Paraguay	1,850	91 (medium)	67	91	94
Peru	2,420	86 (medium)	54	83	95
Suriname	1,000	65 (medium)	53	91	95
Uruguay	5,760	38 (high)	59	98	97
Venezuela	3,020	46 (high)	62	90	92

Sources: 1997 and *1998 World Population Data Sheets,* Population Reference Bureau; and *Human Development Index 1998,* United Nations Development Programme.

social programs as they are in some low-income Caribbean countries.

The United Nations Gender Empowerment Measure (GEM, column 4) measures the extent to which females have opportunities to participate in economic and political life within specific countries. The GEM figures show that only four countries in the entire region rank relatively high on this female empowerment scale: Bahamas (15), Barbados (18), Trinidad and Tobago (17), and Cuba (25). In fact, their GEM rank is significantly higher than their HDI rank. All these countries are in the Caribbean. In these four countries, government supports efforts to provide education and equal opportunity to women. These efforts have in turn resulted in lowering rates of natural increase in these four countries to an average of 0.6, the lowest in the region. When a country has a significantly higher GEM than HDI rank, it can mean that despite economic problems, the society is comparatively open to female participation in public life: education, business, and government. In the Caribbean, women have prominent positions in families, increasingly serve in government and in community organizations, and often have higher literacy rates than do men. Many countries rank quite low on GEM (Chile, Brazil, Paraguay, Peru, Venezuela, etc.), though Mexico and several Central American countries rank in the 30s (of only 104 countries ranked on GEM). Still, all do better than does relatively rich but gender-stratified Kuwait, where education and health opportunities for women are very limited.

To return to the case of Miss Eliza in Jamaica, we can now see that her income of $4000 for a family of four is actually lower than average for that country, but we also know that in her case low income is compensated for by social support customs—exemplified by Miss Eliza looking after and feeding her aged aunt, who then, in return, provides a house and child care for Miss Eliza. It is through such informal reciprocal exchange that people manage to survive and even thrive despite low incomes and declining tax-supported public services.

SUBREGIONS OF MIDDLE AND SOUTH AMERICA

This tour of the subregions of Middle and South America focuses primarily on how the themes of cultural diversity, economic disparity, and environmental issues are reflected somewhat differently from place to place.

The Caribbean

The Caribbean is often misinterpreted by those who visit as tourists. Typically short-term visitors are isolated in enclaves or on cruise ships where they glimpse only tiny swatches of the island landscapes. From that vantage point, it is hard to see beyond the tiny houses and garden plots or quaint narrow streets to the statistical facts and social relationships that make life in the Caribbean so different from what it appears to be.

Most of the island societies (Figure 3.16) have emerged only in the last half century from colonial status to become independent, self-governing entities. These islands, with the exception of Haiti and parts of the Dominican Republic, are no longer the poverty-stricken places they were 30 years ago. Rather they are managing to provide a reasonably high quality of life for their people (see Table 3.3). Children go to school—literacy rates for people under 70 years of age average well over 90 percent. There is basic health care—mothers get prenatal care, nearly all babies are born in hospitals, and infant mortality rates are low (drastically so, compared with what they were even in the 1970s). Life expectancy is in the 70s for most islands. And people are choosing to have fewer children; the overall rate of population increase for the Caribbean is the lowest in Middle and South America. A number of Caribbean islands are in the most prosperous cohort on the Human Development Index and do particularly well on the Gender Empowerment Measure. Returned emigrants often say that the quality of life on many Caribbean islands actually exceeds that of far more materially endowed societies, because life is enhanced by strong community and family support. And then, of course, there is the healthful and beautiful physical environment.

Beyond the beaches and quaint villages there are local civic organizations like the Rotary and Lions clubs, libraries, chambers of commerce, gourmet cooking clubs, garden societies, community associations, and active churches. These organizations practice participatory democracy daily: citizens educate each other about social and environmental issues, and they continuously design and implement solutions to local problems. The progress indicated by the demographic statistics (see Table 3.3) is the result of hard work and civic responsibility, as well as aid from the old colonial powers and Canada (less so from the United States).

Island ministers of government continuously search for ways to turn plantation economies, formerly directed from Europe and North America, into more self-directed, self-sufficient, and flexible entities that can adapt quickly to the perpetually changing markets of the global economy. On the one hand, they are tempted to specialize; but on the other hand, they are wary of the dependency and vulnerability that too much specializa-

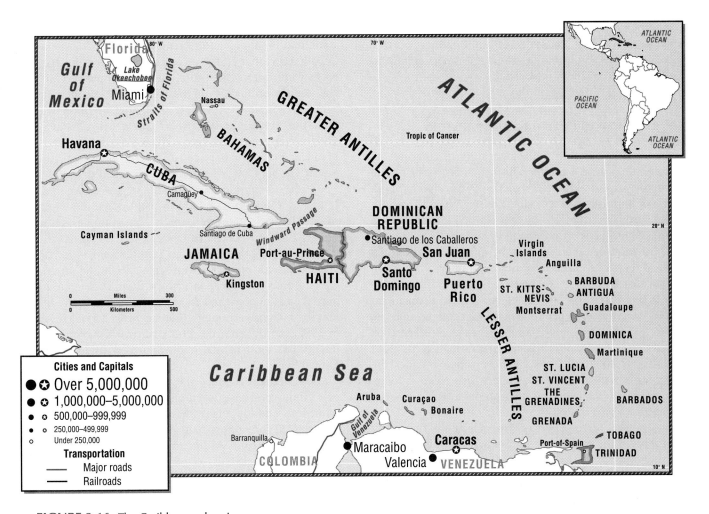

FIGURE 3.16 The Caribbean subregion.

tion can bring. When plantation cultivation of sugar, cotton, and copra died out in the 1950s and 1960s, some islands turned to producing "dessert" crops like bananas and coffee for specially protected markets in Europe. But these protections are likely to disappear once the European Economic Union is complete. Other islands turned to the processing of special resources (like petroleum in Trinidad, bauxite in Jamaica), the assembling and finishing of high-tech products like computer chips or pharmaceuticals, or the processing of computerized data. A number of islands combined one or more of these strategies with tourism development.

In some islands, tourism and related activities contribute as much as 80 percent of the GNP, as was the case in Antigua and Barbuda, Barbados, and the Bahamas in the 1980s. But heavy borrowing to build hotels, airports, water systems, and shopping centers for tourists left some islands with huge debts to pay off. Furthermore, there is a special stress that comes from dealing perpetually with hordes of strangers, especially when they make unflattering assumptions about one's culture and state of well-being. Every year in the mid-1990s, Jamaica (pop. 2.6 million) received visitors numbering twice its population, Antigua and Barbuda (pop. 66,000) hosted more than 4 times its population, and St. Maarten (pop. 20,000), 20 times its population.

Recent studies have suggested that tourism is a chancy development strategy, if heavy borrowing and direct investment from outside are necessary to establish the tourism infrastructure. Outsider owners of airlines, tourist agencies, and hotels, like the colonists of old, tend to export the profits to their home banks rather than reinvest in the host country. When big outside investors control a dominant sector of the economy like tourism, they can wield unseemly control over other island matters as well, such as elections. The potential benefits of tourism are sometimes bled away from local populations by gambling, which was introduced in some islands as a drawing card for tourists in the 1980s. As studies have shown elsewhere, ultimately it is not the tourists who support the gambling industry but the local citizenry. According to gambling executives (personal

145

communication, 1989) Caribbean tourists rarely spend more than several hundred dollars on gambling, per trip; but the local employees of gambling casinos often gamble away their weekly paychecks!

Cuba and Puerto Rico Compared

Cuba and Puerto Rico are interesting to compare because they share a common history until the 1950s and then diverge starkly. After the end of Spanish rule, about 1900, both islands were dominated by North American interests. United States investors owned plantations and other businesses on both islands, and the U.S. government protected their interests by influencing dictatorial local regimes to keep labor organization at a minimum and social unrest under control. By the 1950s, poverty was widespread on both Cuba and Puerto Rico. Infant mortality was at 50 per 1000 or higher, and most people worked as agricultural laborers. Then each island took a different course toward social transformation. In 1959, Cuba experienced a communist revolution under the leadership of Fidel Castro. Puerto Rico meanwhile experienced a capitalist metamorphosis into a high-tech manufacturing center.

Since Castro seized control, Cuba has drastically improved the well-being of its general population in all categories of measurement (life expectancy, literacy, infant mortality), such that by 1990 it had one of the best human well-being records in the entire region (see Table 3.3). Cuba thus proved that, once the requisite investment in human capital is made, poverty and so-cial problems in Latin America are not as intractable as some had thought. Unfortunately, Cuba has been politically repressive in the extreme, forcing out the aristocracy and jailing dissidents. And, economically, Cuba has been inordinately dependent on outside help to achieve its social revolution. The Soviet Union was Cuba's chief sponsor. It provided cheap fuel and generous foreign aid and bought Cuba's main export crop, sugar, at preferential prices. With the demise of the Soviet Union, Cuba's economy has declined sharply.

Cuba's communism, repression of dissent, and potential as a security risk have brought down the wrath of the United States repeatedly. An example is the Helms-Burton Act enacted in 1996, which restricts the interaction of other sovereign states with Cuba, and imposes a trade embargo. Most countries in the Americas and especially those in Europe, have chosen to ignore the restrictions, and that has made a significant difference to Cuba's economy. Tourism grossed $1.5 billion in 1997, mostly from the European market. Nonetheless, Cuba's most natural trading partner would be the United States.

In Puerto Rico since the 1950s, many U.S. "suitcase" industries have taken advantage of generous tax reductions and low Puerto Rican wages to process and assemble all sorts of products for reexport. Puerto Rico is a commonwealth within the United States and its people are U.S. citizens, so many Puerto Ricans migrate to work in the United States. These employment opportunities have done much to improve living conditions on the island, but social investment by the U.S. government has also upgraded the standard of living.

In an effort to attract foreign visitors, Cubans have developed new spaces in Havana designed for tourists, such as the Plaza Carlos Mall built along the waterfront of the Malecon River. [Betty Press/Woodfin Camp & Associates.]

Many Puerto Ricans receive some sort of support payment from the federal government, including health care. The infant mortality rate is now 11.5 (Cuba's is just 7.2), and life expectancy is 74 (Cuba's is 75). The United States subsidizes the Puerto Rican tourism and light industry economy, but outside of flashy San Juan, with it skyscraper tourist hotels, Puerto Rico's landscape reflects stagnation.

Statehood for Puerto Rico, which is desired by some, would mean the end of tax holidays for U.S. companies and hence the end of Puerto Rico's ability to attract assembly plants. Also, many fear that statehood would eventually mean cultural assimilation and the loss of the island's language and Spanish heritage.

Haiti and Barbados Compared

Haiti and Barbados are a study in contrasts. Both spent the colonial era as European possessions with plantation economies, Haiti as a colony of France and Barbados as a colony of Britain. Yet they have had very different experiences and today are far apart in economic and social well-being. Haiti is the poorest nation in the Americas with a rating on the United Nations Human Development Index of 159, while Barbadians have the highest HDI rating in the region.

Haiti, once a French colony, was by the end of the eighteenth century the richest plantation economy in the Caribbean, but the brutality of the French planters sparked an equally brutal revolt by the slaves. The Haitian slave revolt evolved into the earliest independence movement in the entire region. By 1804, Haiti was an independent country.

The former slave reformist leaders were overthrown by brutal and corrupt militarists, who did nothing to reform the exploitative plantation economy. A long series of unstable authoritarian governments was followed eventually by a class-based reign of terror under "Papa Doc," François Duvalier (1957–1986), that pitted the mulatto elite against the black poor. Today Haiti is overwhelmingly rural, with widespread illiteracy, high infant mortality, and badly damaged lands (70 percent of the territory is eroded). Recently, multinational corporations have opened *maquiladora*-like assembly plants employing primarily young women, but the plants are not yet flourishing. Minerals such as bauxite and copper and tin exist, but cost-effective development is not yet possible. A priest and advocate of liberation theology, Jean-Bertrand Aristide, was elected president in 1991. He was unable to stop the long history of violence, and since the early 1990s, the United Nations has maintained peace-keeping troups in Haiti. Several humanitarian aid organizations maintain programs in Haiti.

Far more prosperous Barbados has fewer natural resources and is roughly twice as crowded as Haiti. Bar-

bados has 166 square miles (432 sq km) and 1600 people per square mile (630 per sq km), whereas Haiti has 10,000 square miles (25,000 sq km) and just 708 people per square mile (280 per sq km). But Barbadians are well educated and well fed, and most are homeowners. Barbados has a diversified economy that includes tourism, sugar production, remittances from migrants, and modern industries. Most jobs demand skilled and literate employees. Britain maintains an interest in Barbados and helps it out financially in small ways. Meanwhile, the Barbadian government constantly seeks new employment options for its citizens.

Mexico

Cortez is said to have been at a loss when asked by Queen Isabella to describe Mexico. Now, nearly 500 years later, the task of interpreting Mexico is no easier. Mexicans of today, like those of old, have been given a stage on which to live out their lives, a stage that is so spectacular and full of personality it is not a backdrop for their activities but rather a character in the play. Mexico today is working to fulfill its potential of becoming a reasonably well-managed, middle-income democracy. Most of the efforts along this line, whether private or governmental, are in some way focused on Mexico's relationship with the United States.

The Sierra Madre (the Occidental and the Oriental ranges) form a wide V that extends through the northern two-thirds of Mexico (see Figure 3.1). In the north, the Sierra Madre are blue-gray hills that seem hardly touched by human presence; but farther south, small farmers cultivate a variety of crops on the many facets of the steep and once forested mountains. Between the two mountain ranges lies a high northward-tilting plateau, the Mesa Central. On its undulating arid surfaces, where rainfall is sufficient, cattle and other grazing animals are raised, along with subsistence crops like maize and beans. And where irrigation is possible, wheat and fruit are grown for the North American market. To the south, in the crook of the V, is a high valley surrounded on three sides by lofty snowcapped volcanoes reaching to nearly 18,000 feet (5500 meters). To the east of the volcanoes, the land descends to a wide stretch of humid tropical lowlands along the Caribbean. To the west is the narrow Pacific coast and to the south the deep, hot Balsas Depression, and then more mountains extend all the way to the Isthmus of Tehuantepec and and beyond to Guatemala. The high valley in the V once held the famed Aztec city of Tenochtitlán. Today, it is the site of one of the world's largest urban areas, Mexico City, whose total metropolitan area now holds upwards of 25 million people, more than one-quarter of Mexico's population.

Mexico's formal economy has modernized rapidly in recent decades (see Figures 3.10 and 3.11). Its components are mechanized agriculture, a vastly expanded manufacturing sector, petroleum extraction and refining, tourism, a service and information sector, and the remittances of millions of emigrants working abroad. Mexico's large and varied informal economy employs an undetermined but substantial portion of the population in activities that include craft making, personal services, trash recycling, street vending, and a flourishing black market and crime sector.

There is a geographic pattern to the distribution of these economic sectors. Just 12 percent of Mexico is good agricultural land, and much of that is on hillsides. The biggest agricultural units are large corporate farms, many government subsidized, which have replaced the old, inefficient haciendas and ranches. They produce high-quality meat and produce—citrus, melons, winter vegetables, oil seeds, strawberries, and raspberries—and sorghum for animal feeds. Most of this is for the North American market. Many of these farms are located in the arid north close to the U.S. border. In the tropical lowlands, soil has been drained or irrigated, as necessary, to produce tropical fruits and products like jute, sisal, and tequila. Mexico's convoluted upland landscapes provide many small and specialized niches where a wide variety of crops like sesame seeds, hot peppers, and flowers are grown.

Petroleum refining is located along the Gulf coastal plain. The most important tourism facilities are along the Caribbean and Pacific coastal plains. The service sector, including restaurants, hotels, financial institutions, consulting firms, and museums, is found in every city. As Figure 3.17 illustrates, manufacturing is concentrated along the U.S. border in cities like Tijuana, Mexicali, Ciudad Juárez, and Reynosa, where numerous U.S. firms operate factories called *maquiladoras;* some of these are also in the general vicinity of Mexico City. The informal economy is everywhere, but it is most varied and noticeable in the big cities.

The *Maquiladora* Phenomenon

The term ***maquiladora*** refers to foreign-owned plants that hire people at low wages to assemble manufactured goods. The goods are then returned to the country of origin for sale there or elsewhere. There are thousands of *maquiladoras* along the Mexican-U.S. border (Figure 3.17). Nearly all are branches of American corporations, and the number is growing quickly, as Table 3.4 shows. The border location is popular because of the cheap labor—many of the workers are young unmarried women earning $20 a week or less—and because

FIGURE 3.17 The Mexico subregion. The areas shaded brown are *Maquiladora* zones. [Adapted from David Clawson, *Latin America and the Caribbean* (Dubuque, IA: Wm. C. Brown, 1997), p. 270.]

TABLE 3.4

Rapid growth rate of the *maquiladora* sector

Year	Number of *maquiladoras*	Number of employees
1968	79	17,000
1974	455	75,974
1981	605	130,973
1988	1400	369,489
1990	2042	486,000
1997 (June)	2676	897,354 (up 16% over 1996)

Sources: David L. Clawson, *Latin America and the Caribbean* (Dubuque, IA: Wm. C. Brown, 1997), p. 268; for 1997 data, see *Migration News*, 4, no. 11 (1997). http:\\www.CanadaDallas. org\French\fsw2001\fsw5003.htm.

in. Fast food is way beyond her means. A Big Mac, medium Coke, and fries costs $3.05 and for Ms. Serratos this is a full day's wages. She earns 35 cents an hour wrapping tape around bundles of electrical wires in one of Juárez's assembly plants.

"What people in your country make in an hour, we work a whole day for," says Ms. Serratos, 32. Ana lives with six siblings in a dirt-street suburb of Ciudad Juárez and commutes to work two hours each way on ramshackle buses. "These companies from the U.S. and Japan don't pay people what they ought to. . . . But we have to recognize that they're important for Juárez."

The vast majority of wage earners in Juárez earn little more than Ms. Serratos and are unfamiliar with labor unions. Such low wages don't yield much in tax revenue, hence the tax base of this city of 1.2 million is woefully small. Thus, although drinking water has run out, there is no money for new wells, and it will be 15 years before the streets are blacktopped. The mayor of Juárez notes that the factories pay very low taxes and that tax money goes first to Mexico City. Though he is hoping to attract yet

Mexico has far fewer regulations than the United States on worker safety, environmental protection, and fringe benefits. Mexico also charges much lower taxes. The mostly female laborers migrate from rural locations across Mexico; and the contributions they send to their families give them an economic importance that women in earlier generations did not enjoy.

While Mexico is pleased to have the *maquiladoras* and the jobs they bring, increasingly it is having to deal with negative side effects. The border area is developing serious ground, water, and air pollution problems because of the high concentration of insufficiently regulated factories and unplanned worker settlements, numbering hundreds of thousands. Social problems are also developing. Workers from many backgrounds are crowded into unsanitary living conditions. There are not adequate schools for the increasing numbers of children. Family violence is a growing problem, brought on by the tensions of migration, overcrowded conditions, and changing gender roles (women often can find work more easily than men).

VIGNETTE — Sometimes Ana Serratos pauses outside a McDonald's restaurant in Ciudad Juárez, just across the border from El Paso, Texas; but she resists the temptation to stop

In Nuevo Laredo, Mexico, workers in this sewing factory, leased by R. G. Barry Corporation of Pickerington, Ohio, are making a brand-name slipper for markets in North America and Europe. [Paul S. Howell/Gamma-Liaison.]

more factories, the mayor concludes that the *maquiladora* economy is "creating an enormous mass of wretchedly poor people." [Sam Dillon, *New York Times News Service,* December 1995.]

Foreign Trade

Most of Mexico's trade is now with the United States and Canada. The United States buys 80 percent of Mexico's exports and supplies 70 percent of Mexico's imports. The North American Free Trade Agreement is an ongoing effort to further enhance trade among Mexico, Canada, and the United States. NAFTA means different things to different people; but to the Mexicans it is a chance to attract North American investment in industry and communications and a chance to produce and sell with fewer restrictions in the rich North American market. It is also a way to create jobs for its ever increasing population of young people. From the Mexican perspective, NAFTA is one of a set of important new trading partnerships being set up with nations in both hemispheres. Costa Rica, Venezuela, Colombia, and Chile have recently entered into free trade agreements with Mexico that gradually will remove tariffs. Tariffs in Mexico had run as high as 60 percent on consumer goods. The removal of tariffs will aid Mexico's new Middle and South American trading partners—to them Mexico is a large and relatively prosperous market for their goods—and put a greater choice of products in Mexican stores. Trade with Asia and with Europe is also emerging, but it is now equal to only a tiny portion of Mexico's present level of trade with the United States and Canada.

Population

Mexico's many efforts to industrialize, find jobs for its people, and improve trade relationships are all focused on raising standards of living. Yet all these efforts are endangered by relentless population growth. According to international figures (1998), Mexico now has 95.7 million people, and that number will double in 32 years, a rate of increase that is alarmingly higher than past estimates. Seventy-one percent, or 68 million Mexicans, live in urban places, the majority in large cities. And Mexicans are very young, with 50 percent under 21 and more than one-third the population under the age of 15 (Figure 3.18).

The youth of the Mexican population is both good news and bad. All these young people could develop into energetic and highly productive workers, filling jobs, serving on committees, running local governments, addressing environmental problems, and consuming products and services. But to do so, these young people will

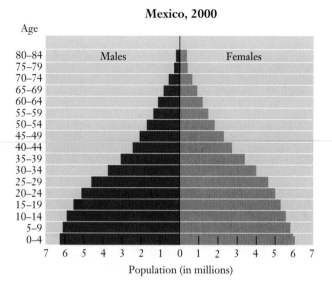

FIGURE 3.18 Mexico population pyramid. [Adapted from U.S. Census Bureau, International Data Base, at http://www.census.gov/cgi-bin/ipc/idbpyry.pl.]

need a healthy childhood and advanced education. Mexico's poor record in providing basic services for its people means that nearly one-half do without adequate sanitation facilities. The infant mortality rate is high, at 34 per 1000 births. Only 65 percent of the eligible students are in school. Mexico needs to be able to spend the coming years upgrading life for the citizens it already has; but without miraculously high economic growth and the dedication of substantial tax money to human services (especially education and health care), living standards for the majority in Mexico are likely to sink, not rise.

Migration

Migration is often a strategy to alleviate problems related to low income. Rapid rural-to-urban migration in Mexico is legendary, and the problems that accompany burgeoning urban populations have been discussed earlier in this chapter. Emigration of Mexicans into North America is also a well-known phenomenon, one that has an enormous impact on Mexico as a nation. On the one hand, the skills of the best and brightest are lost, but on the other, some benefits from their industry are gained.

Consider the following. Unlike Europeans, who, when they came to North America, usually cut their ties with family and native land, Mexicans often remain loyal to their home villages. Their migrations are most often undertaken with the express idea of helping out their own families and communities. A recent paper (1998) by the geographers Dennis Conway and Jeffrey

H. Cohen reports that couples migrating from Native American villages in Mexico often work just long enough at menial jobs in the United States to save a substantial nest egg. Then they return home to build a house (usually a family self-help project) and buy appliances. Afterward, the family lives off that nest egg for several years, while one or both members of the couple renders volunteer community service to the home village—perhaps building schools, serving on the town council, improving the town water system, or refurbishing the town's public spaces. When the money runs out, the man or the couple may migrate again to save another nest egg. Often these civic-minded migrants cycle other members of their family through a menial U.S. job, such as dishwashing, thus keeping the job open for themselves when they need it again.

Their bosses and coworkers in the United States never guess that such unprepossessing, minimum-wage workers are actually influential and public-spirited citizens in their home villages, who use migration and hard work to enhance community living standards and participatory democracy. Of course, all this is possible because of the self-help nature of Mexican communities, where people build houses and schools with their bare hands, and because the Mexican economy is much less affluent than that of the United States. Hence, a few thousand dollars saved in the United States will accomplish a great deal in rural Mexico.

Central America

In Central America, wealth is in the land. Industry accounts for only about 20 percent of the gross domestic product and the region is not rich in mineral resources, so the seven countries of Central America (Figure 3.19) remain dependent on the produce of their plantations, ranches, and small farms. Here the disparity of income takes the form of disparity in the distribution of land. It is not uncommon for 1 or 2 percent of the population to control the vast majority of the productive land as well as the lives of an uneducated mass of laborers and subsistence farmers. The poor of Central America have repeatedly tried to obtain a greater share of the wealth, and in recent years their efforts have led to armed conflict.

Most of the Central American isthmus consists of three physical zones that are not well connected with each other: the narrow Pacific coast, the highland interior, and the long, sloping, rainwashed Caribbean coastal region. Along the narrow Pacific coast mestizo (*ladino* is the local term) laborers work on large plantations

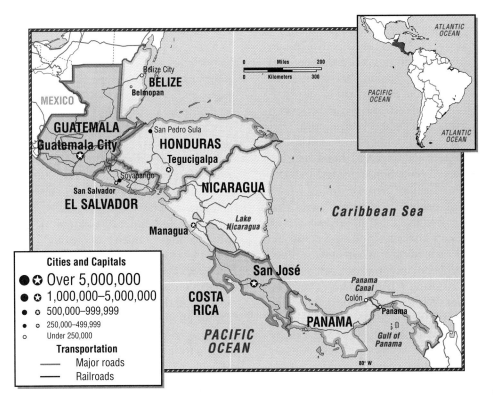

FIGURE 3.19 The Central America subregion.

Some minifundios (tiny farm plots) have been redistributed to needy families in El Salvador. [Tomasz Tomaszewski, *National Geographic.*]

where common crops in the lowlands are sugar, cotton, bananas, and other tropical fruits; coffee is grown in the hills back of the coast. In the highland interior of Guatemala, Honduras, and Nicaragua, Native American people have lived for centuries off subsistence agriculture; but recently, cattle ranching and commercial agriculture have spread into the highlands, displacing them. The humid Caribbean coastal region was previously sparsely occupied by some native people and African-Caribbean people; now it is increasingly the site of resettlement projects for displaced highland small farmers, export-oriented plantations, forestry, and tourism development.

The majority of people in Central America are Native Americans or rural mestizo (ladino) people. Most make a living by doing a variety of things: cultivating their own food and cash crops on their own or rented land or as sharecroppers, and working seasonally as laborers on large farms and plantations. They have experienced centuries of hardship: loss of most of their native lands to elites, virtual slave labor (long hours and low wages), and denial of the most basic of social amenities (clean water, sanitation, health care education, and protection from agricultural chemical poisoning). Although most of these people live in rural villages, they often do not have access to enough cultivable land to meet their needs; the majority of the land is held in huge

tracts—ranches, plantations, and haciendas—by the upper classes. As a result, the small percentage of land accessible to the poor for their own cultivation may have densities of 1000 people or more per square mile.

While there is a general hunger for land among the poor majority, only tiny El Salvador is truly densely populated, with an average of more than 742 people per square mile. In fact, land there is so scarce that people desperate for land have slipped over the border to cultivate in Honduras.

The populations of most Central American countries are growing rapidly, a not uncommon occurrence when dire conditions prevail (Table 3.5). Children are still seen as a labor asset in rural situations, and women have very little education for work outside the home. Minimal improvements in diet and health care have decreased deaths so that now births outnumber deaths 4 or 5 to 1. Still, poverty cannot be attributed directly to overpopulation because it is the unequal distribution of land and wealth that accounts for the dire conditions of life.

In all countries except El Salvador, population is an issue chiefly because growth rates are outstripping efforts to improve standards of living. If access to employment at living wages and to resources (land, clean water, sanitation) and social services (health and education) were equitable, most countries, other than El Salvador, could probably support somewhat larger pop-

TABLE 3.5

Population data on Central America

Country	Population	Population density per square mile	Rate of natural increase (percentage)	Literacy rate (percentage)
Belize	200,000	24	3.3	70
Guatemala	10,000,000	235	2.9	55
Honduras	5,600,000	130	2.8	71
El Salvador	5,900,000	738	2.6	70
Nicaragua	4,600,000	100	2.7	65
Costa Rica	3,600,000	181	2.2	95
Panama	2,700,000	90	1.8	90

Sources: 1998 World Population Data Sheet, 1998, Population Reference Bureau; and *Human Development Report 1998*, United Nations Human Development Programme.

ulations at decent standards of living. But given the realities, continued growth is not a wise course.

Frustrated with governments unresponsive to their plight, Native Americans and other mistreated rural people in Guatemala, Honduras, Nicaragua, and El Salvador began organizing guerrilla movements. In some cases they had the help of Marxist revolutionaries from outside the region. The consequence has been the destructive civil wars that have in recent years plagued Guatemala, Honduras, and El Salvador.

Guatemala, Honduras, and El Salvador

These three countries in Central America remain particularly afflicted with the colonial legacy of unequal distribution of wealth. In Guatemala, just 2 percent of the population holds 80 percent of the land; in El Salvador, 1 percent holds 70 percent of the land; and Honduras, which has the least fertile land of the three, has had a similar landholding pattern. The large plantations and ranches on elite-held land produce products for export to the United States and Europe, including timber, bananas, melons, coffee, cotton, tobacco, shrimp, and cattle, which are an important source of national income.

The extreme deprivation experienced by landless farm workers in these three countries has sparked guer-

rilla movements, as mentioned previously. In the 1980s, protests were particularly strong in Guatemala, which has the largest Native American population of the three. The military government, armed through aid programs from the United States intended to fend off communist insurgents, killed thousands of Indian protestors and drove 150,000 into exile in Mexico. Rigoberta Menchu is a Native American woman who lost her family to this conflict and eventually earned the 1992 Nobel Peace Prize for her efforts to stop government violence against her people. Her autobiographical account attracted public attention to the carnage and was important in awakening worldwide concern. Eventually, after a number of regional peacemakers joined Menchu in bringing international pressure to bear, the Guatemalan Peace Accord was signed in September 1996.

The shortage of farmland for the rural poor has been an important impetus to urban migration in Guatemala, Honduras, and El Salvador. As yet, more than half of the people live in rural areas, but cities in the region attracted an estimated 4 million migrants between 1990 and 1998. Most hope to work in *maquiladoras,* but there are usually more migrants than jobs.

Because so much of the land is owned by only a few, poor farmers are forced to use unwise tactics in wrenching enough from the soil to feed their families. In some places farmers have overused chemicals to control weeds

153

and pests. Each year hundreds of children die from allergies and other effects of chemical poisoning. Land management by the elite is also a problem. Clearing enough land for large-scale agriculture and cattle grazing leads to erosion of stupendous proportions. In Honduras, the reservoir for a large hydroelectric dam built only a few years ago has nearly silted up because of clearing on the surrounding land. Electricity output must now be supplemented with generators run on imported oil.

Nicaragua

Until recently, Nicaragua showed a similar pattern of landownership: a tiny elite held the usual monopoly of land, while the mass of laborers lived in poverty. Political upheaval has succeeded in accomplishing some land reform but not yet in creating a healthy economy.

North American investors have had an interest in the coffee and fruit plantations of the Pacific coastal plain since early in this century. When social unrest threatened the export economy, the United States sent in the marines several times in the early part of the twentieth century. This interference helped the Somoza family establish themselves as dictators in the 1930s. The particularly brutal Somoza regime was finally ousted by the Marxist-leaning Sandinista coup d'état of 1979. The Sandinistas, who eventually won several national elections, embarked on a program of land and agricultural reform, redistributing thousands of acres and downplaying ranching. They also improved general basic education and health services. Soon, however, a debilitating war with "rightest" counterinsurgents (Contras) backed by the communist-wary United States during the Reagan administration undid most of the social progress. A trade embargo further contributed to the ruin of the economy. By the end of the 1980s, Nicaragua was one of the poorest nations in the Western Hemisphere. In 1990, a coalition led by Violetta Chamorro defeated the Sandinistas, who had lost popularity due to their own incomplete reform programs, as well as to weariness with the Contra harassment. Subsequent governments continue to find it difficult to bring Nicaragua some measure of prosperity.

The civil conflicts in Central America gave rise to the unusual phenomenon of women engaging in public protest and activist politics. Although progress comes slowly, the more vocal stance of these women has spurred governments to make a more careful accounting of the contributions that women have been making in society all along. Increasingly, studies are revealing that not only do women head many rural households in Central America but they are essential actors in many sectors of the economy. They do many of the most labor-intensive tasks involved in tending animals, soil management, marketing farm products, procuring firewood, and reforestation. Hence, programs to increase entrepreneurial activity or the environmentally sensitive management of forests and agricultural resources are now recognizing that training women as well as men may yield much better results than the old strategy of training men only.

Costa Rica and Belize

Costa Rica and Belize are exceptions to patterns of elite monopoly and mass poverty. The huge disparities in wealth between colonists and laborers did not develop in Costa Rica, chiefly because the fairly small native population died out soon after the conquest. Without a captive labor supply, the European immigrants to Costa Rica set up small but productive farms that they worked themselves as family units, not unlike early North American family farms. Costa Rica's democratic traditions stretch back to the nineteenth century, and it has one of the region's most sound economies and unusually enlightened elected officials. Investment in human resources has been high. Costa Rica has the subregion's highest literacy rates, and on many scales of comparison the country stands out for its high living standards. Thus, Costa Rica has often been hailed as a beacon for the more troubled nations of Central America.

Both Costa Rica and Belize have been leaders in the environmental movement in Central America. They have established wetland parks along the Caribbean coast, encouraging ecotourism, while at the same time paying some attention to its potentially negative environmental side effects. Costa Rica supports scientific research with several international study centers in its central highlands and lowland rain forests.

Belize, formerly British Honduras, was the sole British colonial foothold on the mainland of Central America. Belize is populated by a variety of people who have chosen or been forced to settle there. A group of mixed African slaves and Carib Indians were brought by the British from the island of St. Vincent in the eastern Caribbean in the 1790s. They are known as the Garifuna, or Black Caribs. North American dissidents moved to Belize in the nineteenth century and were joined by Mennonite farmers from the United States and by African-Caribbean people from the islands who now make a living as agricultural workers, subsistence cultivators, or fisherpeople. Most recently, Spanish- and Mayan-speaking refugees from Guatemala and El Salvador have arrived.

Belize was for years a major source of tropical hardwoods used to make fine furniture and dyes. The forests in the northern part of the country are already used up and logging is now extending deep into the moister southern forests. Ecotourism is promoted as an alternative to timber extraction, but it is increasingly apparent that coral reefs and other coastal zone environments are too fragile to sustain continuous use by ecotourism.

Partly in response to a growing realization that all development brings environmental problems, Belize has begun to establish itself as an offshore banking center and place of registry for cargo ships. This activity brings its own hazards, however: Belize may find itself in the position of abetting illegal activities, if not outright international crime, by laundering ill-gotten money.

Panama

Since early Spanish colonial days, Panama has served as a conduit for moving goods between the Caribbean and the Pacific. In the early days, much of the trip was made by mules and other draft animals. Originally part of Colombia, Panama was created as an independent state under pressure from the United States, which, by the 1890s, wanted to finance the construction of a canal that made use of Gatun Lake for part of the route. The Panama Canal was built primarily with West Indian labor and many West Indians stayed, making Panama a distinctly Caribbean place. The country remained a virtual colony of the United States, which managed the canal and maintained a large military presence there. For many years, those Panamanians employed in the Canal Zone or in canal-related occupations lived a way of life that was heavily influenced by U.S. culture and the U.S. economy; Panama is Central America's wealthiest nation and the canal is the reason. Away from the canal, however, poverty is much more common. Corruption linked to the canal and to the international drug trade led the United States to invade Panama in 1989 in order to squelch the illegal activities of a renegade Panamanian general, Manuel Noriega, who had shadowy connections with drug dealing and with U.S. covert operations in the region.

In 1977, under pressure from Panama, the United States agreed to give the canal back to that country in 1999 and remove itself as a dominant presence. Interestingly, this comes at a time when the canal is becoming obsolete. It is no longer big enough to accommodate the huge cargo container ships of the modern era. Although traffic has not yet slowed, it is no longer growing at previous rates. Plans for updating the canal have been delayed by a number of considerations: importantly, there is no alternative route to use during repairs, except around the tip of South America.

A look at the map reveals that Panama runs east-west, with the canal approximately in the center. The plantation, ranching, and fishing economies of the western part of the country are similar to those of Costa Rica and other neighbors. Eastern Panama is remote and not yet much developed; it is occupied by Native American subsistence farmers. The Pan-American Highway is being completed in this region and the road is bringing change; entrepreneurs hope to use the region for timber and cattle ranching.

The Northern Andes and Caribbean Coast

The five countries in the northernmost part of South America share a Caribbean coastline and extend back into a remote interior of wide river basins and humid uplands (Figure 3.20). Three of the countries, the Guianas, have traditional plantation economies reminiscent of the Caribbean and fascinating multicultural societies made up of descendants of African, East Indian, Pakistani, Dutch, French, and English settlers. The other two countries, Venezuela and Colombia, are interesting because in each the course of events has come to be dominated by a single resource: oil in the case of Venezuela, the coca plant in the case of Colombia.

Guyana, French Guiana, and Suriname

To the north of Brazil are the three small countries known collectively as the Guianas. Like the islands of the Caribbean, they were colonized by several West European powers, one still present, two only recently departed. Guyana gained independence from the British in 1966, and Suriname from the Dutch in 1975. French Guiana is now considered part of France. Today, the common colonial heritage is visible both in the economy and the people. Sugar, rice, and banana plantations established by the Europeans in the coastal areas are still economically important, but logging and the mining of gold, diamonds, and bauxite in the resource-rich highlands are now the leading activities. The population descends mainly from laborers who once worked the plantations.

There are two major cultural groups: Africans, brought in as slaves, and South and Southeast Asians, brought in as indentured servants after the abolition of slavery. Many descendants of Asian indentured servants became poor rice farmers or owners of small businesses. Since independence in both Suriname and Guyana, Asians, despite their numbers, have not participated fully in governments that have been dominated by Africans and remnants of the tiny European elite. These governments proved to be corrupt and often violently repressive toward those opposed to their policies, and after decades of political agitation Asian political parties have risen to prominence in both countries. It is uncertain if the Asian parties will be any more responsible. An unusual economic situation prevails in French Guiana, which has strong ties to the European Union through the extensive facilities for the European space program. These space facilities are located in Guiana due to its year-round warm climate and its solid position as an outlying province of France.

155

FIGURE 3.20 The Northern Andes and Caribbean Coast subregion.

Venezuela and Colombia

Venezuela and Colombia have a Spanish colonial heritage. A small but still dominant European political and economic elite lives mainly in the larger cities of the cooler Andean highlands. Both countries have a predominantly mestizo population. In the case of Colombia, mestizos are employed mainly in agriculture, especially on lowland cattle ranches and on coffee plantations in the uplands. In Venezuela they are employed mainly in industries and the service sector in urban areas. A relatively small African population works primarily on the banana plantations of Colombia's western coastal lowlands, in subsistence agriculture, and on sugar plantations along the Caribbean coast. In all countries of this subregion, small indigenous populations survive, mainly in the lowland Orinoco and Amazon interior, engaged in hunting and gathering and subsistence agriculture.

Venezuela has long been one of the wealthier countries in South America, thanks mainly to its oil industry. That country holds a significant portion of American oil deposits, and oil has been the backbone of the economy since the mid-twentieth century. Most of the wealth

generated has been retained within the 20 percent of the population that forms the middle and upper classes, mainly of European descent. Only modest amounts have gone to badly needed improvements in education, transport, and communications infrastructure that would benefit all Venezuelans. Thus, while the capital city of Caracas is bedecked with gleaming skyscrapers, modern freeways, universities for the elite, and lavish monuments to past leaders, it is also surrounded by shantytowns where most people have poor access to clean drinking water and sanitation, and the schools are substandard.

Despite high oil prices in the early 1980s, Venezuela accumulated a large debt, which it planned to pay off with future oil profits. The pitfalls of dependence on a single resource became vividly clear when oil prices slumped in the late 1980s and the country was plunged into a debt crisis. With prices low, Venezuela's debt mushroomed, inflation skyrocketed, and the poverty rate went from the 40 percent typical of the region to an astonishing 70 percent. The government responded with structural adjustment programs that drastically lowered the living standards of urban populations. Violent riots resulted that left up to 2000 dead in 1989. The 1990s have seen several failed military coups, a president impeached for corruption, as well as rising levels of urban violence and drug trafficking.

Colombia has the distinction of being the murder capital of the world, where some 30,000 people every year are killed in an ongoing civil war that has displaced over 1 million people in the past decade. The current wave of violence is part of a long string of conflicts that have arisen out of the inequalities in the country's social order. Colombia is today the world's second largest exporter of coffee and a major exporter of oil and coal, but elites of European descent have reaped most of the profits and have resisted the redistribution of their extensive landholdings. The civil war is being fought between revolutionary guerrilla bands of poor farmers and both the Colombian military and the private armies of the elite.

The current hostilities, while still basically driven by unequal access to wealth, power, and above all land, are complicated by the involvement of all the warring parties in the country's flourishing drug trade. The trade depends on the coca plant, an ancient Andean crop, whose leaves have traditionally been chewed (a mild dose) as a fatigue and hunger suppressant and as an invigorating tonic and a mild mood enhancer. Today, Colombia's location as the Andean nation closest to the major U.S. drug markets makes it an excellent area for processing coca leaves into the much stronger cocaine (a crystalline extract of coca leaves noted for its euphoric, stimulating, and addicting effects). The coca growers are usually very poor farmers in remote areas, who make a somewhat better income from coca than they would from other crops. Most of the profits are reaped by the drug cartels of Cali and Medellín, which have become world famous for their illicit wealth and power, as well as for their bribery, intimidation, and murder of Colombian government officials. Colombia's president, Ernesto Samper, is thought to have received millions from the major drug cartels in return for regulating in their favor, and the military has used its own planes to transport cocaine. Meanwhile, the private armies of the drug cartels fight side by side with the military against guerrillas who are also sustained by the drug trade. The contest is over land, market monopolies, bribery payments, transport routes, and protection from arrest.

The many poor rural Colombians, both coca growers and regular farmers, have suffered the bulk of the casualties and have been effectively walled off from the outside world. The conflict shows no signs of diminishing, as most leaders favoring peace have been killed off and as guerrilla forces have made steady gains in recent years. The U.S. military has become more deeply involved as part of its own "war on drugs." Predictably, in Colombia, as well as in Venezuela and the Guianas, many skilled and educated young people are emigrating abroad to avoid the violence and uncertainty of their home countries.

The Central Andes

The central Andes, containing the countries of Ecuador, Peru, and Bolivia, is the poorest region in Middle and South America but also a place where hopeful signs of change are emerging (Figure 3.21). On the eve of the Spanish conquest this was the home of the Incas, one of the two great civilizations of the region. Their legacy is reflected in the roughly one-half of the population today that is Native American, the largest proportion in South America.

After its fall to the Spanish, the central Andes, like other parts of the New World, went into a long decline; during this time, a tiny elite prospered while the vast majority sank into poverty. Most of the twentieth century has been marked by failed efforts at social change and resultant violence, but now there are important signs of change in this region. Recent years have seen a decline in violence and a rise in the political involvement of the large indigenous population. In exploring the central Andes we will look at three main regions: the economically dynamic coastal lowlands, the poor and largely Native American highlands, and the resource-rich and environmentally threatened Amazonian lowlands.

The coastal lowlands are located only in Ecuador and Peru, as Bolivia is landlocked. Here the population is mainly mestizo and African. The coast is where the largest, most modern and cosmopolitan cities are; they include Lima, Peru's capital, a commercial center and major site of silver production; and Guayaquil, Ecuador's leading industrial center. While the climate is often dry, especially in Peru, irrigation allows plantations and other forms of export agriculture to thrive along the coast. The production of crops like cotton, tobacco, grapes, citrus, apples, and sugarcane has increased dramatically, but food production for local consumption actually declined 14 percent in Peru between 1985 and 1990. Fishing grounds based on the nutrient-rich Peru Current also sustain a vital fishing industry.

Like other parts of Middle and South America, this region has had to tighten its belt in response to massive government debts acquired through unwise borrowing for development. Structural adjustment programs have been imposed that mandate privatization of state-run industries and streamlining of government. The reforms have brought stronger economic growth but also job losses and social turmoil. Prices for gasoline, electricity, and transport have been dramatically increased as the government tries to raise funds to pay off debts—a policy that hurts urban poor people the most even though they are among the least responsible for the debt. In

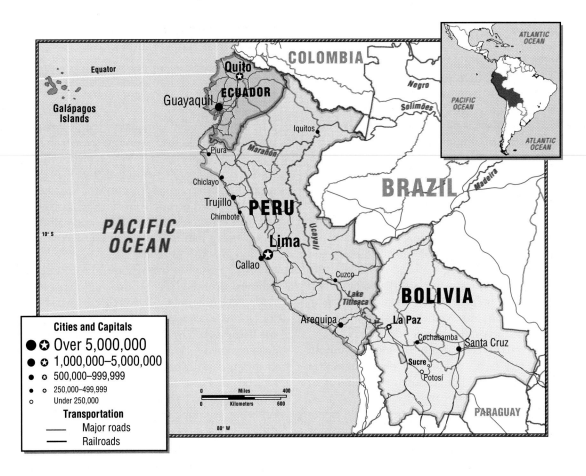

FIGURE 3.21 The Central Andes subregion.

rural coastal areas, SAPs have also removed protections for small-scale farmers, who are now increasingly being pushed out by larger farms and corporations. In Ecuador, protests by working people brought down the government in 1997, and the same might have happened in Peru had it not been for suppression by the military. Nevertheless, the benefits of economic growth and the need to repay debts have kept both countries from changing their policies in response to the unrest.

The highlands are the home of the bulk of the region's indigenous people (see the box "Learning from the Incas"), who for centuries worked on the large haciendas and in the rich mines owned by a small elite class of European descent. Income for most of the Native Americans now comes from subsistence agriculture, sheepherding, and work in mines. Peru extracts copper, lead, and zinc from highland mines; Bolivia mines tin, bauxite, lead, and zinc.

The Amazonian lowlands have traditionally been the home of scattered groups of indigenous people. In recent years this region has been strained by rapid and often destructive development of natural resources. At the forefront of this process are oil and mining companies. Leaky oil pipelines have slowly released amounts of oil that dwarf even the largest offshore spills, and mining processes that use cyanide, a powerful poison, have spoiled entire river systems. Roads built to facilitate resource extraction have opened up this region to massive waves of migration from the highlands and coastal lowlands, and also have brought diseases that decimate local populations.

In the late twentieth century, different strategies of dealing with gross social inequalities have been tried, with varying degrees of success and failure. Bolivia was the first to attempt reform when the government took over the tin mines in the **altiplano** in the 1950s, after a revolution in which the miners' unions played a key role. For several decades, wages were higher and conditions better, but then world prices for tin declined because plastic packaging replaced tin cans at the same time that tin mining intensified across the globe. One result is that the drug trade replaced tin as the major export sector in Bolivia. As in Colombia, the military and the government are extensively involved in the drug trade, even though they publicly condemn it.

In the 1970s, Peru's then military dictatorship sought to improve the lives of indigenous peoples by transforming the haciendas of the elite into state-run

AT THE LOCAL SCALE

Learning from the Incas: Agricultural Restoration in the Peruvian Highlands

Around the ancient Inca capital of Cuzco, in the Peruvian highlands, terraces and canals once supported crops that fed hundreds of thousands of people on what would otherwise have been barren mountain slopes. Much of this infrastructure still remains but was not being used. Some is now being restored, however, thanks mainly to more than two decades of careful research on the part of the British rural development specialist and archaeologist Ann Kendall. Kendall recognized that the Incan agricultural technologies were more advanced than had been thought. The construction of terraces, for example, allows for efficient recy-

cling of nutrients, making high-yield organic cultivation possible. In particular, Kendall found that the Incan use of clay as a flexible, semiwet sealant on both terraces and canals was extremely well adapted to the earthquake-prone environment of the Peruvian highlands because it doesn't break the way concrete does, and cracks tend to reseal themselves. So far, reviving these traditional methods has proved highly productive, allowing some highland peoples who had migrated to lowland cities to return home and take up farming. One canal and its associated terrace system can irrigate enough land to support more than 2000 people.

communes. The experiment soon proved a failure, and the communal lands were eventually redistributed to the poor farmers themselves. After enduring several years of guerrilla insurgency in the highlands, quelled for the moment now, the Peruvian government has avoided reigniting past grievances by supplying highland communities with subsidies and protections from the harsher aspects of SAP reforms that are straining the lowlands.

In Ecuador, the government has not yet challenged elite dominance as in Peru, but a stronger challenge to the status quo may be emerging from the indigenous peoples of the highlands. Based in the highlands, CONAIE, a federation representing all of the country's indigenous groups, has been a strong force fighting for the land rights of Native Americans. CONAIE's support was central to the success of the protests against SAPs, which brought down Ecuador's government in 1997, as members of the federation blocked off roads to many remote highland areas.

The Southern Cone

The countries of Chile, Paraguay, Uruguay, and Argentina have diverse physical environments but remarkably similar histories (Figure 3.22). Although the Southern Cone received little attention from Europe during the time of the Spanish Empire, immigrants arrived in large numbers from Europe in the late nineteenth and early twentieth centuries. The immigrants swamped the surviving Native American populations, except in Paraguay, the only country of the four that has a predominantly mestizo population. Europeans, mainly Germans, Italians, and Irish, were drawn by the temperate climates and by the opportunities available in economies that periodically were especially dynamic, due mainly to their raw materials export sectors. However, when the Southern Cone economies have taken a turn for the worse, social and political upheaval have resulted, often with disastrous consequences.

Indian women lay stones for a road on the outskirts of La Paz in exchange for food. [Stuart Franklin/Magnum Photos.]

FIGURE 3.22 The Southern Cone subregion.

Agriculture has long been a leading economic sector in the Southern Cone. The primary zone is the **pampas,** an area of extensive grasslands and highly fertile soils in northern Argentina and Uruguay. The main products are cattle, for which the region is famous, and grain. Sheep raising continues to dominate Argentina's drier, less fertile southern zone, Patagonia. On the other side of the Andes, in Chile's central zone, the Mediterranean climate supports large-scale fruit production that caters to the winter markets of the Northern Hemisphere. Chile also benefits from considerable mineral wealth, especially in copper.

Although the agricultural and mineral exports of the Southern Cone have created considerable wealth, dependence on these exports has also resulted in instability. Fluctuating prices for raw materials on the global market can send Southern Cone economies into a sudden downturn. This was a major impetus for the push to increase industrial development that occurred in the mid-twentieth century. At first, the new industries were based on processing of agricultural and mineral raw materials, but industry subsequently diversified into a wide range of manufacturing activities. Most were import substitution industries, driven and supported by state policies. However, as discussed earlier, industry never became a leading sector for the region, mainly due to inefficiencies, corruption, and local markets that were too small to support the local industries that, in turn, were not good enough to compete on the global scale.

Given the Southern Cone's often volatile economies, it is not surprising that the distribution of wealth and the principles of economic policy have been a major source of conflict for decades. Despite their considerable resources, these countries have always had substantial impoverished populations. During the mid-twentieth-century industrialization phase (1940s), popular political movements used the region's fairly well-established democratic traditions to demand more economic equality, and each country developed mechanisms for redistributing wealth that did alleviate poverty to some degree: government subsidies for jobs, food, rent, basic health care, and transport, for example. However, when global markets for raw materials produced a downturn for the region in the 1970s, people clamored for more fundamental changes, at times along socialist, communist, or trade unionist lines. In response, militaries, with the support of the elite, took over governments and waged bloody campaigns of repression against the working class and the socialist and communist opposition, in what came to be called the "dirty war." In the years of state-sanctioned terror that followed, 3000 people were killed in Chile and 14,000 to 18,000 in Argentina, and tens of thousands more were tortured for their political beliefs. At the same time, the International Monetary Fund was applying pressure for repayment of the massive debts accumulated under both civilian and military governments. This effectively shifted countries away from wealth redistribution policies and toward free market economic reform.

This process began in Chile in the early 1970s under the military dictatorship of Pinochet; but it did not really get under way in Argentina and Uruguay until the late 1980s and early 1990s, just at the time that a wave of democratization swept through the region. However, popular resistance is forcing these governments to moderate their programs somewhat, as the sale of state-run industries combined with cuts in government payrolls has thrown hundreds of thousands out of work. Meanwhile, cuts in social spending have made life much harder for the increasing number of impoverished people. Ar-

gentina, in particular, has seen serious resistance to further free market reforms: general strikes have periodically crippled the country, and workers from a wide range of industries have shut down plants, blocked roadways, and generally demanded a change of course.

As mentioned earlier, Mercosur (see Figure 3.12) may provide part of the solution to these problems by linking the rather small markets of all Southern Cone countries, plus Brazil, into a single common market. A larger market may help raise the general level of prosperity by nurturing more efficient, well-run industries. Nevertheless, as always, there will be winners and losers. For this reason, Chilean grain farmers object to common market integration for fear of competition from cheaper Argentine and Uruguayan wheat and corn, while Chilean fruit growers and winemakers see greater access to Southern Cone and Brazilian markets as beneficial. On the whole, however, Mercosur seems likely to help economies achieve greater stability. In addition to nurturing more competitive industries, the increased trade between the countries of the region may provide a more reliable alternative to dependence on often unstable global markets.

Brazil

It is hard to know just how to think about Brazil. The observant visitor is quickly caught up in its physical complexity and in the richly exuberant, multicultural quality of Brazilian society (Figure 3.23). Brazil is large, about the same size as the United States; but its landscapes, more than those of North America, show the environmental effects of both colonialism and recent rapid economic development. And the people living in these landscapes reflect the fact that this is a highly stratified society with a small, very wealthy elite, a modest but rising middle class, and a huge majority that live in poverty or just barely above the poverty line. Many dire social problems, such as high crime rates and thousands of abandoned children, spring from the gross inequity in well-being. Travelers find themselves at once caught up and delighted by the flamboyant creativity and elegance of the people but sobered by the obvious hardships under which both the land and the people labor.

Despite Brazil's size, its two main physical features are fairly easy to conceptualize. The huge Amazon Basin in the northern equatorial zone covers about two-thirds of the country. It is widest in the western interior and gathers thousands of streams flowing down from the Andes and the Guiana and Brazilian highlands to form a giant stream that is miles across when it reaches the Atlantic. The other, southern third of the country is occupied by the Brazilian Highlands, a variegated plateau that rises abruptly in an escarpment just

FIGURE 3.23 The Brazil subregion.

back of the Atlantic seaboard 500 miles (800 kilometers) south of the mouth of the Amazon. The northern portion of the plateau is arid; the southern part receives considerably more rainfall. Settlement in Brazil is concentrated in a narrow band along the Atlantic seaboard in the northeast and south through Salvador. Settlement extends deeper inland at Rio de Janiero and farther south through São Paulo, Curitiba, and Portô Alegre, in Brazil's zone of temperate climate.

The Brazilian economy is the largest in Latin America, the eighth largest in the world; and the resources available for development in Brazil are the envy of most nations. Local oil now provides for 60 percent of Brazil's needs, and more has recently been discovered west of Manaus in the Amazon. Minerals—gold, silver, precious gems—have been important since colonial days; but it is industrial minerals—titanium, manganese, chromite, tungsten, and especially iron ore—that are today the most valuable. They are found in many parts of the plateau. Hydroelectric power is widely available for development because of the many rivers and natural waterfalls that descend off the plateau. There has been large-scale agriculture in Brazil for 400 years: in the south, European-style farming of fruits and vegetables; in the northeast, plantations, primarily of sugar, tobacco, cotton, cassava, and oil palm; in the interior dry zones, ranching. Agriculture has some potential to expand; but most of the available land is in the tropical north where soils are fragile. Using the land for agriculture there requires special and sustained attention, and more investment than has been anticipated by recent entrepreneurs.

Brazil is the most highly industrialized country in South America. Most of the industry—steel, motor vehicles, aeronautics, appliances, chemicals, textiles, and shoes—is concentrated in a triangle formed by the huge southeastern cities of São Paulo, Rio de Janiero, and Belo Horizonte. Until the 1990s, the vast majority of Brazil's mining and industrial operations were developed with state capital, and many are still government owned and run. Recently elected Brazilian governments have opted to privatize many government industries and businesses (television stations, power plants, mines, and agricultural land) in an effort to make them more efficient and profitable; and many of them have been sold to foreign investors. In 1997 alone, direct foreign investors spent $23 billion on Brazilian properties; but these sales may be hurting Brazil in the long run because the properties are going at bargain basement prices.

Hyperinflation (running as high as 2000 percent per year) characterized the Brazilian economy for many years. This has made the development of a middle class particularly difficult because their savings continuously lose value as their living costs rise. After 1964, prices rose so fast that people became geared to a situation in which "things" would be worth more the next week than they would be today; hence a buying spree seemed perpetually the wisest course of action. Buying on credit was especially wily because payment time came in the future when the currency would be worth even less. Some stores started taking postdated checks to attract buyers who did not have credit cards. Hyperinflation led Brazil, as a nation, to run up huge debts in the 1980s and early 1990s, just as its private citizens did on credit cards. President Fernando Cardoso, elected in 1994, developed many successful anti-inflationary mea-

sures. In addition to adopting belt-tightening policies, he created a new, stable currency, the real, whose value is tied to the U.S. dollar. The inflation rate was just 5 percent in 1997.

Urbanization

Brazil has a number of large and well-known cities: Rio de Janeiro, São Paulo, Belo Horizonte, Salvador, Recife, Fortaleza, Belém, Manaus, and Brasília. All but Manaus, Brasília, and Belo Horizonte are on the Atlantic perimeter of the country. During the global depression of the 1930s, farm workers throughout the country began migrating into urban areas as world prices for Brazil's agricultural exports (jute, sugar, coffee, cacao, rubber) fell. By 1960, Brazil was 22 percent urban. Since then, efforts to modernize and mechanize agriculture have reduced labor requirements further. Agricultural change pushed people off the land; incipient industrialization pulled them into the cities. During and after the 1960s, huge factories were built with government money. Brazil's competitive edge globally was its cheap labor; and the military governments of that time thought the country's industries could continue to pay very low wages for some time because there was such a surplus of workers drawn from the low-wage countryside.

By 1995, 77 percent of Brazil's population was urban and at least one-third of the urban population, many of them by then unemployed, were living in favelas, the Brazilian urban shantytowns. The poverty in the very hardest hit cities in the northeast rivals that of Haiti, the poorest country in the Americas. Brazilians, however, are intrepid at finding ways to make life worth living. Favela dwellers are famous for their efforts to upgrade their communities through collective action. An example is a religious movement, known as Umbanda, that thrives in the coastal cities from Fortaleza to Rio. Umbanda groups are centered around a male or female spiritual leader. The leader welcomes celebrants into a neighborhood center and evokes the spirits to help people cope with health problems and the ordinary stresses and strains of a life of urban poverty. Drumming, dancing, spirit possession, and psychological support are the central focus. Umbanda grew out of an older African-Brazilian belief system called Condomble, and similar movements are to be found elsewhere in the Americas, including the Caribbean and the United States and Canada. In Brazil, Umbanda appeals to an increasingly wide spectrum of the populace. There are many centers with adherents of different European backgrounds and Native Americans as well.

Rio de Janiero and other cities in Brazil's industrial heartland, the southeast, have districts that are elegant

The two women in lace shawls are in a trance state, having been possessed by the spirits of Oxala and Yemanja during a Batuque ritual. They are greeted and supported by mediums called *fihas de santos*. Batuque ceremonies, like Umbanda and Condomble ceremonies, use mesmerizing drum rhythms to invoke various spirits, including Christian saints. These ceremonies regularly unite large groups of people in a common uplifting experience. [Jacques Jangoux, Brazil.]

and futuristic showplaces, resplendent with the very latest technology and graced with buildings that would put New York, Singapore, or even Tokyo to shame. The stores are filled with artistically designed consumer goods at attractive prices for those with desirable foreign currency. Brazilian planners now acknowledge that, in the rush to develop the most modern of urban landscapes, developers neglected to underwrite the parallel development of a sufficient urban infrastructure. In short supply are sanitation and water systems, up-to-date electrical wiring, transportation facilities, schools, housing, and medical facilities—all necessary to sustain modern business, industry, and a socially healthy urban population. But the Brazilians should not be overly criticized for what in hindsight seems like an obvious error. During the 1970s and 1980s, many world financial institutions thought that building the material accouterments of development—**growth poles**—would start a chain reaction. The office buildings, factories, and shopping centers would efficiently leak prosperity down to the poor, generate the tax money to upgrade the infrastructure, and also send immediate generous profits to the rich. Only very recently are all parties coming to recognize that developing human capital through education, health services, and community development, whether privately or publicly funded, is a primary part of building strong economies.

Brasília

Brasília, the new capital, is one of the most intriguing examples of a growth pole, of the effort to lead development by constructing a spectacular urban environment. Built in the state of Goiás, Brasília lies about 600 miles inland from the glamorous old administrative center of Rio de Janiero. The capital was built in this location for the avowed purpose of encouraging the development of the western highland territories and then, eventually, of Amazonia. The scholar William Schurz has an alternative explanation: moving the capital so far away from the centers of Brazilian society was the most efficient way to trim the badly swollen and highly inefficient government bureaucracy. In any case, the city was designed and built in about three years, beginning in 1957. Symbolism figured more prominently than practicality in the design, which called for the city to be laid out to look from the air like a swept-wing jet plane. There was to be no central business district, but rather shopping zones in each residential area and one large mall. Pedestrian traffic was limited to a few grand promenades; people were expected to move about in cars and taxis. Public buildings were designed for maximum visual and ceremonial drama.

After people had spent several decades actually using this urban landscape, all sorts of interesting things had happened to the formal design. At the parliament, legislative staff and messengers created footpaths where they needed them—through flowerbeds and (with little steps notched in the dirt) up and over landscaped banks—to efficiently connect the administration buildings, bypassing the sweeping esplanades. Commercial districts were retrofitted in and around hotel complexes. Urban workers who couldn't afford taxi fares wore direct footpaths across great green swards of grass. Little hints of the informal economy that characterizes life in the old cities of Brazil began to show up—a vendor here, a manicurist there. And the shantytowns, which the planners had tried hard to eliminate, began to rise relentlessly around the perimeter. Today, life in the shantytowns is so much more interesting than in the sterile environment of Brasília that tour buses take visitors to see them and shop there.

Curitiba

The southern Brazilian city of Curitiba, capital of the grain-producing state of Paraná, is gaining international renown for its environmentally friendly urban planning. Like most other Brazilian cities, Curitiba has mushroomed, doubling its population in just 20 years to over 1.3 million people. Unlike many American cities, North and South, undergoing rapid growth, Curitiba has carefully oriented its expansion around an integrated public transport system. Minibuses bring people from their neighborhoods to terminals where they meet express buses to all parts of the city. The wide expanses of modern urban environments and the lack of good, affordable transportation systems are typical hindrances to the world's urban poor. Being able to get to work quickly and cheaply has helped Curitiba's poor to find and keep jobs.

The city's streets and its many parks and green spaces are kept spotlessly clean and decorated with flowers. The city also has a decentralized public health service. A trash recycling program encourages people in the informal economy to collect specific kinds of trash and sell them to recycling companies.

One goal is to keep migrants from swamping Curitiba's well-designed, environmentally sensitive urban environment with shantytowns. The city first tries to stem the flow by offering free bus tickets back home to new migrants. Twenty-five thousand people have used the tickets. And to accommodate those migrants who come to take what are often short-term jobs in Curitiba's industrial sector, the city is building rural satellite towns, *vilas rural*, where people can live and maintain their agricultural skills by farming small plots when they are in between industrial jobs. In this way, they will be able to feed themselves and possibly some urbanites as well. Financed by the World Bank and the Inter-American Development Bank, 5 *vilas rural* have been built, 15 are under construction, and 60 more are planned. The plan is to accommodate a significant proportion of Paraná's landless farmers in these urban fringe communities, where the advantages of rural and urban life can be enjoyed by those of meager means.

REFLECTIONS ON MIDDLE AND SOUTH AMERICA

Middle and South America were the first regions in the world to undergo European colonialism. In a number of ways, European colonialism in the Americas launched the modern global economic system. It was in the Americas that large-scale extractive practices were inaugurated. Raw materials were shipped at low prices to distant locales where they were turned into high-priced products, while the profits went to Europe. Local people were diverted from producing food and other necessities for themselves to working as low-paid or enslaved labor in the fields and mines. The rules governing private property were set down in societies that had long practiced communal land rights. In the process, the landscapes and settlement patterns of the Americas were reorganized as the focus shifted from producing for local and regional economies to producing for global markets.

After the colonial era, this region continued to serve as a testing ground for economic theories both socialist and capitalist. Mechanized agriculture for export, government-sponsored industrialization to create jobs and to produce substitutes for imports, rural-to-urban migration as a solution to rural poverty, government borrowing for large-scale development projects, broad government subsidies to keep the poor from revolting—all were tried out in Middle and South America. When these measures resulted in catastrophic debt rather than economic growth, belt-tightening structural adjustment policies were tried out as a cure for indebtedness and as a way to quickly reorganize economies and eliminate graft.

Now there are many indications that times are improving for this part of the globe. There is increasing recognition that to be judged successful, development must first change the lives of the majority for the better. Middle and South Americans are beginning to build on their strengths and to invent solutions to problems common in many places around the world. Curitiba, Brazil, seeks simple but humane solutions to rapid urbanization and to the pollution and social disruption it brings. Degraded agricultural lands are being rehabilitated in the Peruvian highlands by the revival of ancient practices. Environmental groups are addressing the root causes of deforestation—demands for forest products in distant markets and unequal distribution of lands and resources at home. And regional trade organizations are emerging with enough strength to negotiate for the good of the region and to fend off self-interested rich outsiders.

As you read other chapters of this book, it might be useful to reflect on the geographic issues of Middle and South America discussed here. For example, notice how Europe's situation today—its wealth, its position as a world leader, and its emerging commitment to help former colonial possessions—is related in part to its colonial experiences, which began in the Americas. You will see that Africa and Asia have experienced some conditions under colonial rule similar to those in the Americas, and more recently they also have felt the sting of SAPs. Southeast Asia, Australia, New Zealand, and Oceania, too, have had comparable experiences as colonies; but in recent decades their "colonizers" have included wealthy Asian capitalists. In the former Soviet Union and Central Asia, outside investors intent on exploiting oil and forest resources may be even more voracious than the conquistadors and their successors once were in the Americas.

165

Selected Themes and Concepts

1. Mountains and volcanoes often form at **subduction zones,** where the edge of one tectonic plate plunges below the edge of another. A long spine of mountains runs down the western edge of Middle and South America, produced by the subduction of three eastward-moving plates—the Pacific, Nazca, and Cocos—under the three westward-moving American plates.

2. There are four main **temperature-altitude zones** commonly used to describe climates in Middle and South America. They are, in order of rising altitude, *tierra caliente* (the "hot lands"), *tierra templada* (the "temperate lands"), *tierra fria* (the "cool lands"), and *tierra helada* (the "frozen lands").

3. The conquest of Middle and South America by the Spanish and Portuguese transformed life in the region. Much of the Native American population died of disease, and new populations were introduced from Europe, Africa, and Asia. During the colonial period, a minority of European descent controlled wealth and power in the region.

4. As a result of conquest and colonization, the region of Middle and South America is now one of cultural complexity. Native American culture remains particularly strong in the highlands of Middle and South America and in the Amazon and Central American lowlands. Many different European cultures, but especially those of Spain and Portugal, have blended with strong cultural strains imported from Africa and with Native American cultures to create a mosaic of **Creole** cultures. South Asian indentured labor brought new influences in the nineteenth and twentieth centuries, and recently East Asian investors and industrialists have joined the cultural mix.

5. **Rural-to-urban migration** has fed the rapid growth of cities in the twentieth century. There are "push" and "pull" reasons for migration. **Push** factors—like loss of agricultural jobs, lack of educational facilities, and rising poverty—impel people to leave the countryside. **Pull** factors—like new opportunities in industry or domestic work or the chance for an education—attract people to the cities.

6. In developing countries, often one city becomes the focus of industrial development and migration. As a result, it grows rapidly to a size much larger than all other cities in the country and becomes the seat of wealth and power. Such cities, called **primate cities,** draw invest-

ment, government services, and talented people away from other cities in the country.

7. Cities are concentrated along coastal zones, with only a few in lowland interiors. Some cities are in upland and highland regions in Mexico and in Central and South America.

8. Disparity in the distribution of income and wealth is more severe in this region than elsewhere on earth, even though this region is not the poorest region overall. Native Americans and other people of color tend to be the poorest.

9. The **extended family** is the basic social institution of Middle and South America. In this region, family members have distinct roles defined by gender. *Marianismo* is a set of values that dictates the behavior of women, who are expected to remain mostly in the home to serve the needs of husband and family. Men measure themselves by the model of *machismo,* which recognizes manliness in the ability to father children, to be master of one's household, and to be an engaging raconteur in the male community.

10. **Liberation theology,** a movement within the Roman Catholic Church, encourages the poor to organize to change their own lives and promotes social and economic reform. **Evangelical Protestantism** is the fastest-growing religious movement in the region. The movement preaches the "gospel of success" to the poor: a life dedicated to Christ will result in prosperity of the body and soul.

11. Since early colonial times, the economies of Middle and South American have been **extractive,** that is, based on the export of unprocessed agricultural and mineral materials.

12. The countries of the region have experimented with different strategies for encouraging economic development. To encourage industrialization, some countries adopted **import substitution** policies. State-owned industries, protected by tariffs on competing imports, tried to fulfill consumer demands. In the 1970s, countries borrowed billions of dollars to fund development projects, such as hydroelectric dams, roads, and mechanized agriculture. When development failed to produce income, countries defaulted on their debts, leading to a **debt crisis.** Major lending institutions imposed **structural adjustment programs (SAPs)** that required debtor countries to lay off government employees, cut back on social spending, and privatize national industries.

13. During the colonial period, intraregional trade was discouraged, which inhibited economic development. Now regional trade agreements, such as **Mercosur,** are breaking down trade barriers among member countries, offering hope for expanded, regionally integrated economic growth.

14. After a history of authoritarian and military rule, all countries in Middle and South America except Cuba now have democratically elected governments. Democracy remains fragile, and corruption continues to be a problem.

15. The region of Middle and South America was one of the first to alert the world to the dangers of environmental deterioration. Deforestation, erosion, loss of species diversity, and urban air pollution are among the environmental issues raised in this region.

Selected Readings

Anderson, Arthur J. O., and Charles E. Dibble, eds. *The War of Conquest—How It Was Waged Here in Mexico: The Aztecs' Own Story as Given to Fr. Bernardino de Sahagun.* Salt Lake City: University of Utah Press, 1978.

Blouet, Brian W., and Oldwyn M. Blouet. *Latin America and the Caribbean—A Systematic and Regional Survey,* 3rd ed. New York: Wiley, 1997.

Butzer, Karl W. The Americas before and after 1492: An introduction of current geographical research. In *Annals of the AAG* 82 (1992): 345–368.

Chaney, Elsa M., and Mary Garcia Castro, eds. *Muchachas No More—Household Workers in Latin America and the Caribbean.* Philadelphia: Temple University Press, 1989.

Chant, Sylvia, ed. *Gender and Migration in Developing Countries.* London: Belhaven Press, 1992.

Clawson, David L. *Latin America and the Caribbean Lands and People.* Dubuque, IA: Wm. C. Brown, 1997.

Cravey, Altha J. *Women and Work in Mexico's Maquiladoras.* Lanham, MD: Rowan and Littlefield, 1998.

Denevan, William M. The pristine myth: The landscape of the Americas in 1492. *Annals of the AAG* 82 (1992): 369–385.

Hansis, Randall. *The Latin Americans: Understanding Their Legacy.* New York: McGraw-Hill, 1997.

Hays-Mitchell, Maureen. Street vending in Peruvian cities: The spatio-temporal behavior of *ambulantes. Professional Geographer* 46 (1994): 425–438.

Keeling, David J. *Buenos Aires: Global Dreams, Local Crises.* New York: Wiley, 1996.

Klak, Thomas. Globalization, neo-liberalism and economic change in Central America and the Caribbean. In *Latin America 2000: Globalization and Modernity,* ed. Robert A. Gwynne and Cristóbal Kay. London: Edward Arnold, 1999.

MacDonald, Gordon J., Daniel L. Nielson, and Marc A. Stern, eds. *Latin American Environmental Policy in International Perspective.* Boulder, CO: Westview Press, 1997.

Meyerson, Julia. *Tambo Life in an Andean Village.* Austin: University of Texas Press, 1990.

Olmos, Margarite Fernandez, and Lizabeth Paravisini-Gebert, eds. *Sacred Possessions: Vodou, Santeria, Obeah, and the Caribbean.* New Brunswick, NJ: Rutgers University Press, 1997.

Parker, Christian. *Popular Religion and Modernization in Latin America: A Different Logic.* Maryknoll, NY: Orbis Books, 1996.

Patai, Daphne. *Brazilian Women Speak: Contemporary Life Stories.* New Brunswick, NJ: Rutgers University Press, 1988.

Rabinovitch, Jonas, and Josef Leitman. Urban planning in Curitiba. *Scientific American,* March 1996, pp. 46–53.

Rengert, George. *The Geography of Illegal Drugs.* Boulder, CO: Westview Press, 1996.

Richardson, Bonham C. *The Caribbean in the Wider World 1492–1992.* Cambridge: Cambridge University Press, 1992.

Sauer, Carl Ortwin. *The Early Spanish Main.* Berkeley: University of California Press, 1966.

Stewart, Douglas Ian. *After the Trees: Living on the Transamazon Highway.* Austin: University of Texas Press, 1994.

Turpin, Jennifer, and Lois Ann Lorentzen. *The Gendered New World Order.* London: Routledge, 1996.

Watts, David. *The West Indies Patterns of Development, Culture and Environmental Change Since 1492.* Cambridge: Cambridge University Press, 1987.

Weatherford, Jack. *Indian Givers: How the Indians of the Americas Transformed the World.* New York: Crown, 1988.

EUROPE

INTRODUCTION TO EUROPE

The Italian journalist Luigi Barzini refers to Europe as those "venerable and illustrious countries occupying the jagged rump of Asia, occasionally pecking at each other like irritable hens." Over the last 500 years, Europeans managed to colonize much of the world, but could not get along back home. The map of Europe today shows many countries, each with its own language and strong identity and each occupying a relatively small space. Until recently, the cultural and political complexity of this region led to almost continuous conflict. Centuries of brutal skirmishes in countless locales across the continent culminated during the twentieth century in two world wars and multiple genocides. This unfathomable bloodshed was followed by nearly 50 years of hostilities known as the **cold war.** During this period, the western part of Europe and the United States—"the West"—faced off against the Soviet Union and its eastern European allies—"the East"—in a battle of ideologies. The West espoused versions of free market capitalism and democracy, and the East centrally planned economies and socialism. Each tried to win nonaligned nations in Latin America, Asia, and Africa to its side.

Now Barzini's "irritable hens" seem to have found a lasting basis for peace: a workable economic union, maybe even one day political union. Will Europe succeed in its current efforts to unite in what is known formally as the European Union (EU)? Can Europe's scrapping culture groups find common ground at last? Analysts differ; a number of outcomes are possible.

The Hungarian writer, humorist, and self-professed anthropologist Dork Zygotian (probably a pseudonym) assesses the prospects of European union from the perspective of a sausage lover. Zygotian writes that when you bite into a Hungarian sausage (*kolbasz*), "great torrents of paprika colored grease and juice should explode into the atmosphere around you. If you eat more than two, you should expect to bite on some piece of bone or possibly find a tooth or hair sometime during your meal. There will be a large yellow gelatinous bit somewhere in your sausage that you should not be able to identify." This is all part of the tasty Hungarian *kolbasz* experience.

But now there is talk that Hungary, long part of the East, will soon be joining the EU, and Zygotian is concerned about the impact such membership will have on his country's sausages, which he rates as Europe's best. He fears that overzealous EU standards of cleanliness and purity will kill the special flavors of Hungarian sausages. Worse, "Eurofication" (his term)

may well leave Hungarians unable to afford their beloved *kolbasz*. Prices in the small, poorer countries are likely to rise to match those of wealthy Germany, France, the Netherlands, and Switzerland.

Maybe sausage lover Zygotian is kidding, but this idea that European unification will erase distinguishing cultural features, encourage boring homogenization, and even diminish well-being comes up seriously again and again. And often the "Euro-skeptics" lack Zygotian's good humor. In this chapter, the geography of Europe is examined in light of two recent significant changes in internal European relationships: the demise of the Soviet Union (accompanied by the end of the cold war), and the steady progress toward European economic union.

Themes to Look for

As you read this chapter, be alert for certain themes that appear repeatedly:

1. Europe's prosperity is due in part to the many benefits it has obtained—and still obtains—from its access to peoples and resources across the globe.

2. European governments play an active role in shaping the economy and city environments, including housing, education, health care, transportation, and overall human well-being. However, there is regional variation in social philosophies and in the degree to which services are provided.

3. The lure of greater prosperity is drawing the countries of Western Europe into union and the countries of Eastern Europe into closer association with Western Europe.

4. Despite increasing union, there are counter-tendencies that work toward disunion: increasing national identity, wary attitudes toward outsiders, and wide differences in economic development and in levels of well-being.

5. European workers are facing increasing competition from workers in developing parts of the world.

6. Europe's dense population and its high rates of consumption are producing ever more worrisome environmental problems. Environmental activism is growing in Europe.

Terms to Be Aware Of

Because important realignments are taking place in Europe, special care is needed in designating the various parts of the region. In this book, Europe is divided into subregions in following way. **North Europe** includes

Iceland, Denmark (including Greenland and the Faroe Islands), Sweden, Norway, Finland, Estonia, Latvia, and Lithuania. **West Europe** includes the United Kingdom, the Republic of Ireland, France, Belgium, Luxembourg, the Netherlands, Germany, Switzerland, and Austria. **South Europe** includes Portugal, Spain, Italy, and Greece. **East and Central Europe,** the largest subregion, includes Poland, the Czech Republic, Slovakia, Hungary, Albania, Bulgaria, Romania, Ukraine, Moldova, and the countries once known as Yugoslavia: Slovenia, Croatia, Bosnia/Herzegovina, Macedonia, Montenegro, and Serbia. The last two now call themselves Yugoslavia. The actual physical location—east, west, north, south—is less important in our subregional scheme than other features like historical, economic, political, and cultural alignments. For example, the countries lying between the Adriatic and the Black Sea (often called the Balkans in the past) are not considered part of South Europe, despite their southerly location, because their cultural history and recent political experience as communist countries have linked them more to East and Central Europe, which is the designation they prefer.

In this book, I have included Estonia, Latvia, Lithuania, Poland, Ukraine, Moldova, Romania, and Bulgaria in Europe; all were recently in the Russian sphere of influence. Some of the countries I have included in East and Central Europe may eventually become members of the EU, but all are sufficiently European culturally and politically to be included in the region.

For convenience, I occasionally use the term *Western Europe* to refer to all the countries that were not part of the experiment with communism in the Soviet Union and Yugoslavia. That is, **Western Europe** will be used for the combined subregions of North Europe (except Estonia, Latvia, and Lithuania), West Europe (except former East Germany), and South Europe. **Eastern Europe** will be used to designate all the countries once part of, or allied with, the former Soviet Union, including those once a part of the former Yugoslavia.

PHYSICAL PATTERNS

Europe is a region of peninsulas upon peninsulas. The entire European region is one giant peninsula extending off the Eurasian continent, and the whole of its very long coastline is itself festooned with peninsular appendages, large and small. Norway and Sweden share one of the bigger appendages, and Norway bris-

tles with hundreds of little peninsulas. In between them are the deep glacier-gouged river mouths called **fiords** for which Norway is so well known. The Iberian Peninsula (shared by Portugal and Spain), Italy, and Greece are other examples of large peninsulas with their own small peninsulas.

All these many fingers jutting into the oceans and seas mean that the warm air blowing in from the ocean penetrates deeply into the landmass. These complex interconnections with the surrounding seas are one reason that the European continent, as a whole, has a relatively mild climate despite its northerly location.

Landforms

Although European landforms are fairly complex, the basic pattern is not hard to learn. The four components are **mountains, uplands, lowlands** (plains and valleys), and **rivers.** Have a look at the map on pages 168–169 and notice first the gold color associated with mountains. You will see a network of mountains that was formed primarily as the result of pressure from the collision of the African Tectonic Plate moving north and the Eurasian Plate moving to the southeast. Europe lies on the westernmost extension of the Eurasian Plate. Europe's largest mountain chain stretches west to east through the middle of the continent, from southern France through Austria and curving southeast into Romania. The Alps are the highest and most central part of this formation. South of this main formation, mountains extend into the peninsulas of Iberia and Italy, and along the Adriatic through Greece. The northernmost mountainous formation is shared by Scotland, Norway, and Sweden. These mountains are old (about the age of the Appalachians in North America) and worn down by glaciers.

A band of low-lying hills and plateaus extends northward from the central mountain zone. These are **uplands,** the term used to describe the transition zone between mountains and lowlands (or plains). This area, crossed by many useful rivers and holding valuable minerals, is the location of many of Europe's industrial cities and densely occupied rural areas. These uplands gradually descend northward into the North European Plain.

The North European Plain is the most extensive landform in Europe. It begins along the Atlantic coast in western France and stretches in a wide band around the north flank of the main European peninsula, reaching across the English Channel and North Sea to take in southern England in the British Isles, southern Sweden, and a part of southern Finland. The plain continues east through Poland and then broadens to the south and north to take in all the land east to the Ural Mountains. The coastal zones of this plain are densely

The Pannonian (or Hungarian) Plain, which is surrounded by mountain ranges, is another of the lowlands of Central Europe. [Mac Goodwin.]

occupied all the way east through Poland. Much of the coast is low lying. In countries such as the Netherlands, people over the last thousand years have transformed the natural seaside marshes and vast river deltas into farmland, pastures, and urban areas by building dikes and draining the land with wind-powered pumps.

The rivers of Europe (see the map on pages 168–169) have aided human use of the continent for thousands of years. As might be expected in such a humid area, there are a number of large rivers linking interior Europe to the surrounding seas. Many of these rivers are navigable well into the upland interior, and they flow sufficiently fast to generate electricity. Several large industrial cities have developed along the estuaries. The Rhine, flowing through the economic heart of Europe, carries the most traffic; and the course it has cut through the Alps and uplands to the North Sea serves also as the route for modern railways and motorways. The delta of the Rhine is so busy with trade and transport activities that it is considered the economic core of Europe. By contrast, the Danube flows from Germany to the southeast, connecting the center of Europe with the Black Sea and passing the important and ancient cities of Vienna, Budapest, and Belgrade on the way.

Europe was once covered by a range of forests and grasslands. Today, forests exist only on the most rugged mountain slopes, in the most northern parts of Scandinavia, and in a few places where reforestation is under way. The dominant vegetation in Europe is now crops and pasture grass. The rest of the land is covered with industrial sites, railways, roadways, parking lots, canals, cities and their suburbs, and parks.

Climate

Europe has three main climate types: marine west coast, Mediterranean, and humid continental (Figure 4.1). The marine west coast climate dominates in northwestern Europe, where the influence of the Atlantic Ocean is strong. A broad warm current called the North Atlantic Drift sweeps north along the eastern coast of North America from the equatorial zones and turns farther east along the coast of Maine toward Europe, carrying with it warm wet air. The warmest part of this current is also called the Gulf Stream. Prevailing winds blow the warm wet air above the Atlantic over northwestern Europe, resulting in a much warmer and wetter climate than is found elsewhere in the world at similar latitudes. That climate has cool summers, mild winters, and consistent rainfall. Moreover, the marine west coast climate extends far inland over the open lowland of the North European Plain, bringing moderate temperatures and rain deep into the Eurasian continent. To handle the rainfall, people in these areas have developed elaborate drainage systems for houses and communities (steep roofs, rain gutters, storm sewers, and drained fields), and they grow crops such as potatoes, beets, turnips, and cabbages that thrive in cool wet conditions.

Farther to the south, the warm Mediterranean climate of hot dry summers and mild rainy winters prevails. In the summer, the Mediterranean is strongly influenced by an atmospheric high-pressure cell that sits over North Africa and the Atlantic at about 30° latitude. The hot dry climate of these areas shifts north over the Mediterranean in the summer, bringing high temperatures, clear skies, and dry periods as far north as the Alps. Major crops, such as olives, citrus fruits, and wheat, must be drought resistant or irrigated. Later in the year, as this high-pressure zone shifts south, cooler temperatures and thunderstorms sweep in off the Atlantic, and the northern Mediterranean climate can resemble the marine west coast climate of northwest Europe. Along the Mediterranean, houses by the sea are often open and airy to afford comfort in the hot, sunny, rainless days of Mediterranean sum-

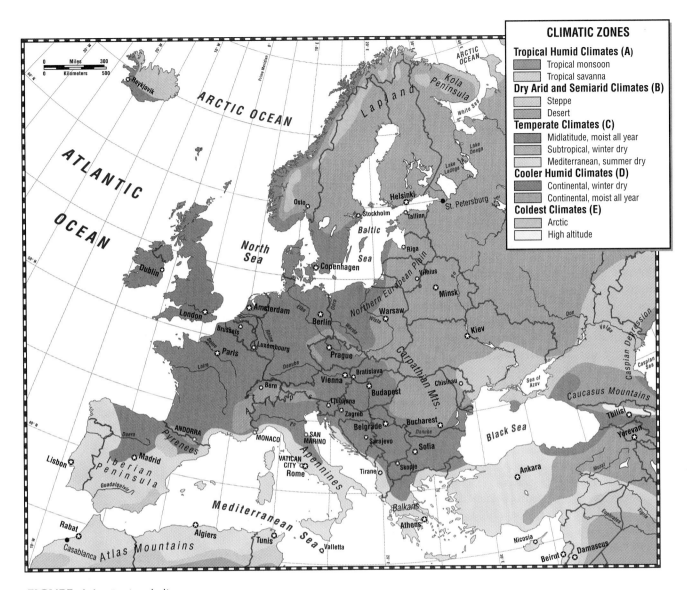

FIGURE 4.1 Regional climate.

mers. Tourists escaping the drab climate of northwest Europe crowd scenic areas, especially beaches.

In eastern Europe and most of Scandinavia, the moderating influences of the Atlantic and Mediterranean are less and the climate is more extreme. Summers are fairly hot in the interior of the continent, although much less so in Scandinavia. Winters are longer and colder the farther north one goes (Scandinavia) or the deeper into areas of what is called humid continental climate (southern Germany, Austria, Hungary). Here, houses tend to be well insulated, with small windows and low ceilings. Crops, where they can be grown at all, must be adapted to much shorter growing seasons. From Napoleon to Hitler, marauders from more temperate climates attempting to expand into this area have been defeated by the harsh winters that blow in from Siberia.

HUMAN PATTERNS

Some grand claims have been made in the name of Europe, and geographers have been among both the most vociferous supporters and the strongest critics of these ideas, as the following two quotations attest:

Europe has been a great teacher of the world. Almost every vital political principle active in the world today had its origin in Europe or its offspring, European North America. . . . [T]he same is true of the arts. Even though other parts of the world have produced rich folk arts, the culture of the West has become dominant. (George F. Hepner and Jesse O. McKee, *World Regional Geography*, p. 144.)

[There is] the [unfortunate] notion that European civilization—"The West"—has had some unique historical advantage, some special quality of race or culture or environment or mind or spirit, which gives this [particular] human community a permanent superiority over all other communities, at all times in history and down to the present. (James Blaut, *The Colonizer's Model of the World,* p. 1.)

We are so used to hearing laudatory assessments of western (European) culture that for most of us it is hard to spot the fallacies. In fact, you may have read the above passages idly, and said to yourself, "So?" In fact, the fallacies lie not in the claim of wide diffusion but rather in the failure to recognize that many European ideas and technologies were synthesized from non-European sources. Most of all, the fallacy lies in the underlying assumption that the ability to dominate militarily, politically, and economically is evidence of overall cultural superiority. It is true that, at least over the last 500 years, Europe, more than any other region, *has* dominated how the rest of the world trades, fights, thinks, and governs itself. Attempts to explain this situation have ranged from racist theories, proclaiming Europeans to be a genetically superior breed of humans, to no less simplistic assertions that Europe's many bays, peninsulas, and navigable rivers have promoted commerce to a greater extent than elsewhere. We may never have a single satisfying answer to the question of why Europe gained the dominance it has. Still, it is worth taking a broad look at the history of this area and to consider just a few of the many developments that have made Europe, for good and bad, unique and so influential in the human experience.

Sources of European Culture

Starting about 10,000 years ago, the practice of agriculture and animal husbandry gradually spread into Europe from the Tigris and Euphrates river valleys in Southwest Asia (also known as Mesopotamia), and from farther east in Central Asia. Wheat, numerous vegetables and fruits, cattle, pigs, sheep, and goats came to Europe from the east. Human settlement increased across Europe as forests were cleared and as other cultural "inventions," such as pottery making, weaving, mining, and metalworking, opened the way for a wider range of economic activity. Many of these innovations had their origins outside Europe, especially in Turkey, Mesopotamia, and Egypt, and some influences came from as far away as China and Mongolia.

The first European civilizations were ancient Greece (800–86 B.C.) and Rome (100 B.C.–A.D. 500). The innovations of these civilizations and their extensive borrowings from other societies formed some of the most important cultural legacies of Europe. Located in southern Europe, Greece and Rome interacted more with the Mediterranean rim, Southwest Asia, and North Africa than with the rest of modern Europe, which was relatively poor and thinly populated. Greek artists, philosophers, and mathematicians were fascinated with the workings of both the natural world and human societies. Later European traditions of science, art, and literature were heavily based on Greek ideals. The Romans, perhaps the greatest borrowers of Greek culture, also left important legacies to Europe. Many Europeans today speak Romance languages, such as Italian, Spanish, and French, which are in large part derived from Latin, the language of the Roman Empire. Roman law established individual ownership of private property as the norm in Europe and aided commerce by instituting the use of contracts in business transactions. Also influential were Roman systems of colonization. The Romans secured newly conquered areas by establishing small settlements, colonies of Roman citizens. These colonies, also based largely on Greek models, were powerful vehicles for the spread of Roman domination into areas such as the Hungarian Plain, North Africa, and Turkey. These areas provided agricultural and other resources to the Roman Empire. This same model of colonization was used when European states laid claim to territory in the Americas and across the globe after 1500.

Islamic civilization was an influence on Europe that often goes unrecognized today. North African Muslims, called Moors, ruled Spain for 600 years, starting in A.D. 711. The Muslim Turks of the Ottoman Empire ruled various parts of the Balkans and Greece from the sixteenth through the early twentieth centuries. Muslim traders in Southwest Asia brought to Europe many goods, food crops, and technologies from China, India, and Africa. Muslim scholars preserved much learning from Greece, Egypt, and other ancient civilizations, and brought Europe its numbering system as well as significant advances in mathematics and medicine. Arab mathematicians, for example, invented both algebra and algorithms, essential elements of the computer age.

Growth and Expansion of Continental Europe

Continental Europe became increasingly important as the Roman Empire declined in the fifth century A.D. and European settlement expanded northward. By about A.D. 900, a social system that came to be known as feudalism had evolved; it provided a viable defense against the Vikings and the nomadic raiders from the Eurasian steppes. The idea was to have a sufficient number of heavily armed, professional fighting men, or knights, on hand at any moment, ready to defend the farmers, called serfs, who cultivated plots of land for them. Over time, some of these knights evolved into an elite class of warrior-aristocrats; they constituted Europe's nobility, and were bound together by a complex web of allegiances obligating them to assist each other in times of war. Often, the lavish lifestyles of the wealthier knights were supported by the labors of the serfs, who were legally barred from ever leaving the lands they cultivated for their protectors. Thus, while Europe's knights conquered kingdoms and empires, most of rural Europe continued to live in poverty. The Spanish later reinvented aspects of this feudal system in the Americas: the Spanish crown expropriated land from Native Americans and granted it to colonists, along with the right to treat the native inhabitants like serfs.

While rural life followed established feudal patterns, Europe's towns were developing new institutions that would exert a huge influence on settlement and commerce in modern Europe. Often founded as trading posts by former raiders, towns were able to maintain independence from the feudal knights of the surrounding countryside. They sheltered craftspeople and merchants who created essential institutions of modern European capitalism, including banks, insurance companies, and corporations. The **town charter** established certain civil rights that were to be enjoyed by all citizens. These strong new social institutions allowed Europe's towns to avoid the severe exploitation of the feudal system and to establish a pace of technological and social change that left the feudal hinterland literally in the "dark ages." This split in European thought between the "exciting urban" and the "behind-the-times rural" still shapes many of our attitudes toward economic development. In former European colonies, for example, urban development often receives more support than rural development, even though the majority of the population may be rural.

The liberating effects of Europe's urban growth would transform the modern world. Since Roman times, the Catholic Church had dominated religion, politics, and daily life throughout much of Europe. However, in the towns of the North European Plain there arose a reform movement that came to be known as the **Protestant Reformation** and that challenged the often elitist Catholic practices. This movement eventually gave birth to more popularly based Protestant sects. Protestantism had its largest impact in the British Isles, northern Europe, and the North European Plain, challenging many established ways of thinking and promoting broader public literacy and education. Another important outgrowth of European town life was the **Renaissance** (French for "rebirth"), a broad cultural movement that drew inspiration from the Greek, Roman, and Islamic civilizations. Renaissance thinkers embarked on explorations into science, politics, commerce, and the arts, and in so doing provided the key underpinnings of modern European culture.

A direct outgrowth of the Renaissance and the Reformation was Europe's **age of exploration.** This was the beginning of a period of accelerated global commerce and cultural exchange that continues to the present in many ways. Portugal, in the fifteenth and sixteenth centuries, took advantage of Renaissance advances in navigation, shipbuilding, and commerce, to round the Horn of Africa and set up a trading empire in Asia and eventually a colony in Brazil. Spain, beginning with the first voyage of Columbus in 1492, founded a vast and profitable American-Pacific empire. By the eighteenth century, however, these empires were beginning to weaken, partly because of reliance on archaic Greco-Roman colonial institutions and a strong alliance with the Catholic Church; these models discouraged social or technological change. Dutch and British empires soon overshadowed the Spanish and Portuguese empires. Influenced by the Protestant emphasis on individualism and innovation, the Dutch and British used less religious and conservative methods of colonial expansion. By the twentieth century, these various European colonial systems had strongly influenced nearly every country in the world. The systems produced great wealth for Europe, often at the expense of destructive political and economic instability in the colonies (Figure 4.2).

An Age of Revolutions

Unlike other civilizations, Europe did not slow its pace of transformation after achieving a relatively high level of development. The Chinese civilization, for example, had dwarfed all others until the seventeenth century, but had then stopped progressing. In contrast to China, the more rich and powerful Europe became, the more the pace of change accelerated. Scholars have developed many theories to explain why this happened. One is the notion that Europe's success was due to its fragmentation into many distinct kingdoms or other geopolitical entities that competed with each other for dominance, thus pushing Europe into a race with itself. Whatever the ultimate causes, Europe's transformation resulted in two major processes that allowed it to continue to change rapidly, namely, the industrial and the democratic revolutions.

Europe's **industrial revolution** was intimately connected with colonial expansion and the age of exploration. Particularly important was the experience of Britain. By the eighteenth century, Britain had transformed itself from an island of only modest resources into a major economic power, with a huge and growing empire, expanding industrial capabilities, and the

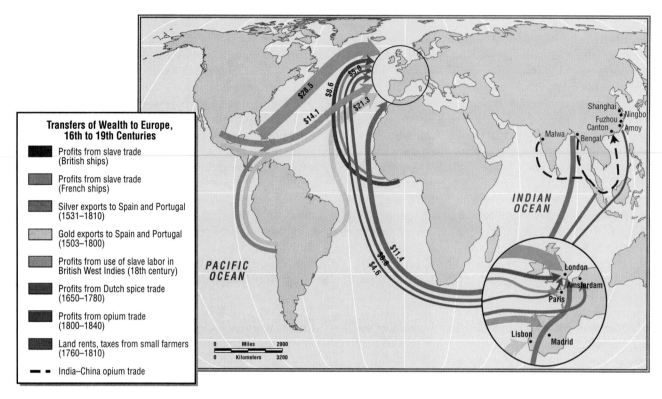

**Transfers of Wealth to Europe,
16th to 19th Centuries**

- Profits from slave trade (British ships)
- Profits from slave trade (French ships)
- Silver exports to Spain and Portugal (1531–1810)
- Gold exports to Spain and Portugal (1503–1800)
- Profits from use of slave labor in British West Indies (18th century)
- Profits from Dutch spice trade (1650–1780)
- Profits from opium trade (1800–1840)
- Land rents, taxes from small farmers (1760–1810)
- - - India–China opium trade

FIGURE 4.2   Transfer of wealth from the colonies back to Europe. The dollar amounts are in billions of current U.S. dollars (total = $101 billion). [Adapted from Alan Thomas, *Third World Atlas* (Washington, DC: Taylor & Francis, 1994), p. 29.]

world's most powerful navy. Britain's empire in India and North America gave it access to a wide range of raw materials and to markets for finished goods. Soon the country was straining to meet a demand for more manufactured goods than it could produce. The challenge was met by introducing mechanization into its in-

dustries, first in textile weaving and then in the production of coal and steel. Eventually, whole cities based on a complex of industries grew up around Britain's coal and iron fields. In time, these industrial technologies spread throughout Europe. Although industrialization began with a substitution of mechanical for human la-

Women and young girls in long, full dresses doing heavy lifting in a massive cotton factory hall with open belts and presses. The scene depicts the nineteenth-century outgrowth of an old association between women and large-scale textile production. In medieval times, lords required women laborers to provide them with a certain amount of cloth every year. Women often wove this cloth in a central location within the castle grounds. [Bettmann/Corbis.]

bor, soon skilled and unskilled factory workers were demanded in huge numbers, triggering steady migrations from the countryside. However, the unsafe working conditions, low wages, and squalid urban slums of Europe's new industrial cities meant that living standards remained low for many people, especially for women, who were offered only the lowest-paying jobs.

In the midst of this industrialization, Europe experienced political and social transformations that redistributed power and eventually wealth more evenly throughout society. The key developments in this process were the rise of the **nation-state,** the advent of **democracy,** and the birth of the **welfare state.** For centuries, Europe's power structure was basically feudal in nature: most territory was dominated by kingdoms whose rulers were held accountable mainly to a small elite of wealthy knights and other nobility. By the eighteenth century, in some kingdoms, especially in western Europe, the political elite was expanding to include the clergy and property owners as well, and kings were forced to accept constitutions that restricted their power. In 1789, a mass movement arose in France out of the tensions created by extreme disparities of wealth in French society. Inspired in part by news of the popular revolution in North America, this movement led to the French Revolution and the first major European inclusion of the common people into the political process. From then on, the concept of the **nation** was increasingly influential in Europe. A nation was conceived of as a large group of people, both rich and poor, living in a specific territory and bound together, in part, by certain common cultural traits, such as a common language. Above all, they are bound by their allegiance to the very idea that they, the people, together form a nation and should ideally be united in a single country, called the nation-state, to which they are loyal and obedient. This new ideology of **nationalism** spread throughout much of western, northern, and southern Europe during the nineteenth century, and throughout eastern Europe in the early twentieth century. It transformed the political scene as individual kingdoms, in the case of France, or collections of kingdoms, as in the case of Germany and Italy, tried to establish the notion that all their people were together a nation.

Later, the role of the common people in the political life of the nation became formalized, with the introduction of democratic institutions. All adults, first men and only after considerable protest women as well, obtained the right to vote on who their leaders should be. This trend toward popular democracy spread from North America to western and northern Europe, to southern, and finally to eastern Europe over the course of the nineteenth and twentieth centuries.

As the common people played an increasingly important role in European society, their demands for an improvement in their standard of living grew. So far, the industrial revolution had resulted in a society plagued by extreme inequities, no longer dominated by kings and knights but by industrialists, bankers, merchants, and their political allies. In western and northern Europe, popular discontent at the persistence of huge inequities was channeled through the democratic process, resulting in various forms of the welfare state. In countries with a welfare state, the government guarantees the basic necessities of life for the poor and the elderly, and mechanisms are in place to establish more harmonious relations between labor unions and employers, all of which has the effect of reducing disparities in wealth and increasing overall prosperity.

Decline and Rebirth

By the early twentieth century, Europe still lacked a system of collective security that could prevent war between its rival nations. In this century, two horribly destructive world wars removed Europe from its position as the dominant region of the world. Germany was seen as an instigator of both wars, and its defeat resulted in a number of enduring changes in Europe. After the end of World War II, in 1945, Germany was partitioned into two parts. West Germany, after a brief occupation by France, the United Kingdom, and the United States, became an independent capitalist democracy, while the Soviet Union (USSR) maintained control over what became East Germany. In fact, the line between East and West Germany became part of what came to be called the **iron curtain,** which separated Western Europe from Eastern Europe. Eastern Europe was integrated into the USSR's sphere of communist states with a form of centrally planned socialism: the state owned all farms and industry and dictated output. This separation of Europe laid the foundation for the cold war between the United States and the USSR. The entire world became a stage on which these two superpowers competed for dominance (Figure 4.3). Once-powerful Europe became subject to the geopolitical manipulation of the superpowers. Yet another manifestation of Europe's decline was the fact that it could no longer control its colonial empires. By the 1960s, most former colonies were independent.

In the decades after World War II, Europe reemerged as a dominant power. Economic reconstruction and industrial growth proceeded rapidly in the capitalist democracies of Western Europe, but more slowly in communist Eastern Europe, which was saddled with inefficient and highly polluting state-run industries. By the late 1980s, much of Eastern Europe was on the brink of abandoning communism, and finally did so with the economic and political collapse of the USSR in 1991. Meanwhile, some of the capitalist

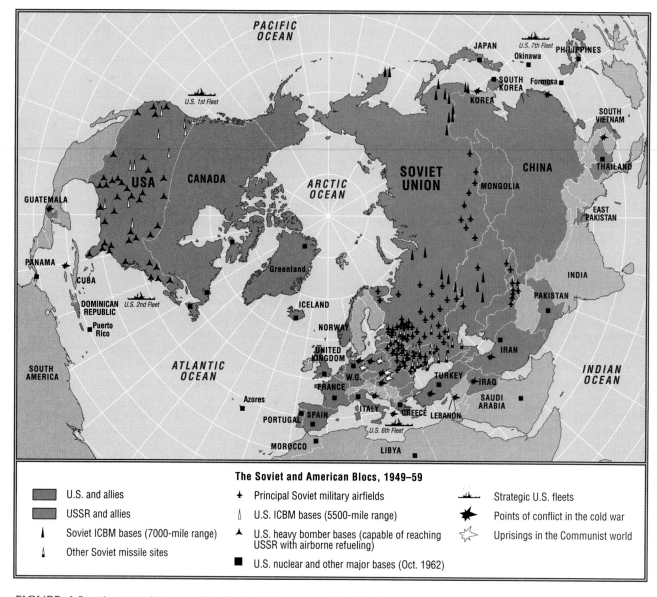

FIGURE 4.3 The United States and the Soviet Union covered the Northern Hemisphere with military installations in an attempt to avert war by striking a balance of power. Notice how the United States and its allies managed to encircle the Soviet Union and China. [Adapted from *Hammond Times Concise Atlas of World History,* 1994, pp. 148–149.]

democracies had been lowering barriers to trade and were becoming increasingly linked economically. This process, begun in the 1950s, eventually led to the establishment of the **European Union (EU)** in 1993. The EU is a supranational institution including most of western, southern, and northern Europe. It encourages **economic integration,** the free movement of people, goods, money, and ideas among member countries. The EU will make it possible for Europe to operate as a unit, much as the United States or Canada does. Increasingly, citizens of EU countries are living

similar lives regardless of their nationality. The EU has reestablished Europe as a world economic power, capable of challenging the dominance of the United States.

Population Patterns

Enumerating just how many people now live in Europe is a bit complex because, as a result of recent political changes, there is no universally agreed-upon eastern border of the region. According to the way Europe is

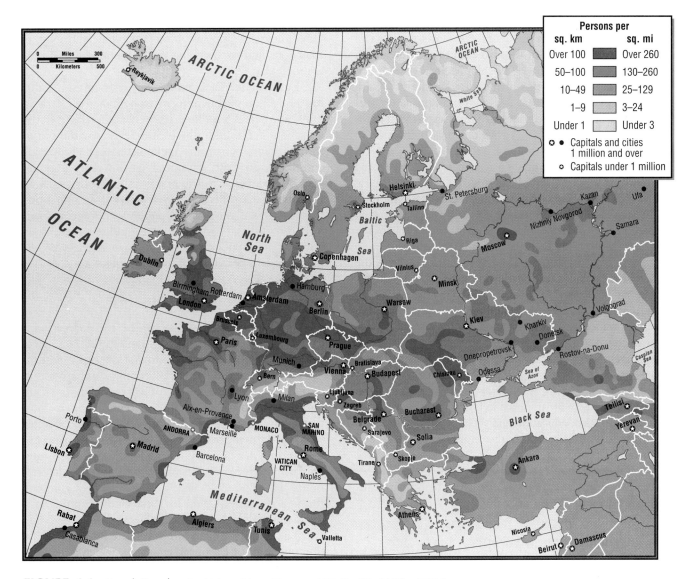

FIGURE 4.4 Population density. [Adapted from *Hammond Citation World Atlas,* 1996.]

defined in this book, there are about 570 million Europeans; and as Figure 4.4 shows, they are unevenly distributed. On the map, the densest settlement in Europe stretches in a disconnected band from the United Kingdom and northwestern France east through the Netherlands and central Germany all the way to Kiev, Chisinau, and Bucharest. Parts of Italy and pockets along the coasts of Portugal, Spain, and southern France are also densely populated. Although North Europe is relatively sparsely inhabited, a glance at the global population map in Chapter 1 will show that, overall, Europe is one of the most densely occupied regions on earth. One might assume that at higher densities there would be fewer resources to go around, so an interesting question is how Europeans maintain their high standards of living.

Population Density and Access to Resources

Population density, in and of itself, says little about how well people are doing in a particular place. If people have access to adequate resources and these resources are allocated fairly among the population, they may live well even at high densities. A region's **resource base** is the selection of raw materials available for domestic use and industrial development: coal, petroleum, iron ore, cotton and wool fiber, food, soil and water, for example. In the case of Europe, the relationship between the population and resource base is not simple. Europe depleted many of its resources, especially forests and minerals, during the early industrial revolution; but for hundreds of years it has had access to a resource base that is global in extent, not confined to Europe. The map in Figure 4.2 shows transfers of wealth to Europe from the sixteenth to the nineteenth centuries. Since about 1500, colonies in the Americas, Africa, and Asia have contributed tremendous wealth to Europe in free or very low-paid labor, in natural resources, and in agricultural products extracted at low costs. This wealth added considerably to the overall standard of living of Europeans and to the ability of Europe to develop an industrial economy. Even the poorest Europeans have benefited.

Take the case of the European chocolate industry. African cacao farmers barely eke out a living growing cacao beans and have little or no power to negotiate the prices they are paid. Meanwhile, European cacao traders grow wealthy from the profits they make in the world cacao market; and European workers in chocolate factories also live very well in comparison to cacao farmers. Some observers would reply that the European cacao traders and chocolate factory workers are rewarded with high income for their higher levels of skill and technology, and for developing the chocolate market in the first place. Critics of global market systems might counter with the observation that the cacao farmers are actually quite skilled, despite little access to schooling; also, education and technology ought not to privilege so overwhelmingly those who trade and process a product, in comparison with those who produce the raw materials—at least not to the point that the producers are too impoverished to feed their families adequately or send their children to school.

Urbanization in Europe

Europe is a region of cities. Even in sparsely settled North Europe, 84 percent of the people live in urban areas. South Europe is least urbanized, with 61 percent living in cities. Many European cities began as trading centers more than a thousand years ago and still bear the architectural marks of medieval life in their quaint centers. Most of these old cities are located on navigable rivers in the interior or along the coasts, because water transport figured prominently (and still does) in Europe's trading patterns.

Since World War II, nearly all cities across Europe have expanded in concentric circles of apartment blocks. Well-developed rail and bus lines link these blocks to each other and to the old central city. Land is scarce and expensive in Europe. Only a small percentage of Europeans live in single-family homes, though the number is growing; these homes tend to be attached or densely arranged on small lots surrounded by walls or fences to ensure privacy and protect small gardens. Rarely does one see the sweeping lawns that North Americans spend so much time grooming. Publicly funded transportation is widely available, so

many people prefer to live in apartments near city centers. They can either walk or take public transport to their jobs and to shopping centers, and can easily do without a car.

Europe contains a number of large cities: London has 11 million people in its metropolitan area, Paris 10 million, Madrid 5 million, Essen 5 million, and Berlin 4 million. Yet, even in these cities, everyday life can be intimate and personal. While deteriorating housing and slums do exist, European city dwellers are very well off compared to the residents of Mexico City or Calcutta, where the majority are very poor and living in shantytowns. Substantial public spending on social welfare systems, sanitation, water, utilities, education, housing, and public transportation accounts for the high standard of living in Europe's cities.

Population Growth Patterns

Though Europe is densely occupied, the population is aging and no longer growing rapidly. In fact, birth rates in Europe are now the lowest on earth, and for the region as a whole there is actually a **negative rate of natural increase** (−0.1). That is, death rates are higher than birth rates. This circumstance is most marked in countries that were once part of, or allied with, the former Soviet Union. In these countries, people are now having very few children, and death rates are fairly high in part because health care has deteriorated. The one-child family is increasingly common throughout Europe, and in West Europe immigrants are the major source of population growth.

The declining birth rate is reflected in the population pyramids of European countries, which look more like lumpy towers than pyramids. The population diagram of Germany (reunited in 1990) is an example (Figure 4.5). The diagram's narrow bottom, somewhat like the trunk of a tree, indicates that since about 1978 very few babies have been born, compared with the rate in the 1950s, 1960s, and 1970s. After World War II, during the years when those now 30 to 50 years of age were born, both Germanys experienced a baby boom. East Germany's baby boom was very modest. In that country, postwar socialist policy required women to work in the newly developing industrial economy; yet women were expected to perform all the domestic duties as well, and there was no social pressure for spouses to help. One way for East German women to lighten the load of the double workday was to have fewer children.

The trend toward fewer children is found in West Germany as well. There, an estimated 25 percent of women are choosing to remain unmarried into their thirties (unmarried motherhood is not common); and 35 to 40 percent of women are choosing to have no children at all. More and more women desire profes-

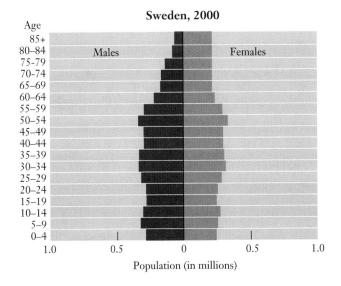

Sweden, 2000

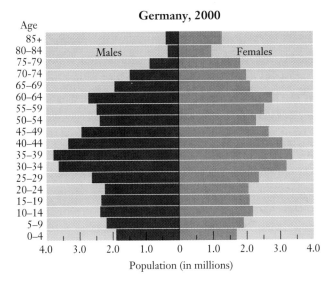

Germany, 2000

FIGURE 4.5 Population pyramids. Notice that the population scales are different for the two countries.
[Adapted from U.S. Census Bureau, International Data Base, at http://www.census.gov/cgi-bin/ipc/idbpyry.pl.]

sional careers, yet the German government makes very few provisions for working mothers: there is little day care available and school days are short, with no lunches provided, so mothers must stay at home. Many women decide to remain unmarried, and even married women are opting against motherhood. Two results are that the vast majority of Germans are over the age of 20 and the population pyramid continues to narrow at the bottom due to the small number of births. If these trends continue, the population will eventually settle down into a stable age structure. The population "pyramid" for Sweden (see Figure 4.5) depicts such an age structure. It resembles an elongated box, with nearly equal numbers from birth through middle age, tapering at the top for the category of advanced old age.

A stable population with a low birth rate has several consequences. While families have extra money for luxury spending, new consumers are not being produced; hence, in time, markets may contract unless immigrants can be attracted. And demands for new laborers, especially the highly skilled, may go unmet, again unless immigration supplies a solution. The number of younger people to provide expensive health care to the very elderly, either personally or through tax payments, is small.

CURRENT GEOGRAPHIC ISSUES

The social, economic, and political geography of Europe is in a particularly unstable state of flux at the turn of the twenty-first century; this is the result of the demise of the Soviet Union, the end of the cold war, and the effort toward economic integration that has produced the European Union. Yet the same circumstances hold out the promise of unprecedented peace and prosperity for Europe, if tensions that may act as roadblocks to unity can be resolved.

The demise of the Soviet Union and the move toward a more open and competitive market system has placed many people throughout East and Central Europe in jeopardy. Many are losing their jobs, living with scarcities of food and other necessities, and falling victim to boiling social turmoil, including a rising crime rate. Old totalitarian restraints are falling away before new, more democratic systems of social control have been established. Meanwhile, in Western Europe, the economic adjustments necessary to make way for closer economic union have produced some of the same effects, especially unemployment; countries have had to give up policies that protected certain sectors, such as farming, in their economies. And now, to make the situation yet more complicated, the relatively poorer countries of the old Soviet bloc are begging to be included in the emerging European Union.

All across Europe, people are nervous about the changes in their familiar way of life, and one result has been the rise of conservative political movements that foster a sort of "circling of the wagons" mentality. Recently, there has been strident talk of excluding "strange" people with unfamiliar ways of life, especially immigrants from outside Europe who are thought to be taking jobs Europeans need. Overall, the signs are good that these tensions can be resolved amicably, but there will be many occasions for the new relationships to deteriorate into open hostility, especially if

181

democratic leaders are not able to preserve an atmosphere of tolerance and mutual understanding.

Sociocultural Issues

These days, all Europeans are having to reconsider what it means to be European and how, with increasing economic integration, they will resolve different regional attitudes toward a wide range of social issues. These issues include how to relate to outsiders, the proper role of nationalism, how to manage changing gender roles, and the role the state should play in human welfare.

Immigrants and European Ideas Toward Outsiders

By the 1960s, the European economy had recovered from the devastation of the war, and there was a labor shortage in many parts of the continent. To fill the empty positions, immigrants were invited into Europe as so-called **guest workers.** These immigrants came primarily from former European colonies (in the West Indies, North Africa, and Southeast Asia), and also from Turkey, Yugoslavia (as it was then), Greece, and the Middle East. The hosts and guests often had different expectations of what this migration would mean in the long run. The Europeans expected the immigrants to earn a nest egg and then go home, whereas the immigrants often found that they wished to stay.

Many guest workers did fulfill host expectations and return home. Often, guest workers from a particular part of the world would crowd together in small apartments, each working several jobs and saving money assiduously. While they worked, they sent money home to support children and the elderly, and they also saved enough to build a house for an extended family on their return. The following are two vignettes from the author's research, describing migrants who for a time took advantage of Europe's relatively high wages and then returned with their earnings to enhance life at home.

VIGNETTE In 1965, in the mountain village of Baker Hill on the island of Montserrat, in the West Indies, Mr. Barzey left his mate and young children in a tiny two-room house he had just built. With money saved from working as a laborer in cotton fields and selling vegetables he grew in the mountains, he paid for passage on a steamer across the Atlantic. After arriving in England, he worked for 12 years without a break in the Kodak plant,

sending home enough money to support his family and to feed a growing savings account in the Montserrat bank. In 1977, Mr. Barzey returned to Montserrat, where he settled back into a life of subsistence agriculture, a dream that had sustained him for more than a decade of long hours in a cold European industrial city. Using part of his nest egg, he built several additions to his home, including a kitchen, bath, and walled flower beds. He christened the additions "Kodak" in honor of the company that had made possible his relative prosperity.

VIGNETTE In 1965, Dusan Andoljsek left his mother and sisters in the village of Velike Poljane in the Dolensko Valley of Slovenia (then part of Yugoslavia) and rode a train to Frankfurt, Germany. There he worked for five years in an auto plant. To avoid the crowded apartment he shared with six others, he asked for as much overtime work as he could get. He regularly wired money home to his mother and sisters, who continued to plant and harvest potatoes in the several family fields surrounding the village. Living standards in Germany impressed Dusan, and he got the idea that they should remodel their 300-year-old home in Velike Poljane with the very latest styles and gadgets. By the time I visited it in 1971, the medieval cottage had a new tile roof. The huge, carved, double front doors, which once led to the passageway for horses and wagons to an inner farm courtyard, now opened onto a wide, elegant hallway tiled in Spanish ceramics. The living room floor was carpeted; the lighted bar cabinet held cut crystal glassware and an impressive array of liqueurs, and a modern stereo system graced a fine, polished credenza. The kitchen had a double stainless steel sink and all the most modern appliances. Yet for all this, through the kitchen window I could see Dusan's elderly mother in her traditional black clothes and head scarf, still digging potatoes by hand.

Not all guest workers take their money and go home willingly. Many have left much more difficult home situations, and some are refugees from civil wars and no longer have homes. Like the vast majority of European immigrants who permanently immigrated to North America from the seventeenth century on, many of these people hope to make their home in a Western European country, raise a family, and eventually become accepted as citizens. The map in Figure 4.6 depicts migration into Europe in the 1990s.

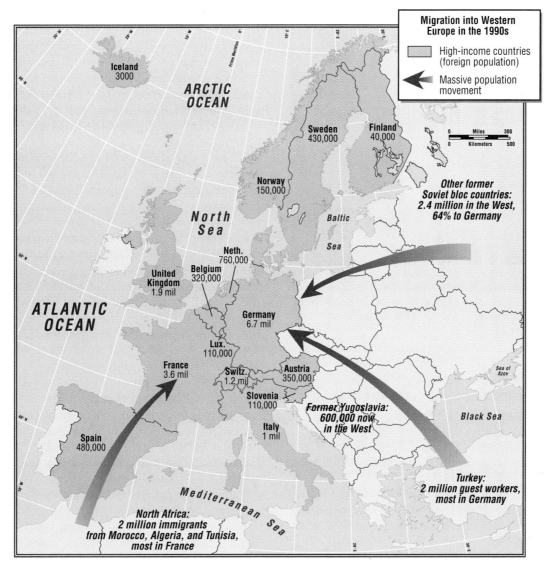

FIGURE 4.6 People flocked to Western Europe in the early 1990s. Some were seeking lives of a better quality or looking for higher-paying jobs or any job. Some were refugees fleeing oppression and ethnic cleansing. [Adapted from *National Geographic,* May 1993, p. 102.]

For their part, the European host countries have very different policies regarding immigrant workers. Some, like the Netherlands, have lenient laws, allowing immigrants from former colonial territories to stay indefinitely while receiving subsidized housing and other social services paralleling those provided for citizens. France provides less adequate housing in informally segregated neighborhoods, and the atmosphere is less welcoming. In Germany and France, right-wing parties now openly speak of driving the immigrants out.

European Ideas on Citizenship. In no European country is it possible to acquire citizenship with anything close to the ease with which immigrants can qualify in the United States or Canada. Germany has received the largest numbers of immigrants and refugees of any EU country; somewhat over 8 percent of its 82 million people are foreign born. Yet Germany makes it extremely difficult for a migrant to become a citizen. Traditionally, the Germans view citizenship as determined primarily by ethnicity. Thus, for example, the descendants of Germans brought to Russia more than 200 years ago by Catherine the Great to farm in the Volga River valley can move to Germany as full citizens. Yet, even if born in Germany, the children and grandchildren of Turkish or North African immigrant workers are not considered citizens. Most are rejected when they apply. Of the more than 2 million people

Turkish migrants relax in Berlin's Tiergarten, the city's central park. A soccer game is under way. By the mid-1990s, one of every eight residents in Berlin was a foreigner. [Gerd Ludwig/National Geographic.]

of Turkish origin who live in Germany and who run upward of 30,000 businesses, less than 1 percent had acquired citizenship as of 1994.

France's regulations on citizenship are somewhat more generous. And the United Kingdom has in the past absorbed many hundreds of thousands of West Indians, Indians, Pakistanis, and Africans. Today, the United Kingdom is debating how to define the several hundred thousand citizens of its few remaining colonies. It is likely that eventually they will be given British citizenship.

A recurring and particularly troublesome theme in European politics is the idea that citizenship should be ethnically based: that "Germany is for the Germans" and "France is for the French." This form of nationalism motivated Germany's Nazis to perpetrate genocide against Jewish people during World War II, and led Spain to repress ethnic Basques and Catalonians until the 1970s. Since the recent end of the cold war, ethnicity has become more important in determining citizenship in Central and East Europe. When Czechoslovakia split into the two countries of Slovakia and the Czech Republic in 1993, ethnic Slovaks became foreigners the instant the deal was signed, no matter how long they had lived in the Czech part of the country.

Rules for Assimilation.   In Europe, "race" and skin color play less of a role in defining the differences between people than does culture. An immigrant from Asia or Africa may be fully accepted into the community if he or she is skilled in European ways, especially in language, and the finer points of manners and deco-

rum. Yet a member of a European minority that has been around thousands of years, such as the Basques in Spain or the Gypsies, will find it nearly impossible to blend into society. In Europe, **assimilation** usually means a comprehensive change of life: the immigrant gives up the lifeways of home—language, dress, family relationships, food, customs, mores, and even religion—and adopts the ways of Germany or France, for example, instead.

The geographer Eva Humbeck studied how Thai women who came to Germany explicitly to marry German men grapple with the demands of assimilation. Since 1990, about 1000 such Thai women a year have arrived in Germany. The expected role of housewife as opposed to career woman is not unfamiliar to the Thai brides, but in Germany they must live in isolation, away from female relatives, who in Thai culture are a woman's best friends. According to Humbeck, the women are generally satisfied with their lot in Germany, but they feel that Germans view Thai culture as inferior; thus they feel constrained to drop all Thai ways, and few Thai wives know one another. Many confess to daydreaming about the Thai hospitality and family conviviality they once enjoyed.

It should be noted that the degree of adjustment expected of immigrants differs remarkably from what is the case in North America. There, the norm is **acculturation** (adaptation to the host culture enough to function effectively and be self-supporting), not total assimilation. Especially in the United States, and also in Canada, immigrants are expected to learn the language and to abide by the laws of the land; in Canada, their right to retain their own language is protected. Beyond that, immigrants are free to keep their native cultures and cuisine. Those who retain native dress and particularly exotic customs may encounter a certain amount of informal discrimination, but they will also find that the laws protect their rights to be different and that much about America—for example, international street festivals or ethnic food fetes—actually encourages a measure of cultural retention.

There are signs that Europeans may be moving toward more acceptance of non-Europeans within their midst. Cross-cultural marriage is increasingly common, and the multiethnic offspring of these marriages will influence their generation's attitudes. Some analysts think that as economic conditions improve with the EU, and as interactions between ethnic groups increase, Europeans will adopt more open attitudes toward other cultures and more flexible notions of citizenship.

European Ideas About Gender

As is the case nearly everywhere on earth, all societies in Europe accept the notion that men and women are innately programmed to perform different functions. European public opinion among both women and men holds that women are simply unable or less able than men to perform the types of work typically done by men; and this view is etched deeply into European social institutions. In most cases, men have greater social status, earn higher pay (Table 4.1), have greater autonomy, and enjoy more freedom of movement through space than do women. To be sure, women can act in male roles. That is, they can work outside the home in certain jobs, such as factory laborers, service workers, teachers, textile producers, architects, physicians, professors, and so forth. However, women already have as-

signed roles—as wife, mother, housewife—that entail full-time domestic work.

When European women work outside the home, men typically do not take on an equal proportion of domestic work in return. When women take up employment outside the home, they must do double duty—paid work and housework. The obligation of women to work both on the job and in the home is referred to as the **"double day."** United Nations research shows that throughout Europe, women's workdays (including time spent in housework) are five to nine hours longer than men's. Although in some European countries, a social welfare system may

TABLE 4.1

Gender statistics from selected countries

Country	Female unemployment, % of total	Male unemployment, % of total	Female pay as percentage of male pay	Percentage of child-care time provided by men
Denmark	14	11	83	36
Iceland	3.6	2.6	90	NA
Norway	5	7	86	29
Belgium	10.7	4.6	75	NA
France	14	10	81	NA
Germany	8	8	76	29
Netherlands	7	6	77	28
United Kingdom	8	12	70	24
Greece	12.9	4.8	78	NA
Italy	17	8	80	NA
Spain	24	10	70	14
Hungary	10.5	7.6	82	36
Poland	14.9	11.8	78	31
Romania	10.7	6.2	NA	NA
Austria	NA	NA	78	NA
Finland	NA	NA	77	25
Ireland	NA	NA	69	NA
Portugal	NA	NA	76	NA
Slovenia	NA	NA	80	NA
Sweden	NA	NA	89	28
Switzerland	NA	NA	68	NA
United States	NA	NA	75	28

NA = not available.

Sources: Data from United Nations, *The World's Women*, 1995, p.108; Joni Seager, *Women of the World Atlas*, 1997, pp. 68–69; Office of Women's Politics, *Preliminary Report from the Republic of Slovenia on Measures Taken for the Abolishment of All Forms of Discrimination Against Women*, 1993, Ljubljana, Slovenia.

provide child care to working women, women burdened by the double day will generally operate with somewhat less efficiency on the job than do men. Also because of the double day, women will often choose employment close to home that offers more flexibility in hours and skills required. These more flexible jobs almost always offer lower pay and less chance for advancement, but not necessarily fewer work hours, than typical male jobs.

How stringently gender roles are imposed in Europe varies a great deal from country to country and region to region. A good way to examine this variability is to look at how the various social welfare systems in Europe view gender roles.

Variability of Social Welfare Concepts Across Europe

The idea of elaborate, tax-supported social welfare systems is much more widely accepted in Europe than in the United States. In fact, the word "welfare" in Europe includes many services to the middle class. A few of these middle-class benefits exist in the United States and Canada (e.g., social security, pension plans, tax-deferred savings programs, mortgage tax deductions) but are not thought of as welfare per se. Europeans generally pay much higher taxes than do Americans, and they expect a wide range of services and safety nets in exchange. Still, Europeans do not

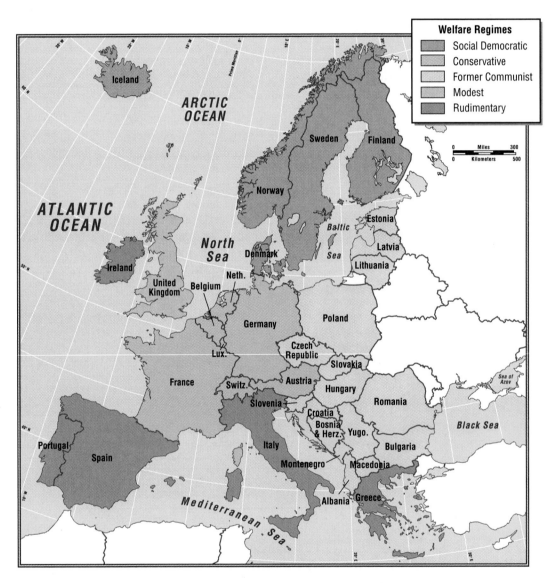

FIGURE 4.7 Many scholars have sought to categorize European countries according to their approaches to welfare, and some have studied how these approaches affect women. This map and the accompanying explanation are derived from several such studies and should be taken only as an informed approximation of the patterns.

agree on just how generous these welfare systems should be, or on their goals. As Figure 4.7 illustrates, there is a great deal of variability across Europe in approaches to welfare.

Here, using the work of the British sociologist Crescy Cannan and others, I have classified the approaches in five basic categories of welfare regimes, linked to particular parts of Europe. You will notice that each regime makes certain assumptions about rightful gender roles. All erroneously assume that the norm is a two-parent family in which men are the breadwinners, despite the fact that in most parts of Europe such families are in the minority. Women often take employment outside the home because of circumstances such as unmarried status, death of a mate, desertion, migration, responsibility for elderly kin, low male wages, and illness.

The **social democratic** welfare regimes in Scandinavia, particularly in Sweden and Iceland, seek to achieve equality across gender and class lines by providing generous benefits to all citizens. Citizens pay high taxes to provide an environment in which every child's potential is realized. At adulthood, every citizen, ideally, will be able to contribute to his or her highest capabilities, and social problems will not develop. Child care is widely available, not just to help women enter the labor market but also to provide the state with a mechanism for instilling values such as good nutrition, the work ethic, and good study habits. Nonetheless, traditional gender roles are still officially emphasized, and in the workplace and public forums women are not yet equal to men (see wage gap indicated in Table 4.1).

Conservative welfare regimes like those found in France, Germany, the Netherlands, Austria, and Switzerland have a conscious goal of providing minimum welfare for all citizens. They tend to preserve status differences in society. Hence, the state intervenes to assist those in need, but it does not see its mission as one of assisting upward mobility. For example, the state would not normally make a college education accessible to the children of poor families; though a university education is often free, there are strict entrance requirements that the poor find hard to pass. On the other hand, many state-supported services, like health care and pension plans, are available to all economic classes. Nonetheless, the welfare system unites with other public institutions to reinforce the idea that women should stay home and take care of children themselves (the so-called "housewife contract"). For example, the half-day school schedule and the lack of school lunches practically compel mothers to stay at home. Thus, many women who work settle for part-time work or jobs with flexible hours. In France, women are more likely to work full time and there is a bit more of the idea that working men and women

share an equal status, but not that they should share equal housework duties.

Communist welfare regimes, in countries like Poland, the Czech Republic, and Hungary before they broke away from the Soviet Union, were in theory comprehensive. Although the bureaucracy that administered benefits was inefficient and the programs unevenly funded, the ideal resembled the "cradle-to-grave" social democratic system in Scandinavia, except that women were pressured to work outside the home. In all the former Eastern bloc countries, women work outside the home in huge numbers, but men have never taken over any significant portion of domestic duties. Women accept nearly full responsibility for the home and all domestic duties. State-supported day care is available, though elderly grandmothers and other female relatives often provide child care. The double day is especially taxing for women in this part of Europe because labor-saving devices are not yet widely available; most people must launder clothes by hand, cook in rudimentary kitchens, and shop for food daily because their small refrigerators cannot hold more than a day's food.

Modest welfare regimes seek to encourage individual responsibility and the work ethic as the norm. A regime of this type has been evolving in the United Kingdom since conservative reforms in the 1980s and 1990s, and is roughly similar to the welfare system in Canada (the U.S. system is less generous). Benefits are modest, just enough for those who qualify to maintain a minimally adequate standard of living; and recipients are often stigmatized in jokes and conversation as being lazy and "on the dole." There is general agreement that welfare encourages dependency, whereas the ideal citizen is characterized by initiative, self-reliance, and personal responsibility in all matters. The state takes the view that it does not have a direct interest in the quality of daily life of its citizens; these matters are of individual choice in a free market. Women are free to work outside the home or not; but the state supports neither option. In actuality, because of pervasive gender role assumptions, women cannot enter the labor market on the same terms as men. Women occupy the lowest-paying factory jobs and the lower echelons of the business and professional sectors. Minimal state-supported child care is provided to help mothers work outside the home, but availability is unpredictable and not everyone qualifies for it.

Rudimentary welfare regimes are found in Portugal, Spain, Italy, Greece, and Ireland, where the accepted position is that citizens do not have inherent rights to government-sponsored welfare support. Local governments provide some services or income support, but the patterns of availability vary widely even within one country. In these countries, the traditional extended family and community are still common. The state assumes that when someone is in need, his or her relatives and friends will intervene to provide needed services, financial support, and care for the young, old, and disabled. The state also assumes that women kin are available to provide child care and other social services free, despite the fact that in South Europe women actually form the bulk of the flexible, low-wage work force. Finally, there is the official assumption that the large informal economy will provide some sort of employment for whoever needs it. Some of these attitudes may be changing in Italy, which has experienced an economic boom in recent years. With more and more women working full time outside the home, some state-supported day care is available for children under five.

As the European Union develops, Europe's social welfare systems will probably become more similar to one another, but it is as yet unclear just which models will prevail. Some suggest that the dominance of the German economy in Europe could mean that the conservative German model for welfare will spread. Others suggest that the entry of more progressive Scandinavian countries into the EU will reinvigorate the commitment to active, less gendered, welfare policies. One crucial factor influencing which models will emerge will be the degree to which women are successful in increasing their representation on policy making bodies in the EU (see the section on women and political power in Europe later in this chapter).

Economic and Political Issues

Almost all economic and political issues in Europe today are in one way or another linked with the efforts to achieve economic union. After World War II, there was a feeling that closer economic ties would prevent the hostilities that had led to two world wars. In 1958, Belgium, Luxembourg, the Netherlands, France, Italy, and West Germany formed the European Economic Community, whose members agreed to eliminate certain tariffs and promote mutual trade and cooperation. In 1993, after decades of preparation, during which an expanded common market removed tariffs and eased the flow of people and goods across national borders, 15 European countries agreed to form the EU. The intention is to lower trade barriers further, improve the climate for large-scale production, make investment capital more freely available, and create a common European currency. Some geographic specialization within the EU is encouraged in order to enable each country to develop to its best advantage. The countries now in the EU are Austria, Belgium, Denmark, Finland, France, Germany, Greece, the Republic of Ireland, Italy, Luxembourg, the Netherlands, Portugal, Spain, Sweden, and the United Kingdom. The plan is to prudently add more countries to their number over time (Figure 4.8).

The European Union

There are now close to 350 million people in the EU (out of a total of 570 million in the whole of Europe). Their combined exports are 40 percent of the world's total, and their average gross national product (GNP) per capita is roughly that of the United States. Although the day is probably far off when the EU economy will be as open as that in the United States, Europe is moving in that direction. Americans can easily appreciate the advantages of being able to move across (state) borders with total ease, of being able to search for jobs across the continent instead of in only one state, and of having a continent-wide market in which to buy and sell. Nonetheless, not all Europeans support the EU. Some countries, especially Britain, resisted joining it out of fear of losing control of their own economies. In all countries, especially the wealthier ones like Germany, France, and the Netherlands, sectors of organized labor have opposed the EU. They fear that workers in wealthier countries will lose jobs, their high wages, and their benefits if industries have the freedom to move to poorer parts of the EU, such as Portugal, Spain, Ireland, and Greece.

At this time, the EU is by no means an association of equals. Germany is the largest country, with 82 million people, and it is considered to be the most stable economy. Its people live well and enjoy many tax-supported social services, although reunification with the nearly bankrupt former East Germany has recently caused some strain. France, with 58.4 million people and a diversified economy, also has a high standard of living. The United Kingdom, with 58.8 million people, has been the international financial center in Europe for hundreds of years and is currently enjoying a time of prosperity. The countries of South Europe (Portugal, Spain, Italy, and Greece), with much smaller populations and a long history of low productivity, have usually been considered poor cousins. Recently, however, Italy and Spain have also begun to prosper, in part because their low wage scales attract industry. Individual EU members are wary that these variable circumstances might jeopardize their own circumstances. At the same time, many are intrigued by union and the benefits it could bring.

Many of the countries of East and Central Europe would like to join the EU, but the transition from centrally planned to free market economies is difficult and slow, and only some are considered strong candidates. Poland, the Czech Republic, Hungary, Estonia, and Slovenia are being groomed for entry. All now trade with the countries of the EU, under tariff-free terms. Nonetheless, their economies are fragile, and western

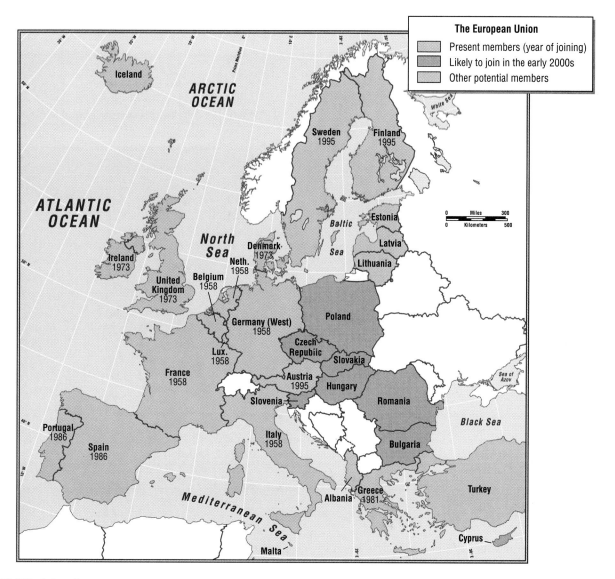

FIGURE 4.8 The European Union (EU) and countries that wish to join.

Europeans are not eager to accept into their midst countries with unresolved problems. Moreover, each new country admitted to the EU has the potential to upset the delicate political and economic balance achieved up to now. As of 1998, the five countries just mentioned were being considered for admission in 2003.

NATO's Role in the European Union. During most of the time since World War II that Europe has been moving toward economic union, the cold war raged as an overarching fact of life. To counterbalance the USSR and its Eastern European allies, the United States, Canada, Western Europe, and Turkey formed a military alliance called the North Atlantic Treaty Organization, or NATO. This experience in NATO with military cooperation and sharing of authority was an important precursor to European economic union.

Now, with the demise of the Soviet Union, NATO's role has become that of a stabilizing institution while Europe adjusts to a new era of cooperation. As cold war contentions fade and international politics become truly global in scale, some foresee NATO expanding its role as a peacekeeper to adjacent regions, such as the Balkans, Central Europe, Russia, and Southwest and Central Asia. A further possibility is that membership in NATO may serve as a stepping stone to membership in the EU, especially for countries once allied with the USSR. Three such countries, Poland, the Czech Republic, and Hungary, joined NATO in 1999.

A Common European Currency. The next step in deepening the level of economic unity in Europe is to create a common currency. At the moment, each

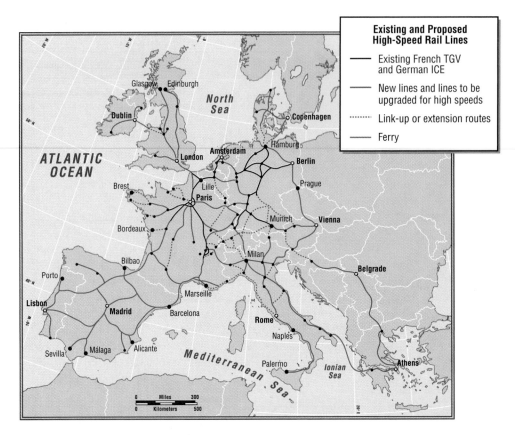

FIGURE 4.9 Existing and proposed high-speed rail lines (as intended by the EU Commission). [Adapted from William H. Berentsen, *Contemporary Europe: A Geographic Analysis* (New York: Wiley, 1997), p. 164.]

European country has its own money, which varies in value from all others. Travelers and international businesses must change currencies every time they go from country to country, and fees are charged for every exchange. To avoid the inconvenience and expense, there is a move to create an entirely new currency, called the euro, to be used by all the countries of the EU. The euro became the official medium of exchange for bookkeeping on January 1, 1999, though it will probably not be widely used in everyday retail transactions until after January 2002. Many countries are attached to their own money, and three EU countries—the United Kingdom, Denmark, and Sweden—have elected not to participate. More especially, they are loath to give up the power of controlling their own economies, which might be lost if everyone uses the same money and money flows freely across borders.

Transportation Infrastructure Development. As European unification proceeds, there is increasing focus on extending transportation networks to draw all Europe together. Europeans have typically emphasized fast rail networks more than automobile highways

(Figure 4.9). Now there is a noticeable movement to less energy-efficient but more flexible motorized vehicles. In 1994, leaders of the EU announced the intention to build **Corridor Five,** a major transportation roadway across southern Europe, stretching from Barcelona east 2000 miles (3500 kilometers) to Kiev in Ukraine. It will match a similar route to the north that now stretches across Germany and carries much of the east-west European trade. The completion of Corridor Five promises to change economic relationships between European countries, drawing more trade to the south and east.

One can now travel by canal and river across the North European Plain from Paris to Warsaw; and a canal now links the Rhine with the Main and Danube rivers. Recently completed work to make the Danube navigable in all seasons means that there is now a 2000-mile (3500-kilometer) waterway linking Rotterdam on the North Sea with the Black Sea, thus the countries of East and Central Europe are brought into closer contact with West and North Europe. Both water and highway links will surely facilitate the eventual inclusion of some of these countries in the EU.

Trends in European Economic Sectors

Europe is one of the wealthiest and most productive regions on earth, but it is facing increasing competition from other regions. A major reason for the effort at economic union is Europeans' desire to secure their position in the world economy.

Industry and Manufacturing. Europe was the birthplace of the industrial revolution, and its industrial growth was enhanced by the local availability of energy, raw materials, relatively cheap labor, and good transport. But times change. Now Europe's competitive edge is being dulled by the very fact that it was first to industrialize. Its laborers and managers are highly paid compared to world standards. Because Europe industrialized early, some of its industrial facilities—its factories and mines, roads and railroads—are becoming obsolete, driving up the costs of production. This is especially true in East and Central Europe, where industrialization came later and standards and efficiency remained below par. Also, modern industry and transport require more sources of energy than are available within the continent. To continue its industrial leadership, Europe will have to find new sources of energy.

Historically, the continent depended heavily on coal for powering industry, providing heating, and generating electricity. Now Europeans tend to use oil, gas, and nuclear power, and increasingly they are dependent on energy from outside the region. For example, Europe now buys some of its gas from Algeria and Russia and much of its oil from the Middle East. Within the region itself there are large oil and gas deposits in the North Sea and under the Netherlands. The North Sea deposit, controlled by Britain and Norway, now supplies a major portion of energy used in Germany and Britain. The Netherlands ships gas to most of West Europe. The use of nuclear power for industry and domestic needs has been more common in Europe than in North America. France, for example, depends on nuclear power more than any other country on earth. Nonetheless, many European countries are now phasing out their use of nuclear energy in response to public concern about safety risks.

Industry in Europe used to be primarily heavy industry, that based on coal and steel production. It was concentrated in the British Midlands and along the Rhine and other major rivers of the North European Plain, close to Europe's main coal fields. In the twentieth century, industry began to diversify and spread into North and South Europe. Figure 4.10 shows these patterns. In the last several decades, industry, much of it high tech, has spread to all major metropolitan areas. Many factors have made industrial location more flexible, including new technology, the expansion of transport systems (especially highways), the easing of trade and migration restrictions in preparation for the EU, and the switch away from coal as a source of energy. Older industrial locations have expanded as well.

Europeans produce a wide range of high-quality products, yet the cost and inefficiency of their production sometimes leaves them uncompetitive in the world market. This is because services to industries such as utilities (phones, energy, water) are expensive, and because of high labor costs, high taxes, and tight environmental and financial regulations. To lower costs, many firms are now establishing branches abroad for the same reasons that American firms have moved to Mexico or Southeast Asia: to take advantage of lower wages, fewer costly environmental regulations, cheaper energy, and proximity to raw materials. Being close to willing customers for the items produced is also an advantage at times. Interestingly, some European firms are finding that moving to the United States saves them money for all these reasons. Such moves may increase unemployment at home, at least for a while.

Agriculture in the Region. Europeans have long been known for their successful farms. Although fewer and fewer people are engaged in full-time farming, most Europeans are eating better than ever before and food is absorbing a smaller percentage of household budgets. In the most troubled parts of East and Central Europe this is not so much the case, however, because many farms remain behind technologically and are unable as yet to produce efficiently for market demands.

To keep their agricultural production high and diversified, Europeans have encouraged farmers to stay on the land by guaranteeing them certain prices for commodities and by providing other government subsidies. These programs have the effect of raising food costs for the consumer. Sometimes subsidies encourage overproduction of a commodity, causing a glut. Europe has then been known to sell these surpluses on the world market, a practice called dumping, which lowers global prices and hurts producers of these same commodities elsewhere around the world, especially in Australia, New Zealand, and the United States.

There is regional specialization in European agriculture, tuned to both climates and cultural preference. For example, the United Kingdom focuses on producing meat and dairy products; in part, this is because its wet, cloudy climate is not ideal for growing field crops but does promote the luxurious growth of grass for grazing. France is also well watered but with more sunshine, and it is Europe's leading agricultural producer. France is an exporter of grains, dairy products, fruits, vegetables, and finished luxury products like wine and fine cheese. The Netherlands, with its mild, cool climate, has some dairy farming and specializes in fine

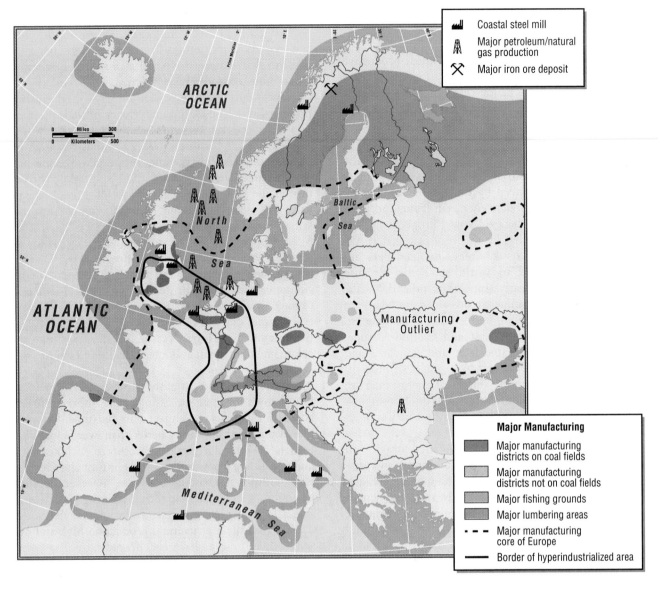

FIGURE 4.10 Europe's principal industrial centers. [Adapted from Terry Jordan, *The European Culture Area* (New York: Harper & Row, 1988), p. 338.]

vegetables and greens. In addition, the Netherlands provides flowers, and its seeds and bulbs are marketed internationally. Farther east in Europe, the more continental climates have colder winters and warmer summers, and farms grow wheat and cold-resistant vegetables like beets and cabbages. In South Europe, the climate is warm and dry during the growing season. There, permanent crops like olives and grapes are more common, but recently Spain and Portugal have begun shipping high-quality produce like tomatoes, peppers, and oranges throughout the continent. These are, however, only general patterns of regional specialization for commercial farmers. Gardening is extraordinarily popular in Europe; people in all countries grow a wide range of crops for their own personal use.

Farms in Europe tend to be smaller and more intensive in production than those in the United States. In the EU, 80 percent of the farmers operate on 159 acres or less: in France, the average is just 61 acres; in the Netherlands, less than 40 acres. (U.S. farms average 469 acres.) The geographer Ingolf Vogeler, who studies European agriculture, points out that these small European farms are disappearing. As is the case in the United States, the trend in Europe is toward larger farms, worked by fewer people. For example, in West Germany between 1950 and 1980, 850,000 tiny farms were folded into larger units. Vogeler points out that more extreme consolidation happened under communism in East and Central Europe, for many of the same reasons. Bigger farms are more efficient; profits

Community gardens, like this one in Ljubljana, Slovenia, dot many urban landscapes in Europe, especially where there are nearby apartment complexes. In many places, gardens rather than lawns are customary for individual homeowners. [Mac Goodwin.]

rise and living standards improve for farm families who remain after consolidation. Mechanization shortens the workday and frees women from drudgery. Children can attend school and prepare for careers outside agriculture, instead of working endlessly in the fields. Farmers have time to learn to become scientific managers who can take advantage of research aimed at improving all aspects of the farm, from soil fertility to marketing.

Now, in East and Central Europe, Vogeler finds that many owners have reclaimed land taken by the Communists for collective farms; but these owners are not farming themselves. They are choosing to rent their land to large corporate farms, which continue to work the big fields used under the old collectivized system. In time, these large farms, revamped into corporations, may give the smaller, more family-oriented farms of Western Europe some stiff competition. They, in turn, will undergo consolidation as the EU reduces the subsidies and price supports that kept them viable.

In coming years, EU farmers are likely to market more goods to the wider world, and EU consumers are likely to buy more food from outside the region. For example, between 1994 and 1996, U.S. food exports to Europe grew by 33 percent to $9 billion; and EU agricultural exports to the United States grew to $6.5 billion. This increase is due in part to international agreements to remove tariffs, but also to the activities of multinational food companies. For example, the American company Archer-Daniels-Midland has food-processing plants in several European countries, while Royal Ahold of the Netherlands owns several American supermarket chains.

Tourism. The long vacation is a European institution. Most workers are allowed at least a month off from the job every year, and many receive five or six weeks. Hence, tourism is a substantial part of the European economy. One job in eight in the European Union is related to tourism, and the industry generates 13.5 percent of the EU's gross domestic product and 15 percent of its taxes.

The seaside is a particularly favorite destination; for decades, Europeans flocked to Portugal, Spain, the south of France, Italy, the Adriatic, and Greece. These were once the poor parts of Europe where, because of low wages and cheap quarters along the sea, tourists could afford a long vacation. Now, the south of France is one of the poshest vacation spots on earth. Spain and Italy are also becoming too expensive for many lower middle-class Europeans. The Adriatic has been inaccessible since the wars in Bosnia and Croatia during the 1990s. As a result, many less affluent Europeans are beginning to visit the Caribbean, especially Cuba, which attracts the working-class European market. EU vacationers increasingly tend to visit one another's countries. Germans travel the most, followed by the British, French, and Italians. Figure 4.11 shows where these travelers went during 1996 and the amount that tourists of each nationality spent while on vacation.

Political Challenges to the European Union

The immigrant and citizenship issues discussed earlier often figure in positions taken by the political right in Europe. Rather than seeing immigrants as adding richness and variety to European life, many right-wing parties see them as taking away jobs and contaminating European culture. This view is indicated in the following quotation from a leader of France's rightist National Front.

If we want to send the Arabs and Africans and Asians back to where they came from, it is not because we hate them, it is because they pollute our national identity and take our jobs. When we have power, we will organize their return. . . . [We] will force companies to pay a tax on foreign workers that will eventually lead to the foreigners losing their positions. (Bruno Megret, deputy director of France's National Front, 1997.)

Some of these groups promote the idea of "Fortress Europe," in which the EU would become a bulwark against so-called cultural corruption. Others oppose the EU entirely, on the grounds that it will dilute or

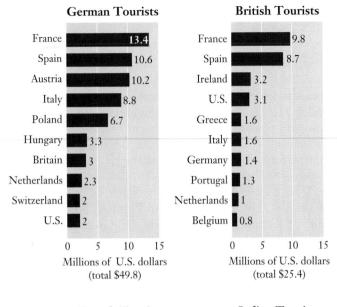

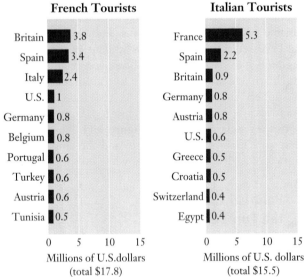

FIGURE 4.11 Destinations for and money spent by selected European tourists in 1996. [Adapted from Sue Truesdell, *New York Times,* April 12, 1998, p. WK5.]

million immigrants were to leave, 3 million unemployed French would find jobs. Demographers say the National Front is wrong. Given present levels of government support for the unemployed, most French would refuse to do the jobs many immigrants take as street sweepers, domestic servants, rest-room attendants, and agricultural laborers. The pay is too low and the work thought to be too demeaning. Furthermore, as France's population ages, taxes paid by the mostly young immigrant workers will be needed to pay the pensions of retiring French workers.

In recent years, the tensions associated with the move toward a more economically integrated Europe have also led to growing support for socialist and other left of center politicians, as well as to increases in the activity of labor unions. This is in large part a reaction against the current tendency of EU policies to abandon the European model of capitalism in favor of the U.S. model of capitalism. In the U.S. model, industries have relatively few obligations to their workers or the communities they are located in; industries are free to move wherever they want, often laying off tens of thousands of workers in the process. Many argue that jobs are easier to create where there are lower taxes and fewer obligations to employees; thus, in the long run unemployment will be less. In contrast, the European model features much stronger labor unions that have been able to demand a more generous welfare state (paid for with higher personal income and business taxes), higher wages, better working conditions, and laws that make it harder for employers to fire their workers. The economies of Germany and North Europe are the most complete examples of the European model. These economies are highly productive, thanks to a well-educated and economically secure work force; and they are functioning smoothly, thanks to a high level of cooperation between labor unions, employers, and the government. Nevertheless, unemployment is higher than in United States, and recent EU policies have exacerbated the problem by making it easier for European companies to move to low-wage areas.

European labor unions have called on the EU to develop plans for creating jobs in order to temper the rise in unemployment. To many European political analysts, the EU member-state elections in the late 1990s signaled popular sentiment in favor of a model that takes worker interests to heart. In those elections, voters in the United Kingdom, France, and Germany elected left-leaning politicians, who typically are supportive of organized labor and social welfare programs. However, most ruling political parties support the overall drift toward less social welfare. The EU remains limited in its ability to address controversial issues like wage rates, social welfare benefits, and unemployment, because the various countries have competing interests that are difficult to resolve.

extinguish distinct national cultures. In either case, the far-right groups arouse considerable anxiety, in part because their brand of extreme nationalism bears resemblance to that of the Nazis and other fascist groups held responsible for World War II. Some right-wing parties are associated with vigilante neo-Nazi groups that perpetrate violence against immigrants and others they perceive as "undesirable," such as homosexuals and Jewish or Muslim people.

Right-wingers have had some success in promoting their policies. The French National Front has successfully linked unemployment and immigrants in the minds of many French citizens, suggesting that if 3

Women and Political Power in Europe

In Europe, the political power and influence of women lags far behind their numbers, as Figure 4.12 demonstrates. In France, women are about 9 percent of elected representatives; they are less than 15 percent in Portugal (13), Italy (10), Ireland (14), the United Kingdom (12), and Greece (6.3). In the United States, they are 11 percent of the elected representatives. In East and Central Europe, the record is similarly low despite policies professing gender equality. Only in North Europe do women come anywhere close to forming 50 percent of the representatives in parliament or the legislature. Throughout the continent, women are also poorly represented in government positions, serving mostly in the lower end of the bureaucracy. Women thus have little voice in the formation of na-

tional policies, even those that directly affect them. They have had to rely on men to push for such legal measures as the right to work, equal job opportunities, and equal wages and fringe benefits. Progress has been slow. For example, French women account for 46 percent of the work force, but earn 20 percent less than men.

One might question why, given the region's overall prosperity, women in Europe have not achieved more equality than is the case. First, although EU policies have officially ended discrimination against women, implementation lags far behind. Also, some analysts point out that, despite efforts at solidarity, women have fewer chances to meet together locally or internationally because of differences born of language, ethnicity, nationality, education level, social background, and geographic separation. Nonetheless, despite underrepresentation, Europe has the greatest proportion of women in elected positions of all world regions, and there are now several pan-European women's commissions that disseminate information on the status of women in the region.

Environmental Issues

Europe's environment is already dramatically changed from what it was before human beings became so active in the region 10,000 or more years ago. Nearly all the original forests are gone, some for more than a thousand years. Europe's seemingly natural landscapes, many of which are unusually beautiful, are in large part the creation of humans who have changed the landforms, the drainage systems, and the plant cover repeatedly over time. In a number of countries, most outstandingly the Netherlands, there are literally no natural landscapes left. So environmentalists in Europe focus more on sustaining livable environments for future generations than sustaining pristine nature into the future.

The Green movement in Europe is a transnational effort to bring the wasteful use of resources and pollution and its consequences to the attention of the general European public. The movement has gained considerable political strength, and many Green principles are incorporated into the policies of the European Union. In some countries, there are Green political parties that successfully present candidates for major office; increasingly, such parties are strong enough to influence national elections, as was the case in Germany in 1998. Throughout Europe, the Green party has succeeded in mounting popular movements to stop or modify environmentally damaging development projects, especially those connected with nuclear power. But beyond political activism, Green ethics influence the daily life of Europeans. The observant

Women in Legislature or Parliament

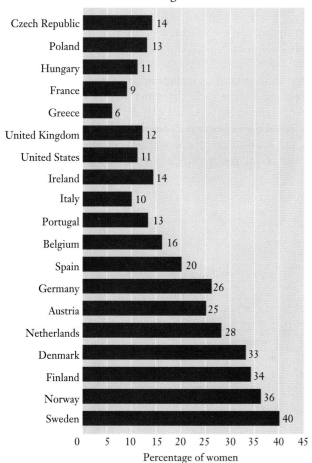

FIGURE 4.12 Percent of women legislators in selected European nations (with U.S. comparison).
[Data from the Gender Empowerment Measure, *1998,* United Nations Development Programme, *Human Development Report* at http://www.undp.org/undp/hdro/98gem.htm.]

American traveler in Europe will notice many ways in which European lifeways result in lower resource consumption: people walk to many of their appointments, their cars are smaller, public transportation is fast and easy to use, people take shorter showers, they live in smaller spaces, the yards of their houses contain vegetable gardens rather than great expanses of grass. Many of these practices are the natural outgrowth of circumstances in the region, and the Green movement has made Europeans further aware of the advantages of curtailed resource use.

The Seas

Europe is surrounded by seas—the Baltic, the North Sea, the Atlantic, the Mediterranean, and the Black Sea. Any pollutants that enter Europe's interior rivers, streams, and canals eventually reach these surrounding seas. Because the Atlantic is such a large body of water and is open to the circulating flow of the world ocean, it is able to disperse most pollutants dumped into it along European shores. The North Sea, a relatively open pouch off the Atlantic, is also able to cleanse itself quickly. On the other hand, the Baltic, Mediterranean, and Black seas are nearly landlocked bodies of water that do not have the power to flush themselves out. All three seas are prone to accumulate pollution, yet all three are surrounded by countries that are at different stages of development, making it difficult for them to cooperate on solutions. Take, for example, the case of the Mediterranean.

It appears to take about 80 years for a complete exchange of water within the Mediterranean Sea. Atlantic water flows in through the narrow Straits of Gibraltar and moves east, evaporating as it goes, so the water at the far eastern end is more saline and heavier. This heavier water sinks and flows back west at a lower depth, and finally exits the Mediterranean, many decades later, back at Gibraltar. The ecology of the sea basin is attuned to this lengthy cycle, but over time the balance has been upset. About 320 million people now live in countries surrounding the Mediterranean. Municipal and rural sewage (75 percent of it untreated), eroded sediment, agricultural chemicals, industrial waste, nuclear contamination, and oil spills are pouring into the Mediterranean. Some of the much beloved resorts in the Mediterranean are no longer safe for swimmers. Many of the pollutants add nitrogen, which causes vast tracts of algae to "bloom," rendering the sea environment inhospitable to natural life-forms and humans alike. Figure 4.13 shows the geographic pattern of Mediterranean pollution.

Relatively rich and industrialized Europe (along the north shore of the Mediterranean) shares the basin with relatively poor North Africa and the Middle East (along the south shore). While most of the pollution is generated in the north, populations are rising rapidly in the south, and soon their sheer numbers will also pose an environmental threat. In 1995, the European Union inaugurated a cooperative movement seeking to link the richer economies of the northern Mediterranean with those of the southern Mediterranean. The two groups

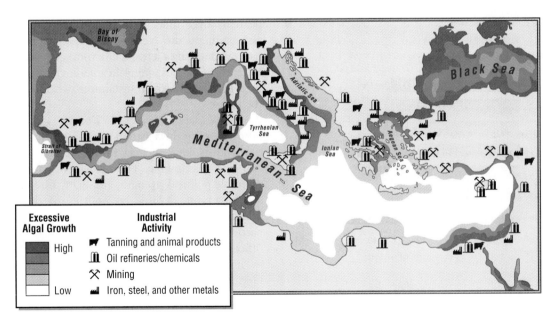

FIGURE 4.13 Sources and types of pollution in the Mediterranean Sea. [Adapted from *The Economist Atlas of the New Europe*, 1992, p. 210.]

are to resolve jointly what kind of development is feasible for the welfare of the entire region. The developed economies on the European side of the sea have sounded the alarm only after they have themselves substantially polluted the water; this fact has left the developing countries of North Africa and the eastern Mediterranean feeling that they are being asked to make sacrifices for the environment that Europe was unwilling to make.

The Rivers

Many of Europe's rivers are navigable deep into the interior of the continent. They have transported people and goods for many hundreds of years (see Figure 4.14), but they are also heavily used for other purposes. Europe's large cities situated along rivers or at their mouths dump municipal waste into the waters, and dams have increasingly been built across rivers to supply hydroelectric energy to cities. It has been difficult to manage the use and cleanup of these rivers rationally because Europe is divided into small countries and many rivers run through or form the border of a number of different countries.

The Danube River is a particularly interesting environmental case study. It rises in the Black Forest of southern Germany and flows east and south past Vienna, Budapest, and Belgrade, passing through or forming the border of seven countries before emptying into the Black Sea. Before the fall of the USSR, Austria, what was then Czechoslovakia, and Hungary had agreed to jointly build two hydroelectric dams across the river; these would have worked in tandem to flush huge volumes of water through turbines twice daily. The project pushed ahead, even though no one had properly calculated the environmental impacts along what had been a relatively unspoiled part of the river.

Then the political climate in Eastern Europe shifted, and in Hungary, remarkably, a new reformist government dismantled the newly built Hungarian portion of the dams and even in part restored the landscape. But Slovakia persevered in the project by diverting the Danube and sending it through a canal and turbines. Now Hungary is suing Slovakia in the World Court because the original riverbed has dried up and species that once occupied the river's wetlands are dying. Meanwhile, agricultural chemicals are polluting a reservoir created upstream of the Slovak dam and are destroying its aquatic life.

Hungary's landmark claim in the World Court could set an important precedent for the many cross-border environmental disputes that are brewing in Europe and beyond. Until now, customary Western law accepted the idea that upstream users have rights over users downstream, a legal concept that has led to many a Wild West movie plot in the United States and

to tensions in several parts of the world where this concept applies. Hungary will argue that shared resources, such as rivers, can be exploited only by mutual consent, and that pollution of a common resource constitutes a breach of human rights.

The Air

Air pollution is produced when large amounts of oil, gas, coal, or wood are burned to power vehicles, heating systems, and machinery, or when industrial processes or accidents release airborne chemicals. It is a significant problem across much of Europe. Reducing energy use and burning fuel more efficiently improve air quality, and European industry has a good record of cleaning up polluting emissions. Nevertheless, there is now a trend everywhere toward increased use of cars and trucks; air pollution will therefore rise.

According to the geographer Brent Yarnal, the former Communist states of East and Central Europe have the world's highest per capita emissions from burning oil and gas. Until belt-tightening began in the transition to market economies, these countries used energy at rates averaging 50 to 150 percent higher than the United States (one of the world's largest per capita users of energy). In Poland in the late 1980s, air quality in the industrial centers was so bad that all young children had to be relocated to rural environments to preserve their health. Bulgaria was the least efficient and most polluting of the lot, and the hope was that restructuring the economy would improve energy efficiency and reduce emissions. Pollution did decrease briefly in Bulgaria after 1990, but only because of economic decline; by the mid 1990s, pollution levels were up again.

Yarnal found that in Bulgaria and elsewhere there is likely to be a long lag until energy use and air pollution are reduced. Reformist organizations that might push for environmental improvements are not well developed. Antipollution activists are reviled for suggesting regulations that might slow economic growth. But heavy pollution has long-term costs: decline in human health, lowering of crop yields, loss of water quality and quantity. Recognizing these costs, the World Bank and private firms are beginning to force change. For example, in the early 1990s, the World Bank encouraged five countries in Eastern Europe—Bulgaria, the former Czechoslovakia, Hungary, Poland, and Romania—to reduce fossil-fuel use; this was to be done by drastically cutting government subsidies that for many years had lowered the costs to consumers and encouraged wasteful use.

One has to ask why the countries of East and Central Europe allowed their environmental situations to reach a state of catastrophe. Part of the reason may be the Marxist theories and policies promoted by the

USSR, which portrayed nature as the handmaiden of social progress, existing only to serve human needs. The Soviet leader Joseph Stalin once said: "We cannot expect charity from Nature. We must tear it from her." Another reason may be that, with only superficial democratic institutions in place during the Soviet era, there was little opportunity for public outrage at pollution to be channeled into constructive political activism and change.

Measures of Human Well-Being

VIGNETTE

The Parvanov family lives in a small apartment outside Sofia, Bulgaria. The family appears to have the material wealth of the middle class: adequate food, a nice home, a car in the garage. But looks are deceiving; there is trouble. Because of recent high rates of inflation, Mr. Parvanov's salary is now worth only U.S. $30 a month, so he moonlights on a construction job. Mrs. Parvanov holds three part-time jobs: she works as a clerk, as an assistant in a building company, and at night machine-knits clothes she sells in the local market. Theodora, the 19-year-old daughter, attends university by day and helps her mother knit at night. Yet with all this effort (six jobs in all), the family earns only about U.S. $100 a month. With this tiny amount they must also support two grandparents whose pensions will no longer cover food, let alone medicine. The car hasn't been driven in months because gasoline is too expensive. They are able to survive only because the Bulgarian government heavily subsidizes the costs of food, rent, and other basic services, a situation that will not last much longer. [Adapted from Robert Frank, Price of ioslation: Impoverished Bulgaria is ready for reform, *Wall Street Journal*, February 28, 1997, p. 1.]

The governor of the central bank in Bulgaria, Lubomire Filipov, says: "Bulgaria likes to think of itself as European, [but] now, our inflation looks more like [it used to in] Latin America, and our debt and poverty looks more like Sudan." In fact, Bulgaria is now Europe's poorest country.

We have already observed that there is considerable disparity in wealth across Europe. Table 4.2 provides the opportunity to compare the well-being of people like the Parvanovs with Europeans in 19 other countries and with people outside the region, in the United States, Japan, and Kuwait. The three indexes are those explained in Chapter 1 and used throughout this book.

In the category of gross national product per capita, you can see that most countries in North and West Europe compare favorably with the United States, Japan and Kuwait. South Europe lies in the middle range of GNP per capita, but East and Central Europe are way down the scale. Their per capita figures are well below those of several of the Middle and South American countries, for example. It is important to note, however, that until recently in East and Central Europe there has not been great disparity in wealth between classes, because the communist system specifically sought to even out the distribution of wealth. As a result, GNP figures for this region are a somewhat more meaningful measure of real well-being than they are in Middle and South America, where class disparities are huge.

In column 3 of the table, the United Nations Human Development Index (HDI) combines three components—life expectancy at birth, educational attainment, and adjusted real income—to arrive at a ranking of 174 countries that is more sensitive to factors other than just income. In many parts of Europe, state subsidies keep prices low and make salaries go further, as had been the case for the Parvanovs in Bulgaria. All countries in North, West, and South Europe (with the exception of Estonia) rank fairly high on the global HDI. North Europe and France stand out, undoubtedly because these countries look after their people with comprehensive social welfare systems. Meanwhile, East and Central Europe rank relatively low because, as the communist system failed, most state-run firms cut jobs, social welfare programs went bankrupt, and environmental quality declined. People lost not only their jobs, but even health care, housing, and food subsidies. Those retaining their jobs saw their salaries rendered meaningless pittances as a result of high inflation rates—as did Mr. Parvanov in Bulgaria. Air and water pollution increased, daily stress mounted, overall quality of life declined drastically, and life expectancies plummeted. All of East and Central Europe ranks lower on the HDI than Argentina (30) and Chile (33) in the Americas. In fact, Albania and Bulgaria are now poorer than many Latin American countries on several indexes.

The Gender Empowerment Measure (GEM, column 4 of Table 4.2) ranks countries by the extent to which females have opportunities to participate in economic and political life. It looks at where women are employed in the economy and the extent to which women participate in society, especially as elected officials. The GEM figures show that North and West Europe, with the notable exceptions of Estonia, Latvia, and France, do better than most countries in empower-

TABLE 4.2

Human well-being rankings of selected European countries

Country	GNP per capita (in U.S. dollars), 1996	Human Development Index (HDI) global rankings, 1998[a]	Gender Empowerment Measure (GEM) global rankings, 1998
Selected countries for comparison			
Japan	40,940	8 (high)	38
Kuwait	17,390 (1997)	54 (high)	75
United States	28,020	4 (high)	11
North Europe			
Denmark	32,100	18 (high)	3
Estonia	3,080	77 (medium)	47
Finland	23,240	6 (high)	5
Iceland	26,580	5 (high)	6
Latvia	2,300	92 (medium)	52
Lithuania	2,280	79 (medium)	Not available
Norway	34,510	3 (high)	2
Sweden	25,710	10 (high)	1
West Europe			
Austria	28,110	13 (high)	10
France	26,270	2 (high)	31
Germany	28,870	19 (high)	8
Luxembourg	45,360	26 (high)	14
Netherlands	25,940	7 (high)	9
Switzerland	44,350	16 (high)	13
United Kingdom	19,600	14 (high)	20
South Europe			
Greece	11,460	20 (high)	51
Italy	19,880	21 (high)	26
Portugal	10,160	33 (high)	22
Spain	14,350	11 (high)	16
East and Central Europe			
Albania	820	105 (medium)	Not available
Bosnia/Herzegovina	Not available	Not available	Not available
Bulgaria	1,190	67 (medium)	43
Czech Republic	4,740	39 (high)	24
Hungary	4,340	47 (high)	30
Moldova	590	113 (medium)	Not available
Poland	3,230	52 (high)	29
Romania	1,600	74 (medium)	64
Slovakia	3,410	42	27
Slovenia	9,240	37 (high)	36
Ukraine	1,200	102 (medium)	Not available
Yugoslavia (Serbia)	Not available	Not available	Not available
Europe (including Belarus and Russia)	13,710	NA[b]	NA
World	5,180	NA	NA

[a]The "high" and "medium" designations indicate where the country ranks among the 174 countries classified into three categories (high, medium, low) by the United Nations.
[b]NA = Not applicable.
Sources: Data from *1998 World Population Data Sheet*, Population Reference Bureau; and *Human Development Report 1998*, United Nations Development Programme.

ing women. Latvia and Estonia's ranks are low because they were long part of the Soviet bloc and retain many features that restrict women. France ranks lower because, in comparison to the rest of West and North Europe, women are more often shut out of upper echelon jobs, are overwhelmingly in low-paid jobs, and hold very few elected positions. Notice that in South Europe, Spain ranks rather high on the GEM, Italy less so. Both countries are changing rapidly as they enjoy an economic boom. Women who had long been overeducated for the lower echelon jobs they held have rushed to take new, more responsible positions; hence, the GEM rankings for these countries are likely to rise. In East and Central Europe, useful statistics have not been collected, in part because of the present turmoil and in part because the issue is not recognized. Specific studies report that now, compared to men, a disproportionate number of women in East and Central Europe are unemployed and sinking into poverty. As state-run firms are sold off and made more efficient, women, who occupy the lowest ranks, are the first to be fired. Policy makers have concluded that men's jobs are more essential than women's jobs.

SUBREGIONS OF EUROPE

The text now looks at the subregions of Europe as separate units and discusses in greater detail some of the issues that presently affect them. The decision about which subregion a particular country should be placed in was based simply on my best judgment of the situation in Europe at this time. Good arguments for other combinations could be made. One could, for example, place the United Kingdom and the Republic of Ireland in North Europe; and Estonia, Latvia, and Lithuania in East and Central Europe.

Every subregion of Europe is undergoing changes; these are linked to the end of cold war politics, the struggles of East and Central European countries to find themselves, moves toward greater economic and political cooperation throughout the region, and global shifts in economic power.

West Europe

Despite their apparent economic success, the countries of West Europe (Figure 4.14)—the United Kingdom, the Republic of Ireland, France, Germany, Belgium, Luxembourg, the Netherlands, Austria, and Switzerland—are confronting several issues that will

affect their development and overall well-being. These include (1) the continuing movement toward economic and political union; (2) the resolution of long-standing cultural and religious conflicts, such as that in Northern Ireland, and recent strife between host countries and immigrant groups; (3) the existence of high unemployment despite general economic growth; and (4) increasing the global competitiveness of Europe's agriculture, industry, and service sectors.

Benelux

Often called the Low Countries or Benelux, Belgium, the Netherlands, and Luxembourg have achieved very high standards of living considering their dense populations. The three countries are well located for trade: they lie close to North Europe and the British Isles and are adjacent to the very active Rhine delta and the industrial heart of Europe. The coastal location of Benelux and its great port cities of Antwerp, Rotterdam, and Amsterdam give these countries easy access to the global marketplace.

International trade has long been at the heart of the economies of Belgium and the Netherlands. Both were active colonizers of tropical zones: Belgium in Africa; the Netherlands in the Caribbean and Southeast Asia. Their economies benefited from the wealth extracted from these places and from the global trade in tropical products, such as spices, chocolate, fruit, wood, and minerals. Private companies based in Benelux still maintain advantageous relationships with the tropical areas, which supply raw materials for European industries. Brussels, the capital of Belgium, was chosen as the seat for European Union headquarters, and the Benelux countries have long played a central role in the EU; as a result, they occasionally find themselves embroiled in conflicts related to both the colonial past and pressures to integrate. The European "chocolate standards war" is a case in point.

In Europe, chocolate is an important luxury product that sells at very high prices. Godiva, for example, a brand loved by American chocoholics, is a Belgian company. Chocolate first enters Europe in the form of dried cacao beans, which are now grown mostly in Africa. Belgium, France, and six other EU nations agree that real chocolate (so labeled) must be made only of cocoa butter derived from cacao beans, with no oil or fat additives. But the United Kingdom, Denmark, and several other countries now routinely add cheaper oils to their mass-produced candy. The EU Commission, charged with defining common manufacturing standards for the entire EU, is trying to bring the different national chocolate traditions into line. It is thought that with open borders, the cheaper chocolate made with oil additives will have an unfair advantage over pure chocolate both in the EU and

FIGURE 4.14 The West Europe subregion.

abroad. Globally, six multinational firms, controlling well over half of all chocolate sales, side with the United Kingdom in arguing that chocolate recipes should not be standardized. The purists, on the other hand, argue that European chocolate stands a better chance of competing in the global market if it is a gourmet product that maintains the highest standards of purity.

West African countries that produce cacao beans favor the prohibition of other oils. Ghana, Cameroon, and Côte d'Ivoire are former European colonies that depend on cacao for at least a quarter of their export earnings. They estimate that the use of even as little as 5 percent of noncocoa oils in the EU will mean a 10 percent drop in world cacao consumption and will dev-

astate their economies. These three African countries have petitioned their former colonizers (Belgium, France, and Britain) to maintain the pure chocolate standards as part of agreements they made to help African economies rebound from colonial exploitation.

The largest Benelux nation, the Netherlands, is particularly noted for having reclaimed for human use land that was previously under the sea (Figure 4.15). One result is that today its landscape is almost entirely a human construct. As populations grew in the Middle Ages and after, people created more livable space by filling in a large natural wetland. To protect themselves from devastating North Sea surges, they built dikes, dug drainage canals, pumped water with windmills, and constructed artificial dunes along the ocean. Today,

FIGURE 4.15 Land reclamation areas in the Netherlands. [Adapted from William H. Berentsen, *Contemporary Europe: A Geographic Analysis* (New York: Wiley, 1997), p. 317.]

These two photographs of the Netherlands, taken from the air, show intensive land use and human manipulation of natural interactions between land and water in coastal zones. The photograph on the left shows part of the port of Rotterdam, looking northwest. Cranes transfer products between river vessels and oceangoing ships. The oil "tank farms" figure prominently in Dutch chemical industries. [Aeroview, Rotterdam.] The photograph on the right shows fields of flower bulbs on raised, drained lands close to the coast. Economically, the flowers, which are sold locally, are merely a by-product of the bulbs, which are marketed internationally. At the top of the picture can be seen the dunes that are the last defense against the sea. They are planted with trees for stabilization. [Aeroview, Rotterdam.]

a train trip through the Netherlands between Amsterdam and Rotterdam takes one past raised rectangular fields crisply edged with narrow drainage ditches and wider transport canals. The fields are filled with commercial flower beds of crocuses, tulips, daffodils, and hyacinths; there are also grazing cattle and vegetable gardens that feed the primarily urban population. There are virtually no pockets of wilderness, yet the landscape has an open, bucolic ambiance. In one vista through the train window, huge cranes at the port of Amsterdam loom in the distance; closer to one side are the high-tech office buildings of a new satellite town. In the foreground, a small fishing boat heads out to sea along a sparkling blue, reed-lined canal; and an elderly woman pushes her bicycle down a rural path, the rear basket stuffed with leeks and flowers.

The Netherlands has 15 million people, who enjoy a high standard of living. Yet it is the most densely settled country in Europe, and there is no land left for suburban expansion without seriously intruding on agricultural space. People now travel great distances to reach their jobs, and long commutes add to the air pollution and miserable traffic jams. There is not nearly enough space for recreation; bucolic as they seem, transport canals and carefully controlled raised fields and pastures are not a venue for picnics and soccer games.

France

France has the shape of a rough hexagon bounded by water on the north and west, mountains on the south and southeast, hills and plateaus on the east, and lowlands on the northeast. This hexagonal shape is centered on the capital city of Paris. It could be said that the cultural and economic life of France centers around Paris as well.

Paris is often called the City of Light because of the elegance of its architecture and urban design and its reputation as a center of culture and intellectual eminence. France's population is concentrated in Paris: together with its suburbs, the city has more than 11 million inhabitants, roughly a fifth of the country's total. It is also the hub of a well-integrated water, rail, and road transport system. Its central location and transport links attract a disproportionate share of trades and businesses: manufacturers of luxury items, designers, high-tech and automotive industries, distributors of fine farm produce; there is a steady stream of workers of all sorts. Several years ago, however, French planners decided that Paris was large enough, and they began diverting development to other parts of the country, especially Toulouse and farther south to the Mediterranean.

France is divided into several distinctive geographic regions. The Mediterranean coast is the site of France's leading port, Marseille, and of the famous French Riviera. Here, development is booming. Tourism, in particular, has inspired the building of marinas, condominiums, and parks that threaten to occupy every inch of waterfront.

To the northeast of Paris, close to Belgium, is an older industrial area around Lille that has been in decline for sometime (see Figure 4.10). Some of its steel, electronics, and aluminum companies have gone under, but others have survived and become more efficient.

To the west and southwest of Paris, toward the Atlantic, are lowland basins that are primarily less densely settled agricultural regions. Here, though wheat and other crops are grown, grapes are an important crop. The Bordeaux region is a leading exporter of French wines. France has the largest agricultural output in the EU and is second only to the United States in agricultural exports. Its climate is mild and humid, though drier to the south; and throughout the country, farmers have found profitable specialties: wheat (ranked fifth in world production), grapes (used to make wine), cheese (second in world production), fruit, olives, sugar beets and other vegetables, and sunflower seed oil (third in world production). Despite its leadership in agricultural production, agriculture accounts for only 8 percent of the national economy and employs only 5 percent of the population. Industry accounts for more than 30 percent and the service sector for 60 percent.

France derived considerable benefit and wealth from a large overseas empire, which it ruled until the mid-twentieth century. There were French colonies in the Caribbean, North America, North Africa, sub-Saharan Africa, Southeast Asia, and the Pacific. Now, many of the citizens of these former colonies live in France and lend to it their skills and a distinguishing multicultural flavor—this, despite the fact that the French are unusually conscious of their distinctive culture and are concerned about protecting what they consider its purity and uniqueness.

Few would quarrel with the idea that French culture has a certain cachet and that France is a worldwide arbiter of taste. People of many different cultural backgrounds accept the idea that the French language is particularly elegant and refined, the pinnacle of sophisticated expression. Furthermore, French style as exemplified in clothing, jewelry, perfume, and interior design is highly sought after, and French culinary arts remain among the most cultivated of cooking traditions. Its sophisticated culture has made France one of the leading tourist attractions on earth. In 1996, France attracted 62.4 million international tourists, more than the population of the entire country (58.6 million). Other Europeans, Americans, and Turks form the majority of tourists in France.

France's strong cultural identity is both a blessing and a curse. Many in France are deeply concerned about what they perceive as a decrease in French prestige in the world, about rising unemployment and falling social welfare benefits, about cultural adulteration from France's former colonies, and about a decline in French industrial competitiveness. Such feelings have resulted in the increasing popular support of the National Front, France's xenophobic right-wing party. But others in France are searching for a new way to think about themselves in a now much wider world—a potentially more egalitarian global community they helped to create.

Germany

The most famous image of Germany of the last several years is that of a happy crowd dismantling the Berlin Wall in 1989. This important symbolic end of the Soviet sphere of influence in East and Central Europe had particular significance for Germany, which for 40 years had been divided into two unequal parts. Russian troops occupied the smaller, eastern third of Germany after World War II and then, in 1949, the Soviets and their German counterparts created East Germany. Over the next several years, perhaps as many as 3 million East Germans migrated to West Germany. To retain the remaining population, the Soviets in 1961 literally walled off the border. East German skilled labor, mineral resources, and industrial capacities were used to buttress the socialist economies and support the military aims of the USSR and its allies.

Because Germany was regarded as the perpetrator of two world wars, West Germany had to tread a careful path after 1945, seeing to its own economic and social reconstruction, rebuilding a prosperous industrial base (see Figure 4.10), and yet not seeming to become too powerful economically or politically. For the most part, West Germany played its complex role successfully. Since the early 1980s, it was a leader in the efforts to construct a united Europe. It bore the biggest financial burden of the unification process.

The fall of the Berlin Wall in 1989 brought new responsibilities to Germany. In 1990, East Germany came home with a suitcase of troubles. Its industries were outdated, inefficient, polluting, and, in large part, not redeemable. Its infrastructure of roads, bridges, dams, hydroelectric plants, nuclear energy plants, waterways, and buildings did not meet the standards of West Europe. They had to be remodeled or dismantled and replaced. Its industrial products had little competitive value on the world market, and German workers from the east, though considered highly competent in the Soviet sphere, were undereducated by West European standards.

Reunified Germany is Europe's most populous country (82 million people) and is a leader in industry and trade, but the costs of absorbing the poor eastern zone have dragged Germany down in many rankings within Europe. In the 1990s, unemployment rose sharply (especially among women) and remained an estimated 10.9 percent in 1998. Not only are there layoffs in the east, but German workers, accustomed to high wages and lavish benefits, are losing jobs as firms move overseas, some to the United States. Daimler Benz recently agreed to open a Mercedes plant in Alabama and bought the Chrysler company in Detroit.

The British Isles: The United Kingdom and the Republic of Ireland

The British Isles, located off the northwest coast of the main European peninsula, are occupied by two countries: the United Kingdom of Great Britain and Northern Ireland (often called Britain, or the United Kingdom), and the Republic of Ireland. The latter was once a colony of Britain and the two countries have long held contrasting positions in the world. Britain is a powerful industrialized country that has experienced a decline in its global influence and wealth. Ireland is a once poor agricultural country that is beginning to find its feet.

In the seventeenth century, Protestant England conquered Catholic Ireland; and after killing and exiling many of the Irish, England settled Lowland Scots and English farmers on the land. The Irish continued to resist and finally, after a long and bitter guerrilla war, the Republic of Ireland gained independence from the United Kingdom in 1921. However, Protestant majorities in six counties in the northeast corner of the island of Ireland voted to remain part of the United Kingdom. In these counties, known collectively as Northern Ireland, Protestants held political control and Catholics, the minority, suffered economic and social discrimination. Catholic nationalists unsuccessfully lobbied for a united Ireland via constitutional means. Various other Catholic groups, the most radical being the Irish Republican Army (IRA), resorted to violence, often against British peacekeeping forces, who were

seen as supporting the Protestants. These tactics were met with reciprocal violence by Protestants. Over 3000 people have been killed since the 1960s.

After many efforts at peace, a peace accord was reached in 1998. The opposing groups were tired of seeing the development of the entire island—especially of Northern Ireland—blighted by the persistent violence. In May 1998, voters in Northern Ireland and the Irish Republic voted overwhelmingly to approve the peace accord: 71 percent voted for the accord in Northern Ireland, and over 90 percent in the Republic of Ireland. Even though problems of implementing the accord remain, voter approval is a huge step forward.

The Republic of Ireland's only physical resources are its soil and abundant rain. This combination has contributed to a continued dependence on agriculture. So has its former relationship with Britain, which for a long time squelched Irish industrialization. As a result, Irish people overall have the lowest per capita income in West Europe. Recently, however, there are signs of change: for the first time, more people are employed in industry than in agriculture. Ireland is attracting foreign companies by offering cheap labor, accessible air transport, low taxes, and financial incentives. These foreign firms have brought in small industries specializing in food processing and the manufacture of chemicals and textiles. Many of them unfortunately are "suitcase" industries: they can be quickly packed up and moved to other locations that offer cheaper labor and less stringent operating conditions.

The United Kingdom, in contrast to Ireland, has been operating from a position of power for many hundreds of years. Like Ireland, the United Kingdom has a mild, wet climate, and a robust agricultural sector, based, in its case, on grazing animals. But the land is more extensive, the mountains are higher, and they contain important mineral resources, particularly coal and iron. Beginning in the seventeenth century, Britain amassed a colonial empire in the Americas, Africa, and Asia that secured access to enormous resources of labor, agricultural potential, minerals, and timber. Britain's colonial and domestic resources were sufficient to make it the leader of the industrial revolution in the early eighteenth century. By the nineteenth century, the British Empire covered nearly one-quarter of the earth's surface. As a result, British culture was diffused far and wide and English became the lingua franca of the world (displacing French).

Its wide international affiliations, set up during the colonial era, positioned Britain to become a center of international finance as the global economy evolved. London is Europe's leading financial center, and it handles 31 percent of the global foreign currency exchange, more than twice that of New York City, its closest rival. But although the United Kingdom remains Europe's financial center, it is no longer Europe's industrial leader. At least since World War II, and some say before, the United Kingdom has been sliding down from its high rank in the world economy toward the position of an average European nation. British manufactured goods no longer competed as well with goods from other world regions where labor and production costs were cheaper. The discovery of oil and gas reserves in the North Sea gave the United Kingdom a cheaper and cleaner source of energy for industry than the coal it had long depended on but did not stop economic decline. In the old industrial heartland, cities like Liverpool and Manchester, and Belfast in Northern Ireland, became extremely depressed.

Beginning in the 1970s, a series of conservative governments tried to make the United Kingdom more competitive by instituting two decades of budget cutbacks, reducing social spending, selling off unprofitable government-run firms, and tightening education budgets. Unemployment rose. Eventually, foreign investment began to pour into the United Kingdom because the skills of the labor force were high compared to the wages people would accept after years of cutbacks.

Britain has now successfully established high-tech industries in parts of the country that previously were not industrial, for example, near Cambridge and west of London in a region now called Silicon Vale. But service industries now dominate the economy. There are new jobs in health care, food services, sales, financial management, insurance, communications, tourism, and entertainment. Even the movie industry has recently discovered that England is a cheap and pleasant place to do film editing and production. Because Britain is accustomed to international activities, it seems well positioned to provide superior services in a globalizing economy; but many of these new jobs are not highly paid. The jobs tend to go to young, educated, multilingual city dwellers, many of them from outside the United Kingdom, and not to middle-aged, unemployed ironworkers and miners left in the old industrial heartland. Because the EU allows the free movement of EU citizens, there are now more than 400,000 foreign nationals working in Greater London alone. Thirty-five percent of the J. P. Morgan brokerage house and bank staff are non-British.

London is also now home to people from across the former British Empire. The Jamaican poet and humorist Louise Bennett used to joke about Britain being "colonized in reverse," referring to the fact that so many from the former colonies now live in the United Kingdom. Indeed, it would be hard to overemphasize the international spirit of London. For example, London has become an intellectual center for the Muslim world. Salman Rushdie, the controversial Indian Muslim writer, lives there; Israelis and Palestinians privately talk about peace there; and the Saudi Arabian government has a strong presence. Take a walk along Queensway and you

A multiracial crowd in London. Overall, Britain is a far more integrated society than is America. Marriage often occurs across ethnic lines and 74 percent of white English people say they would not mind a close relative marrying someone of another race. [Terry E. Eiler/Stock, Boston.]

will find dozens of Arabic bookstores; on a leisurely stroll in nearby Kensington Gardens, you will discover thousands of people from all over the Islamic world who now live, work, and raise their families in London. They are joined by Asian, African, and West Indian families pushing baby carriages and tossing frisbees to older children.

South Europe

Each of the four countries of South Europe (Figure 4.16) has figured prominently in a past era of European history. First Athens, in Greece, and then Rome, in Italy, were seats of empires whose influence extended in wide arcs from the Mediterranean. In the medieval period, from the fifth to the fifteenth centuries, the cities of Venice, Florence, and Genoa were important trading centers. During the sixteenth century, Spain and Portugal developed large empires, primarily in the Americas but also in Asia. As a result, Europe's economy became more global, and the Mediterranean was no longer the center of trade. After Spain and Portugal lost their empires in the nineteenth century, South Europe did not again flourish, though northern Italy and parts of northern Spain remain fairly prosperous. On the whole, the industrial revolution passed South Europe by until recently. Even today, much of the region remains poor by comparison to the rest of the continent. Only the countries of East and Central Europe are worse off. We will take a closer look at Spain and Italy in the sections that follow.

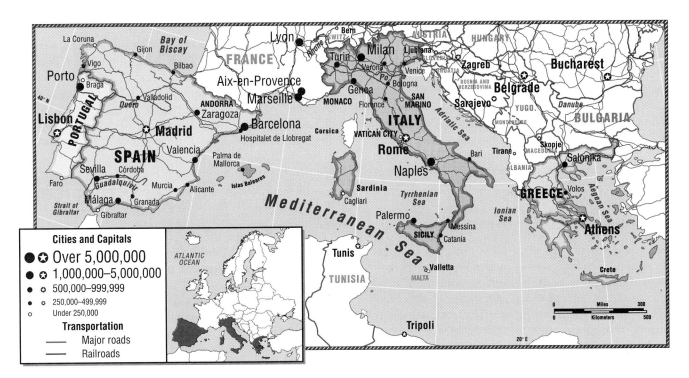

FIGURE 4.16 The South Europe subregion.

Today, South Europe faces a number of complex problems. One concerns agriculture. Areas under irrigation have grown in all of South Europe's countries in recent years, even as agriculture as a whole (measured in terms of percent of GNP and percent of labor force) has declined. Irrigation has increased output and opened up new, semiarid locations for a wide range of crops, particularly in Spain. But, as also in the western United States, irrigation schemes bring problems: water shortages develop, reservoirs become depleted, soil salinity increases over time. Farmers in northern Spain and Portugal complain of water shortages because water originating in that region is transported away by canal to irrigate more arid regions in the south. And Spain has another problem: the newly irrigated farms are producing surpluses beyond EU capacity to consume. The excess food is dumped on the market, to the annoyance of Spain's EU neighbors.

For several decades, tourist money has been bringing new life to the economy. Masses of western and northern Europeans flock to see the monuments of past civilizations and to enjoy the south's warm climate and beautiful beaches. However, tourist money has done little to elevate the lives of poor rural people. While some localities within countries have grown prosperous, perhaps as the site of elegant resorts, many have not. Examples are provided by Greece. Income from tourism has been confined to scenic coastal and island locations, and many rural areas remain poor and isolated. As in much of South Europe, the very quali-

ties that attract tourists to Greece are being threatened by the sheer numbers of visitors and the impact they have on the environment and on rural culture.

While change is underway, many women in South Europe live in situations that are very different from those in North and West Europe. South Europe is kept running by the extended family and informal social networks, especially the region's vast informal economy (including illegal activities). The informal economy and the extended family, while both flexible and adaptable institutions, tend to place burdens on the already disadvantaged. For example, while it is often the male head who arranges for the family to take in elderly members or absorb relatives who have lost their jobs, it is usually women who must find the extra bed, cook the extra food, wash the extra clothes. The average woman often finds herself saddled with such enormous domestic responsibilities that if she must earn money, she can work only part time in a low-paying sweatshop, or at home doing piecework for a factory that wants to avoid employing unionized labor. Even in the modernizing high-tech part of the South Europe economy, the small firms tend to be family based, with women performing many tasks for which they may not be paid and that are not included in any statistics.

Extended families do hold some advantages, especially for women, because they often provide employment within the domestic unit; and they provide security and social support during times of illness, divorce, or unemployment, or in old age. Furthermore, families often pay for members to receive special training or education, though such advantages typically go first to young males. It should be noted, also, that these opportunities tend to contribute to the eventual breakdown of the family unit, since those who have received special training eventually seek employment outside the family firm, often migrating far from home. In North and West Europe, formal welfare systems take care of many social and economic functions performed informally by the extended family in South Europe.

Spain

Spain has recently emerged from centuries of underdevelopment and decades of government by a dictatorship. Today, it is one of the more hopeful countries on the continent, poised to take advantage of opportunities in a more integrated Europe. However, barriers remain high, both physical and political. Mountain ranges slice through the Iberian Peninsula, making travel and commerce difficult. Furthermore, Spain has several distinct cultural regions (Figure 4.17), such as the Basque provinces in the north and Catalonia on the northeast coast; and many people in these regions do not have a commitment to the central government.

After reconquering its land from the Moors in the fifteenth century, Spain itself conquered a huge empire

FIGURE 4.17 The contentious cultural regions of the Iberian Peninsula. [Adapted from Terry Jordan, *The European Culture Area* (New York: Harper & Row, 1988), p. 188.]

in Middle and South America and in the Philippines. For a time it was the wealthiest, most powerful country in Europe. By the late nineteenth century, however, Spain's empire was all but gone and Spain was known as "the Old Man of Europe." A civil war rent the country from 1936 to 1939, followed by 40 years of military dictatorship under General Francisco Franco that kept Spain behind the rest of Europe. Since Franco's death in 1975, Spain has made a cautious transition to democracy under a series of Socialist governments. Catalonia and the city of Madrid are centers of wealth and industry, while the northwestern and southwestern provinces are Spain's poorest regions, with few resources, a shortage of water, and low incomes. The regional disparity of wealth in Spain plus a high level of ethnic loyalty means that a number of provinces—especially Catalonia, Spain's most industrialized region, and the Basque region, also industrialized—often speak of secession. They would like to avoid supporting the poorer regions. A small Basque separatist movement periodically resorts to violence.

Spain joined the EU in 1986. Since then, growth has accelerated with the help of EU funds, foreign investment has increased, and there has been a substantial rise in tourism, especially along the eastern Costa del Sol and in the Balearic Islands; both regions are highly desirable destinations for middle-class European vacationers. Nonetheless, segments of Spanish society have not participated in the new prosperity. Many small farmers in the western provinces and elsewhere remain poor, and urban industrial workers in Madrid and Catalonia have been laid off as a result of factory modernizations. Spain has at times had one of the highest unemployment rates in Europe, and in the late 1990s unemployment still hovered around a startlingly high 20 percent. In times of high unemployment, workers are almost always willing to work for less.

The relatively low wage scales are one reason that Spain is attracting foreign investment from around the world, a strong indicator of a healthy and growing economy. The democratic government appears to be stable. There is an educated and skilled work force, the result of Spain's greater investment in human resources under Socialist governments. Environmental and workplace regulations are modest. Additionally, Spain has good ports on the Atlantic and the Mediterranean and an industrial base that includes food and beverage processing and the production of automobiles, chemicals, metals, machine tools, and textiles. An interesting indicator of growth is Spain's growing investments in its former Latin America colonies: Spanish banks have lent over U.S. $4 billion since 1992 to Cuba, Mexico, and various countries in South America. Spain's telecommunications giant, Telefonica, holds over U.S. $5 billion in Latin American telecommunications companies.

AT THE LOCAL SCALE *The Moorish Legacy in Southern Spain (Andalucía)*

Muslim traders and conquerors (known as Moors) came to Spain in the 700s and stayed until the 1400s. They deeply influenced all aspects of Spanish life.

Tourists from all over the world are drawn to the many remains of Moorish culture in the landscape of southern Spain. Muslim tourists from Southwest Asia often comment about how "at home" they feel in the dry hills and walled courtyards of Andalucía. The palaces and mosques of Córdoba and Granada's Alhambra rank among the worlds greatest architectural marvels. Strong Moorish influences can be heard in flamenco, the world-famous music of Andalucía's Gypsies, and Spanish contains countless Arabic words and sayings. The elaborate multigalleried home built to face inward around a central courtyard garden is a Moorish contribution. Its purpose was to house the extended family and to shield the women of the family from the public spaces (and gazes) of men, an important concept in gender roles in Islam.

Courtyard of the Parador de San Francisco in La Alhambra, Granada, Spain. [Mark D. Phillips/Photo Researchers.]

Italy

Of all the countries of South Europe, Italy is seen as the model for successful development. It is by far the wealthiest in the subregion and is, in fact, the fifth largest economy in the world. Its average income and per capita GNP are higher than those of the United Kingdom (see Table 4.2). Nevertheless, Italy has problems of a political and geographical nature. In particular, there are huge disparities between the rich north and the poor south.

The contrast between the wealth and dynamism of northern Italy and the poverty and stagnation of south-

ern Italy is one of the greatest regional contrasts to be found in any European nation. In Roman times, the situation was reversed: the south and especially the island of Sicily were then the most progressive and productive areas in the Roman Empire, while the Po Valley in the north was an uninhabited, mosquito-infested swamp. The turnaround was slow and steady, as archaic agricultural practices made the south less and less productive, and the urban people of northern Italy converted the Po Valley into a productive agricultural region and Venice into a trading center, beginning in the thirteenth century. Today, the north has one of the most vibrant economies in the world, producing products renowned

209

for their quality and beauty of design—such as Ferrari automobiles, Giorgio Armani clothing, Olivetti office equipment, and a large number of high-quality musical instruments. In Turin, Fiat automobiles produced in a fully robotized plant are shipped throughout Europe; and in Milan, one of the largest cities in Italy, fashion designers have surpassed even their rivals in Paris.

Meanwhile, south of the city of Naples, Italy, is a land of rural poverty. The government has made massive efforts at promoting industry, with little success. Roads and public buildings are unfinished, and empty factory hulks (called "cathedrals of the desert") dot the landscape. The money for development has been dissipated by corrupt officials, misguided policies, and a poorly skilled labor force.

Perhaps the most pervasive aspect of daily life in Italy is the informality of social arrangements. A parent contacts a teacher, an old friend, to make sure a child passes the upcoming exams; a factory worker punches the time card of a perpetually late friend, in return for the free use of a large hall for his daughter's wedding reception. These are the kinds of arrangements that permeate Italian society, making the country both inefficient and apparently corrupt in the larger sense and yet somehow workable and attractive on a personal scale. Possibly as much as 20 to 25 percent of the economic activity takes place in the black market.

Italians seem to have limited faith in the efficacy of government; they have elected several dozen different administrations since 1948. Italy has been a democracy since World War II, and it is a charter member of the EU. Yet it has been mired in bureaucracy for so many decades that a whole other body based on informal relationships, the *sottogoverno*, or "undergovernment," is said to take over whenever a crisis develops. The infa-

mous Mafia has permeated Italian society most deeply in southern Italy, where the absence of effective government is conspicuous. Only recently has the Mafia been recognized as something that people could collectively combat.

Many of these peculiarities of Italy seem to arise from an inherent distrust of any institutions not based on the family or on personal relationships. Most businesses are family-run, even including some of the large corporations of northern Italy; and as discussed earlier, the rudimentary welfare system assumes that strong families and social networks will provide what the state cannot. To many Italians, this system is a fact of life, taken for granted—never mind that it works to the detriment of the poor, whose families and networks can draw on only meager resources.

North Europe

North Europe (Figure 4.18) traditionally has been defined as the countries of Scandinavia—Iceland, Denmark, Norway, Sweden, Finland—and their various dependencies. Greenland and the Faroe Islands are territories of Denmark; Svalbard in the Arctic Ocean is part of Norway. In this text I expand North Europe to include the three Baltic states of Estonia, Latvia, and Lithuania, all part of the USSR until September 1991. The countries of North Europe are linked by their location in the North Atlantic, the North Sea, or the Baltic Sea, and by their intimate connections with the sea as witnessed by their reliance on fishing and ocean trade. In Denmark, for example, all 5.2 million inhabitants live within 52 miles of the sea. The main cities of the region are vibrant ports, such as Copenhagen and

Nestled within 10 miles of Mount Vesuvius, a volcano overdue for an eruption, is Naples. A city of over 1 million inhabitants, it is considered by many the gateway to southern Italy. The beautiful, vibrant city, founded by Greeks in 600 B.C. as Neapolis, has many of the features of the south: violence, drugs, and corruption. Yet it also houses what is perhaps Italy's finest opera house, luxurious palaces and gardens, and the Piazza del Plebiscito. This central square overlooking the Bay of Naples is the background for thousands of wedding portraits for southern Italy's brides. [David A. Harvey/National Geographic.]

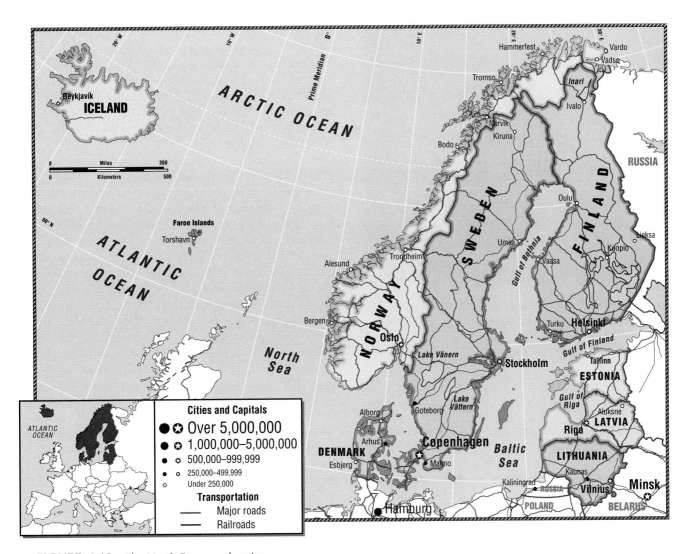

FIGURE 4.18　The North Europe subregion.

Helsinki, that have long been centers of shipbuilding, fishing, warehousing of goods, and legal and financial institutions related to maritime trade. A look at the map at the beginning of this chapter will reveal at least six other main port cities in North Europe.

The North Sea contains important reserves of oil and natural gas. Most of the oil lies along the continental shelf off Norway and England; farther north, Norway and Russia are disputing rights to potential oil reserves in the arm of the Arctic Ocean known as the Norwegian Sea. The fishing grounds of the North Sea, the North Atlantic, and the southern Arctic Ocean are also an important resource for North Europe countries (as well as for several other countries on the Atlantic). In recent decades, however, overexploitation has seriously reduced fishing stock. Right of access to the fishing grounds remains a cause of dispute; but in 1994, the EU created a joint 200-mile coastal exclusive economic zone (EEZ) that ensures equal access and sets

fishing quotas for member states. Although Norway, Iceland, the Faroe Islands, and Greenland are not EU members (Norway declined when invited to join), all have made free trade agreements with the EU.

Aside from maritime trade and fishing, the countries of North Europe have other diverse economies. The successful Scandinavian countries have strong links to the capitalist societies of Western Europe and North America. The Baltic states have many remaining links to Russia, Belarus, and other parts of the former USSR, but are attempting to reorient their economies and societies in varying degrees to the West.

Scandinavia

The Scandinavian countries are rich in resources, which are skillfully exploited. The warmer flatlands of the south are dedicated to agriculture. Denmark, although a small country, produces the preponderance of

Even apartment complexes, such as the Tokarp development in the south-central town of Jönköping, reflect the Swedish sense of modernist simplicity. [Tomasz Tomaszewski/ National Geographic.]

North Europe's poultry, pork, dairy products, wheat, sugar beets, barley, and rye. The well-managed forests of the mountainous north, in Sweden and Finland, produce timber and wood pulp. Norway had been considered poorly endowed in comparison to the rest of Scandinavia, but the discovery of gas and oil under the North Sea in the 1960s and 1970s has been a windfall to that country. The exploitation of these resources dwarfs all other aspects of the economy. Able to supply its own energy needs through hydropower, Norway exports oil and gas to the EU and is now one of Europe's richest countries.

A healthy industrial sector contributes to the region's prosperity. Sweden is the most industrialized nation in North Europe. The Swedes produce most of North Europe's transport equipment and two highly esteemed automobiles, the Saab and the Volvo, as well as furniture and housewares famed for their spare, elegant design. Despite Denmark's agricultural successes, two-thirds of the Danish economy is derived from services (financial and education, for example) and from high-tech manufacturing, construction and building trades, and fisheries. Even Finland, long dependent on timber output, has been entering into modern shipbuilding and mobile communications.

Two important characteristics distinguish the Scandinavian countries from other European nations. The first is the degree to which they embrace strong social welfare systems. The second is the extent to which Scandinavian countries have achieved equality of participation and well-being for men and women. Norway, Sweden, Denmark, Finland, and Iceland hold

five of the top six positions in the United Nations Gender Empowerment Measure (GEM) rankings. As discussed earlier in this chapter, Scandinavian countries have social democratic welfare regimes that seek to provide benefits across class and gender lines at high standards. Sweden's stance on welfare and Norway's record on women's empowerment are illustrative of North Europe's successes.

Social Welfare in Sweden. Sweden's "cradle-to-grave" social welfare system is founded on three concepts that are deeply embedded in Swedish culture. First is the idea of security: all people are entitled to a safe, secure, and predictable way of life, free from discomfort and unpleasantness. Second, the appropriate life is ordered, self-sufficient, and quiet, not marred by efforts to stand out above others. Third, when the first two concepts are practiced as they should be, the ideal society, *folkhem* ("people's home"), is achieved. The three concepts provide insight into why Swedes are willing to pay for a social welfare system that consumes two-thirds of the Swedish government's annual budget (as of 1993 figures) and provides a safety net and stability for every one of the country's 8.8 million people.

Sweden's comprehensive welfare system is possible because it is a prosperous industrialized country. Generous social welfare systems work only in economies that produce substantial surpluses and where a democratic government ensures equitable distribution. While the combination of a strong economy and a strong welfare system has generally worked well in Sweden, there have been problems. In the 1990s, a recession set in when Swedish autos began losing their competitive edge in the global market. In an effort to deal with the economic problems, Swedes elected a more conservative government that promised to reform welfare, cut taxes, and join the EU. But the anxious mood also led to an uncharacteristic rise in Swedish nationalism and some strong feelings against foreigners—both taboo political stances since World War II. By the late 1990s, Sweden was moving slightly back to the left politically.

Equal Rights in Norway. Equal rights for women are closer to being a reality in Norway than in any other country. In 1986, Gro Harlem Brundtland, a physician, became the country's first woman prime minister, and she appointed women to 44 percent of all cabinet posts. Norway became the first country in modern times to have such a high proportion of women in important government policy-making positions. She was reelected and served in the post for 10 years. In 1998, women made up 36 percent of Norway's parliament (second only to Sweden's 40 percent); they held nearly 33 percent of elected positions in municipal government and over 40 percent of posts in county government. Perhaps most indicative of the growing power of women is the fact that in the 1990s, the leaders of Norway's three major political parties are or have been women.

It is not just in politics that near equality in gender has been achieved. Norway was the first country in the world to have an equal-status ombudsperson whose job it is to enforce the 1979 Equal Status Act. This act has a "60–40 rule" requiring a minimum of 40 percent representation by each sex on all public boards and committees. Even though the 40 percent rule has not yet been achieved in all cases, female representation is, on average, over 35 percent for state and municipal agencies. In addition, employment ads are required to be gender neutral, and all advertising must be nondiscriminatory. For example, an advertisement for a car cannot depict a bikini-clad male or female as an eye-catcher. Nude bodies in ads can only be used for products that are directly related to the body in question.

In a break with most societies, much of the recent work on equality in Norway has been directed toward advancing male rights in traditional women's arenas, not the reverse. Men, for example, now have the right to one month of paternity leave to stay home with a new child. This policy recognizes a father's responsibility in child rearing and related family obligations; in addition, it provides a chance for father and child to bond during the early days of life.

The Baltic States

The three small Baltic states of Latvia, Estonia, and Lithuania are situated next to each other on the east coast of the Baltic Sea. Culturally, the countries are distinct, with different languages, myths, histories, and music. Recently they shared the experience of being part of the USSR, but traditionally, their cultural ties are with West and North Europe. Ethnic Estonians, who make up 62 percent of the people in Estonia, are nominally Protestant, with strong links to Finland; they view themselves as Scandinavians. Ethnic Latvians, who are just 50 percent of the population of Latvia, are mostly Lutheran; they see themselves as part of the old German maritime trade tradition. Lithuanians, for their part, are primarily Roman Catholic and also see themselves as a part of old Europe.

Recent ties with the USSR introduced a substantial Slavic influence. To secure its dominance, the USSR settled many ethnic Russians in the main cities of all three countries. Today, Russians are about a third of the population in both Estonia and Latvia, and they wish to keep ties with Russia strong. Significantly, in both countries the indigenous populations are aging because they are reproducing at very low rates. Meanwhile, the Russian minorities are having many more children, and in a few decades could become the dominant culture group. Poles, not Russians, are the dominant minority in Lithuania (somewhat under 20 percent), and ethnic Lithuanians are reproducing fast enough to remain the dominant majority for some time to come.

The Baltic states see national security as their dominant issue, because their strategic position along the Baltic Sea has long attracted the attention of Moscow, which has no easy outlet to the sea except through St. Petersburg. After World War II, all three became Soviet republics by force. The Baltic states are now independent, but the countries of Western Europe

Riga, Latvia's capital, is spread along the Daugava River. Once known as the Paris of the Baltic, the city strives to regain the economic prosperity it once had. The return to private enterprise has helped many small entrepreneurs, but privatization of industrial production is proceeding more slowly.
[Torleif Svensson/The Stock Market.]

213

have been unwilling to commit to military support against any future invasion. They hope to iron out differences with Russia, not antagonize it.

The economic picture for the Baltic states is the most precarious in North Europe. Under Soviet rule, the Russians expropriated their agricultural and industrial facilities and directed them primarily for Russia's benefit. Until 1991, 90 percent of the Baltic states' trade was with other Soviet republics. Since then, in reorganizing their economies, the three countries have moved in different directions.

Estonia has a light industrial base that is relatively easy to reorient. It has undertaken the most radical economic change, moving toward capitalism and increasing its trade with the West, especially Finland and Germany. Of the three, Estonia is the only one to show real economic growth, and its accomplishments have attracted foreign aid and private investors. Heavily industrialized Latvia and Lithuania are still dependent on Russia for the bulk of their trade. Their products do not meet Western standards of quality and their factories are out of date and heavily polluting.

Virtually no consideration was (or is) given to the ecological consequences of industrialization. Perhaps the worst example in Estonia remains the oil shale production facility near Kohtla-Järve in the northeast corner of the country. Smoldering hills of shale residue add to the noxious smoke from the plants. Oily acids seep into the groundwater and into the Baltic, giving coastal fish skin ulcers. It is possible to ignite the chemicals floating on water obtained from wells on nearby farms.

One important block to Lithuanian economic independence is the Russian **exclave** of Kaliningrad (old East Prussia). Kaliningrad is called an exclave because, although it is an actual piece of Russia, it lies far from that country along the Baltic between Lithuania and Poland. A relatively ice-free port, Kaliningrad is headquarters for the Russian Baltic fleet, and it is now also a center where Western businesspeople can go to negotiate with Russians without having to go to Russia. Some call it Russia's Hong Kong. Because Russians must pass through Lithuania to get to Kaliningrad, Russia's strategic interest in Lithuania is unlikely to diminish.

East and Central Europe

No other part of Europe is in a more profound period of change than East and Central Europe (Figure 4.19). In the euphoria at the end of the cold war, many believed that democracy and market forces would turn around the region's sluggish, highly polluting, and inefficient centrally planned economies. Instead, most parts of the region have experienced political turmoil and a drop in the standard of living.

Those Eastern bloc countries with the most resilience have proved to be Slovenia, Poland, the Czech Republic, and Hungary. The last three of these have joined NATO and are in line to join the EU early in the twenty-first century. For the rest of Eastern Europe, adjusting to democracy and the privatization of formerly centrally planned economies has proved complicated. Plagued by corruption and economic chaos, many governments have eased up on their plans for ambitious reforms as they are now struggling merely to maintain civil peace. Not surprisingly, many people are looking back nostalgically to the Communist era, when jobs were stable, health care and education were free, and there was a strong, authoritative government. Except for Slovenia, this is especially

Gray snow floats down from the stacks of the Kunda cement factory in Estonia. As in most other former Soviet nations, environmental degradation in Estonia resulted from the Russian emphasis on industrial output as the key to economic growth and prosperity. [Larry C. Price.]

FIGURE 4.19 The East and Central Europe subregion.

true in all of the republics of the former Yugoslavia, where the end of the cold war brought a collapse of central authority, years of ethnic warfare, hundreds of thousands of deaths, and violence that still continues. Still, many are optimistic about East and Central Europe as a whole. Many of the countries in this region have useful natural resources, both for agriculture and industry, and all have relatively cheap work forces that will probably attract foreign investment once the political scene calms down.

Soviet Legacies in Agriculture and Industry

After World War II, the influence of Soviet central planning dominated the economy of East and Central Europe. In agriculture, governments forced independent farmers to surrender title to their lands, then consolidated those lands into large collective farms. While there were some gains in efficiency, there were also some significant failures. In the worst, 7 million to

215

8 million people died during the human-created Ukrainian famine of the late 1950s. Today, much of the region is still collectivized, as government officials are wary of making changes that could jeopardize food supplies. The cause for concern is lessened, however, by the fact that so many families grow up to half their own food supply in small family gardens. In Ukraine, for example, family garden plots have proliferated in the years since independence, especially in urban areas. Ukraine is very similar to France in size of territory, population, and agricultural productivity (Figure 4.20). Many analysts believe that Ukraine, which produced huge food supplies for the USSR, could eventually dominate the agricultural economy of Europe—but not until its collective farms are extensively modernized.

VIGNETTE Despite the near virtuoso horticulture skills of Ukrainian urban gardeners, some Ukrainian farmers who spent their lives on collective farms have difficulty

making the transition to being private farmers. In Tadani, in western Ukraine, Ivan Mychajlyshyn works on a collective farm herding cows. Although he would like his own place, he seems unwilling to seize the moment. "The people who know how to farm are the old ones," he says. "People like me might go back to it, but we don't know how to work the land. Anyway, there's hardly any equipment." Meanwhile, Vasyl Speiko, age 35, also a farmer in western Ukraine, recently obtained 12 acres of his own, after spending years on the Bukovyna collective farm. So far, the only equipment he can afford is a horse and wagon, but he is optimistic, saying, "I want to know what it's like to be a free man." In working his land, he benefits from the counsel of his aged father, who lost his 61 acres of farmland to the state collective in 1948. [Mike Edwards, After the Soviet Union's collapse—A broken empire, *National Geographic*, March 1993, pp. 49–52.]

FIGURE 4.20 Even though its agricultural output is similar to that of France, Ukraine's manufacturing output is less than one-quarter that of France. The country is still dependent on Russia for most of its energy, and Russia remains the primary market for its grains. [Adapted from Moshe Brawer, *Atlas of Russia and the Independent Republics* (New York: Simon & Schuster, 1994), p. 43.]

Eastern and Central Europe's considerable industrial base is undergoing steady transformation, but it is still burdened by many legacies of the Soviet era: heavy industries that make inefficient use of energy and other resources and hence are highly polluting; a dependence on raw materials imported from the USSR because only a few parts of Eastern and Central Europe are rich in minerals; and an emphasis on coal and steel production rather than consumer-oriented manufacturing and service industries. Of these, industrial pollution has been the overriding problem. For example, in Upper Silesia, Poland's leading coal-producing area, forests have succumbed to acid rain, soils yield contaminated crops, and whole cities are declared unsafe for children. Residents experience birth defects, high rates of cancer, and lowered life expectancies.

The worst environmental disaster occurred in north-central Ukraine. In 1986, the explosion of one of four nuclear reactors at Chernobyl severely contaminated a huge area in northern Ukraine, southern Belarus, and Russia, and spread radiation over much of the eastern part of Europe and Scandinavia. Direct results included 5000 people killed, 30,000 disabled, and 100,000 evacuated from their homes. Yet 15 Chernobyl-style reactors still operate in Ukraine, Russia, and Lithuania, and all are increasing safety risks.

Difficulties and Successes of the Economic Transition. The region is attempting to shift away from central planning toward a free market economy, but progress has been rocky. Today, the process of reform is increasingly bogged down by corruption, the loss of public sector jobs, and the loss of welfare state benefits. The difficulties have prompted political protest movements that challenge the wisdom of becoming more like Western Europe. There have been, however, a number of successful transitions, and other promising developments make democracy and free market reform the most likely path the region will take in the near future.

Corruption worsened during the last years of communism and then mushroomed in the post–cold war era. Involvement by organized crime has plagued the sale of formerly state-owned industries, especially in military-related sectors. One mobster based in Budapest has reportedly taken over virtually the entire Hungarian armaments industry and is selling guns globally. Organized crime as a whole has facilitated the spread of high-tech weapons, possibly including nuclear warheads smuggled from the military bases of the former Soviet Union, to terrorists and countries interested in bolstering their arsenals. Increasingly, politicians have mobster connections, and foreign businesspeople eager to invest in East and Central Europe often pay bribes to organized crime.

Throughout Eastern and Central Europe, many people have suffered directly from the privatization or collapse of state-owned industries. The new private owners commonly refuse to pay any taxes. Coal miners and other industrial workers, in both state and private firms, have gone for months without pay, and many have suffered layoffs or job loss as privatized industries have tried to slim down. The inefficient heavy industries are being closed rather than updated because the funds to remodel them are not available. The closures bring the hardships of unemployment to countries that no longer have social safety nets. Entire populations are suffering as social services have declined. The situation in the once well-funded state hospitals is epitomized by First General Hospital in Sofia, Bulgaria, where doctors try to avoid crowds of patients waiting for treatment. "I can't look them in the eyes anymore," one doctor told a reporter, shuffling into an elevator. "I know we won't be able to treat them." The hospital is running out of all types of medicines and equipment, even intravenous fluids and painkillers. New patients are accepted only in extreme emergencies. Similar conditions prevail in the region's underfunded schools and research facilities. In reaction, scientists, technicians, artists, writers, and highly skilled personnel are leaving to move to wealthier parts of the world.

The advent of democracy has reduced some of the tensions associated with the economic transition, because people have been able to vote out governments whose reforms create high levels of unemployment and inflation. However, the tendency to remove reformers before they can accomplish anything significant has dampened the enthusiasm of potential foreign investors. On the other hand, even crudely practiced democracy is in many cases leading to long-term economic growth and stability by encouraging governments to take a greater interest in the financial security of the population as a whole. In Hungary and the Czech Republic, largely under pressure from voters, plans are taking shape for new national pension systems to replace defunct communist pension plans. New pension systems would give financial stability to people who have worked all their lives and political stability to states that cannot afford to alienate the older generation that labored under communism.

The effect of the economic transition on women has been somewhat ambiguous. The sociologist Alena Heitlinger, who studies gender in both the Czech Republic and the Slovak Republic, writes that under state socialism there was only "pseudo emancipation" of women; none of the attitudes of gender equality was internalized. Working women gained status mainly through a job in a state-run firm, but the traditional patriarchal village beliefs regarding gender roles were retained. Hence, women were given lower-paid "easy work" thought suitable for their sex. This easy work was not actually easy, it just had low status. For example, agriculture was perceived as the most undesirable labor; farming therefore became the task of older women, who often had the use of manual tools only. Urban cleaning jobs, too, were overwhelmingly performed by elderly women. Since the transition, the status of women as a whole seems to have worsened, though economic opportunities for a few have improved. Throughout the region, there is now a push to convert even highly trained professional women to housewives. It is thought that in times of high unemployment, women should give up their jobs to men, despite the fact that in many cases women are a family's sole support. Discrimination based on age and sex is not illegal, and newspaper want ads still contain such statements as "young, attractive females" wanted for sales and secretarial positions and "competent men" for managerial jobs.

Nonetheless, some of those most successful in the privatizing economy are women, as the story of Maria Frangu illustrates.

VIGNETTE

Maria Frangu sells Coca-Cola, Pepsi-Cola, pastries, and coffee out of a tiny shop in the center of Bucharest, Romania. In a few short years, her savings and her assets have increased tenfold, and she is planning to build a house. Maria's success came about because of "the Cola wars." Pepsi-Cola has long been the primary cola available in the Soviet bloc, having set up joint ventures with the Communist regimes back in 1959. Pepsi agreed to work through the state-run bottling and marketing companies, and did not have control over the operations. When the Soviet Union began to disintegrate in the 1980s, Coca-Cola was invited to enter into a joint venture with Romania's largest soft drink bottler; but Coke insisted on control of the operation. The company invested heavily in Romania, spending many millions on new plants and equipment, new uniforms, red-painted Coca-Cola trucks, and marketing. By 1995, Coke had six bottling plants in Romania, 2500 employees, and annual sales of U.S. $120 million. Coke now outsells Pepsi over 2 to 1. Coke's success has opened the way for thousands of small capitalists. A University of South Carolina study in 1994 indicated that at least 23,000 jobs were supported by the sale of Coca-Cola products in Romania. [Nathaniel C. Nash, Coke's great Romanian adventure, *New York Times*, February 26, 1995, pp. 1 and 10.]

Economic Strategies. Many governments are taking a variety of "free market friendly" steps to help their economies grow more quickly. One strategy is to encourage foreign investment. While there have been a number of false starts by investors unaware of the difficulties they would face, there have also been some successes. An example is Poland's joint venture with the French glass company Saint-Gobain to construct one of the world's most modern glass factories. The factory is being built in the south, near the Czech border, in what has been Poland's most polluted region, Silesia. Significantly, it will be one of the most environmentally safe plants of its kind in Europe, with emissions well below the minimum standards set by Germany, the industry leader. All waste glass material will be entirely recycled.

Another way to increase growth is to improve infrastructure, a strategy that Ukraine is adopting with its plans to link up with East and Central Europe and South Europe via the Corridor Five highway. Yet another strategy for growth is to encourage the development of sectors that give countries a **comparative advantage,** wherein a particular specialty is developed to the point that it can successfully compete with rivals. For example, to survive agricultural competition from Ukraine, Slovenia is encouraging its farmers to specialize in organic farming in order to supply Europe's increasingly health-conscious markets. The greater attention to crops and the land that organic farming requires may be easier for Slovene farmers to deliver, since their farms are already fairly small and few chemicals are used.

The cities of East and Central Europe are some of Europe's most distinguished urban places and they are becoming magnets for tourists from America, Japan, and western Europe. One example is Budapest, the capital of Hungary. Situated on the Danube River and built on the remnants of the second- to third-century Roman city of Aquincum, Budapest was one of the seats of the Austro-Hungarian Empire, which ruled Central Europe until World War I. In the 1990s, Budapest was reemerging as one of Europe's finest metropolitan centers, filled with architectural treasures, museums, concert halls, art galleries, discos, cabarets, theaters, and several universities of distinction. And Hungarians have revived their love affair with jazz, called "the music of the imperialists" under the Communist regime. After the change to a market economy in 1989, dozens of jazz clubs opened.

Tourism is increasingly recognized as an important part of a well-rounded market-based economy. The remnants of medieval structures like forts and castles are being refurbished and promoted as tourist attractions. Interesting ethnic expressions of culture can also serve as tourist attractions. As elsewhere in Europe, the Jews of Ukraine hardly exist anymore. Seventeen thou-

Hasidic Jews from the United States and several other countries celebrate Rosh Hashanah in Uman, Ukraine, each year. [Efrem Lukatsky/AP/Wide World Photos.]

sand were killed by the Nazis and the Ukrainian militia in World War II. Yet today, in the small city of Uman, hundreds of black-clad Hasidic Jewish pilgrims come, primarily from the United States, to celebrate Rosh Hashanah, the Jewish New Year, and to remember the thousands of Jews killed there during the Russian October Revolution of 1917 and World War II.

The Balkans: Understanding an Armed Conflict

In 1991, a civil war erupted in the Balkans that has taken the lives of more than 250,000 people. This mountainous region north of Greece is home to a variety of ethnic groups of differing religious faiths. The media have carried many assertions to the effect that violence and ethnic hatred is an age-old way of life in the Balkans. A deeper look shows that ancient ethnic tensions have greatly intensified in recent decades, suggesting that more immediate political and economic factors have made significant contributions to the conflict.

Many of the so-called indigenous ethnic groups of the Balkans were themselves invaders thousands of years ago, coming from Russia, Central Asia, and beyond. These disparate groups jointly occupied the Balkan Peninsula with yet older inhabitants in a patchwork quilt pattern. For the most part, the various ethnic groups managed to live together peacefully, intermarrying, blending, and realigning into new groups. The historian Charles Ingrao argues that coexistence

was even easier in areas like Bosnia, where three or more groups living side by side forestalled any one group from dominating the others. External wars often exacerbated local ethnic tensions, as when the Nazis made an ally of Croatia, pitting it against Slovenia, Serbia, and others. Nevertheless, this activity in the Balkans was no more severe than ethnic rivalries in the rest of Europe.

After World War II, the country of Yugoslavia was formed out of six territories. Five were each dominated by a single ethnic group (Figure 4.21), but in most of them minorities were present. These territories were Serbia, Croatia, Slovenia, Macedonia, and Montenegro. A sixth area, Bosnia, was without a majority ethnic group, although there were substantial populations of Muslims, Serbs, and Croatians. When free elections were held for the first time in 1991, the result was declarations of independence first by Slovenia, then by Croatia, Macedonia, and finally Bosnia. While Slovenia and Macedonia were allowed to separate relatively peacefully, the now much smaller Yugoslavia, composed of Serbia and Montenegro, fought long and protracted wars against Croatia and Bosnia. Serbia in particular was seen as an instigator of conflict, as its vehemently nationalist leadership claimed that Serb-populated territories in Croatia and Bosnia should be in one Serbian-led country. To rid the coveted territory of non-Serbs, some Serbs carried out genocidal "ethnic cleansing" campaigns against civilians, especially against Muslims in Bosnia and Kosovo.

The experiences of the Djukanovic family illustrate how they once got along with people of different ethnicities and then found that for reasons unknown to them the situation changed.

VIGNETTE Mitra Djukanovic and her husband, Dusan, are Serbian farmers who defied Serb leaders and returned to now Muslim-administered territory, their home village of Krtova. Ready for the coming hard winter, they tell their story in front of drying meat smoking over a smoldering tub, and bags of potatoes, walnuts, pickled peppers, and flour. Dusan speaks: "I thought it was time to come back. I stopped worrying about living with Muslims. I lived with them most of my life. . . . My grandfather told me about the old times, and there was never trouble between us and the Muslims here. We all just worked a lot and had nothing. It was equal. Until this war, I never had trouble either. If there is a Muslim government, so what?" [Mike O'Connor, Serbs go home to Bosnia village, defying leaders, *New York Times International*, December 8, 1996, p. 1.]

FIGURE 4.21 The Balkans. [Adapted from *The Economist,* January 24, 1998, special issue, A Survey of the Balkans, p. 4.]

If sentiments like these are common, as most observers say they are, why has there been so much violence between ethnic groups? To understand the recent violence in the former Yugoslavia, it is useful to look at how the political and economic situation of recent decades increased ethnic hostilities where previously there were few.

After the formation of Yugoslavia, Marshal Tito, Yugoslavia's founder and leader until his death in 1980, tried to gloss over ethnic differences by encouraging pan-Yugoslav nationalism and his own cult of personality. While there was ethnic peace during Tito's rule, there was no national dialogue about the benefits of ethnic diversity. Other ethnic groups were made uneasy by the domination of Serbs, the most populous ethnic group in the military and in much of the federal government bureaucracy. Throughout the 1980s, resentment of the Serb-dominated central government increased as the semicentrally planned economy of the country deteriorated. When Slovenia and Croatia, two of the richest territories, voted to declare independence in 1991, local populations were responding less to age-

old hatreds and fierce nationalism than to a deteriorating economy and a government dominated by one ethnic group, the Serbs.

Given the scale of interethnic violence that occurred in the following years, it is not surprising that many, especially outsiders, have seen ethnic hatred as the overriding cause of the civil war. The Serb-dominated government and military of the new, smaller Yugoslavia allowed Slovenia to become separate peacefully, in part because of its strategic location close to the heart of Europe and far from Serbia, in part because there were no significant enclaves of Serbian supporters in Slovenia. But the Yugoslav government feared that unless it made a strong show of force in dealing with Bosnians and Croats, the rest of the non-Serb populations of Yugoslavia would also move to secede and take valuable territory with them. This fear has become a reality, as Kosovo, the ethnic Albanian Muslim-dominated southern area of Yugoslavia, has attempted to secede—perhaps to join Albania, which lies just to the south. Despite the undoubted culpability of the Serbs in starting the conflict and in perpetrating much of the brutality, they cannot be blamed exclusively for all the interethnic violence that has taken place. Albanians, Croats, and Bosnians have used ethnic cleansing in retaliation.

Regardless of the causes of the war, its results have been devastating. By 1996, when peace accords were signed in Dayton, Ohio, the Serbian economy was ruined, and Serbia was actually smaller than before. Unemployment reached 60 percent during the war and inflation was at 20 percent. The GNP per capita, which had been U.S. $2900 for all of Yugoslavia in 1990, was just U.S. $1400 for Serbia in August 1996. In Bosnia, 200,000 people, 5 percent of the population, died in the war; many were the victims of Serbian war crimes. The cosmopolitan city of Sarajevo, as well as countless villages, was destroyed. In Spring 1999, Serbia forced most of the majority Albanian population out of the province of Kosovo. Today the situation is still in flux, with war crime trials proceeding at the World Court in The Hague, the Netherlands.

In their first ever formal military action, NATO forces bombed Serbia in retaliation.

REFLECTIONS ON EUROPE

Europe's position as a center of world economic and political power seems less formidable when the region is viewed close up. Europe is no monolith; its geographic patterns are highly variable. The distribution of wealth, social welfare policies, approaches to environmental issues, treatment of outsiders, and participation of women in public and private affairs are just some of the aspects of life in Europe that reflect this variation.

Many of the issues confronting European people are similar to those encountered elsewhere around the world. For example, the effort at economic integration is exposing European states to the problems of restructuring now faced by so many, much poorer, developing countries. Also, the vicissitudes of dealing with an ever more integrated world economy are apparent on every hand in Europe; and the questions raised, though different in degree of severity, are the same as those raised in Latin America, Asia, and Africa. How can a country retain jobs for its people when there are qualified workers waiting to work for less within relatively easy reach? How can more good jobs be created? How can those less fortunate be helped to a better life while at the same time lessening the drain on public funds by welfare programs? How can poor parts of the region be stimulated to develop? And how can development everywhere be made to conform to the requirements of an increasingly stressed environment? No less complex are the cultural questions of how countries with distinctly different traditions and mores can find sufficient common ground on which to base the economic cooperation that will bring them all greater prosperity. For all its current troubles, Europe's headlong start on development, its already established world leadership, and its heightened awareness of global economic issues brought on by its own efforts at integration— all these factors position Europe to retain its global influence.

From the perspective of people in the Americas, Europe's current preoccupation with economic integration should prove instructive. Many of the same issues will be confronted if the economic integration of the Americas proceeds: the free movement of people, the loss of jobs to low-wage areas, and the need to strengthen and coordinate environmental policies, to name just a few.

The future of the relationship between Europe and the region to be covered in Chapter 5—the Russian Federation, Belarus, Caucasia, and Central Asia—is not clear. Will these two regions increasingly integrate their economies and societies, or will Russia's very serious economic and social problems make it too unattractive a partner? Will new alignments and contentions in Central, South, and East Asia draw Russia away from Europe? These will be among the geographic issues to be discussed in the next chapter.

Selected Themes and Concepts

1. An influential idea in Europe is the idea of the **nation**. A nation is conceived of as a large group of people bound together by common cultural traits and by their allegiance to the idea that they form a united group. The concept has influenced attitudes toward outsiders and the drawing of national boundaries.

2. Europe is one of the most densely occupied regions of the world. Its prosperity is related to the fact that Europe has access to a **resource base** that is global in extent.

3. Social welfare systems in Europe now vary greatly region to region in their philosophies and abundance of benefits. In those states that have generous benefits, guaranteeing basic necessities of life for the poor and the elderly, disparity in wealth distribution is low.

4. Europe is now in a state of flux related to the effort toward European **economic integration,** the demise of the Soviet Union, and the move toward more open and competitive market systems in East and Central Europe.

5. Europe now has a **negative rate of population growth** (−0.1), the lowest on earth. Many people are choosing lifestyles that include only one or no children.

6. Definitions of what it means to be European are changing as various countries confront the ethnic diversity of **guest workers** in their midst and try to define new policies toward outsiders.

7. European women confront many of the same issues that women all over the world confront: the **double day,** low status, low representation in government and policy-making bodies, and fewer employment opportunities than are available to men.

8. Europe's long lead in industrialization is now giving way to competition from abroad, but European countries are taking many measures to compete more efficiently: diversifying, inviting in outside investors, investing abroad, and lowering some restrictions that have discouraged job formation.

9. Europe's agricultural sector is productive and highly diversified, and protected by price guarantees and protected markets.

10. Europe's environment has been drastically modified by human activity. The Green movement is a regionwide effort to educate the public and influence public policy toward measures that will control pollution and wasting of resources.

11. Europe's air, rivers, and seas are particularly afflicted with pollution from domestic and industrial sources. Pollution is particularly a problem in East and Central Europe.

12. Human well-being in Europe varies greatly, but is generally acceptable except in East and Central Europe, where economic and social collapse have produced marked declines in general health and longevity.

Selected Readings

Andrews, Edmund. Great chocolate war reveals dark side of Europe. *New York Times*, October 24, 1997.

Bosworth, Barry P., and Gur Ofer. *Reforming Planned Economies in an Integrating World Economy*. Washington, DC: Brookings Institution, 1995.

Buckwalter, Donald W. Geopolitical legacies and Central European export linkages. *Professional Geographer* 50, no. 1 (February 1998): 57–70.

Cannan, Crescy. From dependence to enterprise? Women and Western welfare states. In *Women and Market Societies*, ed. Barbara Einhorn and Eileen James Yeo. Aldershot, UK: Edward Elgar, 1995.

Cultural Survival Quarterly, Summer 1995, entire issue.

Davies, Norman. *Europe: A History*. New York: Oxford University Press, 1996.

Day, Lincoln H. *The Future of Low Birthrate Populations*. London: Routledge, 1992.

Duncan, Simon. The diverse worlds of European patriarchy. In *Women of the European Union—The Politics of Work and Daily Life*, ed. Maria Dolors Garcia-Ramon and Janice Monk. New York: Routledge, 1996.

Einhorn, Barbara. Ironies of history: Citizenship issues in the new market economies of East Central Europe. In *Women and Market Societies*, ed. Barbara Einhorn and Eileen James Yeo. Aldershot, UK: Edward Elgar, 1995.

Fonseca, Isabel. *Bury Me Standing—The Gypsies and Their Journey*. New York: Vintage Books, 1995.

Garcia-Ramon, Maria Dolors, and Janice Monk, eds. *Women of the European Union—The Politics of Work and Daily Life*. New York: Routledge 1996.

Haub, Carl. *Population Change in the Former Soviet Republics—Population Bulletin* 49, no. 4 (December 1994). Washington, DC: Population Reference Bureau.

Humbeck, Eva. The politics of cultural identity: Thai women in Germany. In *Women of the European Union—The Politics of Work and Daily Life*, ed. Maria Dolors Garcia-Ramon and Janice Monk. New York: Routledge, 1996.

Kaplan, Robert D. *Balkan Ghosts—A Journey Through History*. New York: Vintage Books, 1993.

Koulov, Boian. Political change and environmental policy. In *Bulgaria in Transition*, ed. John Bell. Boulder, CO: Westview Press, 1998.

Lebor, Adam. *A Heart Turned East—Among the Muslims of Europe and America*. London: Warner, 1998.

Lobodzinska, Barbara, ed. *Family, Women, and Employment in Central-Eastern Europe*. Westport, CT: Greenwood Press. 1995.

Pryde, Philip R., ed. *Environmental Resources and Constraints in the Former Soviet Republics*. Boulder, CO: Westview Press, 1995.

Rai, Shirin, Hilary Pilkington, and Annie Phizacklea, eds. *Women in the Face of Change: The Soviet Union, Eastern Europe and China*. London: Routledge, 1992.

Smith, Joan, Immanuel Wallerstein, and Hans-Dieter Evers, eds. *Households and the World-Economy*. Beverly Hills, CA: Sage. 1984.

Terlouw, Kees. A general perspective on the regional development of Europe from 1300 to 1850. *Journal of Historical Geography* 22, no. 2 (1996): 129–146.

Vogeler, Ingolf. Rural landscapes of Eastern Germany. *Annals of the Association of American Geographers* 86 (September 1996): 432–458.

Wolchik, Sharon L. Women's issues in Czechoslovakia in the communist and postcommunist periods. In *Women and Politics Worldwide,* ed. Barbara J. Nelson and Najma Chowdhury. New Haven, CT: Yale University Press, 1994.

Wolf, Eric. *Europe and the People Without History.* Berkeley: University of California Press, 1982.

Yarnal, Brent. Socioeconomic transition and greenhouse-gas emissions from Bulgaria. *Geographical Review* 86 (January 1996): 42–58.

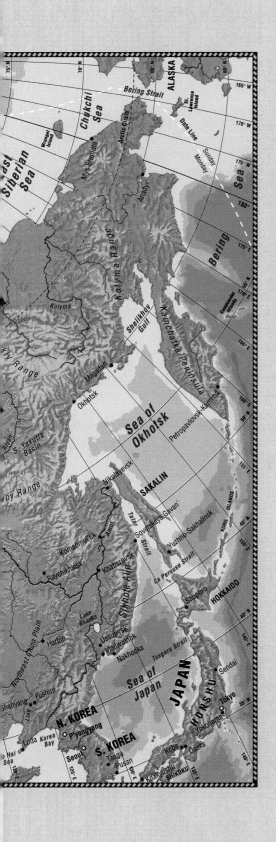

CHAPTER

FIVE

THE RUSSIAN FEDERATION, BELARUS, CAUCASIA, AND CENTRAL ASIA

INTRODUCTION TO RUSSIA AND EURASIA

VIGNETTE

Yuri Ivanovich is ecstatic! In his driveway sits a brand new Lada, the "people's car" of Russia. With a few minor adjustments, it will be humming down the streets of Dubna, a city on the Volga River two hours by train north of Moscow. As is the case in most Russian cities, many Dubna residents do not own a car, and spend their leisure hours walking the miles of greenways that link city parks with the surrounding countryside. But Yuri is deeply into another sort of leisure activity. First he tackles an obvious little detail—the folks at the Lada plant couldn't be bothered to attach the gear lever to the gear box. By the end of the day, Yuri has disassembled a fair amount of his Lada, greased it, and put it all back together. Yuri doesn't mind the trouble, however, even if his car does rattle here and there and looks a bit dated (the Lada is a virtual carbon copy of a 1972 Fiat 124). After 45 years of public transportation and hitchhiking, Yuri, a high school mathematics instructor, is for the first time in his life independently mobile. [Adapted from Russia's car industry: Modernizing the mastodon, *The Economist*, June 10, 1995.]

Yuri lives in a country that has been attempting to change its entire political and economic system in a few short years. The change offers opportunities to many, and a new car to Yuri, but hardships and risks as well. Until a few years ago, Yuri's country was called the Union of Soviet Socialist Republics (USSR). It was by far the largest country on earth, stretching from eastern Europe all the way across Asia to the Pacific Ocean. In December 1991, the USSR ceased to exist. In its place stood 15 independent republics joined in a loose economic alliance. The largest and most powerful was the Russian Federation, consisting of Russia and its federated internal republics. Soon, 5 of the 15—Latvia, Lithuania, and Estonia as well as Ukraine and Moldova—abandoned the alliance. Having chafed under Russian domination for many decades, they turned toward Western Europe. That has left the Russian Federation, Belarus, the three republics of Caucasia (Georgia, Armenia, and Azerbaijan), and the

five republics of Central Asia (Kazakhstan, Kyrgyzstan, Tajikistan, Uzbekistan, Turkmenistan) loosely allied. The demise of the USSR has required a period of adjustment and reorganization across the globe, because so many economic and political relationships were based on the assumption of the cold war that the West (Europe and North America and their allies) and the USSR were locked in a perpetual struggle for power and influence.

Now Russia and the Eurasian republics (those in Caucasia and Central Asia, plus Belarus) are in a state of transition. It is hard to overemphasize the exhilaration, trauma, and confusion of the spatial, cultural, and economic changes that are under way in the former Soviet Union. Imagine that in the space of five years the geography of the United States changed in the following ways. First, old alliances with Canada and with Europe dissolved; then, one-third of the states declared independence and drifted over to what had been viewed as the enemy. Resources the United States had depended on, like prime agricultural land and crucial minerals, now unexpectedly belonged to someone else. Whole sectors of the economy were abruptly declared obsolete; and in the restructuring, hundreds of thousands of people, especially well-educated women, lost jobs and with them a comprehensive support system of housing, daily meals, and medical care. Imagine that in short order the disruptions began to take their toll in the form of earlier deaths for adults (especially men) and sharply rising infant mortality, in episodic food shortages, and in rising lawlessness, especially organized crime. Then, imagine that an old enemy (say, the Soviet Union) began to send emissaries offering to restructure the United States along new lines—their lines.

All this and more began to transpire in the former Soviet Union in the 1990s. Important regions once under its sphere of influence have broken away, while its own internal cohesion is under assault. One should add to all these disturbing changes some positive outcomes: greater freedom of expression and of movement, the right to practice religion openly, and the availability of consumer products in far greater variety and quality than ever before. Meanwhile, all parts of the old union are experiencing a flood of foreign influences, the ultimate impact of which is as yet quite unknown. Russia, Belarus, Caucasia, and Central Asia are today overrun with Western businesspeople and lawyers, rock stars, franchise hawkers, international drug dealers and gun merchants, American environmentalists, computer and cell phone vendors, U.S. Chamber of Commerce delegations—all missionaries in their own way for capitalism and the market economy. Even actual Christian missionaries hold revival meetings and seek converts in many Russian cities.

Themes to Look For

A number of themes are dealt with throughout this chapter. Many of them are associated with the difficulties encountered in economic and political restructuring, for example:

1. Population patterns are changing in response to rising social problems like unemployment and declining health.

2. The move toward more popular participation in government has been fraught with acrimony, threatened coups, and assassinations.

3. There are cultural as well as physical barriers to unity: ethnic groups reasserting cultural identities that were repressed during the Soviet period; vast geographic areas poorly connected by roads and other transport systems.

Terms to Be Aware Of

The term *Russian Federation* refers to what is normally called Russia, plus more than 20 republics that lie within the boundaries of the Russian state. These internal republics are not independent countries but are joined with Russia under an overarching government. They are not to be confused with the external republics like those in Caucasia and Central Asia, which *are* independent countries. Russia is still closely associated economically with the external republics, but their governments are completely separate.

At this time there is no entirely satisfactory name for the whole region. The formal title I have chosen is somewhat cumbersome: the Russian Federation, Belarus, Caucasia, and Central Asia. When referred to within the text, it will be shortened to Russia and the Eurasian republics. The long-term viability of Russia's current linkages with Belarus, Caucasia, and Central Asia, or even with Russia's own easternmost Pacific areas, is in doubt. I anticipate that by the next edition of this book, events will have broken the links joining some parts of this present region and will have forged new connections.

Greater Asia is another term used in this chapter, although sparingly. Greater Asia would encompass Southwest Asia (countries such as Turkey, Iraq, Iran, Afghanistan, and Saudi Arabia), South Asia (Pakistan, India, Bangladesh), Southeast Asia (Burma, Thailand, and Indonesia, for example), and East Asia (including China and Korea). There is a Eurocentric bias inherent in designating all these varied places and peoples simply as "Asian."

PHYSICAL PATTERNS

Landforms

The landforms of the combined region of Russia and the Eurasian republics, though vast in extent, are arranged in a fairly simple pattern, illustrated on the map at the beginning of the chapter. Moving west to east, there are four units roughly equal in size across the northern two-thirds of the region. First, there are two plains: (1) the eastern extension of the North European Plain (European Russia) and (2) the Western Siberian Plain. The two plains are separated by the Ural Mountains. Beyond the Siberian Plain there is (3) an upland zone known as the Central Siberian Plateau and finally (4) a mountainous zone that borders the Pacific, called the Russian Far East. To the south of these territories, from west to east, there is an irregular border of **steppe** lands (semiarid grasslands), barren uplands, and high mountains that separate the region from the southern reaches of the Eurasian continent (Iran, Afghanistan, Pakistan, China, Mongolia, and Korea).

The low, flat extension of the North European Plain rolls east from the Carpathian Mountains in Ukraine and Romania 1200 miles (2000 kilometers) to the Ural Mountains. Rivers have long been important routes for transport in European Russia, and the most important is the Volga, which flows into the Caspian Sea. The Volga River is connected, via canals, lakes,

Barges and tugboats ply the Volga-Baltic waterway.
[James P. Blair/National Geographic.]

and natural tributaries, to many parts of the North European Plain and to the Baltic and White seas in the north and the Black Sea in the southwest.

The Ural Mountains extend in a fairly straight line south from the Arctic Ocean into Kazakhstan. The Urals do not constitute a serious barrier to nature or humans: there are several easy passes across the mountains, and winds carry moisture all the way from the Atlantic and Baltic across the Urals and into Siberia. Much of the once-dense forest that covered the Urals has been used to build and fuel the new industrial cities established in the mountains during the twentieth century.

To the east of the Urals is the great Western Siberian Plain, a primarily marshy lowland that is drained by the Ob River and its tributaries. This lowland tilts almost imperceptibly to the north; hence, the rivers drain into the Arctic Ocean, taking north what could be useful moisture for the dry regions of Central Asia lying to the south. The Central Siberian Plateau and the Russian Far East, beyond, are together the size of the United States. The usefulness of this vast expanse of land is limited, however, by the fact that it lies far to the north and that, like the Ob, the principal rivers drain north into the usually frozen Arctic Ocean.

Along the southern part of European Russia and several areas of Siberia, there is a relatively dry zone that is part of a larger swatch stretching across what some call Greater Asia (from Turkey to Korea). Along the southern limit of this dry zone is a wide, curving band of mountains, including the Caucasus, the Hindu Kush, and those ranges in the east along the northern border of Mongolia and China. These mountains block the movement of warm air and moisture from the south; but their rugged terrain has not seriously deterred cultural influences that have penetrated north and south for literally tens of thousands of years. The peoples on the steppes of central Eurasia and the large numbers of culture groups along the southern and eastern reaches of Eurasia have persistently crisscrossed the mountains, exchanging plants (apples, citrus, onions, wheat, garlic), animals (horses, goats, sheep, and cattle), technologies (rug and tapestry weaving, tent making, agriculture, and animal tending), and belief systems (Islam, Christianity, Judaism, Buddhism).

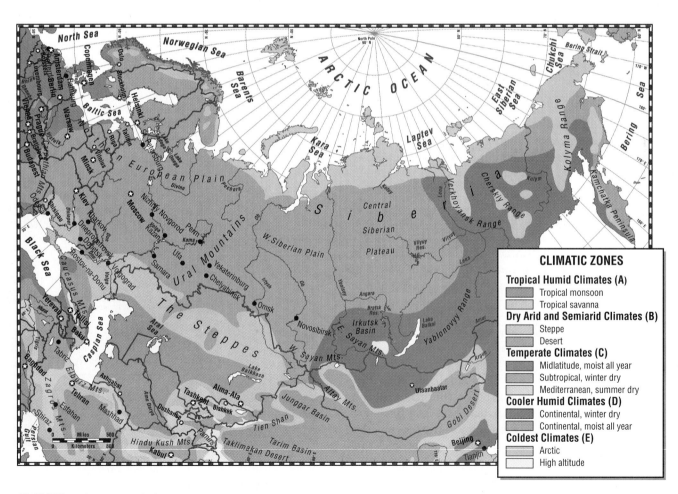

FIGURE 5.1 Regional climate.

Climate

With the exception of Antarctica, no place on earth has as harsh a climate as the northern part of the Eurasian landmass occupied by Russia (Figure 5.1). Here the "seasonal continental breathing" (described in Chapter 1) is dominated by a long, dry, frigid exhaling in winter. A short inhaling in summer brings in only modest amounts of moist, warmer oceanic air from across the mountains to the south or from the Pacific in the east and the Atlantic in the west. Russia's climate is a prime example of continental climate, which means the winters are long and cold, the summers short and cool to hot.

Dry conditions prevail except where moisture is pulled in from distant seas and oceans. The main rainfall for the region comes from storms that blow in off the Atlantic Ocean far to the west. By the time these initially rain-bearing air masses arrive, most of their moisture has been squeezed out over Europe. Nevertheless, sufficient rain reaches the fertile lands of European Russia and the Caucasian republics to make this area the agricultural backbone of the region. The Caucasian mountain zones are some of the only areas in the region where rainfall adequate for agriculture coincides with long growing seasons. These areas were once important sources of fruits and vegetables for the whole Soviet Union.

East of the Caucasus Mountains, the lands of Central Asia have a warm, dry continental climate, with scorching summers and short but intense winters. Agriculture is rarely possible without irrigation, and herding is widely practiced. To the north and northeast of Central Asia are the lands of Siberia, which receive more precipitation but experience a much colder winter. Agriculture is generally not possible, though reindeer are tended; and huge expanses of taiga (northern coniferous forest) cover much of the land. In northern Siberia, temperatures become so low that permafrost (permanently frozen water in the soil and bedrock) exists only a few feet below the surface; tundra, a landscape of mosses, lichens, shrubs, and dwarf trees, predominates.

HUMAN PATTERNS

The core of this entire region has long been European Russia, the most densely populated area and the homeland of the Russians. From here the Russians conquered a large empire of many cultures, which included the whole of the region covered in this chapter. These conquered territories remained under Russian control as part of the Soviet Union. The breakup of the Soviet Union has reversed this gradual process of accretion for the first time in centuries. The transformation has been accompanied by migrations, changes in the population structures, and a decline in well-being, as people seek to adjust to the stress of upheaval.

The Rise of the Russian Empire

For thousands of years, nomads crisscrossed the vast stretches of Eurasia, living on the meat and milk of their herds of sheep, horses, and other grazing animals. They followed the seasonal changes in the wide grasslands stretching from the Black Sea to Lake Baikal. By several thousand years ago, the steppes and their forest fringes were in large part ecologically "full." Only technological innovations, such as the domestication of animals and the development of agriculture, allowed populations to expand. Often nomads, taking advantage of their superior horsemanship and hunting skills, would plunder settled communities. In defense, permanently settled peoples began fortifying their towns.

The archaeologist Jeannine Davis-Kimball, working in the Ural steppes on the border of northern Kazakhstan, found the burial ground of a 14-year-old woman with bowed legs, possibly caused by a life on horseback. Artifacts recovered included arrowheads, a sword, a stone amulet, and shells. The finds are part of the evidence that nomadic women in the past participated fully in the economic life of their culture (herding, hunting, fighting, and playing games—often on horseback), as is the case in nomadic cultures of Tibet and Mongolia today. [Courtesy of Dr. Jeannine Davis-Kimball.]

These towns grew up in two main areas: the dry lands of Central Asia, and the more moist forests that fringed the steppes to the northwest in modern Ukraine and Russia. As early as 5000 years ago, Central Asia was supporting settled communities, even large empires at times, that were enriched by irrigated croplands and by trade along the famed Silk Road (see Figure 9.16), the ancient trading route between China and the Mediterranean.

The settled communities in the forests of European Russia eventually gave rise to the Russian Empire, which would one day dominate both the steppes and Central Asia. Powerful kingdoms arose in these forests after the arrival, about a thousand years ago, of the **Slavs,** a group of farmers who originated between the Dneiper and Vistula rivers, in modern-day Poland, Ukraine, and Belarus. The Slavs expanded east, founding a triad of towns: Kiev, Novgorod, and eventually Moscow. The threat of nomad invasion remained, however; the Mongol armies of Genghis Khan conquered these forested lands in the twelfth century. Moscow's rulers took advantage of their position as tax gatherers for the Mongols to dominate neighboring kingdoms. Eventually they grew powerful enough to end Mongol rule in the late fifteenth century.

By the seventeenth century, Moscow had conquered many former Mongol territories, integrating them into the Russian Empire, which stretched from the Baltic eastward over the thinly populated northern Eurasian landmass to the Pacific. The empire contained huge natural resources and many non-Russian peoples who resented domination. Nonetheless, the Russians continued their expansion, driven partly by the fear of invasion from the steppes and from Europe, and partly by the search for resources and for access to the world's oceans via ports that were not frozen a majority of the time (so-called warm water ports).

The first major non-Slavic area to be annexed was Siberia. Although the Russians borrowed many methods of conquest and administration developed by the Mongols, their expansion into Siberia also resembled the spread of European colonial powers throughout Asia and the Americas. Everywhere, the Russian colonists upheld European notions of private property at the expense of indigenous patterns of land use. Perhaps most significantly, the expansion into Siberia made way for massive migrations of laborers from Russia in the eighteenth and nineteenth centuries. They soon far outnumbered native Siberians. By the mid-nineteenth century, czarist Russia was also conquering Central Asia in order to control its major export crop, cotton. This crop was in high demand in global markets because the American Civil War was disrupting cotton exports from the United States.

The Russian Empire, ruled by the czar (a title derived from "Caesar," the name of the Roman emper-

ors), was highly stratified. The czar and a tiny aristocracy lived in splendor while the vast majority of the people lived in poverty—many as serfs who were essentially slaves. Even though serfdom ended legally in the mid-nineteenth century, the brutal inequalities of Russian society persisted into the twentieth century, and internal opposition grew.

Soviet Russia

Ultimately, in 1917, at the height of Russian suffering during World War I, Czar Nicholas II was overthrown. Within a few months, a faction of revolutionaries call the **Bolsheviks** came to power. Though not very numerous, they were a highly disciplined organization of communists, who were inspired by the writings of the German revolutionary Karl Marx. Marx argued that the societies of Europe were inherently flawed, in that the capitalists, the minority who had large sums of money, exploited the vast majority. Driven by their desire for profit, the capitalists used their ownership of factories, farms, businesses, and other "means of production" to dominate the propertyless masses, who, with no other options, had to work for low wages. To end this domination, Marx called on workers to unite—regardless of religious, ethnic, or other differences—to overthrow the capitalists and establish a completely egalitarian, stateless society.

The Bolshevik leader, Vladimir Lenin, decided that the people of the former Russian Empire needed a transition period of centrally orchestrated drastic change in order to implement Marx's ideas. Accordingly, as in czarist times, power was centralized in Moscow and in the hands of the Russians, who continued to dominate the other peoples of the USSR and to occupy many key positions even in non-Russian areas. The Communist party exercised power through the Moscow-based bureaucracy, and in part through a secret police force (the KGB) that also resembled czarist predecessors. The country was given a new name, the Union of Soviet Socialist Republics, to reflect its composition from a number of ethnically diverse political units.

After Lenin's death, Joseph Stalin's 26-year rule of the Soviet Union (1927–1953) brought a mixture of revolutionary change and despotic brutality that largely set the course for the rest of the USSR's history. Stalin took the revolution to the countryside, forcing farmers to join large state-owned collectives. But Stalin considered heavy industry the main engine of economic growth. The central bureaucracy directed the development of industry and determined what it would produce. During the Great Depression of the 1930s, the Soviet Union's industrial productivity grew steadily as the global economy stagnated; but, as was the case under the czar, much industrialization was geared toward supplying the military. Little attention was paid to the demand for consumer goods and services that would have made life easier for the Russian people. Conversely, Europe and North America at this time were discovering that everyday consumers could be a major source of economic growth. Moscow gave scant consideration to the effects of industrial development on either the natural environment or the health of Soviet citizens. During and after the Stalin regime, Soviet notions of human dominance over nature helped create some of the world's worst industrial disasters and the most polluted and unlivable cities.

The most destructive aspect of Stalin's rule, however, was his relentless and ruthless amassing of personal power through fear. Sometimes called the "Marxist Czar," Stalin silenced almost all opposition to his rule through the use of the secret police, starvation, and mass executions. The lucky ones were those merely sentenced to labor in the frigid cold of Siberia. Stalin's atrocities, which resulted in the death of at least 20 million people, were a major factor in ensuring that the USSR had no real political revolution and that it continued nearly to the end to be governed by authoritarian power structures similar to those used by the czars.

Although the Soviet system continued on for 38 more years after Stalin, deep flaws finally led to its collapse in 1991. Its greatest failure was an inability to generate technological and managerial innovation on a par with the rest of the industrialized world. Its vitality was also sapped by the cold war, which pitted the USSR against the United States in an intense and expensive geopolitical rivalry on a global scale. For a long time, the Soviet state-dominated and centrally planned development provided an alternative model to capitalism for countries emerging from colonialism. The USSR was able to export versions of its revolutionary communism to Eastern Europe, China, Cuba, Vietnam, Nicaragua, and various African nations. Still, the global economic and political order steadily drifted toward the free market democratic model advocated by the United States. Trying to match the global military capacity of the United States, the Soviets diverted more and more funds to the military at the expense of much-needed economic and social development. In addition, a war in Afghanistan, launched to maintain Soviet influence in Central Asia, severely drained morale in the Soviet Union as a whole. Pressure for change increased, ultimately leading to the rise of a reform-minded chief executive, Mikhail Gorbachev, in 1985. Nevertheless, Gorbachev's efforts to revitalize the Soviet economy resulted in little real change. When he made moves to democratize decision making throughout the Soviet Union in the late 1980s, resentment toward the government in Moscow mounted. Strong independence movements grew in popularity in the outlying republics, whose position in the Soviet

Union had been somewhere between that of conquered territories and states within the United States. The Soviet Union dissolved in an atmosphere of economic and political chaos in 1991.

The post-Soviet years have been both exhilarating and troubling. Instead of one massive state, there are now 15 independent republics. Russia is the chief successor of the USSR and still the largest country in the world. While Russia has tried to maintain high levels of influence on the rest of the former Soviet Union, these efforts have foundered due to the consistent inability of the leadership to deal with major problems. The transition to a free market economy has proceeded rapidly and without much planning, leaving once centrally controlled economies drifting on a tortuous track to collapse. The region's already sad record of environmental abuse has worsened in response to intense financial strains. Nevertheless, there are some reasons for hope: the problems of Russia and the Eurasian republics are at least being more openly discussed.

Population Patterns

Most people in Russia and the Eurasian republics live far to the west, in European Russia (Figure 5.2). The settlement pattern in European Russia is the eastward extension of the band of heavy settlement (discussed in Chapter 4) that runs through the North European Plain beginning in Belgium and the Netherlands. A broad area of fairly dense population forms a wedge shape, with its base stretching from the Black Sea in the south to the Baltic in the north. The point of the wedge stretches east past Moscow and across the Urals to the industrial city of Chelyabinsk, thinning noticeably farther east to Novosibirsk in southern Siberia. Generally speaking, the area of greatest population density corresponds to the distribution of good agricultural soils and mineral resources (coal, uranium, natural gas, and petroleum).

A spur of dense settlement extends away from the wedge to the south and east, through the Caucasus region between the Black Sea and the Caspian Sea. The rest of the huge landmass (nearly twice as big as the continental United States) that stretches across Siberia to the Pacific is very sparsely inhabited, with 25 or fewer people per square mile (10 per square kilometer). There are scattered bands of settlement in the Central Asian republics, in the vicinity of Tashkent and along rivers used to irrigate commercial agriculture, principally cotton. There are also a number of industrial cities with several hundred thousand people apiece, scattered across Siberia. Great expanses of Siberia, however, are virtually uninhabited.

The well-being of the population has declined rapidly over the last few years. Before the breakup,

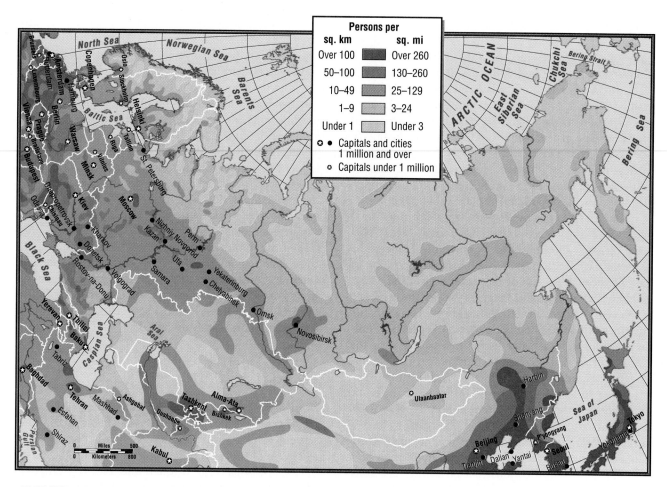

FIGURE 5.2 Population density. [Adapted from *Hammond Citation World Atlas*, 1996.]

Russia, Belarus, Caucasia, and Central Asia were considered "developed" regions, with fairly high standards of well-being; in the 1990s the situation deteriorated significantly (Table 5.1). Not only are infants and children dying in larger numbers, but adult life spans have also contracted markedly. In Russia, male life expectancy declined from 63.9 years in 1990 to 58.9 in 1993 (in 1996 it was 61), while female life expectancy dropped from 74.4 to 71.9 in the same period (in 1996 it was 73). A gap of 12 years between average male and female life expectancy is unheard of elsewhere on earth. Male life spans in the Russian Federation are now the shortest of all industrialized countries. Both males and females in Caucasia have a significantly longer life span than in Russia or Central Asia (see Table 5.1); this may in part be due to a more nutritious diet.

The apparent causes of declining life expectancies are the physical and mental stress caused by lost jobs and social disruption, most notably reflected in increasing rates of alcoholism. Alcohol abuse shortens many lives, especially those of men. Many people are suffering nutritional deficiencies caused by sharply falling in-

comes and scarcities brought on by armed conflict in a number of the republics. The British geographer James Bater has shown that throughout Russia and the Eurasian republics, per capita consumption of basic foodstuffs declined in the mid-1990s. People are eating fewer vegetables; less meat, eggs, and dairy products; and even less bread. The cost of food is taking up as much as half of family budgets. Bater writes: "A diet of bread, pasta products, tea, and the occasional egg or piece of sausage is now the daily reality for literally millions of people, in both cities and rural areas." Though entrepreneurial farmers are supplying attractive fresh food to the best city markets, ordinary people cannot afford to buy it. Those who can, plant gardens; but there is a limit to what they can produce in the small spaces available and during the short growing seasons.

Environmental pollution also plays a large, if as yet poorly understood, role in untimely illness and death. Noxious emissions, heavy metallic pollution of the ground, air, and water, and nuclear contamination may be affecting as much as a third or more of the population. In Central Asia also, life expectancies have re-

TABLE 5.1

National population statistics

Country	Population (millions), 1998	Births per 1000		Fertility rate (no. of children per woman aged 15–45)		Life expectancy at birth, male, 1998	Life expectancy at birth, female, 1998	Infant mortality rate (deaths per 1000 live births)	
		1990	1998	1990	1998			1990	1998
Belarus	10.2	13.9	9	1.9	1.3	62	74	11.9	12
Russia	146.9	13.4	9	1.9	1.2	61	73	17.4	17
Armenia	3.8	24.0	13	2.6	1.6	69	76	18.6	14
Azerbaijan	7.7	26.4	17	2.7	2.1	67	74	23.0	19
Georgia	5.4	17.0	11	2.2	1.6	69	76	15.9	17
Kazakhstan	15.6	21.7	15	2.7	1.9	60	70	26.4	25
Kyrgyzstan	4.7	29.3	22	3.7	2.8	63	71	30.0	28
Tajikistan	6.1	38.8	22	5.1	2.9	65	71	40.7	32
Turkmenistan	4.7	34.2	24	4.2	2.9	62	69	45.2	42
Uzbekistan	24.1	33.7	26	4.1	3.2	66	72	34.6	26
Total	229.2								
United States, included for comparison	270.7	16	15	2.0	2.0	73	79	9.7	7

Sources: 1998 World Population Data Sheet, Population Reference Bureau; and *Population Bulletin*, 49 (December 1996): 48–49.

"My God! She's eating with her eyes!" [From KROKODIL in Russia, March 1997 (republished in *Transitions*, January 1998, p. 93)]

cently fallen for both sexes. The widespread use of toxic chemicals in irrigated cotton cultivation has threatened the health of agricultural workers; and it has helped to pollute river waters and the Caspian Sea. In the industrial cities of European Russia and Siberia, careless handling of industrial waste and inadequate water and sewage treatment endanger health through the pollution of air, water, soil, and food.

Declining birth rates and new migration trends are two other significant changes in population patterns. In the Soviet era, birth rates in Russia and Belarus were already low compared to birth rates in the United States and Europe; since the early 1990s the rates have dropped still further (see Table 5.1). The traditionally high birth rates in the Caucasian and Central Asian republics are also dropping. Surveys show that people are choosing to have fewer children mostly out of concern for the gloomy economic prospects of the near future. In 1992, 75 percent of Russian women who had decided against childbearing cited insufficient income as the reason. Because contraceptives are in short supply and of poor quality, abortion is the method of choice for birth control.

While births are falling, migration rates are rising. Civil unrest or loss of jobs has forced many people into new locales. Many of the people on the move are ethnic Russians who had previously been resettled in the non-Russian republics in order to shift the political balance and secure Russia's grasp on distant resources. Now that the Moscow-supported system of "hardship" pay and special privileges has stopped, and ethnic consciousness is being voiced in the Eurasian republics, many of these Russians are returning to European Russia.

Related to this mounting internal migration is the unusual phenomenon of declining urban populations. In all parts of Russia and the Eurasian republics, except Belarus, urban populations declined by small amounts in the early 1990s. In Caucasus, people apparently moved back to the countryside, perhaps to avoid civil unrest. In Central Asia, once independence was declared, many Russian workers left. But the phenomenon is most marked in the Russian Federation. There, the urban population declined by over 1.2 million. There are many causes: rising urban death rates; the flight from failing industrial cities in Siberia; government programs to resettle the infirm and unemployed

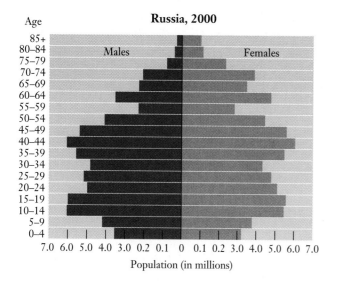

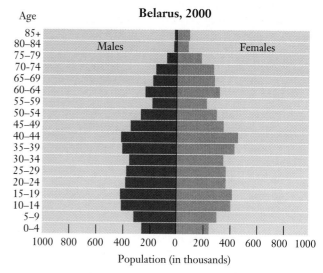

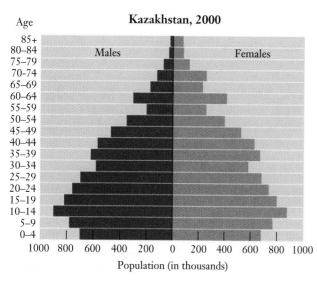

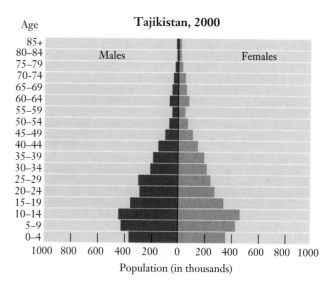

FIGURE 5.3 Population pyramids for Russia, Belarus, Kazakhstan, and Tajikistan. The pyramid for Russia is at a different scale (millions) from the other three (thousands), but this does not affect the pyramid shape. [Adapted from U.S. Census Bureau, International Data Base, at http://www.census.gov/cgi-bin/ipc/idbpyry.pl.]

in southern zones, where they are less expensive to maintain; the exodus from Moscow to rural areas and smaller cities in response to sharply rising living costs; the reclassification of some small towns as rural; and immigration to Europe, Israel, and America.

Population pyramids for the various republics (Figure 5.3) show the overall population trends, while reflecting regionally different patterns of family structure and fertility. Pyramids for Belarus and Russia resemble those of European countries (for example, Germany, as shown in Figure 4.5). They narrow at the bottom, indicating that birth rates are declining. The narrower point at the top for males depicts their much shorter average life span (see Table 5.1). In Central Asia, the bases of the Kazakhstan and Tajikistan pyramids are narrowing as a drop in birth rates accompanies urbanization. But both pyramids still have a wide base, reflecting the higher fertility rates common in a more rural, primarily Muslim society, with a patriarchal family structure. All pyramids have a noticeable "waist" at the 55–59 age group, the result of high death rates and low birth rates during and just after World War II.

CURRENT GEOGRAPHIC ISSUES

The goals of the Soviet experiment begun in 1917 were unique in human history: to reform quickly and totally both a human society and the physical, political, and economic context of that society. Now, in the aftermath of the collapse of the USSR, the people are undertaking a second unique experiment: the transformation of a communist society and a centrally planned economy into its antithesis, a society based on a free market economy. At this point, the process has barely begun and life is proceeding amid considerable chaos. Because so much of what is transpiring in the region today is linked to the economic and political turmoil of the post-Soviet period, I will consider economic and political issues first and then move on to the social, cultural, and environmental consequences of the transition.

Economic and Political Issues

VIGNETTE The kindly, gray-haired teacher tapped the blackboard under the words "profit" and "inventory" as the first graders struggled to pronounce the Russian words. They were reviewing the story of Misha, a bear who opens a honey, berry, and nut store in the forest. He

soon outsmarts the overpriced state-run Golden Beehive Cooperative, becoming first a prosperous bear and eventually the finance minister of the forest. [Adapted from Sarah Koenig, In Russia, teaching tiny capitalists to compete, *New York Times*, February 9, 1997.]

Teaching tiny children capitalist economics in the first grade may seem a bit outlandish, but under the communist system ordinary citizens had little understanding of profit and loss, or of supply and demand, or even of the idea that people have to work hard and take responsibility for their own financial well-being. Now there is a widespread call for public education on the fundamentals of capitalism.

Amazing changes have occurred since the collapse of the Soviet Union, as a region once vehemently opposed to capitalism has, with a few exceptions, made major efforts to become capitalist itself. For the most part, this about-face was necessitated by the deep flaws of the Soviet Union's old "command economy." While some former Soviet states, especially Russia, have ambitiously pursued reform, changes made to the economy have been rapid and haphazard. The result has been economic chaos, expanding corruption, and declining living standards for the majority. Moreover, all the new republics are scrambling to establish new post–cold war relationships with the international community.

The Command Economy

Under the Soviet Union's **command economy,** government bureaucrats planned, spatially allocated, and managed all production and distribution. State-controlled firms monopolized every niche of the economy: agriculture, mining, manufacturing, transport, shipbuilding, construction, retailing, clothing design, tourism, services, and so forth. The goal was to organize life more efficiently, distribute the benefits of development to all regions, and prevent the severe deprivation suffered by so many under the czars. To some extent the task was successfully performed. Although many goods were continually in short supply, the basics, like housing, food, health care, and transport, were provided freely or cheaply to all. Perhaps the greatest triumph of the Russian Revolution was that abject poverty was largely conquered.

Nonetheless, the command economy had deep flaws. The planners in Moscow who formulated the **Gosplan** (state plan) set goals for state firms that were crude in comparison to those set by most private enterprises. In a **capitalist free market economy,** firms try to produce the goods that people want and sell them for a profit, and they continually adjust to market circumstances. The Soviet planners set production quotas for agriculture and industrial enterprises that had to be met regardless of actual demand for particular products. For example, a tire plant had to produce x amount of tires, a dairy farm so many gallons of milk. The planners' calculations were often wrong, and the highly bureaucratic production system nurtured rivalry and corruption that hindered the ability of firms to meet the quotas. Consequently, some goods were produced that were not needed and others were not produced in sufficient quantity. The result was massive gluts and acute scarcities.

Another problem resulted from the ways in which planners tried to boost efficiency. In most capitalist economies, many firms produce similar items and compete with each other to produce the cheapest and highest quality goods. In contrast, the Gosplan often concentrated production in a single factory to minimize the equipment and resources needed for production. But with no competitors, there was little pressure to increase quality and efficiency; many factories and other facilities depended on severely outmoded technologies, sometimes several decades out of date. As a result, they used more resources, produced more pollu-

tion, and were less productive than their counterparts in capitalist free market economies.

The central planners also implemented inefficient, even contradictory, regional economic development policies. Industry was to be widely dispersed in order to reduce regional disparities. These widely dispersed industrial centers were also thought to be easier to defend militarily. In addition, industrial and agricultural development was used to buttress political claims to distant territory. The goal of economic development was also used to justify bringing supposedly inferior culture groups (ethnic minorities) on the periphery into modernized ways of life and into conformity with the dominant socialist ethic. Figure 5.4 shows the distribution of various industrial activities across the USSR after these ideas were implemented. Figure 5.10 shows agricultural distributions.

Soviet efforts to develop Siberia illustrate inherent flaws in these regional development policies. Siberia is a resource-rich territory, but it is also huge and sparsely settled, with few transportation links. It is also remote from the administrative heart of the country and is burdened with a difficult climate. Industries are scattered across thousands of nearly uninhabited miles,

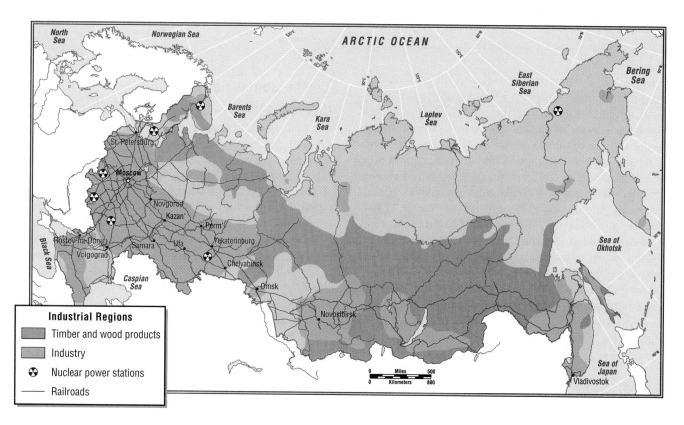

FIGURE 5.4   Principal industrial areas of Russia. [Adapted from Moshe Brawer, *Atlas of Russia and the Independent Republics* (New York: Simon & Schuster, 1994), pp. 32–33.]

yet costs would be lower if resources, factories, labor supplies, and markets were closer together. Furthermore, the Soviet plan to modernize supposedly backward ethnic groups overlooked the fact that those groups were too small to supply the labor required by the new industries. So a labor force had to be attracted (or pushed forcibly) out of European Russia, at considerable expense. Finally, developing remote Siberia required an expensive transport system—most notably the Trans-Siberian Railroad, but also feeder roads. The railway system was never entirely completed and depended heavily on government subsidies.

The great size of the USSR has always posed transportation problems for industry and agriculture, and these are compounded by an array of difficult physical features: long winters, swampy forest lands, and complex upland landscapes, especially in Siberia. Although the USSR is more than two and one-half times the size of the United States, it has less than one-sixth the hard-surface roads and virtually no multilane highways. As Figure 5.9 shows, in European Russia a system of roads, rail lines, and inland waterways is relatively highly developed; farther east, the road network remains sparse (see Figures 5.12 and 5.13). Transport through Siberia is either by air or by rail, the latter chiefly in an east-west direction in a narrow band across southern Siberia where the Trans-Siberian Railroad runs.

Economic Reform

The inefficiencies of the command economy were a major factor in the collapse of the Soviet Union. Since then, Russia has cast about for suitable reform policies. It has by far the largest economy in the region, and its fate is still crucial to the other republics. However, the post-Soviet administration of President Boris Yeltsin has been widely criticized for reforming by decree rather than consulting widely with the public. The administration's reforms have often misfired. Using a strategy described as "shock therapy," the Yeltsin administration rapidly removed many of the key regulating mechanisms of the command economy, such as control over prices. The goal was to usher in a new era in which private entrepreneurs in pursuit of profit would provide the basis for economic growth. However, the removal of price controls set off skyrocketing inflation that wiped out the savings of many people. It became difficult for some to purchase even the necessities, much less to open their own businesses. Most business opportunities were snapped up by people with connections to corrupt officials high in the administrative hierarchy.

By the end of the 1990s, only one-quarter of the Russian economy was in private hands. The complicated mixed economy that has resulted is itself prob-

In an effort to supplement their government pensions (many of which have not been paid for months), some older citizens here at Petrovskiy Zavod sell food to Trans-Siberian Railroad passengers. [Gerd Ludwig/National Geographic.]

lematic. Many large state-owned firms have not privatized because they depend on government subsidies for their survival. The communities they are located in would be devastated if they closed down or fired enough workers to become competitive. These obsolete firms are able to continue operating because remaining bits and pieces of the old central planning agencies in Moscow are still functioning. They thwart reforms and keep the old system limping along.

Meanwhile, the new private enterprise economy is developing alongside. It is made up partly of privatized state firms that focus on the manufacture of basic necessities, and partly of new, smaller entrepreneurial businesses that supply luxuries and conveniences. Some of the small entrepreneurs are legal, but many operate as part of the unregulated, untaxed informal economy. Many ordinary people pushed out of stable jobs by privatization depend on the informal economy for their livelihoods.

To some extent, the new informal economy is an extension of the old one that flourished under communism, when nearly everyone was trying to beat the system. For example, a black market based on currency exchange and the vending of hard-to-find luxuries has long existed. Not too long ago, savvy Western tourists could finance a vacation on the Black Sea with a pair or two of name-brand blue jeans and some chocolate bars. Today, however, the range of "informal" ventures is much more diverse. Many people operate out of their homes, selling cooked foods, assembling telephones, manufacturing eyeglasses, making vodka in their bathtubs, growing plants and packaging seeds, designing (and sometimes pirating) computer software, managing commercial cleaning crews, organizing travel agencies. So much of the economy is in the informal sector that most Russians are better off than the official gross national product figures suggest. For example, the true agricultural output is underreported because so many farmers, still employed on declining collectives, now earn a considerable portion of their income from the private gardens they grow on the fringes of the state farms.

The chief disadvantage of a large informal economy is that the production goes untaxed. For example, homemade vodka now accounts for 70 percent of the Russian market, displacing with lower prices the legitimate vodka that has traditionally been a huge source of tax revenue for the government. As a result, the Russian government does not have enough money to pay the salaries and pensions of workers in the many remaining state firms or to provide many essential public services—such as electricity or garbage collection. Moreover, tax dodging is a way of life even in legitimate private firms (Figure 5.5). Only 49 percent comply even occasionally. The tax laws themselves are rife with loopholes for the well connected.

Widespread corruption has become a major obstacle to economic advancement and effective government. In Moscow and other major cities, the willingness of government officials to be bought off has led to a tremendous rise in organized crime. Throughout Russia, upper-level provincial bureaucrats trade access to exploitable resources for personal gain. This form of corruption, already strong in timber resource areas, has spread to oil and gas areas as well. The potential for political instability and Mafia-style violence scares away legitimate foreign investors. The Russian economy has a much lower rate of foreign investment than do other economies undergoing the transition from central planning to capitalism, such as China or much of Eastern Europe.

VIGNETTE In his early years, Boris K. used to race go-carts, and he even drifted into producing films for a while. Still a young man, Boris now owns several kiosks, which makes him, by most Russian standards, a gangster. Kiosks are highly mobile and modular stores, usually consisting of a large steel box, about twice the size of a dumpster, with windows and a display case. They are usually crammed with a wide variety of goods, ranging from vodka and candy to toilet seats. Capable of being locked up as securely as a safe, kiosks can be loaded onto trucks and transported anywhere overnight. This allows the operators to avoid trouble from the authorities and to take advantage of nearly any public space with commercial potential. These places where kiosks congregate are called *tolkuchkas,* or "places of pushing."

Why the gangster connection? Nearly all kiosks sell some sort of purloined product: counterfeit CDs, fake name brands, stolen property. Few pay taxes. Many are run by toughs who strong-arm other vendors or demand protection money. Some are in dirty, rubble-strewn squares, some are next to pleasant parks; nearly all are temporary, disappearing and reappearing depending on the needs of those who own and supply them, and who is buying what. Many kiosks have names painted on the outside, usually in bright colors and in English. The names reflect their somewhat rebellious and capitalistic nature: "Freedom," "My Valentine," "What You Want?" As Boris puts it, kiosks and their *tolkuchkas* are "spontaneous rackets," very attuned to the market of the moment. [Adapted from Mark Kramer, *Travels with a Hungry Bear: A Journey into the Russian Heartland* (Boston: Houghton Mifflin, 1996), pp. 262–268.]

As a result of these problems with unemployment and corruption, support for reforms is dwindling. The majority of people still depend on the rapidly deteriorating institutions of the command economy. Dissatisfaction grows as ever increasing numbers are laid off or deprived of benefits once provided through the workplace (subsidized food, housing, health care, and education). Many are looking back to the "good old days" of the Soviet era, when living standards were higher, jobs more secure, leaders less blatantly corrupt, and racketeering and social violence far less serious problems. Some opposition leaders are now advocating a more moderate pace of reform. The geographer Philip Pryde,

Taxes Owed to Russia's Federal Government

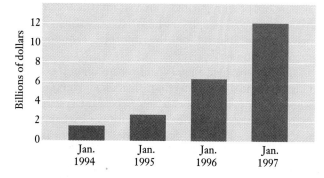

FIGURE 5.5 Even some large companies in Russia do not pay their lawful taxes, and apparently enforcement is barely existent. [Adapted from *New York Times,* February 19, 1997, p. A8.]

Imported (probably smuggled) VCRs and TVs are sold in impromptu, non-tax-paying open markets; this one is in Moscow. They are tended by men affecting, if not actually living, a "Mafioso" style. Police are paid to look the other way. [Gerd Ludwig/National Geographic.]

in his book on the environmental crises in the former Soviet Union, observes that what exists in Russia today is reminiscent of the unregulated laissez-faire capitalism discredited in the capitalist world since the 1930s. Russia has few of the controls on excess that stable free market economies depend on: antitrust or anti-price-fixing legislation, vigorous environmental protection and other regulatory agencies, better business bureaus, and numerous "watchdog" consumers' and citizens' organizations. Many observers emphasize the need for banking and credit institutions that are accessible to ordinary people and would help them establish their own businesses.

Political Reforms

If the task of reforming the economy has been difficult and slow moving, attempts to foster democracy have been even more so. Russia's president, along with the leaders of most other former Soviet republics, has ruled primarily by decree, using legislatures and public referendums mainly as rubber stamps to legitimize decisions already arrived at behind closed doors. To be fair, it is unclear that a majority of the people could have participated more fully in the decision-making process. The last 80 years have not fostered civic responsibility. Even today, ordinary citizens tend to think of political leaders as patriarchs from whom to beg favors. Furthermore, the concept of a society voluntarily taxing itself to raise revenues for necessary services is alien to an inexperienced electorate, which never before had to think about balancing budgets. There is a tendency to look for the heroic (patriarchal) leader who can produce simple solutions to complex problems, and cheaply.

An increasingly debated subject is the status of women and their involvement in politics in the evolving democratic capitalist societies. Although women were granted equal rights under the USSR's constitution, they never wielded much power in government. In 1990, women accounted for 30 percent of Communist party membership, but they made up just 6 percent of the governing Central Committee. Moreover, since the fall of the USSR, women have lost political representation. In Russia today, they still make up only 5.4 percent of those in government offices and only 12 percent of the elected parliamentary representatives.

Many of the independent organizations now seeking to encourage democratic skills among the citizenry have been founded by women. With goals that range from conservative to liberal, these groups themselves exemplify the overall inexperience with democracy; for example, until recently, they had little to do with one another. In 1990 they met jointly under the slogan "Democracy minus women is not democracy" and created an ongoing discussion among women's organizations. Now there is more open debate about violence against women and how gender bias affects the free market economy and entrepreneurial opportunity.

Still, as in most societies, there is ambivalence among women as to just how and when, and toward which goals, they wish to wield the political power of their numbers. There has been little open support for a women's political movement, despite massive evidence of gender discrimination and despite mounting solidarity among women in dealing with the challenges of everyday life. As elsewhere in Europe and in the Americas, women in Russia tend to rely on other women daily and during times of difficulty; yet there is a hesitancy to join together with other women to exert political pressure. They fear that to do so would be taken as evidence of antimale attitudes or as rejection of femininity, ideas most women across the region dismiss.

Geopolitical and Geoeconomic Legacies of the USSR

The division of Soviet territory into numerous newly independent states has required complete renegotiation of all former economic and political arrangements across the region. Russia can no longer control the movement of resources and people, and its continued dominance in the region is precarious. The question of just which geographic units of the old union will stay together, and under what types of agreements, is still unresolved, as is the question of how Russia and the republics of Caucasia and Central Asia will work out new relationships with the outside world.

For decades, Russia had a colonial relationship with its associates in Eastern Europe, the Caucasus, and Central Asia. Russia appropriated their resources in uneven exchanges that left the republics impoverished and dependent. Today, Russia is struggling to maintain what is left of these arrangements. Several former Soviet republics, including the Baltic republics, Ukraine, and Moldova, have already drifted far out of the sphere of Russian influence. Thus, in this book they are included in Europe, and not discussed in this chapter. At the moment, Russia, Belarus, Caucasia, and Central Asia are connected through their economies; but present-day arrangements may not last. For example, the cotton growers of the Central Asian republics currently sell their product to textile mills located within Russia, which export cotton cloth back to Central Asia. In time, Central Asia will most likely build its own cotton mills

and reap the profits of exporting finished textiles to the global marketplace. Central Asia's oil and gas industry currently sells to Russia at prices below those of the global market, but in the future they are likely to sell to China and elsewhere.

For either of these developments to occur, some sticky transport issues will have to be settled. As Figure 5.6 shows, pipelines now deliver oil and natural gas from Caucasia and Central Asia primarily to Russia. As capitalism takes hold, multinational energy companies are pressuring Central Asian countries to permit the building of new, more efficient delivery systems. Routes for roads and pipelines have been proposed through Iran, Afghanistan, China, Caucasia, and Russia, but civil wars and interrepublic hostilities get in the way. Russia no longer has the power to force one solution or another.

How Russia and the Eurasian republics will work out new relationships with the outside world is an

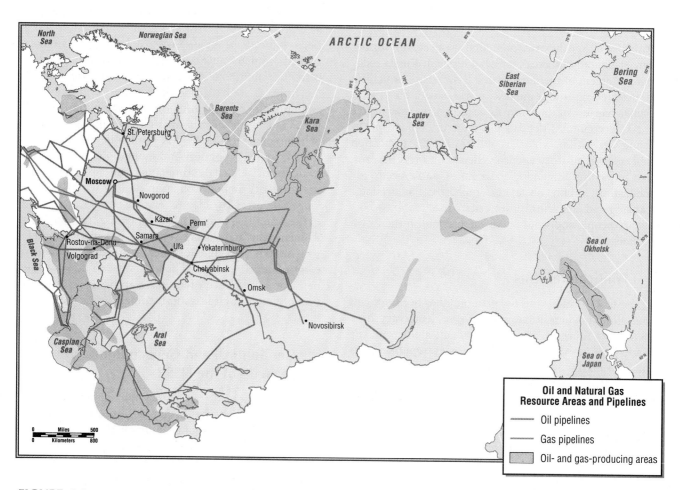

FIGURE 5.6 Oil and natural gas resource areas and pipelines. [Adapted from William H. Berentsen, *Contemporary Europe: A Geographic Analysis* (New York: Wiley, 1997), pp. 625–627.]

equally complicated issue. Having long been regarded as a global superpower, Russia, especially, feels it must salvage some respect in its relationships with Europe and North America. Aware of the danger of disregarding Russia's sensitive ego, the Western powers are slowly trying to bring Russia into closer association. Invitations to join the World Trade Organization and participate more fully in meetings of the Group of Seven industrial nations are meant to compensate Russia for the fact that one of its old cold war foes, the North Atlantic Treaty Organization (NATO), is expanding eastward to include Poland, the Czech Republic, and Hungary. NATO is being redefined as a sort of mutual benefit and peace keeping society, still with a military focus but with definite economic overtones. The unspoken worry that Russia might return to foe status is a major motivation behind current efforts to bring it into the outer periphery of NATO nations.

Of all the unknowns in Russia's future, the question of the military's role is one of the most important. The military was once the most privileged sector of society, and its soldiers had access to goods and services that ordinary citizens could only dream about. Now, after huge funding cuts, the military has been reduced by hundreds of thousands. It now numbers about 1.5 million troops, and personnel are returning from far-flung posts all across Central Asia and Siberia. With few skills, few job prospects, little decent housing for their families, and not even adequate clothing, these former soldiers form a huge reservoir of discontent.

Moreover, the military has no tradition of acquiescing to policies developed through democratic processes; and in their present embarrassed circumstances some leaders of the once-proud military could seek to ally with extremist groups. Already, military coups have been attempted, the most important being a botched coup against Gorbachev in August 1991, which led to the formal dissolution of the USSR. A further worry is that the former Soviet nuclear arsenal could become uncontrollable. Already there is some evidence that nuclear expertise and even some warheads may have been smuggled out of Russia to countries such as North Korea, Iran, and Iraq, whose governments are widely distrusted by the international community.

Measures of Human Well-Being

Since the breakup of the former Soviet Union, average levels of well-being have sunk across the region. Perhaps more important, disparities in well-being have increased both regionally and between individuals as the transition to a market economy creates opportunities for a few and troubles for many. Few statistics are available to prove the widening disparities in

well-being, because they were not collected. But the United Nations Human Development Index (HDI) in Table 5.2 records the current level of well-being. Also in short supply are useful figures comparing the situations of men and women.

Gross national product (GNP) per capita, the most common index used to compare countries, is at best a crude indicator of well-being. In Table 5.2 you can see that whereas the Russian Federation and Belarus have per capita GNPs similar to those of some East and Central Europe countries (Poland, Slovakia), the newly independent republics of Caucasia and Central Asia have particularly low GNP per capita figures. It is hard to believe that these can be figures for developed countries, but when these republics were part of the Soviet Union they were so classified. Most have had significant industrial development but have deteriorated due to an inability to compete outside the protective climate of the command economy. The growing disparity between rich and poor is noteworthy because, formerly, the communist system specifically sought to equalize the distribution of wealth. These low GNP per capita figures mask yet lower figures for the majority; the few newly rich have skewed the figure upward.

In columns 3 and 4 of the table, the HDI combines three components—life expectancy at birth, educational attainment, and adjusted real income—to arrive at a ranking of 174 countries that is more sensitive to elements other than just income. Here, the figures for both 1990 and 1998 reveal that daily life deteriorated badly throughout the region. All the republics sank significantly lower in the HDI rankings: the Russian Federation fell from 37 to 72, Armenia from 47 to 99, Tajikistan from 88 to 118. Of the three components of the HDI, adjusted real income fell the most dramatically, dropping by half in Georgia and Armenia and by one-third in Azerbaijan. The drop is a result of a halt in industrial production and general disruption of economic activity. For the Russian Federation and Belarus, the loss of HDI rank is explained primarily by drops in life expectancy; the decline in life expectancy does not appear in southern Caucasia. Experts attribute the higher death rates in Russia and Belarus to deteriorating health brought on by the stress of lost jobs, overcrowding, lost socialist state safety nets, and such related factors as high inflation.

The United Nations Gender Empowerment Measure (GEM) is not available for Russia and the Eurasian republics. Gender Development Index (GDI) figures are given as a substitute. They are not comparable to GEM, however, since they measure only the extent to which males and females have access to the same basics, like food and health care. The GDI says nothing about the ability of females to have control over their own lives and state of well-being through direct participation in government and society. As

TABLE 5.2

Human well-being rankings of Russia and the Eurasian republics

Country	GNP per capita (in U.S. dollars), 1996	Human Development Index (HDI) global rankings, 1998		Gender Empowerment Measure (GEM) global rankings, 1998
		1990	1998	
Selected countries for comparison				
Japan	40,940		8 (high)	38 (GDI = 13)
United States	28,020		4 (high)	11 (GDI = 6)
Kuwait	19,040 (1997)		54 (high)	75 (GDI =50)
Russian Federation and Belarus				
Russian Federation	2,410	37 (high)	72 (medium)	Not av. (GDI = 53)
Belarus	2,070	38 (high)	68 (medium)	Not av. (GDI = 51)
Caucasia				
Georgia	850	49 (high)	108 (medium)	73 (GDI = 98)
Armenia	630	47 (high)	99 (medium)	Not av. (GDI = 75)
Azerbaijan	480	62 (medium)	110 (medium)	Not av. (GDI = 100)
Central Asian Republics				
Kazakhstan	1,350	54 (high)	93 (medium)	Not av. (GDI = 73)
Turkmenistan	940	66 (medium)	103 (medium)	Not av. (GDI = 87)
Uzbekistan	1,010	80 (medium)	104 (medium)	Not av. (GDI = 86)
Tajikistan	340	88 (medium)	118 (medium)	Not av. (GDI = 106)
Kyrgyzstan	550	83 (medium)	109 (medium)	Not av. (GDI = 97)
World	4,740	NA	NA	NA

Sources: Data from *1998 World Population Data Sheet*, Population Reference Bureau; and *Human Development Report 1998*, United Nations Development Programme.
The high and medium designations indicate where the country ranks among the 174 countries classified into three categories (high, medium, low) by the United Nations.
GDI = Gender Development Index.
Not av. = Not available. NA = Not applicable.

already observed, women have very little real representation in decision-making positions at any level of government. The GDI figures show that women's access to health, education, and equal pay is closer to that of men in Russia and Belarus than in Caucasia and Central Asia; but in no part of the region do the genders approach equality in this regard.

Sociocultural Issues

When the winds of change began to blow in the Soviet Union, political and economic repercussions were expected, but few anticipated the decline in well-being or the social and cultural chaos that has ensued. On the one hand, the new freedoms have encouraged self-expression and individual initiative for some, and the possibility of cultural and religious revival. On the other hand, the loss of structure once provided by the socialist state has resulted not only in loss of livelihood but in loss of housing, food, and health care. In the general disruption, widespread corruption has taken root.

Cultural Dominance of Russia

The Russians always regarded themselves as the heart of the Soviet Union, a point of view that originated with the czars as they extended the Russian Empire over adjacent regions. Throughout the twentieth century, Russians felt closest to the European republics (Ukraine, Moldova, Belarus, and the Baltic states). The Caucasian and Central Asian republics were of interest primarily for the resources they possessed; otherwise, their distinctive cultural features set them apart. Now Russia is left with the company only of those republics that seemed the most alien—in Caucasia and Central Asia, and even they are beginning to pull away.

In the former Soviet Union, ethnically Russian technicians, teachers, and professionals occupied the choice positions in the republics, and Russian culture dominated. Although more than 40 legally recognized languages were spoken throughout the USSR, the Russian language was the language of official business. By the 1980s, the use of minority languages was in decline throughout the USSR. Ancient local customs of non-Russian peoples were suppressed, including family organization, domestic architecture, manner of dress, religion, farming, and foodways. In the school curriculum, Russian culture was presented as the norm. The Russians openly denigrated the Muslim religion and culture of the republics in Caucasia and Central Asia.

The project of making the USSR more culturally unified (more Russian) was linked to the Soviet goal of economic integration. Each part of the USSR was expected to specialize in particular industries or particular agricultural products and to contribute to the centrally planned whole. For example, Ukraine was to be primarily agricultural; the Ural region was to specialize in iron mining and heavy industry; the Kuznetsk Basin, more than 1000 miles to the east in southern Siberia, was to specialize in coking coal. To ensure regional compliance and to provide a skilled labor force, the Soviets resettled Russian people in the peripheral republics. They entered in such large numbers that in several cases, especially in urban centers like Bashkir, Russians vastly outnumbered the local ethnic population.

Cultural Revival in the Post-Soviet Era

As of the late 1990s, all the external republics, including those in Caucasia and Central Asia, were independent countries. All are now trying to reassert their pre-Soviet cultural identities and to reconstitute their economies in order to be less dependent on circumstances they cannot control. Often the result is ethnic clashes as two or more groups assert conflicting claims to territory or resources. But the constructive efforts of individuals like Fahreeden in Uzbekistan are also worthy of note.

VIGNETTE Fahreeden is a taxi driver who operates out of Samarkand, Uzbekistan, in a dusty and battered old Fiat that he starts by hot-wiring. The tires are worn down to the steel fibers and the brakes no longer work. His client today is an American lawyer pursuing an interest in religious history. The destination is Bukhara, Fahreeden's hometown. Bukhara is four hours away, a distance that will bring three flat tires, and five halts by highway police, who expect bribes (baksheesh) every time. Fahreeden and the lawyer have agreed on a fee that includes the anticipated police bribes, flat tires, and a generous luncheon worthy of a Silk Road merchant. The dusty ribbon of road through the semiarid landscape is conveniently punctuated with shops dedicated to tire repair. There are no signs advertising this service, just a bald tire sitting upright along the roadside. As you wait for your tire to be repaired, you may be treated to tea and conversation with the family of the repair person. Eventually, due to missed trains and changed plans, the lawyer will spend the night in the taxi driver's home where, to the guest's surprise, the walls and floors are covered with beautiful and expensive handmade carpets. Dinner, prepared by Fahreeden's wife, Miriam, is shish-kebab, fresh fruit, tomato salad, round loaves of bread, rice pilaf, tea, and lassi (a yogurt-based drink, taken from a common bowl). The guest will sleep in splendor on the same soft rugs on which his meal was graciously served. [From the travels of Ron Leadbetter, personal communication, Autumn 1996.]

Fahreeden's efforts to adapt to the post-Soviet era have led him to reinvent ancient ways of life in Central Asia. As was the case for many in the days of the ancient Silk Road trade, his family income is based on accommodating travelers and merchants and on steering them safely through potentially dangerous territory.

Religion

Although religion had no place in the Soviet state, it has recently revived with a flourish, and many groups and

Resurrecting Christ the Savior Cathedral in Moscow, 1995.
[Gerd Ludwig/National Geographic.]

individuals are rediscovering their religious roots or taking up new beliefs. Attendance at religious services has increased, and many sanctuaries are being restored. In Russia, most people have some ancestral connection to Orthodox Christianity, and Jews form a sizable minority. In the internal republics, many people are Muslims. Most people in the Caucasian and Central Asian republics are Muslims, with the notable exception of Christian Armenia. Buddhists are found in many southern border areas and in the Russian Far East.

Christian fundamentalist sects from the United States are spreading in European Russia. These sects emphasize the role of the individual in the salvation of the soul and also in negotiating the rigors of everyday life. This is a particularly useful message to new capitalists who are relying on their own resources, often for the first time.

VIGNETTE

Valerii, age 35, once a government research scientist, is now one of the new capitalists. He makes a comfortable living in a semilegal import-export niche in the informal economy. Though he has to bribe officials and pay protection money to the *reketiry* (racketeers, or mobsters), his income places his family of three—he, his wife, Nina, aged 30, and their son, Mikhail, 10—well above the living standards of their longtime friends. Nina is the only woman among them who does not work outside the home. Their new wealth, the precariousness of the present economy, and the fact that their friends do

not share their prosperity leave Nina and Valerii uncomfortable and humbled. In search of values that will guide them in this radically new set of circumstances, both have recently been baptized in a Christian fundamentalist sect. They say they chose this particular religious group because it emphasizes the virtues of modesty, honesty, and commitment to hard work. [Adapted from Timo Piirainen, *Towards a New Social Order in Russia: Transforming Structures and Everyday Life* (Aldershot, UK/Brookfield, VT: Dartmouth Press, 1997), pp. 171–179.]

Gender and Opportunities in Free Market Russia

Since 1917, but especially after World War II, there was a push in the Soviet Union to have all women work for wages outside the home. Leninist theory had always argued that women should contribute fully to national development. The post–World War I push to employ women was, however, more an expedient to replace the massive number of male workers killed in the war. In fact, the old patriarchal attitude that the only real role for women is as mothers and keepers of the home persisted. So women did both: worked outside the home and did housework. By the 1970s, 90 percent of able women were working full-time, the highest rate of female paid employment on earth.

For a variety of reasons, the Russian female labor force was, by 1991, on average, more educated than the male (this was not the case in Muslim Central Asia). Women were common in white-collar professions, as economists, accountants, scientists, and technicians. Three out of four physicians were women, one in three were engineers; but many were also laborers in factories and in the fields. Despite their higher qualifications on average, women were seldom found in senior supervisory positions, and as recently as 1996, women workers averaged about 20 percent less than men workers in pay. Table 5.3 shows the percentage of women workers in selected economic sectors and the wages for those sectors as a percent of the national average for all sectors. The table illustrates that in 1991 women were concentrated in sectors that consistently fell below the national wage average. By the late 1990s the situation had changed only in that more women than men had lost their jobs.

As market reforms have resulted in a reduction of jobs, women, including highly qualified professionals, have been laid off in larger numbers than men; and women with children were laid off first (apparently because of their supposed priority role as mothers). By the late 1990s, 70 percent of the registered unem-

TABLE 5.3

Women and wages in selected economic sectors in Russia, 1991

Employment sector	Percentage of workers who are women	Average wage in sector as percent of national average for that sector
Professional occupations		
Medicine	86	69 (all workers in health and social security)
Education and science	73	78 (workers in education) 113 (workers in science)
Planning and accounts	88	93–94 (all workers in administration, credit, and insurance)
Manual occupations		
Trades and catering	89	75
Services	89	76
Communications	84	89
Textiles	83	94
Clothing	93	81

Source: Sue Bridger, Rebecca Kay, and Kathryn Pinnick, *No More Heroines: Russia, Women, and the Market* (London and New York: Routledge, 1996), p. 42.

ployed were women. Mikhail Gorbachev, chairman of the Communist party until the end of 1991, purposely established the precedent for laying women off in preference to men by publicly stating that, since the first role of women is to be domestic, they could best serve their country by returning to the home and leaving the increasingly scarce jobs to men. Many, if not most, of the women so treated were—due to illness, death, or divorce—the sole support of often three generations: themselves, their parents, and their children. In urban Russia, one in two marriages ends in divorce.

Many highly qualified women (physicians, engineers, physicists) are now cooking and cleaning for a living. Some women jettisoned in the economic restructuring are finding new opportunities as entrepreneurs. For example, the Russian women's association, Missiya, has formed a cooperative that promotes home-based craft work to help unemployed women survive the transition period and then find more suitable careers. Many highly qualified women soon found they made more at craft work than they had in their office jobs. One woman engineer commented: "At first

when I was offered home-working I didn't know whether to take it or not. I thought, 'I'm an engineer, for goodness' sake!' But then I agreed to do it and found that I liked it."

Nevertheless, the success of the Missiya cooperative, and other women's support organizations, reinforced some gender stereotypes: that even highly educated women are happiest when employed in domestic activities; that men should by rights have first claim at jobs; and that women-based businesses should focus on the domestic arts (sewing, cooking, the decorative arts), even though such products have a limited market and limited options for expansion.

Unemployment and Loss of Safety Net

Many men have lost their jobs too. And in fact, the number of those who no longer go to work is probably much higher than the official unemployment figures. Numerous state firms simply no longer operate and have no money to pay employees who are still on the

AT THE LOCAL SCALE   *Norilsk*

Norilsk lies 200 miles (320 kilometers) north of the Arctic Circle, atop a rich deposit of minerals: 35 percent of the world's nickel supply, 10 percent of its copper, 40 percent of its platinum. The city's reason for being is Norilsk Nickel, a huge plant that employs 110,000 workers out of a total population of about 270,000. In short, Norilsk is a company town. More than 18,000 of these workers do not work in the plant but are employed in the social services division that manages all the benefits provided to plant workers: housing, health care, saunas, sports clubs, holiday homes in warmer climes, day care centers, cafeterias, and even farms that supply some of the food consumed. In the old centrally planned economy, Norilsk Nickel merely had to produce the needed metals for the nation's industries; any profits went into providing for the workers, who had only been attracted to the bleak, remote area by the well-paying jobs and good social services. The environment is heavily polluted and male life expectancy is just 50 years.

Now, in the more open economy, Norilsk Nickel is no longer viable. A capitalist firm recently acquired 38 percent of the company and it is insisting on efficiencies in all branches, especially the social services division. In 1997, social services ate up all the profits the plant made, an estimated U.S. $260 million, or about U.S. $2000 per worker. Few of the new privately owned firms in Russia and the Eurasian republics provide any social services; and the new joint owners of Norilsk Nickel are trying to persuade the city of Norilsk to take these over now. Whatever happens, the services will shrink drastically or disappear just when many plant workers are likely to be laid off permanently. They will have no jobs, no benefits, and no pensions, and their few savings will have been destroyed by recent high levels of inflation.

Source: The Economist, January 10, 1998, p. 59.

books. Estimates are that in the mid-1990s, three-fifths of the Russian labor force was not being paid in full and on schedule. For years, many families lived on their savings; by now, such savings are depleted. It is thought that by 1996 the true unemployment rate in Russia was in excess of 13 percent overall and 22 percent for young adults aged 18 to 25. The rate of underemployment was much higher. The loss of job and status hits many men especially hard, and many have turned to drinking. Cheap homemade liquor has become the drug of choice for those experiencing the boredom, anxiety, and loss of self-esteem of not working. It is estimated that half the men and perhaps one-third of the women in the region are alcoholics. Death by alcohol poisoning rose 25 percent in the 1990s.

It is especially devastating to lose a job in the former Soviet Union because the social welfare system was organized around the workplace. The job was an individual's link not just to income, but to everything else in life. The state-owned companies were the providers of housing, two main meals a day in the company cafeteria, health care, and day care for children. They were also the center of community and social life. For many, when the job went, there was no alternative safety net. With so many industries now obsolete, in some cases whole cities are facing not just unemployment but the loss of all social benefits for their people. Such is the case in the city of Norilsk in the far

north of the Central Siberian Plateau (see the box "Norilsk").

Crime and Corruption as Sources of Social Instability

The role of corruption in economic and political life has been noted, but perhaps the most dangerous threat posed by rampant crime and corruption is to social stability in Russia and the Eurasian republics. Since independence, gangsters have taken over portions of the economy in every republic, and literally every citizen has to deal daily with the effects of corruption. Recently, an American Fulbright scholar, John G. Stewart, posted to teach public administration ethics in the Caucasian country of Georgia, found himself learning from his students about the roots of corruption in daily life. First, they reminded him that, even before rampant inflation, all government salaries were ridiculously low; a civil servant now earns the equivalent of $10 a month or less. There is no way to live on such incomes, so other means must be found. The government bureaucracy was and is nearly nonfunctional until a bribe is paid; that is one way a civil servant supplements a low salary. Someone who wants to build a building or open a shop can spend months standing in lines to obtain the necessary permits, or can shorten the process with a few well-placed bribes. Additionally, because laws are poorly written and contradictory, the most capable and ambitious people simply ignore restrictions and regulations. There has evolved a general scofflaw attitude of noncompliance with all regulations—even those that might clearly serve the common good, like speed limits, sanitary regulations, or limits on the transport and disposal of nuclear waste.

It was a short step from such ingrained systemic corruption to protection rackets, outright robbery, and violence, especially after cheap weapons became readily available in 1991. A market economy and a democratic society that rely on trust, ability, hard work, and the rule of law cannot flourish in such a setting. Also, it is dangerous for an individual to buck the system because the officials and the police have often been bought off by the gangsters.

Stewart's students worried how they, as future public administrators, could practice ethical values and survive in the real world. Since finishing the public administration course, his 28 Georgian students have set up a support group to help one another implement ethical procedures and to find legitimate supplementary employment, so that bribes need not become part of their income. Georgia's president, Edvard Shevardnadze, also mounted a government-wide campaign against corruption of all types.

Environmental Issues

VIGNETTE — Katerina, a mother of three, lives with her family in Azerbaijan, 20 miles from a Russian-run chemical complex on the Caspian Sea. This is one of dozens of chemical plants and oil and gas refineries that line the Caspian, whose shores are divided among Russia, Azerbaijan, Kazakhstan, Turkmenistan, and Iran. When the breezes are favorable, a step outside in the morning brings only a momentary gasp as one gets used to the throat-catching stench of sulfur or chlorine. But Katerina says that often the air is much worse. Some days, what used to be a welcome, cooling breeze off the Caspian now carries with it an insidious chemical poison. The first sign appears when her three-year-old son's nose starts to bleed, then in a few minutes the older kids get dizzy and they all detect the sulfur odor of spoiling eggs. [Adapted from *The Economist*, supplement on the Caspian, February 7, 1998, p. 12.]

Residents around the Caspian are aware that the refineries and chemical plants are ruining their health, but their leaders do not respond to complaints. The leaders are working to attract potential investors from Europe, America, and Asia, who will greatly increase oil, gas, and chemical production and who will pay a gratuity to the officials in order to seal a deal. When grassroots environmental pressure groups finally organize in the Caspian region, they will have to contend not only with five independent governments but also with a long history of official corruption.

Resources: Distribution and Use

The potential of the natural resources of Russia and the Eurasian republics is considerable. The Russian Federation alone has significant reserves of natural gas, coal, and petroleum, as well as industrial minerals like iron ore, lead, mercury, nickel, platinum, and gold. Russia also has enormous hydropower capacity. It is already the third largest producer of hydropower in the world, and could easily generate yet more. Furthermore, Russia has forest reserves that stretch in a wide band across the northern reaches of the continent. The Eurasian republics share a large deposit of oil and gas that is apparently centered on the Caspian Sea but also extends east toward China. The five independent states that border this sea, as well as Uzbekistan, are frantically jockeying for rights to tap and transport these fossil fuels to the world market.

The environmental degradation associated with the exploitation of these resources is as impressive as the resources themselves. Figure 5.7 shows the distribution in Russia and the Eurasian republics of primary mineral resources as well as the distribution of environmental degradation. Notice that both patterns of distribution cross international borders, making the resolution of pollution issues especially difficult. Much of the pollution shown on the map is associated with the mining and industrial processing of minerals and with the generation of the energy necessary for this processing. Hydropower is the main source of energy for the enormous industrial complexes that produce chemicals, aluminum, steel, nickel, and pulpwood. Many of the largest hydropower plants on earth are in Siberia, two on the Yenisey River alone. Their chief direct environmental impact is **thermal pollution** (unnaturally hot water is returned to the environment) and habitat destruction by dam and reservoir construction. In addition, the industries and the surrounding urban settlements send tons of chemicals and raw sewage into the very rivers that furnish the hydropower.

Recent research suggests that Russian forests play an important role globally in absorbing carbon dioxide, a major by-product of human industrial activity. From the point of view of forest conservation, a fortunate side effect of the fall of the USSR was that forest clearing may have fallen by half in the 1990s. There are two reasons: domestic demand for wood declined, and

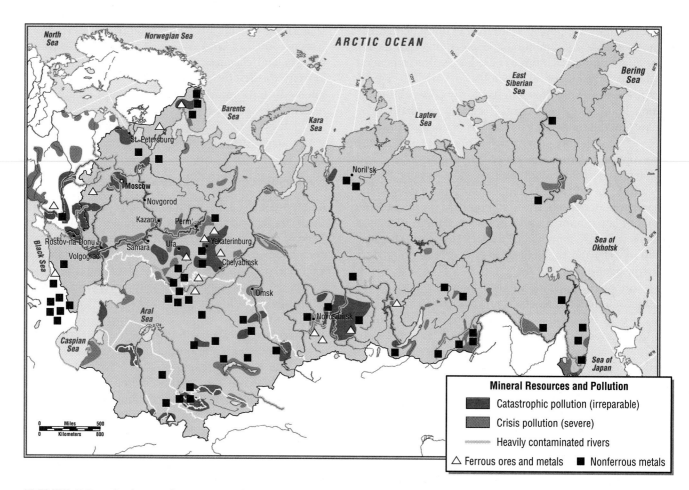

FIGURE 5.7 Chief mineral resources and zones of pollution. [Adapted from James H. Bater, *Russia and the Post-Soviet Scene* (London: Arnold, 1996), pp. 154, 314.]

international prices happened to fall too. The Trans-Siberian Railroad had long charged very low rates to carry logs; after 1991, haulage rates went up significantly. Observers worry that either international thieves will steal remote stands of trees or that soon an economically strapped Russian government will give contracts to private foreign concessionaires for very rapid and unsustainable clear-cutting.

Marxist theory held that only human labor imparted value to goods. Natural resources like forests, minerals, groundwater, rivers, lakes, and wild animals were deemed to have no value until exploited, a view oddly similar to those of the earliest laissez-faire capitalists. To the Soviet planner, nature was a mere servant of industrial and agricultural progress. The grander the evidence of domination, the better, hence the emphasis on huge projects. This view of nature led to the environmental nightmare that is a daily reality for so many people in Russia and the Eurasian republics.

Today in the former Soviet Union, over 35 million people (15 percent of the population) live in areas where the air is dangerous to breathe, birth defects are rampant, and by some estimates only one-third of all schoolchildren are completely healthy. The chaos following the collapse of the Soviet Union largely nullified what little progress had been made toward a more livable environment and sustainable economy. As one Russian environmentalist recently put it: "When people became more involved with their stomachs, they forgot about ecology." Now, instead of one central planning agency, there are 15 independent republics with widely differing policies, and none has the money to correct even a few of the past environmental abuses.

Industrial and Nuclear Pollution

Many Soviet cities were created in the twentieth century. They were built quickly to accommodate industry and to house the rural workers who flocked in from the countryside. The dense concentration of workers, alone, was enough to produce lethal pollution. There are few urban sewer systems and fewer still that actually process and purify the sewage. Many large apartment blocks have the equivalent of septic systems,

Known locally as Atomic Lake, this shimmering place continues to exude radiation. It was created when a nuclear device was exploded in 1965 to make a reservoir northwest of Semey in Kazakhstan. [Gerd Ludwig/National Geographic.]

of rural pollution arose out of the Soviet Union's various nuclear pursuits. In the thinly populated deserts of Kazakhstan, the Soviet military triggered almost 500 nuclear explosions. Local populations, mostly poor Kazakh herders, suffered radiation sickness and birth defects, but were not told the cause until 1989.

Many coastal communities in both Russia and neighboring countries are now concerned about the large amount of nuclear waste that has been dumped at sea. Although the government signed an international antidumping treaty, it sank 14 nuclear reactors and dumped thousands of barrels of radioactive waste in the world's oceans. Known dump sites are in the Arctic Ocean and in the Sea of Okhotsk in the northwestern Pacific.

Pollution has dropped somewhat since independence in 1991, as outmoded factories have either shut down or curtailed production. But the republics are seeking to reinvigorate industrial and agricultural production in order to provide jobs and earn tax revenue for purposes like pollution cleanup. Ironically, when sufficient funds are obtained to reinvigorate production, the pollution cycle will start up again because, as yet, prevention measures are not in place.

Irrigation and the Aral Sea

For thousands of years, the Aral Sea and the two rivers feeding it, the Syr Darya and Amu Darya, sustained human life in a large, arid part of Central Asia. In 1960, the Aral was the fourth largest lake in the world. Through a continuous cycle of incoming fresh water, seepage of groundwater, and evaporation, the Aral encouraged the growth of vegetation and had a moderating influence on the surrounding climate. Now the sea is disappearing. By early 1993, the sea had shrunk in area by over 50 percent and had lost 75 percent of its volume (Figure 5.8). It is expected to shrink further by the turn of the century and to disappear entirely in a decade or two.

Already the shrinkage of the sea has noticeably altered the area's climate. Since the 1960s, the country around the sea has become drier. There is evidence that the summers are 2° to 3° hotter and the growing season is three weeks shorter; winters are 2° cooler and come two weeks earlier. Winds sweeping across the landscape now pick up the newly exposed salt and seabed sediment, creating poisonous dust storms that deposit a deadly cargo of sediment in people's lungs.

How did such a dramatic environmental change happen? The Syr Darya and Amu Darya rivers bring snowmelt from the lofty Hindu Kush and Tien Shan mountains to the southeast. In 1918, planners in Moscow decreed that water diverted from the two rivers would irrigate millions of acres of land in Kazakhstan and Uzbekistan. The idea was to grow

meaning that they rely on the land under and around the block to absorb sewage.

There was little effort to segregate residential areas from industries that produced harmful by-products. This regional concentration of people and industries in the same space exacerbates the polluting effects. The city of Moscow, for example, sits at the center of a huge industrial area. In the region around Moscow, infant mortality and birth defects are particularly high. People in the vicinity are exposed not only to pollution from the huge complex of surrounding industries, but to pollution from many sources that cannot be pinpointed (nonpoint sources). These include untreated automobile exhaust, raw sewage, and agricultural chemicals that drain from fields into the cities' water supplies. In some cities, the source of pollution is easy to spot—a single huge plant may be the basis of the economy, simultaneously providing a livelihood and misery to tens of thousands. The city of Magnitogorsk in the Urals, for example, is the site of the largest steel mill in the world. One in three of its citizens has respiratory problems such as asthma or bronchitis from breathing smoke and airborne chemicals.

Even workers in the countryside have been subjected to urban emissions that have drifted to rural areas. They have also been exposed to fertilizer and pesticide pollution. In Siberia, numerous inland oil spills have contaminated lakes, rivers, and wildlife that provide sustenance for indigenous populations of hunters and fishers. But the most dangerous examples

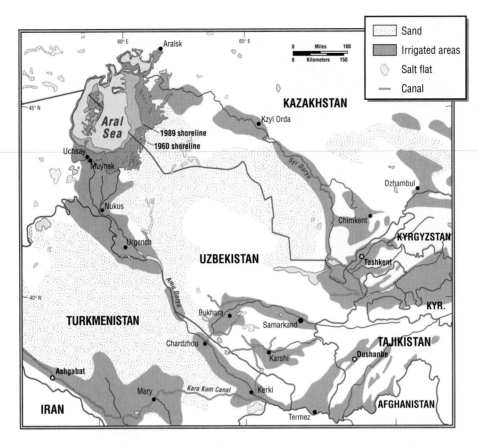

FIGURE 5.8   The decline and disappearance of the Aral Sea. [Adapted from *National Geographic* (February 1990), pp. 72, 80–81.]

cotton to meet Russian textile needs. The plan was so successful that by 1937, Russia had become an exporter of the "white gold." In 1956, millions more acres were put into production in Turkmenistan, irrigated with water brought by an open, 850-mile-long, desert canal fed by the Amu Darya. The canal, which lost a great deal of water through evaporation, was the critical turning point. Within four years, the Aral Sea had measurably declined. Yet, enticed by the income generated by the crops, planners had still more land irrigated. By the early 1980s, no water was reaching the Aral Sea and the shrinkage became dramatic. By early 1990, the Aral had divided into two smaller seas.

The economic benefits of irrigation are hard to resist. Drawing from both rivers, Uzbekistan irrigates 16 percent of its total cropland, most of which grows cotton. That country is the world's fifth largest cotton grower; the crop is the country's leading hard currency earner (representing one-third of its exports) and employs about 40 percent of the national labor force. The situations in Turkmenistan and Kazakhstan differ in details but are comparable.

Despite the economic benefits, the dying sea is exacting a terrible cost in human health. For example, in rural northern Turkmenistan near the Amu Darya, the drinking water is heavily polluted with chemicals applied to the region's cotton fields. Seventy percent of the population suffers from one or more chronic illnesses. But the Turkic Muslims in Karakalpakstan, a separate republic in Uzbekistan at the south end of the Aral Sea, suffer most. Here, 69 out of every 100 persons is incurably ill and, in some villages, life expectancy is 38 years (the national average is 70 years).

What is being done? In Uzbekistan, very little; the government acknowledges the problem but has taken few steps to solve it. In Turkmenistan, any opposition to the still-Communist government is branded counter to national interests, and attempts to raise environmental issues are suppressed. Kazakhstan, the Central Asian republic with perhaps the greatest economic potential, allows far more environmental activism and input than its neighbors; but by itself it can do little to reconcile the people's desire for a better standard of living with the need to halt environmental degradation.

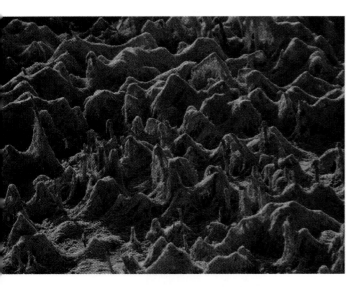

Near the Aral Sea salts left from irrigation cover the stalks of dead cotton plants the water was meant to nourish. [David Turnley/Corbis.]

TABLE 5.4

Countries of the world by descending area size

Country	Square miles (square kilometers)
Russia	6,520,660 (16,889,000)
China	3,601,310 (9,327,000)
Canada	3,560,220 (9,221,000)
United States	3,536,340 (9,160,000)
Brazil	3,265,060 (8,457,000)
Australia	2,951,520 (7,644,000)
India	1,147,950 (2,973,000)

SUBREGIONS OF RUSSIA AND THE EURASIAN REPUBLICS

In this subregional section, the Russian Federation is discussed first because it, especially European Russia, has dominated the entire region for many hundreds of years and its experiences in the post-Soviet era will affect all the adjacent external republics. Even though Belarus is officially independent, it is grouped with the European Russia (western) portion of the Russian Federation because of its location and close affinities to this part of Russia. The themes discussed for the various subregions echo those already discussed for the region at large. Here the reader is provided with a sense of what life is like in the various parts of this unusually large area.

The Russian Federation and Belarus

Within the former USSR, the Russian Federation was the paramount republic in terms of size, cultural dominance, and economic wealth and potential. This has remained the case in the post-Soviet era. The Russian Federation is still the largest country on earth—nearly twice the size of China, Canada, or the United States

(Table 5.4). It is also a leader in population, ranking sixth. In potential natural wealth, it also ranks high.

The Russian Federation consists of much of the territory gradually claimed over the last 500 years by the European Russian state. As it expanded east, eventually reaching the Pacific, Russia absorbed many small ethnic minorities that are now the more than 30 internal republics and so-called autonomous regions. The words *federation* and *autonomous* are both misnomers, since they imply self-government and freedom to terminate the association. The internal republics control some of their own affairs but have little choice in their coalition with Russia. As Figure 5.11 shows, many are tiny **enclaves:** they lie entirely within the borders of Russia.

In the following discussion, the Russian Federation is made up of three parts: European Russia (west of the Urals), the internal republics, and Russia east of the Urals (Siberia and the Russian Far East). In between the first and second parts, the text discusses Belarus.

European (Western) Russia

European Russia is that area of Russia that shares the eastern part of the North European Plain with Latvia, Lithuania, Estonia, Belarus, Ukraine, and Moldova

FIGURE 5.9 European Russia and Belarus.

(Figure 5.9). It is usually considered the heart of Russia, because it is here that early Slavic peoples established what became the Russian Empire, with its center in Moscow. Although it occupies only about one-fifth the total territory of present-day Russia, European Russia has most of the industry, the best agricultural land, and about 70 percent of the population of the Russian Federation (105 million out of 147 million).

The vast majority of western Russians live in cities, their parents and grandparents having been forced off the farms by Stalin's efforts to collectivize agriculture and establish heavy industry. Most moved to one of four major industrial regions chosen by central planners for ease of accessibility and location of crucial minerals. One region centered on Moscow, another in the Ural Mountains and foothills, a third along the Volga River from Kazan to Volgograd, and the fourth just north of the Black Sea around Donetsk. This last region is now mostly in Ukraine and represents a ma-jor loss to Russia, since Ukraine has chosen to turn away from Russia toward greater trade and political alignment with Western Europe.

The most heavily occupied part of European Russia—stretching from St. Petersburg on the Baltic south to Ukraine and on to the forest-steppe zone to the southeast—coincides with that part of the continental interior that has the most bearable climate. Even so, the winters are long and harsh and the summers mild and short, because the region lies so far to the north; Moscow lies on a latitude 100 miles north of Edmonton, Canada.

The best agricultural land is in the southwest of European Russia, between the Black and Caspian seas and along the northern border of Kazakhstan (Figure 5.10). The really prime agricultural land is in Ukraine and Caucasia, which are now independent from Russia. Worries over the loss of access to the agricultural resources of Ukraine and Caucasia will play an important role in Russian policy decisions for years to come.

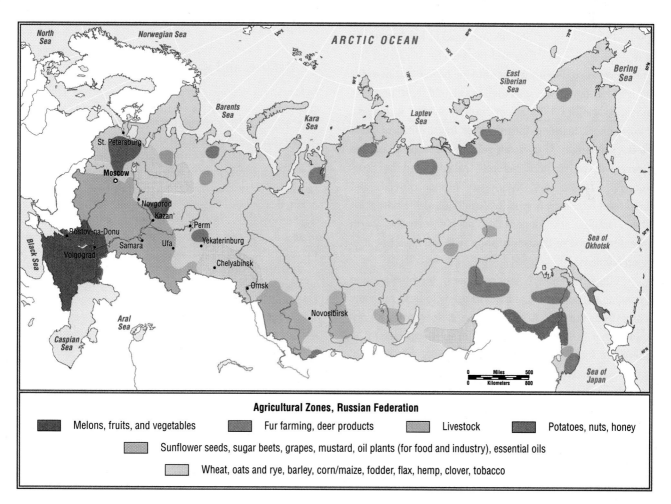

Agricultural Zones, Russian Federation

- Melons, fruits, and vegetables
- Fur farming, deer products
- Livestock
- Potatoes, nuts, honey
- Sunflower seeds, sugar beets, grapes, mustard, oil plants (for food and industry), essential oils
- Wheat, oats and rye, barley, corn/maize, fodder, flax, hemp, clover, tobacco

FIGURE 5.10 The principal agricultural zones of the Russian Federation and Belarus subregion. [Adapted from Moshe Brawer, *Atlas of Russia and the Independent Republics* (New York: Simon & Schuster, 1994), p. 31.]

Moscow remains at the heart of Russian life in the post-communist era. In this city, the selection of goods and food is the best, the nightlife the most exciting. Inflation is the wildest, prices the highest. The criminals are more concentrated, more innovative, and more violent. Entrepreneurial activity is most accepted and rambunctious here, the market economy most developed, and government jobs particularly precarious. By 1992, more than a quarter of Moscow's labor force of 4.4 million was in non-state employment; by 1994, more than half the jobs were in the private sector. The retail sector and small-scale services to the public—like street food vending and sales of inexpensive clothes, home furnishings, and small appliances—created the most jobs (often in the informal economy). Today, for individuals adjusting to the loss of "cradle-to-grave" security, life in Moscow can be painful, or frightening, or exhilarating, or all three, as the following account of the experiences of Natasha and her customers illustrates.

VIGNETTE

Natasha is an engineer in Moscow. She has managed to hold on to her job and the benefits it carries; but inflation has so diminished her buying power that in order to feed her family she sells used household items and secondhand clothes in a street bazaar on the weekends. "Everyone is learning the ropes of this capitalism business," she laughs. "But it can get to be a heavy load. I've never worked so hard before!" Asked about her customers, Natasha says, "Many are former officials and high-level bureaucrats who just can't afford the basics for their families any longer. Old people love the warm sweaters. Some of them who shop with me have to eat in soup kitchens.

"But, you know," she continues, brightening and changing the subject, "the bales of used clothes I buy now come from the U.S. A guy drives a carload from a container ship in Amsterdam harbor every two weeks. And there are lots of sturdy clothes, especially for children, some quite new with the price tags still on; but only occasionally is there a really fashionable item for a woman." [A composite story based on work by Alessandra Stanley, David Remnick, and David Lempert.]

The privatization of real estate in Moscow gives an interesting insight into pre- and post-Soviet circumstances. During the communist era, all housing was state owned and there was a general shortage. Thousands of families were always waiting for housing, some more than 10 years. Most apartments were built after the mid-1950s, in large, shoddily constructed blocks; the units were one to three rooms, housing one to four or more people. But older buildings in the center city contained much more spacious, if bedraggled, dwellings. In 1991, the government allowed people to acquire, free, about 250 square feet (27 square meters) of usable living space per person—about the size of a typical American living room. Most people simply took ownership of the apartments in which they had been living; by 1995, a majority of Muscovites owned their apartments. The market economy quickly took over and a lively real estate market emerged, with specific neighborhoods quickly claiming the best prices. The shortage in housing, combined with a rising wealthy elite, put a premium on large remodeled apartments in the center city, and soon the apartments were selling for U.S. $100,000 to U.S. $250,000. Rents also skyrocketed. Those who could find alternative housing for themselves made tidy sums by simply renting out their inner-city apartments The demand for commercial space to house private businesses took many former dwelling units out of circulation, thus exacerbating the housing shortage.

Belarus and Kaliningrad

Belarus is a globular-shaped country of few resources surrounded by Latvia, Lithuania, Poland, Ukraine, and Russia. In size and terrain Belarus resembles Minnesota: its flat, glaciated landscape is strewn with forests and dotted with thousands of small lakes, streams, and marshes that are replenished by abundant rainfall. Today, much of the land has been cleared and drained for agriculture, mostly on collective farms. The stony soils are not particularly rich; nor, beyond a little oil, are there many useful resources or minerals beneath the surface. Belarus absorbed a large amount of radiation contamination after the Chernobyl nuclear accident in Ukraine. Twenty percent of the agricultural land and 15 percent of the forestland were lost.

Long noted for their passivity and peacefulness, the people of Belarus (now about 10 million) have shown little inclination to the fervent nationalism so common in the vicinity. The country was forced into independence by the collapse of the Soviet Union in 1991, and now actively seeks to reintegrate with Russia. Cultural features and several economic and political factors help explain why. Belarus has been rather thoroughly "Russified" during the twentieth century. Although 80 percent of the population is Belarus (a Slavic group) and only 13 percent Russian, the Russian language predominates and Belarus culture survives only in museums and historical festivals. The urban concrete landscape feels Russian. The Belarus economy remains dominated by state firms that sell to Russia; only a few retail shops are now private. Its important petro-

Kaliningrad's busy port bristles with ship-loading cranes. It is the only year-round ice-free port on Russia's Baltic coast. [Dennis Chamberlin.]

chemical industry depends on Russian oil and gas for raw material. In Russia, Belarus is welcomed by the remaining communists as well as by the military, who see it as a useful buffer state against extension of NATO membership to Poland, and by all those who wish to see the former Soviet "empire" reconstituted.

Kaliningrad is a tiny exclave of Russia that lies beyond Belarus along the Baltic coast between Poland and Lithuania, about 200 miles from the closest Russian point. Acquired from Germany at the end of World War II, Kaliningrad is now 90 percent Russian in population and is an important port on the Baltic for Russia, which has so few year-round outlets to the world's oceans. There has been some talk of making Kaliningrad a duty-free trade zone for the Baltic.

The Internal Republics

Many of the often quite tiny internal republics of Russia are the territories inhabited by particular, non-Russian, ethnic groups. The people who live in these republics trace their origins to Turkic, Tatar, Finnish, Ugric (Hungarian), and Persian groups. Some of the groups are Muslim, some Buddhist, some have animistic beliefs that predate any of the organized religions. Others have converted to Christianity from Islam; and Jewish and Buddhist beliefs are entwined among the Kalmyk people (No. 7 in Figure 5.11), who live along the lower Volga.

The distributions of these groups today are in part the result of forced migration. Imperial Russia repeatedly removed and resettled whole groups in an effort to get at the riches of a particular region. During the Soviet era this trend continued, and, in addition, large

numbers of Russian people were resettled in the midst of the enclaves. The ethnic Russians were usually given the task of modernizing and "civilizing" what were viewed as culturally inferior people. The Russians received the best jobs and housing and they often outnumbered the native people. A handful of truly indigenous people (analogous to Native Alaskans) live in the far northern reaches of Russia, especially in Siberia. Because of the remoteness and harshness of their homelands, they have been spared encroachment; some still hunt, herd reindeer, gather wild plants, and fish.

Today, the many internal republics have a bewildering array of political arrangements with Russia, and their status is continuously being renegotiated republic by republic (see the box "An Ethnic Republic Reasserts Itself"). One should expect to hear the names of these republics in the news over the next decade or two as they work out new relationships with each other and with Russia. The republic of Chechnya (No. 5 in Figure 5.11), for example, was often in the news while Chechen guerrillas drove out the Russian Army in the mid-1990s. In that republic, political conflict and violence, both internal and with its neighbors, still rule.

Russia East of the Urals

Siberia. In popular parlance, Siberia has meant everything east of the Ural Mountains, and this territory is usually divided into three physical zones: the western plain, the middle plateau, and the far eastern mountains (see physical geography section on landforms earlier in this chapter). For our purposes here, "Siberia" refers to only about half the landmass east of

255

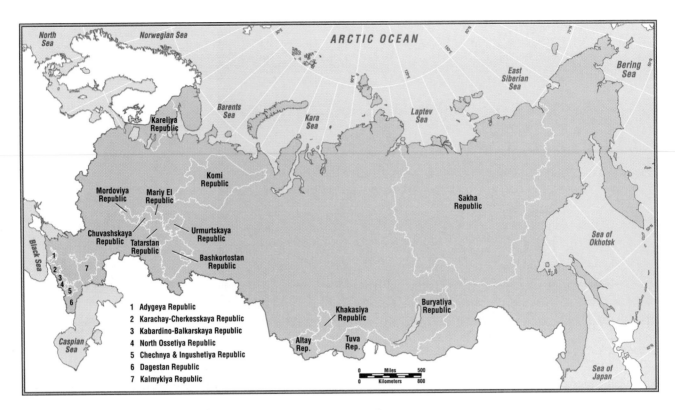

FIGURE 5.11 The 21 internal republics in the Russian Federation subregion are outlined in white. These republics are only somewhat analogous to counties, states, reservations, or territories in the United States. [Adapted from James H. Bater, *Russia and the Post-Soviet Scene* (London: Arnold, 1996), pp. 280–281.]

AT THE LOCAL SCALE   *An Ethnic Republic Reasserts Itself*

Tuva is a narrow mountainous republic just north of Mongolia, with 300,000 people. Traditionally, the Tuva were nomadic herdspeople, who tended camels, reindeer, cattle, sheep, and horses. When the Soviets came in 1944, most were forced to settle in wooden houses, put their children in Russian schools, and join the work force on collective farms or in the coal, asbestos, cobalt, and gold mines. Russian bureaucrats came to run the various collectives, mines, and schools; today, Russians make up one-third of the population.

A few thousand nomads remain active in herding. In the summer they move repeatedly, seeking higher, cooler elevations where the grass is sufficient for their animals. Their homes are yurts, large round felt-covered tents stretched on circles of wooden lattice that contract into a tight bundle for moving. Many Tuva dream of returning to the nomadic life where the work is hard and the feeling of accomplishment great.

Few, however, retain the skills or the ability to face the rigor of the old ways.

Tuva has its own language and its own parliament, but it generates only 18 percent of its national budget. The rest comes from Moscow. Tuva's main export is its music, called "throat singing." The music is based on a distinctive harmonized sound created when one singer produces two notes at once, one a vibrating hum, the other a quaver. Touring throat singers have won the acclaim of Americans and Europeans, and have recorded with well-known musicians such as Ry Cooder. The Tuva president hopes the singers' popularity will protect his republic from any Russian efforts to violently quash a mounting independence movement. "[If something bad happens], we want the world to know where Tuva is and who we are," he told interviewers.

Source: Richard Feynman, http://feynman.com/tuva.

FIGURE 5.12 Siberia.

the Urals: it encompasses the Western Siberian Plain and about half the Central Siberian Plateau (Figure 5.12) The rest of the landmass east to the Pacific is called the Russian Far East.

Siberia is so cold that 60 percent of the land is under permafrost. This vast central portion of the Russian Federation is home to just 33 million people, many of whom have been moved into the region from west of the Urals and who live in the somewhat warmer, southern quarter. For millennia, Siberia was a land of wetlands and quiet, majestic forests; now it is dotted with bleak urban landscapes and industrial squalor, the legacy of the continuing effort to exploit its valuable natural resources.

Among the cities of Siberia are Tobolsk and Novosibirsk (New Siberia). Tobolsk was founded as an outpost of imperial Russia in 1587 by a band of Cossacks (frontiersmen organized into a cavalry unit of the czar's army). The city sits on the vastness of the Siberian wetlands, and remnants of the distinctive old

wooden medieval town architecture still persist. But most of the 100,000 people occupy a Soviet-style concrete city, devoid of artistic flourish. The town's modern growth began with the discovery of oil nearby and the arrival of a rail spur line connecting it to the Trans-Siberian Railroad further to the south. Massive Soviet-style apartment blocks housing thousands of workers express the Soviet vision of the future in Siberia.

Novosibirsk, Siberia's twentieth-century capital, is illustrative of the Soviet policy of claiming space by distributing industries across its huge landmass. The city lies more than 600 miles east, as the crow flies, from Tobolsk; yet, despite few natural resources, this commercial center has the highest concentration of industry between the Urals and the Pacific. Its over 200 heavy-industry plants are renowned for high rates of pollution. As Siberia's financial center, Novosibirsk is now a hotbed of privatization and a focus for outside investors. By the late 1990s, there were nearly 400 joint ventures based in the city, mostly with Chinese,

German, or South Korean partners. Thirty-two U.S. firms, such as Pepsi-Cola, Eastman Kodak, 3M, and Philip Morris, were participating in some of the 11,000 privatized businesses.

The Russian Far East. The Russian Far East is an extensive territory of mountain plateaus with long coastlines on the Pacific and Arctic oceans (Figure 5.13). It makes up slightly over one-third of the entire Russian Federation in area and is nearly two-thirds the size of the United States. The population of 8.16 million is sparsely settled: on average there are just 2.3 persons per square mile (1.3 per square kilometer), compared to 23 for Russia as a whole. Almost 90 percent of the land is covered by permafrost; the coastal volcanic mountains stop the warmer Pacific air from moderating the Arctic cold that spreads deep into the continent.

This region is richly endowed, but difficult to reach. Huge, relatively unexploited stands of timber cover 45 percent of the area; the tree roots grow in the sun-warmed sediment above the permafrost. Soviet central planners, and now private investors, have been attracted by the region's resources of coal, natural gas, oil, tin, antimony, gold, diamonds, iron, and other minerals. But, even more than in lowland Siberia to the west, development has been hampered by the distance from population centers and by the difficult environment; only 1 percent of the territory, mostly along the Pacific coast, is suitable for agriculture.

The Russian Far East is a land of immigrants. Most arrived in the twentieth century, and for some the journey was a trip into exile for a perceived misdeed in the Soviet era. Here, where serfdom never intruded, there is a spirit of independence that is rare elsewhere in Russia. The earlier immigrants worked at timber and

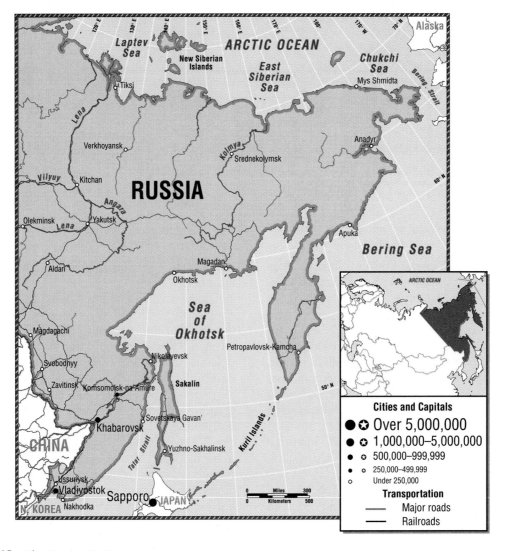

FIGURE 5.13 The Russian Far East.

mineral extraction and in isolated industrial enclaves; more recently, immigrants have headed for cities along the Pacific coast. The Russian Far East today is 75 percent urban. Most people now live along the Pacific coast, especially in Nakhodka and Vladivostok.

Although there are only a few Pacific coast cities, the influx of people and the clearing of forests have radically changed the fragile natural habitat, endangering many species of plants and animals. Such is the case for both the Siberian tiger and the cranes of the Amur River basin. Siberian tigers once ranged throughout eastern Russia, China, and Korea. Now they are threatened not only by loss of habitat, but also by the market for their fur and by Asian folk beliefs. Poachers receive $100 a pound for pulverized tiger bones, which are thought to increase the sexual prowess of men. By one estimate, only 430 tigers remain. Four species of rare cranes, birds that live and breed in wetlands, are threatened by timber harvesting on both the Heilongjian (Chinese) and Siberian sides of the Amur, which is the world's largest remaining unbridged and undammed river. Though forestry is now in a slump, both China and Siberia have plans to drastically increase timber extraction and development of the Amur.

The people of the Russian Far East are those most likely to profit greatly in the transition to a market economy and freer international trade. Already, by the late 1990s, there were more than 900 joint ventures in operation, and trade grows annually. China, just across the Amur River, accounts for nearly 50 percent of the foreign trade, much of it by Han Chinese entrepreneurs who have recently settled in Heilongjiang. Japan, a rich country but poor in natural resources, accounts for 20 percent of the trade, and that is likely to grow. Some geographers and economists forecast that, because of its rich resource reserves and its location so far from the Russian core, the Russian Far East will eventually integrate economically with other Pacific Rim nations, perhaps detaching itself from European Russia.

Caucasia

Caucasia is surely one of the most ethnically complex places on earth. Between the Black Sea and the Caspian Sea, in a mountainous space the size of California, live more than 50 ethnic groups: Armenians, Chechens, Ossetians, Karachays, Abkhazians, Georgians, to name but a few (Figure 5.14). Some groups are tiny (the Ginukh, for example, number just 200), some are large (the Turkic Azerbaijanis number over 6 million). Some are Orthodox Christians, many are Muslims; Gypsies pass through; there are Jews; and some groups retain ancient elements of local animistic religions. Many of the ethnic groups in Caucasia are remnants of ancient migrations. For thousands of years, Caucasia was a stopping

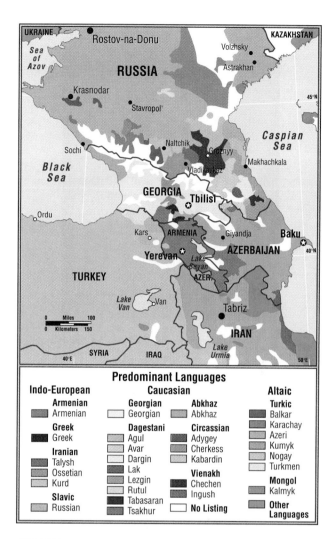

FIGURE 5.14 The diversity of ethnolinguistic groups in the Caucasian subregion illustrates the cultural complexity of the area. [Adapted from http://www.geocities.com/southbeach/marina/6150/ethno.jpg.]

point for nomadic peoples moving between the Central Asian steppes, the Mediterranean, and Europe. Other ethnic enclaves were created more recently by Soviet-forced relocation of troublesome minorities. Today many Caucasians maintain ties to Europe and North America, where hundreds of thousands of emigrants from the region live.

The region is located around the rugged spine of the Caucasus Mountains, which stretches between the Black Sea and the Caspian Sea. The boundary between the Russian Federation to the north and the three external republics to the south runs along the mountains' central spine. The northern flank, lying within the Russian Federation, consists of relatively gentle foothills and level steppes. Russians are the dominant population to the north, but such groups as the Chechens, Dagestanis, Ossetians, and Nagay are found there as well.

Jazz in Azerbaijan. Aziza Mustafa Zadeh is an Azerbaijani singer and jazz pianist, popular in Europe and the eastern Mediterranean. Her version of jazz is inspired by *mugam*, an ancient, mesmerizing modal system of traditional music from Caucasia. [Courtesy of Aziza Mustafa Zadeh.]

On the southern flank of the mountains, in what is known as Transcaucasia, is a band of subtropical intermontane valleys. The valleys, as well as low coastal plains and high volcanic plateaus, are occupied by the external republics of Georgia, Armenia, and Azerbaijan. Most of the people live in the intermontane valleys (see Figure 5.2). These are treasured pieces of real estate, blessed with warm temperatures and abundant moisture coming from off the Black and Caspian seas. In these favorable conditions, farmers can grow crops, such as citrus fruits, that can be produced in no other part of the vast Russian and Eurasian expanse. Before 1991, most of Soviet citrus and tea came from Georgia, as did much of its grapes and wine.

In Caucasia, a single ethnic group is often split up into fragments living in several different republics. Although ethnic strife has been common, it is often fomented by larger powers—Turkey, Russia, Iran— seeking access to strategic military installations and agricultural and mineral resources. After the Soviet collapse in 1991, the three culturally distinct republics of Georgia, Azerbaijan, and Armenia obtained independence as nation-states. Then, very quickly, several other ethnic groups took up arms to obtain their own independent territories: the Abkhazians and the South Ossetians against Georgia; the Chechens against Russia. In a few years of fighting, many thousands have died. In

the conflict over Nagorno Karabakh—a Christian Armenian mountainous enclave in Muslim Azerbaijan— 15,000 died before a truce was signed in 1994.

Oil has joined cultural differences as a source of conflict in Caucasia. Estimates of Caspian oil reserves vary widely from 28 billion barrels to 200 billion barrels. The "oil game" has been blamed for various things: coup attempts in Azerbaijan, part of the Armenian-Azerbaijani conflict; Chechnya's war with Russia; a thriving arms trade; and several attempts on the life of Georgia's president, Edvard Shevardnadze. A major issue is how to get the oil out of Caucasia safely and into the world market. Pipelines? Trucks? Ocean tankers? All require safe passage across difficult terrain and through several hostile republics. A consortium of Western oil companies is considering several pipeline routes to the Black Sea through Chechnya and Russia and through Georgia.

The Central Asian Republics

Kazakhs, now where is the land on which you have lived since the Kazakh tribe was formed?

They drove you off and put the land under the Russians.

Only the salt lakes and waterless plain are left to us.
                                        —*Duwlat-uli, "Kazakh Lands"*

Since the fall of 1991, following nearly 12 decades of Russian colonialism, five independent nations have emerged in Central Asia: Kazakhstan, Kirghizstan, Tajikistan, Turkmenistan, and Uzbekistan (Figure 5.15). Consistent with the mosaic of cultures that is found here, each of these new nations has a language and traditions that are recognizably different from those of the others. Yet all of them draw on the deep, common traditions of this ancient region, of which Islam is only one. Central Asia is poised for change brought on, especially, by the exploitation of new oil and gas reserves and by the rise of ethnic and Islamic religious sensitivies.

Central Asia is situated deep in the center of the Eurasian continent, in the rain shadow of the lofty southern mountains. Its dry continental climate is a reflection of this location. What rain there is falls mainly in the north, on the Kazakh plain, where wide grasslands support limited agriculture and large herds of sheep, goats, and horses. In the south are deserts crossed by rivers carrying glacial meltwater from the high peaks still further south. These rivers are tapped to irrigate huge fields of cotton and smaller fields of wheat and other grains. In many areas of the south, gardens are attached to houses and walled to protect

FIGURE 5.15   The Central Asian subregion.

against desiccating winds. They nurture apricots, peaches, apples (apricots and apples were first domesticated in Central Asia), and many types of melon.

Civilization flourished in Central Asia long before it did in lands to the north. The ancient Silk Road passed through the region. This continuous ribbon of traders connecting China with the fringes of Europe operated for thousands of years, diffusing ideas and technology from place to place. Modern versions of ancient trading cities still dot the land: Bukhara, renowned as a center of Islamic learning and culture; and Samarkand, which has been in existence for 5000 years. The commerce of the Silk Road died down by the fifteenth century; Central Asia, bypassed by trade now carried by sea routes, then entered a long period of stagnation.

By the mid-nineteenth century, Central Asia was increasingly under the sway of czarist Russia. The czars' primary interest was the region's major export

crop, cotton. In a pattern similar to that seen in colonized places elsewhere around the world, the Russian administration set up modern mechanized textile mills; these quickly put out of business small-scale textile firms that employed people to do traditional cotton and silk weaving. The new installations, often located in entirely modern Russian towns built alongside railroad lines, benefited only a few Central Asians. In rural areas, cotton fields replaced the wheat fields that previously had fed local people. People therefore suffered occasional famines whenever they could not afford imported food or when supplies were interrupted.

Russian domination intensified during the Soviet era. Only a few Central Asians were eventually allowed to join the Communist party, and they were thoroughly "Russified"—molded to accept Russian values and perspectives. Islam, though officially tolerated, was eroded by the government's promotion of atheism and

One of the most remarkable cultural traditions of Central Asia is carpet weaving, an art practiced primarily by women and children. The carpets probably originated as the highly portable and useful furnishings of nomadic yurts and *gers* (tents); there are many different types and styles. Each region and culture group has distinctive patterns, with particular combinations of colors. The practice of weaving rugs stretches from interior China to Caucasia, Turkey, and the Balkans. The rug pictured here is an Ersari from Turkmenistan. [Courtesy of Charles W. Jacobsen, Inc., Syracuse, NY.]

not changed, however. Russian influence remains strong, although it is balanced somewhat by growing international interest in the region's oil and gas wealth. Islam remains relatively subdued, with Iranian-style fundamentalism thus far not very influential. Poverty remains widespread and health standards are the lowest in the former USSR. While there is a general sense that democracy and free markets are the wave of the future, authoritarian Soviet-style government remains the norm.

A particularly troubling legacy survives in the borderlands of Central Asia, where Soviet efforts to divide ethnic groups (the better to control them) live on. There are, for example, pockets of Tajiks in Uzbekistan, or Kazakhs in Turkmenistan. Hence, current relations between some Central Asian nations are plagued by **irredentism,** the name for the situation when a country or ethnic group makes claims to territory held by another country and demands its return.

Despite the overall slow pace of change and the difficulties of transition, the Central Asian republics appear to be finding their "free market legs" fairly quickly. As the Russians leave, the people of Central Asia are taking up old market-based skills that have been part of their heritage since the ancient Silk Road days, when trade and long-distance travel were the heart of the economy. For example, a blossoming, largely contraband, trade in consumer goods and illegal substances from drugs to guns goes on with Iran, Afghanistan, and China. (See references to the revival

by restrictions on Islamic worship, pilgrimage to Mecca, and access to mosques.

Nonetheless, the Soviet era did benefit some Central Asians. The patriarchal landholding system was partially dismantled and some poor sharecroppers were given land. Health care improved, and literacy expanded dramatically: from under 10 percent in 1915 to over 50 percent by 1959. Although even under the Russians, Central Asian women have had little access to schooling, they gained greater freedom because they were encouraged by the state to work outside the home. But their main opportunities were low-paying jobs in cotton fields and factories, with few opportunities for advancement.

In the years since independence in 1991, Islam has made a comeback and there has been a revival of Central Asian languages and culture. Many things have

Once Kazakhstan gained independence in 1991, ethnic Kazakhs returned home from self-imposed exile in Mongolia. Kazakhs and Mongolians share a cultural history of nomadic herding. The portable yurt homes are visible in the background. [Gerd Ludwig/National Geographic.]

of the Silk Road and the ancient market at Kashgar in Chapter 9.) There are also chances to render services such as food, transport, and accommodations to tourists and traveling businesspeople who hope to set up legitimate concerns in the region. Turkmenistan is already finding a market for its oil and gas in Iran; and Iran is establishing a free trade zone along its north border with Turkmenistan. Iran feels certain that shoppers will once again materialize from across the steppes, as they have for thousands of years.

REFLECTIONS ON THE RUSSIAN FEDERATION, BELARUS, CAUCASIA, AND CENTRAL ASIA

The region comprising the Russian Federation, Belarus, Caucasia, and Central Asia is bound to go through wrenching changes over the next several years. In a decade it may no longer be appropriate to combine these particular political units into one region. But just how the future will look is unclear. No set of countries has ever attempted such a rapid transformation to a free market economy by peaceful means. Perhaps more than for most regions, it is useful here to prognosticate a bit about the future. The following comments are derived in part from the ideas of Daniel Yergin and Thane Gustafson (in *Russia in 2010*). They have attempted to anticipate how the former USSR will evolve in the future.

As the command economy recedes and localities take over the direction of their own destinies, regional differences and disparities will increase. It is likely that Russia will maintain its paramount position in the region, yet its power could be weakened if the Russian Far East breaks away, or the internal republics rebel, or a powerful European Union excludes Russia while including many of the old Soviet satellites.

Second, it seems likely that the state will remain especially strong in most republics and that participatory democracies will evolve only slowly. Although some individuals are eager to learn from the West, there is widespread and understandable resistance to rapid culture change and to too much influence from abroad. Some places, like Georgia and the Russian Far East, may embrace democracy rapidly—Georgia because of its pro-democracy leadership, and the Russian Far East because of a certain pioneer spirit and promising economic potential.

Most republics in the region will probably have a love-hate relationship with the West for some years to come: embracing many aspects of market economies and democracy with enthusiasm, while mourning the loss of certain civilities and welfare guarantees of the old system. Rising crime, violence, and fraud, associated either with the breakdown of the old system or the introduction of capitalism, will surely alienate many from the West. The Central Asian republics may sort out the nuances of the market economy more rapidly because of the long heritage of entrepreneurial trade in the region. On the other hand, parochial ethnic rivalries, the secular influences of capitalism, and discord over changing roles for women in Central Asia may become the nexus of anti-West, anticapitalist feeling.

All parts of the region will be hampered for years to come by the aging and inefficient industrial infrastructure and by serious environmental pollution. The poorer, less developed republics with oil and gas resources may be able to attract new money for investment in the latest, less polluting technology. Underdevelopment has limited the extent of pollution thus far. On a bright note, the technological revolution may enable most regions to leapfrog over stages of development and thereby save costly investment dollars. For example, the cell phone could save building an expensive telecommunications network.

The changes of the last few years have awakened some women to the features of post-Soviet society that keep them from equitable access to jobs and pay and from equitable domestic duties. There are increasing signs that some women are organizing for change across ethnic and class lines. Men and women in the region have a particularly challenging future as they deal with all that the move toward a market economy entails: lost jobs, obsolete skills, loss of social safety nets formerly associated with the workplace, and changing gender roles—as well as the exhilarating opportunities for greater self-expression and material well-being that market economies can provide.

Selected Themes and Concepts

1. Russia and the Eurasian republics form a huge territory that stretches across the northern reaches of the Eurasian continent from the Baltic to the Pacific. The climate of this massive region is harsh, either especially cold or, in the south, dry.

2. Europeans (especially the Slavs) and the Central Asian nomads have interacted for thousands of years to create a complex pattern of cultures. During the last several hundred years the Russian culture group has dominated the entire region, operating out of their traditional homeland surrounding Moscow.

3. The population center of this region is in European Russia. The rest of the region is thinly settled, but there are large industrial cities widely spaced toward the east into the lowland plains of western Siberia. Urban centers are also growing in the Russian Far East along the Pacific.

4. Since the breakup of the Soviet Union, average living standards have declined as the socialist support system providing the basics of employment, housing, food, and health care has disintegrated. Nutrition and birth rates have declined and death rates risen.

5. After the USSR dissolved in 1991, some powerful factions wished to replace the communist **command economy** with a **free market** or **capitalist** economy. Some state-owned enterprises were sold to private investors, often from abroad, and citizens were allowed to buy their dwellings. With the abrupt move to capitalism, however, many state enterprises could no longer compete. Many lost the ability to pay their workers, who often turned to the informal economy to make a hand-to-mouth living.

6. Economic and political relationships between Russia and the Caucasian and Central Asian republics are in the process of being renegotiated. The trend is toward greater political autonomy and control over resources and production on the part of the republics. The overall result is a lessening of the power of Russia.

7. The non-Russian internal republics and the ethnic groups in Caucasia and Central Asia are showing a renewed interest in reasserting their pre-Soviet cultural identities. Many are finding within their cultural heritage elements that help them participate in the emerging capitalist economy.

8. Bringing women into the mainstream work force was a particular goal of the communist revolution. By the 1980s, 90 percent of working-age women were employed outside the home, and Russian women had, on average, a higher education level than men. Nonetheless, they earned less than their male counterparts. During the reform era a disproportionate number of women were laid off. By the late 1990s, 70 percent of the unemployed were women.

9. The resource inventory of Russia and the Eurasian republics is huge, with especially plentiful oil, gas, other mineral, and forest resources. Who will have access to these resources is now in contention. Agricultural land and water are in short supply. Cultivable land is found primarily in European Russia and Caucasia. Irrigation has made Central Asian lands temporarily cultivable, but the environmental effects of irrigation and chemical fertilizer use have been detrimental.

Selected Readings

Allworth, Edward, ed. *Central Asia—130 Years of Russian Dominance, A Historical Overview*, 3rd ed. Durham, NC: Duke University Press, 1994.

Aslund, Anders. *How Russia Became a Market Economy*. Washington, DC: Brookings Institution, 1995.

Barr, Donald A., and Mark G. Field. The current state of health care in the former Soviet Union: Implications for health care policy and reform. *American Journal of Public Health* 86 (March 1996): 307–312.

Bater, James H. *Russia and the Post-Soviet Scene—A Geographical Perspective*. London: Arnold, 1996.

Bridger, Sue, Rebecca Kay, and Kathryn Pinnick. *No More Heroines? Russia, Women and the Market*. London: Routledge, 1996.

Citrin, Daniel A., and Ashok K. Lahiri, eds. *Policy Experience and Issues in the Baltics, Russia, and Other Countries of the Former Soviet Union*. Washington, DC: International Monetary Fund, 1995.

Clark, Miles, and James P. Blair (photographer). A Russian voyage—From the White to the Black Sea. *National Geographic* 185 (June 1994): 114–138.

Clarke, Simon, ed. *Management and Industry in Russia—Formal and Informal Relations in the Period of Transition*. Hants, UK: Edward Elgar, 1995.

Crowe, David M. *A History of the Gypsies of Eastern Europe and Russia*. New York: St. Martin's Press, 1995.

Dadrian, Vahakn N. *History of the Armenian Genocide—Ethnic Conflict from the Balkans to Anatolia to the Caucasus.* Providence, RI: Berghahn Books, 1995.

Dutkina, Galina. *Moscow Days—Life and Hard Times in the New Russia.* New York: Kodansha International, 1996.

Hunter, Shireen. Islam in post-independence Central Asia: Internal and external dimensions. *Journal of Islamic Studies* 7, no. 2 (1996): 287–303.

Kramer, Mark. *Travels with a Hungry Bear—A Journey to the Russian Heartland.* Boston: Houghton Mifflin, 1996.

Lempert, David H. *Daily Life in a Crumbling Empire—The Absorption of Russia into the World Economy*, vol. 1. Boulder, CO: East European Monographs, 1996.

Lenczowski, George. The Caspian oil and gas basin: A new source of wealth? *Middle East Policy* 5 (January 1997): 111–119.

Mandelbaum, Michael. Westernizing Russia and China. *Foreign Affairs* (May/June 1997): 80–95.

Minakir, Pavel A., and Gregory L. Freeze, eds. *The Russian Far East—An Economic Handbook.* Armonk, NY: M. E. Sharpe, 1994.

Olcott, Martha Brill. *The Kazakhs*, 2nd ed. Hoover Institution Press, 1995.

Pryde, Philip R., ed. *Environmental Resources in the Former Soviet Republics.* Boulder, Press, 1995.

Rasputin, Valentin. *Siberia, Siberia.* Translated by Margaret Winchell and Gerald Mikkelson. Evanston, IL: Northwestern University Press, 1996.

Richards, Susan. *Epics of Everyday Life—Encounters in a Changing Russia.* New York: Viking, 1991.

Schuster, Mike. The Islamic comeback in Central Asia. *All Things Considered.* National Public Radio, December 12, 1996. Can be heard on the NPR www site.

Schuster, Mike. The Silk Road. *All Things Considered.* National Public Radio (1998): 10/29 #9; 10/31 #2; 11/8 #5; 11/12 #19. Can be heard on the NPR www site.

Stewart, John G. Student attitudes toward systemic corruption: Teaching ethics in the Republic of Georgia. *Journal of Public Administration Education* 3 (1997): 1–12.

Yergin, Daniel, and Thane Gustafson. *Russia in 2010 and What It Means for the World.* New York: Random House, 1993.

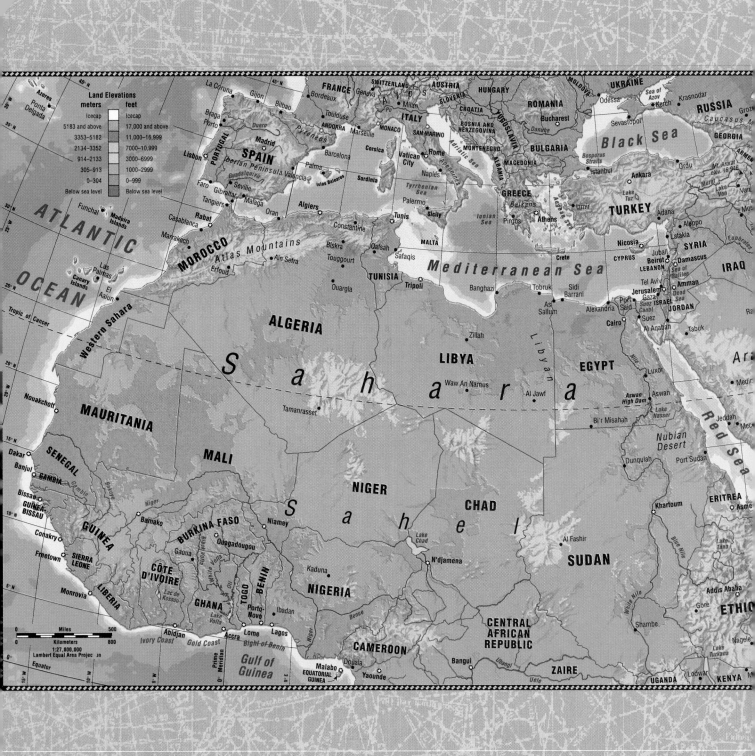

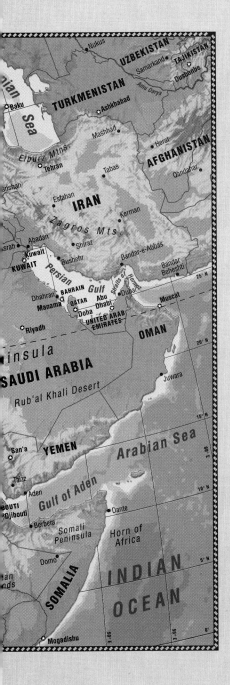

NORTH
AFRICA
AND
SOUTHWEST
ASIA

INTRODUCTION TO NORTH AFRICA AND SOUTHWEST ASIA

When Nabila Benkiran, a 38-year-old mother of five, goes to the beach in Rabat, Morocco, she goes in "a homespun waterproof tunic and pants—to keep her modesty intact and to spare men any temptations." Other women go in tiny bikinis, while still others sit in full-length djellabas too unwieldy for swimming. Just a generation ago, no women would have been allowed at the beach at all in Morocco or elsewhere in this region. These contrasts in beach attire reflect the varying circumstances in which women live across the region of North Africa and Southwest Asia.

In some places in this region, the spaces women may legitimately occupy are tightly controlled, and their access to education, health care, careers, and activities outside the home are restricted. In other places, gender roles are somewhat less firm. Many women dress no differently from European women. While women like Nabila observe strict religious rules that require them to remain mostly secluded at home, other women are working to change family law that keeps women in the legal status of minors. In reality, the contentions over women's roles, spaces, and dress are part of wider debates over how these soci-

eties will construct themselves, what roles democratic consensus and religiously inspired leadership will play, and what to do about demoralizing cultural intrusions from outside the region, especially from Europe and America.

All 23 countries in the region have achieved political independence only in the twentieth century, many not until after World War II. Most were tyrannized by European colonial administrations, and several had to throw off foreign domination assertively. Many found it necessary to fend off foreign efforts to appropriate the region's resources (especially oil and gas) and to dominate their institutions: schools, universities, government systems, military establishments, even religious practices. As a result, people in the region may mistrust Europe and the United States, and see a need to protect their culture from outside influences.

In turn, this region has long been the subject of particularly insidious misrepresentation and unwarranted generalizations, both frequent by-products of colonialism. Too often, outsiders seize on single issues as defining the entire region—the Arab-Israeli conflict, for example. Or their mental images of a space nearly twice the size of the United States are sketchy and blurred, so that they erroneously equate life in Morocco with that in Saudi Arabia or Sudan or Iran. In fact, despite common features of arid climate and a general religious preference for Islam, there is much geographic and cultural variety across this region. Oil is present in abundance in some places but totally absent in others. In some parts of the region, nearly everyone lives in a city; in other parts, rural life is dominant. In some countries, civil laws are heavily influenced by religious law; others have secular legal systems. Women may be active in public life and prominent in government, or they may lead secluded domestic lives. And across the region ethnicity varies greatly.

Themes to Look For

You may notice several themes appearing repeatedly as you read this chapter. Among them are the following:

1. The dominance of Islamic culture: a major source of debate in the region is the degree to which Islamic beliefs should influence government, law, gender roles, and behavior in general.

2. The impact of oil, particularly in the oil-rich countries of the Persian Gulf: oil has provided wealth for a few, but the economy remains undiversified, dependent on oil or a few other resources only.

Muslim women enjoying a day at the beach near Syria's busy Mediterranean port of Latakia. [Ed Kashi.]

3. The attempt to make a desert region inhabitable for an increasing population: how to obtain water and expand agriculture are two burning and interrelated issues.

Terms to Be Aware Of

The term **Middle East** is not used in this chapter because of the Eurocentric bias it carries; the term is symptomatic of the tendency to lump the whole of Asia together, differentiating it only by its distance from Europe (near, middle, far). Furthermore, the term does not normally include the western sections of North Africa or eastern portions of Southwest Asia—Iran, for example. On the other hand, the reader should know that some people who live in the region do use the term themselves. The terms **Islamist** and **Islamic fundamentalist** are now being used for those Muslims who favor a religiously based state that incorporates strictly enforced Islamic principles as part of the legal system.

PHYSICAL PATTERNS

Climate

No other region in the world is as pervasively dry as North Africa and Southwest Asia (Figure 6.1). Circling the planet, between roughly 20° and 30° latitude north and south, is a global belt of dry air that cuts right through this region, creating desert climates in the Sahara, the Arabian Peninsula, Iraq, and Iran. The Sahara's size and southerly location make it a particularly hot desert; in some places, temperatures can reach 130° in the shade. In the nearly total absence of heat-retaining water or vegetation, nighttime temperatures can drop quickly to below freezing. Nevertheless, in even the driest zones, humans survive at scattered oases where they maintain groves of drought-resistant date

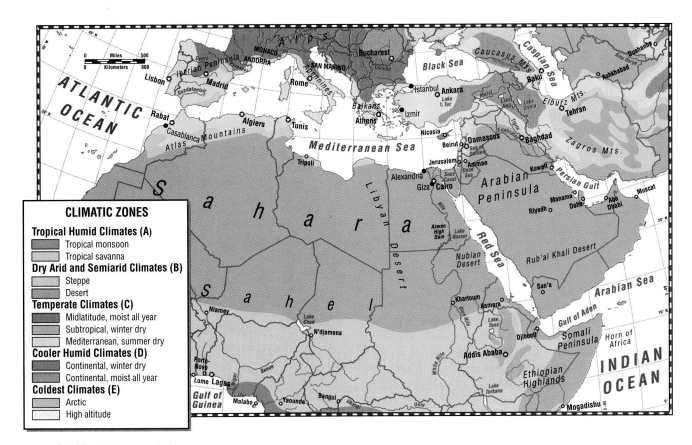

FIGURE 6.1 Regional climate.

Climate change has repeatedly affected human settlement over the millennia. Grazing animals depicted in caves like this at Tassili 'n Agger, Algeria, in the heart of the Sahara, could not have lived here under present conditions. [Pierre Boulat/Woodfin Camp & Associates.]

and east, spreads the great Sahara Desert, where rain falls rarely, and unpredictably.

Africa and Southwest Asia are separated by a rift formed where two tectonic plates are moving away from each other. The rift, which began to form about 12 million years ago, is now occupied by the Red Sea. In the southwest corner of Arabia, mountains bordering the rift rise to 12,000 feet, and the precipitation they capture from moisture-laden monsoon winds crossing central Africa is the primary source of rain for the entire peninsula.

Behind these mountains, to the east, lies the great desert Rub'al Khali. Like the Sahara, it is virtually devoid of vegetation. Strong winds drive sand into every crevice and move huge dunes across the landscape. The dunes of the Rub'al Khali are the world's largest; some are more than 2000 feet high. To protect themselves from the persistent winds, blowing sands, and temperatures that vary radically from day to night, desert dwellers line their tents with animal skins, rugs, and tapestries.

palms and some irrigated field crops. Desert inhabitants often wear light-colored loose, flowing robes that reflect the sunlight during the day and provide insulation against cold at night.

On the margins of the desert to the north and south, enough rain falls to nurture grass and some trees. Too dry for cultivation, these areas have long been the prime herding lands of the region's nomads, such as the Berbers in North Africa and the Bedouins of the steppes and deserts on the Arabian Peninsula.

Landforms and Vegetation

The undulating surfaces of desert and steppe lands cover most of North Africa and Saudi Arabia. Fringes of mountains, located here and there across the region, capture moisture and make possible the survival and even flourishing of humans, plants, and animals. In northwest Africa, the Atlas Mountains stretch from Morocco on the Atlantic to Tunis on the Mediterranean. They block and lift the moisture-laden winds off the Atlantic, creating the conditions for rainfall that may measure more than 50 inches a year in some places. Snowfall is sufficient in places to support a skiing industry. Behind these mountains, to the south

A wadi is a dry riverbed in the desert. This is Wadi Rum in Jordan. [Adam Woolfitt/Woodfin Camp & Associates.]

270

The landforms of Southwest Asia are more complex than those of North Africa and Arabia. The great desert peninsula of Arabia on the Arabian Plate is rotating to the northeast, away from the African Plate. Where it collides with Asia, it is pushing up the widely spaced mountains and plateaus of Turkey and the Zagros Mountains in Iran. Mountainous Turkey receives considerable rainfall from the moisture masses that pass over Europe from the Atlantic Ocean. But by the time this air reaches the mountains of Iran, to the southeast of Turkey, only a little moisture remains. The interior of Iran is thus very dry.

There are only three rivers of major distinction in this entire region, and all have attracted human settlement for thousands of years. The Nile flows north from the central East African highlands across mostly arid Sudan and desert Egypt to a large delta on the Mediterranean. The Euphrates and Tigris rivers both begin in the mountains of Turkey and flow to the southeast to the swamps of the Shatt al Arab estuary terminating in the Persian Gulf. Most other streams in the region flow only during certain times of the year.

Although this region was home to some of the very earliest agricultural societies, today agriculture is possible only in a few places. In areas along the Mediterranean coast, where rain can be counted on during the winter, people grow citrus fruits, grapes, olives, and many vegetables, often using irrigation. In the valleys of the major rivers, seasonal flooding and newly introduced irrigation methods provide water for crops such as cotton, wheat, and barley. In occasional oases, and in a few places where groundwater is pumped to the surface with the help of high-tech equipment, a variety of crops may be grown, including dates, melons, apricots, and vegetables.

HUMAN PATTERNS

In this area of ancient human occupation, the origins of cultural practices are often obscure and subject to misconceptions. For instance, a common belief is that particular practices regarding women, like seclusion and veiling, originated with Islam. Yet scholars have found evidence that these practices predate Islam. Nor are the antiforeign attitudes often associated with Islam today inherent to that religion. On the contrary, past Islamic empires have been known for their cosmopolitan culture and tolerance of foreign ways. Antiforeign sentiment is a much more recent phenomenon, coming after years of self-interested European and U.S. interference in the affairs of the region. Given the tremendous transformations that the region has gone through in recent decades, the people of this region are understandably interested in controlling the process of change to suit their preferences.

Agricultural Beginnings

Between 20,000 and 10,000 years ago, nomadic peoples began to settle down in one of the earliest known agricultural communities in the world, those located in the uplands of the Tigris and Euphrates river systems (in modern Turkey) and in the Zagros Mountains of modern Iran (Figure 6.2). Somewhat later cultivators settled along the Nile River (in modern Egypt and Sudan). In these places, they found bountiful environments, plentiful fresh water, open forests and grasslands, abundant wild grains, goats, wild cattle and other large animals, as well as rich fishing. As these peoples settled in, their emerging arts of domesticating plants and animals allowed them to build more elaborate settlements and societies that were eventually based on widespread irrigated agriculture.

Some also think that this period in human history may mark the institutionalization of markedly different roles for men and women. As societies became more complicated, people with specialized skills were needed to act variously as farmers, engineers, builders, administrators, and scholars. Although undoubtedly there were many exceptions, it seems likely that men filled many of the new positions in public life, while women took over the domestic duties that increased in complexity and importance as settlements grew and family size expanded. The theory is that men took over the more public roles because they could better endure the heavy labor required in some occupations; women, on the other hand, were tethered to the home place by the need to bear, nurse, and care for several small children, particularly as human fertility increased along with improved food yields.

Agriculture was also early in the upper Nile Valley, west in the Maghreb (northwest Africa), and east in Persia (modern Iran). In adjacent steppe zones, societies of nomadic animal herders traded meat, milk, hides, and other animal products for the grain and manufactured goods of the settled areas. At times, however, nomadic tribes would band together, sweep over agricultural settlements with devastating cavalry raids, and set themselves up as a ruling class. These ruling nomads had a tendency to adopt much of the culture of the sedentary peoples they conquered; after a few generations they became almost indistinguishable from them. In time, they themselves became vulnerable to defeat by new waves of nomadic peoples. Nevertheless, some rulers tried to maintain their military traditions by constantly expanding their domains, a practice that occasionally led to the creation of vast but unwieldy empires.

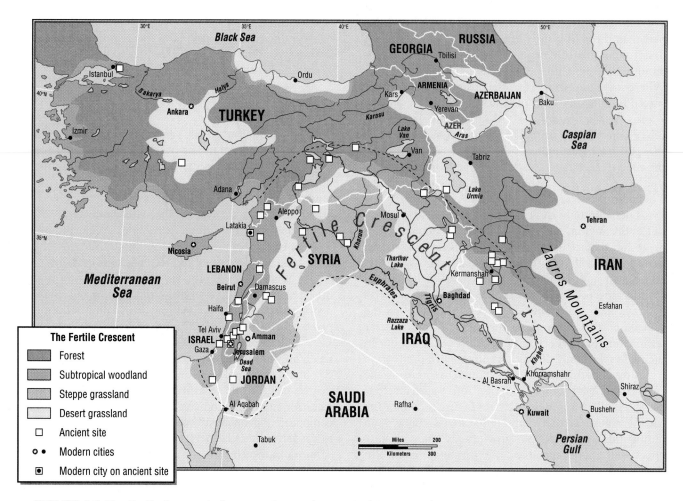

FIGURE 6.2 The Fertile Crescent is the name given to the area in this region where people first domesticated plants. It is an arc extending from the eastern Mediterranean coast into the mountains of southern Turkey and curving to the lands along the Tigris-Euphrates rivers and the Zagros Mountains. [Adapted from Bruce Smith, *The Emergence of Agriculture* (New York: Scientific American Library, 1995), p. 50.]

The Coming of Islam

According to tradition, the archangel Gabriel revealed the principles of Islam, the dominant religion of this region, to the Prophet Muhammad in the seventh century A.D. Muhammad was a merchant and caravan manager in the small trading town of Mecca near the Red Sea. Islam was, and is, considered an outgrowth of Judaism and Christianity, both of which originated in the settled areas of present-day Israel and Palestine. Muhammad himself claimed to be merely the last in a long series of great prophets, which included Abraham, Moses, and Jesus. Just as their teachings were recorded in the Bible, Muhammad's were written down in the **Qur'an** (or Koran), the holy book of Islam. Similarly, just as Jerusalem was the central holy place for Jews and Christians, Muhammad's hometown of Mecca became the most holy place of Islam. (Jerusalem is also a

holy city for Muslims, the place from where the Prophet Muhammad ascended into heaven.) Throughout the history of Islam, Arabia has maintained its central place in the Islamic world through the tradition of the **hajj,** the pilgrimage to the city of Mecca that all Muslims are encouraged to undertake at least once in a lifetime.

The nomads of the Arabian Peninsula, the Bedouins, were among the first converts to Islam. They were already spreading the faith and creating a vast Islamic sphere of influence by the time of Muhammad's death in A.D. 632. Over the next several centuries, their traders and armies conquered most of North Africa and Southwest Asia as well as Spain (Figure 6.3). Through similar waves of trade and conquest, the Islamic faith eventually spread to Turkey, the Balkans, and across Central Asia to western China; by sea, it was carried to Indonesia and Malaysia, some

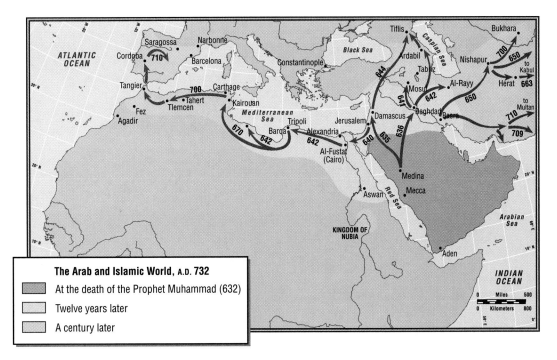

The Arab and Islamic World, A.D. 732

At the death of the Prophet Muhammad (632)

Twelve years later

A century later

FIGURE 6.3 By 732 (the Prophet Muhammad died in 632), Arabs, bearing Islam, had conquered most of the lands immediately around the Mediterranean and had spread well into Southwest Asia. [Adapted from Rafic Boustani and Philippe Fargues, *The Atlas of the Arab World: Geopolitics and Society* (New York: Facts on File, 1991).]

parts of the Philippines, and southeastern China. These areas are still predominantly Islamic today, with the exception of Spain, some parts of the Balkans, and southeast China.

While Europe languished in the so-called Dark Ages, Muslim geographers traveled extensively throughout Asia and Africa, making important contributions to centers of world learning in Alexandria, Baghdad, Damascus, and Toledo (in Spain). These centers were sustained by vibrant economies that benefited from the early Islamic development of financial institutions and practices, such as banks, trusts, checks, and receipts. From India, Muslims imported the useful mathematical concept of the zero, further advancing trade, record keeping, and scientific knowledge in the region. Islamic medicine drew on a wide variety of traditions that had their origins from China to West Africa; it was considered superior to the medicine practiced in Europe until the nineteenth century.

From the eleventh to the fifteenth century, the Arab-dominated Islamic empire fell into decay and was conquered by the Mongols and other peoples. Meanwhile, the greatest Islamic empire the world has ever known, the Ottoman Empire, was forged by the nomadic herders of western Turkey. By the fifteenth century, the Ottoman Muslims had defeated the Christian Byzantine Empire, renaming the capital city of Constantinople "Istanbul." Very soon they controlled most of the eastern Mediterranean, Egypt, and Mesopotamia. The Ottoman Empire inherited the political and religious institutions of Islam from the late Arab empire, although it was known for greater religious tolerance within its borders. Asserting influence in the name of Islam, the Ottomans took over much of central Europe in the sixteenth century. Prospering from the productivity of its many different peoples, and drawing on trading networks that stretched from Central Europe to Algeria to the Indian Ocean, Istanbul became a cosmopolitan capital, outshining most European cities until the nineteenth century.

Western Domination

The Ottoman Empire ultimately withered in the face of a Europe made powerful by the industrial revolution. Throughout the eighteenth and nineteenth centuries, North African lands changed from Ottoman to European control; World War I brought the death of the empire. The Ottomans had allied with Germany, and after the war ended in defeat for that nation, all Ottoman lands outside Turkey fell under British,

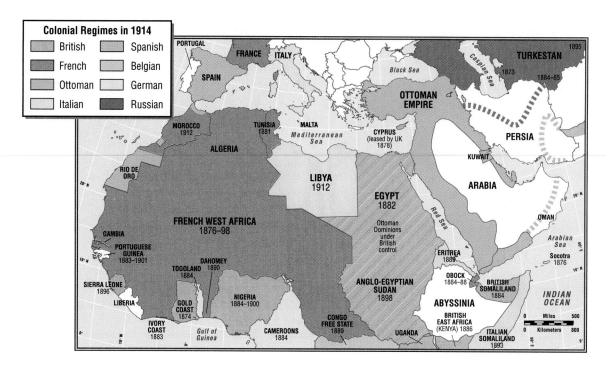

FIGURE 6.4 European powers controlled most of this region at the onset of World War I. Fifty years later, virtually all of the nations were independent, and the map of Southwest Asia had been redrawn to include Jordan, Israel, Lebanon, Syria, Iraq, and the new states of the Arabian Peninsula. [Adapted from *Hammond Times Concise Atlas of World History,* 1994, pp. 100–101.]

French, Italian, or Russian influence (Figure 6.4). The years of European colonialism in North Africa and Southwest Asia, lasting in many places from the first quarter of the nineteenth century to the mid-twentieth century, were tremendously influential. In some cases, European powers ruled directly, as did France in Algeria, Syria, and Lebanon, and Britain in Egypt, Iraq, Kuwait, and Palestine. In other cases, Europe, and increasingly the United States, simply manipulated local politics to their own advantage. These Western powers maneuvered normal power struggles within countries so that elites came to power who would favor European and U.S. access to oil and other resources. This interference set the stage—in countries like Iran, Saudi Arabia, Libya, and Turkey—for highly authoritarian governments that were backed by Western powers. The efforts of such governments were often not directed first to the welfare of their people and the development of their economies but to benefiting their own class and to the accumulation of wealth.

The region achieved independence from overt foreign domination during the mid-twentieth century. Nevertheless, foreign influence remained strong in many countries. For example, in Iran and Saudi Arabia, where vast oil deposits became especially lucrative by

mid-century, European and U.S. oil companies played a key role in deciding who ruled the countries. In both, an extremely wealthy elite hoarded oil revenues. Throughout the region, oil money was not primarily used to industrialize or improve general well-being. Rather, it was often spent on opulent living for the elite or invested abroad in such things as shopping malls and resorts in the United States, and banks and department stores in the United Kingdom. The region remained dependent on Europe and North America for the technology needed to exploit oil and to begin the mechanization of manufacturing, transportation, and agriculture. The elite bought their consumer goods and luxury items in London and Paris. During this period, disparity in wealth increased dramatically.

Today, the region is experiencing some attempts at economic, political, and environmental reform, although a number of problems are complicating these efforts. The region's regimes remain authoritarian and elite dominated. Long-needed economic reform for a more equitable distribution of wealth has just started in most countries. Such efforts include reducing bloated and inefficient bureaucracies, reallocating agricultural land, privatizing state-run industries, and diffusing the power of patriarchal figures. So far, however, the reforms have done little to increase economic diversification, reduce overdependence on oil, increase jobs for growing populations, or decentralize political power. Hence, governments are vulnerable to criticism from revolutionary movements. The movement with the fastest-growing influence across the region is the so-called Islamic fundamentalist movement, referred to in this book as "Islamist." The Islamist movement builds on the discontent of the poor and the unemployed and on disenchantment with Western influences, while appealing to religious piety—devotion and reverence to Islam. As problems of wealth disparity and joblessness intensify, they bring increased levels of violence and social chaos. In this atmosphere, it is becoming more difficult to address the region's very serious environmental problems, which include various types of pollution and an impending shortage of water.

Population Patterns

The great size and aridity of this region have had important implications for human settlement and interaction. Although it is nearly twice as large as the United

States, the spaces that are useful for agriculture and settlement are tiny by comparison. The land must support 100 million more people than the United States; therefore, actual population densities in livable space can be quite high. Meanwhile, vast tracts of desert are virtually uninhabited. The population map (Figure 6.5) demonstrates that people live mostly along coastal zones and river valleys and in mountain zones that capture orographic rainfall. Efforts are being made to extend livable space into the desert, but this may require extremely costly and environmentally questionable solutions to the problems of water scarcity and soil infertility.

In the last decades, human fertility rates across the region have fallen dramatically. In the 1960s, when most women married shortly after reaching puberty, they had on average close to nine children each in some countries. Now, women marry on average by age 21 and go to school for more than a year or two; the average number of children is just four per woman. But this fertility rate is still higher than the world average (only Africa's is higher); the result is that, for a number of the most populous countries in the region, well over 40 percent of the population is under the age of 15

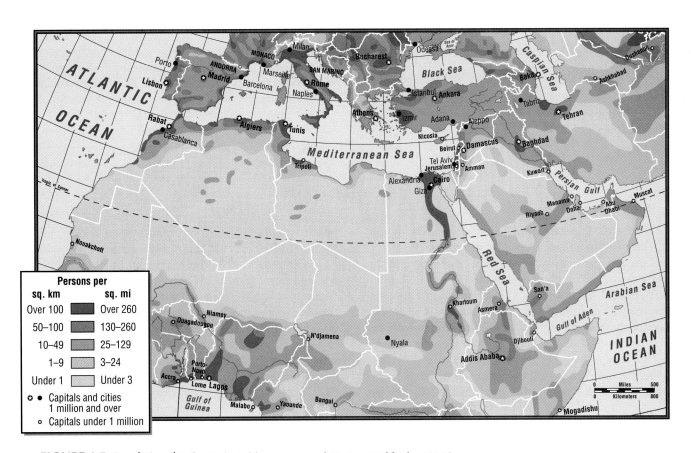

FIGURE 6.5 Population density. [Adapted from *Hammond Citation World Atlas,* 1996.]

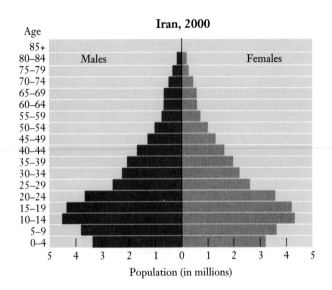

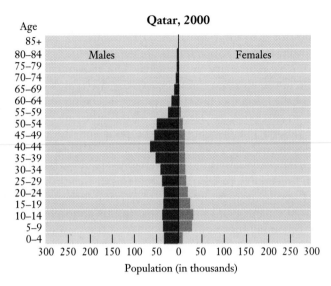

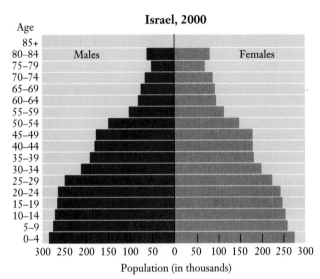

FIGURE 6.6 Population pyramids for Iran, Qatar, and Israel. The population pyramid of Iran is at a different scale (millions) from that of Israel and Qatar (thousands). Observe that Iran has had significantly fewer births over the last ten years, and that Qatar's pyramid is skewed by the presence of numerous male guest workers in the 25- to 54-age groups and by missing females in the 0- to 4-age group. [Adapted from U.S. Census Bureau, International Data Base, at http://www.census.gov/cgi-bin/ipc/idbpyry.pl.]

(Figure 6.6). Population will continue to grow rapidly as these children reach reproductive age.

At present rates of growth, the population of the region, now 395 million, will double to 790 million by the year 2030. It is difficult to imagine how the area will support the additional people. Fresh water is already in extremely short supply, and most countries must import food at great cost. Furthermore, 32 million more jobs would have to be created within the next decade to employ the added population—compared to just 4.5 million needed in Europe; that figure will be higher yet unless women continue to stay out of the labor market. As Figure 6.7 shows, across the region (except for Morocco and Turkey) less than 25 percent of women work outside the home, and in most of North Africa and Saudi Arabia less than 16 percent do so. If the sta-

tus of women evolves more quickly than anticipated, the demand for jobs will drastically increase.

Within the region, there is the idea that the industrialized world (Europe, North America, Japan, parts of Oceania) is overly concerned with population growth in the developing world, and promotes population control elsewhere so that it can continue to consume more than its share of the world's resources. On the other hand, some leaders in the region (especially in Algeria, Egypt, Iran, Morocco, Sudan, Tunisia, Turkey, and Jordan) see the wisdom of population control. Most specialists in Islamic law say that limiting family size is acceptable for a wide variety of reasons, so long as the motive is not to shirk parenthood altogether or to avoid having girl children. As a method of birth control, abortion is not common, but it is permitted.

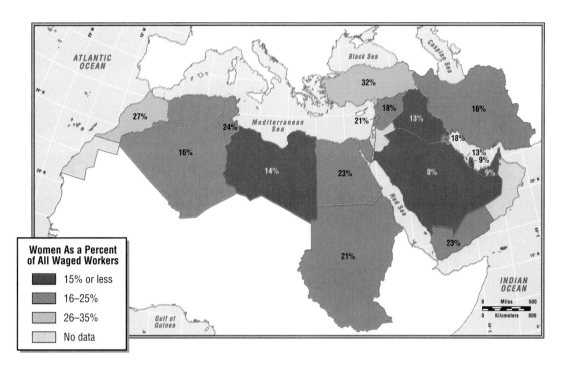

FIGURE 6.7 Percent of women who are wage-earning workers. [Adapted from Joni Seager, *Women in the World: An International Atlas* (New York: Viking Penguin, 1997), pp. 66–67.]

Gender Roles and Population Growth

In societies such as those of this region, fertility rates remain high, despite a decline in labor-intensive agriculture of the sort that depends on children as a labor supply. In such cases, gender inequality may be part of the explanation. If men have a much higher education level than do women (which is the case across the region; see Table 6.1), greater access to employment, and greater power to make family and community decisions, children become an overwhelmingly important source of power for women, and thus there is a desire among women to have many. On the other hand, especially in urban contexts, when women have opportunities outside the home—for obtaining knowledge, or wages, or prestige on the job, or for participating in political activity—they almost always choose to have fewer children. Furthermore, when women are restricted to the home (secluded) and undereducated, they have little chance to generate wealth and to enhance the prospects and reputation of the family. Hence, in societies with stark gender differences and seclusion customs, like those in North Africa and Southwest Asia, there is a deeply entrenched cultural preference for sons, who because of their wider opportunities can enhance family wealth and social standing.

Families often continue having children until they have a sufficient number of sons.

Migration and Urbanization

At present, across the region of North Africa and Southwest Asia, migration is an increasingly common phenomenon. Because jobs are hard to find, especially for those with some education, many millions have migrated to other parts of the world in search of work. Most of those leaving the region are young men, because women typically do not travel widely. Several million immigrants are guest workers in Europe; in 1990, Turks alone numbered more than 2 million. Of these, many intend to return home, in part because it is difficult to gain citizenship in European countries. In the meantime, they send remittances to their families in North Africa or Turkey or Lebanon, significantly increasing local standards of living.

In some parts of the region **in-migration** is the trend. In the last decades, the oil-rich states of the Arabian Peninsula have imported large numbers of guest workers. When oil revenues poured in after price rises in the 1970s, the money was used to rapidly modernize all aspects of life. Their own people were either undereducated for the jobs created or culturally conditioned not to accept the strictures of daily work

TABLE 6.1

Adult literacy

	Percent literate, female	Percent literate, male		Percent literate, female	Percent literate, male
Northern Tier of Southwest Asia			**Egypt and Sudan**		
Turkey	72.4	91.7	Egypt	38.9	63.6
Iraq	44.9	70.7	Sudan	34.6	57.7
Iran	59.3	77.7			
			The Maghreb and Libya		
Eastern Mediterranean			Western Sahara	—	—
Syria	55.8	85.7	Morocco	31	56.6
Lebanon	90.3	94.7	Algeria	49.1	73.9
Israel	93	97	Tunisia	54.6	78.6
Jordan	79.4	93.4	Libya	63	87.9
The Arabian Peninsula			**For Comparison**		
Saudi Arabia	50.3	71.5	United States	99.0	99.0
Yemen	39	39	Brazil	83.2	83.3
Oman	46	71	Portugal	87	92.5
United Arab Emierates (UAE)	79.8	78.9	World	71.5	83.7
Qatar	79.9	79.2			
Bahrain	79.4	89.1			
Kuwait	74.9	82.2			

Source: Gender-Related Development Index (GDI), *Human Development Report 1998*, United Nations Development Programme.

schedules. By 1990, nearly 70 percent of the peninsula's labor force were immigrants! They built roads, government buildings, housing, schools, universities and technical colleges, water desalinizing plants, ancillary oil and gas industries, and high-tech irrigation systems; and they ran the systems once completed.

Immigrant workers in the Arabian Peninsula came from all over the world, but there was a preference for Muslims. Several hundred thousand workers—some technically skilled, many willing to do manual labor—came from Palestinian refugee camps in Lebanon and Syria, others from Egypt. In the 1980s, 1.5 million came from Pakistan alone. Many, especially female domestic workers, came from Islamic countries in the Far East. Studies among Indonesian Muslim female migrants revealed that they were attracted to Saudi Arabia not only by the relatively high wages, but also by the chance to make the pilgrimage to the holy cities of Mecca and Medina. Most had little prior understand-

ing of female seclusion customs in Saudi Arabia. The Texan Martha Kirk, the wife of an agricultural specialist employed by the Saudis, in her description of five years living on an irrigated wheat farm in Saudi Arabia, noted the many Filipino and Sri Lankan female servants. They were silent, shadowy figures, serving tea and waving incense burners during lavish, women-only parties in the harems of desert palaces and in urban villas in the city of Riyadh. Kirk also described the many male migrant workers she encountered: Turks drove bulldozers, Mexicans set up pumps and dug wells, Pakistanis and Americans specialized in grain cultivation, other Americans set up dairies, Palestinians worked in construction and as farmhands.

Immigrant workers in the Arabian Peninsula will probably not become permanent residents. During and after the Gulf War in 1991, millions of foreign workers left the Gulf states in a rush. Although many have returned, some Arabian Peninsula governments are now trying to persuade their own people to fill the vacated positions. The loss of income to the families of the migrant workers returning to refugee camps in Syria or to rural villages in Indonesia, Turkey, Mexico, and Egypt has often meant a return to drastically lower standards of living.

Israel is also a site of high in-migration, but here those arriving are Jews settling permanently in Israel, many fleeing persecution. They began coming to Palestine after World War I and in huge numbers just after World War II when Israel was created in 1948. The most recent surge of immigration was in the 1990s, when 300,000 Jews were allowed to leave the former Soviet Union. Another 25,000 fled from Ethiopia. Despite already crowded conditions, Israel encourages Jewish immigrants because it is thought that a large population will keep the country from being swamped by hostile surrounding Arab countries.

Internal migration from rural villages to urban areas has also been an important pattern within the region. Until recently, most people lived in small settlements; but by 1990, nearly 60 percent of the region's people lived in urban areas (Figure 6.8). There are now more than 120 cities with more than 100,000 people, 24 of them with more than 1 million people. New settlers must often build their own dwellings hastily in peripheral shantytowns, where basic services like clean water and sewage disposal are missing.

Refugees

Hundreds of thousands of refugees are to be found across North Africa, throughout the eastern Mediterranean, and on into Turkey and Iraq. Usually they are fleeing wars or environmental disasters like earthquakes or long-term drought. In recent years, many nomads became refugees when new national borders cut off seasonal migration routes. When Israel was created on territory occupied by Palestinians, as many as 2 million Palestinians were displaced to refugee camps in Lebanon, Syria, Jordan, the West Bank, and the Gaza Strip. However, as of 1999, the country with the world's largest refugee population is Iran, which shelters 1.4 million Afghans and 600,000 Iraqis. An even larger group of people remain within their home countries but are unable, usually because of civil unrest, to occupy their homelands. Sudan has 4 million such displaced persons living in camps.

Refugee camps often become semipermanent communities of stateless people, in which whole generations are born, mature, and die. The residents may show enormous ingenuity in creating a community and an informal economy under dire conditions. Nevertheless, the toll in social disorder is high. Children rarely receive enough schooling. Years of hopelessness and extreme inconvenience take their toll on youths and adults, alike, leading some to violence. Moreover,

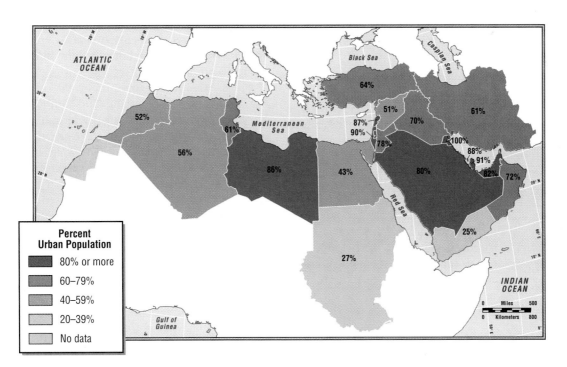

FIGURE 6.8 Percent of urban population for each country. [Data from *1998 World Population Data Sheet*, Population Reference Bureau.]

Al Salaam is a desert refugee camp near Khartoum, Sudan, for those who fled to the city from the south. Water is trucked in daily and distributed in plastic cans. [Robert Caputo/Aurora and Quanta Productions.]

even when international organizations contribute money for basic sustenance, large numbers of refugees represent a huge expense for their host countries.

CURRENT GEOGRAPHIC ISSUES

Despite the variety of physical landscapes, level of development, political and economic systems, and gender relations in the region of North Africa and Southwest Asia, some common themes and institutions are broadly shared; and they are key to an understanding of the social, political, and economic dynamics of the region.

Sociocultural Issues

The countries of North Africa and Southwest Asia are all undergoing social changes that may be better understood by looking at specific issues and circumstances. Here we examine religion, family, gender roles and female seclusion, the lives of children, and cultural diversity as reflected in language.

Religion in Daily Life

More than 93 percent of the people of this region subscribe to Islam, at least nominally. The religion focuses primarily on how to live daily life through its teaching of the five **Pillars of Islamic Practice** (see the box).

All but the first Pillar are literally things to do, rather than articles of faith. Islamic practice is thus a consistent part of daily life in ways rarely experienced in the West, where the practice of religion is usually set aside for certain times and spaces.

Beyond these Five Pillars, Islamic religious law, called **shari'a** (the correct path), guides daily life according to the **Qur'an.** Some believe that no other legal code is necessary in an Islamic society. There are, however, numerous interpretations of just what behavior meets the requirements of shari'a and what does not. The Islamic community is split into two major groups, with differing interpretations of shari'a: **Sunni** Muslims, who today account for 90 percent of the world community of Islam; and **Shi'ite** (or Shi'a) Muslims, who are found primarily in Iran. Even within each of these groups, though, there are many different interpretations of shari'a. Those currently labeled **Islamists** (fundamentalists) have arisen in both Sunni and Shi'ite traditions. Though they all tend to hark back to what are thought to be more strict interpretations of the Qur'an, Islamists vary greatly in the perspectives and fervor they bring to their causes. Nevertheless, all are reacting, to some extent, against what they regard as dangerous Western secular influences on Islamic society.

Islam does not recognize a separation of religion and the state as this is understood in the West. In several of the countries in this region—Saudi Arabia and Iran, for example—the state is the defender and even enforcer of religion. These are **theocratic states.** In such countries, Islam is the officially accepted religion, the leaders must be Muslim and divinely guided, and the legal system is based on shari'a. Other countries—Algeria, Egypt, Morocco, Iraq, Turkey, and Tunisia—

CULTURAL INSIGHT   *The Five Pillars of Islamic Practice*

1.   A testimony of belief in Allah as the only God, and in Muhammad as His Messenger (Prophet).

2.   Daily prayer at one or more of five times during the day (daybreak, noon, midafternoon, sunset, and evening). Prayer, though an individual activity, is often done in a group and in a mosque.

3.   Obligatory fasting (no food or drink) during the daylight hours of the month-long Ramadan, followed by a light celebratory family meal.

4.   Obligatory almsgiving *(zakat)*, in the form of a progressive "tax" of at least 2.5 percent that increases as wealth increases. The alms are given to Muslims in

need. *Zakat* is based on the recognition of the injustice of economic inequity; though usually an individual act, the idea of government-enforced *zakat* is coming back in certain Islamic republics.

5.   Pilgrimage (hajj) to the Islamic holy places, especially Mecca, during the twelfth month of the Islamic calendar. Rituals shared with the devout of all backgrounds, from across the world, reinforce the concept of *umma*, the transcultural community of believers.

Source: Adapted from Carolyn Fluehr-Lobban, *Islamic Society in Practice* (Gainesville: University of Florida Press, 1994).

---

have declared themselves **secular states.** In these countries there is, theoretically, no state religion and no direct influence of religion on affairs of state. In reality, however, across the region, religion is more an obvious part of daily political and social life than in Europe and the Americas. Except in Israel, political leaders even in declared secular states are at least nominally Muslim, and Islam plays a role in the affairs of governments. Still, as elsewhere, there is great variation in the stringency with which people practice their religion. Many people do not strictly observe the Five Pillars or shari'a, and believe a secular state is best; yet they consider themselves Muslim.

Ancient settlements of Christians and Jews are also to be found in this region, many of them predating the spread of Islam. After the establishment of Israel in 1948, more than 400,000 Jews left North Africa to settle in Israel. Christian communities, often dating from the Roman era, exist in Egypt, Sudan, Jordan, Lebanon, Iraq, and Turkey.

Family and Group Values

As in the United States and Canada, the issue of family values is also being discussed throughout North Africa and Southwest Asia. Here, though, the traditional multigeneration, patriarchal family is still very much the norm. Nonetheless, patterns are changing; families are becoming smaller, and several generations less often live together in the same households.

In Islamic culture, the family is both a physical space and a functional grouping. Physically, the family space is usually a walled compound that focuses inward, where food, shelter, and companionship are provided. The size and details of these compounds vary according to class and geographic location. The family group consists of kin that span several generations and may include elderly parents, adult siblings and cousins, and their children. A system of interlocking duties, obligations, and benefits, often along gender lines, provides a role for each individual and solidarity for the whole. All accomplishments or misdeeds become part of a family's heritage. Membership in a family carries reciprocal responsibilities, and a complex system of informal social pressure ensures that no one becomes an obvious slacker. Whether a member receives just a meal or something as grand as a university education from pooled resources (most often made available to males), the recipient knows that some measure of repayment will come due, eventually.

Gendered Roles, Gendered Spaces

Carefully specified gender roles are common in many cultures. Particularly strict versions of these roles have been perpetuated in Islamic culture, even though they probably originated long before Islam. The differences in gender roles are reflected in the organization of space within the home and within the larger society. In both rural and urban settings, men and boys go forth into **public spaces**—the town square, shops, fields, the market. Here, men not only make a living, they also continuously transact alliances with other men up and down the social ladder in order to negotiate a host of arrangements that will advance the interests of their particular families. It is through such networks that people get the best price for an appliance or a car, find a mate for a son or daughter, obtain a job or admittance to professional school, find some scarce item, or unsnarl a particularly nasty bureaucratic problem. For any favors they receive, they incur future obligations; and if they are successful, they also garner considerable respect and prestige within their own family.

By contrast, women usually inhabit secluded **domestic spaces.** Although the standards of seclusion vary greatly, and women are seen in public in large numbers in some parts of the region, in most parts the idea is that women should not be in public places except when on serious business; in many parts, women in public are to be accompanied by a male relative. In some parts of the region, seclusion is most strictly enforced in relatively more affluent, urban neighborhoods. Rural women are less secluded, because they have many tasks they simply must perform outside the home: agricultural labor, carrying water, gathering firewood, and marketing. Although women are regarded as the rightful keepers of the home and the guardians and teachers of young children, the rules governing secluded women make some seemingly negative assumptions about the female sex. Women are thought to be

less responsible when out on their own, less capable of logic than men, more ruled by emotion, more likely to forget facts, and more likely to fall victim to sexual temptation.

In the more secular Islamic societies, women regularly engage in a range of activities that place them in public spaces. And, increasingly, female doctors, lawyers, and teachers and businesswomen are found in even the most conservative societies. Figure 6.9 shows the various levels of restrictions on women across the region. Some are officially sanctioned, and some are the result of social pressures.

Architecture, window treatments, and clothing are elements of material culture designed to help seclude women from the public gaze. In all parts of this region, homes are very private places, centered on an interior courtyard where household work is performed and family life takes place. The private female space within the home is usually this courtyard. Only male relatives may enter. For the upper classes in urban places, female space may be an upstairs set of rooms with latticework or shutters at the windows. Here it is possible to look out at street life, and for breezes to pass through, but not to be seen.

The veil allows a woman to carry her seclusion around with her, and thus it actually expands the space she may safely occupy. Some garments totally cover the person, including the face; some allow alluring eyes to

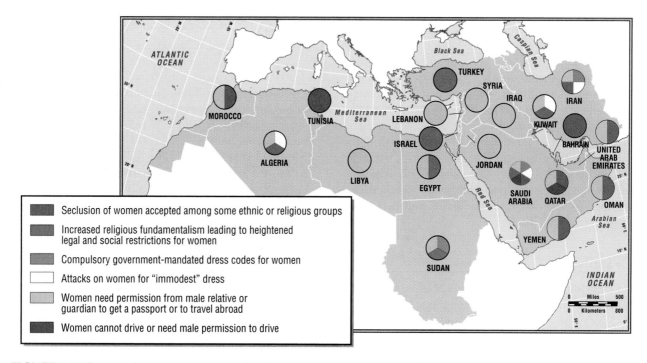

FIGURE 6.9 The map shows the restrictions placed on women in the countries of North Africa and Southwest Asia. [Adapted from Joni Seager, *Women in the World: An International Atlas* (New York: Viking Penguin, 1997), pp. 28–29.]

This house in Jeddah, Saudi Arabia, exhibits numerous versions of louvered and latticed bays that allow women to observe life on the streets from seclusion. Such architectural details are found wherever Islam has been an influence. [Hubertus Kanus/Photo Researchers.]

be seen; and some are a mere head covering. Among women who have worn the all-encompassing chador (full body veil), there are those who find that it offers an intriguing anonymity and satisfying privacy from the gaze of strangers. Women who wear the hijab, a loose long dress and a scarf that leaves the face exposed, talk of liking the signal it sends to all that here is a devout Muslim woman. Paradoxically, many women throughout the region (including the mother of Iran's President Khatami) wear high-fashion Western clothes under the chador or hijab.

VIGNETTE   The veil has played a changing role in Egypt. Egyptian women were among the first to take off their veils, when two Arab feminists returned from an international meeting in 1923 and discarded their veils in the Cairo train station. They started a trend that lasted until recently, when some Cairenes began veiling with an enthusiasm brought on by a desire to assert Muslim identity and make a statement against Westernization.

Stores selling veils are often found in shopping malls. But for women who think of the veil as providing a chance for a fashion statement, Wafeya Sadek runs an Islamic designer-veil studio out of her home in Cairo.

Women who find the black cloak unattractive come from across the city to buy a custom-made veil. A best-seller is a leopard print veil, favored by young women for day wear. Some of her designs for evening seem to call for the type of bold individualism that is frowned on in Islam, for example, a close-fitting black bonnet topped with a wildly colorful cock's comb of velvet. Operating in the informal economy, Madame Sadek counts on word-of-mouth advertising. [Adapted from the writings of Amy Dockser Marcus, *Wall Street Journal,* May 1, 1997.]

There is considerable controversy over the origin of female seclusion. Many scholars of Islam, male and female, say these ideas do not derive from the teachings of the Prophet Muhammad. On the contrary, the Prophet advocated equal treatment of male and female children. His first wife, Khadija, was an independent businesswoman whose council he frequently sought. Muhammad did suggest that both genders dress modestly; but the veiling and seclusion of women were not specified, and Muslim women did not cover their faces in his presence. The Qur'an contains only the barest hint about veiling and nothing on seclusion.

Some modern scholars of Islam now state that interpretations of the Prophet Muhammad's sayings were influenced by the severely restrictive customs of non-Islamic cultures that were conquered by Arab Muslims in the first few centuries after the Prophet's death. Recently, Muslim scholars have shown that interpreta-

There are numerous versions of the veil. These are Bedouin women from Saudi Arabia. [David Austen/ Woodfin Camp & Associates.]

tions of Islamic law regarding female rights have gotten more conservative just during the twentieth century. For Western readers, it is important to remember that European women had to wait more than a thousand years to acquire property-holding rights that were guaranteed by the Qur'an as far back as A.D. 700. The Qur'an allows women, married or not, to manage their own property. It was not until 1870 that British laws broke the custom of putting all the wealth that a woman brought to a marriage under her husband's control. Similar state laws in the United States were changed only after pressure for equal rights in the 1960s.

The Lives of Children

Two sweeping statements can be made about the lives of children in the Islamic cultures of North Africa and Southwest Asia. First, their daily lives take place overwhelmingly within the family circle. Girls and boys spend their time within the home space with adult female relatives, and with siblings and cousins of both sexes. Even teenaged boys identify more with family than with age peers. Only the poorest of children play in the streets. In rural areas, before puberty, girls often have considerable **spatial freedom** as they go about their chores in the village. The geographer Cindi Katz found that until puberty, rural Sudanese Muslim girls have considerably more spatial freedom than do girls of similar ages in the urban United States, where

they now are rarely allowed to range through their own neighborhoods.

The second observation is that the lives of children in this region, like those of so many around the world, are now being circumscribed by school and TV. Most children go to school (girls for at least a few years, many boys for a decade or more), and in most urban areas even the poorest families have access to a TV. Furthermore, the set is often on all day, in part because it provides a window on the world for secluded women. TV may serve either as a reinforcer of traditional culture or as a vehicle for secular values, depending on which channels are watched.

Minorities and Language

Arabic is now the official language in all countries of this region except Iran, Turkey, and Israel; but this language uniformity masks considerable cultural diversity. There are numerous minorities within the region who have their own languages: Berbers, Tuareg, Sudanese, Nilotics, and Nubians, to name a few in North Africa; and Kurds and Turkomans in Southwest Asia. There are also many dialects of Arabic that indicate deep cultural differences. Dialects are disappearing, however, in this era of modern communications as Arabic is becoming standardized by broadcasters. More importantly, Arabic is replacing the languages of the minorities. Meanwhile, the use of French and English as second languages is

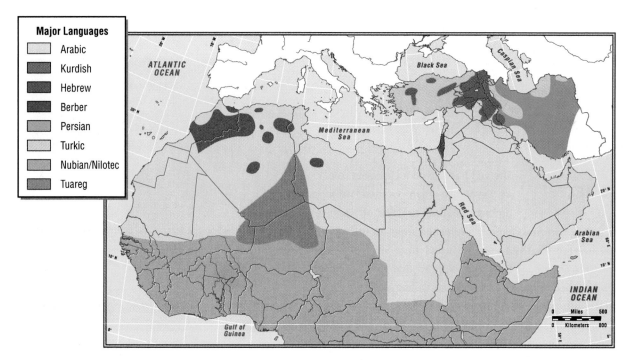

FIGURE 6.10 Major languages of the region. [Adapted from Charles Lindholm, *This Islamic Middle East: An Historical Anthropology* (Oxford: Blackwell, 1996), p. 9.]

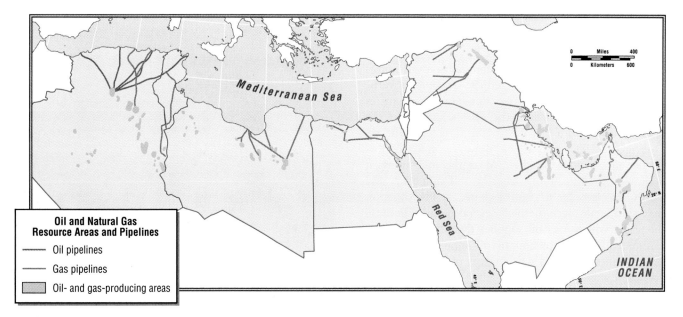

FIGURE 6.11 Oil and natural gas fields and pipelines in the region. [Adapted from Rafic Boustani and Philippe Farques, *The Atlas of the Arab World—Geopolitics and Society* (New York: Facts on File, 1990), pp. 85, 88, 89.]

also very common. Figure 6.10 shows the distribution of languages in North Africa and Southwest Asia.

Economic and Political Issues

There are major economic and political barriers to peace and prosperity within the region today. Oil wealth is limited to a few elites; most people are relatively poor farmers, herders, or low-wage urban workers. The economic base of the region is unstable because oil and agricultural commodities are subject to wide price fluctuations on world markets. New bases of economic development are badly needed, but so far a more diverse range of industries has not developed. Meanwhile, hard times loom on the horizon for many poorer non-oil-producing countries as large national debts are forcing governments to restructure their economies.

The Oil Economy

This region contains the world's largest known petroleum (oil and gas) reserves, located mainly around the Persian Gulf (Figure 6.11). Thus, the petroleum wealth so frequently associated with this region is concentrated mostly in the area around the Persian Gulf: Saudi Arabia, Kuwait, Iran, Iraq, Oman, Qatar, and the United Arab Emirates. Much of the region remains poor and highly dependent on agriculture or herding. Oil and gas are also found in Algeria, Tunisia, and Libya.

European and North American companies were the first to exploit the region's oil reserves, early in the twentieth century. They acquired the resource at bargain prices. Real control of oil reserves was not assumed by the governments of the region until the 1970s, when oil industries were declared the property of the state. At the same time, oil-producing countries united to form a cartel called **OPEC**—the Organization of Petroleum Exporting Countries. Its members include all the oil states previously listed, plus Venezuela, Indonesia, and Nigeria. OPEC members cooperated in restricting oil production, thereby significantly raising its price on world markets. Prices rose swiftly from less than U.S. $3/barrel before 1973 to a peak of U.S. $34/barrel in 1981.

While these price rises (so-called oil shocks) strained the economies of both the industrialized and developing worlds, they were a huge boon to the OPEC countries. However, rather than generating broad prosperity, the oil wealth has mainly benefited the friends and families of the politically powerful. For the most part, they have spent their money on luxury items or have invested it abroad in more stable and profitable economies. As a result, the oil-rich countries have, like their poorer neighbors, remained dependent on the industrialized world for their technology and manufactured goods.

Because the OPEC countries did not invest sufficiently in human resources (education and health care) or in developing technical and natural resources, they were unable to generate anything approaching an industrial revolution. Nevertheless, oil did bring significant benefits to the region as a whole. Laborers and highly trained professionals were hired to improve the Persian Gulf's transport and communications infrastructure, as well as its health, educational, and governmental systems. Even people from non-oil countries were able to share a little in the wealth, as many of the laborers came from Egypt, Jordan, Syria, and Turkey. During the 1980s and 1990s, however, much of this oil-driven growth slowed down as the industrialized countries became more energy self-sufficient and OPEC was less able to control oil prices. The situation may shift again over the next several decades because oil prices will rise as oil supplies dwindle worldwide. Ultimately, total depletion of oil supplies will force these countries to find new sources of income or risk economic ruin.

A desert-irrigated wheat field in Saudi Arabia.
[Ray Ellis/Photo Researchers.]

Agriculture

The tending of grazing animals was the economic mainstay of the region for thousands of years; but crop agriculture in the region was confined to river valleys and to coastal areas where mountain ridges captured orographic rainfall. Grains, cotton, and sugarcane are raised in the Nile Valley, and grains and fruit in the Tigris and Euphrates river valleys. Citrus fruits, olives, wine grapes, and dates thrive on the northern coasts of Africa. The farmers of Yemen and Oman grow coffee trees and grains. Israelis and Palestinians grow vegetables and fruits. Turkish farmers produce cotton, tobacco, sugar beets, and livestock; and Iranians grow rice, barley, wheat, nuts, tea, tobacco, and livestock. More recently, ambitious irrigation schemes are expanding agriculture to neighboring areas that had not been able to support large-scale cropping. Examples are in Libya, Egypt, Turkey, and Iraq.

These attempts at expansion have not always been well conceived. Many state-sponsored irrigation projects have damaged soil fertility through **salinization.** This happens when large amounts of water evaporate, leaving behind dissolved salts and other minerals that inhibit plant growth over time. Israel has developed more efficient techniques of drip irrigation that curtail salinization; but poorer states have been unable to afford the technology, and other wealthy states have been wary of becoming dependent on a technology developed by a country they distrust. The region's numerous political tensions have convinced many governments that they should try for self-sufficiency in food production no matter what the expense. To that end, some oil-rich governments have frittered away huge amounts of money on shortsighted and poorly engineered development schemes. Saudi Arabia and Libya are pumping up massive volumes of precious ground-

water at highly unsustainable rates to grow crops for home use and export. Saudi Arabia has even used the hugely expensive process of desalinating seawater to provide irrigation for wheat fields. Wheat grown this way costs ten times what it could have been bought for on the world market.

Among the often unnoticed losers in state-led development are rural women and nomadic herders. For thousands of years, women have participated in the planting, tending, and harvesting of crops. Most projects introducing new technologies have been aimed at men, however. As a result, women's status and freedom in rural society declines and they are excluded from access to cash. Nomadic herders have similarly lost financial and spatial independence. In establishing large irrigated agriculture projects, many governments may monopolize water sources previously available to the herders, or may require the nomads to settle permanently in order to provide a labor pool for these projects. Herders are also forced to settle down because their tendency to cross national borders in search of grazing lands and water is perceived as a national security threat. Finally, nomads are hard to tax or to control in other ways, such as enforcing compulsory school attendance for children.

Attempts at Diversification

Greater **economic diversification** (a wider array of economic activities) could bring broader prosperity and stability. Few countries in the region, however, have developed diversified economies. Perhaps the most successful is Israel. For the region, that country has a particularly solid manufacturing base, and its goods and those of its modern agricultural sector are exported worldwide. Turkey, Egypt, Morocco, and Tunisia are also starting to develop more diversified economies, although they are not as far along.

Economic diversification has not occurred more widely for a variety of reasons. For decades the state, not the private sector, has driven economic development. This is partly because ruling elites have wanted to maximize their power. It is also because, in the postcolonial era, the state has been viewed as a leader in spurring the development of local industries that were discouraged by colonial regimes eager to sell their products to the region. State-owned enterprises (textiles, toilet paper, cement, processed food) were protected from foreign competition by tariffs and other trade barriers. However, a number of problems frustrated the goal of achieving widespread industrialization. Industries overprotected from foreign competition and free local competition produced shoddy and expensive products with limited export potential. Meanwhile, the extension of governmental control into so many parts of the economy nurtured corruption.

In recent decades, expensive blunders in state-led development have saddled the poorer governments of the region with crippling debt burdens. As a result, they have been forced to cut back their role in the economy. This trend has been under way since the 1970s, when international lending institutions, such as the International Monetary Fund and the World Bank imposed **structural adjustment programs (SAPS).** In return for guarantees of additional loans and for rescheduling the payments on existing debts, governments were forced to shift away from state-led development and toward free market capitalist development. States privatized and streamlined their state-owned industries, removed import barriers, and reduced subsidies. While there have been benefits from SAPs, they have often had a negative impact on poor people. In Egypt, for example, poverty doubled in rural areas and increased by half in urban areas in the 1980s. Reductions in food and housing subsidies have pushed millions into the informal economy. Hundreds of thousands now eke out a living on the streets of Cairo; many streets are now so clogged with vendors that traffic cannot pass through. Over 6 million live in illegal "squatter" communities on the outskirts of the city, without sanitation and other services. Throughout the region, governments in similar situations are increasingly depending on international nongovernmental organizations (NGOs) to provide services and diffuse mounting tensions. However, the resources of NGOs are proving too small; and as living standards continue to fall, rioting and violence are becoming more common.

A Tangle of Hostilities

A complex tangle of hostilities hinders needed changes in the region. Many of these hostilities are in part the legacy of a long history of outside interference in regional politics. In the early twentieth century, Britain and France carved up non-Turkish parts of the Ottoman Empire and parts of North Africa into a number of small countries dependent on the colonial powers for defense and trade. Many countries today are legacies of this era of strong colonial influence, including the oil-rich Persian Gulf monarchies of Kuwait, Saudi Arabia, Bahrain, Qatar, and the United Arab Emirates (UAE). Because of their small size and population, these states have repeatedly called for European or U.S. involvement in the region to protect them from larger neighbors, such as Iran and Iraq.

A case in point is the Gulf War, the most massive war ever in the region. Over 1.2 million people died as a result of this war and its aftermath. The conflict started when Iraq invaded Kuwait in August 1990. Kuwait had been unwilling to restrain its oil production in accordance with OPEC guidelines. Kuwait's behavior was driving down the price of oil on global markets at a time when Iraq was badly in need of oil revenues to fund its recovery from a horribly destructive eight-year-long war with Iran. It is believed that Iraq's need to boost oil prices was a major factor in the invasion. Iraq's decision to invade Kuwait, rather than pursue diplomacy, ultimately proved disastrous, however; it brought on retaliation from a UN force led by the United States. The direct result was the deaths of over 100,000 Iraqis and a full withdrawal from Kuwait.

Despite its victory, the United States is frequently criticized throughout the region for having rejected several opportunities to solve the conflict peacefully. In the years following the war, Iraq's refusal to give up its lethal chemical weapons, capable of killing on a massive scale, led the UN to impose the most crippling economic sanctions ever leveled against a country. The resulting shortages of food, medicine, and other necessities have caused massive deaths of civilians, especially children; yet the intended goal of weakening of the Iraqi regime has not been achieved.

Perhaps the thorniest legacy of the colonial period is the **Israeli-Palestinian conflict,** which has spawned several major wars and innumerable skirmishes. This conflict is described more fully on pages 302–305. The Israeli-Palestinian conflict is a tremendous obstacle to political and economic cooperation. Israel has the most modern and diversified economy in the entire region, thanks to a constant influx of relatively well-educated and well-connected Jewish immigrants and to the country's own excellent educational institutions. Many Israelis would like to see their country become a major source of investment and technology for the region's poor but potentially growing economies. Although this possibility seemed to be gaining momentum, in recent years it has been derailed by mounting hostilities.

Another significant obstacle to improved economic relations within the region and with other parts of the world is a history of terrorism. Turkey, Iran, Iraq, Libya, Egypt, Israel, Jordan, Lebanon, and Algeria have all experienced politically motivated bombings that have taken a high toll in lives, almost always of innocent bystanders. Iran, Iraq, and Libya are suspected of having instigated bombings outside the region, in places such as the New York World Trade Center in 1993 and in the air over Lockerbie, Scotland, in 1988 when a jumbo jet flying to the United States exploded.

Islamism and Democracy

Today, many people fear that Islamist extremism, also known as **Islamism,** is the greatest threat to the region's political instability. Islamist movements are grassroots religious revivals-cum-political campaigns, whose energies are consumed in trying to take control of national governments currently dominated by more or less secular parties. Many governments in the region appear willing to sacrifice democracy in order to repress Islamist movements. Yet, in their repression of usually peaceful, popular movements, they may increase the chances of violent revolutionary upheaval.

Understanding the popular base of Islamism as a movement can yield insights into its strength. Many recruits are young men from lower-class neighborhoods in the region's largest cities. Others are descendants of poor farmers and nomads who were forced off their land and into the city by state-sponsored development programs and imported labor-saving agricultural technologies. Refugee camps in Palestine and elsewhere are also sources of recruits. Given the crowded, polluted, and often chaotic living conditions in cities such as Cairo or Algiers, it is not surprising that many of the younger generation have come to question the basic philosophy of the governments under which they live. Many Islamist activists, especially the leaders, come from the large pool of recent university graduates, both male and female, who are frustrated at not finding employment and disenchanted with foreign interference in the region. Meanwhile, many Islamist leaders are respected religious men who offer seemingly simple solutions to the region's problems. They say all will be well if people return to strictly interpreted versions of Islam and eschew secularism. Perhaps the greatest support for Islamism is gained by appealing to the widespread discontent of millions of increasingly poor people, whose plight has been worsened by SAPs. Although more and more people are drawn to the radical alternatives proposed by the

Islamists, the movement is primarily country based and not internationally coordinated.

Algeria's recent history illustrates the dangers of using political repression to safeguard against extremist movements. Since independence in 1962, Algeria has been ruled by a single-party Socialist dictatorship that represses all viable opposition. In 1991, the Islamists won the first free elections by an overwhelming margin. A peaceful transfer of power could have diffused the pent-up discontent of many Algerians, but instead there was a military takeover motivated largely by fears that the newly elected government would pursue an extreme path. Algeria's coup, however, plunged the country into a devastating civil war. The conflict has allowed the Islamist opposition to become more radical as it gains support.

Many governments are using the threat of Islamism as an excuse to keep political power in the hands of a small, wealthy elite. Nonetheless, there are powerful forces of change at work, of which Islamism is only one. As more people become educated, fewer are content to submit passively to policies imposed by distant, inefficient, and often corrupt regimes. Ethnic minority movements, women's organizations, and students and workers returning from abroad have increasingly been voices for change throughout the region.

Measures of Human Well-Being

The gross national product per capita is a crude indicator of the actual state of well-being, but nonetheless gives some sense of the distribution of wealth across the region. Looking at Table 6.2, the reader can see that the pattern of wealth as measured by GNP per capita (column 2) is uneven. The primary oil-producing nations (Saudi Arabia, Iran, the UAE, Kuwait, Libya) and Israel have high GNP per capita figures. Many other countries in the region are well below the world average of about U.S. $5000. Even politically influential countries like Turkey and Egypt are below the world average. GNP per capita does not indicate the internal distribution of a country's wealth, but is only an average. Because most countries in this region have highly stratified societies, many are living on an income much lower than that listed, while a very few people are extremely rich.

The United Nations Human Development Index (HDI; column 3 of the table) combines three components—life expectancy at birth, educational attainment, and adjusted real income—to arrive at a ranking of 174 countries that is more sensitive to factors other than just income. The reader may remember the case of Kuwait, from other chapters. Despite its high GNP, Kuwait suffers rather badly on the HDI in comparison to nearly all developed countries in the world, primarily because of low literacy rates, especially among adult

TABLE 6.2

Human well-being rankings of countries in Northwest Africa and Southwest Asia

Country	GNP per capita (in U.S. dollars), 1996[a]	Human Development Index (HDI) global rankings, 1998[a]	Gender Empowerment Measure (GEM) and Gender-Related Development Index (GDI) global rankings, 1998[b]
Selected countries for comparison			
Japan	40,940	8 (high)	38 (GDI = 13)
United States	28,020	4 (high)	11 (GDI = 6)
Mexico	3,670	49 (high)	37 (GDI = 49)
Northern Tier of Southwest Asia			
Turkey	2,830	69 (medium)	85 (GDI = 55)
Iraq	Not av.	127 (medium)	Not av. (GDI = 127)
Iran	Not av.	78 (medium)	87 (GDI = 92)
Eastern Mediterranean			
Syria	1,160	81 (medium)	79 (GDI = 94)
Lebanon	2,970	66 (medium)	Not av. (GDI = 68)
Israel	15,870	22 (high)	32 (GDI = 22)
Jordan	1,650	87 (medium)	97 (GDI = 90)
The Arabian Peninsula			
Saudi Arabia	7,040[c]	70 (medium)	Not av. (GDI = 102)
Yemen	380	151 (low)	Not av. (GDI = 143)
Oman	4,820[c]	71 (medium)	Not av. (GDI = 104)
United Arab Emirates (UAE)	17,400[c]	48 (high)	92 (GDI = 66)
Qatar	11,600[c]	57 (high)	Not av. (GDI = 67)
Bahrain	7,840[c]	43 (high)	Not av. (GDI = 60)
Kuwait	17,390[c]	54 (high)	75 (GDI = 58)
Egypt and Sudan			
Egypt	1,080	112 (medium)	88 (GDI = 111)
Sudan	Not av.	157 (low)	96 (GDI = 151)
The Maghreb and Libya			
Western Sahara	Not av.	Not av.	Not av. (GDI = not av.)
Morocco	1,290	125 (medium)	82 (GDI = 96)
Algeria	1,520	82 (medium)	93 (GDI = 96)
Tunisia	1,930	83 (medium)	74 (GDI = 68)
Libya	Not av.	64 (medium)	Not av. (GDI = 79)
World	5,180	NA	NA

[a] Total ranked in world = 174.
[b] Total ranked in world = 104 (no data for many).
[c] Indicates 1997 data.
NA = Not applicable; Not av. = Not available.
Sources: Data from *1998 World Population Data Sheet*, Population Reference Bureau; and *Human Development Report 1998*, United Nations Development Programme.

women. Until very recently, education has been available to only a minority of females. Thus, there is a huge population of older illiterate women in the Arab states. Israel is the only country in this region with both a high GNP per capita and a high HDI rank (24). Notice that some of Israel's closest neighbors (Syria, Lebanon, Jordan, and Egypt) rank fairly low on both the GNP index and the HDI. Israel's ranking reflects the fact that the country has made a special effort to provide the basics of a decent life, including income, shelter, food, education, and health care, to all—regardless of race or sex. Israel has a culture marked by a strong emphasis on education, and it has drawn highly educated immigrants from around the world. But Israel has also been a major recipient of U.S. and private donor aid since its creation shortly after World War II. Its neighbors, other than Egypt, have not.

The Gender Empowerment Measure (GEM; column 4) ranks countries by the extent to which women have opportunities to participate in economic and political life. For a variety of reasons, the statistics necessary to calculate GEM are not available for more than one-third of the countries in this region. As already observed, the region is characterized by rather stark differences between gender roles; and, despite the importance of women in the home, they do not participate in policy-making debates in the larger society. Many of even those countries for which GEM data is available are far down in the rankings and are lower in GEM than HDI (Turkey, Iran, Israel, Jordan, the UAE, Kuwait, Algeria); this is a clear indication of neglect of women's well-being. Israel's relatively high GEM rank of 32 is the result of its direct efforts to include females in all aspects of society, including the armed forces. But, even in Israel, women hold only 8 percent of parliamentary seats.

Where GEM rankings are missing, the Gender-related Development Index (GDI) is used. This index only measures the access of males and and females to health care, education, and income. It does not measure the extent to which males and females actually participate in policy formation and decision making within a country.

Environmental Issues

The Islamic scholar and World Bank executive Ismail Serageldin writes that the Qur'an contains numerous references to the role of humans as stewards of the earth. These references are interpreted to mean that humans have the right to use the earth's resources, but only within the general limitations placed against greed and personal ambition in Islam.

In actual practice, Muslims are like people in all societies across time: they have not always followed their own religious teachings and cared for the earth. Urban crowding, mechanized agriculture, and a general drift toward materialism have resulted in pollution, species extinctions, and degraded environments. Although environmental issues are not yet at the forefront of public debates, they are emerging and are among the concerns of some Islamist critics of modern secular society. The combination of rising expectations for ever higher standards of living, and concern over rapid population growth and a natural setting that offers only a limited selection of resources, suggests that environmental issues will increasingly move onto center stage.

In this section we look at two issues: water availability and use and sustainable development.

Water Issues

Many of the region's current environmental issues are somehow linked to its arid climate. Cultural attitudes toward water differ greatly from those of North Americans. Here, people expect to use very little water, and they have devised many strategies for living with low water availability. They design their traditional buildings to maximize shade and conserve moisture; they capture mountain snowmelt and move it to dry fields and villages in underground water conduits *(qanats)*; they bathe, typically, in public baths; and everyone practices countless recycling techniques, such as using bathwater to irrigate.

Despite a long tradition of careful water use, a number of factors have exacerbated the water shortage over the last few decades. Modernization has brought new ways to use water: in household plumbing, sewage treatment, industrial cooling and cleaning, and mechanized, irrigated agriculture. Moreover, the number of people who must share scarce water resources is growing rapidly. If natural supplies of water remain more or less constant in this region, yet water use rises, will supplies no longer meet basic needs? Experts have established that for a country to maintain human health and support general development, it must have no less than 1000 cubic meters of water available per capita per year. Figure 6.12 shows that in 1990, 10 countries in the region already fell well below this standard. By the year 2050, 6 more countries will be below the standard, leaving only 5 of the 21 countries of the region with 1000 cubic meters of available water per capita per year.

The biggest use of water throughout the region is for irrigated agriculture. A typical country, such as Tunisia, uses 89 percent of the water it withdraws for agriculture, 9 percent for domestic purposes, and 3 percent for industrial uses. In comparison, the United States uses 42 percent for agriculture, 13 percent for domestic purposes, and 45 percent for industry. Irrigation water evaporates quickly and leaves dissolved

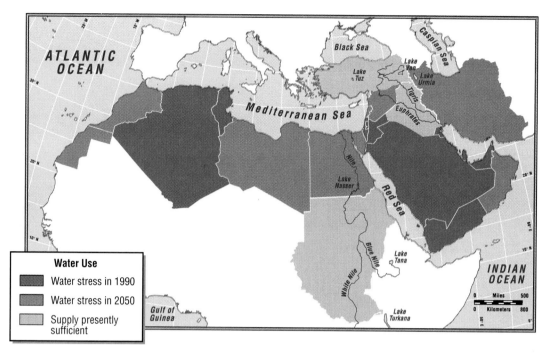

FIGURE 6.12 An annual minimum of 1000 cubic meters of water per capita is considered essential to maintain public health and to support development. The 10 countries colored brown do not have enough water to meet this minimum requirement and therefore are already under water stress. At current levels of water use, almost every country in the region will have the same problem by 2050 (those colored tan), and perhaps sooner if the populations continue to grow as rapidly as they have in recent years. Only Sudan, Turkey, and Iraq are likely to have sufficient water. [Data from *World Resources 1996–97* (New York: Oxford University Press, 1996), pp. 302–303.]

salts on the surface of the soil (soil salinization), rendering it sterile eventually. The low volume of water in rivers and streams is quickly polluted by chemical fertilizers applied to the soils to enhance fertility. Even strategies to increase the supply of water—damming of rivers, desalinization, groundwater pumping—create their own problems: water is wasted through evaporation or leakage; the production and use of energy for desalinization creates air pollution; and land subsides as the water table sinks.

The most ambitious efforts to increase water supplies have been the construction of dams and reservoirs in major river systems: on the Euphrates, the Tigris, the Jordan, and the Nile (see the box "Turkey's Anatolian River Basin Project"). These projects all raise questions about the rights of downstream and upstream water users. Dams that halt the ebb and flow of rivers remove water from huge tracts of land downstream. Just as serious, they stop the deposition of silt during seasonal flooding, which formerly enhanced soil fertility. International laws governing water rights along river systems evolved in regions, mainly Europe, where water was plentiful. Under existing laws, it is possible for a country to dam a river that flows through its territory, with little or no consideration of those downstream or upstream. Downstream countries in arid zones may have little recourse short of war when their source of water is cut off.

Dams create problems for the host countries as well. The huge artificial reservoir created upstream of a dam floods villages, fields, wildlife, and evidence of the historic heritage. The silt that used to be carried downstream may fill up the reservoir behind the dam in just a few years. In a warm climate, the standing water is a natural host for mosquitoes, carrying debilitating diseases like malaria, and for dangerous parasites like hookworm and schistosome species. Also, huge volumes of water will be lost from the reservoir through evaporation; and soil repeatedly saturated and dried out will eventually become salty and infertile. Salinized soil and the accumulation of silt behind dams thwarted the great agricultural economies of the Tigris and Euphrates and Nile river basins in ancient times. More recently, the Aswan High Dam project on the Nile in Egypt and numerous dam projects along the Tigris and Euphrates in Iraq have experienced most of these problems.

291

AT THE LOCAL SCALE   *Turkey's Anatolian River Basin Project*

The Euphrates River is very much on the mind of the water engineer Olcay Unver, a native of Turkey. After years of study and work in Texas, he is back home managing the massive Anatolian river basin project (Figure 6.13), similar in many ways to the Tennessee Valley project in the United States, one of its models. The Euphrates River begins life as trickles of melting snow in the mountains of Turkey, then gathers power from a number of tributaries as it flows southeast through the Anatolian plateau and then through Syria and Iraq. In Iraq, the Euphrates is joined by a second major river, the Tigris. The two run roughly parallel for hundreds of miles, joining just before they reach the Persian Gulf.

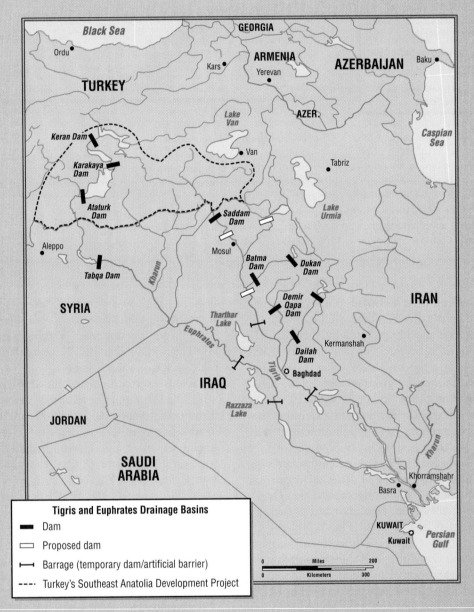

FIGURE 6.13 Dams of the Tigris-Euphrates drainage basins. [Adapted from Christine Drake, Water resource conflicts in the Middle East, *Journal of Geography* (January/February 1997): 7.]

The project Olcay Unver is managing was begun as a series of 22 dams to reserve Euphrates waters in Turkey for irrigation and hydropower generation; 19 plants are planned. Now the enterprise has broadened to include reforestation, farming courses, the establishment of fisheries, and provision of social services like literacy training, health care, and women's centers. Mr. Unver describes the project, in this heretofore neglected southeastern part of Turkey, as "an integrated socioeconomic development project which aims to enhance the standard of living in this area."

As important as the Anatolian project may be to Turkey, its effects on Syria and Iraq downstream could be disastrous. If completed as planned, the project will reduce the Euphrates flow to Syria by 30 to 50 percent within the next several decades. Moreover, the water will be polluted after having been used for irrigated agriculture in Turkey and infused with fertilizers, pesticides, and salts. Syria, whose population will double in just 25 years, depends on the Euphrates for at least half of its water, and Syria also plans to use more of the Euphrates flow for irrigation. Iraq is the last to receive the river water and the most vulnerable. Iraq claims 570 cubic meters of water per second as its rightful share of the Euphrates' flow; but Syria plans to release only 290 cubic meters of water that will be yet further degraded.

Source: Adapted from Stephen Kinzer, Restoring the Fertile Crescent to its former glory, *New York Times*, May 29, 1997; and Christine Drake, Water resource conflicts in the Middle East, *Journal of Geography* (January/February 1977): 4–12.

Sustainable Development

As is the case elsewhere on earth, environmentally sustainable development strategies—those that do not compromise the prospects of future generations—are only just emerging in this region. Among the most effective are those that are small in scale and focused on the needs of a single community. An example is the case of the Zabbaleen, an ethnic group in Cairo, Egypt, that has long earned a living by camping at urban dump sites and sorting through refuse looking for recyclable items. They perform a useful service, but their occupation puts them (especially children) at great risk from disease as well as injuries from broken glass and metal. In the 1980s, several NGOs began helping the Zabbaleen to improve conditions in their settlements. With a small loan, they purchased machinery that converts rags and plastic into reusable materials, which bring higher income than reselling unprocessed materials. Also, improved compost systems allowed the Zabbaleen to recycle organic food and animal wastes into salable products, while clearing the streets of refuse they had previously ignored. The hope is that people throughout the region can, on their own, reclaim and sustain environments without waiting for policy decisions from government bureaucracies.

Among the sustainability issues commonly reported in this region is **desertification.** The United Nations defines desertification as a set of ecological changes that turn nondesert lands into deserts. These changes include the loss of soil moisture, the degradation of vegetation, the erosion of soil by wind, and the formation of sand dunes on formerly vegetated land. These changes can be brought on by long-term climatic change, by relatively short-term climate variability, or by human activity that in one way or another reduces moisture. Desertification is occurring in a wide range of locations across the globe. Estimates of how much usable land is being lost to desert vary, but the ecologist and author G. Tyler Miller writes that globally, every year, 23,000 square miles (60,000 square kilometers) become new desert.

It is the human processes leading to desertification that are of greatest concern; and in the region of North Africa and Southwest Asia, nomadic herders are most often blamed for mounting desertification. They are said to overstock rangelands and allow their animals to overgraze. With little grass remaining, the soil is unable to retain moisture. Studies are showing that the real story is more complicated. The geographer and veterinarian Diana Davis found that herders are normally careful to manage their herds so that the grassland on which they depend is not destroyed. In her research among herders in Morocco, Davis observed that herdspeople were more likely to decrease rather than increase their herds when times were good. Their indigenous knowledge of range ecology led to management practices that accord well with the arid environment. A wide range of economic changes has probably contributed to a general drying of grasslands bordering the Sahara, including the depletion of groundwater for urban use and irrigated agriculture, the encouragement of settled cattle ranching by international development agencies, and programs that encourage pastoral nomads to settle permanently and take up modern lifeways which include greater per capita use of water.

SUBREGIONS OF NORTH AFRICA AND SOUTHWEST ASIA

Deciding which countries to group with others in subregions is a particularly difficult task for this region. Where, for example, does Egypt belong: in the discussion of conflicts in the eastern Mediterranean? with Libya and the rest of North Africa? or with the Sudan as part of the Nile River valley/drainage? Here, Egypt is placed with the Sudan, since the Nile is treated as a primary theme. As you read and reason through the subregions below, you may develop supporting arguments for subregional alignments or groupings other than the ones used here.

The Maghreb (Northwest Africa)

Many readers may already have formed intriguing images of North Africa, often from old movies: Berber or Tuareg camel caravans moving exotic goods across the

Modern high-rise complex in Tripoli, Libya. [P. Robert/Sygma.]

Sahara from Timbuktu to Tripoli or Tangiers; the Barbary Coast pirates; Rommel, the "Desert Fox"; the lovers played by Humphrey Bogart and Ingrid Bergman in the movie *Casablanca*. These fleeting images—some real, some fantasy, some merely exaggerated—are of the western part of North Africa, what Arabs call "the Maghreb" (the place of the sunset). The reality of the Maghreb is much more complex, however, than Western images.

The countries of the Maghreb stretch along the North African coast from Morocco to Libya (Figure 6.14). They share a number of geographic features. Most people live along a narrow coastal zone facing either the Atlantic Ocean or the Mediterranean Sea. Most of this zone, except for Libya in the east, is backed by the Atlas Mountains. These mountains trigger sufficient rainfall to foster export-oriented agriculture, despite the overall arid nature of the climate. Each country's interior is flanked by the huge expanse of the Sahara Desert.

All countries of the Maghreb have had long and changing relationships with Europe: they went through a period of domination by Europe that lasted well into the twentieth century and by some measures has not yet ended. The people of North Africa have become acculturated and have taken on European ways (more so than some wish were the case). They depend on Europe as a market for exports—especially oil, gas, and agricultural produce—and as a source of jobs. Now they are seeking an identity that will be grounded less in Europe and more in their own distinctive heritage.

The concentration of settlement and economic activities along the narrow coastal zone is a defining geographic fact about this region (see Figure 6.5). Life is lived primarily in the cities that line the Atlantic and Mediterranean shores—Casablanca, Rabat, Tangiers, Algiers, Tunis, Tripoli—and in the towns and villages that link them. The architecture, spatial organization, and urban life of these cities mark them as cultural transition zones, links between African and Arab lands and Europe. Today, the economy of the Maghreb remains tied to Europe. The cities, beaches, and numerous historic sites attract millions of European tourists every year who come to enjoy a culture markedly different from their own and to buy North African products for their homes: fine leather goods, textiles, handmade rugs, sheepskins, brass and wood furnishings, and paintings. The agricultural lands of the Maghreb are located in warm moist zones strategically located close to Europe, where there is a strong demand for Mediterranean food crops: olives, olive oil, citrus, melons, tomatoes, peppers, dates, grains, and fish. Agriculture employs about one-quarter of the population. With few exceptions, most farms are large, relatively modern operations that use irrigation, mechanization, and chemicals to enhance production.

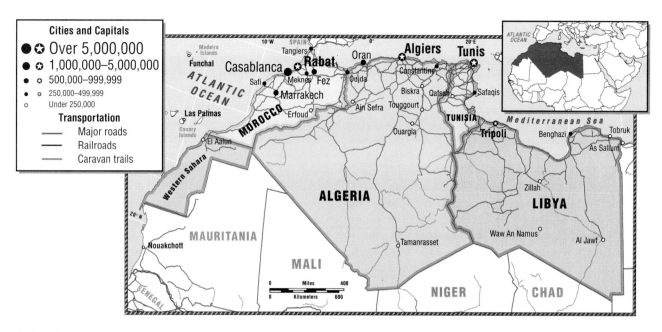

FIGURE 6.14 The Maghreb subregion (Northwest Africa).

Oil, gas, and water are three crucial resources that will figure prominently in the Maghreb's future. Only Algeria, Tunisia, and Libya have notable oil and gas reserves. Libya and Algeria supply about one-quarter of the oil and gas used by the European Union. Oil makes up almost 99 percent of Libya's total exports, and the revenues have raised the standard of living for most of Libya's 5.6 million people. It also finances state-owned industries that supply domestic needs.

In the Maghreb, the debate raised by Islamism has turned particularly hostile. As the historian John Ruedy puts it, for those people who were Westernized during the colonial era, and who now make up the educated middle class, independence from Europe meant the right to establish their own secular nations. Now the Islamist movement seeks to undermine independent secular states by associating them in a negative way with European colonial domination. For these activists, Islamism is a positive cultural identity and an antidote to Eurocentric attitudes. These strict interpreters of Islam are challenging current definitions of democracy across the Maghreb, seeking to reassert Islamic law. Secular leaders and many citizens who are religious but who prefer a secular government are fearful of the outcome.

Modern life in Algeria is centered on the coast; inland, strategies for living in and with the desert persist. At Souf, an oasis in the Algerian Sahara, farmers plant date palms. The roots reach down for the water located near the surface in depressions between the dunes. The farmers also build fences against the prevailing winds, creating wavelike patterns in the sand. Sand collects against the fences, building higher dunes and further sheltering the trees from the desiccating wind. [Georg Gerster/Photo Researchers.]

Women of the Maghreb experience a variety of social attitudes. For women who eschew seclusion, Tunisia may be the most desirable Arab country in which to live. As a secular state, Tunisia has abolished polygamy and recognized the equal right of either spouse to seek divorce. It also requires mutual spousal obligation in household management and child care, and no longer permits preteen girls to marry. Tunisia requires equal pay for equal jobs, has increased the penalties for spousal abuse, and has created a fund guaranteeing alimony for divorced women and their children. While political representation is far from equal (women hold just 7 percent of the parliamentary seats), gains are being made. Women hold 23 percent of the country's judgeships and head 1500 businesses, managing 13 percent of those in greater Tunis.

Violence in Algeria

Algeria, with 28 million people, is arguably the Maghreb's most troubled country. In 1992, the military-influenced Socialist government declared parliamentary elections to be null and void, because the Islamic Salvation Front, a conservative Islamist party, had made a strong showing. Leaders of the party were jailed. Since then, Islamism has made major advances. While some of its advocates have joined religious social service agencies and worked to upgrade life in shantytowns, others have taken a more militant, even violent course. By 1998, terrorists claiming Islamist affiliations had killed at least 80,000 people, many of them rural villagers. The violence has traumatized the society and ruined the already strained economy.

After a violent independence struggle with France, won in 1962, Algeria's economy retained colonial aspects. The European colonists had owned large modern farms on the best land, producing dates, wine, olives, fruit, and vegetables for export. The new Socialist government expropriated these farms, and they ended up in the hands of the Algerian elite, either as private holdings or as large cooperatives. Meanwhile, most of the large agricultural population remain on small, poor holdings. These small producers are 25 percent of the labor force but produce only 12 percent of GNP. A division has developed between the well-off who replaced the Europeans in positions requiring skills and education, and those who remained poor, with only a few years of education. Although there are exceptions, the well-off, generally speaking, are the people now often labeled as secular; the poor are the people to whom Islamism makes a strong appeal.

Nearly half the economy is state owned; and overall, the system does not stimulate innovation, growth, or job creation. Unemployment in 1998 was 80 percent or higher among under-30 urban dwellers. The government, democratic in name only and referred to as "the Power," relies on a strong military that routinely uses political arrest and torture and forbids even peaceful protests. In recent years, large numbers of partially educated, jobless young people have become increasingly frustrated, claiming they live under *hogra*, a word meaning being both excluded and held in contempt by the larger society.

During the 1990s, Algeria undertook major economic structural adjustment: the country privatized many industries and attempted to reattract foreign investment in the hopes that jobs would thereby be created. But structural adjustment often results in hardship for the poorest until the economy takes off. GNP per capita fell from U.S. $2400 in 1990 to less than U.S. $1600 in 1997. During this time, brutal terrorist attacks by extremist factions of Islamists increased.

CULTURAL INSIGHT   *Algeria's Dangerous Political Music*

Algeria is the home of *rai*, a musical form born in the 1920s among poor urban youth. In the early years, rai was frankly Western, with lyrics often about pleasure, wine, women, and sex. But like calypso music in the Caribbean, rai songs began to celebrate political dissent and youthful rebellion. Many young French colonists and tourists liked the music and it was imported into France. After the revolution, the early Algerian government became somewhat puritanical and tried to ban rai. Later, in the 1980s, controls were relaxed and the music revived. In the 1990s, however, both Islamists and conservative French dislike rai. Islamists object to the secular qualities, and some extremists have killed rai musicians. Conservative French associate it with the hundreds of thousands of North Africans living and working in France, whom they see as posing a threat to French ways of life.

Source: Joan Gross, David McMurray, and Ted Swedenburg, Rai, rap, and Ramadan nights: Franco-Maghribi cultural identities. In *Political Islam*, ed. Joel Beinin and Joe Stork (Berkeley: University of California Press, 1997), pp. 257–268.

They began with attacks against the military and police shortly after the nullified election in 1992. They then targeted educated and working women not observing seclusion and/or not wearing the veil; several thousand such women have now been killed. Then, even journalists sympathetic to the Islamist movement, who merely reported on the violence, became targets. Even musicians and artists came under attack (see the box "Algeria's Dangerous Political Music"). The attacks eventually spread to rural villages, and whole communities were massacred with apparently no attention paid to political or religious affiliation. By mid-1997, public sentiment was turning strongly against Islamic fundamentalism. In a more or less fair election in June 1997, moderate Islamists, espousing nonviolence, won nearly one-third of the seats in the National Assembly. But the unexplained massacres continued. Usually the rationale behind the killings is unclear, but some Algerians feel strongly that some civilian massacres and attacks on women have actually been staged by the government to discredit the Islamic underground.

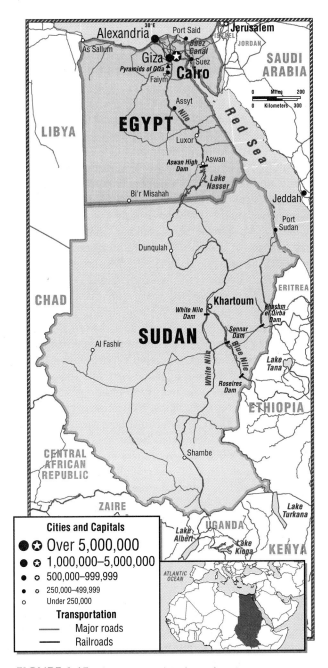

FIGURE 6.15 The Egypt and Sudan subregion.

The Nile: Sudan and Egypt

The Nile River begins its trip north to the Mediterranean in the hills of Uganda and Ethiopia in central East Africa. But the main part of the Nile River system is shared by the countries of Sudan and Egypt (Figure 6.15), and for them it is the chief source of water. Although these two countries have the Nile River, an arid climate, and Islam in common (Egypt is 94 percent Muslim, Sudan 70 percent), they are a study in cultural and physical contrasts. Egypt, despite troubling social, economic, and environmental issues, plays an influential role in global affairs, while Sudan struggles with civil war and remains relatively untouched by development.

Egyptians are mostly Arab, although some are Bedouins and Nubians; and there are many smaller groups from around the Mediterranean: Italians, Greeks, Lebanese, and Syrians. The Copts are Christians, descendants of the very earliest followers of Christ. Sudan is more culturally diverse than Egypt. About one-third of its people are Arab and one-half are African (especially Dinka).

Sudan

Sudan, slightly more than one-quarter the size of the United States, is the largest country in this region and the largest in all Africa. Yet it has only about one-half the population of Egypt. The country has three distinct and progressively drier environmental zones. The upland south, called the Sudd (the first zone), consists

of vast swamps fed by rivers bringing water from the high rainfall regions of central Africa. North of the Sudd, the much drier steppes and hills of central Sudan (the second zone) are home to animal herders. Toward the north, the Sahara (the third zone) begins, stretching all the way through Egypt to the Mediterranean. Most of the 28 million Sudanese live in a narrow strip of rural villages along the main stream of the Nile and its two chief tributaries (the White Nile and the Blue

Nile). Between the two tributaries, irrigated fields produce cotton for export. Sudan's only cities are clustered around the famed capital of Khartoum, where the White and Blue Niles join.

There is animosity between south and north Sudan that has roots deep in the past and is fed by more recent events. Islam did not spread to the upland south until the end of the nineteenth century, when Egyptians, backed by the British, subdued that part of the country. Sudan then became a joint Protectorate of Britain and Egypt until independence in 1955. The southern Sudanese are either Christian or hold various indigenous beliefs. They have long feared the more numerous Muslim, Arabic-speaking Sudanese of the north, since for thousands of years northerners raided the south for slaves. In 1983, the Muslim-dominated government decided to make Sudan a completely Islamic state and imposed shari'a on the millions of non-Muslim southerners. Women, the most directly affected, were permitted to continue to work as nurses and primary school teachers but were barred from jobs in higher education and the civil service. They could no longer travel without a male escort, and many were abused by the various militia groups that operate in the country and in refugee camps. In protest over Muslim domination, southern Sudan launched a war.

The hostilities devastated Sudan. Several hundred thousand were killed; and the situation worsened after a series of droughts and floods brought the death toll to over 1 million. Two million people are now refugees.

Egypt

In Egypt, the Nile flows more than 800 miles north in a slightly meandering track to its massive delta along the Mediterranean. The valley and delta of the Nile are virtually the only habitable parts of the country. Ninety-six percent of Egypt is desert. Yet agriculture along the banks of the Nile has fed the country and provided high-quality cotton for textiles for thousands of years.

The Nile's flow is no longer unimpeded. At the border with Sudan, the river is captured by a 300-mile-long artificial reservoir, Lake Nasser, that stretches back from the Aswan High Dam, completed in 1970 (see Figure 6.15). The Aswan controls flooding along the lower Nile and produces hydropower for Egypt's cities and industries. North of (below) the Aswan, the riverine environment is now greatly modified. Irrigation canals keep some fields in nearly continuous production, and the alluvial plain is no longer replenished every year with a fresh load of sediment from upstream. Instead, fertilizers are used to maintain fertility.

Principal crops, now almost all irrigated, are cotton, grains, vegetables, and sugarcane, as well as animal feed. Egypt's population is growing so fast that al-

though the cities are ballooning, the actual number of people still living and working on the land has increased as well. Nonetheless, the Nile fields are no longer sufficient to feed Egypt's 65 million people, and food must be imported.

VIGNETTE   Mohammed Abdel Wahaab Wad has just spent a week in jail for protesting the loss of the land his family has leased for several generations. In the 1950s, land was taken from the rich and redistributed to poor farmers at very low rents so that they would be able to support their families. Now a new law is reversing the process—the result of SAPs suggested by the World Bank and the International Monetary Fund. The aim is to increase the productivity of land by cultivating it in large tracts managed with machinery. This reorganization of the agricultural system is expected to boost Egypt's ability to feed itself and grow export crops like cotton and rice. The change in land holding is expected to affect 900,000 tenant farmers, like Mr. Wad, who have continued to use labor-intensive techniques to cultivate crops of vegetables and wheat just sufficient to feed themselves. Mr. Wad, who has to support three wives and 11 children, has never before even been asked for rent for the eight acres he occupies on the edge of the Sahara, northwest of the Aswan Dam. Now the new law says that the owner can ask the family to leave. The owner of the land, Gamal Azzam, a member of the urban aristocracy, is adamant that he will recover his land and that the Wad family must go. Worries are growing that in the short run armed conflict will break out, and that in the long run the result will be a rush to the already crowded cities and a period of malnutrition for many while the agricultural system is reorganized around mechanized production. [From Douglas Jehl, Egypt's farmers resist end of freeze on rents, *New York Times*, December 27, 1997, p. A5.]

Egypt's two main cities, Cairo and Alexandria, are both in the Nile delta region. Cairo, at the head of the delta, has 14 million people in its environs and is one of the most densely populated cities on earth. Egypt's crowded delta faces many environmental problems. First there is the crisis of water availability. In 1995, Egypt became one of the countries with less than 1000 cubic meters of water per capita per year (see map in Figure 6.12). Also, the delta waters that irrigate some of Egypt's best land harbor a freshwater parasite that produces a disease called schistosomiasis (also known as bilharzia). The parasite infests humans, causing internal bleeding, debilitating exhaustion, and eventual death. One in 12 Egyptians is infected. For those who must work in the water, prevention is difficult and treatment, with the drug praziquantel, is expensive.

Also worrisome is industrial pollution. Less than 10 miles outside and upwind from Cairo is a major industrial complex that recycles used car batteries collected from all over Europe. Here, the employees break down the batteries to recover the lead. While recycling is laudable, there are virtually no pollution controls on the lead smelters. These send lead concentrations 30 times higher than the world health standards mandate into the air that blows across Cairo. Lead affects brain development and, ultimately, intelligence. Some children's playgrounds in Cairo are so polluted they would be considered hazardous waste sites in the United States.

In the 1990s, Egypt's economy, long plagued with stagnation, inflation, and unemployment, appeared to be turning around. After years of structural adjustment, inflation was brought under some control, and foreign investment in industry is rushing in: Microsoft, Owens-

Corning, McDonald's, American Express banking and investment divisions, Lowenbrau of Germany, and three German automakers, to name a few.

For the ordinary working people of Egypt, however, this flashy development does not translate quickly into prosperity. Export industries are weak; unemployment sits at around 20 percent and may rise as population grows. In part because of the general social and political malaise, but also because of personal values, many of Egypt's young people are attracted to Islamism. Overall, conservative interpretations of Islam seem to be gaining popularity; and as already discussed, many young women are choosing to wear the veil as a sign of their piety.

The Arabian Peninsula

The desert peninsula of Arabia has few natural attributes to encourage human settlement, and today large areas remain virtually uninhabited (Figure 6.16). The largest country, Saudi Arabia, has a population density

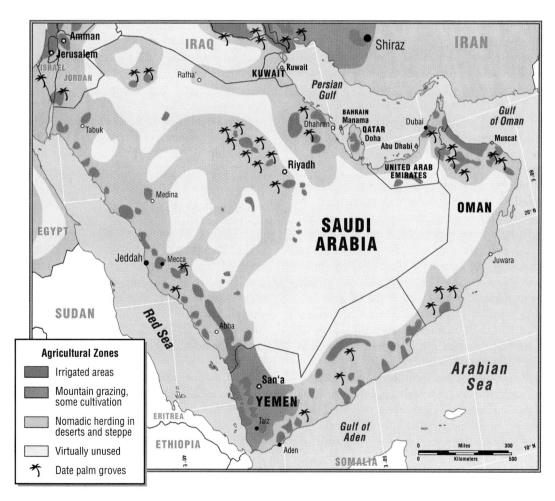

FIGURE 6.16 The Arabian Peninsula subregion.

of only 24 people per square mile (15 per square kilometer). The land is persistently dry and barren of vegetation over large areas. Streams flow only after sporadic rainstorms that may not come again for years. In the interior, it is not unusual for temperatures to go from 54°C (130°F) at midday to below freezing (0°C, −32°F) at night. Nature has given the peninsula one significant resource, however: oil. More than 65 percent of the world's proven oil reserves are found in the countries bordering the Persian Gulf. Saudi Arabia has, by far, the largest quantity, with approximately 25 percent of the world's reserves.

Traditionally, control of the land was divided among several tribal groups led by patriarchal leaders called **sheiks.** The sheiks were based in desert oasis towns and in the uplands and mountains bordering the Red Sea. The tribespeople were either nomadic herders, who traveled over wide areas in search of pasture and water for their flocks, or poor farmers settled where rainfall or groundwater supported crops. Additional income was provided by trade that crossed the desert via camel caravans and by money spent by those on holy pilgrimages to Mecca.

In the twentieth century, the sheiks of the Saud family, in cooperation with conservative religious leaders, consolidated the tribal groups to form an absolutist monarchy, called Saudi Arabia. It now occupies the large midsection of the peninsula. Six much smaller Arab states are ruled by tribes that resisted the Saudi expansion; these occupy the peninsula's eastern and southern margins. The Saud family consolidated its power just as reserves of oil and gas were becoming exportable resources for Arabia. The resulting wealth has added greatly to their power and prestige.

Despite the overall conservative nature of Arab society, oil money has brought enormous changes to landscapes, populations, material culture, and social relationships. Where once there were mud brick towns and camel herds, there now are a number of large modern cities served by airports and taxis. The population has doubled and tripled, to 43.6 million. Pickup trucks have replaced camels (camels are often transported in the back of pickups!); irrigated agriculture has made the peninsula nearly self-sufficient in food; education is now promoted for young girls as well as boys; and more and more women work outside their homes, usually in work spaces secluded from men.

The other, smaller nations on the Arabian Peninsula have varying profiles. Kuwait and the UAE, each with close to 10 percent of the world's oil reserves, are rapidly modernizing and are very affluent, but their societies remain conservative. Yemen occupies about one-quarter the space of Saudi Arabia but has a population nearly as large (16 million); it has only small and as yet undeveloped oil reserves. Yemen's

standard of living remains the lowest on the peninsula (see Table 6.2). Oman and Qatar have modest oil and gas reserves, but they are sufficient to generate relatively high standards of living. Bahrain is virtually a city-state. It generates income not from its tiny oil reserves but from services related to oil production and transport, and from providing entertainment and manufactured goods for neighboring wealthy Saudis.

In 1971, the major oil-producing countries banded together as OPEC to manage global oil prices. Oil income in Saudi Arabia alone shot up from U.S. $2.7 billion in 1971 to U.S. $110 billion in 1981. In this era of fabulous prosperity, those peninsula countries that had significant oil (Saudi Arabia, the UAE, Kuwait) sharply increased investment in some aspects of the national infrastructure: roads, new cities, irrigated agriculture, and petrochemical industries. As a result of rapid development, their own consumption of energy rose steeply; in 1994, Qatar and the UAE used twice as much oil per capita as the United States. Some oil revenue went into higher technical education for elite males primarily and some elite females. But until the 1990s, investments to upgrade the skills of the majority of Arab citizens were not emphasized. Instead, Arab leaders imported laborers and technicians for many projects from neighboring countries, the Americas, and especially Southeast Asia. These outsiders, who for the most part are kept socially segregated from Arab peoples, soon made up about one-quarter of the total peninsula population.

The countries of Saudi Arabia and Yemen are described in somewhat more detail in order to show something of the geographic variety of the Arabian Peninsula.

Saudi Arabia

This country occupies a prestigious position in Islam. It is the site of two of Islam's three holy shrines or sanctuaries: Mecca, the birthplace of the Prophet Muhammad and of Islam; and Medina, site of the Prophet's mosque and his burial place. One of the Five Pillars of Islam is that all Muslims make a pilgrimage (the hajj) to the two holy cities at least once in a lifetime. Each year, a large private sector service industry organizes and oversees the five- to seven-day hajj for more than 2.5 million foreign visitors during the month of Dhu al-Hijja on the Muslim lunar calendar. Although oil now overshadows the hajj as a source of national income, the event is economically important to the country, just as Christmas is in Western countries.

Government in the Kingdom of Saudi Arabia is not based on popular participation. The laws of the land are shari'a, and recent legislation establishes an independent judiciary based on Islamic principles. The

A rare glimpse of the Grand Mosque in Mecca, at the height of the pilgrimage season. [Mohamed Lounes, Gamma-Liaison.]

government, consisting of the king, tribal leaders, and members of the royal family, hears the voice of the people only as it filters through various levels of sheiks, who look after local districts. This patriarchal form of government relies on Islamic principles, such as the Fourth Pillar of obligatory almsgiving, to ensure that all members of the society are looked after. Abject poverty is rarely experienced. On the other hand, this method of government does not allow for open dissent; and large segments of society—women, those not part of the Saudi family, minorities, and foreign guest workers—are left out of the decision-making process.

Yemen

Yemen lies at the southwest corner of the Arabian Peninsula, where relatively "moist" uplands and mountains make cultivation possible. For more than 2000 years, people have farmed terraces growing coffee, cereals, vegetables, and a shrub called *qat* whose leaves produce a mild narcotic when chewed. Yemen's situation differs considerably from that of other Arab states. It lacks significant oil reserves and so is looking to diversified development as a way to support its large and uneducated population. Along the southern coast of the Arabian Sea, a broad valley known as the Hadramaut is now the focus of modernized agriculture. Yemen's port city of Aden, one of the best harbors in the region, is being developed by the Port Authority of Singapore in Southeast Asia. The focus will be on transferring cargo from container ships to lighter vessels headed up the Red Sea to the Mediterranean through the narrow Suez Canal, or to small regional carriers that take cargo to East Africa and the Persian Gulf.

VIGNETTE

Raufa Hassan, 38 years old, with a Ph.D. in social communications from the University of Paris, is Yemen's most outspoken feminist. Her goal is to help women learn how to vote independently; and Yemen's Islamist party, Islah, supports her efforts. Despite having the right to vote, Yemeni women's lives are not conducive to political participation. Nearly 70 percent of the population is still rural, and in rural areas only 1 in 10 women is literate. Typically, girls stay home and work rather than go to school. Women perform many essential tasks in the rural economy, like herding cattle, grinding wheat, and carrying water. After marriage, it is not unusual for a woman to bear as many as 12 children (7 is average). Dr. Hassan found that husbands generally keep their wives' and daughters' voter registration certificates because both parties believe the women would be likely to lose them; as a result, men often control whether or not a woman votes.

Sheik Ahmed Abdulrahman Jahaf, whose daughter is running for parliament, worries that what he calls the "backward villagers" will think ill of his daughter. Although he notes that an educated woman like his daughter is more attractive as a bride, still, he feels: "The nature of women leads us to the conclusion that a woman's right place is home." In these waters, Dr. Hassan wades carefully, always getting the sheiks' permission before she talks to the village women; but the sheiks, too, seem to be changing their views lately. They see they must begin to respond to their peoples' demands, both men and women, if they wish to stay in power. There is even recognition that if they support the women's right to vote and encourage them to do so, the sheiks' own sons may profit in future elections when female voters are more numerous. [Adapted from Daniel Pearl, Yemen steers a path toward democracy with some surprises, *Wall Street Journal*, March 28, 1997, pp. A1, A11.]

The Eastern Mediterranean

Perhaps no other part of Southwest Asia and North Africa has shown as much promise, or has been torn by as much conflict, as the area occupied by Jordan, Lebanon, Syria, and Israel. Yet if tensions were resolved, this area could become an economic leader.

The countries of the Eastern Mediterranean (Figure 6.17) all have considerable economic potential. One state, Israel, is already technologically advanced and broadly prosperous; another, Lebanon, was similarly developed and prosperous until a civil war disrupted the economy. The countries of this subregion are strategically located adjacent to the rich markets of Europe and the potential markets of Central Asia and the Gulf states. Their climate makes them suitable for tourism and semitropical agriculture. Jordan already exports vegetables, citrus fruits, bananas, and olive products; if irrigation water can be found, Syria could do likewise. Syria lost an important trading partner when the Soviet Union broke apart, but private investors, especially from the Gulf states, are helping the country expand into a variety of industrial sectors: pharmaceuticals, food processing, and textiles, in addition to gas and oil production.

Jordan, Lebanon, Syria, and the Palestinian people (who have no actual political state but live within these three countries and Israel) have all been preoccupied in recent decades with political and armed conflict centered on the establishment of the state of Israel, but encompassing wider issues. The Arab-Israeli conflict spilled over Lebanon's borders in the 1970s and ignited discord between Christian and Muslim Arabs. Syria has tensions with most of its neighbors, notably with Iraq and Turkey over water and with Israel over possession of the Golan Heights. The core of the conflict, however, centers around Israel and the Palestinians.

Israel has the best-educated, most prosperous, and best-cared-for population in the region, thanks largely to the strong work ethic of Jewish immigrants, substantial U.S. foreign aid (Egypt and Israel have been the largest recipients of U.S. foreign aid for several decades), a pool of unusually well-educated immigrants, and high levels of investment by the worldwide Jewish community. There are a range of sophisticated industries located along the coast, between the large port city of Tel Aviv and Haifa. Israeli engineering is world renowned; and Israeli innovations in cultivating arid land have spread to the Americas, Africa, and Asia. Some argue that Israel could be a model of development for neighboring countries that remain poor despite having much more land and resources than Israel. However, the country has been involved in a continuing conflict with its neighbors since its very emergence.

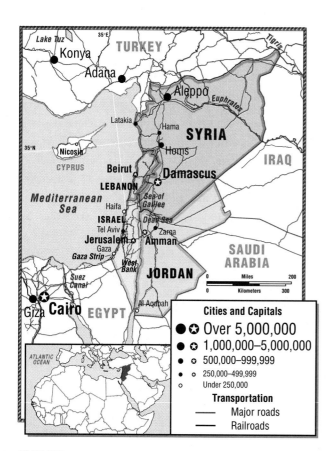

FIGURE 6.17 The Eastern Mediterranean subregion.

The Emergence of Israel

This area of ancient human habitation contains major holy places for Jews, Christians, and Muslims, a fact that has much to do with the wars and violence that have plagued the region since the end of World War II. However, the former colonial powers of Britain and France played an equally, if not more, significant role in the creation of tension in this political hot spot. The origins of the Israeli-Palestinian conflict are a case in point.

When the Ottoman Empire was dissolved after World War I, the League of Nations (precursor to the United Nations) allotted the territory the empire had held at the eastern end of the Mediterranean to France and England. Syria and Lebanon went to France as mandated territories, Jordan and Palestine to Britain. In 1946, Syria and Lebanon became independent republics and Jordan an independent kingdom. A different fate awaited Palestine. Britain mandated that Palestinian lands would be used to create a new state, Israel, as a Jewish homeland. The Jews had been without a homeland since being forced out of the eastern Mediterranean after the fall of the Roman Empire and during the Christian Crusades in the Middle Ages. The Jews were dispersed throughout Europe, North Africa, and Asia. Many encountered persistent discrimination through the ages, especially in Eastern Europe, where occasionally whole villages would be murdered in **pogroms** (episodes of ethnic cleansing). When the Jews left Israel, a thousand years ago and more, the land was reoccupied by a predominantly Muslim people who by 1990 called themselves Palestinians.

In 1947, after World War II, the Western powers were searching for a place to settle the tens of thousands of Jewish refugees who were still in displaced persons camps in Europe. These people were understandably desperate to leave, as most had narrowly escaped death in the Nazi gas chambers that had claimed 6 million victims. Although some were taken in by England, France, the United States, and South America, no country stepped forward to offer a home to all. Meanwhile, the idea of European Jews migrating to the ancestral homeland once known as Israel had been gaining popularity since the idea was proposed in nineteenth-century Austria. Calling themselves

Zionists, a small group of Jews had begun purchasing land from landed Palestinian villagers. But most Palestinians were not landowners. Those displaced were often poor cultivators and herdspeople who had long-standing customary rights to use bits of land for their fields, pastures, and villages. They had little understanding of Palestine as being their own country or ethnic homeland. It was simply all they had ever known, the familiar site of their lives.

By 1946, strong sentiment had built among the world's Jews that a homeland in Palestine should be created, and many Jews already in Palestine took up arms to convince the British of their cause. Slowly awakening to what was happening, the Palestinians began to feel pangs of nationalism. They and their primarily Muslim supporters in the region fiercely objected to the formation of Israel and defended their rights to land that they had occupied for centuries. Nevertheless, in 1948, British, European, and U.S. sentiment sided with the Jews, and Palestine was partitioned: a portion going to create the new state of Israel, and other portions going to Jordan and to Egypt.

The warfare and violence that have since plagued the region began in 1949 on the very day that the last British soldier left. Amazingly, these wars saw Israel not only repeatedly defeat alliances of its much larger neighbors, including Egypt, Syria, and Jordan, but also expand Israeli control into territories long claimed by these neighbors. As a result of the frequent warfare, hundreds of thousands of Palestinians fled or were removed to refugee camps. Israel, for its part, repeatedly assured the Palestinians that they were welcome to live

AT THE LOCAL SCALE   *Palestinians in Israel*

About 1 million Palestinian Arabs live as full citizens within the state of Israel; but they feel their minority status daily in this land that is 82 percent Jewish. How do Palestinian children learn about their own history? Until the 1993 peace agreements, Israel had controlled the teaching of Palestinian history, geography, and culture, and banned any content that criticized Israel's perspective. Since then, the Palestinian Authority created to administer self-rule, has been allowed to produce its own textbooks for primary and secondary school children. Palestinian textbook writers walk a thin line between the political reality of Israel and the dream of a Palestinian territory. The books contain poems and biographies of Palestinian writers and other artists, and depict the Palestinian flag and anthem,

once banned by the Israelis. Historical accounts reveal some aspects of the Palestinian resistance movement against Israel; but no mention is made of guerrilla leaders or violent activities. Yasir Arafat, the militant advocate of Palestinian self-determination, is depicted mildly as the current head of the Palestinian Authority. No mention is made of old Jewish ties to the land of Israel, nor are there accounts of the biblical kingdoms. The history jumps directly from pre-Jewish Canaan to the Muslim conquests in the seventh century A.D.

Source: Joel Greenberg, Palestinian maps for a state that doesn't exist, *New York Times*, June 27, 1997. http://search.nytimes.com/search/daily/bin/fastweb?getdoc + site + site + 27060 + 76 + WAAA + June%7E27, 1997.

and work in Israel as Muslims (see the box "Palestinians in Israel"). Many did so, and many thousands more entered Israel daily to work and then return to villages and refugee camps at night. However, the tide of anti-Israeli sentiment became ever stronger in the region. Throughout the mid-1980s and early 1990s, the Palestinian people, many of whom had by then lived in refugee camps for 40 years or more, mounted a prolonged uprising against Israel, known as the **intifada.** With the 1993 peace accords, the Palestinians acknowledged the right of Israel to exist; but many obstacles to the resolution of the Israeli-Palestinian conflict remain

to be overcome. The maps in Figure 6.18 show the progression of changes in territory since the 1920s.

The 1993 Oslo Agreement allows for shared Israeli and Palestinian control. By 1998, Palestinians controlled patches of the West Bank territory and most of Gaza. If peace is to succeed, the question of how to make the sacred city of Jerusalem accessible peacefully to Muslims, Jews, and Christians will have to be resolved. Muslims revere the city as the place where Muhammad ascended to heaven, although they do not put it on a par with Mecca. Jews and Christians both see the city as central to their faith. Another bone of Israeli-Palestinian con-

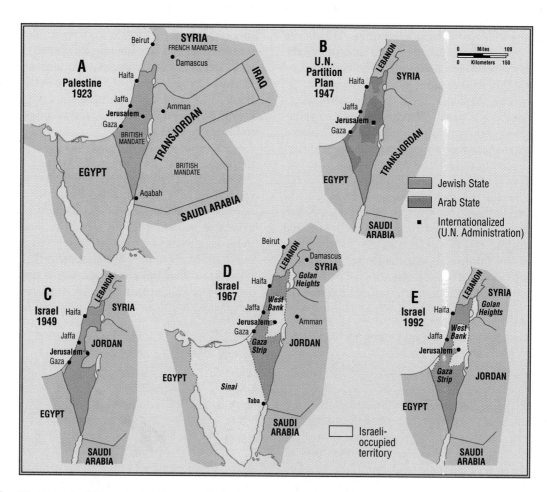

FIGURE 6.18 (A) In the 1920s, the British controlled what is now Israel and Jordan. (B) Following World War II, plans for creating Jewish and Palestinian (Arab) states were developed by the United Nations. (C) But the Jewish settlers did not agree; they fought and won a war, creating the country of Israel. (D) Many of Israel's Arab neighbors were totally opposed to an Israeli state and through war attempted to eliminate Israel. In 1967, Israel soundly defeated combined Arab forces and took control over the Sinai, Gaza, the Golan Heights, and the West Bank. (E) In subsequent peace accords, the Sinai was returned to Egypt, but Israel has maintained control over Golan and the West Bank, which the Israelis claim are essential to their own security. The Palestinians now have some autonomy in Gaza and the West Bank and would like more territory as living space. [Adapted from Colbert C. Held, *Middle East Patterns—Places, Peoples, and Politics* (Boulder, CO: Westview Press, 1994), p. 184.]

tention is the allocation of scarce water resources in this arid and densely occupied space. The two populations are growing—Israelis due to immigration and Palestinians due to high birth rates—and both claim the right to pump water from the same dwindling rivers and aquifers. Finally, land itself continues to be a central issue. A major part of the 1993 peace accord was Israel's promise to stop settling Jews in the disputed "occupied territories." These originally predominantly Palestinian areas, consisting of the Gaza Strip and parts of the West Bank of the Jordan River, had been taken by Israel in the 1967 war. Since then, Israel has established hundreds of Jewish settlements, mainly on the West Bank, as part of its efforts to make room for new immigrants. Periodically, Palestinian groups have retaliated with terrorist bombing campaigns in Israeli cities. Israel often counters with an economic blockade against Palestinian areas. The blockades hurt ordinary Palestinians, who are prevented from reaching their places of employment in Israel.

Religious Fundamentalism in Israel

It is primarily conservative religious forces in Israel that have pushed to continue settlements on the West Bank; more secular groups favor rapprochement with the Palestinians. In a speech on May 14, 1997, marking Israel's independence day, Ammon Shahak, then Israeli Army Chief of Staff, noted that the country is experiencing a division within its society between the religious and the secular reminiscent of the secular/Islamist division being experienced by many predominantly Muslim countries in the region. Shahak observed that, surprisingly, current crucial struggles in the region are not between Arabs and Jews and not between countries, but within countries (Algeria, Turkey, Morocco, Egypt, Iran, Israel). Since 1993, the issue is no longer whether Israel will exist, but rather how Israel and the Arabs can normalize relations so that they can address common environmental, social, and economic issues. Now, the greatest roadblocks to real progress are the factions within the protagonist countries, not hostilities between them.

Thomas Friedman, writing in the *New York Times*, agrees that the real struggle over Jerusalem is between Jews who see Jerusalem as a city of pluralism and tolerance and Jews who want to preserve it as a haven against modernization and secularization. He writes that feelings are now so polarized in Israel that there is discussion of dividing the country. Jerusalem would become the capital of an ultra-Orthodox Israel and Tel Aviv the capital of a secular state. The ultra-Orthodox Jews in Israel see the peace process in much the same light that Islamists in Algeria see Pizza Huts and smutty cable television videos. All are viewed as forces pushing toward Western secular values and loss of cultural identity.

The Northeast: Turkey, Iran, and Iraq

Turkey, Iraq, and Iran (Figure 6.19) are culturally and historically distinct; in each country a different language is spoken: Farsi in Iran, Turkish in Turkey, and Arabic in Iraq. Yet they share a number of features. Each, at different times in the past, was the seat of a great empire. Each was deeply affected by the spread of Islam, which is now the religion of over 97 percent of the people. At present, each occupies the attention of Europe and the United States because of location, resources, or potential threats. All have some common concerns, such as how to allocate scarce water and how to treat the large Kurdish minority. Moreover each country has gone through a radical transformation at the hands of idealistic governments, though the paths pursued have varied dramatically.

Turkey

Turkey looks toward Europe more than any other country in the region does, with the possible exception of Israel. A strong faction within the country seeks to join the European Union, and many Turks have spent years in Europe as guest workers. Once the core of the Ottoman Empire, Turkey's government undertook a path of radical Europeanization following the fall of the empire after World War I. While dramatic transformations have taken place, backlashes and simple inertia have blunted many changes. Islam, once deemphasized to the point of being suppressed, is making a comeback. Similarly, although a state-sponsored industrial revolution has proceeded in western Turkey, much of eastern Turkey remains relatively poor and strongly oriented toward agriculture.

Turkey straddles the Bosporus, a narrow passage from the Black Sea to the Mediterranean that is often overly dramatized as the separation between Europe and Asia. During the cold war, Turkey's location made it a strategic member of the North Atlantic Treaty Organization (NATO), an alliance of European countries and the United States whose mission was to contain Russia. Now, in the post-Soviet era, this same location gives Turkey potential advantages if economic links open up between Europe, the Caucasus, and Central Asia. The U.S. Commerce Department has listed Turkey as one of the world's 10 largest emerging markets. Istanbul, already a booming city of over 10 million, is now the regional headquarters for hundreds of international companies. There are over 250 U.S.-based companies alone, virtually all of them joint ventures of one kind or another: Coca-Cola, IBM, Eastman Kodak, Kraft Foods, Levi Straus, and Citibank, to name a few.

Turkey's future is linked to its ability to manage relatively abundant water resources. With its mountainous topography, Turkey receives the most rainfall of any country in the region, and the headwaters of the economically and politically significant Tigris and Euphrates rivers are in the mountains of southeastern Turkey. As the new irrigation and power generation systems on the Euphrates come on line (see the preceding section on environmental issues), production of cotton, grains, fruits and vegetables, soybeans, and seed oils will increase dramatically. Agriculture employs half the work force and accounts for 20 percent of Turkey's exports (mostly cotton and luxury food items).

The cheap hydropower will also enhance industry, which already accounts for 80 percent of exports. Though up until now Turkey has been hampered by a lack of energy, the country's diversified economy still manages to produce a wide variety of goods, including steel, textiles, leather goods, cement, automobiles, and tires, all of which are exported to Europe and Central Asia. With its already strong industrial base, upheld by a well-trained work force,

hydropower could put Turkey into position for rapid growth. However, Turkey's plans to appropriate a lion's share of the Euphrates' flow places the country in an antagonistic position vis-à-vis its neighbors to the southeast.

Perhaps the greatest obstacle to the stability of Turkey is the country's ongoing civil war with the Kurdish minority. The Kurds are tribal peoples who have lived in the mountain borderlands of Iran, Iraq, and Turkey (see Figure 6.19) for at least 3000 years. The division of the Ottoman Empire by France and Britain dispersed their lands among Turkey, Iran, Iraq, and Syria, leaving the Kurds without a state of their own. All these states have hostile relations with their Kurdish minorities. In Turkey, the conflict has escalated to the point of continuous armed strife and repression of noncombatant Kurds. Turkey's harsh treatment of the minority may well block its entrance into the European Union.

Iran

Like Turkey, Iran has natural resources, a strategic location, and a large population that could make it a re-

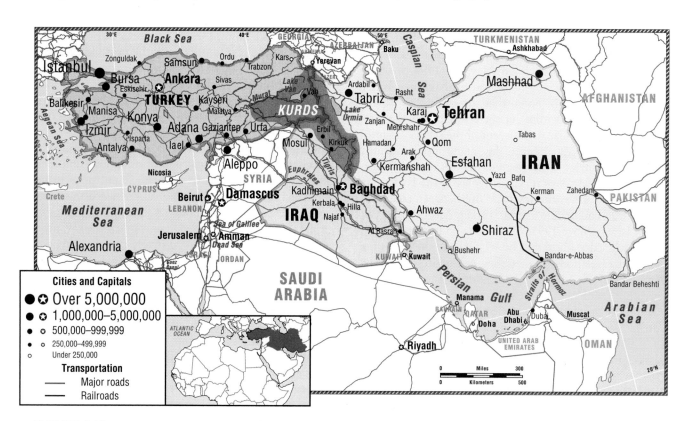

FIGURE 6.19 The Kurds and the Northeast subregion. The Kurdish people retain their own language and culture. Today, there may be 25 million Kurds, half of whom live in southeastern Turkey. Roughly 7 million live in Iran, over 3.5 million in Iraq, close to a million in Syria, 300,000 in Armenia, 330,000 in Germany, 60,000 in Lebanon; and others are scattered elsewhere. [Adapted from Edgar O'Ballance, *The Kurdish Struggle 1920–1994* (New York: St. Martin's Press, 1996), p. 235.]

CULTURAL INSIGHT   *The Turkish Narghile*

One of life's simple pleasures for many retired Turks is relaxing with friends in one of Istanbul's salons dedicated to the narghile, a Turkish water pipe. The pipe base is a bell-shaped, water-filled, glass bottle that sits on the floor next to a patron. An intricately engineered brass neck screws onto the bottle and connects with a pipe bowl and a long (5 to 6 feet) flexible smoking tube and mouthpiece. The aficionado puts a plug of strong Turkish tobacco in the bowl. The server then places one or two red-hot coals on the tobacco and the smoker puffs away; the smoke reaches the mouth only after bubbling through the water, where it is cooled and some particles removed. It takes one to two hours to smoke a pipeful; meanwhile, the male patrons (a few women partake occasionally) sip tea or coffee (no alcohol), play dominoes or backgammon, and enjoy the companionship of old friends.

Men meet at a social club in Istanbul, Turkey, to enjoy conversation and the narghile water pipe. [Robert Frerck/Woodfin Camp & Associates.]

gional economic power. Iran is an energy linchpin, because it holds 9 percent of proven global oil reserves and 15 percent of the natural gas reserves. Yet social and economic turmoil have long held the country back.

Iran has a theocratic government that is based in large measure on Islamism. The theocracy was formed in 1979 under the leadership of the Ayatollah Khomeini, a Shi'ite spiritual leader who led the revolution against the previous ruler, Shah Reza Pahlavi. Pahlavi's father had seized the country in the 1920s and introduced secular and economic reforms patterned after those in Turkey. Reza Pahlavi continued Europeanization, but his emphasis on military might and royal grandeur tended to overshadow any genuine efforts at agricultural reform and industrialization. With the Iranian revolution of 1979, the situation in Iran changed rapidly. Resistance to the new theocratic state was crushed by massive imprisonments and executions. Among those most affected were women. Many women had lived emancipated lives under the shah's reforms, studying abroad and returning to serve in important government posts. Now all women past puberty had to wear long black chadors, and they could not travel in public alone, or drive, or work at most jobs. Yet even some highly educated women supported the return to seclusion, seeing it as a way to counter the unwelcome effects of Western influence.

The turmoil of revolution was followed by a decade of isolation brought on by war with Iraq. Today, punitive economic sanctions imposed by the United States and Europe in response to Iran's suspected funding of terrorism are still in place, and the government has only begun to work toward economic diversification. Many products that people depend on must be imported. The country's out-of-date transport system is being updated (see the box "The Bandar Express") so that Iran can begin again to participate in trade with its Arab and Central Asian neighbors. Agriculture remains Iran's weakest economic sector; even though one-third of the work force are farmers, Iran must import a large part of its food. Elections in May 1997 brought the landslide victory of a moderate leader, Mohammad Khatami. His election success is credited to women and young voters who were attracted by his subtle hints that he favored reform.

Iraq

Iraq, more than any other country in the region, is in a state of crisis. Once an oil-rich Socialist state, the country has suffered from the devastation of two wars: the war with Iran (see the box "The Iran-Iraq War,

1980–1988") and the war with Kuwait (the Gulf War of 1990–1991). Ten years of severe economic sanctions imposed by Europe and the United States have crippled the country. Once the sanctions are lifted, Iraq's oil reserves will finance reconstruction, but the country that emerges will be significantly poorer and more behind the times than it might have been.

Most of Iraq's people live in the area of productive farmland in the country's eastern half, on the alluvial plain of the Tigris and Euphrates rivers. Sunnis reside in the northern two-thirds of the plain, around the capital of Baghdad. About 4 million Kurds, who are also Sunni Muslims, live in the northern mountains in the border regions with Turkey and Iran. The southern third of the country is occupied by at least 10 million Shi'ite Muslims, concentrated around Basra at the head of the Persian Gulf. Iraq's main oil fields are also in the south.

Iraq, home to one of the earliest farming societies on earth, was carved out by Britain and the Arab sheiks from the dying Ottoman Empire after World War I. Iraq remained a British mandate until 1932, when it became an independent monarchy. Although most of the Iraqi people are Shi'ite Muslims, since 1932 the government, and most of the wealth, have been controlled by Sunni Muslims, who are about one-third of the population. Like many governments in the region, the Iraqi monarchy maintained strong alliances with Britain and the United States and gradually lost touch with its people. A tiny minority monopolized the wealth generated by increasing oil production but invested little in development. In 1958, a group of young officers overthrew the government, creating a secular Socialist republic that prospered over the next 20 years despite occasional political disruptions. Large proven oil reserves (second in size behind Saudi Arabia) became the basis of a very profitable state-owned oil industry, and the profits from oil financed a growing industrial base. Agriculture on

the ancient farmlands of the Tigris and Euphrates alluvial plain also prospered. The proceeds from oil and agriculture produced a decent standard of living for most people, who benefited from excellent government-sponsored education and health care systems.

At the end of the twentieth century, however, the people of Iraq are suffering terribly. The economy, strained by the long war with Iran, has been kept moribund by international sanctions that prevent the sale of the country's oil. These were imposed after the brief but highly destructive Gulf War with the United States and its European and Arab allies (see page 287). The sanctions have hit the poor and children the hardest. The economy has contracted to the point that unemployed doctors and lawyers are working as street vendors. Yet the impact on a privileged minority has been blunted because the government was able to form alliances with smugglers who bring in supplies from neighboring Jordan and Syria. Smugglers are forming a new economic elite; many are desert people with a knowledge of ancient transport routes into Jordan and Syria. Another group of the newly rich are buying up state-owned industries at bargain prices. Money from such sales has enabled the regime to survive.

The situation in Iraq raises important ethical questions. How shall the global community handle cases of abuse of power within countries when normal avenues of censure prove ineffective? Is it best to allow the situation to deteriorate to the point that the people themselves rise up against a despot? Or does such a strategy lead to unconscionable loss of life and resources? At what point can the world community pass judgment on one country alleged to have developed chemical and biological weapons (so-called weapons of mass destruction) when those standing in judgment have themselves breached the principles they are now enforcing? For example, the United States and European nations have for years researched and developed weapons designed

AT THE LOCAL SCALE *The Bandar Express*

The Bandar Express is an Iranian train that runs from Tehran to Iran's main port city on the Persian Gulf, Bandar-e-Abbas. As part of its economic recovery, Iran is building an extensive rail network connecting all the major towns and cities. The most recently completed link to the Turkmenistan border now connects, indirectly, the countries of the old Silk Road to the sea at Bandar-e-Abbas. Already, trainloads of Uzbeki and

Kazakhi cotton are reaching the port; and autos, refrigerators, and other consumer goods make the return trip from duty-free Dubai, just across the gulf. A newer, shorter direct route is being planned across the arid central Iranian Plateau.

Source: The Economist, June 21, 1997, pp. 49–50.

AT THE REGIONAL SCALE   *The Iran-Iraq War, 1980–1988*

In 1980, the Iraqi president, Saddam Hussein, invaded Iran, apparently thinking that the country was in such chaos that he could acquire territory along the Shatt al Arab estuary and the fertile lowlands between the Zagros Mountains and the Tigris River. Hussein calculated correctly that other countries would not come to Iran's aid. The historian Bernard Lewis explains the many issues. There was an ethnic dimension: Arabs against Persians; a sectarian side: Shi'ite Muslims versus Sunni Muslims; and an economic side over who was to control oil. It was also a war between the Islamism of Iran and the secularism of Iraq. And it was a political war: a battle over territory and regional domination. There was also a geopolitical dimension, in that the United States and Arab countries that feared the spread of Islamism from Iran helped to

equip and finance Hussein. But Hussein, expecting a relatively quick victory, had not realized the extent to which Iranian leaders were willing to use the bodies of their religiously inspired young men against the war machine of Iraq. Iran lost hundreds of thousands of lives, many of them young boys barely past puberty. Eventually, with heavy financing from wealthy Arab neighbors and with U.S. weaponry, logistical, and intelligence support, Hussein forced Iran to the peace table. Hussein himself emerged in a marginally better position, but both Iran and Iraq's infrastructure and oil industry were left in serious disrepair.

Source: Bernard Lewis, *The Middle East: A Brief History of the Last 2000 Years* (New York: Scribner's, 1995), pp. 368–369.

•

to kill en masse. Given that it is a violation of international law to seek the removal of a head of state surreptitiously and to destabilize a country purposely, is it ethical for the United States and Europe to seek the same goal through economic sanctions, which hurt the poor more than the offending despot?

REFLECTIONS ON NORTH AFRICA AND SOUTHWEST ASIA

The region of North Africa and Southwest Asia meanders across portions of two continents, yet nevertheless demonstrates considerable spatial cohesion. People in this part of the world deal with common environmental conditions defined primarily by water scarcity; settlement patterns reflect the necessity to locate close to the few water sources available. The people also share an important cultural feature: the religion of Islam. Although interpreted differently from place to place, Islam nonetheless unites by virtue of its central Five Pillars of Islamic Practice. In all parts of the region,

there is tension between strict adherence to Islam and more secular ways of life. And everywhere, gender roles are at the heart of social debate, because these roles raise such basic questions about how individuals will relate to family and society.

Additionally, most of the region has endured some form of foreign domination over the last several hundred years; and it is presently in transition from outside control to systems of governance and economic development that are regionally or locally oriented. Though not united since the Ottoman Empire, the 23 countries included here share long histories that intersect richly and repeatedly and often violently. They have begun to set up associations like OPEC that work for common goals. Although the nations of North Africa and Southwest Asia are far from achieving economic or political union, the possibilities are gaining attention.

The next edition of this book may well show that this region has re-sorted itself. Iran may by then fit better with Central Asia, Afghanistan, and Pakistan, if present Iranian development plans succeed. Turkey may be more closely associated with Europe if secular forces win out; or it may be aligned with Central Asia and Iran if Islamist forces become dominant. Though it seems unlikely just now, North Africa might begin to see its future as more closely linked with European Mediterranean countries, a possibility envisioned by those in southern Europe who see intriguing economic possibilities and who worry about pollution in the

Mediterranean (see Chapter 4). The trends to look for in the news regarding this region are a growing environmental movement, political maneuverings over water rights, efforts to develop participatory democracy interwoven with further efforts to establish Islamist

governments, a continuation of the decline in birth rates, and slow but relentless redefinitions of gender roles. As always, the geographic patterns of these trends will be uneven but related to earlier social and physical patterns.

Selected Themes and Concepts

1. More than 93 percent of the people subscribe to the **Islamic religion,** and it is the dominant religion in all countries but Israel.

2. Some countries have adopted **theocratic states** that require all leaders to be Muslim and all citizens to follow Islamic law. In other countries, the **secular states,** there is theoretically no state religion and no direct influence of religion on affairs of state. **Islamism,** a fundamentalist movement, is particularly influential.

3. Throughout the region, men tend to occupy **public spaces** (the workplace, the mosque, and the marketplace), whereas women occupy **domestic spaces** (the home). In some parts of the region, women's movements, behavior, and ability to work outside the home are severely restricted.

4. Both **in-migration** and out-migration are important. The oil-rich countries have imported laborers from within the region and from Southeast Asia and

the Americas, while young men from poorer countries may move to European countries as guest workers.

5. Rich petroleum deposits (oil and gas) are located along the Persian Gulf and in some places along the northern coast of Africa. Petroleum wealth has been used to fund the luxurious lifestyles of a small elite and build communications and transportation infrastructure. But the economies of most countries remain undiversified.

6. The region has recently endured instances of hostility between states—Iran versus Iraq, Iraq versus the Gulf states and the United States, Israel versus the Palestinians—and within countries—in Egypt and Sudan, Algeria and Lebanon.

7. The shortage of water is a looming environmental issue. Attempts to obtain water through aquifer pumping and dam construction create their own environmental difficulties, while the use of water in irrigation may lead to soil **salinization** and loss of fertility.

Selected Readings

Afkhami, Mahnaz, ed. *Faith and Freedom: Women's Human Rights in the Muslim World.* Syracuse, NY: Syracuse University Press, 1995.

Arab World Online at http://www.awo.net/

Badran, Margot. *Feminists, Islam, and Nation—Gender and the Making of Modern Egypt.* Princeton, NJ: Princeton University Press, 1995.

Bascom, Johnathan. The peasant economy of refugee resettlement in eastern Sudan. *Annals of the Association of American Geographers* 83, no. 2 (1993): 320–346.

Beinin, Joel, and Joe Stork, eds. *Political Islam—Essays from Middle East Report.* Berkeley: University of California Press, 1997.

Benton, Kathy. Many contradictions: Women and Islamists in Turkey. *Muslim World* 86, no. 2 (April 1996): 106–127.

Brooks, Geraldine. *Nine Parts of Desire—The Hidden World of Islamic Women.* New York: Anchor Books/Doubleday, 1995.

Burr, J. Millard, and Robert O. Collins. *Requiem for the Sudan—War, Drought, and Disaster Relief on the Nile.* Boulder, CO: Westview Press, 1995.

Davis, Diana. Gender, indigenous knowledge, and pastoral resource use in Morocco. *Geographical Review* 86, no. 2 (1996): 284–288.

Drake, Christine. Water resource conflicts in the Middle East. *Journal of Geography* (January/February 1997): 4–12.

Falah, Ghazi. The 1948 Israeli-Palestinian war and its aftermath: The transformation and de-signification of Palestine's cultural landscape. *Annals of the Association of American Geographers* 86, no. 2 (1996): 256–285.

Fuller, Graham E., and Ian O. Lesser. Persian Gulf myths. *Foreign Affairs,* May/June 1997, pp. 42–52.

Katz, Cindi. Sow what you know: The struggle for social reproduction in rural Sudan. *Annals of the Association of American Geographers* 81, no. 3 (1991): 488–514.

Kirk, Martha. *Green Sands—My Five Years in the Saudi Desert.* Lubbock: Texas Tech University Press, 1994.

Langewiesche, William. *Sahara Unveiled—A Journey Across the Desert.* New York: Pantheon, 1996.

Lightfoot, Dale R., and James A. Miller. Sijilmassa. The rise and fall of a walled oasis in medieval Morocco. *Annals of the Association of American Geographers* 86, no. 1 (1996): 78–101.

Mackey, Sandra, with W. Scott Harrop. *The Iranians—Persia, Islam and the Soul of a Nation.* New York: Dutton, 1996.

Majok, Aggrey Ayuen, and Calvin W. Schwabe. *Development Among Africa's Migratory Pastoralists.* Westport, CT: Bergin & Garvey, 1996.

Malik, Lynda P. Social and cultural determinants of the gender gap in higher education in the Islamic world. *Journal of Asian and African Studies* 30, nos. 3–4 (1995): 181–193.

Malley, Robert. *The Call from Algeria—Third Worldism, Revolution, and the Turn to Islam.* Berkeley: University of California Press, 1996.

Mama, Amina. *Beyond the Masks—Race, Gender and Subjectivity.* London: Routledge, 1995.

Monshipouri, Mahmood. Islamism, civil society, and the democracy conundrum. *Muslim World* 86, no. 1 (January 1997): 54–66.

O'Ballance, Edgar. *The Kurdish Struggle 1920–94.* New York: St. Martin's Press, 1996.

O'Conner, Anthony. *Poverty in Africa—A Geographical Approach.* London: Belhaven Press, 1991.

Ruedy, John, ed. *Islamism and Secularism in North Africa.* New York: St. Martin's Press, 1994.

Tessler, Mark, and Jolene Jesse. Gender and support for Islamist movements: Evidence from Egypt, Kuwait and Palestine. *Muslim World* 86, no. 2 (April 1996): 200–217.

Wikan, Unni. *Tomorrow, God Willing—Self-Made Destinies in Cairo.* Chicago: University of Chicago Press, 1996.

SUB-
SAHARAN
AFRICA

INTRODUCTION TO AFRICA

*I*n the harbour of Mombasa lay a rusty German cargo-steamer, homeward bound. Upon the deck there stood a tall wooden case, and above the edge of the case rose the heads of two Giraffes. They were . . . coming from Portuguese East Africa and were going to Hamburg, to a traveling menagerie.

The Giraffes turned their delicate heads from one side to the other, as if they were surprised, which they might well be. They had not seen the Sea before. They could only just have room to stand in the narrow case. The world had suddenly shrunk, changed and closed round them.

They could not know or imagine the degradation to which they were sailing. For they were proud and innocent creatures, gentle amblers of the great plains; they had not the least knowledge of captivity, cold, stench, smoke, and mange, nor of the terrible boredom in a world in which nothing is ever happening.

In the long years before them, will the Giraffes sometimes dream of their lost country . . . the grass and the thorn-trees, the rivers and water-holes and the blue mountains? . . . Where have the other Giraffes gone to, that were side by side with them when they cantered over the undulating land?

—*Isak Dinesen*, Out of Africa

It has been more than 500 years since Europeans began colonizing Africa in order to use and remove the continent's animals, people, minerals, and agricultural products. The net flow of wealth is still out of Africa. Although colonialism is finished, **neocolonialism** thrives—the practice whereby rich countries of the world continue to reap Africa's wealth by extracting minerals, exploiting the soil through unsustainable commercial agriculture, and employing its inexpensive labor. An example is provided by the fishing industry of tiny Guinea-Bissau, a country that ranks near the bottom on the United Nations Human Development Index (161 out of 174). It lies on the west coast of Africa, adjacent to the rich Canary Current. In 1996, 97 percent of the fish catch in Guinea-Bissau waters was taken and sold abroad by high-tech foreign fishing fleets from Japan, Korea, Russia, Spain, and Portugal. The owners of these fleets paid just U.S. $11 million a year to Guinea-Bissau for licenses to take a catch worth U.S. $130 million annually.

Deals like this one have been the rule across Africa for 500 years and more. Little surprise, then, that Africa is now impoverished. The per capita poverty of Africans in the lands south of the Sahara is exceeded only by that of South Asians. And from time to time, ethnic conflict, often arising over access to resources, has turned the generally low standards of living into outright destitution.

European colonists did much to set up the circumstances for Africa's current poverty and scattered disharmonies. When European colonists went to Africa, they did so to extract resources at low cost from a foreign place, and secondarily to create markets in the colony for products manufactured in the "mother" country. To facilitate their plan, they found it expedient to remove the traditional chiefs and to install their own handpicked leaders. They uprooted vast numbers of people and transformed family structures, all in order to control resources and to create a labor pool.

Today there are many hopeful signs that well-being for the majority can be enhanced and conflict resolved. Africa south of the Sahara consists of 46 countries and about 600 million people in a landmass that could contain three Chinas. Within that space, there is room for a great deal of complexity in resources and variety in solutions to Africa's chief problems of poverty and political conflict. African observers say that many countries, especially those in eastern and southern Africa, are making significant progress. In recent years, a number of Africans have emerged who

Giraffes at home in Okavango Delta, Botswana.
[Frans Lanting/Minden Pictures.]

are now recognized as among the best leaders the world has to offer: UN Secretary-General Kofi Annan from Ghana; South Africa's former president, Nelson Mandela, and its former archbishop, Desmond Tutu; and the late Nigerian writer Ken Saro-Wiwa, to name but four.

Themes to Look For

Several themes are developed in this chapter. Among the most important are

1.   The roots of African poverty

2.   Patterns in the modern era that perpetuate the circumstances of colonialism

3.   Changing ecological relationships

4.   The role of African population dynamics and disease in slowing improvements in standards of living

5.   The increasing role of Africans in defining the region's problems and designing their solutions

Terms and Attitudes to Be Aware Of

The language used to report on Africa has been particularly prone to **ethnocentrism,** the belief in the superiority of one's own cultural perspective. This tendency to use ethnocentric language has subconsciously extended many of the prejudices of the colonial era. There is now a movement to purge colonial terminology from depictions of Africa, because these terms too often are based on European misperceptions of cultures very different from their own. Words like *tribe* and *tribalism*, *primitive*, *savage*, and *fetish* all have legitimacy in some circumstances, but in reference to Africa they are, for the most part, too loaded to be useful. In this book, we use **ethnic group** and **ethnicity** to refer to groups of people and the culture they share. *Civilization* is another term often misused in relation to Africa. Only certain people were thought to be civilized; and examples were said to be the people of ancient China and Greece, Mesopotamia, the Indus Valley, the Maya and Inca empires in the Americas, and most of Europe since A.D. 1000 or so. Meanwhile, Africa was classified as uncivilized. By now, most scholars recognize just how narrow this European concept of civilization is. First, Africa had several ancient societies that fit common definitions of civilization. Second, African cultural practices that seemed to indicate savagery to the Europeans were often grossly misunderstood. Moreover, so-called civilized societies in Europe and elsewhere were seldom evaluated closely

enough to reveal how much they themselves were shored up by brutish behavior and the savage exploitation of underclasses.

PHYSICAL PATTERNS

Landforms

Geologists almost always place Africa at the center of the ancient megacontinent of Pangaea. In simulations of continental drift over the last 200 million years, continents break off from Africa and move away: North America to the northwest, South America to the west, India to the northeast. As Africa loses all this "baggage" of continent-sized pieces, it readjusts its situation only a bit, drifting gently into Southwest Asia. Africa continues to sit at more or less the same place on the globe's surface and continues to break its connection to the Arabian Plate at the Red Sea. Still all one plate, Africa is, however, in the process of breaking up further, at least along its eastern flank. There, two major rifts marked by chains of lakes are now well developed. The Somali Plate will be the next to go, perhaps in another 30 million years or so.

Perhaps because Africa has been more or less stable over time, its landforms are today exceptionally uniform. The whole continent can be envisioned as a raised platform bordered by fairly narrow and uniform coastlines and covered by an ancient mantle of rock in various states of weathering. The platform slopes downward to the north. Thus the southeastern third of the continent is an upland region with several substantial mountain ranges, while the northwestern two-thirds of the continent is a lower-lying landscape, interrupted only here and there by uplands and mountains. These landforms have hindered transport within Africa and connections to the outside world. Routes from the plateau to the coast must negotiate steep escarpments around the rim of the continent, and the long uniform coastlines have few natural harbors.

Climate

Most of sub-Saharan Africa has a tropical climate (Figure 7.1), and temperatures generally stay above 64°F year-round everywhere except at the more temperate southern tip of the continent. African climates differ more by rainfall than temperature.

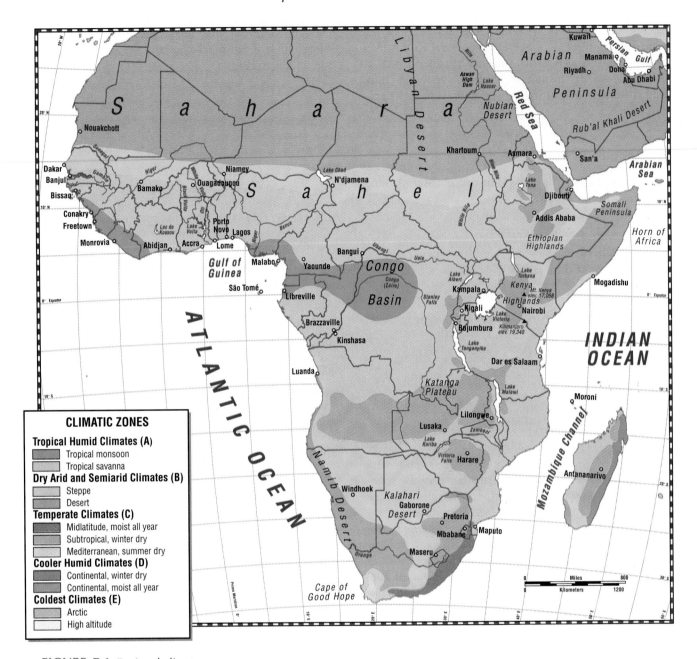

FIGURE 7.1 Regional climate.

Most rainfall comes to Africa by way of the **intertropical convergence zone (ITCZ)**, a band of atmospheric currents circling the globe roughly around the equator (Figure 7.2). At the ITCZ, warm winds converge from both north and south. These winds push against each other, causing air to rise in altitude, cool, and release moisture in the form of rain. The effects of the ITCZ are most evident in central and western Africa near the equator. There the frequent rainfall nurtures the dense vegetation of tropical rain forests.

The ITCZ shifts north and south seasonally, generally following the area of the earth's surface that has the highest average temperatures at any given time.

The tilt of the earth's axis causes the most direct rays from the sun to fall in a band that sweeps into the Northern Hemisphere during its summer (June–September) and into the Southern Hemisphere during its summer (December–March). Hence, during the height of the Southern Hemisphere summer in January, the ITCZ might bring rain far enough south to water the grasslands of Botswana, while during the height of the Northern Hemisphere summer in August, the ITCZ brings rain as far north as the fringes of the Sahara (the Sahel). Beyond both of these extremities, a belt of descending dry air blocks the effects of the ITCZ and creates the deserts found in

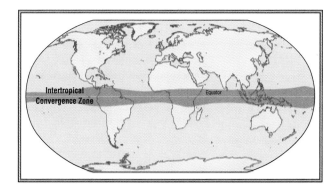

FIGURE 7.2 Intertropical convergence zone. [Adapted from Tom L. McKnight, *Physical Geography* (Upper Saddle River, NJ: Prentice Hall, 1996), p.125.]

Africa and other continents at roughly 30° north and south latitude. Across central Africa, in between the wet equatorial rain forests and the dry scrub of the deserts, there are mirror image bands of ecosystems that take advantage of the varying amounts of rainfall. Two examples of these ecosystems—the seasonally dry tropical forest and the moist savanna, where tall grasses and trees intermingle—have been used for agriculture for thousands of years.

This described banded pattern of ecosystems is modified along the eastern coast from Tanzania to Somalia. Air currents blowing north along the east coast of Africa keep ITCZ-related rainfall away from the Horn of Africa; consequently, this is one of the driest parts of the continent.

The climate of Africa presents a number of challenges to human beings. Insects and parasites that breed prolifically in warm wet climate zones cause serious debilitating diseases, such as river blindness, schistosomiasis, and malaria. In the drier tropical climates, water is often in short supply for drinking, farming, and keeping animals; and the soils, lacking organic matter, are not particularly fertile, even if irrigated. In humid areas, cultivated soil easily loses its fertility. Wherever both temperature and moisture are high, **organic matter** (the remains of any living things) in the soil decays rapidly and the nutrients released are quickly absorbed by surrounding plants or **leached** (washed) out into groundwater and runoff. In a standing forest, the detritus shed every day decays and provides a continual source of nutrients for the growth of plants. If the forest is removed, this source of nutrients is gone and the soil quickly deteriorates. The minerals are leached out and soil particles washed downslope. The direct rays of the sun bake the soil into a permanently hard surface called **laterite.**

Over the ages, cultivators in the wet tropics have learned several strategies to maintain soil quality. They clear only small patches, an acre or two at a time. They use the cleared vegetation as "fertilizer," sometimes burning it to release nutrients. And they plant their gardens as a sort of miniature forest with many species—often 20 or more per garden—of different sizes, shapes, and requirements that cover the soil quickly to prevent the creation of laterite in the hot sun. Because the soil quickly loses fertility, the small plots produce well only for two or three years and are then allowed to go back to forest for several decades. Typically, commercial agriculture that depends on large, clean-cleared fields and long-term production has not succeeded in tropical zones. Even chemical fertilizers cannot maintain fertility.

There is evidence that Africa has experienced repeated changes in climate over the last 20,000 years and that a new, drier cycle is starting. Since the 1970s, droughts have been frequent. They may simply be a consequence of the natural cycle; but increasingly, scientists think that the cause of some present climatic changes is global warming linked to the rising levels of greenhouse gases produced in the industrialized parts of the world. Scientists expect present climatic patterns in Africa to intensify: hot, wet places will become hotter and wetter; hot, dry places will become hotter and drier. Grasslands on the desert margins will become deserts; low-lying coastal areas will be inundated by seawater rising because of melting glaciers at the poles. Because so many Africans live in arid or low-lying zones, as much as one-quarter of the population could find their homelands becoming uninhabitable.

HUMAN PATTERNS

A general ignorance of Africa's past and of its peoples and customs has seemingly always prevailed. Even Greek and Roman explorers, barred from complete access by the Sahara, did not leave accurate descriptions of this part of the world. Later, the Europeans who began the Atlantic slave trade in the 1500s resisted new information that did not jibe with their preconceptions. For example, news of the substantial and elegantly planned city of Benin in West Africa, encountered by European explorers in the 1500s, never became part of Europe's image of Africa. Even today, most people in the rich countries of the world seldom study Africa's past. The current lack of interest is probably linked to the widespread belief that the region as a whole is unimportant in the global economy, because at this point it is relatively poor and makes only small contributions to world commerce. Yet, over the course

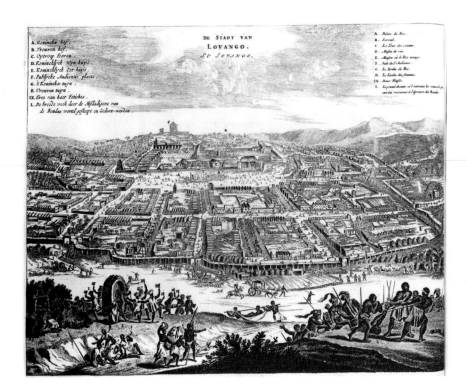

Loango was a sizable coastal city (just north of present-day Point Noir, the Congo) in 1686 when Olfert Dapper, a seventeenth-century Dutch explorer, drew it. Little of it remains today. [From *African Civilizations* by Graham Connah, Cambridge University Press, 1987. Original source: O. Dapper, *Description de l'Afrique . . . Traduite du Flamand,* Chez Wolfgang, Waesberge, Boom & van Someren, Amsterdam 1686: 320–321. John Carter Brown Library, Brown University.]

of time, Africa has made tremendous contributions in resources and human labor to the wealth of other regions, usually for little or no compensation. Understanding how Africa came to be so exploited sheds much light on the modern world and its problems.

The Peopling of Africa

Africa is the ancient home of the human race. By about 400,000 years ago, the close ancestors of humans *(Homo erectus)* had moved out of Africa and across Eurasia. Anatomically modern *Homo sapiens sapiens* evolved in Africa between 200,000 and 100,000 years ago. By 90,000 years ago, modern humans had reached what are now North Africa and Israel; and from there, they spread throughout the Eastern Mediterranean area and then into Europe and Asia.

Although further research may change the picture, it appears that people from equatorial Africa and areas to the south remained essentially hunters and gatherers until about 4000 years ago. Then agriculturalists from the Ethiopian-Sudanese Highlands began moving south into East Africa. About the same time, Bantu-speaking people from coastal West Africa, who specialized in wet tropical cultivation, began moving south and east through the tropical forests of the Congo River Basin. Within a thousand years, descendants of people from both agricultural centers were converging and migrating southeasterly into southern Africa, displacing the local hunter-gatherers.

Several influential centers made up of dozens of linked communities developed in the forest and the savanna. One was the empire of Ghana, located not near the modern country of that name but north of the headwaters of the Niger River. During the eleventh to the thirteenth centuries, Muslim traders from North Africa converted to Islam several West African kingdoms, such as those of Ghana, Mali, and Hausaland, in what is now northern Nigeria. These converts periodically sent huge entourages on the pilgrimage to Mecca, where their opulence was a source of wonder.

In East Africa, trading cities along the coastline of the Indian Ocean were linked in a huge annual cycle of regional trade, stretching north to the Persian Gulf and east to India, Southeast Asia, and even China. In both East and West Africa, major components of trade were ivory, iron, gold, and slaves. It is estimated that between A.D. 600 and 1900, close to 9 million Africans were exported to the Islamic areas around the Mediterranean; cities in both West and East Africa reflected Arabic, and eventually Islamic, influence.

Iron smelting, including the making of steel, has long been practiced in the highlands of eastern central Africa and at Jenno-Jeno in West Africa. By the fifteenth century, a remarkable agricultural and mining-based civilization had developed in the highlands of Zimbabwe. In these highlands, nineteenth-century British explorers discovered thousands of massive stone ruins, tens of thousands of mine shafts, and even fragments of Chinese pottery. European archaeologists of the time did not believe that indigenous African civi-

The archaeological ruins of The Enclosure at Great Zimbabwe are surrounded by the ruins of numerous other structures. [Don L. Boroughs/The Image Works.]

went primarily to plantations in South America and the Caribbean; about one-quarter were sent to the plantations of southern North America.

Slavery severely drained the African interior of human resources and set in motion a host of damaging social responses that are even now not well understood. Slavery also fostered dependence on European goods and technologies (especially guns used by raiding kingdoms) and ships. Much African culture survived the cruelties of slavery, however, to enrich the language, cuisine, religion, literature, music, agricultural technology, and art of other world regions, especially the Americas.

The Scramble to Colonize Africa

European involvement in Africa gradually increased, culminating in the establishment of formal colonies in the late nineteenth century. The British transatlantic slave trade was officially stopped by 1809, but other European nations continued trading in slaves until 1865. By that time they had found that it was more profitable to use African labor *in Africa* in order to extract raw materials for Europe's growing markets. European interests extended inland to include the exploitation of fertile agricultural zones and areas of mineral wealth, and places with large populations to serve as sources of labor.

Colonial powers competed avidly for territory and resources. To prevent the eruption of armed conflicts between them, it became necessary to establish clear boundaries between the claimed African territories. The result was the virtually complete seizure and partition of the continent by the time of World War I (Figure 7.3). There was no consultation with Africans in the partitioning of their continent, and only two African countries retained independence: Liberia and Ethiopia. Otto von Bismarck, the German chancellor who in 1884 convened the Berlin Conference, at which the competing powers first gerrymandered Africa, declared: "My map of Africa lies in Europe." With some notable exceptions, the boundaries of most African countries today derive from the colonial boundaries set up between 1884 and 1916 by European treaties. This fact continues to lie at the root of many of Africa's current problems.

There were a few basic patterns in the European domination of Africa during the colonial period. The geographer Robert Stock identifies three:

lizations could exist, let alone have trading links to China, so they credited the Zimbabwe culture to outsiders. Among their outlandish ideas was the theory that the ruins and mines belonged to the biblical King Solomon or the Queen of Sheba.

The Coming of the Europeans

The course of African history shifted dramatically in the fourteenth century, when Portuguese sailing ships began to appear off the West African coast. The names given this coast by Portuguese and other early European maritime powers reflected their interests in trading Africa's resources: "the Gold Coast," "the Ivory Coast," "the Pepper Coast," and "the Slave Coast." The Portuguese, British, Dutch, and French took slaves in a fashion far beyond anything Africa had experienced before, either internally or in the course of the Islamic and Asian slave trade. Europeans established forts on the west coast and enlisted nearby African kingdoms, supplied with European rifles, to make slave raids into the interior. As in the pre-European slave trade, some of the captives were taken from enemy kingdoms in battle; however, many more were kidnapped from peaceful ethnic groups in the forest and savanna. Most slaves traded in the international market were male, as the raiding kingdoms preferred to keep captured women for their reproductive capacities. Over a period of almost 400 years, some 13 million captives were packed aboard ships, most destined for the plantation economies of the Americas. Up to a quarter of the human cargo died at sea in the cramped and filthy ships. The 9 or 10 million who arrived in the Americas

1. European settlers occupied land on a large scale only in a few places. These were mainly areas with especially attractive resources or where the climate was considered comfortable by Europeans—such as the relatively cool highlands of Kenya or the upland plateau of

319

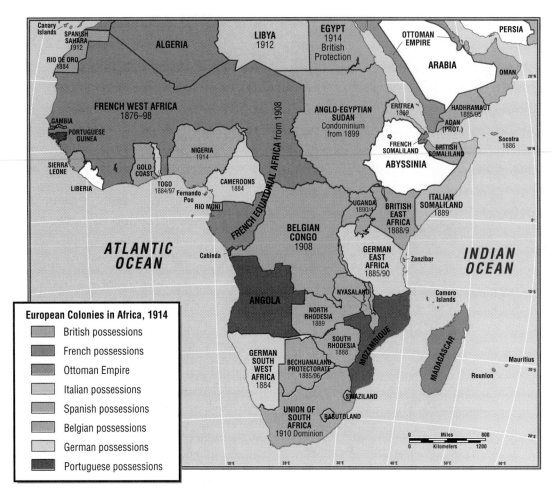

FIGURE 7.3 The European colonies of Africa in 1914. The dates on the map indicate the time of officially recognized control by the colonizing powers. [Adapted from Alan Thomas, *Third World Atlas* (Washington, DC: Taylor and Francis, 1994), p. 43.]

South Africa. Here, Europeans forced indigenous farmers and herders onto marginal land in reservations or made them labor on white-owned farms and plantations. Areas taken over by Europeans were privileged, in that taxes were kept low and roads were constructed to provide ready access to local and global markets.

2. African farmers of small plots remained in many densely populated agricultural regions and in locations considered disagreeable by Europeans. They were often encouraged or directed to switch from food crops to export crops. Some adapted eagerly, in the hope of becoming wealthier; some changed grudgingly because of the need to pay taxes in cash to the colonial regimes. Many experienced malnutrition as more and more land was shifted from food to cash crops or livestock production. Despite wrenching change to their economies, these areas of indigenous farming received little assistance from Europeans. Transportation was only modestly upgraded; and Africans were often

forced to pay higher taxes than the Europeans who had taken their land.

3. Remote areas that were difficult to exploit economically were treated as "labor reserves." Young men were often removed from these areas and put to work on government projects such as railroad construction, where they were separated from their families and subjected to dangerous working conditions, and received very low pay. Many died from nutrition-related diseases, as they were not given sufficient food and were not allowed the time to grow or hunt their own. In the Belgian Congo, as many as 10 million died in this way during the reign of King Leopold of Belgium (1865–1909). (The Belgian Congo became an independent country that was called Zaire until the mid-1990s, then the Democratic Republic of the Congo. Hereafter in this book it is referred to as Zaire/Congo, to distinguish it from the Republic of the Congo and from the natural area known as the Congo.)

In all areas colonized by Europe, the main objectives of colonial administrations were to extract the most raw materials possible, create markets for European manufactures, and keep the costs and the commitments of government at an absolute minimum. It is useful to examine the case of South Africa to appreciate how the European incursion into Africa led to the expropriation of land, the subjugation of African peoples, and, in this case, the infamous system of apartheid.

Shortly after the Dutch took possession of the Cape of Good Hope from the Portuguese in the 1650s, the first significant migrations of Europeans to Africa occurred. These Dutch immigrant farmers, called Boers, practiced herding and farming techniques that used large tracts of land. As they spread into the interior, the Boers pushed indigenous people off their land, despite strong resistance. The Boers enslaved laborers elsewhere in Africa and brought them to work on their farms. After the British took possession of South Africa in 1795 and then outlawed slavery in 1834, large numbers of Boers migrated to the northeast, to elude British control, in what was called the "Great Trek." In these interior areas, conflicts with Africans were often intense and violent. Then the discovery of extremely rich diamond mines in the 1860s and gold mines in the 1880s secured the economic future of this land, which became known as the Orange Free State (OFS) and the Transvaal. Africans were often forced to work in the mines for minimal wages, under unsafe working conditions, and to live in unsanitary compounds that travelers of the time likened to large cages. Eager to claim the wealth of these mines, Britain invaded the OFS and the Transvaal in 1899, waging the bloody Boer War that gave them brief control of the mines until resistance by Boer nationalists forced the granting of independence to all of South Africa in 1910.

In 1948, the enactment of apartheid laws reinforced the long-standing segregated society of the Boers. These laws required all but whites to carry passbooks and live in racially segregated rural townships, specific urban sections, or in workers' dormitories attached to mines and industries. Eighty percent of the land was reserved for the use of Europeans, who were only 15 percent of the population. All blacks were also assigned to ethnic-based "homelands" that were considered independent enclaves within the borders of, but not part of, South Africa. African people were similarly treated in other areas, such as Northern and Southern Rhodesia (modern Zambia and Zimbabwe), Tanzania, and Kenya.

Overt resistance to the apartheid system began in the 1960s and grew steadily despite heavy-handed repression. The protesters, many of them mere schoolchildren, were aided by international pressure and economic sanctions. Finally, in the 1990s, the white-dominated government began to negotiate majority rule, which arrived in 1994 with the election of the African statesman Nelson Mandela as president.

The Aftermath of Independence

In Africa, the era of formal European colonialism was relatively short. In most places it lasted for about 75 years, from roughly 1890 to 1965. Nevertheless, the history of Africa since 1960 reveals the deep influence of the colonial period. Like their colonial predecessors, most independent African governments remained authoritarian, antidemocratic, and dominated by privileged and Europeanized elites, although some African governments have recently become more democratic. African economies continue to depend overwhelmingly on the export of raw materials.

Thus Africa enters the twenty-first century with a complex mixture of enduring legacies from the past and looming challenges in the future. Although Africa has been liberated from colonial domination, its future is still very strongly influenced by the world's wealthier countries. It remains inextricably linked to the global economy, where it has long operated at a disadvantage. Meanwhile, poverty is expanding rapidly as solutions to Africa's problems are slow to come. At present, Africa faces declining economic productivity, severe periodic drought and famine, major health problems, including the world's worst AIDS epidemic, and the challenge of having the fastest-growing population on earth. The brightest spot in Africa's future is that the recent decades of rapid and often wrenching change have made many people more willing to consider innovative alternatives to conventional solutions. Perhaps more than any other region of the world, Africa needs a new plan of action for the future.

Population Patterns

A look at the population density map of the continent of Africa (Figure 7.4) will surprise many American readers, who may have the erroneous impression that Africa is particularly densely populated. In fact, people are very unevenly, but generally sparsely, distributed across the continent. Only a few places exhibit the densities that are widespread in Europe, India, and China. Nonetheless, there are serious population issues in Africa. Some countries like Rwanda, Burundi, and Nigeria have pockets of very high density but few resources to support these people; this is sometimes because the resources have been diverted to serve the needs of others outside the region. And in a number of countries, population growth rates are now so high that they sap the power of the society to develop adequate educational and health infrastructures. The result is that living standards actually sink rather than rise.

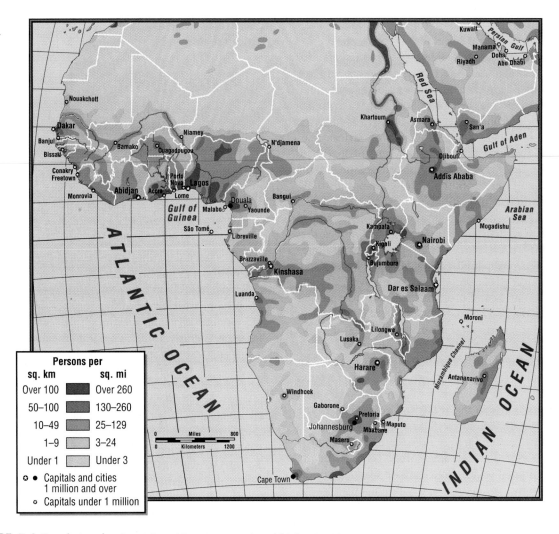

FIGURE 7.4 Population density. [Adapted from *Hammond World Atlas,* 1996.]

Defining Density

To some extent, whether population is dense or sparse depends on a region's carrying capacity. **Carrying capacity** refers to the maximum number of people a given territory can support sustainably with food, water, and other essential resources. There are several environmental factors that affect the carrying capacities of African lands. In some persistently arid places, the shortage of water limits the possibilities for cultivation or grazing. In some persistently wet places, the leached soils cannot sustain long-term cultivation. Some places with alternating wet and dry seasons may be able to support fairly dense populations, provided people have devised ways to use land and water sustainably. Some otherwise useful African ecological zones are not fully inhabited because they harbor diseases like sleeping sickness (borne by tsetse flies) and malaria (mosquito-borne).

Ultimately, the carrying capacity of any place is affected by cultural, social, economic, and political fac-

tors rather than just simple physical features. For example, in most of Africa, people are largely dependent on the local agricultural carrying capacity of the land for a subsistence living. In such cases, many fewer people can be adequately supported than would be the case if there were sufficient wealth to purchase food, building materials, industrial raw materials, and so forth from elsewhere. Think of an American suburban family of four on a half-acre lot, supporting themselves on the adults' salaries of between $50,000 and $100,000. In some of the poorest parts of Africa, rural densities actually exceed American suburban densities by a good bit. But the Africans must live off their land, whereas American suburbanites do not depend on their lawns and flower gardens for subsistence. A typical rural African family of seven or eight subsists almost entirely on 0.4 hectare (about 1 acre) of land, often with no reliable outside source of cash. In trying to understand Africa's difficulties, it is good to remind ourselves that we in wealthy societies (Europe, North America,

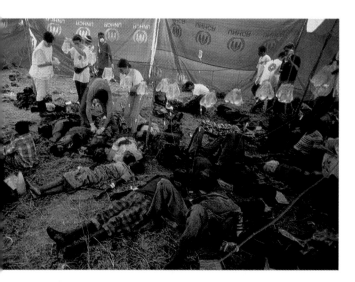

Exhausted and dehydrated Rwandan refugees receive emergency rehydration therapy at a refugee camp in Zaire run by the United Nations High Commission for Refugees. [Courtesy of UNHCR.]

Australia, Japan) tap into resources across the globe (including Africa), often at prices that are favorable to us. Hence, our standard of living is only partially linked to the carrying capacity of our own environments. For this reason, we can live in cities that are both dense and affluent. On the other hand, the vast majority of people in Africa, like many in Asia and in Central and South America, have much less access to resources in distant lands; this is because, for a variety of reasons, they are not able to generate the necessary political power or cash to acquire them.

Unusual circumstances may place additional burdens on a given carrying capacity. For example, war or oppression often creates refugees. Over the last decade of the twentieth century, in such places as Somalia, Ethiopia, Uganda, Liberia, Sierra Leone, Rwanda, and Mozambique, refugees have poured back and forth across borders in panic to escape **genocide**—the deliberate destruction of an ethnic, racial, or political group—instigated by rival political factions. According to the Population Reference Bureau (1998), the African continent has about half the world's refugee population (including persons displaced within a country). Official figures, however, are well below the actual numbers. Demographers estimate that about three-quarters of these refugees are women and children. As horrible as is the burden for the refugees, the burden for the country of refuge is also severe. Even with help from international agencies, the hosts find their own development plans derailed by the arrival of so many distressed people, who must be fed, sheltered, and given health care. Large portions of economic aid to Africa have

been diverted to deal with the emergency needs of refugees.

Population Growth

African populations are growing faster than any others on earth (Figure 7.5). In the last 47 years, the population of Africa south of the Sahara has more than tripled, reaching nearly 624 million in 1998. This rapid growth is the main threat to human well-being in places where the carrying capacity has already been reached or exceeded. In some places, Africa's already low standards of living are actually declining further. The addition of ever more individuals to feed and educate and house and vaccinate and eventually employ is outstripping even the best efforts to improve nutrition, education, housing, health care, and employment possibilities. UN projections for sub-Saharan Africa show the number of primary school students (aged 6–11) increasing, from 76.9 million in 1985 to 144.2 million in 2005 and to 195.3 million in 2025.

The geographer Ezekiel Kalipeni has found that people across Africa are not yet choosing to have smaller families because they view children as an essential and age-old link between the past and the future. Childlessness is a tragedy. Not only do children ensure a family's genetic and spiritual survival, they still do much of the work on family farms; and in a region of

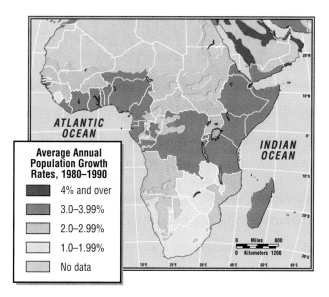

FIGURE 7.5 As a whole, Africa's population is growing at nearly twice the world average; death rates are declining and fertility is only in slow decline. The impact of AIDS, however, will be to reduce growth rates in several countries over the next decade (see Figure 7.6). [Adapted from Farzaneh Roudi and Lori Ashford, *Men and Family Planning in Africa* (Washington, DC: Population Reference Bureau, 1996), p. 3.]

323

high infant death rates, parents produce many offspring in hopes of raising a few to maturity. In short, in most places in Africa, the demographic transition—the sharp decline in births that usually accompanies economic development—is not yet happening. But in a handful of countries—Kenya, South Africa, Namibia, Zimbabwe, and Botswana—circumstances have changed sufficiently to make smaller families desirable. First, in these few places, education of women has improved and gender role restrictions have been relaxed a bit (as measured by the United Nations Gender Empowerment Measure); hence, women are choosing to use contraception because they have options beyond motherhood. Second, because infant mortality is now relatively low, parents can expect their two or three children to live to adulthood.

VIGNETTE

Mary, a Kenyan farmer, has just had her third son. Mary's mate and father of her children works in a distant city and visits the family only several weeks a year. He uses his earnings to support himself and to buy occasional nonessentials for the family. Mary tells an interviewer that three children are sufficient for happiness and so today, at age 29, she is having her tubes tied. She has only one cow and a small piece of land that can't be further divided, so all she can give her kids is an education. Mary says that she won't be able to afford to educate more than three. Such attitudes are spreading in Kenya, where population is growing so fast that there is not sufficient food, health care, or work. Mary is planning to augment her farm income through entrepreneurial activity. She has applied recently for a small loan (U.S. $150) to start a sanitary-pit toilet business. The success of her business could mean not only that her children will become well educated but also that she herself will gain prestige and, as the mother of a relatively small family, become a role model. [Adapted from Jeffrey Goldberg, *New York Times Magazine*, March 2, 1997, p. 39; and *World Resources*, 1996–97, p. 5.]

A number of factors have proved to be active in reducing family size in any culture. The longer people put off having sex, the fewer children they will have; and the more education parents have, the fewer children they will desire. Communication between husband and wife turns out to be especially crucial; surveys reveal men often actually wish they had fewer children, and if encouraged they would suggest birth control to their wives.

Breast-feeding biologically retards fertility, and in some African ethnic groups it is the custom to abstain from sex for several years after a birth. On the other hand, polygamous relationships, which are rather common in parts of Africa (see the section on gender relationships), produce more children than monogamies. Perhaps a certain competition is set up between the wives. In addition, men who choose polygamy tend to be less well educated and to be especially interested in having lots of children as a status symbol, children traditionally being a source of wealth.

Settlement Patterns, Rural and Urban

Sub-Saharan Africa is a rural region. Over 70 percent of the population still live in village settings, making it and South Asia by far the most rural areas in the world. There are thousands of versions of the African village, with many different house types and schemes for village arrangement, all depending on the cultural heritage of the inhabitants. But there are some constants in African villages. People usually live in extended family compounds, consisting of several houses arranged around a common space in which most activities take place. Sometimes these compounds stand alone in a dispersed pattern across an agricultural landscape; sometimes they are compactly grouped with other compounds and surrounded by family-designated fields. Villages, and the compounds that make them up, are economic units, with agricultural labor carefully apportioned by custom.

VIGNETTE

African villages usually have a head. In some cultures, the head is autocratic; in others, decisions are reached through consensus. Traditionally, the head has looked after both the civic and the spiritual well-being of the community. Twenty-two-year-old Chief Sinqobile Mabhena succeeded her father as head of the Ndebele village of Nswazi in Zimbabwe in December 1996. Her father suggested her as his successor before he died, and she was the villagers' choice. Nonetheless, there was strong opposition from those who objected to a woman sitting in judgment of men accused of wrongdoing, or becoming privy to the secret knowledge normally presided over by a chief. It took a year to iron out the difficulties. Among the items on the agenda at her first village meeting were a discussion of why rain has been sparse and how to cure the problem, who should receive more agricultural land, and who should be sent to a shrine to inform the ancestors that the old chief had died and she was taking his place.

As a teacher in a nearby college, Chief Mabhena has a number of educational goals for her village, including a new high school and a poultry cooperative. She does not see herself as a fighter for women's rights so much as a practitioner of them. When asked how she reconciles traditional beliefs that charms will bring rain or cure illness with her knowledge as a trained teacher, she says: "In every subject I teach, there must be an aspect of culture. The children need that. I am for [the charms] if [they] will improve things." [Adapted from Donald G. McNeil, Jr., *Zimbabwe tribal elders air a chief complaint*, New York Times, January 12, 1997, p. 1.]

Although village life remains the norm, in the late twentieth century African cities grew very fast indeed. The growth rate—more than 4 percent a year—exceeds even the rates of Asian and Latin American cities, which are about 3 percent and 2.5 percent, respectively. In the 1960s, only 15 percent of Africans south of the Sahara lived in cities; now about 30 percent do. The cities have attracted such massive migration for at least two reasons. Life in rural villages and towns offers little in terms of jobs and upward mobility, while cities beckon because of the widely held misconception that life there offers quick access to money and prestige.

As is often the case in developing countries, most African countries have one very large city, usually the capital, which attracts virtually all migration. (The primate city phenomenon is discussed on pages 121 and 481.) For example, Kampala, Uganda, is almost 10 times the size of the next largest city in that country. The population of another typical primate city,

Kinshasa in Zaire/Congo, has soared from 450,000 in 1960 to a projected 4.35 million in 2000. Lagos, Nigeria, had a population of 230,000 in 1950 but will be 48 times bigger in 2000. Such rapid and concentrated urbanization within a country means that the urban infrastructure—housing, sewage treatment, schools, utilities, and transport—is overwhelmed. Typically, governments have paid little attention to the housing needs of the throngs of poor urban migrants. Most migrants have had to construct their own shanties on illegally occupied land, using what would be discarded as trash in North America, Europe, or Japan. They live in vast squatter settlements surrounding the older urban centers. Transport in such huge and shapeless settlements is a jumble of government bus routes and private vehicles that ply no fixed route. Individuals often have to travel long hours to reach distant jobs. They spend a good deal of their travel time moving at a snail's pace through extremely congested traffic.

Public Health Issues

Africa's greatest public health issue is the HIV/AIDS epidemic now building in a large number of countries. By 1996, Africa had an estimated 66 percent of the then worldwide total of 30 million HIV-positive cases (Figure 7.6). Among the wealthiest countries on earth, less than 0.1 percent of the adult population is infected with HIV/AIDS. In North America, the figure is 1.9 percent; but in Botswana and Zambia, for example, 25 percent of the adults are infected, and in Uganda 14 percent. The disease threatens to change population growth and life expectancy patterns drastically across the continent. For example, in Zimbabwe, an estimated 900,000—nearly 25 percent of the adult population—were infected with

The closely packed houses in a shantytown near downtown Lagos, Nigeria, leave little room for ventilation in the tropical heat. The dwellings surround a parking lot for the cars of office workers.
[L. Gilbert/Sygma.]

325

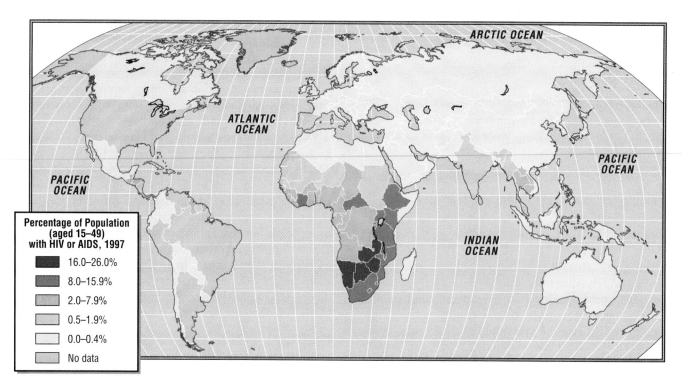

FIGURE 7.6 Africa contains the countries with the highest percentage of people ages 15 to 49 infected with HIV or suffering from AIDS. [Adapted from *New York Times,* June 24, 1998, p. 1.]

HIV in 1994. According to a Population Reference Bureau report issued in 1997, AIDS will probably reduce life expectancy there from the 1997 level of 51 to just 33 by the year 2010. Had HIV/AIDS not occurred, Zimbabwe could have achieved a life expectancy of 69.9 by 2010; instead, the rate may fall to what it was 200 years ago. Zimbabwe's population growth rate was already dropping quickly in the mid-1990s, primarily in response to rising standards of living; now HIV/AIDS is expected to actually reduce the total population. Zimbabwe is estimated to have a negative growth rate of −0.5 by 2010. The demographic effects of HIV/AIDS are expected to be comparably dramatic in such countries as Uganda, Nigeria, Kenya, Burkina Faso, Rwanda, Zaire, Tanzania, Ethiopia, and South Africa.

In Africa, AIDS is a heterosexual phenomenon: four-fifths of the world's women with AIDS are in Africa. Many of them are young mothers infected by their husbands, who may visit sex workers when they travel for work or business. In some cities, literally 100 percent of the sex workers are infected. In Uganda, one-quarter of married urban women, who are normally considered at low risk, are HIV-positive. Because AIDS manifests itself slowly in its victims, controlling the epidemic is particularly difficult. UN officials suspect that 90 percent of African carriers of HIV do not learn they have been infected until several years have passed.

During this time, they may produce infected children and pass the disease to several other adults. The overwhelming majority of infected Africans cannot afford the costly combination of drugs that keeps victims alive in places like North America, Europe, and Japan.

The present rapid spread of HIV/AIDS in Africa is related to many circumstances, which, in turn, are related to rapid urbanization. With the improvement in transportation between cities and the countryside, bus and truck drivers are thought to be major spreaders of the disease, helped along by urban migrants coming home for visits. In today's mobile urban world, young men and women encounter each other more often without the community pressure that would have precluded intimacy in the past. Women are often subjected to coerced sex, and have great difficulty insisting that their mates use condoms. Men tend to feel that it is their prerogative to have multiple partners. A popular belief is that only sex with a mature woman can cause AIDS, so very young girls are increasingly sought out as sex partners. For many poor women, occasional sex work is part of what they do to survive economically.

Is AIDS nature's diabolical plot to reduce Africa's population? Demographers predict that in the end, the total population will only be about 5 percent lower than it would have been without AIDS (Figure 7.7).

**Effect of AIDS on (A) Population Growth and
(B) Life Expectancy in Sub-Saharan Africa, 2010**

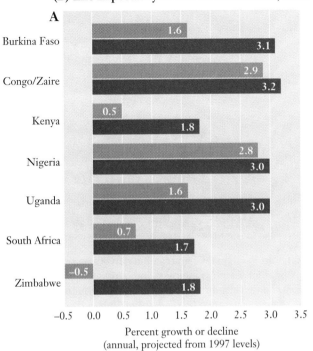

A

Percent growth or decline
(annual, projected from 1997 levels)

With AIDS

Without AIDS

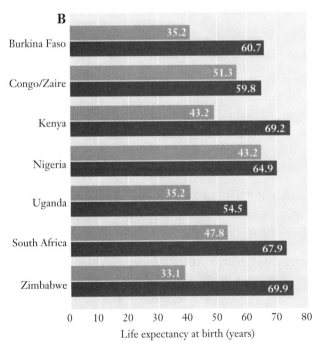

B

Life expectancy at birth (years)

FIGURE 7.7 By 2010, in sub-Saharan Africa, AIDS is expected to reduce both population growth and life expectancy in many countries. [Adapted from S. Jay Olshansky et al., Infectious diseases—New and ancient threats to world health, *Population Bulletin*, 52, no. 2 (July 1997): 20.]

But the social consequences are enormous. Young adults, parents, teachers, and trained professionals are lost in the prime of their lives to a slow, agonizing death. Elderly grandparents have to provide for orphaned dependent children (who may also be infected). Time, money, and energy are being channeled to HIV/AIDS treatment and away from education and from the control of other diseases like schistosomiasis. This parasitic affliction, spread by organisms that breed in standing fresh water (like that associated with dam and irrigation projects), now affects as many as 10 percent of Africans; it leaves them listless, often unable to work, and susceptible to other infections. Malaria, river blindness, cholera, and the Ebola virus are other serious and life-threatening infectious and parasitic diseases that are being neglected in the wake of AIDS.

CURRENT GEOGRAPHIC ISSUES

As we have learned, after the year 1500, Europeans reorganized African social and economic institutions and human/environment relationships, first via the slave trade and then through colonization. Because the effects of the colonial era in Africa run deep, in many cases it is too soon to tell just how African countries will find ways to become socially, economically, and politically viable. Still, many researchers are optimistic about the future. A broad consensus is developing that Africa's prospects will improve if development policies give Africans the power to seek their own solutions.

Sociocultural Issues

It is impossible to generalize about the African continent because there are so many environments, political systems, and ethnic groups. The following selection of cultural issues is meant only as a sample of what one might study further. And in each case, the discussion gives only one or two perspectives when there may be dozens or hundreds.

Traditional village life, both material and spiritual, has adapted to influences first from the Muslim north and then from European colonizers. Religious traditions in Africa are often an interesting blend of indigenous practices and Islamic or Christian traditions. Colonialism had a devastating impact on family structure and gender roles, as men increasingly had to stop participating in village agriculture, and it became primarily the women's responsibility. Now urban life has added new challenges to traditional African ways of living.

Religion

Religion plays a particularly active role in African daily life. The region's rich and complex religious traditions derive from three main strains: the indigenous belief systems, and two systems of belief introduced from outside, Islam and Christianity. Hinduism is a third introduced religion, but its impact is felt primarily in spots along Africa's east coast and on the coastal islands, where there are significant East Indian or mixed African-Indian populations.

Indigenous Belief Systems.   Traditional African religions have probably the most ancient heritage of any on earth. African beliefs and rituals seek to bring the vast host of departed ancestors into contact with people now alive, who, in turn, are the connecting links in a timeless community that stretches into the future. The future is reached only if present family members procreate and in other ways perpetuate the family heritage. The people in a living community are usually led by a powerful man, or occasionally a powerful woman, who combines the roles of politician, patriarch or matriarch, and spiritual leader.

According to traditional African beliefs, the spirits of the deceased are all around, in trees and streams and art objects. In return for respect (expressed through ritual), these spirits offer protection from life's vicissitudes and from the ill will of others. Rosalind Hackett, a scholar of African religions and art, writes that "African religions are far more pragmatically oriented than Western religions, being concerned with explaining, predicting and controlling misfortune, sickness and accidents. [They give believers a way] to make sense of and act upon adverse forces in their public and private lives." African religions remain fluid and adaptable to changing circumstances. Osun, the god of water, long credited with healing powers, is now invoked also for those suffering economic woes caused by structural adjustment measures imposed by the International Monetary Fund.

Religious beliefs in Africa are not static, but continually evolve as new influences are encountered. Hence, if Africans convert to another religion, they commonly retain parts of their indigenous religious heritage and blend them with aspects of the new faith, creating a new entity—a process sometimes erroneously referred to as syncretism (Figure 7.8). From such a blending of Roman Catholicism and African beliefs in the Americas there developed new belief systems known as Voodou in Haiti or Obeah in Jamaica, Condomble in Brazil, and more recently Santeria in Cuba, Puerto Rico, and North America. Missionaries of the established churches—Roman Catholic, Episcopal, Baptist, and so

Coffin art in Ghana. Ghana's coffin carvers accomplish an apparent seamless interweaving of religion, art, and modern life. They are experts at artistically interpreting the life of the deceased: a Mercedes Benz for a chauffeur, a plane for a pilot, a boat for a fishing fleet captain. The coffin carver's art is highly sought after by rich and poor, who may commission a coffin long before death comes, often spending their life savings to buy a niche in the cultural memory of the community. [Carol Beckwith and Angela Fisher/Robert Estall Photo Library, UK.]

forth—often refused to allow Africans to incorporate their folk beliefs. This rejection helped to spawn independent, charismatic Christian sects that suited African needs for religions which represented their culture and their experience, rather than those of Europe or America. These independent churches have given rise to the "gospel of success" churches now growing so quickly in Africa (see the box "The Gospel of Success").

Islam and Christianity in Africa.   Islam began to extend into Africa south of the Sahara, especially in East Africa, soon after Muhammad's death in 632. As Figure 7.8 shows, Islam is now the predominant religion throughout North Africa and in much of West and East Africa, including the coastal zone along the Indian Ocean where Islamic traders were especially active. When the British entered East Africa to colonize it in the late 1800s, they obtained the help of Islamic leaders in administering the countryside and towns, especially in the drier northern areas. The descendants of these Islamic administrators are still politically powerful in Nigeria and some other parts of West Africa.

Christianity spread into sub-Saharan Africa to a significant degree, starting in the nineteenth century, when Methodist missionaries became active along the coast of West Africa. Today, Christianity is prevalent

AT THE REGIONAL SCALE   *The Gospel of Success*

We first encountered the "gospel of success" in Chapter 3 on Middle and South America. In Africa, this adaptable version of evangelical Christianity melds certain aspects of Christianity and capitalism with the Central and West African beliefs in the importance of sacrificial gifts to ancestors and in miracles. The message is simple. According to preachers like those at the Miracle Center in Kinshasa, Zaire/Congo: "The Bible says that God will materially aid those who give to Him. . . . We are not only a church, we are an enterprise. In our traditional culture you have to make a sacrifice to powerful forces if you want to get results. It is the same here." The supplicants accept the message that generous gifts to such churches will bring divine intervention in their miseries, whether physical or spiritual. They donate food, television sets, clothing, and money—one woman gave three months' salary in the hope that God would find her a new husband. The collection plates are large plastic bags. By combining spiritual ministration with a touch of hucksterism, the leaders of this largely urban movement receive the respect and adulation Africans used to reserve for rural village leaders.

Like all religious belief systems, the gospel of success is probably best understood within its cultural context. Many of the believers, new to the city, feel bereft

Worshipers at the Miracle Center in Kinshasa, Zaire/Congo. [Robert Grossman/Sygma.]

and are seeking a supportive community to replace that left behind. Material dues are viewed as not that far removed from the labor and goods previously donated to maintain one's standing in a village compound.

---

along the coast of West Africa and in Central and Southern Africa; and Christians are an important minority or the majority in much of East Africa. Colonial administrators in the British-held territories discouraged missionaries from going north into Muslim territory because Islamic leaders were already aiding the colonization process. Christian missionaries in Central and Southern Africa found a useful niche as providers of the education and health services that colonial administrators had neglected. Very recently, old-line established churches have begun doing particularly well in East and West Africa. The Church of England (Anglican) has been growing so rapidly in Kenya, Uganda, and Nigeria that by 2000 there will be more Anglicans in these countries than in the United Kingdom. African Anglicans appear to favor a conservative stance on social issues—they are against women priests and the acceptance of homosexuals—but they are often liberal on economic issues. For example, in 1998, African Anglican bishops persuaded the world-

wide Anglican Communion to oppose holding the world's poor countries to crippling debt payments. The Anglican Church in Africa appeals to the educated urban middle class, whereas modern evangelical versions of Christianity are gaining ground among less educated, more recent urban migrants (see the box "The Gospel of Success").

Gender Relationships in Work and Reproduction

All the evidence points to long-standing African traditions of fairly strict division of labor and responsibilities between men and women. The exact allocation by gender of work and power and family wealth varies from subregion to subregion; overall, however, women are responsible for domestic activities, including bearing and caring for children, caring for the sick and elderly, and caring for the house. They do about 90 percent of the water carrying and 80 percent of collecting

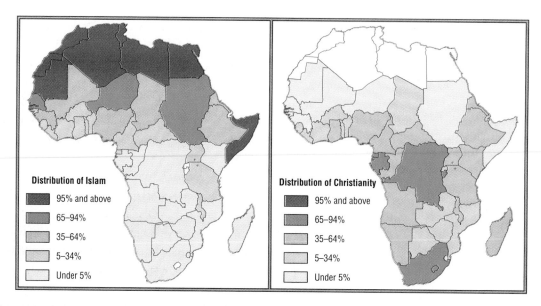

FIGURE 7.8 Traditional belief systems persist in varying degrees across Africa, even in those areas that are heavily Muslim or Christian. As others elsewhere in the world have done, many African peoples have integrated traditional beliefs and practices with Islam and Christianity. [Adapted from Robert Stock, *Africa South of the Sahara—A Geographic Interpretation* (New York: Guilford Press, 1995), p. 50.]

firewood; and they produce and prepare nearly all food. Labor studies show that women handle about 50 percent of the care of livestock, and that where there are small agricultural surpluses or handcrafted items to trade, women transport and sell them in the market. Throughout Africa, married couples tend to keep separate accounts and manage their earnings as individuals, so when a wife sells her husband's produce at market, she will usually give the proceeds to him for his use.

Men are normally responsible for preparing all land for cultivation, a job that entails clearing, burning, and turning the soil. In the fields intended to produce food for family use, women take over the sowing, weeding, and general tending as well as the harvesting and processing of the crops. In those fields where cash crops are grown, men perform most of the work. Women may help with weeding and harvesting these fields, but it is usually understood that any earnings belong to the man. In cases where husbands, in search of cash income, have migrated to work in the mines or in urban jobs, women take over nearly all agricultural work. Studies have shown that women are the majority of agricultural laborers in Africa and contribute about 70 percent of the total time spent on African agriculture. They tend to work with few labor-saving devices, and during their reproductive years often do field labor with a child strapped on their backs.

At least in rural areas, African men, on average, do not have as many responsibilities as women, nor do they work as hard or for as many hours. The reasons

why are complicated. Many African men are extremely hardworking and labor under tremendous hardships, including unusually long commutes. Nonetheless, as the geographer Robert Stock observes, rural African women not only have the "double day" that women in industrial societies have, but a "double double day," in that so much of their work entails backbreaking physical labor and time-consuming treks for water and fuel.

The retreat of men from virtually all activities related to supporting domestic life seems to have started with European colonialism. At that time, men became increasingly engaged in cash-earning activities, as laborers or as cash-crop cultivators. At first, this was in order to meet the colonial administration requirement that taxes be paid in currency; later it was to pay for school fees, basic electricity, certain consumer goods, and even food, when access to land was lost due to agricultural modernization. European Christians colonized Africa during the Victorian era, when the prevailing idea in Europe was that women were lesser creatures who should remain in the home and have their affairs managed by husbands. This idea facilitated the colonial policy in Africa of recruiting men for cultivating cash crops and doing work for wages, while leaving women to shoulder all the domestic work as well as what had formerly been the shared work of subsistence agriculture.

In the precolonial past, there were social controls that tempered the effects of male domination over women's lives. Most marriages were social alliances be-

330

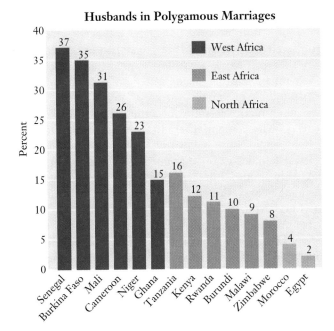

Husbands in Polygamous Marriages

FIGURE 7.9 Polygyny is less common in East Africa than in West Africa, and uncommon in Southern African families. [Adapted from Farzaneh Roudi and Lori Ashford, *Men and Family Planning in Africa* (Washington, DC: Population Reference Bureau, 1996), p. 7.]

tween families; therefore, husbands and wives spent most of their time doing their tasks with family members of their own sex rather than with each other. Traditional gender relationships were modified wherever Muslim culture first and European Christian culture later were introduced into Africa south of the Sahara. In most cases, it seems that the power of men increased and women lost options. The Muslim proviso that women be restricted to domestic spaces deprived them of autonomy and the power to move about, seize opportunities, trade in the markets, and so forth. In Islamic Africa, the strong patriarchy and the practice of **polygyny**—the taking by a man of more than one wife at a time—leave many lesser wives in servitude, with few legal rights. It should be noted that having multiple wives is actually much more common in Africa south of the Sahara than it is in North Africa. This is because the custom of polygyny predates Islam by a good bit. Nonetheless, as Figure 7.9 shows, even in Africa those who practice polygyny are a minority.

VIGNETTE

The majority of women in West Africa and elsewhere on the continent adhere to traditional roles like those just described. They are married often by age 15, after which point they have little freedom and enormous responsibilities. But some young urban women are establishing what may become a pattern indicative of the future. The anthropologist Miriam Goheen includes the following stories (paraphrased here) among those of many educated, self-supporting young women in Cameroon, who are choosing not to marry until and if they find the right "modern" man who shares their ambitions and their convictions that husbands and wives should share everything equally.

Ida is a vibrant, outgoing woman in her mid-20s with a hearty laugh and a quick intelligence. Her father is a wealthy businessman who has married several wives. Ida lives with her mother in her grandfather's busy and hospitable compound in a small city. She has finished secondary school and worked for the coffee cooperative for two years. Now she is an assistant in a community development office where she is known for her competence. Well connected, Ida has become active in local women's politics. She has just had her second child and chooses to say little about the father(s) of her children. She jokes about the competencies of men, or rather the lack thereof, and treats them in the same warm, offhand, friendly but firm manner that she treats her four-year-old son. "While she clearly enjoys the company of men, she doesn't seem intent on marrying in the near future."

Mary lives with her father and two younger siblings in the town of Kimbo', works long hours at the hospital, and is a primary source of income for the family. She says she is determined in her decision not to marry in the traditional manner (monogamously or polygynously) and become subservient to the man of the household. Arriving home from work, she sinks into an overstuffed chair in the living room of her father's compound, rubs her feet, and calls for her young son to fetch a Fanta (a brand of soft drink). With a quiet intensity, she defends her decision not to be married unless she finds a compatible well-educated mate . . . until then she will just stay as she is and raise her son in her father's family. In the late afternoon she joins her younger sisters in the kitchen, where they will prepare the evening meal and share the daily gossip. [Adapted from Miriam Goheen, *Men Own the Fields, Women Own the Crops* (Madison: University of Wisconsin Press, 1996), pp. 187–189.]

It is important to note that the middle-class women described in the vignettes are the rare women with sufficient education and social standing to reject millennia-old gender roles. The prosperous extended families of these young women have made it possible for them to elude the storm of disgrace that would meet a poor rural woman who gave birth out of wedlock. This author's fieldwork (1993) among middle-class women in the West Indies indicates that the same pattern of professional women choosing single parenthood is already well established there. Again, the women who are able to achieve, despite (they might say *because of*) single parenthood, almost always have the backing of several strong older women in the family who give guidance on many levels and help with child care.

Female Genital Excision

A perplexing practice is widespread in at least 27 countries throughout the central portion of the African continent (Figure 7.10). Known as female circumcision, the practice actually amounts to the removal, usually without anesthesia, of the labia and the clitoris (to do away with the possibility of sexual stimulation) and often the stitching nearly shut of the vulva (infibulation). All these actions, done in part or in total, result in the irremediable removal of a healthy organ; many physicians therefore refer to the practice as **female genital mutilation.** The custom, which was reported by

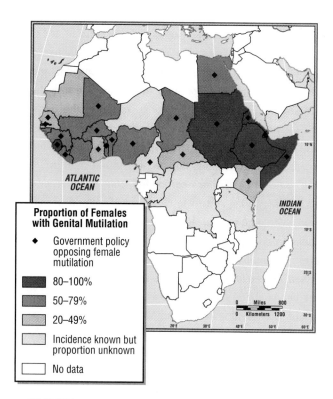

Proportion of Females with Genital Mutilation

♦ Government policy opposing female mutilation

■ 80–100%

■ 50–79%

■ 20–49%

□ Incidence known but proportion unknown

□ No data

FIGURE 7.10 Female genital mutilation occurs all across the center of the African continent in spite of government policies against the practice. [Adapted from Joni Seager, *The State of Women in the World: An International Atlas* (London: Penguin, 1997), p. 53.]

Herodotus in 500 B.C., predates Islam and is practiced by some Muslims, Christians, and followers of traditional religions. It is probably linked to efforts to ensure that a female is a virgin when married (hence not pregnant by another male), but there are many complex symbolic meanings.

The practice has now become the focus of a controversial movement to eradicate it. In some culture groups, such as the Kikuyu of Kenya, nearly 100 percent of females were "circumcised" 40 years ago; today, only about 40 percent of Kikuyu schoolgirls have been. It is now thought that as many as 130 million girls and women presently living in Africa have undergone the procedure (2 million a year, 6000 per day). The practice also takes place surreptitiously among African émigrés in Europe, North America, and elsewhere. For those who have undergone female genital excision, urination and menstruation are difficult, intercourse painful, and childbirth particularly devastating, because the scarred flesh is inelastic. Many African and world leaders, men and women, have concluded that the practice constitutes an extreme human rights abuse; but because the custom is deeply ingrained in value systems, the most successful eradication campaigns have emphasized the threat posed to a woman's health. Beyond the debilitating side effects just mentioned, recent research shows that the practice leaves women exceptionally susceptible to HIV infection.

There is another side to the story. Defenders of the custom refer to its symbolic importance as ritual purification; and often girls who have not undergone excision are considered unclean and unmarriageable. The *New York Times* reporter Celia W. Dugger writes of interviewing a 12-year-old in Côte d'Ivoire, who said that more than anything she wants to be "cut down there," gesturing to her lap. All her friends have had it done, and afterward they are showered with gifts and money and there is a huge celebration for relatives and friends. The father of the child said if he did not have it done, he would not be allowed to speak in village meetings and no man would marry her. Nonetheless, the child's mother, who has undergone excision, says she hates the custom because it deprives a woman of sexual sensitivity.

Ethnicity and Language

Robert Stock writes that in Africa it is better to use the term **ethnicity** to refer to culturally distinct groups rather than *tribe* and *tribalism*, which for too long have been used to connote primitive feuding. Ethnicity refers to the shared language, cultural traditions, and political and economic institutions of a group. The term does not refer to race or color, only to culture. Most ethnic groups have a core territory in which they

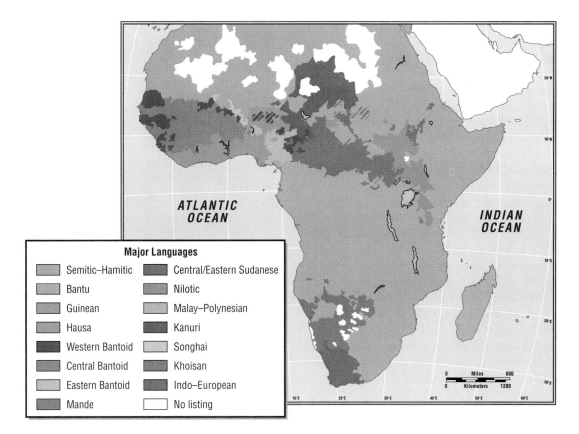

Major Languages

- Semitic–Hamitic
- Bantu
- Guinean
- Hausa
- Western Bantoid
- Central Bantoid
- Eastern Bantoid
- Mande
- Central/Eastern Sudanese
- Nilotic
- Malay–Polynesian
- Kanuri
- Songhai
- Khoisan
- Indo–European
- No listing

FIGURE 7.11 Major languages of Africa. [Adapted from Edward F. Bergman and William H. Renwick, *Introduction to Geography—People, Places, and Environment* (Englewood Cliffs, NJ: Prentice Hall, 1999), p. 256.]

have traditionally lived; but very rarely do groups occupy discrete and exclusive spaces. Often, several groups will share a space, perhaps practicing different but complementary ways of life and using different resources. For example, one ethnic group might be subsistence cultivators, another might be animal herders on adjacent grasslands, and a third group craft specialists working as weavers or smiths. People can share ethnic identity but have little in common culturally; for example, in Kenya, Kikuyu villagers and Kikuyu urbanites who reside in Nairobi live very different lives. In other cases, people may be very similar culturally but identify themselves as being from different ethnic groups; for example, Hutu and Tutsi cattle farmers in Rwanda share an occupation and similar ways of life but think of themselves as very different in ethnicity. Some countries in Africa have only one or two ethnic groups; others, like Nigeria, Tanzania, and Cameroon, have many groups. Nigeria has three groups of about equal size: the Hausa, Igbo, and Yoruba, each with about 25 million people; but there are hundreds of smaller groups. The vast majority of African ethnic groups have peaceful and supportive relationships with each other.

Language is, to a large extent, correlated with ethnicity. More than a thousand languages, falling into more than a hundred language groups (Figure 7.11), are spoken in Africa. Some are spoken by only a few dozen people, others, like Hausa, by several million. Language use is always in flux, so some African languages are now dying out. They are being replaced by those that suit people's needs better, or at least have become politically dominant. Increasingly a few **lingua francas** (languages of trade) are taking over: Swahili and Arabic in East Africa, Hausa in West Africa. In addition, the former colonial languages of English and French are widely used in commerce, education, and technology.

Economic and Political Issues

Africa cannot continue to produce what it does not consume and consume what it does not produce.
    —*Ali Mazrui,* The Africans

Sub-Saharan Africa faces one of the most serious economic crises it has ever experienced. After years of declining output and shrinking economies, most Africans are poorer today than they were in the 1960s. Moreover, the value of the region's output as a whole is tiny in comparison to the output of more technologically advanced areas. Today, some 600 million sub-Saharan Africans produce commercially exchanged goods and services worth about as much as those produced by the 16 million people of the Netherlands. (This figure does not include many aspects of the African informal economy.) In part, Africa's economic crisis is a result of its precarious position in the world economy as an exporter of raw materials—chiefly agricultural products and minerals—for which prices are low and unstable. Furthermore, many countries in Africa compete with each other by producing the same products. These patterns developed during the colonial era, when Africa supplied raw materials to European industries. An additional problem is that virtually overnight, technology can render African products obsolete, as was the case when synthetic fibers replaced copper in telephone systems.

Since independence, African governments have tried to reduce reliance on exports of raw materials, but most efforts have been unfruitful. Corruption and mistakes by African leaders have been partly to blame, and so have economic policies required by the international finance community. Africans are pursuing alternative strategies to strengthen their local and regional economies, but these efforts provide only partial solutions. The current crisis demands deep changes both in Africa and in its economic relations with the rest of the world.

Africa's political instability contributes to its economic problems. That instability is largely an outgrowth of the social disruptions and authoritarian legacies of colonialism, as well as interference related to the cold war. After decades of dictatorship, ethnic strife, and elite dominance, many African countries are experiencing a transition toward more democratic forms of government. Although Africa's democratic gains remain shallow and fragile, many hope that democracy will provide the stability needed for economic development.

Botswana: A Case Study

Since independence in 1966, Botswana has been touted as a rising economic star in Africa. The gross national product per capita was U.S. $69 in 1966; by 1997, it was U.S. $3020, second only in the southern part of Africa to South Africa (at U.S. $3160). More significantly, the nation's Human Development Index ranking is 71, the highest by far for Africa south of the Sahara. How is an arid, landlocked country able to prosper to this extent? To what extent does the general population share in the country's wealth?

Botswana's wealth is mineral based. Diamond deposits were found shortly after independence, and by

The Jwaneng mine in Botswana is one of the world's richest. The diamond-laden earth is loaded into trucks and taken to a treatment plant for crushing and sifting. The diamonds are then separated into industrial and gem-quality stones. [Peter Essick/Aurora and Quanta Productions.]

1995 Botswana was the world's third largest diamond producer and first in output value. The country also derives income from deposits of gold, soda ash and potash, copper, nickel, and coal. Diamonds are the mainstay, however, and account for over 63 percent of government revenues and 80 percent of export dollars. When such wealth is statistically apportioned among just 1.5 million people, the per capita gross national product (GNP) is understandably high by African standards.

The actual allocation of wealth in Botswana is uneven. Less than 1 percent of the people have become very wealthy, and perhaps as many as 20 percent have reasonably well paying positions in government or the mining industry. The remaining 80 percent work in agriculture, and most suffer dire poverty. The lot of the poor is made worse because some of the newly wealthy people have purchased productive land for large-scale cattle ranching. Owners of small farms who sell their land to cattle ranchers have more cash temporarily, but they are pushed onto less productive lands. As meat production (much of it is exported) has increased, overall food production has decreased. The country produces only 50 percent of the food needed to feed its population; the rest has to be imported, and one-third comes in as food aid. So even though there is an appearance of wealth, only a small percentage of the population does well. The vast majority are, if anything, less prosperous.

Botswana's experience illustrates some of the pitfalls of basing development on extractive activities and of measuring success by GNP per capita. Some African and outside observers are suggesting that development success be measured more by how the lives of the majority are improved, not by volume and value of exports.

Independence: The Difficulties of Change

After independence, the economies of most African countries still centered around the export of one or two raw materials, and this pattern has continued (Figure 7.12). Southern Africa exports a wide range of minerals and produces 27 percent of the world's gold and 50 percent of its platinum. West Africa exports oil (Nigeria) and produces about half of the world's cocoa beans, nearly all of which supply the European market. Peanuts and fish are other West African exports. East Africa exports small percentages of the world produc-

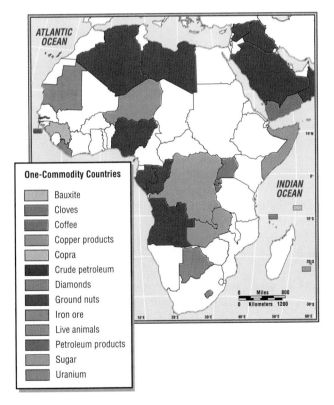

FIGURE 7.12 Most exports from African countries are shipped as raw materials (metallic ores and timber, for example) that require further processing and manufacturing before they become consumer products. And most countries have only between one and four of these primary products and hence are dependent on just a few finite resources. This map depicts those countries that depend on just one commodity for more than 50 percent of their export earnings. [Adapted from George Kurian, ed., *Atlas of the Third World* (New York: Facts on File, 1992), p. 76.]

tion of copra, oil palm, and soybeans; Central Africa exports some tropical hardwoods. At the time of independence, outsiders still owned African industries and invested the profits not in Africa but in Europe or America. Efforts to remedy this situation met with a mixture of success and failure. To increase its control over the economy, the government of Côte d'Ivoire entered into joint ventures with foreign companies as a majority partner. Kenya broke up coffee plantations formerly owned by Europeans and sold the land to small-scale coffee growers whose standard of living subsequently greatly improved. Other efforts were less successful. Socialist Ghana's large state-owned factories operated at only a fraction of their capacity. In socialist Tanzania, rural people were forced to resettle in semi-communal villages that were notoriously unproductive. Not even the successful efforts managed to alter fundamentally Africa's position in the world economy.

South Africa was an exception to the general pattern. This country managed to create a large and diversified economy, producing a total output that is today only slightly less valuable than the output of all other sub-Saharan African countries combined. A major factor in South Africa's success is that for centuries there has been a large European population with the skills and connections to foster economic development within that country. The colonial governments served the interests of the Dutch (Boer) and English settlers of South Africa more than they did those of black Africans; and in 1910, these settlers became the rulers of an independent South Africa. The country produced many lucrative local spin-off industries, such as the refining of minerals, gemstones, and metals from the country's rich mines. These spin-off enterprises kept more profits in the country, allowing the construction of a large industrial economy. Nonetheless, South Africa's small white minority enjoyed most of the profits. While a few black South Africans benefited from relatively high wages, the majority were exploited at least as ruthlessly as elsewhere on the continent.

The Current Economic Crisis

Sub-Saharan Africa's weak position in the world economy is more evident today than ever before. Global prices for its raw materials have been steadily falling for several decades, largely due to a glut of such materials. Production has increased within Africa and in relatively poor countries elsewhere, while the consumption of raw materials has failed to expand to meet supply. Meanwhile, prices have risen for imported manufactured goods, including the machinery required by mines and the fertilizers, special seeds, equipment, and pesticides required by modernizing farms and plantations. Most countries have found it increasingly difficult to pay back loans extended to them to pay for mechanized agriculture, small industries, hydroelectric plants, roads, and so forth.

In the early 1980s, the major international banks and financial institutions that had made the loans to African governments developed a plan to obtain repayment. Working through the World Bank and the International Monetary Fund, the lending institutions threatened to cut off all loans to the debtor countries unless they enacted specific packages of economic reform called structural adjustment programs (SAPs). SAPs try to increase government revenues by reducing state interference in the economy. The theory is that economies guided solely by free market mechanisms will better allocate investment money and resources, be more vibrant and entrepreneurial, and hence be able to produce more tax revenue with which to pay off the loans. To raise money, governments are also required to slash their own payrolls by cutting health care, education, training, and other social service programs.

SAPs have accomplished some good. They tightened up bookkeeping procedures and thereby curtailed corruption and waste in the bureaucracies. They cut the power of the elite to commandeer resources for their own profit. They did away with inefficient and corrupt state agencies that were cheating farmers in getting their crops to market. And they stopped the practice of capping food prices to appease urban dwellers, so that now local food producers receive fair prices for their crops and are encouraged to produce more. SAPs closed state-owned monopolies in industries and services; and they have opened up some sectors of the economy to medium- and small-scale entrepreneurs. They have also made tax collection more efficient. But they have made it harder for the poor majority to make a decent living and stay healthy, and they have failed to reduce the debt burden. The debt has continued to grow, despite the fact that the region as a whole is now spending more on debt payments than on all health care and education—more than U.S. $13 billion a year.

One reason the debt persists is that SAPs have generally eliminated more jobs than they have created. To maximize revenues and achieve greater efficiency, governments have sold off state-owned businesses to the private sector and removed protections for local industries. Both steps usually bring firings and layoffs. Additional jobs have been lost as large state bureaucracies have been significantly reduced. Contrary to SAP theory, foreign investment did not pour into Africa once the cuts had been made. Investors have been discouraged by problems that SAPs have either ignored or made worse: an undereducated work force, political instability, and poorly developed water, transport, health, and utilities infrastructures. The result has been rising unemployment, the descent of more than two-thirds of the population into poverty, and considerable social unrest. Foreign investment in Africa remains less than in any other world region. Only South Africa, which did not have to endure SAPs, has attracted significant investment.

Because the policies promoting structural adjustment are highly complex, we will look at their effects on a number of different aspects of sub-Saharan African societies, including agriculture, industry, and the informal economy. Then we will look at some of the alternatives to SAPs.

Agriculture

SAPs have especially affected the agriculture sector, which employs 70 percent or more of Africans in one way or another. The programs encourage the growing of export crops, such as cocoa, sugar, bananas, and oil palms, by lowering taxes on profits, decreasing government regulation, and providing loans for equipment and land. But at the same time, the profitability of food production for Africa's own use has been reduced in a number of ways. One way is through **currency devaluation,** a policy central to structural adjustment. This lowers the value of African currencies relative to the U.S. dollar, the Japanese yen, or other currencies of global trade. Devaluation promotes the sale of African export crops by making them cheaper relative to the world market, but it also makes all imports more expensive. Therefore, farmers who grow for the internal food market must spend much more on imported seeds, fertilizers, pesticides, and farm equipment. With the shift to export production, many farmers no longer have the time or space to grow their own food, so Africans as a whole must pay for expensive imported food instead. Meanwhile, SAPs have mandated production increases in so many competing countries that prices for agricultural export crops have come down, eroding farm incomes.

In some countries, land has deliberately been taken away from local people and turned over to foreign-owned export-agriculture ventures; this brings criticisms that SAPs are a return to colonial exploitation. For example, throughout Southern Africa (e.g., Zimbabwe, Zambia, Mozambique), wealthy white Afrikaner (of Dutch descent) plantation owners emigrating from South Africa have taken some of the best lands to set up large, technologically sophisticated fruit-growing and juice-processing facilities. In most cases, smaller-scale local farmers have lost access to land they were renting and have become laborers or sharecroppers on the new plantations. Here they are often paid little and must endure abusive treatment. Farmers who remain self-employed often find themselves displaced onto less productive marginal land.

SAPs encouraged large-scale forest clearing and the use of mechanized equipment, chemical fertilizers and pesticides, and often irrigation. These techniques produced some short-term gains, but for many farmers they became prohibitively expensive after SAP currency devaluations. They also proved to be of doubtful sustainability; in the high moisture and high humidity of many African environments, soils do not remain fertile under continuous use. Furthermore, agricultural scientists, with their European and U.S. backgrounds, missed the fact that in Africa women grow most of the food for family consumption. Hence, they did not consult women or include them in development projects, except possibly as field laborers. The displacement of women from the land and the focus on cash crops had an unforeseen consequence. Between 1961 and 1995, per capita food production in Africa declined by 12 percent; it is thus the only region on earth where people are eating less well than they used to.

The overwhelming emphasis that SAPs place on the energy- and resource-intensive farming techniques common in the United States and Europe flies in the face of growing evidence that indigenous African farming techniques are more sustainable and better adapted to African conditions. In Nigeria, Dr. Bede Okigbo, a botanist at the International Institute of Tropical Agriculture (IITA) in Ibadan, was eventually able to make aid officials hear what he had long known to be true: that traditional farmers (many of them women), growing complex tropical gardens, were actually skilled systems analysts who could successfully cultivate 50 or more species of plants at one time, sustainably producing more than enough food for their families on a continual basis. "At IITA we were working at a much simpler level than the local farmer," says Okigbo. "We [could only advise] about one or two systems, while they had to deal with something far more complex."

Industry

Africa's debt crisis was in part triggered by attempts prompted by the World Bank to develop industries for export rather than domestic markets. For example, in the 1980s, in Tanzania, the World Bank financed a shoe factory that was to use Tanzania's large supply of animal hides to manufacture high-fashion shoes for the European market. Machines for this type of footwear had to be imported at high cost; but due to a host of miscalculations, the factory never managed to produce suitable shoes for Europe. The machines were incapable of producing shoes Africans would care to wear, even though the market for good shoes in Africa is huge. The unused factory deteriorated, but Tanzania was still expected to repay the cost to the World Bank.

The trend toward export-oriented industry was furthered in other ways. For example, SAP policies encouraged the massive Maputo Corridor highway project between South Africa and Mozambique. This road connects mainly ports, plantations, and mines, bypassing local communities whose farm-to-market roads remain in disrepair. In Ghana, foreign-owned mining companies are taking land away from local farmers and pushing out the small-scale mining sector, diverting money away from local economies. In the textile industries of Tanzania, Zimbabwe, and Uganda, SAP-inspired reductions in tariffs on foreign textiles from Asia have led to factory closings and massive job losses. Throughout Africa, currency devaluations have made imported equipment and spare parts for locally focused industries prohibitively expensive.

Whether export-oriented manufacturing industries can succeed is uncertain. The rich industrialized countries place tariffs on African manufactured goods such as footwear and clothing, so Africa lacks access to prosperous, stable markets. Instead, it is often assumed that Africa should sell its products to other poor regions where markets are highly unstable. All in all, the various strategies dictated by SAPs have resulted in hardship for Africa's working people: lower wages, lost jobs, lost social services, deteriorating working conditions. For many, the escape hatch has been the informal economy.

The Informal Economy

With regular employment difficult to find, many Africans are turning to the informal economy. Most people perform useful and productive activities, like selling craft items, prepared food, or vegetables grown in one of Africa's thousands of prolific urban gardens. But others make a living more nefariously, by smuggling scarce or illegal items, such as drugs, weapons, endangered animals, or ivory.

In most African cities, informal trade once supplied perhaps a third to a half of all employment. Now it often provides more than two-thirds. Informal employment has provided some relief from abject poverty, but it cannot resolve the overarching problems of African economies. The informal economy is very difficult to tax: it does not help pay for government services or repay debt. Moreover, its profits are unreliable, even declining. More and more people compete to sell goods and services to populations whose disposable incomes are falling.

One result is a decline in living standards that is disproportionately severe for women and children. As large numbers of men have lost their jobs in factories or the civil service, they have crowded into the streets and bazaars as vendors, displacing the women and young people who formerly dominated there. Women and children have then turned to contract work manufacturing clothing, shoes, or other items in their homes. Often they work long hours for little pay, using chemicals or techniques that are hazardous to their health. With families disintegrating under the pressure of economic hardship, some women turn to prostitution, putting themselves at high risk of contracting AIDS. Meanwhile, more and more children must fend for themselves on the streets. Cities like Nairobi, Kenya, which had very few street children even 15 years ago, now have tens of thousands.

Alternative Paths to Economic Development

For many reasons, Africans are considering regional economic integration along the lines of the European Union, South America's Mercosur, or Southeast Asia's ASEAN. Many African countries, especially in West Africa, are simply too small to function efficiently in the world economy. Their national markets and resource bases are not large enough to nurture a significant industrial base. Hence these countries have remained heavily dependent on Europe, especially the former colonial powers, for most of their trade. A measure of this dependency is that only 4 percent of the total trade of Africa south of the Sahara consists of trade between African countries. But internal trade links can be difficult to establish. The necessary transport and communication networks are not in place. Air travel and even long-distance telephone calls from one African country to another often must go by way of Europe, and roads are bad even between major cities. All of this makes doing business in Africa about 50 percent more expensive than it is in Asia.

Throughout Africa, there have been bad experiences with surrendering authority on economic policy formation to distant IMF and World Bank officials. Governments are therefore hesitant to surrender what little

Women returning from market at Kisangani, Zaire/Congo, pass by Tshopo Falls on a tributary of the Congo River. [Tom Friedmann/Photo Researchers.]

power they still have to a new regional bureaucracy that would implement economic integration. Nonetheless, there are a number of subregional organizations working toward economic integration. Two of the best known are the Economic Community of West African States (ECOWAS) and the Southern African Development Community (SADC). SADC has major projects under way that are linking both transport and communications infrastructures. ECOWAS, dominated by the regime in Nigeria, has worked toward alleviating tariffs, forming a common currency, and forging cooperation between former British and French colonies. In East Africa, there is the Preferential Trade Area (PTA), which is dominated by Kenya and Tanzania but looks toward eventual greater cooperation with Southern Africa.

Another promising alternative development strategy for Africa is **grassroots rural economic development,** which provides sustainable livelihoods in the countryside. One of the most promising ideas is **self-reliant development,** which features small-scale development schemes in rural areas that focus on local skills, create local jobs, produce products or services for local consumption, and maintain local control so participants retain a sense of ownership. One district in Kenya has over 500, mostly women's, self-help groups. They terrace land, build water tanks, and plant trees. They form farm cooperatives for small-scale producers of poultry, honey, dairy products, and crafts or for those engaged in fishing. They also build houses, schools, and barns; run bookshops, nurseries, and restaurants; or form credit societies. Nonetheless, there are limitations to such efforts. For one thing, they require facilitators with extraordinary skill in managing people. Moreover, in recent years the success of locally funded self-reliant strategies has tempted governments to ignore the needs of rural communities for financial support.

Examining the issue of rural transport illustrates how an African perspective and a focus on local needs might suggest transport improvements that differ remarkably from those advocated by large external development agencies. When non-Africans hear that transport facilities in Africa are underdeveloped, they usually think big: roads, railroads, airports, buses, and the like. But a recent study analyzing transport on a local level—the time spent, the distances traveled, the loads carried—discovered that women handled a major part of village transport and that most of the goods moved were carried on their heads. Women "head up" firewood gathered in forests and water from wells to their homes, and goods going to markets. Eighty-seven percent of this domestic load bearing is on foot; and on average, an adult woman moves the equivalent of 20 kilograms (44 pounds) over 2 kilometers (1.25 miles) a day, spending about 1.5 hours a day at the tasks. Men tend to carry much less of these local burdens. In Kasama, Zambia, for example, an adult woman transports the equivalent of 35.7 tons a year in comparison to 7.1 tons transported by the typical man, no matter what his conveyance. Yet even when development agencies have examined transport at the household and village level, they have focused exclusively upon transport by men, suggesting bicycles, wheelbarrows, donkey carts, and pickup trucks to help men out. As forests are depleted and water becomes more scarce, the time, loads, and distances traveled by women are increasing. Mothers most often recruit their daughters to help them carry their loads, thus cutting into their time in school.

Tiny changes can make big differences in people's lives. Giving women access to low-tech transport like donkeys and bicycles might free some of their time for more education and perhaps for small-scale entrepreneurial activities.

Political Problems: Colonial Legacies and African Adaptations

Few places in the world today seem as politically turbulent as Africa. The media bring us reports of civil wars, of genocide in Rwanda, of military despots who execute members of the opposition, and of presidents like Zaire/Congo's Mobutu Sese Seko, who plundered the national treasury for decades while millions of Zaireans went without food, shelter, health care, and education. Africa's civil wars are in part a legacy of European-created borders and disrupted economies, and in part the results of Africa's own ethnic and regional discrimination. Fortunately, there are some reasons for optimism on the horizon. Political and economic shifts are shaking the power of entrenched elites, forcing them to allow democratic freedoms that, in the future, may bring more responsible government.

In 1990, 45 percent of the population of sub-Saharan Africa was considered at risk of suffering as a result of armed conflicts of some sort. In many ways, the prevalence of conflict is related to Africa's national borders, which were imposed by Europeans during the colonial era (Figure 7.13). Some ethnic groups were split by national boundaries, and other very different and sometimes hostile groups were thrown together in the same country. In too many cases, years of carnage followed independence, as African governments, though

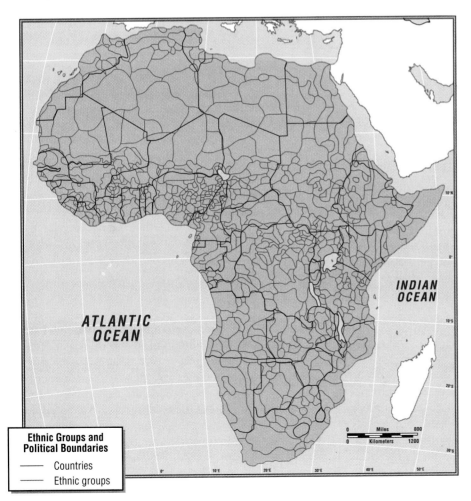

ATLANTIC OCEAN

INDIAN OCEAN

Ethnic Groups and Political Boundaries
—— Countries
—— Ethnic groups

FIGURE 7.13 The map shows the large number of distinct ethnic groups spread across the continent of Africa. Observe that ethnic group boundaries match political boundaries in only a few places. [Adapted from James M. Rubenstein, *An Introduction to Human Geography* (Upper Saddle River, NJ: Prentice Hall, 1999), p. 246.]

less racist than their colonial predecessors, nonetheless often practiced ethnic discrimination. Civil wars arose out of attempts to crush ethnic/regional separatist movements in Nigeria, Zaire/Congo, and Somalia, and out of general repression of disadvantaged minorities in too many cases to mention. The state even sponsored interethnic violence bordering on genocide in Zaire/Congo, Uganda, Rwanda, and Burundi. Often, conflicts were worsened by military establishments that were only loosely under the control of civilian governments or that seized the state itself—as in Nigeria, Liberia, and Sierra Leone. Africans and non-Africans must share the blame for these tragedies. Most notably, the cold war between the United States and the Soviet Union deepened and prolonged conflicts in Angola, Mozambique, Namibia, Zaire/Congo, Ethiopia, and Somalia, just to name a few.

In many independent African countries, power has been wielded by African elites who have continued colonial traditions of authoritarian and corrupt rule. In many African countries, a single political party has a monopoly on power, and any viable political opposition is repressed. Often the elites who control these parties argue that the open political debates of Western democracies are out of sync with African traditions of communal identity and collective decision making. Similarly, elites, building on African traditions of patronage, have warped these traditions to create huge, inefficient government bureaucracies, encouraging rampant corruption that has penetrated to the highest levels. For example, in Nigeria, which has the largest economy in sub-Saharan Africa next to South Africa, political and economic elites have appropriated immense wealth from the country's large oil industry. Hence most Nigerians are no better off than any other Africans. When poor Nigerians get in the way of oil profits, for example by asking for compensation for damages created by oil spills, they often suffer brutal government repression. In Ogoniland, the southern province where most of the country's oil reserves lie, protests against pollution have been met with government campaigns of terror, murder, and the execution of protest leaders, such as the writer Ken Saro-Wiwa.

Shifts in African Geopolitics

In recent years, a number of positive developments have shown that sub-Saharan Africa could become a more stable and democratic region. Signs of progress are especially visible in the southern part of the region. For years, the white-dominated government of South Africa tried to prolong white rule throughout Southern Africa. When that failed, it supported rebellions

During the Mozambique civil war, the world's arms makers supplied enough weapons to arm nearly every person in the country with a rifle. Over 6 million AK-47s alone entered Mozambique (a country with only 18 million people). In a recent move to reduce guns among the population, the Anglican Church began buying back the weapons in a "Guns for Plowshares" program. Guns are exchanged for tools and agricultural implements, sewing machines, bicycles, schoolbooks, and other useful items. The weapons are immediately destroyed. On any given day, one might encounter the unlikely sight of a church employee sawing guns in half in the churchyard. [Joao Silva/Sygma.]

against the successor governments headed by black Africans. Now that white political control has ended in South Africa, the country's leaders are pursuing more friendly and cooperative relations with neighboring countries, bringing greater stability to Southern Africa as a whole. The end of the cold war is also aiding political reform, although the picture is still complicated. Civil wars in a number of countries have died down somewhat, as opposing sides can no longer secure military aid by playing off the U.S.-Soviet antagonism. On the other hand, Africa now receives less foreign aid as

AT THE REGIONAL SCALE   *African Women in Politics*

Successful development efforts focused on women have often led to greater political activism and democratic participation by women. Once empowered economically, women better understand the forces that stand in the way of progress, and they gain the self-confidence to collaborate in tackling larger issues. The following is paraphrased from an article by James C. McKinley, Jr.:

Charity Kaluki Ngilu (pronounced GEE-loo) *will never forget the day she became a professional politician. She was washing dishes in her kitchen in Kitui, about 75 miles east of [Nairobi, Kenya], when she saw a group of women approaching the backdoor with leafy branches in their hands.*

The women had worked with her to build better waterworks and health clinics in the town. Mrs. Ngilu answered the knock on the door, drying her hands on an apron. The women said they wanted her to run for Parliament in Kenya's first multi-party elections.

"I said, 'You are joking,'" she recalled.

That was five years ago. Mrs. Ngilu not only beat the governing party's incumbent, but since then has become a thorn in the side of President Daniel arap Moi, criticizing his government for doing little or nothing for the poor, especially women.

On July 6, 1997, she announced that she would run for the presidency. She was the first woman to run for President in Kenya, a country not known for women's equality. She faced an uphill fight, because, as in most of Africa, Kenyan women are not likely to vote at all, and men are not likely to support female candidates in sufficient numbers. Nevertheless, many men supported her because they felt she was capable of making bigger changes than a man, since her very candidacy was a blow to convention. Though she didn't win, she made an important statement with her campaign, which focused on repealing colonial-era laws that enable the president to cripple opposition effectively by jailing dissidents and breaking up political demonstrations.

Source: Adapted from James C. McKinley, Jr., A woman to run in Kenya? One says, "Why not?" *New York Times,* August 3, 1997, p. 3.

more resources are being directed toward promoting capitalist development in Eastern Europe. The drop in aid, along with Africa's deepening economic crisis, has contributed to urban protest movements that have threatened governments throughout Africa.

Nevertheless, more discontent is being freely and openly expressed today in the form of legal opposition parties. There is hope for a "second independence" as repressive, corrupt ruling elites are replaced or moderated by parties enjoying the electoral support of the majority of the people; this is occurring in South Africa. At least one encouraging statistic supports such hopes: in 1990 only four sub-Saharan countries were pluralist democracies; during the 1990s, 47 states promised or allowed multiparty elections. By the end of the century, even Nigeria, long under a military dictatorship, held elections. There remained several states, including Ethiopia, Rwanda, and Zaire/Congo, where violence or open warfare rendered fair elections impossible.

In view of the daily suffering of Africa's people, it is not unusual for observers to wonder if African governments shouldn't meet basic needs like food, shelter, and health care before they open up the electoral process to citizens. The question implies that undemocratic governments could meet these immediate needs better than elected governments. But the Nobel Prize–winning economist Amartya Sen, of Harvard University, disagrees. He points out that famine is rarely a problem in independent democratic countries where there is a free press. If there are no forums for public criticism of leaders, no chance for an opposition to speak, no chance to "throw the bums out" at election time, those who rule don't have to worry about being accountable for the consequences of bad or corrupt policies. Famines never kill the rulers, so bad rulers have little incentive to cure the problems. It is probably no accident that Zimbabwe and Botswana, where democracy is beginning to flourish, have successfully prevented famine and raised standards of living. In comparison, Zaire/Congo, Rwanda, and Ethiopia, with repressive dictatorships, have not only fallen far short of meeting basic needs but have descended into horrendous civil violence. In actuality, as the box "African Women in Politics" shows, the processes of development and democratization probably work best when they go hand in hand.

TABLE 7.1

Human well-being rankings of countries in sub-Saharan Africa

Country	GNP per capita (in U.S. dollars), 1996	Human Development Index (HDI)[a] global rankings, 1998	Gender Empowerment Measure (GEM) global rankings, 1998	Gender-Related Development Index (GDI)[b] global rankings, 1998	Female literacy (percentage), 1995	Male literacy (percentage), 1995
Selected countries for comparison						
Japan	$40,940	8 (high)	38	13	99	99
United States	28,020	4 (high)	11	6	99	99
Kuwait	17,390 (1995)	54 (high)	75	50	77.3	73.4
West Africa						
Benin	350	145 (low)	Not av.	135	26	49
Burkina Faso	230	172 (low)	77	161	9	29
Cape Verde Isles	1,010	117 (medium)	57	107	64	81
Côte d'Ivoire	660	148 (low)	Not av.	141	30	50
Gambia	Not av.	165 (low)	94	154	25	53
Ghana	360	133 (low)	Not av.	121	64	76
Guinea	560	167 (low)	Not av.	157	22	50
Guinea-Bissau	250	164 (low)	Not av.	153	42	68
Mali	240	171 (low)	72	160	23	39
Mauritania	470	149 (low)	101	138	26	50
Niger	200	173 (low)	102	162	7	21
Nigeria	240	142 (low)	Not av.	133	47	67
Liberia	Not av.	Not av. (low)	Not av.	Not av.	Not av.	Not av.
Senegal	570	158 (low)	Not av.	149	23	43
Sierra Leone	200	174 (low)	Not av.	163	18	45
Togo	300	144 (low)	99	136	37	67
Central Africa						
Cameroon	610	132 (low)	86	124	52	75
Central African Republic	310	154 (low)	98	142	52	68
Chad	160	163 (low)	Not av.	152	35	62
Congo, Republic of the	640	128 (medium)	Not av.	117	67	83
Equatorial Guinea	530	135 (low)	90	126	68	90
Gabon	3,950	120 (medium)	Not av.	112	53	74
São Tomé and Príncipe	330	121 (medium)	Not av.	Not av.	Not av.	Not av.
Zaire/Congo	130	143 (low)	Not av	132	68	87

TABLE 7.1 (CONTINUED)

Human well-being rankings of countries in sub-Saharan Africa

Country	GNP per capita (in U.S. dollars), 1996	Human Development Index (HDI)[a] global rankings, 1998	Gender Empowerment Measure (GEM) global rankings, 1998	Gender-Related Development Index (GDI)[b] global rankings, 1998	Female literacy (percentage), 1995	Male literacy (percentage), 1995
Horn of Africa						
Djibouti	Not av.	162 (low)	Not av.	Not av.	Not av.	Not av.
Eritrea	Not av.	168 (low)	Not av.	155	25	25
Ethiopia	100	169 (low)	Not av.	158	25	46
Somalia	Not av.	Not av.	Not av.	Not av.	Not av.	Not av.
East Africa						
Burundi	170	170 (low)	Not av.	159	23	49
Kenya	320	137 (low)	Not av.	122	70	86
Rwanda	Not av.	Not av. (low)	Not av.	Not av.	Not av.	Not av.
Tanzania	170	150 (low)	Not av.	137	57	79
Uganda	300	160 (low)	Not av.	146	50	72
East African Islands						
Comoros	450	141 (low)	Not av.	130	50	64
Madagascar	230	153 (low)	Not av.	139	46	46
Mauritius	3,380	61 (high)	49	54	79	87
Seychelles	6,850	56 (high)	Not av.	Not av.	Not av.	Not av.
Southern Africa						
Angola	270	156 (low)	Not av.	145	29	56
Botswana	3,020 in 1997	97 (medium)	48	85	60	81
Lesotho	660	134 (low)	50	123	62	81
Malawi	180	161 (low)	89	150	42	72
Mozambique	80	166 (low)	55	156	18	52
Namibia	2,250	107 (medium)	Not av.	99	74	78
Swaziland	1,210	115 (medium)	63	105	76	78
South Africa	3,160	89 (medium)	23	74	82	82
Zambia	360	146 (low)	81	134	71	86
Zimbabwe	610	130 (medium)	56	118	80	90

Sources: Human Development Report 1998, United Nations Development Programme; and *1998 World Population Data Sheet*, Population Reference Bureau.

[a] The high, medium, and low designations in column 3 (HDI) indicate where the country ranks if the 174 countries are classified into just three categories.

[b] Total GDI ranked in world 163.

Not av. = Not available.

Measures of Human Well-Being

When looking at the very low gross national product per capita figures in Africa (Table 7.1, column 2), it is a relief to remember that GNP is, at best, only a crude indicator of the actual state of well-being. Still, these figures indicate a desperately poor continent where people survive by sharing through reciprocal exchange, by working in the informal economy, by growing their own food, by conserving in a host of inventive ways, and by severely limiting all cash consumption. Within the low range of GNP per capita figures, there is still considerable variation. Botswana, Gabon, Mauritius, Cape Verde, Namibia, South Africa, Swaziland, and the Seychelles are all above U.S. $1000 per year, but together they account for less than 10 percent of Africa's population; and within these countries there is a wide spread in income.

In column 3 of the table, the Human Development Index combines three components—life expectancy at birth, educational attainment, and adjusted real income—to arrive at a ranking of 174 countries that is more sensitive to factors other than just income. Virtually all African countries rank in the lowest third of world nations. With such low GNP figures, there is little tax money to invest in human capital: basic health care, sanitation, and education. The literacy figures (columns 5 and 6) show both the generally low level of education and the discrimination against women. Structural adjustment programs have contributed to actual declines in well-being over the last decade or so by diverting social service money to debt repayment. During the 1980s, per capita government spending on health care fell, and the introduction of fees limited the number of people who could afford care. A result has been higher death rates during and after childbirth, for both mothers and infants. Spending on education fell from U.S. $11 billion to U.S. $7 billion. When school fees were introduced, enrollment in elementary schools fell from 77.1 to 66.7 percent.

The Gender Empowerment Measure (GEM, column 4 of Table 7.1) ranks countries by the extent to which females have opportunities to participate in economic and political life. For a variety of reasons (some related to the low status of women in African countries), the statistics necessary to calculate GEM are not available for many countries. Many that are ranked on GEM are far down in the rankings. But some countries rank relatively high: Botswana, Lesotho, Mozambique, South Africa, and Zimbabwe. In these countries, a rather high proportion of women are employed in professional and technical positions. Moreover, in these same countries, women occupy some seats in parliament—Botswana 9 percent, Lesotho 11 percent, Mozambique 25 percent, South Africa 23 percent, and Zimbabwe 15 percent—so they may be able to influence future policies regarding women.

Because GEM statistics are missing for so many countries in this region, we have included a column for the Gender-Related Development Index (GDI) as we did for some countries in Chapter 6. This index measures only the access of men and women to health care, education, and income, but not the degree to which they participate in public policy formulation and decision making.

Environmental Issues

With more than 50 percent of the population profoundly poor, the first order of environmental business is to find sufficient resources to upgrade standards of living and then sustain them. Admittedly, Africa poses some of the most difficult human/environment problems ever encountered. In some areas with large populations, the carrying capacity of the environment is stretched thin because soils are not well suited for intensive agriculture or because water is scarce. There are pockets of extremely high population density where poverty is deeply entrenched, and other areas where prosperity seems just around the corner.

Addressing environmental problems in Africa is complicated by the fact that this continent has a unique and priceless complex of plant and animal species warranting preservation and protection. Yet this issue of conservation cannot really be separated from African human well-being issues. If the condition of Africa's people declines yet further, the habitats that support endangered plants and animals will surely be victims too. Hence the wisest planners, increasingly Africans instead of outsiders, design strategies that will both provide basic human needs and address Africa's environmental issues. Just a sampling of such issues are discussed here.

Desertification

There is little doubt that parts of Africa are now in a natural cycle of increased aridity. The results are most dramatic in the region called the **Sahel** (Arabic for "shore" of the desert), a band of arid grassland (between 200 and 400 miles wide) that runs east-west along the southern edge of the Sahara. Over the last century, the Sahel has shifted significantly to the south, in a process called **desertification** by which arid conditions spread to places that previously were quite moist (Figure 7.14). For example, the *World Geographic Atlas* (Bayer) in 1953 showed Lake Chad situated in a tropical rain forest environment south of the southern edge of the Sahel. By 1998, the Sahara itself was encroaching on Lake Chad. This shift of aridity to the south—

and its opposite, the shift of moister conditions to the north—is part of a long-term natural cycle; but human activity may be speeding up the cycle and broadening the area affected.

The Sahel and other dry grasslands in Africa are what geographers call **fragile environments** because, due to generally low rainfall (10–20 inches, or 25–50 centimeters, per year) and low levels of organic matter in the soil, the usual vegetative cover has reached the limits of its endurance. Any further stress, like fire, plowing, or intensive grazing of animals, may cause the dry grasses to give way to species like tough bunchgrass and thorny shrubs that are more tolerant of stress. These species do not cover the soil as well, they allow rain to evaporate more quickly, and they are not useful for grazing. Soon, the denuded soil is blown away by the wind, and the remaining sands pile into dunes as the grassland shifts to a more desertlike state.

Indigenous animal herders are frequently blamed for desertification. Although overgrazing can be the trigger for this process, natural cycles are often the underlying cause of change. Furthermore, development agencies have at times mistakenly advised animal herders to give up raising traditional animals like camels and goats in favor of cattle to be sold to distant urban markets. Preparing cattle for market can place greater stress on the grasslands than more traditional practices. The conditions for desertification can also be set up when high-tech equipment drills borehole wells around which nomads and their herds settle permanently; this leads to overgrazing. Desertification can also occur when marginal lands are cleared and plowed for agriculture. A few years of irrigated agriculture in a dry environment can leave the soil poisoned by water-borne minerals that are left behind as crystals when the irrigation water evaporates. The overharvesting of trees and shrubs for fuel also contributes to a general drying out of the soil and the advance of desertlike conditions.

Forest Resources

The destruction of tropical rain forests is a worldwide phenomenon. In Africa, it is estimated that 1.15 million square miles (3 million square kilometers)—more than 60 percent of the original rain forest—is gone. Most of the loss is attributed to the demand for farmland and fuelwood by growing populations, especially in West Africa. Thus far, Africa earns little from its valuable hardwoods. What logs are harvested are sold as raw wood. If the trees were cut according to scientific logging principles and processed in Africa into refined wood products, the financial return would be much greater. The most extensive remaining tracts of African rain forest lie in Zaire/Congo. There, scientific forest management is not practiced at all. Untrained commercial exploitation is merely awaiting an end to warfare and the building of better roads.

Dry forests—those that lose their leaves during the dry season—once covered nearly twice as much territory as the rain forest. They are being destroyed at nearly the same rate. Dry-forest products are used for building materials, furniture, and medicinal cures, but their greatest use is as fuelwood. Africans still use wood or charcoal—a prepared wood product that burns at a higher heat than wood—for nearly all domestic and industrial energy. Making and selling charcoal is an important niche in the informal economy of most African countries; and much of the wood is harvested free as a

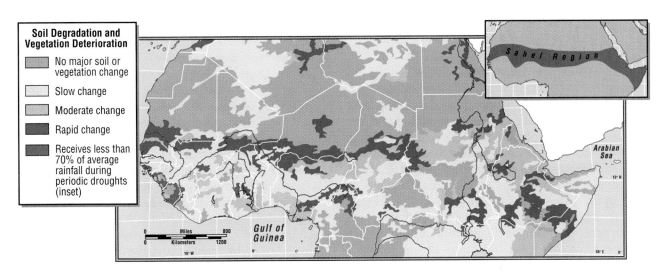

FIGURE 7.14 Areas susceptible to desertification in Africa. The changes are toward aridity. [Adapted from John L. Allen, *Student Atlas of Environmental Issues* (Guilford, CT: Dushkin/McGraw-Hill, 1997), p. 110.]

commodity held in common. Even in urban areas, wood and charcoal remain the cheapest fuels available. In Nigeria, which has large reserves of oil, most people cannot afford petroleum products as fuel; Nigeria is the leading fuelwood producer in Africa.

For a decade or more, many Africans have recognized the need to curtail the use of wood for fuel. Fast-growing trees are being planted for fuelwood. Development planners have tried to come up with fuel-efficient stoves, but users find the stoves lack the convenience and nostalgic associations of old-fashioned cooking fires. To save wood resources, Africans may eventually have to consider alternative energy sources—hydropower, bottled gas, solar, wind—to meet their growing energy needs.

Tropical Disease

Tropical pests that produce disease have long plagued Africans, their animals, and their crops. Examples are the tsetse fly, whose bite infects people with incurable sleeping sickness and transmits an illness fatal to cattle; the mosquito, which spreads malaria; corn borers that destroy fields of corn; and cattle ticks. To fight these diseases, African men and women are setting up and staffing research institutes like the International Centre of Insect Physiology and Ecology (ICIPE) in Kenya. Here, the search is for natural, genetic, and microbial controls for insects like the tsetse fly. ICIPE scientists are looking for solutions that are at once high tech and grassroots—ideas that will both cure problems and create sustainable livelihoods for African people. Indigenous people receive the crucial jobs implementing projects. For example, young Masai warriors are now the technicians who develop and maintain tsetse-fly traps near Lake Magadi in Kenya's Rift Valley.

Wildlife

Africa's wildlife has an important role to play in improving the lives of the continent's human populations. Many Africans depend on wild game and fish as their main source of protein. Africa's wildlife also forms the basis for several important economic activities. There is growing interest in game farming because wild animals have resistance to certain diseases, are adjusted to the climate, and can withstand occasional droughts or heat waves better than domesticated animals. African animal products like skins, taxidermy specimens, and ivory have been important exports to places like Europe, China, and America for thousands of years. Live animals, like the giraffes boxed up for shipment to Germany referred to at the beginning of this chapter, have supplied the world's zoos. At times, this trade in animal parts and in live animals threatens the survival of some species. Now television programs document-

ing the diminishing numbers of gorillas, elephants, lions, zebras, and giraffes or the decline of rain forests and grasslands have raised public concern over Africa's diminishing wildlife heritage.

Water

In a growing number of African countries, per capita supplies of water are declining rapidly. In many parts of arid Africa, water is being pumped from aquifers faster than it is being replaced by nature; it is being diverted from natural wetlands for agricultural, domestic, and industrial uses; and it is being polluted by salinization, human waste, and chemical poisons. Large development projects may divert water for industrial, agricultural, or urban uses; this leaves rural people in arid lands with insufficient water and causes complex ecosystems to be lost. Kenya, for example, has only 635 cubic meters of water per capita, compared to the accepted global standard of 1000; its water supply is expected to drop to just 190 cubic meters per capita by the year 2050.

Safe water is hard to come by, even in the moist zones of the continent, rural or urban. Most households must carry in all their water from springs, wells, pools, or streams; in urban areas, water is drawn from standpipes. Following long-standing tradition, women are the almost universal procurers of water. As sources become depleted or polluted, women must walk farther and farther to collect safe water. The difficulty of carrying water limits the amounts available for people's needs, and illness is spread when insufficient water is used to clean dishes, diapers, clothing, and other materials. Because plumbing and sewage treatment are usually not available, even in cities, human wastes often find their way into water sources.

Saving what is now being lost is perhaps the greatest source of "new" water for most places on earth. Agriculture accounts for about 70 percent of global water use. In Africa, many large agricultural projects use irrigation, and most modern irrigation systems lose a great deal of water through leakage and evaporation: water often runs through unlined open ditches and is sent into fields via sluices or sprinklers. In addition, standing pools are sources of disease. Some development thinkers are saying that the solutions to Africa's water problems may lie less in high-tech applications than in rediscovering folk ideas about water conservation that fit with local customs. A decade or two ago, African women who delivered irrigation water directly to the roots of their needy plants via human water brigades were laughed at. Now, the rationale for these practices (and the camaraderie they nourish) are better appreciated. The installation of "old-fashioned" sanitary roof catchments and cisterns in place of complex piped delivery systems can save construction costs and water, as can sanitary hand-flushed pit toilets in place of public sewer systems.

At present, the two goals of sustainable development and structural adjustment are often in conflict. When people are as poor as they are in Africa, structural adjustment often drives them and their governments to spend down environmental capital just to stave off imminent disaster. In other words, they use or export their resources at grossly unsustainable rates for prices that are much too low, just in order to survive.

SUBREGIONS OF SUB-SAHARAN AFRICA

This text divides sub-Saharan Africa into five subregions that predominantly reflect geographic location. Factors such as the current geopolitical situation and tradition have also guided the placement of a particu-

lar country. Chad, for example, could have been discussed with the arid countries of northern West Africa, along with Niger and Mali. I have placed it in Central Africa, chiefly because most of Chad's people live in the far southern reaches of the country and are closer in culture to Cameroon and the Central African Republic.

West Africa

West Africa occupies the bulge on the west side of the African continent. It comprises 15 countries, as indicated on the map in Figure 7.15. It is bordered by the Sahara on the north, by the Atlantic Ocean on the west and south, and by Lake Chad and the mountains of Cameroon on the east. The region can be thought of as a series of horizontal ribbons of physical zones: dry in the north, moist in the south; economic activities: herding in the north, farming in the south; and, to some extent, religions and cultures: Muslim in the north, Christian in the south. And yet, most of these cultural and physical features do not have distinct boundaries but rather zones of transition and exchange.

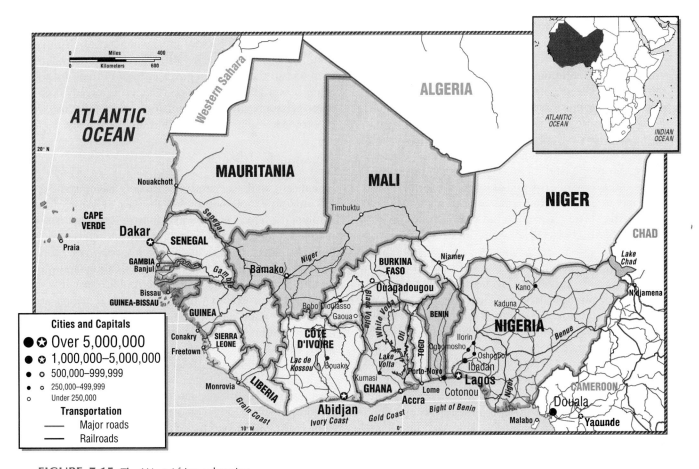

FIGURE 7.15 The West Africa subregion.

Across West Africa, from west to east, stretches a variegated belt of vegetation zones that reflect the south-north moisture zones. Remnants of tropical rain forests still exist along the Atlantic coast of countries like Côte d'Ivoire, Ghana, and Nigeria. To the north, this moist environment grades into drier woodland mixed with savanna (grassland). Further north still, as the environment gets drier, the trees thin out and the savanna dominates. The savanna grades into the yet drier Sahel environment of arid grasslands. In the northern parts of Mali, Niger, and Mauritania, the arid land becomes actual desert, part of the Sahara.

Although people of many different cultures live in this series of environments, all have had to deal with the opportunities and challenges it offers agriculture and animal herding. Along the coast, and inland where rainfall is abundant, crops like coffee, cacao, yams, oil palms, corn, bananas, sugarcane, and cassava are common. Further inland, the crop complex is adapted to the drier climate: millet, peanuts, cotton, and sesame grow in the savanna environments. Cattle are also tended here and north into the Sahel; further south, however, the threat of tsetse flies prevents cattle raising. People in the Sahel and Sahara are generally not able to cultivate the land, except along the Niger River during the summer rains. Food, other than that provided by animals and the fields along the riverbanks, must be imported from coastal zones, places like Gambia and Senegal.

The West African environments have dried out as more and more people have cleared the forests and woodlands for cultivation and to obtain cooking fuel. Forest cover no longer blocks sunlight and wind. As a result, sunlight evaporates moisture, and desiccating desert winds blow south all the way to the coast. The drying out of the land is exacerbated by the recurrence of a natural cycle of drought. As a result, the ribbons of differing vegetation running west to east are not as distinct as they once were, and even coastal zones on occasion experience dry, dusty conditions reminiscent of the Sahel.

As mentioned, the geographies of religion, ethnicity, and race in West Africa to some extent repeat the north-south physical patterns. Generally, the north is Muslim and the south is a mix of Christian and traditional religions, though Islamic influence now extends into the southeast section (especially Nigeria). The ethnic distribution patterns in West Africa are particularly complex because seasonal and permanent migration has been important for thousands of years. There are some large ethnic groups, like the Hausa and Yoruba (see the subsection on Nigeria) and the Fulani and Malinka (also called Mandingoes). These groups live in many different zones, in both rural and urban contexts, and in a number of different countries. There are hundreds of smaller ethnic groups, each with its own language (see Figure 7.16). The Muslim traders who converted the people of the north to Islam were generally Caucasian people who came from Egypt, North Africa, and beyond. Hence, many people in the north have light skin; those in the south tend to have dark skin.

The boundaries of these countries today derive from those that Portuguese, French, and British colonizers set for their own purposes. These boundaries often cut across ethnic group patterns, making it difficult for people to maintain connections and interrupting natural economic flows. The economy of each country is often more linked to its European colonizer than to neighboring territories. Nonetheless, the region remains informally interdependent because laborers migrate from the poorer states to the wealthier and send money home to their families. In this way, the people perpetuate the long-standing informal economic integration of West Africa.

All the states in this subregion belong to the Economic Organization of West African States, which was founded to promote freer trade. Many hope that it will foster closer cooperation on many levels to alleviate West Africa's poverty and prevent occasional bloody conflicts. In 1996, ECOWAS, led by Nigeria's military dictatorship, intervened to quiet civil violence in Liberia; and in 1997, it restored the democratically elected president of Sierra Leone when a coup deposed him. Some worry that ECOWAS may become the instrument of the Nigerian government to extend its political power across the region. Nigeria is already dominant economically because of its large population, its oil reserves, and its relatively diversified economy.

Nigeria

The most populous country in Africa is Nigeria, and its 121 million people outnumber the rest of West Africa combined. Nigeria is a country of extremes. The size of its economy, 90 percent of it derived from oil, is second only to that of South Africa. Yet Nigeria's per capita GNP is only U.S. $240 (1998). There is a tiny and very wealthy elite, and a small, growing middle class able to afford some luxuries; but the vast majority of people are exceedingly poor. The nation now offers universal primary education and has numerous universities and colleges, yet the literacy rate is only 47 percent for women and 67 percent for men. Illiteracy is particularly high in the Muslim north. Christian missionaries established a strong tradition of basic education in the south. Despite its considerable wealth, the country ranks near the bottom (137 out of 174) of the HDI.

Like the whole of the region, Nigeria is a nation of cultural complexity (Figure 7.16). There are four main ethnic groups. The Muslim Hausa (21 percent of the population) and Fulani (9 percent) have until recently

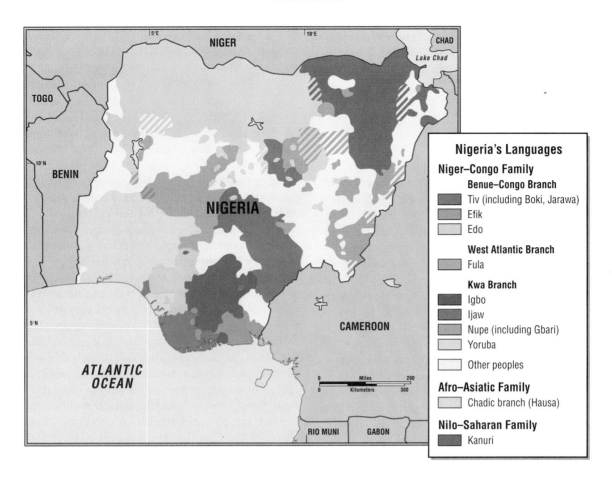

FIGURE 7.16 Nigeria's languages reflect the variety of ethnic groups in the country. The main languages are indicated in color, but many smaller groups speak distinct languages or Creole dialects not shown on this map. [Adapted from James M. Rubenstein, *An Introduction to Human Geography* (Upper Saddle River, NJ: Prentice Hall, 1999), p. 167.]

lived mostly in the north, where the moist grassland grades into dry savanna and then semidesert. The Hausa, once traders, dryland farmers, and animal herders, have dominated both the government of Nigeria and the military since independence. The Yoruba (20 percent) live in southwest Nigeria in the moister woodland and grassland environments. The Igbo (17 percent) are centered in the southeast in and near the tropical rain forest zone. Hundreds of other ethnic groups live among and between the larger groups; the government recognizes 250 distinct languages. Nigeria is still a primarily rural country, with only 16 percent of the people considered urban; yet the wealth of the country is mostly in the cities.

There has been little pretense of democracy in Nigeria, and virtually every form of protest or opposition has been put down violently. In 1966, the slaughter of 30,000 Igbos ignited the three-year Biafran War, in which a portion of eastern Nigeria unsuccessfully tried to secede and over 200,000 people died. University students have suffered beatings, imprisonment,

and death for protesting social and political conditions; and the universities have been shut down for years at a time. During the 1990s, the military government of Nigeria imprisoned Mashood Abiola, the duly elected head of state. In 1995, the world community was outraged by the summary execution of the writer Ken Saro-Wiwa, who had led a protest of the Ogoni people. Much of Nigeria's oil is located on Ogoni lands, yet the Ogoni have received little benefit, and oil extraction has polluted their lands.

Oil is Nigeria's primary resource. Nigeria has the potential to be the richest country in Africa, but its oil resources have been mismanaged to enrich military leaders and foreign oil companies. High oil prices in the 1970s encouraged the government to overspend on expanded social services and construction of the new federal capital at Abuja, in the center of the country. There was heavy borrowing against future oil revenues, but little was invested in productive activities like agriculture or industry. Soon the growing cities became increasingly dependent on imported food. When oil prices later fell, basic social services and new development projects had to be cut back or abandoned as Nigeria fell behind in debt payments and became subject to SAPs.

Water Management in Mali and Niger

Mali and Niger—each with populations of about 10 million—lie primarily in the northern Sahel and Sahara climatic zones. The desert prevails in the northern parts of both countries; but in the southernmost sections, the Niger River waters valuable habitats that change with the seasons. The Niger is the most important river of West Africa. It carries summer floodwaters northeast into the normally arid, clay-lined lowlands of Mali and Niger. There the waters spread out into a mosaic of lakes and streams that nourish wetlands. For a few short months of the year (June through September), these wetlands ensure the livelihoods of millions of fishers, farmers, and pastoralists who share the territory in carefully synchronized patterns of land use that have survived for millennia. These desert wetlands produce eight times as much plant matter per acre as the average wheat field and provide seasonal pasture for millions of cattle, goats, and sheep—the highest density of herds in all of Africa.

The Niger's waters have not yet been harnessed by dams, but some international experts are advising the governments of Mali and Niger to dam the river and channel it into agricultural projects. Such projects would probably better feed the overwhelmingly poor people of Mali and Niger. Although 80 percent of the people are farmers, because of population pressure those living in these countries must rely on imported food to survive. But the dams will forever change the seasonal rise and fall of the river that for millennia has supported an intricate mix of wildlife and human uses. The impact will be felt in Europe also, because the Niger is a seasonal migration stopover for birds that summer north of the Mediterranean.

Central Africa

If one were to look at a map of Africa without any prior knowledge, one might reasonably expect the countries of Central Africa (Cameroon, the Central African Republic, Chad, Congo, Gabon, São Tomé and Príncipe, and Zaire/Congo) to be the hub of continental activity, the true center around which life on the continent is organized (Figure 7.17). Such is not the case. Paradoxically, Central Africa is peripheral to larger patterns on the continent. Its dense tropical forests, tropical diseases and difficult terrain make it the least accessible part of the continent.

Central Africa consists of a core of wet tropical forest. This physical region is called the Congo, after the river that flows through it. It is bounded to the north and south by a broad band of drier tropical forest. The forests have cut Central Africa off from the rest of the continent for centuries, and much of the region remains inaccessible. There are virtually no maintained roads. The physical features of the land and tropical diseases inhibit the development of transportation, commercial agriculture, and even mining. Moreover, the natural ecology of the forest does not lend itself to long-term cash-crop agriculture. Most people are subsistence farmers living in rural settings along the river courses and the occasional railroad line. Cities are only beginning to grow, fed mainly by people escaping civil violence in the countryside.

Central Africa is one of the most undeveloped regions on the continent—in part because of its physical features and in part because corruption and the persistence of violence discourage most entrepreneurs of goodwill, African or outsider. Although this subregion possesses significant mineral and forest wealth, a long string of corrupt governments has pocketed the profits, and smugglers of minerals and other resources have leaked the potential wealth to outsiders. Its colonial heritage has contributed not a little to the region's difficulties. The Belgian and French colonial regimes left a terrible legacy of violence. A chronicler of the 1890s recorded that after a group of Africans rebelled against the French, their heads were used as a decoration around a flower bed in front of a French official's home.

Central Africa is an overlapping ethnic mosaic, made up of groups speaking some 700 languages. In addition, the artificial political borders imposed by the Europeans and their policy of deliberately pitting Africans against each other exacerbated tensions between ethnic groups. Indigenous governance systems were disrupted when Europeans removed chiefs and installed new leaders who would do their bidding. In this way, long-standing traditional restraints on unwise leadership were lost, thus opening the door for the type of power abuses that have developed in the twentieth century.

Most of the countries of Central Africa received their independence in the 1960s, but the Europeans stayed on to continue their economic (and political) domination. Tax-free profits were sent home to France, Belgium, or Spain; and rarely was anything reinvested in Africa. With no money to develop an infrastructure, no experience with multiparty democracy, and no educated constituency, many Central African countries ran into trouble. (See the discussion of Zaire/Congo for an example.) Political upheavals were accompanied by downward-spiraling economies. In some countries, like Zaire/Congo, Equatorial Guinea, and Chad, the aver-

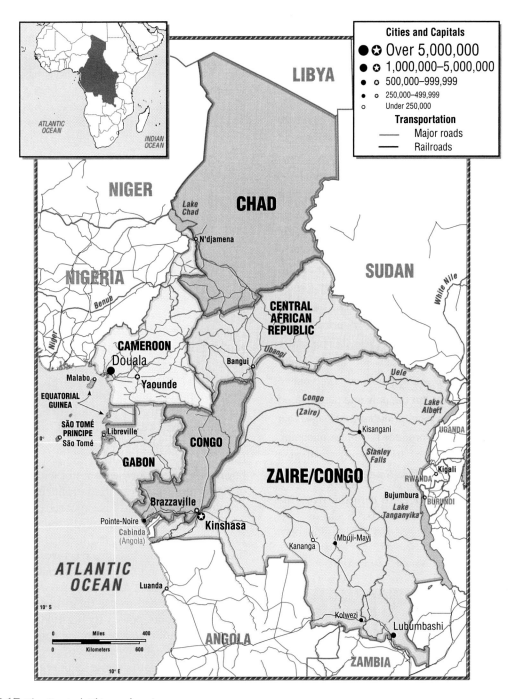

FIGURE 7.17 The Central Africa subregion.

age person's purchasing power is notably less now than it was some decades ago. These countries have little tax revenue to call on because of tax concessions to foreigners as well as government graft. So maintenance of roads, railroads, waterways, telephone networks, electricity grids, and buildings is negligible. Industries, both government and private, cannot survive for lack of electricity and raw materials. People are so poor that there is little market for any type of consumer product.

Zaire/Congo: A Case Study

VIGNETTE

Two women in Kisangani: *"Se debrouiller"*—"Make do with what you have"—is the way of life for Mauwa Funidi, 45, the first college graduate in her once prominent family. Now Mauwa sells small bags of charcoal on the street in Kisangani, Zaire/Congo, to earn a few pennies to help support her extended family. She still holds her real job, that of university librarian, which paid U.S. $300/month in 1976, but after decades of inflation pays her just U.S. $11/month in 1997. The university library is empty, the windows are broken, books and other publications are rotting in the humidity. Thirty years ago education was celebrated in Kisangani. Now there are not only no funds for the university, but the government stopped funding kindergarten through twelfth grade. The majority of children do not finish primary school, as their families cannot afford the U.S. $7 a month tuition.

Alphonsine shares a two-room, tin-roofed mud house with a dirt floor and no water or power with her seven-year-old son and teenage brother and sister. Alphonsine, aged 25 and unmarried, is a devout practicing Roman Catholic who takes Communion weekly and prays for help in feeding her family. She is the family's primary support and has been employed for two years as a sex worker at the local Take-a-Peek bar, the only job that provides enough to feed her son and younger siblings. "Everyone in the family criticizes me, but I'm the only one putting food on the table," she says. The local priest acknowledges that "the Congo's long slide has produced a moral quagmire that is at least as wretched as its economy." [Adapted from Nicholas Kristof, *New York Times,* May 20, 1997, p. A10].

Mauwa in her defunct library, Kisangani, Zaire/Congo.
[Stephen Crowley/NYT Pictures.]

Virtually all of Zaire/Congo's 47 million inhabitants are in circumstances not dissimilar to those of Alphonsine's family. The average GNP per capita is U.S. $130 a year. Yet the country has an enormous wealth of untouched natural resources: copper, gold, diamonds, and other minerals; and it has enough undeveloped hydroelectric resources to supply power to every household and those of some neighboring countries, as well.

What happened in Zaire/Congo is a direct result of the following: European colonization, the cold war, and the desire of local leaders to stay in power and enrich themselves. When independence came in 1960, severe political and economic collapse was imminent as Belgian technocrats withdrew, leaving untrained Congolese in charge. The new government of Patrice Lumumba tried to address the inequalities produced by the colonial era by nationalizing foreign-owned companies so that the profits could be kept in the country. These strategies, reminiscent of communism, adopted during the height of the cold war, led to intervention from outside. The USSR supported and armed Lumumba's pro-socialist movement, and the Western allies supported and armed opposing politicians, like the extraordinarily corrupt Mobutu Sese Seko.

After five years of violent political struggle, Mobutu Sese Seko seized power. Once firmly established, Mobutu nationalized the country's institutions, businesses, and industries, but not with the intention of using the previously exported profits for the good of the people. Rather, he and his supporters began extracting personal wealth from the newly reorganized ventures. Foreign experts, trained technicians, and capital left in droves. The country's infrastructure, economy, educational system, food supply, and social structure started on a rapid decline. As conditions worsened, Mobutu and his cronies had to use their money and their paid army to hold onto power. By the 1990s, the vast majority of Zairean/Congolese peoples had reached bottom. Mobutu was finally overthrown in 1997 by Laurence Kabila, a new dictator whose inept regime led to widening strife in Central Africa. By 1999, Angola, Namibia, Zimbabwe, Chad, Rwanda, and Uganda all had troops on Zaire/Congo's soil and were competing for parts of its territory and resources.

The Horn of Africa

The Horn of Africa (Djibouti, Eritrea, Ethiopia, and Somalia) is the easternmost part of the continent and wraps around the southern tip of the Arabian Peninsula (Figure 7.18). Two sharply contrasting physical zones—agriculturally productive farmlands in the highland west and an arid east—are reflected in two basic strategies for gaining a livelihood.

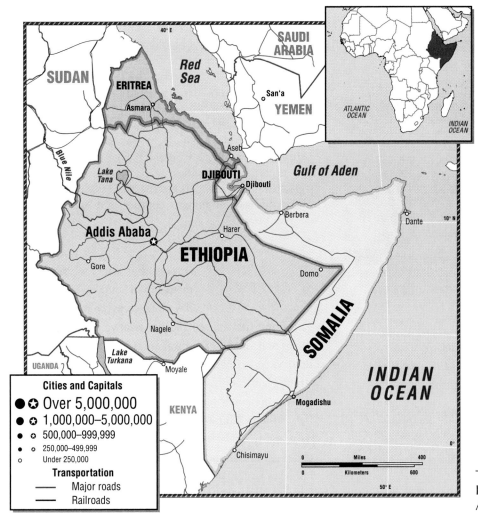

FIGURE 7.18 The Horn of Africa subregion.

The tectonic rift filled by the Red Sea has a lesser counterpart, known as the Rift Valley, which extends southwest through the Horn and into East Africa. The western part of the subregion, in the vicinity of the rift, is an area of mountains and plateaus called the Ethiopian-Sudanese Highlands, ranging from 4000 to over 10,000 feet. These highlands are drained by deep river valleys, including the valley where the headwaters of the Blue Nile lie. This upland area, where rain falls during the summer, contains a mixture of environments that vary with elevation. To the east and south of the Ethiopian-Sudanese Highlands is a broad arid apron that descends to the Indian Ocean and the Gulf of Aden. In this coastal zone there are few rivers and large stretches of sand and salt deserts. Traditionally, Muslim herders made a meager living from animal herding and precarious oasis cultivation.

The Amhara and Gurage ethnic groups of the highlands are known for their particularly complex and productive systems of **mixed agriculture,** meaning that they raise cattle and use the manure to fertilize a wide variety of crops that are finely tuned to particu-larly fragile environments. Pastures and fields are rotated in a systematic fashion. Agronomists have recently begun to appreciate the precision and scientific validity of these ancient and specialized African mixed agriculture systems, now threatened by development schemes and population pressure.

VIGNETTE Kadija and Hassain Saide Adem have a 4-hectare farm 400 kilometers (150 miles) north of Addis Ababa, the capital of Ethiopia. They grow sorghum mostly and some corn. The Adems's sorghum plants are 15 feet tall; the heads of the plants contain seeds that are landraces, the genetic descendants of plants carefully nurtured for thousands of years.

Hassain says he grows the landraces rather than purchase the seeds because he is impressed with the results. He once raised 29 stalks of sorghum from a single seed. His wife, Kadija, usually sorts the seeds, determining

In this Italian-built factory in Asmara, Eritrea's capital, women make shoes for foreign markets. Eritrea has new laws guaranteeing gender equality: women now have the right to divorce, to vote, to acquire and own land, and to work outside the home. [Robert Caputo/Aurora & Quanta Productions.]

which are best for planting, for storing, and for cooking. Successes like those experienced by this farm couple are especially important as Ethiopia attempts to resolve the decades of economic and social disruption that have drastically reduced agricultural productivity. [Adapted from Pattie Lacroix, Ethiopia's living laboratory of biodiversity, International Development Research Centre of Canada, 1995, at http://www.idrc.ca/books/reports/12ethiop.html.]

Ethiopia is a true multicultural state; more than 70 percent of its 58.7 million people come from three main groups: the Oromo (40 percent), the Amhara (25 percent), and the Tigre (7 percent). The various political factions are aligned with different ethnic groups. The Amhara had been politically dominant for several centuries until, in 1991, the Tigrayan minority took over. About 50 percent of Ethiopians are Muslim, 40 percent Christian (mostly Coptic, but some Roman Catholic and Protestant), and the remainder primarily animist.

Somalia, a V-shaped country with its point jutting into the Indian Ocean, occupies the majority of the low, arid coastal territory. Somalia's population of 10.2 million is virtually all ethnically Somali, and 99 percent Sunni Muslim. They are aligned in six principal clans that have engaged in violent rivalry for power over the last decade. Political turmoil has created refugees who cannot be productive, and it has blocked access to some lands that are crucial to the food production system, causing land that is available to be overused. Population has increased significantly in all countries of the African Horn, but Somalia has seen the largest increase. In these arid countries, growing populations are especially difficult to accommodate because of the scarcity of water and other resources, and because the complex agricultural system requires careful management to remain productive. Ethiopia, Eritrea, and Somalia have suffered famines in the last two decades, only partly as a result of significant periods of decreased rainfall and very much because of human conflict and environmental degradation.

VIGNETTE During the wars of the 1990s, many urban Somalis fled the everyday violence perpetrated by armed gangs and looters, seeking the relative peace of smaller towns and villages. The rural areas were less prone to random violence because they were under the control of strong clan leaders. After her husband was killed trying to protect the family home from looters in the Somalian capital of Mogadishu, Halima Farah Jibril took her four children and what few remaining possessions she could carry, and went to the north coastal town of Bossaso in her clan homeland. Because Halima knew no one in the town when she arrived, the family has to live in a tent, and she makes a meager living selling cups of tea to passersby. But the family lives in peace, without fear of stray bullets from marauding bands.

Bossaso is a relatively peaceful town of 80,000, with a growing economy. Most of its inhabitants are refugees like Halima Jibril's family. It is controlled by a council of clan elders, who meet regularly, usually behind closed doors, to decide on issues of public interest. They have become an effective government, in that most infrastructure necessities (water, power, communication facilities, roads, the port, and markets) are functioning well and expanding. It is too early to tell how long clan rule will effectively replace national government in Somalia. [Adapted from James Mckinley, Jr., *New York Times,* June 22, 1997, p. 3].

East Africa

East Africa (Figure 7.19) has long been united culturally and economically by its dependence on a trade network focused on the Indian Ocean. Today, it is famous for its wildlife and national parks, both of which are threatened by an expanding and needy population.

Physically, East Africa consists of three distinct zones: (1) The mountain and lake country of the Rift Valley stretches through Kenya and curves around the western edges of Uganda, Rwanda, Burundi, and Tanzania. The valley is covered primarily with temperate and tropical savanna, although patches of forest remain on the high slopes and in Tanzania's southwest. (2) A broad coastal zone stretches from the uplands to the sea and is also covered primarily with savanna grasses. (3) Islands to the east consist of Madagascar, the largest and most varied in environment, and the Comoros, the Seychelles, and Mauritius, groups of smaller islands that arc hundreds of miles around the northern half of Madagascar.

Most rural people make a living by cattle herding, particularly in the dry savanna of the north. Herding and cultivation are combined in the wetter central uplands of Kenya and the woodland of Tanzania's south. A mixture of shifting subsistence and plantation cultivation sustains populations toward the south. The main economic activity of the coastal zone, however, is oceanic trade.

For thousands of years, people around the Indian Ocean—from China, Indonesia, Malaysia, India, Persia (Iran), Arabia, and Africa—have met and traded along this shore. The result has been a grand blending

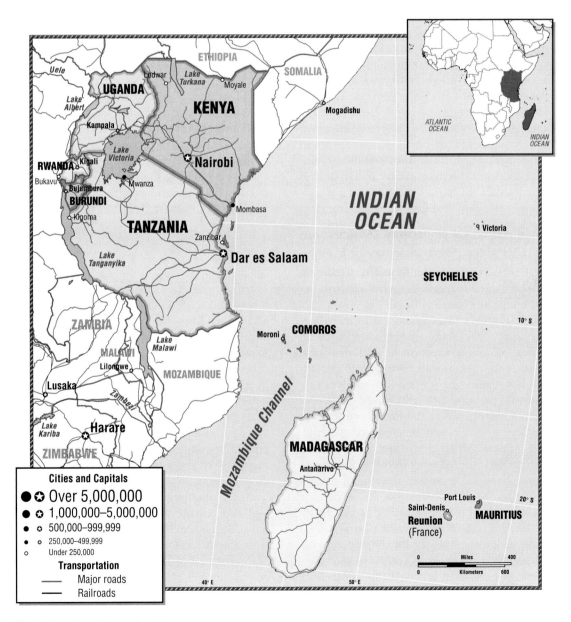

FIGURE 7.19 The East Africa subregion.

of human genetics, culture, plants, animals, and languages. In the sixth century, Arab traders brought Islam to East Africa, where it remains a dominant influence. Traders speaking Swahili, a lingua franca that pragmatically blends Arabic and African languages, established networks that acted as a link between the coast and the interior. These networks penetrated deep into the farming and herding areas of the savanna, and into the semifeudalistic cultures of the "Great Lakes" area. The East African islands participated in this trade, and they show the effects of cultural blending even more than the mainland.

As far back as ancient times, trade in this part of Africa focused on two commodities—slaves and ivory. By the early nineteenth century, the depletion of elephant herds, hunted for ivory, and changing attitudes toward slavery had sent the region into stagnation, making British and French colonial penetration easier. By the turn of the twentieth century, East Africa was undergoing colonial reorganization. Native highland farmers in Kenya were relocated to make way for European coffee plantations, while herders, like the Masai in Kenya and Tanzania, were displaced from the savanna. Their lands became "game reserves," designed to protect the savanna wildlife for the use of European hunters and tourists. Meanwhile, British "indirect rule" in Uganda, and a similar German system in Tanzania as well as Belgian system in Rwanda and Burundi, gave local African elites the responsibility for collecting taxes and drafting laborers for various colonial construction projects. In Rwanda and Burundi, the elite Tutsi were thereby empowered to take advantage of the more numerous Hutu. This practice destabilized long-standing relations between these two groups and was in part responsible for ethnic bloodshed in the 1990s.

Kenya and Tanzania have turned the former colonial game reserves into some of the finest national parks in Africa, offering protection to wild elephants, giraffes, zebras, and lions, as well as many less spectacular but no less significant species. Tourism, mostly connected to wildlife parks, accounts for 20 percent of foreign exchange earnings, but the future of the parks is precarious due to competing demands for the land.

Kenya is the wealthiest and most industrialized country in East Africa, producing cement, petroleum products, autos, beer, and processed food. Yet it still remains one of the poorest countries in the world (see Table 7.1). Government policies resettled black African farmers on formerly European-owned plantations in the highlands, giving the country a strong base in export agriculture (coffee, tea, sugarcane, corn, and sisal). Nomadic peoples have fared less well than agriculturists. Policies for managing the national wildlife parks have allowed tsetse-fly infestations to spread into the local pastoralists' herds; and in a dispute between cultivators and herders over scarce water, the government has sided with the farmers, even to the point of policing the nomadic herders from armed helicopters.

Agriculture brings in a fair amount of money, but the country's dependence on this sector has also created problems. One is related to population growth. In the mid-twentieth century, populations throughout East Africa began to grow extremely rapidly. In 1946, Kenya had just 5 million people; by the late 1990s, it had 28 million trying to eke out an existence from the same land and resource base. In the past, the primarily arid land, when managed according to traditional customs (herding, subsistence cultivation, and trade), could adequately support relatively small populations. Today its carrying capacity is seriously stressed. Competition for cultivable land has pushed thousands of people out of the more fertile uplands into the drier and more fragile savannas that had been communal rangelands and habitats for wild animals. Now the small plowed plots are only marginally productive and have displaced nomads, elephants, impala, and giraffes alike. While Kenyans try desperately to increase agricultural production, volatile world market prices for some export crops in recent years have sent the national economy plunging. These problems are threatening Kenyan and Tanzanian game reserves and parks. Population pressure has forced farmers to plow under and overgraze wildland buffer zones surrounding the parks. Hungry people have begun to poach park animals for food, and there is now a large underground trade in bush-meat.

The Islands

Madagascar, lying off the East African coast, is the fourth largest island in the world; the other three are Greenland, New Guinea, and Borneo. Its unique plant and animal life—the result of diffusion from mainland Africa and Asia—is highly prized by biologists and greatly threatened by environmental degradation. The other East African island nations—the Comoros, the Seychelles, and Mauritius—are much smaller and their habitats are less complex. All the islands have a cosmopolitan ethnic makeup, the result of thousands of years of trade across the Indian Ocean and of further cultural mixing that took place during European (primarily French and British) colonialism. During the colonial era, these islands supported large European-owned plantations, with labor brought in from Asia and the African mainland. More recently, islanders have begun developing tourism that draws visitors from the Indian Ocean area, as well as from Europe.

Southern Africa

Optimistic voices are being raised in Southern Africa these days. Just a few years ago, racial conflict in South

Africa, the largest and wealthiest country in this region, dominated the news. Now racial reconciliation is taking place within South Africa, and the competent work of Nelson Mandela's government, the country's first led by indigenous Africans, is bringing an air of cautious confidence to the entire region.

Southern Africa consists of Angola, Zambia, Malawi, Mozambique, Zimbabwe, Botswana, South Africa, Swaziland, and Lesotho (Figure 7.20). Southern Africa is a plateau ringed on three sides by mountains and a narrow lowland coastal strip. In its center is the Kalahari Desert, but Southern Africa, for the most part, is a land of savannas and open woodland. Population density is light, with the highest densities in the southeastern part of South Africa (see Figure 7.4). Africa's mineral wealth is concentrated in this part of the continent: there are rich deposits of diamonds, gold, chrome, copper, uranium, and coal.

Angola and Mozambique are both former Portuguese colonies. Their wars of independence evolved into civil wars between Marxist governments and rebels supported by South Africa and the United States. Mozambique ended its civil war in 1994; and in 1996 the once devastated economy experienced one of the highest rates of growth on the continent. But in Angola the fighting continues. The officially recognized Marxist-influenced government holds the coastal regions where most Angolans live and where

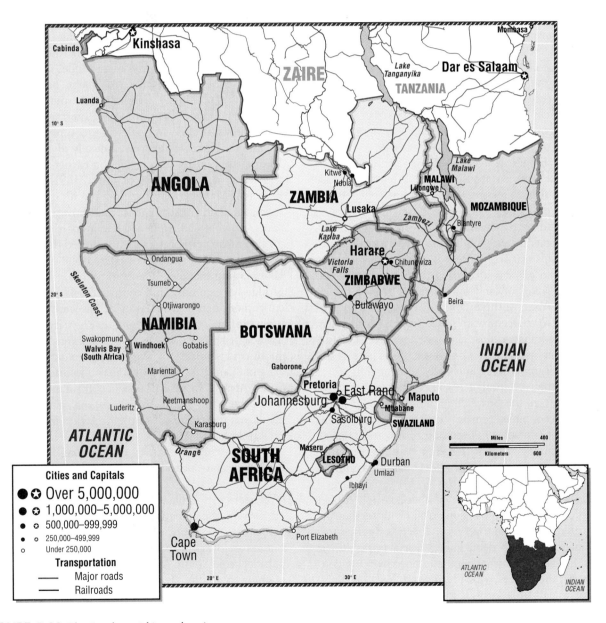

FIGURE 7.20 The Southern Africa subregion.

the country's oil and fishing resources are found. The opposition, known as Union for the Total Independence of Angola (UNITA), draws its strength from among the Ovimbundu-speaking people in the south-central plateau, where gold, diamonds, uranium, and manganese are located. UNITA held the upper hand for years, controlling 70 percent of the country. It previously garnered support from the now defunct Mobutu regime in Zaire/Congo and from the sales of diamonds and other resources. In early 1998, UNITA and the Angolan government agreed to a peace treaty, but episodic violence continued in the countryside.

The three interior countries of Malawi, Zimbabwe, and Zambia are still overwhelmingly rural. Agriculture and related food-processing industries form the basis of life for most people and a major portion of exports. Recently, however, agriculture has emerged as a problem, and the case of Malawi is illustrative. Until recently, Malawi had sufficient food and surpluses for export; but in the 1980s, land productivity began to fall as a result of declining fertility from overuse. Part of the problem lies in the fact that after independence came in 1964, the government chose to focus on large-estate agriculture to produce cash crops (tobacco, tea, sugar) for export. Fragile tropical soils that ordinarily need years of rest between crops were expected to produce continually. After a few years, the soil was depleted and production on plantations declined. Smallholders, who had lost land to commercial producers, found themselves with insufficient land for the necessary fallow periods. The historian F. Jeffress Ramsay writes that, by the 1990s, 86 percent of Malawi rural households had less than 5 acres of land on which to grow food for themselves. Yet it is these same smallholders who produce nearly 70 percent of the food for rural and urban people. The country must also now feed over 600,000 refugees from Mozambique's civil war.

Today, Zambia and Zimbabwe are struggling to reconstitute their cultural heritage after generations of colonialism (see the box "The Thumb Piano"). However, their economies remain focused on extractive industries. In Zimbabwe, chromium, gold, coal, nickel, and silver mining accounts for 40 percent of the country's exports; a newly opened (1994) platinum mine is expected to make Zimbabwe the world's second largest producer, after South Africa. Zambia has rich copper resources and has been a major world producer, but the industry lost money in the 1990s. The loss was due to a combination of high debt, falling world prices in the 1980s, inefficient management, and poor working conditions for the miners, which resulted in low productivity. Botswana's situation is discussed as a case study in the section on economic and political issues earlier in this chapter (see page 334).

Majority Rule Comes to South Africa

South Africa is about twice the size of Texas, with a population of 39 million people. Seventy-five percent of these are of African descent, 14 percent are of European background, 2 percent are of Indian extraction, and the rest are of mixed descent. After more than 300 years of colonization by Europeans and rule by the white minority, free elections were held in 1994 and black Africans took over the government. The end of white minority rule came after nearly 50 years of strict segregation by color, a system known as apartheid.

South Africa is a country of beautiful and dramatic vistas. Just inland of its long coastline lie uplands and mountains that afford dramatic views of the coast and the ocean. The interior is a high rolling plateau reminiscent of the Great Plains in North America. South Africa is entirely within the midlatitudes and has consistently cool temperatures that range between 60°F and 70°F (16°–20°C). The extreme southern coastal area around Cape Town has a Mediterranean climate: cool and wet in the winter, dry in the summer.

South Africa has long been deeply divided by race. As discussed in the history section earlier in the chapter, white supremacy lasted from 1652 until 1994. President Mandela was unyielding in his efforts to heal the racial divide, insisting that the country first face the reality of what had happened under apartheid and then forgive those perpetrators who admitted their deeds.

South Africa is now considered one of the world's 10 emerging markets. The country has a balanced and productive economy that contributes 45 percent of the entire continent's production. It has built competitive industries in communications, energy, transport, and finance (it has a world-class stock market), and supplies goods and services to neighboring countries (80 percent of Namibia's and Botswana's imports come from South Africa). In return, products from all over Africa have permeated South Africa's markets, and many people across the region of southern Africa are dependent on jobs in South Africa.

The Angolan peace treaty, economic successes in Zimbabwe and Botswana, and reconciliation and political and economic progress in South Africa have prompted forecasters to speculate that this region, more than any other, holds the potential to lead Africa into a more prosperous age. Certainly, poverty is still widespread and resources are overstressed. But with creative leadership and outside help, South Africa and a few of its neighbors might even go directly from agrarian economies into the incipient information age of the twenty-first century, leapfrogging over the industrial phase experienced by Europe, North America, and Japan.

CULTURAL INSIGHT   *The Thumb Piano*

In Zimbabwe, the Shona people have considered the mbira (thumb piano) a core element of their culture for several hundred years. The mbira plays both a sa-

Thumb piano. [Jose Azel/Contact/Woodfin Camp & Associates.]

cred and a secular role in society. Practitioners use it in bira ceremonies to contact the spiritual realm. In the 1970s, the mbira was one of the principal instruments used in the subtle songs and traditional parables of protest against white rule. These songs infuriated members of the white Rhodesian government because they could not understand them. Missionaries viewed the music as pagan and tried to ban it. But now it is once again used extensively both for entertainment and to lift the spirits.

Musicians play the mbira by depressing and releasing the ends of the finely tuned metal keys with their thumbnails. The keys vibrate against the carefully crafted wooden resonator and produce warm, metallic tones that add mysterious, melodious sounds to any composition. There are many different styles of mbiras, and the number of keys can range between 8 and 52. While many modern instruments are box-shaped affairs, traditional mbiras are made of resonant calabash bowls.

Source: Adapted from *Dandemutande* magazine, at http://www.africaonline.com/AfricaOnline/music/zimbabwe.html.

REFLECTIONS ON SUB-SAHARAN AFRICA

Late one evening, in a restaurant in Central Europe, after a lengthy conversation that danced lightly over some of the earth's perplexing problems, my colleague leaned across the elegant white linen tablecloth and queried: "But don't you think that Africa is, after all, better off for having been colonized by Europeans?"

How to reply to such a question? Africa, the ancient home of the human race, is of all regions on earth today the one in greatest need of attention. Africa is poor and, by some measures, getting poorer. Yet, to the casual observer, the explanations for Africa's poverty are not immediately apparent. Africa is blessed with many kinds of resources: agricultural, mineral, and forest. Nonetheless, its income from these resources is low. And although most of Africa is not densely occupied, rapid population growth is thwarting efforts

to improve standards of living. Africa's people work hard, but their productivity, at least as measured by the standards of the developed world, is low.

An understanding of the reasons for Africa's present poverty and its social and political instability begins to emerge only through an exploration of its history over the last several centuries of European colonialism and from a careful analysis of how that history is still affecting the organization of African economies and African societies. Under colonialism, Africans were methodically removed from control of their own societies, and their places and peoples were turned to the service of distant locales. Even now, after colonialism is officially over, outsiders continue to consider African resources as available for the taking at less than a fair price. As an example, remember the case of the international fishing fleet off Guinea-Bissau, mentioned in the introduction to this chapter. In view of all this, it is hard to believe that anyone would think Africa is better off for having been colonized.

Africans are only beginning to devise new development strategies and political institutions to replace the ones imposed by outsiders over the last 500 years.

Africa today remains a continent of countries created out of foreign perceptions of how Africans should be organized politically; but wider visions are now being articulated by African statesmen. Pan-African movements for economic integration and regional cooperation to control violence are emerging.

It is tempting to suggest that next should come an era when the rest of the world leaves Africa to the Africans. But that may be too simplistic a view. Although Africa had plenty of help getting into its current predicament, and outsiders have prospered from its stolen wealth, it has never been the recipient of much development aid. Europe, America, and Japan together give about U.S. $16.2 billion a year to sub-Saharan Africa, of which the United States gives only about 4 percent, or U.S. $665 million annually. Egypt alone gets U.S. $2.4 billion from the United States, or about 15 percent of total U.S. foreign aid. Just 7 percent of this total goes to all of sub-Saharan Africa. This figure is far less than Americans reap in profits from private investment in Africa. For example, in 1996, the Coca-Cola Corporation alone took profits of roughly $83 million from African operations.

Many economists who support the idea of development based to some reasonable degree on free markets and entrepreneurship, think it behooves the wealthy nations to financially support Africa's comeback. This would help Africans reach the point where they are more prosperous and can themselves become a market for imported products. Experts in and out of Africa are independently reaching the conclusion that some combination of the following strategies is needed. First, as recently suggested by the bishops of the Anglican Church and the Pope, the developed world should cancel African debt. This step would divert debt payments to public investment in social services (education, health care) and stop the destructive effects of SAPs. Second, the developed world should lower tariffs against African manufactured products so as to foster indigenous industries. Finally, more basic development assistance for the enhancement of education, health care, and technical skills is in order. The consensus is that the developed world should not abandon Africa now but rather should listen to and support African voices on how best to turn the genius of the African people to the task of solving Africa's problems. For years, some African leaders and others with deep experience on the continent have pleaded that aid be designed to take advantage of indigenous skills and knowledge, that development planning address local needs as defined and managed by local expertise. This is a fundamentally conservative perspective, which invests faith in the ability of people to ultimately look out for themselves.

Selected Themes and Concepts

1. Most of sub-Saharan Africa has a tropical climate that varies primarily by amounts of rainfall, distance from the equator, and the annual north-south movements of the **intertropical convergence zone.**

2. Africa's arid ecosystems are particularly **fragile environments** because intense use by humans almost always results in loss of yet more moisture.

3. Africa has been particularly adversely affected by European colonialism and continues to endure **neocolonialism**—the circumstance whereby non-Africans have relatively inexpensive access to resources that are exported, usually in an unrefined state. The profits from resource extraction tend to go into foreign accounts rather than to be invested in African development.

4. The era of formal European colonialism lasted less than 100 years, but it resulted in widespread reorganization of African economies and settlement patterns and the dislocation and separation of families in order to address the labor and resource needs of colonial enterprises like mining and plantation agriculture.

5. During the cold war, newly independent African countries were often courted and armed by either the United States or the USSR, as these two powers competed for global dominance. Many of the conflicts now, or recently, in progress in Africa stem from these European and American interventions.

6. Africa is not particularly densely populated. Its population problems stem from rapid growth that threatens to exceed the land's **carrying capacity**—the number of people the environment and economic systems can support.

7. Most countries in Africa rank low in global standards of living. However, although poverty remains widespread, there are definite patterns, with some countries providing a decent life for most citizens.

8. Debilitating diseases of several sorts afflict a large number of Africans. AIDS is only one and thus far not the most deadly. In Africa, AIDS is a heterosexual phenomenon: four-fifths of the world's women with AIDS are in Africa. Many of them are young mothers infected by their husbands.

9. International development agencies like the World Bank have often encouraged African countries to go into debt to implement development schemes, only to find that, due to bad planning, the schemes are unworkable. Structural adjustment programs are aimed at belt-tightening so that government revenue can be increased and debts can be paid. SAPs often have the most debilitating effect on the poorest.

10. Women do much of the work on the domestic and village levels in Africa, and are subject to particularly severe gender discrimination. These circumstances are thought to be in part the result of colonial reorganization of indigenous African economies to facilitate resource extraction.

Selected Readings

Bass, Thomas A. *Camping with the Prince and Other Tales of Science in Africa.* New York: Penguin, 1991.

Blakely, Thomas D., Walter E. A. van Beek, and Dennis L. Thomson, eds. *Religion in Africa—Experience and Expression.* London and Portsmouth, NH: James Currey and Heinemann, 1994.

Blunt, Alison. *Travel, Gender, and Imperialism—Mary Kingsley and West Africa.* New York: Guilford Press, 1994.

Chapman, Graham P., and Kathleen M. Baker, eds. *The Changing Geography of Africa and the Middle East.* London: Routledge, 1992.

Clarke, John I. *Sierra Leone in Maps: Graphic Perspective of a Developing Country.* New York: Africana, 1972.

Dale, Richard. *Botswana's Search for Autonomy in Southern Africa.* Westport, CT: Greenwood Press, 1995.

De Villiers, Marq, and Sheila Hirtle. *Into Africa—A Journey Through the Ancient Empires.* Toronto: Key Porter Books, 1997.

Dorkenoo, Efua. *Cutting the Rose—Female Genital Mutilation: The Practice and Its Prevention.* London: Minority Rights Group, 1994.

Gade, Daniel W. Madagascar and nondevelopment. *Focus* (October 1995): 14–21.

Gellar, Sheldon. *Senegal: An African Nation Between Islam and the West.* Boulder, CO: Westview Press, 1995.

Goheen, Miriam. *Men Own the Fields, Women Own the Crops—Gender and Power in the Cameroon Grassfields.* Madison: University of Wisconsin Press, 1996.

Grosz-Ngate, Maria, and Omari H. Kokole, eds. *Gendered Encounters—Challenging Cultural Boundaries and Social Hierarchies in Africa.* London: Routledge, 1997.

Hackett, Rosalind I. J., ed. *New Religious Movements in Nigeria.* Lewiston/Queenston, NY: Edwin Mellen Press, 1987.

Iliffe, John. *Africans—The History of a Continent.* Cambridge: Cambridge University Press, 1995.

Kalipeni, Ezekiel. The fertility transition in Africa. *Geographical Review* (July 1995): 286–300.

Kelly, Sean. *America's Tyrant—The CIA and Mobutu of Zaire—How the United States Put Mobutu in Power, Protected Him from His Enemies, Helped Him Become One of the Richest Men in the World, and Lived to Regret It.* Washington, DC: American University Press, 1993.

Lelyveld, John. *Move Your Shadow.* New York: Penguin, 1985.

McEwan, Cheryl. Paradise or pandemonium? West African landscapes in the travel accounts of Victorian women. *Journal of Historical Geography* 22, no. 1 (1996): 68–83.

Moore, Henrietta L., and Megan Vaughan. *Cutting Down Trees—Gender, Nutrition and Agricultural Change in the Northern Province of Zambia, 1890–1990.* Portsmouth, NH: Heinemann, 1993.

Nugent, Paul. *Big Men, Small Boys and Politics in Ghana—Power, Ideology and the Burden of History, 1982–1994.* London: Pinter, 1995.

Rocheleau, Dianne, Barbara Thomas-Slayter, and Esther Wangari, eds. *Feminist Political Ecology—Global Issues and Local Experiences.* London: Routledge, 1996.

Sanneh, Lamin. *The Crown and the Turban—Muslims and West African Pluralism.* Boulder, CO: Westview Press, 1997.

Somah, Syrulwa L. *Historical Settlement of Liberia and Its Environmental Impact.* Lanham, MD: University Press of America, 1995.

Walker, Alice, and Pratibha Parmar. *Warrior Marks—Female Genital Mutilation and the Sexual Blinding of Women.* New York: Harcourt Brace, 1993.

Wright, Donald R. *The World and a Very Small Place in Africa.* Armonk, NY: M. E. Sharpe, 1997.

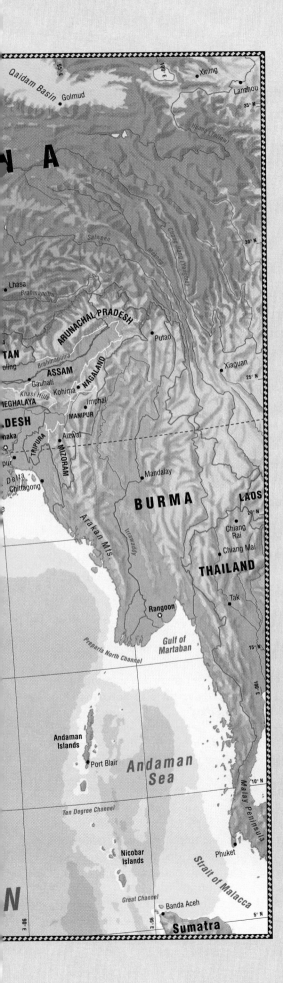

CHAPTER

EIGHT

SOUTH ASIA

INTRODUCTION TO SOUTH ASIA

*T*he Ganges delta is "an unexpectedly beautiful land, with a soft languor and gentle rhythm of its own," writes Richard Critchfield, who has studied village life in more than a dozen countries. "Mist hangs over the endless sea of rice paddies like steam over a vat." By day, the village of Joypur, "with just over fifteen hundred people in a hundred and forty families [lay] steamy and somnolent in the sun—its busy activity off in the fields, or hidden from view in the women's courtyards. Chickens scratched for grain, naked children played in the dust, . . . a tailor sat cross-legged before an ancient sewing machine.

Several generations of a North Indian family, from the village of Dharamkot in Himachal Pradesh province, enjoy each other's company. [David Morgan.]

"At dusk the village came to life . . . the men came to settle in groups before one of the open pavilions and talk—rich, warm Bengali talk, argumentative and humorous, fervent and excited in gossip, protest and indignation. The men were barefoot and clad only in saronglike longis—from habit and the high price of cloth. A few still had rags tied about their coarse black hair against the day's fierce sun or sudden monsoon rains. . . . Most were undernourished, though a few robust figures stood out—like muscular Rashid, respected as the best farmer in Joypur, or silver-haired Abdur, the head of the cooperative society."

In the enclosed women's quarters lamps flicker and the chirping of cicadas rises from the fields. In one such quarter, Mishri is finishing up her day by the dying cooking fire as her year-old son tunnels his way into her sari to nurse himself to sleep. Mishri lives in this tiny world bounded by the walls of the courtyard she shares with her husband and five children and several of her husband's kin. Almost all her activity takes place here, in seclusion. Her village, though Hindu, has long ago adopted the Muslim practice of purdah, *in which women keep themselves apart from male gazes and community life. Mishri meets with two women friends every day to talk. She is devoted to her husband; and out of respect never says his name aloud.*

—Adapted from Richard Critchfield, Villages, *pp. 71–72; and Faith D'Aluisio and Peter Menzel,* Women in the Material World, *p. 115*

South Asia may be the best-defined region in the world outside of the Americas. Physically, it is bounded by the sea on the south and by very obvious mountainous zones on the north. Culturally and politically it is enormously complex, and yet there are amazing unifying features: the village is one; the common experience of British colonialism is another.

The vast majority of South Asians—about 75 percent—live in rural areas, in hundreds of thousands of villages, and most of these people would recognize elements of life in Joypur. The village way of life unites the region and renders tolerable its extravagant cultural complexity. Even many of those now living in South Asia's giant cities were born in a village or visit one regularly. In fact, were one to observe life carefully in a city like Madras or Peshawar, one would discover that the city is hardly that at all, but rather thousands of tightly compacted reconstituted villages.

South Asia is physically smaller by far than Africa; South Asia would fit five times into Africa. Yet, with nearly 1.3 billion people, it has twice the population.

The countries that make up the region are Afghanistan and Pakistan in the northwest, the Himalayan states of Nepal and Bhutan, Bangladesh in the northeast, India, Sri Lanka, and several sets of islands in the Arabian and Bengal seas.

Themes to Look For

Themes to follow in this region are:

1. The importance of village life

2. The residual influence of British colonization

3. The ancient and layered pattern of multiple cultural influences—prehistoric indigenous, Dravidian, Aryan, Hindu, Islamic, Buddhist, Malayan, and British.

4. An extreme disparity of wealth

5. Rapid population growth among the very poor majority

The complexity of the region results in a good bit of confusion and internal conflict; and yet, for all its troubles, South Asia has a spirit that is vibrant and inventive and often cheerfully good-natured.

PHYSICAL PATTERNS

Landforms

The Indian subcontinent and its surrounding territory make up some of the most spectacular landforms on earth. This region illustrates dramatically what can happen when two tectonic plates collide.

About 180 million years ago, India broke free of the eastern edge of the African continent and floated to the northeast. About 60 million years ago, it began to collide with Eurasia and became a giant peninsula jutting into the Indian Ocean. As the relentless pushing from the south continued, both the leading (northern) edge of India and the southern edge of Eurasia crumpled and buckled. The massive Himalayan mountain range, rising more than 28,000 feet (8500 meters), was formed out of this collision, but the effects extended far beyond them. To the west and east of the Indian landmass, the pressure pushed curved crinkles into the "fabric" of Eurasia. These crinkles became, in the west, the Hindu Kush, the Pamirs, and the other mountains of Pakistan and Afghanistan; in the east, they became the mountains of far eastern India and adjacent Burma,

China, and Thailand. In response to the continuous compression, the Tibetan Plateau rose up behind the Himalayas to more than 15,000 feet (4500 meters) in some places. Land elsewhere in Asia, as far north as Siberia, responded by arching, bending, and cracking.

South of the Himalayas, the central portions of the huge triangle of the Indian subcontinent form the Ganges river basin and south of that the Deccan Plateau. The plateau is an area of modest uplands 1000 to 2000 feet (300 to 600 meters) high interspersed with river valleys. This upland region is bounded by two moderately high mountain ranges, the Eastern and Western Ghats. They descend to a lengthy but narrow coastline interrupted by extensive river deltas and alluvial plains. The river valleys and coastal zones are densely occupied; the uplands only slightly less so.

Climate

The end of the dry season [April and May] is cruel in South Asia. It marks the beginning of a brief lull that is soon overtaken by the annual monsoon rains. In the lowlands of eastern India and Bangladesh, temperatures in the shade are routinely above a hundred degrees; the heat causes dirt roads to become so parched that they are soon covered in several inches of loose dirt and sand. Tornadoes wreak havoc, killing hundreds and flattening entire villages. Even the wind provides little relief, as it whips up sandstorms, making it impossible to see farther than six feet in any direction. Inhaling the sand and dust leads to widespread respiratory problems that cause many to spend long stretches of the summer ill.

This is also a time of hunger, as with each passing day thousands of rural families consume the last of their household stock of grain from the previous harvest and join the millions of others who must buy their food. Each new entrant into the market nudges the price of grain up a little more, pushing millions from two meals a day to one, from 90 percent of the minimal caloric intake needed to sustain life, to 70 percent.

—Alex Counts, Give Us Credit, *p. 69*

From mid June to the end of October is the time of the river. Not only are the rivers full to bursting, but the rains pour down so relentlessly and the clouds are so close to village roofs that all the earth smells damp and mildewed, and green and yellow moss creeps up every wall and tree. . . . Cattle and goats become aquatic, chickens are placed in baskets on roofs, and boats are

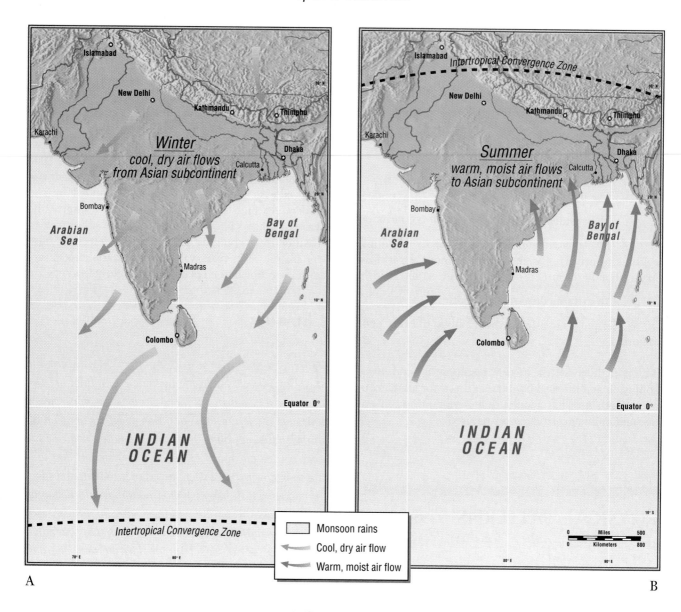

A

B

C

FIGURE 8.1 (A) In the winter, cold, dry air blows from the continent across India toward the ITCZ much farther south. (B) The ITCZ moves to the north of India in the summer, picking up huge amounts of moisture from the ocean, which it then deposits over India. (C) Moisture-laden monsoon air from the cooler ocean rises when it hits the warmer land, and is pushed up still further when it encounters mountains, releasing copious rain in the summer.

loaded with valuables and tied to houses. Cooking fires are impossible . . . so the staples [are] precooked rice, a dry lentil called dal, *and jackfruit, a large smelly melon that ripens on trees during this season. . . . Because most villages are built on artificial mounds raised above the fields, as the floods rise villages become tiny islands, . . . self-sustaining outpost[s] cut off from civilization . . . for most of three months of the year.*

—*James Novak,* Bangladesh:
Reflections on the Water, *pp. 24–25*

These two passages describe the dramatic contrasts between South Asia's **summer** and **winter monsoons**, or seasons (Figure 8.1). As described in Chapter 1, somewhat cooler moisture-laden air moves from the ocean over the land in summer (comparable to inhaling in breathing), whereas cool dry air moves from land to sea in winter (comparable to exhaling). Though this process happens across the globe, the massive size of the Eurasian landmass greatly intensifies it. The monsoon brings plentiful rain in the summer, and that process is amplified by yet another process taking place at the equator.

Air masses moving south from the Northern Hemisphere and north from the Southern Hemisphere converge at the equator. This warm moisture-laden air rises upward, forming clouds that, as they rise and cool, produce copious precipitation. This belt of warm rising air circling the earth around the equator is called the intertropical convergence zone, or ITCZ (see Figure 7.2). In the northern summer, the ITCZ shifts north of the equator; in winter, it shifts south of the equator. Climatologists now think that the powerful "inhalation" of the Eurasian landmass in summer actually bends the ITCZ belt near the Horn of Africa. This bending allows the ITCZ to move north rapidly over the Indian Ocean, picking up enormous amounts of moisture that are then deposited throughout Asia.

The monsoons and the ITCZ are major influences on South Asia's climate (Figure 8.2). In June, the ITCZ-generated warm moist air first hits the mountainous Western Ghats and Sri Lanka's central highlands. The rising air mass cools as it moves over the mountains, releasing rainfall that nurtures dense tropical rain forests. After dumping huge amounts of rain, the air mass is reduced in moisture, and somewhat less (but still significant) rain falls to the east of the Western Ghats. Once on the other side of India, the monsoon gathers more moisture and power in its northward sweep up the Bay of Bengal, sometimes turning into a tropical cyclone. Once the monsoon system reaches the hot plains of West Bengal and Bangladesh in July, rising air causes strong updrafts in the moist atmosphere. These updrafts create massive,

thunderous cumulonimbus rain clouds that drench and then flood the parched countryside. Precipitation is especially intense in the foothills of the Himalayas. There, the northeastern Indian state of Meghalaya has the highest average annual rainfall in the world: about 35 feet (10.9 meters). Rainfall diminishes to the west of Nepal, but seasonal rain is still significant in a band paralleling the Himalayas that reaches across northern India all the way to northern Pakistan. The variations in rainfall are reflected in the varying climate zones (see Figure 8.2).

By November, the cooling Eurasian landmass is sending cooler drier air to South Asia. This cooler air from the north pushes the warm wet air back south to the Indian Ocean. Although very little rain falls during this winter monsoon, parts of South India and Sri Lanka receive winter rains as the ITCZ drops moisture picked up on its now southward pass over the Bay of Bengal.

Monsoon rains deposit enormous amounts of moisture over the Himalayas, much of it in the form of snow and ice. Meltwater feeds the headwaters of the three river systems that figure prominently in the region: the Indus, the Ganges, and the Brahmaputra. All three rivers actually begin within 100 miles (150 kilometers) of each other in the Himalaya highlands near the Tibet/Nepal/India borders. The Ganges flows generally south through the mountains and then east across the Ganges plain to the Bay of Bengal. The Brahmaputra flows first east, then south, and then west to join the Ganges in forming the giant delta of Bengal. The Indus in the far west takes a southwesterly course across arid Pakistan and empties into the Arabian Sea. These rivers and many of the tributaries that feed them are actively wearing down the surface of the Himalayas; they carry an enormous load of silt, especially during the rainy season when their volume is increased drastically. Their velocity slows when they reach the lowlands, and much of the sediment settles out. It is then repeatedly picked up and redeposited by successive floods. As is illustrated in the Brahmaputra diagram (Figure 8.3), this seasonally replenished silt nourishes much of the agricultural production in the densely occupied plains of Bangladesh. The same is true on the Ganges and Indus plains.

HUMAN PATTERNS

Over the millennia, a variety of groups have migrated into South Asia, many of them invaders who conquered peoples already there. The result has been a

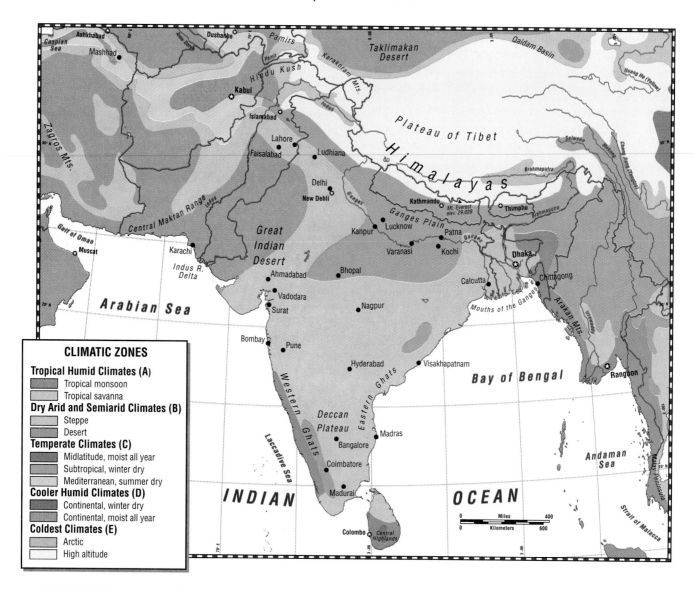

FIGURE 8.2 Regional climate.

level of cultural diversity that few other world regions can equal. Today, this diversity makes South Asia one of the most politically contentious places in the world.

The most recent invaders were the British, who established a colonial empire here in the eighteenth century and remained until the middle of the twentieth. This British era has left a number of legacies that affect deeply how South Asians relate to the outside world and interact with each other. Today the chief threats to the region are those originating from within.

A Series of Invasions

The first recorded invaders into South Asia were the so-called **Aryans,** who stormed into the Indus Valley and Punjab from Central and Southwest Asia perhaps

as early as 6000 years ago. Many scholars believe that the Aryans instituted the hugely influential **caste system.** The caste system divides society into a hierarchy of distinct social units of greatly varying status. Although the system is weakening today, traditionally a person is born into a given caste and generally cannot change that designation. Over time, the caste system may have weakened South Asia's ability to resist invaders. Rules barring contact between castes made for weak armies, and certain castes were easily co-opted into the ruling structures of invaders. In particular, the highest priestly castes, known as the Brahmins, served as advisers and administrators to foreign conquerors. Under Brahmin influence, invaders often adopted many of the cultural attributes, including the caste system itself, that had made the South Asians vulnerable to conquest in the first place. Thus, over generations,

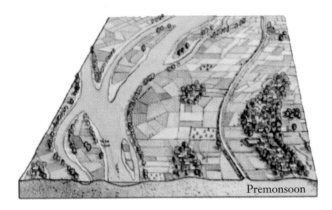

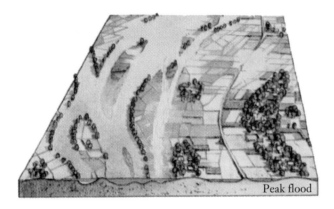

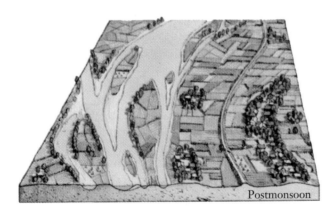

The great fortress at Agra, built 1565–1571, had walls 22 meters high enclosing an area about 2.5 kilometers in circumference. [JHC Wilson/Robert Harding Picture Library.]

FIGURE 8.3 In the premonsoon stage (top) the Brahmaputra River in Bangladesh flows in multiple channels across the flat plain. During peak flood stage (middle), the great volume of water jumps the banks and spreads across fields, towns, and roads. It cuts new channels, leaving some places cut off from the mainland. In the postmonsoon stage (bottom), the river has returned to its banks but some of the new channels persist, changing the lay of the land. As the river recedes, it leaves silt and algae that provide nourishment to the land. New ponds and lakes are formed, filled with fish. The farmers learn to adapt their home sites to an ever changing landscape. Throughout much of the nation farmers are able to produce rice and vegetables nearly year-round (see photo on page 402). [Adapted from *National Geographic,* June 1993, p. 125.]

as invaders settled into their role as a caste of ruling elites, their realms became more vulnerable to waves of new invaders.

Some of the most significant invaders were Islamic peoples from Central and Southwest Asia. Muslim invasions started around A.D. 1000 and reached their height in the sixteenth century, when the **Moguls** conquered a vast empire, covering most of the region between 1526 and 1857. The primary legacy left by the Moguls and other Islamic peoples are the more than 300 million Muslims now living in South Asia. A few are the descendants of the Moguls themselves; most descend from Hindus who converted to Islam for a variety of reasons, including a wish to escape life as members of low-status castes. Today Islam is central to the national character of three countries in the region: Afghanistan, Pakistan, and Bangladesh. In India, Muslims are the largest religious minority, making up about one-eighth of the population.

South Asia's most recent and influential invader was Great Britain. That nation was already a strong trading presence in the 1750s and ruled most of South Asia directly from 1857 to 1947.

The Legacies of Colonial Rule

British rule profoundly influenced South Asia politically, socially, and economically. The British Empire used the region's resources for its own benefit, often to the detriment of South Asia. A typical example of the process is provided by a look at the textile industry of Bengal—modern day Bangladesh and the Indian state

369

of West Bengal. This was one of Britain's first inroads into South Asian economies. Long known for their high-quality muslin cotton cloth, Bengali weavers initially benefited from the greater access British traders gave them to overseas markets in Asia, the Americas, and the European continent, as well as in Britain itself. However, as Britain's own highly mechanized textile industry developed during the eighteenth century, cheaper British cloth replaced Bengali muslin, first on world markets and eventually throughout South Asia as well. Thus, as one British colonial official put it, while the mills of Yorkshire prospered, "the bones of Bengali weavers bleached the plains of India."

What little development that did take place in South Asia was allowed only if it benefited Britain. Continental Europe and the United States, and later Japan, used protective tariffs to provide a shield against cheaper imported British manufactured goods. But the British prohibited protective tariffs in South Asia; hence, British competition ruined many established South Asian industries and forced their workers to return to agricultural pursuits. For the remainder of the colonial period, Britain encouraged the production mainly of agricultural raw materials, such as cotton, jute (a fiber used in making gunnysacks and rope), tea, sugar, and indigo; these were intended to supply its own growing industries and fit in with British consumption patterns.

Another example of how colonialism distorted development in South Asia is the building of railroads in India. Thousands of miles of track were built, but almost all the locomotives, cars, and rails were made in Britain, which thus received a boost for its coal, steel, and manufacturing industries. The railroads were not primarily intended to be a transport network linking South Asian places. Rather, they were intended as a series of lines to carry raw materials to ports and transport British manufactured goods back for sale in the hinterlands of South Asia. Nonetheless, internal linkages were eventually made.

The economic historian Dietmar Rothermund argues that this British emphasis on inhibiting and reversing Indian industrial development in order to suit its own needs not only deprived local economies of profitable industries but also encouraged population growth, now such a prominent issue in all of South Asia. Poor farmers produced as many children as possible, both for farm labor and as insurance against destitution in their old age. Had they moved from being farmers to being industrial workers and entrepreneurs, they might have opted, like their counterparts elsewhere, for smaller families; and they might simply have saved their earnings to provide for their old age.

Nonetheless, there were some benefits from the British Empire. British irrigation projects aided some farmers; and a few areas prospered from trade with the rest of the empire, especially the large British-built cities on the coast, such as Bombay (now officially returned to its precolonial name of Mumbai), Calcutta, and Madras. The railroad did boost trade between parts of South Asia, and it greatly eased the burden of personal transport. In addition, English became a common language for South Asians of widely different backgrounds, assisting both trade and cross-cultural understanding. Moreover, most of today's South Asian governments are based largely on institutions put in place by the British to administer their vast empire. It is true that South Asian governments have inherited many of the shortcomings of their colonial forbears, such as highly bureaucratic procedures, a resistance to change, and a tendency to remain distant and aloof from the people they govern. Nonetheless, these governments have proved functional. In particular, democratic government, though it was not instituted on a large scale until the final years of the empire, has provided people with an outlet for voicing their concerns and has enabled numerous peaceful transitions of elected governments.

Perhaps the most enduring and damaging legacy of colonial rule was the tragic partition of British India into the independent countries of India and Pakistan in 1947 (Figure 8.4). As part of the independence agreement, it was decided that northwestern and northeastern India, where the population was predominantly Muslim, would become a single country. This new country, Pakistan, thus consisted of two parts, known as East and West Pakistan, separated by all of northern India. Though both India and Pakistan maintained secular constitutions, with no official religious affiliation, the general understanding was that Pakistan was to be a Muslim majority country and that India would would have a Hindu majority. Fearing that they would be persecuted if they did not move, millions of Hindus migrated from their ancestral homes in Pakistan to India; similarly, Muslims left their homes in India for Pakistan. In the process families and communities were divided, and up to a million people were killed in innumerable skirmishes between the two religious groups.

Many historians argue that partition could have been avoided had it not been for deliberate British efforts throughout the colonial era to heighten tensions between South Asian Muslims and Hindus, thus creating a role for themselves as indispensable and benevolent mediators. There is much evidence of these so-called divide and rule tactics. In many localities, it was common for British administrators to favor the interests of minority communities in order to weaken the power of the majority community, which could have threatened British authority. At the national scale, the British worked out political deals with Muslim leaders

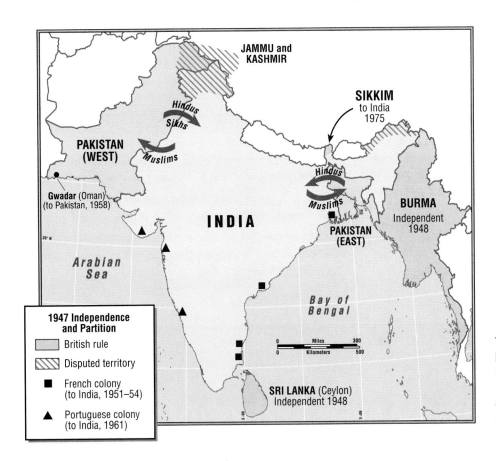

FIGURE 8.4 The breakup of Britain's South Asian colonies in 1947 with the partition of India and Pakistan. [Adapted from *National Geographic,* May 1997, p. 18.]

as a way of weakening Muslim support for the Indian Congress party, which led the independence movement and claimed to represent the interests of both Muslims and Hindus. In the independence era, the painful legacy of partition spawned two major wars between India and Pakistan. Relations between the two countries remain strained to this day.

Since Independence

In the 50 years since the departure of the British, South Asians have experienced both progress and setbacks. With invasion from without no longer a realistic threat, the region's people have increasingly benefited from self-rule. Democracy has expanded steadily, if somewhat slowly. The last major monarchy, the tiny Himalayan kingdom of Bhutan, is in the process of giving its people the vote. India has maintained its status as the world's most populous democracy and has relentlessly dismantled age-old traditions that held back poor low-caste Hindus and other disadvantaged groups. Agricultural advances have brought relative prosperity to a few rural areas; and a small but increasing number of educated Indians are reaping the economic benefits of the global growth in information technology. Nonetheless, all South Asian countries have continued to suffer from low levels of economic development, with a collective gross national product per capita of U.S. $384 (as of 1998). This is the lowest average for any world region.

If threats from outside the region have diminished, the threat of violence originating from within has steadily risen. After 1947, East and West Pakistan, despite their common religion, struggled to overcome their stark cultural differences and wide spatial separation. East Pakistan was the most populous, and through the export of primary products was the chief earner of the country's foreign exchange. West Pakistan dominated in government and military positions. As a result of a bloody civil war in 1971, Pakistan was divided and East Pakistan became the independent country of Bangladesh. In the years since, civil wars have plagued Sri Lanka, Afghanistan, and parts of India; and the possibility of nuclear confrontation between Pakistan and India has loomed ominously on the horizon. Future threats to the region's stability may result from stresses that a huge and still growing population place on the region's already precarious natural environment. Hence, despite the considerable gains of the past, South Asia is one of the world's two poorest regions and potentially one of the most unstable.

Population Patterns

Although Africa has absolutely the fastest-growing population on earth, South Asia is already so densely populated (Figure 8.5) and continues to grow so quickly that the consequences are to be seen everywhere in the landscape. At night, homeless sleepers occupy virtually all urban public spaces; commuters cling to the outside of packed buses as they groan through the streets of New Delhi; rural hills are denuded of trees and bushes because people have cut wood for cooking and grass for animal fodder; crowded urban shantytowns have but a few water spigots for thousands of residents. And nearly everywhere, there are people, throngs of people.

South Asia has several of the world's largest cities—Bombay with 13 million, Calcutta with 11 million, Delhi with 8 million, Dhaka with 7 million—and the stream of migrants from the countryside seems never-ending. But the stream can only increase because thus far less than 30 percent of the population is urban.

VIGNETTE One of the consequences of South Asia's rapid urban growth is that the cities have become so crowded that housing has long since been exhausted and many people simply live on the streets. In a National Public Radio interview in August 1997, an Indian journalist re-

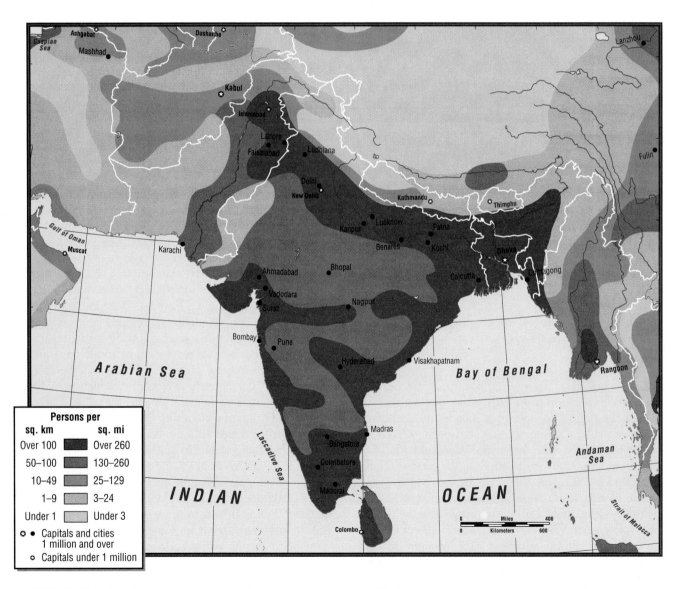

FIGURE 8.5 Population density. [Adapted from *Hammond Citation World Atlas,* 1996.]

A rickshaw bicycle and driver in Delhi. [Lindsay Hebberd/Woodfin Camp & Associates.]

called once impulsively asking a bicycle rickshaw driver about himself as he peddled her through Delhi. He replied that his belongings—a second set of clothes, a bowl, and a sleeping mat—were under the seat where she was sitting. He had come to Delhi 14 years before from the countryside and he had never found a home. He knew virtually no one; he had few friends and no family; and no one had ever inquired about him before. He worked virtually around the clock and slept here and there for two hours at a time. [Gagan Gill, National Public Radio, Weekend Edition, August 16, 1997.]

As a region, South Asia already has more people (1.3 billion) than China (1.25 billion). By 2020, India alone is expected to overtake China, whose growth rate (1.0) is half that of India's (1.9). This rapid growth rate puts a huge strain on efforts to improve life for South Asians. The Indian economy, while not particularly efficient, has nonetheless grown at a steady rate for several decades; but every year India adds more than 18 million people, approximately the population of the state of Texas, to its ranks. To accommodate these new Indians adequately, every single year the country would need to build 127,000 new village schools, hire 373,000 new schoolteachers (50 students per teacher), build 2.5 million new homes (7 people per home), create 4 million jobs, and produce 180 million new bushels of grain and vegetables. Only in food production has India come close to keeping pace with population growth, although its ability to continue doing so is precarious. The high-tech agriculture responsible for growing adequate yields may not be sustainable because of high costs and impacts on the environment and soils. In all other categories, India falls further and further behind, despite respectable economic growth.

South Asia has been trying to reduce births since 1952. India spends over a billion dollars a year on population programs, and it pays for nearly all these programs itself. Fertility rates have indeed declined in India and Bangladesh, and especially in Sri Lanka, although hardly at all in Pakistan and Nepal (Figure 8.6). Why does population continue to boom despite such efforts? The answers are no different from those reported elsewhere in this text.

First, in Pakistan, for example, a look at the population pyramid (Figure 8.7) shows that a huge portion of the population is in the early reproductive years, so

FIGURE 8.6 Some South Asian countries have experienced large declines in fertility rates in the last 30 years. [Adapted from *A Demographic Portrait of South and Southeast Asia* (Washington, DC: Population Reference Bureau, 1994), p. 8.]

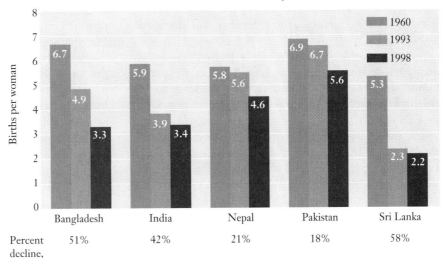

Decline in Total Fertility Rates

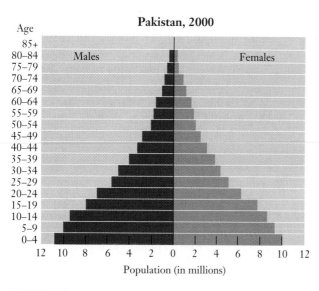
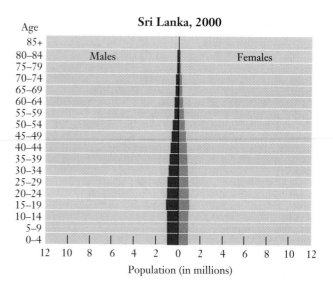

FIGURE 8.7 Population pyramids for Pakistan and Sri Lanka in the year 2000. [Adapted from U.S. Census Bureau, *International Data Base,* at http://www.census.gov/cgi-bin/ipc/idbpyry.pl.]

even a one-child-per-couple policy would result in growth for years to come. Of equal importance, poor, uneducated people see children as their only source of wealth. Babies not only bring joy, they quickly become productive family members: three-year-olds are already able to perform some useful tasks, and ten- or twelve-year-olds pull their weight, quite literally, in the fields, or even accomplish highly skilled tasks like carpet weaving (see the box "Should Children Work?"). Grown children are the only retirement plan that most South Asians will ever have. Because of precarious health circumstances, infant mortality rates hover around 75 per 1000 live births; only sub-Saharan Africa's are higher. Couples, therefore, want to have as many children as possible in order to see some reach maturity. The pyramid for Sri Lanka, on the other hand, shows a situation where fertility has declined significantly.

As we have observed elsewhere in this book, the economic factors encouraging large families are compounded by the fact that patriarchal societies place a premium on sons and, for the most part, do not educate daughters. Most couples want at least two sons, and a run of sons often brings on the desire for yet more because of the wealth and the secure old age they represent to the parents. Meanwhile, women have few ways to achieve a sense of fulfillment except that of prolific motherhood; a popular toast to a new bride is "May you be the mother of a hundred sons."

Even the middle class becomes caught up in the desire for sons. Many couples patronize high-tech labs

that specialize in identifying the sex of an unborn fetus, with the intention of aborting one that is female. This method, and the even less savory practices of neglecting girl children and of female infanticide, have resulted in the odd circumstance that across India adult men outnumber women. The 1991 census showed 929 females to every 1000 males, whereas, due to their longer natural life span, adult women usually outnumber men. In India, women outnumber men only in the state of Kerala—1048 women for every 1000 males.

Indian social scientists explain the exception of Kerala by noting that there the entire population is more educated. Literacy is 90 percent, whereas, for India as a whole, literacy rates are 39 percent for women and 64 percent for men. In Kerala, the elected Communist state government has for many years emphasized education and broad-based health care for all. Females are less likely to be thought a liability because, through education, they are equipped for work outside the home. Education is also credited with the fact that 63 percent of women in Kerala use contraception; in India as a whole, the rate is only 41 percent. Sri Lanka has also been successful in bringing down population growth rates by focusing on basic literacy (Figure 8.8).

It is well known that education, especially of women, but also of men, reduces the incentives for large families. Educated women are able to add significantly to family incomes and to the well-being of elderly parents, thus countering the overwhelming preference for sons. Yet India, on average, spends just U.S. $9 per capita annually on education, and very

AT THE REGIONAL SCALE   *Should Children Work?*

In recent years, a number of reports have raised questions regarding the exploitation of child labor in Asia, especially in the handwoven carpet industry. Carpet weaving is an ancient artistic and economic enterprise in Central and South Asia and in parts of East Asia, too. Traditionally it has been family ·based, with women and children the weavers and men the merchants. But it is Indian middlemen and foreign traders from Europe and America who make the big money. Competition from cheap labor in Iran and China keeps wages low for the actual weavers. For thousands of years, young children have learned the weaving skill and thereby become proud members of the family production unit. Now, children need to attend school to learn skills that will serve them in contemporary society. Meanwhile, the demand for fine handwoven carpets remains strong throughout the developed world.

Is there a problem with the use of child labor in South Asia, or is this a nonissue, the result of different cultural perceptions of what childhood should be? To what extent is this an issue of grinding poverty, rather than outright exploitation? What about children who work in polluted environments, such as the leather tanning industry, where barefoot children stand in dangerous chemicals while making safety boots for American workers? These are questions that the United Nations and South Asian governments are now addressing in an active program to curb child labor abuses, while remaining sensitive to the positive experience that learning a skill and being part of a family production unit can be for a child. In India, there is now a national system to certify that exported carpets are made in shops where the children go to school, have an adequate midday meal, and receive basic health care. Such carpets will bear the label KALEEN.

If abuses can be eliminated, the custom of child labor is likely to continue because it has significant benefits, both psychological and economic, to children and

Two young boys tie knots at a carpet loom in India.
[Cary Wolinsky/Stock, Boston.]

their families. Until the modern era, such work was considered an important part of a child's training for adulthood, even in the United States and Europe. Some experts argue that it is the lack of meaningful roles for children that leads to juvenile crime.

little of that on girls. In comparison, Korea, where prosperity has leapt upward and family size has shrunk, spends about $130 per capita annually, whereas the state of Tennessee (ranked 48th in the United States in education spending per capita) spends $2757. Paradoxically, although education has the power to bring fertility rates down quickly, the ever increasing costs of rapid population growth make education harder and harder to provide. The most crucial fact, however, is that, given their social and economic circumstances, large families still seem desirable to many South Asians.

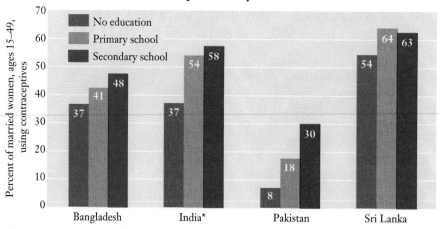

Contraceptive Use by Level of Education

FIGURE 8.8 The positive relationship between education and use of contraception is virtually universal. In South Asia, women with at least some education use contraception at higher rates than women with no education. In countries like Pakistan, where overall use is low, education drastically changes a woman's attitude toward contraception. In countries where education and contraception use are already fairly high, as in Sri Lanka, some education still increases the rate of use significantly (10 percent), but the effects of yet further education—through secondary school, for example—are negligible. [Adapted from *A Demographic Portrait of South and Southeast Asia.* (Washington, DC: Population Reference Bureau, 1994), p. 18.]

CURRENT GEOGRAPHIC ISSUES

The selection of geographic issues in South Asia presented here includes both those that characterize the region and make it distinctive—language, religion, caste—and those that are receiving current coverage in the international press—economic change and disparities, relative degrees of democratization, gender, high-tech industrialization, and innovative development strategies like microcredit. Again, colonialism played a role in setting the stage for the present, as it did in Central and South America, Southwest Asia, and Africa; but there are some differences. The Europeans left South Asia, for the most part, in the 1940s. Their imprint certainly remains; but 50 years have passed, and in that time South Asians have modified their situation drastically. Many problems still seem insurmountable, but progress on many levels is also not hard to find.

Sociocultural Issues

Part of the delightful challenge of learning about South Asia is to spot the connections between cultural aspects of life: religion, food, caste, gender. These links exist in all societies, but here, perhaps because of the venerable age and overlapping of cultural features, when connections are revealed they can be particularly illuminating.

Language and Ethnicity

In South Asia everyone is a minority. The Indian writer and diplomat Shashi Tharoor observes that his own country illustrates this point eloquently:

A Hindi-speaking male from the Gangetic plain state of Uttar Pradesh might cherish the illusion that he represents the "majority community," . . . but he does not. As a Hindu he belongs to the faith adhered to by some 82 percent of the population, but a majority of the country does not speak Hindi; a majority does not hail from Uttar Pradesh; and if he were visiting, say, Kerala, he would discover that a majority is not even male. . . . Our archetypal Hindu has only to step off a train and mingle with the polyglot polychrome crowds thronging any of India's five major metropolises to realize how much of a minority he really is. Even his Hinduism is no guarantee of majorityhood, because his caste automatically places him in a minority as well: if he is a Brahmin, 90 percent of his fellow Indians are not; if he is a Yadav [member of the Yadav caste], 85 percent of Indians are not, and so on." (Shashi Tharoor, *India: From Midnight to Millennium*, p. 112.)

There are a large number of distinct ethnic groups in South Asia, and many of them have their own languages, dialects, and subdialects. In India alone, 17 languages are officially recognized, but there are actually hundreds of separate languages and literally thousands of dialects. Figure 8.9 shows the complexity of the distribution of languages in South Asia. That complexity is the result of the great age of settlement, long periods of isolation, and, especially, the movement of people. The several patches of lavender indicate some of the most ancient culture groups in India. The languages colored with tones of gold, brown, and yellow are linked to several groups of Indo-Aryan people who entered South Asia from Central Asia at different times.

Hindi, an ancient Indo-Aryan language derived in part from Sanskrit, is understood by about 50 percent of the population, primarily because of the popularity of romantic Hindi-language movies. But it is not the first language of the majority; no Indian language can make that claim. English is a common second language. It was for years the language of the colonial bureaucracy and remains a language used on the job by professional people across the region. From 10 to 15 percent know how to speak, read, and write English.

Religion

The main religious traditions that have influenced South Asia are Hinduism, Islam, Buddhism, Sikhism, Jainism, and Christianity. The geographic distribution of the adherents of these various faiths is uneven, as the

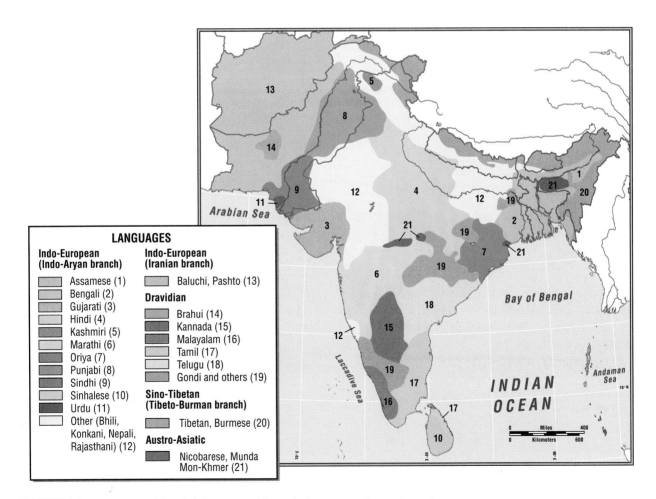

FIGURE 8.9 Languages of South Asia. [Adapted from Alisdair Rogers, ed., *Peoples and Cultures* (New York: Oxford University Press, 1992), p. 204.]

377

map in Figure 8.10 shows. **Hindus** are by far the most numerous; they account for 740 million people, 700 million of them in India. The 300 million Muslims form the majority in Afghanistan, Pakistan, Bangladesh, and the Maldives. They are also a large and important minority in India (somewhat over 118 million), living mostly in the northwest and northeast, but also scattered throughout the country. **Buddhists** are only 1 percent of the population—a majority only in Bhutan and Sri Lanka. **Sikhs** (about 18 million) are mainly in Punjab but are found elsewhere, and their influence is greater than their numbers because they specialize in military and police careers. Sikhism combines aspects of Islam and Hinduism but rejects the caste system. There is a legend that Christians first arrived in the far south Indian state of Kerala with St. Thomas, the Apostle, in the first century. Today they are a small minority within India, as well as in Sri Lanka, Pakistan, and Bangladesh. Throughout the region, and especially in central and northeastern India, there are indigenous people whose occupation of the area is so ancient that they are considered aboriginal inhabitants. These people hold animist beliefs, which often also incorporate aspects of Hinduism, Islam, Buddhism, or Christianity.

The different religious traditions of South Asia have deeply affected one another, and this is especially true of the two largest faiths. Where Hindus have lived in close association with Muslims, they have absorbed Muslim customs, such as purdah (female seclusion). For their part, Muslims have adopted some of the Hindu ideas of caste into their social organization. Despite the fact that Muslims make up only 11 percent of the Indian population, the political and social dynamics between Hindus and Muslims are enormously complex. The great independence leaders Mohandas Gandhi and Jawaharlal Nehru both emphasized the common cause that united Muslim and Hindu Indians: throwing off British colonial rule. Since independence, members of the Muslim upper class have been prominent in Indian national government and the military; Muslim generals served India willingly, even in its wars with Pakistan after partition. In the upper echelons of society, Hindus and Muslims often amicably share social space, including neighborhoods, cocktail parties, recreational facilities, and clubs. In urban areas, middle-class people of both faiths willingly share apartment blocks and schools, and occasionally marry each other.

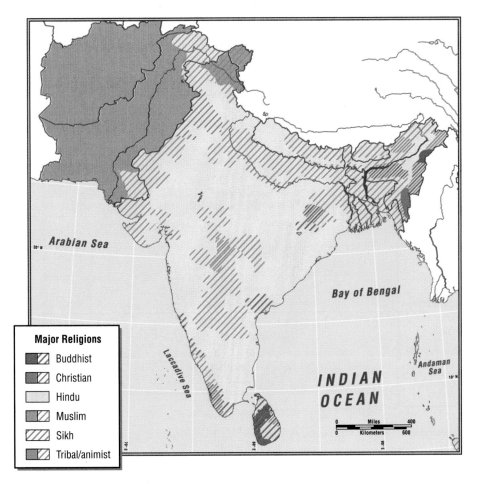

FIGURE 8.10 Religions in South Asia. [Adapted from Gordon Johnson, *Cultural Atlas of India* (New York: Facts on File, 1996), p. 56.]

But there is an opposite side to the Hindu-Muslim relationship. Especially in rural India, some upper- and middle-caste Hindus have been known to regard Muslims as members of low-status castes. Fueling this perception is the fact that whole low-caste Hindu villages sometimes convert to Islam to escape the hardships of being low caste. It doesn't always work because Muslims are still perceived as having low social status. Often, religious rules about food are the source of contention. Hindus regard the cow as sacred and use its products with reverence: milk for food and dried excrement for fuel. They never kill cows for food or hides. Muslims, on the other hand, run slaughterhouses and tanneries, eat beef, and use cowhide to make shoes and other items.

The Hindu-Muslim relationship is no less complex in Bangladesh. After the separation of Bangladesh from Pakistan, most upper-class Muslims moved to Pakistan, leaving Bangladesh with a preponderance of poor Muslim farmers. Meanwhile, many of the Hindu landowners remained, and some lower-caste Hindus converted to Islam. In Bangladesh villages, the Muslims are usually in a majority, but the Hindus are often somewhat wealthier and perhaps a bit disdainful of them. While the two groups may coexist amicably for many years, there is a definite "them" and "us" attitude abroad that could quickly disintegrate into so-called **communal conflict,** a widely used euphemism for religion-based violence.

VIGNETTE

The sociologist Beth Roy, a specialist in conflict resolution, recounts an incident in Panipur, Bangladesh, in her book *Some Trouble with Cows*. The incident started when a Muslim farmer carelessly allowed one of his cows to eat the lentil field of a Hindu. The Hindu complained, and when the Muslim reacted complacently, the Hindu seized the offending cow. By nightfall, Hindus had allied themselves with the Hindu lentil farmer and Muslims with the owner of the cow. More Muslims and Hindus converged from the surrounding area, and soon there were thousands of potential combatants lined up facing each other. Fights broke out. The police were called. In the end, a few died in what all described as a riot, and relationships in the village were forever molded by the incident. In the words of Roy, the dispute "delineat[ed] distinctions of caste, class, and [religious] culture so complex they intertwine[d] like columbines climbing on an ancient wall." [Adapted from Beth Roy, *Some Trouble with Cows—Making Sense of Social Conflict* (Berkeley: University of California Press, 1994), pp. 18–19.]

Caste

The ancient caste system for dividing and assigning hierarchies in society seems alien to Euro-Americans, and yet customs of social division and inequality are common in both Europe and America. In fact, all human groups have deeply ingrained concepts of relative social status. The old often have more authority than the young; or, conversely, as in U.S. pop culture, the young sometimes outrank the old. In many situations in Europe and America, men still have more influence than women. Nearly everywhere on earth, **social differentiation** is indicated by clothes, hairstyle, manner of speaking, material possessions, space occupied, residential location, and religion. In America, something so simple as the use of "ain't" or "youse" or a certain kind of headgear (baseball cap, motorcycle helmet, straw hat) gives immediate and profound information about one's origins or point of view. In some quarters, race still carries overtones closely akin to those of caste in South Asia. So, in fact, South Asia's customs associated with caste are not beyond comprehension to outsiders.

Caste is primarily a custom associated with Hindu India, but ideas associated with caste have been absorbed into Muslim and Buddhist culture, too. A person is born into a given caste, and that happenstance largely defines the individual's experience for a lifetime—where one will live, where and what one can eat and drink, with whom one will associate, one's marriage partner, and one's livelihood (see the box "Food Customs in South Asia"). There are four main categories of caste and many hundreds of subcategories that vary from place to place. Brahmins, the priestly (and warrior) caste, are the most privileged. Then, in descending rank, are farmers and merchants, or Vaishya; laborers and artisans known as Sudras; and the Harijan, also called Dalits or Untouchables, who are actually considered to be so lowly as to have no caste. The Harijan perform tasks thought to be the most despicable—killing animals, tanning hides, sweeping, and cleaning. The numerous subcastes are often associated with a certain place, such as a village or a neighborhood in a city, and with a particular language or dialect.

Across India there are many variations on the caste system, with different names in different places (and somewhat different ranks) for those who are shoemakers, or scholars, or healers. Despite regional variation, divisions between castes and the rules governing contact and avoidance became extremely rigid. But when a person stays in the recognized space of his or her caste, the individual is enclosed in a comfortable circle of families and friends that becomes a mutual aid society in times of trouble. This cohesion within castes and attachment to place help to explain the persistence of a system that seems to put such a burden of shame on

CULTURAL INSIGHT   *Food Customs in South Asia*

Customs governing food and its preparation reveal ways in which religion and caste remain an active force in the everyday life of South Asia. The best known of India's food rules is that Hindus do not eat beef. In Afghanistan, Pakistan, and Bangladesh it is pork that is prohibited. But there are countless other regulations that vary from place to place.

The long tradition of highly seasoned, meatless cuisine in South Asia is particularly strong in southern India. Many notions of purity and pollution surround the preparation of food in South Asia. According to tradition, Hindus should not accept food prepared by anyone

from a lower caste; and only the right hand is to carry food to the mouth, because the left hand is reserved for cleaning the body after defecating, hence is ritually impure. Menstruating women are also not allowed to prepare food. These taboos are fading in urban areas where caste and gender rules are now less important.

In rural areas, where the vast majority of South Asians still reside, the serving of food is also culturally prescribed. Women and girls eat after men and boys, a practice that often leaves them undernourished, and accounts in part for the fact that female children die more often than male children.

the lower ranks. Until caste was challenged during India's independence movement, there was relatively little friction between castes.

Caste is disappearing as a force in everyday life wherever people are able to separate themselves from their ancestral villages, occupations, and caste-related dialects. Individuals who migrate far from home and disappear into the anonymity of city life can sometimes profess to be a member of a higher caste. Now, with the many changes that have come with independence, all the members of some subcastes have upgraded themselves by abandoning a stigmatized occupation like fishing and acquiring land so they can farm instead, a more prestigious occupation.

In the twentieth century, Mohandas Gandhi, India's leader for independence (see the box "The Founder of Nonviolent Protest"), began an official effort to eliminate the caste system as the organizing principal of daily life and of social relationships. In the late 1940s, India began an affirmative action program that reserves a portion of government jobs, spaces in higher education, and parliamentary seats for the lowest castes and "outcastes." The latter, Harijans and Dalits (Untouchables), now constitute approximately 16 percent of the Indian population. Another group protected by affirmative action laws are descendants of the aboriginal inhabitants (or ethnic minorities), who account for about 8 percent of the population. Together, both groups are guaranteed 22.5 percent of the government jobs and 15 percent of the parliamentary seats.

Among the educated in urban areas, the campaign has been remarkably successful. Dalits are now power-

ful officials throughout the country. In 1997, the 21-member cabinet of Prime Minister H. D. Deve Gowda, himself a member of a low agricultural subcaste, contained just two members of upper castes. Members of high and low castes now ride the city buses side by side, eat together in restaurants, use the same rest rooms, and drink from the same water fountains. More remarkably, caste is disappearing as the crucial factor in finding a marriage partner. Newspaper matrimonial ads, which in cities substitute for the arranged marriage, frequently bear the proviso that "caste is no bar." Nonetheless, it would be folly to conclude that caste is now irrelevant in India. In rural areas, where the majority of Indians still reside, the divisions of caste remain prevalent.

Geographic Patterns in the Status of Women

The overall status of women in South Asia is extraordinarily low, despite the fact that there is a tiny minority of highly successful women in business, academia, medicine, politics, law, and law enforcement—some in very high positions of power. Throughout the region, the vast majority of women are partners in marriages in which they have very little power. Girls are often married off as very young children, and then continue to live with their parents until puberty. At age 12 or so, a girl abruptly leaves the home of her parents and joins her husband in his family compound, where she becomes a source of labor for her mother-in-law. Most junior brides serve as domestic servants for many years until they have produced enough children to have their

CULTURAL INSIGHT   *The Founder of Nonviolent Protest*

Mohandas Gandhi's influence has transformed civil society everywhere on earth. Gandhi (1869–1948) came from a wealthy merchant family in Gujarat, in Northwest India, where relations between Hindus, Muslims, and Jains (a small and influential group that accepts some aspects of Hinduism) were warm, and where social reform was an important theme of community life. British colonialism had failed to penetrate Gujarat significantly; the region was prosperous and little affected by Western culture. After studying law in England, Gandhi had difficulty finding his niche back home and ended up being posted to South Africa, where discrimination based on race was stark. For 20 years he worked on social reform and developed a personal philosophy of self-control and nonviolence. In protesting the treatment of both Africans and Indians by the white South African government, Gandhi developed the strategy of gathering a large group of sympa-

thizers to publicly, but peacefully, break a discriminatory law—first notifying the authorities of the coming demonstration. If the authorities ignored the act, the demonstrators would have made their point and the law would have been rendered moot. If the authorities used force to break up the demonstration, the government's moral sway was undermined.

Gandhi later used his nonviolent techniques in India against the British, and he is considered the father of Indian independence. He did not support the partition into Muslim Pakistan and Hindu India, and greatly lamented the bloodshed that followed. Nonviolence as a social reform technique has since diffused around the world. It has been used successfully in the civil rights movement in the United States, in labor movements in Asia, in the women's movement worldwide, and, especially, in South Africa to bring an end to apartheid.

---

own crew of small helpers, at which point they gain a bit of prestige and a measure of autonomy. Their power is increased when they become mothers-in-law in their own right. But the death of a husband can completely deprive a woman of all support and even of her home and children and reputation. Widows are frequently ritually scorned and blamed for their husbands' death. Widows rarely remarry and, in some areas, become enslaved to their in-laws or are cast out in the street to beg.

Purdah is the practice of concealing women from the eyes of nonfamily men, especially during their reproductive years. It is a part of many women's lives in rural villages in areas of South Asia where Islam is the main religion. Absorbed into Hindu culture, purdah is less strong where the influences of Islam are weak— that is, among Hindus in central and south India and in the larger cities of India, Bangladesh, and Pakistan, especially among highly educated upper-caste women. The custom is also not observed by the aboriginal people of the region, many of whom live in northeast India, or by low-caste Hindus throughout the region. Purdah is, however, sometimes a mark of prestige for those castes that are making an effort to upgrade their overall status, since the ability to seclude women signals the possession of surplus wealth. Purdah accounts for the fact that relatively few women in the north and northwest of India participate in agricultural labor, be-

cause work in the fields would put them in view of nonfamily males.

There is geographic variability in the relative well-being of women in South Asia. Women in Afghanistan have arguably the most difficult lives since an archconservative Islamist movement, the Taliban, became the government there in the late 1990s. The Taliban is made up in large part of uneducated young Muslim men, many of them mujahedeen (resistance fighters) in the recent Afghan war with Russia. They see the liberalization of women's roles as particularly dangerous to traditional Muslim Afghan ways of life. The Taliban favor the extreme seclusion of females: women are not to work outside the home or attend school, and they must wear a completely concealing heavy black veil whenever out of the house. The Taliban have even decreed that women shall not make a sound as they walk, as the sound of their footsteps is distracting and potentially erotic to men.

Women in Bangladesh are also having a difficult time with purdah. Women must now answer to Islamist village councils, called *salish*, which operate with apparent impunity outside the Bangladesh constitution as community court and punishment agencies. According to investigations conducted by Amnesty International in 1996, very young women have been stoned to death for alleged relationships with men in which they had no choice. In several cases, the victims, as young as 13, had

Lattice screens known as *jalee* are an architectural feature in areas where women are in purdah. *Jalee* allow ventilation and let in light, but shield women from the view of strangers. [Lindsay Hebberd/Woodfin Camp & Associates.]

gotten pregnant after being raped by village men, who were not punished. In addition, literally hundreds of nongovernmental agencies (NGOs) that provide schooling, health care, family-planning services, or development aid to women have been sacked and burned after Islamist clerks issued **fatwas**—legal opinions based on interpretations of Muslim law—against them. Islamist leaders have said publicly that NGOs like the famous Grameen Bank, known for its small loans to poor rural women, "alienate women from their proper social roles and Islamic lifestyle," and hence should be banned. Village courts have reportedly carried out similar patterns of violence against women in Pakistan.

The Islamist leaders are correct in their assumption that there are NGOs that seek to diminish the influence of purdah customs, which keep women illiterate and confined to their houses, without the ability to earn their own income. The idea is that freeing women from these strictures will in the short term improve the educational attainments of children and the health and nutrition of families. Experience has shown that with even a little education, women seek a way to make some income and generally invest their earnings in food, medicine, and schooling for their children. In the long term, freeing women from purdah will also encourage lower fertility, because women will channel their energies less to reproduction and more to activities like business, innovative agriculture, recycling of resources, teaching, and other service occupations. Figure 8.11 shows the extent to which women are now literate in India.

In India, sanctions against women comparable to those found in Bangladesh and Afghanistan sometimes occur, but constitutional protections are more likely to be enforced, at least after the fact. In the 1980s, the then Prime Minister Rajiv Gandhi introduced the concept of *panchayate raj* (village government) to encourage gender equality in village life. These local councils differ from the impromptu Bangladeshi *salish* not only because they have official standing but especially because 30 percent of the seats are reserved for women. Support is growing for legislation that would reserve one-third of the seats of the lower house of the Indian parliament and of state assemblies for women for a 15-year trial period. After that time, it is hoped, women will have achieved the political experience to win elections without the aid of quotas.

Urban professional women in Pakistan, Sri Lanka, and India are beginning to enjoy opportunities and acceptance unknown to rural women and not accorded until recently even to many women in Europe or the Americas. In the cities of Karachi, Delhi, Bombay, Bangalore, and Madras there is a growing number of highly successful businesswomen, female directors of companies, highly qualified technicians, high-ranking academics, and women who serve prominently in government. As the experiences of one cosmopolitan urbanite illustrate:

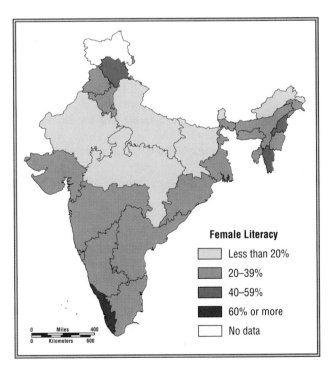

Female Literacy

- Less than 20%
- 20–39%
- 40–59%
- 60% or more
- No data

FIGURE 8.11 Female literacy is less than 40 percent in most of India. [Adapted from Bina Agarwal, Gender, environment, and poverty interlinks: Regional variations and temporal shifts in rural India, 1971–91, *World Development* 25 (1997): 32.]

Living in Karachi [Pakistan, a city of 10 million] is like living in London in terms of the freedoms women are allowed. . . . More and more you're seeing middle-class women entering the workplace alongside their brothers to help supplement the family income. These women are finding jobs in . . . trade and services, sales and marketing, secretarial work. This is a huge change from ten years ago, when these sorts of job opportunities didn't exist simply because those sectors hadn't begun to develop. Everything in this country changes according to economics. (Shomaila Loan, as quoted in John McCarry, The Promise of Pakistan, National Geographic, October 1997, pp. 64–65.)

The Cultural Context of Bride Burning and Female Infanticide

For some years now, a practice in India called "bride burning" or "dowry killing" has been reported, in which a husband and his relatives stage an "accidental" kitchen fire that kills his wife. Her death enables the widower to marry again and collect the dowry that, by custom, comes with a wife. The government of India released figures in 1987 that affirmed 1786 such deaths in that year alone; and the numbers have been rising every year throughout the 1980s and early 1990s. In some cases, the threat of bride burning is used to extort further dowry from a wife's family.

Changing customs regarding dowry appear to be a factor in the growing incidence of both bride burning and female infanticide in India. Among the lower castes, paying a **bride price** was the custom until recently: a groom paid the family of the bride a relatively small sum that symbolized the loss of their daughter's work to their family economy and the gain of her labor to his. **Dowry,** on the other hand, was common in the upper castes where women observed purdah. With her ability to work inhibited by seclusion, an upper-caste female was a liability who had to be unloaded for a price, and her family paid the groom a dowry. Oddly enough, the custom of dowry was reinforced with increasing education (for males) and family affluence. Young men came to feel that their diplomas increased their worth as husbands. This gave them the power to demand larger and larger dowries. Soon the practice filtered down to the lower castes, and now the poorest of families who have daughters are crippled by the dowries they must pay to get their girls married. This duty is taken extremely seriously, since the stigma of having an unmarried daughter is huge. For an increasing minority of families, the birth of more than one daughter threatens the family with hopeless impoverishment. Such families often view the birth of a daughter as a calamity; second and third daughters may be fed a poisonous substance soon after birth. The circumstances that lead parents to take such a step are illustrated in the following example.

VIGNETTE

Muya and Mohan were married and had one girl. They worked as agricultural laborers and together earned $350 a year. Muya was paid half as much as Mohan for the same work. The couple lived on an acre of land they cultivated for themselves, and owned a cow. Mohan's mother lived with them and the four shared a collection of neat mud huts surrounded by coconut trees. They were just well enough off to plan for a brighter future. They had managed to save enough money in the bank so that when their daughter was old enough they could pay the going dowry rate, an amount equal to what the two of them earned in a year. This outlay of money would be balanced by the dowry any future son would receive upon marriage. When Muya became pregnant again (she knew nothing about birth control technology), they decided that they could not afford the dowry for a second girl. Thus, if a girl were born they would "put her to sleep." Eventually, Muya delivered a girl after four hours of labor. The next day the family gathered and fed the baby cow's milk laced with five sleeping pills. Then they buried the child along the road in view of the surrounding hills. [Adapted from Elisabeth Bumiller, *May You Be the Mother of a Hundred Sons* (New York: Fawcett Columbine, 1990), pp. 110–112.]

Economic Issues

South Asia is a region of startling economic contrasts, where it is possible for a country to foster a growing computer software industry and a space program, and at the same time be home to hundreds of millions of desperately poor people. These extremes reflect the propensity of South Asian economies to favor the interests of a privileged minority over those of the poor majority. While the British colonial system deepened the extent of South Asia's poverty, and widened the gap between rich and poor, the current wealth disparities in the region have much to do with economic policies favored by post-independence-era leaders. Despite the region's celebrated democratic traditions, the poor have largely been left out of the political process and bypassed or hurt by economic reforms. Meanwhile, frustration has mounted among the poor. The results have been the scapegoating of particular culture groups, mob violence in some areas, and threats to the overall stability of the region.

Agriculture

Figure 8.12 shows the distribution of agricultural zones for South Asia. Rice is the main crop wherever rainfall is plentiful, especially in the flat Ganges basin and on terraced mountain slopes around the southern rim of India. Rice occupies about one-third of the land planted in grain. Wheat, grown in the west central and northwest of the region, is the second most important crop, and its cultivation is spreading with the use of irrigation systems. Other grains include millet and grain sorghum. Cotton remains an important cash crop and is often grown with the aid of irrigation. Animal grazing is predominant in the dry areas of Northwest India, Pakistan, and Afghanistan.

Until recent years, agriculture in this region remained largely based on traditional small-scale systems that managed to feed families in good years but often not in years of drought or floods. Moreover, these largely subsistence systems did not produce sufficient surpluses for the region's growing cities, which increasingly existed on imported food. Large-scale mechanized agriculture, where it existed, was aimed at producing export crops like cotton, flax, jute, tea, and rice.

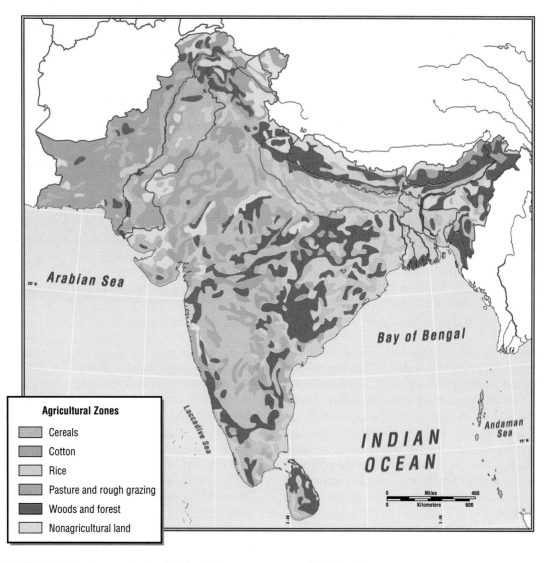

FIGURE 8.12 Agricultural zones in South Asia. Afghanistan is not included on the map because, after years of conflict, not much is known of the current details of existing agricultural patterns. Overall, Afghanistan is primarily pastoral (nomadic herding), with some cultivation of wheat, fruits, nuts, and unknown amounts of opium poppies and marijuana in the river valleys. [Adapted from Gordon Johnson, *Cultural Atlas of India* (New York: Facts on File, 1996), p. 34.].

Most of South Asia's agricultural land is still cultivated by hand; and overall agricultural development has been bypassed in favor of industrial development, especially in India.

Over the last several decades, there have been some important improvements in South Asian food production. Beginning in the late 1960s a so-called **green revolution** boosted grain harvests dramatically through the use of new seeds and fertilizers, mechanized equipment, irrigation, pesticides, and herbicides. One result is that Pakistan, for example, is now self-sufficient in wheat, rice, and sugarcane, and produces surpluses for export. India has needed to import grains only occasionally when drought diminished harvests. However, the main beneficiaries of the green revolution innovations have not been those who need them most. Some multinational food conglomerates have profited. Among farmers, only those who can afford to pay for new technologies have benefited from the increased yields. Poorer farmers, unable to afford the seeds, fertilizers, pesticides, and new equipment, have often been forced off their land and into low-wage farm labor or sharecropping; or they have been forced into the cities, where they have a hard time finding jobs of any sort. Moreover, while the new technologies result in dramatically higher production rates, the increased food supplies tend to bypass the poorest (and hungriest). They are sold instead to the cities or even exported; some South Asian rice finds its way to specialty stores in the United States. South Asian governments place a high priority on ensuring a sufficient supply of food to the cities, because urban unrest poses a greater threat to the interests of government and the middle and upper classes than rural unrest.

Industry over Agriculture

After independence from Britain in 1947, agriculture continued to be neglected on the development agendas of ambitious new leaders. Influenced by socialist ideas, they concluded that agriculture was incapable of supplying the growth and technological innovation that poor countries needed. Instead, government involvement in industrialization was considered necessary to ensure the levels of job creation that would cure poverty. The new South Asian leaders engineered government takeovers of the industries they believed to be the linchpins of a strong economy: namely, steel, coal, transport, communications, and a wide range of manufacturing and processing industries.

There was some impressive growth in the early years of independence. This was enough to make India the eighth most industrialized country in the world in terms of the relative output of the industrial sector compared to other sectors. But for the most part, South Asian economic policies failed to meet

As the numbers of Indians with a bit of disposable income increases (estimates are that this may be as many as 200 million people), opportunities for all kinds of entrepreneurial capitalism increase. Indian pharmaceutical companies are eyeing this group as potential consumers of basic modern medicines like aspirin, cough syrup, and ointments. [Pablo Bartholomew/Gamma-Liaison.]

their goals. The emphasis on industry was ill suited to countries that had been primarily agricultural for years. In India, for example, governments sank huge amounts of money into a relatively small industrial sector that even today employs only 15 percent of the population, while agriculture employs 70 percent. Only a small portion of the population directly benefited, so industrialization failed to increase South Asia's overall prosperity significantly. Another problem was that the measures governments took to boost industries often nurtured inefficiency and ignored market incentives. One policy has been for industries to employ as many people as possible, even if they are not needed. So, for example, it still takes 250,000 Indian workers to produce the same amount of steel as 8000 Japanese workers; and Indian steel is thus more expensive. In addition, decisions about what products particular manufacturing industries should produce have been made by ill-informed government bureaucrats rather than driven by consumer demand. Items that would aid daily life for the poor majority are produced only in small quantities. These would be items such as cheap cooking pots, buckets, cheap, sturdy bicycles, and simple tools. Meanwhile, there is a relative abundance of more middle-class items, such as vacuum cleaners, watches, TVs, kitchen appliances, and cars; yet only a very few can afford to purchase them.

Economic Reform

Today, much of South Asia is undergoing a wave of economic reforms intended to make the various national economies more efficient and productive. But it is unclear whether these will in the end benefit the vast majority of the poor. India's reforms, or structural adjustment programs (SAPs), begun in 1991, are aimed at privatizing industries, removing government regulation, and opening up the economy to foreign goods and foreign investment. This more competitive situation has undoubtedly increased productivity in the export and industry sectors of the economy. As a result, rates of economic growth are now higher—5 to 8 percent compared with 3 to 4 percent before the reforms. Most of the new growth, however, has occurred in the Indian Ocean states of Maharashtra, Gujarat, and Karnataka. The rest of the country lags far behind. Moreover, like SAPs in Middle and South America and Africa, the new policies are producing wider disparity in income; most gains are confined to a middle class now estimated to be nearly 25 percent of the population. Meanwhile, hundreds of thousands of state employees have been fired as governments sell off state-owned industries to private buyers who seek efficiency rather than maximum employment for India's multitudes. Over the course of the reform period, rural poverty rates—in India that portion of the population that cannot afford to eat a basic minimum diet—have increased. In 1988, in rural India, 39.2 percent of the population was in poverty. By 1992, the rural poverty rate was 43.47 percent.

Agriculture still receives less attention and less investment than industry, and few efforts have been made to provide other economic opportunities to rural areas. The nutrition of poor people throughout the country has declined because food subsidies have been removed, a particularly dangerous situation in a country where as many as 320 million are at risk of malnutrition. Similar economic reforms have taken place in Pakistan and Bangladesh, with similar results.

Innovative Help for the Poor

In recent years, some promising strategies for helping poor people have been developed in South Asia. One of these is **microcredit,** a program that makes very small loans available to poor entrepreneurs in both rural and urban areas. Throughout South Asia, and indeed in much of the world, poor people have a difficult time obtaining loans. The poor do not have much collateral, so lending to them seems risky; nor do they need very large sums, so lending to them is unprofitable. Hence, the poor must rely on small-scale moneylenders who often charge extremely high interest rates of 30 percent or more *per month*. In the late

1970s, Mohammed Yunnis, an economics professor in Bangladesh, responded to this problem by starting the Grameen Bank, or "People's Bank," which makes small loans mostly to people in rural villages. Loans often pay for the start-up costs of small businesses, such as chicken raising or small-scale egg production or construction of pit toilets. The problem of collateral is overcome by having potential borrowers arrange themselves in small groups that are responsible as a whole for paying back the loans. If one member fails to pay back a loan, then the group as a whole will be denied loans in the future. This system, based on weekly meetings, creates incentives for mutual support between group members as well as peer pressure to repay loans. The weekly meetings are often the only time that women borrowers leave the confines of home, and are their first contacts with non-kin women (and sometimes even non-kin men). The repayment rate on the loans is extremely high, averaging around 98 percent—much higher than most banks obtain. Hence the Grameen Bank can afford to charge interest rates of around 13 to 14 percent per year, much lower than those of village moneylenders.

Women have turned out to be the most successful loan recipients in the microcredit system. And researchers have found that loans to women have a distinctive multiplier effect, which can enhance life in a whole community. If men's incomes are boosted, because of traditions regarding male social obligations much of their income goes into luxury purchases, such as cigarettes and alcohol for peers and village leaders. But women tend to spend extra income on improving family nutrition and health care, and on sending children to school. Women who earn their own incomes are also more likely to use birth control. They are less influenced by patriarchal attitudes that encourage the production of as many male children as possible. So far, the Grameen Bank has been an enormous success in Bangladesh, where it has loaned over U.S. $1.8 billion to more than 2 million borrowers. Similar microcredit projects have been established in India and Pakistan, and throughout Africa, Middle and South America, North America, and Europe.

Political Issues

South Asia is often praised as a bastion of democracy that serves as an example of political enlightenment to the rest of the developing world. It is true that democracy, at least in India and Bangladesh, has peacefully resolved many conflicts, smoothed numerous potentially bloody transitions of power, and nurtured vibrant public debate over the issues of the day. There has also been, however, much tension resulting from the incorporation of older nondemocratic traditions, such as a form of favoritism known as the patron–client relationship. While democracy would probably never have worked had it not incorporated some of what existed before, the patron–client system has increasingly warped South Asian democracy. Recently, religious nationalism has brought on hate-based campaigns that threaten overall peaceful relations within India and between India and Pakistan.

Patrons and Clients

The **patron–client** relationship is a form of unequal reciprocity, not written into any constitution, that nonetheless characterizes almost all important political interactions in the region. One way to examine the workings of the system is to observe its imprint on the landscape. In South Asian villages today, most land and other resources are monopolized by a single wealthy dominant group, usually a high caste in a Hindu village or a respected clan, or "lineage," in a Muslim or other non-Hindu village. The leaders of this dominant group act as patrons, providing the rest of the villagers (their clients) with resources in the form of food, clothing, and money. They may also provide protection from hostile forces. In return, the clients provide their labor, skilled services, and political loyalty to the patrons. The differences in status between patron and clients are visible in the hierarchical arrangement of the village: in house size, in access to water, and in the arrangement of fields. Similar versions of this relationship are found in government bureaucracies and political parties. Subordinates act as clients, giving services and allegiance to their superiors. The superiors, in return, act as patrons, offering resources and career advancement. Patron–client relationships also link the business community with political parties, as businesspeople become the clients of influential politicians in return for opportunities to make money. Clients make payments, resembling bribes, to their patrons, and such payments may form a major part of the incomes of politicians and bureaucrats.

Some argue that the patronage system is now essential for the effective functioning of democracy in South Asia because it facilitates village and neighborhood connections to governments and political parties. People's lives are made better as a result of the attention paid to them by officials who want their support. Others observe that rational planning cannot be achieved through bribes. Hence, the landscape is littered with a hodgepodge of buildings and projects that cater to the needs of small groups but are ill-suited to each other and may work at cross-purposes for the larger society.

Rising concern over the degree of corruption at the highest levels of government is increasingly a subject covered by the relatively free press. Wealthy entre-preneurs lavish ever larger bribes on government patrons, for which they receive access to immense state-controlled resources and exemption from many regulations. In the process, the great majority of people who cannot bribe at such a scale are shut out of the development process.

Religious Nationalism

Increasingly, people disgusted with corruption are joining religious nationalist movements and regional separatist movements because they see such movements as purifying sources of morality. Although most people in South Asia live under formally secular governments, **religious nationalism** has long been a reality, shaping relations between people and their governments. Religious nationalists believe that a particular religion is strongly connected to a particular territory, perhaps even to the exclusion of other religions, and that those who share a belief should have their own political unit that they control—be it a neighborhood, part of a country, or a separate country. Although both India and Pakistan were formally created as a secular states, India is generally thought of as a Hindu state, and Pakistan, and now also Bangladesh, as Muslim states. Many strongly associate their religion with their national identity. Since partition, religious nationalism has periodically fueled wars and conflicts between India and Pakistan over disputed territories. Moreover, political parties based on religious nationalism have gained popularity throughout South Asia. They are thought of as forces that will purge corruption and violence, despite the fact that these parties are usually only slightly less corrupt and certainly no less violent than other parties (see the box "Babar's Mosque"). Religious nationalism, then, is a major contributor to South Asia's level of conflict.

Regional Political Conflicts

The worst armed conflicts in South Asia today are **regional conflicts.** These occur when a regional ethnic or religious minority actively resists the authority of national governments, which they see as controlled by a majority that deprives them of a voice in their own government. Two regional conflicts in the neighboring Indian states of Punjab and Kashmir have both religious and political components and carry a high potential to destabilize the region. They are the heart of on-again–off again hostilities between India and Pakistan.

In Punjab, the Sikh community has long pressed for greater recognition of its distinct religious and ethnic identity and for greater regional autonomy within India. Sikhism arose in the fifteenth century as a Hindu reformist movement that espouses belief in one God, high ethical standards, and meditation. It rejects the

AT THE REGIONAL SCALE

Babar's Mosque—The Geography of Religious Nationalism

Proponents of religious nationalism often try to gain mass support through political campaigns that interweave history and mythology with the South Asian landscape. In late 1992 and early 1993, a series of riots occurred throughout South Asia that were the culmination of a long campaign waged by India's leading Hindu nationalist party, the Bharatiya Janata party (BJP). The trigger for the riots was the destruction of a Muslim mosque in the town of Ayodhya, in Uttar Pradesh. The mosque had been built by the Mogul emperor Babar during his early invasions of India in the sixteenth century, supposedly on the ruins of a Hindu temple believed by local residents to mark the birthplace of the Hindu god Ram. After years of campaigning for the mosque's destruction, the BJP finally succeeded in late 1992, with the help of a highly organized Hindu mob of 300,000. The destruction led to riots that ripped through most major northern Indian cities. Mobs, commanded by urban Hindu nationalist political parties, burned and looted selected Muslim businesses and homes, often with the complicity of the police. Nearly 5000 people died. The location of the riots reflected the urban base of Hindu nationalist parties; and their highly organized criminal actions reflected the violent gangster-style tactics that are becoming increasingly common on the South Asian political scene. In retaliation, Muslim mobs in Bangladesh and Pakistan harassed Hindu communities and destroyed their temples.

caste system but retains other Hindu beliefs, and now also incorporates some Muslim beliefs. There have long been tensions between Sikhs and Hindus in Punjab over access to land and water and the control of religious sites. After supporting India in its war with Pakistan, Sikhs successfully agitated for the creation of two states out of Punjab: one, a Sikh majority state called Punjab, and the other, a Hindu majority state called Haryana. Since then, however, Sikhs have felt alienated from the rest of India because their state has often been governed by leaders appointed by the national government in New Delhi, rather than by democratically elected candidates. Matters came to a head in 1983–1984, when the members of a militant Sikh group barricaded themselves in the holiest Sikh shrine, the Golden Temple in Amritsar, which they then used as a base of operations to agitate for Sikh political autonomy. In 1984, the Indian government attacked the shrine, killed the militants, damaged the temple, and thereby deeply alienated the Sikh community. Shortly thereafter, Prime Minister Indira Gandhi, who had called for the attack, was assassinated by two of her Sikh body guards. Riots throughout India over the next few days resulted in the deaths of more than 2700 Sikhs, who are a wealthy and influential minority in many cities outside of Punjab. Since this low point, conditions have improved somewhat, but government forces and Sikh militants continue to battle periodically in parts of Punjab.

The roots of conflict in Kashmir reach back to India's partition in 1947. Pakistan invaded the Muslim majority state when it showed signs of joining India. The ensuing war resulted in a tenuous cease-fire line (Figure 8.13). The two countries are technically still waiting for a UN decision on where the final border will be, but Pakistan effectively controls thinly peopled mountain areas in the north and one-third of the densely populated Vale of Kashmir. India holds the rest and maintains an ominous presence of more than 500,000 troops. Civil war has erupted repeatedly over the years, and as many as 20,000 people have been killed. As in Punjab, much of the conflict has centered around the right of Kashmiris to elect their own state leaders; this is a right the national government in New Delhi has frequently denied by appointing its own favorites. Throughout the 1980s, Kashmiri guerrillas carried out bombings and assassinations, to which the Indian government responded with blunt counterattacks notorious for killing large numbers of civilians. Sporadic fighting between India and Pakistan continues along the cease-fire line, where at one location the two countries intermittently clash in the world's highest battle zone, at an altitude of 20,000 feet (6000 meters).

Both countries continued to test nuclear weapons as recently as 1998. Many international security analysts believe that, of all the world's disputes, the conflict in Kashmir is the most likely to result in the use of nu-

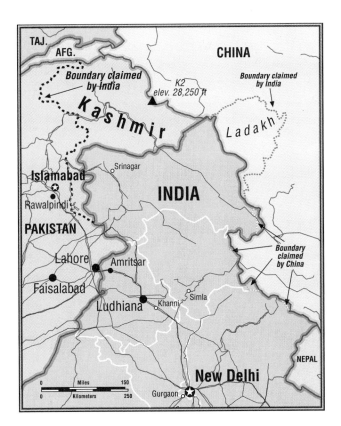

FIGURE 8.13 The Kashmir areas of dispute between India and Pakistan. Less well known and (currently) less volatile areas of border disputes between India and China are also shown. [Adapted from *National Geographic,* May 1997, p. 19.]

clear weapons, because of the religious fervor of the protagonists.

The Future of Democracy

While there are many political "hot spots" in South Asia as a whole, there are a number of reasons to expect greater tranquillity in the future. There are signs that democracy is expanding, making better government a real possibility. For example, in India, the Congress party had ruled with only a few years of interruption since 1947. However, by the 1990s a much more competitive multiparty arena was taking shape, and voters were increasingly less tolerant of corruption and violence. While, in the short run, this has meant greater influence for Hindu nationalists, it has also led to fairer and more peaceful elections, and a clearer focus on giving opportunity to disadvantaged groups. Meanwhile in Pakistan and Bangladesh, after years of military dictatorship, democratic elections are occurring with some regularity; and in Nepal a more freely elected legislature and a reduction of the king's power is giving the people a greater voice in society.

Measures of Human Well-Being

I have emphasized throughout this book that gross national product (GNP) per capita (Table 8.1, column 2), the most common index used to compare countries, is at best a crude indicator of well-being. GNP per capita in South Asia is the lowest on earth. People in South Asia are, for the most part, extremely poor. Many actually live on less than the amounts indicated in the table, because the existence of some very rich South Asians raises the average. South Asians practice extreme frugality and resourcefulness to survive: they recycle nearly everything, hence their villages are, for the most part, "spic-and-span" places; they are entrepreneurs in the informal economy; they grow their own food whenever possible; and they strictly limit cash expenditures by setting up reciprocal exchange agreements with each other.

As Table 8.1 shows, a few places in South Asia fare a bit better than the others; but they represent only a tiny proportion of the more than 1 billion people in the whole region. The GNP per capita of the Maldive Islands is boosted by income from tourism. Sri Lanka's higher GNP per capita is a result of a physical environment favorable to agriculture (tea is a chief product) and the presence of exportable minerals. But most importantly, a history of investing in the education and health of its citizens has helped to equalize wealth distribution in Sri Lanka. That country would probably be yet more prosperous if unrest between the Tamil and Singhalese ethnic groups had not hindered development.

On the United Nations Human Development Index (HDI; see Table 8.1, column 3), three components—life expectancy at birth, educational attainment, and adjusted real income—are combined to arrive at a ranking of 174 countries. Virtually all South Asian countries rank in the lowest third of world nations on the HDI, that is, those countries that rank over 130. Since South Asia accounts for about one-quarter of the earth's population, the numbers of poor are staggering. Both life expectancy and literacy figures are low, especially for women. As in Africa, governments have not provided even the most basic of services. In India, only half the eligible children are in school; in Pakistan, only one-quarter; and in Afghanistan, just one-eighth. In Pakistan and Afghanistan, and even in Sri Lanka, less than half the population has access to safe drinking water. In India, Bangladesh, and the Himalayan states, clean water is available to about 80 percent of the people; but in the entire region sanitary toilets, including outhouses and pit toilets, are only available to less than 25 percent of the population. Even as development proceeds in South Asia, the likelihood is that the gap between rich and poor will continue to grow. Most wealth

TABLE 8.1

Human well-being rankings of countries in South Asia

Country	GNP per capita (in U.S. dollars), 1996	Human Development Index (HDI) global rankings, 1998[a]	Gender Empowerment Measure (GEM) global rankings, 1998[b]	Female literacy (percentage), 1995	Male literacy (percentage), 1995	Life expectancy 1995
Selected countries for comparison						
Japan	40,940	8 (high)	38	99	99	79.6
United States	28,020	4 (high)	11	99	99	76.1
Kuwait	17,390 (1995)	54 (high)	75	75	82	74
South Asia						
Afghanistan	Not av.	Not av. (low)	Not av.	15	47	46
Bangladesh	260	147 (low)	80	26	49	59
Bhutan	390	155 (low)	Not av.	28	56	66
India	380	139 (low)	95	38	65	59
Maldives	1,080	95 (medium)	76	93	93	62
Nepal	210	152 (low)	Not av.	14	41	55
Pakistan	480	138 (low)	100	24	50	58
Sri Lanka	740	90 (medium)	72	87	93	72

[a]The high, medium, and low designations in column 3 (HDI) indicate where the country ranks among the 174 countries classified.
[b]Only 104 ranked in the world.
Not av. = Not available.
Sources: Human Development Report 1998, United Nations Human Development Programme; and *1998 World Population Data Sheet*, Population Reference Bureau.

is being created in the middle and upper classes, and their spending and reinvestment tend not to be of the type that creates jobs for the poorest or enhances their well-being in other ways.

The United Nations Gender Empowerment Measure (GEM; see Table 8.1, column 4) ranks countries by the extent to which women have opportunities to participate in economic and political life. All the countries in South Asia for which figures are available are in, or very close to, the bottom quarter of the countries ranked. For Afghanistan, Bhutan, and Nepal, figures are not even available; it is safe to assume that these missing figures would also be low. In South Asia, there are virtually no bright spots on the GEM for

women; remember that in Africa, several countries rank in the 40s and 50s. The fact that several heads of state in South Asian countries (Pakistan, India, and Bangladesh) have been women should not be taken as an indication of a general rise in the status of women.

Environmental Issues

In 1973, in the Chamoli district of Uttar Pradesh, India, a sporting goods manufacturer wanted to cut down a grove of ash trees so that his factory, in the distant city of Allahabad, could use the wood to make tennis racquets. The trees were sacred to nearby villagers, however, and when their protests were ignored, a group of local women took a dramatic action that became a symbol of the struggle to protect South Asia's environmental quality. When the loggers came, they found the women hugging the trees and refusing to let go until the threat to their grove had passed. Soon the sports manufacturer located another grove. The women's action grew into the "Chipko movement" (literally, the "stick to" movement), which has spread to other forest areas, slowing down deforestation and increasing ecological awareness.

Deforestation

The Chipko movement is a reaction to a pattern found throughout South Asia, in which the resources of rural areas are channeled to urban industries without considering the needs of local peoples. The proponents of the "social forestry movement" argue that management of forest resources should be turned over to local communities. They say that people living at the edge of forests possess complex local knowledge of these ecosystems, gained over generations—knowledge about which plants are useful for building materials, for food, for medicinal use, and as fuelwood. These people have the incentive to manage carefully, because they want their progeny to benefit from forests for generations to come. In contrast, the government forestry departments typically shut local people out of their traditional forestlands, forcing them to depend on smaller and more marginal common-access lands that may now contain only a very few of the useful species.

The fact is, though, that burgeoning local populations themselves carry out much deforestation in order to obtain ever more firewood and fodder for animals. It is difficult to enlist impoverished people on the side of conservation. Their need for employment predisposes them to collaborate with poachers of rare forest products. Moreover, the powerful industrial and government interests that monopolize forest reserves are not likely to yield control easily to local people. Despite these problems, a number of environmental groups have been able to take direct actions to reforest denuded landscapes.

Water Issues

One of the most controversial environmental issues in South Asia today is the battle between India and Bangladesh over access to the waters of the Ganges River. In recent years, during the dry season, India has diverted 60 percent of the Ganges flow to Calcutta to flush out places where the river is silting up and ham-

pering trade. This practice deprives Bangladesh of normal flow. Less water is available for irrigation, causing crop yields to fall; and salt water from the Bay of Bengal penetrates inland, ruining fields. The diversion has also created major alterations in Bangladesh's coastline, damaging the small-scale fishing industry. Thus, to serve the needs of Calcutta's 11 million people the livelihoods of 40 million have been put at risk, triggering massive protests in Bangladesh. Now India has signed a treaty promising to reduce the scale of the diversions, yet they have not been reduced. As with other serious environmental problems, a solution has been hard to reach because the population affected is not only poor and rural but located in a different region—in this case a different country—from the politicians and bureaucrats who are in a position to respond to the protests.

Women who must wash clothes in the water course flowing through Bombay's Dharavi section, Asia's largest slum, have a difficult time because garbage and raw sewage pollute the water daily. [Steve McCurry/National Geographic.]

Massive protests have drawn national and international attention to the problems created by hydroelectric dams. Perhaps the most successful of the protest movements has been one directed against dams being built on the Narmada River in central India. As many as 320,000 people are being relocated to make room for new reservoirs. The law required government agents to provide land of equal or better value to displaced peoples, but resistance hardened when that land turned out to be barely arable. Facing starvation on these new lands, the farmers and their families returned to their old villages and fields in 1989 and eventually marched, 80,000 strong, on the capital in New Delhi; there they demanded that the project be halted. This and other protests culminated in a 1993 decision by India's supreme court to turn down U.S. $450 million in loans for the Narmada project to be provided by the World Bank. Nonetheless, after a brief hiatus, construction has resumed, largely in response to pressure from the state government of Gujarat. Most of the more prosperous farmers who stand to benefit from the irrigation waters provided by the project live in Gujarat. Even so, the "Save the Narmada" movement has persuaded the international aid community to demand environmental impact studies more frequently. No such study was provided for the Narmada hydroproject.

Water purity is an issue in historic pilgrimage towns such as Benares (also known as Varanasi), where each year millions of Hindus come to die, be cremated, and have their ashes scattered over the adjacent Ganges River. As the number of such final pilgrimages has increased, wood for the cremation fires has become scarce, and incompletely cremated bodies are being dumped into the river, where they pollute water used for drinking, cooking, and bathing. The government has sponsored campaigns to discourage cremation and other ritual uses of the Ganges, but so far little has changed.

Elsewhere, the water, and the air as well, may be endangered by industrial activity. In 1984, an explosion in a pesticide plant in Bhopal, India, produced a gas that killed at least 3000 people and severely damaged the lungs of 50,000 more. The explosion was largely the result of negligence on the part of the U.S.-based Union Carbide Corporation, which owned the plant, and the local Indian employees who ran it. In response to the tragedy, the Indian government launched an ambitious campaign to clean up poorly regulated factories that spill toxic effluents into rivers, often along with the untreated sewage from thousands of towns and cities. Nonetheless, by the late 1980s these plans were foundering, hindered by corruption and resistance from industry.

SUBREGIONS OF SOUTH ASIA

The following subregional geographies group areas of South Asia roughly according to their physical and cultural similarities. In several cases, the text groups parts of India with adjacent countries. This is true in the Himalayan region, in northeastern South Asia, and in the southernmost South Asian region, where parts of India and the country of Sri Lanka are treated as a subregion. Among the themes that emerge in the following sections are

1. The physical diversity of the region
2. The pervasive rural quality of life for most
3. The very large and distinctive cities
4. The still small but growing industrial economy of the region
5. The lingering religious and ethnic conflict that is exacerbated by lack of economic opportunities

Afghanistan and Pakistan

Afghanistan and Pakistan (Figure 8.14) are combined for consideration here because they share landforms and a history. These mountainous countries comprise the lands through which so many cultural influences have passed into the rest of South Asia: Indo-Aryan migrations in prehistory, the diffusion of Islam after A.D. 1000, and the Mogul invasion beginning in the sixteenth century and lasting through most of the eighteenth century. Today both countries are primarily Muslim and rural; 82 percent of Afghanistan's population is rural, as is 72 percent of Pakistan's. Both countries must cope with arid environments, scarce resources, and the need to find ways to provide rapidly growing populations with higher standards of living.

The landscapes of Afghanistan and Pakistan are best imagined in the context of the tectonic crash between India and Eurasia. At either end of the Himalayan mountain mass the crash created curved crinkles in the Eurasian landmass. The lofty Hindu Kush, Pamir, and Karakoram mountains of Afghanistan and Pakistan are the western manifestation of these crinkles. The system of high mountains and intervening valleys swoops away from the Himalayas and bends down to the southeast

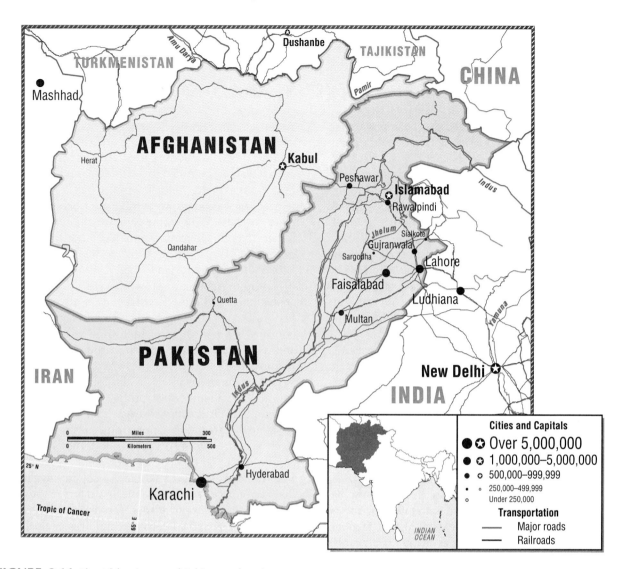

FIGURE 8.14 The Afghanistan and Pakistan subregion.

toward the Arabian Sea. Afghanistan, landlocked between Pakistan on the east, Iran on the west, and Central Asia to the north, is entirely within this mountain system. Pakistan has two contrasting landforms: the north, west, and southwest are in the mountain zone just described (see the chapter opening map on pages 362–363); the central and southeastern sections are arid lowlands watered by the Indus River and its tributaries.

Afghanistan

Afghanistan's Hindu Kush mountains in the north fan out into lower mountains and hills, and then into plains to the north, west, and south. In these gentler but arid landscapes, characterized by sparsely vegetated steep meadows and pasture land, most of the country's people struggle to earn a subsistence living based on

grazing and some cultivation; the main crops are wheat, fruit, and nuts.

There are more than 24 million Afghans, and 43 percent of them are 14 years of age or younger. Life expectancy is only 46 years, yet the population is growing by 2.5 percent per year. Women bear seven children on average. Generally, low life expectancy and a high birth rate are the markers of an extremely poor country.

The less mountainous regions to the north, west, and south are associated with the three main ethnic divisions of the country. To the north are people who share culture and language traditions with people of Central Asia: Turkmen and Uzbeks. To the west, the Tajik and Hazara people are more closely aligned with Iranian culture and languages. And to the south, the Pashto-speaking Pathans are culturally akin to groups

393

further south across the Pakistan border. The various ethnic groups have remained separate and competitive, but they share for the most part conservative religious and social attitudes.

Political debate became polarized in the 1970s between urban elites who favored industrialization and democratic reforms, and rural conservative religious leaders whose positions as landholders and ethnic leaders were threatened by the proposed reforms. Some urban elites allied with the Soviets, who, fearing that a civil war would destabilize their southern borders, invaded Afghanistan in 1979. The United States, Pakistan, and Iran supported the opposing guerrilla movement formed by rural conservatives—a collection of warlords strongly influenced by Islamist thought and known as mujahedeen. The Soviets eventually gave up and left, and the rural conservatives defeated the forces of the promodern urban elites.

In the early 1990s, a radical religious-political military movement emerged, called the Taliban. The Taliban are for the most part illiterate young men from remote villages, many in southern Afghanistan. They see their role as controlling corruption and bringing stability and peace by enforcing the shari'a, the Islamic social and penal code. They have taken particular aim at urban women, upon whom they are now enforcing seclusion and the completely concealing chador. By the late 1990s, the Taliban controlled two-thirds of the country, including the capital, Kabul, and were moving north.

The traditional rural subsistence economy has proved remarkably resilient and self-sufficient in the face of continuing hostility between Afghan factions. Women have often taken over, as many male farmers and herders leave periodically to fight. Many of the men have not returned alive, leaving women increasingly in charge of family subsistence. In order to finance arms purchases, many farmers are now producing hashish, opium, and heroin on a large scale.

Pakistan

Although not much bigger in area than Afghanistan, Pakistan, with a population of 137.8 million, has five times as many people. Pakistanis live primarily in villages. Some are sprinkled throughout the arid mountain districts associated with herding and subsistence agriculture, but it is the lowlands that have attracted most settlement. Here, the ebb and flow of the Indus and its tributaries during the wet and dry monsoons form the rhythm of agricultural life. The river brings fertilizing silt during flood stage and provides water to irrigate millions of cultivated acres during the dry season.

Pakistan enjoyed an overall economic growth of 6 percent a year in the 1980s and early 1990s. This growth was fueled substantially by agriculture in the Pakistani Punjab area, where cash crops such as cotton, wheat, rice, and sugarcane are grown on large tracts of irrigated land. Nevertheless, Pakistan is in trouble economically and, by some estimates, headed toward bankruptcy. In 1996, the International Monetary Fund withheld U.S. $70 million of a loan because of governmental mismanagement and apparent fudging on budgetary figures. Currently, over 70 percent of the national budget goes to pay off debt and to finance Pakistan's standing military of over half a million and its nuclear weapons program. Partly because of this huge investment in nonproductive military activities rather than in education and basic health care, per capita GNP is only U.S. $480—above India's U.S. $380 but lower than China's U.S. $750.

Despite economic growth, wealth is inequitably apportioned and most Pakistanis do not see the benefits of the growth. The productive farmland of Punjab is owned by a small elite. Industries based on textiles and yarn making are growing around the cities of Lahore and Karachi. But the wealth generated is not passed on to the workers in the form of high wages; and the reinvestment of profits in Pakistan is low. Beyond this, international drug dealing is a major activity, and corruption among officials is widespread. Arif Nizami, editor of the Lahore newspaper *The Nation*, is quoted by the *New York Times* correspondent John Burns as saying: "Pakistan is a country where millions cannot get two square meals a day, yet the prime minister has a fleet of planes, flies to his place in the country in a personal helicopter, and lives in a palace to shame the White House."

Himalayan Country

The northern border of South Asia is the Himalayan mountain chain. It stretches in a broad convex curve from Kashmir in the far northwest to the eastern border with Burma. Here, there is another set of crinkled mountains curving to the southeast—the counterpart of the mountains of Afghanistan and Pakistan. People in this region (see Figure 8.15) must deal with rugged mountain terrain, a harsh climate, and a diversity of environments.

The map that begins this chapter shows the mountainous zone running from west to east through the northern borderlands of India and continuing through Nepal and Bhutan. India actually extends east in a narrow corridor running between Bhutan to the north and Bangladesh to the south, and then balloons out in a far eastern lobe. Physically, this mostly mountainous region grades from relatively dry in the west to wet in the east, because the main monsoon winds move up the Bay of

FIGURE 8.15 The Himalayan country subregion.

Bengal and hit the east first and hardest. Culturally, the region is Muslim in the west, Hindu and Buddhist in the middle. Indigenous beliefs are important throughout but are especially strong in the far eastern part.

Life in this region is dominated by the spectacular mountain landscape. This strip of Himalayan territory can be viewed as having three zones: (1) the high Himalayas, (2) the foothills and lower mountains to the south, and (3) a narrow strip of southern lowlands running along the base of the mountains. This band of lowlands is actually the northern fringe of the Ganges River plain in the west and the narrow Assam valley of the Brahmaputra River in the east. Although some people manage to live in the high Himalayas, most of the population lives in the foothills, where they cultivate subsistence strips in the valleys or herd sheep and cattle on the hills. This area is so rural in character that the capital city of Thimphu, with 27,000 inhabitants, is the largest town in Bhutan; and the capital city of Nepal, Kathmandu, has just 52,000 people.

Throughout the region, but especially in valleys in the high mountains and foothills, pockets of indigenous cultures continue living in traditional ways, isolated from daily contact with the broader culture. There are many such groups in places like the Indian state of Arunachal Pradesh, at the eastern end of the region. Many indigenous groups have a unique language, as in Arunachal Pradesh, where a population of under 1 million speaks more than 50 languages. Despite language differences, these peoples have learned to survive in the difficult mountain habitat by relying on each other. An example of this reciprocity between cultures comes from central Nepal, where two indigenous groups engage in a complex cycle of trade that links them with both Tibet and India (see the box "Salt for Grain and Beans").

Most people in the Himalayan mountain region are very poor. Statistics for the various Indian states in this region hover near those of Nepal, which has an annual per capita GNP of just U.S. $210. In Nepal, the average life expectancy is 54, literacy is about 40 percent, and some 65 percent of the children under three years of age are malnourished. At present, only 18 percent of the land is cultivated, and the country's high altitude and convoluted topography make expansion unlikely. The government's strategy, therefore, is to improve crop productivity and lower the population growth rate.

The Indian state of Arunachal Pradesh is one of the region's more prosperous areas. Moist air flowing north off the Bay of Bengal brings plentiful rain as it lifts over the mountains. This is one of the most pristine regions in India. Forest cover is abundant, and a dazzling array of flora and fauna occupies habitats in descending elevations: glacial terrain, alpine meadows, subtropical mountain forests, and fertile floodplains. Conditions at different altitudes are so good for

395

AT THE LOCAL SCALE   *Salt for Grain and Beans*

The Dolpo-pa people are yak herders and caravan traders who live in the high, arid part of Nepal. In that difficult environment they can produce only enough barley and corn to feed themselves for half a year. Through trade, the Dolpo-pa parlay a half year's supply of grain into food sufficient to feed them for a whole year. At the end of the summer harvest, they load a portion of their grain onto yaks and head for Tibet. There, they trade grain to Tibetan nomads in return for salt, a commodity in short supply in Nepal. They leave some of the salt in their village for their own use; the rest they carry on to Rong-pa villages in the central Nepal foothills. They then trade this salt for enough grain to last them through the winter. Bargaining is fierce, and it can take days before a price is agreed upon, averaging between 3 and 5 measures of corn for 1 measure of salt. Their trading season ends in November, so the Dolpo-pa usually winter over in a convenient field, paying for the privilege.

The Rong-pa people are sheep and goat herders, and salt is a necessary nutrient both for them and their animals. In recent years, the Dolpo-pa, because of salt shortages in Tibet, have not brought out enough salt to meet all the Rong-pa needs. The Rong-pa, therefore, load goats and sheep with bags of red beans and set out for Bhotechaur, where they meet Indian traders at a large bazaar and trade their beans for iodized Indian salt; a good price is 1 measure of beans for 3 measures of salt. Often they will also sell a sheep or two to buy cloth, or perhaps a copper pan, to take home.

Source: Adapted from Eric Valli, Himalayan caravans, *National Geographic,* December 1993, pp. 5–35.

The Dolpo-pa people trading with Tibetan nomads. [Eric Valli.]

cultivation that lemons, oranges, cherries, peaches, and a variety of plants native to South America—pineapple, papaya, guava, beans, maize, and potatoes—are now grown commercially for shipment to upscale specialty stores in Indian cities.

Cool and dry Kashmir at the far western end of this region, adjacent to Pakistan, is known for the extrafine goat-hair fiber used in the manufacture of expensive cashmere sweaters. The exotically beautiful land of the Karakoram Mountains includes K2, the second highest peak in the world. One normally fearless trekker described the experience of merely looking *up* at the Karakoram Mountains as panic-inducing. Despite its beauty and exotic appeal, Kashmir is the fourth poorest state in India, in part because of continuing war (see the discussion on page 388).

Northwest India

Northwest India stretches almost a thousand miles from the Punjab/Rajasthan border with Pakistan to somewhat east of the famous city of Benares (Varanasi) on the Ganges (Figure 8.16). It is dry country, yet

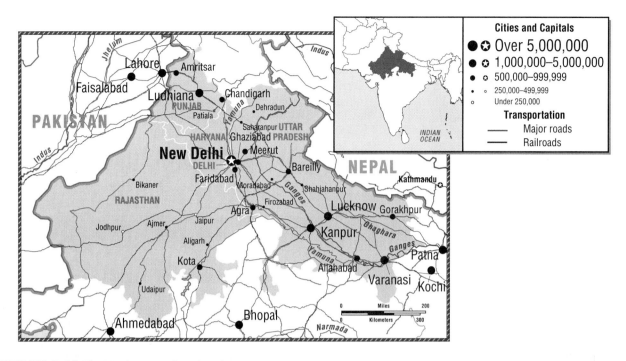

FIGURE 8.16 The Northwest India subregion.

contains some of the wealthiest and most fertile areas in India.

In the west of this subregion, there is so little rainfall that houses can safely be made of mud with flat roofs. Widely spaced cedars and oaks are the only trees, and the landscape has a dusty khaki color. Yet filling the landscape between the trees are fields of barley and wheat, potatoes, and sugarcane, plowed by villagers using oxen and humpbacked cattle. Along the northern reaches of this region (Punjab and Uttar Pradesh), the deficient rainfall is compensated for by rivers descending from the Himalayas. The most important is the Ganges; its many tributaries flow east and water the whole of Uttar Pradesh, bringing not only moisture but fresh soil from the mountains.

The western half of the region contains one of India's poorest states, Rajasthan, as well as its wealthiest, Punjab. Strategically situated in the path of

In the Rabari village of Bhopavand, Gujarat, camels are taken out to graze nearby. Many Rabari still lead a partially nomadic life, traveling northward through Rajasthan and across the Great Indian Desert in the dry season. [Dilip Mehta/Contact Press Images.]

397

invaders trying to penetrate into India from Central and Southwest Asia, Rajasthan was for over a thousand years home to warrior princes ensconced in fortresses and palaces. They fought one another more often than a common enemy. Rajasthan, with only a few fertile valleys, is dominated by the Thar (Great Indian) Desert in the west, which covers more than a third of the state. Seminomadic herders of goats and camels still cross the desert with their animals. Perhaps the best known are the Rabari. Originally a caste of camel herders and dung gatherers, today the Rabari, about 250,000 strong, continue their annual migrations during the dry season in search of green pastures. As they travel, they trade or sell animal dung for grazing rights, thus keeping farmers' fields fertile. By the 1990s, however, with rising populations there were more and more small farmers occupying former pasturelands. Although they want the dung, they cannot afford to lose one bit of greenery to the passing herds, so the ecological reciprocity between herders and farmers is being lost.

In this arid state, less than 1 percent of the land is arable, yet agriculture, poor as it is, produces 50 percent of the state's domestic product. It is not surprising that the per capita GNP is just U.S. $140. Crops include rice, barley, wheat, oilseeds, peas and beans, cotton, and tobacco. A thriving tourist industry, focused on the exotic palaces and fortresses of the past, accounts for much of the other half of the domestic product.

Punjab, also heavily dependent on agriculture, has double the per capita GNP of Rajasthan (U.S. $307). The differences in wealth are accounted for in part by differences in physical geography. Rajasthan is a desert; Punjab receives water and fresh soil carried down by rivers from the mountains. While Rajasthan is about three times the size of Punjab, only 1 percent of its land is cultivated. Nearly 85 percent of Punjab's land is cultivated, and it is particularly productive. In 1994–1995, Punjab alone provided 62 percent of India's food reserves. The usual crops are maize, potatoes, sugarcane, peas and beans, onions, and mustard.

While agriculture is the most important economic activity throughout the region and the employer of about 75 percent of the people, industry is also important in the city-state of Delhi and in the Ganges River plain. Here and elsewhere in the region, typical industries are sugar refining and the manufacture of cotton cloth and yarn, cement, and glass. People also make craft items and hand-knotted wool carpets. Urban areas have more modern forms of industry. For example, in the city of Chandigarh there are 15 medium-size and large-scale industrial facilities that produce electronic and biomedical equipment, household appliances, tractor parts, and cement tiles and pipes.

That portion of the Ganges River plain that lies within this region is considered the home of Hinduism. Every 12 years, provided astrologers say the time is right, India's largest religious festival takes place there. Millions of Hindus converge on the Uttar Pradesh city of Allahabad (not a Muslim name, incidentally) to bathe at the confluence of the Ganga and Yamuna rivers as an act of devotion. This area is also the center of Hindu conservative activism. Periodically there is violence against Muslims who, in this part of India, make up about 15 percent of the population.

Delhi

The city-state of Delhi, about eight times the size of Washington, D.C., in population, is located approximately in the center of the region and is the site of New Delhi, India's capital. Built by the British in 1931, New Delhi is the eighth city to arise in the territory; the remnants of all eight remain today. Delhi has all the problems one might expect of a big city in a country as poor as India. With already well over 10 million people, it is the focus of a continuing migration stream. Most of the new arrivals have left nearby states to escape conflict or poverty or both. The city is also home to refugees who fled Tibet to escape Chinese oppression, and to those who fled the Afghan war. Although per capita income in Delhi is average for the country, at U.S. $371, actual incomes are much lower for most; Delhi's tiny minority of the very wealthy pulls up the average. The low literacy rate, just 75 percent, is in part due to the continual arrival of migrants from poor rural areas, but Delhi also has far fewer schools than necessary for its population. In fact, the city has difficulty providing even the most basic services: there are not sufficient water, power, or sewer facilities, and 75 percent of the city structures violate local building standards. Many people have no buildings to inhabit at all; they live in shanties constructed from refuse.

Pollution is a particular concern: Delhi has been designated the world's fourth most polluted metropolitan area. The annual death rate from pollution-caused illness has reached 7500. One estimate is that on any given day, each citizen inhales the toxic equivalent of 20 cigarettes. Most of the pollution comes from the over 3 million unregulated motor vehicles. Taxis, trucks, buses, motorized rickshaws and scooters, most without pollution control devices, all compete for space, for cargo, and for passengers.

Despite this grim picture of life in Delhi, the big change here and across India is that the middle class is growing. Now estimated to be one-quarter of the population, or 250 million people, the Indian middle class is nearly as large as the total U.S. population. This significant change in the geographic and economic landscape has happened primarily since 1980, and it has brought a vibrancy to India and to Delhi. The global market economy, evident across the nation, is especially visible in cities like Delhi, where clubs, department stores, boutiques, cinemas and video parlors, and brand names like McDonald's, Louis Vuitton, Nike, and Hermès are common.

Northeastern South Asia

Northeastern South Asia, in strong contrast to arid Northwest India, has a wet tropical climate. Look at the map (Figure 8.17) and notice that the states of Bihar and West Bengal, the country of Bangladesh, and the far eastern provinces of India cluster at the north end of the Bay of Bengal. Their dominant shared features are two rivers, the Ganges and the Brahmaputra, and the giant delta region created by these rivers. The abundance of water and fertile land has nourished a population that is now among the densest on earth, often struggling to support itself in the overcrowded conditions.

The Ganges/Brahmaputra river delta is the largest on earth. Every year, the two rivers deposit enormous quantities of silt, building up the fluid landmass so that the delta extends farther and farther out into the bay. The rivulets of the bay repeatedly change course, until it is periodically flushed out by a huge tropical storm (a cyclone in 1991 left 130,000 delta dwellers dead). The people of the delta have learned never to regard their land as permanent (see Figure 8.3). Their dwellings, means of transport, and livelihoods are adapted to drastic seasonal changes in water level and shifting deposits of silt. Villages on river terraces are clusters of houses on mounds, surrounded by lush green forests and fields. The houses are intricately woven from bamboo and palm material, with sloping thatched roofs able to withstand heavy rainfall. In the lowlands, the houses are usually raised on posts above the high-water line. Transport is by small boats; people fish during the wet season and farm when the land emerges from floods. Even beyond the delta per se, most people have to cope with flooding at some time of the year, either when the monsoon rains come or, in the foothills of the Himalayas, when the spring snowmelt in the mountains swells rivers beyond their banks.

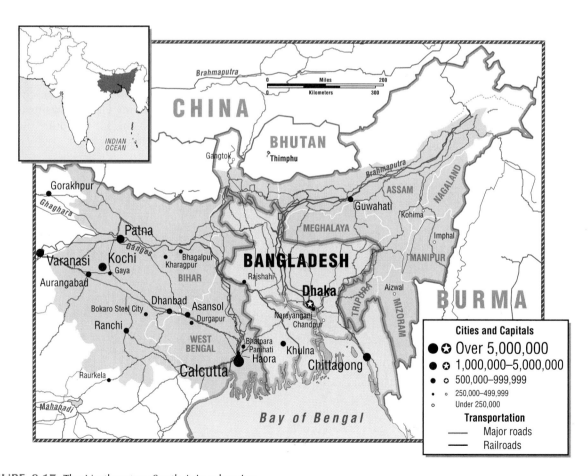

FIGURE 8.17 The Northeastern South Asia subregion.

West Bengal and Bihar

The Ganges River and the delta play a spiritually sustaining as well as a life-sustaining role in the western part of the subregion, the Indian states of Bihar and West Bengal. Most Hindus try to come to the river sometime in their lives to bathe, and many millions of funeral pyres are burned along its banks every year. Thus, the western portion of the region (especially Bihar) looms large as a Hindu pilgrimage site. But Buddhists also revere the area. The city of Bodhgaya in Bihar is Buddhism's most important pilgrimage site. Just outside the Mahabodhi Temple is an old bo tree that is believed to be a direct descendant of the tree under which Buddha was meditating when he attained enlightenment.

With a population of over 68 million packed into an area slightly larger than Maine, West Bengal is India's most densely occupied state: 1982 people per square mile (762 people per square kilometer). Its population has been swelled by Hindu migration from Bangladesh since partition; even more Hindu immigrants have come in from the western, predominantly Muslim, Indian states. The result is a mix of cultures that is frequently at odds: there are Hindu/Muslim religious riots and disputes over land occupied by new migrants. Nearly 75 percent of the people in this crowded state make a living in agriculture, yet agriculture accounts for only 35 percent of domestic production. In addition to growing food for their own consumption, many work as rice and jute cultivators or tea pickers, all labor-intensive activities. Twenty-five percent of India's tea comes from West Bengal—the plant is grown in the far north of the state around

Darjeeling, a name well known to tea drinkers. Each leaf must be selected and picked by hand, and it is often women and children who do this work. One result of a dense population dependent on agriculture is that continuous intensive cultivation often severely overstresses the land, and soil fertility declines over time. Also, surrounding woodlands are depleted by impoverished farm laborers who must gather firewood because they cannot afford kerosene.

Calcutta.   Calcutta, one of the most famous cities on earth, is in the delta region of West Bengal. This giant city of 12 million people is known for its legendary beggars, pestilential gutters, Mother Theresa's ministrations to the poor at Nirmal Hriday (Home for Dying Destitutes), and outrageously opulent, but crumbling, marble palaces. Calcutta was built on a swampy riverbank in 1690 and served as the first capital of British India. But its sumptuous colonial-built environment, substantially upgraded in the nineteenth century, has become lost in squatters' settlements that surround the city and have invaded its parks and boulevards. It is often characterized as a city in such a state of decline that nothing can be done. The reasons for Calcutta's decline are economic and social, brought on by massive immigration since 1947. But also, outmoded regulations limit entrepreneurism and incentives to improve private property. For example, under rent controls presently in place, a Calcuttan can pay as little as U.S. $1.40 a month for a four-room apartment and pass the lease down to the next generation. Many of the city's educated young people are leaving Calcutta, a situation that is beginning to cause problems for the future survival of the city.

This street scene in Calcutta shows a small marketplace and several modes of transportation. Relics of European influence are visible in the architecture. [Steve McCurry/ National Geographic.]

Somraj Kundu, a 20-year-old who has been accepted for graduate studies at Oxford, in England, indicates there are four main reasons he is leaving Calcutta: the breakdown of traditional extended families; the much too rapid increase in population as immigrants pour in; corruption at many levels (one can bribe an official to get a passport or a professor to avoid receiving a low grade in a course); and, perhaps most important, the lack of opportunity for economic advancement for him and others like him.

Eastern India

Eastern India has two physically distinct regions: the river valley of the Brahmaputra as it descends from the Himalayas, and the mountainous uplands stretching south of the river between Burma on the east and Bangladesh on the west. Although migrants have recently arrived from across South Asia, traditionally this region has been occupied by ancient indigenous groups that are related to the hill people of Burma, Tibet, and China.

The Indian state of Assam encompasses the river valley of the Brahmaputra, eastern India's most populated and most productive area. Hindu Assamese are two-thirds of the population of 29 million, and indigenous Tibeto-Burmese ethnic groups make up another 16 percent. The rest are recent migrants. To reduce the proportion and influence of the Assamese people, who objected to being under central Indian control, the Indian government has made large tracts of land available to people from outside: for example, Bengali Muslim refugees fleeing the civil war in Pakistan in 1971, Nepali dairy herders, and Sikh merchants. There were violent disputes in the late 1970s and early 1980s between Assamese and the new ethnic groups, and between Assam and India; the disputes continue, even though the violence has lessened.

More than half the people in Assam work in agriculture, growing and producing food; another 10 percent are employed on tea plantations or in forestry (forests cover about 25 percent of the land area). Two-thirds of the cultivated land is in rice; but tea is the main cash crop, and Assam produces half of India's tea. Furthermore, by the 1990s, Assam's oil and natural gas accounted for more than half that produced in all of India. Given India's shortage of energy, this alone explains India's political actions in Assam.

Colorful names like "land of jewels" and "abode of the clouds" convey the exotic beauty of the emerald valleys, blue lakes, dense forests, carpets of flowers, and azure, undulating hills in the mountainous sections of eastern India that surround Assam. Here, people produce for themselves primarily: 80 percent or more of the inhabitants make a living from the land. Many practice a particularly complex version of traditional

tropical horticulture specifically adapted to the region; others cultivate rice on permanently terraced fields.

Much of the population is composed of indigenous ethnic groups. In one area the size of New Jersey, for example, the majority of the 1.2 million inhabitants are from one of 16 indigenous ethnic groups. In some places, more than half the indigenous population is Christian, the result of English colonization in the late nineteenth and twentieth centuries. At that time, ethnic minorities adopted Christianity, in part as a hedge against the encroachment of Hindu power. Although literacy rates are not high in most of the region, the state of Mizoram ranks second in India, at 82 percent, because of the influence of Christian missionary schools.

Bangladesh

Bangladesh is not so much a land upon water as water upon a land. One-third of Bangladesh's physical space of fifty-five thousand square miles is comprised of water in the dry season, while in the rainy season up to 70 percent is submerged. Water is the central reality of Bangladesh, just as its shortage is the central reality of Saudi Arabia. At least 10 percent of the people live in boats, up to 40 percent depend on the sea and rivers for a livelihood, and 100 percent depend on rain and floods for food. Water is the main source of protein, the major provider of crop fertilizer and transport, and unquestionably the greatest source of wealth. Bangladesh's main crops—rice, jute, and tea—cannot exist without huge amounts of water.

—James J. Novak, Bangladesh, *pp. 22–23*

Today, Bangladesh is one of South Asia's poorest countries; only Bhutan and Nepal rank lower on most indexes. It is also one of the region's most populous democracies and the world's most densely populated agricultural nation. Over 122 million live in an area slightly smaller than Alabama. Population density is 2432 people per square mile—in the United States it is 75; yet all but 18 percent of these people are in rural areas, trying to live as farmers on a severely overcrowded land. Some 50 million people live below the poverty line, meaning that their daily caloric intake is below 2122, the minimum standard for adults.

Although desperately poor, the country is better off at the end of the twentieth century than it was just a few short years ago. The percentage of rural people living in poverty dropped 9 percent in the years from 1989 to 1994, according to the U.S. Agency for International Development. There has been a significant reduction in fertility rates, from 7 children per

401

Called *nodi bhanga lok* ("people of the broken river"), the people who occupy the constantly shifting silt of the Ganges delta region are looked down upon by more permanent settlers on slightly higher ground. Because they must so often flee rising flood water, they are known to be less secure financially and are thought to lack qualities of thrift and good citizenship that come from living in one place for a lifetime. The delta floods come from these sources: the Ganges, the Brahmaputra, and storms that sweep up the Bay of Bengal. [James Blair/National Geographic.]

woman in 1974 to 3.6 in 1997. This drop is attributed in large part to increased education and use of contraceptives, both funded primarily by foreign aid. Infant mortality has also dropped from 128 per 1000 in 1986 to 77 per 1000 in 1997. Economically, there are signs that the textile industry, once the source of considerable wealth in Bangladesh, is reviving. Bangladesh now ships more than U.S. $2 billion worth of garments to the United States and Europe annually. Although Bangladesh remains in distress, there is no reason to conclude that further progress is not possible. In fact, Bangladeshi innovation in microcredit is contributing to progress among the poor in many countries through the model provided by its Grameen Bank, discussed on page 386.

Central India

The central Indian subregion stretches across the widest part of India, from Gujarat in the west to Orissa in the east (Figure 8.18). It contains both India's last untouched natural areas and much of the country's industrialized area.

Some of India's most significant environmental battles are being fought in the highlands of this subregion. Central India has most of India's remaining forest cover and a concentration of national parks and sanctuaries (most notably the tiger reserve). Yet already the forest cover is merely patchy, not continuous; and areas between patches are densely occupied by humans in dispersed rural villages. The isolation of small populations of wild plants or animals in forest patches weakens the gene pools, and extinction becomes inevitable, even if somewhat delayed by protection. In recognition of this problem, there are plans now to reconstitute

corridors between parks. Estimates of future human population growth, however, do not bode well for the future of wildlife anywhere in this subregion.

Central India is notable for its several industrial areas. The state of Gujarat in the far west corner, on the Arabian Sea, has light industries in all of its major cities. Gujarat's service and industrial sectors account for 71 percent of its domestic production; the rate is

In Ahmadabad, a member of the Self-Employed Women's Association signs a withdrawal slip with her fingerprint as she is not able to read or write. This trade union has 220,000 members. In addition to helping set up bank accounts, the association provides child care, job training, legal assistance, and other services. [Steve McCurry/National Geographic.]

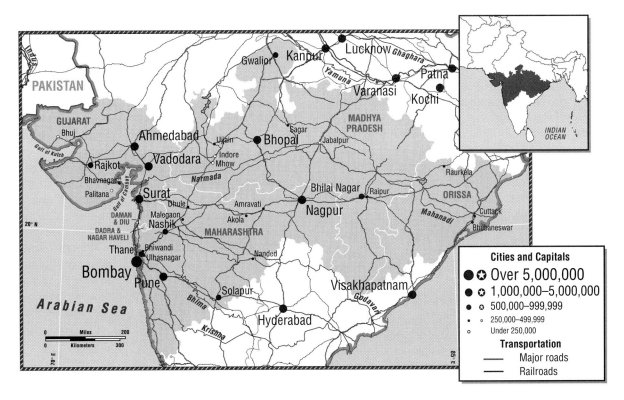

FIGURE 8.18 The Central India subregion.

even higher, at 77 percent, in the neighboring state of Maharashtra. Even the central plateau and eastern areas, although more rural in character, have pockets of industrial activity. An example is the city of Indore, a commercial and industrial hub whose residents think of it as a mini-Bombay. Although currently in decline, cotton textiles remain the city's main product. Other enterprises include oilseed extraction, machine tools, bicycles, electronics, iron, and steel. Indore also produces about one-third of all *Namkeen*, a popular variety of spicy cracker-like snacks made in India and sold in specialty food stores around the world. Nearby, the town of Pithampur, known as India's Detroit, houses several automobile plants, a steel plant, and small appliance factories. Industry and urbanization are clearly connected, and in fact the western part of the region is exceptionally urbanized for India. In Gujarat, more than 35 percent of the people live in urban areas; and in Maharashtra, the location of the megacity Bombay, the figure is about 40 percent.

Even though this region might be considered newly industrializing, it too can lose to the mobile global economy. The city of Ahmadabad, in Gujarat, with 4.8 million people, used to be known as the "Manchester of India" because of its large textile mills. Although the Arvind denim mills are still in operation, most of the old mills are closed today, having lost out to newer mills and cheaper labor elsewhere in Asia.

Bombay

Bombay is the name by which most know Maharashtra's capital, but since 1995 its official name has been Mumbai, after the Hindu goddess Mumba. In the sixteenth century, when a local sultan gave the bay, with its seven small islands, to the Portuguese, it became known as Bom Bahia, or "Beautiful Bay." Eventually the British joined the islands with bridges and landfill and built the largest deepwater harbor on India's west coast. Bombay, with 13 million people, is now India's largest and most prosperous city. It hosts India's largest stock exchange and the nation's reserve bank. It pays about a third of the taxes collected in the entire country and brings in nearly 40 percent of India's trade revenue; and its per capita production is three times that of Delhi. Yet the wealth is not readily visible. By some estimates, lack of housing has reduced half the population to living on the streets.

Bombay boasts Asia's largest slum. The community of Dharavi houses over 600,000 people on less than 1 square mile. Although most in Dharavi have no plumbing, people work at three or four jobs, and the community is known for its inventive entrepreneurs. One young man, for example, collects and sells aluminum cans that once held ghee, India's form of butter fat. He says he makes about 15,000 rupees a month (U.S. $480), nearly twice that of the average college professor in India, and much more than he made as a truck driver. Hence, despite widespread poverty and ethnic and religious tensions, Bombay has more than a few success stories.

Bombay is known popularly in India as "Bollywood" because it produces popular Hindi movies portraying love, betrayal, and family conflicts. The stories, played out on lavish sets and accompanied by popular music and dance, serve to temporarily distract the huge audiences from the rigors and disappointments of daily life. Bombay produces many more films than Hollywood, on much smaller budgets. The stars make six or more films a year and are so popular that movie posters are everywhere, in public and private spaces alike.

Southern South Asia

Southern South Asia (Figure 8.19) resembles the rest of the region, in that the majority of people work in agriculture—ranging from about 70 percent in the west to somewhat more than 50 percent in the east of the subregion. The cultural mix here, however, sets it apart. It is the center of ancient Dravidian cultures and languages that predate Indo-European influences. Also, this region exhibits influences that grow out of its long sea-trading heritage, especially with Arabs and Southeast Asians. Most in the region are Hindu (90 percent); Buddhists are a strong minority, and Muslim influence is relatively weak.

This part of India is particularly well watered and well suited for growing tobacco and rice, but also peanuts, chilies, limes, cotton, and castor-oil plants (the source of an intestinal medicine and skin lubricant). The southwestern coast of India is a narrow coastal plain backed by the Western Ghats. The sea-facing slopes of these mountains, just back of the coast, are some of the wettest in India; they support teak, rosewood, and sandalwood, all highly valued furniture woods. A substantial part of the Deccan Plateau, a series of uplands to the east, is also forested. Here, dry deciduous forest yields woods like teak, eucalyptus, cashew, and bamboo. Several large rivers and numerous tributaries flow toward the east across this plateau and form rich deltas along the lengthy and fertile coastal plain facing east to the Bay of Bengal.

A New Silicon Valley

These days, an air of excitement surrounds the Indian state of Karnataka in southwestern India, particularly

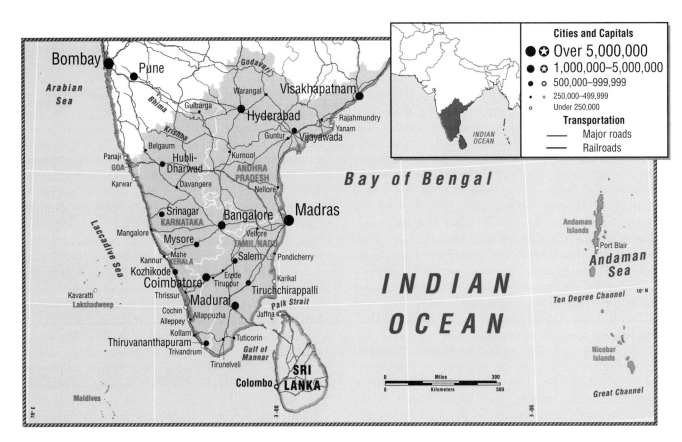

FIGURE 8.19 The Southern South Asia subregion.

the city of Bangalore. Although overall adult literacy is just 56 percent, Bangalore holds what is probably India's highest concentration of scientists and technicians, universities, colleges, and technical schools. In and around the city, India's "Silicon Valley" is developing.

Many Indians have earned graduate computer engineering degrees abroad at places like MIT and Harvard in Boston, and have returned home to Bangalore to found India's fast-growing computer industry. With Bangalore in the lead, Karnataka illustrates that it is possible to go directly from an agricultural economy to the information age. Some believe that India is poised to become a high-tech nation without adhering to the standard economic principle that to develop economically a place must have a solid local market for its own products. Bangalore is now a major worldwide center for software development, despite the fact that India has very poor telephone communications and one of the world's lowest concentrations of computers: 7 per 10,000 people. The world average is 250 per 10,000; Singapore has 1070 per 10,000, and the United States 2500 per 10,000. Lacking a sufficient home market, Bangalore sells its products on the other side of the world.

Although per capita income in Bangalore is only a few dollars higher than India's average of $380, it seems poised to go higher, quickly. There are now more than a dozen industrial parks outside Bangalore, housing such firms as Hewlett-Packard, Compaq, American Express, Citibank, Reebok, and IBM, and employing thousands of highly educated Indian computer experts and engineers. Besides developing new software for the international market, these people maintain many of the everyday systems that govern financial life in the United States. For example, while you are sleeping, a software specialist in Bangalore may be fixing the glitch in the automatic teller machine that ate your bank card yesterday.

The Special Case of Kerala

Kerala is a well-watered, primarily coastal state in far southwestern India. It is frequently cited as an aberration on the Indian subcontinent because its people enjoy a higher standard of human well-being than the rest of the country. Literacy rates are the highest in the whole of South Asia, at close to 100 percent. Women enjoy relatively high status and outnumber men in the population—there are no "missing females" as elsewhere in India. Moreover, women actively participate in the economy and are far less secluded than elsewhere. Standards of health are also better in Kerala.

Just why Kerala stands out in these ways is not entirely understood, but the state has a relatively unique history. Its traditional family organization gives considerable power to women; for example, a husband often resides with his wife's family (a pattern also found in Southeast Asia), instead of the reverse. The concept of female seclusion, while present, is less stringently practiced. Agriculture employs less than half of the population; instead, fishing has long figured prominently in the state economy. This livelihood strategy leaves women in charge of families while men are away at sea, and it gives women even more power because in Kerala tradition assigns to them the jobs of processing and selling the catch (see the box "Kerala's Fishing Industry").

Other features of life in Kerala that may have added to the openness of society and to greater freedom for women include significant contact with the outside world. Beginning thousands of years ago, traders from around the Indian Ocean, and especially Southeast Asia, made calls along the Malabar coast, possibly bringing other ideas about gender roles. Then, in the first century A.D., the Apostle Thomas is said to have come to spread Christianity. Eventually Muslims brought their faith by sea, as well. The state's 29.1 million people have a history of cultural and religious pluralism that seems to have led to somewhat more tolerance than in neighboring states. Still, some groups, especially fisherfolk, experience a pervasive sort of discrimination. Fishers are one of the very lowest Hindu castes, and there is a broad unwritten assumption that they will always be an underclass.

Sri Lanka

Sri Lanka, known as Ceylon until 1972, is a large island country off India's southeast coast that is known for its beauty. From the coastal plains, covered with rice paddies and with nut and spice trees, the land rises to hills where tea and coconut plantations are common. At the center is a mountain massif that reaches nearly 8202 feet (2500 meters) at its highest elevation. The southwest monsoons bring abundant moisture to the mountains, giving rise to forests and several unnavigable rivers that produce hydroelectric power. Close to 30 percent of the land is cultivated and just over 25 percent remains forested. Despite its inordinate beauty, Sri Lanka has suffered particularly vicious civil unrest that grew out of ethnic rivalry and high unemployment.

The original hunter-gatherers and rice cultivators of Sri Lanka, today known as Veddas, were joined several thousand years ago by settlers from northern India who built numerous city-kingdoms. Today known as Sinhalese, these Indians make up about 74 percent of the population of 18.7 million. The Sinhalese brought Buddhism to Sri Lanka, and today 70 percent of the people (most of them Sinhalese) are Buddhist. Because of Sri Lanka's location in the center of the Indian Ocean, it has also been influenced by traders from China, Southeast Asia, Africa, and Arabia. Sri Lankan

405

AT THE LOCAL SCALE   *Kerala's Fishing Industry*

The geographer Holly Hapke has studied how recent structural changes in the fishing industry of Kerala have changed family economics among Christian fisherfolk in and around Trivandrum, in the far south. Prior to Independence in 1947, fishing in Kerala was carried out almost entirely on a small scale. Thousands of fishermen worked from boats that held crews of from one to forty men. The catches were small and consisted of multiple species of fish. Once the boats had returned, the wives of the fishermen sorted and cleaned the catches, then sold the fish on the beach to wholesalers or in town at the market. Therefore, unlike most women elsewhere in South Asia, Kerala fishwives regularly dealt with the public as businesswomen; at the same time, they performed their multiple household and child-raising tasks.

In the 1950s, the Indian government hoped to improve the incomes of Kerala's fisherfolk by increasing the catch for the local market. It introduced large mechanized vessels to villages north of Trivandrum. Very soon, the project shifted to harvesting prawns for the world market; but mechanization spread to the fishing economy elsewhere along the coast. By the mid-1970s, the mechanized fleet was encroaching on traditional fishermen, damaging their gear, and competing for their catch. The intensification of fishing has led to declining fish stocks and pronounced declines in income for Trivandrum's fishing villages, which continue to use traditional technology. Men no longer bring in sufficient fish harvests; hence the women no longer have fish to clean and sell. While the men occasionally find wage labor in the now mechanized fishing industry, the role of preparing and marketing the catch has shifted out of the reach of women into the hands of male fish brokers. Yet, because the fishermen are no longer bringing in sufficient income, the families have become increasingly dependent on the women's earnings. The women, therefore, have shifted to buying fish from wholesalers and then reselling them in the market or to regular customers, all the while keeping up with their household duties. To compete as fish vendors against the larger operators, the women must

Selling fish in a Trivandrum neighborhood market. [Holly Hapke.]

themselves deal in larger volumes; this requires investment cash, which they must borrow at the high rates charged by moneylenders. The exorbitant interest depletes the women's earning, leaving them operating on the margins, with their family economies at risk.

Hapke concludes that state planners ignored women's roles in processing and marketing the fish catch; when the system was reorganized, women were left out entirely. They must now bear more of the responsibility for their family incomes, but they have little access to institutional and societal supports. Despite their considerable entrepreneurial spirit, without more attention their situation is likely to worsen as the traditional sector disappears.

Source: Adapted from Holly M. Hapke, *Fish Mongers, Markets, and Mechanization: Gender and the Economic Transformation of an Indian Fishery* (Syracuse, NY: Syracuse University, 1996).

Jewelry stores line a portion of Sea Street in Colombo, the capital of Sri Lanka. Gemstones have long been one of Sri Lanka's resources, and polishing and setting them is a major industry. Other businesses include textiles, clothing, and, increasingly, tourism. Britain, Germany, and the United States are Sri Lanka's primary export trading partners. [Steve McCurry/National Geographic.]

traders were among the many groups that participated in early East African trading centers.

About 1000 years ago, Dravidian people from southern India, known as Tamils, began migrating to Sri Lanka; by the thirteenth century they had established a Hindu kingdom in the north part of the island. Their numbers increased in the nineteenth century when many poor Tamils from Tamil Nadu in southeast India were brought in to work on British-managed tea, coffee, and rubber plantations. Known as Sri Lankan Tamils (to distinguish them from those in Tamil Nadu), they make up about 12 percent of the population of Sri Lanka. The Tamils have done well in Sri Lanka, dominating the entrepreneurial sectors of the economy.

Sri Lanka once had a thriving economy, led by a vibrant agricultural sector, and a government that made significant investments in health care and education for both rural and urban areas. It was thought to be poised to become one of Asia's "tigers." However, conditions in rural areas took a drastic turn for the worse in the 1960s as declining prices for the chief agricultural exports of tea, rubber, and coconuts prompted the government to shift investment away from rural development and toward urban manufacturing and textile industries. The resulting high levels of rural underemployment were a major factor in an insurrection by the Tamil population in the north, which began to agitate, sometimes through terrorism, for

separation from the Sinhalese areas in the south. Meanwhile, urban industrial development has lagged despite efforts to create a free trade zone to attract industries. International investors have been scared off by repeated episodes of terrorist bombings.

REFLECTIONS ON SOUTH ASIA

Conflicting images of life in South Asia abound. The writer Elisabeth Bumiller, who has written about women in India, made a comment that could be paraphrased to cover the entire region. She suggested that any one statement made about a region as complex as South Asia can be matched by an opposite statement that is equally as true. For example, South Asia has some of the largest and most crowded cities on earth, yet more than 70 percent of the population lives in rural villages. Poverty is endemic and the gaps between rich and poor are widening, but South Asia is also the home of one of the most potentially empowering and far-reaching development strategies ever conceived—microcredit. Although telephones are missing from most homes, the high-tech information age is in full flourish. And while religious conflict between Muslims and Hindus threatens to precipitate nuclear war between Pakistan and India, the region is a mecca for those seeking spiritual enlightenment. It is also the home of the highly effective strategy of nonviolent social protest, begun by Mohandas Gandhi and adopted by advocates for human rights in the American South, in South Africa, and in Beijing's Tiananmen Square. And one more contrast out of many could be cited: India is the world's largest democracy, yet it is also a place where religious intolerance has led to thousands of deaths in the last few years. Even more important, in South Asian democracies, a person's sex significantly determines whether that person has access to sufficient food, education, income, opportunity, and, indeed, to life itself.

Perhaps one of the most provocative characteristics of South Asia is that it is a region that comments eloquently on itself, and in the process adds to the enlightenment of others. Many Indian and Bengali writers make the best-seller lists in Europe and North America. Most have something to add to the global conversation on poverty, human rights, and development. The Bengali Nobel laureate Rabindranath Tagore wrote prophetically before his death in 1941

407

about the need for South Asia to assess carefully its Western-led development trajectory:

We have for over a century been dragged by the prosperous West behind its chariot, choked by the dust, deafened by the noise, humbled by our own helplessness and overwhelmed by the speed. We agreed to acknowledge that this chariot-drive was progress, and the progress was civilization. If we ever ventured to ask, "progress towards what, and progress for whom", it was considered to be peculiarly and ridiculously Oriental to entertain such [reservations] about the absoluteness of progress. Of late, a voice has come to us to take count not only of the scientific perfection of the chariot but of the depth of the ditches lying in its path. (Rabindranath Tagore, Crisis of civilization. In Collected Works of Rabindranath Tagore, *vol. 18.)*

It took more than three decades for Tagore's critique of development policy to gain wider acceptance.

The "progress for whom" question is only now being asked in the highest halls of policy formation at the World Bank or the United Nations. Strategies for aiming development at the poorest, rather than at those who are already reasonably well off, are only now being invented; and as we have seen, South Asians are some of the most innovative thinkers along these lines. Readers have only to check the newspapers in their towns and cities to discover small groups of cooperative borrowers meeting regularly to support and encourage each other in entrepreneurial ventures, emulating their million-plus counterparts in the Grameen Bank in Bangladesh, where microcredit got its start.

So at the close of a chapter about a region that is arguably the poorest on earth, it is illuminating to note that this region is also a leader in inventive ideas for development as well as provocative thought about the present trajectory of human society.

Selected Themes and Concepts

1. About 75 percent of the people of South Asia live in one of the hundreds of thousands of villages in this region.

2. South Asia has experienced many cultural influences from outside the region: some, like Hinduism and Islam, were brought by invaders; others, like Buddhism and Christianity, were the result of more peaceful diffusion.

3. The yearly **monsoon** climate cycles of South Asia are important influences on the organization of daily life and economic activities. For much of the region there are distinct wet and dry seasons.

4. British colonial rule had a pervasive influence, and the effects are still to be found in many aspects of South Asian life. An important consequence of British colonization in India was the undermining of South Asian indigenous industries, especially cotton cloth manufacture. India became instead a producer of raw materials for mechanized textile production in Britain.

5. High population densities and rapid population growth make it difficult for South Asian countries to improve the well-being of their people. Economic factors encourage large families, and cultural attitudes also contribute to high birth rates.

6. The main religious traditions that have influenced South Asia are Hinduism, Islam, Buddhism, Sikhism,

Jainism, and Christianity. The different religious traditions of South Asia have deeply affected one another; and this is especially true of the two largest faiths: Islam and Hinduism.

7. **Caste** is a custom associated primarily with Hindu India, but ideas associated with caste have been absorbed into Muslim and Buddhist culture, too. Caste is disappearing as a force in everyday life wherever people are able to separate themselves from their ancestral villages, occupations, and caste-related dialects.

8. The overall status of women in South Asia is extraordinarily low. This fact is attested to by literacy rates, female survival rates, gender ratios in the adult population, preference for sons, violence against females, and purdah, a custom that keeps women from participating in paid employment and government work.

9. Agricultural development has been neglected in favor of industry. In the 1990s, South Asian countries reversed a policy of government intervention in industry. The resultant move toward more efficient, competitive industries has eliminated many industrial jobs.

10. One of the most promising strategies for helping poor people, **microcredit,** was developed in South Asia and has been diffused globally.

11. South Asian countries are formally secular, but **religious nationalism** is a strong countercurrent.

Religious nationalists believe that a certain religion is connected to a particular territory and that those who share a belief should have their own political unit they control.

12. South Asia is plagued by a number of **regional conflicts** between factions within the region. One is that between India and Pakistan, another is that between Muslims and Hindus, a third is that between the Tamils and Sinhalese in Sri Lanka.

13. On human well-being scales, South Asians do not fair well. Most countries in this region rank at the bottom. South Asians survive and even flourish in many cases because of extremely frugal living habits that allow them to make the most of all resources available to them.

Selected Readings

Amin, Sajeda. The poverty-purdah trap in rural Bangladesh: Implications for women's roles in the family. *Development and Change* 28 (1997): 213–233.

Bagwe, Anjali. *Of Woman Caste—The Experience of Gender in Rural India.* Atlantic Highlands, NJ: Zed Books, 1995.

Bhalla, A. S. *Uneven Development in the Third World—A Study of China and India.* New York: St. Martin's Press, 1995.

Brauns, Claus-Dieter, and Lorenz G. Loffler. *Mru—Hill People on the Border of Bangladesh.* Basel: Birkhauser Verlag, 1989.

Bumiller, Elisabeth. *May You Be the Mother of a Hundred Sons—A Journey Among the Women of India.* New York: Fawcett Columbine, 1991.

Counts, Alex. *Give Us Credit.* New York: Times Books/Random House, 1996.

David, Kenneth, ed. *The New Wind—Changing Identities in South Asia.* The Hague: Mouton, 1977.

Dutt, Ashok K., S. P. Chatterjee, and M. Margaret Geib. *India in Maps.* Dubuque, IA: Kendall/Hunt, 1976.

Emadi, Hafizullah. The state and rural-based rebellion in Afghanistan. *Central Asian Survey* 15, no. 2 (1996): 201–211.

Gamburd, Michele Ruth. Sri Lanka's "army of housemaids": Control of remittances and gender transformations. *Anthropolgica* 37 (1995): 49–88.

Gunnell, Yanni. Comparative regional geography in India and West Africa: Soils, landforms and economic theory in agricultural development strategies. *Geographical Journal* 163 (March 1997): 38–46.

Guthman, Julie. Representing crisis: The theory of Himalayan environmental degradation and the project of development in post-Rana Nepal. *Development and Change* 28 (1997): 45–69.

Johnson, Gordon. *Cultural Atlas of India—India, Pakistan, Nepal, Bhutan, Bangladesh and Sri Lanka.* New York: Facts on File, 1996.

Magnus, Ralph H. Afghanistan in 1996. *Asian Survey* (February 1997): 111–117.

Mohanti, Prafulla. *Changing Village, Changing Life.* New York: Viking, 1990.

Novak, James. J. *Bangladesh—Reflections on the Water.* Bloomington: Indiana University Press, 1993.

Paz, Octavio. *In Light of India.* New York: Harcourt Brace, 1995.

Raju, Saraswati, and Deipica Bagchi, eds. *Women and Work in South Asia—Regional Patterns and Perspectives.* London: Routledge, 1993.

Rangan, Haripriya. Property vs control: The state and forest management in the Indian Himalaya. *Development and Change* 28 (1997): 71–94.

Rashid, Ahmed. Subversive—When it's Islam versus soap opera, Mohammed hasn't got a chance. *New York Times Magazine,* June 8, 1997, p. 78.

Risso, Patricia. *Merchants and Faith: Muslim Commerce and Culture in the Indian Ocean.* Boulder, CO: Westview Press, 1995.

Rothermund, Dietmar. *Liberalising India: Progress and Problems. South Asian Studies No. 29.* Columbia, MO: South Asia Books, 1996.

Roy, Beth. *Some Trouble with Cows—Making Sense of Social Conflict.* Berkeley: University of California Press, 1994.

Schuler, Sidney Ruth, Syed Mesbahuddin Hashemi, and Ann P. Riley. The influence of women's changing roles and status in Bangladesh's fertility transition: Evidence from a study of credit programs and contraceptive use. *World Development* 25, no. 4 (1997): 563–575.

Tharoor, Shashi. *India from Midnight to Millennium.* New York: Arcade, 1997.

Thompson, Paul M., and Parvin Sultana. Distributional and social aspects of flood control in Bangladesh. *Geographical Journal* 162 (March 1996): 1–13.

Land Elevations

meters		feet
Icecap		Icecap
5183 and above		17,000 and above
3353–5182		11,000–16,999
2134–3352		7000–10,999
914–2133		3000–6999
305–913		1000–2999
0–304		0–999
Below sea level		Below sea level

Miles
0   300

Kilometers
0   500
1:20,354,000
Albers Equal Area Projection

EAST ASIA

INTRODUCTION TO EAST ASIA

VIGNETTE

Eighteen-year-old Hong Xiaohui (Hong is her family name) and two friends eagerly signed up when the labor officials came to her remote farming village in Sichuan Province. They had come to hire workers for Mattel, Inc.'s, Barbie Doll factory in Changan, a factory town in Southern China, between Guangzhou (Canton) and Hong Kong.

When the bus left a few days later, it held 100 young women. Most had never left their home villages before, but now they were on a 1200-mile trip that would take five days, most of it along bumpy, winding roads. Exhaust fumes and little ventilation would bring constant nausea. Nearly all were short of cash; but most had a supply of food provided by anxious mothers: sugarcane, bags of oranges, salted duck eggs, peanuts, and bottles of orange soda. Chatting with her friends, Xiaohui says, "I've always itched to get away from home. Life there is empty. I want to be independent. I want to learn something so I can come back and change things." These are the sentiments of migrants through all time.

On the fifth day, the bus reaches Changan. In a few years the city has grown in population from 30,000 to 180,000. The Mattel Barbie Doll factory is in the middle of town, in a modern white building known locally as "Paradise of Girls" because nearly all 3500 employees are female. Within a day, Xiaohui has completed training, signed a three-year contract, and is learning how to put either brown or blonde hair into Barbie Doll heads of varying skin color. The pay is 200 yuan a month (about U.S. $24), considerably less than the 350 yuan the recruiters had promised. Xiaohui learns by asking around that no one earns more than 400 yuan.

When a reporter inquires, the Mattel officials say only, "We're confident that we provide these workers with a better standard of living than they would have without Mattel." [Adapted from Kathy Chen, Boom-town bound, *Wall Street Journal,* October 29, 1996, pp. 1, A6.]

This brief description of Hong Xiaohui's first trip to China's booming southeast coast illustrates some of the rapid changes that are sweeping the whole of East Asia. Here we see rural villagers from one of China's poor interior provinces rushing to a coastal city. Not only will they labor at the low-income end of the global economy, many will deprive themselves in order to send remittances home to poor relatives. They are among the millions who are making East Asia's coastal cities among the biggest and most rapidly growing on earth. Meanwhile, although the remittances help, poor rural interior provinces are deprived of the energy, initiative, and leadership of their young adults. This story also hints at the changing gender roles throughout East Asia. Though many of the old restrictions on women persist, increasingly it is young women who are the workers in the factories of multinational firms like Mattel. Women have always been a major source of labor in China, but until the Communist revolution of 1949, they labored without wages on the farm and within the home. Now women are earning wages, but the low pay hints at continuing gender discrimination and at the wide disparity of wealth that has been characteristic in China for thousands of years. We will take up Hong Xiaohui's story again in the economic issues section.

Home to nearly one-quarter of humanity, East Asia is a vast territory stretching from the Taklimakan Desert in the far west to Japan's rainy Pacific coastline; and from the frigid mountains of Mongolia in the north to the steaming subtropical forests of China's southeast coastal provinces. The East Asian region consists of the countries of China, Mongolia, North Korea, South Korea, Japan, and Taiwan. Today, East Asia is home to several of the world's most rapidly growing economies; and that alone makes it of interest. It is also the most populous world region and is among the most precarious environmentally. For all of these reasons, East Asia will figure prominently in global relationships for years to come.

Themes to Look For

These trends in the economy, migration, population, and the environment of East Asia are reflected in the following themes, which appear repeatedly throughout this chapter:

1.   Free market economies are growing rapidly throughout the region, pioneered by Japan.

2.   Ancient Chinese forms of government and philosophy have influenced the entire region, including the development of the economy, the dominance of bureaucracies, and gender roles. Yet countries such as Japan and China have incorporated these influences in very different ways.

3.   The heavily populated heartland of China, in the east—the home of the Han Chinese majority—

dominates the more culturally diverse western hinterlands of China.

4. Regional disparities in wealth are growing within China, as inland rural areas lose people and resources to the booming cites on the coast.

5. Huge populations are putting strain on the environment, with consequences such as floods, dangerous levels of pollution, and overcrowding.

Terms to Be Aware Of

Whenever possible, I will give place names in English transliterations of the appropriate Asian language; also, redundancies will be avoided. For example, *he* and *jiang* are both Chinese words for "river." Hence the Yellow River (so called because it is yellowed by the heavy sediment load it carries) is the Huang He, and the Yangtze River is the Chang Jiang. There is no need to add the term *river* to either name; it is already there. Pinyin forms of Chinese place names are now commonplace. For example, the city once called Peking in English is Beijing, Canton is Guangzhou, the region known as Manchuria is here referred to simply as the Northeast, Tibet is Xizang, though the native people of Xizang will be referred to as Tibetan.

of horticulture and animal husbandry to get plants and animals to flourish in difficult conditions.

A simple way to visualize the varied landforms of East Asia is to think of them as analogous to the shapes that would be formed in a huge carpet if a grand piano (standing in for the Indian subcontinent) were shoved deeply into one side of it. The mountain ranges, plateaus, depressions, fissures, and bulges across Eurasia are thought to be the result of the slow-motion collision of the Indian subcontinent with the southern side of Eurasia roughly 50 million years ago. The Himalaya Mountains are the most dramatic result of the collision; and on the north side of the Himalayas, the Xizang-Qinghai Plateau (the Northern, or Tibetan, Plateau, depicted in rust and lavender on the map at the beginning of the chapter) absorbed some of the pressure by bulging upward and spreading outward to the northeast. To the north of the plateau, in Xinjiang the land responded by sinking to form various basins like the Qaidam Basin and the sea-level Tarim Basin in the Taklimakan Desert. Further north, it buckled again to form the mountains on either side of the Dzungar Basin and those of northern Mongolia and southern Siberia. To the east and west of the Himalayan impact zone are the wrinkled mountain and valley formations that curve away to the southwest and southeast from the Xizang-Qinghai Plateau.

PHYSICAL PATTERNS

A quick look at the map of East Asia reveals that the topography is perhaps the most rugged in the world, consisting of a wide range of complex landforms produced by powerful tectonic forces. We will learn that East Asia's climate is a dynamic balance between huge forces of land and sea, and that the variety of ecosystems that evolved over the millennia, now greatly affected by rapidly expanding human populations, still contains many important and unique habitats.

Landforms

There are few flat surfaces to be found in the rugged landscapes of East Asia; and many of those that do exist are too dry or too cold to be very useful to humans. The large numbers of people who occupy the region have had to be particularly inventive in creating spaces for agriculture. They have cleared and terraced whole mountain ranges by hand, irrigated drylands with water from melted snow, drained wetlands using elaborate levees and dams, and applied their complex knowledge

In the midst of the Taklimakan Desert, international petroleum company trucks are driving to a remote oil field that has potential reserves far greater than those in the United States. [Reza/National Geographic.]

The landforms of East Asia form four steps. The top step is the Xizang-Qinghai Plateau. The second step down is a broad expanse of basins, plateaus, and low mountain ranges—depicted in deep yellow and light greens on the map at the beginning of this chapter. These include the deep dry basins and deserts of Xinjiang to the north of Xizang-Qinghai and the broad, rolling highland grasslands and deserts of the Mongolian Plateau northeast of Xinjiang. South of the Mongolian Plateau, this step also includes the upper portions of China's two great river basins through which flow the Huang He and Chang Jiang. Yet further to the south is the rugged Yunnan Plateau, where the topography is dominated by the deeply folded mountain and valley system mentioned above, which bends south through the Southeast Asian peninsula.

The third step, directly east of this upland zone, consists mainly of broad coastal plains and the deltas of China's great rivers (shown in green on the map), with the intervening low mountains and hills (shown as yellow patches on the green areas on the map). Starting from the south is a series of three large river basins: the Xi Jiang (Pearl) basin, the massive Chang Jiang basin, and the Huang He basin on the North China Plain. As the Huang He carried massive deposits of silt down from the Loess Plateau, it built the North China Plain into the Gulf of Bo Hai. The far northeast of China (Heilonajiang, Jilin, and Liaoning), the Korean Peninsula, and the westernmost parts of southern Siberia are also part of this third step.

The fourth step consists of the continental shelf, covered by the waters of the Yellow Sea, the East China Sea, and the South China Sea. Numerous islands—Hong Kong, Hainan, and Taiwan—are anchored on this continental shelf, all part of the Asian landmass. The same is not quite the case with the islands of Japan, which rise out of the waters of the northwestern Pacific. These rugged islands, lying squarely on the Pacific "Ring of Fire," where the Pacific Tectonic Plate grinds into the Eurasian Plate, are volcanic in origin. The dramatic volcano Mount Fuji is perhaps Japan's most recognizable symbol. The entire Japanese island chain is particularly vulnerable to disastrous eruptions and earthquakes.

Climate

East Asia has two contrasting climate zones (Figure 9.1): one is the dry continental west; the other is the more complex monsoon east. Recall from Chapter 1 that *monsoon* refers to the seasonal reversal of surface winds that flow from the north in winter and from the south in summer across the southeastern quadrant of Asia.

The Dry Continental Western Zone

The western, or dry, zone lies in the interior of the East Asian continental landmass. Because land heats up and cools off more rapidly than large bodies of water, locations in the middle of large bodies of land in the midlatitudes tend to experience extreme cold in winter and extreme heat in summer. The western part of China is a classic and extreme example of a continental climate. This part of China includes the Mongolian Plateau, the basins of Xinjiang, and the Xizang-Qinghai Plateau—all very dry and all extremely cold in winter and extremely hot during the day in summer. Summer nights can also be cold because there is too little vegetation or cloud cover to retain the warmth of the sun after nightfall. Heat is lost so rapidly that variations between summer daytime and nighttime temperatures may be as much as 100°F (55°C).

Grasslands and deserts of several varieties cover most of the land in this dry region. Only scattered forests grow on the few relatively well-watered mountain slopes and in protected valleys supplied with water by snowmelt. In all of East Asia, humans and their impact are least conspicuous in the large, uninhabited portions of the deserts of Xizang, the Tarim Basin in Xinjiang, and the Mongolian Plateau. The grasslands of Mongolia and basins of far northwest China traditionally supported only scattered tribes of nomadic herders. However, they are increasingly being turned over to more intensive uses, like irrigated agriculture in the Taklimakan and Dzungar basins. In Mongolia, many nomads now live on large-scale, stationary, livestock cooperatives, also supported with irrigation.

The Monsoon East

The monsoon climates of the east are influenced by the extreme continental climate of the huge Eurasian landmass in the winter and the more moderate maritime climate of the surrounding seas and oceans in the summer. In what is commonly called the "winter monsoon," dry frigid arctic air sweeps down through East Asia, giving the Mongolian Plateau, the North China Plain, and China's northeast a long bitter winter. The winter monsoon also causes occasional freezes in southern China. Central and southern China have shorter, less severe winters because they are protected from the advancing arctic air by the east-west ranges of the Qin Ling Mountains and because they lie close to the warm waters of the South China Sea.

In the summer months, the summer monsoon pulls in warm tropical air from the Pacific Ocean and its adjacent seas (see Figure 8.1). The warm monsoon air picks up a huge amount of moisture from ocean waters, which is then deposited on the land as seasonal rains. As the East Asian summer monsoon moves to-

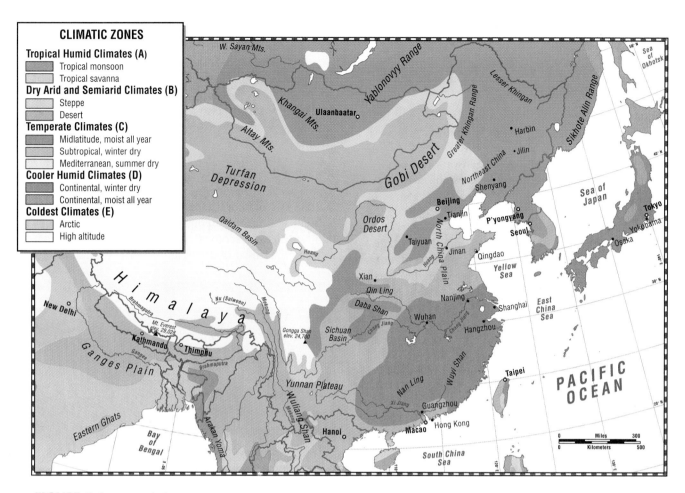

FIGURE 9.1 Regional climate.

ward the northwest, it must cross numerous mountain ranges and must displace a massive amount of cooler air; hence, its effect is weakened in that direction. Thus the Xi Jiang basin in the far southeast is drenched with rain and enjoys warm weather for most of the year, while the Chang Jiang basin, which lies in central China to the north of the Nan Ling Mountains, receives only about five months of the summer monsoon. The North China Plain, north of the Qin Ling range, receives only about three months of monsoon rains. Very little monsoon rain makes it to the southern Mongolian Plateau or to Inner Mongolia; and the far northwest is also left out.

China's far northeast, and Korea and Japan have a wetter climate because of their proximity to the sea. However, they still have hot summers and cold winters because of their northerly location and exposure to the continental effects of the Eurasian landmass. Japan and the more southerly Taiwan actually receive monsoon rains twice: once in the spring when the main rains move toward the land, and again in autumn as the winter monsoon forces the warm air off the continent and over the coastal seas. The warm air, in retreat, again

picks up moisture that is then deposited on the islands. Japan, however, has a much longer and more severe winter than semitropical Taiwan; and much of Japan's autumn rain comes as snowfall.

The eastern areas of the Asian landmass, watered by the seasonal rains, once supported rich forests with an amazing array of plant and animal life, much of it unique to East Asia. The character of the forests changed from north to south: coniferous forests covered the far northeast and graded to deciduous broad-leafed forests in Korea, Japan, and the North China Plain. Broad-leafed evergreen forests and even tropical rain forests grew in the south. Over the past two or three millennia, however, agriculture has transformed the landscape. Many lowland ecosystems were wiped out as farmers expanded into any flat or hilly, well-watered or irrigable land. Hills and low mountainsides were rarely left covered with undisturbed forest; rather, they were logged continuously, or planted in orchards, or completely cleared and terraced for agriculture. Today, the few undisturbed natural areas in the humid zone are remote, deeply convoluted, and increasingly threatened by development.

HUMAN PATTERNS

East Asia is a region of ancient civilizations and dramatic transformations. Settled agricultural societies have flourished in China for over 4000 years; and as early as 2000 years ago, the basic institutions of government that still exist today were established there. Until the twentieth century, China was the source of wealth, technology, and culture for the people of the region.

For most of East Asian history, only the rich agricultural areas in eastern China were considered to be part of China proper. This area, centered on the North China Plain, is the heartland of China, which was unified under successive empires. Bordering it were the lands of inner Asia. Extending to the north and west, these lands, home to Mongolian peoples, were considered alien and uncivilized by the Chinese. The dry continental climate there was unsuitable for crop-based agriculture. Yet these huge territories were ideal for nomadic animal herding, and the nomads, for their part, pitied the Chinese farmers who were tied to a particular place for a lifetime. On East Asia's eastern fringe, the Korean Peninsula and the islands of Japan and Taiwan were profoundly influenced by the culture of China, but were isolated enough so that each developed distinctive cultures and usually maintained political independence. These characteristics proved crucial during the twentieth century, when these areas (except for North Korea) leaped ahead of China economically and militarily, in part by integrating European influences that China disdained.

The Beginnings of Chinese Civilization

While humans and their ancestors have lived in East Asia for hundreds of thousands of years, the earliest complex civilizations appeared in north China after 2000 B.C. Here, agricultural societies developed a political and land use system that was basically feudal. A small militarized aristocracy controlled vast estates on which the mass of the population worked and lived as impoverished farmers and laborers. The landowners usually owed allegiance to one of the petty kingdoms that dotted north China. However, they were relatively self-sufficient and well defended with private armies, and often proved insubordinate to central authority.

Between 400 and 221 B.C., a new order emerged that eradicated feudalism and laid the foundations for the great Chinese empires that for thousands of years dominated East Asia. Following a long period of war between the petty kingdoms of north China, a single kingdom emerged as dominant. What gave this kingdom, known as the Qin dynasty, its edge was the use of a trained and salaried bureaucracy to extend the monarch's authority into the countryside. The old feudal alliance system was scrapped, and the estates of the aristocracy were divided into small units and sold to the previously semi-enslaved farmers. The kingdom's agricultural output increased, for two reasons. The people worked harder to farm land they now owned; and the salaried bureaucracy that replaced their former masters was more responsible in building and maintaining levees, reservoirs, and other public works that reduced the threat of floods and other natural disasters.

After unifying China in 211 B.C., Qin Shi Huang became its emperor. One of his numerous public works, which included China's Great Wall, was the creation of a life-size terra-cotta army of thousands filling a vast underground chamber that became his mausoleum. Since 1974, archaeologists have been excavating, restoring, and preserving this site, which attracts over 2 million visitors a year. [Wally McNamee/Woodfin Camp & Associates.]

Although the Qin empire was short-lived, subsequent empires maintained its bureaucratic ruling methods, which proved essential to the governing of China as a whole for 2000 years.

Confucianism

Closely related to China's bureaucratic ruling tradition is the philosophy of **Confucianism.** Confucius, who lived about 2500 years ago, taught that the best organizational model for the state and society was a hierarchy modeled after the patriarchal family. In the Chinese extended family, the oldest male was the seat of authority; all others were aligned under him according to age and sex. Extending these conventions, Confucianism held that commoners would obey imperial officials, and everyone would obey the emperor. As the supreme human being, the emperor was seen as the source of all order and civilization—in a sense, the grand patriarch of all China.

Over the centuries, this Confucian elitist and patriarchal ideology (not really a religion but certainly a value system) penetrated the most intimate crevices of Chinese society, altering its social, economic, and political geography in profound ways, and circumscribing the lives of the masses at the base of the hierarchical pyramid. An early literary interpretation of the ideal woman gives a sense of how this system rested on the subjugation of women, confining them to the domestic space of the home and almost always placing them under the authority of others. A student of Confucius wrote: "A woman's duties are to cook the five grains, heat the wine, look after her parents-in-law, make clothes, and that is all! When she is young, she must submit to her parents. After her marriage, she must submit to her husband. When she is widowed, she must submit to her son."

One reason that Confucian ideology had such an impact on China's human geography was that it conveniently served the best interests of the political and economic elite. Imperial officials and their families gained access to power only by entering the bureaucracy, a process that demanded an expensive education based on familiarity with the Confucian classics. Thus, for more than 2000 years, Confucian policies and attitudes, as interpreted by the elite, dominated China, transforming both the social order and the ways in which resources were used and developed. Elites claimed the produce raised by impoverished farmers and the wealth produced by artisans and craft workers. Merchant wealth was limited wherever possible. In parable and folklore, merchants were characterized as a necessary evil, greedy and disruptive of the social order, while the lowly farmer was heralded, but not rewarded. For 2000 years, the expropriation of farmers' wealth and the curtailment of merchants' prosperity resulted in little incentive or investment capital for agricultural improvements, industrialization, or entrepreneurialism.

While Confucian bureaucracy allowed empires to expand, its weaknesses nurtured imperial decline. A large tax burden on the farmers led to periodic revolts. These revolts weakened imperial stability, and invasions of nomadic peoples from what is today Mongolia and western China often dealt the final blow to successive Chinese empires. Nomadic invaders actually founded two of China's great empires (Figure 9.2).

By the tenth century, China had the world's wealthiest economy, its largest cities, and the highest living standards. When the Venetian trader Marco Polo wrote about his visit to China between 1271 and 1295, Europeans were stunned to learn that the then imperial city of Hangzhou (near modern Shanghai) was 100 miles in circumference, had a population of 900,000, was dotted with parks and served by a sewer system, had a large canal system, and supported several principal markets, each frequented daily by 40,000 to 50,000 people. Wares included rhinoceros horns from Bengal, ivory from India and Africa, coral, agate, pearls, crystal, rare woods, and spices.

China's achievements in this era were impressive. Improved strains of rice allowed dense farming populations to expand throughout southern China and supported larger urban industrial populations. Metallurgy flourished; for example, as early as 1078, people in north China were producing twice as much iron as people in England did 700 years later, in 1778. Innovation was not lacking either: Chinese inventions included papermaking, printing, paper currency, gunpowder, and improved shipbuilding techniques. Nevertheless, the overall pace of change in China remained slow compared to what would occur later during Europe's industrial revolution. In part, the slow pace of change was the result of a continued focus on agriculture and the failure of a large commercially oriented middle class to develop. With commerce still not a respected occupation according to Confucian philosophy, trade did not develop rapidly nor did it nurture vibrant entrepreneurialism. The overwhelmingly conservative nature of the Chinese empires, as well as their periodic collapse, meant that in their hands technologies progressed slowly. Thus, despite the high level of technology that China attained early on, the level was eventually surpassed by Europe in the eighteenth century.

Rising European Influence

By the mid-1500s, Spanish and Portuguese traders had found their way to East Asian ports. They brought a strong interest in commerce and a number of new food

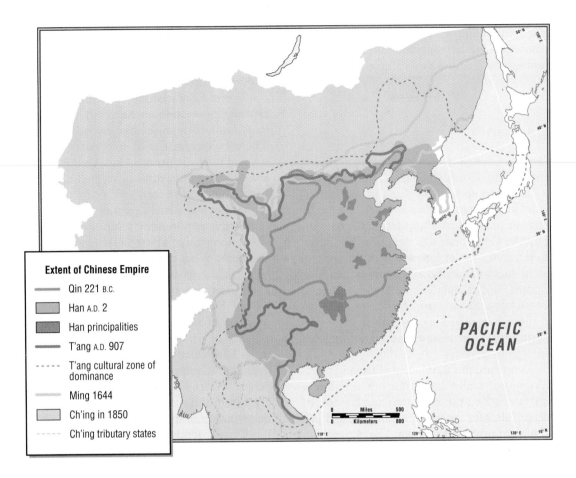

Extent of Chinese Empire

Qin 221 B.C.

Han A.D. 2

Han principalities

T'ang A.D. 907

T'ang cultural zone of dominance

Ming 1644

Ch'ing in 1850

Ch'ing tributary states

FIGURE 9.2 The extent of Chinese empires, 221 B.C.–1850. The Chinese state expanded and contracted throughout its history; the colors on the map indicate the extent of its dominion at various times. [Adapted from *Hammond Times Concise Atlas of World History,* 1994.]

crops from the Americas, such as corn, peppers, and potatoes. The earliest visible European impact on East Asia was a rapid rise in the Chinese population. While the Confucian bias toward agriculture had always nurtured large populations (estimated at 120 million by A.D. 1000), after 1500 the new food crops fueled steady population growth. By the mid-1800s, China's population stood at over 400 million, and many Chinese were migrating to the frontiers of the empire: to Yunnan in southwestern China and to the northeast. By the nineteenth century, European influence had increased markedly as foreign merchants lobbied to get access to the huge China market. Between 1839 and 1860, Qing dynasty leaders tried to fight off the European incursion in what were called the Opium Wars. The Chinese were trying to prevent British merchants from exchanging opium for Chinese wares like fine silks and fine ceramic dinnerware much sought after in Britain.

In the nineteenth century, the Qing dynasty's authority declined rapidly. After China was defeated in a series of conflicts with Britain and France, most of the country was carved up into "spheres of influence." In these, certain Western powers, notably Britain, France, Germany, and Russia, established trading interests; this was especially the case in port cities like Shanghai, which became a British enclave. The final blow to China's preeminence within East Asia came, however, in 1895 when a rapidly modernizing Japan won a spectacular naval victory over China in the Sino-Japanese War. After its defeat by the Japanese in 1895, the Qing empire made only halfhearted attempts at modernization, and collapsed in 1912 after a coup d'état. Until the communist takeover in 1949, much of China was governed by provincial warlords in rural areas, and a mixture of Chinese and Western administrative agencies in the major cities. During this era, in the new Western-style universities, radical ideologies gained popularity as intellectuals searched for a new basis of political authority to replace Confucianism. Of particular interest were various forms of socialism and communism.

Revolution Comes to China

Two rival reformist groups arose in the early twentieth century. One was the Nationalist party, known as the Kuomintang, or KMT, led by Chiang Kai-shek. The KMT united the country in 1924 and at first reorganized it along the socialist political and economic lines envisioned by Lenin in the Soviet Union. After 1927, however, the KMT increasingly became the party of the urban upper and middle classes. The rival group, the Chinese Communist party (CCP), appealed most to the far more numerous rural laborers. Japan took advantage of these internal struggles to take over northeast China (Manchuria) in 1931. Then, in 1937, while the Western powers were concerned with European fascism, Japan invaded China, conquering most of its important cities and coastal provinces. For a while, the KMT and CCP tried to unite against this common enemy, but once Japan surrendered to the Allied forces at the end of World War II in 1945, all common ground between the two Chinese reformist parties was lost. Although the KMT was backed by the United States (then particularly preoccupied with opposing communist movements), it was quickly pushed out of the country by the now very popular CCP, led by Mao Zedong. The KMT and many of its urban supporters fled to Taiwan. There they formed a government-in-exile that remained bitterly opposed to the Communist government on the mainland.

Although Japan's East Asian empire proved short lived, the country's rapid transformation astounded many throughout the region and the world. In the mid-nineteenth century, Japan was a feudal, technologically less developed society, seen by many as merely a backwater of China. However, a group of forward-thinking leaders was able to adapt Western economic and political models to Japanese culture so successfully that by the early twentieth century Japan was on a par with most major European powers. Japan's lack of resources was a major factor that inspired its leaders to attempt to take over most of East and Southeast Asia before and during World War II. The years following the war saw Japan rebuild itself to become the second largest economy in the world and an important source of investment money throughout East Asia and globally as well.

The end of World War II brought dramatic changes to Korea and Taiwan also. Shortly after the war, Korea was torn apart by a civil war. The result was a communist North Korea, allied with the Soviet Union and China, and a capitalist South Korea, allied with the United States. Both Taiwan and South Korea embarked on a style of capitalist economic development that emulated Japan with some success.

On the Chinese mainland, Mao Zedong's tactics of revolutionary mobilization among the rural majority made the newly established People's Republic of China the most powerful and expansionist government China had ever had. The Communist party assumed total control over the economy; established a dominant presence in the outlying areas of the Northeast, Inner Mongolia, and lands to the west known as Xinjiang; and launched a brutal occupation of Xizang (Tibet). The People's Republic was in many ways similar to a traditional Chinese dynasty. The Confucian bureaucracy was replaced by the Chinese Communist party, and Mao Zedong became a sort of emperor with unquestioned authority over the party, the military, and virtually all other aspects of government.

The Communist revolution substantially changed Chinese society. The chief early beneficiaries were the mass of Chinese farmers and landless laborers. It would be hard to exaggerate the desperate plight of the Chinese people on the eve of the revolution in 1949. Huge numbers lived in grinding poverty, famine was frequent, massive floods regularly devastated villages and farmland, and infant mortality rates were exceedingly high. For the millions outside the small middle and upper classes, life was short and miserable. The vast majority of women and girls were held in low social esteem and spent their lives in unrelenting servitude.

The revolution drastically changed this picture. Land and wealth were reallocated, often—although certainly not always—resulting in improved standards of living for those who needed it most. Heroic efforts were made to improve agricultural production and to ameliorate the age-old twin afflictions of floods and droughts. Huge numbers of Chinese, regardless of age, class, and sex, were mobilized to construct massive public works projects almost entirely by hand. Chinese laborers terraced, and reterraced, mountainsides by hand; and they unclogged silted waterways by means of bucket brigades. They built roads across difficult terrain with virtually no machinery. The famed "barefoot doctors"—people with rudimentary medical training—dispensed basic medical care, midwife services, and nutritional advice to the remotest locations. Schools were built in the smallest of villages. Opportunities for women opened up, and some of the worst abuses against them stopped. Until recent decades, famine had taken place somewhere in the country every few years. Since the mid-1970s, however, China has managed to feed its own, only occasionally having to buy grain on the world market or accept food aid. The vast majority of Chinese who are old enough to have witnessed the changes say that, materially, life is now better by far than before the revolution.

Nonetheless, the progress made under Communist party rule has come at enormous human and environmental costs. Millions died needlessly, persecuted for dissenting from party policies, or they were killed by famine or other avoidable disasters that resulted from the rush to fulfill poorly planned development objectives. In like fashion, China's considerable natural resources have been sacrificed to a short-sighted vision of progress.

In the aftermath of famine and other disasters, some Communist leaders tried to liberalize the economy, only to be purged themselves as Mao Zedong scrambled to stay in power. One ploy was the initiation in 1966 of the Cultural Revolution; this series of highly politicized and destructive mass campaigns so disrupted Chinese society that by Mao's death in 1976 the Communists had been thoroughly discredited. Two years later, a new leadership formed around Deng Xiaoping. In the early 1980s, he initiated a series of reforms that liberalized China's economy in the direction of more capitalist norms, at the same time maintaining Communist political control. In the late 1980s, however, protests among students and workers for democratic freedoms prompted violent repression by the government. At the close of the twentieth century, many observers are concerned that the strains of rapid economic growth may create further instability in China that could spill over to neighboring countries.

Population Patterns

China, with 1.2 billion people, has more than one-fifth the world's population. Today, most urban couples are limited by law to one child (but some still have two), and the Chinese are now reproducing at a rate considerably lower than the world average: 17 births per 1000 yearly, as opposed to the world average of 23 per 1000. Nevertheless, China's numbers will continue to grow for years to come, simply because so many Chinese are just entering their reproductive years. If the one-child family pattern expands, which is not now the case, there is some hope of curtailing growth significantly. With relatively fewer births, the median age will rise fairly quickly; by 2005, the average age may be as high as 38. As the population ages, China's growth will eventually slow and possibly even stop—but not until perhaps the year 2050, and only after millions more are added. A halt in growth depends on continued and improved compliance with control measures.

Population Density

As you can readily see from a look at the population map of China (Figure 9.3), people are not evenly distributed on the land. In fact, many parts of China are very lightly settled because they are extremely dry or cold or the terrain is very rugged. Ninety percent of China's people are clustered on only one-sixth of the total land; from this land they extract a very high level of agricultural production, though with considerable environmental costs. People are especially densely concentrated in the North China Plain, the middle and lower Chang Jiang basin, the delta of the Xi Jiang in South China, and the Sichuan Basin.

In these parts of China, grain production per acre can exceed that of the American Midwest. Yet, in China, due to much lower standards of living, 500 to 600 people may subsist on a plot of 500 acres (202 hectares), which in America would provide income for just a family of five or six people. And the ratio of people to units of productive land is growing rapidly. In some parts of China there are six times more people on productive farmland today than there were just 50 years ago. The concern is that China will lose its newly gained ability to feed itself.

CURRENT GEOGRAPHIC ISSUES

In modern times, the people of East Asia, and the Chinese people in particular, are dealing with geographic issues similar to those facing people all over the world. Previously in this book, we have seen that in many parts of the world there is concern over the size and growth of the human population. Then there is the matter of how to provide an acceptable standard of living for that population. What are the best economic strategies for achieving that standard of living? Can the physical environment support the standard desired? There is the matter of equity. The opportunity to participate in political processes is unevenly distributed geographically and within the ranks of society. In fact, in some parts of the world, there is no agreement that equity and participatory democracy should be goals at all.

In the twentieth century, the Chinese people have tried some innovative, indeed drastic, solutions to these problems. Mongolia's path has resembled China's, and until recently so has North Korea's. But Japan, South Korea, and Taiwan have taken the capitalist route and have achieved material prosperity and economic leadership throughout Asia. Nonetheless, they still face some of the same geographic issues as China, especially those related to rapid urbanization, changing family and gender relationships, democratic participation, and deteriorating environments. In this chapter, I address political and economic issues first; this is because in centrally planned China, Mongolia, and North Korea, as well as in capitalist Japan, South Korea, and Taiwan—where economic crises have lately loomed—

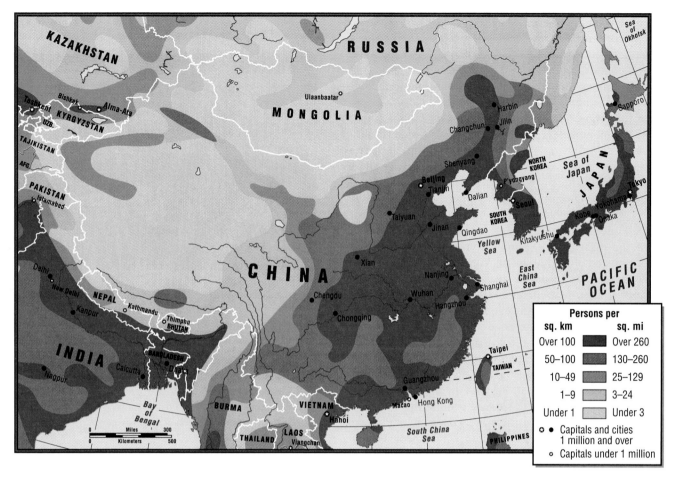

FIGURE 9.3 Population density. [Adapted from *Hammond Citation World Atlas,* 1996.]

these issues have an especially pervasive effect on social and cultural issues.

Political and Economic Issues

Major economic and political changes are afoot in East Asia today. China and Mongolia are moving away from centrally planned socialist economies toward more capitalist systems. Japan, South Korea, and Taiwan have long had strong capitalist economies. In the 1990s, however, growth in these three countries slowed, partly in response to internal problems and partly in response to the financial problems in Southeast Asia, an important trading partner to all three. North Korea, which remains committed to central planning, is doing so badly that its population is thought to be suffering serious malnutrition.

Politically, all countries of the region have been dominated by powerful state bureaucracies; but Japan, South Korea, and Taiwan have all been formal democracies for many decades. Nonetheless, the level of public participation in decision making is relatively low.

Mongolia is struggling to make the transition from authoritarianism to democracy, while China and North Korea have made no formal moves in this direction. Most observers agree, however, that moves toward more public participation in day-to-day decision and policy making, as well as in elections, are likely in most East Asian countries in the future.

Contrasting Bureaucracies

Strong state bureaucracies characterize all governments in the region. While the universal presence of such bureaucracies is indicative of marked cultural similarities among all East Asian countries, there are also notable differences between these bureaucratic systems, which derive from the unique historical circumstances within each country.

The power and respect accorded government bureaucracies in East Asia is unique. In Japan, a bureaucrat who leaves the government to take up a job in private industry is said to have "descended from heaven," meaning that he has left the prestigious for the mundane. Some have argued that Confucianism and related cultural traditions are the main reason that government officials are accorded this high degree of respect. Confucianism long ago established the philosophical and political framework for powerful bureaucratic governments in China, Taiwan, and Korea; and it encouraged self-sacrifice by the individual for the overall good of the group. In Japan, the influence of Confucianism is less; nonetheless, cultural models also require individual subordination to the will of the group. In the recent past, the various country bureaucracies have evolved in different ways while maintaining the tradition of strong central control.

Widespread fear of Western domination permeated mid-nineteenth-century Japan, mostly in response to the disorder and humiliation that China suffered during and after the Opium Wars. In 1861, a group of young leaders managed to unify Japan militarily and steer it in a new direction. This movement became known as the Meiji restoration. In order to speed the pace and efficiency of change, they chose authoritarian political models that allowed only minimal public input. Over time, power within the government shifted more and more toward the bureaucracy and the military. As it established an East Asian empire, Japan imposed this bureaucratic structure militarily on Korea and Taiwan as well. In these two countries, the model featured especially strong colonial bureaucracies that facilitated the domination of local peoples. When Japan withdrew from Taiwan and Korea at the end of World War II, the bureaucracies had been functioning effectively for several decades. Successor governments have kept them in place.

In China, North Korea, and Mongolia, Communist governments all used powerful bureaucracies to revolutionize their societies. Chinese Communist bureaucrats had almost total power over the economy, because the state claimed ownership of all land and resources. In contrast, Japan's bureaucrats did not have total power but strongly influenced economic activity by giving advice to private enterprise and arranging financing. As we will see, these two different models for government management led to different trajectories of economic and social development in the various East Asian countries.

Economic Transitions and Crises

In the decades since World War II, East Asia has been characterized by contrasting economic systems: the centrally planned communism of China, Mongolia, and North Korea and the free market capitalism of Japan, Taiwan, and South Korea. Recently, the differences between countries seem to be diminishing, as China and Mongolia move toward more capitalist economic models. This transition has not been without its

In Kyushu's Fukuoka Prefecture, a highly mechanized Toyota plant turns out a hardtop model for the domestic market. Here precision robot arms weld the car bodies. [Mike Yamashita/Woodfin Camp & Associates.]

pitfalls, however. And even capitalist Japan and South Korea have recently faced economic crisis.

The Capitalist Countries. Throughout the nineteenth century, the economies of Japan, Korea, and Taiwan were minuscule compared to China's. Then, during the twentieth century all three grew tremendously; today, Japan's economy is the second largest in the world. It is four and a half times larger than China's, even though Japan has only one-tenth the population of China. South Korea, with one-twenty-sixth the population of China, has the world's twelfth largest economy. Tiny Taiwan's economy is one-third as large as mainland China's. For the most part, the credit for this achievement belongs to Japan, which developed the models of government-guided capitalism that these three countries used to reach prosperity. In accordance with these models, a strong state bureaucracy helped wealthy private capitalists to start industrial enterprises that became the foundation of early economic development in Japan and, later, Taiwan and South Korea. The government assistance included advice, financial assistance, and protection from competition, both internal and external.

In the mid-1990s, however, the Japanese model showed signs of strain, and by the end of the decade Japan's economy was shrinking by several percentage points a year. Japan's economic problems are linked to the crisis in Southeast Asia that began in the late 1990s (discussed in Chapter 10), because 45 percent of Japan's exports go to Southeast Asian countries and Japan is the single biggest investor in Southeast Asian ventures; it owns interests in agriculture, forestry, manufacturing, mining, and tourism. When companies in Southeast Asia began to close because of bad debts, Japanese investors lost money. Similarly, when millions of Southeast Asians lost their jobs, they could no longer afford the products of Japanese companies. These companies began to go bankrupt.

Corruption is also part of the economic crisis in Japan. The long-standing close relationship between government and industry had nurtured favoritism on a grand scale. Politicians often encouraged economic development projects within Japan that were not needed, because the projects brought money and jobs to voters in their home constituencies. For example, many rural areas in Japan now have elaborate transportation infrastructures, far beyond the needs of the small rural populations. Another problem was that Japan overexpanded its productive capacity. Between 1988 and 1992, Japan expanded its ability to produce by an amount equal to the entire economy of France—just when the demand for that output began to contract at home and abroad. Bureaucrats, who had nurtured enterprises with advice and financial support, were often unwilling to let them go bankrupt, even when they were being poorly managed or no longer had potential. Instead, the Japanese government forced banks to make large loans to troubled firms. Eventually, both the firms and the banks went bankrupt. Korea and Taiwan have undergone financial crises similar to Japan's, though Taiwan has suffered less, largely because it has been more willing to let its unviable enterprises go bankrupt.

Many see the Japanese financial crisis as linked also to the fact that Japanese workers have been overly protected and not encouraged to perform at their full potential. Good workers are rewarded with job security rather than higher pay, a policy that has encouraged conformity at the expense of innovation and creativity. As a result, the Japanese model depends largely on technologies developed elsewhere, usually in North America and Europe. Another consequence of the relatively low wages is that middle- and lower-class Japanese consumers cannot buy many of the high-quality items they themselves produce, whereas their counterparts in other industrialized economies make up a huge internal market for locally made wares. Japanese high-end goods are sold instead to consumers in North America and Europe. Many argue that these qualities of the Japanese model make it inherently unstable, as it renders a country dependent on foreign technology and on just a few large external markets. Should the economies of North America and Europe falter, so would the economies of all countries following the Japanese model. It is therefore argued that workers in Taiwan, South Korea, and Japan should be paid more, with raises contingent on performance, so that there will be incentives for workers in these countries to generate more of their own technological innovations. Also, more prosperous workers would create an internal market for domestic products, thus stabilizing the economy.

The Communist Countries. The communist economic systems of China, Mongolia, and North Korea emerged in the mid-twentieth century. Following World War II, all three countries abolished private property, and the state took control of virtually every aspect of the economy. Many saw this course as the only way to salvage societies that had been badly damaged by a grossly self-centered elite, by foreign colonial domination, and by civil war. The broad, sweeping changes ultimately proved less successful than hoped.

When the Communist party first came to power in China in 1949, its top priority was to greatly improve both agricultural and industrial production. The first strategy was land reform, which to the Communists meant taking large unproductive tracts out of the hands of landlords and putting them into the hands of the millions of landless farmers. By the early 1950s, much of China's agricultural land was divided up into tiny plots. But it soon became clear that this system was also inefficient. The farmers needed to produce enough to feed people who were being drawn out of agriculture to work in the many expanding industries. It was decided to band smallholders into cooperatives. They could then share their labor and pool their resources to acquire tractors and other technological aids to increase agricultural production. In time, these cooperatives were banded together into full-scale communes averaging 1600 households. The communes, at least in theory, took over all aspects of life. They were the basis of political organization (all within the Communist party), and they provided health care and education. In addition, the communes were responsible for building rural industries to supply themselves with items like fertilizers, gunnysacks, pottery, and small machinery. They also had to fulfill the ambitious expectations of the leaders in Beijing for better flood control, expanded irrigation systems, and the generation of surplus funds for investment elsewhere.

The system had several problems. Farmers had to spend so much time building roads, levees, and drainage ditches, or working in the new rural industries, that they had much less time to actually farm. Compounding the problem, local Communist party administrators often reported that harvests were larger than they actually were, to impress their superiors in Beijing. The leaders in Beijing responded by requiring larger grain shipments to the cities, creating food shortages in the countryside. These measures pushed the system to its limits in the late 1950s, during the "Great Leap Forward." The result was a massive famine and death by starvation for 30 million people.

Industrial production beyond that of small farm-linked industries was focused on heavy industry, not on consumer goods. The leadership felt that China needed first to upgrade its infrastructure—to build roads, railways, dams—all requiring heavy equipment. So the emphasis was on mining for coal and other minerals, on producing iron and steel, and on building heavy machinery. Funds for industrial development were obtained from the already inefficient agricultural sector in several ways. Agricultural zones were required to sell their crops to the state at artificially low prices. The state kept any profits gained in the reselling process. In addition, the state diverted to industrialization funds that had been earmarked for agricultural improvements; other funds for industry came from profits in mining and forestry, and from savings on workers' wages, which were kept very low.

By design, most people in Communist China were not allowed the means to consume more than the bare necessities. On the other hand, nearly everyone was guaranteed a job for life and the means to obtain the basic essentials. As was the case with the Japanese model, the emphasis on job security rather than on rewarding creativity and hard work led to overwhelming conformity and a lack of innovation. Hence, the level of overall productivity remained low. This problem characterized industry in Mongolia and North Korea as well.

China's Policies for Regional Development

One peculiar aspect of China's communist phase has been its attempt to reduce regional variations in prosperity. For centuries, agricultural and herding areas in the interior, especially those in more remote areas to the west, had been much poorer than the coastal areas to the east, where industries and trade were concentrated. After the revolution, the Communist leadership instituted a policy of **regional self-sufficiency:** it encouraged each region to develop independently, building agricultural and industrial sectors of equal strength, in the hope of creating jobs and evening out the national distribution of income. Government funds were used to establish industries in nearly every province, regardless of practicality. For example, a steel industry was established in Inner Mongolia at great expense when other provinces already had steel industries that could have been improved with far greater payoff. Similarly, agriculture was extended into marginal physical environments far from markets, often where continuous irrigation was necessary or where growing seasons were very short. Huge mechanized grain farms were developed on cleared forest lands

in far north Heilongjiang, when the same effort elsewhere would have yielded better results and the forests could have been saved for other purposes. This policy of regional self-sufficiency was also responsible for programs that encouraged individual communities to develop backyard smelters, or kilns, or tool and die factories, or their own tiny tractor factories. Certainly these efforts were a tribute to community ingenuity, but ultimately they were a waste of time, resources, and environmental quality.

Another reason for encouraging dispersion of industry across China and regional self-sufficiency was linked to the cold war. It was thought that a dispersed pattern of industrial development and the ability of each region to feed itself would foil an enemy's effort to quickly destroy China's productive capacity.

Market Reforms

In the late 1970s, the failures of China's communist economic policies caused the country's leadership to pursue a more efficient and market-oriented economy. The reform strategies fell into three main categories, all linked to some extent: (1) economic decision making was decentralized; (2) market principles (competition, efficiency, pricing according to demand, and incentives) were implemented; and (3) regional specialization rather than regional self-sufficiency was encouraged.

The decentralization of decision making resulted in what have come to be called the **responsibility systems,** in which managers of many state-owned enterprises were given the rights and responsibilities to make their operations work efficiently. The responsibility systems were linked to the introduction of market principles, in that managers could now size up a situation and redesign an operation to meet a need. In addition, they could set the prices for goods and services according to supply and demand, thus resolving many inefficiencies. To some extent, anyone could create a new enterprise. Those who made money could then use it for consumption or to reinvest. The reforms have increased regional specialization, as managers and entrepreneurs (sometimes with assistance from the state) take advantage of the different resources and opportunities offered by different areas of the country. The Chinese economy has become more productive overall, and many have achieved greater prosperity; the per capita gross national product has more than doubled, from U.S. $300 in the mid-1980s to U.S. $750 by the late 1990s. But the reform of state-owned enterprises has gone slowly. Many still flounder along, using resources inefficiently, making unmarketable products, and adding to pollution problems. And rural workers' wages are falling far behind those in urban areas, thus increasing the rural/urban contrast in standards of living.

Trends in Agriculture. The market reforms have brought new opportunities to some agricultural sectors. Throughout China, farmers have been encouraged to organize family-sized or larger entrepreneurial operations that meet the local food demand. Regional specialization in agriculture is increasing on a number of fronts. Those farmers close to cities are producing for the urban markets. Instead of selling the grain they grow, an increasing number are using the grain to feed animals to satisfy a rising demand for meat among the affluent. In places where growing seasons are long enough, such as the far southern provinces of Yunnan and Guangdong, farmers are now producing fresh produce for distant markets in northern cities.

There is a danger that these new developments could compromise China's **food stability,** its ability to supply sufficient food consistently to all the people. Pressures on the food production system are increasing for the following reasons. Agriculture is only possible on a portion of China's vast territory because much of the land is too cold, too dry, or too steep (Figure 9.4). China's huge population has already stretched the productive capacity of many fertile zones well beyond sustainability, yet demands are increasing. As urban populations grow more affluent, their taste for meat and for fresh fruit and vegetables will place an added burden on China's agricultural land. The raising of animals for meat especially requires more land and resources than

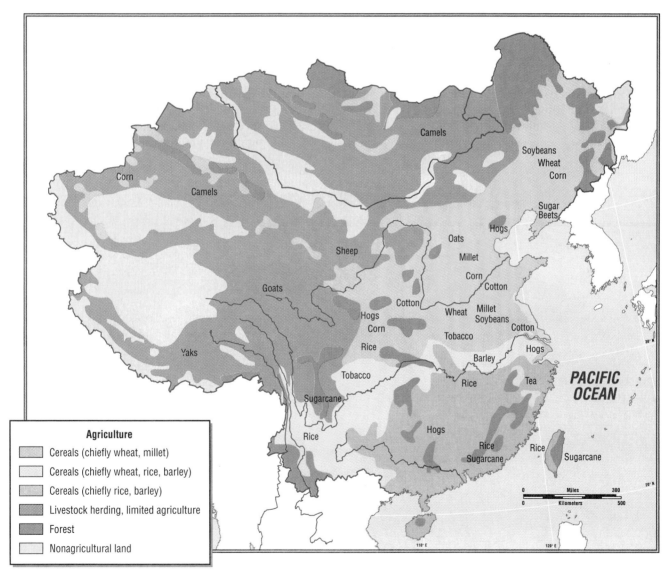

FIGURE 9.4 China's agricultural zones. [Adapted from *Hammond Citation World Atlas,* 1996.]

the more plant-based agriculture of the past. As agriculture mechanizes and agricultural collectives close, farm laborers are losing their jobs and many will not have access to land to grow their own food. They are likely to flee to the already overburdened cities looking for work. The result may be a markedly larger, mostly urban population, dependent on a food production system that meets the needs of the more affluent but does not provide nutritious food at low enough prices for the masses.

A Market Focus for Rural Enterprises.   One of the most remarkable recent developments has been the growth in entrepreneurial rural enterprises that may do everything from operating coal mines to making plastic flowers to assembling high-tech electronics. These enterprises have become the mainstay of many rural economies, especially in the eastern and southern provinces of Jiangsu, Fujian, and Guangdong. These enterprises may still be township or village collectives, though some are privately owned; but they have in common that they leave major decisions to managers (not the collective) and price their products according to the market. Rural enterprises have bloomed so quickly and successfully that they now constitute a quarter of the economy and may actually produce over

half the industrial output and 40 percent of the exports. Statistics are not easy to come by; but it is known that such enterprises now employ more than 125 million people, more than the Chinese government itself, and account for more than 30 percent of farm household income.

Problems are brewing with the rural enterprises. Environmental pollution and corruption have accompanied their growth, in no small part because the rural enterprises are largely unregulated. In the mountains west of Beijing, for example, where many such industries are located, pollution exceeds that in the city. Clouds of exhaust from trucks linking the rural industries with markets contaminate the air. Paper mills pollute the waterways, farmers' fields, and aquifers. Some managers have paid off officials to ignore the breaching of regulations and pilfering of funds, and most try to evade taxes. The government, while moving to enact legislation that could lessen these problems, is wary of driving rural enterprises out of business, because the whole country is now dependent on their success.

Regional Disparities.   Since China's market reforms, long-term disparities in wealth between the country's regions are once again increasing, as is indicated by the map in Figure 9.5. Remote provinces like Xizang

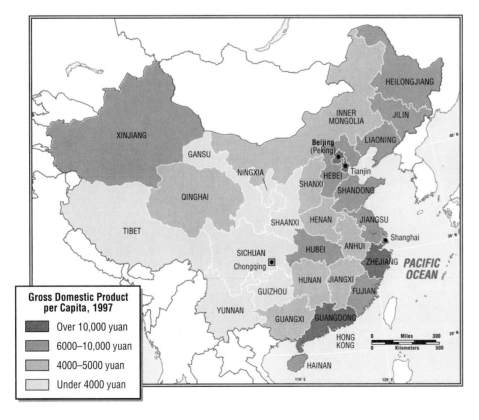

FIGURE 9.5 Regional disparity in wealth. U.S. $1.00 = 8.28 yuan (May 18, 1999). [Adapted from *The Economist,* January 16, 1999, p. 40.]

(Tibet) or Yunnan, or those with little mineral or agricultural wealth, such as Inner Mongolia or Qinghai, have lost special support from the central government, yet have had difficulty generating rural enterprises. Increasingly, so many young people and skilled laborers are leaving the interior provinces (often without official permission) that the only ones left in some rural communities are children, some women, and the very old. Meanwhile, the eastern and southern coastal provinces, with their larger cities, more developed infrastructure, skilled work forces, and ready access to the sea, are enriching themselves through manufacturing industries and foreign trade.

Special Economic Zones. Central to the economic success of the coastal region has been the establishment of **Special Economic Zones (SEZs)** and related **Economic and Technical Development Zones**

(ETDZs) that now stretch into the interior of China (Figure 9.6). In the early 1980s, China selected five coastal cities—Zhuhai, Shantou, and Shenzhen in Guangdong Province (near Hong Kong), Xiamen in Fujian, and Hainan Island—to function as free trade zones, able to practice free market policies and management methods that were unavailable to the rest of the country. Foreign investors and their companies are allowed income tax breaks and reductions of import duties, and they may take their profits out of China. In the years since their establishment, these SEZs have been successful in bringing in international investors, attracting industry, and spawning related activities such as insurance, commerce, and information-gathering and consulting services.

The SEZ concept has been expanded to cover many more cities along the coastal zone and inland. Shanghai, for example, long a window on the outside

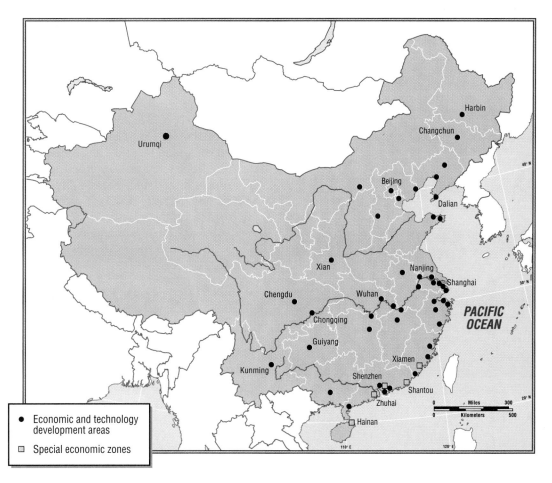

FIGURE 9.6 China's Special Economic Zones (SEZs) and Economic and Technology Development Zones (ETDZs).
[Adapted from http://www.harper.cc.il.us/~mhealy/geogres/maps/eagif/chsez.gif and http://www.sezo.gov.cn/eindex.htm.]

world for China, was chosen to spearhead the expansion of free trade zones up the Chang Jiang all the way to Chongqing. By the late 1990s, the Chinese authorities had applied the SEZ concept to 32 state-level locations (ETDZs) in the interior of China, stretching all the way to Urumqi in Xinjiang Province. These zones are proving tremendously popular with international investors and multinational companies eager to establish footholds in a country with such a huge pool of cheap labor and such a large number of potential consumers. Today the original SEZs and related development zones (there are now at least 48 altogether) are major **growth poles** in the country, meaning their success is drawing yet more investment and migration. Internal migration is still not freely allowed in China. Nevertheless, many migrate illegally, and coastal cities like Shenzhen, Qingdao, Wenzhou, and Changan are pulling skilled people from the rest of the country at an enormous rate. In the space of 20 years many coastal cities (SEZs and more recent designations) have grown from mid-sized towns or even villages to become some of the largest cities in the country.

First and foremost among the SEZs is Shenzhen, which is strategically located at the neck of the Hong Kong peninsula. Hong Kong was one of the very first European trading posts in China, and while under British control it grew into one of the wealthiest and most dynamic trading cities in the world. Britain's lease on Hong Kong ran out in 1997, and the territory reverted to Chinese control. In preparation for this shift, Shenzhen and neighboring SEZs were established as places that could absorb some of Hong Kong's commercial energy. Long before the takeover, Hong Kong was already an important financial link between China and the rest of the world, with billions of investment dollars flowing through Hong Kong to Shenzhen and the rest of China's SEZs. Much of this money has come from Taiwan. Having no formal political relations with China, the Taiwanese have had to invest in China via Hong Kong for most of the era of market reforms.

Hong Xiaohui's Story Continues. In the opening vignette we met Hong Xiaohui, from Sichuan, who is representative of millions of young migrants who every day leave sheltered rural village life to work in the highly competitive industrial zones of the SEZs. Many come intending not only to succeed as individuals but to send money home to impoverished families and possibly one day return to help their home communities improve. Hong Xiaohui traveled 1200 miles by bus to a job in the Barbie Doll factory in Changan, where she learned she would be paid 200 yuan, or 43 percent less than the labor recruiter had promised in Sichuan. We return now to her story because Ms. Hong's triumphs and travails over the first year are illustrative of how life is going for the migrants from the hinterlands who have come to China's booming coastal cities.

Trucks from Hong Kong wait to pass through the portal into Shenzhen SEZ. [Mike Yamashita/Woodfin Camp & Associates.]

VIGNETTE

When she first arrived in Changan, Ms. Hong learned that, in addition to the lower pay than she had been promised, the shifts at Mattel were usually 12 hours, with no overtime pay and just one day off a month. More important, when Ms. Hong rapidly mastered her task of putting hair on Barbie Dolls, she began to entertain dreams of becoming a supervisor, only to find that such a position might require sexual favors to the plant manager. With an income equaling just U.S. $24 a month, Ms. Hong and her fellow workers could only afford a crowded dormitory room and canteen food. There were 11 women in one small concrete room with a tiny bath.

In less than two months, Ms. Hong broke her contract with Mattel and returned home to her village in

Sichuan where, using ideas and the assertiveness she had gained from her time in the south, she opened a kebab stand and in just one month made 10 times her investment of U.S. $12. Soon she also opened a Hot Pot soup shop in her family home. But Ms. Hong yearned to return to the south coast to seek employment on her own. So, leaving the kebab shop to her sister and brother-in-law, she eventually went again to Changan. In one year, the city had grown by 20 percent and now had 1400 foreign companies trying to hire labor. To find a job, Ms. Hong asked one of her old friends to act as a guarantor on her behalf. In a matter of days she had a job in a Japanese-owned factory and also one for her sister, who rushed to Changan, leaving her husband and baby in Sichuan. The sisters quickly made friends with several young women from different parts of China, and together they enjoyed an active urban social life hampered only by a tight budget and their generally conservative village ways. In just a year from Ms. Hong's first trip to Changan, she was making enough to live relatively comfortably, though still in a crowded dormitory. She was sending money home to her parents and once again saving to start a business. This time she dreamed of opening a karaoke bar back in her village. [Adapted from Kathy Chen, *Wall Street Journal*, July 9, 1997]

Hong Xiaohui's story illustrates why the central government in Beijing thinks of southeastern China as "the golden coast," and why they hope it will become a model for the rest of the country. Yet there are worries. Policing the activities of thousands of foreign firms is already an impossible task for the Beijing government. Finding ways to tax and yet not discourage petty capitalists like Ms. Hong is difficult. Just housing the flood of migrants, or providing them with sanitation and needed transportation, is expensive and poses environmental problems. Developing the infrastructure of the coastal zone fast enough to accommodate all these new residents will bleed resources away from places where life is still unbearably hard. As a result, yet more will flee to the cities from the interior and the regional disparity of wealth will increase.

One of the most visible and potentially dangerous results of the reforms is the growing number of impoverished and unemployed people now crowding into China's cities. Chinese citizens are not allowed to migrate at will and must always obtain a permit to go to a particular place; yet this regulation is increasingly flouted. A growing concern for the government is this so-called **floating population,** made up of jobless or underemployed people who have, without permission, left

economically depressed rural areas for the cities and are now unaccounted for. By some estimates they may number 100 million people, many virtually homeless. Though some find work and are a source of support for rural relatives, many are suspected of per-petrating petty crime waves. Moreover, there is the worry that these "floating" masses may form a base for social instability. Some large industrial towns already have 20 percent unemployment, a figure that is likely to rise. Mongolia is facing similar dilemmas as it, too, implements market reforms. Meanwhile, even in the much wealthier economies of Japan and South Korea, the recent recession has also created large numbers of unemployed.

Sociocultural Issues

Since the late 1970s, Chinese society has slowly begun to address some of the problems that the communist period left unresolved or exacerbated. Although many of these issues have economic, political, and environmental aspects, in this section I focus on the social and cultural facets of three issues: (1) strategies for making impersonal capitalist systems meet China's needs; (2) the interlinkings of population patterns and gender attitudes, and the related subject of changing family, work, and gender relationships; and (3) the treatment of minorities. The main focus is on China, but where appropriate I discuss these issues in Mongolia, Taiwan, North and South Korea, and Japan.

Cultural Adaptation to Capitalism: Doing Business with Strangers

China's embrace of capitalism amounts to another episode of radical social engineering analogous to the Communist revolution. Although doing business for profit was part of Chinese culture long before the revolution, 50 years have intervened since that event. Now, in addition to reorienting their ways of life away from the communist model, China's industrial laborers and newly minted entrepreneurs must manage the risks of doing business with strangers. Those who have spent a lifetime in rural villages must for the first time travel to distant cities to find a job or negotiate deals; or they have to hire competent and efficient workers from among masses of unfamiliar applicants, or deal with impersonal financial institutions. Surprisingly, however, there are ancient cultural institutions that are useful in the modern business era. One venerable institution that is newly useful is the third-party **guarantor,** who vouches for the honesty and reliability of one person in his or her dealings with another party.

The preference in the past for dealing with family members or fellow villagers grew out of the desire to keep risk at a minimum. Guarantors were used for all manner of negotiations when parties to a deal did not know each other. For instance, before the revolution, a person new to Shanghai who wished employment in a bank, department store, or factory needed a guarantor—someone who would convince the employer that the prospective employee was properly skilled and sufficiently honest. The guarantor also protected the employee to some extent from exploitation. These days, ideally, one still first seeks out business associates who are known in some way—people from the same region, if nothing else. But when two total strangers must do business, the *xinyong,* or trustworthiness and financial solvency of each party, is vouched for by the *xinyong* of a professional guarantor. The guarantor is paid for this service and, if things go wrong, is obliged at least to mediate and sometimes to cover losses. Once you appreciate the role of the guarantor as one who assumes (for a price) the risk in business deals—which in simpler times was taken on by the family—it is easier to appreciate Asian business practices. In China, the Koreas, Japan, and Taiwan, guarantors or similar functionaries play a role in nearly every aspect of business dealings, from finding a factory job to building a skyscraper. Some Western businesspeople, perhaps feeling shut out by the system, tend to view guarantors as evidence of favoritism and cronyism, even corruption. Others simply find themselves a guarantor.

Population Policies, Gender Attitudes, and the East Asian Family

In the 1970s, when nearly five children were born per woman aged 15 to 45, Chinese leaders realized that the rapidly rising population was sapping China's ability to progress. Strict population control measures were deemed necessary, and by 1980 China had adopted a policy of one child per family.

From its inauguration, Chinese demographers and the population at large realized that this one-child policy would dramatically affect family life and the social fabric. Were it effectively enforced, within one generation the kinship categories of sibling, cousin, aunt and uncle, and sister- and brother-in-law would disappear from all families that complied. This would be a major loss in a society that placed great value on the extended family. But it was the prospect of the one child being a daughter, and forever precluding the possibility of having a son, that caused the most despair. Despite strong conditioning by the Communist revolution that the sexes should be considered equal, patriarchal ideas that sons are preferable remain strong to this day. These ideas are based in part on the belief that only a son can inherit property, pass on the family heritage, and provide sufficient income for aging parents, even though daughters or daughters-in-law were always expected to provide the daily personal care of the aged. For years, the makers of Chinese social policy have been seeking

to overturn these prejudices by empowering women economically and socially. The thought is that female children will be just as desirable as males when it is clear that well-trained, powerful daughters can bring honor to the family name and earn sufficient income for their families.

Whatever their sex, the offspring of one-child families have no kinfolk with whom to share tasks when they reach adulthood. They experience an increased burden of both child care and elder care. And in China, the elderly are especially dependent on the younger generation. There was never a state-wide pension system; pensions are even less common since the closing of many collectives during the economic reforms of the 1980s and 1990s. Hence, as the single-child family spreads through the generations, the elderly will remain dependent on their solitary offspring.

With all these negative effects of the one-child policy, despite being the most common family form it has never been very popular. From time to time, the government has offered different incentives to young couples in different parts of the country. In some urban areas, couples who have only one child receive a monthly subsidy and a housing allowance. In other areas, complying couples receive special chances for promotion. Some who have additional children may lose these benefits, receive demotions, and have to pay a fine; in the case of others, their infractions may be ignored. Some Chinese, especially in rural areas, have extra children and simply pay the fines, which when enforced can be several times the annual income of both parents. Some ethnic minorities are officially exempted from family-size restrictions, presumably to answer political charges that the majority Han ethnic group is

This army officer enjoys some moments with his only child, a son. [Alain le Garsmeur/Panos Pictures.]

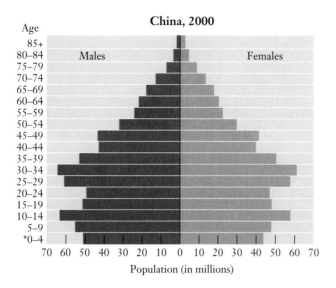
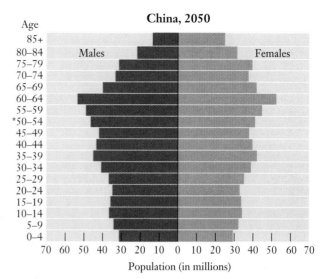

FIGURE 9.7 The population pyramid on the left shows China's sex and age distributions in the year 2000, while the one on the right shows them projected to the year 2050 (based on a low estimate of China's growth rate). China's population growth rate does appear to be under control. Note, however, that people who are 4 and under in the year 2000 will, by the time they reach the 50–54 age group (see asterisks), have a much larger number of elderly people to care for than 50-year-olds today. [Adapted from U.S. Census Bureau, International Data Base, at http://www.census.gov/cgi-bin/ipc/idbpyry.pl.]

too dominant. Still, there is evidence that family-size limits have been imposed on ethnic Tibetan women, many of whom have been forced to have abortions.

There is no doubt that population control has been successful. Between 1950 and 1990, the Chinese birth rate dropped dramatically; and the one-child family is now in the majority. Much of the drop in fertility is the result of modernization of life in China. In almost all situations, people who learn to read, move to the city, and take up a lifestyle based on cash income will choose to have fewer children because in the new urban circumstances children are expensive. They do not help to produce income as they did on the farm.

The population pyramid at the left in Figure 9.7 reflects two sharp past declines in birth rates. The first took place during the Great Leap Forward (1959–1961), when policy errors resulted in famine, and malnutrition led to lower fertility. The second is the result of the strict population control efforts in the early 1980s. In the mid-1980s, birth rates increased when market reforms of many sorts were instituted. Into the 1990s, increasing prosperity prompted some Chinese to have two or more children despite official sanctions. It is too soon to tell, but it looks as though another significant decline in birth rates may have begun by 1998.

The pyramid shows one other interesting phenomenon. If one looks very carefully, it appears that for 50 years or more the number of male infants born (or reported) has significantly exceeded the number of female infants. The pyramid shows that among those 0–4 years of age, there were 43 million girls and 51 million boys, indicating a deficit of about 8 million girls. The question of what happened to the girls has several possible answers. Given the preference for male offspring, the births of these girls may simply have gone unreported as families hoped to conceal the girl and try again for a boy. There are plentiful anecdotes of girls being raised secretly or even disguised as boys; and adoption records indicate that girls are given up for adoption much more often than boys. Or the girl babies may have died in early infancy, either through benign neglect or actual infanticide. Finally, some parents have access to technology that can be used to identify the sex of their unborn babies, and there is evidence that in China, as elsewhere around the world, some of these parents will chose to abort a female fetus.

Elsewhere in East Asia, small families are also now the norm, and population growth rates hover around China's rate of 1.0 percent. Japan has the lowest rate, at 0.2 percent (one-third the rate in the United States); Mongolia has the highest, at 1.6 percent. Rates of marriage remain high throughout the region and divorce rates are low. The smaller families and increasing opportunities for women outside the home mean that family life and gender roles are changing everywhere.

AT THE LOCAL SCALE   *Chinese Marriage Customs in Cities and Villages*

In most cities in China today, a new couple must apply for housing long before they can marry. Since women are not allowed to apply for housing until they have worked for a firm for 15 years, the couple will apply through the man's job. While they wait to obtain housing, they try to acquire the necessary household goods. It is said that the man must provide the "48 legs and the whole chicken." This saying refers to the fact that the full furnishings for an apartment have 48 legs in total (the bed has 4 legs, two bedside stands 8 legs, and so forth). The "whole chicken" is a play on words: *ji* is the Chinese word for chicken and is a homonym (same sound, different meaning) for machine. Hence, the "whole chicken" refers to all the household appliances from the sewing machine and television to the stove and refrigerator. Meanwhile, the woman must provide the "soft goods," like bed-clothes, kitchen and laundry equipment, and a new set of clothes for herself. The husband's contribution usually is far greater than that of the bride, a holdover from the prerevolutionary idea of the **bride price,** a sum paid by a groom to the parents of the bride to compensate them for the costs of raising her and the loss of her labor.

Family, Work, and Gender Relationships in Industrialized East Asia

In Japan, Taiwan, and South Korea, the institution of marriage must meet the needs of urban life because close to 80 percent of the population live in cities. Life in a small city apartment is very different for a couple than life among a host of relatives in a farming village. Nonetheless, in these urbanized countries the woman still performs most domestic duties and dedicates herself primarily to looking after her husband and children. Often she has responsibility also for the care of elderly parents or parents-in-law. Surveys of women in these three countries who do work outside the home show that most do not desire a job with full responsibilities. Although there is a small but growing group of career-oriented young women who are as ambitious as men, even many university-educated married women say they wish to earn only supplementary income for the household.

One reason that family life has been assigned to women to manage is that jobs in these industrial economies are particularly demanding. Workdays are long and commutes often add more than three hours to the time away from home. Of even more consequence is the "culture of work" in Japan, Taiwan, and South Korea, which is based on male camaraderie and demands an especially high level of loyalty to the firm. In Japan, for example, a firm will have a corporate song, a corporate exercise program, and a strict dress code. After work, leisure time is to be spent with business colleagues. Management is a vertical hierarchy that is accessible only to those who are perceived as most diligent. Rivalry between firms is often so strong that it elicits a siege mentality among workers. It is considered disloyal to refuse overtime, and a man who takes off early to spend time with his wife or to help her with child raising or care of the elderly is not a "real man." Women, when hired, are there to support men as secretaries and assistants, not to participate as full members of corporate teams.

By the late 1990s, the East Asian urban family structure was being publicly challenged, and not least by men themselves. In Tokyo, a group calling itself Men Concerned about Child Care meets regularly to discuss ways to participate more fully in home and community life. Another group has formed to lobby for four-hour workdays for both men and women, so that both can spend time with the family. This group has also filed lawsuits against employers who routinely require employees to accept job transfers to distant locations where they cannot take their families. These soul-searching movements may result in some important alterations in gender and work roles. It is particularly significant that urban men are the ones challenging the extremes of the lockstep East Asian work ethic. They are at once the group that has been most regimented and most deprived of personal time and family life, and the group that has the power to change the system.

Minorities in China, Taiwan, and Japan

Cultural diversity exists throughout East Asia despite the fact that most countries have one dominant ethnic group. In China, for example, 93 percent of the population call themselves "people of the Han." The name harks back some 2000 years to the Han dynasty, but it gained currency only in the early twentieth century when nationalist leaders were trying to create a mass

Chinese identity. The term *Han* does not denote an ethnic group, but rather connotes a general and unspecified pride in Chinese culture and a sense of superiority over ethnic minorities and outsiders. The main language of the Han is Mandarin, though there are many dialects. (All versions of Chinese use the same system of writing.) The Han are, overwhelmingly, rural agriculturists; about 75 percent of them still live in the countryside, primarily in the eastern half of the country.

Since China is such a populous country (1.2 billion people), the non-Han minorities, though only 7 percent of the population, still amount to more than 87 million people. There are more than 55 different minority groups scattered across the vast expanse of China; but as Figure 9.8 shows, most live outside the Han heartland of eastern China. They are located in the hinterlands: in the borderlands with Mongolia and Russia in the north and with Central Asia and Pakistan in the west; in Xinjiang and Xizang (Tibet); and in the south, in the mountains that lead to Southeast Asia. Theoretically, the largest minority groups have been granted autonomous status and can manage their own affairs. In practice, however, the Han-dominated Communist party has not allowed self-government. Beijing has controlled the fate of the minorities, especially those who live in zones that are believed to pose security risks or that have resources of interest to the central economy.

One such zone is far northwest China, where Turkic-speaking peoples live: the Kirghiz, Kasakhs, Tajiks, and Uygurs, many of whom remain nomadic. The Beijing government has sent troops and hundreds of thousands of Han settlers to this area of China. These outsiders manage mineral extraction and run military bases, facilities for nuclear testing, and power generation. Communist party officials are frank in their assertion that an important role of these Han settlers is to dilute the power of minorities within their own lands and to assist these minorities in ridding themselves of "unacceptable" cultural practices and distinctive national identities. In the case of the Turkic-speaking peoples, cultural assimilation to Han ways includes giving up Islam. Although assimilation may be the long-term outcome, for now there has been a rebirth of Islamic culture, inspired in part by the resurgence of Central Asia in the aftermath of the Soviet decline. Trade across the borders between Turkic peoples has been revived. The old Silk Road market of Kashgar is back in business. Islamic prayers are once again heard five times a day, Muslim women are again wearing Islamic dress, and Islamic architectural traditions are being revived.

The growing worldwide Islamic movement has raised Beijing's anxieties because there are other Muslim peoples in China. The Hui are the descendants of ancient Muslim traders who plied the Silk Road

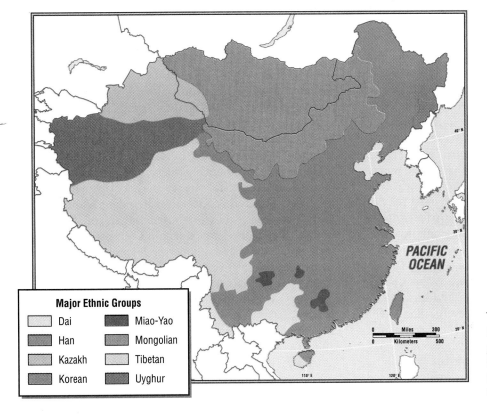

FIGURE 9.8 The many ethnic groups of China. [Adapted from Chiao-min Hsieh and Jean Kan Hsieh, *China—A Provincial Atlas* (New York: Macmillan, 1995), p. 12.]

Major Ethnic Groups

Dai	Miao-Yao
Han	Mongolian
Kazakh	Tibetan
Korean	Uyghur

At the market in Kashgar (now called Kashi), an ancient Silk Road city, you can still buy a camel, a fine oriental rug, the original bagel, an endangered-animal skin, a haircut, or you can get your teeth fixed. [Reza/National Geographic.]

and monks in thousands of monasteries, and a religious nobility. That society was dismantled and the monasteries destroyed. Hundreds of thousands of Han were then settled in the midst of Tibetan cities, where they were expected to acculturate the Tibetans to Han ways. Urban Tibetans are on the verge of becoming minorities within their own principal cities.

In China's far southeast, in Yunnan Province, there are more than 20 groups of ancient native peoples, such as the Bai, Yi, Miao, Yao, Dai, and Zhuang. These peoples speak many different languages and live in remote areas tucked away in the deeply folded mountains. Many of these groups appear to have ethnolinguistic connections to the Tibeto-Burman people, and others to Thai and Cambodian people. Interestingly, discrimination against women is less common than it is in Han culture areas. A crucial difference may be that among several groups, most notably the Dai, men move in with the wife's family at marriage and provide her family with labor or income. A husband inherits from his wife's family rather than from his birth family. In contrast, in most of China, a woman traditionally leaves her birth family and moves to her husband's family compound, where she works under the direction of her mother-in-law. Anthropologists think it is not a coincidence that, contrary to elsewhere in the country, the minorities in Yunnan value female children just as highly as males. Similar patterns of family structure and gender values are noted among indigenous peoples in Southeast Asia, as discussed in Chapter 10.

In Taiwan and adjacent islands, the Han account for 95 percent of the population; but there are also 60 minority groups. Nine of these are aboriginal groups that have been in Taiwan for thousands of years. Their languages are akin to Austronesian and they have some cultural characteristics—certain types of weaving, the making of bark cloth, iron smithing, and agricultural and hunting customs—that indicate a strong connection to ancient cultures in far Southeast Asia and the Pacific. Mountain dwellers have resisted assimilation better than plains dwellers, and all are now protected and may live in mountain reserves, if they chose. But increasingly, these Taiwanese aboriginal peoples, who in 1994 numbered 365,000, are attending schools and participating in mainstream urbanized and modernized Taiwan life. Hence native cultures, embodied in languages, beliefs, skills, and modes of family support, are dying out. Like native groups in other societies worldwide, their average incomes lag far behind those of the majority; in addition, acute social problems typical of the underclass everywhere (alcoholism, low self-esteem, unemployment, undereducation, poverty) afflict the aborigines of Taiwan.

Japan has a particularly strong sense of cultural solidarity and a tendency to suppress difference. Nonetheless, there are several cultural minorities in

across Central Asia from Europe to Kashi (Kashgar) to Xian. They still live as a distinct group on the Loess Plateau. Another group of 9 million Hui lives in southeast China, in and near Fujian Province. They are the descendants of Muslim traders who made their way to China from Malaysia during the twelfth century. The Hui, who have a long tradition of commercial activity, are particularly successful in China's new capitalist climate. They are using their money not only for conspicuous consumption but also to generously fund their mosques and revive religious instruction.

Tibet was forced into the Chinese realm and renamed Xizang when Chinese troops invaded in 1950. Repression has been particularly severe there. The spiritual leader of the Tibetans, the Dalai Lama, was forced into exile in India, along with thousands of followers. The Chinese army treated the remaining Tibetans brutally. Traditional Tibetan society entailed complex interdependencies among herdspeople, nuns

Japan and, not surprisingly in a country that prizes sameness, they have suffered considerable discrimination. There remain about 2 million Burakumin, who once specialized in butchering and leather working and in ancient times were held in very low esteem. Attitudes toward them can still take on racist tones, and as a result the Burakumin tend to deny their cultural background. A smaller and more distinctive group are the Ainu. Now numbering only about 16,000, the Ainu are a Caucasian group physically distinguished from Japanese by their light skin, heavy beards, and thick wavy hair. They are thought to have come many thousands of years ago from the northern Asian steppes. The Ainu, who lived by hunting and fishing, and some cultivation, once occupied the northern part of Honshu as well as Hokkaido islands; but they are being displaced by forestry and other development activities. Today there are very few full-blooded Ainu because, despite prejudice, they have been steadily absorbed into the mainstream population.

Measures of Human Well-Being

More than most regions on earth, there is extreme variance from country to country in East Asia on all indexes of human well-being. Table 9.1 combines several indicators that are widely used by international agencies to compare how different countries are doing in providing basic health care and welfare for their citizens.

As pointed out many times in this text, human well-being is a complicated concept that draws on

TABLE 9.1

Human well-being rankings of East Asian countries

Country	GNP per capita (in U.S. dollars), 1996	Human Development Index (HDI) global rankings, 1998[a]	Gender Empowerment Measure (GEM) global rankings, 1998[b]	Female literacy (percentage), 1995	Male literacy (percentage), 1995	Life expectancy, 1995
Selected countries for comparison						
United States	28,020	4	11	99	99	76
Kuwait	19,040 (1995)	54	75	75	82	72
East Asia						
China	750	106	33	73	90	71
(Hong Kong[c])	24,290	25 (high)	Not av.	88	96	79
Japan	40,940	8 (high)	38	99	99	80
Korea, North	Not av.[d]	75	Not av.	95	95	66
Korea, South	10,610	30 (high)	83	97	99	74
Macao[c]	Not av.	Not av.	Not av.	Not av.	Not av.	80
Mongolia	360	101	Not av.	75.6	87.8	57
Taiwan[c]	Not av.	Not av.	Not av.	Not av.	Not av.	75

[a]The high designations in column 3 (HDI) indicate where the country ranks among the 174 countries classified into three categories (high, medium, low) by the United Nations.
[b]Only 104 ranked in the world.
[c]Data constructed from several sources.
[d]Not av. = not available.
Sources: Human Development Report 1998, United Nations Development Programme; and *1998 World Population Data Sheet*, Population Reference Bureau.

social, cultural, and political factors as much as economic ones. Using the crude indicator of well-being, gross national product (GNP) per capita (Table 9.1, column 2), we see a variance from U.S. $360 per capita per year in Mongolia to U.S. $40,940 per capita per year in Japan. This is the widest spread found in any world region. China's figure of U.S. $750 per capita provides a similar contrast to Japan's high figure, especially when one remembers the great size of the Chinese population. Yet the apparently enormous disparity of wealth is somewhat misleading. Acting according to long-standing socialist philosophies, both Mongolia and China provide basic necessities for their citizens. That these services level out the disparities at least a little is attested to by rankings on the United Nations Human Development Index (HDI), which measures basic well-being. Whereas Japan's per capita income is 54 times greater than China's, Japan's rank on the HDI is only 13 times greater than China's and 12 times greater than Mongolia's. In fact, mass poverty such as that found in India or Bangladesh, or during famine in Africa, has not existed in China or Mongolia for several decades. Both now fall in the medium category of human development.

United Nations Gender Empowerment Measure (GEM) figures are missing for several countries, but notice that China outranks Japan by several points. There have been concerted efforts to eliminate gender bias in the Chinese workplace, whereas in Japan that is not the case. Notice also, that both Japan (38) and China (33) greatly outrank South Korea (83). South Korean society still harbors many repressive attitudes toward women.

Since 1978, China has made gigantic strides in improving life for the vast majority. Infant mortality has fallen dramatically, and life expectancy has risen from 63 to 71. These advances are the result of efforts to improve basic health care delivery, including massive immunization and family-planning programs, programs to control infectious and parasitic disease, and improved nutrition. Also contributing to well-being are better housing, improved water quality, and literacy training. Then there has been the general effort to alleviate poverty by creating jobs through industrialization, expanded agricultural production, and improved transportation facilities. Only remote and very poor areas have not participated fully in the general improvement in well-being.

Environmental Issues: China

China's remarkable record of improved well-being is now slipping, due to the very activities that brought the dramatic turnaround. It is now apparent that China has the most severe environmental problems on the planet, so severe that they could prevent future progress. Industrialization, improved transport, increased agricultural production, better housing, widespread home heating, and urbanization are producing environmental effects that are causing degenerative conditions like asthma, chronic bronchitis, and intestinal diseases, and cancer of many sorts. Adding to the problems is population growth that, despite vigorous efforts at birth control, is still significant.

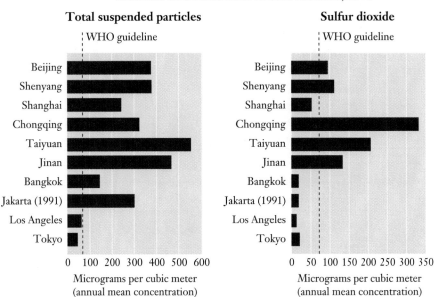

FIGURE 9.9 Air pollution concentrations in selected Chinese and world cities, 1995. [Adapted from *World Resources 1998–99* (New York: Oxford University Press, 1998), p. 117.]

Air Quality

Since the late 1970s, industrial output has been growing at the rate of 18 percent annually. Such rapidly developing industry uses huge amounts of energy. China's consumption of fossil fuel energy has risen more than 150 percent. Since 1977, coal consumption has doubled; coal now fulfills 75 percent of China's energy needs. The use of oil and gas and other sources of energy is also increasing, as is shown in Figure 9.9.

Coal burning is the primary cause of China's poor air quality and is blamed for a critical toll in respiratory ailments. Coal burning releases two types of emissions at high levels: suspended particulates and sulfur dioxide. In Chinese cities, these emissions can exceed World Health Organization guidelines by 10 times. Figure 9.9 shows emission levels of particulates and sulfur dioxide for a number of Chinese cities and compares them with those of other large world cities.

The geographic pattern of air pollution in China correlates with population density and urbanization. The lightly populated plateaus and mountains to the north, northwest, and west are troubled with air pollution primarily in urban areas where industries are concentrated and there are large numbers of homes to be heated. In the Sichuan Basin and in most of eastern China, air pollution is prevalent in both cities and rural areas. Air pollution is the worst in northeastern China, since homes and industries are in close proximity and both depend heavily on coal for fuel. Less heating is necessary in the warmer climate of southeastern China. But the air is still laden with sulfur and suspended particles because there are many industries here and because a softer, highly polluting coal is burned. Since precipitation rates are higher in the south, air pollution is converted into water pollution; the rain absorbs sulfur in the air and becomes acid rain, which is known to affect many species of plants and animals adversely.

Throughout eastern China, large numbers of people are exposed to high levels of gaseous emissions from vehicles. The use of personal cars has hardly begun—in Beijing the number of vehicles is just one-tenth the number in Tokyo or Los Angeles. Nevertheless, pollution attributable to vehicles in Beijing even now equals that of Los Angeles. The explanation lies in out-of-date technology. Most of China's vehicles are fueled with leaded gasoline, and lead emissions can reach 14 to 25 times the suggested maximum per vehicle. Chinese cars also emit 6 to 12 times more carbon monoxide than foreign vehicles.

Even cooking practices contribute to poor air quality. As Table 9.2 shows, air quality can be serious indoors as a result of the use of unventilated coal and gas cookers. Homes in some rural areas may have indoor pollution that is worse than the outdoor pollution in cities. The effects of indoor pollution are concentrated in women and children, who in winter spend most of their time inside.

Water: Too Much and Too Little

Like many places in the world, China suffers from having too much water at times in some locations and too little in others. During the summer monsoon, huge amounts of rain are deposited on the land, often causing catastrophic floods along the rivers and their tributaries. Flooding is a common and particularly severe problem along the Chang Jiang and Huang He. Engineers constructed elaborate systems of dikes, dams, reservoirs, and artificial lakes to help control flooding as well as provide water for irrigation and power for industry and urban populations. Since 1949, for example, the government has built 120,000 miles of dikes.

TABLE 9.2

Indoor air pollution in selected urban and rural places

Place	Urban/ rural	Indoor particulates (micrograms per cubic meter)
Shanghai	Urban	500–1000
Beijing	Urban	17–1100[a]
Shenyang	Urban	125–270
Taiyuan	Urban	300–1000
Harbin	Urban	390–610[a]
Guangzhou	Urban	460
Chengdu	Urban	270–700[a]
Yunnan	Rural	270–5100
Beijing	Rural	400–1300
Jilin	Rural	1000–1200[a]
Hebei	Rural	1900–2500[a]
Inner Mongolia	Rural	400–1600[a]

[a] Particles less than 10 micrometers in size.

Sources: World Resources, 1998–99 (New York: Oxford University Press, 1998), p. 119; and *Health and Environment in Sustainable Development: Five Years After the Earth Summit* (Geneva: World Health Organization, 1997), p. 86.

Despite these efforts, the flood control system failed repeatedly in the late 1990s. Along the Chang Jiang, heavy rains in June and July of 1996 caused some of the worst flooding in two centuries. Several thousand people died and millions were still homeless months later. Crops, which were ready for harvest, lay dead and rotting. Much of the farmland and essential fish-farming facilities remained unusable for months. This situation was repeated with even more severity in the summer of 1998.

Further north, along the Huang He, the rains are less heavy, but still the waters are reaching the highest levels ever recorded because silt is building up in the riverbed. The situation is so precarious that silt must be removed by hand to avert burst levees that, potentially, could kill over 1 million people.

Flooding is a natural phenomenon, but in China, as in many other places, it is exacerbated by human activities. Many environmental scientists attribute the sharp rise in worldwide deaths and damages from floods in the last three decades to deforestation, land cultivation, urbanization, mining, and overgrazing—all human activities which remove water-absorbing soil and vegetation. Another suggested factor is a change in rainfall patterns caused by global warming, the result of fossil fuel burning.

At the other end of the water availability scale, droughts happen somewhere in China every year and often cause more suffering and damage than any other natural hazard. Droughts are triggered by periods of abnormally low rainfall and abnormally high temperatures, with attendant higher evaporation rates. They are made worse by many of the same human factors that exacerbate floods—overgrazing, irrigation, deforestation, global warming, overpopulation, and urbanization. When people begin living in or farming dry environments, as many millions have done in China in the twentieth century, they increase evaporation rates by clearing natural vegetation and they obtain water by tapping into underground aquifers. Ecological forecasters indicate that northern China, parts of the western United States, and other naturally dry areas of the world that are experiencing increased human pressure are likely to confront severe water shortages in the next several decades.

Water use in China falls into three basic categories. Industries use 7 percent; public use (domestic and municipal) accounts for 6 percent; and agriculture uses the remaining 87 percent. As a measure of comparison, in the United States industry uses 11 percent of the water; another 38 percent is used to cool power plants; domestic and municipal uses account for 10 percent; and agriculture uses 41 percent. China's allocations resemble those of arid Tunisia in North Africa, which uses 3 percent of its water for industry, 9 percent for domestic uses, and 88 percent for agriculture.

It takes 20 to 40 tons of water to produce a single ton of steel; and 1200 to 1700 tons to produce a single ton of textile fiber. Thus, perhaps the most serious water problems in China stem from headlong development and unplanned urbanization. The result has been both water scarcity in cities and water pollution in cities and the countryside. Some of the worst water polluters are the village enterprises that have been so important in creating jobs and alleviating rural poverty since 1978. The United Nations reports that in China's cities, water shortages are curtailing industrial production by more than U.S. $10 billion a year and causing health problems with costs that amount to U.S. $4 billion. Fully one-third of the population does not have safe drinking water. Raw sewage and chemical pollution, much of it from synthetic nitrogen fertilizers, have contaminated lakes, reservoirs, and 29,000 miles of China's waterways. Only 24 percent of the Chinese population have access to adequate sanitation; in rural areas 90 percent of the people have only latrines or more primitive facilities. In the east, coastal cities have used up underground reserves to the extent that new construction is collapsing on subsiding land, and salt water is intruding into water supplies. Some Chinese scientists estimate that one-half the groundwater supplying Chinese cities is contaminated.

At both the national and local levels, people in China are taking steps to alleviate the problems. The 1998 floods along the Chang Jiang, coming so soon on the heels of the 1996 floods, inspired a major public protest against inept planning and enforcement, acknowledged by the government. One result was the start of an incipient Green movement, which could potentially lead to greater democratic participation in other venues. High literacy rates and a freer press are creating an informed public that is beginning to press for environmental cleanup. Although only 30 percent of urban water is now recycled, many of China's cities are taking steps to improve recycling procedures. And a system of permits, incentives, and penalties aimed at removing pollutants from industrial wastewater discharge is being woven into the fabric of Chinese industry and farming at all levels. Ultimately, this processed water will be safe to use elsewhere.

But even the solutions have their own negative environmental effects. For example, some of China's rivers are being diverted (at least partially) to provide water for growing metropolitan areas. River diversion has made possible stricter control of groundwater usage: those who use more than their planned allotment are fined, while those who save water are rewarded. In the Loess Plateau, water from the Huang He is being diverted to several growing cities. On the less positive side, river diversion deprives downstream users, like farmers and small villages, of water; and it destroys natural biological habitats.

AT THE LOCAL SCALE   *The Three Gorges Dam*

The Chang Jiang carries about two-thirds of all goods shipped on China's inland waterways. Before the first locks and dams were built at Gezhouba above Yichang in the 1980s, barges, junks, and tugs going upstream to Sichuan could not handle the grade and the current at certain points, so they had to be winched up with human power. Crews of as many as 200 men were harnessed to long towlines of braided bamboo extending from the bow of the boat to the shore. "For the whole month's work we were paid three silver dollars in addition to our food," reported one tow crewman when interviewed in the 1980s, "but we had to furnish our own towing harness and sandals."

A work force of more than 100,000, most working only with their hands, constructed the Gezhouba lock and dam. The lock improved navigation, and the 21 Gezhouba dam turbines generate three times what the entire Chinese supply of electricity was in 1949; but the supply of electricity is now woefully insufficient. The Three Gorges Dam (see map at beginning of the chapter), which thus far (1999) is the largest engineering project ever undertaken on earth, will not only supply much needed energy but is intended to control the flooding of the middle and lower Chang Jiang basin. While the new dam is expected to save millions of lives and much property, the floods of 1996 and 1998 that devastated the middle basin around Wuhan came from monsoon rains that fell below, not above, the dams. Nor will the clean hydropower generated at Three Gorges be sufficient to meet the burgeoning demand, so the massive chemical pollution that comes from burning 50 million tons of coal a year will continue.

As with similar large dams in the United States, Egypt, and Brazil, there are numerous negative human and ecological effects from the Chang Jiang dam projects. The Three Gorges Dam reservoir will create a 370-mile-long (600 kilometer) lake and drown 62,000 acres (250 square kilometers) of farmland, 13 major cities, 140 large towns, 800 factories, and hundreds of small villages—displacing over 1.2 million people. It will also inundate many hundreds of archaeological sites that cannot be reclaimed sufficiently before the flooding starts. One example, among many, of ecologi-

cal losses is the giant sturgeon, weighing as much as three-quarters of a ton. The sturgeon used to swim in huge numbers more than 1000 miles up the Chang Jiang past the Three Gorges to spawn. Now the reproductive process of the sturgeon has been irretrievably interrupted. Hundreds of other species of plants and animals will be affected, but there is little money allotted to fund research or salvage efforts.

The productive rural landscape and the city in the background are typical of the places that will be flooded by the Three Gorges Dam. [Alexis Duclos/Gamma-Liaison.]

The Guangzhou Brewery in Guangdong Province illustrates the working of new pollution control measures. It became a private enterprise in 1991 and, after entering into a joint venture with a Hong Kong brewery, became a profitable business producing over 100,000 tons of beer annually. Since its inception, however, it had been discharging wastewater into the Xi Jiang (Pearl River) estuary. In 1980, China began implementing its first environmental policies. The brewery, then still a state-owned enterprise, obtained a permit and began paying fees that allowed it to discharge pollutants. Five years later, the company constructed a wastewater treatment plant that was expanded in 1988. Since the 1991 joint venture, the company has met discharge standards and has not paid any pollutant fees.

Even though the Guangzhou Brewery is now discharging acceptably clean water, a financial study conducted in 1993 points up one of the problems that all governments face as they try to deal with the conflicting goals of development and environmental protection. From a purely financial perspective, building the wastewater treatment plant was not a good decision for the Guangzhou Brewery: the costs of building, operating, and maintaining the plant were higher than the pollutant discharge fees they would have been assessed over the same time period. Until recently, the brewery cleanup project might have been abandoned after such revelations; in fact, pollutant discharge fees across China are too low to encourage the development of cleaner processes. Environmental awareness among the Chinese public is increasing, but as yet the public only occasionally exerts enough pressure to force the private sector to continue expensive water-quality projects.

Environmental Issues Elsewhere in East Asia

Many environmental issues found in China also exist elsewhere in East Asia. However, normally, Japan, the Koreas, and Taiwan do not suffer water deficits because they are located in the wet northwestern Pacific. On the other hand, Mongolians have always had to cope with arid conditions. Mongolia lost hundreds of thousands of acres to forest fires in the late 1990s. North Korea has suffered flooding as an immediate consequence of deforestation, and soil depletion as a long-term consequence. That country has also recently suffered a series of devastating crop failures related to environmental mismanagement, and it is thought that many thousands have died.

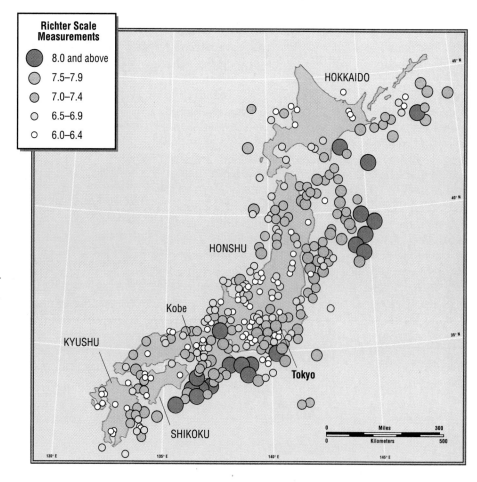

FIGURE 9.10 Dozens of severe earthquakes (above 6.0 on the Richter Scale) have devastated Japan since the year 599. For example, the 1995 Kobe earthquake, which measured 6.8, leveled much of the city and killed over 6000 people. On the map the larger and darker the circle, the higher the scale and the greater the intensity. [Adapted from *New York Times,* January 13, 1998, p. B14.]

The ills of water and air pollution connected with modern agriculture, industrialization, and urbanized living are present in all these countries, but to varying degrees. Mongolia and North Korea have lower overall levels of pollution only because they are not yet heavily industrialized. In Japan, Taiwan, and South Korea, air pollution in the largest cities—most notably Tokyo and Osaka, Taipei, and Seoul—and in adjacent industrial zones is severe enough to pose public health risks. Only in the last several decades have these three countries been paying significant attention to industrially based pollution of all sorts. Legislation is being passed and enforcement increased; but the fact remains that, here as elsewhere around the globe, high population density and rising lifestyle expectations make it difficult to improve environmental quality. Taiwan's case is cited as an example.

Taiwan's extreme population density of 1555 per square mile (600 per square kilometer) has exacerbated pollution and related environmental problems. In the far north, around the metropolitan area of Taipei, where seven cities in the vicinity contain a total of 3.26 million people, densities can rise to 5000 or more per square mile (2000+ per square kilometer). As standards of living have increased, so has per capita consumption of water, sewage facilities, energy, and material possessions of all sorts.

The Taiwanese possess four motor vehicles for every five people, adults and children included. That is more than 16.5 million exhaust-producing vehicles, both cars and motorcycles. Add to this the fact that there are three registered factories for every square kilometer, all spewing forth waste gasses, and it should come as no surprise that Taiwan has some of the dirtiest air on earth—publicly acknowledged by the government as six times dirtier than that of the United States or Europe.

In the category of natural hazards, Japan is a special case. Its location along the northwestern edge of the Pacific Ring of Fire means that it has many volcanoes (Figure 9.10), and experiences earthquakes and tidal waves **(tsunamis)** related to the collision between the Eurasian Plate and the Pacific Plate. These phenomena are a constant threat in Japan, especially in heavily populated zones.

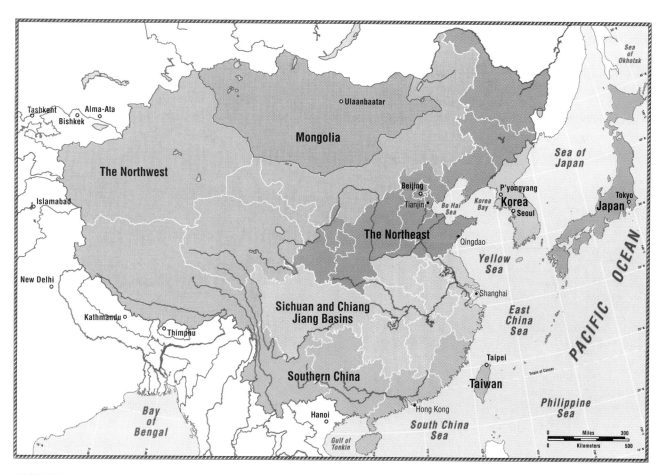

FIGURE 9.11 Subregions of East Asia.

441

SUBREGIONS OF EAST ASIA

Over the course of history, China has been officially divided into provinces, which have changed in size and shape according to shifting alignments of power. The China scholar Mark Elvin suggests that for purposes of organizing one's accumulating knowledge of the country, it is useful to divide it into a relatively small number of regions. Here, I have decided on four such regions (Figure 9.11). As is almost always the case in geography, these regions are not all chosen according to precisely the same set of criteria. Rather, the delineation of each region is based on a set of physical and human factors that make sense for that region's particular situation.

In addition to the four subregions of China, there are four others in this chapter: Taiwan, Japan, North and South Korea as one subregion, and Mongolia.

China's Northeast

The Loess Plateau and the North China Plain in China's Northeast are the ancient heartland of China (Figure 9.12). For thousands of years before the time of Christ, the ancient city of Chang'an (not to be confused with Changan in South China)—near modern Xian in the southeastern Loess Plateau—was an imperial capital and cultural center for peoples of both the

Loess Plateau and the North China Plain. After A.D. 900, the center of Chinese civilization shifted down onto the North China Plain, but the Loess Plateau remained a crucial part of China. The cities of Chang'an and then Xian were the eastern terminus of the lucrative Silk Road trade that connected China with Central Asia and Europe since at least the time of the Roman Empire. In addition, the Loess Plateau acted as a buffer between the more populous plain in the east and the arid areas to the west and north occupied by often hostile nomadic herders.

The Loess Plateau and the North China Plain are linked physically as well as culturally. Both are covered by fine yellowish **loess,** or windblown soil. Millennia of dust storms have picked the loess up off the surfaces of the Gobi and other deserts to the north and west, then carried it east. The loess has drifted into what used to be deep mountain valleys in Shanxi and Shaanxi provinces, creating an undulating plateau. In a perhaps even more massive earthmoving process, the Huang He has transported enormous amounts of loess sediment from the Loess Plateau to the coastal plain. Over the millennia, this river has created the North China Plain by depositing its heavy load of loess sediment in what was once a much larger Gulf of Bo Hai.

The Loess Plateau. This dry upland region is sheltered from the moisture-bearing monsoon rains by higher surrounding mountains. An unusually diverse mixture of peoples from all over Central Asia and East Asia have found it a fertile, though challenging, place

In some places in Shanxi Province, like this hillside, the loess is so thick and firm that people build energy-efficient cavelike houses in it.
[United Nations World Food Program, Beijing.]

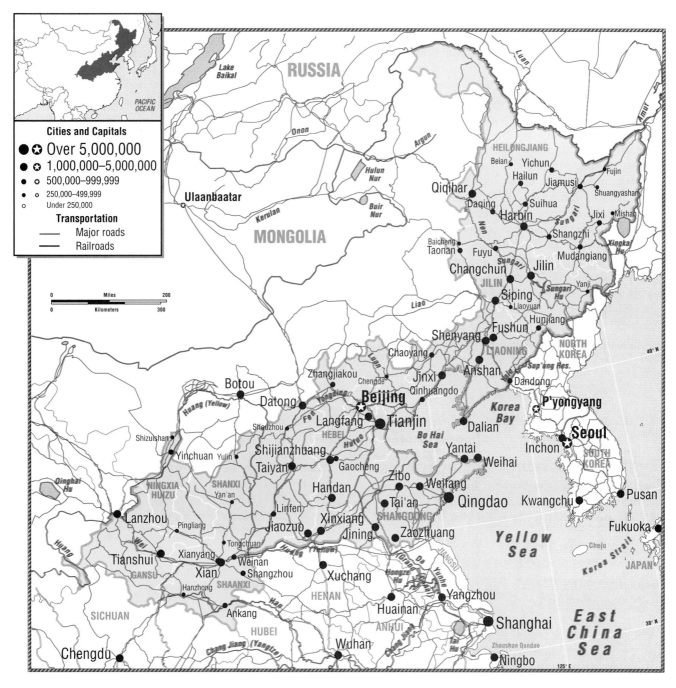

FIGURE 9.12 China's Northeast subregion.

to farm and herd. The plateau is populous and productive. Many of the inhabitants farm cotton and millet in irrigated valley bottoms or raise sheep on the drier grassy uplands. China's largest coal reserves, also found here, have supplied crucial energy to the nation's industrial sectors.

Among the many culture groups that share the plateau are the Hui, a Muslim people thought to be a mixture of traders from Central Asia, and the Han of

China. Mongols, Tibetans, and Kazakhs also occupy the plateau. Today, Chang'an/Xian, with 2 million citizens, is an industrial center producing steel, chemicals, and textiles; but it retains its multicultural features.

Soil erosion is a particularly severe problem here. Thousands of years of human occupation have stripped the land of ancient forests, leaving only grasses to stabilize the loess. Because the loess is so thick, hundreds of feet deep in many areas, deep gullies form after torrential rains. Such gullies now cover much of the landscape. Although hillsides have been terraced for agriculture, they are prone to landslides, so many of them are no longer farmed. For decades, the government has maintained a reforestation campaign to stabilize slopes, and the new forests are spreading. But cropland is too badly needed to put all the land in forests.

The North China Plain. The North China Plain is the largest and most populous expanse of flat, cultivatable land in China. Since the sixth century, it has been home to most of the imperial dynasties. From this seat, the Han Chinese have dominated the longest, spreading through the various river basins of China.

Today the North China Plain is one of the most densely populated spaces in the country: it has an average of more than 1400 people per square mile (550 per square kilometer); a total of more than 370 million people—more people than live in the whole of North America—live in a space about the size of France. The majority are farmers working the relatively small fields that cover the plain. They produce wheat primarily, which grows well in the relatively dry climate. The food

historian E. N. Anderson says of the North China Plain that there is not one square inch of natural cover left. The forests that once covered the plain were cut down millennia ago, and now the only trees that survive are those around temples or planted as windbreaks.

The Huang He (Figure 9.13) is the most important physical feature of the North China Plain. The river is a major transport artery that provides some irrigation water but is particularly known for its disastrous floods. After its descent from the Loess Plateau, the river's speed is drastically reduced on the flat surface of the plain and its load of silt begins to settle out. The silt steadily raises the level of the riverbed year after year until it is so high that the river, usually during the spring surge, seeks lower ground. If it breaks out of the levee, it spreads out across the surrounding plain in a flood. The Huang He has cut many new channels over time, as can be seen on the map in Figure 9.13. The resulting floods are in one sense a gift that endows the plain with a new layer of fertile soil as much as a yard (meter) thick; but over 3000 years of recorded history, some 1500 floods have wiped out crops, brought famine for millions, and destroyed whole cities. For

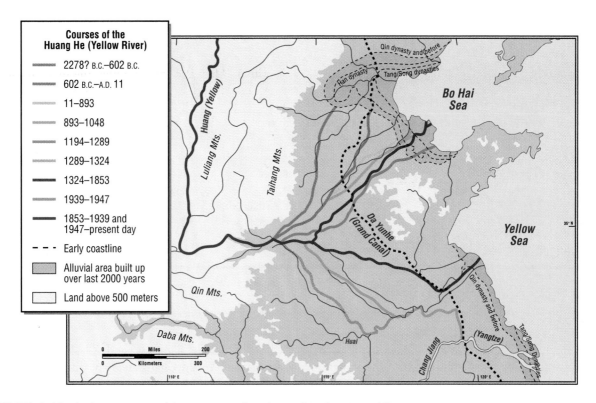

FIGURE 9.13 The lower course of the Huang He has changed its direction of flow many times over the last several thousand years. In 2000 B.C., it flowed north and entered the Gulf of Bo Hai south of Beijing. Then it repeatedly shifted to the east and then southeast like the hand of a clock until it joined the Huai and then cut south all the way to the delta at Shanghai. [Adapted from Caroline Blunden and Mark Elvin, *Cultural Atlas of China,* rev. ed. (New York: Checkmark Books, 1998), p. 16.]

these reasons, the river is referred to as both the "Mother of China" and "China's sorrow."

Far Northeast China.   The far northeast corner of China, also known as Manchuria, has long been considered a peripheral region, partly because of its location and partly because of its harsh climate. The winters are long and bitterly cold, the summers short and hot. The frost-free season is often less than 120 days, so agriculture is precarious. Nonetheless, Manchuria has become increasingly important for its agriculture and natural resources. The region is endowed with fertile plains, sufficient rainfall that comes primarily in the summer, thickly forested uplands, and mineral resources of oil, coal, gas, gold, copper, lead, and zinc. Heilongjian, the most northerly province, is today covered with huge state farms where wheat, corn, soybeans, sunflowers (for oil), and beets are grown. With the discovery of oil at Daqing, it has become the country's leading oil and gas producer. The rich mineral base is the foundation for a growing industrial sector. The huge iron and steel complex in Anshan produces more than 20 percent of the national output.

Development in the Northeast has been helped by its extensive rail network, first begun by the Russians. In the nineteenth century, the Russians built a part of the Siberia-to-Vladivostok railway through the fishing village of Harbin in Heilonjiang. It is now a city of more than 4 million. Today, the rail and road facilities in the region are the best in China.

Beijing and Tianjin.   Beijing, China's capital city, lies between the North China Plain and the far northeast (Manchuria). It is the administrative headquarters of the People's Republic of China, has several of the nation's most prestigious universities, and, with the nearby port city of Tianjin, is becoming an industrial center. Some of the grandest Chinese architectural masterpieces have been preserved there, notably the "Forbidden City," the former imperial headquarters. Nonetheless, Beijing has lost some of its character under the Communists, who have torn down many older monuments. Supposedly, the demolition was intended to improve the flow of traffic, but it also served to blot out some of China's politically out-of-fashion history.

Central China: The Sichuan and Chang Jiang Basins

This region of China is a sequence of three river basins that drain into the Chang Jiang (Figure 9.14). Like so many of Eurasia's rivers, the Chang Jiang starts in the Xizang-Qinghai Central China Plateau. It becomes part of the mainstream of Chinese life when it skirts the southeastern rim of the Red Basin in Sichuan

Province. From there, the Chang Jiang hurtles through the Witch Mountains (Wu Shan) to China's densely occupied central plain (the Middle and Lower basins); from here it takes a winding course to the Pacific, exiting in a huge delta on which sits the famous trading city of Shanghai.

Sichuan Province.   Sichuan is China's most populous province, with 107.2 million people, and one of the best endowed with resources. It has rich soil, a hospitable climate, inventive cultivators, and sufficient natural resources to support diversified industry. Of all the provinces of China, Sichuan perhaps best embodies the revolutionary ideal of complementary agricultural and industrial sectors.

The heart of the province is the Sichuan, or Red, Basin, so named because of the underlying red sandstone. This is a fertile region of hills and plains, crossed by many rivers that drain south toward the Chang Jiang. The shape and angle of the Sichuan Basin set up the conditions for a milder and wetter climate than is usually the case for such a midlatitude, continental location. The basin is tilted toward the south and therefore receives comparatively direct sun rays during much of the year; overall temperatures are therefore higher than would be expected. Furthermore, the basin is surrounded by mountains that are highest in the north and west (rising to 24,000 feet, or 7500 meters), so they form a barrier against the arctic blasts in winter. They also trap and hold the moist warm air moving up from the southeast all year round. For these reasons, the climate of Sichuan is generally mild and humid, and the basin is so often cloaked in fog or low cloud cover that it is said: "A Sichuan dog will bark at the sun."

For the last several thousand years, the basin has been home to a dense population of relatively affluent farmers. They have cleared the native forests, manicured the landscape, and channeled the rivers into an intricate system of irrigation streams. Only a few patches of old-growth forest are left in the uplands and mountains. The geographer Chiao-Min Hsieh vividly describes how the wet "rice fields in [the lowlands] are shaped like squares on a chessboard. Everywhere one can hear water gurgling like music as it brings life and growth to the farms."

The use of irrigation in such a wet climate may seem puzzling, but it is actually an effort to maximize production. By diverting the river water into many small sluiceways, the farmers can control flooding and make water available during the winter dry season, when temperatures are still high enough for cultivation to take place. Furthermore, this is a region where **wet rice cultivation** is practiced. This type of rice production, which results in particularly prolific yields, requires that the roots of the plant be submerged in water

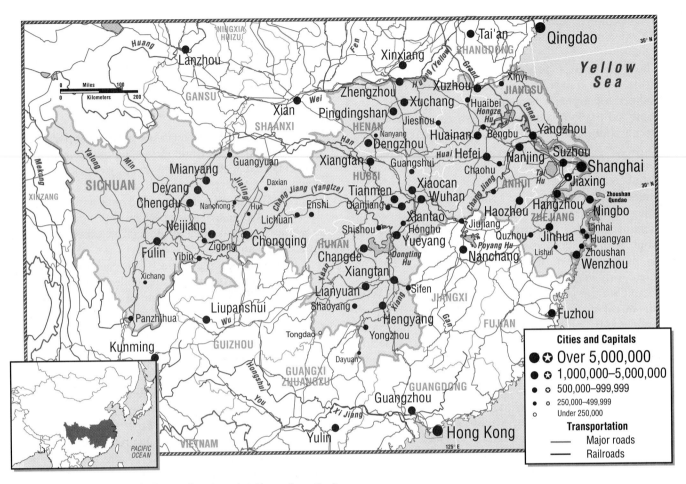

FIGURE 9.14 Central China subregion: the Chang Jiang Basin.

for part of the growing season. It would be risky to depend solely on rainfall to keep the rice paddies filled.

Most of the people of Sichuan live in rural areas in the basin, where the population density is more than 800 per square mile (500 per square kilometer). Their crops are rice, wheat, maize, barley, sweet potatoes, rapeseed, sugarcane, tobacco and tung (oil) trees. Farmers raise silkworms, pigs, and fowl as a sideline; and the mountain pastures to the west of the basin support cattle, yaks, sheep, and horses, which produce hides, skins, and wool. Many of the mountain herders are Tibetan (Sichuan has the largest group of Tibetans outside Tibet—close to 1 million).

The two main cities of the Sichuan Basin are Chengdu, the capital, and Chongqing. Chengdu, with a population approaching 5 million, is an ancient trading center; it still functions as such, being a main hub for national rail and highway service. Chengdu is also home to a good bit of light industry, especially food processing and the manufacturing of textiles and precision instruments. Chongqing has a population of well over 3 million. It is a large industrial city with thousands of factories. Its iron and steel manufacturers and

machine-building industries take advantage of Sichuan's rich deposits of iron, coal, copper, and lead.

Sichuan's historic ability to support its dense population has earned the region a reputation as an extraordinarily productive place, but as population grows and as expectations for yet more affluence increase, degradation of the environment may escalate to intolerable levels. For example, sulfur dioxide emissions in Chongqing in 1995, measured in micrograms per cubic meter, were five times the guidelines recommended by the World Health Organization. A side effect of the basin's tendency to retain warm moist air is that industrial and vehicle emissions build up to produce especially high levels of pollution. Water quality is also a problem; much is polluted with agricultural runoff, and in Chengdu only 37 percent of the population is connected to any sort of sewer system.

Sichuan's age-old connection with the outside world has been the Chang Jiang. The river used to leave the basin in the southeast in a turbulent rush through the famous Three Gorges of the Wu Shan. Now, however, it must first pass through a huge reservoir stretching from Chongqing to the new Three

AT THE LOCAL SCALE   *Silk and Sericulture*

Silk has long been an important crop in the Sichuan Basin, in the lower Chang Jiang basin, and in the Xi Jiang basin in the south. Silk cloth has figured importantly in China's interaction with the outside world—indeed, it gave its name to the Silk Road trade with Central Asia and Europe. Silk production spread to Japan in the seventh century and is now an activity in many parts of Southeastern Asia. Although its overall role is now greatly reduced, both because China has turned to other industries and because fabrics made of artificial fibers and cotton have largely replaced silk fabrics, silk is still an important commodity in Chinese commerce.

The silk fiber is produced by caterpillars (of the Bombyx moth family) that produce a fine, strong, continuous fiber from which they spin a cocoon. The cater-pillars are raised from eggs; the cultivation of the silk-producing caterpillar is called sericulture. The caterpillars are fed on mulberry leaves; the caterpillars that hatch from one ounce of eggs will consume the leaves of 25 to 30 trees! To make silk, the completed cocoons, with the caterpillar inside, are plunged into hot water to kill the creature. Then the cocoons are carefully dried and unspun so the fiber can be used to weave cloth.

People who tend the cocoons must take great care to control temperatures, humidity, and disease. Losses of 70 percent of the product are not uncommon, though technical assistance has improved production. Sericulture is primarily a sideline cottage industry run by women—one of the ways that Chinese women, and now women throughout East Asia, have gained access to their own cash.

Gorges dam. Then it must hurdle the dam and pass through an older reservoir and dam known as the Gezhouba just above the central plain.

The Middle Basin. After the Chang Jiang emerges from its concrete shackles in the Three Gorges, it traverses an ancient, undulating lake bed that is interrupted in many places with low hills. This is the middle basin of the Chang Jiang. It and the river's lower basin, leading to the coast, are rich agricultural regions dotted with industrial cities.

The lake bed of the middle basin has been silted in with **alluvium** (riverborne sediment) carried down from the Sichuan Basin. Other rivers entering the basin from the north and south bring in loads of alluvium and significant volumes of water, which are added to the main channel. The Chang Jiang system carries a huge amount of sediment—as much as 186 million cubic yards (143 million cubic meters) per year—past the large industrial city of Wuhan.

At the beginning of its trip through the middle basin, the river is still 960 miles (1800 kilometers) from the coast, but it has already descended to just 130 feet (40 meters) above sea level. The rest of its trip is a very slow descent, and the volume of water contained in the river changes drastically from season to season. In winter, before the spring monsoons, levels are low. A trip down the river is boring because one travels between high mud banks topped with earthen levees. In summer, the river and its tributaries and lakes are flooded, and boat traffic rides high. One can see over the levees that line the riverbanks. They are meant to protect wide areas of agricultural land from floods like the disastrous ones of the late 1990s.

The climate of the middle basin, while not as salubrious as Sichuan's, is milder than that of the North China Plain. The Qin Ling Mountains, extending eastward across the northern limits of the basin, block some of the cold northern winter winds; they also trap warm wet southern breezes, so the basin retains significant moisture most of the year. The growing seasons are long, nine months in the north and ten in the south. The natural forest cover has long since been removed to make agricultural land for the ever increasing rural population. Summer crops are rice, cotton, corn and soybeans; winter crops include barley, wheat, rapeseed, sesame seed, and broad beans.

The Lower Basin. The lower basin of the Chang Jiang lies on the coastal plain. As the river approaches the Pacific, it turns north, skirting some uplands around the city of Nanjing. It then turns east, depositing the last of its sediment load in a giant delta. The old and rapidly reviving trading city of Shanghai sits at the delta's outer limits.

There are more than 400 million people in the hinterland drained by the lower Chang Jiang and its tributaries. In the past, many were farmers, growing wheat and rice, but more and more are migrating to the many industrialized cities of the region. Shanghai

AT THE LOCAL SCALE · *Shanghai's Urban Environment*

Shanghai has a long history as a trend setter, a penchant that is here illustrated by three current phenomena: a very uncommunist mania for stock trading, the popularity of pajamas as street fashions, and tentative experiments with alternative sexual identity for some.

The Secrets of Wall Street was one of the hottest titles in bookstores in Shanghai in the late 1990s. Housewives, barmaids, and bureaucrats were buying the book, taking investment courses, and placing orders at automated brokerage machines or trading via the telephone. Shanghai investors tend to be highly speculative in their approach, most holding a stock for only a short time.

As an arbiter of fashion, Shanghai has long been a leader; but until recently, it was only the wealthy who indulged in the effort to stay abreast of trends. In the late 1990s, however, ordinary Shanghai people began to participate in an extraordinary fashion statement by wearing pajamas on the street. Pastel printed, light cotton pajamas became the leisure-time garment of choice for males and females, young and old. The reason? Comfort, convenience, and good looks were the explanations given. In Shanghai's steamy climate, the light cotton fabric is undeniably comfortable. And for many migrants newly employed in urban firms, the ability to afford pajamas is a statement about well-being and upward mobility.

Shanghai is also introducing China to a more broadminded multicultural approach to modern living. Although sexual orientation has rarely been negotiable in China in the past, many gay and lesbian young people are now finding that Shanghai offers them their first opportunity to live their preference openly. Official tolerance of gay and lesbian sexual identity is quietly growing, to the point where there are now public gathering

Shanghai's Pudong New Area, a complex of industrial parks, high-rise apartments, foreign factories, and housing developments. [Stuart Franklin/Magnum Photos.]

spots, restaurants, and bars where people can meet openly—one a park across from a police precinct station. Emboldened by the accepting atmosphere of the city, some gays and lesbians are choosing to tell their friends and coworkers. Some report that heterosexual friends accept them with little notice; most, however, are hesitant to tell their families back in the villages, where sexual discussions of any sort are considered in exceedingly poor taste.

Source: Adapted from *Wall Street Journal*, August 17, 1997; and *New York Times*, August 6 and September 2, 1997.

overshadows all these cities in importance. For many centuries, Shanghai's location facing the East China Sea, with the whole of Central China at its back, has positioned the city well to participate in whatever international trade was allowed. When the British forced trade on China in the 1800s, Shanghai became their seat. Before the Communist revolution, Shanghai was among the most refined and elegant cities on earth, home to well-educated literati, wealthy traders, connoisseurs of fine antiquities—and a goodly portion of

underworld figures, as well. After the revolution, the Communists designated the city as the nexus of capitalist corruption and it fell into disgrace.

Shanghai is well situated to take advantage of the changes that began in the 1980s; and by now the whole of the Shanghai region is busy building factories, workers' apartment blocks, international banks, fancy apartment houses, and elegant postmodern style villas. Today, some of the Overseas Chinese—those who fled the repression of the Communist party for places like

Taiwan, Singapore, and Kuala Lumpur—are coming back to invest in everything from television and discotheques to factories, shopping centers, and entertainment parks. And Americans are coming, too, hoping to find joint ventures with Chinese partners.

China's Northwest

The northern and western interior provinces have long been thought of as the periphery of China (Figure 9.15). Here the land is especially dry and often cold, and the cultures are heavily influenced by the ancient and persistent economy of pastoral nomadism. Populations are widely dispersed and settled agriculture is usually dependent on irrigation. Much of this interior is designated as autonomous regions rather than as provinces because of the high percentage of ethnic populations. The designation as autonomous has not meant, however, that these people have power over their own affairs.

Inner Mongolia.   Inner Mongolia, which lies on the southern periphery of the Gobi Desert, is physically and culturally, but not politically, an extension of Mongolia proper. The nomadic herders of Mongolia proper, and hence those of Inner Mongolia, have long been feared by the Han Chinese, who isolated the Mongolians from the rest of the mainland by building the Great Wall. Here, as elsewhere in minority areas, the Chinese have tried to keep the 2 million people of Inner Mongolia pacified by settling Han migrants, now numbering around 17 million, among them. The newcomers, who are overwhelmingly urban dwellers, have

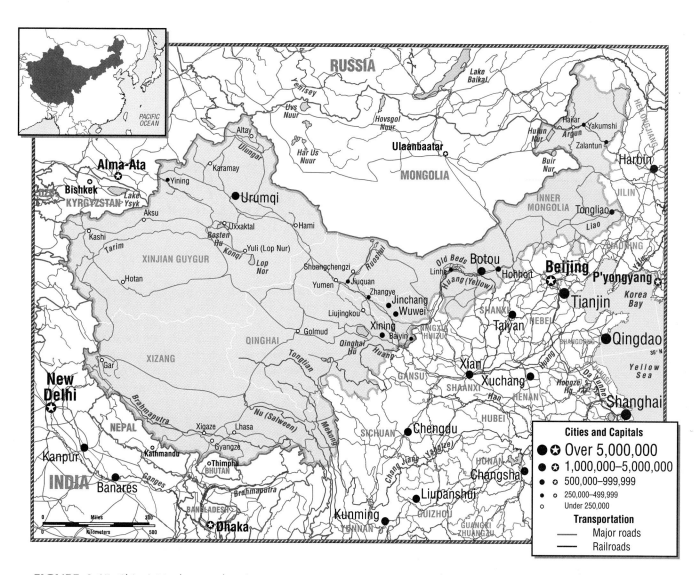

FIGURE 9.15 China's Northwest subregion.

swamped the native Mongols. Within the last 40 years Hohhot, the capital, has grown from a one-bus village to a modern city of 800,000 inhabitants.

Whereas the traditional economy of Inner Mongolia was the raising and breeding of sheep, cattle, horses, and camels, here, as in other interior zones, the Chinese Communist party has encouraged diversified development. So Inner Mongolia now grows grain and other cash crops and is developing its mineral resources. It also boasts one of the biggest iron and steel production facilities in the country. It is in these new economic activities that most of the Han migrants are employed.

Xinjiang. The Xinjiang Uygur Autonomous Region, in the far northwest of China, is the largest of all provinces and autonomous regions. It accounts for one-sixth of Chinese territory. Considered remarkably remote from eastern China, it is now, paradoxically, becoming a region of lively trade and enterprise.

Xinjiang has only 16 million indigenous inhabitants, and their roots lie mainly in Central Asia. The most numerous, at 8 million, are the Turkic-speaking Uygurs; there are also Mongols, Persian-speaking Tajiks, Kazakhs, Kinghiz, Manchu-speaking Xibe, Hui, and new migrants of Han Chinese origin. The peoples native to the region once made their living as nomadic

herders and animal traders, moving with their herds and living in **yurts** or *gers* like those used in the Mongolian culture area: round, heavy felt tents stretched over collapsible willow frames. These cozy houses can be folded and carried on horseback or in horse-drawn carts. In the last decades, many of these peoples have gone to work in the emerging oil industry and now live in apartments. At least 6 million Han migrants live primarily in the cities and work as bureaucrats or in the oil, gas, or atomic industries.

Xinjiang consists of two dry basins: the Tarim Basin occupied by the Taklimakan Desert, and the smaller Dzungar (Junggar) Basin to the northeast. Both are virtually surrounded by 13,000-ft-high (4000-meter-high) mountains topped with snow and glaciers. In this distant corner of China, far from the world's oceans, rainfall is exceedingly sparse; and snow- and glaciermelt from the high mountain peaks is an important source of moisture. Much of the meltwater makes its way to underground rivers, where it is protected from the high rates of evaporation on the surface. Long ago, people built conduits called **qanats**, deep below the surface to carry groundwater dozens of miles to where it was needed. *Qanats* have made some of the hottest and driest places on earth productive. The Turfan Depression, situated between the Dzungar and the Tarim basins, is a case in point. Temperatures often reach 104°F (40°C), and evaporation rates are phenomenal; but because the *qanats* bring irrigation water, it produces some of China's best luxury foods: melons, grapes, apples, and pears.

Xinjiang was once centrally located in the global economic system on the Silk Road (Figure 9.16). Traders carried Chinese and Central Asian products (silk, rugs, spices and herbs, ceramics) over the Silk Road to Europe, where they were exchanged for gold and silver. Today, the province is recovering some of its ancient economic vitality.

Xinjiang is now one of a growing number of places on earth where the local and the global, the very ancient and the very modern, confront each other daily. Herdspeople still living in yurts and *gers* dwell under high-tension electric wires that supply new oil rigs. Tajik women weave traditional rugs that are sold to merchants who fly from New Jersey to the ancient trading city of Kashgar for the Sunday market, which can draw more than 100,000 shoppers (see the photo on page 434). With the breakup of the Soviet Union, citizens of the new republics of Central Asia are eager to return to their entrepreneurial trading heritage; and China is welcoming them and attracting others by giving special economic zone status to cities like Kashgar and Ürümqi.

Xizang and Qinghai Plateaus. Situated in the far west of China, Xizang and Qinghai are stepped

In Yining, northwest Xinjiang, a Kazakh girl plays "kiss the maiden." In the game, a suitor gallops after the girl and tries to steal a kiss; if he succeeds, she chases him and tries to beat him with a whip. The contest tests the riding skills of both future spouses. [Jay Dickman.]

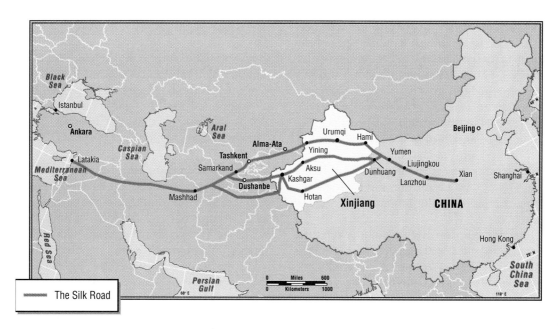

FIGURE 9.16 The ancient Silk Road. [Adapted from *National Geographic,* March 1996, pp. 14–15.]

plateaus, averaging 13,000 feet (4000 meters) and 10,000 feet (3000 meters) above sea level, respectively. They are surrounded by mountains soaring thousands of feet higher. Xizang and Qinghai are noted for the distinctive Tibetan Buddhist culture, which has dominated traditional life since the seventh century. The Tibetan form of Buddhism sees humanity as characterized by a series of opposites: masculine and feminine, active and passive, intellectual and intuitive. Many Tibetan young people, male and female, spend several years in monastic life before marrying and having families. Older Tibetans may return to the monasteries. Tibetan Buddhists revere the Dalai Lama as their leader. He is seen to be the present reincarnation of the first such leader, who emerged in the fifteenth century.

Xizang and Qinghai have rather cold, dry climates (late June can feel like March does on the American Great Plains) because they lie so high and because the Himalaya Mountains to the south block warm wet air from moving in. Along the southern rim of Xizang and elsewhere across the plateaus, snowmelt and rainfall are sufficient to support a short growing season for barley and vegetables like peas and broad beans, and to form the headwaters of some very important rivers— the Indus, Ganges, Brahmaputra, Nu (Salween), Irrawaddy, Mekong, Chang Jiang, and Huang He.

Traditionally, the economy of the Xizang-Qinghai Plateaus has been based on the raising of grazing animals. The yak is the main draft animal, and it also provides meat, milk, butter, cheese, hide, fur, hair, and

dung and butterfat for fuel and light. Other animals of economic importance are sheep, horses, donkeys, cattle, and the dog. Animal husbandry on the sparse grasses of the plateaus has required a mobile way of life so that the animals can be taken to the best available grasses at different times of the year. Yet, for several decades, the government has pressured herdspeople to settle in permanent locations so that their wealth can be taxed, their children schooled, their sick cared for, and dissidents curtailed. Still, throughout the plateaus, many native (non-Han) peoples continue to live solitary lifestyles as they have for centuries, occasionally adopting some of the accouterments of modern life and adapting to its restrictions.

By the 1990s, the Beijing government was trying the strategy of overwhelming Xizang (Tibet) with secular social and economic modernization instead of with military force. China is attempting to bring its economic boom to Xizang by granting hundreds of millions of dollars and trying to attract trade and tourism to this remote province. China sees this as part of its overall strategy to make the entire country an economically and socially integrated whole. Schools and roads are being built and the job markets opened up to young people. Increasingly, Tibetans are accepting the continuation of a Chinese presence and are channeling their Tibetan cultural pride into efforts to preserve the Tibetan language and religion.

Women have always had a relatively high position in traditional Tibetan society. Among the nomadic herders, they were free to have more than one husband, just as men were free to have more than one wife. Also, as with some other minority groups in China, ancient marriage customs call for the husband to join the wife's family. This custom alone allowed women to attain a higher status than among the Han. Buddhism introduced patriarchal attitudes from outside Xizang, yet encouraged female independence. At any given time, up to one-third of the male population was living a short-term monastic life, so Tibetan Buddhist women have been particularly self-sufficient, often spending days herding on horseback as well as performing most other daily duties that support community life.

In the modern era, the women of the Xizang-Qinghai plateaus fare less well than they have under traditional lifeways. Chinese culture has typically regarded the women of the western minorities as barbarian, precisely because gender roles were not clearly defined: they rode horses and worked alongside the men in herding and agricultural activities. An effect of residual Confucian ideas in modern policy is often that the highest paying technical or supervisory jobs go to men, while the low-paying, labor-intensive jobs, such as those in agriculture and factories, go to women.

Southern China

Southern China has two distinct sections: the mountainous and mostly rural provinces of Yunnan and Guizhou to the southwest and the coastal provinces of Guangxi, Guangdong, and Fujian to the southeast, where the booming cities of China's evolving economic revolution are located.

The Yunnan-Guizhou Plateau. The Yunnan-Guizhou Plateau is noted for its natural beauty and wild climate, and for being the home of numerous indigenous groups that are culturally distinct from the Han Chinese. The plateau is a rough, mountainous land of deeply folded north-south–trending mountains that carry the headwaters of the Mekong, Nu (Salween), and Irrawaddy rivers (Figure 9.17). Its heavily forested valleys may be as deep as 5000 feet (1500 meters), yet only one-quarter of a mile (400 meters) across. People can call to one another across the valleys; and yet it would take more than a day's difficult trip to reach the other side. In some places, rope and bamboo bridges have been slung across the chasms. The landforms here are unstable and earthquakes do heavy damage to the care-

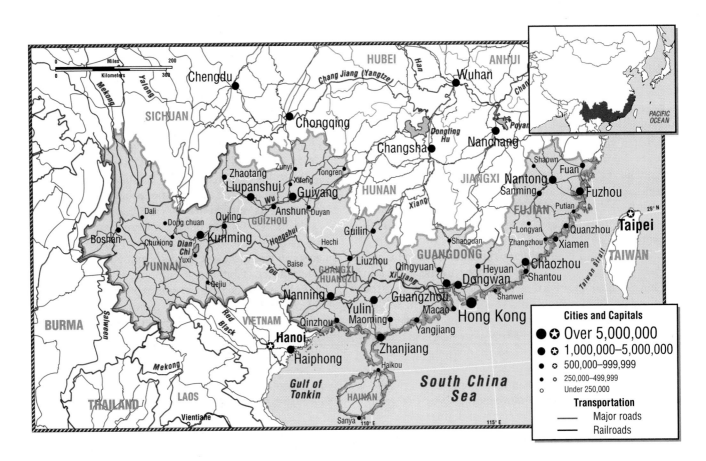

FIGURE 9.17 The Southern China subregion.

Rainy and warm Yunnan Province is increasingly important nationally for its market gardening and small-animal raising. Here a family transports its wares in the produce baskets typical of the subregion. [Eastcott/Momatiuk/Woodfin Camp & Associates.]

fully constructed rice paddy terraces, which must be absolutely level to receive gravity-fed irrigation water.

The lower parts of the plateau, to the east, are composed of karst, or limestone, deposits that are eroded by water to form fantastic landscapes of sharp jagged peaks jutting out from surrounding flat valleys. This phenomenon is found in its most extreme case in Yunnan, where there is a karst "forest" of 90-foot-high jagged limestone columns interspersed with lakes.

The valuable natural resources of the Yunnan-Guizhou Plateau are primarily biotic. Yunnan Province is one of the most heavily forested regions in the country. Although Yunnan is required to supply wood for China's industrialization (25 percent of China's forests have been clear-cut in just three decades), it still has many untouched zones. Yunnan is called "The National Botanical Garden" because it is home to many of

China's native plant species and one-third of China's bird species (400 or more). Both flora and fauna are now in trouble. A British team of biologists traveling in Yunnan in the mid-1980s reported that by then "birds were absent even in the reserves," presumably due to recent human disturbance of the habitat. Until the 1970s, the tropical forests of far south Yunnan harbored elephants, bears, porcupines, gibbons, and boa constrictors.

The Southeast Coast. The southeast coastal zone of China has long been a window to the outside world. Very likely it was the coastal fishing culture that first encouraged contact with strangers on the high seas and provided the opportunity to trade. Arab traders began coming to this part of China more than 1200 years ago; by the fifteenth century, some of the first Europeans in the region described a necklace of flourishing trading towns all along the coast. People from this region have long ventured out to seek their fortunes throughout Southeast Asia and beyond. The overwhelming majority of Overseas Chinese, living in places from Singapore to West Africa, London, São Paulo, Brazil, and Atlanta, Georgia, have their roots along China's southeast coast. Even today, fisherfolk sailing the legendary junks meet officially forbidden trading partners from Taiwan and Vietnam and elsewhere, far out to sea. In the 1980s, the central government of China decided to take advantage of this long tradition of outside contact by designating several of the old coastal fishing towns as SEZs, anticipating that they would quickly grow into major trading cities. This designation gives them special rights to conduct business with the outside world and allows them to create conditions that will attract foreign investors.

The southeast coastal region is separated from the Chang Jiang basins and the rest of China to the north by a broad, rugged, generally east-west–trending mass of mountains. The principal river, the Xi Jiang, is joined by several tributaries to form one large delta below the city of Guangzhou (Canton). The lowlands along the rivers and deltas are subtropical in climate and have a perpetual growing season. The rich delta sediment and the interior hinterland are used to cultivate sugarcane, tea, fruit, vegetables, herbs, mulberry trees for sericulture (raising of silk worms), and timber—products that are sold in the various SEZs and exported to global markets.

Guangzhou has long been the most important trading center in South China; but since the nineteenth century, Hong Kong (Xianggang)—which until 1997 was a British crown colony—has posed stiff competition. Now there are at least five other trading and manufacturing centers along the south coast that have SEZ status: Xiamen in Fujian Province; Shantou in far eastern Guangzhou Province; Shenzhen, adjacent to

453

Hong Kong; Zhuhai, close to the old Portuguese trading colony of Macao; and Haikou, on Hainan Island (see Figure 9.6).

Hong Kong. Hong Kong, one of the most densely populated cities on earth, has packed its 6.4 million people into just 23 square miles (60 square kilometers) of the territory's total of 380 square miles (1000 square kilometers). This very small place has the world's eighth largest trading economy and the world's largest container port; it is the world's largest producer of timepieces. Figures like these are what have enabled Hong Kong's populace to achieve an annual gross domestic product per capita of more than U.S. $24,000, with an annual economic growth of 4.6 percent in 1995. In July 1997, Hong Kong's niche as a British trading enclave came to an end when the 150-year lease agreement ran out. There had been considerable worry that China would absorb Hong Kong and no longer allow it the economic freedoms it had enjoyed. However, Hong Kong has long played an important role as China's unofficial link to the outside world of global trade; some 60 percent of foreign investment in China was funneled through Hong Kong before 1997. The conclusion is that dramatic change is unlikely; but given the very obvious success of numerous cities along China's Pacific coast, from Macao in the south to Shanghai, Hong Kong will no longer occupy the privileged position it has in the past.

Taiwan

In the late nineteenth century, Taiwan (also once known as Formosa) was a poor agricultural island on the periphery of the Chinese Qing empire. In 1895, Japan annexed Taiwan as a colony and exploited its resources for half a century. Then, in 1949, the Chinese Nationalists (the Kuomintang) lost to the Communists and had to flee the mainland. They chose to settle in Taiwan, against the opposition of the indigenous peoples, and renamed the island the Republic of China (ROC). Taiwan became home to the exiled government of Chiang Kai-shek and more than a million migrants from the mainland. Over the course of the next 50 years, it has become a modern, crowded, and highly industrialized society that is playing a leading role in the rapid transformation of East Asian economies.

Taiwan lies across the Taiwan Strait from southeast China (Figure 9.18). With an area of 14,000 square miles (36,000 square kilometers) and more than 21 million people, Taiwan has a population density of over 1500 people per square mile (600 per square kilometer). Shaped somewhat like a leaf, the island has a mountainous spine running from the northeast to the southern tip. A rather steep escarpment faces east, and

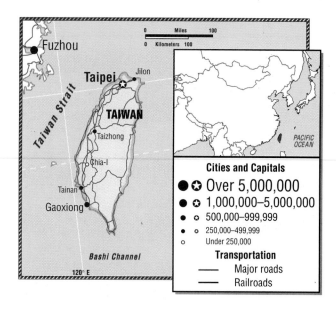

FIGURE 9.18 The Taiwan subregion.

a long, more gentle slope faces west. Most of the population lives on the western side, especially in lower elevations along the coastal plain. Increasingly, as farming declines as an occupation, people are concentrated in a few urban centers. The greatest concentration is in the far north surrounding Taipei, the capital.

Taiwan, despite its small size and small population, is one of the economic tigers of the Asia-Pacific region. It is fourteenth globally in the size of its foreign trade, and the GNP per capita in 1994 was higher than $13,900. After the Communist revolution in China, Taiwan took advantage of its ardent anti-Communist stance, its burgeoning refugee population, and its geographical location so close to the worrisome mainland to draw aid and investment from Europe and America. The island's economy quickly changed from one in which 90 percent of the population was agricultural to one in which most of the people lived in or near cities and worked in industries; many of these industries made products for Taiwan's impressive export markets. Then slowly the emphasis changed again, from labor-intensive industries to high-technology and service industries requiring education and skill.

By the mid-1990s, the domestic economy was expanding rapidly and local buyers were absorbing a major proportion of Taiwan's own production—home appliances, electronics (including the latest in computers and related communications devices), automobiles, motorcycles, and synthetic textiles. This high rate of consumption was made possible in part by a neat pirouette performed by the Taiwanese. As Taiwan lost its labor-intensive industries to cheaper labor markets throughout Asia—including its old nemesis, the mainland of

AT THE LOCAL SCALE   *Leisure Time in Taiwan*

A social issue in Taiwan that many urban dwellers around the world can relate to is the lack of leisure time and of the spaces in which to enjoy it. Almost all Taiwan employers expect people to work a half day on Saturday. This fact, and gridlock traffic, seriously limit the enjoyment of leisure time on Taiwan. And places to go are scarce, as well. Taipei and the surrounding densely packed cities have very few public spaces, besides the crowded streets, where people can relax and spend time together or be alone. There are a few national parks, but dense traffic makes them inaccessible. It is not unusual for a family to set out early to visit such a park, only to give up and return home after spending a half day in stalled traffic breathing exhaust fumes. A result is that increasingly Taiwanese urban dwellers (the vast majority of the population) spend their leisure time inside, either watching videos at home or visiting high-tech entertainment centers, karaoke bars, and restaurants.

Source: Arthur Zich, The other China changes course—Taiwan, *National Geographic*, November 1993, pp. 2–33.

A family masked against air pollution go for a drive in a park, Kaohsiung, southwestern Taiwan. [Jodi Cobb/National Geographic.]

China—individual Taiwanese invested their savings in the very places that were giving them such stiff competition, like the new SEZs in South China. Estimates are that in the mid-1990s, Taiwanese businesses invested around U.S. $25 billion in China. Hence, Taiwan remained competitive as a rapidly growing economy with strong export markets, and also profited from dealing with the less advanced, but emerging economies in the vicinity.

Life for Taiwanese women has changed radically since the 1950s; women then made up less than one-third of the high school students and their social status reflected Confucian values. After World War II, many Taiwanese women left their homes in towns and villages across the island and took low-paying urban factory jobs in the textile and garment industries that fueled Taiwan's economy. By the 1990s, Taiwanese women had equal access to education, at least through the high school level; 40 percent worked outside the home; and they were choosing to have only one or two children. Nonetheless, women are still greatly underrepresented in supervisory and management positions throughout the government bureaucracy and in private firms, and very few are politicians.

Official publications in Taiwan still refer to the whole of mainland China as a renegade part of the

Technology and electronics industries are a core of Taiwan's capitalist economy. Stan Shih, CEO and chairman of Acer, displays products ready for shipping in the company plant in Taipei. [Lincoln Potter/Gamma-Liaison.]

Republic of China. Meanwhile, China also refuses to recognize Taiwan, except as a renegade province. Yet oddly, both the mainland and Taiwan expect reunification. Taiwanese people are worried about this prospect, for there have been no agreements to date that would guarantee Taiwan's autonomy at any level.

Today a hotly debated question in Taiwan is, what is the republic's likely future role in the wider world? As mainland China emerges as a world power with a huge population and enormous market potential, tiny Taiwan can no longer keep up the fiction that it speaks for (or is) China. Inevitably, its voice on the world stage is becoming muffled. On the other hand, Taiwan is perfectly located to participate in the development of mainland markets and in related efforts to integrate the Asia-Pacific economy.

Japan

Japan has for some time enjoyed the reputation of being an unusually resourceful country, one that overcame crippling defeat at the end of World War II and a limited base of natural assets to become one of the world's leading industrial economies and a principal player in the economies of Asia, Oceania, and the Americas. Japan's success in overcoming its handicaps and its innovative approach to industrial organization have made it a role model for both developing and developed countries alike. Nonetheless, in the late 1990s Japan faltered. As Southeast Asia entered a difficult era of economic and social reform, Japan felt the repercussions of lost markets and precarious investments in that region. At home, the exposure of cronyism and corruption, the failure of a number of banks and industries, and the awakening of modest social reform movements promised some changes in Japan's heretofore sleek image.

Landforms, Climate, and Vegetation

The Japanese Archipelago is a chain of four main islands and hundreds of small ones (Figure 9.19). Most are volcanic and mountainous, rising steeply out of the highly unstable zone where the Pacific, Philippine, and Eurasian plates grind into each other. Prone to severe earthquakes, seismic sea waves (tidal waves), and disastrous tropical storms, and so mountainous that only 18 percent of its land can be cultivated, Japan might seem an unlikely place to find 126 million people living in affluent comfort.

Japan stretches over latitudes roughly comparable to those between Nova Scotia and Florida (46°– 24° N); and, although half a world away, it has a climate similar to the east coast of North America. The climate is cool on the far northern island of Hokkaido, temperate on the island of Honshu, and tropical in the southern Ryuku Islands. Despite the moderating effect of surrounding oceans, the extreme seasonal climatic shifts of nearby continental East Asia give Japan a more extreme seasonal variation in temperature than would be the case if it lay farther out to sea.

The large central island of Honshu is the most mountainous and heavily forested island and the most densely populated. Having gained access to forest products in Southeast Asia and beyond, Japan has been able to keep much of its forests in reserves. Today the interior mountains of Honshu (and Hokkaido) remain largely forested. The few flat lowlands and coastal areas of north and south Honshu were once intensively cultivated and supported a dense rural population. Industrial cities now fill many of these same lowlands, especially in the south. Tokyo-Yokohama is the largest urban agglomeration in the world, at 26.2 million; it lies on the Kanto Plain on the east-central coast. Kobe-

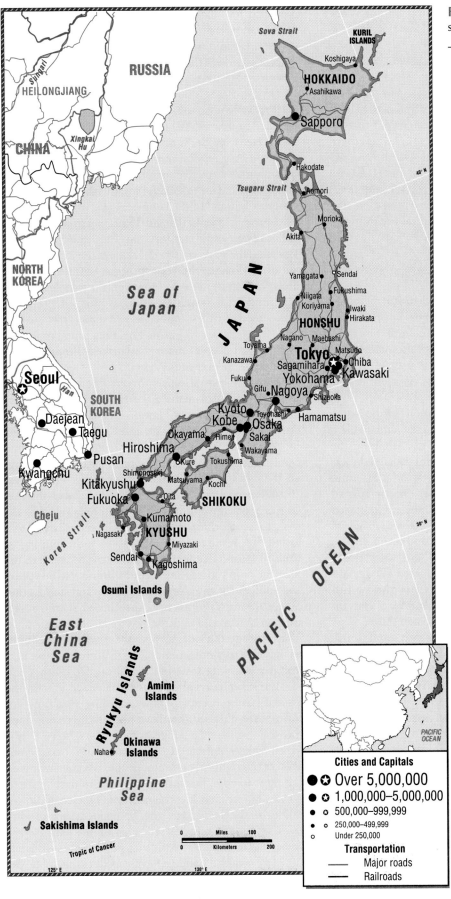

FIGURE 9.19 The Japan subregion.

Cities and Capitals

● ✪ Over 5,000,000
● ✪ 1,000,000–5,000,000
• ✪ 500,000–999,999
· ✪ 250,000–499,999
○ Under 250,000

Transportation

—— Major roads
—— Railroads

Osaka, Japan's second largest city at 10.6 million, is one of several major urban areas located on the flatlands that ring the Inland Sea.

Japan's other three main islands are the most northerly and least populated island, Hokkaido, and two southern, smaller islands, Kyushu and Shikoku. The northern slopes of Kyushu and Shikoku islands, facing the Inland Sea, have narrow ribbons put to agricultural, industrial, and urban uses. The southern slopes are more rural and agricultural. Off of Kyushu's southern tip, the very small, mountainous Ryuku Islands stretch out in a 650-mile (1000-kilometer) chain. Although many areas are densely settled, the Ryuku Islands are considered a poor rural backwater of the four big islands.

Japan's Rise to Economic Power

Over the past 2000 years, influences from mainland East Asia have joined with indigenous Japanese elements to give the islands a distinctive culture. Since the mid-nineteenth century, Japan has also integrated Western influences in ways that led to a type of colonial expansion affecting much of East Asia and culminating in World War II.

Starting around A.D. 300, migrations from Korea transformed Japan. The Japanese imperial Yamato clan, still recognized today as the oldest royal family in the world, has Korean roots. As the Yamato expanded their power, the indigenous peoples of Japan (the Ainu, Burakumin, and others) were driven north toward Hokkaido. The Yamato imported Chinese Confucian philosophy and administration practices, as well as Buddhism and Chinese writing, arts, and technologies. As a result, everyday life and land use were transformed. Eventually, clan rivalries distracted the Yamato emperors, and their rule disintegrated in the twelfth century. Until the mid-nineteenth century, a class of military warriors called samurai dominated Japan.

During the seventeenth, eighteenth, and nineteenth centuries, advances in rice farming allowed the growth of larger urban populations. Meanwhile, in cities like Edo and Osaka, craft industries produced increasingly profitable items for export to the Asian mainland, and Japan developed banking and commercial infrastructures that were superior to those of most countries of the time. Much like the free towns of late feudal Europe, Japanese cities flourished.

In 1853, a U.S. mission succeeded in forcing Japan to open up to trade, thereby disgracing Japan's leaders in the eyes of its people. In 1867, a small group of European-influenced reformist samurai from western Japan overthrew the government. The samurai cooperated brilliantly to create a powerful and forward-thinking government. Its large investments in education helped to create a skilled industrial work force by 1900.

The next few decades witnessed the rise of the world's first Asian industrialized nation. By the early twentieth century, Japan's inexpensive manufactured goods were entering markets throughout East Asia, and its military was on a par with that of the European powers.

In the 1930s, military leaders launched Japan on a destructive course of overseas expansion throughout East and Southeast Asia (Figure 9.20). Geography was a major factor in the creation of Japan's empire, as the country's only modest natural resources made overseas expansion an attractive option for supporting a growing population and an expanding industrial economy. Japan annexed Taiwan (1895) and Korea (1910), and extended its control in the 1930s and 1940s to cover the North China Plain and territory up the Chang Jiang to Wuhan. Japan invested in developing the export potential of all three territories and began to do the same in much of Southeast Asia. However, the people in these colonized areas benefited little, as most of the products—food, textiles, minerals and other raw materials—were shipped to Japan. The often brutal treatment of colonized peoples made the Japanese Empire one of the most hated ever in the region.

Japanese expansionism overreached itself in late 1941, when Japan made a daring assault on the U.S. base at Pearl Harbor in Hawaii. The United States declared war and eventually defeated Japan in the Pacific. In 1945, after four years of brutal air, sea, and ground combat, the United States dropped two atomic bombs on the cities of Hiroshima and Nagasaki, killing over 200,000 people and bringing an instant end to the war. One rationale given for the use of atom bombs was the wish to avoid the projected 2 million casualties that would have resulted from an invasion of the four big islands of Japan. The bombing was also a response to the Soviet Union's increasing interest in the Pacific region and subsequent invasion of Korea. To forestall further Soviet advances in East Asia, the United States chose a weapon that would end the war as quickly as possible. This strategy did not prevent the Soviet Union from having a strong influence in North Korea for the next four decades.

For seven years after the end of World War II, the United States occupied Japan. During this time reforms were imposed that have profoundly transformed the country. Fundamental human rights were established by law, replacing Confucian customs that did not protect the rights of common people. Women obtained the right to vote, and a new constitution decentralized power by making the democratically elected lower house of the legislature the preeminent law-making body. Economic reforms set Japan on the path toward achieving one of the world's most equitable distributions of wealth. Land reforms made it possible for farmers to own, not rent, their fields, giving Japan an economically stable agricultural population.

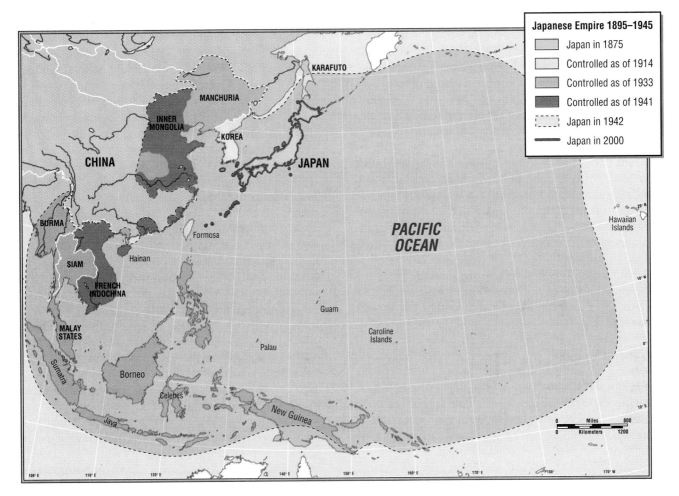

FIGURE 9.20 Japan expansions, 1875–1942. [Adapted from *Hammond Times Concise Atlas of World History,* 1994.]

As a condition of surrender, Japan was made to renounce war formally and give up all but purely defensive armed forces. The Japanese people, who felt they had been betrayed by their military leaders, generally supported this move. Japan came firmly under the protection of the United States, which was soon preoccupied with the spread of communism from China and Russia. As part of its cold war strategy, the United States placed large military bases on a number of Japanese islands. Thus relieved from the cost of maintaining its own military, Japan focused on increasing its commercial influence throughout East Asia and the world.

Over the next half century, Japan rebuilt itself into one of the world's wealthiest and most influential nations. For much of the postwar period, Japan's economy grew at roughly 10 percent a year, with heavy industry and manufacturing the leading sectors. The worldwide geographic impact of Japan's "economic miracle" has been, and continues to be, immense. Resources from seemingly everywhere are shipped to Japan: minerals and ore from Africa; coal and steel

from Australia; timber from the Philippines, Indonesia, Malaysia (see Figure 10.12), Canada, and the United States; and oil from Southwest Asia. These raw materials are then turned into inexpensive yet high-quality manufactured goods that soon were in demand throughout the world. Japan's profits from these industries have often been invested abroad in factories, hotels, and resorts, thus securing multiple market niches for the country. Meanwhile, Japan has been loath to allow much foreign investment or foreign trade within its borders.

Many are now arguing that the economic and political model that Japan developed and used so successfully has outlived its usefulness. Indeed, the Japan of today is an increasingly different place from the Japan of the economic miracle. Urban populations, though affluent by most standards, are growing uneasy. Long forced, in the interest of rapid economic growth, to endure extended workdays, overcrowding, pollution, high prices, and only modest buying power, Japanese people are agitating for changes that will improve their living standards. Greater participation of women in the work force and the need for more creative and innovative employees are leading to changes in the workplace. Moreover, increased life expectancy is producing an aging population. The increasingly large proportion of the elderly will soon require more social spending, which will further burden the working-age population.

Internationally, the rising economic power of China promises opportunity for Japanese investors, but China could also pose a competitive threat in the marketplace, or if it chooses territorial expansion, a military threat. This possibility could one day motivate Japan to reassess its nonmilitary status and strategic alliance with the United States. Meanwhile, the United States is pushing Japan to remove its barriers against foreign imports. Since 1950, Japan's access to North American markets has been a major factor in its economic rise, but it has consistently blocked incoming trade. The end of the twentieth century has brought the Japanese people no reduction in worries.

The Many Faces of Japan

Perhaps more than any other country on earth, Japan is renowned for its ability to confound foreigners. In an attempt to penetrate some of Japan's cultural complexity, we will look at several aspects of Japan, including agriculture, urban life, the home, and work.

Agriculture. With 126 million people and only 18 percent of its land suitable for agriculture, Japan has nearly the largest ratio of people to farmland in the world. More than 7000 people depend on each square mile of cultivated land. Thus, rice terraces march up hillsides that even in China or Korea would be planted in orchards or left forested.

While the agricultural way of life looms large in Japanese national identity, today only 4 percent of the population farms. Japanese farms are increasingly highly mechanized, and in terms of output per acre they are highly productive. But the produce is some of the most expensive in the world. A single cantaloupe can cost as much as U.S. $10, a head of lettuce U.S. $5, a pound of beef more than U.S. $50. These high prices are in part a reflection of the very superior quality, but they are also the result of government efforts to keep Japan self-sufficient in food production. The government gives huge subsidies to farmers to persuade them to stay on the land. These payments discourage competition, as do trade barriers that keep imported food out. The system is increasingly unpopular with urbanites, who are aware that imported food would be much cheaper.

Urban Japan. Japan's major cities, long the driving force behind its rapid industrialization, are nearly all along the coastal perimeter. Here they can easily import raw materials and export finished products, and ideas from the outside world can penetrate more easily, aiding technological advancement and cultural synthesis. Tokyo, for example, has the world's largest stock exchange, numerous centers for research and development, and some of the world's most beautiful modern architecture. Nonetheless, Japanese cities are some of the least livable in the world. Overcrowding is among the world's worst. In Tokyo it is not uncommon for a middle-class family of four, plus a grandparent or two, to live in a one-bedroom apartment. Japanese cities cannot expand to relieve crowding because they are hemmed in by surrounding mountains and the ocean, and by regulations protecting Japan's scarce agricultural lands. But perhaps the greatest causes of overcrowding are corruption and lack of competition in the construction industry, which keep housing in short supply. Although pressure for change is growing, most Japanese stoically endure minuscule, astronomically priced apartments and long commutes to work. It is common to travel two or even three hours one way in trains that are so overcrowded that stations employ "shovers," who physically push as many passengers as possible into a single car.

The greatest source of discomfort to urban dwellers is pollution. Several cities have endured major episodes of poisoning from mercury and PCBs, and all large cities have chronic air pollution from automobiles and factories, as well as noise pollution. In the 1970s, grassroots campaigns at the local level led to the first serious government efforts to limit pollution and to establish a moderately effective environmental agency.

The Home. Japanese domestic space is known for its simple, elegant aesthetics and its highly functional use of space. Traditional homes are made of wood and usually roofed with heavy tiles. Even in larger rural homes, interior space is much less than most Westerners are accustomed to. The three or four rooms of a typical middle-class home are used for many purposes during the course of the day: they are transformed as needed by sliding doors of paper and wood or by folding, decorative room dividers. Furniture is simple, with much of family life centered on a low table and floor cushions. Sleeping is done on a firm mattress, called a futon, which is often rolled out on whatever floor space is available. Meals are usually prepared in very small kitchens, now furnished with many electric appliances. Almost every Japanese family has a color TV, and many have automobiles.

Work. Renowned for their hard work and high-quality output, most Japanese are intensely devoted to their jobs. The lives of many people are shaped by the companies that employ them. The employer provides

The suburbs of Japanese cities are densely packed with family homes. During the day, housewives go about their many shopping, laundry, childcare, and eldercare duties. [Michal Heron/Woodfin Camp & Associates.]

lifetime employment, regular paid vacations, a pension upon retirement, and often subsidized housing. Some companies even have a graveyard for employees. Job-hopping is considered reprehensible, and loyalty is reinforced by personnel management that instills camaraderie and conformity. Individualism is regarded as selfish, and innovation is actually frowned on. Often, employees who have good ideas will sit on them for several years before presenting them or will give credit to someone else. The Japanese language does not even have a word for entrepreneur; only recently has it become a buzz-word in Japanese.

Recently, some younger college graduates have turned away from the lifetime job in favor of temporary employment. Called "freeters," they move from job to job, earning what they need, then taking a break to pursue other interests. They settle for a lower standard of living and give up job-related benefits; but they are also unencumbered by contracts and do not feel compelled to grovel before their superiors or work overtime. This more free-lance approach to the world of work allows time for entrepreneurial activity, and many of these mavericks are starting independent, low-budget enterprises. But this path is also full of risk: the old loyalty system makes repeatedly finding a job difficult. Firms are often unwilling to hire someone who has worked for a competing company.

Japanese manufacturers do excel at creating highly efficient spatial arrangements of firms, and their practices have been imitated globally. Firms that supply components such as engine parts for automobiles often are clustered around a single internationally renowned company where final assembly takes place. The close proximity allows suppliers to deliver their products "just in time," literally minutes before they are needed. Defects in production runs can be spotted more quickly, so fewer defective parts are produced and less space is taken up by warehouses. This so-called kanban system has influenced economic geography globally. Rather than out-sourcing parts to cheap labor pools in developing countries, many firms now seek to locate the assembly of both components and final products in a single area, either abroad or at home.

The kanban system, however, has also given Japan a sort of dual economy. The high-status final assembly firms give better wages and benefits, and more secure employment than do the supplier firms. Supplier firms tend to hire more women, who are almost always given lower pay. Often, though they actually work more than full time, these women are formally classed as part-time workers and receive no benefits.

Korea, North and South

The Korean Peninsula has been the source of some of the most enduring international tensions in East Asia. After centuries of unity under one government, the peninsula is now divided between communist and inward-looking North Korea and capitalist, more cosmopolitan, and newly democratic South Korea.

Physically, Korea juts out from the Asian continent like a thumb (Figure 9.21). Two rivers, the Yalu (Amnok in Korean) and the Tumen, separate the peninsula from the Chinese mainland and a small area of Russian Siberia. A chaotic jumble of low-lying mountains covers much of North Korea and stretches along the east into South Korea, covering nearly 70 percent of the peninsula. In this mountainous zone there is little level land for settlement, and ground communication from valley to valley is difficult. Along the western side of Korea, alluvial plains slope toward the Yellow Sea, and most people live on these western slopes and plains. Although the peninsula is surrounded by water, its climate is essentially continental because it lies so close to the huge Asian landmass. The same cyclic monsoon that "inhales" and "exhales" over the Asian continent (see pages 414–415) brings hot wet summers and cold dry winters.

The Creation of Two Koreas

Scholars think that present-day Koreans are descended primarily from people who migrated in from the Altai Mountains in western Mongolia. The Korean language appears to be most closely akin to languages from this region. Other ethnic groups—Chinese, Manchurians,

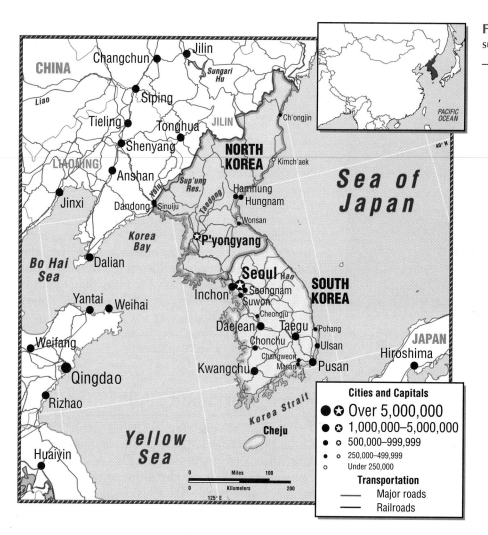

FIGURE 9.21 The Korea subregion.

Japanese, and Mongols—have migrated into the peninsula and influenced events there significantly.

Korea was a unified country as early as A.D. 668. Chinese Confucian values and Buddhism have influenced its educational, political, and legal systems. Korea is noted for early advances in mathematics and medicine, and for a system of printing by movable type; this form of printing, developed by 1234, predated the Gutenberg press in Europe by 200 years. From 1910 to 1945, Japan occupied Korea and treated it as a colony: a source of cheap minerals and agricultural raw materials for Japan's own growing manufacturing centers. Resentment grew in Korea and nationalist sentiment increased. Western ideas, including communism, flooded into Korea, competing with the more traditional Confucian and Buddhist beliefs. Labor unions and other social movements developed, which remain influential to this day.

As World War II was drawing to an end in August 1945, the Soviet Union declared war against Japan and invaded Manchuria and the northern part of Korea. Rather than allow the entire country to come under Soviet control, the United States brought the war to a rapid close and proposed dividing Korea at the 38th parallel. The United States took control of the southern half of this peninsula and the Soviet Union the northern half. Over the next few years, the United States held elections in the south, recognized South Korea's independence, and withdrew its troops. Meanwhile, in the north, the Korean and Soviet Communists constructed a robust military and political structure. In June 1950, North Korean forces attacked the south. The United States soon came to the south's defense, leading a UN force that fought a three-year war against North Korea, the Soviet Union, and China. The Korean War brought huge losses of life on both sides and utter devastation of the peninsula's infrastructure.

Although an armistice brought the fighting to an end in 1953, north and south each adopted a vociferous nationalist stance that has amounted to 50 years of hostile competition. Both elaborated on the ancient Korean concept of *chuche*, which means "the right to govern yourself in your own way." In North Korea, *chuche* is interpreted as unquestioned loyalty to the

A North Korean woman and grandchild walk along the garden paths in a farm village in Hwanghe Province.
[Caritas/POOL/AP/Wide World Photos.]

Great Leader (there is no pretense of democracy), and a general "leave-us-alone" sentiment that occasionally takes the form of military threats to South Korea and its allies, especially Japan. North Korea, still run by a Communist dictatorship, remains isolated, in a defensive posture, and increasingly poor. In South Korea, *chuche* has come to mean vigorous individualism, coupled with pride and loyalty to one's own people. Social criticism and even violent protest are allowed, with the understanding that one's ultimate loyalty still lies with South Korea. After a series of military dictatorships,

South Korea held democratic elections in 1987. Politically, South Korea allied itself with the United States, Japan, and Europe, and sought economic revival through foreign aid and capitalist development.

Gender Roles

The cultural history of Korea bears a certain resemblance to that of China, primarily because both countries have been shaped by Confucian thought. Society is organized hierarchically; authority accrues to elder males, and in all public situations women are expected to be subservient to men. Parents prefer to have sons over daughters, in part because they believe sons will provide better income for them in their old age and that sons' wives will provide the necessary personal care. Within the household, women wield financial power, even to the point of controlling men's spending. Yet this responsibility often means that women must make insufficient funds stretch so that the earning power of the husband will not be questioned and the family lose face. Women are responsible for most of the household work, even though most women in both North and South Korea now work outside the home. Men are expected to maintain the family's more public social and economic connections. After work, they meet along the streets and in shops to drink, eat, tell stories, play games, and make personal connections that can facilitate everyday life for the entire family.

Contrasting Economies

Table 9.3 gives some indication of the present-day differences between North and South Korea. Economically

TABLE 9.3

Comparative statistics for North and South Korea

	Land area (sq mi)	Population (per sq mi)	HDI rank	Population	Percent natural increase	Infant mortality per 1000 (live births)	Life expectancy
North Korea	46,490	477	75	22,200,000	1.9	39	66
South Korea	38,120	1218	30	46,400,000	0.9	11	74

Sources: 1998 World Population Data Sheet, Population Reference Bureau; and Human Development Report 1998, United Nations Development Programme.

they differ dramatically. North Korea has better physical resources for industrial development, including forests and deposits of coal and iron ore. Its many rivers descending from the mountains have considerable potential for generating hydroelectric power. South Korea has better resources for agriculture, given its flatter terrain and slightly warmer climate, which make possible the double cropping of rice and millet. Nevertheless, in recent decades South Korea has surpassed North Korea not only in agricultural production, but especially in industrial development. Its manufacturing industries now export goods throughout the world. A major economic impetus has been the development of huge corporations known as *chaebol.* South Korea's governments have assisted the *chaebol* by making credit easily available and by allowing the purchase of foreign technology patents so that Koreans could specialize in product quality and marketing, rather than in inventing. Today there are numerous facilities that produce consumer electronic equipment (televisions, stereos, computers, videocassette recorders, and microwave ovens), as well as cars, ships, vehicles, clothing, shoes, and iron and steel. Nevertheless, *chaebol* have come under increasing criticism in recent years, because the close connections to the government have led to corruption. Unwise loans and investments have destabilized the South Korean economy. Despite these problems, the South Korean system worked well enough so that today most South Koreans, who were extremely poor at the end of the Korean War, can now afford the products they formerly only exported. For example, even in rural areas where incomes are low, 90 percent of households have a refrigerator, an electric rice cooker, and a propane gas range, and many have telephones and color television sets.

North Korea has seen a few benefits from communist economic policies, particularly the widespread availability of basic health care and education. In general, however, its economy is in an alarming state of deterioration. Its industries are inefficient, its workers poorly motivated; and since the demise of the Soviet Union, North Korea has suffered a loss of markets, raw materials, fuel, and technical training. Agriculture has been failing for several years, and recurrent cycles of floods and droughts have brought on extensive famine. Though the government has been unwilling to release much information, it is possible that up to 2 million people have died of hunger. The government has responded ineffectively to this dire situation. Collectives remain the dominant form of agricultural production, and only very small plots are allowed for private production of vegetables and fruit, and raising small animals. Nevertheless, small farms are so popular (and apparently profitable) that by the mid-1990s virtually every spare inch of land, including playgrounds and parks, was cultivated in vegetables.

Mongolia

VIGNETTE As their truck descended onto a broad plain within the high Altai Mountains of Mongolia, the visitors saw two horsemen herding hundreds of sheep. One of the two horsemen, a sun-tanned man in his 60s, rode over, dismounted, and greeted the two Americans (and their interpreter) with a smile and a query as to their state of health. He wore a traditional knee-length coat, fastened at the side and the shoulder with buttons and belted with a silk sash. His black leather boots were in a Western style. Anthropologists Cynthia Beall and Melvyn Goldstein were to learn that his easy, confident demeanor was typical of Mongolians. He seemed amused to have found these strangers popping up among the sheep on this normally lonely sweep of grazing land.

They had spoken for only a few moments when the Mongolian herder said cheerfully, "You know, I heard on the radio that your Foreign Minister Baker has visited our capital and that our two countries are now friends. That is good. Please come to visit my camp later. It's not far from [where you are headed]. We can talk more then. I have many questions to ask you about America, and I have a lot to say about [how things are changing in Mongolia]."

In their book, *The Changing World of Mongolia's Nomads* (1994), Melvyn Goldstein and Cynthia Beall admit that this encounter shattered their assumptions that Mongolians would be wary of outsiders, hesitant to express themselves, and unaware of the outside world.

Mongolia is a sovereign country of about 2.25 million people (Figure 9.22). They occupy a territory so large that the average density is nearly the lowest on earth, at 3.6 persons per square mile (1.4 persons per square kilometer). For thousands of years, the economy has been based on the nomadic herding of five kinds of animals: sheep, goats, camels, horses, and cattle (yaks). Today, at least one-third of the population are still engaged in rural activities in some way related to this traditional lifestyle.

For more than 60 years (1924–1989), Mongolia was a Communist country under the Mongolian People's Revolutionary Party, which looked to the Soviet Union for guidance. Russian advisers and technicians wielded considerable influence in organizing the economy and resources into a system of central planning. During this time, Mongolia was partially industrialized and the old extended family households were turned into collectives. Some continued to herd

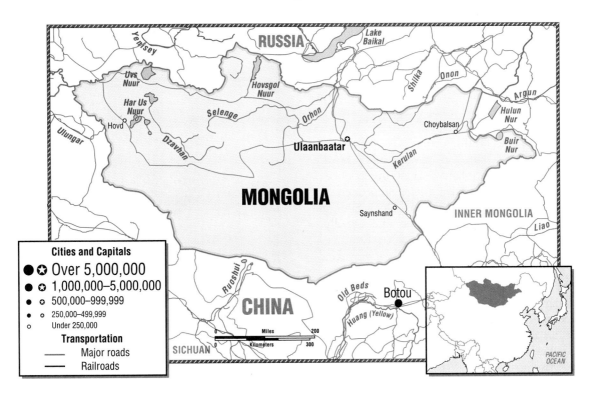

FIGURE 9.22 The Mongolia subregion.

animals, others engaged in sedentary livestock production, and some farmed crops. During this era, an elaborate system of social services subsidized by the Soviets was introduced; it included health care, education, and pensions. Poverty was rare. Then, in 1989, Mongolians decided to do away with central planning and follow a market system. The move to a market economy has been a difficult transition, accompanied by the loss of support from an increasingly stressed Soviet Union. The general quality of life is lower now than under communism.

Physical Geography

The Mongolian Plateau lies in the heart of Central Asia, directly north of China and south of Siberia. It is high, cold, and dry, with an extreme continental climate. The physical geography of Mongolia can be broken down into four major zones. In the extreme south and extending to the border with China is the Gobi Desert. This is actually a very dry grassland that grades into true desert in especially dry years or when overgrazed. To the east and northeast of the Gobi is a huge, rolling, somewhat moister grassland. The remaining two zones are Mongolia's two primary mountain ranges: the forested Hangai (Khangai) in north-central Mongolia and the grass- and shrub-covered Altai (Altay) sweeping around west and south and into the Gobi Desert in the southeast.

History

No one is sure just where the ancestors of the Mongolians came from, but it is safe to say that they descend from groups of people who have occupied the massive mountains and plains of Central Asia for more than 40,000 years. Scholars have noted that **nomadic pastoralism**—the tending of grazing animals—is one of the most complex agricultural traditions ever invented by humans—one that dates at least as far back as the cultivation of plants (10,000 to 8000 years). Not only do nomadic herders understand the complex biological characteristics of the animals they breed, but they must know intimately the ecology, the seasonal changes in vegetation, and the physical geography of the land they traverse with their herds. Mongolian pastoralists have perfected management systems and technologies, like the portable *ger*, that make possible frequent moves of whole communities and hundreds of animals over the course of the year.

At the beginning of the twentieth century, after long years of serfdom under Manchurian rule, Mongolians were among some of the poorest people in Asia. Profits from herding went to the feudal elite, and trade was monopolized by Chinese merchants who sent their profits home rather than investing in Mongolian development. In 1921, after considerable turmoil, Mongolian independence from China was declared, and some years later a Communist revolution took

465

place. Sixty-five years of deep social reform and close connection with Russia began.

Communism brought the end of feudalism, and in time the nomadic herder economy was reorganized along socialist lines without drastic disturbance of traditional lifeways. By 1989, there was nearly universal education through middle school, and adult literacy reached 93 percent. Health care was available as it never had been before: life expectancy rose drastically, and the previously high infant mortality figures began to drop. The nomadic herder who impressed the American anthropologists Melvyn Goldstein and Cynthia Beall in the early 1990s was undoubtedly a beneficiary of these educational and social reforms.

Gender Roles

In the long-ago days of the Mongol Empire (fourteenth century), women may have enjoyed a status more or less equal to that of men, but they lost their more egalitarian position with the introduction of Lamaist Buddhism in the sixteenth century and the start of Manchurian rule in the seventeenth century. Nevertheless, in the pastoral economy of today, men and women share many tasks. Women often breed animals and tend the mothers and their young, preserve meat and milk, and produce numerous essentials from animal hides and hair, including felt, yarn, and furs. Men do many of these tasks also. Women provide the materials for house (*ger*) construction, and also the furnishings for the interiors. Both boys and girls are taught to ride horseback at an early age, and they help in the herding activities. As they mature, women become more responsible than men for routines of daily life: care of children, food preparation and serving, home maintenance, and care of the elderly and infirm. Men are primarily engaged in managing the pasturing of the herds and arranging the marketing of the animals and by-products; and they undertake other activities—such as the occasional planting of grain crops like barley and wheat—that are carried out beyond the home compound.

The condition of Mongolian women rose rapidly under communism. The daily work of women herders was valued, and like their husbands they were eligible for pensions as they aged. Women could leave destructive marriages because there was support for them and their children. A few women became teachers, judges, and party officials; and soon they were better represented in institutions of higher education.

Economic and Gender Issues

By 1985, nomadic herding and forestry accounted for less than 18 percent of the produced national income and somewhat less than 30 percent of the labor force.

Mongolia is one of the most youthful countries in the world. Half the population is under 21 and three-fourths under 35. As new democracy and capitalism get off to a rocky start, the urban landscape of Ulaanbaatar still features yurts (*gers*), the traditional nomadic pastoral form of housing. [Thierry Falise/Gamma-Liaison.]

Like the USSR and China, Mongolia emphasized the development of mining and heavy industry; by 1985, mining and industry, communications, transport, and construction accounted for about 48 percent of the produced national income and one-third of the labor force.

At the end of the 1980s, the disintegration of the USSR brought drastic social and economic changes. In particular, Mongolia became the first Communist country in Asia to make a commitment to the development of a market economy. The transition to a market economy has not gone smoothly. With the disappearance of Soviet support, the chief export market and source of imports vanished and new connections had to be made. The highly trained Soviet managers went, too, leaving behind few Mongolians trained to replace them—a phenomenon similar to that when a colony is abruptly freed. With the loss of export markets have come layoffs and factory closings. Even the nomadic herders have experienced a serious decline in their standard of living, despite the fact that they are self-sufficient in food and shelter production. Nationally, the incomes of both men and women dropped by 30 percent; by 1995, more than one-quarter of the population lived in poverty. The funds to support the elaborate human services infrastructure were suddenly cut to the bone. Between 1990 and 1992, total public expenditure dropped by 58 percent, but education was cut by 69 percent. Kindergartens and rural boarding schools closed, and many older students left school to help their families cope with the new circumstances. Many young adults remain unemployed and rootless, turning to substance abuse for solace. Street children have lately proliferated in Ulaanbaatar, the outcasts of disintegrating families.

As a result of the jolting changes of the past decade, women may be losing some of the progress they had enjoyed. Especially distressing is the report that women have lost their voice in officialdom. Few women even ran for election when that became possible, and elected reformers have eliminated legal protections for females in the new laws. For example, the proposed Family Code Law assigns inheritance of animals and land leasing rights only to sons.

Nonetheless, women's networks are developing to regain equity in access to education, jobs, health care, housing, legal protections, and credit. And there are many reports of successful efforts by women entrepreneurs: an out-of-work truck mechanic received a small loan and put herself and her brothers to work repairing trucks. A woman who used to make sausages in a state-run meat plant now makes sausages in her kitchen, employing 14 of her fellow workers. She peddles the sausages on the streets. As in so many other countries moving from communism to a market economy, the informal economy of street peddlers and small-scale service people seems to be on the verge of a boom.

REFLECTIONS ON EAST ASIA

The opening up of China to market forces and to outside influences presents huge economic opportunities to other East Asian countries. Most have already begun investing in the rapidly growing industrial coastal zones, the SEZs. But the present tendency to hang so many regional hopes on China's debut into capitalism could backfire. It is not at all clear yet how the rapid social changes going on in China will be worked out politically either within the country or internationally. Will economic liberalization lead to more political freedom for ordinary people and more public input in things like environmental policy? Will China's emerging policies toward Hong Kong and Taiwan be those that bring continued rapid economic growth, social

change, and outside contact, or will they bring a reversion to greater control of economic forces and of people, and a break with the international community?

Leadership within the region is in question. Residual animosities linger toward Japan for the excesses it committed during its imperial period before and during World War II. Whether Japan retains the confidence of fellow Asians and a leadership role in East and Southeast Asia may depend on how it deals with its own internal financial crises and whether it opens its own markets to its neighbors. China may bolster its position as regional leader if it decides to woo the interest of the Overseas Chinese, many of whom were forced to leave China during the revolution but have since prospered in Taiwan, or Singapore, or Malaysia. Politically, there is no clear leader in the effort to bring more participatory democracy to East Asia. Although variations on parliamentary democracy appear to be gaining as the dominant political system in East Asia, the actual distribution of power tends overwhelmingly to remain with a male elite.

A combination of factors all related to present population control will affect the future. These factors include shrinking family size, the increase in the relative numbers of the retired and elderly, and the fact that women are no longer available to stay home to care for children and elders. To cope with these changes, governments may have to spend more on social services and be content with slower economic growth. The most emphasized population issue in East Asia today is the need to curtail population growth; yet the issue that may most influence the future is that of finding a way to care for large numbers of aging people.

There is also the matter of how East Asia will deal with the world's cultural diversity. Barring a major reversal of policy on the part of China, contact between all of East Asia and the rest of the world will increase significantly. Not only will outsiders from all backgrounds be more prominent, but women and minority groups within each country are bound to become more politically assertive. A possible outcome is that East Asian society will become more welcoming to other cultures and to the idea of women acting in expanded roles.

Finally, East Asia, along with the rest of the industrialized world, will be considering how to balance the desire for a clean, safe environment with the desire to lead consumer lifestyles. In this regard, the tremendous talents of innovation and synthesis found throughout East Asia may be called on even more in the future than they have in the past.

467

Selected Themes and Concepts

1. The landforms of East Asia can be visualized as a series of steps descending from the Xizang-Qinghai Plateau.

2. East Asia has two contrasting climate zones: the dry continental west and the monsoon east.

3. The philosophy of **Confucianism** teaches that the best organizational model for the state and society is a hierarchy modeled after the patriarchal family. Confucianism has influenced both family and government structure throughout the region.

4. Ninety percent of China's people are concentrated on one-sixth of the land, in the eastern part of the country. This is China's heartland, the center from which the country has been governed for thousands of years. This is also China's most highly productive agricultural region.

5. China's hinterland is the west and north. In this less densely settled area, including Mongolia, people have traditionally practiced **nomadic pastoralism** (the raising of grazing animals) and some farming.

6. The region has in the past been split between two economic models. Japan, South Korea, and Taiwan practice a model of free market capitalism developed by Japan. China, Mongolia, and North Korea practice a form of communism influenced by the Soviet Union. Now Mongolia and China are making the transition to more free market economies.

7. China's strategies for market reform include the **responsibility system,** giving the managers of state-owned enterprises the right and responsibility to make their operations work efficiently, and the designation of **Special Economic Zones (SEZs),** selected cities and surrounding areas that encourage foreign investment.

8. The Chinese Communists implemented a policy of **regional self-sufficiency:** each region was expected to build agricultural and industrial sectors of equal strength to even out the national distribution of income. Now this policy is being abandoned, and disparities of wealth are growing between inland rural regions of China and the booming cities of the coast. A **floating population,** of jobless or underemployed people, has left economically depressed rural areas for the cities.

9. China is the most populous country in the world, and Japan and Taiwan are densely populated as well. Most East Asian countries have dramatically lowered their fertility rates, as a result of urbanization and industrialization and, in the case of China, a policy of one child per family. A future consequence will be an aging population with few children to care for the elderly.

10. The countries of China, Japan, and Taiwan all have single dominant ethnic groups that share the country with a diversity of other ethnic groups in an often uneasy relationship. These minority ethnic groups often live in peripheral areas—in the mountains or hinterlands—although in Japan and Taiwan many individual members of such groups are becoming absorbed into the dominant society.

11. The Chinese people have battled floods and droughts for centuries. Today the threat is more severe than ever owing to human activities that remove water-absorbing soil and vegetation.

Selected Readings

Bell, Linda S. For better, for worse: Women and the world market in rural China. *Modern China* 20, no. 2 (1994): 180–210.

Bih-er, Chou, and Cal Clark and Janet Clark. *Women in Taiwan Politics: Overcoming Barriers to Women's Participation in a Modernizing Society.* Boulder, CO: Lynne Rienner, 1990.

Blunden, Caroline, and Mark Elvin. *Cultural Atlas of China,* rev. ed. New York: Facts on File, 1998.

Cannon, Terry, and Alan Jenkins. *The Geography of Contemporary China: The Impact of Deng Xiaoping's Decade.* London: Routledge, 1990.

Duara, Prasenjit. *Rescuing History from the Nation: Questioning Narratives of Modern China.* Chicago: University of Chicago Press, 1995.

Einhorn, Barbara, and Eileen Janes Yeo, eds. *Women and Market Societies: Crisis and Opportunity.* Aldershot, U.K.: Edward Elgar, 1995.

Fairbank, John King. *China, a New History.* Cambridge, MA: Belknap Press of Harvard University Press, 1992.

Fan, C. Cindy. Economic opportunities and internal migration: A case study of Guangdong Province, China. *Professional Geographer* 48, no. 1 (1996): 28–45.

Fitzgerald, Stephen. *China and the Overseas Chinese: A Study of Peking's Changing Policy 1949–1970.* Cambridge: Cambridge University Press, 1972.

Gernet, Jacques. *Daily Life in China on the Eve of the Mongol Invasion 1250–1276*, trans. H. M. Wright. New York: Macmillan, 1962.

Goldstein, Melvyn C., and Cynthia M. Beall. *Nomads of Western Tibet: The Survival of a Way of Life*. Berkeley: University of California Press, 1990.

Griffin, Keith, ed. *Poverty and the Transition to a Market Economy in Mongolia*. New York: St. Martin's Press, 1995.

Jaschok, Maria, and Suzanne Miers. *Women and Chinese Patriarchy*. London: Zed, 1994.

Kim Elaine H., and Chungmoo Choi, eds. *Dangerous Women — Gender & Korean Nationalism*. New York: Routledge, 1998.

Kulp, Daniel Harrison II. *Country Life in South China — The Sociology of Familism*. Vol. 1. *Phenix Village, Kwantung, China*. Taipei, Taiwan: Ch'eng-Wen, 1966.

Lieberthal, Kenneth G., Shuen-fu Lin, and Ernest P. Young, eds. *Constructing China — The Interaction of Culture and Economics*. Ann Arbor: Center for Chinese Studies, University of Michigan, 1997.

Mackerras, Colin, and Amanda Yorke. *The Cambridge Handbook of Contemporary China*. Cambridge: Cambridge University Press, 1991.

Naughton, Barry. *Growing Out of the Plan: Chinese Economic Reform, 1978–1993*. Cambridge: Cambridge University Press, 1995.

Overmyer, Daniel L. *Religions of China: The World as a Living System*. San Francisco: Harper & Row, 1986.

Pope, Geoffrey G. Ancient Asia's cutting edge. *Natural History* 102, no. 5 (1993):54–59.

Reingold, Edwin M. *Chrysanthemums and Thorns — The Untold Story of Modern Japan*. New York: St. Martin's Press, 1992.

Schell, Orville. *To Get Rich Is Glorious: China in the Eighties*. New York: Pantheon, 1984.

Sinkule, Barbara J., and Leonard Ortolano. *Implementing Environmental Policy in China*. Westport, CT: Praeger, 1995.

Smith, Christopher J. *China People and Places in the Land of One Billion*. Boulder, CO: Westview Press, 1991.

Stafford, Charles. *The Roads of Chinese Childhood: Learning and Identification in Angang* [Taiwan]. Cambridge: Cambridge University Press, 1995.

Strassberg, Richard E., trans. *Inscribed Landscapes: Travel Writing from Imperial China*. Berkeley: University of California Press, 1994.

Theroux, Paul. *Riding the Iron Rooster: By Train Through China*. New York: Putnam's, 1988.

Tian, Gang. The emergence of Shanghai's role as entrepot center since the mid-1980s. *Journal of Contemporary China*, no. 4 (1994): 3–27.

Wong, How Man, and Adel A. Dajani. *Islamic Frontiers of China: Silk Road Images*. London: Scorpion, 1990.

Woronoff, Jon. *The Japanese Social Crisis*. New York: St. Martin's Press, 1997.

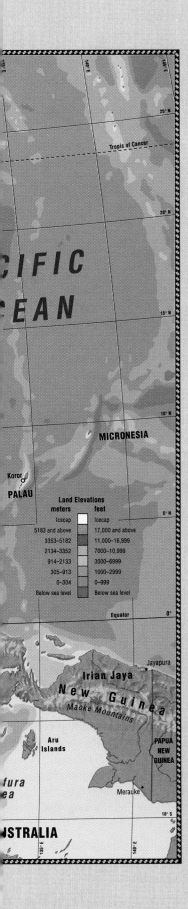

CHAPTER

TEN

SOUTHEAST ASIA

INTRODUCTION TO SOUTHEAST ASIA

Planeloads of customers, tourists, and businesspeople fly in from Japan, Germany, Australia, and the United States. They land in Bangkok, Hanoi, Jakarta, and a host of other Southeast Asian cities. All are eager to partake in some way of Southeast Asia's economic miracle. But among the travelers are those coming to fulfill fantasies—sexual fantasies that apparently can be lived out in this region of the world better than in any other. In Ho Chi Minh City (Saigon), rickshaws take passengers to hotels and business meetings, but they also take them to the brothels, bars, and massage parlors where the girls (and boys) are. Diminutive sex workers with waist-length hair, mini dresses, and elbow-length gloves ride Honda motorbikes, calling out enticingly to prospective customers.

To begin a regional chapter with a reference to the geography of the sex trade might be an obvious and odious ploy to gain readership were it not the case that, at least in the popular press, the regional image of Southeast Asia is very much caught up in international sex tourism. Even government officials have recognized the importance of sex work in the region. Serving on a panel discussion of global tourism, a Thai official states that it is sex workers "who attract most of the tourists. . . . They have saved our economy from bankruptcy, really." Whether or not that is actually true, the sex tourists are coming in ever increasing numbers. Tourism as a whole increased in Thailand from 250,000 in 1965 to more than 4 million a year by 1990.

General economic growth in Southeast Asia has been phenomenal over the last several decades, as laborers have left the countryside to obtain low-wage work in clothing, shoe, and appliance factories. Part of the economic growth across the region has been the sex trade. This trade, usually based on the work of young women and girls (but also young men and boys), raises dozens of questions relevant to all sectors of the economy. These questions concern the meaning and goals of development, the use of human resources, and the geography of gender, human rights, disease, and work environments. Indeed, as the geographer Jonathan Rigg observes, Southeast Asia is a stage on which the relative merits and detriments of all kinds of development are being debated.

This chapter is not about the geography of the sex trade. To be sure, the subject comes up now and then, but a more central theme of the chapter is to ask the reader to reflect on the real costs of all the "commodities" Southeast Asia sells, whether trees, or athletic shoes, or shirts, or its young women and men and children. The extreme exploitation in the Southeast Asian sex trade is a metaphor for many other aspects of commerce and consumption based on unfair transactions—not just in Southeast Asia, but in the wider world. As Jeremy Seabrook, whose narratives on cities in the developing world are cited often in this chapter, observes: "The buyers and the shoppers in the malls and galleries of the world . . . are . . . safeguarded from any knowledge of the real cost of the commodities their money procures for them. . . . One young woman I met in a garment factory in Jakarta suggested every item should have a 'price of pain' printed on it, so that people would know how many tears and how much sweat are stitched into every article."

Themes to Look For

Since the late 1970s, Southeast Asia has been cast as a model of rapid development that other regions might emulate. By the late 1990s, that role was called into serious question because of a wide range of problems: economic recession, evidence of widespread corruption and cronyism among officials and private businesspeople, and environmental problems. In this chapter I cover these issues as well as the more long-term cultural and social issues that reflect life in this region. The themes of this chapter include the following:

1. Many distinct culture groups have lived side by side for centuries in Southeast Asia, absorbing a spectrum of cultural influences from outside, yet retaining their uniqueness.

2. Human strategies for managing physical resources have been influenced by social and economic factors, but also by the tropical environment. The rich soils of river valleys and deltas, and the tropical rain forests in the uplands and islands, have been intensively used. Large numbers of people are supported, but there have been consequences ranging from soil erosion to flooding.

3. The countries of the region range from primarily agricultural lands just beginning to modernize (Laos, Cambodia) to fiercely competitive economic "tigers" with significant industrialization (Indonesia, Malaysia, Thailand, Singapore). Throughout the region, workers as a group endure low wages and unhealthful working conditions.

4. Although family structure contains a patriarchal overlay, it has some unique features that give the wife more power than in many other world regions.

Terms to Be Aware Of

Many of the region's inhabitants want to dispense with place-names that connote past colonial status. Numerous names that are familiar to Westerners are not the names now preferred by the people of the region. In this book I generally use the place-name officially preferred by the locality. In some cases I have used the now-preferred name and given the older, more familiar, Western name in parentheses. In the case of Burma and Cambodia, however, I have made an exception to this practice: Burma is the old name, now being revived, for Myanmar; and Cambodia, the older name for Kampuchea, is also now being revived. Hence, *Burma* and *Cambodia* are used in this text.

PHYSICAL PATTERNS

Landforms

Southeast Asia is a region of peninsulas and islands. Although the region stretches over a space nearly as extensive as Europe, most of that space is ocean. In fact, the area of all the land in Southeast Asia amounts to less than half of that in the contiguous United States. There is a large mainland peninsula, sometimes called Indochina, that extends to the south of China. It is occupied by Burma, Thailand, Laos, Cambodia, and Vietnam. This peninsula then itself sprouts an especially long, thin peninsular appendage that is shared by outlying parts of Burma, Thailand, a part of Malaysia, and the city-state of Singapore at the tip. To the south and east of the peninsulas lies a group, or **archipelago,** of large and small islands, fanning out over an area bigger than the continental United States. They are grouped into the countries of Malaysia, Indonesia—Indonesia alone has some 17,000 islands—and the Philippines—comprising 7000 islands. The independent country of Brunei shares the large island of Borneo with Malaysia and Indonesia. All this region except the northernmost part of Burma lies within the tropics, with the islands lying on, and to both sides of, the equator.

The irregular shape and topography of Southeast Asia are the result of the same tectonic forces that were unleashed when India left the African Plate and crashed into Eurasia (discussed first in Chapter 8). India now lies at the northern end of the roughly semicircular Indian-Australian Plate, which is pushing under the Eurasian Plate (see Figure 1.8). The collision has pushed up the Himalaya Mountains and, to the east and west of the crash zone, has forced up bunches of wrinkles in the land as though one had kicked into a throw rug. The eastern wrinkles are a series of ridges and gorges that bend out of the Tibetan Plateau and turn south. They then fan out to the west and east, creating wider valleys in the south, toward the sea. Each valley between the ridges hosts a river: the Irrawaddy, the Salween, the Mekong, and others. These are the landforms of Burma, Thailand, Laos, and Vietnam.

Much of island Southeast Asia actually sits on a submerged lobe of the Eurasian Plate, extending south from the main bulk of the plate. In fact, the curve formed by the Indonesian islands of New Guinea, East Timor, Bali, Java, and Sumatra conforms approximately to the shape of the lobe's leading edge. As the Indian-Australian Plate plunges beneath the Eurasian Plate along this curve, the process has generated hundreds of volcanoes, especially on the islands of Sumatra and Java. Volcanoes are also being created in the Philippines, where the Philippine Plate (part of the Pacific Plate) is pushing against the eastern edge of the Eurasian Plate's southern lobe. The volcanoes of the Philippines are part of the Pacific "Ring of Fire" (see page 21). Volcanic explosions, and the aftermath of mud flows and landslides, endanger and complicate the lives of many in Southeast Asia. In the long run, however, the volcanic material creates new land and provides minerals that can enrich the soil for farmers.

The now submerged shelf of the Eurasian continent that extends under the Southeast Asian peninsulas and islands was above sea level during recurring ice ages, when the world's water was taken up by glaciers (Figure 10.1). The exposed shelf, known as Sundaland, allowed ancient humans and Asian land animals (elephants, tigers, rhinoceros, proboscis monkeys, and orangutans) to travel south into the islands of Southeast Asia. Sundaland remained exposed until about 16,000 years ago. A second exposed continental shelf, known as Wallacea, was attached to Australia and stopped just off the eastern edge of the present-day island of Bali. Sundaland and Wallacea never met because they were, and are, separated by a deep ocean trench known as Huxley's Line. This trench extends north from Bali through the Macassar Strait and along the western side of the Philippines. Humans using watercraft were probably the only major land creatures to cross the gap; dogs, however, appear to have made the trip with them. They made their way to New Guinea and Australia. But Balinese tigers, for example, were not able to spread east, and Australian kangaroos could not move west.

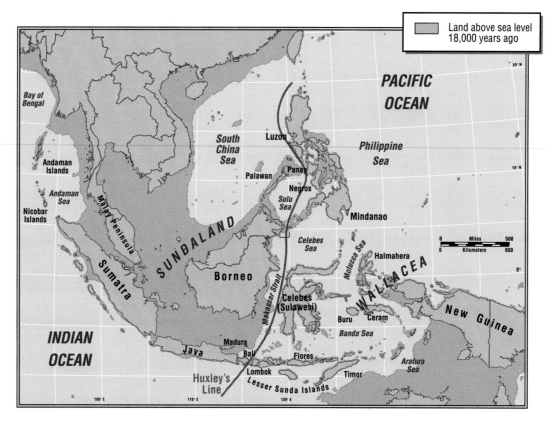

FIGURE 10.1 Sundaland and Wallacea 18,000 years ago. [Adapted from Victor T. King, *The Peoples of Borneo* (Oxford: Blackwell, 1993), p. 63.]

Climate

The tropical climate of this region is distinguished by continuous warm temperatures in the lowlands—consistently above 65°F—and heavy rain (Figure 10.2). The rainfall is the result of two major processes: the continental "breathing" (see Chapter 1) that brings the monsoons; and the intertropical convergence zone (ITCZ), a band of rising warm air circling the earth roughly around the equator (see Figure 7.2). The wet summer monsoon occurs from May to October, when the warming up of the Eurasian landmass sucks moist air in from the surrounding seas. Between November and April there is a long dry season on the mainland, when the seasonal cooling of Eurasia causes dry air from the inner continent to blow out toward the sea. However, for the many islands of Southeast Asia, the winter can also be wet, because the air that blows out from the continent picks up moisture again as it passes over the seas. The air releases its moisture as rain after ascending high enough to cool down. With rains coming from both the monsoon and the ITCZ, island Southeast Asia receives copious rain year-round, enough to support dense tropical vegetation over much of the landscape, and is one of the wettest regions of the world.

Periodically, the normal patterns of rainfall are interrupted, especially in island Southeast Asia; serious drought is the result. In recent years these periodic droughts, which occur on an 8- to 13-year-long cycle, have been recognized as part of the El Niño phenomenon (see Figure 11.3). In an El Niño event, the usual patterns of circulation in the Pacific are reversed. Ocean temperatures are cooler than usual in the west near Southeast Asia. Instead of warm wet air rising and condensing as rainfall, cool drier air sits at the ocean surface. In 1997, an El Niño event brought drought and cool temperatures to the countries of Malaysia and Indonesia. Crops failed, springs and streams dried up, and the heavy cool air prevented air pollution from venting into the upper atmosphere, especially the pollution caused by auto and industry exhaust and forest fires. The result was the worst case of widespread air contamination ever experienced in the region.

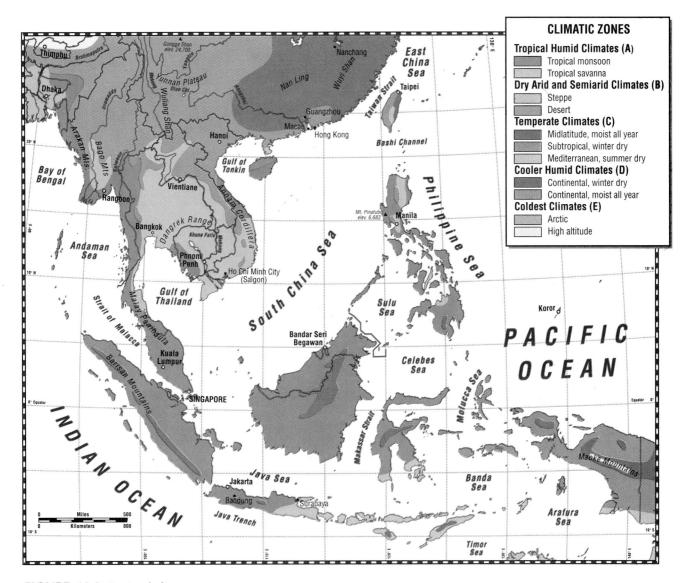

FIGURE 10.2 Regional climate.

The soils in Southeast Asia are typical of the tropics: although not particularly fertile, they will support dense and prolific vegetation when left undisturbed for long periods. The high temperatures and damp conditions promote the rapid decay of **detritus**—dead plant material and insects—and the quick release of useful minerals. These minerals are taken up directly by the living forest system rather than enriching the soil. Some of the world's most impressive rain forests thrived in this region until very recently. Today the forests are being cleared at record rates, especially by multinational logging companies, but also by local people seeking farmland (see the section on deforestation later in this chapter, papes 495–496). Often the refuse is burned, another cause of serious air pollution.

HUMAN PATTERNS

Southeast Asia's position as a group of islands and peninsulas surrounded by seas has for centuries made it easily accessible to ocean trade and cultural influence from outside. First settled by migrations from the Eurasian continent, it later came under the influence of Arab, Indian, Chinese, and European colonizers. In the twentieth century, the region emerged from a long period of colonial domination ready to profit from selling manufactured goods to its former colonizers. Its

Dayak farmer Abdur Rani plants cassava in a section of Kalimantan rain forest ravaged earlier by loggers. The haze—like that which covered most of Indonesia, Malaysia, and parts of other Southeast Asian countries in 1997—is smoke from forest fires. [Michael Yamashita/Woodfin Camp & Associates.]

economic success has not yet been enough to catapult the majority out of poverty, but signs of the region's industrialization are declining birth rates (the demographic transition), growing urbanization, and rising rates of literacy.

The Peopling of Southeast Asia

The modern indigenous populations of Southeast Asia stem from two migrations widely separated in time. The first of these migrations, a group of hunters and gatherers called Australo-Melanesians, moved from southern Eurasia into the exposed landmass of Sundaland about 60,000 years ago. They were the ancestors of the indigenous peoples of New Guinea and Australia, and their descendants still live elsewhere in the region as well, in small pockets throughout mainland and island Southeast Asia. The second migration began about 5000 years ago, when a culture of skilled farmers and seafarers from South China, named Austronesians, migrated first to Taiwan, then to the Philippines, and then into island Southeast Asia and the Malay Peninsula. Other groups of these Austronesians appear to have moved southward along the coast of China and Vietnam. Some of these sea travelers eventually moved westward, to southern India and as far as Madagascar off the east coast of Africa. They also moved eastward, to the far reaches of the Pacific islands (see Chapter 11). It is important to observe that there are today no clear biological or geographic boundaries between the descendants of the early Australo-Melanesians and the more recent Austronesians. Rather, there is a gradual grading from one to the other, the result of continual intermixing of peoples in Southeast Asia.

Further Cultural Influences

Southeast Asia has continued to be shaped by a steady stream of cultural influences from outside the region. These influences were so numerous in part because the sea that touches or surrounds all the countries except Laos brought ships and travelers. The shifting winds of the monsoon also played a role. In the spring and summer, the monsoon winds blowing from the west carried seaborne traders, religious teachers, and occasionally even invading armies from the coasts of India and Arabia. These newcomers brought religions—Hinduism, Buddhism, and Islam—and goods, such as cotton textiles, mangoes, and tamarinds, deep into the Indonesian archipelago. The traders and teachers penetrated the islands and as far as Cambodia, Laos, Vietnam, and China on the mainland. The blending of these many cultural influences is obvious in the region today.

The merchant ships sailed home on the monsoon winds of autumn and winter that blow from the northeast. They carried Southeast Asia's people, as well as spices, bananas, sugarcane, silks, domesticated pigs and chickens, and other goods to the wider world. China was also influential, especially in Vietnam, which it ruled on and off for centuries. After the tenth century, Vietnam resisted conquest, becoming a major bulwark that kept China's empire from expanding into the rest of the region. Yet another strong influence has been Islam. That religion came to the region mainly through South Asia, after India fell to Muslim conquests in the thirteenth century. Today Islam is a major religion in the region, and Indonesia has the world's largest Muslim population.

Colonialism

Over the last five centuries, Europe, Japan, and the United States have been among the foreign areas influencing Southeast Asia. All three established colonies or quasi-colonies in the region (Figure 10.3). The Portuguese were drawn to Southeast Asia's fabled spice trade in the fifteenth century. Sailing around Africa, they reached India in 1498 and Sumatra, Indonesia, by 1515. While their better ships and weapons gave them an advantage, their anti-Islamic and pro-Catholic policies provoked strong resistance in Southeast Asia. Meanwhile, by 1540 the Spanish had established trade links across the Pacific between the Philippines and their colonies in the Americas, especially Mexico. Like the Portuguese, they practiced a style of colonial domination grounded in Catholicism; they met less resistance, however, because their attitude toward non-Christians was more relaxed. The Spanish ruled the Philippines for 400 years, and as a result that archipel-

ago is the most deeply Westernized and certainly the most Catholic part of Southeast Asia.

The Dutch were the most economically successful of the European colonial powers in Southeast Asia. From the sixteenth to the nineteenth centuries, under the auspices of the Dutch East India Company, they extended their control of trade over most of what is today called Indonesia. Their privately chartered trading company was headquartered in Batavia (now Jakarta) on the island of Java. Dutch colonists were far less interested in territory than in profits, and they avoided direct administrative rule by placing local leaders in charge; in exchange for this, they obtained exclusive trading rights. The Dutch were renowned for their often bloody extermination of Southeast Asian competitors. Eventually, they became interested in export cash crops, primarily coffee, sugar, and indigo. In the nineteenth century, the Dutch diverted farmers from producing their own food to working unpaid in Dutch enterprises, especially plantations. Severe famines were the periodic result. Resistance to the Dutch often took the form of Islamic religious movements, and the rise of these movements hastened the spread of Islam throughout Indonesia. As in South Africa, the Dutch settlers made little effort to spread Christianity.

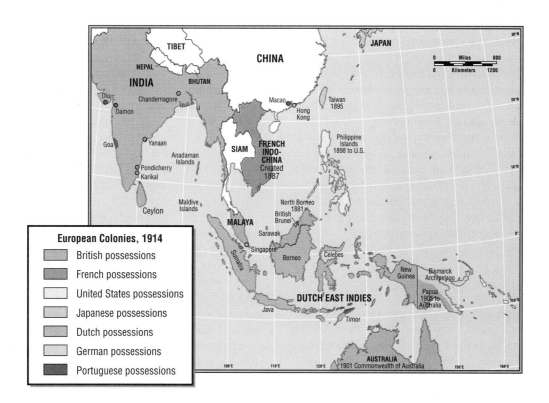

FIGURE 10.3 European colonies in Southeast Asia, 1914. [Adapted from *Hammond Times Concise Atlas of World History,* 1994, p. 101.]

The British were only slightly less ruthless and commercially motivated than their Dutch rivals. In the early nineteenth century, the British East India Company, operating with government and military powers sanctioned by the British Crown, controlled a few key ports on the Malay Peninsula. The British held these ports both for their trade value and to protect the Strait of Malacca, through which passed trade between China and Britain's empire in India. Britain extended its rule over the rest of modern Malaysia after the commercial benefits of tin mines and plantations in the interior were demonstrated in the late nineteenth century. Once Malaysia came under their rule, the British argued that Malays, and in fact all "Orientals," were incapable of governing themselves effectively and needed a "benevolent" European power to rule over them. Similar justifications were offered for the violent wars that culminated in the annexation of Burma to British India in 1885. The actual motivation for the British takeover of Burma was to gain access to trade routes to China and to extensive stands of tropical hardwoods.

In the early seventeenth century, French Catholic missionaries began actively seeking converts in Indochina, which was the name given to the eastern mainland area—comprising the modern states of Vietnam, Cambodia, and Laos. The French eventually colonized the region in the late nineteenth century, spurred on by rivalry with Britain and other European powers for greater access to the markets of nearby China.

In all of Southeast Asia, the only country to remain independent was Thailand. Like Japan, it protected its sovereignty by undergoing a massive drive toward European-style modernization; and it was adept at using diplomacy to prevent European conquest. Another factor in Thailand's ability to maintain sovereignty was that Britain and France both wanted a neutral **buffer zone** (a territory separating adversaries) between their colonial possessions on mainland Southeast Asia. This was in order to lessen the possibility for direct confrontation between the two colonial powers.

Struggles for Independence

Agitation against colonial rule began in the late nineteenth century, when Filipinos fought first against Spain and then, after the United States took control of the Philippines in 1899, against the Americans. However, independence for the Philippines and the rest of Southeast Asia had to wait until the end of World War II. By then, Europe's ability to administer its colonies was badly damaged. In part this was because of the devastation caused by the war, and in part also because, during the war, Japan had exploded the

myth of European superiority by conquering most of Southeast Asia. By the mid-1950s, the colonial powers had granted self-government to most of the region. Only Malaysia and Singapore had to wait until the early 1960s to become independent.

The most bitter battle for independence took place in the French-controlled territories of Vietnam, Laos, and Cambodia. Although all three became nominally independent in 1949, France retained political and economic power. Various nationalist leaders led resistance to continued French domination. While these leaders did not begin as communists, and in fact shared ancient antipathies toward China for its previous efforts to dominate the region, the resistance leaders accepted military assistance from now communist China and the Soviet Union when the French refused to release control. Thus the cold war was brought to mainland Southeast Asia.

By the mid-1950s, the French were losing what had become a guerrilla war centered in Vietnam. In 1954 the United States, increasingly worried about the spread of international communism, stepped in and eventually took over the Vietnam War. The resistance leaders held control of the northern half of Vietnam, while contesting control of the southern half with the United States and a U.S.-supported South Vietnamese government. After several years of brutal conflict, U.S. public opinion forced the U.S. withdrawal from the conflict in 1973. Many in the United States were turned against the war by nightly broadcasts showing gruesome pictures of burning children and village massacres, and by the loss of their own sons, as well as by revelations of the ineptness of U.S. officials. The war finally ended in 1975. During the Vietnam War more than 4.5 million people died in Indochina, including more than 58,000 Americans. Another 4.5 million on both sides were wounded, and bombs, napalm, and defoliants ruined much of the Vietnamese environment.

While the withdrawal of its forces in 1973 ranks as one of the most profound upsets in U.S. history, the suffering of Vietnam and its neighbors, Cambodia and Laos, continued. The United States imposed economic sanctions against Vietnam that lasted until 1993 and crippled its recovery from the war. Moreover, the war spilled over the border into Cambodia, where a particularly rabid revolutionary faction seized control in the mid-1970s. The apparent goal of the Khmer Rouge, as these revolutionaries were called, was to impose their ideological vision of rural communist society, which entailed destroying virtually all traces of the European colonial era. Their vision cost the lives of 2 million people who resisted, or one-quarter of the Cambodian population. Vietnam invaded Cambodia in an effort to drive out the Khmer Rouge, but in the process visited yet more suffering on the people. Laos, Cambodia's neighbor to the north, was also drawn into the conflict. Hostilities continue to occur from time to time.

Although the independence era has brought violence to some areas, it has also brought relative peace and economic development to much of Southeast Asia. Since the 1960s, the economies of Thailand, Malaysia, Singapore, Indonesia, and the Philippines have grown considerably, aided largely by industries that export manufactured products to the rich countries of the world. Some critics regard this situation as a form of neocolonialism, because the countries of the region remain dependent on markets in distant wealthy nations and often compete with each other to sell their products to their former colonizers. This stiff competition often results in wages that are too low to provide a decent standard of living, and in skimping on pollution controls and worker safety regulations.

Peaceful relations among these countries have been encouraged by high levels of political and economic cooperation, a trend that should increase with the institution of a regional free trade zone planned for soon after the year 2000. However, not everyone has benefited equally. Elites with connections to government officials have profited immensely, and much of the region's prosperity is based on the exploitation of cheap labor. Moreover, unprecedented losses of natural habitat and high levels of pollution have accompanied rapid economic growth. As the millennium approached, these problems converged and threatened a number of countries with financial disaster.

Population Patterns

Today more than half a billion people occupy the peninsulas and islands of Southeast Asia. Twice as many people as live in the United States are packed into a land area half its size. A look at the population map in Figure 10.4 reveals, however, that several parts of the region are only lightly populated. Few people live in the upland reaches of Burma, Thailand, and northern Laos; on the island of Borneo (Kalimantan); in southern Sumatra; in most of the Celebes (Sulawesi); or in Irian Jaya, the Indonesian part of New Guinea.

Most of the people of Southeast Asia live in patches of particularly dense rural settlement. These densely settled areas are located in the river deltas of the mainland, in coastal Vietnam, in the Philippines, on the island of Java, and surrounding urban areas across the region. The cities of Southeast Asia are among the most crowded on earth. Manila packs 10.2 million people into a confined urban space in the

northern Philippines, giving it a population density of 54,000 people per square mile (20,000 per square kilometer). Jakarta, on the west end of the island of Java, in Indonesia, is nearly three times as dense as Manila; it has 130,000 people per square mile (50,000 per square kilometer). Southeast Asia's young population is likely to keep growing even as family sizes shrink; 36 percent are 15 years old or younger and have not yet begun to reproduce. Given Southeast Asia's relatively small landmass, the rising level of consumer demand, and the fragility of its tropical environments, it seems likely that population pressure on land, soil, water, and forest resources will remain a major public issue for many years.

Population Dynamics

Overall, Southeast Asians are having smaller families than they used to, but the patterns are highly variable. In some places, fertility rates have declined sharply since the 1960s, as Figure 10.5 shows. Singapore, an unusually wealthy city-state, had a fertility rate in 1998 below replacement level: 1.7 children per adult woman. It continues to grow, however, because Singapore attracts a steady stream of highly skilled immigrants. Thailand has the next lowest fertility rate in the region: 2.0. It is very poor compared to Singapore, with just one-tenth the income per capita, but literacy for women is high, and employment opportunities and freedom of movement are widespread.

The cases of two extremely poor countries in the region show the more usual correlation between poverty and high fertility. In Cambodia and Laos, women average five or more children each, and infant mortality rates are about 100 per 1000 births; Malaysia's is just 10, Thailand's 25. Vietnam is similarly impoverished, yet has a lower fertility rate (2.3) and infant mortality rate (38), which continue to drop. This is explained by the fact that Vietnam, as a Socialist state, provides basic education and health care regardless of income. Meanwhile, the rapidly growing economy is attracting foreign investment; hence employment for women is expanding, replacing childbearing as the central role in their lives.

The use of birth control in Southeast Asia (55 percent) is significantly more prevalent than in South Asia (40 percent). Generally speaking, fertility tends to drop when access to health services, education, jobs, and housing improves (Figure 10.6). It is highly likely that fertility rates would drop further if birth control technology were more readily available. In several of the most populous countries, including Indonesia, the Philippines, and Vietnam, over half the women say they do not want to become pregnant again, yet many do not yet have access to effective contraception.

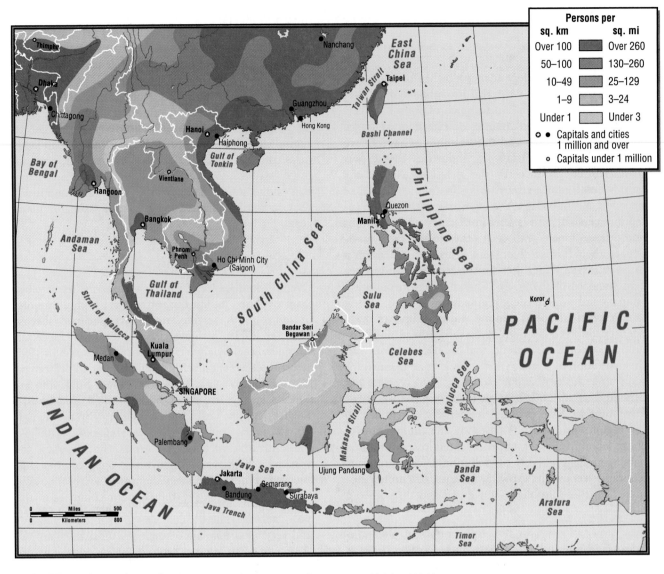

FIGURE 10.4 Population density. [Adapted from *Hammond Citation World Atlas*, 1996.]

Southeast Asia's AIDS Tragedy

VIGNETTE In the crematorium in Lopburi, Thailand, dozens of fist-sized white cotton bags sit unclaimed at the foot of the gilded statue of Buddha. The Buddhist monk in charge of the hospice, himself infected with HIV, explains that the ashes stay there because the families are afraid to take them for fear of getting sick themselves.

HIV infection is growing across Southeast Asia, but at present Thailand and Burma have the highest rates of infection. In Thailand, the center of the sex trade industry in the region, as many as 2 percent of the adult population may already be infected. Many think that the disease may soon increase rapidly in places that are as yet only lightly affected. There are several reasons for this gloomy forecast. Southeast Asian societies have a number of religious traditions, especially Islam and Catholicism, which strictly limit sexuality and discussions of it. At the same time, there are ancient, popularly accepted traditions—animism, Buddhism, and Hinduism—that allow a fair amount of latitude in sexual practices. The conservative religious leaders restrict public sex education and AIDS prevention programs, but popular customs reinforce sexual experimentation at least among some parts of the population. In Thailand, for example, a visit to a brothel has long been a sort of rite of passage for young Thai men, and brothels are found in most neighborhoods. Just as in South Asia and Africa, truck drivers commonly spread AIDS because they travel far from home

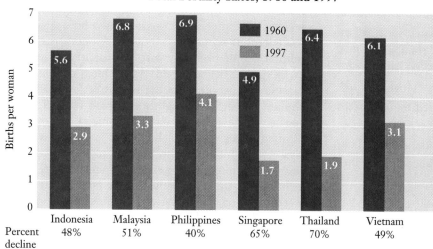

Total Fertility Rates, 1960 and 1997

Births per woman

Indonesia 48% — 5.6 (1960), 2.9 (1997)
Malaysia 51% — 6.8 (1960), 3.3 (1997)
Philippines 40% — 6.9 (1960), 4.1 (1997)
Singapore 65% — 4.9 (1960), 1.7 (1997)
Thailand 70% — 6.4 (1960), 1.9 (1997)
Vietnam 49% — 6.1 (1960), 3.1 (1997)

Percent decline

FIGURE 10.5 Total fertility rates declined from 1960 to 1997 for several Southeast Asian countries. The percentage decline for each country is indicated below the name of the country. [Adapted from *A Demographic Portrait of South and Southeast Asia* (Washington, DC: Population Reference Bureau, 1994), p. 9; and 1997 *World Population Data Sheet,* Population Reference Bureau.]

and may have sexual partners in several different locales. In Thailand, a rigorous government education campaign to use condoms is reducing infection rates. Meanwhile, Buddhist monks are running hospices for those stricken with the disease.

Although AIDS is treatable, the drug regimen costs about U.S. $15,000 a year—far beyond the reach of the vast majority in Southeast Asia. Most cannot even afford to be tested, so they spread the disease unknowingly.

Migration

Rural to urban migration is an important phenomenon in Southeast Asia as elsewhere in the world. The region as a whole is 35 percent urban, but Malaysia is 57 percent urban, the Philippines 47 percent, and the city-state of Singapore 100 percent urban. Often the

focus of migration is the capital, which may quickly become a **primate city,** in that it is two or three times the size of other cities in the country. Rarely can such cities provide sufficient jobs, housing, and services to the new arrivals. Individuals or families leave rural areas to escape deteriorating conditions in the countryside: often they have lost their access to land for subsistence cultivation and must obtain cash to buy what they previously provided for themselves; these are the **push factors** in migration. People are attracted to the city by the higher living standards they expect to find there; these are the **pull factors.** They usually leave behind very young and very aged relatives whom they must then support with earnings sent home, called **remittances.** The primate cities of Southeast Asia, like Singapore, Jakarta, Kuala Lumpur, and Bangkok, are magnets for such migrants.

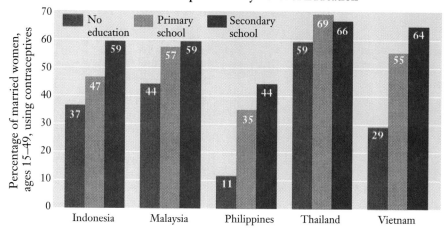

Contraceptive Use by Level of Education

Percentage of married women, ages 15–49, using contraceptives

No education / Primary school / Secondary school

Indonesia — 37, 47, 59
Malaysia — 44, 57, 59
Philippines — 11, 35, 44
Thailand — 59, 69, 66
Vietnam — 29, 55, 64

FIGURE 10.6 Contraceptive use generally rises with level of education. [Adapted from *A Demographic Portrait of South and Southeast Asia* (Washington, DC: Population Reference Bureau, 1994), p. 19.]

VIGNETTE

Mak and Lin, husband and wife (he 33, she 27), left their two sons in the care of her parents in a village north of Bangkok, Thailand. With their rural wages they could not afford even their oldest son's school fees; yet they hoped to educate both boys, even though that was not the custom. So Mak and Lin traveled by bus for 10 hours to reach Bangkok, where after several anxious days they both found grueling work unloading bags of flour from ships in the harbor. When they finished the day, they walked miles to their quarters in one part of a tiny houseboat anchored, with thousands of others, on the Chao Phraya River. That river is Bangkok's site of low-income housing, the city's source of water, its primary transport artery, and sewer. Mak and Lin had to step gingerly across dozens of boats to get to theirs, intruding repeatedly on the privacy of their fellow river dwellers. They bathed in the dangerously polluted river, washed their sweaty, floury work clothes by hand, and cooked their dinner of rice over a Coleman burner. Their only entertainment was provided by the private lives of their too numerous and too near-at-hand neighbors, who were often drunk on cheap liquor. For two years, Mak and Lin sent remittances to their family and managed to save enough to buy a bicycle, to pay the school fees, and to tide them over for several months at home. Glad to be out of Bangkok, both nevertheless agreed that they would eventually go back if they couldn't find work near their village.

To alleviate rural unemployment, to forestall migration to the crowded cities, and for a variety of other reasons, governments in Southeast Asia have developed **resettlement schemes** to move large numbers of agricultural people from one part of a country to another. In Indonesia, beginning in 1904, Dutch colonists began moving people from the islands of Java, Bali, and Madura to land only lightly occupied by indigenous people in the outer islands of Sumatra, Kalimantan (Borneo), Sulawesi (Celebes), and present-day Irian Jaya. These immigrants were to supply labor for plantation crops intended for export. Much larger resettlement efforts on these same islands began after 1950. Over 4 million people have been moved, making this one of the largest land resettlement schemes ever on earth.

The rationale for resettlement in Indonesia has changed over time from promoting food production, especially national self-sufficiency in rice, to more general goals of regional development, national integration, and population redistribution. Government policy in Indonesia is to assimilate Indonesia's outlying indigenous culture groups into the mainstream society; this is accomplished by placing migrants among them from the densely occupied cultural heartland, especially Javanese. It is also Indonesian policy to disperse people from the crowded core (western Java) to avoid political unrest. Many thousands of people not part of the formal resettlement schemes have joined the stream of people to the outer islands. The results have been unfortunate. In some cases, thousands of migrants moving onto the lands of indigenous peoples have destroyed delicate ecological adaptations. Many

Designated SP6, this new settlement carved out of the Irian Jaya rain forest is part of the government's resettlement program. People who elect to move here receive a one-way air ticket, a house, five acres of land, and a year's supply of rice. Over 200,000 people have taken the offer. [George Steinmetz.]

thousands of acres of forest have been cleared for agricultural resettlement in areas where the tropical soils were too fragile to sustain cultivation for more than a year or two. Serious environmental damage, ethnic discord, and breaches of human rights have been common.

Extraregional migration, or migration to countries outside the region, is also important in Southeast Asia. It may be either short term or permanent. Recently, women have constituted a major proportion of these migrants. In the Philippines, women emigrants now outnumber men, and many are skilled nurses and technicians who work in European and North American cities and in the Middle East. Many Southeast Asian Muslim women (chiefly from the Philippines and Indonesia) have become part of the "maid trade" of 1 million or more who work in the homes of wealthy citizens in the Middle East, especially in Saudi Arabia, Kuwait, and Oman (see Figure 10.7). Between 1983 and 1988, 193,000 Indonesian women went as maids to Saudi Arabia alone.

Skilled male workers from Southeast Asia are especially well known in the world merchant marine (see the vignette on page 39, Chapter 1). There they typically serve in the lower echelons of shipboard occupations, working as seamen, cooks, or engine mechanics.

In recent years, some have been able to advance to officer status.

In this region, as in others, **forced migration** still plays a role in the movement of people (Figure 10.8), and war is perhaps the most prevalent cause. During the last half of the twentieth century, many millions of mainland Southeast Asians fled into neighboring states in attempts to escape protracted conflict. Thailand, Laos, and Cambodia, especially, received many refugees during and after the Vietnam War.

A particular form of forced migration is connected to sexual tourism. Sexual tourism is in some ways an extension of the sexual entertainment industry that served foreign military troops stationed in Asia after World War II and during and after the conflicts in Korea and Vietnam. Now civilian men arrive from across the globe to live out their fantasies during a few weeks of vacation in Thailand or Vietnam or the Philippines. One result is that girls and women have been sold by their families or kidnapped into prostitution. For example, demographers estimate that 20,000 to 30,000 Burmese girls taken against their will (some as young as 12) are working in Thai brothels; their wages are too low to make buying their own freedom possible. In the course of their work, they are routinely exposed to physical abuse and to sexually transmitted diseases, including HIV.

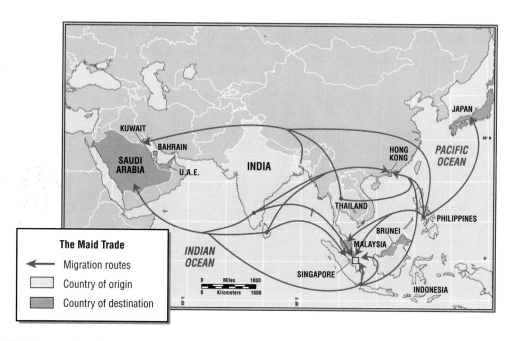

FIGURE 10.7 The "maid trade." In 1996, between 1 million and 1.5 million Southeast Asian women were working elsewhere in Asia and in the Middle East as foreign domestic workers. Educated women from Southeast Asia also migrate and send remittances home. Malaysia and Singapore are, in turn, destinations for women from India, Sri Lanka, Indonesia, and the Philippines. [Adapted from Joni Seager, *Women in the World: An International Atlas* (London: Penguin, 1997), p. 65.]

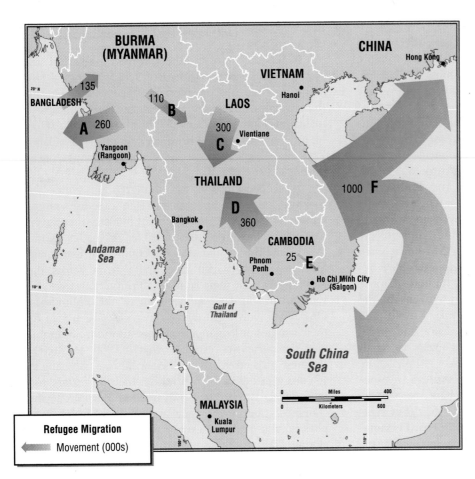

FIGURE 10.8 Refugees fled violence in Burma, Laos, Cambodia, and Vietnam in the decades following the end of the Vietnam War. (A) 1992–1995: Rohingya Muslims fled Burma to Bangladesh, but about half have since returned. (B) 1995: Burma refugees in Thailand. (C) 1973–1975: Laotians fled communism. (D) 1979–1993: Cambodian refugees in Thailand. (E) 1995: Cambodian refugees in Vietnam. (F) 1975–1989: Boat people from Vietnam. [Adapted from Jonathan Rigg, *Southeast Asia* (London: Routledge, 1997), p. 130.]

CURRENT GEOGRAPHIC ISSUES

Exploring geographic issues in Southeast Asia is a particularly illuminating enterprise because of the many forces, past and present, that have brought such rich diversity to the place. Because the region has developed rapidly since World War II, Southeast Asia is frequently cited as a proving ground for development strategies. Attitudes about family size and gender roles are changing in response to new economic circumstances. The cultural complexity of southeast Asia, which is the next topic of discussion, supplies people in the region with an array of strategies for responding to rapid and pervasive change.

Sociocultural Issues

In a book on world regions, one might expect to begin observing patterns repeating themselves from region to region. Certainly, some themes identified elsewhere around the world are to be found in Southeast Asia as well: a history of colonial rule, present uneven development and disparity of wealth, expanding links to the global economy, and a wide array of culture groups and religions. Nonetheless, there are some surprises. Southeast Asia has a cultural and social repertoire that has a distinctly different flavor from all other regions; and, of course, the space it occupies is unique.

Cultural Pluralism

Anthropologists like to say that Southeast Asia is a place of **cultural complexity.** They mean that it is inhabited by groups of people from many different backgrounds who have lived together for a long time yet have remained distinct. As we have observed, the oldest inhabitants were the Australo-Melanesians, who began to arrive some 60,000 years ago. Their descendants now live primarily in the forests of Borneo and New Guinea. Far more numerous today are the descendants of Austronesians, those people who began moving from the South China mainland into the islands about 5000 years ago. Now usually referred to as *indigenous peoples* or *tribals* (a term I am not using), these people are to be found across the region from northern Thailand to southern Indonesia. Many Southeast

Asians are now a cultural and biological mix of indigenous peoples and other ethnic groups from across Eurasia and even East Africa. Immigrants have arrived, in particular, from Arabia, Central Asia, greater India, China, Japan, Korea, and Europe.

Southeast Asia entered an era of increasing interaction with the entire globe when Europeans began colonizing the region after 1500. Most recently, the cultural mix of Southeast Asia has been broadened by ideas from around the world like free market capitalism, communism, nationalism, consumerism, and environmentalism. These ideas and the material culture associated with them, from advertising to motorbikes to green politics and spandex, have also modified the life and landscapes of Southeast Asia.

One might expect that by now Southeast Asia would be a **melting pot.** But until very recently, most groups had not intermingled sufficiently to lose their separate identities. In some countries in this region, dozens of different languages are spoken, people practice many different religions, and neighboring families may trace their roots back to remarkably different racial and ethnic origins. Today, the barriers separating groups are falling as modernization and industrialization processes draw large numbers into the cities and resettlement projects move several ethnic groups together onto newly opened lands. Migration and cross-cultural mating are creating ethnically mixed groups who are unsure of their heritage and may never have seen their ancestral landscapes.

One group, prominent beyond its numbers, is the so-called Overseas Chinese. Small groups of traders from southern and coastal China have been active in Southeast Asia for thousands of years; some got their start as fisherfolk who met their customers on the high seas. Over the centuries there has been a constant trickle of these Chinese immigrants. After China's Communist revolution (1949), many of those fleeing China sought permanent homes in Southeast Asia's trading centers (Table 10.1). Today they are artisans, merchants, middlemen, bankers, transport owners, developers and laborers.

The Chinese in Southeast Asia have the reputation of being rich and influential yet strongly loyal to their own group, often importing kin as employees rather than hiring local people. Some think they should be forced to change their habits, assimilate, and, especially, hire non-Chinese. Occasionally the proponents of these ideas have turned to violence. During the economic recession beginning in 1997, ethnic Chinese merchants were frequent victims of violence on the island of Java; rioters there, protesting rapidly rising prices, sought scapegoats. But overall, Chinese commercial activity throughout the region has reinforced the perception that they are diligent and clever businesspeople.

Religious Pluralism

The major religious traditions of Southeast Asia include Hinduism, Buddhism, Confucianism and Taoism,

Look very closely at the bag the young woman is carrying, and the drink the young man is holding, as they pause amid manicured rice fields in Indonesia. [Ian Lloyd/Black Star.]

TABLE 10.1

Ethnic Chinese in Southeast Asia

Country	Total (millions)	Percent
Indonesia	7.2	3.8
Thailand	5.8	10
Malaysia	5.2	28
Singapore	2.0	70
Burma	1.5	3.4
Vietnam	0.96	1.4
Philippines	0.8	1.3
Laos	0.008	1.3
Cambodia	0.33	4.0
Brunei	0.075	25

Source: Jonathan Rigg, *Southeast Asia* (New York: Routledge, 1997), p. 123.

Islam, Christianity, and animism (Figure 10.9). Of these, only animism is native to the region. **Animism** is the belief system of the rural subsistence cultivators and forest-dwelling peoples, primarily in central Borneo, the Molucca Islands, and Irian Jaya in New Guinea. For animists, natural features like trees, rivers, crop plants, and the rains carry spiritual meaning and are the focus of festivals and rituals to mark the seasons.

The other religions were brought in by immigrants, traders, colonists, and missionaries, and all have undergone change as a result of exposure to one another and to the traditional animist beliefs. Filipino Catholics and other Christians in Burma and Thailand (the Karen hill people, for instance) believe in spirits, and they daily practice rituals that have their roots in animism. Often, missionaries for Christianity or Islam deliberately pointed out ways in which the new faith was similar to indigenous beliefs. Hindus and Christians in Indonesia, surrounded as they are by Muslims, have absorbed many ideas from Islam, such as the seclusion of women. On the other hand, Muslims have absorbed ideas and customs from indigenous belief systems, especially ideas about kinship and marriage, illustrated in the following vignette.

VIGNETTE

Marta is a *dukun*, a woman who prepares a bride for a traditional Javanese wedding. Nearly all Javanese are Muslims, but Islam does not have elaborate marriage ceremonies, so colorful animist rituals have survived. Usually, those marrying each other have never met, their families having worked out the match. Hence the first meeting at the wedding ceremony is surrounded by a great deal of mystery. Marta's job is to reinforce this mystery and to prepare the couple for a life together. She bathes and perfumes the bride, puts on her makeup, and dresses her, all the while making offerings to the spirits of the bride's ancestors and counseling her on how to behave as a wife and how to avoid being dominated by her husband.

The groom, meanwhile, is undergoing ceremonies that prepare him for marriage. Each will sign the marriage certificate before they meet. In the traditional Javanese view, it is best that a young couple not be in love; hence they will not fall out of love. Rather, from the start they will hold each other at arm's length, not investing all their emotional capital in a relationship that is bound to change over the course of the decades as they mature and their family grows up. Marta's role is to create a magically reinforced bond between these two strangers. After marriage, as before, a man's closest friends will continue to be his male age mates and kin, and a woman's will continue to be her female friends and kin.

Divorce is fairly common among Muslim people in Malaysia and Indonesia, who often go through one or two marriages early in life before they settle into a stable relationship. While the prevalence of divorce is lamented, it is not considered outrageous. Apparently, ancient indigenous customs allowed for mating flexibility early in life. [Adapted from Walter Williams, *Javanese Lives* (Piscataway, NJ: Rutgers University Press, 1991), pp. 128–134.]

The map of religious patterns in Southeast Asia (see Figure 10.9) reveals an island–mainland division. Buddhism is dominant on the mainland, especially in Burma, Thailand, and Cambodia. In Vietnam, people practice a mix of Buddhist, Confucian, and Taoist beliefs originating in China. In the islands of Malaysia and Indonesia, Islam is dominant and is growing in the southern Philippines. In the islands, Christianity is second in importance but is dominant on only a few eastern Indonesian islands and in the Philippines north of Mindanao. Catholicism was imported to the Philippines by the Spanish colonists who arrived there to open the trans-Pacific trade with Mexico in the 1540s. Hinduism was much more widespread long ago but is now found only in small patches, chiefly on the islands of Bali and Lombok, east of Java. Traditional beliefs persist across

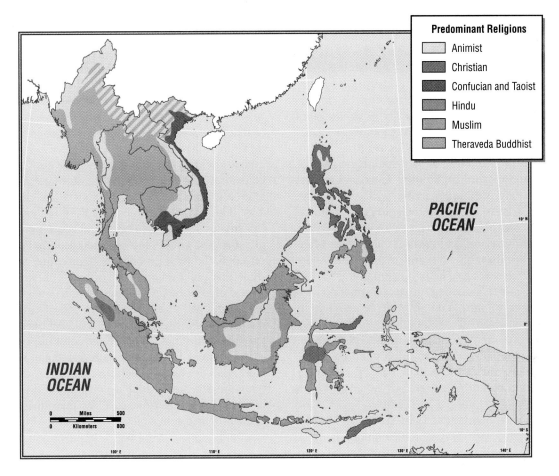

FIGURE 10.9 Religions of Southeast Asia. [Adapted from Alisdair Rogers, ed., *Peoples and Cultures* (New York: Oxford University Press, 1992), p. 222.]

the region, being especially important in Laos and northern Burma, central Borneo, and New Guinea.

Family, Work, and Gender

Family organization in Southeast Asia is variable, as one might expect in a region of so many cultures. Nevertheless, some distinctive themes emerge that are remarkably different from the patriarchal patterns found elsewhere. There is, however, a patriarchal overlay that derives from many sources: Islam, Hinduism, and Christianity, to name a few. Here are some interesting points about family life in Southeast Asia.

Couples Tend to Live with the Wife's Parents. Throughout the region, it is common for a newly married couple to reside with the wife's parents, or at least be most closely associated with them. This ancient family structure survives today even where Islam is the dominant religion. Along with this custom there is a whole range of behavioral rules that go a long way to-

ward empowering the woman in a marriage, despite some basic patriarchal attitudes. Consider this: a family is headed by the oldest surviving male, usually the bride's father. Only when he dies does he pass on his wealth and power as authority figure to his son-in-law, the husband of his oldest daughter, not to his own son! (A son goes to live with his wife's parents and inherits from them.) Hence, a husband may live for many years as a subordinate in his father-in-law's home. Instead of the wife being the outsider under the hegemony of her mother-in-law, as in Southwest Asia, China, India, and elsewhere, it is the husband who must kowtow. There is an inevitable tension between the wife's father and the son-in-law, which is addressed by the custom that the two shall practice ritual avoidance. Communication between them is managed by the bride, and this alone gives her power that brides in Muslim families never have in India or Southwest Asia. She passes messages and even money back and forth between the two; hence, she has access to a wealth of information crucial to the family and has the opportunity to influence each of the men.

Urban Families Tend to Be Nuclear in the Early Years of a Marriage. In urban families influenced by modernization, the young couple may choose to live apart from the extended family. This arrangement takes the pressure off the husband in daily life; but because this nuclear family unit is often entirely dependent on itself for support, wives usually work for wages outside the home. The drawback of this compact family structure, as many young families are now finding out in Europe and America, is that there is no pool of extended kin (grandparents, siblings, aunts, and uncles) available to help working parents with child care. There are not even any kin or neighbors to be hired for child care and housework because most women are themselves out working, and great grandmothers often live back in the village. By the same token, elderly parents are left with no one to help in maintaining the old family home; increasingly, tiny urban apartments must accommodate a young family and one or more aged grandparents in need of care. On the brighter side, working grandmothers in their vigorous middle years, can often substantially help their adult children financially, a point first made in Chapter 1 in the report on the social function of menopause.

Family Money Management Is in Women's Hands. "Women are good with money" is a common saying in Indonesia. The social researchers Hannah Papanek and Laurel Schwede have written about working women and money in Indonesia. Women in that country must take into account the high divorce rate: already, in the 1970s, 38 percent of urban women over the age of 35 and 43 percent of rural women had been married more than once. Thus, Indonesian women often start planning at the beginning of their marriage for the eventuality of having to support themselves. They tend to keep their spending low; and in 70 percent of the families studied by Papanek and Schwede, women were the family money managers.

Work Patterns

When describing changing patterns of work in Southeast Asia, it is impossible to say simply that there is a shift from agricultural to industrial or from rural to urban. The processes of change are far more complex. Agriculture is changing from small-plot family farming to large-scale commercial operations; fewer, but more highly skilled, workers are therefore needed. Rural communities are evolving from inward-looking, self-sufficient places to communities that produce crops primarily for export—rice or bananas, for example. People cycle in and out of rural areas, spending a few years in urban factory work, then returning for an interlude of village life. And the statistics indicate that many remain registered as rural even when they are ac-

tually living in the city. For example, in 1992, 72 percent of the population of Indonesia identified themselves as rural, yet only 56 percent of the labor force worked in agriculture. Households counted as rural in the census may include several individuals who live and work in cities and return only on weekends, if then.

A related emerging pattern is that, despite customs of female seclusion, young single women migrants from rural areas have become the employees of choice in export-oriented industries, as they have in Mexico and China (see Chapters 3 and 9). Groups of girls often migrate together and live several to a room, close to their jobs. The geographer Jonathan Rigg has analyzed several studies done in the region and concludes that bosses prefer to hire young single women because they are perceived as the least problematic employees. Statistics do show that, at least for now, women will work for low wages, will not complain about poor and unsafe working conditions, will accept being restricted to certain jobs on the basis of their sex, and are not as likely as men to agitate for promotions. But the situation varies from country to country; for example, female Filipino workers are more assertive than Malaysians. Also, the work conditions are less dominated by male authority figures in U.S.- and European-owned firms than in Japanese- or Korean-owned companies.

Economic and Political Issues

The Dance of the Tigers

Since the mid-1980s, Southeast Asia has had some of the highest rates of economic growth of any region in the world. Indeed, several countries have earned a reputation as economic "tigers," aggressively on the make and poised to leap into a new era of prosperity. In Malaysia, Thailand, Indonesia, the Philippines, and increasingly in Vietnam, gross national product figures have soared and poverty has been significantly reduced. Many countries that once struggled to feed themselves are now exporting rice as well as a range of increasingly valuable manufactured goods. These dynamic economies are fueled by the hard work of millions of people for whom poverty is a not so distant memory. For many, indeed, it is still a painful reality, as the fierce competitiveness of the tiger economies often comes at the cost of low wages and unhealthful working conditions.

Agriculture

Most Southeast Asians (65 percent) live in rural villages. Agriculture figures as part of the support of most rural people (Figure 10.10), even though many also fish, make and sell crafts, or work part time for wages. Agriculture also yields important products for export

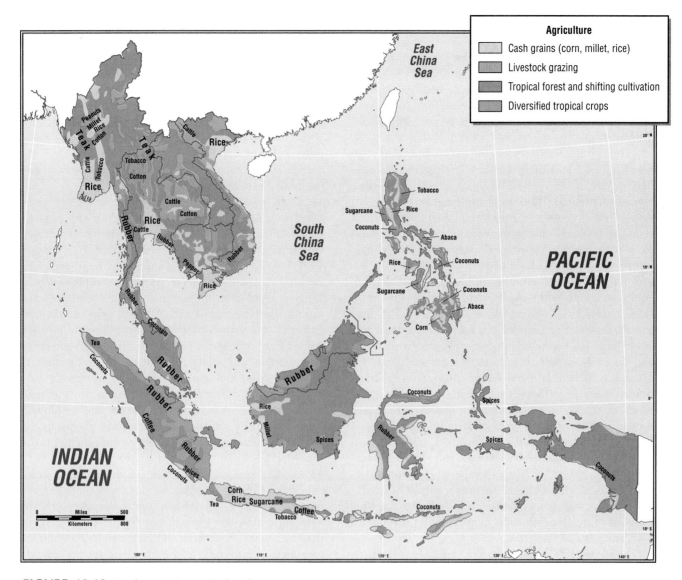

FIGURE 10.10 Southeast Asian agricultural patterns. [Adapted from *Hammond Citation World Atlas,* 1996, pp. 74, 83, 84.]

(especially rice and rubber) and provides important components of urban diets (rice, fruits and vegetables, fish, meat, and dairy products).

Several forms of agriculture are practiced in Southeast Asia. So-called **slash-and-burn, or shifting, cultivation** is an ancient form of multicrop gardening using small plots. It is used on rain forest lands that do not support more intensive types of agriculture. It is practiced today by subsistence farmers in the hills and uplands of the mainland and in coastal Sumatra, Borneo, the Celebes, the southern Philippines, and Irian Jaya. Another venerable and highly productive form of agriculture in the region is **wet rice,** or **paddy, cultivation.** Wet rice cultivation entails the hand planting (usually by women) of rice seedlings in flooded fields that are first cultivated (usu-

ally by men) with hand-guided plows pulled by water buffalo. Laborers terrace and bank the soil by hand to create multiple adjacent ponds on a hillside or plain. They then deliver water to these paddies, usually by directing natural runoff or by pumping water from streams. Wet rice cultivation has transformed landscapes throughout Southeast Asia (see the photo on page 485). It is practiced in river valleys and deltas where rivers bring a yearly supply of silt, and on rich volcanic soils on islands like Java, Sumatra, and the Philippines. While the environmental effects—in the form of forest clearing, landform manipulation, and waterlogging of soils—are extensive, this form of agriculture is sustainable over long periods. It is frequently cited as a prime example of nature being harnessed in the service of humans.

489

Many people are now abandoning paddy cultivation to look for work in the cities. Many of the fields, now worked mostly on the weekends, are prepared quickly with a type of tractor ("iron buffalo"), and rice is broadcast into the paddy, not hand-planted as seedlings. Weeding and the maintenance of water systems and terraces are increasingly neglected, and yields are lower.

During the recent years of prosperity, many of Southeast Asia's farming families left the countryside because their farms were bought up by corporate-owned plantations. The result has been a transformation of rural ecology. **Commercial farming** of such crops as rubber, bananas, pineapples, and rice entails clear-cutting of forests, deep plowing of the soil, planting of usually one species of crop plant, bolstering of soil fertility with chemicals, the use of mechanized equipment, and, in the case of rice, the management of large quantities of water. Labor requirements in this so-called "green revolution" are low, and the emphasis is on large-scale production for cities and for export and on quick profits, not on long-term sustainability. Many commercial farmers of food crops have achieved dramatic boosts in harvests by using high-yield crop races (especially in the case of rice), the result of green revolution research. *All* types of farming, except some forms of small-scale shifting cultivation, entail loss of forest resources, loss of wild animal and plant habitats, and increased use of water. Large-scale commercial farming leads, in addition, to displacement of traditional farmers and forest dwellers, soil erosion and loss of soil fertility, flooding, and chemical pollution of land and groundwater resources.

Poor farmers usually cannot afford to become green revolution farmers or consumers; many can neither grow sufficient food for themselves nor afford to buy it. On the other hand, the millions in Southeast Asian cities need this food, and for many it is affordable.

Industrialization

While growth has been widespread throughout the region, there are large gaps in wealth between countries and significant differences in the types of enterprises that dominate their economies. Generally the poorer countries, such as Vietnam, Laos, Burma, and Cambodia, as well as the more rural parts of the other countries, are primarily dependent on agriculture and forestry. In some rural areas, however, construction and maintenance jobs on projects such as new hydroelectric dams are raising incomes; and in cities and towns, garment and shoe making, food processing, and many types of light manufacturing are expanding. In the urban and suburban areas of the wealthier countries, such as Thailand, Malaysia, and Singapore, and a few areas in Indonesia and the Philippines, more elaborate types of manufacturing are

important: automobile assembly, the refining of chemicals and petroleum, and the making of computers and other electronic equipment. In many ways the star of economic growth in the region is Singapore. That city-state has been an important center of trade since its days as a nineteenth-century free port created by the British. Today Singapore is considered a developed country, with a well-established financial sector, a burgeoning computer software industry, a world-class airline, and the world's busiest harbor where goods are moved from one shipping line to another.

Not everyone has benefited equally from Southeast Asia's "economic miracle." In the region's new factories and other enterprises, it is not unusual for employees to work 10 to 12 hours a day 7 days a week for less than the legal minimum wage and with no benefits. In most of the countries, employers routinely repress labor unions that agitate for better conditions, bribing local and national governments to look the other way. International pressure to improve working conditions has been only moderately effective. For example, in the late 1990s, the U.S. shoe manufacturing firm Nike became the focus of worldwide outrage over the treatment of its workers in Vietnam, Indonesia, and elsewhere across Asia; the employees were frequently exposed to hazardous chemicals, as well as physical abuse and psychological cruelty on the job. In 1991, Nike laborers in Vietnam were paid U.S. $1.06 a day and the production cost for a pair of Nike shoes was U.S. $5.60. Meanwhile, the retail sale price in America was $75. While some improvements in working conditions were made, Nike avoided making major changes by shifting the blame onto subcontractors located in Taiwan and Korea who set up and administered the factories.

The Association of Southeast Asian Nations

Southeast Asian countries trade on a much larger scale with the rich countries of the world than they do with each other. They export food, timber products, minerals, processed commodities, manufactured finished goods and components to Japan, Australia, New Zealand, Europe, and the United States. They import manufactured products that they do not make themselves, including high-fashion consumer products, industrial materials, machinery, and parts. Trade with each other is hard because they all export similar goods. It is hoped that establishing a region-wide free trade zone might stimulate more internal exchange. Such a free trade zone is already being planned by the Association of Southeast Asian Nations, or **ASEAN,** an increasingly important bulwark of both economic growth and political cooperation within the region. Started in 1967 as an anticommunist, anti-China association, ASEAN has long focused on nonconfrontational accords that strengthen regional cooperation. An example is the now established Southeast Asian Nuclear Weapons–Free Zone. Currently, ASEAN is putting together a regional trade block patterned after the North American Free Trade Agreement and the European Union.

Economic Crisis: The Perils of Globalization and Rapid Growth

Beginning in 1997, a financial crisis swept the region, forcing millions back into poverty and creating tensions that shook Southeast Asia's political order. A major factor triggering the crisis was the rapid shift of most Southeast Asian states to less regulated, more free market economies. Since the 1960s, national governments had controlled most investment in the region. They tried to nurture economic development that would be stable over the long term, promoting manufacturing and agricultural enterprises. For the most part, the result was strong and sustained economic growth. Under pressure from foreign governments and multinational corporations, by the early 1990s most governments were opening up the economy, especially in the crucial financial sector. Banks were given greater freedom to determine what kind of investments they would make and the ability to accept money from foreign investors. Soon, Southeast Asian banks were flooded with huge amounts of money from investors in the rich countries of the world, who hoped to profit from the region's growing economies. To make quick profits, the bankers invested in risky ventures such as real estate, high-rise office building construction, and the stock market. As a result, by the mid-1990s many cities had a glut of office space, U.S. $20 billion of which was unsold in the city of Bangkok, Thailand, alone. A further consequence was that the stock prices of many companies were inflated far beyond their real value.

Another factor contributing to the crisis was a kind of corruption called **crony capitalism.** In most Southeast Asian countries, high-level politicians, bankers, and wealthy entrepreneurs often have close personal relationships or are part of the same extended family. Often these personal connections encourage corruption, as they did, for example, in Indonesia. For decades, the most lucrative government contracts and entrepreneurial opportunities were reserved for the children of former President Suharto, who ruled Indonesia from 1967 to 1997 (see the box "Building Cars in Asia"). His children are now some of the wealthiest people in Southeast Asia. With the opening of Southeast Asian economies to foreign investors, this kind of corruption expanded considerably as foreign investment money was easily diverted to bribery or unnecessary projects that glorified political leaders.

The cumulative effect of crony capitalism and the pursuit of quick returns on risky investments was that many ventures failed to produce profits at all. In response, foreign investors withdrew their money on a massive scale. Before the crisis, in 1996, there was a net inflow of U.S. $96 billion to Southeast Asia's leading economies as well as to South Korea, which also was to be hit by the crisis. In 1997, there was a net outflow of U.S. $12 billion. The panicked withdrawal created the crippling scarcity of investment money that has been the most immediate cause of the continuation of the crisis.

The Southeast Asian economic crisis has had a number of disturbing consequences. The biggest losers have been low-income people who did nothing to create the crisis. A decline in the value of most Southeast Asian currencies has caused prices to rise for imported food and consumer goods, on which many urban people depend, and for fertilizers and pesticides, which agriculture requires. As prices rise, consumption is curtailed, firms can no longer make ends meet, and many workers face layoffs and firings. Many urban workers no longer have families farming in the countryside to whom they can return during hard times. In Indonesia, for example, during the crisis rates of poverty have climbed from roughly 11 to 60 percent. Frequent outbreaks of rioting, looting, and general violence have troubled urban and rural areas.

The International Monetary Fund (IMF) has made a major effort to keep the region from sliding deeper into recession. The IMF implemented a bailout package worth some U.S. $65 billion in 1998, much of it used to rescue banks. The IMF considers the banks essential to the region's economic stability, while critics argue that the bailout gives these banks little incentive to improve on their disastrous record. Since the bailout is to be repaid with tax dollars, low-income people will suffer cuts in health care, education, and food subsidies for years to come.

The bailout package (amounting to structural adjustment strategies discussed in Chapters 3 and 7) requires countries to reduce tariffs and other mechanisms that protect many economic sectors. The goal is to lessen corruption and increase efficiency in order to win back the confidence of foreign investors. However, critics point out that too great a dependence on foreign investment leaves the region open to a recurrence of a panicked withdrawal of funds. Critics also argue that if foreign investors take over the most profitable sectors, the profits could leave the developing economies rather than be reinvested at home.

Resentment Toward the Overseas Chinese

Many low- and middle-income people who have been hurt by the recent financial crisis blame their sorrows

AT THE REGIONAL SCALE   *Building Cars in Asia*

Prior to the Asian recession of the late 1990s, many of the world's largest auto manufacturers had established factories in Southeast Asia in anticipation of widespread prosperity that could make family autos a possibility for a large portion of the population (Figure 10.11). But in Indonesia, GM, Ford Chrysler, Toyota, and Honda lost the ability to compete when in 1995 Suharto announced that his son Hutomo and KIA Motors of South Korea would build a "National Car." The car company was to be exempted from duties on imported Korean parts and thus the auto could be sold for thousands of dollars less than those of competitors. Furthermore, the car would be required for government fleets, guaranteeing a market.

KIA Motors went bankrupt in the Korean recession of 1996, and the IMF bailout for Indonesia stopped all special tax and customs privileges for the National Car project in January 1998. The future of car markets in Southeast Asia remains shaky for all makers in view of the general economic downturn. The small motorbike remains the vehicle of choice for most.

Source: Adapted from Philip Shenon, For Asian nation's first family financial empire is in peril, *New York Times*, January 16, 1998; and Robyn Meredith, Auto giants build a glut of Asian plants, just as demand falls, *New York Times*, November 5, 1997.

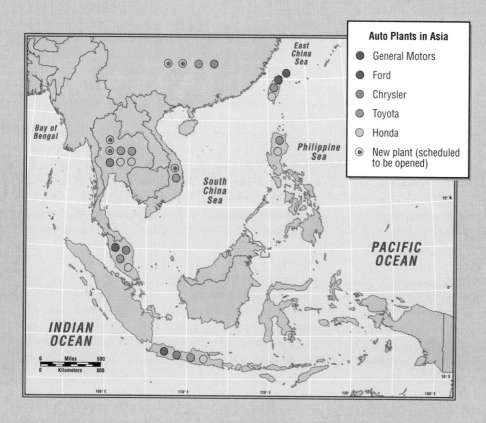

FIGURE 10.11 Automobile plants already built or under construction by leading car makers. [Adapted from *New York Times*, November 5, 1997, p. 1.]

on the Overseas Chinese. The Chinese are more prosperous, and with their region-wide connections and access to start-up money they are able to take advantage of the new growth sectors of modernizing economies. Sometimes new Chinese-owned enterprises have put out of business older, more traditional

establishments that many local people depend on. For example, in the town of Klaten in central Java (Indonesia), an open-air bazaar where local Indonesians once sold a variety of goods has been shut down to make way for a government-sponsored air-conditioned shopping mall. The store rents are so expensive that only the Chinese can afford them. Since the economic crisis, resentment against the Chinese has brought a wave of violence. Chinese people have been assaulted, their temples desecrated, and their homes and businesses destroyed.

Pressures for Democracy

The cultural diversity of Southeast Asia poses twin political threats to democratic government in the region: on the one hand, diversity may become so great that a nation could literally lose its center and fall apart; on the other hand, one culture group may become dominant and impose its will on the rest.

Although the demands for a greater public voice in the political process are strong in Southeast Asia, there are significant barriers. Undemocratic Socialist regimes control several countries—Burma, Laos, and Vietnam, for example. Democracy is kept at a minimum even in slightly wealthier and more free market countries, such as Indonesia; it is virtually nonexistent in the rich city-state of Singapore. Some Southeast Asian leaders, such as Singapore's former prime minister Lee Quan Yue,

have argued that "Asian values" are not compatible with Western ideas of democracy. Asian values are supposedly grounded on the Confucian-based view that individuals should be submissive to authority. Hence, it is argued, Asian countries should avoid the highly contentious public discourse of electoral politics. (For more on this view of Asian values, see the box "*Pancasila*, Indonesia's National Ideology").

This position fails to account for the many people living under undemocratic, authoritarian regimes who have rebelled, even at the risk of their lives. In the 1970s, for example, some 200,000 died in East Timor as they resisted annexation to Indonesia, then under the dictatorial rule of President Suharto. Significant pressure for democracy has accompanied economic development in several countries. In Thailand, for example, years of economic growth have increased literacy levels and awareness of the democratic privileges observed in many other countries. In recent years, Thais have successfully agitated for laws that reduce corruption and provide for regular elections. In Indonesia, after three decades of semidictatorial rule by President Suharto, massive demonstrations in the wake of the

AT THE LOCAL SCALE   Pancasila, *Indonesia's National Ideology*

Indonesia is the largest country in the region and the most fragmented—it comprises 3000 inhabited islands stretching over 3000 miles (8000 kilometers) of ocean. By all calculations, it is the most culturally diverse, with dozens of ethnic groups and multiple religions. Until after World War II, Indonesia was not a national state but rather a loose assemblage of distinct island cultures, which Dutch colonists managed to hold together as the Netherlands East Indies. When Indonesia became a state in 1945, its first president, Sukarno, hoped to forge a new nation out of disparate parts. To that end, he articulated a famous and controversial national philosophy known as **Pancasila,** based on tolerance, particularly in matters of religion.

The five precepts of *Pancasila* are belief in God and the observance of conformity, corporatism, consensus, and harmony. It is easy to see that all four of these words could be interpreted to discourage dissent or even loyal opposition; and they seem to require a sort of perpetual "cheerleading" stance. For some, the strength of *Pancasila* is that it ensures that there will never be either an Islamic or a Communist state.

Others note the chilling effect that the philosophy has had on participatory democracy (the two political parties are state controlled) and on criticism of the president and of the army that does his bidding. And, in fact, there has been no orderly democratic change of government for many years. Sukarno was in power from 1945 until he was deposed by Suharto in 1965. Suharto declared himself president and was in power until forced to step down in 1997. He named a successor rather than call elections.

An example of how *Pancasila* intrudes into the daily life of the people and counters democratic ideals is provided by the state-sponsored women's organization Dharma Wanita (Women's Duty). Modeled on an organization of American military wives, membership is obligatory for all women government employees and wives of government employees. The purpose is to teach women to serve as good wives and to support their husbands' careers, no matter what their actual marital or career status. There is a chapter in every government office, and women hold office in Dharma Wanita according to the husband's position in an organization.

region's economic crisis led to Suharto's resignation and the promise of democratic elections.

Measures of Human Well-Being

Human well-being is a complicated concept that is determined by sociocultural and political factors as much as by economic ones. As pointed out many times in this book, gross national product per capita (Table 10.2, column 2) is the most common index used to compare countries; but it is at best a crude indicator of well-being. In some regions of the world, such as in Africa south of the Sahara and in South Asia, GNP figures are for the most part low everywhere. In Southeast Asia, by contrast, GNP figures vary radically from very high in Singapore, to moderately high in Brunei, Malaysia, and Thailand, to very low in Cambodia, Laos, and Vietnam. The two countries with the highest figures,

TABLE 10.2

Human well-being rankings of countries in Southeast Asia

Country	GNP per capita (in U.S. dollars), 1996	Human Development Index (HDI) global rankings, 1998[a]	Gender Empowerment Measure (GEM) global rankings, 1998[b]	Female literacy (percentage), 1995	Male literacy (percentage), 1995
Selected countries for comparison					
Japan	40,940	8 (high)	38	99	99
United States	28,020	4 (high)	11	99	99
Kuwait	19,040 (1995)	54 (high)	75	75	82
Southeast Asia					
Brunei	$8,800 (1995 GDP[c])	35 (high)	Not av.	83	93
Burma (Myanmar)	$660 (1995 GDP)	131 (low)	Not av.	78	88
Cambodia	300	140 (low)	Not av.	53	80
Indonesia	1,080	96 (medium)	70	78	90
Laos	400	136 (low)	Not av.	44	69
Malaysia	4,370	60 (high)	45	78	89
Philippines	1,160	98 (medium)	46	94	95
Singapore	30,550	28 (high)	42	86	96
Thailand	2,960	59 (high)	60	92	96
Vietnam	290	122 (medium)	Not av.	91	97

[a]The high and medium designations indicate where the country ranks among the 174 countries classified into three categories (high, medium, low) by the United Nations.
[b]Total ranked in the world = 104 (no data for many).
[c]GDP = gross domestic product, used because GNP unavailable.
Not av. = Not available.
Sources: Human Development Report 1998, United Nations Human Development Programme; and *1998 World Population Data Sheet*, Population Reference Bureau.

Singapore and Brunei (in the latter, a measure of gross domestic product), actually do have widespread prosperity. In Singapore the wealth is derived from high-end technological manufacturing, financial services, oil refining, and oceanic transshipment services. Unemployment is low, and poverty unusual. The wealth of Brunei comes entirely from oil and gas. There is virtually no poverty, and most social services are provided free. Elsewhere in the region, GNP figures mask wide variations in well-being. To survive, those with the lowest incomes depend on subsistence cultivation, reciprocal exchange of labor and services, and the informal economy. But, as was the case in Africa and South Asia, often these very poor people live in close proximity to a vastly better-off minority who live in fine houses, travel widely, and consume at high levels. The mainland countries of Vietnam, Laos, and Cambodia are the poorest in Southeast Asia, in large part because of protracted war. Their economies, especially that of Vietnam, are expected to improve as low wages attract foreign investment.

In Southeast Asia, there is a good bit of variance in ratings on the United Nations Human Development Index (HDI) scale (Table 10.2, column 3), which combines information on adjusted real income with information on life expectancy at birth and educational attainment. Singapore's HDI rank is very high indeed (28), whereas Cambodia (140), Laos (136), and Burma (131) all rank in the bottom third, globally. In those countries with the lowest HDI rankings (Laos and Cambodia), literacy figures are exceptionally low, especially for women. Governments in these countries have not provided even the most basic education and health care services. Laos spends only U.S. $6 per capita on education, compared to U.S. $179 per capita in Malaysia. Indonesia is also surprisingly low, at just U.S. $16 per capita.

United Nations Gender Empowerment Measure (GEM) figures are missing for five countries: Brunei, Burma, Cambodia, Laos, and Vietnam. Even very well-off countries can have relatively low GEM rankings, as do both Japan (38) and Kuwait (75) at the top of the table. Singapore (42) ranks the highest in the region; here, women have many opportunities for employment, though at lower wage scales than men. In Malaysia (45) and the Philippines (46), a few well-connected women have access to some high-ranking jobs as administrators and as professional and technical workers. Many Filipino women obtained experience working as bureaucrats and in private companies that served the U.S. military until several large American military bases were closed. Now, many well-educated and experienced Filipino women, especially in the health-related fields, are migrating to work in the United States or other wealthy nations (see Figure 10.7). Elsewhere in the region, most women lag well behind men in education level, wages, and access to jobs. Still, compared to South Asia and Africa, women are gaining some ground toward equal treatment. All but Indonesia and Thailand rank in the top half of the 104 countries ranked on GEM.

Environmental Issues

Virtually everywhere in Southeast Asia, environments are deteriorating rapidly as a result of population pressure and commercial activities like mining, logging, and commercial agriculture. Most Southeast Asian countries are rich in resources: timber and other forest products, minerals (gold, diamonds, tin, and copper), and fertile soils. These resources are being rapidly depleted—often extracted by foreign-owned companies and sold abroad, with only a fraction of the profits being reinvested in the host countries. In this region as elsewhere, when issues about environment are raised, it pays to follow the global connections, especially who is buying extracted resources. The following example illustrates this.

People in Europe and North America (like me) may inadvertently be part of the problem. We have beautiful tropical hardwood paneling in our dens, purchased at an attractively low price at the local branch of a large home improvement warehouse, or we use computer paper by the case. We are all on the demand side of the Southeast Asian resource equation. Though we live far from Southeast Asia, we often support our lifestyles with their resources. In the United States, for example, we consume 690 pounds (313 kilograms) of paper per capita (the highest rate in the world); Japan's rate is 500 pounds (225 kilograms); and most of Europe consumes between 220 and 440 pounds (100 and 200 kilograms). Most Southeast Asian countries consume under 67 pounds (30 kilograms) per capita. Singapore is an exception, consuming 450 pounds (218 kilograms) of paper per person. Much of the wood fiber in paper products comes from Brazil, the Philippines, Indonesia, or a host of other tropical pulpwood producers. The map in Figure 10.12 shows the destinations for Indonesia's timber products. While we have paid a price for our paneling and paper, we must ask if it was a fair price, especially in light of the environmental damage that results from logging.

Deforestation

Environmentalists estimate that between 13 and 19 square miles (3000 to 5000 hectares) of Southeast Asia's rain forests are destroyed each day, a rate 50 percent faster than in the Amazon. About 20 percent of the forests are destroyed by legal logging, road and pipeline construction, and utilities installation. Another

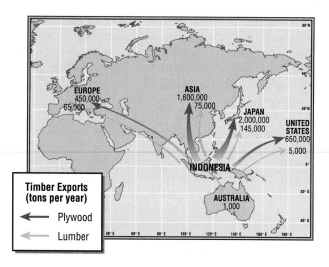

FIGURE 10.12 Annual timber exports from Indonesia. [Adapted from map insert, *Indonesia,* Cartographic Division, National Geographic Society, February 1996.]

forest cover, water moves across the landscape too rapidly to be absorbed, carrying away topsoil. Watercourses cut new gullies and ravines in the uplands, and deposit tons of silt in the lowlands.

The case of the Philippines can serve as an example of a widespread phenomenon. In 1900, 75 percent of the Philippines were covered with untouched, **old-growth forest.** By 1990, only 2.3 percent of the country was so forested. In 1991, 3000 people on the island of Leyte were killed by floods blamed on illegal logging that had been allowed by corrupt officials. In the Philippines, original forests are now confined to ribbonlike patches on higher mountainous terrain. **Secondary forest** will regrow after the first cutting if conditions are right, although it will not have the diversity of species of the original forest. On Sumatra, and in Sarawak and Kalimantan on Borneo, even secondary forest has disappeared, and in many places former forest lands are so degraded that they are useless for agriculture.

25 percent are destroyed for resettlement schemes. Fifty-five percent disappear to gain land for commercial agriculture and shifting cultivation. Indirectly, much of the deforestation is linked to population growth and poverty. The loss of forest cover leads to erosion, flooding, water pollution, degradation of soil, loss of wildlife habitat, and injustice to indigenous forest dwellers and subsistence farmers who once used the forest in more or less sustainable ways. Companies that have legal rights to log the land over a period of 25 years sometimes choose to "cut and run" in just a few months; they thus avoid living up to already woefully ineffective conservation agreements. Illegal logging often outpaces legal logging, and its impact on the environment is even worse because it is done in secret at breakneck speed, with no attention to preserving natural habitat.

Traditional, nonintensive tropical horticulture techniques on forested lands were especially effective and sustainable in Southeast Asia when the population was only about 10 million, as it probably was in about 1800. Until the early twentieth century, population density remained low enough to allow for the use of small cultivation plots and long fallow periods, during which the forest could fill in the clearings. But recently, population has grown astonishingly quickly. For example, in the 19 years between 1973 and 1992, the population increased by 48 percent, from 317 million to 469 million. It now stands at 501 million. To feed the increased numbers, people have expanded cultivation onto the steepest of slopes. Trees are cut down for sale and to make room for farmland. Erosion is drastically changing the shape of the denuded land. Without a

Mining

Probably the extractive activity most disruptive to the land is mechanical strip mining. This technique is increasingly used in Southeast Asia to extract minerals like copper, silver, and gold. The land is cleared of forest, and heavy equipment then peels away the layers of soil and rocks until the desired mineral is exposed. In the United States, companies must take measures to rehabilitate the landscapes they bulldoze, and they must dispose of mining and processing waste without polluting watercourses. Strip-mined land can never be truly restored, however, and despite regulations, many mining operations in the United States are still serious polluters. One reason that international mining companies are interested in Southeast Asia is that environmental regulations do not exist or are unenforced.

The most publicized mine in the region is the 13,000-foot (4000-meter) open-pit multimineral mine on Grasberg Mountain in Irian Jaya. The mountain contains the world's largest known gold reserve. Each day in 1996, the Freeport international consortium (with strong ties to firms in the United States) extracted U.S. $7.2 million worth of copper, gold, and silver from this mine; Freeport, Irian Jaya's largest foreign taxpayer, now has contracts to mine over 9 million acres (3.6 million hectares) in the mountain range. Mining will continue here for at least another century, according to Freeport President George Mealey. Local villagers, however, complain that they have been driven off their land without compensation. And the Komoro, who live on the coast, claim that tailings from the mines have polluted the Aikwa River, causing flooding and ruining their stands of sago palm.

The Freeport-McMoRan Grasberg open-pit mine.
[George Steinmetz.]

In Indonesia (Kalimantan and Irian Jaya) and the Philippines (Mindanao), national armed forces have been called out to quell protests against loss of native habitats to mining operations. Such clashes reflect the conflict between the interests of local, often remote, politically weak forest-dwelling peoples (and traditional cultivators) on the one hand, and, on the other, national governments bent on rapid economic development.

Air Pollution

Usually we think of islands in the sea as pristine places where the air is invigorating. But twice in the 1990s,

the islands of Southeast Asia have been hit with a putrid and persistent cloud of pollution; this occurred most recently in the fall of 1997. Although large cities like Kuala Lumpur and Jakarta were the worst affected, air pollutants surged beyond safe levels even in remote parts of the islands (Figure 10.13). People were urged to wear masks, and airplanes could not land. One plane crash is thought to have been caused by the smog.

The immediate cause of the poisonous haze was smoke from fires set on forestland recently logged and now being prepared for fast-growing trees for palm oil or paper pulp production. Unfavorable winds, drought, and a delayed monsoon seem to have conspired to spread the burning. A high-pressure air mass (posssibly linked to El Niño) kept the smoky haze and the region's normal industrial air pollution from diffusing as usual into the upper atmosphere. The ASEAN environmental ministers meeting to deal with the crisis had to move their meeting to avoid the unhealthful air.

Energy Production

There is a huge unmet need for energy in Asia generally. With 60 percent of the world's population, Asia as a whole now uses about one-quarter of the world's energy. Long brownouts are common in the largest Asian cities, and power shortages are cited as a leading obstacle to development. Many of the poorest countries of Southeast Asia are building dams, some to provide irrigation water, and most to generate power that they plan to sell to more rapidly developing neighbors. For example, landlocked Laos, one of the poorest countries in Asia, hopes to develop hydropower to sell to Thailand.

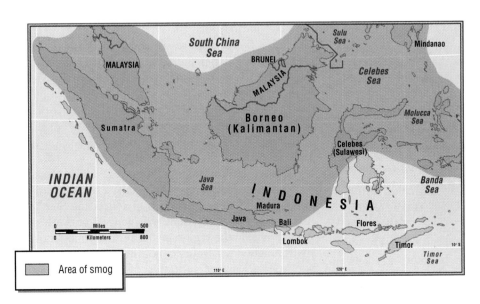

FIGURE 10.13 Extent of the smog that covered the region during September and October 1997. [Adapted from *The Economist,* September 27, 1997, p. 40.]

Swedish and Norwegian investors are privately financing a 210-megawatt hydroelectric dam being built as a profit-making operation in Laos on the Theun River, a tributary of the Mekong. Laos will receive a share of income from the power sales but will not use the electricity itself. Laotian village people living near the dam sites will bear the environmental costs. By blocking the natural flow of water, dams stop the seasonal deposition of silt downstream that refreshes crop soil. Also, the turbines transfer heat to water flowing downstream, ruining plant and animal habitats. Flooding behind the dam may destroy valuable human and natural habitats; the standing reservoir water may leak into geological structures, polluting aquifers or causing erosion at some distance from the dam itself. The new availability of irrigation water may stimulate agricultural clearing nearby. Reservoirs may rapidly silt up, making water storage and power generation impossible. There is little incentive for the investors in far-away Sweden and Norway to pay for mitigating environmental impacts they will never experience and that will probably not affect their profits until the damage is done.

Urbanization and Industrialization

Southeast Asia is home to some remarkably densely populated and rapidly growing cities. Urban environments lack the basics of housing, sanitation facilities, and safe drinking water. The factories that attract migrants dispense industrial wastes into rivers that bubble with stinking gases. Proliferating motor vehicles render breathing by pedestrians a dangerous proposition. Rain passing through polluted air picks up chemicals and delivers them to soil and groundwater. In the cities and beyond, this acid rain threatens aquatic life, human health, and the garden plants meant to feed city people. The following description by the author Jeremy Seabrook demonstrates one way in which Jakarta's environmental problems intersect with its informal economies. Like Washington, D.C., Jakarta tries to relieve exhaust pollution and traffic congestion by requiring carpooling.

VIGNETTE Traffic regulations in Jakarta insist that on some streets no car may carry fewer than three occupants. At the entrances to such streets wait the "jockeys," young boys who will provide a driver with the necessary number of passengers. The driver pays the boys 500 rupiah for the ride, and then drops them on the other side of the restricted area, where they may make the return trip with another needy driver. From time to time the boys are rounded up, banned, fined, imprisoned, sometimes beaten by the police. But they always return. In fact, the traffic generates a great deal of employment. Young men and women at the traffic lights, wearing masks against the pollution, sell bottled water, candy, and cigarettes. Most are financing their education. Other young men earn a living by stopping the traffic on main roads to enable vehicles to pass out of small side turnings. By placing himself bodily in front of the oncoming vehicles, a young man stops traffic long enough to allow the cars from side streets to join the mainstream of vehicles. The grateful driver gives 100, sometimes 500 rupiah. [Adapted from Jeremy Seabrook, *In the Cities of the South* (London: Verso, 1996), p. 296.]

Although there has been little locally based mass environmental activism, individuals across the region are developing an understanding of the systems that have brought about such serious circumstances. Jeremy Seabrook recounts standing by the polluted Chao Phraya River in Bangkok and being joined by an elderly gentleman who explained:

In Thailand we used to use banana leaves as plates and to wrap food. Then we could discard them in the streets and fields because they were natural products that decayed, fertilized the fields, left no pollution. Now we buy buns in polystyrene containers, Coke in plastic bottles; but we still treat these things as if they were natural products and throw them down in the streets and streams. We haven't noticed yet that it is not the same, and that is why Bangkok is drowning in a sea of filth. (From In the Cities of the South, *pp. 296–297.)*

Some suggest that the repeated occurrence of preventable disasters like the air pollution crisis of 1997 highlights the weaknesses of social institutions. Environmental regulations are not strongly enforced, and those who pay bribes may avoid them entirely. Meanwhile, the political systems do not encourage public debate. Throughout the region, great value is placed on gentle consensual persuasion as embodied in the principles of *Pancasila* in Indonesia (see box on page 493) not on legal sanctions. This is especially true regarding environmental issues, which, as elsewhere in the world, consistently take a back seat to development. Ultimately, success in addressing Southeast Asia's environmental issues will depend on both consumers outside the region giving serious thought to the environmental consequences of their purchases and the Southeast Asian general public becoming more aware of how they can change unsustainable development policies.

SUBREGIONS OF SOUTHEAST ASIA

The subregions of Southeast Asia share a number of features. All have tropical environments that support rice paddy cultivation wherever soil is rich enough. Most also have dense rain forests that are the tempting target of logging operations. The subregions share many of the same cultural features: the influences of Islam, the Overseas Chinese, and colonialism are widespread. Yet the subregions are distinct in many ways as well. One obvious difference is the pace of modernization.

Another interesting difference to watch out for concerns how the countries have responded to the ethnic diversity within their borders—whether cultural differences are tolerated or people are encouraged to conform to one standard; whether groups participate equally in wealth and power or one or two groups dominate. Achieving national unity is a major concern in the region, but it is striven for in very different ways.

Mainland Southeast Asia: Thailand and Burma

Burma and Thailand occupy the major portion of the Southeast Asian mainland and share the long slender peninsula that reaches south to Malaysia and Singapore (Figure 10.14). Although the two countries share adjacent space and similar physical environments, Burma is poor and dependent on agriculture, while Thailand is rapidly industrializing.

The landforms of Burma and northeast Thailand consist of a series of ridges and gorges that bend out of the Tibetan Plateau and descend to the southeast, spreading out across the Indochina Peninsula. Rivers like the Irrawaddy and the Salween, which get their start far to the north on the Tibetan Plateau, flow south through narrow valleys to the huge delta at the southern tip of Burma or the large plain in central Thailand. Most agriculture takes place in the Burmese interior lowlands and in central Thailand's large plain, flanked by the Chao Phraya River in the west and the Mekong in the east.

The mountains of the northern reaches of these two countries received ancient migrations from southern China, Tibet, and eastern India; the rugged topography has protected these indigenous peoples—Shans, Karens, Mons, Chins, and Kachins—from outside influence. Hence traditional ways of life, including animistic beliefs, are common. The valleys and lowlands to the south in Burma, and the large central plain in

Thailand, are places of urban development, Buddhism, and modernization. Burma is named for the Burmans, who constitute about 70 percent of the population and live primarily in the lowlands. Thailand is named for the Thais, a diverse group of indigenous peoples who originated in southern China.

From 70 to 80 percent of the world's remaining teakwood is still growing in the interior uplands of Burma. A single tree can be worth U.S. $200,000. Other resources include oil, tin, antimony, zinc, copper, tungsten, limestone and marble, precious stones, and natural gas. With an estimated per capita annual income of U.S. $660, and an HDI of 133, Burma ranks as one of the region's poorest countries. About 75 percent of the people still live in rural villages and the economy is primarily based on rural activities: cultivation of paddy rice, corn, oilseed, sugarcane, and pulses; and logging of teak and other tropical hardwoods. Burma is thought to be the world's largest producer of illicit opium and is the probable source for over 60 percent of the heroin imported into the United States. Opium is the major source of income for a number of indigenous ethnic groups, especially the Wa. Now this group is also manufacturing synthetic drugs, especially methamphetamine. They protect their territory with surface-to-air missiles. Those who are persuaded to stop growing poppies experience a 90 percent drop in income.

The military government of Burma has manipulated the drug traffic and even harvested poppies, especially in the lightly settled uplands and mountains near the Thai border. When indigenous inhabitants have protested, they have been silenced by resettlement and by killing and plundering. One tactic used by the military is to capture ethnic women and young girls and smuggle them into prostitution rings in Thai cities. There are over 100,000 refugees from Burmese military violence in camps in Thailand and Bangladesh. In 1997, international forces applied economic sanctions against the military government, including a U.S. embargo on future investment in Burma.

Thailand is much more urbanized and developed than Burma. During the boom years of the mid-1990s, it was known as one of the Asian "tiger" economies, meaning that it was rapidly approaching widespread modernization and prosperity. It has been a matter of pride in Thailand that the country avoided being colonized by European nations and that it has been able to transform itself from a traditional agricultural society into a modern nation. But this self-image of Thailand is not entirely accurate. While Thailand's rapid industrialization and phenomenal urban growth are impressive, for 70 percent of the people life is still rural and agricultural. Meanwhile, the majority of the nearly 20 million who live in urban areas find themselves in extremely crowded, polluted, and often impoverished conditions.

499

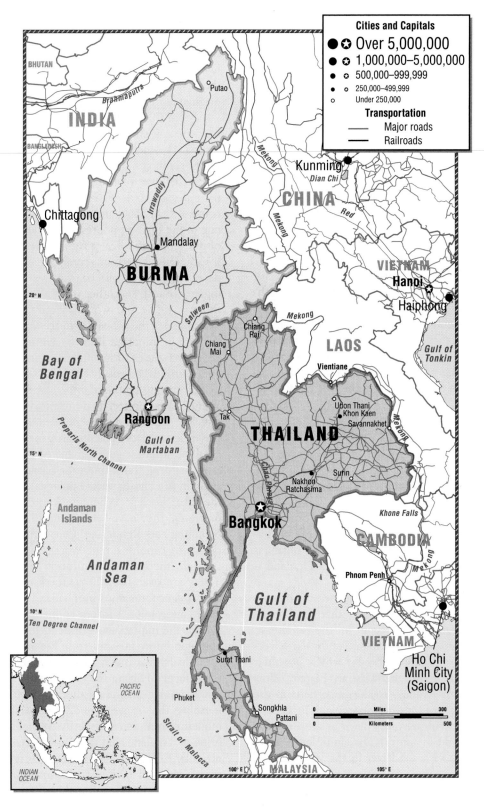

FIGURE 10.14 The Mainland Southeast Asia: Thailand and Burma (Myanmar) subregion.

Is Thailand an Economic Tiger?

According to the World Bank, between 1985 and 1994 Thailand had the world's fastest-growing economy, averaging a GNP per capita annual growth of 8.2 percent. At the same time, the country kept unemployment relatively low for a developing country—at 6 percent—and inflation in check at 5 percent or lower. The growth rate climbed, despite the fact that the majority of working people are still farmers who, according to official statistics, produce only 11 percent of the nation's wealth. (Remember, though, that much of what farmers, especially women, produce is not covered in the statistics.) The Bangkok metropolitan area, which lies at the head of the Gulf of Thailand, can lay claim to 50 percent of the country's wealth and 10 percent of its population. It can thus be considered a primate city. But cities elsewhere in Thailand are also growing and attracting investment: Chiang Mai in the north, Khon Kaen in the east, Surat Thani on the south peninsula. And despite the significant downturn in the economy in 1996–1998, the country still has a growing middle class with money to spend and invest.

VIGNETTE The life circumstances of Buaphet Khuenkaew illustrate a standard of living not uncommon among Thai people who live on the urban fringe. Many retain some agricultural ways of life while tapping into the opportunities for employment in the city. Also illustrated are several points made earlier about typical family organization, residence patterns, and the relative autonomy of women in Southeast Asia, as compared to other places in Asia.

Buaphet, 35, lives in Ban Muang Wa, a village near the northern city of Chiang Mai. She married at 18 and has two children, a son, 10, and a daughter, 17. She is a Buddhist with a sixth-grade education, and is both a homemaker and a seamstress. Six days a week she drives the family motor scooter 30 minutes to her job in Chiang Mai, where she sews buttonholes in men's shirts for 2800 baht (U.S. $118) a month. The children perform weekday household chores when they return from school.

Buaphet's husband, Boontham, is a farmer who is about five years older than she. The couple knew each other before they were married. He would visit her at her parents' home, and eventually they fell in love. One day he and his parents came to the house with a bride price of 10,000 baht ($420) in gold and asked to marry her. She accepted. They used the gold to build their house on land owned by her mother, across the street from where she was born. They have electricity and a small television set.

Buaphet shares the morning meal with her family before setting off to work. [Joanna Pinneo/Material World.]

Drinking water comes from a well and is filtered through stones and stored in ceramic jars. Many household activities, including bathing, washing clothes, and washing dinner dishes, take place outside, but meals are eaten inside. Though her husband feels men are rightly regarded as superior in Thai society, Buaphet reports that she and her husband have an egalitarian marriage in which all decisions are joint. Nonetheless, they do not spend their leisure time together. Buaphet says she is happy with her life but also regularly complains about not having appliances and more up-to-date furnishings like her friends have. [Adapted from Faith D'Alusio and Peter Menzel, *Women in the Material World* (San Francisco: Sierra Club Books, 1996), pp. 228–239.]

Industrialization has had unanticipated detrimental side effects in Thailand. Thousands of rural people have been drawn to the cities seeking jobs, status, and an improved quality of life. Many arrive only to find a difficult existence and meager earnings, like the Bangkok migrants Mak and Lin described earlier. The *Asiaweek* reporters Catherine Shepherd and Julian Gearing tell the story of Luan Srisongpong, a 33-year-old farmer from the southeast province of Ubon Ratchathani. He, along with 20,000 others, is a member of the Assembly of the Poor, a protest group that has convened three times since 1995 on the streets of Bangkok to protest living and working conditions. Many are protesting the fact that large development programs, like the Yadana pipeline (see the box "The Yadana Project"), forced them off the land and into the

AT THE LOCAL SCALE   *The Yadana Project: A Natural Gas Joint Venture*

Bangkok, Thailand, needs power. Neighboring Burma has natural gas reserves. The Yadana natural gas field, located some 43 miles off Burma's coast in the Andaman Sea, contains reserves of some 5 trillion cubic feet (142 billion cubic meters). These reserves are being tapped in a joint venture led by Total of France (holding a 31 percent interest), UNOCAL of California (28 percent), the Burmese government oil company (15 percent), and the Petroleum Authority of Thailand (26 percent). The liquefied petroleum gas (LPG) will be piped to the port at Daminseik, Burma; from there it will then pass through 155 miles (248 kilometers) of buried pipeline to a power plant outside Bangkok. Beginning in 1998 and continuing for the next 30 years, the gas from the Yadana field is expected to generate up to 2800 megawatts of electricity for Bangkok (a megawatt is the amount of electricity required to light 10,000 100-watt lightbulbs). By way of comparison, San Francisco, Berkeley, and Oakland, California, together require about 1300 megawatts for residential use.

Burma will gain a natural gas facility near Rangoon that will provide 125 million cubic feet (3.6 million cubic meters) a day for domestic consumption. It will also get an electric generating plant using the gas, and an accompanying fertilizer plant (fertilizer is a by-product of LPG production). Burma will also receive U.S. $200 million annually from Thailand for the natural gas; Thailand will pay another U.S. $200 million a year to Total of France and UNOCAL. The project has additional benefits for Burma: the creation of 2000 high-wage jobs; much-improved medical care and renovated hospitals; new schools; newly built or improved roads; improved village water systems; electricity; and several village-scale development projects, primarily focused on the breeding of pigs, chickens, shrimp, and cattle for profit. Burmese villagers displaced by the pipeline are to be compensated.

As good as all this sounds for Burma, a major problem remains. Burma is ruled by a military government that has committed numerous human rights violations. In acquiring land for the pipeline, the Burmese government is thought to have used forced labor and to have moved whole villages forcibly. Meanwhile, the environment is being severely affected by clearing and bulldozing for the pipeline construction. At shareholder meetings, critics in the United States have been protesting UNOCAL's position. They have filed court cases suggesting that the company is indirectly involved in human rights abuses the Burmese government may have committed against its own citizens in connection with the Yadana pipeline project. UNOCAL's position is that it is simply an oil company and is not involved in nor should be held accountable for political developments. They argue that their expenditures to bring jobs and improvements in quality of life to local villagers should outweigh other negative effects.

The United States and the international environmental movements are trying to raise the intertwined issues of natural preservation, rights of indigenous peoples, and environmental justice in regard to the Yadana pipeline project through the U.S. courts. This effort presents an interesting model for future activism. One thing to consider, however, is that multinational corporations can avoid such sanctions simply by not registering in countries that wish to hold them accountable.

city. Some protesters are farmers who suffer from food price controls meant to quiet hungry urban workers. Others are objecting to factory layoffs, which ensue when industries outproduce their markets or move to parts of Asia that have yet cheaper labor. The Assembly of the Poor is effective: half its list of problems has been sorted out to their satisfaction. The fact that public protest is permitted and acceded to in Thailand is noteworthy, because protest is forbidden in Burma and many other parts of the region.

The geographer Jim Glassman challenges the idea that Thailand is in fact an Asian tiger. First, its infrastructure is far from developed: the number of paved roads lags far behind other middle-income countries; a second international airport is needed; and there are only six telephone lines per 100 people. (Incidentally, as in rapidly modernizing parts of the old Soviet Union, the cellular phone industry is leaping into the breach; there are now more than 3 million cellular phones in the country.) But Glassman's main point is that too large a percentage of Thailand's population is not participating in prosperity, and the levels of income disparity are increasing. Unlike Korea and Taiwan, the state has not played a significant role in addressing economic and social inequalities by devoting sufficient funds to education, basic health care, and housing.

Even though Thailand has literacy rates above 92 percent, education levels are minimal. Only 33 percent of the children move into secondary school and just a tiny minority go on to higher education. As a result, Thailand's workers are less able to compete on the global wage market, and there is a deficit of highly trained scientists and engineers compared to countries like the Philippines and Malaysia. Glassman adds that Thailand received little foreign aid compared to Korea and Taiwan, which during the cold war era, received massive U.S. aid that went toward education and infrastructure improvements and some land reform.

The geographers Joni Seager and Jonathan Rigg have separately noted that labor unions are particularly weak in Thailand, and that part of the reason is that, as in so many countries, the new industrial workers are overwhelmingly women, who have little experience with protest and little social power. Furthermore, most of the challenge presented to private elites has focused on their monopoly of resources, not on such things as raising taxes to support public education or improve the urban infrastructure—housing, sewage, water, sanitation, or traffic control. Neither the high-profile protest by Buddhist monks on behalf of the environment nor the protests of the Assembly of the Poor have made a strongly reasoned challenge to the elite and to the present trajectory of development.

Mainland Southeast Asia: Vietnam, Laos, Cambodia

On the map in Figure 10.15, the three countries of Vietnam, Laos, and Cambodia appear to be ideally suited for peaceful cooperation, sharing as they do the Mekong River and its delta on the southeast peninsula of Eurasia. Nonetheless, the three have suffered a disruptive century of war that has pitted them against each other. Until after World War II, all three were colonies known together as French Indochina. All three have fought a long struggle to make the transition from colonies controlled by the French to viable independent nations. In the 1990s, they remained essentially Communist states; yet free market capitalism has been allowed in measured doses. Now visitors and investors are arriving; and once somber city streets are abuzz with people and enterprise.

A long curved spine of mountains runs through Laos and into Vietnam. In the south, these mountains are flanked on the east by the broad alluvial plain of Cambodia and on the west by the long coastline and fertile river deltas of Vietnam. The rugged mountainous country in the north is the least densely occupied area in Southeast Asia. Laos, almost entirely mountainous, has only 59 people per square mile (22 per square kilometer). Most of the region's population is in the

People who live along the Mekong River in Cambodia and Vietnam usually build their houses on stilts, because during the rainy season the river can rise 10 or more feet (3 meters), broadening into a lazy flow 2 to 3 miles wide.
[Michael Yamashita/Woodfin Camp & Associates.]

Mekong River delta and coastal zones of Vietnam. There, people take advantage of the wet tropical climate and flat terrain to cultivate rice. Throughout the subregion, at least 75 percent of the people support themselves as subsistence farmers. In Cambodia, only 13 percent of the people live in cities.

The Mekong River is the region's major transport artery. It originates in China, high on the Tibetan Plateau, then flows through Laos, central Cambodia, and far southern Vietnam. This part of the region is a large wetland formed by the Mekong delta. Here, people live in houses on stilts, as in the Ganges delta, in order to weather the seasonal floods. Until recently,

503

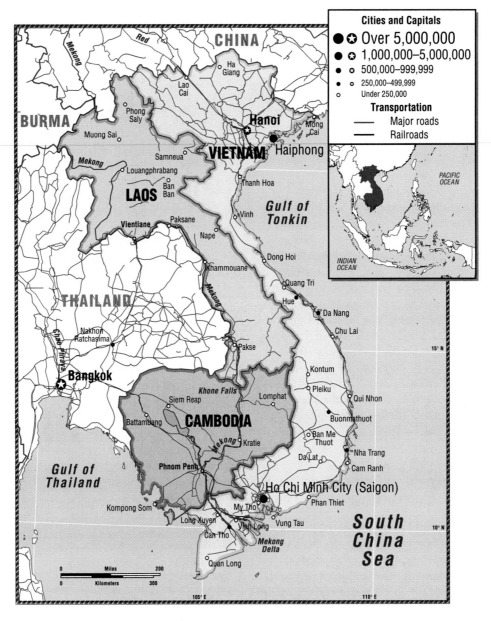

FIGURE 10.15 The Mainland Southeast Asia: Vietnam, Laos, and Cambodia subregion.

the Mekong River had but one bridge for auto traffic, and one dam, located in Yunnan, China, and completed in 1995. China now has plans for eight Mekong dams and several bridges on its side of the border. In Laos, a hydroelectric plant is to go in above the capital, Vientiane (see discussion in the section on energy production, pages 497–498), where it will block river transport routes. Perhaps the dams will not all be built. The multinational United Nations Mekong River Commission is reconsidering plans in light of the ecological problems created by similar giant river projects in Hungary (on the Danube), Turkey (the Euphrates), and India (the Narmada); these are discussed in Chapters 4, 6, and 8.

Thailand, immediately to their west, is the main trading partner of Laos and Cambodia. Thai investors are interested in resources like timber, gypsum, tin, gold, precious gems, and hydropower, and the production of rice, vegetables, coffee, sugarcane, and cotton for export. Some are hoping to promote the Mekong basin as a destination for European tourists. Despite the regional economic downturn in the late 1990s, all three countries, but especially Vietnam, appear to be entering a period of rapid economic growth.

Vietnam

Vietnam is a long slender country with nearly 1000 miles of coastline along the South China Sea. Both the northern and southern extremities of the country are marked by deltas that are important rice-growing regions: the Red River delta in the north and the Mekong River delta in the south. Vietnam is by far the most populous of the three eastern countries of the Southeast Asian mainland. It has a population of 75.1 million, 20 percent of whom are urban; Laos, in contrast, has 5.3 million and Cambodia 10.8.

After the Americans left in 1973 (see page 478), the Communist government, assisted by the Soviet Union, began an aggressive investment in health care, basic nutrition, and basic education. In the 1990s, only about 214 people out of every 100,000 attended college, but most have completed elementary school and literacy is about 90 percent for both women and men. Since 80 percent of the people are cultivators living in rural situations, their extensive knowledge is of practical things: plants, animals, home building and maintenance, fishing, medicinal herbs, and related matters. The Vietnamese have a national flair for excellent cuisine. When times are good, the dinner table is filled with artfully prepared fish, vegetables, herbs, rice, and fruits.

Vietnam has mineral resources (phosphates, coal, manganese, offshore oil) and at one time had a lush forest cover, much of which was destroyed by defoliants in the latter years of the Vietnam War. Despite its resources, Vietnam's economy languished for nearly two decades after the war, in part because the United States imposed an economic blockade, and in part because of the inefficiencies of communism. In the mid-1980s, the Hanoi leadership began introducing elements of capitalism in a program called ***doi moi,*** which was very similar to **perestroika** in Russia—meaning economic and bureaucratic restructuring. With the lifting of the U.S. embargo in 1994, firms from all over the world began moving into Vietnam. By the late 1990s, about 90 percent of the nation's labor force worked in the private sector. Today's agricultural products include rice, corn, potatoes, coffee, tea, soybeans, rubber, fish, and animal products. The extractive sector of the economy includes mining, oil production, and fishing; the industrial sector comprises production of cement and fertilizers, and food processing; manufacturing includes the making of textiles and clothing. The service sector is growing as well, with a significant emphasis on tourism, which attracts middle-class Europeans and Asians.

The factors that have brought some economic improvement are causing considerable dislocation elsewhere in the economy. As we have seen in other parts of the postcommunist world, the diversion of government investment away from state firms and social welfare spending and into free market–related investment usually means an initial and often severe downward pressure on general standards of living. For example, in the late 1990s small-scale Vietnamese farmers felt the

Vietnam's capital city of Hanoi is home to over 3 million people. The city's tree-lined streets and architecture retain a French colonial flavor. The 1911 opera house in a central square at the end of the boulevard serves today as the municipal theater. [David Allen Harvey/National Geographic.]

505

squeeze when their taxes were raised and some of their lands were confiscated to be used in foreign-funded enterprises like an oil refinery or a golf course.

Island and Peninsula Southeast Asia: Malaysia and Singapore

Malaysia and its neighbors Singapore and Brunei are the most economically successful countries in Southeast Asia. Malaysia was created in 1963 by combining the previously independent Federation of Malaya (the lower portion of the Malay Peninsula) with Singapore at the very tip, and the territories of Sarawak and Sabah on the north coast of the large island of Borneo to the east (Figure 10.16). All had been British colonies since the nineteenth century. In 1965, the city-state of Singapore became independent from Malaysia. The tiny and wealthy sultanate of Brunei, also on the north coast of the island of Borneo, refused to join Malaysia and remained a British colony until independence in 1984. Brunei does not release statistics, but its citizens probably have a per capita income close to U.S. $8000, and virtually all citizens have a high standard of living supported by wealth from oil and natural gas. A look at the human well-being table (Table 10.2) will confirm

that Singapore is one of the wealthiest countries on earth. And Malaysia, though much less wealthy than the other two, still ranks as a high-income country.

Malaysia

Malaysia is home to 21 million ethnically diverse peoples. Most live in West Malaysia, the portion of Malaysia at the end of the Malay Peninsula that has 40 percent of the land area and 86 percent of the people. Nearly 60 percent of Malaysia's people are Malay, who are nearly all Muslims. Ethnic Chinese comprise 29 percent of the people, and they are mostly Buddhist. Eight percent are Tamil- and English-speaking Indian Hindus. The remaining 2 percent are forest-dwelling indigenous peoples who live primarily on Borneo. Until the 1970s, conflicts among these groups divided the country socially and economically. Malaysians have worked hard to improve relationships among these groups, and they have had noteworthy success.

Throughout most of its history, West Malaysia was inhabited by Malay people and a small percentage of Tamil-speaking Indians. The Indians were traders who plied the Strait of Malacca, the ancient route from India to the South China Sea. Even before the eastward spread of Islam (in the thirteenth century), Arab traders of the ninth and tenth centuries began using this route, stopping at small fishing villages along the

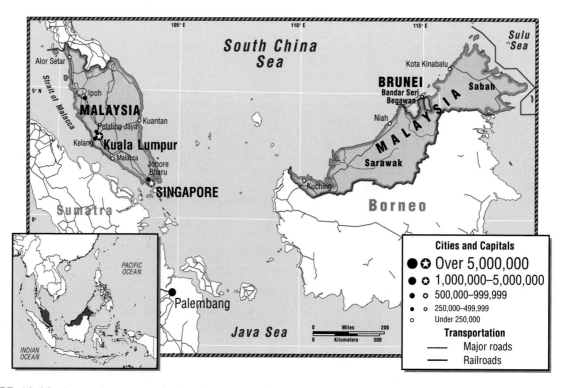

FIGURE 10.16 The Southeast Asia Island and Peninsula subregion.

Members of some of Malaysia's culture groups can be seen in the capital city, Kuala Lumpur, which has slightly more than 1 million inhabitants. [Stuart Franklin/Magnum Photos.]

way to replenish their ships. By 1400, virtually all ethnic Malay inhabitants had converted to Islam.

During the colonial era, the English brought in Chinese Buddhists to work as laborers on their West Malaysian plantations. The Chinese eventually became merchants and financiers; and the Indians succeeded in the professions and small businesses. The far more numerous Malays remained poor village farmers and plantation laborers. The English maintained control over their Southeast Asian colonies by promoting ethnic, religious, and economic rivalries. As economic disparities widened, animosities between the groups increased. After independence, animosities exploded in 1969 with the onset of widespread rioting by the poor. Political rights were suspended, and it took two years for the situation to calm. The violence so shocked and frightened Malaysians that they agreed to address some of its fundamental social and economic causes.

After a decade of discussions among all groups, Malaysia launched a long-term affirmative action program in the early 1980s. Its core was the new economic policy (NEP), designed to help the Malays and indigenous peoples gain economic advancement. The policy required Chinese business owners to have Malay partners. It set quotas increasing Malay access to schools and universities and to public jobs. As the plan evolved in the 1980s, the goal became to bring Malaysia to the status of a fully developed nation by the year 2020. The program has succeeded in narrowing the social and economic inequalities. A sense of nationhood and national pride has developed. One measure of success in building nationhood is the fact that during the reform period, when the rights of indigenous Malays

were being championed, the prime minister was Mahathir Mohamad, of Indian heritage. *Asiaweek*, a regional newsmagazine, reported that in late 1997 the real standard of living in Malaysia—adjusted for per capita purchasing power—was nearly U.S. $10,000, more than double what it was at the beginning of the 1990s.

Nonetheless, poverty is still prominent in the landscapes of Malaysia. In the capital of Kuala Lumpur, at least one-fifth of the total population are squatters, amounting to several hundred thousand people. Most of the squatters reside on land, but many live in raft houses on rivers or bays. Rafts are an ingenious way of overcoming the acute housing shortage. In 1993, the geographer Asmah Ahmad studied urban raft dwellers in Malaysia and found that the typical domicile is a wood structure 36 feet × 24 feet (11 meters × 7.3 meters), with a zinc roof. A rear platform provides space for domestic chores, and a wooden plank gives access to the river bank. People often cultivate fast-growing crops like sweet potatoes on the riverbank, so if moving is necessary, not too much will be lost.

The economy of Malaysia has traditionally rested on export products like palm oil, rubber, tin, and iron ore. But much of the growth of the 1990s has come from Japanese and U.S. investment in manufacturing, especially electronics, and from oil extracted from offshore wells in the South China Sea. Timber exports, too, are important, and the cleared land is developed into additional palm oil and rubber tree plantations. Now Malaysia is banking on a new multi-billion-dollar, high-tech manufacturing, supercorridor 10 miles wide by 30 miles long (16 by 48 kilometers) just south of Kuala Lumpur. It is designed to become Southeast Asia's Silicon Valley, not unlike Bangalore in India (see Chapter 8), to help leapfrog the nation into a prosperous twenty-first century.

Like many Asian economic tigers, Malaysia is subject to roller-coaster economic patterns. Currency values and stock market prices may fluctuate widely. Overall, however, it does seem that Malaysia is more balanced economically and its wealth distributed more equitably than is the case for many of its neighbors. In spite of downturns, Malaysia seems likely to achieve increasing prosperity.

Singapore

Singapore occupies a hot, flat, humid island just off the southern tip of the Malay Peninsula. It is a totally urban society. Its 3.5 million inhabitants live together at a density of over 14,500 people per square mile (5600 per square kilometer). Singaporeans seem to share the notion that making money is a worthy goal. Capitalism reigns, but there is strict government control over virtually all aspects of society.

Ethnically, Singapore is overwhelmingly Chinese (77.5 percent). Malay people account for 14.2 percent, Indians 7.1 percent, and 1.2 percent of the population is mixed. Singapore is religiously diverse: 42 percent are Buddhist or Taoist, 18 percent Christian, 16 percent Islamic, and 5 percent Hindu; the rest include Sikhs, Jews, and Zoroastrians. The government encourages unity among this diversity: Singapore officially subscribes to a national ethic not unlike *Pancasila* in Indonesia. The nation commands ultimate allegiance; loyalty is to be given next to the community, and then to the family, which is recognized as the basic unit of society. Individual rights are to be respected; but the emphasis is on shared values, community consensus not conflict, and racial and religious harmony.

Singapore has a meticulously planned cityscape with little congestion and safe, clean streets. Permits are required for virtually any activity, including having a car radio, owning a copier, working as a journalist, having a satellite dish, being a sex worker, or performing as a busker—a street artisan or entertainer. Eighty percent of the people live in government-built housing, and workers are required to contribute up to 25 percent of their wages to a government-run pension fund. Home care of the elderly, however, is the responsibility of the family and is enforced by law. Each child,

on average, receives 10 years of education and can continue further if grades and exam scores are high enough. Literacy averages over 90 percent. Law and order is strict, too. A few years ago, a U.S. teenager was publicly caned for spray painting graffiti. Drug users are severely punished, and pushers are sentenced either to life imprisonment or death. But virtually all Singapore citizens seem to have accepted this control and strictness in return for the next highest per capita income in Asia after Japan.

Island Southeast Asia: Indonesia

Indonesia is a recent amalgamation of island groups, which before the colonial era never thought of themselves as a unit (Figure 10.17). Rivalry between island peoples remains strong, and many resent the growing dominance of the Javanese in government and business. The resentment is a serious threat to continued unity.

The archipelago of Indonesia consists of the large islands of Sumatra and Java; the Lesser Sunda Islands (Bali, Lombok, Flores, Timor, and many more) to the east of Java; Kalimantan, which shares Borneo with

FIGURE 10.17 The Indonesia subregion. Many of the Indonesian island names have changed in the past three decades. I am using the Indonesian names in this book, but here I include in parentheses the name better known in the West; for example, Sulawesi (Celebes).

Malaysia and Brunei; Irian Jaya on the western half of New Guinea; the Celebes (Sulawesi) Islands; and the Molucca Islands. In all, there are some 17,000 islands, but many of them are small uninhabited bits of coral reef. The term *Indonesia* was conceived by James Logan, an Englishman residing in Singapore in 1850. He combined two Greek words, *indos* (Indian) and *nesoi* (islands), to create the name. Indonesians themselves now refer to the archipelago as *tanah air kita*, meaning "Our Land and Water." This name conveys a sense of the environment of the archipelago but falsely indicates a universal feeling of togetherness and environmental concern.

Java and Sumatra are the two most economically productive islands. They are home to 80 percent of the population. Java alone has 60 percent of the nation's 204 million people, but only 7 percent of the country's available land. Over thousands of years, the ash from Java's 17 volcanoes has made the soil rich and productive, capable of supporting large numbers of people. Another 21 percent of the people live on the adjacent volcanic island of Sumatra. Recently, nearly 3 million people were resettled from Java to Sumatra, most under government sponsorship. In fact, the resettlement of Javanese to other islands in Indonesia is an increasingly contentious issue. Many indigenous peoples suspect a government plot to inundate them with Javanese culture and Javanese concepts of economic development in order to gain access to and profiteer from indigenously held natural resources.

Two members of the Dani, a Papuan indigenous group in Irian Jaya, try to adjust to urban life in Wamena, a highland trading town. The Dani have little in common with recent Muslim migrants from Java, who were promised acreage carved out of the Dani's forested lands. [George Steinmetz.]

Harvesting the Rain Forest

Indonesia contains close to 40 percent of the Southeast Asian total landmass. In about 1800, it had only 10 million people. At that time, it boasted huge tropical rain forests that contained more than 4000 species of trees and at least 1500 bird and 500 mammal species—including large mammals like Asian elephants, tigers, rhinoceros, proboscis monkeys, and orangutans. Now, 200 years later, Indonesia has 20 times the population (204 million) and much less forest.

Rain forests still cover more than 56 percent of the Indonesian total landmass, but logging operations and commercial farming strip at least 4700 square miles (12,000 square kilometers) of rain forest a year—twice Brazil's rate of rain forest destruction. Only a few individuals of the larger mammal species are left in the shrinking habitat. The government says it recognizes the importance of the forests and claims to have protected nearly 80 percent with legislation. In fact, some 30 national parks and 150 nature preserves protect only about 10 percent of the forest habitat; lack of government personnel, weak enforcement of regulations, and absence of environmental awareness jeopardize conservation efforts outside these protected areas.

Official government policy is to seek managed growth and environmental protection through a "sustainable development" policy of discouraging the export of logs, per se. Wood is not exported as raw timber; rather, local factories turn harvested trees into products for export. The most commonly made product is plywood from the sought-after dipterocarp, the dominant hardwood in the forest canopy. This strategy does create jobs for Indonesians, who, the government argues, might otherwise be clear-cutting the forest for subsistence farming.

Timber harvesting in Kalimantan and Irian Jaya is a representative example of timber operations throughout Southeast Asia. Kalimantan is the southern part of the island of Borneo, and Irian Jaya is the western section of the island of New Guinea. Both are only lightly occupied. Kalimantan has about 10.5 million people and Irian Jaya has about 2 million. About one-third of Indonesia's forests are on Kalimantan. In the mid-1980s, East Kalimantan province supplied 30 percent of the country's timber. Some 85 percent of Irian Jaya is covered in rain forest and thick mangrove swamp. The central mountains of Irian Jaya reach as high as 16,000 feet and contain Asia's only tropical glacier.

These two places are wet, warm, and mountainous. Such tropical environments are at their most productive and sustainable when supporting their natural vegetative cover. They do not easily sustain large populations or support, without damage, profit-making exploitation.

Logging companies have obtained leases to huge tracts of rain forest for timber operations on Kalimantan and Irian Jaya. These companies are usually foreign owned, sometimes in partnership with Javanese companies controlled by political leaders. The favored method of operation is clear-cutting: the loggers cut down every tree in an area instead of taking only the valuable species and preserving the forest in some form. Clear-cutting is fast and gives quick profits. It lets companies avoid the supervision of human rights advocates and environmentalists, which would come with more long-term forestry efforts. The indigenous peoples who live in the forest are driven off the land and often resettled near state-owned factories affiliated with the timber interests or on newly developed state rubber plantations. In either case, they become a source of cheap, compliant labor. Sometimes settlers from overcrowded rural and urban areas (transmigrants) are also brought in to more quickly "civilize" the indigenous peoples. The transmigrants are expected to cultivate the newly cleared land, work for which they may have no prior experience.

In this way, the now deforested land becomes **contested space** between displaced indigenous peoples and incoming settlers. The government's argument that it provides jobs is true, strictly speaking. But the habitat is degraded beyond repair, and people are left in impoverishing circumstances, in tiny shacks on muddy tracts of land, with little sense of community. The central government invokes the principles of *Pancasila*, arguing that resettlement unifies the people as Indonesians by eliminating ways of life that are different from the government's vision. The policy is applauded as nation-building by those who see homogenization of Indonesia's cultural diversity as desirable.

Urban Factories

"Levi Closes Two Plants in Knox; 2,221 Laid Off" reads the bold headline of the Knoxville, Tennessee, *News-Sentinel* for Tuesday, November 4, 1997. Levi Strauss insists that the jobs are not moving overseas and that it will still make 55 percent of its jeans in the United States. The closings are necessary, they say, because current production levels are higher than demand. But among labor leaders and workers there is speculation about the role played by overseas garment production in regions like Southeast Asia.

Levi Strauss is one of several multinational companies prominent in the Jakarta area of Indonesia. The

Shantytowns, like this one on the outskirts of Jayapura, the capital of Irian Jaya, rise on the outskirts of most Indonesian cities as thousands of rural people flock to cities looking for jobs. Notice the mosque. Jayapura is a city of over 310,000 people. On any given day, an interisland ferry may arrive with another 2000 people—peddlers, contract laborers, students, sex workers, and soldiers—looking for work. [George Steinmetz.]

company prides itself on insisting on fair labor practices for its foreign employees and for workers of Levi Strauss subcontractors (small companies that make snaps or buttons or other garment parts). In Indonesia, many of the garment subcontractors are Korean owned. Working conditions and wages at these companies are far below U.S. standards. Levi Strauss (and other companies, like Nike and Reebok) has a code of conduct it issues to subcontractors, but the subcontracts almost always go to the lowest bidder, regardless of code enforcement.

The writer Jeremy Seabrook observes that Levi Strauss, like other companies, reacts only when the poor labor practices of its subcontractors are publicized. In one case, for example, rather than try to enforce its code of conduct and improve working conditions, Levi Strauss canceled the contract with the offender and went to another company that has not (yet) received bad publicity.

VIGNETTE   **Hira and Mirim are two single women in their 20s who work in a Singapore-owned Jakarta garment factory that was once a Levi Strauss subcontractor. The contract was voided because of bad publicity, but the factory stayed in operation by supplying garments to other companies. In 1994, the two women earned the minimum**

Indonesian wage of 3800 rupiah (U.S. $1.80) a day. Their factory has an uninsulated metal roof and is crammed with 200 workers. There is only one toilet. The women are often forced to work an additional six hours overtime to fill an order. For this they earn the equivalent of 10 cents an hour. There is no allowance for food, transportation, or health care.. According to Seabrook, independent observers say that to meet basic needs in Jakarta, people need to earn a minimum of U.S. $5 a day.

Hira and Mirim share a single room of 60 square feet (six square meters) in the upper story of a slum shack that costs them U.S. $8 a month each. The toilet is down the street a bit, on the edge of a foul, black canal; usually there is no flush water in it when they arrive home at four in the afternoon on a normal working day. Besides, the toilets are surrounded by only chest-high wooden slats and there are too many curious people around. The two women usually have to wait until well after dark for the water to come back on and to gain a bit of privacy. To avoid hunger pangs, they must each spend a minimum of U.S. $24 a month on food and water. To maintain basic nutrition, they need to spend more. Thus, their minimum essential needs of food, water, and shelter cost them each about U.S. $32 a month out of their U.S. $45 monthly take-home pay. Like the vast majority of their coworkers, Hira and Mirim come from villages in central Java. They migrated to further their education and make something of their lives. They do not return home because they are embarrassed that they have not accomplished what they set out to do and would bring shame on their families.

Island Southeast Asia: The Philippines

If ethnic diversity sometimes leads to conflict, is a country where most people belong to the same ethnic groups likely to be more peaceful and egalitarian? Not necessarily, is the answer if one looks at the Philippines. Ninety-five percent of Filipinos are Malays, and yet the country is one of the most contentious in the region and has the most unequal distribution of wealth.

The Philippine Islands, lying at the northeastern reach of the Malay Archipelago, consist of more than 7000 islands spread over about 500,000 square miles (1.3 million square kilometers) of ocean (Figure 10.18). The two largest are Mindanao in the south and Luzon in the north. Together, they make up about two-thirds of the total landmass, which is about the size of Arizona. The Philippine Islands, part of the Pacific Ring of Fire, are volcanic in origin. The violent erup-

tion of Mount Pinatubo in June 1991 devastated 154 square miles (400 square kilometers) and blanketed most of Southeast Asia with ash. Volcanologists had predicted the eruption and precautions were taken, so although more than a million people were threatened, only 250 died. A history of volcanic eruptions has blessed the Philippines with relatively fertile soil and rich mineral deposits (gold, copper, iron, chromate, and several other elements). Vast stands of timber were once another important resource, but the forests have been seriously plundered in recent years. Despite formal agreements to harvest wood over 25-year periods, several foreign-owned timber companies in the 1990s clear-cut their allotments in a few months.

In 1898, when the Philippines became a U.S. protectorate, it had 7 million people. Now, just 100 years later, it has more than 73 million. Population density has increased from 63 to 638 people per square mile (246 per square kilometer). Close to 50 percent of these people live in cities, a high proportion for this region. The Philippines contains one of the largest and most densely settled urban agglomerations on earth. The metropolitan area of Manila, the country's capital, has a population of at least 11 million. Urban densities exceed 50,000 people per square mile (20,000 per square kilometer). Probably at least one-quarter of the people living in these cities can be classed as poor, and many are unemployed squatters living in shelters built out of scraps. Some of the newest urban dwellers are people displaced by the eruption of Mount Pinatubo in 1991. Others are those displaced by rapid deforestation, dam projects, and the mechanization of commercial agriculture. The masses of urban poor in the Philippines represent a particular political and civil threat, because the people's faith in the government has not yet been restored since the excesses of Ferdinand Marcos's dictatorial regime (1965–1986).

The radical increase in population density might alone cause social problems, but Philippine society is also complex culturally. Within the Malay majority, there are at least 60 distinct ethnic groups. Another 2 percent are Chinese, and the remaining 3 percent include Europeans, Americans, other Asians, and indigenous peoples. Most Philippine people are Roman Catholic (83 percent), a result of nearly 400 years as a Spanish colony.

In the Philippines, as elsewhere in Southeast Asia, wealth is apportioned along ethnic and religious lines. The vast majority of the wealthy are descendants of Spanish (and Spanish-Filipino) plantation landowners, or of Chinese business and financial people. It is estimated that 30 percent of the top 500 corporations in the islands are controlled today by ethnic Chinese-Filipino people (of Chinese extraction but resident in the Philippines for generations). This group comprises less than 1 percent of the population. The poor are

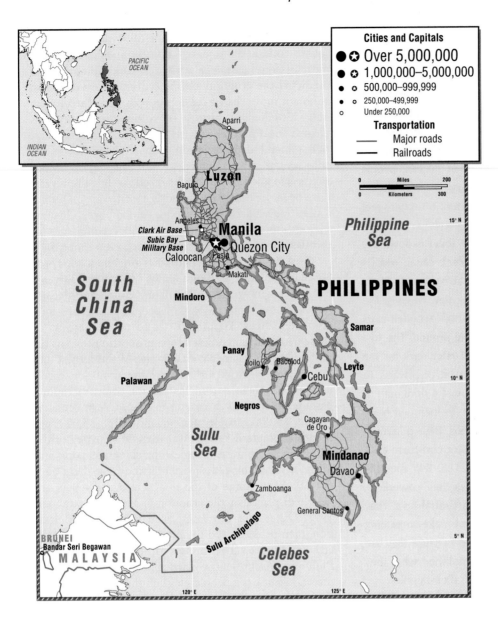

Cities and Capitals
- ●○ Over 5,000,000
- ●○ 1,000,000–5,000,000
- ● ○ 500,000–999,999
- ● ○ 250,000–499,999
- ○ Under 250,000

Transportation
— Major roads
— Railroads

FIGURE 10.18 The Philippines subregion.

overwhelmingly Malay people, and, in the southern islands, they are often Muslim as well.

By 1972, family conglomerates controlled 78 percent of all corporate wealth in the Philippines. But, unlike Malaysia, the Philippine government of the 1970s did not embark on a new economic policy to give the more disadvantaged ethnic groups access to jobs and education. Instead, after protests erupted in the early 1970s, President Marcos declared martial law (1972) and managed to hang on to power for another 14 years until he was overthrown. During that time and since, there has been little progress in job creation and wealth redistribution. The Philippines still spends comparatively little on education for its populace, just U.S. $25 per capita in 1993.

Violent social unrest has been very much a part of life in the Philippines. Filipinos are keenly aware that a better social and political system is possible, in part be-

cause the long association with the United States (first as a protectorate, later as the site for large U.S. military installations) gave the Philippine people a window on the outside world. It was often a dirty window, in that some of the worst aspects of U.S. culture were imported (drug use, sex work, wasteful consumerism), especially around the six U.S. military bases. Nonetheless, the Subic Bay Naval Base alone employed 32,000 local people and indirectly created 200,000 jobs. Many of the workers, especially women office workers, were exposed to information, education, and opportunities to migrate that other Southeast Asians have not had. Furthermore, some of the urban protest strategies employed in the United States have been brought to the Philippines by liberation theology Catholics and by community developers.

Geographers are often interested in the strategies used to gain and maintain control of contested space. Denis Murphy, coordinator of Urban Poor Associates, is an American who helps urban squatters foil government eviction plans in Manila. He notes that the urban poor in cities like Manila form ad hoc organizations to take care of each other and to challenge those who would displace them—be it government, developers, the police, or the military. In an area of Manila called Bulaklak, meaning "flower," the squatters, in an effort to foil urban developers, built their own houses and named all the streets after flowers. They then embarked on a self-financed project to develop a drainage system and to mark individual lots, even though ultimate land ownership is questionable. Each house contributes 5000 pesos (U.S. $200) for the project, apportioned over a 15-year period. As of 1996, construction was under way on the drainage system. Nonetheless, Bulaklak risks violent demolition, a common fate of squatter settlements in Manila and elsewhere. Murphy believes that although the squatters' movement is not motivated by socialist ideology, they represent a threat because they demonstrate their ability to construct autonomous, egalitarian alternatives to the status quo.

In their efforts to settle social unrest and attract investment, Marcos's successors have been hampered by the triple economic disasters of the Mount Pinatubo eruption, the closing of the American military bases, and a drastic cut in U.S. foreign aid in 1993. One of the few bright spots in the Philippine economy is the success of microcredit programs. The successes of these small entrepreneurs are illustrative of the spirit that Denis Murphy talks about and that too often remains untapped in the closed-off Philippine society.

VIGNETTE

When Jesusa Ocampo made her first batch of *macapuno* candy for sale 14 years ago, she had no idea that the exercise would one day grow into a full-fledged business. Neighbors snapped up all 20 packets of her coconut-based sweet. It wasn't long before Ocampo was making over 100 packets of candy daily. There was just one problem: she was too poor to pay for the expansion needed to meet rising demand. Then a friend told her about a microcredit program financed by the Philippine government. Beginning with a loan of just U.S. $145 obtained through a local cooperative, Ocampo gradually built up her mom-and-pop operation. She flourished and so did her credit rating. In the spring of 1997, she obtained a loan of U.S. $3000, her nineteenth loan. She and her family are now building their own home on land they have purchased outside Manila.

The case of the Philippines shows how bad leadership and corrupt government can hold a country back.

Despite the rampant sale of its timber resources, the economy has been slow to grow. The agricultural sector—rice, coconuts, corn, sugarcane, bananas, pineapples, mangos, and fish and animals—has remained relatively constant over the past 20 years, hovering between 22 and 25 percent of the total economy but employing 55 percent of the labor force. In 1993, industry accounted for 33 percent of the economy and services 45 percent; but perhaps the most meaningful figure is that 30 percent of the population is un- or underemployed. *Asiaweek* magazine reports that in terms of purchasing power, per capita income in the Philippines is twice that (or more) of Laos, Burma, Vietnam, and Cambodia, but less than Indonesia's. These numbers suggest that the Philippine economy is still controlled by a relatively small oligarchy. The oligarchy discourages entrepreneurial initiatives like the Bulaklak project.

Paradoxically, because the Philippines remained underdeveloped longer than its neighbors, the country has been less affected than others by the financial crisis and turmoil of the late 1990s across most of the region. Foreign investors are now building facilities, construction in Manila is growing, and on the former U.S. naval base at Subic Bay, an industrial park rises. Some economists predict that because the Philippines is starting from behind, it may lead most of its neighbors in terms of real economic growth at the millennium.

REFLECTIONS ON SOUTHEAST ASIA

For years, Southeast Asia has been touted as a model of fast, efficient development, following the peerless example of Japan. Many countries in Southeast Asia—especially Malaysia, Thailand, Singapore, and Indonesia—have grown more quickly and consistently than countries in any other developing region. By comparison with Latin America, the distribution of wealth has been far more equitable, as Table 10.3 shows.

Southeast Asia is often held up as a model to regions like Latin America or Africa south of the Sahara, in terms of rate of growth, distribution of wealth, and rate of personal savings. But, it is important to note that what is often called the miracle of Southeast Asian development is almost always calculated in economic terms. Those who do not think only in economic terms (geographers, political scientists, anthropologists) have advocated a more thorough analysis of the miracle.

513

TABLE 10.3

Income spread ratio of selected countries in Middle and South America and Southeast Asia

Country	Income spread ratio*
Brazil	32.1
Peru	29.2
Chile	18.3
Mexico	13.6
Costa Rica	12.7
Malaysia	11.7
Singapore	9.6
Thailand	9.3
Philippines	7.4
Vietnam	5.6
Indonesia	4.9

*The higher the number, the greater the spread between the income of the wealthiest 20 percent and the income of the poorest 20 percent.
Source: Wealth, poverty, and social investment table, *Human Development Report 1996*, p. 170, United Nations Human Development Programme.

They would also look at how rapid economic progress affects the environment, human rights and political participation, investment in social programs and education, families, and the status of women. In fact, according to the UN rankings of countries on overall human development (the HDI), Latin America has an overall better showing, averaging in the 50s. Southeast Asian countries rank in the 90s, with the largest country, Indonesia, ranking at 96.

For a time it looked like human and environmental issues were not likely to receive much attention in Southeast Asia. Then in the late 1990s, the situation began to shift. A major economic downturn in conjunction with an alarming environmental episode—a persistent poisonous haze throughout island Southeast Asia—turned attention to factors that had escaped notice for some time. Threatening economic recession precipitated appalling revelations of bad loans based on widespread corrupt practices in high places. Under scrutiny, the poisonous smog was shown to be the result of rampant environmental exploitation, including clear-cutting of timber and burning for plantation cultivation as well as industrial and vehicle emissions. Soon it looked as if the region's competitive edge had been founded on wildly unsustainable practices. None of the information was really new; it was just that the supposed economic prowess of the region had always overridden indications that all was not well.

But will crisis in Southeast Asia lead to a different definition of development, to a recognition that the means of development—democratic participation and widespread access to opportunity and information—are more important than such ends as quick profits and high mass consumption? Certainly the people of the region have amply demonstrated that they have the fortitude to work hard, but it seems possible that the national philosophies of conformity and harmony may thwart deep reforms. If the economic and environmental issues are seriously addressed, the region may very well pull off another miracle. Thus far, no other region in the world has achieved both social and physically sustainable development.

Selected Themes and Concepts

1. Southeast Asia is a large region, with a moist tropical climate, made up of peninsulas of various sizes and several archipelagos containing numerous islands, large and small. Much of the surface area of the region is ocean.

2. The present indigenous inhabitants of Southeast Asia are descendants of two ancient migrations. The Australo-Melanesians came about 60,000 years ago; the Austronesians came about 5000 years ago from the vicinity of the South China coast.

3. Southeast Asia's position, surrounded by seas, has for centuries made it easily accessible to trade and cultural influence from outside. Hindu and Muslim traders, the Chinese, and European colonizers were perhaps the most important of these influences.

4. Since the 1960s, the economies of Thailand, Malaysia, Singapore, Indonesia, and the Philippines have grown considerably, aided largely by industries that export manufactured products to the rich countries of the world. Much of the region's prosperity is based on the employment of cheap labor and the unsustainable use of natural resources, particularly timber, minerals, and soil.

5. Most of the people live in patches of particularly dense rural settlement. About 35 percent of the population live in the numerous urban areas across the region that are among the most densely occupied cities on earth.

6. While family size is shrinking in the region, the youth of the population means populations will grow for many years to come.

7. Several types of migration are responsible for major changes in the region: rural-to-urban migration, government resettlement schemes, forced migration, and extraregional migration.

8. Despite patriarchal customs, women play central roles in Southeast Asian families and have considerable autonomy. Divorce rates are high.

9. From the mid-1980s to the mid-1990s, Southeast Asia's high rates of economic growth earned many countries reputations as economic "tigers," aggressively on the make and leaping into a new era of prosperity. By the late 1990s, many were heavily in debt with declining prospects, at least in the near term.

10. The cultural diversity of Southeast Asia poses twin political threats to democratic government in the region: diversity may make consensus impossible or one culture group may impose its will on the rest. Governments have attempted to resolve the political problem of diversity by devising national philosophies that encourage conformity and harmony, sometimes with the effect that dissent is violently and undemocratically repressed.

11. Within the region of Southeast Asia there is great variance in levels of well-being, from very rich in Singapore and among the upper classes in the urban areas of most countries to very poor in war-ravaged places like Laos and Cambodia.

Selected Readings

Atkinson, Jane Monnig, and Shelly Errington, eds. *Power and Difference: Gender in Island Southeast Asia.* Stanford, CA: Stanford University Press, 1990.

Barry, Kathleen, ed. *Vietnam's Women in Transition.* New York: St. Martin's Press, 1996.

Bercuson, Kenneth, with Robert G. Carling, Aasim M. Husain, Thomas Rumbaugh, and Rachel van Elkan. *Singapore: A Case Study in Rapid Development.* Washington, D.C.: International Monetary Fund, 1995.

Bernard, Stephane, and Rodolphe De Koninck. The retreat of the forest in Southeast Asia: A cartographic assessment. *Singapore Journal of Tropical Geography* 17, no. 1 (1996): 1–14.

Bourdet, Yves. Laos in 1996—Please don't rush in. *Asian Survey* 37, no. 1 (January 1997): 72–77.

Brookfield, Harold, ed., with Loene Doube and Barbara Banks. *Transformation with Industrialization in Peninsular Malaysia.* Kuala Lumpur: Oxford University Press, 1994.

Cartier, Carolyn L. Creating historic open space in Melaka. From the American Geographical Society, at http://www.elibrary.com/...42850221x0y628:0001:D000, 1993.

Christie, Clive J. *A Modern History of Southeast Asia: Decolonization, Nationalism and Separatism.* London: I. B. Tauris, 1996.

Cleary, Mark, and Shuang Yann Wong. *Oil, Economic Development and Diversification in Brunei Darussalam.* New York: St. Martin's Press, 1994.

De Koninck, Rodolphe. *Malay Peasants Coping with the World—Breaking the Community Circle?* Singapore: Institute of Southeast Asian Studies, 1992.

Fforde, Adam, and Stefan de Vylder. *From Plan to Market—The Economic Transition in Vietnam.* Boulder, CO: Westview Press, 1996.

Howard, Michael, ed. *Asia's Environmental Crisis.* Boulder, CO: Westview Press, 1993.

Karim, Wazir Jahan. *"Male and Female" in Developing Southeast Asia.* Washington, DC: Berg, 1995.

Murray, Alison J. *No Money, No Honey—A Study of Street Traders and Prostitutes in Jakarta.* Singapore: Oxford University Press, 1991.

Myanmar's virgins! *New York Times Magazine*, June 29, 1997, p. 13.

Odzer, Cleo. *Patpong Sisters—An American Woman's View of the Bangkok Sex World.* New York: Arcade, 1994.

Parnwell, Michael J. G., and Raymond L. Bryant, eds. *Environmental Change in South-East Asia—People, Politics, and Sustainable Development.* London: Routledge, 1996.

Peletz, Michael G. *Reason and Passion—Representations of Gender in a Malay Society.* Berkeley: University of California Press, 1996.

Rajakru, Dang. The state, family and industrial development: The Singapore case. *Journal of Contemporary Asia* 26, no. 1 (1996): 3–27.

Rigg, Jonathan. *Southeast Asia—Human Landscape of Modernization and Development.* New York: Routledge, 1997.

SarDesai, D. R. *Southeast Asia: Past and Present,* 4th ed. Boulder, CO: Westview Press, 1997.

Seabrook, Jeremy. *In the Cities of the South—Scenes from a Developing World.* London: Verso, 1996.

Sellato, Bernard. *Nomads of the Borneo Rainforest—The Economics, Politics and Ideology of Settling Down.* Honolulu: University of Hawaii Press, 1994.

Williams, Walter L. *Javanese Lives: Women and Men in Modern Indonesian Society.* Piscataway, NJ: Rutgers University Press, 1991.

Winichakul, Thongchai. *Siam Mapped—A History of the Geo-Body of a Nation.* Honolulu: University of Hawaii Press, 1994.

Wolf, Diane Lauren. *Factory Daughters—Gender, Household Dynamics, and Rural Industrialization in Java.* Berkeley: University of California Press, 1992.

Wurfel, David, and Bruce Burton, eds. *Southeast Asia in the New World Order—The Politcal Economy of a Dynamic Region.* New York: St. Martin's Press, 1996.

CHAPTER

ELEVEN

OCEANIA:

AUSTRALIA,

NEW ZEALAND,

AND THE

PACIFIC

INTRODUCTION TO OCEANIA

Pacific islanders, wrote the anthropologist Bronislaw Malinowski, have created a tradition around their outrigger canoes. They adorn them with the best carvings; they color and decorate them. The canoes, with a long main hull and an outrigger float for stability, are constructed of extremely light material, which gives the craft great buoyancy. The canoes hug the surface of the water and are far less subject to capsizing than "any sea-going European craft." An outrigger canoe "skims the surface, gliding up and down the waves, now hidden by the crests, now riding on top of them." When on a calm day the fresh breeze rises to fill the sail and the canoe lifts its outrigger out of the water, racing along, flinging spray to the right and left, "there is no mistaking the keen enjoyment." The canoe is revered as a powerful contrivance for the mastery of nature that allows its creators "to cross perilous seas to distant places."

The name **Oceania** conveys the role that the Pacific Ocean has played in defining the possibilities and limitations of life in this region, comprising Australia, New Zealand, and the Pacific islands. If there is one theme that knits Oceania together as a region through time, it is the human urge to travel. It is a theme that stretches back 60,000 years to an ancient people in Southeast Asia (the Australo-Melanesians), who one day decided to move on. Their descendants, and a second wave of migrants some 5000 years ago (the Austronesians), eventually settled Australia and New Zealand and thousands of islands in the Pacific. Since 1800, hundreds of thousands of Europeans have made the ocean voyage to Australia and New Zealand—far fewer to the Pacific islands—motivated by the simple need to make a life for themselves. This theme of travel in Oceania is as immediate as yesterday's flight carrying rugby players from the Marquesas to New Zealand for a championship game or an excited college student from Saipan in the Northern Mariana Islands to take her graduate record exam in Guam.

A look at the globe reveals that the Pacific Ocean covers more than a quarter of the earth's surface. The central and southwestern Pacific is the locus of the region we call Oceania. This part of the Pacific contains the continent of Australia and more than 20,000 islands, many of which are uninhabited atolls barely rising above the surface of the sea. Setting Australia aside for a moment, the single island of New Guinea and the two islands of New Zealand account for

90 percent of the land area in the Pacific. The other 10 percent is shared among thousands of islands lying mostly in the central and southern Pacific. For many of these islands, the nearest neighbor is more than 600 miles (1000 kilometers) away. Despite its great size, Oceania contains only 30 million people. Partly for this reason I have decided not to include the usual treatment of the subregions—Australia, New Zealand, and the Pacific islands—at the end of the chapter. Instead, I have written about these subregions in the various issues sections.

Themes to Look For

More than some other regions in this book, Oceania gives us a pleasant, but not trouble-free, image of the future. The people of the Pacific have developed an attitude or point of view they call "the Pacific Way." It has different meanings in different parts of the region; but wherever it is present, the attitude has inspired some useful ways of dealing with life. The themes that characterize this region are

1. The growth of Pacific regional consciousness based on cultural diversity

2. An increasing orientation toward trade and social interaction with Asia and a decreasing emphasis on European roots

3. A growing recognition of environmental issues

4. An increasing attention to the rights of indigenous peoples

5. A familiarity with mobility (and tourism) and the consequences of bringing people of disparate backgrounds into close contact

PHYSICAL PATTERNS

The huge expanse of the Pacific plays a role of supreme importance in this region. The movement of the water and its varying temperatures influence climates in all the region's landmasses. For living things, the Pacific serves as a link between lands that are widely separated. Humans have long used the ocean as an avenue for communication, for visiting, trading, and raiding. For the region's inhabitants, sea life is a source of food; and in the modern era it is a source of income, as catches are sold in the global market. But the wide expanses of water have also acted as a barrier, profoundly limiting the natural diffusion of plant and ani-

This is an atoll in the Tuamotu Archipelago of French Polynesia. As is the case here, usually the circular shape of an atoll's submerged crater is not intact, so the parts form a sort of necklace of flat islands around a central lagoon. Often the necklace surrounds one or more islands that are the remnants of the old volcanic core. Some of these lagoons are home to *Pinctada margarifera,* the black-lipped pearl oyster, which produces famous black pearls. [David Doubilet.]

mal species, and keeping Pacific islanders isolated from each other. The vast ocean has imposed solitude and has fostered self-sufficiency and subsistence economies well into the modern era.

Island Formation

The islands of the Pacific were created by a variety of processes related to the movement of tectonic plates. Some islands are part of the "Ring of Fire," the belt of frequent volcanic eruptions and earthquakes circling the Pacific; Central America and California are a part of this belt. Many of the Pacific islands were created in boundary zones where the plates are either colliding or pulling apart. For example, the Marianas chain east of the Philippines are volcanoes formed when one plate plunged beneath another. The two much larger islands of New Zealand were created when the eastern edge of the Indian-Australian Plate was thrust upward by its convergence with the Antarctic Plate.

There are two basic types of islands: atolls and high islands. **Atolls** are low-lying islands formed of coral reefs, which are made up of the skeletons of tiny living creatures called coral polyps. These islands are arranged in the form of a circle because the polyps build their reefs on the rims of submerged craters of undersea volcanoes. As a consequence of their low elevation, these islands tend to have only a small range of environments. **High islands** are most often volcanoes that rise above the sea into mountainous, rocky formations that contain a rich variety of environments. The Hawaiian Islands, Tahiti, the Samoa Islands, and Easter Island are examples of high islands (Figure 11.1). These mid-Pacific islands were created when magma pushed up through weakened spots in the earth's crust called "hot spots."

Continent Formation

The biggest landmasses of the Pacific are the frozen continent of Antarctica (not considered here) and the ancient continent of Australia at the southwest perimeter of the Pacific. The continent of Australia is composed of some of the oldest rock on earth and has been a more or less stable landmass for more than 200 million years, with very little volcanism and only an occasional, mild earthquake. Once a part of Pangaea, the ancient supercontinent, Australia broke free and drifted to where it eventually collided with the plate on which Southeast Asia sits. The impact created the mountainous island of New Guinea; downwarping created the lowland that is now filled with sea between New Guinea and Australia.

Australia is shaped roughly like a dinner plate, with a lumpy, irregular rim and two portions missing: one in the north (the Gulf of Carpentaria) and one in the south (the Great Australian Bight). The center of the plate is the great lowland Australian desert. The lumpy rim is made up of uplands: the Eastern Highlands are the highest and most complex of these. Over the millennia, fierce winds have worn Australia's landforms into low, rounded formations, some quite spectacular.

Off the northeastern coast of the continent lies the Great Barrier Reef, which stretches in an irregular arc for more than 1000 miles (1600 kilometers). The tiny, calcium-rich coral polyps that make up the reef exist in an abundance beyond enumeration. They are extremely fragile and unable to live in water that is too cold, or too full of sediment, or polluted. This giant reef interrupts the west-flowing ocean currents in the South Pacific circulation pattern, shunting warm water to the south. In and around the reef there is a great profusion of aquatic environments, some protected and warm, some cool and wildly active with pounding surf.

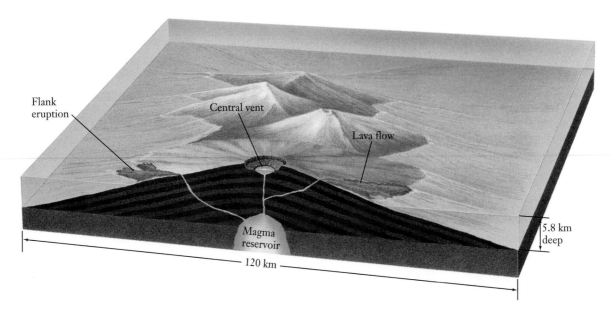

FIGURE 11.1 Some islands in the Pacific, like the Hawaiian chain, are formed by shield volcanoes. As this model of Mauna Loa on the Big Island of Hawaii illustrates, magma bursts through "hot spots," or weaknesses, in the surface of a plate. Wide, thin layers of lava spread from the point of eruption, slowly building undersea mountains that emerge as islands. [Adapted from Frank Press and Raymond Siever, *Understanding Earth,* 2nd ed. (New York: W. H. Freeman, 1998), p. 111.]

Climate

Although the Pacific stretches nearly from pole to pole, it is primarily a tropical ocean. It is widest through its tropical zones, and most of the islands of Oceania lie within, or close to, the tropics. The tepid water temperatures of the central Pacific bring year-round mild climates to nearly all the inhabited parts of the region (Figure 11.2). The southernmost reaches of Australia and New Zealand have the greatest seasonal variability in temperatures.

With the exception of the huge, low-lying landmass of Australia, most of Oceania is warm and humid nearly all the time. New Zealand and the high islands of the

Uluru (Ayers Rock) and the nearby Olgas of central Australia are smooth remnants of ancient sedimentary rock mountains that have resisted erosion. These sites are held sacred by central Australian Aborigines. They are also among the most popular tourist destinations. [Susan Metros.]

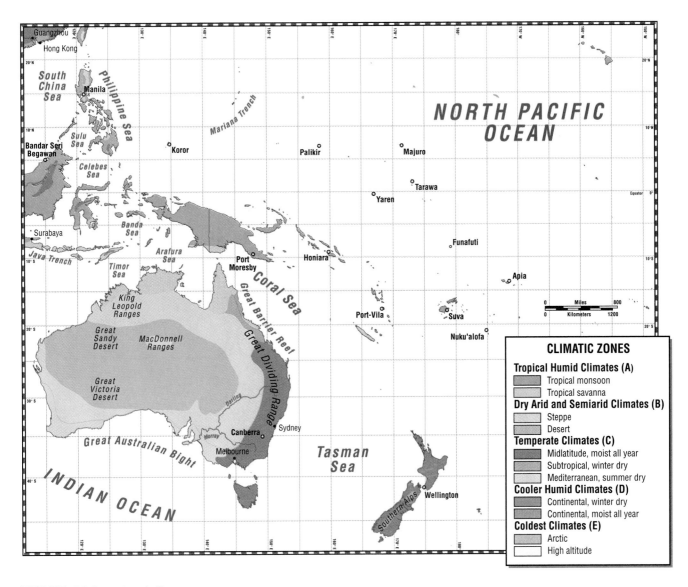

FIGURE 11.2 Regional climate.

Pacific receive copious rainfall and support dense forest vegetation Most travelers approaching New Zealand, either by air or by sea, notice a distinctive long white cloud that stretches above the two islands. A thousand years ago, Polynesian settlers called the Maori noticed this phenomenon, too, when they first encountered New Zealand; and so they named the place Aotearoa, "the long white cloud." The distinctive mass of moisture is brought in by the legendary roaring forties, powerful westerly air and ocean currents that speed around the far Southern Hemisphere virtually unimpeded by landmasses. These westerly winds deposit 130 inches (325 centimeters) of rain a year in the New Zealand highlands and 30+ inches (75+ centimeters) on the coastal lowlands. At the southern tip of North Island, New Zealand's capital, Wellington, has 118 days a year when the wind blows more than 40 miles (64 kilometers) an hour; cabbages have to be staked to the ground or they will blow away.

The low-lying islands across the region do not provide sufficient uplift for regular rainfall, and as a result they tend to have no surface fresh water and little vegetation, though the air is moist. Australia's landforms and climate are remarkably different from New Zealand's mountainous topography and wet temperate climate. Two-thirds of the continent of Australia is overwhelmingly dry. That large dry portion receives less than 20 inches (50 centimeters) of rain a year (see Figure 11.2). The Eastern Highlands block the movement of moist westward-moving air; they deflect it to the south so that rain does not reach the interior but is abundant along the eastern slopes of the highlands. During the

521

southern summer, the fringes of the monsoon that operates over Southeast Asia and Eurasia bring moister conditions (from 20 to 80 inches, or 50 to 200 centimeters, a year) across the Australian north coast and around to the far southeast. Australia is so arid that there is only one major river system—in the temperate southeast, where most Australians live. There the Darling and Murray river systems drain one-seventh of the continent and flow into the ocean at Adelaide. A measure of the overall dryness of Australia is that the entire annual flow of this river system is equal to just one day's flow of the Amazon in Brazil.

Every 8 to 13 years, a number of changes take place in the circulation of air and water in the Pacific (Figure 11.3). These changes, which are not yet well understood, have been given the name **El Niño.** Normally (A in Figure 11.3), water in the eastern Pacific (the Peru side) is cooler than water in the western Pacific (the New Guinea/Australia side). In an El Niño event, the reverse is true (B in Figure 11.3): ocean temperatures (and those of the air above the water) are cooler than usual in the west, warmer in the east. Instead of warm wet air rising over the mountains of New Guinea and condensing as rainfall, the cool drier air sits at the ocean surface. The result is less cloud cover and less rainfall. The El Niño event of 1997–1998 illustrates the effects. By December 1997, New Guinea had received very little rainfall for almost a year. Crops failed, springs and streams dried up, and fires broke out in tinder-dry forests. The cloudless sky allowed heat to radiate upward from elevations above 7200 feet (2200 meters), so there were stretches of a week or more when temperatures went below freezing at night. Meanwhile, along the coasts of North, Central, and South America, the warmer than usual weather brought unusually strong storms, high ocean surges, and a lot of wind and rainfall.

Flora and Fauna

Oceania's composition as a region of islands has had a special effect on its animal and plant life. Many species are **endemic,** that is, they exist in a particular place and nowhere else on earth. This is especially true for Australia, but many Pacific islands also have endemic species.

Plant and Animal Life in Australia. The uniqueness of Australia's plant and animal life is the result of the long physical isolation of the continent, its large size, its relatively homogeneous landforms, and the strikingly arid climate. Since Australia broke away from the supercontinent of Pangaea about 100 million years ago, its plant and animal species have evolved in isolation. The "homegrown" Australian species evolved to fill not only the humid zones similar to those on

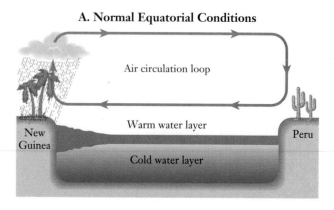

A. Normal Equatorial Conditions

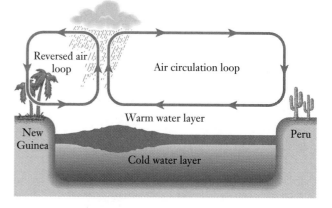

B. Developing El Niño Conditions

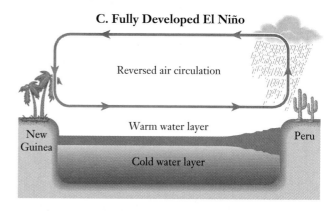

C. Fully Developed El Niño

FIGURE 11.3 The El Niño phenomenon. [Adapted from Environmental Dynamics Research, Inc., 1998.]

Pangaea, but all the various arid niches that eventually dominated the Australian landscape.

One spectacular result of the long isolation has been the development of over 144 living species of marsupial mammals. **Marsupials** are mammals that give birth to their young at a very immature stage and then nurture them in a pouch equipped with nipples. The most famous marsupials are the kangaroos; other species include wallabies, wombats, phalangers, the tiger cat, possums, the koala, numbats, and bandicoots.

These different types of marsupials fill niches elsewhere occupied by rats, badgers, moles, cats, wolves, ungulates (grazers), and bears. One other type of mammal is exclusive to Australia and New Guinea. These are the **monotremes**, egg-laying mammals that include the duck-billed platypus and the spiny anteater.

Birds are also unusually varied; parrot species are especially diverse. Some of the 750 species of birds known on the continent migrate in and out, but more than 325 species are endemic. Since birds had few natural predators in Australia, they rarely needed to make quick escapes; several species, therefore, lost the ability to fly. The large emu and cassowary are examples of flightless birds. Since their arrival in the late eighteenth century, Europeans have introduced many more animals from Europe and elsewhere, often with dire consequences for native species.

Most of Australia's endemic plant species are adapted to dry conditions. Many of the plants have deep taproots to draw moisture from groundwater and small, hard, shiny (sclerophyll) leaves to reflect heat and to hold moisture. Much of the continent has only grass- and scrubland, with bits of open woodland; there are only a very few true forests—in the Eastern Highlands and in Tasmania (Figure 11.4). Two plant genera account for nearly all the forest and woodland plants. They are the *Eucalyptus* (450 species, often called "gum trees") and the *Acacia* (900 species, often called "wattles").

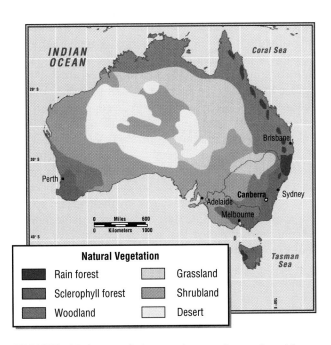

FIGURE 11.4 Australia's natural vegetation. [Adapted from Tom L. McKnight, *Oceania* (Englewood Cliffs, NJ: Prentice Hall, 1995), p. 28.]

Plant and Animal Life in New Zealand and the Pacific Islands. Generally speaking, the distribution of land animals and plants is richest in the western Pacific, near the larger landmasses of New Guinea, New Zealand, and Australia. The variety thins out to the east, where the islands are smaller and farther apart. While the natural vegetation of New Zealand and of the high islands in the Pacific is abundant and is mostly dense rain forest, the fauna in New Zealand and the Pacific islands are often described as simply "absent" because there are no indigenous land mammals, no reptiles to speak of, and only a few species of frogs. The reason for this is that New Zealand and the islands were never connected to the landmass of Eurasia as were Southeast Asia and Australia. There was never a land bridge that animals (and humans) could cross. On the other hand, birds in New Zealand are numerous and varied, especially waterfowl. New Zealand is the home of the kiwi, a flightless bird, and, in the past, of the huge moa. Some species of this bird grew 12 feet high. The moa was a major source of food until it was hunted into extinction before Europeans arrived. Today, New Zealand is the country most characterized by introduced species of mammals, fish, and fowl. Nearly all were brought in by European settlers.

The prehuman biogeography of the Pacific islands has long interested those who study evolution and the diffusion of plants and animals. Islands have to snare their plant and animal populations from the sea and air around them. Birds and large storms drop seeds and spores. Dead logs and other debris from storms convey small animals, seeds, and plant shoots from larger islands and continents to distant atolls and volcanic islands. Some seeds, like large, buoyant coconuts, can float to a random destination on their own. Then, in a complicated process, these organisms "colonize" their new home. For example, coconut trees accomplish the long process of moving from the beach to inland locations by dropping the coconuts of each succeeding generation onto ever slightly higher ground. Over time, plant and animal colonizers may evolve into new species that are endemic to one island.

High, wet islands generally have more and varied species because their more complex environmental mosaics provide niches for a wider range of wayfarers; they provide a greater range of circumstances for evolutionary change. The flora and fauna are also modified by human inhabitants. In prehistoric times, settlers exploring by canoe out of Asia carried with them garden plants like taro, bananas, and breadfruit, and animals like pigs, chickens, and dogs—as well as less desirable passengers like rats, fleas, and diseases. Today, human activities from tourism to military exercises to city building continue to change the plants and animals of the Pacific islands.

HUMAN PATTERNS

The story of humans in Oceania begins in ancient times with a series of fantastic voyages across incredible space. In historical times, the region has experienced European colonialism that resembles colonialism in other world regions in its exploitation of resources and treatment of indigenous people. Oceania is now interacting more and more with Asia, its nearest neighbor, but a region that until recently has exerted only indirect influence.

The Peopling of Oceania

The longest surviving inhabitants of Oceania are Australia's Aborigines. The ancestors of the Aborigines migrated from Southeast Asia as early as 60,000 years ago, over the Sundaland landmass that was exposed during the ice ages (see Figure 10.1). Amazingly, some memory of this ancient journey may be preserved in Aboriginal oral traditions, which recall mountains and other geographic features that are now submerged under water. At around the same time the Aborigines were settling Australia, related groups were settling nearby areas. These were the Melanesians, so named for their relatively dark skin tones, a result of high levels of protective melanin pigment. The Melanesians spread throughout New Guinea and other nearby islands, giving this region its name, Melanesia. Like the Aborigines, they survived mostly by hunting, gathering, and fishing, though some groups also practiced agriculture.

Much later, about 4000 to 5000 years ago, linguistically related groups called Austronesians continued the settlement of the Pacific, migrating out of what is now southern China. By about a thousand years ago, the Austronesians had spread throughout the remaining islands of the Pacific, sometimes mixing with the Melanesian peoples they encountered (Figure 11.5). The Austronesians were renowned for their ability not only to survive at sea but also to navigate over vast, featureless distances by using the stars and "reading the waves"; they were also fishers, hunter-gatherers, and cultivators who developed complex cultures and maintained trading relationships among their far-flung islands. Micronesia refers to the small islands lying east of the Philippines and north of the equator. Polynesia refers to the numerous islands lying in an irregular triangle formed by New Zealand, Hawaii, and Easter Island in the far eastern Pacific.

In the millennia intervening since first settlement, humans have continued to circulate throughout Oceania.

Some apparently set out because their own space was too full of people or food reserves were declining, or because they wanted a life of greater freedom. Just as likely, Pacific peoples were also enticed to new locales by the same lures that later attracted some of the more romantic Europeans: sparkling beaches, beautiful people, scented breezes, and lovely landscapes.

Arrival of the Europeans

The earliest recorded contact between Pacific peoples and Europeans took place in 1521, when the first Europeans to cross the Pacific, led by the Portuguese explorer Ferdinand Magellan, landed on the island of Guam in Micronesia. That encounter ended badly. The islanders, intrigued by European vessels, tried to claim a small skiff. For this crime, Magellan had his men kill the offenders and burn the village to the ground. By the 1540s, the Spanish had set up a lucrative trade route between Manila in the Philippines and Acapulco in Mexico. Explorers from other European states followed, at first taking an interest mainly in the region's valuable spices. The British and French explored extensively in the eighteenth century, but the region was not formally divided among the colonial powers until the nineteenth century. By this time, the United States, Germany, and even Japan had joined France and Britain in taking over parts of Oceania.

Many enduring notions about the Pacific arose from the European explorations of the eighteenth and nineteenth centuries. This was a period of intense questioning in Europe as to whether or not civilization actually improves the quality of life for human beings. Some Europeans argued that civilization corrupted and debased people. This point of view in part grew out of the negative effects of industrialization in Europe, where crowded, dirty, impersonal, often crime-ridden cities were proliferating. Romanticists glorified what they termed "primitive" people, living in distant places supposedly untouched by corrupting influences; they coined the term *noble savage* to describe such people. Pacific explorers were influenced by these ideas and often spoke of the people they encountered as being in a pristine state of nature that was more conducive to virtuous moral conduct. Europeans were caught off guard when, from time to time, the islanders rebelled, armed themselves, and attacked those who would take their lands and resources. Usually, when this happened, the Europeans quickly changed their opinions, referring to the "noble savages" as brutish and debased.

The realities of life in Oceania were much more balanced than the positive and negative extremes that Europeans saw. In Australia, and on New Guinea and the larger islands of the rest of Melanesia, a relatively

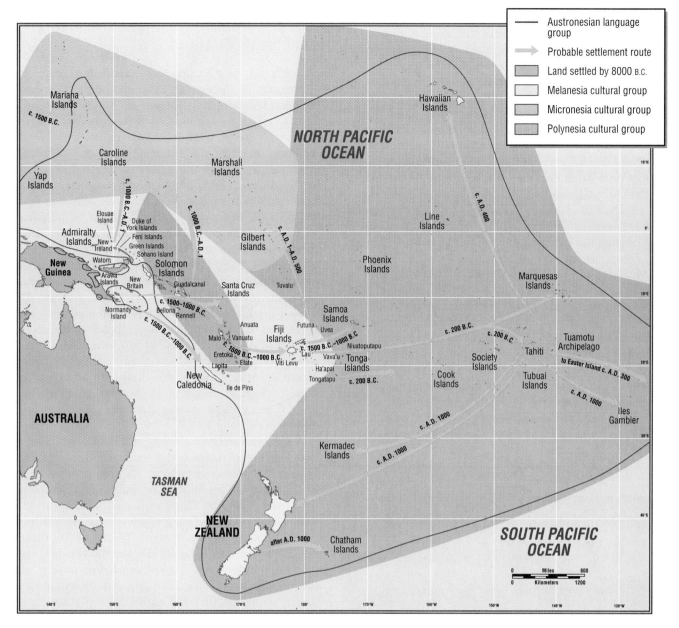

FIGURE 11.5 Modern *Homo sapiens,* scholars argue, reached coastal New Guinea about the same time they reached Australia, about 60,000 years ago. By about 25,000 years ago, people were spread across a large part of New Guinea and had even begun moving across the ocean to nearby Pacific islands. Archaeologists have found a site on Buka in the northern Solomon Islands dated to about 26,000 years ago. Movement into the more distant Pacific islands apparently began with the arrival of the Austronesians, who reached the Philippines from southern China 5000 years ago and New Guinea shortly thereafter. This map shows the divisions of Pacific islands into Melanesia, Micronesia, and Polynesia. [Adapted from Richard Nile and Christian Clerk, *Cultural Atlas of Australia, New Zealand and the South Pacific* (New York: Facts on File, 1996), pp. 58–59.]

plentiful resource base offered the possibility for people to live in small, simple societies, less subject to the stratification and class tensions of so much of the world. Land and resources were more scarce on the smaller islands of Micronesia and Polynesia. On these islands, many societies were **hierarchical,** with ruling elites at the top and outcasts and slaves at the bottom. Moreover, many of the peoples of Oceania were in a frequent state of antagonism, and warfare was not uncommon; but hostilities were often settled ritualistically and by means of annual tribute-paying ceremonies, rather than by resorting to actual violence. Individual rulers rarely amassed large territories or controlled them for long.

Perhaps the most enduring departure from reality made by Europeans was their characterization of the women of Pacific islands as gentle, simple, compliant love objects; tourist brochures still promote this myth. Though there is ample evidence to suggest that Pacific islanders did have more sexual partners in a lifetime than their European counterparts, the reports of unrestrained sexuality related by European sailors were influenced by the exaggerated fantasies one might expect from individuals living with all-male crews for months at a time. The notes of Captain James Cook are typical: "No women I ever met were less reserved. Indeed, it appeared to me, that they visited us with no other view, than to make a surrender of their persons."

Over the years, such notions about Pacific women have been encouraged by the paintings and prints of Gauguin, the writings of the novelist Herman Melville (*Typee*), the studies of the anthropologist Margaret Mead (*Coming of Age in Samoa*), as well as by movies and musicals such as *South Pacific*. In reality, gender roles in the Pacific varied considerably from those in Europe. Women often exercised a good bit of power in family and clan, power that increased with motherhood and advancing age. In Polynesia, a women could achieve the rank of ruling chief in her own right, not just as the consort of a male chief. In everyday life in Polynesia, men were the primary cultivators of food as well as the usual cooks. Women were primarily craftspeople. And, in Micronesia, lineage was established through women, not men.

Arearea "Amusement" by Gauguin, 1892. The painting is of Tahitian women rendered in a European Romantic pastoral style that emphasizes their gentle, compliant demeanor.
[Musée d'Orsay, Paris, Photograph by Erich Lessing, Art Resource, New York.]

The Colonization of Australia and New Zealand

Though all of Oceania has experienced rule by Europeans or Americans at some point, the most Westernized parts of the region are Australia and New Zealand. The colonization of these two countries by the British has resulted in many parallels with North America. In fact, the major impetus for "settling" Australia came from the American Revolution, which deprived Britain of a place to send its convicts. In early nineteenth-century Britain, a relatively minor theft—for example, of food or a piglet—might be punished with a term of seven years hard labor in Australia. After their time was up, most former convicts chose to stay in Australia. They were joined by a much larger group of free immigrants from the British Isles who came in waves up to World War II. Nevertheless, the steady flow of English and Irish convicts lasted until 1868 and is credited with having had a huge impact on the development of Australia; it resulted in a society with a rustic self-image and an egalitarian spirit similar to that of North America. Comparable things are often said of New Zealand. It, too, had an overwhelmingly British population, though it was colonized later and was never a penal colony.

Another similarity among Australia, New Zealand, and North America was the treatment of indigenous peoples by European settlers. Native peoples were killed outright, annihilated by infectious diseases to which they had little immunity, or were shifted to the margins of society. The few who lived on territory deemed undesirable by Europeans were able to maintain their traditional way of life; but the vast majority who survived lived and worked in grinding poverty, either in urban slums or on cattle and sheep ranches. Today, native peoples still suffer from pervasive discrimination and all the accompanying maladies of an underclass, such as alcoholism and malnutrition. Even so, some progress is being made toward improving their lives. New Zealand has made great strides in appreciating the culture and rights of its native Maori population; Australia is beginning to do the same in relation to the Aborigines, though in Australia there is vocal resistance to this project among some of European background.

Oceania's Growing Ties with Asia

Over the course of the twentieth century, Oceania's relationship with the rest of the world has changed at least three times: from a predominantly European focus, to identification with the United States and Canada, to its currently emerging linkage with Asia. Up until roughly World War II, the colonial system gave the region a European orientation. In most places, the economy depended largely on the export of raw materials to Europe. Thus, even when independence was gained, as it was in Australia in 1901 and in New Zealand in 1907, people remained strongly tied to their "mother countries." During World War II, however, the European powers could provide only token resistance to Japan's invasion of much of the Pacific and bombing of northern Australia. Hence, after the war, Oceania increasingly became oriented toward the United States, which was now the dominant power in the Pacific and throughout much of Asia as well. Although U.S. dominance did not sever the economic linkages with Europe, U.S. investment became increasingly important to the economies of Asia and Oceania. Both Australia and New Zealand joined with the United States in a cold war military alliance known as ANZUS. Both fought alongside the United States in Korea and Vietnam, suffering considerable casualties and experiencing significant antiwar movements at home. U.S. cultural influence was strong also, as its products, technologies, and movies and pop music penetrated much of Oceania.

Nevertheless, by the 1970s a shift was taking place as Oceania became steadily drawn into the growing economies of Asia. In one sense this development was long overdue, given the proximity of Asia and its potential as a market for Oceania's raw materials. Many Pacific islands have significant Chinese, Japanese, Filipino, and Indian minorities; and even the small Asian minorities of Australia and New Zealand are increasing. Since the 1960s, Australia's thriving mineral export sector has become increasingly geared toward supplying Japan's burgeoning manufacturing industries. Similarly, since the 1970s New Zealand's wool and dairy exports have gone mostly to Asian markets. As we shall see, these transformations are accompanied by considerable cultural and economic strains. Nonetheless, despite occasional backlashes against "Asianization," Australia, New Zealand, and the rest of Oceania are becoming more open to Asian influences.

Population Patterns

Southeast Asia has more than half a billion people, and East Asia well over a billion. By comparison, just over 30 million people are spread over Oceania's huge portion of the earth's surface—from New Guinea and Australia to Hawaii. The Pacific islands, including Hawaii, have somewhat over 8 million people, while Australia has 18.7 and New Zealand 3.8 million.

As the population map (Figure 11.6) indicates, the people of this region are unevenly distributed. Most Australians live in a string of cities along the east and southeast coast—Brisbane, Newcastle, Sydney,

Canberra, Melbourne, Adelaide—and on the southwest tip of the continent in and around the city of Perth. Australia and New Zealand have the highest percentage of city dwellers outside Europe—85 percent in both cases. The vast majority of people live in modern, affluent cities and work in a range of occupations typical of highly industrialized societies. New Zealand has one very large city, Auckland, and a string of medium-sized cities on both the North and South islands. Nonetheless, overall densities in both countries are low: Australia averages just 6 people per square mile and New Zealand 35 per square mile.

The smaller islands of the Pacific are much less urbanized, and some are sparsely settled or completely uninhabited. On the other hand, some of the smallest Pacific islands, like the Marshall Islands and Tuvalu, have between 800 and 1000 people per square mile (375 to 386 per square kilometer). The highest density is found on the tiny island of Nauru, with 1130 people per square mile (430 per square kilometer). People on Nauru live in relative prosperity on the proceeds of the mining of phosphate derived from eons of bird droppings. The phosphate is exported for use in the manufacture of fertilizer.

There are two divergent patterns of population profiles in Oceania. The Pacific islands tend to have high fertility rates, between 2.5 and 6.7 children per woman. Their populations are young, with 30 to 50 percent under the age of 15 and just 3 to 5 percent elderly. In contrast, the population profiles of Australia and New Zealand closely resemble those of North America, Europe, and Japan. Women there average less than two children, and people tend to live into their mid- to late 70s. The overall trend throughout the region, however—though this is just beginning in the Pacific—is toward smaller families and aging populations.

CURRENT GEOGRAPHIC ISSUES

Many current geographic issues in Oceania are related to the transition now under way from European to Asian and inter-Pacific cultural influence. This change in cultural orientation is in turn related to the larger transition to a global economy now under way everywhere. The old relationships were built on historical factors—like Australia's and New Zealand's settlement by Europeans. In contrast, the new relationships are influenced more by practical financial and spatial considerations, such as physical proximity to Asia. Hence

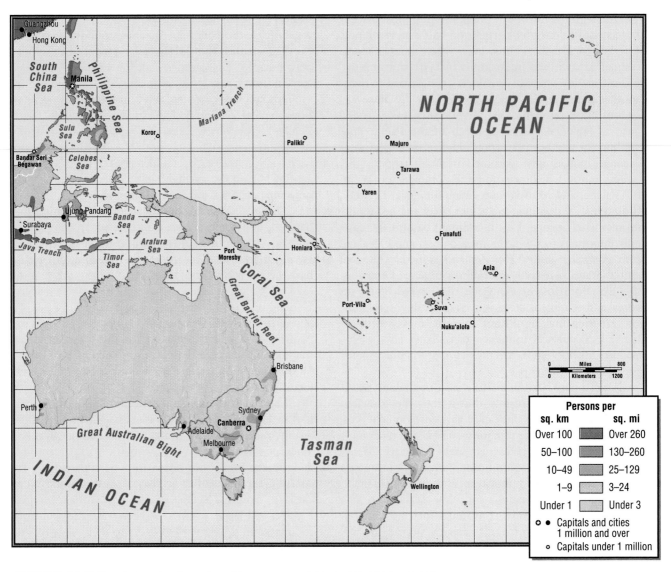

FIGURE 11.6 Population density. [Adapted from *Hammond Citation World Atlas,* 1996.]

Australia now trades more with Asia and less with Europe; and New Zealand, while continuing to trade mostly with Australia, finds increasing opportunities in Asia and the Pacific. But there is yet more to consider. Emerging technologies like E-mail and the Internet and rapid air travel are encouraging greater cultural sensitivity and the modification of old prejudices. One result is that New Zealand and the Pacific islands are able to find common philosophical grounds for closer relationships, including the renewal of a cherished Polynesian (as well as European) cultural heritage and the fostering of greater environmental awareness.

Sociocultural Issues

The cultural sea change away from Europe and toward Asia and the Pacific has been accompanied by new re-

spect for indigenous peoples: the Aborigines of Australia, the Maori of New Zealand, and the Melanesian, Micronesian, and Polynesian peoples of the Pacific islands. The growing sense of regional economic common ground with Asia has also heightened awareness of the attractions of Asian culture.

Ethnic Roots Reexamined

Until very recently, the people of Australia and New Zealand often thought of themselves as Europeans in exile, and they frequently considered their lives incomplete until they had made a pilgrimage to the British Isles or the European continent. Louise Mack in her book, *An Australian Girl in London* (1902), wrote: "[We] Australians [are] packed away there at the other end of the world, shut off from all that is great in art and music, but born with a passionate craving to see, and hear and come close to these [European] great things and their home[land]s."

These longings for Europe encouraged Australians and New Zealanders to think of themselves as transients in their own countries, as separate from the region in which they resided; such feelings were accompanied by racist attitudes toward the Aborigines and Maori. The historian Stephen H. Roberts managed to write a history of settlement in Australia without even mentioning the Aborigines. In a later book, *The Squatting Age in Australia*, published in 1935, he noted of the Aborigines: "It was quite useless to treat them fairly, since they were completely amoral and usually incapable of sincere and prolonged gratitude." The idea was abroad that both Australia and New Zealand should preserve white culture in this nether region of the Southern Hemisphere, warding off not only indigenous peoples but also Pacific islanders and Asians in general. Hence, in the 1920s, migrants from Asia and the Pacific were legally barred. Trading patterns further reinforced connections to Europe: up until World War II, the United Kingdom was the prime trading partner of both New Zealand and Australia.

When migration from the British Isles slowed after World War II, in the mid-1940s, both Australia and New Zealand began to lure immigrants from southern Europe. Hundreds of thousands came from Greece,

parts of the former Yugoslavia, and Italy. The arrival of these non-English-speaking people began a shift toward more multicultural societies. In the 1960s the "whites only" immigration policies were set aside, and migration from China, India, Vietnam, South Africa, and elsewhere in the Pacific was allowed. As a result, important shifts are under way in the ethnic makeup of the populations of Australia and New Zealand. Australia is now among the most ethnically diverse countries on earth (Figure 11.7). In both Australia and New Zealand, immigrants from Asia, especially from Vietnam and China, are a significant portion of new arrivals. Nonetheless, Asians remain a small percentage of the population in both countries (less than 7 percent in Australia). People of European descent are declining as a proportion of the population but are expected to remain the most numerous segment throughout the twenty-first century.

The population makeup is also changing in another respect. In Australia, for the first time in recent memory, those who claim indigenous origins are increasing. Before Europeans came at the end of the eighteenth century, the sole inhabitants were about 300,000 Aborigines. In the intervening two centuries, the overall population has grown to more than 18 million, but the Aboriginal population, just 2 percent of that total, is barely bigger than it was in 1800. Therefore, it was a

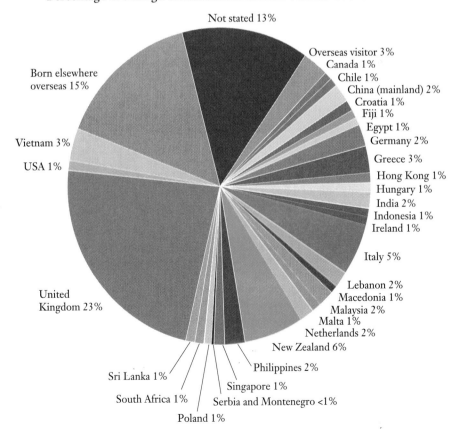

Percentage of Foreign-born Australians from Various Countries

FIGURE 11.7 Australia's cultural diversity. About 74 percent (13.2 million) of Australia's population were born in the country; the rest of the people were born in many other places, making Australia one of the world's most culturally diverse nations. The chart, based on the 1996 census, shows the birthplace of the 26 percent of Australia's residents born elsewhere. [Data from 1997 Commonwealth of Australia, http://www.abs.gov.au/websitedbs/c311215.~sf.]

surprise when, between 1991 and 1996, those claiming Aboriginal origins rose by 33 percent. In New Zealand, those claiming Maori background rose by 20 percent. These increases are thought to be linked in two ways to changing attitudes toward indigenous peoples in the region. Many people now understand better that colonial attitudes are in large part responsible for the low social standing and impoverished state of indigenous peoples. Hence, those who have Aboriginal or Maori origins are more willing to claim them. Another result is that mating relationships between European and indigenous peoples are more common and more open, and thus the number of those with mixed heritage is increasing.

In 1988, during a two-hundredth anniversary celebration of the founding of white Australia, a contingent of some 15,000 Aborigines protested that there was nothing for them to celebrate. During the same 200 years, they had been excluded from their ancestral lands, from basic civil rights, and even from the national consciousness. Into the 1960s, Aborigines had only limited rights of citizenship, and it was even illegal for them to have a drink of alcohol. Up until 1993, Aborigines were thought to have no prior claim to any land in Australia. In the late eighteenth century, the British had deemed the Aborigines too primitive to have concepts of land tenure, since their nomadic cultures had "no fixed abodes, fields or flocks, nor any internal hierarchical differentiation." After the Australian High Court declared this position void in 1993, Aboriginal groups began to win some land claims, mostly on land in the arid interior previously claimed only by the Australian government.

In New Zealand, relations between the majority European-derived population and the indigenous Maori have proceeded somewhat more amicably. Today, New Zealand proudly portrays itself as a harmonious multicultural society. Yet there is deep ambivalence about the foundations of this supposed harmony. The geographer Eric Pawson writes that when the Maori signed the Waitangi Treaty with the British in 1840 and accepted European "guns, goods and money," they thought they were granting rights of land usage in return for a trading relationship. The Maori did not regard land as a tradable commodity, but rather as an "asset of the people as a whole," used by families and larger kin groups to fulfill needs. Pawson writes: "To the Maori the land was sacred . . . [and] the features of land and water bodies were woven through with spiritual meaning and the Maori creation myth." On the other hand, the British assumed that the treaty gave them *exclusive* rights to Maori lands on which to settle surplus British population, and from which to extract wealth through farming, mining, and forestry. Therein lay the grounds for a conflict that has resulted in loss for the Maori.

In the 50 years after 1840, the Maori went from occupying all of New Zealand to occupying just 16.2

There were many different Aboriginal groups across Australia when the Europeans invaded, but all seem to have based their moral laws and daily customs on the idea that the spiritual and physical worlds were intricately related. The dead are everywhere present in spirit, and they guide the living in how to relate to the physical environment. "Dreamtime" refers to the time of creation when the spiritual connections to rocks, rivers, deserts, plants, and animals were made clear. This representation (in Kakadu National Park, Northern Territory) is of Djawok, a creator who left his image of a cuckoo on this rock. Aboriginal people who have remained close to their heritage still read the landscape as complex sign systems conveying spiritual meaning. Particular tribal groups associate with particular animals or landscape features from which they gather solace and inspiration. When people die, they are said to "go into the country." [Belinda Wright/National Geographic.]

percent; by 1950, they occupied just 6.6 percent. European settlers and the government owned and occupied the rest. Maori numbers shrank from a probable 120,000 in the early 1800s to just 42,000 in 1900; and they came to occupy the lowest and most impoverished rung of New Zealand society. In the 1990s, however, the Maori began to reclaim their culture, and they established a tribunal that forcefully advances Maori interests through the courts. New Zealand's efforts to right past wrongs and bring greater equality and social participation to the Maori and other minority groups in the country were formalized in 1996, when the government agreed to settle several long-standing Maori land claims.

By 1996, Maori numbers had rebounded to 523,000, a number that includes many who previously hid, but are now proud to claim, their Maori origins. Many New Zealanders now embrace the Maori component of their cultural heritage; overall, New Zealand may lead the world in addressing past mistreatment of indigenous peoples. Nonetheless, the Maori still have high unemployment, lower educational attainments, and poorer health than the population as a whole.

Forging Unity in Oceania

In embracing its Maori roots, New Zealand has in effect also begun to embrace its connection to the wider Pacific, especially Polynesia. While immigration into New Zealand has continued to be dominated by people from the United Kingdom, the second largest influx has come from the Pacific islands. Auckland now has the largest Polynesian population of any city in the world.

A sense of unity with Oceania as a whole is developing throughout the region, as people become appreciative of the region's cultural complexity and begin to cooperate in a range of activities, from schooling to sports to environmental activism. One way unity is manifest is through interisland travel. Today, people fly much more often than they travel by sea; they usually go in small planes, carrying from 5 to 30 passengers, from the outlying islands to hubs like Fiji, where jumbo jets can be caught to Auckland or Melbourne or Honolulu. Cook Islanders call these little planes "the canoes of the modern age." New Zealanders migrate to Australia to teach or train. A businessman from the Kiribati group in Polynesia flies to take a short course at the University of the South Pacific in Fiji. A Cook Islands teacher takes graduate training in Hawaii in reading disabilities. And who funds all this travel, especially in the island Pacific? Many do so themselves. An individual may earn money by selling food or handmade crafts at public events. A popular way for a group to get the plane fares together is to sell raffle tickets for baskets of food or a bicycle. There may be plenty of customers in one's own extended family. Governments help, too, with scholarships to the various universities in Australia, New Zealand, Hawaii, or Fiji; but one is often placed on a waiting list for these grants, so a college education may come later in life, when one is 30 or 40.

Several other trends are encouraging a growing sense of unity throughout the region: the use of pidgin languages, a movement called the Pacific Way, and the popularity of sports.

Languages in Oceania. The Pacific islands, and most notably Melanesia, have a rich variety of languages. In some cases, islands in a single chain will have several different languages. A case in point is Vanuatu, a chain of 80 mostly high volcanic islands to the east of northern Australia. At least 108 languages are spoken by a population of just 180,000—averaging one language for every 1600 people! New Guinea is the largest, most populous, and most ethnically diverse island in the Pacific. There, no less than 800 languages are spoken by a populace of 4.1 million. Languages are both an important part of cultural identity for a community and a serious hindrance to cross-cultural understanding.

In Melanesia, and elsewhere in the Pacific, the need for communication with the wider world is served by several **pidgin** languages that are sufficiently similar to be mutually intelligible. Pidgins are made up of words borrowed from the several languages of people involved in trading relationships. They can grow over time into fairly complete languages, capable of fine nuances in expression; when a particular pidgin is in such common use that mothers talk to their children in it, then it can literally be called a "mother tongue." In Papua New Guinea, pidgin is the official language.

The imposition of European languages on Oceania extinguished a number of native tongues. For example, there were 500 or more Aboriginal languages in Australia at the time of first contact; most are now gone. It is around the issues of reviving and preserving indigenous languages that an effort at regional solidarity known as the **Pacific Way** has crystallized.

The Pacific Way. *The Pacific Way* is a term used since 1970 to convey the idea that Pacific islanders and their governments have a regional identity, which grows out of their own particular social experience. It includes the idea that Pacific islanders have the ability to control their own development and solve their own problems. The idea of the Pacific Way first emerged when Pacific peoples were grappling with the problems presented by colonial-dominated school curricula, which suppressed the use of native languages and often depicted the region as peripheral and backward. They developed the Pacific Way as a philosophy to guide them in writing their own school texts. It embodied the idea that Pacific island children should first learn about their own cultures and places before they studied Britain or France or the United States. Increasingly, this idea has grown into an integrated approach to economic development and environmental issues, and an emphasis on consensus as a traditional approach to problem solving. The concept in some ways resembles *pancasila* in Southeast Asia (see Chapter 10), and it has some of the same potential for abuses. But there have been constructive steps to implement the Pacific Way. The South Pacific Regional Environmental Program (SPREP), in existence since 1980, emphasizes pan-regional cooperation and grassroots environmental education. The geographer Carolyn Koroa of the University of the South Pacific in Fiji reports that the organization is extraordinarily egalitarian and that SPREP programs routinely incorporate traditional environmental knowledge into efforts to promote sustainable livelihoods, many based on traditional crafts.

Sports as a Unifying Force. Sports and games are a major feature of daily life throughout the Pacific. Surfing evolved in Hawaii from ancient navigation customs that matched human wits with the power of the ocean. Sporting traditions introduced from outside have been embraced and modified to suit local needs. The Scottish game of golf is a favorite of Japanese and South Korean tourists in Hawaii, Tahiti, and Guam. On hundreds of Pacific islands and in Australia and New Zealand, the rugby field, the volleyball court, and the cricket pitch are important centers of community activity. Baseball is a favorite in the parts of Micronesia that were U.S. Trust Territories. Sports competitions, including native dance, are the single most common and resilient link among the countries of Oceania. Such competitions encourage regional identity and provide the motivation for extensive travel by ordinary citizens back and forth across the region and to sports venues in other parts of the world. The South Pacific Games, featuring soccer, boxing, tennis, golf, and netball, among other sports, are held every four years. The Micronesians hold periodic games that incorporate many traditional tests of skill, like spearfishing, climbing coconut trees, and outrigger canoe racing.

In New Zealand, Maori and Samoan cultures are central to that country's world dominance in rugby. At the beginning of a game, the players perform the Maori war dance, the Haka, to arouse feelings of aggression. Many of the New Zealand players are Samoan in origin; Samoans are Polynesians, noted for their size, strength, and acuity in games of skill. In Oceania, as in societies the world over—in North America, the Caribbean, Africa, Europe, South Asia—sports have smoothed the way for multicultural acceptance, especially at the Olympic level. Nonetheless, here as elsewhere, there is a danger that a particular group can be tagged as good at sports yet still find full participation in society blocked.

Gender Roles

There is great variation in gender roles in Oceania, and throughout the region they are changing significantly.

In the Trobriand Islands near New Guinea, the British game of cricket has been reformulated to include local traditions. Village teams of as many as 60 men dress in traditional garments and decorate their bodies in ways that are reminiscent of British cricket uniforms, like white kneesocks; yet they also include elements of magical decoration. Chants and dances are part of Trobriand cricket matches. The matches can go on for weeks, and they attract crowds of young onlookers, as seen in this picture.
[Robert Harding Picture Library, London.]

Over the last few decades in Australia and New Zealand, women's access to jobs and policy making positions has improved. Among the results is that Australian women bureaucrats have been credited with materially improving the living conditions of the poorest segments of Australian society. Increasingly, young women are choosing careers and do not marry until their 30s. In New Zealand, nearly half (48 percent) of women aged 24 to 29 are not married, nor are 26 percent of those aged 30 to 34. Often these women have mates but choose not to marry them. Nonetheless, Australian and New Zealand societies continue to reinforce the housewife role for women in a variety of ways. For example, the expectation is that women, not men, will interrupt their careers to stay home to care for young or very old family members.

Recent research has shown that, historically, gender roles and relationships varied in the Pacific from island to island and were in a continual state of flux. Furthermore, gender roles change over the course of life. Today, many young women fulfill traditional roles as wives and mothers and practice a wide range of domestic crafts like weaving and basketry in addition to child rearing. Then, in middle age, they may return to school and take up careers. Some Pacific women, with the aid of government scholarships, may pursue higher education or job training that takes them far from the villages where they raised their children, yet their incomes often get shared with children and grandchildren. (The reader is reminded of the social function of menopause discussed in Chapter 1.) Accumulating age and experience may boost Pacific women into community positions of considerable power.

The New Zealand geographer Camilla Cockerton reports that throughout their lives Pacific women contribute significantly to family economies through the formal and informal economy. Most traders in marketplaces are women, and the items they sell are usually made and transported by women. Yet, like women in all world regions, they experience difficulty in obtaining credit for their businesses. For example, of the 2039 loans approved by the Agricultural Bank of Papua New Guinea in January 1991, only 91 went to women (.04 percent). Cockerton also reports that Pacific women who migrate play a huge role in Pacific economies, sending larger remittances to their home countries than men do, despite their lower incomes.

On the Cape York Peninsula, Queensland, a ringer, or station hand, takes a break before heading home at the end of the workday. [Sam Abell/National Geographic.]

Being a Man: Persistence and Change

Because of its cultural diversity, Oceania encompasses many acceptable roles for men, but popular male images throughout the region are those of supermasculinity. In the Pacific, males traditionally were cultivators, fishermen, and masters of seafaring. In Polynesia, they also were responsible for many aspects of food preparation, including cooking. Now men fill many positions, but idealized male images continue to be associated with vigorous activities such as rugby, cricket, and canoe building and navigating.

In Australia and New Zealand, the cult of the supermasculine white working-class settler has long had prominence in the national mythologies. Only recently have the stories of female immigrants, men of ordinary demeanor, Aboriginal laborers, or the many early Chinese settlers come to public attention. In New Zealand, the classic male settler was a farmer and herdsman; in Australia he was, more often, an itinerant laborer—stockman, sheepshearer, cane cutter, or dig-

ger (miner). This drifter of multiple skills went from large farm to large farm (called stations in Australia) or from mine to mine, working hard but sporadically, gambling, then working again, until he had sufficient money or experience to make it in the city. There he often felt ill at ease and chafed to return to the wilds. Now immortalized in songs, novels, and films such as the Crocodile Dundee movie series, and in American TV advertisements, these men are portrayed as a rough and nomadic tribe, with a laid-back, laconic sense of humor (see the box "Waltzing Matilda"). Although they may have had families somewhere, they traveled as loners, often outnumbering women in a given place by 100 to one. Not surprisingly, male camaraderie, a demonstrated loyalty to their "mates" (male friends), and frequent brawls dominated their social life. No small part of this characterization derived from the fact that many of Australia's first immigrants were convicts who seized the opportunity for a new identity and measure of freedom "down under."

CULTURAL INSIGHT *Waltzing Matilda*

The term *swagman* encompasses the many types of itinerant laborers who wandered across the outback in search of work. Carrying all his possessions on his person (often in a swag on a stick) and walking, bicycling, or hitching rides, the swagman, rather than being denigrated as a tramp or hobo—as was the case with such itinerants in North America—was immortalized in the words of the famous Australian song "Waltzing Matilda." The words were composed by A. B. ("Banjo") Paterson in the 1890s. The tune was first played in about 1894.

The song requires a bit of deciphering. "To waltz Matilda" means to take to the road with a bedroll, which was often given a girl's name as an ironic reference to the scarcity of women. A billabong is a section of still water adjacent to a river (an oxbow lake) where water usually stays longer than in the watercourse itself. A billy is a tin can used for boiling water to make tea or soup. A coolibah is a type of eucalyptus tree that grows beside billabongs. A jumbuck is a sheep; and a tucker-bag is a sack in which a swagman carried his food supply. In Australia, squatters usually got claim to the land they settled on, and the authorities backed them up against incursions by swagmen.

Once a jolly swagman camped by a billabong
Under the shade of a coolibah tree
And he sang as he watched and waited 'til his billy
 boiled
You'll come a-waltzing Matilda with me

(refrain)
Waltzing Matilda, Waltzing Matilda
You'll come a-waltzing Matilda with me
And he sang as he watched and waited 'til his billy
 boiled
You'll come a-waltzing Matilda with me

Down came a jumbuck to dri-ink at that billabong
Up jumped the swagman and grabbed him with
 glee
And he sang as he stuffed that jumbuck in his
 tucker-bag
You'll come a-waltzing Matilda with me
(refrain)

Up rode the squatter, mounted on his
 thoroughbred
Up rode the troopers, one, two, three
"Where's that jolly jumbuck You've got in your
 tucker-bag?"
You'll come a-waltzing Matilda with me
(refrain)

Up jumped the swagman and sprang into that
 billabong
"You'll never take me alive!", said he
And his ghost may be heard as you pass by that
 billabong
"You'll come a-waltzing Matilda with me
(refrain)

Today, as part of larger efforts to recognize the diversity of Australian society, new ways of life for men are emerging, which are breaking down the national image of the isolated male loner. Nonetheless, the old, problematic model persists and remains prominent in the public images of Australian businessmen, politicians, and movie stars.

Economic and Political Issues

Although the reorientation away from Europe and toward Asia and the Pacific has many cultural ramifications, the process is largely driven by economic forces like trade, tourism, and migration.

Export Economies

For decades, natural resource riches and agricultural products have been the backbone of the national economies of Australia and New Zealand. Australia, for example, supplies about 25 percent of the world's wool; it is the world's largest supplier of coking coal used in steel manufacturing; it is first in bauxite production, third in gold, and fourth in nickel. But neither of the two countries has been a major supplier of the more profitable manufactured goods. Rather, such goods are produced in industrialized economies far away from Australia and New Zealand. There are several reasons why. First, the domestic markets in both countries are so small that they do not support the type of competition among manufacturers that would result in quality improvement. Second, most of their major trading partners only want raw materials, in order to supply their own industries. Japan, for example, now buys more from Australia than do the United States and Europe combined—but almost all purchases are raw materials. A third reason is that Japan and other Asian markets have restrictive import policies, so Australia cannot sell many of its own manufactures in those markets.

New Zealand has attempted to create better international markets for its agricultural products by lowering transportation costs and by producing luxury products. Milk is sold as whole milk powder, whey, and casein because these forms are cheap to ship. Fine dairy products (butter and cheese) and exotic gourmet foods like venison and bright green, lemon-banana-tasting kiwi fruit have found markets in Europe, Asia, and North and South America. New Zealand is now the world's leading exporter of dairy products.

The Pacific islands also depend on raw natural resources for their exports. But there is a major difference between their economies and those of Australia and New Zealand: on many of the islands, subsistence lifestyles are still common. On the island of Fiji, for example, part-time subsistence agriculture engages more than 60 percent of the population. But a desire for modern amenities has made it imperative to find methods of generating cash. In this regard, cash crop or plantation agriculture is less important than it used to be. On Fiji, sugar and other cash crops—copra, cacao, rice, and timber—make up about 22 percent of the economy. Today tourism is the primary source of income in the Pacific, and fisheries and seafood products are second.

New Orientations

The increasing influence of Asia in Oceania is seen most clearly in economics. Throughout the Pacific, Asians dominate the tourist trade, making a vital contribution to Pacific economies and impacting local land use tremendously. For example, an important segment of the Honolulu tourist infrastructure—hotels, golf courses, specialty shopping centers, import shops, nightclubs—is geared to visitors from Japan. In addition, increasing numbers of Asians are taking up residence in the region. Hence, in Hawaii, for example, the strongest force favoring reorientation toward Asia in the future may come from the simple fact that Asians now make up about 60 percent of the population, outnumbering both native Pacific islanders and Westerners.

The rise in Asian influence is also seen in the increasing exports of raw materials to Asia. In the Pacific, coconut, forest resources, and fish products industries

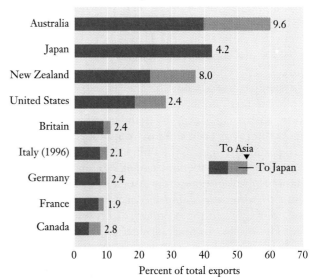

Exports to Asia, 1997

FIGURE 11.8 Exports to Asia from selected countries. [Adapted from *The Economist,* June 13, 1998, p. 69.]

sell mostly to Asian markets; increasingly, these industries are controlled by Asian companies. The products of Australian and New Zealand farms—wool, dairy products, meat, and hides— once found a ready market in Britain but are now clothing and feeding wealthy Asian populations. Australian coal and iron are supplying the rapidly growing Asian manufacturing industries. Figure 11.8 shows exports to Asia from selected countries as a percentage of total exports and of gross domestic product (GDP). Also shown is the proportion going just to Japan. Australia sells 60 percent of its exports to Asia, and New Zealand sells 40 percent. Meanwhile, Oceania is a major market for exports from Japan, South Korea, Taiwan, Singapore, Malaysia, Thailand, and Indonesia. While Asia's growing influence in the region is associated with increasing prosperity, such extreme dependence upon Asian markets for imports and exports has made the region increasingly vulnerable to economic downturns in Asia.

Tourism in Oceania: The Hawaiian Case

Tourism is a growing part of the economy throughout Oceania, but perhaps nowhere in the region are the issues raised by tourism clearer than in Hawaii. Travel and tourism is the largest industry in Hawaii and produces 24.3 percent of the gross state product (GSP). By way of comparison, travel and tourism accounts for 10.8 percent of GDP worldwide. In 1997 alone, this segment of Hawaii's economy provided 176,450 jobs, employed nearly one-third of Hawaii's work force, and accounted for $9.8 billion in output.

In the early 1990s, the Hawaiian economy began to falter, and one of the reasons was a decline in tourism. The chief factor contributing to this decline was the general decline of the Japanese economy. While the total number of visitors to Hawaii has been slowly increasing since 1994, the point of origin of these visitors has been shifting from North America to Asia, particularly Japan, the Philippines, Indonesia, and South Korea. In 1995, for example, 40.3 percent of all visitors to Hawaii came from Asia, mostly from Japan. Thus, the dramatic slump in Asian economies in the late 1990s affected the economy of Hawaii in a major way. The decline in tourism hurt not only the tourist industry (travel companies, airlines, hotels, restaurants, tour companies, and so forth) but also the construction industry, which had been thriving on the building of office towers, condominiums, hotels, and resort/retirement facilities.

Many of the islands in Oceania are also dependent on tourism for significant parts of their income, so economic troubles in Asia caused declines in their economies, too. Guam, in Micronesia, for example, depends on middle- and lower-class Japanese and South Koreans—laborers, clerks, students, midlevel management, and assembly line workers—for its tourism clientele. In 1995, over 1.3 million tourists came to Guam, 77 percent from Japan and 14 percent from South Korea. During the recession in Asia in the late 1990s, several hundred thousand Japanese and South Koreans cut the yearly Guam vacation from their budgets—a loss to Guam of several hundred million dollars per year.

While tourism is important to Pacific economies, it can threaten the way of life of local people. An example is provided by a recent effort to build a retirement home for mainlanders near Honolulu. In the early 1990s, the national officials of a major U.S. Protestant denomination voted to build a retirement home for their church members on the island of Oahu in Hawaii. The idea was to acquire land and build a multilevel care facility to which members from the mainland could retire, living independently until they needed nursing home care. This type of relocation retirement to sunny climes is often called "residential tourism." The church officials proceeded by looking for affordable land, close to Honolulu yet with landscapes of rural tropical beauty. They found a suitable tract in Pauoa Valley, one of the last valleys near Honolulu where rural people of Native Hawaiian origins still live in extended family compounds and grow their traditional gardens.

In earlier years, the Pauoa land might have been acquired and the facility built before the public had

Archaeologists Tom Dye and Mac Goodwin assist Pauoa Valley residents to establish the archaeological features of the valley. The residents were successful in fending off the acquisition of their land by a mainland-based church to be used for a retirement home for their church members. [Conrad "Mac" Goodwin.]

time to reflect on the development's impact. But this time, Native Hawaiians and their supporters led a public discussion that linked the retirement home plan to past episodes of colonialism, especially to indigenous land rights issues and environmental justice. They pointed out that Pauoa Valley people live as *ohana*, that is, as members of a traditional Hawaiian community. While many work in Honolulu, they still grow much of their own food, and still hunt and gather in the adjacent forest. They are surrounded with the stone ruins of sacred sites and burial grounds from the pre-European days; and they believe that trees and other natural features are inhabited by spirits and that those who lived long ago still visit now and then. The residents have a general feeling of living a special way in a special place. Were the Native Hawaiians the only inhabitants, their solidarity and Hawaiian laws regarding such matters would protect the land against sale; but new immigrants from North America and Asia now share the valley, and some were eager to sell. Yet, if the retirement home was built, life would change irreversibly even for those residents who chose not to sell. The ecology and ambiance of the valley would be transformed by the introduction of a large complex with 141 apartments and a 106-bed nursing home, large concrete parking lots, and manicured grounds. Once the church officials understood the issues raised by the Native Hawaiians, they decided to build the retirement home on the mainland rather than in Pauoa Valley.

The Stresses of Reorientation to Asia

The move toward greater trade with Asia has posed challenges for Oceania. Throughout the region, local industries that previously enjoyed protected trade with Europe now face competition from much larger firms in Asia. In the tiny islands of the Pacific, economic growth is hindered by small resource bases, small populations, and remote locations. While many islands have economies based on tourism, mineral resources, and sugar, coconut, and other cash crops, few have any significant manufacturing industries. Hence they must import manufactured goods from Asia. What few Pacific manufacturers there are have to mount aggressive "buy Pacific" appeals to maintain markets for their wares, which almost always carry higher prices than imports.

Australia and New Zealand are also experiencing significant stress as a result of competition from Asia. Their export sectors—mainly wool, cattle, dairy products, coal, and metals—have maintained a competitive edge largely through mechanization; thus they employ only a small proportion of the population. Most people are employed in other sectors of the economy, such as services or manufacturing. The manufacturing and service sectors have grown despite relatively small domestic demand, partially because they have benefited from government subsidies, tariffs, and other barriers to foreign investment. Today, as trade barriers fall worldwide, and as Asian manufacturing industries continue to become more competitive, Australia and New Zealand are under increasing pressure to reform their economies by reducing the number of employees, streamlining operations, and eliminating subsidies and tariffs.

Reform measures have been especially traumatic to the Australian and New Zealand labor movements, which historically have been some of the world's strongest. Australian coal miners' unions successfully agitated for the world's first 35-hour workweek. Other labor unions won a minimum wage, pensions, and aid to families with children long before such programs were enacted in many other industrialized countries. For decades these arrangements were highly successful, as both Australia and New Zealand enjoyed living standards comparable to North America and a relatively egalitarian distribution of income. Since the 1970s, however, competition from Asia has meant that increasing numbers of workers have lost jobs and many hard-won benefits. In Australia, unemployment has risen from 2 percent in the 1960s to between 8.5 to 9.5 percent in the 1990s. Meanwhile, social spending has been cut across the board in order to deal with mounting government deficits. All this has contributed to rising income disparity in recent years.

Social tensions related to the reorientation toward Asia are especially pronounced in New Zealand. Due to its small size and limited resource base (Figure

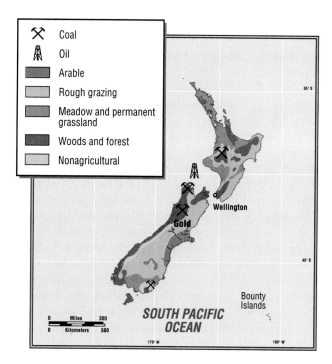

FIGURE 11.9 Land use and natural resources of New Zealand. [Adapted from Richard Nile and Christian Clerk, *Cultural Atlas of Australia, New Zealand and the South Pacific* (New York: Facts on File, 1996), p. 194.]

11.9), New Zealand has always had a harder time competing in world markets than has Australia. For decades, it managed well by selling its major exports of wool, meat, and dairy products to the United Kingdom on preferential trading terms. However, when Britain joined the Common Market in 1973, the other members insisted that the United Kingdom curtail its protected agricultural imports from New Zealand, which France felt competed unfairly with its own agricultural products. The loss of the U.K. market sent New Zealand's economy into decline. By the mid-1980s, the government was forced to cut agricultural subsidies, funding for the welfare state, and the government payroll. At the same time, New Zealand's "whites only" immigration policies were dropped and the doors were opened to Asian immigrants, especially wealthy professionals who, it was hoped, would reinvigorate the economy with their savings and investments. The new immigration policy has resulted in considerable tensions; there is some resentment of the presence of wealthy immigrants at a time when many New Zealanders themselves are jobless or strapped for cash.

The Future: A Mixed Asian and European Orientation?

Despite the powerful forces pushing Oceania toward Asia, there are important factors still favoring a strong

Western presence. The economic recession that swept through Asia in the late 1990s highlighted the need for Oceania to maintain contacts with the economies of Europe and the United States because they are more stable. Yet another factor is the lingering fear of Chinese aggression, justified to some extent by expansionist motions that China has made in the South China Sea, toward Taiwan and the potentially oil-rich Spratly Islands. Moreover, Australia and New Zealand will in all likelihood retain a cultural affinity with the West for generations to come. In the Pacific, several islands, especially those in the northwest of the region (Micronesia), may be strongly drawn into the Asian sphere. But lingering colonialism will prevent others from straying very far from a Western orientation. Both the United States and France maintain possessions in Polynesia and Micronesia, and any desire for independence has not been sufficient to override the financial benefits of aid, subsidies, and investment money from the former colonial powers. Hence, as Oceania is being steadily drawn closer to Asia, strong ties remain with the United States and Europe.

Measures of Human Well-Being

The overall status of human well-being in Oceania is probably higher than the statistics indicate, especially for the Pacific islands, because there subsistence agriculture and reciprocal exchange remain important in the everyday economy. Statistics for Australia, New Zealand, and several of the larger islands of the Pacific are easy to come by; but data for many of the smaller island groups is missing or only partially available. The reader should keep in mind that the sizes and populations of many of the island states are very small.

As discussed throughout the text, gross national product per capita (column 2, in Table 11.1) is at best a crude indicator of well-being. Oceania, like most other regions, has a wide variation in GNP per capita. Australia and New Zealand provide their citizens with a high standard of living that is further enhanced by publicly financed programs. This high standard of living is demonstrated by, for example, long life expectancy and high literacy rates, and the fact that 67 percent of the dwellings in Australia are owned by their occupants. Generally the Pacific islands have relatively low GNP or GDP figures. Still, compared to many places in Asia and Africa, even the lowest figures of U.S. $800 to U.S. $1000 probably support an adequate standard of living for most people. On many Pacific islands, people still rely on fishing and subsistence cultivation, even while embracing some aspects of the cash economy. Also, GNP or GDP figures do not reflect the often thriving informal economies of these countries or the high rate of remittances from family members overseas; both are important sources of contributions to household income. As a result, Pacific islanders can have a safe and healthy life on relatively little formal income. Some have called this state of affairs **subsistence affluence,** meaning that diets can be luxurious but access to cash limited, thus precluding the purchase of manufactured goods. If there is poverty, it is in lack of access to information and opportunity, related to isolation. But computers and the revolution in global communications networks are already alleviating this situation for some island groups.

Places like the Solomon Islands, on the other hand, which once had vibrant local cultures, now find that in comparison to other parts of Oceania they are poor and undereducated. They have high birth rates (a fertility rate of 5.7) and have little economic potential other than attracting foreign aid; promoting export agriculture, fishing, or forestry; or encouraging tourism. In the developed economies of Australia and New Zealand, the urban poor—who tend to have Aboriginal or Maori origins—may have higher incomes than Pacific islanders but much lower standards of living. In the cities there is little they can do to supplement their incomes with self-produced food or other necessities. This is also the case for the urban poor in cities throughout the Pacific, such as Port Moresby in Papua New Guinea, Suva in Fiji, Papeete in Tahiti, and Honolulu in Hawaii.

In column 3 of Table 11.1, the United Nations Human Development Index (HDI) is not particularly useful for the region of Oceania. Notably, Australia and New Zealand rank high, fifteenth and ninth, respectively. Hawaii is not ranked because it is part of the United States. If it were, Hawaii would have a higher score than the United States as a whole (which is ranked fourth behind Canada, France, and Norway) because in life expectancy, educational attainment, and income it ranks among the top 10 of the U.S. states. Fiji, in Melanesia, has a respectable ranking of 47; but all the others ranked by the United Nations are in the bottom half. Their low rankings are in part the result of low investment in education and health, and the difficulty of providing advanced training to very small populations. The problems of providing medical care to remote populations lower average life expectancy. Stiff competition for all nonagricultural jobs keeps wages low.

Most Pacific island countries, thanks to aid from former colonial rulers, generally have good primary health care programs; an exception is interior Papua New Guinea. Nevertheless, changing diets (more sugar and fat) and lifestyles (more sedentary) have provoked an increase in diseases such as diabetes and heart disease. A result is significantly lower life expectancies. Specialized, high-tech health care facilities are generally not to be found outside New Zealand, Australia, and Hawaii.

The United Nations Gender Empowerment Measure figures (GEM, column 4 of Table 11.1) are missing for most of the Pacific islands; but where they are available, some interesting patterns emerge. Of the places ranked, Papua New Guinea and the Solomon Islands, although they rank low in GNP and on the HDI, do better on the GEM. Part of the explanation is that these indigenous cultures do not traditionally exclude women from decision making or devalue their economic contribution. Also, women tend to partici-

pate successfully in the informal economy. Of the developed states in Oceania, Australia and New Zealand gained rank on the GEM as contrasted to the HDI. In Australia, improved conditions are due in part to an assertive movement by female middle-class civil servants, labeled "femocrats," to make the social service bureaucracy more responsive to the needs of poor women and children. New Zealand's high rank on gender empowerment (4) is due to the high percentage of women in parliament (21 percent of the seats) and the fact that

TABLE 11.1

Human well-being rankings of selected countries in Oceania

Country	GNP per capita (in U.S. dollars), 1996	Human Development Index (HDI) global rankings, 1998[a]	Gender Empowerment Measure (GEM) global rankings, 1998	Female literacy (percentage), 1995	Male literacy (percentage), 1995	Life expectancy, 1998
Selected countries for comparison						
Japan	40,940	8 (high)	38	99	99	79.6
United States	28,020	4 (high)	11	99	99	76.1
Kuwait	19,040 (1997)	54 (high)	75	75	82	75
Australia	20,090	15 (high)	12	99.0	99.0	78
Melanesia (selected units)						
Fiji	2,470	47 (high)	78	89	94	63
Papua New Guinea	1,150	126 (medium)	91	63	81	56
Solomon Islands	900	123 (medium)	Not av.	62	62	70
Vanuatu	1,290	124 (medium)	Not av.	Not av.	Not av.	63
New Caledonia	(GDP 8,000)	Not av.	Not av.	Not av.	Not av.	72
Micronesia (selected units)						
Guam	(GDP 14,000)	Not av.	Not av.	99	99	74
Federated States of Micronesia	2,070	Not av.	Not av.	88	91	66
Kiribati	8,100	Not av.	Not av.	Not av.	Not av.	62

[a]The high and medium designations indicate where the country ranks among the 174 countries classified into three categories (high, medium, low) by the United Nations.
Not av. = Not available.
Sources: Human Development Report 1998, United Nations Development Programme; and *1998 World Population Data Sheet*, Population Reference Bureau.

(Continued)

TABLE 11.1 (CONTINUED)

Country	GNP per capita (in U.S. dollars), 1996	Human Development Index (HDI) global rankings, 1998[a]	Gender Empowerment Measure (GEM) global rankings, 1998	Female literacy (percentage), 1995	Male literacy (percentage), 1995	Life expectancy, 1998
Micronesia (selected units)						
Marshall Islands	1,890	Not av.	Not av.	88	100	62
Northern Marianas	(GDP 10,500)	Not av.	Not av.	96	97	67
Nauru	(GDP 10,000)	Not av.	Not av.	Not av.	Not av.	67
Palau	(GDP 5,000)	Not av.	Not av.	90	93	67
Polynesia (selected units)						
French Polynesia	(GDP 8,000)	Shares French rank of 2 (high)	Shares French rank of 31	98	98	70
Hawaii	28,020	Shares U.S. rank of 4 (high)	Shares U.S. rank of 11	99	99	77
Tonga	(GDP 2,160)	Not av.	Not av.	100	100	69
Tuvalu	(GDP 800)			Not av.	Not av.	63
Western Samoa	1,170	88 (medium)	Not av.	97	97	65
American Samoa	(GDP 2,600)			97	98	73
New Zealand	15,720	9 (high)	4	99.0	99.0	72

one-third of administrators and managers and nearly half the professional and technical workers are women. In 1997, New Zealand acquired a woman prime minister when Transportation Minister Jenny Shippey became head of the ruling party.

Environmental Issues

A case could be made for saying that in Oceania there is more public involvement in environmental issues than in any other region in the world. Despite its relatively small population, Oceania faces many serious environmental problems. The human introduction of many nonnative species has ravaged the region's unique ecosystems; so has the expansion of human populations themselves. Even remote areas have been subject to intense pollution from mining and the testing of nuclear weapons. Finally, global environmental crises related to climate change and ozone depletion are particularly threatening to this region.

There is also a more positive side to environmental issues in Oceania. In many areas, a revived pride in cultural heritage has encouraged Pacific islanders and other indigenous peoples to become active in Green movements. As cultural allegiances shift away from distant Europe, local cultures may provide a basis for more sustainable lifestyles. Because environmental conditions vary across the region, this text addresses Oceania's environmental issues regionally.

Australia: Human Settlement in an Arid Land

Unique organisms found nowhere else occupy many niches in Australia's unusually arid environments. Since settlement by Europeans, after 1788, many of Australia's native plants and animals have been displaced or even driven to extinction by nonnative species. At least 41 bird and mammal species and more than 100 plant species have become extinct; in all likelihood many more disappeared before they were biologically classified. European rabbits are among the most destructive of the introduced species. They were brought to Australia by early British settlers who enjoyed hunting and eating them. Since rabbits have no natural predators in Australia, they multiplied at an incredible rate. Rabbits eat many local plants, destroying the food supply for indigenous species, and they dig holes to live in, which create considerable soil erosion. Attempts to control the rabbit population, by introducing European foxes and cats, only made the problem worse. The vigorous European species drove many native predators to extinction without having much impact on the rabbit population. In recent years, diseases intentionally introduced for the purpose have wiped out as much as 90 percent of the rabbit population. However, this strategy has also created new problems. Without rabbits to eat, cats and foxes prey more on indigenous species. Hence the eradication of cats and foxes has been stepped up as well. Meanwhile, some rabbits have proved resistant to disease, and the rabbit population may rebound.

Agriculture has also had a huge impact on Australian ecosystems. Because the climate is arid and soils infertile, the dominant land use in Australia (but not the most lucrative sector of the economy) remains the grazing of introduced species, primarily sheep, but also cattle. More than 15 percent of the land is given over to grazing, and ranchers increasingly use irrigation, herbicides, and pesticides to extend the seasonal availability of pastureland. Crop agriculture is limited to just 6 percent of the total land, most of that in the southeast. Crops, too, now rely on irrigation and chemicals. One result is that natural underground water reserves are receding. Another is that many rivers and lakes have become polluted by agricultural chemicals and the algae that feed off them.

The dingo fence: The world's longest fence snakes for 3307 miles between South Australia and New South Wales. Made of tough wire attached to wood posts, it separates the dingo dog indigenous to Australia from sheep herds. A single dingo can kill up to 50 sheep in one night of marauding. The fence requires constant patrolling and mending, but the dingoes' sheep killing has been reduced dramatically. Kangaroos, the dingoes' natural prey, have learned to live on the sheep side of the fence, where their population has increased. Kangaroos compete with sheep for the same scarce grass and water. [Medford Taylor/National Geographic.]

In an overwhelmingly urban place like Australia (Figure 11.10), urban activities may create environmental issues. As observed previously, Australia's major cities form a series of nodes along the east and southeast coasts from Brisbane to Adelaide. The nodes themselves are of fairly low density, but they are connected by dispersed towns and coastal developments. As a result, there is nearly universal dependence on the private car for transport. That dependence has a variety of impacts. Not only do streets and parking lots consume space, they reduce the amount of rainfall that can be absorbed by the soil, increasing flooding and

FIGURE 11.10 Australia's urban concentrations.

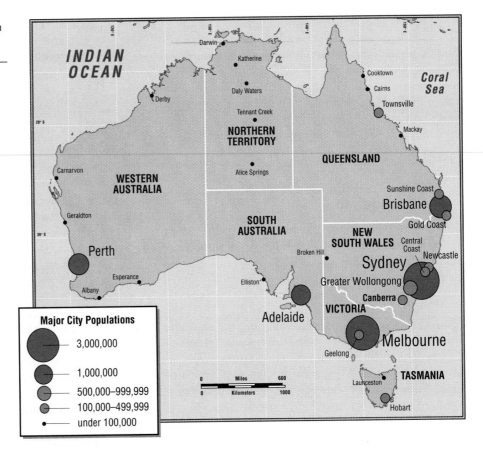

erosion. The cars also need fuel, so per capita energy consumption in urban Australia is high, just below that of the United States. Consequently, per capita greenhouse emissions are higher than in any other industrialized country except the United States and Luxembourg; and photochemical smog and chemical haze are common.

Another problem associated with large urban populations is water scarcity. Domestic per capita water consumption has risen markedly over the last 25 years, due mostly to lifestyle changes: more flushing toilets, more washing machines, more showers, more irrigation of ornamental plants and crops. Australians have had to build giant water storage facilities, which have displaced natural habitats and diverted the natural flow of streams.

New Zealand: Loss of Forest and Wildlife

New Zealand has many of the same environmental concerns as Australia: loss of endemic plants and animals, pollution, water shortages. The differences in concerns result from the country's different set of physical and human features. There were no humans in New Zealand until just about 1000 years ago, when Polynesian Maori people settled there. At the time of their arrival, dense midlatitude rain forest covered 85 percent of the land. The Maori were cultivators, who brought in yams, taros, and sweet potatoes, as well as other nonindigenous plants and birds. By the time of European contact, forest clearing and overhunting by the Maori had already degraded the environment and driven several species of the moa bird to extinction. There is also archaeological evidence that intensive competition for resources had led to warfare.

As in Australia, European settlement in New Zealand drastically intensified land use. Today, just 23 percent of the country remains forested. Most has been cleared for pastures and cropland. Grazing has become so widespread that today there are 15 times as many sheep as people, and 3 times as many cattle. Meanwhile, European agriculture brought many new crops and inadvertently introduced damaging pests. Soils exposed by the clearing of forests proved thin and acidic, and ranchers buttressed them with chemicals to maintain pastures. As in Australia, chemicals have seriously polluted waterways. New Zealand's environment has become hostile to many native species. Ranches, farms, roads, cities, and towns claim more than 90 percent of the lowland area, resulting in unusually high extinction rates for endemic plants and animals.

The Pacific Islands: At the Mercy of Global Trends

Though widely dispersed, the Pacific islands share a number of environmental concerns and opportunities. Their small sizes, often tiny populations, and insignificant influence on the global economy give them little say about international forces that nonetheless affect their environments. Mining, nuclear pollution, ozone depletion, global warming, the globalization of economies, and increasing tourism all have environmental side effects.

Pollution from mining has proved a problem for Papua New Guinea. Two mines in particular have had devastating effects on the country's environment. Both mines were operated by Australian mining companies that took advantage of poorly enforced or nonexistent environmental codes to dump huge amounts of mine waste in rivers. As a consequence, entire river systems have been devastated, displacing indigenous subsistence cultivators. In the case of the Ok Tedi gold mine in mainland Papua New Guinea, local landowners are suing the Australian mining company, BHP, for U.S. $4 billion. The case of the copper mine on the island of Bougainville (part of Papua New Guinea) is somewhat further from resolution. In the late 1980s and in the 1990s, resistance to the mine grew into a war for independence from Papua New Guinea, which claims the

Supermarkets, like this one in Tari in the Papua New Guinea highlands, are rearranging the ways people have traditionally obtained food and other goods. The stores are doing away with long-established personal trading networks and are rapidly bringing the impersonal global economy into one of the last frontiers on the planet. [Sassoon/Robert Harding Picture Library, London.]

island. While the mine is now closed and peace negotiations are under way, the future is uncertain. Meanwhile, the mining industry has displaced indigenous peoples into the cash economies of rapidly built market towns where their subsistence skills are of little use.

Another major environmental issue for the Pacific islands is nuclear pollution from weapons tests and reactor waste. During World War II, U.S. nuclear bomb experiments destroyed Bikini atoll in the Marshall Islands and caused cancer among islanders. Similarly, French Polynesia has suffered 180 nuclear weapons tests and numerous shipments of nuclear waste from France; this has resulted in widespread cancer, infertility, birth defects, and miscarriages among the native population. One response to this pollution is the establishment of the South Pacific Nuclear Free Zone. Most independent countries in Oceania have signed an agreement that bans weapons testing and waste dumping on their lands. The agreement has not been signed by U.S. territories, such as the Marshall Islands, or by French Polynesia. Dumping and weapons testing continue. Japan, North Korea, South Korea, France, and the United States have all explored the possibility of depositing their radioactive waste in the Marshall Islands.

Global warming, which is expected to result in rising sea levels, is of obvious concern to islands that already barely rise above the waves (Figure 11.11). Many of the lowest-lying atolls will simply disappear under water if seas rise the 4 inches (10 centimeters) per decade predicted by the International Panel on Climate Change. Other islands, some already very crowded, will be severely reduced in area and made more vulnerable to storm surges and cyclones. Pacific peoples have little direct control over the forces that appear to be causing such precarious circumstances, as they themselves produce only a very small percentage of the earth's greenhouse gases.

The whole of Oceania is particularly affected by depletion of the ozone layer. This is a layer existing in the upper atmosphere that contains a type of oxygen molecule called ozone; ozone filters out biologically harmful ultraviolet (UV) radiation emitted by the sun. Since the mid-1980s, a hole in the ozone layer has periodically appeared over Antarctica. It is being caused by a class of manufactured chemicals called chlorofluorocarbons (CFCs), which float up to the ozone layer and destroy it. The hole enables increasing amounts of UV radiation to reach the surface of the earth. The higher amounts of UV radiation are likely to increase levels of skin cancer. Australia already has the highest incidence of skin cancer of any country in the world, explained by the fact that its largely white, transplanted population, with little protective skin pigment, lives under intense sunlight. Higher levels of UV radiation will also probably increase the incidence of eye disease

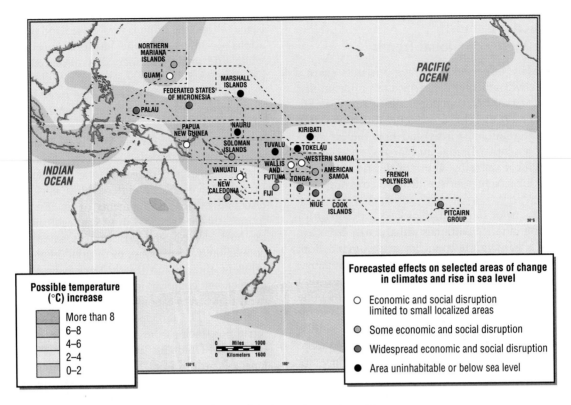

FIGURE 11.11 Climate change in the region due to global warming. [Adapted from Richard Nile and Christian Clerk, *Cultural Atlas of Australia, New Zealand and the South Pacific* (New York: Facts on File, 1996), p. 223.]

and weaken the immune systems of a variety of organisms, including humans. UV radiation could also decrease agricultural and marine productivity.

The Law of the Sea Treaty is an example of how the globalization of island economies has thwarted environmental protection. The treaty allows islands to claim rights to sea resources 200 miles out from the shore. Island countries can now make money by licensing foreign fishing fleets from Japan, South Korea, Russia, or the United States to fish within the 200-mile limits; but protecting the fisheries from overfishing by licensees has turned out to be an enforcement nightmare. Similar problems have risen in controlling the exploitation by foreign companies of under-the-sea mineral deposits.

Even tourism, which until recently was considered a "clean" industry, has now been revealed to create environmental problems. Foreign-owned tourism enterprises have often accelerated the loss of wetlands and worsened beach erosion. Tourism increases the use of scarce water resources and the production of sewage, as well as the consumption of environmentally polluting products, such as gasoline, kerosene, fertilizers, plastics, and paper.

Despite the increasingly serious environmental problems facing the Pacific islands, there are a few bright spots on the horizon. As discussed previously, in the sociocultural issues section, there is increasing support for the Pacific Way, which conveys the idea that Pacific islanders and their governments have a regional identity and a consensus-based approach to dealing with their problems.

REFLECTIONS ON OCEANIA

One way to assess Oceania and its future prospects is to think of it in relation to its nearest neighbors. We have noted in other chapters the economic vigor of East and Southeast Asian economies, the energy and potential they seem to have for future expansion, and the possibility that they will either subvert or pull along other economies around the globe. We have also considered the many challenges Asian economies face, not the least of which are cronyism, corruption, and inattention to environmental issues. Will Oceania's economic relationships with Asia leave it wealthier and more secure, or in a more precarious economic state?

Some have suggested that Oceania might effectively implement the Pacific Way. They are encouraged by Oceania's somewhat superior environmental record, its leadership in the movement to ban nuclear weapons, and the strength of Pacific indigenous cultures. The concept of the Pacific Way is only just emerging; it seems, however, to hold considerable promise in the post–cold war era, when many are in a mood to demilitarize and to find less wasteful lifestyles and something grander than national chauvinism. The Pacific Way is based on ancient Pacific techniques for conflict resolution through cooperation and consensus.

It is, in fact, more of an ideal and a legend than a reality, since traditional Pacific cultures were not particularly democratic. But it seems that most parts of Oceania are at a stage where cooperation and consensus may seem desirable. Most Pacific islands are redefining their relationships with former colonial governments and choosing independence of some sort; at the same time, they recognize that they can hardly go it alone as tiny states. Meanwhile, Australia and New Zealand are newly aware of their "Pacificness." Why not, then, become a region with a splendid mission—a place where value is placed on sustainable development, where affluence is defined in nonmaterial ways, where the primary goal is to enhance human and social capital, and where collaboration and common consent are honored.

Selected Themes and Concepts

1. Oceania consists of Australia, New Zealand, and a huge number of islands spread over a large portion of the Pacific Ocean. The oceanic islands may be circular **atolls,** formed by coral reefs growing on the rims of volcanoes, or **high islands,** formed by the volcanoes themselves.

2. The vast Pacific Ocean plays a major role in the climate of Oceania and since prehistoric times has been the route for human communication. Its great size has imposed solitude and fostered self-sufficiency.

3. Oceania was populated by three waves of migrants. First, the Australo-Melanesians arrived about 60,000 years ago; then the Austronesians, about 5000 years ago; and finally the Europeans, beginning around 1800. A fourth wave, Asians, began moving in during the nineteenth and twentieth centuries.

4. Oceania's composition as a region of islands has had a special effect on its animal and plant life. Many species are **endemic,** that is, they exist in a particular place and nowhere else on earth.

5. Over the course of the twentieth century, Oceania's relationship with the rest of the world has changed at least three times—from a predominantly European focus, to identification with the United States during and after World War II, and now to its currently emerging linkage with Asia.

6. **The Pacific Way** is a phrase that conveys the idea that Pacific islanders and their governments have a regional identity, which grows out of their own particular social experience. Overcoming European judgments that the Pacific was peripheral and backward, Pacific peoples now take pride in their ability to control their own development and solve their own problems.

7. The overall status of human well-being in Oceania is probably higher than the statistics indicate, especially for the Pacific islands, because of **subsistence affluence.** This means that the people eat well by growing their own food and live comfortably, but have little cash to purchase manufactured goods.

8. Despite their high levels of wealth and well-being, Australia and New Zealand remain primarily producers and exporters of raw materials, both agricultural and mineral.

9. The Pacific islands also depend on raw natural resources for their exports. A major difference between their economies and those of Australia and New Zealand is that on many islands subsistence lifestyles are still common.

10. Since settlement by Europeans, after 1788, many of Australia's native plants and animals have been displaced or even driven to extinction by nonnative species. The same can be said of New Zealand and the Pacific islands.

11. The Pacific islands are affected by a number of environmental problems that originate in the world's industrialized economies: mining and nuclear pollution, ozone depletion and global warming, the effects of overuse of resources linked to the global reach of rich economies, and increasing tourism.

Selected Readings

Brewis, Alexandra. *Lives on the Line—Women and Ecology on a Pacific Atoll.* Fort Worth, TX: Harcourt Brace, 1996.

Buck, Elizabeth. *Paradise Remade—The Politics of Culture and History in Hawaii.* Philadelphia: Temple University Press, 1993.

Cockerton, Camilla. Women. In *The Pacific Islands: Environment and Society,* ed. Moshe Rapaport. Honolulu: Bess Press, 1999, pp. 305–314.

Colbert, Evelyn. *The Pacific Islands—Paths to the Present.* Boulder, CO: Westview Press, 1997.

Crocombe, Ron. Geopolitical change in the Pacific islands. In *Global Geopolitical Change and the Asia Pacific—A Regional Prespective,* ed. Dennis Rumley et al. Hampshire, UK: Avebury, 1996, pp. 282–300.

Eisenstein, Hester. *Inside Agitators—Australian Femocrats and the State.* Philadelphia: Temple University Press, 1996.

Feinberg, Richard, ed. *Seafaring in the Contemporary Pacific Islands—Studies in Continuity and Change.* DeKalb: Northern Illinois Press, 1995.

Flanagan, Tom. Traditional owners fight Jabiluka mine, in the *Green Left Weekly,* from the Internet at http://www.peg.apc.org/~stan/278/278p5.htm. 1997.

Hayashida, Roanald Hideo. Papua New Guinea in 1996—Problems in the homestretch. *Asian Survey* 37, no. 2 (February 1997): 199–203.

Hviding, Edvard. *Guardians of Marovo Lagoon—Practice, Place and Politics in Maritime Melanesia.* Honolulu: University of Hawaii, 1996.

Jolly, Margaret. *Women of the Place—Kastom, Colonialism, and Gender in Vanuatu.* Switzerland: Harwood, 1994.

Jolly, Margaret; and Martha Macintyre, eds. *Family and Gender in the Pacific—Domestic Contradictions and the Colonial Impact.* Cambridge: Cambridge University Press. 1989.

Kapferer, Judith. *Being All Equal—Identity, Difference and Australian Cultural Practice.* Oxford: Berg. 1996.

Linnekin, Jocelyn. *Sacred Queens and Women of Consequence—Rank, Gender, and Colonialism in the Hawaiian Islands.* Ann Arbor: University of Michigan Press, 1990.

McKnight, Tom L. *Oceania—The Geography of Australia, New Zealand, and the Pacific Islands.* Englewood Cliffs, NJ: Prentice Hall, 1995.

Mitchell, Andrew. *The Fragile South Pacific—An Ecological Odyssey.* Austin: University of Texas Press, 1990.

Morton, Helen. *Becoming Tongan—An Ethnography of Childhood.* Honolulu: University of Hawaii Press, 1996.

Nile, Richard, and Christian Clerk. *Cultural Atlas of Australia, New Zealand and the South Pacific.* New York: Facts on File, 1996.

Pawson, Eric. Two New Zealands: Maori and European. In *Inventing Places,* ed. Kay Anderson and Fay Gale. Melbourne: Longman Cheshire, 1992.

Pesman, Ros. *Duty Free—Australian Women Abroad.* Melbourne: Oxford University Press, 1996.

Polk, Susan. Once Were Warriors, a film review, from the Internet, at http://technoculture.mira.net.au/sponce.htm. 1995.

Price, Lary W. Hedge and shelterbelts on the Canterbury Plains, New Zealand: Transformation of an antipodean landscape. *Annals of the Association of American Geographers* 83, no. 1 (1993): 119–140.

Robillard, Albert B., ed. *Social Change in the Pacific Islands.* London: Kegan Paul International, 1992.

READING MAPS

Have you ever considered how much information is necessary to draw just one map of the countries of the world? Thousands of miles of intricate coastlines must be drawn, as well as frequently changing borders and place names. A good political map will often include hundreds of labeled cities, rivers, oceans, seas and gulfs, mountain ranges, and deserts. The map reader may become so caught up in the map that he or she fails to appreciate much of this information. To make the best and fullest use of any map, it is helpful to develop a few basic map-reading skills.

It is always essential to read any **title, caption,** or **legend.** The legend is the box that tells you what the symbols mean or what the colors represent. It may be simple or complex, but its purpose is to show you how to make sense of the map.

SCALE

It is always important to notice the **scale** of a map. Scale refers to the relationship between the distances on the map and the actual distances on the surface of the earth. Usually the scale is constant for the whole map and is stated in one of several ways near the bottom of the map. One method is to provide a numerical ratio showing what one unit of measure on the map equals in the same units on the face of the earth. For example, 1:1,000,000, or the fraction 1/1,000,000, means that one unit on the map equals one million of the same units on the face of the earth. That is, one inch on the map equals one million inches on the face of the earth, and one centimeter on the map equals one million centimeters on the face of the earth. Other maps may express scale using a phrase such as "one inch equals sixteen miles" or "one centimeter equals ten kilometers." Alternatively, a simple bar may express the same information visually:

```
0    10    20    30    40    50 km
|____|____|____|____|____|
```

In the accompanying maps of the Caribbean (Figure A1), you can see how the change in scale affects the detail on the map. Notice that as the amount of area shown on a map becomes larger, the amount of detail that can be shown decreases.

LONGITUDE AND LATITUDE

Most maps contain **lines of latitude and longitude,** which are useful for establishing a position on the map relative to other points on the globe. These lines are purely a human invention developed by European cartographers so that early European navigators could more easily locate themselves on a map when far out at sea with no visible landmarks and only the stars and the passage of time to orient them. Lines of longitude run from pole to pole, lines of latitude run parallel to the equator. It is important to note the ways in which these two sets of lines are different from each other. Lines of longitude (also called **meridians**) come closer together as they move away from the equator, and they all meet at the poles. These lines of longitude are all the same length (half the circumference of the globe). On the other hand, lines of latitude (also called **parallels**) circle the globe, but they do not meet. The only latitude line that spans the full circumference of the globe is the equator; the rest of the latitude lines describe ever smaller circles of the globe to the north and the south of the equator, and the poles are marked with just a point (Figure A2).

Both kinds of lines, latitude and longitude, describe some part of a circle and are measured in degrees. As in all circles, there are 360 degrees in each circle of latitude and longitude, 180 for each hemisphere. The space between degrees has 60 minutes, and each minute has 60 seconds. But remember that these are measures of relative space on a circle, not time, or even real distance.

The **prime meridian,** which is labeled zero degrees longitude, runs from the North Pole through Greenwich, England, to the South Pole. The half of the globe's surface west of the prime meridian is called the Western Hemisphere, the half to the east, the Eastern Hemisphere. The longitude lines moving both east and west from the prime meridian are labeled by

A. The scale of this map is 1:3,000,000

B. The scale of this map is 1:15,000,000

C. The scale of this map is 1:45,000,000

FIGURE A1   Examples of Scale from the Eastern Caribbean. Map A is of Guadeloupe and Dominica in the eastern Caribbean. The scale of 1:3,000,000 makes it possible to show towns, a few roads, and a few landforms, but not much else. Map B is at a scale of 1:13,000,000. You can see much more of the eastern Caribbean, but the only detail that can be shown is the shape of the islands and the location of the capital cities. Map C, at a scale of 1:50,000,000, shows most of the Caribbean Sea and its general location between North, South, and Central America, but now the eastern Caribbean islands are too small to clearly identify. [Adapted from *The Longman Atlas for Caribbean Examinations,* 2nd ed. (Essex, UK: Addison Wesley Longman, 1998), p. 4.]

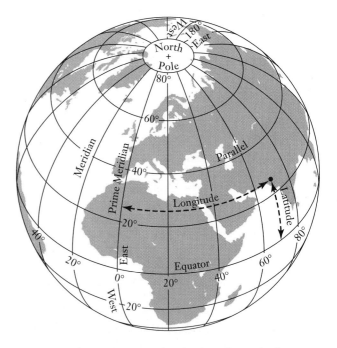

FIGURE A2   Summary of Latitude and Longitude. Lines of longitude (meridians) extend north and south of the equator. The distance between lines of longitude decreases steadily toward the poles, where they all meet. All lines of latitude are parallel, hence do not meet. They are equally spaced north and south of the equator and meet the longitude lines at right angles. The only line of latitude that is the complete circumference of the earth is the equator; all other lines of latitude describe ever smaller circles heading away from the equator. For example, the 60th lines of latitude (parallels) north and south are one-half the circumference of the equator. [Adapted from *The New Comparative World Atlas* (Maplewood, NJ: Hammond, 1997), p. 6.]

their distance in degrees from the prime meridian, from 1 to 180 degrees. Thus there are, for example, a longitude line 20 degrees east of the prime meridian and another 20 degrees west of the prime meridian; they are distinguished by the labels "east" and "west," and are written "20°E" and "20°W." The longitude line at 180 degrees, which runs through the Pacific, is used as the international date line; this is where the calendar day begins. The equator is zero degrees latitude; the poles are at 90 degrees north and south.

Lines of longitude and latitude run perpendicular to each other, intersecting at right angles; hence they form a grid that can be used to designate the location of a place. In Figure A1, for example, in Map A you can see that the island of Marie Galante lies just south of the parallel (or line of latitude) at 16 degrees north and just about 17 minutes to the west of the meridian (or line of longitude) at 61 degrees west. The position of Marie Galante's north coast is 16°N, 61°17′ W.

MAP PROJECTIONS

All maps must deal with the problem of showing the spherically shaped earth on a flat piece of paper, and it is important to understand the limitations of the different strategies devised. It is easy to appreciate the problems of distortion that would result if one were to draw the map of the earth on an orange, then peel the orange and try to flatten out the orange-peel map and transfer the map exactly to a flat piece of paper.

The various systems devised for showing the round surface of the earth on flat paper are called **projections.** All projections entail some sort of distortion. For maps of small parts of the earth's surface the distortion is minimal, but developing a projection for the whole surface of the earth that minimizes distortion is much more challenging. A popular world map projection is the **Mercator projection** (Figure A3A), now rarely used by geographers because of its gross distortion toward the poles. Named after the Flemish cartographer Gerhardus Mercator (1512–1594), this projection stretched the poles out, depicting them as long lines equal in length to the equator. It is not hard to imagine the distortion that results: Greenland, for example, appears about as large as Africa, despite the fact that it is actually about one-sixth Africa's size. Nevertheless, Mercator's projection is still useful for navigation (for which it was developed) because it portrays the shapes of landmasses more or less accurately. Also, a straight line between two points on this map gives the compass direction between them. This type of projection can be safely used for parts of the globe

that are within 15 degrees south or north of the equator because the distortion in this range is minimal.

Today there are many projections of the earth's surface onto a flat plane. All distort either the size or shape of the land and sea surfaces. One of the most popular projections is **Goode's interrupted homolosine projection** (Figure A3B). This projection flattens the earth rather like an orange peel, thus preserving some of the size and shape of the landmasses, but snipping up the oceans. Also popular is the **Robinson projection** (Figure A3C), which sacrifices poleward accuracy for an uninterrupted view of lands and oceans. In this book we often use the Robinson projection for world maps.

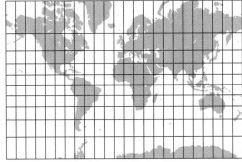

A. Mercator Projection

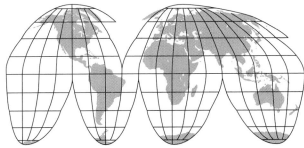

B. Goode's Interrupted Homolosine Projection

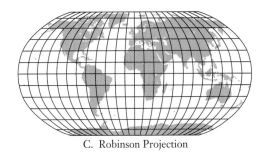

C. Robinson Projection

FIGURE A3 Three Common Map Projections. Mercator Land Robinson projections.[Adapted from *The New Comparative World Atlas* (Maplewood, NJ: Hammond, 1997), pp. 6–7.] Goode's interrupted homolosine projection. [Adapted from *Goode's World Atlas,* 19th ed. (Rand McNally, 1995), p. x.]

It is interesting to note how most currently popular world projections reflect the European origin of modern cartography. Europe or North America is usually placed near the center of the map, where distortion is minimal, while other population centers, such as East Asia, are placed at the highly distorted periphery. These days there is a need for world maps that center on different parts of the globe. For example, much of the earth's economic activity is now taking place in and around Japan, Korea, China, Taiwan, and Southeast Asia; hence, for discussions of this activity maps are needed that focus on these regions but still include the rest of the world in the periphery. Similarly, political developments in the Middle East or in Southwest Asia can best be depicted graphically on world maps that center on Palestine or Iraq.

APPENDIX B
POPULATION DATA BY COUNTRY

The following table of population data reproduces most of the data in the *1998 World Population Data Sheet*, published by the Population Reference Bureau. This table lists data for individual countries and also for world regions. Notice that many of the world regions are equivalent to those in this textbook, but that there are some notable differences.

	Population mid-1998 (millions)	Births per 1000 pop.	Deaths per 1000 pop.	Natural increase (annual, %)	"Doubling time" in years at current rate[a]	Projected population (millions) 2025	Infant mortality rate[b]	Total fertility rate[c]	Percentage of population of age <15	65+	Life expectancy at birth (years) Total	Male	Female	Data available code[d]	Percent urban	Percentage of women ages 15–19 giving birth each year	Percentage of married women using contraception All methods	Modern methods[e]	Government view of birth rate[f]	GNP per capita, 1996 (U.S.$)	Land area (sq mi)	Population/ sq mi
WORLD	5,926	23	9	1.4	49	8,082	58	2.9	32	7	66	64	68	—[g]	44	6	56	51	—	$5,180	—	—
AFRICA	763	40	15	2.5	27	1,288	91	5.6	44	3	52	50	53	—	31	12	22	17	—	650	—	—
SUB-SAHARAN AFRICA	624	42	16	2.6	2.7	1,076	96	6.0	45	3	48	47	50	—	27	14	17	11	—	510	—	—
NORTHERN AFRICA	167	29	8	2.2	32	259	59	4.0	39	4	65	63	67	—	47	6	41	37	—	1,280	—	—
Algeria	30.2	31	7	2.4	29	47.3	44	4.4	39	4	67	66	68	C	56	5	47	43	H	1,520	919,591	33
Egypt	65.5	28	6	2.2	32	95.8	63	3.6	39	4	67	65	69	B	43	6	48	46	H	1,080	384,344	171
Libya	5.7	45	8	3.7	19	14.2	60	6.3	50	2	65	62	67	C	86	14	—	—	S	—	679,359	8
Morocco	27.7	24	7	1.8	40	41.2	62	3.3	36	5	72	69	74	B	52	4	50	42	H	1,290	172,317	161
Sudan	28.5	35	14	2.1	33	46.9	70	5.0	43	3	51	50	52	C	27	6	10	7	H	—	917,375	31
Tunisia	9.5	26	6	1.9	36	13.5	35	3.2	35	5	68	67	69	B	61	2	60	49	H	1,930	59,985	158
Western Sahara	0.2	47	18	2.9	24	0.4	150	6.9	—	—	47	46	48	D	—	13	—	—	—	—	102,700	2
WESTERN AFRICA	228	45	16	2.9	24	409	92	6.4	46	3	50	49	52	—	24	15	13	6	—	310	—	—
Benin	6.0	45	14	3.2	22	12.4	94	6.3	49	3	54	51	56	B	36	12	16	3	S	350	42,710	139
Burkina Faso	11.3	47	18	2.9	24	21.4	94	6.9	49	3	47	46	47	C	15	15	8	4	H	230	105,637	107
Cape Verde	0.4	36	8	2.9	24	0.5	52	5.3	45	6	70	66	73	C	44	10	—	—	H	1,010	1,556	257
Côte d'Ivoire	15.6	39	13	2.6	27	26.1	89	5.7	45	3	52	51	54	B	46	15	11	4	S	660	122,780	127
Gambia	1.2	43	19	2.4	29	2.0	90	5.9	44	3	45	43	47	B	37	18	12	7	H	—	3,861	309
Ghana	18.9	40	12	2.9	24	36.3	66	5.5	45	3	56	54	58	C	35	12	20	10	H	360	87,853	215
Guinea	7.5	43	19	2.4	29	13.1	153	5.7	47	3	45	43	47	C	29	16	2	1	H	560	94,873	79
Guinea-Bissau	1.1	42	22	2.1	34	1.9	141	5.8	42	4	43	41	44	C	22	19	—	—	H	250	10,857	104
Liberia	2.8	43	12	3.1	22	6.5	108	6.2	42	4	59	56	61	C	45	17	6	5	H	—	37,189	75
Mali	10.1	51	20	3.1	23	22.6	123	6.7	47	3	46	45	47	C	26	19	7	5	H	240	471,116	21
Mauritania	2.5	40	14	2.5	27	4.4	101	5.4	43	3	52	50	53	C	54	13	3	1	S	470	395,838	6
Niger	10.1	53	19	3.4	21	22.4	123	7.4	48	2	47	45	48	B	15	23	4	2	H	200	489,073	21
Nigeria	121.8	45	15	3.0	23	203.4	84	6.5	46	3	50	49	52	C	16	15	15	7	H	240	351,649	346
Senegal	9.0	43	16	2.7	26	17.0	68	5.7	45	3	49	48	50	B	42	10	13	8	H	570	74,336	122
Sierra Leone	4.6	49	30	1.9	36	8.2	195	6.5	44	3	34	33	36	C	36	21	—	—	H	200	27,653	166
Togo	4.9	46	11	3.6	19	11.0	84	6.8	46	3	58	56	60	C	31	15	12	3	S	300	21,000	234
EASTERN AFRICA	233	42	18	2.4	29	379	104	6.0	46	3	44	43	45	—	21	13	18	12	—	230	—	—
Burundi	5.5	43	18	2.5	28	10.5	105	6.6	47	3	46	44	47	D	5	6	9	1	H	170	9,915	558
Comoros	0.5	37	10	2.7	25	1.2	77	5.1	47	3	59	57	62	B	29	7	21	11	H	450	861	634
Djibouti	0.7	39	16	2.3	30	1.1	115	5.8	41	3	48	47	50	D	81	3	—	—	S	—	8,950	73

	Population mid-1998 (millions)	Births per 1000 pop.	Deaths per 1000 pop.	Natural increase (annual, %)	"Doubling time" in years at current rate[a]	Projected population (millions) 2025	Infant mortality rate[b]	Total fertility rate[c]	Percentage of population of age <15	Percentage of population of age 65+	Life expectancy at birth (years) Total	Male	Female	Data available code[d]	Percent urban	Percentage of women ages 15–19 giving birth each year	Percentage of married women using contraception All methods	Modern methods[e]	Government view of birth rate[f]	GNP per capita, 1996 (U.S.$)	Land area (sq mi)	Population/ sq. mi
Eritrea	3.8	43	13	3.0	23	8.4	82	6.1	44	3	54	52	57	C	16	13	8	4	H	—	38,996	99
Ethiopia	58.4	46	21	2.5	28	98.8	128	7.0	46	3	42	41	42	C	16	12	4	3	H	100	386,100	151
Kenya	28.3	33	13	2.0	35	34.8	62	4.5	46	3	49	48	49	B	27	9	33	27	H	320	219,745	129
Madagascar	14.0	44	14	3.0	23	28.4	96	6.0	47	3	52	51	53	B	22	16	19	10	H	250	224,533	62
Malawi	9.8	42	24	1.7	41	10.9	140	5.9	48	3	36	36	36	C	20	14	22	14	H	180	36,324	269
Mauritius	1.2	17	7	1.0	69	1.4	21	2.0	27	6	70	67	74	A	43	4	75	60	S	3,710	784	1,483
Mozambique	18.6	41	19	2.2	32	33.3	134	5.6	46	2	44	43	46	C	28	17	6	5	H	80	302,737	62
Reunion	0.7	21	5	1.6	44	1.0	9	2.3	30	6	74	70	79	B	73	4	73	67	—	—	965	721
Rwanda	8.0	39	18	2.1	33	12.2	114	6.0	47	2	43	43	44	D	5	6	21	13	H	190	9,525	835
Seychelles	0.1	21	7	1.4	51	0.1	7	2.1	31	7	70	65	76	B	59	4	—	—	H	6,850	174	432
Somalia	10.7	50	19	3.2	22	23.7	122	7.0	48	3	47	45	49	C	24	21	—	—	S	—	242,216	44
Tanzania	30.6	42	17	2.5	28	50.7	100	5.7	46	3	47	45	49	B	21	13	20	13	H	170	341,154	90
Uganda	21.0	48	21	2.7	26	33.5	81	6.9	47	3	40	40	41	B	14	20	15	8	H	300	77,085	273
Zambia	9.5	42	23	1.9	36	16.2	109	6.1	45	3	37	37	38	B	39	16	26	14	H	360	287,023	33
Zimbabwe	11.0	35	20	1.5	46	12.4	53	4.4	44	3	40	40	40	B	31	10	48	42	H	610	149,363	74
MIDDLE AFRICA	90	46	16	3.1	23	187	103	6.5	46	3	49	48	51	—	34	18	9	3	—	300	—	—
Angola	12.0	51	19	3.2	22	25.5	124	7.2	48	3	47	45	48	D	42	24	—	—	H	270	481,351	25
Cameroon	14.3	41	13	2.8	25	28.5	65	5.9	44	4	55	53	56	C	44	16	16	4	H	610	179,691	80
Central African Republic	3.4	38	17	2.1	33	5.5	97	5.1	42	4	46	44	48	B	39	16	15	3	H	310	240,533	14
Chad	7.4	50	17	3.3	21	14.4	110	6.6	44	4	48	45	50	B	22	19	4	1	S	160	486,178	15
Congo	2.7	39	17	2.3	31	4.2	107	5.1	46	3	47	45	49	C	58	11	—	—	H	640	131,853	20
Congo, Dem. Rep. of (Zaire)	49.0	48	16	3.2	22	105.7	106	6.6	47	3	49	47	51	C	29	17	8	3	S	130	875,309	56
Equatorial Guinea	0.4	44	18	2.6	27	0.8	117	5.9	43	4	48	46	50	C	37	19	—	—	S	530	10,830	40
Gabon	1.2	35	15	2.0	35	2.1	94	5.0	38	6	54	52	55	C	73	16	—	—	L	3,950	99,486	12
Sao Tome and Principe	0.2	43	9	3.4	20	0.3	51	6.2	47	4	64	62	65	B	46	14	—	—	H	330	293	511

[a]The number of years it will take for the population to double assuming a constant rate of natural increase, based on the unrounded rate of natural increase.

[b]The annual number of deaths of infants under age 1 per 1000 live births. Rates shown with decimals indicate completely registered national statistics, whereas those without are estimates. Rates shown in italics are based on less than 50 annual infant deaths and, as a result, are subject to considerable yearly variability.

[c]Average number of children born to a woman during her lifetime.

[d]A = completed data . . . D = little or no data.

[e]"Modern" methods include clinic and supply methods, such as the pill, IUD, condom, and sterilization.

[f]H = too high; S = satisfactory; L = too low.

[g]— indicates data unavailable or inapplicable.

[h]z = less than 0.5 percent.

Source: Population Reference Bureau, 1998.

(continued)

APP B-3

	Population mid-1998 (millions)	Births per 1000 pop.	Deaths per 1000 pop.	Natural increase (annual, %)	"Doubling time" in years at current rate[a]	Projected population (millions) 2025	Infant mortality rate[b]	Total fertility rate[c]	Percentage of population of age <15	Percentage of population of age 65+	Life expectancy at birth (years) Total	Male	Female	Data available code[d]	Percent urban	Percentage of women ages 15-19 giving birth each year	Percentage of married women using contraception All methods	Modern methods[e]	Government view of birth rate[f]	GNP per capita, 1996 (U.S.$.)	Land area (sq mi)	Population/ sq mi
SOUTHERN AFRICA	45	28	12	1.7	42	54	55	3.5	36	4	56	54	58	—	53	10	49	48	—	3,280	—	—
Botswana	1.4	33	21	1.2	56	1.6	60	4.3	43	5	41	40	42	B	48	8	33	32	H	—	218,815	6
Lesotho	2.1	33	12	2.1	33	2.7	80	4.3	42	4	56	54	58	C	16	6	23	19	H	660	11,718	178
Namibia	1.6	36	20	1.7	42	2.3	68	5.1	42	4	42	42	42	B	27	10	29	26	H	2,250	317,873	5
South Africa	38.9	27	11	1.6	43	45.3	52	3.3	35	4	58	55	60	C	57	11	53	52	H	3,520	471,444	82
Swaziland	1.0	43	10	3.3	21	1.6	72	5.6	49	2	39	38	41	C	22	6	21	19	H	1,210	6,641	145
NORTH AMERICA	301	14	8	0.6	117	376	7	2.0	21	13	76	73	79	—	75	5	71	68	—	27,100	—	—
Canada	30.6	12	7	0.5	136	40.3	6.3	1.6	20	12	78	75	81	A	77	2	—	—	S	19,020	3,558,080	9
United States	270.2	15	9	0.6	116	335.1	7.0	2.0	22	13	76	73	79	A	75	5	71	68	S	28,020	3,536,340	76
MIDDLE & SOUTH AMERICA	500	25	7	1.8	38	697	36	3.0	34	5	69	66	72	—	72	8	67	58	—	3,710	—	—
CENTRAL AMERICA	132	29	5	2.3	30	197	32	3.4	37	4	71	68	74	—	66	8	60	52	—	3,090	—	—
Belize	0.2	33	6	2.7	26	0.4	34	4.1	42	5	72	70	74	B	51	10	47	42	H	2,700	8,803	27
Costa Rica	3.5	23	4	1.9	36	5.6	11.8	2.8	33	5	76	73	78	B	44	8	75	65	H	2,640	19,714	179
El Salvador	5.8	29	4	2.5	28	8.8	41	3.9	39	5	69	65	72	B	50	12	53	48	H	1,700	8,000	724
Guatemala	11.6	38	7	3.1	23	19.8	51	5.1	44	3	65	63	68	C	38	13	31	27	H	1,470	41,865	277
Honduras	5.9	33	6	2.8	25	9.7	42	4.4	42	3	68	66	71	B	44	9	50	41	H	660	43,201	137
Mexico	97.5	27	5	2.2	32	140.0	28	3.1	36	4	72	69	75	B	74	7	65	56	H	3,670	736,946	132
Nicaragua	4.8	38	6	3.2	22	8.5	46	4.6	44	3	66	63	68	B	63	16	49	45	H	380	46,873	102
Panama	2.8	23	5	1.8	39	3.7	22	2.7	33	5	74	71	77	B	55	7	—	—		3,080	28,737	96
CARIBBEAN	37	22	8	1.4	48	48	40	2.8	31	7	68	66	71	—	60	8	55	51	—	—	—	—
Antigua and Barbuda	0.1	17	5	1.2	59	0.1	18	1.7	30	6	74	71	76	B	36	7	53	51	S	7,330	170	394
Bahamas	0.3	23	6	1.7	42	0.4	19.0	2.0	32	5	72	68	75	A	86	5	65	63	S	—	3,865	76
Barbados	0.3	14	9	0.5	130	0.3	14.2	1.7	24	11	75	73	77	A	38	6	55	53	S	—	166	1,596
Cuba	11.1	14	7	0.6	107	11.8	7.2	1.4	22	9	75	74	77	C	74	6	70	68	S	—	42,402	262
Dominica	0.1	19	8	1.1	61	0.1	16.2	2.0	—	—	—	—	—	A	—	5	50	48	H	3,090	290	256
Dominican Republic	8.3	27	6	2.1	32	11.3	47	3.2	36	4	70	68	72	B	62	11	64	59	H	1,600	18,680	446
Grenada	0.1	29	6	2.3	30	0.2	12	3.8	38	6	71	68	73	B	32	10	54	49	H	2,880	131	731
Guadeloupe	0.4	18	6	1.2	58	0.5	7.9	2.0	26	9	77	73	80	A	99	3	—	—	H	—	653	673
Haiti	7.5	34	13	2.1	33	12.5	74	4.8	40	4	51	49	53	C	33	8	18	14	H	310	10,641	708
Jamaica	2.6	23	6	1.8	40	3.2	16	3.0	32	7	71	70	73	B	50	11	66	60	H	1,600	4,181	613

	Population mid-1998 (millions)	Births per 1000 pop.	Deaths per 1000 pop.	Natural increase (annual, %)	"Doubling time" in years at current rate[a]	Projected population (millions) 2025	Infant mortality rate[b]	Total fertility rate[c]	Percentage of population of age <15	65+	Life expectancy at birth (years) Total	Male	Female	Data available code[d]	Percent urban	Percentage of women ages 15–19 giving birth each year	Percentage of married women using contraception All methods	Modern methods[e]	Government view of birth rate[f]	GNP per capita, 1996 (U.S.$.)	Land area (sq mi)	Population/ sq. mi
Martinique	0.4	15	6	0.9	75	0.5	6	1.7	24	11	78	75	82	C	81	3	—	—	—	—	409	982
Netherlands Antilles	0.2	19	7	1.2	59	0.3	6.3	2.2	27	7	75	72	78	A	90	5	—	—	—	—	309	690
Puerto Rico	3.9	18	8	1.0	71	4.4	11.5	2.1	27	10	74	70	79	A	71	8	—	—	H	—	3,421	1,129
St. Kitts-Nevis	0.04	19	9	1.0	69	0.1	25	2.6	34	10	67	64	70	C	43	7	—	—	H	5,870	139	302
Saint Lucia	0.1	25	6	1.9	36	0.2	18.0	2.7	37	6	71	68	75	A	48	8	47	46	H	3,500	236	628
St. Vincent and the Grenadines	0.1	22	7	1.6	44	0.2	19	2.4	37	6	73	71	74	C	25	5	58	55	H	2,370	151	797
Trinidad and Tobago	1.3	15	7	0.8	86	1.5	17.1	1.9	29	6	71	68	73	A	65	5	53	44	H	3,870	1,981	646
SOUTH AMERICA	331	24	7	1.7	42	453	37	2.8	33	6	69	66	72	—	76	8	72	62	—	4,110	—	—
Argentina	36.1	19	8	1.1	62	47.2	22.2	2.5	29	9	72	69	76	A	89	6	—	—	S	8,380	1,056,637	34
Bolivia	8.0	36	10	2.6	27	13.2	75	4.8	41	4	60	57	63	B	58	9	45	18	S	830	418,680	19
Brazil	162.1	22	8	1.4	48	208.2	43	2.5	32	6	67	64	71	B	76	9	77	70	S	4,400	3,265,062	50
Chile	14.8	19	6	1.4	50	19.5	11.1	2.4	29	7	75	72	78	A	85	7	—	—	S	4,860	289,112	51
Colombia	38.6	27	6	2.1	33	58.3	28	3.0	33	4	69	65	73	B	71	9	72	59	S	2,140	401,042	96
Ecuador	12.2	28	6	2.2	31	17.8	40	3.6	36	4	69	66	71	B	61	9	57	46	H	1,500	106,888	114
French Guiana	0.2	30	4	2.5	27	0.3	14	3.7	36	4	74	71	77	C	—	11	—	—	—	—	34,035	5
Guyana	0.7	24	7	1.7	40	0.7	63	2.7	35	4	66	63	69	C	36	5	—	—	S	690	76,004	9
Paraguay	5.2	32	6	2.7	26	9.4	27	4.4	41	4	69	66	71	B	52	11	51	41	S	1,850	153,398	34
Peru	26.1	28	6	2.2	32	39.2	43	3.5	35	4	69	67	71	B	71	8	64	41	H	2,420	494,208	53
Suriname	0.4	24	6	1.8	39	0.5	29	2.6	34	5	70	68	73	D	70	5	—	—	S	1,000	60,232	7
Uruguay	3.2	18	10	0.8	88	3.8	19.6	2.4	25	12	75	72	78	A	90	5	—	—	L	5,760	67,494	47
Venezuela	23.3	26	5	2.1	33	34.8	20.9	3.1	38	4	72	70	75	A	86	8	—	—	S	3,020	340,560	68
OCEANIA	30	18	7	1.1	63	40	28	2.4	27	10	73	71	76	—	71	3	67	62	—	15,430	—	—
Australia	18.7	14	7	0.7	101	23.5	5.3	1.8	21	12	78	75	81	A	85	2	76	72	S	20,090	2,951,521	6
Fed. States of Micronesia	0.1	33	8	2.6	27	0.2	46	4.7	44	4	66	65	67	C	27	5	—	—	H	2,070	270	422
Fiji	0.8	24	6	1.8	39	1.6	17	2.8	38	3	63	61	65	C	46	4	—	—	H	2,470	7,054	114
French Polynesia	0.2	23	5	1.8	39	0.4	11	3.1	36	3	70	68	72	C	54	7	—	—	—	—	1,413	162
Guam	0.2	28	4	2.4	29	0.2	9.1	3.4	30	4	74	72	76	A	38	9	—	—	—	—	212	700
Marshall Islands	0.1	43	7	3.6	19	0.2	26	6.7	51	3	62	60	63	B	65	15	—	—	H	1,890	70	901
New Caledonia	0.2	22	5	1.7	41	0.3	8	2.8	31	5	72	68	76	B	71	3	—	—	—	—	7,058	29
New Zealand	3.8	15	7	0.8	87	4.3	6.7	2.0	23	12	72	69	75	A	85	3	—	—	S	15,720	103,471	37
Palau	0.02	23	7	1.6	43	0.02	25	2.5	30	5	67	—	—	C	69	4	—	—	—	—	190	90
Papua-New Guinea	4.3	34	10	2.4	29	7.7	77	4.8	40	2	56	56	57	C	15	8	26	20	H	1,150	174,849	25

(continued)

	Population mid-1998 (millions)	Births per 1000 pop.	Deaths per 1000 pop.	Natural increase (annual, %)	"Doubling time" in years at current rate[a]	Projected population (millions) 2025	Infant mortality rate[b]	Total fertility rate[b]	Percentage of population of age <15	65+	Life expectancy at birth (years) Total	Male	Female	Data available code[d]	Percent urban	Percentage of women ages 15–19 giving birth each year	Percentage of married women using contraception All methods	Modern methods[e]	Government view of birth rate[f]	GNP per capita, 1996 (U.S.$)	Land area (sq mi)	Population/ sq mi
Solomon Islands	0.4	37	4	3.2	21	0.9	28	5.4	47	3	70	68	73	C	13	9	—	—	H	900	10,807	38
Vanuatu	0.2	35	7	2.8	25	0.3	41	4.7	46	4	63	—	—	C	18	7	—	—	S	1,290	4,707	38
Western Samoa	0.2	29	5	2.4	29	0.3	21	4.2	41	4	65	64	—	C	21	2	—	—	H	1,170	1,090	166
ASIA	3,604	23	8	1.5	46	4,965	57	2.8	32	6	65	64	67	—	34	4	60	54	—	2,490	—	—
ASIA (Excl. China)	2,361	26	8	1.8	39	3,404	66	3.3	35	5	63	62	64	—	36	6	47	39	—	3,500	—	—
WESTERN ASIA	182	28	7	2.2	32	303	54	4.0	37	5	67	65	69	—	64	7	41	—	—	—	—	—
Armenia	3.8	13	7	0.6	112	4.1	14	1.6	28	8	73	69	76	B	67	6	22	—	S	630	10,888	349
Azerbaijan	7.7	17	6	1.1	62	9.7	19	2.1	35	6	70	67	74	B	52	3	17	—	S	480	33,436	230
Bahrain	0.6	23	3	2.0	35	0.9	14	3.2	31	2	69	68	71	B	88	3	62	31	S	—	266	2,387
Cyprus	0.7	15	8	0.7	96	1.0	8	2.1	25	11	78	75	80	C	68	2	—	—	L	—	3,568	210
Gaza	1.1	52	6	4.6	15	3.0	33	7.4	50	3	72	70	74	D	—	—	34	25	—	—	—	—
Georgia	5.4	11	7	0.4	173	5.1	17	1.6	24	10	73	69	76	B	56	5	17	—	S	850	26,911	202
Iraq	21.8	38	10	2.8	25	41.6	127	5.7	43	3	59	58	60	C	70	5	18	10	L	—	168,869	129
Israel	6.0	21	7	1.5	47	8.1	6.7	2.9	30	9	78	76	80	A	90	2	—	—	L	15,870	7,961	751
Jordan	4.6	30	5	2.5	28	10.0	34	4.4	41	2	68	66	70	B	78	4	53	38	H	1,650	34,336	134
Kuwait	1.9	25	2	2.3	30	3.0	10	3.2	29	1	72	72	73	B	100	3	35	32	S	—	6,880	271
Lebanon	4.1	23	7	1.6	42	5.6	34	2.3	34	6	70	68	73	D	87	4	—	—	S	2,970	3,950	1,030
Oman	2.5	44	5	3.9	18	6.5	27	7.1	47	4	70	68	72	B	72	9	24	18	S	—	82,031	31
Qatar	0.5	19	2	1.7	42	0.7	12	4.1	27	1	71	69	74	B	91	7	26	24	S	—	4,247	125
Saudi Arabia	20.2	35	5	3.1	23	42.6	29	6.4	42	4	70	68	71	C	80	12	—	—	S	—	829,996	24
Syria	15.6	33	6	2.8	25	26.3	35	4.6	45	3	67	67	68	B	51	12	40	28	S	1,160	70,958	220
Turkey	64.8	22	7	1.6	45	88.0	42	2.6	31	5	68	66	71	B	64	5	63	35	S	2,830	297,154	218
United Arab Emirates	2.7	24	2	2.2	32	3.8	11	4.9	30	2	74	73	75	C	82	4	28	24	S	—	32,278	84
West Bank	1.8	40	6	3.4	21	3.9	27	5.4	45	4	72	70	74	D	—	—	51	34	H	—	—	—
Yemen	15.8	44	11	3.3	21	39.0	77	7.3	47	4	58	57	60	B	25	8	7	6	H	380	203,849	77
SOUTH CENTRAL ASIA	1,442	28	9	1.9	36	2,155	74	3.6	37	4	59	59	60	—	27	7	41	36	—	410	—	—
Afghanistan	24.8	43	18	2.5	28	48.0	150	6.1	41	3	46	46	45	D	18	10	—	—	H	—	251,772	98
Bangladesh	123.4	27	8	1.8	38	165.6	82	3.3	43	3	59	59	58	B	16	15	49	42	H	260	50,260	2,454
Bhutan	0.8	40	9	3.1	22	1.5	71	5.6	43	2	66	—	—	D	15	8	—	—	H	390	18,147	44
India	988.7	27	9	1.9	37	1,441.2	72	3.4	36	5	59	59	59	B	26	7	41	36	H	380	1,147,950	861
Iran	64.1	24	6	1.8	38	92.5	35	3.0	40	4	67	67	68	B	61	6	73	56	H	—	631,660	102
Kazakstan	15.6	15	10	0.5	133	18.7	25	1.9	30	7	65	60	70	B	56	5	59	46	S	1,350	1,031,170	15
Kyrgyzstan	4.7	22	8	1.5	48	7.0	28	2.8	37	6	67	63	71	B	34	8	60	49	S	550	74,054	63
Maldives	0.3	42	9	3.3	21	0.6	30	6.4	46	3	62	63	61	B	25	7	—	23	S	1,080	116	2,435
Nepal	23.7	33	11	2.2	32	39.5	79	4.6	43	4	55	55	54	B	10	13	29	26	H	210	52,819	449
Pakistan	141.9	39	11	2.8	25	258.1	91	5.6	41	4	58	58	59	C	28	7	18	13	H	480	297,637	477

	Population mid-1998 (millions)	Births per 1000 pop.	Deaths per 1000 pop.	Natural increase (annual, %)	"Doubling time" in years at current rate[a]	Projected population (millions) 2025	Infant mortality rate[b]	Total fertility rate[c]	% pop. age <15	% pop. age 65+	Life expectancy Total	Male	Female	Data available code[d]	Percent urban	% women ages 15–19 giving birth each year	Married women using contraception — All methods	Modern methods[e]	Government view of birth rate[f]	GNP per capita, 1996 (U.S.$)	Land area (sq mi)	Population/ sq. mi
Sri Lanka	18.9	19	6	1.3	53	24.1	16.5	2.2	35	4	72	70	74	B	22	3	66	44	H	740	24,954	757
Tajikistan	6.1	22	5	1.7	41	9.3	32	2.9	40	4	68	65	71	B	28	3	21	—	H	340	54,286	113
Turkmenistan	4.7	24	7	1.7	41	6.1	42	2.9	39	4	66	62	69	B	45	2	20	—	S	940	181,440	26
Uzbekistan	24.1	26	6	2.0	35	42.3	26	3.2	41	4	70	66	72	B	38	6	56	51	S	1,010	159,938	151
SOUTHEAST ASIA	512	24	8	1.6	42	709	55	2.9	35	4	64	62	67	—	35	5	55	47	—	1,580	—	—
Brunei	0.3	25	3	2.2	32	0.5	8.4	3.4	34	3	71	70	73	A	67	4	—	—	S	—	2,035	155
Cambodia	10.8	38	14	2.4	29	17.0	116	5.2	44	4	52	50	53	D	14	6	—	—	H	300	68,154	158
Indonesia	207.4	24	8	1.5	45	275.2	66	2.7	34	4	62	60	64	B	37	6	55	52	H	1,080	705,189	294
Laos	5.3	42	14	2.8	25	9.8	97	5.9	45	3	54	52	55	C	19	10	—	—	S	400	89,112	59
Malaysia	22.2	26	5	2.1	33	37.0	10	3.2	35	4	72	70	75	B	57	2	48	31	H	4,370	126,853	175
Myanmar (Burma)	47.1	30	10	2.0	35	67.8	83	3.8	36	4	61	60	62	C	25	5	17	14	H	1,160	253,880	185
Philippines	75.3	30	7	2.3	30	116.8	34	3.7	38	4	66	63	69	B	47	5	48	30	H	1,160	115,124	654
Singapore	3.9	15	5	1.1	65	4.2	3.8	1.7	23	7	77	74	80	A	100	1	65	—	L	30,550	236	16,415
Thailand	61.1	17	7	1.1	64	71.6	25	2.0	27	5	69	67	72	B	31	4	72	70	H	2,960	197,255	310
Vietnam	78.5	19	7	1.2	57	109.5	38	2.3	40	5	67	65	69	B	20	3	75	56	H	290	125,672	625
EAST ASIA	1,469	16	7	0.9	74	1,798	29	1.8	25	7	72	69	74	B	37	1	81	78	—	4,750	—	—
China	1,242.5	17	7	1.0	69	1,561.4	31	1.8	26	6	71	69	73	B	30	1	83	81	S	750	3,600,930	345
China, Hong Kong	6.7	9	5	0.4	161	7.8	4.0	1.1	18	10	79	76	82	A	—	1	82	75	—	24,290	382	16,383
Japan	126.4	10	7	0.2	330	120.9	3.8	1.4	15	16	80	77	84	A	78	z[h]	64	57	L	40,940	145,375	869
Korea, North	22.2	18	9	0.9	75	26.1	39	1.9	28	6	66	63	69	C	59	z	—	—	S	—	46,490	477
Korea, South	46.4	16	6	1.0	68	52.7	11	1.7	22	6	74	70	77	B	79	z	77	66	S	10,610	38,120	1,218
Macao	0.5	13	3	1.0	71	0.6	5	1.5	25	7	80	77	83	B	97	1	—	—	S	—	8	59,700
Mongolia	2.4	24	7	1.6	42	3.3	49	3.1	36	4	57	—	—	C	57	5	57	41	S	360	604,826	4
Taiwan	21.7	15	6	1.0	73	25.4	6.7	1.7	23	8	75	72	78	A	75	2	—	—	S	13,710	13,970	1,555
EUROPE	728	10	11	-0.1	—	715	10	1.4	19	14	73	69	77	—	71	2	—	—	—	—	—	—
NORTHERN EUROPE	95	12	11	0.1	535	99	6	1.7	19	16	76	73	79	—	84	2	68	—	—	20,320	—	—
Denmark	5.3	13	11	0.2	431	5.6	5.8	1.8	18	16	75	73	78	A	85	1	78	71	S	32,100	16,382	324
Estonia	1.4	9	13	-0.4	—	1.2	10	1.3	20	14	68	62	74	B	70	3	36	—	L	3,080	16,320	88
Finland	5.2	12	10	0.2	377	5.2	3.5	1.7	19	17	77	73	81	A	65	1	—	—	S	23,240	117,602	44
Iceland	0.3	15	7	0.9	82	0.3	5.5	2.0	24	11	78	76	81	A	92	2	—	—	S	26,580	38,707	7
Ireland	3.7	14	9	0.5	133	3.8	5.5	1.9	23	11	75	72	78	A	57	2	—	—	S	17,110	26,598	138
Latvia	2.4	8	14	-0.6	—	2.0	16	1.2	20	14	70	64	76	B	69	3	32	—	L	2,300	23,958	102
Lithuania	3.7	11	12	-0.1	—	3.5	10	1.4	21	12	71	65	76	B	68	4	20	—	S	2,280	25,019	148
Norway	4.4	14	10	0.3	201	4.9	4.0	1.8	20	16	78	75	81	A	74	1	76	65	S	34,510	118,467	37
Sweden	8.9	10	11	-0.0	—	9.3	3.9	1.6	19	17	79	77	82	A	83	1	—	—	S	25,710	158,927	56
United Kingdom	59.1	13	11	0.2	433	62.6	6.1	1.7	19	16	77	74	80	A	90	3	72	65	S	19,600	93,282	634

(continued)

APP B-7

	Population mid-1998 (millions)	Births per 1000 pop.	Deaths per 1000 pop.	Natural increase (annual, %)	"Doubling time" in years at current rate[a]	Projected population 2025 (millions)	Infant mortality rate[b]	Total fertility rate[c]	Percentage of population of age <15	Percentage of population of age 65+	Life expectancy at birth (years) Total	Male	Female	Data available code[d]	Percent urban	Percentage of women ages 15-19 giving birth each year	Percentage of married women using contraception All methods	Modern methods[e]	Government view of birth rate[f]	GNP per capita, 1996 (U.S.$.)	Land area (sq mi)	Population/ sq mi
WESTERN EUROPE	183	11	10	0.1	517	184	5	1.5	18	15	77	74	81	—	79	1	75	70	—	28,250	—	—
Austria	8.1	11	10	0.1	990	8.3	4.8	1.4	17	15	77	74	80	A	65	2	—	—	S	28,110	31,942	253
Belgium	10.2	12	10	0.1	529	10.3	5.8	1.6	18	16	77	74	81	A	97	1	—	—	S	26,440	11,790	866
France	58.8	12	9	0.3	210	64.2	5.1	1.7	19	16	78	74	82	A	74	1	75	68	L	26,270	212,394	277
Germany	82.3	10	10	-0.1	—	76.1	4.9	1.3	16	15	77	73	80	A	85	1	75	72	L	28,870	134,853	610
Liechtenstein	0.03	13	7	0.6	124	0.04	7.4	1.5	19	10	72	67	78	A	—	1	—	—	S	—	62	502
Luxembourg	0.4	14	9	0.4	161	0.5	4.9	1.8	19	14	76	73	79	A	86	1	—	—	L	45,360	1,000	427
Monaco	0.03	20	17	0.3	239	0.04	3.9	—	—	—	—	—	—	C	—	—	—	—	—	—	—	—
Netherlands	15.7	12	9	0.3	210	17.3	5.7	1.5	18	13	78	75	80	A	61	z	74	71	S	25,940	13,097	1,197
Switzerland	7.1	12	9	0.3	248	7.5	4.7	1.5	18	16	79	76	82	A	68	z	—	—	L	44,350	15,270	466
EASTERN EUROPE	307	9	13	-0.4	—	290	15	1.3	20	13	68	63	74	—	68	4	57	—	—	2,350	—	—
Belarus	10.2	9	13	-0.4	—	9.8	12	1.3	21	13	68	62	74	B	69	4	50	42	S	2,070	80,108	127
Bulgaria	8.3	9	14	-0.5	—	7.9	15.6	1.2	17	15	71	67	75	A	68	5	—	—	L	1,190	42,683	194
Czech Republic	10.3	9	11	-0.2	—	10.2	5.9	1.2	18	14	74	71	77	A	77	2	69	45	S	4,740	29,838	345
Hungary	10.1	10	14	-0.4	—	9.3	10.0	1.4	18	14	70	66	75	A	63	3	73	68	L	4,340	35,653	284
Moldova	4.2	12	12	0.1	1,386	4.9	20	1.8	26	9	66	62	70	B	46	6	22	—	S	590	12,730	330
Poland	38.7	11	10	0.1	630	40.8	12.2	1.6	22	11	72	68	77	A	62	2	—	—	S	3,230	117,537	329
Romania	22.5	10	12	-0.2	—	19.7	22.6	1.3	19	13	69	65	73	A	55	4	57	14	L	1,600	88,934	253
Russia	146.9	9	14	-0.5	—	134.6	17	1.2	20	12	67	61	73	B	73	5	67	49	L	2,410	6,520,656	23
Slovakia	5.4	11	10	0.2	408	5.3	10.2	1.5	22	11	73	69	77	A	57	3	74	42	S	3,410	18,564	291
Ukraine	50.3	9	15	-0.6	—	47.0	14	1.3	20	14	68	62	73	B	68	5	23	—	L	1,200	223,687	225
SOUTHERN EUROPE	144	10	9	0.1	853	143	8	1.3	17	15	77	73	80	—	61	1	—	—	—	15,290	—	—
Albania	3.3	17	5	1.2	58	4.6	20.4	2.0	34	6	72	70	76	A	37	1	—	—	S	820	10,579	312
Andorra	0.1	11	3	0.8	89	0.1	2.9	1.7	16	11	79	76	82	C	63	—	—	—	S	—	—	—
Bosnia-Herzegovina	4.0	13	7	0.6	124	4.3	—	1.5	23	7	72	70	75	D	40	—	—	—	S	—	19,691	203
Croatia	4.2	12	11	0.1	990	4.2	8.0	1.6	19	12	72	69	76	A	54	2	—	—	L	3,800	21,591	193
Greece	10.5	10	10	0.0	6,931	10.2	8.1	1.3	16	16	78	75	80	A	59	1	—	—	L	11,460	49,768	211
Italy	57.7	9	9	-0.0	—	54.8	5.8	1.2	15	17	78	75	81	A	67	1	—	—	S	19,880	113,537	508
Macedonia	2.0	16	8	0.8	90	2.3	16.4	2.1	26	9	71	69	73	A	60	4	—	—	H	990	9,819	208
Malta	0.4	13	7	0.6	120	0.4	10.7	2.1	22	12	77	75	80	B	89	1	86	43	S	—	124	3,035
Portugal	10.0	11	11	0.0	2,310	9.4	6.9	1.4	17	15	75	71	79	A	48	2	—	—	L	10,160	35,502	280
San Marino	0.03	11	7	0.4	161	0.03	10.6	1.3	15	15	76	73	79	C	89	—	—	—	S	—	23	1,122
Slovenia	2.0	9	9	0.0	—	2.0	4.7	1.3	18	13	75	71	78	A	50	1	92	57	L	9,240	7,768	255
Spain	39.4	9	9	0.0	1,733	39.0	4.7	1.2	16	16	77	73	81	A	64	1	72	69	S	14,350	192,834	204
Yugoslavia	10.6	13	11	0.2	289	11.4	14	1.8	22	12	72	70	75	D	51	3	—	—	S	—	39,382	270

acculturation adaptation of a minority culture to the host culture enough to function effectively and be self-supporting; cultural borrowing

acid rain acidic water that has formed through the interaction of rainwater or moisture in the air with sulfur dioxide and nitrogen oxides emitted during the burning of fossil fuels

age distribution or **structure** the proportion of the total population in each age group

air pressure the force exerted by air molecules in a specific unit of space on the air outside it

alluvium riverborne sediment

altiplano an area of high plains in the central Andes of South America

animism belief system in which natural features carry spiritual meaning

archipelago a group, often a chain, of islands

arctic/high-altitude climate the coldest climate, and often one of the driest, found at very high altitude and near the poles

arid climate a climate of little rainfall, and often huge swings of temperature between hot days and cold nights, found in the subtropics and midlatitudes

Aryans an ancient people of Southwest Asia, the first recorded invaders into South Asia

assimilation loss of old ways of life and adoption of the lifeways of another culture

Association of Southeast Asian Nations (ASEAN) an organization of Southeast Asian governments established to further economic growth and political cooperation

atolls low-lying islands, often arranged in a circle, formed of coral reefs built on the rims of the submerged craters of undersea volcanoes

average population density the average number of people per unit area

bipedalism the ability to walk upright on two legs

Bolsheviks an organization of communists who came to power during the Russian Revolution

bride price price paid by a groom to the family of the bride, the opposite of **dowry**

Buddhism religion of Asia founded in the sixth century B.C. that emphasizes modest living and peaceful self-reflection leading to enlightenment; spread from north India to all parts of Asia

capital wealth in the form of money or property used to produce more wealth

capitalist free market economy an economic system in which privately owned firms produce and sell goods for a profit

carrying capacity the maximum number of people that a given territory can support sustainably with food, water, and other essential resources

cartography the making of maps

caste system division of society into a hierarchy of distinct social units of greatly varying status

centrally planned economy see **command economy**

chaebol name given to huge corporations in South Korea that are protected by the government

climatology the study of long-term weather patterns

cold war the contest that pit the United States and Western Europe, espousing free market capitalism and democracy, against the former USSR and its allies, promoting a centrally planned economy and socialist state

colony distant lands acquired by a more powerful country for economic exploitation

command economy an economy in which government bureaucrats plan, spatially allocate, and manage all production and distribution

commercial farming large-scale production of single crops usually involving large cleared fields, deep plowing, chemical fertilizers, mechanized equipment, and (often) irrigation

communal conflict a euphemism for religion-based violence in South Asia

communist welfare regimes the type of welfare regime that once existed in the former communist countries of Europe, intended to provide comprehensive "cradle to grave" security, and in which women were pressured to work outside the home

comparative advantage the economic advantage obtained by developing a particular specialty that outcompetes rivals

Confucianism Chinese philosophy that teaches that the best organizational model for the state and society is a hierarchy based on the model of the patriarchal family

conglomerate company business organization that has interests in loosely related enterprises across the globe

conservative welfare regimes welfare regimes that provide only minimum support services for only the most destitute citizens

contested space any area that several groups claim or want to use in different ways, such as the Amazon or Palestine

cool humid climate moist climate with extremes of temperature, hot in summer and very cold in the winter, found in continental interiors; droughts are rare

Corridor Five a major transportation roadway planned and partially constructed across southern Europe

Creole a new culture formed from the amalgamation of an indigenous culture with immigrant cultures; specifically, that which developed in the colonial period in Middle and South America

crony capitalism a type of corruption in which politicians, bankers, and entrepreneurs, sometimes members of the same family, have close personal as well as business relationships

cultural complexity the cultural identity characteristic of a region where groups of people from many different backgrounds have lived together for a long time, yet have remained distinct

cultural diversity differences in ideas, technologies, and institutions among culture groups

cultural hearth a supposed figurative ancient center of cultural innovation from which ideas and material diffused

cultural marker a characteristic that helps to define a culture group

culturally defined difference a deeply ingrained difference between the sexes or classes of people that is not biological but is instigated by the culture

culture a set of ideas, materials, and institutions that a group of people has invented and passed on to subsequent generations

culture group a group of people who share a set of beliefs, a way of life, a technology, and usually a place

currency devaluation the lowering of a currency's value relative to the U.S. dollar, the Japanese yen, the European euro, or other currency of global trade

debt crisis the inability of many countries during the 1980s to repay massive debts owed to foreign banks, which then resolved that they would no longer lend to debtor nations unless the governments agreed to meet the criteria set by **structural adjustment programs (SAPs)**

delta the triangular-shaped plain of sediment that forms where a river meets the sea

democracy a form of government in which people have the power to govern themselves by direct rule or through elected representatives

demographic transition the change from high birth and death rates to low birth and death rates that usually accompanies a cluster of other changes such as change from a subsistence to a cash economy, increasing education rates, and urbanization

demography the study of population patterns and changes in those patterns

deposition the settling out of rock and soil particles from slowing wind or water

desert area characterized by a climate of low rainfall and by little vegetation

desertification a set of ecological changes that turn nondesert lands into deserts

detritus dead plant and animal material that has accumulated on the ground

development economic efforts to improve standards of living, such as industrialization, mechanized agriculture and transport, and urbanization

doi moi economic and bureaucratic restructuring in Vietnam

domestic spaces spaces in the home (as opposed to public spaces)

double day the longer workday of women with jobs outside the home who also work as family caretakers, housekeepers, and cooks at home

dowry price paid by the family of a bride to the groom; opposite of **bride price**

dry forests forests in which the trees lose their leaves during the dry season

earthquake catastrophic shaking of the landscape, often caused by the shifting and friction of tectonic plates

Economic and Technical Development Zones (ETDZs) zones in China with fewer restrictions on foreign business, established to encourage foreign investment and economic growth

economic core the dominant economic region within a larger region

economic development efforts to improve standards of living through industrialization, mechanized agriculture and transport, and urbanization

economic diversification the expansion of an economy to include a wider array of economic activities

economic integration the free movement of people, goods, money, and ideas among countries

economy the forum where people make their living, including the spatial, social, and political aspects of how resources are recognized, extracted, exchanged, transformed, and relocated

ecotourism nature-oriented vacations often taken in endangered and remote landscapes usually by travelers from industrialized nations

El Niño periodic climate-altering changes, especially in the circulation of the Pacific Ocean, now understood to operate at a global scale

emigration the movement of people out of a region

enclaves quasi-autonomous internal political units

that lie entirely within the borders of a single country

endemic belonging or restricted to a particular place

erosion process by which fragmented rock and soil are moved over a distance primarily by wind and water

ethnic group see **culture group**

ethnicity the quality of belonging to a particular culture group

ethnocentrism the belief in the superiority of one's own cultural perspective

European Union (EU) a supranational institution including most of West, South, and North Europe, established to bring economic integration to member countries

evangelical Protestantism a Christian movement that focuses on personal salvation and empowerment of the individual through miraculous healing and transformation; some practitioners preach the "gospel of success" to the poor, that a life dedicated to Christ will result in prosperity of the body and soul

exchange barter or trade for money, goods, or services

exclave an integral portion of a country that lies entirely outside its main borders

extended families families consisting of related individuals beyond the nuclear family of parents and children

external processes (geophysical) landform-shaping process that originate at the surface of the earth, such as weathering, mass wasting, and erosion

extraction the acquisition of a material resource through mining, logging, agriculture, or other means

extraregional migration movement of people to countries outside their region of origin

fatwas legal opinions based on interpretations of Muslim law

female genital mutilation the removal of the labia and the clitoris and often the stitching nearly shut of the vulva

fiords deep glacier-gouged river mouths

floating population jobless or underemployed people who have left economically depressed rural areas for the cities and move about looking for work

floodplain the flat land around a river where sediment is deposited during flooding

food stability the state of consistently sufficient food for an entire population

forced migration movement of people against their desire

formal economy all aspects of the economy that take place in official channels

fragile environments areas where, because of particularly delicate natural balances, human pressure may result in long-term or irreversible damage to plant and animal life

free trade movement of goods and capital without government restrictions

frontal precipitation rainfall caused by the interaction of large air masses of roughly constant temperature

gender structure the proportion of males and females in each age group of a population

genocide the deliberate destruction of an ethnic, racial, or political group

gentrification rehabilitation and upgrading of city neighborhoods to attract the middle class

geography the study of the earth's surface and the processes that shape it, both physical and human

geomorphology the study of landforms

geopolitics the use of strategies by countries to ensure that their best interests are served

ger a round, heavy felt tent stretched over collapsible willow frames used by nomadic herders in northwest China (see also **yurt**)

global economy the worldwide system in which goods, services, and labor are exchanged

global region the entire world treated as a single region

global warming the predicted warming of the earth's climate as atmospheric levels of greenhouse gases increase

globalization the process of economic integration on a worldwide scale

Gosplan state agency that set economic goals for state firms in the Soviet Union

grassroots rural economic development programs established to provide sustainable livelihoods in the countryside

Green Revolution increases in food production brought about through the use of new seeds, fertilizers, mechanized equipment, irrigation, pesticides, and herbicides

greenhouse gas gas emissions, resulting from burning wood and fossil fuel, that absorb heat radiated from the surface of the earth and thereby contribute to global warming

gross domestic product (GDP) the market value of all goods and services, produced by workers and capital within a particular nation's borders, that are purchased for use within a given year

gross national product (GNP) per capita the total value of all goods and services produced by the citizens and capital of a country in a given year, regardless of where the production takes place; if divided by the number of people in the country, the figure becomes a per capita number

growth pole zones of development whose success draws yet more investment and migration to a region

guarantor in China, a third party who vouches for the honesty and reliability of one person in his or her dealings with another party

guest workers immigrants from outside Europe, often from former colonies, who came to Europe (often temporarily) to fill empty jobs; Europeans expect them to return home when no longer needed

hacienda large agricultural estate in Middle or South America, more common in the past; usually not specialized by crop and not focused on market production

hajj pilgrimage to the city of Mecca that all Muslims are encouraged to undertake at least once in a lifetime

hazardous waste toxic substances such as those generated by nuclear power generation, mining, incinerators, and industry

hierarchical societies social structures formed of groups ranked according to power, prestige, and wealth, with ruling elites at the top and laborers (in the past outcasts and slaves) at the bottom

high islands high-rising islands that are most often volcanoes rising from the sea into mountainous rocky formations

Hindus adherents of Hinduism, a religion of South Asia

hinterland rural areas surrounding cities and usually connected to them economically and socially

Hispanic a loose ethnic term that refers to all Spanish-speaking people from Latin America and Spain; equivalent to **Latino**

import quota limit on the amount of a given item that may be imported over a period of time

import substitution industrialization a form of industrialization involving the use of public funds to set up factories to produce goods that previously had been imported

in-migration the movement of people into a region from outside it; the same as immigration

industrial revolution the transformation from an agrarian society to an industrial one

informal economy all aspects of the economy that take place outside official channels

infrastructure the built environment including industrial plants, power and other utilities, waste treatment plants, port facilities, and interurban rail and interstate highway systems

institutions all of the associations, formal and informal, that help people get along together

internal processes (geophysical) processes, like those of plate tectonics, that originate deep beneath the surface of the earth

interstate highway system federally subsidized network of highways in the United States

intertropical convergence zone (ITCZ) a band of atmospheric currents circling the globe roughly around the equator. Warm winds converge from both north and south at the ITZC, pushing air upward and causing copious rainfall. The ITCZ moves north in the Northern Hemisphere's summer and south in the Southern Hemisphere's summer.

intifada Palestinian uprising against Israel

iron curtain the boundary between Western and Eastern Europe during the cold war

irredentism the policy of claiming territory held by another because it is inhabited by ethnically or politically related people.

Islamism a grassroots movement to replace secular governments and civil law with those guided by Islamic principles

Islamists fundamentalist Muslims who favor a religiously based state that incorporates conservative interpretation of the Qur'an and strictly enforced Islamic principles as part of the legal system

Israel-Palestine conflict long-running conflict over the control of territory between Israel and Palestinians who live in Israel-occupied territory

J curve the graphical depiction of the exponential growth of human population; exponential growth begins slowly and increases rapidly, so the resulting curve resembles a J

landraces the genetic descendants of indigenous plants carefully selected for favorable characteristics for thousands of years

laterite permanently hard surface left when minerals in tropical soils are leached away

Latino a loose ethnic term that refers to all Spanish-speaking people from Middle and South America and Spain; equivalent to **Hispanic**

leaching the washing out into groundwater of soil minerals and nutrients released into soil by decaying organic matter

liberation theology a movement within the Roman Catholic Church that uses the teachings of Christ to encourage the poor to organize to change their own lives and the rich to promote social and economic reform

lingua franca a language used to communicate by people who don't speak one another's native languages

loess windblown dust that forms deep soils in North America, Central Europe, and China

lowlands plains and valleys

machismo a set of values that defines manliness in Middle and South America

magma molten rock and gases from the earth's interior

maquiladoras in Mexico, foreign-owned factories, often located in towns just over the border from U.S. towns, that hire people at low wages to assemble manufactured goods that are then sent elsewhere for sale; now also used for similar firms in other parts of Mexico and Middle America

marianismo a set of values that defines the proper social roles for women in Middle and South America

marine west coast climate climate noted for frequent drizzling rain

marsupials mammals, such as kangaroos, that give birth to their young at a very immature stage and then nurture them in a pouch equipped with nipples

mass wasting process in which loosened rock and soil move down a slope due to gravity

material culture all the things, living and inert, that humans use

Mediterranean climate climate with dry summers, wet winters, and moderate temperatures

Megalopolis the band of urbanization along the eastern United States seaboard from Boston to Washington, D.C.

melting pot the intermingling of groups from different backgrounds sufficiently so that the groups lose their separate identities

Mercosur a regional free trade association in South America

mestizos people who are racially and culturally a blend of Native American and European roots

microcredit a program that makes very small loans available to poor entrepreneurs

Middle East alternative term for parts of North Africa and Southwest Asia

midlatitude temperate climate climate with all-year rain, short, mild winters, and long, hot summers

migration movement of people from one place to another

mixed agriculture the raising of a variety of crops and animals in a single farm often to take advantage of several environmental niches

modest welfare regimes welfare regimes that seek to encourage individual responsibility and the work ethic as the norm, providing help only in emergencies and to the particularly unfortunate; often a stigma attaches to accepting help

Moguls Muslim invaders of South Asia

monotremes egg-laying mammals such as the platypus

monsoon opposing winter and summer patterns of atmospheric and moisture movement in South, Southeast, and parts of East Asia. Warm wet air coming in from the ocean brings copious rainfall during the summer monsoons; cool dry air moves south and east out of Eurasia in winter.

multinational corporation a business organization that operates extraction, production, and distribution facilities in multiple countries

nation group of people who share a language, culture, political philosophy, and usually a territory

nation-state political unit, or country, formed by people who share a language, culture, and political philosophy

nationalism devotion to the interests or culture of a particular country or nation (cultural group); the idea that a group of people living in a specific territory and sharing cultural traits should be united in a single country to which they are loyal and obedient

natural increase rate population growth measured as the excess of births over deaths per 1000 individuals per year; the effects of emigration and immigration are not included

negative rate of natural increase the rate of natural decrease that occurs when death rates exceed birth rates, as is happening in some parts of Europe, where the population is aging and one or no children per family is the norm

neocolonialism the practice whereby wealthy countries of the world reap the wealth of poorer countries through contracts and circumstances that favor the wealthy countries

New World all of the Americas

nomadic pastoralism a way of life and economy centered around the tending of grazing animals that are moved seasonally to gain access to the best grasses

nuclear family a family group consisting of a father and mother and their children

old-growth forests forests that have never been logged

Old World Eurasia, Africa, and Oceania

OPEC (Organization of Petroleum Exporting Countries) a cartel of oil-producing countries (Algeria, Gabon, Indonesia, Iran, Iraq, Kuwait, Libya, Nigeria, Qatar, Saudi Arabia, the United Arab Emirates, and Venezuela) established to regulate the production of oil and natural gas

organic matter the remains of any living thing

orographic rainfall rainfall produced when a moving moist air mass encounters a mountain range, rises, cools, and releases condensed moisture that falls as rain

Pacific Way the idea that Pacific islanders have a regional identity and a way of handling matters peacefully, which grows out of their own particular social experience

paddy cultivation a prolific type of rice production, which requires that the roots of the plants be submerged in water during the first part of the growing season

pampas extensive grasslands with highly fertile soils in northern Argentina and Uruguay

Pancasila Indonesian national philosophy based on tolerance, particularly in matters of religion, and centered around the five precepts of belief in God and the observance of conformity, corporatism, consensus, and harmony

Pangaea hypothesis the proposal that about 200 million years ago all continents were joined in a single vast continent, called Pangaea

parliamentary system a democratic system of government consisting of an executive branch (prime minister and cabinet) and a legislature (parliament)

patron-client relationship a form of unequal reciprocity practiced in political interactions in Asia in which a higher-status patron provides resources, protection, or opportunities to a lower-status client in return for loyalty, services, or payment

perestroika economic and bureaucratic restructuring in the Soviet Union during the 1980s

permeable national borders borders subject to large numbers of legal crossings, often as a result of transborder economies

pidgin (1) a language used for trading that contains made-up words borrowed from the several languages of people involved in trading relationships; (2) one of the made-up words in such a language

Pillars of Islamic Practice Islamic teachings on how to live daily life

plantation a large estate or farm on which a large group of resident laborers grow (and partially process) a single cash crop

plate tectonics a theory proposing that the earth's surface is composed of large plates that float on top of an underlying layer of molten rock; the movement and interaction of the plates create many of the large features of the earth's surface, particularly mountains

pluralistic state political unit in which power is shared among several ethnic groups

pogroms episodes of persecution, ethnic cleansing, and sometimes massacre, especially conducted against European Jews

polyandry the taking by a woman of more than one husband at a time

polygamy the practice of having more than one spouse at a time

polygyny the taking by a man of more than one wife at a time

primary or extractive sector economic activity that extracts resources from the earth

primate city a city that is vastly larger than all others in a country and in which economic and political activity is centered

Protestant Reformation a European reform ("protest") movement that challenged Catholic practices in the sixteenth century, resulting in the establishment of Protestant churches.

public spaces the workplaces and marketplaces, as opposed to domestic (home and private) spaces

pull migration factors reasons for people to migrate to a new place

purdah the perpetual concealment of women from the public at large and from men not of their family

push migration factors reasons for people to move from the region they are living in

pyroclastic flow volcanic eruptions consisting of a blast of superheated rocks, ash, and gas that moves at great speed

qanats usually ancient underground conduits for irrigation water, used in North Africa and Southwest Asia

quaternary sector economic sector that deals primarily with manipulation of information (knowledge)

Québecois French Canadian ethnic group

Qur'an (or **Koran**) the holy book of Islam

racism negative assessment of people, often those who look different, primarily on the basis of skin color and other physical features

rain shadow the side of a mountain range, facing away from the prevailing winds, where rain does not fall as much

ranch a large farm where livestock (usually grazing animals) is raised

rate of natural increase rate of population growth measured as excess of births over deaths per 1000 individuals per year, without regard for the effects of migration

region a unit of the earth's surface that contains distinct patterns of physical features or of human development

regional conflict a conflict created by the resistance of a regional ethnic or religious minority to the authority of a national or state government

regional geography analysis of the geographic characteristics of particular places

regional self-sufficiency economic policy that encourages each region to develop independently in the hope of evening out the national distribution of production and income

religious nationalism the belief that a certain religion is strongly connected to a particular territory, and that adherents should have political power in that territory

remittances earnings sent home by immigrant workers

Renaissance a broad European cultural movement in the fourteenth through sixteenth centuries that drew inspiration from the Greek, Roman, and Islamic civilizations, marking the transition from medieval to modern times

resettlement schemes plans to move large numbers of people from one part of a country to another

resource anything that is recognized as useful, such as mineral ores, forest products, skills, or brainpower

resource base the selection of raw materials and human skills available in a region for domestic use and industrial development

responsibility systems the rights and responsibilities given to the managers of Chinese state-owned enterprises to make their operations work efficiently

Ring of Fire the tectonic plate junctures around the edges of the Pacific Ocean, characterized by volcanoes and earthquakes

rudimentary welfare regimes regimes in which citizens do not have inherent rights to government-sponsored welfare support; there may be some funds and services for the destitute

rural to urban migration movement of people from rural areas to the cities

Sahel a band of arid grassland that runs east-west along the southern edge of the Sahara Desert; the Sahel shifts north and south due to natural climatic cycles that are as yet poorly understood

salinization damage to soil caused by the evaporation of water, which leaves behind salts and other minerals

secondary forests forests that grow back after the first cutting, often with decreased diversity of species

secondary or **industrial sector** economic sector that transforms raw materials into manufactured goods

secular states countries that have no state religion and in which religion has no direct influence on affairs of state or civil law

secularism a way of life informed by values that do not derive from any one religious tradition

self-reliant development small-scale development schemes in rural areas that focus on developing local skills, creating local jobs, producing products or services for local consumption, and maintaining local control so participants retain a sense of ownership

semiarid climate climate of some (usually seasonal) rainfall, with vegetation (usually grass and shrubs) adapted to scarce moisture

shari'a Islamic religious law

sheiks patriarchal leaders of tribal groups in the Arabian Peninsula

shifting cultivation multicrop gardening using land prepared by cutting and burning small plots of rain forest; the cultivator moves to a new plot of land after soil fertility is exhausted in a few years

Shi'ite the smaller of the two major groups of Muslims

Sikhs adherents of Sikhism, a religion of South Asia

slash-and-burn cultivation multicrop gardening using land prepared by cutting and burning small plots of rain forest

Slavs a group of farmers who originated between the Dnieper and Vistula rivers, in what is now Poland, Ukraine, and Belarus

smog a combination of industrial air pollution and car exhaust (*smo*ke + f*og*)

social democratic welfare regimes welfare regimes that seek to achieve equality across gender and class lines by providing generous benefits to all citizens in housing, education, nutrition, and other areas.

social differentiation relative status, as indicated by clothes, speaking style, possessions, or religion

social structures culturally defined ways of organizing society, the family, gender roles, race relations, religious observance, and interactions with government

spatial analysis the study of how people or things or ideas are, or are not, related to one another across space

spatial development, lopsided concentration of wealth and power in one place or particular places

spatial freedom ability to move about without restrictions

Special Economic Zones (SEZs) free trade zones within China

steppes a semiarid, grass-covered plain; the term is usually used for the region north of Central Asia and the region of central North America

structural adjustment programs (SAPs) belt-tightening measures implemented in debtor nations meant to release money for loan repayment

subduction the sliding of one lithospheric (tectonic) plate under another

subregion a division of a world region that has one or more characteristics that distinguish it from the larger region

subsidy monetary assistance granted by a government to an individual or group in support of an activity like farming or housing construction that is viewed as being in the public interest

subsistence affluence life based on home-grown and gathered food as well as hunting and fishing and on relatively little cash income; South Pacific islanders use the term to describe their lifestyle

subsistence agriculture small-scale agriculture or horticulture that produces most or all of the nutritional needs of the producers

subtropical temperate climate climate having short, mild, dry winters and long, hot, wet summers

Sunni the larger of the two major groups of Muslims

sustainable development efforts to improve standards of living in ways that will not jeopardize those of future generations

tariff tax on imported goods usually intended to protect home industries

temperature-altitude zones changing climate zones

ascending a mountain, caused by the decrease in temperature with increasing altitude

tertiary or **service sector** economic activity that amounts to doing services for others

theocratic states countries that require all government leaders to subscribe to a state religion and all citizens to follow certain rules decreed by that religion

thermal inversion a warm mass of stagnant air that is temporarily trapped beneath cooler heavy air

thermal pollution the return of unnaturally hot water to the environment, as by water-cooled nuclear power plants or industrial processes

tierra caliente low-lying "hot lands" in Middle and South America

tierra fria "cool lands" at relatively high elevation in Middle and South America

tierra helada very high elevation "frozen lands" in Middle and South America

tierra templada "temperate lands" with year-round springlike climates at moderate elevations (usually between *caliente* and *fria* zones) in Middle and South America

town charter in Europe in the Middle Ages, an agreement that established certain civil rights that were to be enjoyed by all citizens of a town

trade bloc association of usually neighboring countries that have set up free trade agreements

tropical wet climate climate of consistently warm temperatures in which rain usually falls every afternoon and just before dawn; seasonally dry periods may be experienced

tsunamis large ocean waves caused by earthquakes

uplands the hilly or plateau transition zone between lowlands or plains and mountains

vilas rural rural satellite towns of industrial cities

weathering process in which rocks are physically or chemically broken up

welfare state a country in which the government assumes primary responsibility for the health care, education, employment, and general well-being of the population

wet/dry tropical climate climate in which rain falls seasonally as monsoons

wet rice cultivation a prolific type of rice production that requires that the roots of the plants be submerged in water for part of the growing season

world region one of the largest divisions of the globe, such as East Asia or North America

xerophytic species plants that are adapted in several possible ways (e.g., shiny tough leaves, deep roots) to dry conditions

xinyong in China, the trustworthiness and financial solvency of a party doing business

yurt round, heavy felt tents stretched over collapsible willow frames used by nomadic herders in northwest China, Mongolia, and Central Asia (see also *ger*)

Zionists European Jews who worked to create a Jewish homeland (Zion) on lands once occupied by their ancestors in Palestine

PRONUNCIATION GUIDE

This pronunciation guide shows how to pronounce the place names, names of culture groups, many of the foreign terms, and the names of important people mentioned in the preceding chapters. The terms are taken from the text rather than the maps. The sounds of vowels are represented by the following system, which is meant to provide an intuitive sense of how to pronounce a term:

KEY TO VOWELS

A	PAT	p*a*t
AH	PAH-puh	p*a*pa
AU	PAUT	p*ou*t
AW	PAW	p*aw*
AY	PAY	p*a*te
EE	PEET	p*ea*t
EH	PEHT	p*e*t
IE	PIE	p*ye*
IH	PIHT	p*i*t
OH	POHP	p*o*pe
OO	POOT	p*u*t
	["oo" as in book]	
OO	POOCH	p*oo*ch
UH	PUHT	p*u*tt
AHR	PAHRT	p*a*rt
AIR	PAIR	p*air*
OHR	POHR	p*our*
OOR	POOR	p*oor*
URR	PURR	p*urr*

Chapter 1   INTRODUCTION

Pangaea (pan-JEE-uh)

Chapter 2   NORTH AMERICA

Adirondack Mountains (ad-uh-RAHN-dak)
Appalachia (ap-uh-LACH-uh)
Appalachian Mountains (ap-uh-LACH-uhn)
Bering Strait (BAIR-ing)
Cahokia (ku-HOH-kee-uh)
Cherokee (CHAIR-uh-kee)
Choctaw (CHAWK-taw)
Cree (KREE)
Dubuque (duh-BYOOK)
Hispanic (hihss-PAN-ihk)
Kankakee (KANG-kuh-kee)
Kootenai (KOOT-uh-nee)
Labrador (LAB-ruh-dohr)

Laredo (luh-RAY-doh)
Latino (lah-TEE-noh)
Louisville (LOO-uh-vuhl/LOO-ee-vihl)
Megalopolis (meh-guh-LAW-puh-lihss)
Mesabi (muh-SAH-bee)
métis (may-TEE)
Mohawk (MOH-hawk)
New Orleans (noo OHR-luhnz/noo ohr-LEENZ)
Newfoundland (noo-fuhnd-LAND)
Nogales (noh-GAH-layss)
Nova Scotia (NOH-vuh SKOH-shuh)
Ogallala (oh-gu-LAHL-uh)
Ottawa (AW-tuh-waw)
Québec (kay-BEHK)
Québecois (kay-behk-WAH)
Rio Grande (ree-oh GRAND)
Salish (SAY-lihsh)
San Diego (san dee-AY-goh)
San Francisco (san fran-SIHSS-koh)
Santa Barbara (san-tuh BAHR-bruh)
Sault Ste. Marie (SOO SAYNT muh-REE)
Seattle (see-AT-uhl)
taiga (TYE-guh)
Toronto (tuh-RAWN-toh)
Tuscarora (tuhss-kuh-ROHR-uh)
Valdez (val-DEEZ)
Vancouver (van-KOO-vurr)

Chapter 3   MIDDLE AND SOUTH AMERICA

Acapulco (ah-kah-POOL-koh)
altiplano (ahl-tee-PLAH-noh)
Amazon River (AM-uh-zahn)
Amazonia (am-uh-ZOH-nee-uh)
Andes (AN-deez)
Antigua and Barbuda (an-TEE-guh; bahr-BOO-duh)
Argentina (ahr-juhn-TEE-nuh)
Aristide, Jean-Bertrand   [ah-ree-STEED,
      ZHAW(N) bair-TRAH(N)]
Atacama Desert (ah-tuh-KAH-muh)

Aztec (AZ-tehk)
Bahamas (buh-HAH-muhz)
Balsas Depression (BAHL-suhss)
Barbados (bahr-BAY-dohss)
Barbuda (bahr-BOO-duh)
Belém (buh-LAYM)
Belize (buh-LEEZ)
Belo Horizonte (BEH-loo aw-rih-ZAWN-teh
    ["oo" as in "book"])
Bolivia (boh-LIHV-ee-ah)
Brasília (bruh-ZIHL-yuh)
Brazil (bruh-ZIHL)
British Honduras (hawn-DOOR-ahss)
Buenos Aires (BWAY-nohss IE-rehss)
Cali (KAH-lee)
Calypso (kuh-LIHP-soh)
Caracas (kah-RAH-kahs)
Caribbean (kuh-RIH-bee-uhn)
Castro, Fidel (KAH-stroh, fee-DEHL)
Ceará (seh-ah-RAH)
Chamorro, Violetta (chah-MOHR-oh,
    vee-oh-LEHT-ah)
Chiapas (chee-AH-pahss)
Chile (CHEE-leh)
Ciudad Juárez (see-oo-DAHD HWAHR-ehss)
Cocos Plate (KOH-kohss)
Colombia (koh-LOHM-bee-ah)
Cortez, Hernando (kohr-TEHZ,
    air-NAHN-doh)
Costa Rica (KOHSS-tah REE-kah)
Cuba (KOO-bah/KYOO-buh)
Curitiba (koor-ee-TEE-bah)
Cuzco (KOOZ-koh)
Dominican Republic (doh-MIH-nih-kuhn)
Duvallier, François (doo-VAHL-yay,
    frahnts-WAH)
Ecuador (EHK-wah-dohr)
El Niño (el NEEN-yoh)
El Salvador (ehl sahl-vah-DOHR)
Fortaleza (fohr-tah-LAY-zah)
French Guiana (gee-AHN-ah)
Garifuna (gahr-ee-FOO-nah)
Gatun lake (gah-TOON)
Goiás (goy-AHSS)
Greater Antilles (an-TIL-eez)
Grenada (gruh-NAY-duh)
Grenadines (GREHN-uh-deenz)
Guadeloupe (gwah-duh-LOOP)
Guatemala (gwah-teh-MAH-lah)
Guayaquil (gwah-yah-KEEL)
Guiana Highlands (gee-AHN-ah)
Guyana (gye-AHN-uh)
hacienda (hah-see-EN-dah)
Haiti (HAY-tee)
Havana (ah-VAHN-ah/huh-VAN-uh)
Hispaniola (hihs-puhn-YOH-luh)

Honduras (ohn-DOO-rahss/hawn-DOOR-uhss)
Inca (ING-kuh)
Iquitos (ih-KEE-tohss)
Jamaica (juh-MAY-kuh)
La Paz (lah PAHSS)
Lake Titicaca (tee-tee-KAH-kah)
Lima (LEE-muh)
machismo (mah-CHEEZ-moh)
Managua (mah-NAH-gwah)
Manaus (mah-NAUS)
maquiladora (mah-kee-lah-DOH-rah)
marianismo (mah-ree-ah-NEEZ-moh)
Martinique (mahr-tih-NEEK)
Maya (MAH-yuh)
Medellín (meh-deh-YEEN)
Mesa Central (MAY-zah sehn-TRAHL)
mestizo (mehs-TEE-zoh)
Mexicali (meh-hee-KAH-lee)
Mexico (MEH-hee-koh/MEHK-sih-koh)
Minas Gerais (MEE-nahss zhuh-RIESS)
minifundios (mih-nee-FOON-dee-ohss
    ["oo" as in "book"])
Montego Bay (mawn-TEE-goh)
Montserrat (mohnt-srat)
mulatto (moo-LAH-toh)
Nazca Plate (NAHZ-kuh)
Netherlands Antilles (an-TIL-eez)
Nicaragua (nee-kah-RAH-gwah)
Nogales (noh-GAH-layss)
Noriega, Manuel (nohr-ee-AY-gah,
    mahn-WEHL)
Nuevo Laredo (NWAY-voh lah-RAY-doh)
Orinoco River (ohr-ee-NOH-koh)
pampas (PAHM-pahss)
Panama (PA-nuh-mah)
Paraguay (PAHR-uh-gwaiy)
Paraná River (pah-rah-NAH)
pardo (PAHR-doh)
Patagonia (pa-tuh-GOHN-yuh)
Peru (peh-ROO)
Peten (peh-TEHN)
Pinochet, Augusto (pee-noh-CHAY, au-GOOSS-toh
    ["oo" as in "book"])
Pizarro, Francisco (pee-ZAHR-oh,
    frahn-SEESS-koh)
Pôrto Alegre (POHR-too ah-LEHG-reh)
Potosí (poh-toh-SEE)
Puebla (PWEHB-lah)
Puerto Rico (PWAIR-toh REE-koh/
    POHR-toh REE-koh)
pyroclastic flow (pye-roh-KLAS-tihk)
Quetzalcoatl (keht-sahl-koh-AHT-uhl)
Quito (KEE-toh)
Recife (reh-SEE-feh)
Reynosa (ray-NOH-sah)
Rio de Janeiro (REE-oh dih zhuh-NAY-roh)

Río de la Plata (REE-oh dih lah PLAH-tah)
Río Negro (REE-oh NAY-groh)
Sahagún, Bernardino de (sah-hah-GOON, bair-nahr-DEE-noh deh)
Salinas, Carlos (sah-LEE-nahss, KAHR-lohss)
Salvador (sahl-vah-DOHR)
Samoza, Anastacio (sah-MOH-zah, ah-nah-STAH-see-oh)
Samper, Ernesto (sahm-PAIR, air-NEHSS-toh)
San Juan (sahn HWAHN)
Sandinista (sahn-dee-NEESS-tah)
São Paolo (sau PAU-loh)
Sierra Madre (see-AIR-ah MAHD-ray)
Soufrière (soo-free-AIR)
St. Kitts and Nevis (KIHTSS; NEH-vihss)
St. Lucia (LOO-shuh)
St. Maarten (MAHR-tuhn)
Suriname (soo-rih-NAHM)
Tarahumara (tahr-ah-hoo-MAHR-ah)
Tehuantepec (teh-WAHN-teh-pehk)
Tenochtitlán (teh-nawch-teet-LAHN)
tierra caliente (tee-AIR-ah cah-lee-EHN-tay)
Tierra del Fuego (tee-AIR-ah dehl FWAY-goh)
tierra fria (tee-AIR-ah FREE-uh)
tierra helada (tee-AIR-ah ay-LAH-dah)
tierra templada (tee-AIR-ah temp-LAH-dah)
Tijuana (tee-HWAH-nah)
Tordesillas (tohr-day-SEE-yahss)
Trinidad (TRIH-nih-dad)
Trinidad and Tobago (toh-BAY-goh)
Umbanda (oom-BAHN-dah)
Urubamba (oo-roo-BAHM-bah)
Uruguay (OO-roo-gwaiy)
Venezuela (veh-neh-ZWAY-lah)
Veracruz (va-rah-CROOSS)
vilas rural (VEE-lahss roo-RAHL)
Yanomamo (yah-noh-MAH-moh)

Chapter 4 **EUROPE**

Adriatic Sea (ay-dree-AT-ihk)
Albania (ahl-BAY-nee-ah)
Alhambra (ahl-HAHM-brah)
Amsterdam (AM-sturr-dam)
Andalucía (ahn-dah-loo-THEE-ah)
Antwerp (AHN-twurrp)
Athens (ATH-ihnz)
Austria (AW-stree-uh)
Balearic Islands (bah-lee-AIR-ihk)
Balkans (BAHL-kuhnz)
Baltic Sea (BAHL-tihk)
Basque (BASK)
Belfast (BEHL-fast)
Belgium (BEHL-juhm)
Belgrade (BEHL-grahd)

Benelux (BEHN-uh-luhks)
Bordeaux (bohr-DOH)
Bosnia (BAWZ-nee-uh)
Bosnia-Herzegovina (hairt-suh-goh-VEE-nuh)
Brundtland, Gro Harlem (BROONT-lahnd, GROH HAHR-lehm ["oo" as in "book"])
Brussels (BRUH-suhlz)
Bucharest (BOO-kuh-rehst)
Budapest (BOO-duh-pehsht)
Bukovyna (boo-KOH-vee-nuh)
Bulgaria (buhl-GAIR-ee-uh)
Carpathian Mountains (kahr-PAY-thee-uhn)
Catalonia (kaht-uh-LOH-nee-uh)
Chernobyl (chyair-NOH-bihl)
Chrisnau (KREESS-nau)
Copenhagen (KOH-puhn-hay-guhn)
Córdova (KOHR-doh-vah)
Costa del Sol (KOH-stah dehl SOHL)
Croatia (kroh-AY-shuh)
Czech Republic (CHEHK)
Czechoslovakia (chehk-oh-sloh-VAH-kee-ah)
Danube River (DAN-yoob)
Daugava River (DAU-gah-vah)
Dnieper River (DNYEH-purr)
Dolensko Valley (doh-LYEHN-skoh)
Essen (EHSS-uhn)
Estonia (ehss-TOH-nee-uh)
Faroe Islands (FAHR-oh)
Finland (FIHN-luhnd)
fiord (FYOHRD)
Florence (FLOHR-uhntss)
folkhem (FOHLK-hehm)
Frankfurt (FRAHNGK-fohrt)
Genoa (JEHN-oh-uh)
Gibraltar (jih-BRAHL-turr)
Granada (grah-NAH-dah)
Gypsy (JIHP-see)
Hague, The (HAYG)
Hasidic (hah-SEE-dihk)
Helsinki (hehl-SIHNG-kee)
Herzegovina (hairt-suh-goh-VEE-nuh)
Hungary (HUHNG-guh-ree)
Iberia (eye-BEER-ee-uh)
Islam (ihz-LAHM)
Jönköping (YEHN-keh-pihng)
Kaliningrad (kah-LYIH-nihn-graht)
Kiev (KEE-ehf)
Kohtla-Järva (KOHT-luh YAIR-vuh)
Kosovo (KOHSS-uh-voh)
Krajina (kreye-EE-nuh)
Krtova (krah-TOH-vuh)
Latvia (LAT-vee-uh)
Lille (LEEL)
Lithuania (lihth-oo-AY-nee-uh)
Ljubljana (lyoo-BLYAH-nuh)
Lockerbee (LAW-kurr-bee)

Luxembourg (LOOK-suhm-boork
  [first "oo" as in "book"])
Macedonia (mass-ih-DOH-nee-uh)
Madrid (mah-DRIHD)
Mafia (MAH-fee-ah)
Main River (MINE)
Marseilles (mahr-SAY)
Mediterranean Sea (meh-dih-tuh-RAY-nee-uhn)
Milan (mih-LAHN)
Moldova (mohl-DOH-vuh)
Montenegro (mawn-tih-NEH-groh)
Moor (MOOR)
Moscow (MAW-scau)
Mt. Vesuvius (veh-SOO-vee-uhss)
Muslim (MOOZ-lihm ["oo" as in "book"])
Naples (NAY-puhlz)
Nazi (NAHT-see)
Neapolis (nay-AH-poh-leess)
Ottoman (AW-tuh-muhn)
Oxford (AWKS-furrd)
Pannonian Plain (puh-NOH-nee-uhn)
Piazza del Plebiscito (PYAHT-suh dehl
  pleh-bih-SHEE-toh)
Po River (POH)
Portugal (POHR-chuh-guhl)
Renaissance (REHN-uh-sahnss)
Rhine River (RINE)
Riga (REE-guh)
Riviera (rih-vee-AIR-uh)
Romania (roh-MAY-nee-uh)
Rosh Hashanah (RAWSH hah-SHAH-nah)
Rotterdam (RAWT-urr-dam)
Sarajevo (sah-rah-YAY-voh)
Scandinavia (skan-dih-NAY-vee-uh)
Scotland (SKAWT-luhnd)
Serbia (SURR-bee-uh)
Sicily (SIHSS-uh-lee)
Silesia (sih-LEE-zhuh)
Slovakia (sloh-VAH-kee-uh)
Slovenia (sloh-VEE-nee-uh)
Sofia (soh-FEE-uh)
sottogoverno (soh-toh-goh-VAIR-noh)
Svalbard (SVAHL-bahr)
Tadani (tuh-DAH-nee)
Tito, Marshall (TEE-toh)
Tokarp (TOH-kahrp)
Toledo (toh-LAY-doh)
Toulouse (too-LOOZ)
Turin (TOOR-ihn)
Ukraine (yoo-KRAYN)
Uman (oo-MAHN)
Ural Mountains (YOOR-uhl)
Velike Poljane (vyeh-LEE-kyeh poh-LYAHN-eh)
Venice (VEH-nihss)
Vienna (vee-EHN-uh)
Vistula River (VIHSS-choo-luh ["oo" as in "book"])

Warsaw (WOHR-saw)
Yugoslavia (yoo-goh-SLAH-vee-uh)

Chapter 5   THE RUSSIA FEDERATION, BELARUS, CAUCASIA, AND CENTRAL ASIA

Amu Darya (AH-moo DAHR-yah)
Amur River (AH-moor)
Aral Sea (AHR-uhl)
Armenia (ahr-MEE-nee-uh)
Azerbaijan (ah-zair-bye-JAHN)
Baikal, Lake (bie-KAHL)
baksheesh (bak-SHEESH)
Baltic Sea (BAWL-tihk)
Bashkir (bahsh-KEER)
Belarus (byeh-lah-ROOS)
Bering Strait (BAIR-ihng)
Bolshevik (BOHL-shuh-vihk)
Bukhara (boo-KAH-rah)
Caspian Sea (KASS-pee-uhn)
Caucasia (kaw-KAY-zhuh)
Caucasus Mountains (KAW-kuh-suhss)
Chechnya (chyehch-NYAH)
Chelyabinsk (chyehl-yah-BEENSK)
czar (ZAHR)
Dnieper River (DNYEH-purr)
Donetsk (duh-NYEHTSK)
Dubna (DOOB-nah)
Eurasia (yoo-RAY-shuh)
Genghis Khan (JEHNG-gihss KAHN/GEHNG-gihss KAHN)
Georgia (JOHR-jah)
ger (GURR)
Gorbachev, Mikhail (gohr-buh-CHAWF, mee-KILE)
Kaliningrad (kah-LYIH-nihn-graht)
Kalmyk (kuhl-MIHK)
Karachay (kahr-ah-CHYE)
Karakalpakstan (kahr-ah-kahl-pahk-STAN)
Kashgar (kahsh-GAHR)
Kazakhstan (kah-zahk-STAHN)
Kazan (kuh-ZAHN)
Kiev (kyee-EHF)
Kuznetsk Basin (kooz-NYEHTSK ["oo" as in "book"])
Kyrgyzstan (keer-gihz-STAHN)
Lenin, Vladimir (LYEH-nyihn, vlah-DEE-meer)
Magnitogorsk (mahg-nyee-tuh-GOHRSK)
Marx, Karl (MAHRKS, KAHRL)
Moscow (MAWSS-kau)
mugam (MOO-gahm)
Muslim (MOOZ-lihm ["oo" as in "book"])
Nagorno Karabakh (nah-GOHR-noh kah-rah-BAHK)
Nakhodka (nah-KAWD-kuh)
Nicholas II (NEE-koh-lahss)
Norilsk (nuh-REELSK)
Novgorod (NAWV-guh-ruht)
Novosibirsk (noh-voh-sih-BEERSK)

Ob River (AWB)
oblast (OH-blahsst)
Okhotsk (oh-KAWTSK)
okrug (OH-kroog ["oo" as in "book"])
perestroika (pyeh-ryih-STROY-kah)
pilaf (PEE-lahf)
reketiry (ryeh-kyeh-TEE-ree)
Samarkand (sah-mahr-KAHNT)
Semey (seh-MAY)
Shevardnadze, Edvard (shyeh-vahrd-NAHD-zyeh,
    EHD-vahrd)
shish-kebab (SHEESH kuh-bahb)
Siberia (sye-BEER-ee-uh)
Soviet Union (SOH-vyeht)
Stalin, Joseph (STAH-lihn, YOH-sehf)
Syr Darya (SEER DAHR-yah)
taiga (TYE-gah)
Tajikistan (tah-jee-kyih-STAHN)
Tashkent (tahsh-KEHNT)
Tatar (TAH-turr)
Tobolsk (toh-BOHLSK)
tolkuchka (tohl-KOOCH-kah)
Transcaucasia (tranz-kaw-KAY-zhuh)
Turkmenistan (turrk-mehn-ih-STAHN)
Tuva (TOO-vah)
Ural Mountains (YOOR-uhl)
Uzbekistan (ooz-behk-ih-STAHN)
Vistula River (VIHSS-choo-luh ["oo" as in "book"])
Vladivostok (vluh-dyuh-vuh-STAWK)
Volga River (VOHL-guh)
Volgograd (vuhl-guh-GRAHT)
Yeltsin, Boris (YEHLT-sihn, BOHR-ihss)
Yenisey River (yih-nih-SYAY)
yurt (YURRT)

Chapter 6   NORTH AFRICA AND
SOUTHWEST ASIA

Aden (AH-duhn)
Al Salaam (ahl sah-LAHM)
Alexandria (al-ihk-SAN-dree-uh)
Algeria (ahl-JEER-ee-uh)
Algiers (ahl-JEERZ)
Allah (AH-luh)
Anatolia (an-uh-TOH-lee-uh)
Arabia (uh-RAY-bee-uh)
Arafat, Yasir (AHR-uh-faht, YAH-seer)
Aswan High Dam (ahss-WAHN)
ayatollah (eye-yah-TOH-lah)
Baghdad (bahg-DAHD/BAG-dad)
Bahrain (bah-RAYN)
Bandar Abbas (BAHN-dahr AH-buhss)
Barbary Coast (BAHR-buh-ree)
Basra (BAHZ-rah)
Bedouin (BEHD-oo-ihn)
Berber (BURR-burr)

Bosporus (BAWSS-puh-ruhss)
Byzantine Empire (BIHZ-uhn-teen)
Cairo (KYE-roh)
Canaan (KAY-nuhn)
Casablanca (kah-suh-BLAHNG-kuh)
Caspian Sea (KASS-pee-uhn)
chador (chah-DOHR)
Constantinople (kawn-stan-tih-NOH-puhl)
Coptic Christians (KAWP-tihk)
Damascus (duh-MASS-kuhs)
Dinka (DIHNG-kuh)
djellaba (jeh-LAH-buh)
Dubai (doo-BYE)
El Oued (ehl oh-WEHD)
Euphrates River (yoo-FRAY-teez)
Farsi (FAHR-see)
Gaza Strip (GAH-zah)
Golan Heights (GOH-lahn)
Hadramaut Valley (hah-drah-MAWT)
hajj (HAHJ)
hijab (hee-JAHB)
Hindu Kush (HIHN-doo KOOSH
    [second "oo" as in "book"])
Hussein, Saddam (hoo-SAYN, sah-DAHM)
Intifada (ihn-tih-FAH-duh)
Iran (ih-RAHN)
Iraq (ih-RAHK)
Islam (ihz-LAHM)
Israel (IHZ-ree-uhl)
Istanbul (ihss-STAHN-bool / ihss-tahn-BOOL
    ["oo" as in "book"])
Jeddah (JEHD-uh)
Jerusalem (juh-ROO-suh-lehm)
Jordan (JOHR-duhn)
Khartoum (kahr-TOOM)
Khatami, Mohammad (kah-TAH-mee)
Khomeini, Ruholla (koh-MAY-nee, roo-HAWL-uh)
Koran (koo-RAHN ["oo" as in "book"])
Kurd (KURRD)
Kuwait (koo-WAYT)
Lake Nasser (NAH-surr)
Lebanon (LEH-buh-nuhn)
Libya (LIH-bee-uh)
Maghreb (MAH-gruhb)
Mecca (MEH-kuh)
Medina (meh-DEE-nuh)
Mediterranean Sea (meh-dih-tuh-RAY-nee-uhn)
Mesopotamia (meh-suh-puh-TAY-mee-uh)
Mongol (MAWNG-gohl)
Morocco (muh-RAW-koh)
Muhammad (moo-HAHM-ihd ["oo" as in "book"])
Muslim (MOOZ-lihm ["oo" as in "book"])
nargile (NAHR-guh-leh)
Nilotic (nye-LAW-tihk)
Nubian (NOO-bee-uhn)
Oman (oh-MAHN)

Ottoman Empire (AW-tuh-muhn)
Pahlavi, Reza (PAH-luh-vee, RAY-zah)
Palestine (PAL-uh-stien)
Persia (PURR-zhuh)
pogrom (puh-GRAWM)
qanat (KAH-naht)
qat (KAHT)
Qatar (KAH-tahr)
Qur'an (koo-RAHN ["oo" as in "book"])
Rabat (rah-BAHT)
Rai (RYE)
Ramadan (rahm-uh-DAHN)
Riyadh (ree-YAHD)
Rubal Khali (roob ahl KAH-lee)
Sahara (suh-HAHR-uh)
Saud (sah-OOD)
Saudi Arabia (sah-OO-dee uh-RAY-bee-uh)
shah (SHAH)
Shari'a (shah-REE-ah)
Shatt al Arab (SHAHT ahl AHR-uhb)
sheik (SHAYK)
Shia (SHEE-uh)
Shi'ite (SHEE-eyt)
Sinai Peninsula (SYE-nye)
Sudan (soo-DAN)
Sudd (SOOD)
Suez Canal (SOO-ehz)
Sunni (SOO-nee)
Syria (SEER-ee-uh)
Tangier (tahn-JEER)
Tassili 'n Agger (tah-see-LEE nah-JAIR)
Tehran (teh-RAHN)
Tel Aviv (tehl ah-VEEV)
Tien Shan (TYEHN SHAHN)
Tigris River (TYE-grihss)
Tripoli (TRIH-puh-lee)
Tuareg (TWAH-rehg)
Tunis (TOO-nihss)
Tunisia (too-NEE-zhuh)
Turkomen (TURR-kuh-mehn)
Umma (OO-muh)
United Arab Emirates (EHM-uh-ruhts)
wadi (WAH-dee)
Wadi Mugshin (WAH-dee moog-SHEEN
    ["oo" as in "book"])
Yemen (YEH-muhn)
Zabbaleen (zah-bah-LEEN)
Zagros Mountains (ZAH-grohss)
Zakat (zah-KAHT)

Chapter 7 SUB-SAHARAN AFRICA

Abuja (ah-BOO-jah)
Addis Ababa (AH-dihss AH-buh-bah)
Aden, Gulf of (AH-duhn)
Afrikaner (af-rih-KAH-nurr)

Amhara (ahm-HAHR-uh)
Angola (ang-GOH-luh)
apartheid (uh-PAHRT-hyt)
Asmara (ahz-MAHR-ah)
Bantu (BAN-too)
Belgian Congo (KAWNG-goh)
Benin (beh-NEEN)
Biafra (bee-AH-fruh)
Boer (BOHR)
Bossaso (boh-SAH-soh)
Botswana (bawt-SWAH-nah)
Burkina Faso (burr-KEEN-uh FAH-soh)
Burundi (boo-ROON-dee [both "oo" as in "book"])
Cameroon (kahm-uh-ROON)
Cape Verde Islands (VAIR-day)
Chad (CHAD)
Comoros (KOHM-uh-rohz)
Congo (KAWNG-goh)
Côte d'Ivoire (KOHT deev-WAHR)
Dinesen, Isak (DEE-nih-suhn, EE-zahk)
Djibouti (jih-BOO-tee)
Eritrea (air-ih-TREE-uh)
Ethiopia (ee-thee-OH-pee-uh)
Fulani (foo-LAH-nee)
Gabon (gah-BOHN)
Gambia (GAHM-bee-uh)
Ghana (GAH-nah)
Guinea (GIH-nee)
Guinea-Bissau (GIH-nee bih-SAU)
Hausa (HAU-zuh)
Hausaland (HAU-zuh-land)
Hutu (HOO-too)
Igbo (IHG-boh)
Jwaneng (JWAY-nehng)
Kalahari Desert (kah-lah-HAH-ree)
Kampala (kahm-PAH-luh)
Kasama (kah-SAH-muh)
Kenya (KEHN-yuh)
Kikuyu (kih-KOO-yoo)
Kimbo (KEEM-boh)
Kinshasa (kihn-SHAH-suh)
Kisangani (kee-sahn-GAH-nee)
Kitui (kee-TOO-ee)
Lagos (LAH-gohss)
Lake Magadi (mah-GAH-dee)
laterite (LA-turr-eyt)
Lesotho (leh-SOO-too)
Liberia (lye-BEER-ee-uh)
Limpopo River (lihm-POH-poh)
Loango (loh-AHNG-goh)
Lumumba, Patrice (loo-MOOM-buh, pah-TREESS
    [both "oo" as in "book"])
Madagascar (mad-uh-GASS-kurr)
Malawi (muh-LAH-wee)
Mali (MAH-lee)
Malinka (mah-LIHNG-kuh)

Mandela, Nelson (man-DEHL-uh)
Mandingo (man-DIHNG-goh)
Maputo (muh-POO-toh)
Masai (mah-SYE)
Mauritania (mawr-ih-TAY-nee-uh)
Mauritius (maw-RIHSH-uhss)
M'Baka (uhm-BAH-kuh)
Mbira (uhm-BEER-uh)
Mobutu Sese Seko (moh-BOO-too SAY-see SAY-koh)
Mogadishu (moh-guh-DEE-shoo)
Mombasa (mawm-BAH-suh)
Mozambique (moh-zuhm-BEEK)
Nairobi (nye-ROH-bee)
Namibia (nuh-MIHB-ee-uh)
Niger (NYE-jurr)
Nswazi (uhn-SWAH-zee)
Obeah (OH-bee-uh)
Ogoni (oh-GOH-nee)
Ogoniland (oh-GOH-nee-land)
Okavango Delta (oh-kuh-VAHNG-goh)
Oromo (oh-ROH-moh)
Ovimbundu (oh-vihm-BOON-doo
    [first "oo" as in "book"])
Point Noir [PWA(N) NWAHR]
polygyny (puh-LIHJ-uh-nee)
Rwanda (roo-AHN-duh)
Sahara (suh-HAHR-uh)
Sahel (suh-HAYL)
Santeria (sahn-tuh-REE-uh)
São Tomé y Príncipe (sau too-MAY ee PREEN-see-peh)
Saro-Wiwa, Ken (SAHR-oh WEE-wah)
Senegal (SEHN-ih-gahl)
Seychelles (say-SHEHLZ)
Shona (SHOH-nuh)
Sierra Leone (see-AIR-uh lee-OHN)
Somalia (soh-MAHL-ee-uh)
Swahili (swah-HEE-lee)
Swaziland (SWAH-zee-land)
Tanzania (tan-zuh-NEE-uh)
Tigre (tee-GRAY)
Timbuktu (tihm-book-TOO [first "oo" as in "book"])
Togo (TOH-goh)
Transvaal (tranz-VAHL)
tsetse (TSEH-tsee)
Tshopo Falls (TCHOH-poh)
Tutsi (TOOT-see)
Tutu, Desmond (TOO-too)
Voudon (voo-DAWN)
Yoruba (YOH-roo-bah ["oo" as in "book"])
Zaire (zah-EER)
Zambia (ZAM-bee-uh)
Zimbabwe (zihm-BAHB-way)

Chapter 8 SOUTH ASIA

Agra (AH-gruh)
Ahmadabad (AH-muh-duh-bahd)

Allahabad (ah-luh-huh-BAHD)
Amritsar (ahm-RIHT-surr)
Arabian Sea (uh-RAY-bee-uhn)
Arunachal Pradesh (ah-ROON-ah-chahl prah-DAYSH
    ["oo" as in "book"])
Aryan (AIR-ee-uhn)
Assam (ah-SAHM)
Ayodhya (ah-YOHD-yah)
Bangalore (bang-guh-LOHR)
Bangladesh (bahng-gluh-DEHSH)
Benares (beh-NAHR-ehss)
Bengal (behn-GAHL)
Bhopal (boh-PAHL)
Bhopavand (boh-pah-VAHND)
Bhotechaur (boh-teh-CHAWR)
Bhutan (boo-TAHN)
Bihar (bee-HAHR)
Bo (BOH)
Bodhgaya (boh-duh-GAH-yah)
Bom Bahia (bohm bah-EE-ah)
Bombay (bawm-BAY)
Brahmaputra River (brah-mah-POO-truh)
Brahmin (BRAH-mihn)
Ceylon (say-LAWN)
Chamoli (chuhm-OH-lee)
Chandigarh (CHUHN-dih-gurr)
Chipko Movement (CHIHP-koh)
Colombo (koh-LOHM-boh)
Dalit (DAH-liht)
Darjeeling (dahr-JEE-lihng)
Deccan Plateau (DEHK-uhn)
Delhi (DEHL-ee)
Dhaka (DAHK-uh)
Dharamkot (duh-RUHM-koht)
Dharavi (duh-RAH-vee)
Dolpo-pa (DOHL-poh-pah)
Dravidian (drah-VIHD-ee-uhn)
fatwa (FAHT-wah)
Gandhi, Indira (GAHN-dee, ihn-DEER-ah)
Gandhi, Mohandas (GAHN-dee, moh-HAHN-dahss)
Ganges River (GAN-jeez)
Ghats Mountains (GAHTSS)
ghee (GEE)
Gujarat (GOO-juh-raht)
Harijan (HAH-ree-jahn)
Haryana (hahr-YAH-nah)
Himachal Pradesh (hih-MAH-chahl prah-DAYSH)
Himalayan Mountains (hih-MAHL-ee-uhn/
    hih-muh-LAY-uhn)
Hindi (HIHN-dee)
Hindu (HIHN-doo)
Hindu Kush (HIHN-doo KOOSH
    [second "oo" as in "book"])
Hindustan (hihn-doo-STAHN)
Indore (ihn-DOHR)
Indus River (IHN-duhss)

Jainism (JYE-nihz-uhm)
Joypur (joy-POOR)
Karachi (kuh-RAH-chee)
Karakoram Mountains (kahr-uh-KOHR-uhm)
Karnataka (kahr-nah-TAH-kah)
Kashmir (kash-MEER)
Kerala (KAIR-uh-luh)
Lahore (luh-HOHR)
longi (lohn-ZEE)
Madras (muh-DRAHSS)
Mahabodhi Temple (mah-hah-BOH-dee)
Maharashtra (mah-hah-RAHSH-trah)
Malabar (MAL-uh-bahr)
Maldives (mawl-DEEVZ)
Meghalaya (mehg-AH-lah-yah)
Mizoram (mee-ZOH-rahm)
Mogul (MOO-guhl)
mujahadeen (moo-jah-hu-DEEN)
Mumbai (moom-BYE ["oo" as in "book"])
nankeen (nan-KEEN)
Narmada River (nahr-MAH-duh)
Nehru, Jawaharlal (NAY-roo, jah-wah-HAHR-lahl)
Nepal (neh-PAHL)
New Delhi (DEHL-ee)
Nirmal Hriday (NEER-mahl HREE-day)
nodi bhanga lok (NOH-dee BAHNG-gah LAWK)
Orissa (oh-RIH-sah)
Pakistan (pah-kih-STAHN)
Pamir Mountains (pah-MEER)
panchayate raj (pahn-chah-YAH-teh RAHJ)
Panipur (pahn-ee-POOR)
Pashto (PAHSH-toh)
Pathan (puh-TAHN)
Peshawar (peh-SHAH-wurr)
Pithampur (pee-tahm-POOR)
Punjab (poon-JAHB ["oo" as in "book"])
purdah (PURR-duh)
Rabari (rah-BAHR-ee)
Rajasthan (rah-jah-STAHN)
Rong-pa (RAWNG-pah)
salish (SAH-lihsh)
Sanskrit (SAN-skriht)
Shari'a (shah-REE-ah)
Sikh (SEEK)
Sikkim (SIHK-ihm)
Sinhalese (sihn-huh-LEEZ)
Sri Lanka (shree LAHNG-kah)
Sudra (SOO-druh)
Tajik (tah-JEEK)
Taliban (TAHL-ee-bahn)
Tamil (TAH-mihl)
Tamil Nadu (TAH-mihl NAH-doo)
Thar Desert (TAHR)
Thimphu (THIHM-boo)
Trivandrum (trih-VAHN-druhm)

Udaipur (oo-dye-POOR)
Uttar Pradesh (OO-turr prah-DAYSH)
Vaishya (VYE-shyuh)
Varanasi (vuh-RAH-nuh-see)
Vedda (VEHD-uh)
Yamuna River (yah-MOO-nah)

Chapter 9 EAST ASIA

Ainu (IE-noo)
Altai Mountains (AHL-tye)
Amnok River (AHM-NAWK)
Amur River (ah-MOOR)
Bai (BYE)
Beijing (BAY-JYIHNG)
Bo Hai, Gulf of (BOH-HYE)
Canton (KAHN-tawn)
Chaebol (CHYE-BOHL)
Chang Jiang (CHAHNG JYAHNG)
Changan (CHAHNG-AHN)
Chengdu (CHUHNG-DOO)
Chiang Kai-shek (JYAHNG KYE-SHEHK)
Chongqing (CHOHNG-CHIHNG)
chuche (CHOO-cheh)
Confucianism (kuhn-FYOO-shuhn-ihz-uhm)
Dalai Lama (DAH-lye LAH-mah)
Dai (DIE)
Daqing (DAH-CHIHNG)
Deng Xiaoping (DUHNG SHYAU-PIHNG)
Dzungar Basin (DZOONG-GAHR ["oo" as in "book"])
Edo (AYD-oh)
Fujian (FOO-JYAHN)
Fukuoka (foo-koo-OH-kah)
ger (GURR)
Gezhouba (GUH-JOH-BAH)
Gobi Desert (GOH-bee)
Guangdong (GWAHNG-DAWNG)
Guangxi (GWAHNG-SHEE)
Guangzhou (GWAHNG-JOH)
Guizhou (GWEE-JOH)
Haikou (HYE-KOH)
Hainan (HYE-NAHN)
Han (HAHN)
Hangai Mountains (HAHNG-GIE)
Hangzhou (HAHNG-JOH)
Harbin (HAHR-BIHN)
he (HUH)
Hebei (HUH-BAY)
Heilongjiang (HYE-LAWNG-JYAHNG)
Himalayan Mountains (hih-MAHL-yuhn/
  hih-muh-LAY-uhn)
Hiroshima (hih-ROH-shih-muh)
Hokkaido (haw-KYE-doh)
Honshu (HAWN-shoo)
Huang He (HWAHNG HUH)

Hui (HWEE)
Hun (HUHN)
ji (JEE)
jiang (JYAHNG)
Jiangsu (JYAHNG-SOO)
Jilin (JEE-LIHN)
Kanto Plain (KAHN-TOH)
Kaohsiung (GAU-SHYOONG ["oo" as in "book"])
Kashgar (kahsh-GAHR)
Kobe (KOH-bay)
Kunming (KOON-MIHNG ["oo" as in "book"])
Kuomintang (KWOH-mihn-TAHNG)
Kyushu (KYOO-shoo)
Lijiang (LEE-JYAHNG)
Loess Plateau (LUHS)
Macao (muh-KAU)
Manchu (MAN-CHOO)
Manchuria (man-CHOOR-ee-uh)
Mandarin (MAN-duh-rihn)
Mao Zedong (MAU DZUH-DAWNG)
Meiji (MAY-jee)
Miao (MYAU)
Mongolia (mawng-GOH-lee-uh)
Mt. Fuji (FOO-jee)
Nagasaki (nah-guh-SAH-kee)
Nan Ling Mountains (NAHN LIHNG)
Nanjing (NAHN-JYIHNG)
Ordos Desert (OHR-dohss)
Osaka (oh-SAH-kah)
Peking (PEE-KIHNG)
Pudong (POO-DAWNG)
Qaidam Basin (KYE-DAHM)
qanat (KAH-naht)
Qin (CHIHN)
Qin Ling Mountains (CHIHN LIHNG)
Qingdao (CHIHNG-DAU)
Qinghai (CHIHNG-HYE)
Ryukyu Islands (RYOO-kyoo)
Seoul (SOHL)
Shaanxi (SHAH-AHN-ZHEE)
Shanghai (SHAHNG-HYE)
Shantou (SHAHN-TOH)
Shanxi (SHAHN-SHEE)
Shenyang (SHUHN-YAHNG)
Shenzhen (SHUHN-JUHN)
Shikoku (SHE-kaw-koo)
Sichuan (ZIH-CHWAHN)
Taipei (TYE-PAY)
Taiwan (TYE-WAHN)
Taiyuan (TYE-YUAHN)
Takla Mountains (TAHK-luh)
Taklimakan Desert (TAHK-luh-muh-KAHN)
Tarim Basin (TAH-REEM)
Tianjin (TYAHN-JIHN)
Tibet (tih-BEHT)

Tien Shan (TYEHN SHAHN)
Tienanmen Square (TYEHN-AHN-MUHN)
Tokyo (TOH-kee-oh)
Tumen River (TOO-MUHN)
Turfan Depression (TOOR-FAHN)
Ulaan Baatar (OO-lahn BAH-tawr)
Urumqi (OO-ROOM-CHEE [both "oo" as in "book"])
Uygur (WEE-gurr)
Wenzhou (WUHN-JOH)
Wu Shan (WOO SHAHN)
Wuhan (WOO-HAHN)
Xi Jiang (SHEE JYAHNG)
Xiamen (SHYAH-MUHN)
Xian (SHEE-AHN)
Xianggang (SHYAHNG-GAHNG)
Xibe (SHEE-BUH)
Xijang (SHEE-JAHNG)
Xinjiang (SHEEN-JYAHNG)
Xinjiang Uygur (SHEEN-JYAHNG WEE-gurr)
Xizang (SHEE-DZAHNG)
Yalu River (YAH-LOO)
Yamato (YAH-mah-toh)
Yangtze River (YAHNG-TSUH)
Yi (YEE)
Yichang (YEE-CHAHNG)
Yokohama (yoh-kaw-HAH-mah)
Yunnan-Guizhou (YOO-NAHN GWEE-JOH)
Yunnan Plateau (YOO-NAHN)
yurt (YURRT)
Zhuang (JWAHNG)
Zhuhai (JOO-HYE)

Chapter 10   SOUTHEAST ASIA

Aikwa River (IKE-wah)
Andaman Sea (AN-duh-muhn)
Austronesian (aw-stroh-NEE-zhuhn)
Bali (BAH-lee)
Ban Muang Wa (BAHN MWAHNG WAH)
Bangkok (bang-KAWK)
Batavia (buh-TAY-vee-uh)
Borneo (BOHR-nee-oh)
Brunei (broo-NYE)
Burma (BURR-muh)
Cambodia (kam-BOH-dee-uh)
Celebes (seh-LAY-behss)
Chao Phraya River (chau prah-YAH)
Chiang Mai (CHYAHNG MYE)
Chin (CHIHN)
Dayak (DYE-ak)
Dharma Wanita (DAHR-muh wah-NEE-tuh)
doi moi (DOY MOY)
East Timor (TEE-mohr)
El Niño (ehl NEEN-yoh)
Filipino (fihl-ih-PEE-noh)

Flores (FLOH-rehs)
Grasberg Mountain (GRASS-burg)
Hanoi (hah-NOY)
Ho Chi Minh City (HOH CHEE-MIHN)
Indonesia (ihn-doh-NEE-zhuh)
Irian Jaya (EER-ee-ahn JYE-yah)
Irrawaddy River (eer-uh-WAWD-ee)
Jakarta (juh-KAHR-tuh)
Java (JAH-vuh)
Jayapura (jye-yuh-POOR-uh)
Kalimantan (KAH-LEE-MAHN-TAHN)
Kampuchea (kam-poo-CHEE-uh)
Karen (kuh-REHN)
Khmer Rouge (KMAIR ROOZH)
Khon Kaen (KAWN GAN)
Klaten (KLAH-tehn)
Kuala Lumpur (KWAH-luh loom-POOR
    [first "oo" as in "book"])
Laos (LAH-ohss)
Lee Quan Yue (LEE KWAHN YWEH)
Lombok (lawm-BAWK)
Lopburi (LAWP-BOO-REE)
Luzon (loo-ZAWN)
Makassar Strait (muh-KASS-urr)
Madura (mah-DOOR-uh)
Malacca Straits (mah-LAHK-uh)
Malay (muh-LAY)
Malaysia (mah-LAY-zhuh)
Manila (mah-NIHL-uh)
Marcos, Ferdinand (MAHR-kohss, FAIR-dee-nahnd)
Mekong River (MAY-KAWNG)
Mindanao (mihn-dah-NAU)
Molucca Sea and Islands (maw-LOOK-uh
    ["oo" as in "book"])
Mon (MOHN)
Mt. Pinatubo (pee-nah-TOO-boh)
Myanmar (myahn-MAHR)
New Guinea (GIH-nee)
Pancasila (pahng-kuh-SEE-luh)
Philippines (FIHL-uh-peenz)
Rangoon (rahn-GOON)
Sabah (SAH-bah)
Saigon (sye-GAWN)
Salween River (SAHL-ween)
Sarawak (suh-RAH-wahk)
Shan (SHAHN)
Singapore (SIHNG-uh-pohr)
Suharto (soo-HAHR-toh)
Sulawesi (soo-lah-WAY-see)
Sumatra (soo-MAH-truh)
Sunda Islands (SOON-duh ["oo" as in "book"])
Sundaland (SOON-duh-luhnd ["oo" as in "book"])
Surat Thani (suh-RAHT TAH-nee)
Thailand (TYE-land)
Vientiane (vyehn-TYAHN)
Wa (WAH)

Wallacea (woh-LAH-see-yuh)
Zoroastrian (zohr-oh-ASS-tree-uhn)

Chapter 11 OCEANIA: AUSTRALIA, NEW ZEALAND, AND THE PACIFIC

Aborigine (ab-uh-RIHJ-uh-nee)
Adelaide (AD-uh-layd)
Aoraki (ah-oh-RAH-kee)
Aotearoa (ah-oh-tay-ah-ROH-ah)
Auckland (AWK-luhnd)
Australia (aw-STRAYL-yuh)
Austronesian (aw-stroh-NEE-zhuhn)
Ayers Rock (AIRS)
billabong (BIHL-uh-bawng)
Bougainville (boo-gahn-VEEL)
Brisbane (BRIHZ-buhn)
Buka (BOO-kah)
Canberra (KAN-burr-uh)
Carpentaria, Gulf of (kahr-puhn-TAIR-ee-uh)
coolibah (KOO-luh-bah)
Fiji (FEE-jee)
Gauguin, Paul [goh-GA(N)]
Haka (HAH-kah)
jumbuck (JUHM-buhk)
Kiribati (keer-ih-BAH-tee)
Maori (MAU-ree)
Marianas (mahr-ee-AH-nahss)
Marquesas (mahr-KAY-zahss)
Mauna Loa (MAU-nah LOH-ah)
Melanesia (mehl-uh-NEE-zhuh)
Micronesia (mie-kroh-NEE-zhuh)
Nauru (NAU-roo)
Oahu (oh-AH-hoo)
Oceania (oh-shee-AN-ee-uh)
ohana (oh-HAH-nah)
Olgas (OHL-guhss)
Palau (pah-LAU)
Papeete (pah-pee-AY-tay)
Papua New Guinea (PAH-poo-ah)
Pauoa Valley (PAU-oh-ah)
Polynesia (pawl-ih-NEE-zhuh)
Port Moresby (MOHRZ-bee)
Saipan (sie-PAHN)
Samoa (sah-MOH-ah)
Spratly Islands (SPRAT-lee)
Sundaland (SOON-duh-luhnd ["oo" as in "book"])
Suva (SOO-vah)
Tahiti (tah-HEE-tee)
Tonga (TAWNG-gah)
Trobriand Islands (TROH-bree-uhnd)
Tuamotu Archipelago (too-uh-MOH-too)
Tuvalu (too-VAH-loo)
Uluru (oo-LOO-roo)
Vanuatu (vah-noo-AH-too)
Waitangi (wie-TAHNG-gee)

BIBLIOGRAPHY

In writing this textbook, we consulted hundreds of reference materials from many sources—university, public, and private libraries; newspapers and magazines worldwide; public radio and television news programs and special features; hundreds of sites from the World Wide Web (Internet); and conversations, e-mails, and other correspondence with dozens of our colleagues. In the citations that follow, we list the main references used in our research, including all sources cited in the text and many that are not specifically cited.

The citations are divided into two main groups. The first are the references for each chapter, listed by chapter. The second group are more general references that pertain to the book as a whole.

With respect to the WWW/Internet references, we have done our best to make the URLs/Web addresses as current as possible; that is, at the time this list was prepared (May 1999), all of the URL addresses were available (unless otherwise noted). But as anyone who has used the Internet knows, URL addresses change or are discontinued often without any warning or forwarding address. We apologize for instances in which this has occurred. We may be able to provide assistance in locating the original source. Contact us at cmgoodwin@icx.net.

CHAPTER SOURCES

Chapter 1 Geography: An Exploration of Connections

Anderson, E. N. *The Food of China*. New Haven, CT: Yale University Press, 1988.

Aynsley, R. M., W. Melbourne, and B. J. Vickery. *Architectural Aerodynamics*. London, UK: Applied Science, 1997.

Bechtel, Robert B. *Environment and Behavior: An Introduction*. Thousand Oaks, CA: Sage, 1997.

Bilsborrow, Richard E., sci. ed. *Internal Migration of Women in Developing Countries: Proceedings of the United Nations Expert Meeting on the Feminization of Internal Migration, Aguascalientes, Mexico, 22–25 October 1991*. New York: United Nations Department for Economic and Social Information and Policy Analysis, 1993.

Blumberg, Rae Lesser, Cathy A. Rakowski, Irene Tinker, and Michael Monteon, eds. *EnGENDERing Wealth and Well-Being: Empowerment for Global Change*. Boulder, CO: Westview Press, 1995.

Boserup, Ester. *Woman's Role in Economic Development*. London: Allen and Unwin, 1970.

Bowers, C. A. *Educating for an Ecologically Sustainable Culture: Rethinking Moral Education, Creativity, Intelligence, and Other Modern Orthodoxies*. Albany: State University of New York Press, 1995.

Boyd, Andrew. *An Atlas of World Affairs*, 10th ed. London and New York: Routledge, 1998.

Braidotti, Rosi, Ewa Charkiewicz, Sabine Hausler, and Saskia Wieringa. *Women, the Environment and Sustainable Development: Towards a Theoretical Synthesis*. London: Zed Books in association with INSTRAW, 1994.

Brandt, Barbara. *Whole Life Economics: Revaluing Daily Life*. Philadelphia: New Society, 1995.

Chatterjee, Pratap, and Matthias Finger. *The Earth Brokers: Power, Politics and World Development*. New York: Routledge, 1994.

Christopherson, Susan. Changing Women's Status in a Global Economy. Pp. 191–205, in *Geographies of Global Change* (R. J. Johnston, Peter J. Taylor, and Michael J. Watts, eds.). Oxford, UK: Blackwell, 1995.

Cohen, Joel E. *How Many People Can the Earth Support?* New York: W. W. Norton, 1995.

Commission on Environment and Development. *Our Common Future*. New York: Oxford University Press, 1987.

Crush, Jonathan. *Power of Development*. London and New York: Routledge, 1995.

Culture Front. Summer 1997.

Day, Lincoln H. *The Future of Low-Birthrate Populations*. London: Routledge, 1992.

de Blij, H. J., and Peter O. Muller. *Physical Geography of the Global Environment*. New York: Wiley, 1996.

Diamond, Jered. Why Women Change? *Discover*, July 1996, pp. 130–137.

Dubeck, Paula J., and Kathryn Borman. *Women and Work: A Handbook*. New York and London: Garland, 1996.

Editors at Rand McNally. *Goode's World Atlas*, 19th ed. New York: Rand McNally, 1995.

Ellen, Roy, and Katsuyoshi Fukui, eds. *Redefining Nature: Ecology, Culture and Domestication*. Oxford, UK, and Washington, DC: Berg (Oxford International), 1996.

Feher, Joseph, compiler and designer. *Hawaii: A Pictorial History*. Honolulu: Bishop Museum Press, 1969.

Field, Graham. *Economic Growth and Political Change in Asia*. New York: St. Martin's Press, 1995.

Fisher, James S. *Geography and Development: A World Regional Approach*. Englewood Cliffs, NJ: Prentice Hall, 1995.

Fitzgerald, Stephen. *China and the Overseas Chinese: A Study of Peking's Changing Policy 1949–1970.* Cambridge, UK: Cambridge University Press, 1972.

Flint, David. *China: On the Map.* Austin, TX: Raintree Steck-Vaughn, 1994.

Grove, Richard H. *Green Imperialism: Colonial Expansion, Tropical Island Edens and the Origins of Environmentalism, 1600–1860.* Cambridge, UK: Cambridge University Press, 1995.

Islam, Iyanatul, and Anis Chowdhury. *Asia-Pacific Economies: A Survey.* London and New York: Routledge, 1997.

Jackson, Peter. *Maps of Meaning: An Introduction to Cultural Geography.* London: Unwin Hyman, 1989.

Jackson, Peter, and Jan Penrose, eds. *Constructions of Race, Place and Nation.* London: UCL Press, 1993.

Jackson, Richard H., and Lloyd E. Hudman. *Regional Geography: Issues for Today*, 3rd ed. New York: Wiley, 1990.

Jaquette, Jane S. Women in Power: From Tokenism to Critical Mass. *Foreign Policy* (Fall 1997): 23–37.

Johnston, R. J., Peter J. Taylor, and Michael J. Watts, eds. *Geographies of Global Change: Remapping the World in the Late Twentieth Century.* Oxford, UK, and Cambridge, MA: Blackwell, 1995.

Jones, Carol. Cited in footnote, p. 167, in *Women in Hong Kong* (Veronica Pearson and Benjamin K. P. Leung, eds.). Oxford, UK, and New York: Oxford Unviersity Press, 1995.

Kobayashi, Audrey, and Suzanne Mackenzie, eds. *Remaking Human Geography.* Boston: Unwin Hyman, 1989.

Kommers, Piet A. M., Scott Grabinger, and Joanna C. Dunlap, eds. *Hypermedia Learning Environments: Instructional Design and Integration.* Mahwah, NJ: Erlbaum, 1996.

Krishnan, Rajaram, Jonathan M. Harris, and Neva R. Goodwin, eds. *A Survey of Ecological Economics.* Washington, DC: Island Press, 1995.

Lewenhak, Sheila. *The Revaluation of Women's Work.* London: Earthscan, 1992 (1988).

Light, Andrew, and Jonathan M. Smith, eds. *Space, Place, and Environmental Ethics.* Lanham, MD: Rowman & Littlefield, 1997.

Linden, Eugene. The Exploding Cities of the Developing World. *Foreign Affairs* (January–February 1996): 52–65.

Lopez, George A., Jackie G. Smith, and Ron Pagnucco. The Global Tide. *Bulletin of the Atomic Scientists* (July/August 1995): 33–39.

MacNeish, Richard S. *The Origins of Agriculture and Settled Life.* Norman and London: University of Oklahoma Press, 1992.

Marsh, George Perkins. *Man and Nature.* Cambridge, MA: Belkap Press of Harvard University Press, 1965 (1864).

Mazur, Laurie Ann, ed. *Beyond the Numbers: A Reader on Population, Consumption, and the Environment.* Washington, DC: Island Press, 1994.

McAfee, Kathy. *Storm Signals: Structural Adjustment and Development Alternatives in the Caribbean.* Boston: South End Press, 1991.

Merchant, Carolyn. *Earthcare: Women and the Environment.* New York: Routledge, 1995.

Miller, G. Tyler, Jr. *Environmental Science: Sustaining the Earth.* Belmont, CA: Wadsworth, 1993.

Miller, G. Tyler, Jr. *Living in the Environment: Principles, Connections, and Solutions*, 8th ed. Belmont, CA: Wadsworth, 1994.

Milton, Kay, ed. *Environmentalism: The View from Anthropology.* London: Routledge, 1993.

Mirkinson, Judith. Red Light, Green Light: The Global Trafficking of Women. *Breakthrough*, a political journal publication by Prairie Fire Organizing Committee, 1994.

Moos, Viviane. India's Women. *Culture Front* (Summer 1997): 17–24.

Nelson, Barbara J., and Najma Chowdhury, eds. *Women and Politics Worldwide.* New Haven, CT, and London: Yale University Press, 1994.

Newman, James L. *The Peopling of Africa: A Geographic Interpretation.* New Haven. CT: Yale University Press, 1995.

Nussbaum, Martha C., and Glover Jonathan, eds. *Women, Culture, and Development: A Study in Human Capabilities.* Oxford, UK: Clarendon Press, 1995.

Pacione, Michael, ed. *The Geography of the Third World: Progress and Prospect.* London: Routledge, 1988.

Park, Chris C. *Sacred Worlds: An Introduction to Geography and Religion.* London and New York: Routledge, 1994.

Press, Frank, and Raymond Siever. *Understanding Earth.* New York: W. H. Freeman, 1994.

Rao, Aruna, Mary B. Anderson, and Catherine A. Overholt, eds. *Gender Analysis in Development Planning: A Case Book.* West Hartford, CT: Kumarian Press, 1991.

Rodda, Annabel. *Women and the Environment.* London and New Jersey: Zed Books, 1991.

Rose, Gillian. *Feminism and Geography: The Limits of Geographical Knowledge.* Cambridge, UK: Polity Press, 1993.

Rule, Wilma, and Joseph F. Zimmerman, eds. *Electoral Systems in Comparative Perspective: Their Impact on Women and Minorities.* Westport, CT, and London: Greenwood Press, 1994.

Rutt, Richard. *James Scarth Gale and His History of the Korean People.* Seoul: Royal Asiatic Society Korean Branch by Seoul Computer Press, 1972.

Schumacher, E. F. *Small Is Beautiful.* New York: Harper & Row, 1973.

Seager, Joni. *Earth Follies: Coming to Feminist Terms with the Global Environmental Crisis.* New York: Routledge, 1993.

Smith, Bruce D. *The Emergence of Agriculture.* New York: Scientific American Library, 1995.

Tannahill, Reay. *Food in History.* New York: Crown, 1988.

Taplin, Ruth. *Economic Development and the Role of Women: An Interdisciplinary Approach.* Hants, UK: Avebury, 1989.

Taylor, Timothy. *The Prehistory of Sex.* New York: Bantam Books, 1996.

Tuan, Yi-Fu. *Escapism.* Baltimore, MD: Johns Hopkins University Press, 1998.

United Nations Development Programme. Available at: http://www.undp.org. The Human Development Reports cited through the text are on the Web at http://www.undp.org/undp/hdro.

Waring, Marilyn. *If Women Counted: A New Feminist Economics.* San Francisco: Harper & Row, 1988.

Wegener, Alfred. in *Understanding Earth* (Frank Press and Raymond Siever, eds.), 2nd ed. New York: W. H. Freeman, 1998, pp. 22–23.

Weiskel, Timothy. Can Humanity Survive Unrestricted Population Growth? In *Annual Editions Global Issues 96/97*. Guilford, CT: Dushkin Publishing Group/Brown & Benchmark, 1996.

Wilson, Deborah S., and Christine Moneera Laennec, eds. *Bodily Discursions: Genders, Representations, Technologies.* Albany: State University of New York Press, 1997.

World Bank. *Social Indicators of Development 1991–1992.* Baltimore, MD, and London: Johns Hopkins University Press, 1992.

World Bank. Available at: http://www.worldbank.org/html/Welcome.html.

World Resources Institute. *World Resources 1994–95: People and the Environment: Resource Consumption, Population Growth, Women.* New York: Oxford University Press, 1994.

World Resources Institute. Available at: http://www.wri.org.

Zweers, Wim, and Jan J. Boersema, eds. *Ecology, Technology and Culture.* Cambridge, UK: White Horse Press, 1994.

Chapter 2 North America

Aiken, Charles S. *The Cotton Plantation South Since the Civil War.* Baltimore, MD: Johns Hopkins University Press, 1998.

American Farm Bureau. *Farm Facts: For the Record.* Washington, DC, 1996. Available at: http://www.fb.com/today/farmfacts/ftr.html.

Birdsall, Stephen S., and John W. Florin. *Regional Landscapes of the United States and Canada*, 4th ed. New York: Wiley, 1992.

Blackburn, Robin. *The Making of New World Slavery: From the Baroque to the Creole.* London: Verso, 1997.

Bland, Stephen, Stephen Krajewski, and Henry S. Yu. North American Business Integration. Pp. 199–204, in *Annual Editions International Business 96/97* (Fred Maidment, ed.). Guilford, CT: Dushkin Publishing Group/Brown & Benchmark, 1996.

Blouet, Brian W., and Frederick C. Luebke, eds. *The Great Plains: Environment and Culture.* Lincoln, NB, and London: University of Nebraska Press, 1977.

Bryson, Ken. *Household and Family Characteristics: March 1995.* Current Population Reports. Washington, DC: U.S. Census Bureau, 1996. Available at: http://www.census.gov/prod/2/pop/p20/p20-488.pdf.

Bullard, Robert D. *Dumping in Dixie: Race, Class and Environmental Quality.* Boulder, CO: Westview Press, 1994.

Butzer, Karl W., ed. The Americas Before and After 1492: Current Geographical Research. *Annals of the Association of American Geographers 82*, no. 3 (September 1992).

Canby, Thomas Y. Earthquake—Prelude to the Big One? *National Geographic*, May 1990, pp. 76–105.

Carney, George O., ed. *Fast Food, Stock Cars and Rock-n-Roll: Place and Space in American Pop Culture.* Lanham, MD: Rowman & Littlefield, 1995.

Carpenter, Allan, and Carl Provorse. *The World Almanac of the U.S.A.* Mahwah, NJ: World Almanac Books, 1996.

Conniff, Richard. Toronto. *National Geographic*, June 1996, pp. 121–139.

Cooper, Marc. The Heartland's Raw Deal: How Meatpacking Is Creating a New Immigrant Underclass. *The Nation*, February 3, 1997, pp. 11–18.

Corner, James, and Alex S. MacLean. *Taking Measures Across the American Landscape.* New Haven, CT: Yale University Press, 1996.

Crutsinger, Martin. Conflicting Views Cloud True Impact of NAFTA. *Knoxville News-Sentinel*, July 8, 1997, p. C1.

Darragh, Ian. Quebec's Quandary. *National Geographic*, November 1997, pp. 46–67.

del Pinal, Jorge, and Audrey Singer. Generations of Diversity: Latinos in the United States. *Population Bulletin 52*, No. 3 (1997).

Dobnik, Verena, and Ted Anthony. Robbed of Childhood. *The Knoxville News-Sentinel*, December 21, 1997, pp. D1, D4.

Doyle, Roger. *1994 Atlas of Contemporary America.* New York: Facts on File, 1994.

Dubeck, Paula J., and Kathryn Borman. *Women and Work: A Handbook.* New York and London: Garland, 1996.

Egan, Timothy. New Prosperity Brings New Conflict to Indian Country. *The New York Times*, March 8, 1998, pp. 1, 22.

Einhorn, Barbara, and Eileen Janes Yeo, eds. *Women and Market Societies: Crisis and Opportunity.* Aldershot, UK, and Brookfield, VT: Edward Elgar, 1995.

Emerson, Bo. Violence Feeds 'Redneck', Gun-Toting Image. *The Atlanta Journal-Constitution*, March 29, 1998, p. A8.

Fagan, Brian M. *Ancient North America*, 2nd ed. New York: Thames and Hudson, 1995.

Faulkner's Mississippi. *National Geographic*, March 1989, pp. 313–339.

Faux, Jeff. Is the American Economic Model the Answer? *The American Prospect*, no. 19 (Fall 1994): 74–81. Available at: http://epn.org/prospect/19/19faux.html.

Feder, Barnaby J. Sowing Preservation. *The New York Times*, March 20, 1997, pp. D1–D19.

Fellmann, Jerome, Arthur Getis, and Judith Getis. *Human Geography.* Dubuque, IA: Brown & Benchmark, 1997.

Garreau, Joel. *The Nine Nations of North America.* Boston: Houghton Mifflin, 1981.

Garrett, Wilbur E., ed. *Historical Atlas of the United States.* Washington, DC: National Geographic Society, 1988.

Getis, Arthur, and Judith Getis, eds. *The United States and Canada: The Land and the People.* Dubuque, IA: Wm. C. Brown, 1995.

Gottman, Jean. *Megalopolis: The Urbanized Northeastern Seaboard of the United States.* New York: Twentieth Century Fund, 1961.

Gottmann, Jean. *Megalopolis Revisited: 25 Years Later.* College Park: University of Maryland Institute for Urban Studies, 1987.

Gottmann, Jean, and Robert A. Harper, eds. *Since Megalopolis: The Urban Writings of Jean Gottmann.* Baltimore, MD: Johns Hopkins University Press, 1990.

Grant, Richard, and Jan Nijman. Historical Changes in U.S. and Japanese Foreign Aid to the Asia-Pacific Region. *Annals of the American Association of Geographers 87*, no. 1 (1997): 32–51.

Hanson, Susan, and G. Pratt. *Gender, Work, and Space.* New York: Routledge, 1995.

Hastedt, Glen P., ed. *Annual Editions American Foreign Policy 95/96.* Guilford, CT: Dushkin Publishing Group, 1995.

Henrietta, James A., W. E. Brownlee, David Brody, and Susan Ware. *America's History*, 2nd ed. New York: Worth, 1993.

Hobbs, Frank B., with Bonnie L. Damon. *65+ in the United States. P23-190 Current Population Reports: Special Studies.* Washington, DC: U.S. Census Bureau, 1994. Available at: http://www.census.gov/prod/1/pop//p23-190p23-190.html.

Hudson, John. *Making the Corn Belt: A Geographic History of Middle-Western Agriculture.* Bloomington, IN: Indiana University Press, 1994.

Jackson, John Brinckerhoff. *A Sense of Place, A Sense of Time.* New Haven, CT: Yale University Press, 1994.

Janelle, Donald G. *Geographical Snapshots of North America.* New York: Guilford Press, 1992.

Johnson, Tim, ed. *Spirit Capture: Photographs from The National Museum of the American Indian.* Washington, DC: Smithsonian Institution, 1998.

Kaplan, David. Two Nations in Search of a State: Canada's Ambivalent Spatial Identities. *Annals of the American Association of Geographers 84*, no. 4 (1994): 585–606.

Klinkenborg, Verlyn. A Farming Revolution. *National Geographic*, December 1995, pp. 61–89.

Kromm, David E. Low Water in the American High Plains. Pp. 136–141, in *Annual Editions Geography 93/94.* Guilford, CT: Dushkin Publishing Group, 1993.

Krugman, Paul R. *Peddling Prosperity: Economic Sense and Nonsense in an Age of Diminished Expectations.* New York: W. W. Norton, 1995.

Kunstler, James Howard. *The Geography of Nowhere: The Rise and Decline of America's Man-made Landscape.* New York: Simon & Schuster, Touchstone, 1994.

Lange, Linda. Toronto. *The Knoxville News-Sentinel*, January 11, 1998, pp. E1, E4.

Leckie, Gloria J. Female Farmers in Canada, 1971–1986. *Professional Geographer* (May 1993): 180–193.

Ley, David. *The New Middle Class and the Remaking of the Central City.* New York: Oxford University Press, 1997.

Lippard, Lucie. *The Lure of the Local: Senses of Place in a Multi-centered Society.* New York: New Press, 1997.

Long, Michael. Central Pennsylvania, My Hometown. *National Geographic*, June 1994, pp. 32–59.

Lynch, Kevin. *What Time Is This Place?* Cambridge, MA: MIT Press, 1982.

Martin, Philip, and Elizabeth Midgley. Immigration to the United States: Journey to an Uncertain Destination. *Population Bulletin 49*, no. 2 (September 1994).

Mattson, Catherine M., and Mark T. Mattson. *Contemporary Atlas of the United States.* New York: Macmillan, 1990.

McHugh, Kevin E. Hispanic Migration and Population Redistribution in the United States. *Professional Geographer* (November 1989): 429–439.

McKnight, Tom L. *Regional Geography of the United States and Canada.* Englewood Cliffs, NJ: Prentice Hall, 1992.

Miller, G. Tyler, Jr. *Living in the Environment*, 8th ed. Belmont, CA: Wadsworth, 1994.

Morris, Willie. *Yazoo: Integration in a Deep-Southern Town.* New York: Harper's Magazine Press, 1971.

Murphy, Richard McGill. Seinfeld Masala. *The New York Times:* Magazine section, October 19, 1997, p. 72.

Native American Heritage Map. Washington, DC: National Geographic Society, 1991.

Newman, Cathy. North Carolina's Piedmont. *National Geographic*, March 1995, pp. 114–138.

Norman, Geoffrey. The Cherokee: Two Nations, One People. *National Geographic*, May 1995, pp. 72–97.

Parfit, Michael. Powwow. *National Geographic*, June 1994, pp. 88–113.

Paterson, J. H. *North America: A Geography of the United States and Canada*, 9th ed. New York: Oxford University Press, 1994.

Press, Frank, and Raymond Siever. *Understanding Earth.* New York: W. H. Freeman, 1997.

Ralston, Jeannie. In the Heart of Appalachia. *National Geographic*, February 1993, pp. 112–136.

Rand McNally. *1998 Commercial Atlas and Marketing Guide*, 129th ed. New York: Rand McNally, 1998.

Rawlings, Steve W. Changing U.S. Family Composition 1970–1995. *U.S. Census Briefs: Households and Families.* Washington, DC: U.S. Census Bureau, 1995.

Rengert, George F. *The Geography of Illegal Drugs.* Boulder, CO: Westview Press, 1996.

Richburg, Keith B. *Out of America: A Black Man Confronts Africa.* New York: Basic Books, 1997.

Rimer, Sara. Rural Elderly Create Vital Communities as Young Leave Void. *The New York Times*, February 2, 1998, pp. A1, A14.

Rocheleau, Dianne, Barbara Thomas-Slayter, and Esther Wangari, eds. *Feminist Political Ecology: Global Issues and Local Experiences.* London and New York: Routledge, 1996.

Said, Edward W. *Orientalism.* New York: Vintage Books, 1979.

Scheuerman, Richard, and John Clement. *Palouse Country: A Land and Its People.* College Place, WA: Color Press, 1993.

Seager, Joni. Hysterical Housewives and Other Mad Women. Pp. 271–283, in *Feminist Political Ecology* (Dianne Rocheleau, Barbara Thomas-Slayter, and Esther Wangari, eds.). London: Routledge, 1996.

Simmons, I. G. *Biogeography: Natural and Cultural.* London: Arnold, 1979.

Smith, Griffin. The Cajuns: Still Loving Life. *National Geographic*, October 1990, pp. 40–65.

Sokolov, Raymond. *Why We Eat What We Eat: How the Encounter Between the New World and the Old World Changed the Way Everyone on the Planet Eats.* New York: Summit Books, 1991.

Spencer, Jon Michael. *The New Colored People: The Mixed-Race Movement in America.* New York: New York University Press, 1997.

Stratton, Joanna L. *Pioneer Women: Voices from the Kansas Frontier.* New York: Simon & Schuster, Touchstone, 1981.

Stumberg, Robert. NAFTA Rewrites Status of States. Pp. 130–135, in *Annual Editions American Foreign Policy 95/96* (Glen P. Hastedt, ed.). Guilford, CT: Dushkin Publishing Group, 1995.

Thomas, R. L., and E. P. Neufield. Hemispheric Prospects: NAFTA Changes the Game. Pp. 40–44, in *Annual Editions International Business 96/97* (Fred Maidment, ed.). Guilford, CT: Dushkin Publishing Group/Brown & Benchmark, 1996.

Thompson, Jon. Cotton, King of Fibers. *National Geographic*, June 1994, pp. 60–87.

A Town That Needs Pity: Lefors, Texas. *The New York Times: Sunday Magazine* section, January 5, 1997, p. 9.

Trudeau, Pierre. As quoted in Common Ground, Different Dream. Priit J. Vesilind. *National Geographic*, February 1990, p. 97.

United Nations Development Programme. *Human Development Report 1996*. New York: United Nations Development Programme, 1996.

U.S. Census Bureau. *State Age-Sex Population Estimates Consistent with Census Advisory CB94-43* and *Population Projections for States, by Age, Sex, Race, and Hispanic Origin: 1993 to 2020*, Current Population Reports. Washington, DC: U.S. Census Bureau, 1994.

U.S. Census Bureau. *Sixty-five Plus in the United States*, Statistical Brief. Washington, DC: U.S. Census Bureau, 1995. Available at: http://www.census.gov/socdemo/www/agebrief.html.

Van Dyke, Jere. Growing Up in East Harlem. *National Geographic*, May 1990, pp. 52–75.

Walker III, William O., ed. *Drugs in the Western Hemisphere: An Odyssey of Cultures in Conflict*, Jaguar Books on Latin America, No. 12. Wilmington, DE: Scholar Resources, 1996.

Wallace, Anthony F. C. *Rockdale: The Growth of an American Village in the Early Industrial Revolution*. New York: Knopf, 1980.

Weatherford, Jack. *Indian Givers: How the Indians of the Americas Transformed the World*. New York: Crown, 1988.

Wilson, Deborah S., and Christine Moneera Laennec, eds. *Bodily Discursions: Genders, Representations, Technologies*. Albany: State University of New York Press, 1997.

Wilson, William Julius. *When Works Disappears: The World of the New Urban Poor*. New York: Knopf, 1996.

World Bank. *Monitoring Environmental Progress: A Report on Work in Progress*. Washington, DC: World Bank, 1995.

World Bank. *Sustainability and the Wealth of Nations: First Steps in an Ongoing Journey*, Preliminary Draft, September 30, 1995. Washington, DC: World Bank, 1995.

Zelinsky, Wilbur. *The Cultural Geography of the United States*, rev. ed. Englewood Cliffs, NJ: Prentice Hall, 1992.

Zwingle, Erla. Ogallala Aquifer Wellspring of the High Plains. *National Geographic*, March 1993, pp. 80–109.

Chapter 3 Middle and South America

Allen, John L. *Student Atlas of Economic Development*. Guilford, CT: Dushkin/McGraw-Hill, 1997.

Anderson, Arthur J. O., and Charles E. Dibble. *The War of Conquest: How It Was Waged Here in Mexico—The Aztecs' Own Story as Given to Fr. Bernardino de Sahagun, Rendering into Modern English by Anderson and Dibble*. Salt Lake City: University of Utah Press, 1978.

Behar, Ruth. *Translated Woman: Crossing the Border with Esperanza's Story*. Boston: Beacon Press, 1993.

Blackburn, Robin. *The Making of New World Slavery: From the Baroque to the Creole*. London: Verso, 1997.

Blouet, Brian W., and Olwyn M. Blouet. *Latin America: An Introductory Survey*. New York: Wiley, 1982.

Blouet, Brian W., and Olwyn M. Blouet. *Latin America and the Caribbean: A Systematic and Regional Survey*, 3rd ed. New York: Wiley, 1997.

Bose, Christine E., and Edna Acosta-Belen, eds. *Women in the Latin American Development Process*. Philadelphia: Temple University Press, 1995.

Bowen, Sally. Bringing the Inca Canals Back to Life. *People and the Planet 5*, no. 1 (1996). Available at: http://www.oneworld.org/patp/vol5/feature2.html.

British Information Services, Foreign and Commonwealth Office. Economic Reform in Cuba. Pp. 229–232, in *Global Studies Latin America* (Paul B. Goodwin, Jr., ed.), 7th ed. Guilford, CT: Dushkin Publishing Group/Brown & Benchmark, 1966.

Burges, Sean W. Strength in Numbers: Latin American Trade Blocs, a Free Trade Area of the Americas and the Problem of Economic Development. *Council of Hemispheric Affairs (COHA) Occasional Paper*, vol. 2, April 1, 1998. Available at: http://www.coha.org/nletter/coha2-1.html.

Burgos-Debray, Elisabeth, ed. *I, Rigoberta Menchú: An Indian Woman in Guatemala*. London: Verso, 1983.

Butzer, Karl W. The Americas Before and After 1492: An Introduction of Current Geographical Research. *Annals of the Association of American Geographers 82*, no. 3 (1992): 345–368.

Campbell, Alan Tormaid. *Getting to Know Waiwai: An Amazonian Ethnography*. London: Routledge, 1994.

Chaney, Elsa M., and Mary Garcia Castro, eds. *Muchachas No More: Household Workers in Latin America and the Caribbean*. Philadelphia: Temple University Press, 1989.

Chant, Sylvia, ed. *Gender and Migration in Developing Countries*. London and New York: Belhaven Press, 1992.

Clawson, David L. *Latin America and the Caribbean Lands and Peoples*. Dubuque, IA: Wm. C. Brown, 1997.

Clusener-Godt, M., and I. Sachs, eds. *Brazilian Perspectives on Sustainable Development of the Amazon Region*. Paris and New York: UNESCO and Parthenon, 1995.

Conway, Dennis, and Jeffrey H. Cohen. Consequences of Migration and Remittances for Mexican Trans-national Communities. *Economic Geography 74*, no. 1 (1998): 26–44.

Cowell, Noel M., and Ian Boxill, eds. *Human Resource Management: A Caribbean Perspective*. Kingston, Jamaica: Canoe Press of UWI, 1995.

Cravey, Altha J. *Women and Work in Mexico's Maquiladoras*. Lanham, MD: Rowman & Littlefield, 1998.

Davis, William Columbus. *Warnings from the Far South: Democracy versus Dictatorship in Uruguay, Argentina, and Chile*. Westport, CT: Praeger, 1995.

Dee, Elaine Evans, guest curator. *Frederic E. Church: Under Changing Skies—Oil Sketches and Drawings from the Collection of the Cooper-Hewitt, National Museum of Design, Smithsonian Institution*. Philadelphia: Smith-Edwards-Dunlop, 1992.

Denevan, William M. The Pristine Myth: The Landscape of the Americas in 1492. *Annals of the Association of American Geographers 82*, no. 3 (1992): 369–385.

de Sahagun, Bernardino. *Conquest of New Spain 1585 Revision*. Salt Lake City: University of Utah Press, 1989.

Dillon, Sam. Big Mac? Not for Maquiladoras Workers. New York Times News Service, December 5, 1995, at: http://www.latino.com/news/macc1205.html.

Edmonson, Munro S., ed. *Sixteenth-Century Mexico: The Work of Sahagun*. Albuquerque: University of New Mexico Press, 1974.

Gade, Daniel W. Landscape, System, and Identity in the Post-Conquest Andes. *Annals of the Association of American Geographers 82*, no. 3 (1992): 460–477.

Garrard-Burnett, Virginia, and David Stoll, eds. *Rethinking Protestantism in Latin America*. Philadelphia: Temple University Press, 1993.

Garrett, Wilbur E. La Ruta Maya. *National Geographic*, October 1989, pp. 424–479.

Goodwin, Paul B., Jr. *Global Studies Latin America*, 4th ed. Guilford, CT: Dushkin/McGraw-Hill, 1990.

Goodwin, Paul B., Jr. *Global Studies Latin America*, 6th ed. Guilford, CT: Dushkin Publishing Group, 1994.

Goodwin, Paul B., Jr. *Global Studies Latin America*, 7th ed. Guilford, CT: Dushkin Publishing Group/Brown & Benchmark, 1996.

Goodwin, Paul B., Jr. *Global Studies Latin America*, 8th ed. Guilford, CT: Dushkin/McGraw-Hill, 1998.

Gwynne, Robert N., and Cristobal Kay, eds. *Latin America Transformed: Globalization and Modernity*. New York: Oxford University Press, 1999.

Hansis, Randall. *The Latin Americans: Understanding Their Legacy*. New York: McGraw-Hill, 1997.

Hays-Mitchell, Maureen. Street Vending in Peruvian Cities: The Spatio-temporal Behavior of Ambulantes. *Professional Geographer 46*, no. 4 (1994): 425–438.

Jacquette, Jane S., ed. *The Women's Movement in Latin America: Participation and Democracy*. Boulder, CO: Westview Press, 1994.

Jelin, Elizabeth, ed. *Women and Social Change in Latin America*. London: UNRISD and Zed Books, 1990.

Keeling, David J. *Buenos Aires: Global Dreams, Local Crises*. Chichester, UK, and New York: Wiley, 1996.

Kermath, Brian, and Lydia M. Pulsipher. *Guide to Food Plants Now Used in the Americas*. Washington, DC: Smithsonian Press. Forthcoming.

Kirdar, Uner, ed. *Cities Fit for People*. New York: United Nations, 1997.

Lavrin, Asuncion. *Women, Feminism, and Social Change in Argentina, Chile, and Uruguay 1890–1940*. Lincoln and London: University of Nebraska Press, 1995.

Lockhart, Douglas G., David Drakakis-Smith, and John Schembri, eds. *The Development Process in Small Island States*. London: Routledge, 1993.

Lombardi, Cathryn L., and John V. Lombardi, with K. Lynn Stoner. *Latin American History: A Teaching Atlas*. Madison: University of Wisconsin Press, 1983.

Lovell, W. George. Heavy Shadows and Black Night: Disease and Depopulation in Colonial Spanish America. *Annals of the Association of American Geographers 82*, no. 3 (1992): 426–443.

MacDonald, Gordon J., Daniel L. Nielson, and Marc A. Stern, eds. *Latin American Environmental Policy in International Perspective*. Boulder, CO: Westview Press, 1997.

Maingot, Anthony P. Haiti: The Political Rot Within. Pp. 223–228, in *Global Studies Latin America* (Paul B. Goodwin, Jr., ed.), 7th ed. Guilford, CT: Dushkin Publishing Group/Brown & Benchmark, 1996.

Mexico: Maquiladoras, Remittances. *Migration News 7*, no. 11 (November 1997). Available at: http://migration.ucdavis.edu/By-Month/MN-Vol-4-97/Nov.html#RTFToC8.

Meyerson, Julia. *Tambo Life in an Andean Village*. Austin: University of Texas Press, 1990.

Momsen, Janet Henshall. *Women and Development in the Third World*. London: Routledge, 1991.

Nelson, Barbara J., and Najma Chowdhury, eds. *Women and Politics Worldwide*. New Haven, CT, and London: Yale University Press, 1994.

Nussbaum, Martha C., and Glover Jonathan, eds. *Women, Culture, and Development: A Study in Human Capabilities*. Oxford, UK: Clarendon Press, 1995.

Olmos, Margarite Fernandez, and Lizabeth Paravisini-Gebert, eds. *Sacred Possessions: Vodou, Santeria, Obeah, and the Caribbean*. New Brunswick, NJ: Rutgers University Press, 1997.

Organization of American Historians. *Restoring Women to History* (rev. ed.)*: Teaching Packets for Integrating Women's History into Courses on Africa, Asia, Latin America and the Caribbean, and the Middle East*. Bloomington, IN: Organization of American Historians, 1990.

Parker, Christian. *Popular Religion and Modernization in Latin America: A Different Logic*. Maryknoll, NY: Orbis Books, 1996.

Patai, Daphne. *Brazilian Women Speak: Contemporary Life Stories*. New Brunswick, NJ: Rutgers University Press, 1988.

Premdas, Ralph R. *Ethnic Conflict and Development: The Case of Guyana*. Aldershot, UK: Avebury, 1995.

Radcliffe, Sarah A., and Sallie Westwood, eds. *"Viva" Women and Popular Protest in Latin America*. London and New York: Routledge, 1993.

Rengert, George F. *The Geography of Illegal Drugs*. Boulder, CO: Westview Press, 1996.

Richardson, Bonham C. *The Caribbean in the Wider World 1492–1992*. Cambridge, UK: Cambridge University Press, 1992.

Sabloff, Jeremy A. *The New Archaeology and the Ancient Maya*. New York: Scientific American Library, 1990.

Safa, Helen I. *The Myth of the Male Breadwinner: Women and Industrialization in the Caribbean*. Boulder, CO: Westview Press, 1995.

Sauer, Carl Ortwin. *The Early Spanish Main*. Berkeley: University of California Press, 1966.

Schurz, William Lytle. *Latin America: A Descriptive Survey*. New York: Dutton, 1963.

Scott, Alison MacEwen. *Divisions and Solidarities: Gender, Class and Employment in Latin America*. London: Routledge, 1994.

Serivio Paz y Justicia Uruguay. *Uruguay Nunca Mas: Human Rights Violations 1972–1985*. Philadelphia: Temple University Press, 1992.

Sherlock, P. M. *West Indies: New Nations and Peoples*. New York: Walker, 1966.

Smith, Lois M., and Alfred Padula. *Sex and Revolution: Women in Socialist Cuba*. New York and Oxford, UK: Oxford University Press, 1996.

Stewart, Douglas Ian. *After the Trees: Living on the Transamazon Highway.* Austin: University of Texas Press, 1994.

Stolcke, Verena. Conquered Women. In *Report on the Americas: Inventing America 1492–1992.* Ann Arbor, MI. *NAVLA 24*, no. 5 (1991): 23–28, 39.

Van Cott, Donna Lee, ed. *Indigenous Peoples and Democracy in Latin America.* New York: St. Martin's Press, 1994.

Watts, David. *The West Indies Patterns of Development, Culture and Environmental Change Since 1492.* Cambridge, UK: Cambridge University Press, 1987.

Weatherford, Jack. *Indian Givers: How the Indians of the Americas Transformed the World.* New York: Crown,1988.

West, Robert C., and John P. Augelli. *Middle America: Its Lands and Peoples,* 3rd ed. Englewood Cliffs, NJ: Prentice Hall, 1989.

Wheat, Andrew. The Fall of the Peso and the Mexican "Miracle." *Multinational Monitor,* April 1995. Available at: http://www.essential.org/monitor/hyper/issues/1995/04/mm0495_06.html.

Wheat, Andrew. Toxic Bananas. *Multinational Monitor 17,* no. 9 (September 1996). Available at: http://www.essential.org/monitor/hyper/mm0996.04.html.

Yeager, Gertrude M., ed. *Confronting Change, Challenging Tradition: Women in Latin American History.* Wilmington, DE: Scholarly Resources, 1994.

Chapter 4 Europe

Abercrombie, Thomas J. The Velvet Divorce—Czecho Slovakia. *National Geographic,* September 1993, pp. 2–37.

Anachkova, Bistra. Women in Bulgaria. Pp. 55–68, in *Family, Women, and Employment in Central-Eastern Europe* (Barbara Lobodzinska, ed.). Westport, CT: Greenwood Press, 1995.

Anderson, Bonnie S., and Judith P. Zinsser. *A History of Their Own: Women in Europe from Prehistory to the Present,* Vol. 1. New York: Harper & Row, 1988.

Anderson, Mikael Skou, and Duncan Liefferink, eds. *European Environmental Policy: The Pioneers.* Manchester, UK: Manchester University Press, 1997.

Andrews, Edmund. Great Chocolate War Reveals Dark Side of Europe. *The New York Times,* October 24, 1997.

Anonymous (by request). Kosova, the Quiet Siege. *Cultural Survival Quarterly* (Summer 1995): 34–42.

Associated Press. Man's Hunting Skills Older Than Believed. *The Knoxville News-Sentinel,* February 28, 1997, p. A9.

Barzini, Luigi. *The Europeans.* Middlesex, UK: Penguin, 1983.

Bateman, Milford, ed. *Business Cultures in Central and Eastern Europe.* Oxford, UK: Butterworth-Heinemann, 1997.

Bell, Daniel. The Future of Europe: Beyond the Year 2000. Pp. 172–176, in *Global Issues 95/96. Annual Editions.* Guilford, CT: Dushkin Publishing Group/Brown & Benchmark, 1995.

Bell, John D., ed. *Bulgaria in Transition: Politics, Economics, Society, and Culture After Communism.* Boulder, CO: Westview Press, 1998.

Berentsen, William H., ed. *Contemporary Europe: A Geographic Analysis,* 7th ed. New York: Wiley, 1997.

Black, Antony. *Guilds and Civil Society in European Political Thought from the Twelfth Century to the Present.* London: Methuen, 1984.

Blanning, T. C. W., ed. *The Oxford Illustrated History of Modern Europe.* Oxford, UK: Oxford University Press, 1996.

Blaut, J. M. *The Colonizer's Model of the World.* New York: Guilford Press, 1993.

Bogucki, Peter. *The Neolithic Mosaic on the North European Plain.* Available at: http://www.princeton.edu/~bogucki/mosaic.html. See also http://www.princeton.edu/~bogucki.

Bosworth, Barry P., and Gur Ofer. *Reforming Planned Economies in an Integrating World Economy.* Washington, DC: Brookings Institution, 1995.

Bradshaw, Michael. *A World Regional Geography: The New Global Order.* Madison, WI: Brown & Benchmark, 1997.

Brawer, Moshe. *Atlas of Russia and the Independent Republics.* New York: Simon & Schuster, 1994.

Bridenthal, Renate, and Claudia Koonz. *Becoming Visible: Women in European History.* Boston: Houghton Mifflin, 1977.

Brzezinski, Zbigniew. The Great Transformation. Pp. 90–100, in *World Politics 95/96: Annual Editions.* Guilford, CT: Dushkin Publishing Group/Brown & Benchmark, 1995.

Buckwalter, Donald W. Geopolitical Legacies and Central European Export Linkages. *Professional Geographer* (February 1998): 57–70.

Burg, Steven L. Why Yugoslavia Fell Apart. Pp. 195–201, in *Global Issues 95/96. Annual editions.* Guilford, CT: Dushkin Publishing Group/Brown & Benchmark, 1995.

Bystydzienski, Jill M. Norway: Achieving World-record Women's Representation in Government. Pp. 55–64, in *Electoral Systems in Comparative Perspective: Their Impact on Women and Minorities* (Wilma Rule and Joseph F. Zimmerman, eds.). Westport, CT: Greenwood Press, 1994.

Cannan, Crescy. From Dependence to Enterprise? Women and Western Welfare States. *Women and Market Societies: Crisis and Opportunity* (Barbara Einhorn and Eileen Janes Yeo, eds.). Aldershot, UK, and Brookfield, VT: Edward Elgar, 1995.

Carter, Erica. *How German Is She? Postwar West German Reconstruction and the Consuming Woman.* Ann Arbor: University of Michigan Press, 1997.

Central Intelligence Agency:
  Albania. The World Fact Book 1998. Washington, DC, 1998. Available at: http://www.odci.gov/cia/publications/factbook/al.html.
  Croatia. The World Fact Book 1998. Washington, DC, 1998. Available at: http://www.odci.gov/cia/publications/factbook/hr.html.
  Slovenia. The World Fact Book 1998. Washington DC, 1998. Available at: http://www.odci.gov/cia/publications/factbook/si.html.

Cermakova, Marie. Women and Family: The Czech Version of Development and Chances for Improvement. Pp. 75–85, in *Family, Women, and Employment in Central-Eastern Europe* (Barbara Lobodzinska, ed.). Westport CT: Greenwood Press, 1995.

Clarke, Jonathan G. "The Eurocorps" Making a Fresh Start in Europe. Pp. 79–81, in *World Politics 95/96: Annual Editions.* Guilford, CT: Dushkin Publishing Group/Brown & Benchmark, 1995.

Cohen, Roger. For France, Sagging Self-image and Esprit. *The New York Times:* International section, February 11, 1997, p. A8.

Cole, John. *Geography of the World's Major Regions.* London and New York: Routledge, 1996.

Corrin, Chris. *Magyar Women: Hungarian Women's Lives, 1960s–1990s.* New York: St. Martin's Press, 1994.

Crossette, Barbara. Surprises in the Global Tourism Boom. *The New York Times,* April 12, 1998, p. WK5.

Danforth, Kenneth C. Yugoslavia: A House Much Divided. *National Geographic,* August 1990, pp. 92–123.

Danforth, Loring M. The Macedonian Minority of Northern Greece. *Cultural Survival Quarterly* (Summer 1995): 64–70.

Davidson, Fiona M. Integration and Disintegration: A Political Geography of the European Union. *Journal of Geography* (March/April 1997): 69–75.

Davies, Norman. *Europe: A History.* Oxford, UK: Oxford University Press, 1996.

Day, Lincoln H. *The Future of Low-birthrate Populations.* London and New York: Routledge, 1992.

Denmark Ministry of Environment and Energy. *Denmark's Nature and Environment Policy 1995.* Copenhagen: Denmark Ministry of Foreign Affairs, 1996. Available at: http://www.mem.dk/publikationer/RED/GBRED/index.htm.

Denmark Ministry of Foreign Affairs. *Denmark in a Nutshell.* Copenhagen: Denmark Ministry of Foreign Affairs, 1999. Available at: http://www.um.dk/english.

Dina, Adriana, and Matthew Rowntree. Moldova. Pp. 193–203, in *Environmental Resources and Constraints in the Former Soviet Republics* (Philip R. Pryde, ed.). Boulder, CO: Westview Press, 1995.

Dreifelds, Juris. Latvia. Pp. 109–123, in *Environmental Resources and Constraints in the Former Soviet Republics* (Philip R. Pryde, ed.). Boulder, CO: Westview Press, 1995.

Dukes, Paul. *A History of Europe 1648–1948: The Arrival, the Rise, the Fall.* Hampshire, UK: Macmillan, 1985.

Duncan, Simon. The Diverse Worlds of European Patriarchy. *Women of the European Union: The Politics of Work and Daily Life* (Maria Dolors Garcia-Ramon and Janice Monk, eds.). London and New York: Routledge, 1996.

Dundes, Alan, ed. *The Walled-Up Wife.* Madison: University of Wisconsin Press, 1996.

Eastern European Decisions. Hong Kong: Harrington Kilbride, 1993.

The Economist. Atlas of the New Europe. New York: Henry Holt, 1992.

The Economist:
    In the Slav Shadowlands. May 20, 1995, pp. 47–49.
    Romania and Bulgaria: Those South-eastern Laggards. October 19, 1996, pp. 54–56.
    Europe's Fish: Norway's Lessons. October 19, 1996, p. 58.
    Norway: Post Brundtland. October 26, 1996, p. 65.
    Romania: Fingers Crossed. November 23, 1996, p. 57.
    Europe: A Balkan Spring. January 4, 1997, pp. 47–48.
    Slovenia: Bridging Europe. January 11, 1997, p. 49.
    Albania: Chaos or Worse. March 8, 1997, pp. 57–58.

Editors of McDonald's Corporation. *The Annual McDonald's Corporation 1995 Annual Report.* Oak Brook, IL: McDonald's Corporation, 1996.

Editors of National Geographic. In Focus: Bosnia. *National Geographic,* June 1996, pp. 48–61.

Edwards, Mike. After the Soviet Union's Collapse—A Broken Empire. *National Geographic,* March 1993, pp. 2–53.

Edwards, Mike, and Sisse Brimberg (photos). Searching for the Scythians. *National Geographic,* September 1996, pp. 54–79.

Edwards, Mike, and Gerd Ludwig (photos). Living with the Monster Chernobyl. *National Geographic,* August 1994, pp. 100–115.

Eglesz, Krisztina, designer. *Welcome to Budapest.* Budapest: BudaNet, Inc/Kft. Subsidiary Euro Business Network. Available at: http://www.budapest.com.

Einhorn, Barbara. Ironies of History: Citizenship Issues in the New Market Economies of East Central Europe. Pp. 217–233, in *Women and Market Societies* (Barbara Einhorn and Eileen Janes Yeo, eds.). Aldershot, UK: Edward Elgar, 1995.

Elan Skis. (1998). Available at: http://www.elanskis.com.

Fagan, Brian M. *Men of the Earth: An Introduction to World Prehistory.* Boston: Little, Brown, 1974.

Faroe Islands. *Descriptive Account of the Faroe Islands.* 1996. Available at: http://www.sleipnir.fo/faroe/FAROE5.HTM.

Fonseca, Isabel. *Bury Me Standing: The Gypsies and Their Journey.* New York: Vintage Books, 1996.

Frank, Robert. Price of Isolation: Impoverished Bulgaria Is Ready to Reform—Seven Years Too Late. *The Wall Street Journal,* February 28, 1997.

Garcia-Ramon, Maria Dolors, and Janice Monk, eds. *Women of the European Union: The Politics of Work and Daily Life.* London and New York: Routledge, 1996.

Garrett, Wilbur E. Where Did We Come From? *National Geographic,* October 1988, pp. 434–437.

Global Issues 96/97: Annual Editions. Guilford, CT: Dushkin Publishing Group/Brown & Benchmark, 1996.

Goldman, Milton F. *Global Studies The Soviet Union and Eastern Europe,* 3rd ed. Guilford, CT: Dushkin Publishing Group, 1990.

Goldman, Milton F. Eastern Europe. In *Global Studies The Soviet Union and Eastern Europe,* 3rd ed., pp. 72–143. Guilford, CT: Dushkin Publishing Group, 1990.

Goldman, Milton F. *Global Studies Russia, the Eurasian Republics, and Central/Eastern Europe,* 6th ed. Guilford, CT: Dushkin Publishing Group/Brown & Benchmark, 1996.

Goldman, Milton F. *Global Studies Russia, the Eurasian Republics, and Central/Eastern Europe,* 7th ed. Guilford, CT: Dushkin/McGraw-Hill, 1999.

Gore, Rick. The Dawn of Humans: Neandertals. *National Geographic,* January 1996, pp. 2–35.

Gosar, Anton. Slovenia: Selected Topics in Political Geography. Pp. 7–9, in *Slovenia: A Gateway to Central Europe.* Ljubljana: Association of Geographical Societies of Slovenia, 1996.

Greenland Tourism a/s. *Visiting Greenland.* 1998. Available at: http://www.greenland-guide.dk/gt/intro-03.htm.

Harsanyi, Doina Pasca. Participation of Women in the Work Force: The Case of Romania. Pp. 213–217, in *Family, Women, and Employment in Central-Eastern Europe* (Barbara Lobodzinska, ed.). Westport, CT: Greenwood Press, 1995.

Haub, Carl. *Population Change in the Former Soviet Republics, Population Bulletin 49,* no. 4 (December 1994). Washington, DC: Population Reference Bureau, 1994.

Hayden, Robert. Serbian and Croatian Nationalism and the Wars in Yugoslavia. *Cultural Survival Quarterly* (Summer 1995): 25–28.

Heitlinger, Alena. Women's Equality, Work, and Family in the Czech Republic. Pp. 87–99, in *Family, Women, and Employment in Central-Eastern Europe* (Barbara Lobodzinska, ed.). Westport, CT: Greenwood Press, 1995.

Hellig, Gerhard, Thomas Buttner, and Wolfgang Lutz. *Germany's Population: Turbulent Past, Uncertain Future, Population Bulletin 45*, no. 4 (December 1990). Washington, DC: Population Reference Bureau, 1990.

Hepner, George F., and Jesse O. McKee. *World Regional Geography: A Global Approach*. St. Paul, MN: West, 1992.

Hoffman, George W., ed. *Europe in the 1990s: A Geographic Analysis*, 6th ed. New York: Wiley, 1989.

Hughes, H. Stuart, and James Wilkinson. *Contemporary Europe: A History*, 6th ed. Englewood Cliffs, NJ: Prentice Hall, 1987.

Humbeck, Eva. The Politics of Cultural Identity: Thai Women in Germany. *Women of the European Union: The Politics of Work and Daily Life* (Maria Dolors Garcia-Ramon and Janice Monk, eds.). London and New York: Routledge, 1996.

Information and Documentation Centre for Geography of the Netherlands, Utrecht. *Compact Geography of the Netherlands*. The Hague: Ministry of Foreign Affairs and Zoetermeer: Ministry of Education, Culture and Science, 1994.

Ingrao, Charles. *Wesleyan Magazine* (1996). No further information available.

Ipiewak, Kuba. Constitution—Now Comes the Hard Part. *The Warsaw Voice*, April 13, 1997. Available at: http://www.warsawvoice.com.pl/v442/News00.html.

Jogan, Maca. Redomestication of Women and Democratization in Postsocialist Slovenia. Pp. 229–236, in *Family, Women, and Employment in Central-Eastern Europe* (Barbara Lobodzinska, ed.). Westport, CT: Greenwood Press, 1995.

Jordan, Terry G. *The European Culture Area: A Systematic Geography*. New York: Harper & Row, 1988.

Juric, Igor. Koper: Maritime Gateway to Central Europe. Pp. 33–41, in *Slovenia: A Gateway to Central Europe*. Ljubljana: Association of Geographical Societies of Slovenia, 1996.

Kaplan, Robert D. *Balkan Ghosts: A Journey Through History*. New York: Vintage Books/Random House, 1994.

King, Russell, Lindsay Proudfoot, and Bernard Smith, eds. *The Mediterranean: Environment and Society*. London: Arnold, 1997.

Klarer, Jurg, and Bedrich Moldan, eds. *The Environmental Challenge for Central European Economies in Transition*. New York: Wiley, 1997.

Klejn, Zbigniew. Senior Citizens—Adrift on Golden Pond. *The Warsaw Voice*: Society section, April 13, 1997. Available at: http://www.warsawvoice.com.pl/v442/Soc01.html.

Kofman, Eleonore, and Rosemary Sales. Geography of Gender and Welfare in Europe. In *Women of the European Union: The Politics of Work and Daily Life* (Maria Dolors Garcia-Ramon and Janice Monk, eds.). London and New York: Routledge, 1996.

Koulov, Boian. Political Change and Environmental Policy. *Bulgaria in Transition: Politics, Economics, Society, and Culture After Communism* (John D. Bell, ed.). Boulder, CO: Westview Press, 1998.

Leeman, Sue. DNA of 9,000-Year-Old Skeleton Linked to That of Teacher in England. *The Knoxville News-Sentinel*, March 9, 1997, p. A10.

Levathes, Louise E. Iceland: Life Under the Glaciers. *National Geographic*, February 1987, pp. 184–215.

Lewin, Roger. *The Origin of Modern Humans*. New York: Scientific American Library, 1993.

Lewis, Paul. In the World's Parliaments, Women Are Still a Small Minority. *The New York Times:* International section, March 16, 1997, p. 7.

Lobodzinska, Barbara, ed. *Family, Women, and Employment in Central-Eastern Europe*. Westport, CT: Greenwood Press, 1995.

Lockhart, Douglas G., David Drakakis-Smith, and John Schembri, eds. *The Development Process in Small Island States*. London: Routledge, 1993.

Lyall, Sarah. For British Health System, Grim Prognosis. *The New York Times:* International section, February/March, 1997.

Mazurkiewicz, Ludwik. *Human Geography in Eastern Europe and the Former Soviet Union*. London and New York: Belhaven Press and Halsted Press, 1992.

McNeill, William H. *The Shape of European History*. New York: Oxford University Press, 1974.

Mead, Walter Russell. Waiting for the Market. *Worth* (April 1997): 41–46.

Megret, Bruno. As quoted in Roger Cohen, For France, Sagging Self-Image and Esprit. *The New York Times:* International section, February 11, 1997, p. A8.

Milic, Andjelka. Women and Work in Former Yugoslavia and Their Present Situation. Pp. 237–244, in *Family, Women, and Employment in Central-Eastern Europe* (Barbara Lobodzinska, ed.). Westport, CT: Greenwood Press, 1995.

Ministère des Affaires Étrangères. *The European Union*, February 1996. Available at: http://www.france.diplomatie.fr/frmonde/euro/sommaire.gb.html.
Social Europe. Chapter 12.
Europe and the Environment. Chapter 18.
The European Union and the Central and Eastern European Countries. Chapter 27.
The European Union and the Developing Countries. Chapter 28

Mobius, Helga. *Woman of the Baroque Age*. Montclair, NJ: Abner Schram, 1984.

Moe, Mogens. *Environmental Administration in Denmark*, Environmental News No. 17, 1995. Copenhagen: Danish Environmental Protection Agency, Ministry of Environment and Energy. Available at: http://www.mst.dk/books/moe/contents.htm.

Moisi, Dominique, and Michael Mertes. Europe's Map, Compass, and Horizon. Pp. 74–78, in *World Politics 95/96: Annual Editions*. Guilford, CT: Dushkin Publishing Group/Brown & Benchmark, 1995.

Moore, Jenny, and Eleanor Scott, eds. *Invisible People and Processes: Writing Gender and Childhood into European Archaeology*. London and New York: Leicester University Press, 1997.

Morkhagen, Pernille Lonne. *The Position of Women in Norway.* Oslo: ODIN–Nytt fra Norge for the Ministry of Foreign Affairs, 1996. Available at: http://odin.dep.no/ud/nornytt/uda-147.html.

Mowat, R. C. *Decline and Renewal: Europe Ancient and Modern.* Oxford, UK: New Cherwell Press, 1991.

Nash, Nathaniel C. Coke's Great Romanian Adventure. *The New York Times,* February 26, 1995, sec. 3, pp. 1, 10.

National Geographic Society. *Peoples and Places of the Past: The National Geographic Illustrated Cultural Atlas of the Ancient World.* Washington, DC: National Geographic Society, 1983.

National Geographic Society, Cartographic Division, Dawn of Humans Map and Graphic Pullout. *National Geographic,* February 1997.

Norwegian Board of Health. *Womens Health in Norway.* Oslo: Falch Infotek, for Norwegian Board of Health, 1995. Available at: http://odin.dep.no/shd/publ/health/index.htm.

O'Connor, Mike. Serbs Go Home to Bosnia Village, Defying Leaders. *The New York Times:* International section, December 8, 1996.

Perlez, Jane. *The New York Times:*

  Romania's Communist Legacy: 'Abortion Culture.' International section: November 21, 1996.

  Albania Is Cast Adrift. Week in Review, March 23, 1997, p. 3.

  Ship of Dreams Goes Under in Poland. International section: March 29, 1997, p. 4L.

Pryde, Philip R., ed. *Environmental Resources and Constraints in the Former Soviet Republics.* Boulder, CO: Westview Press, 1995.

Putman, John J. The Search for Modern Humans. *National Geographic,* October 1988, pp. 438–481.

Rai, Shirin, Hilary Pilkington, and Annie Phizacklea, eds. *Women in the Face of Change: The Soviet Union, Eastern Europe and China.* London: Routledge, 1992.

Ratajczyk, Andrzej, and Polfloat Saint-Gobain. *The Warsaw Voice,* April 13, 1997. Available at: http://www.warsawvoice.com.pl/v442/Busi00.html.

Reeves, Joy B. Women, Work, and Family in Former Yugoslavia. Pp. 245–258, in *Family, Women, and Employment in Central-Eastern Europe* (Barbara Lobodzinska, ed.). Westport, CT: Greenwood Press, 1995.

Relethford, John. *The Human Species: An Introduction of Biological Anthropology.* Mountain View, CA: Mayfield, 1990.

Rigaud, Jean-Philippe, Sisse Brimberg (photos), and Norbert Aujoulat (photos). Art Treasures from the Ice Age Lascaux Cave. *National Geographic,* October 1988, pp. 482–499.

Roberts, David. The Ice Man Lone Voyager from the Copper Age. *National Geographic,* June 1993, pp. 36–67.

Sibley, David. *Geographies of Exclusion: Society and Difference in the West.* London and New York: Routledge, 1995.

Simons, Marlise. It's That Feeling of Being Watched. *The New York Times:* International section, February 21, 1997, p. A4.

Slovenian Economic Mirror. An English translation of *Ekonomsko Ogledalo,* derived from data published by Statistical Office of the Republic of Slovenia. Ljubljana: Institute of Macroeconomic Analysis and Development of the Republic of Slovenia, 1996–1999. Available at: http://www.sigov.si:90/zmar/arhiv/ankazalo.html.

Smith, Geoffrey. Euro-What? Pp. 209–212, in *Global Issues 93/94: Annual Editions.* Guilford, CT: Dushkin Publishing Group/Brown & Benchmark, 1993.

Smyser, W. R. Dateline Berlin: Germany's New Vision. Pp. 82–89, in *World Politics 95/96: Annual Editions.* Guilford, CT: Dushkin Publishing Group/Brown & Benchmark, 1995.

Soca'a, Jerzy. Tourism: The Yanks Are Coming (and the Brits, and the Frogs). *The Warsaw Voice:* Business section, April 13, 1997. Available at: http://www.warsawvoice.com.pl/v442/Busi05.html.

Soot, Siim. Estonia. Pp. 95–108, in *Environmental Resources and Constraints in the Former Soviet Republics* (Philip R. Pryde, ed.). Boulder, CO: Westview Press, 1995.

Stanley, Alessandra. The Finns, East-West Headwaiters, Feel Ill-Served. *The New York Times:* International section, March 19, 1997.

Stebelsky, Ihor. Ukraine. Pp. 141–158, in *Environmental Resources and Constraints in the Former Soviet Republics* (Philip R. Pryde, ed.). Boulder, CO: Westview Press, 1995.

Tamas, Veres, webmaster and designer. *Night Life: A Hungarian Night Life Directory.* Budapest: Internet Hungary, 1995. Available at: http://hungary1.com/nights.html.

Terlouw, Kees. A general perspective on the regional development of Europe from 1300 to 1850. *Journal of Historical Geography 22,* no. 2 (1996): 129–146.

Thomas, Alan, Ben Crow, Paul Frenz, Tom Hewitt, Sabrina Kassam, and Steven Treagust. *Third World Atlas,* 2nd ed. Washington, DC: Taylor & Francis, 1994.

Truesdell, Sue. Graphics for Crossette, Barbara. Surprises in the Global Tourism Boom. *The New York Times,* April 12, 1998, p. WK5.

van Heuven, Marten. Rehabilitating Serbia. Pp. 101–105, in *World Politics 95/96 Annual Editions.* Guilford CT: Dushkin Publishing Group/Brown & Benchmark, 1995.

Vesilind, Priit J. Macedonia Caught in the Middle. *National Geographic,* March 1996, pp. 118–139.

Vogeler, Ingolf. State Hegemony in Transforming the Rural Landscapes of Eastern Germany: 1945–1994. *Annals of the Association of American Geographers 86,* no. 3 (1996): 432–458.

Warmenhoven, Henri J. *Global Studies Western Europe,* 2nd ed. Guilford, CT: Dushkin Publishing Group, 1991.

Weaver, Kenneth F. Stones, Bones, and Early Man: The Search for Our Ancestors. *National Geographic,* November 1985, pp. 560–629.

White, Peter T., and Ed Kashi (photos). Crimea: Pearl of a Fallen Empire. *National Geographic,* September 1994, pp. 96–119.

Whitney, Craig R. French Basques Dream of Autonomy. *The New York Times:* International section, February 14, 1997.

Whitney, Craig R. Pity the Poor Eurocrat, Who Can Do No Right. *The New York Times:* International section, Feb/Mar??, 1997.

Wolchik, Sharon L. Women's Issues in Czechoslovakia in the Communist and Postcommunist Periods. Pp. 210–225, in *Women and Politics Worldwide* (Barbara J. Nelson and Najma Chowdhury, eds.). New Haven, CT: Yale University Press, 1994.

Wolf, Eric. *Europe and the People Without History*. Berkeley, CA: Ewha Womans University Press, 1982.

Yanofsky, David. Hungarian Rhapsody: In Budapest, a Thousand Jazzy Flowers Bloom. *Munich Found Magazine* (1996). http://www.munichfound.de/issues/1996/7/articles/Travel/TBudapest.html. Not currently available.

Yarnal, Brent. Socioeconomic Transition and Greenhouse-Gas Emissions from Bulgaria. *The Geographical Review 86*, no. 1 (January 1996): 42–58.

Yugoslavia: A Compilation of Information About Yugoslavia Developed by the Government of the Republic of Yugoslavia (Serbia/Montenegro), 1997. Available at: http://www.yugoslavia.com/Culture/HTML/. Not currently available.

Zygotian, Dork. *Hungarian Report Digest: Resource the International Property Database* (April 1997). http://www.isys.hu/hrep/9704/10.htm. URL no longer available.

Chapter 5 The Russian Federation, Belarus, Caucasia, and Central Asia

Abdinov, Ahmad. Education in Azerbaijan: The Challenges of Transition. *Azerbaijan International*, Winter (1996). Available at: http://azer.com/AIWeb/Categories/Magazinehtml/44.folder/44.articles/44.education.html.

Allworth, Edward A. *The Modern Uzbeks from the Fourteenth Century to the Present*. Stanford, CA: Hoover Institution Press, Stanford University, 1990.

Allworth, Edward, ed. *Central Asia: 130 Years of Russian Dominance, A Historical Overview*, 3rd ed. Durham, NC: Duke University Press, 1994.

Aslund, Anders. *How Russia Become a Market Economy*. Washington, DC: Brookings Institution, 1995.

Azerbaijan International. Comprehensive Azerbaijan Web site. Available at: http://azer.com.

Azerbaijani Oil Consortium. *Oil Consortium Agreement with Azerbaijan*. Washington, DC: American University, 1997. Available at: http://gurukul.ucc.american.edu/TED/AZERI.HTM.

Bacirenko, A. A cartoon in *Krokodil* in Russia. March 1997. Republished in *Transactions* (January 1998): 93.

Barr, Donald A., and Mark G. Field. The Current State of Health Care in the Former Soviet Union: Implications for Health Care Policy and Reform. *American Journal of Public Health* (March 1996): 307–312.

Bateman, Milford, ed. *Business Cultures in Central and Eastern Europe*. Oxford, UK: Butterworth-Heinemann, 1997.

Bater, James H. *Russia and the Post-Soviet Scene: A Geographical Perspective*. London: Arnold, 1996.

Belt, Don. An Arctic Breakthrough. *National Geographic*, February 1997, pp. 36–57.

Berentsen, William H., ed. *Contemporary Europe: A Geographic Analysis*, 7th ed. New York: Wiley, 1997.

Blair, Betty. Azerbaijan International Operating Company: Two Years and Moving Forward, Interview with President Terry Adams. *Azerbaijan International* (Winter 1996). Available at: http://azer.com/AIWeb/Categories/Magazinehtml/44.folder/44.articles/44.aioc.html.

Braund, David. *Georgia in Antiquity: A History of Colchis and Transcaucasian Iberia 550 B.C.–A.D. 562*. Oxford, UK: Clarendon Press, 1994.

Brawer, Moshe. *Atlas of Russia and the Independent Republics*. New York: Simon & Schuster, 1994.

Bridger, Sue, Rebecca Kay, and Kathryn Pinnick. *No More Heroines? Russia, Women and the Market*. London: Routledge, 1996.

Calder, Joshua. *Aral Sea Loss and Cotton* (ARAL Case). Available at: http://gurukul.ucc.american.edu/TED/Aral.htm.

Carmichael, Joel. *An Illustrated History of Russia*. New York: Reyanl & Company, 1960.

Citrin, Daniel A., and Ashok K. Lahiri, eds. *Policy Experience and Issues in the Baltics, Russia, and Other Countries of the Former Soviet Union*. Washington, DC: International Monetary Fund, 1995.

Clark, Miles, and James P. Blair (photos). A Russian Voyage: From the White to the Black Sea. *National Geographic*, June 1994, pp. 114–138.

Clarke, Simon, ed. *Management and Industry in Russia: Formal and Informal Relations in the Period of Transition*. Hants, UK: Edward Elgar, 1995.

Cobb, Charles E., Jr., and Michael S. Yamashita (photos). Storm Watch over the Kurils. *National Geographic*, October 1996, pp. 48–67.

Commander, Simon, and Fabrizio Coricelli, eds. *Unemployment, Restructuring, and the Labor Market in Eastern Europe and Russia*. Washington DC: World Bank, 1995.

Crowe, David M. *A History of the Gypsies of Eastern Europe and Russia*. New York: St. Martin's Press, 1995.

Dadrian, Vahakn N. *History of the Armenian Genocide: Ethnic Conflict from the Balkans to Anatolia to the Caucasus*. Providence, RI: Berghahn Books, 1995.

Davis-Kimball, Jeannine. Warrior Women of the Eurasian Steppes. *Archaeology* (January/February 1997): 44–48.

Dina, Adriana, and Matthew Rowntree. Moldova. Pp. 193–203, in *Environmental Resources and Constraints in the Former Soviet Republics* (Philip R. Pryde, ed.). Boulder, CO: Westview Press, 1995.

Doder, Dusko, and Peter Essick (photos). The Bolshevik Revolution: Experiment That Failed. *National Geographic*, October 1992, pp. 110–130.

Dutkina, Galina. *Moscow Days: Life and Hard Times in the New Russia*. New York: Kodansha International, 1996.

The Economist:
Norisk. January 10, 1998, p. 59.
Supplement on the Caspian. February 7, 1998.

Economist Intelligence Unit. *Russia: Country Report—4th Quarter 1994*. London: Economist Intelligence Unit, 1994.

Edwards, Mike. *National Geographic:*
After the Soviet Union's Collapse: A Broken Empire. March 1993, pp. 2–53.
In Focus: The Fractured Caucasus. February 1996, pp. 126–131.
Sons of Genghis: The Great Khans. February 1997, pp. 2–35.

Edwards, Mike, and Sisse Brimberg (photos). Searching for the Scythians. *National Geographic*, September 1996, pp. 54–79.

Edwards, Mike, and Gerd Ludwig (photos). *National Geographic.*
 Pollution in the Former U.S.S.R.—Lethal Legacy. August 1994, pp. 70–99.
 Living with the Monster Chernobyl. August 1994, pp. 100–115.

Edwards, Mike, and Steve Raymer (photos). *National Geographic:*
 Ukraine. May 1987, pp. 594–631.
 Chernobyl—One Year After. May 1987, pp. 632–653.
 Siberia—In from the Cold. March 1990, pp. 2–39.

Ellis, William S., and David C. Turnley (photos). The Aral: A Soviet Sea Lies Dying. *National Geographic*, February 1990, pp. 70–93.

Environment and Natural Resource Information Network (ENRIN), Central and Eastern Europe (1999). Available at: http://www.grida.no/prog/cee/enrin/index.htm.

Erlandger, Steven. Russian Chief Stays in the Saddle. *The New York Times:* International section, March 23, 1997, p. 4.

Ethnolinguistic Groups in the Caucasas Region—Map. Available at: http://www.geocities.com/southbeach/marina/6150/ethno.jpg.

Fagan, Brian M. *Men of the Earth: An Introduction to World Prehistory.* Boston: Little, Brown, 1974.

Feynman, Richard. *Tuva* on the Internet: http://feynman.com/tuva/.

Frye, Richard N. *The Heritage of Central Asia: From Antiquity to the Turkish Expansion.* Princeton, NJ: Markus Wiener, 1996.

Garrett, Wilbur E., and Steve Raymer (photos). Air Bridge to Siberia. *National Geographic*, October 1988, pp. 504–509.

Georgia Ministry of the Environment. *Georgia: The Black Sea.* 1996. Available at: http://www.parliament.ge/SOEGEO/english/blacksea/blacksea.htm.

Goldman, Milton F. *Global Studies the Soviet Union and Eastern Europe*, 3rd ed. Guilford, CT: Dushkin Publishing Group, 1990.

Goldman, Milton F. *Global Studies Russia, the Eurasian Republics, and Central/Eastern Europe*, 6th ed. Guilford, CT: Dushkin Publishing Group/Brown & Benchmark, 1996.

Goldman, Milton F. *Global Studies Russia, the Eurasian Republics, and Central/Eastern Europe*, 7th ed. Guilford, CT: Dushkin/McGraw-Hill, 1999.

Goldstein, Darra. *The Georgian Feast: The Vibrant Culture and Savory Food of the Republic of Georgia.* New York: HarperCollins, 1993.

Gore, Rick, Kenneth Garrett (photos), and John Sibbick (art). The Dawn of Humans: Expanding Worlds. *National Geographic*, May 1997.

Harcave, Sidney. *Russia: A History.* Chicago: Lippincott, 1959.

Haub, Carl. *Population Change in the Former Soviet Republics, Population Bulletin 49*, no. 4 (December). Washington, DC: Population Reference Bureau, 1994.

Hodgson, Bryan, and Sarah Leen (photos). Russia's Land of Fire and Ice: Kamchatka. *National Geographic*, April 1994, pp. 42–67.

Hornocker, Maurice, and Marc Moritsch (photos). Siberian Tigers. *National Geographic*, February 1997, pp. 101–109.

Hunter, Shireen. Islam in Post-Independence Central Asia: Internal and External Dimensions. *Journal of Islamic Studies 7*, no. 2 (1996): 287–303.

Jacobsen, Charles W. *Oriental Rugs: A Complete Guide.* Tokyo: Charles E. Tuttle, 1979 (1962).

Judge, Joesph. Peoples of the Arctic. *National Geographic 163*, no. 2 (1983): 144–149.

Kerblay, Basile. *Modern Soviet Society* (translated by Rupert Swyer). New York: Pantheon, 1983.

Kochurov, Boris L. European Russia. Pp. 41–60, in *Environmental Resources and Constraints in the Former Soviet Republics* (Philip R. Pryde, ed.). Boulder, CO: Westview Press, 1995.

Koenig, Sarah. In Russia, Teaching Tiny Capitalists to Compete. *The New York Times*, February 9, 1997, p. 3.

Kramer, Mark. *Travels with a Hungry Bear: A Journey into the Russian Heartland.* Boston: Houghton Mifflin, 1996.

Leadbetter, Ron. Tour of Soviet Lands Rewards the Resolute. *The Knoxville News-Sentinel*, January 19, 1997, pp. E4, E7.

Lempert, David H. *Daily Life in a Crumbling Empire: The Absorption of Russia into the World Economy*, Vol. 1. Boulder, CO: East European Monographs, 1996.

Lenczowski, George. The Caspian Oil and Gas Basin: A New Source of Wealth? *Middle East Policy 5*, no. 1 (1997): 111–119.

Mandelbaum, Michael. Westernizing Russia and China. *Foreign Affairs* (May/June 1997): 80–95.

Micklin, Philip. Turkmenistan. Pp. 275–288, in *Environmental Resources and Constraints in the Former Soviet Republics* (Philip R. Pryde, ed.). Boulder, CO: Westview Press, 1995.

Minakir, Pavel A., and Gregory L. Freeze, eds. *The Russian Far East: An Economic Handbook.* Armonk, NY: M. E. Sharpe, 1994.

Novello, Adriano Alpago, Giulio Jeni, Agopik Mauoukian, Alberto Pensa, Gabriella Uluhogian, and B. Levon. *The Armenians: 2000 Years of Art and Architecture.* Paris: Bookking International, 1995 (1985).

Olcott, Martha Brill. *The Kazakhs*, 2nd ed. Stanford, CA: Hoover Institution Press, Stanford University, 1995 (1987).

Olson, Robert. The Kurdish Question and Chechnya: Turkish and Russian Foreign Policies Since the Gulf War. *Mid East Policy 4*, no. 3 (1996): 106–118.

Pakulski, Jan. *World Bank Supports Water Supply Project Near Aral Sea Disaster Zone in Uzbekistan*, Press release from the World Bank. Washington, DC: World Bank, 1996. Available at: http://www.worldbank.org/html/extdr/extme/1119.htm.

Piirainen, Timo. *Towards A New Social Order in Russia.* Aldershot, UK: Dartmouth, 1997.

Pilkington, Hilary, ed. *Gender, Generation and Identity in Contemporary Russia.* London and New York: Routledge, 1996.

Pope, Hugh. Great Game II: Oil Companies Rush into the Caucasus to Tap the Caspian. *The Wall Street Journal*, April 25, 1997, pp. A1, A8.

Pryde, Philip R., ed. *Environmental Resources and Constraints in the Former Soviet Republics.* Boulder, CO: Westview Press, 1995.

Pryde, Philip R. Russia: An Overview of the Deterioration. Pp. 25–40, in *Environmental Resources and Constraints in the Former Soviet Republics* (Philip R. Pryde, ed.). Boulder, CO: Westview Press, 1995.

Pushkareva, Natalia. *Women in Russian History from the Tenth* to the Twentieth Century (translated and edited by Eve Levin). Armonk, NY: M. E. Sharpe, 1997.

Putman, John J. The Search for Modern Humans. National Geographic, October 1988, pp. 438–481.

Quigley, Howard B., and Maurice G. Hornocker (photos). Saving Siberia's Tigers. National Geographic, July 1993, pp. 38–47.

Rai, Shirin, Hilary Pilkington, and Annie Phizacklea, eds. Women in the Face of Change: The Soviet Union, Eastern Europe and China. London: Routledge, 1992.

Rasputin, Valentin. Siberia, Siberia (translated by Margaret Winchell and Gerald Mikkelson). Evanston, IL: Northwestern University Press, 1996.

Raymer, Steve. The Bolshevik Revolution: Experiment That Failed. National Geographic, December 1993, pp. 96–121.

Remnick, David. Moscow: The New Revolution. National Geographic, April 1997, pp. 78–103.

Renne, Tanya, ed. Ana's Land: Sisterhood in Eastern Europe. Boulder, CO: Westview Press, 1997.

Richards, Lynn. Georgia. Pp. 205–220, in Environmental Resources and Constraints in the Former Soviet Republics (Philip R. Pryde, ed.). Boulder, CO: Westview Press, 1995.

Richards, Susan. Epics of Everyday Life: Encounters in a Changing Russia. New York: Viking, 1991.

Rotkirch, Anna, and Elina Haavio-Mannila, eds. Women's Voices in Russia Today. Aldershot, UK: Dartmouth, 1996.

Russian National Tourist Office. Baikal: The Pearl of Siberia, 1996–1997. Available at: http://www.interknowledge.com/russia/baikal01.htm.

Rythkeu, Yuri, and Dean Conger (photos). People of the Long Spring. National Geographic 163, no. 2 (1983): 206–223.

Scherbakova, Anna, and Scott Monroe. The Urals and Siberia. Pp. 61–78, in Environmental Resources and Constraints in the Former Soviet Republics (Philip R. Pryde, ed.). Boulder, CO: Westview Press, 1995.

Siberia Culture Economy Business, 1996. http://ieie.nsc.ru. Site no longer up.

Smith, David R. Kazakhstan. Pp. 251–274, in Environmental Resources and Constraints in the Former Soviet Republics (Philip R. Pryde, ed.). Boulder, CO: Westview Press, 1995.

Soros Foundation. Central Eurasian Projects. Available at: http://www.soros.org/ceu.html and http://www.soros.org/central_eurasia.html.

Specter, Michael. The Cloakrooms of Russia, the Dens of Dragons. The New York Times: International section, November 21, 1996.

Stanley, Alessandra. Democracy in Russia: Women's Lib Is Just Cosmetic. The New York Times, May 11, 1997.

Stebelsky, Ihor. Ukraine. Pp. 141–158, in Environmental Resources and Constraints in the Former Soviet Republics (Philip R. Pryde, ed.). Boulder, CO: Westview Press, 1995.

Stewart, John G. Student Attitudes Toward Systemic Corruption: Teaching Ethics in the Republic of Georgia. Journal of Public Administration Education 3 (1997): 1–12.

Strand, Holly. The Russian Far East. Pp. 79–94, in Environmental Resources and Constraints in the Former Soviet Republics (Philip R. Pryde, ed.). Boulder, CO: Westview Press, 1995.

Swietochowski, Tadeusz. Russia and Azerbaijan: A Borderland in Transition. New York: Columbia University Press, 1995.

Thompson, Jon, and Cary Wolinsky (photos). Inside the Kremlin and Its Imperial Treasures. National Geographic, January 1990, pp. 62–105.

Tolkatchev, A. Caspian Sea-Level Rise: An Environmental Emergency. Paris: IOC Secretariat, UNESCO, 1996. Available at: http://www.nbi.ac.uk/psmsl/gb2/tolkatchev.html.

United Nations Development Programme. Yerevan, 1996. Armenia Human Development Report 1996. Yerevan, Armenia: UNDP, 1996. Available at: http://www.arminco.com/Armenia/HDR.

United Nations Environment Program, 1999. Available at: http://www.grida.no/index.htm.

Valesyan, Armen L. Armenia. Pp. 221–234, in Environmental Resources and Constraints in the Former Soviet Republics (Philip R. Pryde, ed.). Boulder, CO: Westview Press, 1995.

Vaudon, Jean-Pierre, and Pierre Perrin (photos). Last Days of the Gulag? National Geographic, March 1990, pp. 40–49.

Vesilind, Priit J., and Dennis Chamberlin (photos). Kaliningrad: Coping with a German Past and a Russian Future. National Geographic, March 1997, pp. 110–123.

White, Peter T., and Ed Kashi (photos). Crimea: Pearl of a Fallen Empire. National Geographic, September 1994, pp. 96–119.

Wolfson, Zeev, and Zia Daniell. Azerbaijan. Pp. 235–250, in Environmental Resources and Constraints in the Former Soviet Republics (Philip R. Pryde, ed.). Boulder, CO: Westview Press, 1995.

Yergin, Daniel, and Thane Gustafson. Russia 2010 and What It Means for the World. New York: Random House, 1993.

Zadeh, Aziza Mustafa, with Betty Blair. Aziza Mustafa Zadeh: Jazz, Mugam and Other Essentials of My Life. Azerbaijan International, Winter 1996. Available at: http://azer.com/AIWeb/Categories/MusicSection/AudioPages/Aziza/aziza.html.

Chapter 6 North Africa and Southwest Asia

Abercrombie, Thomas J., and Jodi Cobb (photos). Jordan: Kingdom in the Middle. National Geographic, February 1984, pp. 236–267.

Abercrombie, Thomas J., and Steve Raymer (photos). The Persian Gulf: Living in Harm's Way. National Geographic, May 1988, pp. 648–671.

Abu-Lughod, Lila. Islamist Notions of Democracy. Pp. 269–282, in Political Islam (Joel Beinin and Joe Stork, eds.). Berkeley: University of California Press, 1997.

Afkhami, Mahnaz, ed. Faith and Freedom: Women's Human Rights in the Muslim World. Syracuse, NY: Syracuse University Press, 1995.

Ajayi, J. F. Ade, and Michael Crowder, eds. Historical Atlas of Africa. London: Longman, 1985.

Alireza, Marianne, and Jodi Cobb (photos). Women of Saudi Arabia. National Geographic, October 1987, pp. 422–453.

Allen, Thomas B., and Reza (photos). Turkey Struggles for Balance. National Geographic, May 1994, pp. 2–36.

Al Munajjed, Mona. Women in Saudi Arabia Today. New York: St. Martin's Press, 1997.

Amuzegar, Jahangir. Adjusting to Sanctions. Foreign Affairs (May/June 1997): 31–41.

Arab World Online. *Country Profiles.* 1996–1997. Available at: http://www.awo.net/country/overview.

Atiyeh, George N., and Ibrahim M. Oweiss, eds. *Arab Civilization: Challenges and Responses—Studies in Honor of Constantine K. Zurayk.* Albany: State University of New York Press, 1988.

Badran, Margot. *Feminists, Islam, and Nation: Gender and the Making of Modern Egypt.* Princeton, NJ: Princeton University Press, 1995.

Bascom, Johnathan. The Peasant Economy of Refugee Resettlement in Eastern Sudan. *Annals of the Association of American Geographers 83,* no. 2 (1993): 320–346.

Beinin, Joel, and Joe Stork, eds. *Political Islam: Essays from Middle East Report.* Berkeley: University of California Press, 1997.

Bekkar, Rabia. Interview with Hannah Davis Taieb. Islamist Notions of Democracy. Pp. 283–291, in *Political Islam* (Joel Beinin and Joe Stork, eds.). Berkeley: University of California Press, 1997.

Belt, Don, and Annie Griffiths Belt (photos). Israel's Galilee: Living in the Shadow of Peace. *National Geographic,* June 1995, pp. 62–87.

Benton, Kathy. Many Contradictions: Women and Islamists in Turkey. *The Muslim World 86,* no. 2 (April 1996): 106–127.

Bernstein, Henry, Ben Crow, Maureen Mackintosh, and Charlotte Martin. *The Food Question: Profits versus People.* New York: Monthly Review Press, 1990.

Blake, Gerald, John Dewdney, and Jonathan Mitchell. *The Cambridge Atlas of the Middle East and North Africa.* Cambridge, UK: Cambridge University Press, 1987.

Bosworth, C.E., Charles Issawi, Roger Savory, and A.L. Udovitch, eds. *The Islamic World from Classical to Modern Times: Essays in Honor of Bernard Lewis.* Princeton, NJ: Darwin Press, 1989.

Boulding, Elise, ed. *Building Peace in the Middle East: Challenges for States and Civil Societies.* Boulder, CO: Lynne Rienner, 1993.

Boustani, Rafic, and Philippe Fargues. *The Atlas of the Arab World Geopolitics and Society.* New York: Facts on File, 1991.

Brett, Michael, and Elizabeth Fentress. *The Berbers.* London: Blackwell, 1996.

Brooks, Geraldine. *Nine Parts of Desire: The Hidden World of Islamic Women.* New York: Anchor Books/Doubleday, 1995.

Brzezinski, Zbigniew, Brent Scowcroft, and Richard Murphy. Differentiated Containment. *Foreign Affairs* (May/June 1997): 20–30.

Burr, J. Millard, and Robert O. Collins. *Requiem for the Sudan: War, Drought, and Disaster Relief on the Nile.* Boulder, CO: Westview Press, 1995.

Butt, Gerald. *A Rock and a Hard Place: Origins of Arab-Western Conflict in the Middle East.* London: HarperCollins, 1994.

Campbell, Colin J., and Jean H. Laherrère. The End of Cheap Oil. *Scientific American,* March 1998, pp. 78–83.

Caputo, Robert. Tradegy Stalks the Horn of Africa. *National Geographic,* August 1993, pp. 88–122.

Chapman, Graham P., and Kathleen M. Baker, eds. *The Changing Geography of Africa and the Middle East.* London: Routledge, 1992.

CNN staff. 30 Villagers Butchered in Algeria. *CNN Interactive—World News,* May 15, 1997. Available at: http://www.cnn.com/WORLD/9705/15/briefs/algeria.massacre/index.html.

Cobb, Charles E., Jr., and Robert Caputo (photos). Eritrea Wins the Peace. *National Geographic,* June 1996, pp. 82–105.

Country Profiles and Other Information. 1996–1997. Available at: http://www.arab.net.

Dathorne, O. R. *Asian Voyages: Two Thousand Years of Constructing the Other.* Westport, CT: Bergin & Garvey, 1996.

Davis, Diana. Gender, Indigenous Knowledge, and Pastoral Resource Use in Morocco. *The Geographical Review 86,* no. 2 (1996): 284–288.

Deeb, Marius K. Militant Islam and Its Critics: The Case of Libya. Pp. 187–197, in *Islamism and Secularism in North Africa* (John Reedy, ed.). New York: St. Martin's Press, 1994.

de Villiers, Marq, and Sheila Hirtle. *Into Africa: A Journey Through the Ancient Empires.* Toronto: Key Porter Books, 1997.

Doubilet, David. The Desert Sea. *National Geographic,* November 1993, pp. 60–87.

Drake, Christine. Water Resource Conflicts in the Middle East. *Journal of Geography* (January/February 1997): 4–12.

The Economist:
The Blessings of Religion. April 9, 1994, p. 45.
Egypt: Better and Worse. April 9, 1994, p. 48.

El-Baz, Farouk, with James P. Blair and Calude E. Petrone (photos). Finding a Pharaoh's Funeral Bark. *National Geographic,* April 1988, pp. 513–533.

Ellis, William S., and Steve McCurry (photos). Africa's Sahel: The Stricken Land. *National Geographic,* August 1987, pp. 140–179.

El-Naggar, Said, ed. *Economic Development of the Arab Countries: Selected Issues.* Washington, DC: International Monetary Fund, 1993.

El-Rian, Mohamed A. Middle Eastern Economies' External Environment: What Lies Ahead? *Middle East Policy 4,* no. 3 (March 1996): 137–146.

El Saadawi, Nawal. *The Nawal El Saadawi Reader.* London and New York: Zed Books, 1997.

Emmett, Chad F. The Capital Cities of Jerusalem. *The Geographical Review 86,* no. 2 (1996): 233–258.

Endale, DersEh. *Changing Patterns of Employment and Unemployment in Africa. World Development Studies 7.* Helsinki: United Nations University World Institute for Development Economics Research, 1995.

Entelis, John P., ed. *Islam, Democracy, and the State in North Africa.* Bloomington: Indiana University Press, 1997.

Esposito, John. Political Islam: Beyond the Green Menace. Pp. 79–84, in *Developing World 97/98: Annual Editions.* Guilford, CT: Dushkin Publishing Group/Brown & Benchmark, 1997 (1994).

Euro Mediterranean Sciences and Technology Space. *European Union Development Plans: Mediterranean Area.* 1996–1998 (updated 1999). Available at: http://www.jrc.es/projects/euromed/EC/DGXI/DGXI.html#3.

Fagan, Brian M. *Men of the Earth: An Introduction to World Prehistory.* Boston: Little, Brown, 1974.

Faksh, Mahmud A. *The Future of Islam in the Middle East: Fundamentalism in Egypt, Algeria, and Saudi Arabia.* Westport, CT: Praeger, 1997.

Falah, Ghazi. The 1948 Israeli-Palestinian War and Its Aftermath: The Transformation and De-signification of Palestine's Cultural Landscape. *Annals of the American Association of Geographers 86*, no. 2 (1996): 256–285.

Fluehr-Lobban, Carolyn. *Islamic Society in Practice.* Gainesville: University Press of Florida, 1994.

Friedman, Thomas L. The War Within. *The New York Times,* May 15, 1997. Available at: http://search.nytimes.com/search/daily/bin/fastweb?getdoc+site+site+91+13+wAAA+%22The%7EWar%7EWithin%22%7EMay%7E15.

Frye, Richard N. *The Heritage of Central Asia: From Antiquity to the Turkish Expansion.* Princeton, NJ: Markus Wiener, 1996.

Fuller, Graaham E., and Ian O. Lesser. Persian Gulf Myths. *Foreign Affairs* (May/June 1997): 42–52.

Furley, Oliver, ed. *Conflict in Africa,* Tauris Academic Studies. London: I. B. Tauris, 1995.

Ghadbian, Najib. *Democratization and the Islamist Challenge in the Arab World.* Boulder, CO: Westview Press, 1997.

Ghoreishi, Ahmad, and Dariush Sahedi. Prospects for Regime Change in Iran. *Middle East Policy 5,* no. 1 (January 1997): 85–101.

Goldschmidt, Arthur, Jr. *A Concise History of the Middle East,* 4th ed. Boulder, CO: Westview Press, 1991.

Gorkin, Michael, and Rafiqa Othman. *Three Mothers, Three Daughters: Palestinian Women's Stories.* Berkeley: University of California Press, 1996.

Gourevitch, Philip. The Vanishing: How the Congo Became Zaire, and Zaire Became the Congo. *The New Yorker,* June 2, 1997, pp. 50–53.

Greenberg, Joel. Palestinian Maps for a State That Doesn't Exist. *The New York Times,* June 27, 1997. Available at: http://search.nytimes.com/search/daily/bin/fastweb?getdoc+site+site+27060+76+wAAA+June%7E27.

Gross, Joan, David McMurray, and Ted Swedenburg. Rai, Rap, and Ramadan Nights: Franco-Maghribi Cultural Identities. Pp. 257–268, in *Political Islam* (Joel Beinin and Joe Stork, eds.). Berkeley: University of California Press, 1997.

Haddad, Yvonne Yazbeck, and John L. Esposito, eds. *Islam, Gender and Social Change.* New York and Oxford, UK: Oxford University Press, 1998.

Hapgood, Fred, and George Steinmetz (photos). The Quest for Oil. *National Geographic,* August 1989, pp. 226–259.

Held, Colbert C. *Middle East Patterns: Places, Peoples, and Politics,* 2nd ed. Boulder, CO: Westview Press, 1994.

Hobbs, Joseph J. Speaking with People in Egypt's St. Katherine National Park. *The Geographical Review,* January 1996, pp. 1–21.

Hohlfelder, Robert L., Bill Curtsinger (photos), and J. Robert Teringo (paintings). Ceasarea Maritima: Herod the Great's City on the Sea. *National Geographic,* February 1987, pp. 261–280.

Hutchinson, Sharon E. *Nuer Dilemmas: Coping with Money, War and the State.* Berkeley: University of California Press, 1996.

The Indian Express staff. Quick Takes—Forty Ultras Killed in Algeria. *The Indian Express,* March 14, 1997. http://www.expressindia.com/ie/daily/19970314/07350403.html. No longer available.

Jehl, Douglas. *The New York Times:*
Yes, This Is the Nile, but Don't Go Near the Water. International section: March 25, 1997.
Under the Cairo Sun, the Leaden Skies Can Kill. International section: April 4, 1997.
Qatar's Treasure-Trove of Gas. July 23, 1997, pp. 1, 6.
Egypt's Farmers Resist End of Freeze on Rents. December 27, 1997, p. A5.

Joffe, George, ed. *North Africa: Nation, State, and Region.* London: Routledge, 1993.

Joffe, George. The Conflict in the Western Sahara. Pp. 110–133, in *Conflict in Africa,* Tauris Academic Studies (Oliver Furley, ed.). London: I. B. Tauris, 1995.

Joyce, Miriam. *The Sultanate of Oman: A Twentieth Century History.* Westport, CT: Praeger, 1995.

Kane, Eileen. *Seeing for Yourself: Research Handbook for Girls' Education in Africa.* Washington, DC: World Bank, 1995.

Katz, Cindi. Sow What You Know: The Struggle for Social Reproduction in Rural Sudan. *Annals of the Association of American Geographers 81,* no. 3 (1991): 488–514.

Kazemi, Farhad, and R.D. McChesney, eds. *A Way Prepared: Essays on Islamic Culture in Honor of Richard Bayly Winder.* New York: New York University Press, 1988.

Kendall, Timothy, Enrico Ferorelli (photos) and James M. Gurney (paintings). Kingdom of Kush. *National Geographic,* November 1990, pp. 96–125.

Keohane, Alan. *Bedouin: Nomads of the Desert.* London: Kyle Cathie Limited, 1994.

King, Russell, Lindsay Proudfoot, and Bernard Smith, eds. *The Mediterranean: Environment and Society.* London: Arnold, 1997.

Kinzer, Stephen. *The New York Times:*
Turkey Finds European Union Door Slow to Open. International section: February 23, 1997.
Turkey's Military Gives Islamic Leaders a Warning in Defense of Secularism. March 2, 1997, p. A6.
Kurdish Rebels in Turkey Are Down but Not Out. March 3, 1997, pp. 1, 3.
Europeans Shut the Door on Turkey's Membership in Union. March 27, 1997, p. A13.
Restoring the Fertile Crescent to Its Former Glory. International section: May 29, 1997.
Istanbul Journal: Inhale the Pleasure of an Unhurried Ottoman Past. International section: June 10, 1997.

Kirk, Martha. *Green Sands: My Five Years in the Saudi Desert.* Lubbock: Texas Tech University Press, 1994.

Kramer, Gudrun. Islamist Notions of Democracy. Pp. 71–82, in *Political Islam* (Joel Beinin and Joe Stork, eds.). Berkeley: University of California Press, 1997.

Kwamena-poh, M., J. Tosh, R. Waller, and M. Tidy. *African History in Maps.* Harlow, Essex, UK: Longman, 1987 (1982).

Lancaster, John. A Ray of Hope in Bloody Algeria. *The Washington Post,* June 13, 1997.

Langewiesche, William. *Sahara Unveiled: A Journey Across the Desert.* New York: Pantheon, 1996.

LaTeef, Nelda. *Women of Lebanon: Interviews with Champions for Peace.* Jefferson, NC: McFarland, 1997.

Lewis, Bernard. *The Middle East: A Brief History of the Last 2000 Years.* New York: Scribner's, 1995.

Lewis, Bernard. *The Middle East: 2000 Years of History from the Rise of Christianity to the Present Day.* London: Weidenfeld & Nicolson, 1995.

Lhote, Henri, and Kazuyoshi Nomachi (photos). Oasis of Art in the Sahara. *National Geographic,* August 1987, pp. 180–191.

Lightfoot, Dale R., and James A. Miller. Sijilmassa: The Rise and Fall of a Walled Oasis in Medieval Morocco. *Annals of the Association of American Geographers 86,* no. 1 (1996): 78–101.

Lindholm, Charles. *The Islamic Middle East: An Historical Anthropology.* Oxford, UK: Blackwell, 1996.

Long, David E. *The Kingdom of Saudi Arabia.* Gainesville: University Press of Florida, 1997.

Mackey, Sandra, with W. Scott Harrop. *The Iranians: Persia, Islam and the Soul of a Nation.* New York: Dutton, 1996.

Maier, John. *Desert Songs: Western Images of Morocco and Moroccoan Images of the West.* Albany: State University of New York Press, 1996.

Mairson, Alan, and Annie Griffiths Belt (photos). The Three Faces of Jerusalem. *National Geographic,* April 1996, pp. 2–51.

Majok, Aggrey Ayuen, and Calvin W. Schwabe. *Development Among Africa's Migratory Pastoralists.* Westport, CT: Bergin & Garvey, 1996.

Malik, Lynda P. Social and Cultural Determinants of the Gender Gap in Higher Education in the Islamic World. *Journal of Asian and African Studies 30,* nos. 3–4 (1995): 181–193.

Malley, Robert. *The Call from Algeria: Third Worldism, Revolution, and the Turn to Islam.* Berkeley: University of California Press, 1996.

Mama, Amina. *Beyond the Masks: Race, Gender and Subjectivity.* London: Routledge, 1995.

Manners, Ian R. Constructing the Image of a City: The Representation of Constantinople in Christopher Buondelmonti's Liber Insularum Archipelagi. *Annals of the Association of American Geographers 87,* no. 1 (1997): 72–102.

Marcus, Amy Dockser. *The Wall Street Journal:*
 Rising Sphinx: Egypt Quickly Turns an Investment Famine into Times of Plenty. April 10, 1997, pp. 1, A6.
 The Veil Is Old Hat, but Muslim Women Give It New Vogue. May 1, 1997, pp. 1, A6.

Margulies, Ronnie, and Ergin Yildizoglu. The Resurgence of Islam and the Welfare Party in Turkey. Pp. 144–153, in *Political Islam* (Joel Beinin and Joe Stork, eds.). Berkeley: University of California Press, 1997.

Marsden, Peter. *The Taliban: War, Religion and the New Order in Afghanistan.* London and New York: Zed Books, 1998.

Masters, C. D., D. H. Root, and R. M. Turner. *World of Petroleum,* February 1999. Available at: http://energy.er. usgs.gov/products/papers/World_oil/source/index.htm.

Meiselas, Susan, with Martin van Bruinessen. *Kurdistan: In the Shadow of History.* New York: Random House, 1997.

Metz, Helen Chapin, ed. *Algeria: A Country Study.* Washington, DC: Library of Congress, 1994.

Metz, Helen Chapin, ed. *Persian Gulf States: Country Studies.* Washington, DC: Library of Congress, 1994.

Miller, G. Tyler, Jr. *Living in the Environment: Principles, Connections, and Solutions,* 8th ed. Belmont, CA: Wadsworth, 1994.

Miller, Peter, and Victor R. Boswell, Jr. (photos). Riddle of the Pyramid Boats. *National Geographic,* April 1988, pp. 534–550.

Monshipouri, Mahmood. Review article: Islamism, Civil Society, and the Democracy Conundrum. *The Muslim World 87* (January 1997): 54–66.

Moors, Annelies. *Women, Property and Islam: Palestinian Experiences, 1920–1990.* Cambridge, UK: Cambridge University Press, 1995.

Nanji, Azim A. *The Muslim Almanac: A Reference Work on the History, Faith, Culture and Peoples of Islam.* New York: Gale Research, 1996.

O'Ballance, Edgar. *The Kurdish Struggle 1920–94.* New York: St. Martin's Press, 1996.

O'Conner, Anthony. *Poverty in Africa: A Geographical Approach.* London: Belhaven Press, 1991.

Olcott, Martha Brill. *Central Asia's New States: Independence, Foreign Policy, and Regional Security.* Washington, DC: United States of Peace Press, 1996.

Olson, Robert. The Kurdish Question and Chechnya: Turkish and Russian Foreign Policies Since the Gulf War. *Mid East Policy 4,* no. 3 (March 1996): 106–118.

Oneworld. *Western Sahara.* 1996. Available at: http://www.oneworld.org/guides/sahara/land.html.

Organization of American Historians. *Restoring Women to History* (rev. ed.), *Teaching Packets for Integrating Women's History into Courses on Africa, Asia, Latin America and the Caribbean, and the Middle East.* Bloomington, IN: Organization of American Historians, 1990.

Ossman, Susan. *Picturing Casablanca: Portrait of Power in a Modern City.* Berkeley: University of California Press, 1994.

OXFAM. *Living in the Refugee Camps.* 1996. Available at: http://heiwww.unige.ch/arso/05–3.htm.

Pampanini, Andrea H. *Cities from the Arabian Desert: The Building of Jubail and Yanbu in Saudi Arabia.* Westport, CT: Praeger, 1997.

Pearl, Daniel. Yemen Steers a Path Toward Democracy with Some Surprises. *The Wall Street Journal,* March 28, 1997, pp. 1, A11.

Pope, Hugh. Crossroads City: Istanbul's Location Again Makes It Crucial to the Entire Region. *The Wall Street Journal.* March 27, 1997, pp. 1, A10.

Prussin, Labelle. *African Nomadic Architecture: Space, Place and Gender.* Washington, DC, and London: Smithsonian Institution Press and the National Museum of African Art, 1995.

Raffer, Kunibert, and M. A. Mohamed Salih, eds. *The Least Developed and the Oil-Rich Arab Countries: Dependence, Interdependence or Patronage?* New York: St. Martin's Press, 1992.

Ramsay, E. Jeffress. *Africa: Global Studies,* 6th ed. Guilford, CT: Dushkin Publishing Group/Brown & Benchmark, 1995.

Randal, Jonathan C. *After Such Knowledge, What Forgiveness? My Encounters with Kurdistan.* New York: Farrar, Strauss & Giroux, 1997.

Raven, Susan. *Rome in Africa*, 3rd ed. London: Routledge, 1993.

Rice, Michael. *The Archaeology of the Arabian Gulf c.5000–323 B.C.* London: Routledge, 1994.

Roberts, David, and Jose Azel (photos). Mali's Dogon: Below the Cliff of Tombs. *National Geographic*, October 1990, pp. 100–128.

Roberts, David, and Kenneth Garrett (photos). Age of Pyramids. *National Geographic*, January 1995, pp. 2–67.

Rogers, Alisdair. *Peoples and Cultures.* Oxford, UK: Oxford University Press, 1992.

Roudi, Farzaneh. Oman. *Population Today* (May 1997): 7.

Roudi, Farzaneh, and Lori Ashford. *Men and Family Planning in Africa.* Washington, DC: Population Reference Bureau, 1996.

Ruedy, John, ed. *Islamism and Secularism in North Africa.* New York: St. Martin's Press, 1994.

Salahaddeen, Mohamed. *The Turkish Clash of Secularism and Sharia in Al Madina.* February 24, 1997. Available at: http://www.arab.net/arabview/articles/salahaddeen3.html.

Segal, Aaron. Future Options for Jerusalem. *Journal of Asian and African Studies 30*, nos. 3–4 (1995): 194–210.

Serageldin, Ismail. Faith, Development and the Built Environment of Muslims. Pp. 465–474, in *The Muslim Almanac* (Azim A. Nanji, ed.). New York: Gales Research, 1996.

Severy, Merle, and James L. Stanfield (photos). The World of Suleyman the Magnificant. *National Geographic*, November 1987, pp. 552–601.

Shahin, Emad Eldin. *Political Ascent: Contemporary Islamic Movements in North Africa.* Boulder, CO: Westview Press, 1997.

Simons, Geoff. *Libya: The Struggle for Survival*, 2nd ed. London: Macmillan, 1996 (1993).

Slyomovics, Susan. "Hassiba Ben Bouali, If You Could See Our Algeria": Women and Public Space in Algeria. Pp. 211–219, in *Political Islam* (Joel Beinin and Joe Stork, eds.). Berkeley: University of California Press, 1997.

Smith, Bruce D. *The Emergence of Agriculture.* New York: Scientific American Library, 1995.

Sonbol, Amira El Azhary, ed. *Women, the Family, and Divorce Laws in Islamic History.* Syracuse, NY: Syracuse University Press, 1996.

Spencer, William. *Global Studies: The Middle East*, 6th ed. Guilford, CT: Dushkin Publishing Group/Brown & Benchmark, 1996.

Spencer, William. *Global Studies: The Middle East*, 7th ed. Guilford, CT: Dushkin/McGraw-Hill, 1998.

Talhami, Ghada. Introduction to Women in the Islamic Maelstrom. *The Muslim World 86*, no. 2 (April 1996): 103–105.

Tessler, Mark, and Jolene Jesse. Gender and Support for Islamist Movements: Evidence from Egypt, Kuwait and Palestine. *The Muslim World 86*, no. 2 (April 1996): 200–217.

Theroux, Peter, and Ed Kashi (photos). Syria: Behind the Mask. *National Geographic*, July 1996, pp. 106–131.

Theroux, Peter, and Reza (photos). Cairo: Clamorous Heart of Egypt. *National Geographic*, April 1993, pp. 38–69.

Times of India, staff writers. 5 Women Killed in Algeria for Not Covering Their Heads. *The Times of India*, January 15, 1997. http://www.timesofindia.com/150197/home4.htm. No longer available.

Tunisia. 1999. Available at: http://www.tunisiaonline.com.

U.S. Department of State. *Western Sahara Country Report on Human Rights Practices for 1996.* Washington, DC: Bureau of Democracy, Human Rights, and Labor, 1997. Available at: http://www.state.gov/www/global/human_rights/1996_hrp_report/wsahara.html.

Vesilind, Priit J., and Ed Kashi (photos). Water: The Middle East's Critical Resource. *National Geographic*, May 1993, pp. 38–72.

Virtual Tours of the Maghreb. 1997. Available at: http://www.maghreb.net/countries.

Walther, Wiebke. *Woman in Islam.* Montclair, NJ: Abner Schram, 1981.

Washington Post staff writer. Algeria's Nightmare. *The Washington Post*, June 8, 1997, p. C08.

Wenner, Manfred W. *The Yemen Arab Republic: Development and Change in an Ancient Land.* Boulder, CO: Westview Press, 1991.

Wescoat, James L., Jr. Muslim Contributions to Geography and Environmental Ethics: The Challenges of Comparison and Pluralism. Pp. 91–116, in *Space, Place, and Environmental Ethics* (Andrew Light and Jonathan M. Smith, eds.). Lanham, MD: Rowman & Littlefield, 1997.

Wescoat, James L., Jr. The 'Right of Thirst' for Animals in Islamic Law: A Comparative Approach. *Environment and Planning D: Society and Space 13* (1995): 637–654.

Western Sahara Factbook. 1996. Available at: http://www.arabworld.com/factbook/eh.htm.

Weyland, Petra. *Inside the Third World Village.* London: Routledge, 1993.

Wikan, Unni. *Tomorrow, God Willing: Self-Made Destinies in Cairo.* Chicago: University of Chicago Press, 1996.

World Resources Institute with the United Nations Environment and Development Programmes. *World Resources 1994–95.* New York: Oxford University Press, 1994.

Zwingle, Erla, and Bruno Barbey (photos). Morocco: North Africa's Timeless Mosaic. *National Geographic*, October 1996, pp. 98–125.

Chapter 7 Sub-Saharan Africa

Africa Music: Zimbabwe, 1997. Available at: http://www.africaonline.com/AfricaOnline/music/zimbabwe.html.

Ajayi, J. F. Ade, and Michael Crowder, eds. *Historical Atlas of Africa.* London: Longman, 1985.

Ajayi, J. F. Ade, and J. D. Y. Peel, eds. *People and Empires in African History: Essays in Memory of Michael Crowder.* London: Longman, 1992.

Altman, Lawrence K. Parts of Africa Showing H.I.V. in 1 in 4 Adults. *The New York Times*, June 24, 1998, pp. 1, A6.

Atsimadja, Felicite Awassi. The Changing Geography of Central Africa. Pp. 52–79, in *The Changing Geography of Africa and the Middle East* (Graham P. Chapman and Kathleen M. Baker, eds.). London and New York: Routledge, 1992.

Badran, Margot. *Feminists, Islam, and Nation: Gender and the Making of Modern Egypt.* Princeton, NJ: Princeton University Press, 1995.

Baker, Kathleen. The Changing Geography of West Africa. Pp. 80–113, in *The Changing Geography of Africa and the Middle East* (Graham P. Chapman and Kathleen M. Baker, eds.). London and New York: Routledge, 1992.

Bayer, Herbert. *World Geographic Atlas: A Composite of Man's Environment.* Container Corporation of America, Chicago, 1953.

Biggs, David. *This Is Cape Town.* Cape Town, South Africa: Struik, 1993.

Blakely, Thomas D., Walter E. A. van Beek, and Dennis L. Thomson, eds. *Religion in Africa: Experience and Expression.* London and Portsmouth, NH: James Currey and Heinemann, 1994.

Blunt, Alison. *Travel, Gender, and Imperialism: Mary Kingsley and West Africa.* New York: Guilford Press, 1994.

Botswana History and People, 1996. Available at: http://www.interknowledge.com/botswana/index.html.

Boyd, William. In Memoriam: Death of a Writer. *The New Yorker,* November 27, 1995, pp. 51–55.

Brown, Michael Barratt. *Africa's Choices: After Thirty Years of the World Bank.* Boulder, CO: Westview Press, 1996.

Brun, Ole, and Arne Kalland, eds. *Asian Perceptions of Nature: A Critical Approach.* Surrey, UK: Curzon Press, 1995.

Chant, Sylvia, ed. *Gender and Migration in Developing Countries.* London and New York: Belhaven Press, 1992.

Chapman, Graham P., and Kathleen M. Baker, eds. *The Changing Geography of Africa and the Middle East.* London: Routledge, 1992.

Chingono, Mark F. *The State, Violence and Development: The Political Economy of War in Mozambique, 1975–1992.* Aldershot, UK: Avebury, 1996.

Clarke, John I. *Sierra Leone in Maps: Graphic Perspective of a Developing Country.* New York: Africana, 1972.

Cobb, Charles E., Jr., and Robert Caputo (photos). Eritrea Wins the Peace. *National Geographic,* June 1996, pp. 82–105.

Conrad, David C., and Barbara E. Frank, eds. *Status and Identity in West Africa: Nyamakalaw of Mande.* Bloomington: Indiana University Press, 1995.

Coquery-Vidrovitch, Catherine. *African Women: A Modern History* (translated by Beth Gillian Raps). Boulder, CO: Westview Press, 1997.

Cross, Nigel, and Rhiannon Barker, eds. *At the Desert's Edge: Oral Stories from the Sahel.* London: Panos, 1994.

Crush, Jonathan. *Power of Development.* London and New York: Routledge, 1995.

Curtin, Philip D. *The Atlantic Slave Trade: A Census.* Madison: University of Wisconsin Press, 1969.

Dale, Richard. *Botswana's Search for Autonomy in Southern Africa.* Westport, CT: Greenwood Press, 1995.

Daley, Suzanne. In Mozambique, Guns for Plowshares and Bicycles. *The New York Times:* International section, March 2, 1997, p. 3.

D'Aluisio, Faith, and Peter Menzel. *Women in the Material World.* San Francisco: Sierra Club Books, 1996.

Dandemutande magazine. Available at: http://www.africaonline.com/AfricaOnline/music/zimbabwe.html.

Deng, Francis M., Sadikiel Kimaro, Terrence Lyons, Donald Rothchild, and I. William Zartman. *Sovereignty as Responsibility: Conflict Management in Africa.* Washington, DC: Brookings Instutution, 1996.

de Villiers, Marq, and Sheila Hirtle. *Into Africa: A Journey Through the Ancient Empires.* Toronto: Key Porter Books, 1997.

Dinesen, Isak. *Out of Africa.* As quoted in Isak Dinesen's *Africa: Images of the Wild Continent from the Writer's Life and Words.* San Francisco: Sierra Club Books, 1985.

Donnan, Hastings, and Thomas M. Wilson, eds. *Border Approaches: Anthropological Perspectives on Frontiers.* Lanham, MD: University Press of America, 1994.

Dorkenoo, Efua. *Cutting the Rose: Female Genital Mutilation: The Practice and Its Prevention.* London: Minority Rights Group, 1994.

Dubois, Felix. *Timbuctoo: The Mysterious* (translated by Diana White). New York: Negro University Press, 1969.

Dugger, Celia W. Genital Cutting Africa: Slow to Challenge an Ancient Ritual. *The New York Times.* October, 5, 1996.

Duke, Lynne. Africa Inching to Renewal from Economic Stagnation. *The Washington Post,* August 15, 1997, p. A01.

The Economist.
France and Africa: Why Were They There? January 11, 1997, p. 40.
Angola: Arm-Twisting. January 11, 1997, pp. 41–42.
Angola: Still Waiting for Peace. March 29, 1997, p. 48.
Angola: UNITA's End? June 7, 1997, p. 44.
Mozambique: Bending the Rules. June 28, 1997, p. 44.
Liberia: Wooing Warriors. July 12, 1997, p. 40.
Liberia: Farewell, Guns? July 26, 1997, p. 39.

Ejime, Paul. African Military Chiefs Meet on Sierra Leone. *Panafrican News Agency,* August 26, 1997. Available at: http://www.africanews.org/pana/news/19970826/feat28.html.

Ejime, Paul. West Africans Continue Isolation of Freetown Junta. *Panafrican News Agency,* August 27, 1997. Available at: http://www.africanews.org/pana/news/19970827/feat10.html.

Euro Mediterranean Sciences and Technology Space. *European Union Development Plans: Mediterranean Area.* 1996–1998 (updated 1999). Available at: http://www.jrc.es/projects/euromed/EC/DGXI/DGXI.html#3.

Fagan, Brian M. *Men of the Earth: An Introduction to World Prehistory.* Boston: Little, Brown, 1974.

French, Howard W. *The New York Times:*
The Ritual Slaves of Ghana: Young and Female. January 20, 1997, pp. A1, A5.
Africa's Culture War: Old Customs, New Values. February 2, 1997.
Kinshasa Journal. June 24, 1997.

Gade, Daniel W. Madagascar and Nondevelopment. *Focus* (October 1985): 14–21.

Gellar, Sheldon. *Senegal: An African Nation Between Islam and the West.* Boulder, CO: Westview Press, 1995.

Goheen, Miriam. *Men Own the Fields, Women Own the Crops: Gender and Power in the Cameroon Grassfields.* Madison: University of Wisconsin Press, 1996.

Goldberg, Jeffrey. *New York Times Magazine,* March 2, 1997, p. 39.

Gordimer, Nadine. *July's People.* New York: Viking Press, 1981.

Gottlieb, Alma, and Philip Graham. *Parallel Worlds: An Anthropologist and a Writer Encounter Africa.* New York: Crown, 1993.

Gourevitch, Philip. The Vanishing: How the Congo Became Zaire, and Zaire Became the Congo. *The New Yorker,* June 2, 1997, pp. 50–53.

Gregory, Robert G. *South Asians in East Africa: An Economic and Social History 1890–1980.* Boulder, CO: Westview Press, 1993.

Griffiths, Ieuan Ll. *The African Inheritance.* London: Routledge, 1995.

Grosz-Ngate, Maria, and Omari H. Kokole, eds. *Gendered Encounters: Challenging Cultural Boundaries and Social Hierarchies in Africa.* New York and London: Routledge, 1997.

Groulx, Michel. Reforesting the Sahel: Tree Seeds Research in Burkina Faso. March 4, 1997. Available at: http://www.idrc.ca/books/reports/1997/23–01e.html.

Groulx, Michel. Preserving Traditional Agricultural Knowledge. March 4, 1997. Available at: http://www.idrc.ca/books/reports/1997/23–02e.html.

Hackett, Rosalind I. J., ed. *New Religious Movements in Nigeria.* Lewiston/Queenston: Edwin Mellen Press, 1987.

Hackett, Rosalind I. J. *Religion in Calabar: The Religious Life and History of a Nigerian Town.* Berlin and New York: Mouton/de Gruyter, 1989.

Hackett, Rosalind I. J. *Art and Religion in Africa.* London: Cassell, 1996.

Hanson, John H. *Migration, Jihad, and Muslim Authority in West Africa: The Futanke Colonies in Karta.* Bloomington: Indiana University Press, 1996.

Harrison, David. *The White Tribe of Africa: South Africa in Perspective.* Berkeley: University of California Press, 1981.

Haugh, Robert F. *Nadine Gordimer.* New York: Twayne, 1974.

Hay, Margaret Jean, and Sharon Stichter, eds. *African Women South of the Saraha.* London: Longman Scientific & Technical, 1995 (1984).

Hay, Margaret Jean, and Sharon Stichter, eds. *African Women South of the Sahara,* 2nd ed. Essex, UK: Longman Scientific & Technical, 1995 (1984).

Herzenhorn, David M. Fela, 58, Nigerian Musician and Political Dissident. *The New York Times,* August 4, 1997. Available at: http://www.nytimes.com/yr/mo/day/news/national/obit-fela.html.

Heyser, Noeleen, James V. Riker, and Antonio B. Quizon, eds. *Government-NGO Relations in Asia: Prospects and Challenges for People-Centered Development.* Kuala Lumpur: Asian and Pacific Development Center, 1995.

Iliffe, John. *Africans: The History of a Continent.* Cambridge, UK: Cambridge University Press, 1995.

Iyam, David Uru. *The Broken Hoe: Cultural Reconfiguration in Biase, Southeast Nigeria.* Chicago: University of Chicago Press, 1995.

Johanson, Donald, with Enrico Fererelli (photos) and John Gurche (art). Face-to-Face with Lucy's Family. *National Geographic,* March 1996, pp. 96–117.

Kalipeni, Ezekiel. The Fertility Transition in Africa. *The Geopgraphical Review* (July 1995): 286–300.

Kelly, Sean. *America's Tyrant: The CIA and Mobutu of Zaire: How the United States Put Mobutu in Power, Protected Him from His Enemies, Helped Him Become One of the Richest Men in the World, and Lived to Regret It.* Washington, DC: American University Press, 1993.

Kirk-Greene, Anthony, and Daniel Back, eds. *State and Society in Francophone Africa Since Independence.* New York: St. Martin's Press, 1995.

Kristof, Nicholas D. In Congo, a New Era with Old Burdens. *The New York Times,* May 20, 1997. Available at: http://search.nytimes.com/search/daily/bin/fastweb?getdoc+site+site+26819+0+wAAA+Kisangani%7EMay%7E20.

Kukah, Matthew Hassan, and Toyin Falola. *Religious Militancy and Self Assertion: Islam and Politics in Nigeria.* Aldershot, UK: Avebury, 1996.

Kwamena-poh, M., J. Tosh, R. Waller, and M. Tidy. *African History in Maps.* Harlow, Essex, UK: Longman, 1987 (1982).

Lacroix, Pattie. *Ethiopia's Living Laboratory of Biodiversity.* 1995. Available at: http://www.idrc.ca/books/reports/12ethiop.html.

Lamb, David. *The Africans.* New York: Random House, 1982.

Lange, Karen. In Liberia, the People Chose an Awful Hope for Peace. *The Washington Post,* August 10, 1997, p. CO4.

Lanting, Frans. *A World Out of Time: Madagascar.* New York: Aperture, 1990.

Lelyveld, John. *Move Your Shadow.* New York: Time Books, 1985.

Lemon, Anthony, ed. *The Geography of Change in South Africa.* New York: Wiley, 1995.

Lewis, Anthony. Mandela the Pol. *The New York Times:* Magazine section, March 23, 1997, pp. 40–45, 52–54, 73–79.

Lindstrom, Joel, and Catherine Heising. Mai Chi's Music. *Dandemutande* magazine (March 1997). Available at: http://www.dandemutande.com/mag_mai.htm.

Lobban, Richard A., Jr. *Cape Verde: Crioulo Colony to Independent Nation.* Boulder, CO: Westview Press, 1995.

Malan, Rian. *My Traitor's Heart: A South African Exile Returns to Face His Country, His Tribe, and His Conscience.* New York: Atlantic Monthly Press, 1990.

Mauritius Island. Available at: http://www.maurinet.com/mauritius.html.

Mazrui, Ali A., ed. *The Africans.* New York: Praeger, 1986.

McEwan, Cheryl. Paradise or Pandemonium? West African Landscapes in the Travel Accounts of Victorian Women. *Journal of Historical Geography* 22, no. 1 (1996): 68–83.

McIntosh, Roderick J. Africa's Storied Past. *Archaeology* (May/June 1999): 54–60.

McKinley, James C., Jr. *The New York Times:*
In One Somali Town, Clan Rule Has Brought Peace. International section: June 22, 1997, p. 3.

A Woman to Run in Kenya? One Says, Why Not? August 3, 1997, p. 3.

McNeil, Donald G., Jr. Zimbabwe Tribal Elders Air a Chief Complaint. *The New York Times,* January 12, 1997, p. 1.

Meditz, Sandra W., and Tim Merrill. *Zaire: A Country Study.* Washington, DC: U.S. Government Printing Office, 1994.

Metz, Helen Chapin, ed. *Somalia: A Country Study.* Washington, DC: U.S. Government Printing Office, 1993.

Metz, Helen Chapin, ed. *Indian Ocean: Five Island Countries.* Washington, DC: U.S. Government Printing Office, 1995.

Momsen, Janet Henshall. *Women and Development in the Third World.* London: Routledge, 1991.

Moore, Henrietta L., and Megan Vaughan. *Cutting Down Trees: Gender, Nutrition and Agricultural Change in the Northern Province of Zambia 1890–1990.* Portsmouth, NH: Heinemann, 1993.

Murray, Jocelyn, ed. *Cultural Atlas of Africa*, rev. ed. New York: Checkmark Books, 1998.

Namibia Political Environment. 1997. Available at: http://www.tradeport.org/ts/countries/namibia/political.shtml.

Newman, James L. *The Peopling of Africa: A Geographic Interpretation.* New Haven, CT: Yale University Press, 1995.

Nugent, Paul. *Big Men, Small Boys and Politics in Ghana: Power, Ideology and the Burden of History, 1982–1994.* London: Pinter, 1995.

Nugent, Paul, and A. I. Asiwaju, eds. *African Boundaries: Barriers, Conduits and Opportunities.* London: Pinter, 1996.

Nussbaum, Martha C., and Glover Jonathan, eds. *Women, Culture, and Development: A Study in Human Capabilities.* Oxford, UK: Clarendon Press, 1995.

O'Connor, Anthony. *Poverty in Africa: A Geographical Approach.* London: Belhaven Press, 1991.

O'Connor, Anthony. The Changing Geography of Eastern Africa. Pp. 114–138, in *The Changing Geography of Africa and the Middle East* (Graham P. Chapman and Kathleen M. Baker, eds.). London and New York: Routledge, 1992.

Ofcansky, Thomas P. *Uganda: Tarnished Pearl of Africa.* Boulder, CO: Westview Press, 1996.

Ofcansky, Thomas P., and LaVerle Berry, eds. *Ethiopia: A Country Study.* Washington, DC: U.S. Government Printing Office, 1993.

Oliver, Roland, and Anthony Atmore. *Africa Since 1800.* Cambridge, UK: Cambridge University Press, 1994.

Olshansky, S. Jay. *Infectious Diseases: New and Ancient Threats to World Health. Population Bulletin 52*, no. 2, July 1997.

Organization of American Historians. *Restoring Women to History* (rev. ed.), *Teaching Packets for Integrating Women's History into Courses on Africa, Asia, Latin America and the Caribbean, and the Middle East.* Bloomington, IN: Organization of American Historians, 1990.

Osirim, Mary J. The Dilemmas of Modern Development: Structural Adjustment and Women Microentrepreneurs in Nigeria and Zimbabwe. Pp. 127–146, in *The Gendered New World Order* (Jennifer Turpin and Lois Ann Lorentzen, eds.). New York and London: Routledge, 1996.

Palriwala, Rajni, and Carla Risseeuw, eds. *Shifting Circles of Support: Contextualizing Gender and Kinship in South Asia and Sub-Saharan Africa.* Walnut Creek, CA: Altamira Press, 1996.

Potts, Deborah. The Changing Geography of Southern Africa. Pp. 12–51, in *The Changing Geography of Africa and the Middle East* (Graham P. Chapman and Kathleen M. Baker, eds.). London and New York: Routledge, 1992.

Ramsay, F. Jeffress. *Global Studies Africa*, 6th ed. Guilford, CT: Dushkin Publishing Group/Brown & Benchmark, 1995.

Ramsay, F. Jeffress. *Global Studies Africa*, 7th ed. Guilford, CT: Dushkin/McGraw-Hill, 1997.

Republic of Namibia On Line: http://www.republicofnamibia.com/index.html.

Robertson, Struan. *The Cold Choice: Pictures of a South African Reality.* Grand Rapids, MI: Wm. B. Eerdmans, 1991.

Romero, Patricia W., ed. *Women's Voices on Africa: A Century of Travel Writings.* Princeton, NJ: Markus Wiener, 1992.

Roudi, Farzaneh, and Lori Ashford. *Men and Family Planning in Africa.* Washington, DC: Population Reference Bureau, 1996.

Rupert, James. Election May Signal an End to Liberia's Seven Years of Upheaval. *The Washington Post* (Foreign Service), July 28, 1997, p. A14.

Sanneh, Lamin. *The Crown and the Turban: Muslims and West African Pluralism.* Boulder, CO: Westview Press, 1997.

Sen, Amartya. Is Democracy a Luxury? Who Has Famines? Box 2.6 (p. 58), in *Human Development Report 1996.* New York: Oxford University Press, 1996.

Sharp, Lesley A. *The Possessed and Dispossessed: Spirits, Identity and Power in a Madagascar Migrant Town.* Berkeley: University of California Press, 1993.

Somah, Syrulwa L. *Historical Settlement of Liberia and Its Environmental Impact.* Lanham, MD: University Press of America, 1995.

Spear, Thomas. *Mountain Farmers: Moral Economics of Land and Agricultural Development in Arusha and Meru.* Berkeley: University of California Press, 1997.

Stager, Curt, and Chris Johns (photos). Africa's Great Rift. *National Geographic*, May 1990, pp. 2–41.

Stock, Robert. *Africa South of the Sahara: A Geographical Interpretation.* New York: Guilford Press, 1995.

Thomas-Slayter, Barbara, Dianne Rocheleau, et al. *Gender, Environment, and Development in Kenya: A Grassroots Perspective.* Boulder, CO: Lynne Rienner, 1995.

Thompson, Leonard. *A History of South Africa*, rev. ed. New Haven, CT: Yale University Press, 1995.

Turle, Gillies, and Peter Beard and Mark Greenberg (photos). *The Art of the Maasai: 300 Newly Discovered Objects and Works of Art.* New York: Knopf, 1992.

Turpin, Jennifer, and Lois Ann Lorentzen, eds. *The Gendered New World Order: Militarism, Development, and the Environment.* New York and London: Routledge, 1996.

U.S. Department of State. *Country Reports on Human Rights Practices for 1997.* Washington, DC: Bureau of Democracy, Human Rights, and Labor, 1998. Available at: http://www.state.gov/www/global/human_rights/1997_hrp_report/97hrp_report_africa.html.

Walker, Alice, and Pratibha Parmar. *Warrior Marks: Female Genital Mutilation and the Sexual Blinding of Women.* New York: Harcourt Brace, 1993.

Williams, Pat, and Toyin Falola. *Religious Impact on the Nation State: The Nigerian Predicament.* Aldershot, UK: Avebury, 1995.

Woodward, Peter, and Murray Forsyth, eds. *Conflict and Peace in the Horn of Africa: Federalism and Its Alternatives.* Aldershot, UK: Dartmouth, 1994.

Wright, Donald R. *The World and a Very Small Place in Africa.* Armonk, NY: M. E. Sharpe, 1997.

Chapter 8 **South Asia**

Adams, Vincanne. *Tigers of the Snow and Other Virtual Sherpas: An Ethnography of Himalayan Encounters.* Princeton, NJ: Princeton University Press, 1996.

Addleton, Jonathan S. *Some Far and Distant Place*. Athens: University of Georgia Press, 1997.

Agarwal, Bina. Gender, Environment, and Poverty Interlinks: Regional Variations and Temporal Shifts in Rural India, 1971–91. *World Development 25*, no. 1 (1997): 23–52.

Ahmed, Akbar S. *Jinna, Pakistan and Islamic Identity*. London and New York: Routledge, 1997.

Alauddin, Mohammad, and Clement Allen Tisdell. *The Environment and Economic Development in South Asia: An Overview Concentrating on Bangladesh*. Hampshire and London: Macmillan, 1998.

Allchin, F. R. *The Archaeology of Early Historic South Asia: The Emergence of Cities and States*. Cambridge, UK: Cambridge University Press, 1995.

Amin, Sajeda. The Poverty-Purdah Trap in Rural Bangladesh: Implications for Women's Roles in the Family. *Development and Change 28* (1997): 213–233.

Amnesty International. *Bangladesh: Fundamental Rights of Women Violated with Virtual Impunity*. Material provided by the International Secretariat, Amnesty International, 1994. Available at: http://www.amnesty.org/ailib/aipub/1994/ASA/130994.ASA.txt.

Amnesty International. *Asia Pacific Regional Summary. Amnesty International 1997 Annual Report*. Available at: http://www.amnesty.org/ailib/aipub/1997/ASA.

Amnesty International. *Women in Afghanistan: The Violations Continue*, June 1997. Available at: http://www.amnesty.org/ailib/aipub/1997/ASA/31100597.htm.

Arden, Harvey, and Raghubir Singh (photos). Searching for India Along the Grand Trunk Road. *National Geographic*, May 1990, pp. 118–138.

Arif, General Khalid Mahmud. *Working with Zia: Pakistan's Power Politics 1977–1988*. Karachi: Oxford University Press, 1995.

Aryasinha, Ravinatha. Maldives, Sri Lanka and the "India Factor." *Himal*, March 1997. Available at: http://www.south-asia.com/himal/1997/Mar/cov-mal.htm.

Associated Press. Rural poor to get mobile phones in Bangladesh. *The Knoxville News-Sentinel*, April 6, 1997, p. D8.

Bagwe, Anjali. *Of Woman Caste: The Experience of Gender in Rural India*. Atlantic Highlands, NJ: Zed Books, 1995.

Behera, Navnita Chadha. Making and Unmaking Identities. *Himal*, November 1996. Available at: http://www.south-asia.com/himal/November/identity.htm.

Bergman, Edward F., and William H. Renwick. *Introduction to Geography: People, Places, and Environment*. Upper Saddle River, NJ: Prentice Hall, 1999.

Best, Alan C. G., and H. J. de Blij. *African Survey*. New York: Wiley, 1977.

Bhalla, A. S. *Uneven Development in the Third World: A Study of China and India*. New York: St. Martin's Press, 1995.

Bond, Constance, and Raghubir Singh (photos). Buckle Up for the Ride of Your Life. *Smithsonian*, May 1992, pp. 114–121.

Borstein, David. *The Price of a Dream*. New York: Simon & Schuster, 1996.

Brass, Paul R. *The Politics of India Since Independence*, Vol. 4. *The New Cambridge History of India*. Cambridge, UK: Cambridge University Press, 1994.

Brauns, Claus-Dieter, and Lorenz G. Loffler. *Mru: Hill People on the Border of Bangladesh*. Berlin: Birkhaeuser, 1989.

Brun, Ole, and Arne Kalland, eds. *Asian Perceptions of Nature: A Critical Approach*. Surrey, UK: Curzon Press, 1995.

Bumiller, Elisabeth. *May You Be the Mother of a Hundred Sons: A Journey Among the Women of India*. New York: Fawcett Columbine, 1990.

Burns, John. Radio interview with Terry Gross on *Fresh Air*, National Public Radio, January 14, 1997.

Burns, John F. In India's Golden Moment, Voices from the Past. Also, Pakistan at 50: Much to Be Proud Of, Much to Regret and Pakistan's P.M. Says His Country Is at Last on Track. *The New York Times*, August 15, 1997. Available at: http://www.nytimes.com/yr/mo/day/news/world/india-celebrate.html. Available now only for a fee.

Burns, John F. *The New York Times:*

    The West in Afghanistan, Before and After. February 18, 1996, p. E5.

    Denial and Taboo Blinding India to the Horror of Its AIDS Scourge. September 22, 1996, p. 1.

    India Air Disaster's Aftermath Is Mix of Callousness and Pity. November 16, 1996.

    Sharing Ganges Waters, India and Bangladesh Test the Depth of Cooperation. May 25, 1997, p. 6.

    For Kashmir Hostage's Wife, an Anguished Search. July 6, 1997, p. 3.

    Lowest-Caste Hindu Takes Office as India's President. July 26, 1997.

    Would-Be Afghan Rulers Find Their Islamic Steamroller Halted. July 27, 1997, pp. 1, 4.

    A Mere 50 Years of Freedom. August 10, 1997, pp. 13, 18.

    India's 5 Decades of Progress and Pain. August 14, 1997, pp. 1, 10.

    Pakistan's Bitter Roots, and Modest Hopes. August 15, 1997, A1, A12.

    In a Stalemate, Afghan Foes Reload. August 24, 1997, p. 8.

Centre for Monitoring Indian Economy. *India Economic and Business Overview*. Statistical sheets on each state prepared for the Economic Coordination Unit, Ministry of External Affairs, 1995. Available at: http://www.genius.net/indolink/Consulate/iebo/main.htm.

Chakrapani, C., and S. Vijaya Kumar, eds. *Changing Status and Role of Women in Indian Society*. New Delhi: M D Publications, 1994.

Chant, Sylvia, ed. *Gender and Migration in Developing Countries*. London and New York: Belhaven Press, 1992.

Choudhury, Dilara, and Al Masud Hasanuzzaman. Political Decision-Making in Bangladesh and the Role of Women. *Asian Profile 25*, no. 1 (February, 1997): 53–69.

Cobb, Charles E., Jr., and James P. Blair. Bangladesh: When the Water Comes. *National Geographic*, June 1993, pp. 118–134.

Counts, Alex. *Give Us Credit*. New York: Times Books/Random House, 1996.

Critchfield, Richard. *Villages*. Garden City, NY: Anchor Books, Anchor Press/Doubleday, 1983.

Crook, Clive. India's Economy: Work in Progress. A special insert. *The Economist*, February 22, 1997.

Crossette, Barbara. Crumbling Calcutta Begins to Clean Itself Up. *The New York Times:* International section, September 12, 1997.

Custers, Peter. *Capital Accumulation and Women's Labour in Asian Economies*. London and New York: Zed Books, 1997.

Daley, Suzanne. In Mozambique, Guns for Plowshares and Bicycles. *The New York Times*, March 2, 1997, p. 2.

D'Aluisio, Faith, and Peter Menzel. *Women in the Material World*. San Francisco: Sierra Club Books, 1996.

David, Kenneth, ed. *The New Wind: Changing Identities in South Asia*. The Hague and Paris: Mouton, 1977.

Davidson, Robyn, and Dilip Mehta (photos). Wandering with India's Rabari. *National Geographic*, September 1993, pp. 64–93.

Davies, C. Colin. *An Historical Atlas of the Indian Peninsula*. Oxford, UK: Oxford University Press, 1959.

Dugger, Celia W. New York Indians and Pakistanis Have No Problems with Each Other. *The New York Times*, August 15, 1997. Available at: http://www.nytimes.com/yr/mo/day/news/national/ny-india-pakistan.html. Currently only available for a fee.

Dundes, Alan, ed. *The Walled-Up Wife*. Madison: University of Wisconsin Press, 1996.

Dutt, Ashok K., S. P. Chatterjee, and M. Margaret Geib. *India in Maps*. Dubuque, IA: Kendall/Hunt, 1976.

The Economist. Islam's Many Faces. May 31, 1997, p. 16.

Edwards, Mike, and Roland Michaud (photos). "Paradise on Earth": When the Moguls Ruled India. *National Geographic*, April 1985, pp. 460–533.

Ejaz, Manzur. Psyche Warfare—The Dynamics of the Indo-Pakistani Conflict Have to Be Understood, Largely, in North-Subcontinental Context. *Himal*, July–August 1997. Available at: http://www.south-asia.com/himal/1997/Aug/psyche.htm.

Ejaz, Manzur. Wilting of the People's Party of Pakistan. *Himal*, March 1997. Available at: http://www.himalmag.com/97mar/opi-wil.htm.

Emadi, Hafizullah. The State and Rural-Based Rebellion in Afghanistan. *Central Asian Survey 15*, no. 2 (1996): 201–211.

Engel, Peter. Stairways to Heaven. *Natural History*, June 1993, pp. 48–56.

Erdosy, George, ed. *The Indo-Aryans of Ancient South Asia*. Berlin and New York: de Gruyter, 1995.

Farmer, B. H. *An Introduction to South Asia*, 2nd ed. London and New York: Routledge, 1993.

French, Howard W. For Congo's Elmer Gantrys, Flocks to Be Fleeced. *The New York Times*, International section, June 24, 1997.

Frye, Richard N. *The Heritage of Central Asia: From Antiquity to the Turkish Expansion*. Princeton, NJ: Markus Wiener, 1996.

Gadgil, Madhav, and Ramachandra Guha. *Ecology and Equity: The Use and Abuse of Nature in Contemporary India*. London and New York: Routledge, 1995.

Gain, Philip. Rockless Country: Bangladesh. *Himal*, March 1997. Available at: http://www.south-asia.com/himal/1997/Mar/photo.htm.

Galeotti, Mark. *Afghanistan: The Soviet Union's Last War*. London: Frank Cass, 1995.

Gamburd, Michele Ruth. Sri Lanka's "Army of Housemaids": Control of Remittances and Gender Transformations. *Anthropologica 37* (1995): 49–88.

Ganguly, Sumit. *The Origins of War in South Asia: Indo-Pakistani Conflicts Since 1947*. Boulder, CO: Westview Press, 1994.

Ganguly, Sumit. India in 1996: A Year of Upheaval. *Asian Survey 37*, no. 2 (February 1997): 126–135.

Gill, Gagan. *Weekend Edition*. National Public Radio. August 16, 1997. Transcript can be ordered from http://programs.npr.org/npr2/PrgDisp.cfm?PrgDate=08/16/97&PrgID=7.

Gollings, John (photos), and text by John M. Fritz and George Michell. *City of Victory: Vijayanagara: The Medieval Hindu Capital*. New York: Aperture, 1991.

Good, Anthony. *The Female Bridegroom: A Comparative Study of Life-Crisis Rituals in South India and Sri Lanka*. Oxford, UK: Clarendon Press, 1991.

Gujarat: Wildlife: Wild Life Sanctuaries. Junagadh: Sasan Gir. 1999. Available at: http://www.gujarattourism.com/cow.html.

Gunnell, Yanni. Comparative Regional Geography in India and West Africa: Soils, Landforms and Economic Theory in Agricultural Development Strategies. *The Geographical Journal 163* (March 1997): 38–46.

Guthman, Julie. Representing Crisis: The Theory of Himalayan Environmental Degradation and the Project of Development in Post-Rana Nepal. *Development and Change 28* (1997): 45–69.

Hachhethu, Krishna. Nepal in 1996: Experimenting with a Coalition Government. *Asian Survey 37*, no. 2 (February 1997): 149–154.

Haddad, Yvonne Yazbeck, and John L. Esposito, eds. *Islam, Gender and Social Change*. New York and Oxford, UK: Oxford University Press, 1998.

Hanson Cooke Ltd. *Sri Lanka*. 1997. Available at: http://www.tcol.co.uk/srilanka.

Hapke, Holly M. *Fish Mongers, Markets, and Mechanization: Gender and the Economic Transformation of an Indian Fishery*. Syracuse, NY: Syracuse University Press, 1996.

Hapke, Holly M. *Petty Traders, Development and Household Survival in an Indian Fishery*. Paper presented at the 92nd Annual Meeting of the Association of American Geographers, Charlotte, NC, April 8–14, 1996.

Harden, Blaine. To Ghana's 'Earth Magicians,' Burial Is a Form of Art. *The Washington Post*, November 28, 1988, p. A11.

Hasan, Mubashir. Caught in the Nationalist Web. *Himal*, April 1997. Available at: http://www.south-asia.com/himal/April/opinion.htm.

Hazarika, Sanjoy. Refugees Within, Refugees Without. *Himal*, April 1997. Available at: http://www.south-asia.com/himal/1997/Apr/chakma.htm.

Heiderer, Tony. Sacred Space, Sacred Time: India's Maha Kumbh Mela Draws Millions. *National Geographic*, May 1990, pp. 106–117.

Heitzman, James, and Robert L. Worden, eds. *India: A Country Study*. Washington, DC: U.S. Goverment Printing Office, 1996.

Heyser, Noeleen, James V. Riker, and Antonio B. Quizon, eds. *Government-NGO Relations in Asia: Prospects and Challenges for People-Centered Development*. Kuala Lumpur: Asian and Pacific Development Center, 1995.

Hiebert, Fredrik T. South Asia from a Central Asian perspective. Pp. 192–205, in *The Indo-Aryans of Ancient South Asia* (George Erdosy, ed.). Berlin and New York: de Gruyter, 1995.

Hoon, Vineeta. *Living on the Move: Bhotiyas of the Kumaon Himalaya*. Walnut Creek, CA: Altamira Press, 1996.

Huque, Ahmed Shafiqul. The Impact of Colonialism: Thoughts on Politics and Governance in Bangladesh. *Asian Affairs 28*, no. 1 (February: 1997): 15–27.

Hussain, Syed Talat. A Middle-Man in Place. *Himal*, November 1996. Available at: http://www.south-asia.com/himal/November/middle.htm.

Hutt, Michael. Bhutan in 1996: Continuing Stress. *Asian Survey 37* (February 1997) 155–159.

India still lagging potential as major player on world energy markets. *Oil & Gas Journal*, February 12, 1996, pp. 19–22.

Information on Gujarat, 1999. Available at: http://www.gujaratindia.com/index1.html.

Ingram, Derek. The Wonder and the Agony of India's 50 Years. *Gemini News Service*, August 15, 1997. Available at: http://www.oneworld.org/gemini/aug97/women.html. Page no longer up.

Isaacs, Harold R. *Scratches on Our Minds: American Images of China and India.* Armonk, NY: M. E. Sharpe, 1980 (1958).

Islamic Army Routs a Rival, Taking Most of Afghanistan. *The New York Times*, May 25, 1997, p. 4.

Jalal, Ayesha. *Democracy and Authoritarianism in South Asia: A Comparative and Historical Perspective.* Cambridge, UK: Cambridge University Press, 1995.

Jamison, Stephanie W. *Sacrificed Wife, Sacrificer's Wife: Women, Ritual, and Hospitality in Ancient India.* New York: Oxford University Press, 1996.

Janah, Sunil. *The Tribals of India.* Calcutta: Oxford University Press, 1993.

Johnson, Gordon. *Cultural Atlas of India: India, Pakistan, Nepal, Bhutan, Bangladesh and Sri Lanka.* New York: Facts on File, 1996.

Joshi, D. K. Two Faced Parties Set for Battle on Women's Seats. *Gemini News Service*, August 19 1997. Available at: http://www.oneworld.org/gemini/aug97/women.html. Page no longer up.

Kabeer, Naila. Women, Wages and Intra-Household Power Relations in Urban Bangladesh. *Development and Change 28* (1997): 261–302.

Kalbfuss, Elisabeth. Kingdom Summons Up the Power to Break Free. *Gemini News Service*, June 13, 1996. http://www.oneworld.org/gemini/june/bhutan1.html. Page no longer up.

Kalita, J., and Sanjib Barman. Assam: A Peek into the Chest of Culture and Tradition; History in a Nutshell; Economics at a Glance; and Some Economic Information, 1996–1999. Available at: http://www.assam.org/assam/geography/administration.html.

The Kathmandu Post. Available at: http://www.south-asia.com/Ktmpost/1997/Sep/Sep3/sep3–hd.htm.

Local news: Kaleidoscope. September 3, 1997.

Nepal economy. September 3, 1997.

Opposition MPs Gherao Speaker. September 3, 1997.

Khanal, Prakash. Debt-Slaves Struggle to Escape the Landlords' Grip. *Gemini News Service*, August 26, 1997. http://www.oneworld.org/gemini/aug97/nepal.html. Page no longer up.

Kochanek, Stanley A. Bangladesh in 1996: The 25th Year of Independence. *Asian Survey 37* (February 1997): 136–142.

Kristof, Nicholas D. *The New York Times:*

For Third World, Water Is Still a Deadly Drink. January 9, 1997, pp. 1, A8.

In Congo, a New Era with Old Burdens. May 20, 1997, pp. 1, A10.

Why Africa Can Thrive Like Asia. May 25, 1997: WK1.

In Congo, Drivers Find They Can't Get There from Here. International section: July 5, 1997.

Kundu, Somraj. As cited by Barbara Crossette. Crumbling Calcutta Begins to Clean Itself Up. *The New York Times*, September 12: International section.

Kurian, George, ed. *Atlas of the Third World.* New York: Facts on File, 1992.

Lamb, Alastair. *Kashmir: A Disputed Legacy 1846–1990.* Hertingfordbury, Hertfordshire, UK: Roxford Books, 1991.

LaPorte, Robert, Jr. Pakistan in 1996: Starting Over Again. *Asian Survey 37* (February 1997): 118–125.

Lin, Sharai G., and Madan C. Paul. Bangladeshi Migrants in Delhi: Social Insecurity, State Power, and Captive Vote Banks. *Bulletin of Concerned Asian Scholars 27*, no. 1 (1995): 3–20.

Loyd, Anthony. A Market in Human Remains. *The New York Times:* Magazine section, January 12, 1997, pp. 30–32.

Ludden, David, ed. *Contesting the Nation: Religion, Community, and the Politics of Democracy in India.* Philadelphia: University of Pennsylvania Press, 1996.

Mackenzie, Richard, and Steve McCurry (photos). Afghanistan's Uneasy Peace. *National Geographic*, October 1993, pp. 58–89.

MacKinnon, John, and Nigel Hicks (photos). *Wild China.* Cambridge, MA: MIT Press, 1996.

Madan, T.N. *Pathways: Approaches to the Study of Society in India.* Delhi: Oxford University Press, 1994.

Madhya Pradesh. *The Heart of India*, 1999. Available at: http://www.cs.colostate.edu/~malaiya/mp.html..

Magnus, Ralph H. Afghanistan in 1996. *Asian Survey* (February 1997): 111–117.

Maharashtra Tourism. 1999. Available at: http://www.maharashtra.gov.in.

Mahmood, Cynthia Keppley. *Fighting for Faith and Nations: Dialogues with Sikh Militants.* Philadelphia: University of Pennsylvania Press, 1996.

Mahmud, Simeen. Women's Work in Urban Bangladesh: Is There an Economic Rationale? *Development and Change 28* (1997): 235–260.

Maley, William. The Dynamics of Regime Transition in Afghanistan. *Central Asian Survey 16*, no. 2 (1997): 167–184.

Malik, Lynda P. Social and Cultural Determinants of the Gender Gap in Higher Education in the Islamic World. *Journal of Asian American Studies 30*, nos. 3–4 (1995): 181–193.

Maniku, Ahmend Ali. One System or Two? (Maldives). *Orbit*, No. 58, 1995. Available at: http://www.oneworld.org/vso/pubs/orbit/orbit58/educate.htm.

McCarry, John, and Steve McCurry (photos). Bombay: India's Capital of Hope. *National Geographic*, March 1995, pp. 42–67.

McCarry, John, and Ed Kashi (photos). The Promise of Pakistan. *National Geographic*, no. 10 (1997): 48–73.

McKnight, Tom L. *Physical Geography: A Landscape Appreciation*, 5th ed. Upper Saddle River, NJ: Prentice Hall, 1996.

McKnight, Tom L. *Physical Geography: A Landscape Appreciation*, 6th ed. Upper Saddle River, NJ: Prentice Hall, 1998.

McLeod, W. H. *The Sikhs: History, Religion, and Society*. New York: Columbia University Press, 1989.

Meet Jalil Ahmed Ansarj. Successful Owner of a Carpet Manufacturing Unit. And Former "Child Labourer." Available at: http://india.indiagov.org/social/child/childlabour.htm.

Mehta, Gita. *Snakes and Ladders: Glimpses of Modern India*. New York: Anchor Books/Doubleday, 1997.

Metz, Helen Chapin, ed. *Indian Ocean: Five Island Countries*. Washington, DC: U.S. Government Printing Office, 1995.

Miller, Peter, and Raghubir Singh (photos). Kerala: Jewel of India's Malabar Coast. *National Geographic*, May 1988, pp. 592–617.

Ministry of External Affairs, Government of India. *India: 50 Years of Independence. Sections on each State and Union Territory*. 1997. Available at: http://india.indiagov.org/states.

Mitra, Subrata K., and R. Alison Lewis, eds. *Subnational Movements in South Asia*. Boulder, CO: Westview Press, 1996.

Mohanti, Prafulla. *Changing Village, Changing Life*. New York: Viking, 1990.

Moos, Viviane. India's Women. *Culture Front* (Summer 1997): 17–24.

Mukhopadhyay, Carol Chapnick, and Susan Seymour. *Women, Education, and Family Structure in India*. Boulder, CO, and San Francisco: Westview Press, 1994.

Mustaga, Waqar. Where Children Shoulder the Burden of Education. *Gemini News Service*, July (1997). http://www.oneworld.org/gemini/july97/pakistan2.html. Page no longer up.

Nabi, Farjad. The Comeback of Urdu Cinema . . . Not. *Himal*, March 1997. Available at: http://www.south-asia.com/himal/March/urdufilm.htm.

Nath, Dilip C., and Giti Goswami. Determinants of Breast-Feeding Patterns in an Urban Society of India. *Human Biology 69*, no. 4 (August 1997): 557–573.

Neville, Adrian. Blue Lagoons. *Orbit*, no. 58 1995. Available at: http://www.oneworld.org/vso/pubs/orbit/orbit58/lagoons.htm.

Norton, James H.K. *Global Studies India and South Asia*, 2nd ed. Guilford, CT: Dushkin Publishing Group/Brown & Benchmark, 1995.

Norton, James H. K. *Global Studies India and South Asia*, 3rd ed. Guilford, CT: Dushkin/McGraw-Hill, 1997.

Novak, James J. *Bangladesh: Reflections on the Water*. Bloomington: Indiana University Press, 1993.

Nussbaum, Martha C., and Glover Jonathan, eds. *Women, Culture, and Development: A Study in Human Capabilities*. Oxford, UK: Clarendon Press, 1995.

Palriwala, Rajni, and Carla Risseeuw, eds. *Shifting Circles of Support: Contextualizing Gender and Kinship in South Asia and Sub-Saharan Africa*. Walnut Creek, CA: Altamira Press, 1996.

Patra, Priyadarsan. *Orissa*. A Web page maintained by Priyadarsan Patra, 1996–1997. Available at: http://www.cs.utexas.edu/users/darshan/ORISSA.

Paz, Octavio. *In Light of India*. New York: Harcourt Brace, 1995.

Perera, Sasanka. Sri Lanka's South Still Smoulders. *Himal*, May 1997. Available at: http://www.south-asia.com/himal/May/srilanka.htm.

Permanent Mission of the Republic of Maldives to the United Nations. The Republic of Maldives Economy and Environment. 1997. Available at: http://www.undp.org/missions/maldives/maldives.htm.

Piano.Symgrp. The Democratic Socialist Republic of Sri Lanka, 1996, 1999. Available at: http://piano.symgrp.com/srilanka/sle_geninfo.html.

Population Reference Bureau. *A Demographic Portrait of South and Southeast Asia Chartbook*. Washington, DC: International Programs, Population Reference Bureau, 1997.

Price, Pamela G. *Kingship and Political Practice in Colonial India*. Cambridge, UK: Cambridge University Press, 1996.

Rajashekara, H. M. The Nature of Indian Federalism: A Critique. *Asian Survey 37*, no. 3 (March 1997): 245–253.

Raju, Saraswati, and Deipica Bagchi, eds. *Women and Work in South Asia: Regional Patterns and Perspectives*. London: Routledge, 1993.

Rangan, Haripriya. Property vs Control: The State and Forest Management in the Indian Himalaya. *Development and Change 28* (1997): 71–94.

Rasheed, Salma. Health and Safety. *Orbit*, no. 58, 1995. Available at: http://www.oneworld.org/vso/pubs/orbit/orbit58/health.htm.

Rashid, Ahmed. Subversive: When It's Islam versus Soap Opera, Mohammed Hasn't Got a Chance. *The New York Times:* Magazine section, June 8, 1997, p. 78.

Rashid, Salman. Belligerent Villagers of Khunjerab. *Himal*, March 1997. Available at: http://www.himalmag.com/97mar/b-belli.htm.

Rashiduzzman, M. Political Unrest and Democracy in Bangladesh. *Asian Survey 37*, no. 3 (March 1997): 254–268.

Ridgeway, Rick, and Nicholas Devore III (photos). Park at the Top of the World. *National Geographic*, June 1982, pp. 704–725.

Risso, Patricia. *Merchants and Faith: Muslim Commerce and Culture in the Indian Ocean*. Boulder, CO: Westview Press, 1995.

Rowell, Galen. Annapurna: Sanctuary for the Himalaya. *National Geographic*, September 1989, pp. 391–405.

Rowell, Galen, and Barbara Cushman Rowell. Baltistan: The 20th Century Comes to Shangri-la. *National Geographic*, October 1987, pp. 526–550.

Roy, Beth. *Some Trouble with Cows: Making Sense of Social Conflict*. Berkeley: University of California Press, 1994.

Rubenstein, James M. *An Introduction to Human Geography*. Upper Saddle River, NJ: Prentice Hall, 1999.

Rubin, Barnett R. *The Fragmentation of Afghanistan: State Formation and Collapse in the International System*. New Haven, CT: Yale University Press, 1995.

Sarker, Abu Elias. Clientelism and Local Government in Bangladesh: A Study in Relations. *Asian Profile 25*, no. 2 (April 1997): 151–164.

Savada, Andrea Matles, ed. *Nepal and Bhutan Country Studies*. Washington, DC: U.S. Government Printing Office, 1993.

Schaffer, Howard B. Sri Lanka in 1996: Promise and Disappointment. *Asian Survey 37*, no.2 (February 1997): 143–148.

Schofield, Victoria. *Kashmir in the Crossfire*. London and New York: I. B. Tauris, 1996.

Schuler, Sidney Ruth, Syed Mesbahuddin Hashemi, and Ann P. Riley. The Influence of Women's Changing Roles and Status in Bangladesh's Fertility Transition: Evidence from a Study of Credit Programs and Contreceptive Use. *World Development 25*, no. 4 (1997): 563–575.

Seabrook, Jeremy. *In the Cities of the South: Scenes from a Developing World*. London and New York: Verso, 1996.

Sex Worker Myths India: Nepal. *Himal*, May 1997. Available at: http://www.south-asia.com/himal/May/sworker.htm

Shaffer, Jim G., and Diane A. Lichtenstein. The Concepts of "Cultural Tradition" and "Palaeoethnicity" in South Asian Archaeology. Pp 126–154, in *The Indo-Aryans of Ancient South Asia* (George Erdosy, ed.). Berlin and New York: de Gruyter, 1995.

Shah, Nasra M., ed. *Pakistani Women: A Socioeconomic and Demographic Profile*. Islamabad: Pakistan Institute of Development Economics, 1986.

Shamin, Arif. Pakistan's Music Scene: Would Billo or Chief Saab Approve? *Himal*, April 1997. Available at: http://www.south-asia.com/himal/April/billo.htm.

Sharma, Sudhindra. How Hindu Is the Other Hindu-Stan? *Himal*, May 1997. Available at: http://www.south-asia.com/himal/May/howhindu.htm.

Singh, Chandra Pal. Towards a New Equilibrium: India, the Asia-Pacific and Global Geopolitical Change. Pp. 260–281, in *Global Geopolitical Change and the Asia-Pacific: A Regional Perspective* (Dennis Rumley, Tatsuya Chiba, Akihiko Takagi, and Yoriko Fukushima, eds.). Aldershot, UK: Avebury, 1996.

Singh, Raghubir. *Benaras: Sacred City of India*. New York: Thames and Hudson, 1987.

Solomon, Charmaine. *The Complete Asian Cookbook*. New York: McGraw-Hill, 1976.

South South Asia. *Himal*, March 1997. Available at: http://www.south-asia.com/himal/1997/Mar/south.htm.

Stremlau, John. Dateline Bangalore: Third World Technopolis. *Foreign Policy* (Spring 1996): 152–168.

Tagore, Rabindranath. Crisis of Civilization. *Collected Works of Rabindranath Tagore*. Vol. 18, pp. 45, 120. Shantiniketan, India: Vishya Bharati. 1961. As quoted in *Human Development Report*, 1996. New York: Oxford University Press, 1996.

Thakur, Ramesh. India in the World: Neither Rich, Powerful, nor Principled. *Foreign Affairs 76*, no. 4 (July–August 1997): 15–22.

Tharoor, Shashi. *India: From Midnight to Millennium*. New York: Arcade, 1997.

Thompson, Paul M., and Parvin Sultana. Distributional and Social Aspects of Flood Control in Bangladesh. *The Geographical Journal, 162*, no. 1 (March 1996): 1–13.

Tumbahamphe, S. M., and B. Bhattarai. *Trafficking of Women in South Asia*. 1996–1997. Available at: http://www.ecouncil.ac.cr/about/contrib/women/youth/english.

ul Haq, Mahbub. The Subcontinent of Sub-Saharan Asia. *Himal*, March 1997. Available at: http://www.south-asia.com/himal/March/cover.htm.

UNESCO. *Women's Participation in Higher Education: China, Nepal and the Philippines*. Bangkok: UNESCO Principal Regional Office for Asia and the Pacific, 1990.

USAID. *Bangladesh's Emerging Success Story in Population and Family Planning*. 1996. Available at: http://www.info.usaid.gov/countries/bd/populat.txt.

USAID. *The USAID FY 1998 Congressional Presentation: Bangladesh, India, Nepal, and Sri Lanka*. 1997. Available at: http://www.info.usaid.gov/pubs/cp98/ane.

U.S. Bureau of Public Affairs, U.S. State Department. Background Notes, Maldives, June 1996. Available at: http://www.state.gov/www/background_notes/maldives_0696_bgn.html.

U.S. Census Bureau. *Statistical Indicators on Women: An Asian Perspective*, Statistical Brief. Washington, DC: U.S. Census Bureau, November 1993.

Valli, Eric, and Diane Summers. Honey Hunters of Nepal. *National Geographic*, November 1988, pp. 660–671.

Valli, Eric, and Diane Summers. Himalayan Caravans. *National Geographic*, December 1993, pp. 5–36.

Van der Veer, Peter, ed. *Nation and Migration: The Politics of Space in the South Asian Diaspora*. Philadelphia: University of Pennsylvania Press, 1995.

Varma, Mitu. Servant as Murderer. *Himal*, February 1997. Available at: http://www.south-asia.com/himal/Feb/servant.htm.

Vesilind, Priit J., and Steve McCurry (photos). Sri Lanka. *National Geographic*, January 1997, pp. 110–133.

Visweswaran, Kamala. *Fictions of Feminist Ethnography*. Minneapolis: University of Minnesota Press, 1994.

Wahid, Abu N. M., and Charles E. Weis, eds. *The Economy of Bangladesh: Problems and Prospects*. New York: Greenwood, 1996.

Wallace, Bret. *Losing Asia: Modernization and the Culture of Development*. Baltimore, MD: Johns Hopkins University Press, 1996.

Ward, Geoffrey C., and Steve McCurry (photos). India: Fifty Years of Independence. *National Geographic*, May 1997, pp. 1–57.

Watkins, Joanne C. *Spirited Women: Gender, Religion, and Cultural Identity in the Nepal Himalaya*. New York: Columbia University Press, 1996.

Weinbaum, Marvin G. *Afghanistan and the Politics of Pakistan*, UFSI Field Staff Reports No. 7. University Field Staff International, 1990–1991.

Wheeler, Kate. Dense, Complex Calcutta. *The New York Times*, August 10, 1997, p. 12.

Wimaladasa, Vilma. Daylight Robbery Replaces the Midnight Tap on the Door. *Gemini News Service*, August 26 (1997). http://www.oneworld.org/gemini/aug97/srilanka.html. Page not currently available.

Wirsing, Robert G. *India, Pakistan, and the Kashmir Dispute: On Regional Conflict and Its Resolution*. New York: St. Martin's Press, 1994.

Wirsing, Robert G. Pakistan's Security in the "New World Order": Going from Bad to Worse? *Asian Affairs 23*, no. 2 (1996): 101–126.

Zaheer, Hasan. *The Separation of East Pakistan: The Rise and Realization of Bengali Muslim Nationalism*. Karachi: Oxford University Press, 1994.

Chapter 9 East Asia

Akiner, Shirin, ed. *Mongolia Today*. London and New York: Kegan Paul International, 1991.

Alcock, John. Of Pandas and Politics. *Natural History 102*, no. 4 (1993): 88–89.

Allen, Thomas B., and Reza (photos). Xinjiang. *National Geographic 189*, no. 3 (1996): 2–43.

Allen, Thomas B., and Reza (photos). The Silk Road's Lost World. *National Geographic 189*, no. 3 (1996): 44–51.

Anderson, E. N. *The Food of China*. New Haven, CT: Yale University Press, 1988.

Arnold, Eve. *In China*. New York: Knopf, 1980.

Avery, Martha. *Women of Mongolia*. Seattle: Asian Art and Archaeology in association with University of Washington Press, 1996.

Bailey, Jackson H. *Ordinary People, Extraordinary Lives: Political and Economic Change in a Tohoku Village*. Honolulu: University of Hawaii Press, 1991.

Baker, Hugh. The Minorities. In *China: The Land, the Cities, the People, the Culture, the Present* (Derek Maitland, ed.). New York: Exeter Books, 1982.

Barfield, Claude E., ed. *Expanding U.S.-Asian Trade and Investment—New Challenges and Policy Options*. Washington, DC: AEI Press (American Enterprise Institute), 1997.

Baskin, Wade, ed. *Classics in Chinese Philosophy*. New York: Philosophical Library, 1972.

Beasley, W. G. *The Rise of Modern Japan*, 2nd ed. London: Weidenfeld & Nicolson, 1995 (1990).

Bell, Linda S. For Better, for Worse: Women and the World Market in Rural China. *Modern China 20*, no. 2 (1994): 180–210.

Berger, Mark T., and Douglas A. Borer, eds. *The Rise of East Asia: Critical Visions of the Pacific Century*. New York and London: Routledge, 1997.

Berstein, Gail Lee, ed. *Recreating Japanese Women 1600–1945*. Berkeley: University of California Press, 1991.

Bhalla, A. S. *Uneven Development in the Third World: A Study of China and India*. New York: St. Martin's Press, 1995.

Bih-er, Chou, Cal Clark, and Janet Clark. *Women in Taiwan Politics: Overcoming Barriers to Women's Participation in a Modernizing Society*. Boulder, CO, and London: Lynne Rienner, 1990.

Blunden, Caroline, and Mark Elvin. *Cultural Atlas of China*. New York: Facts on File, 1983.

Booth, Alan. *Looking for the Lost: Journeys Through a Vanishing Japan*. Tokyo: Kodansha International, 1995.

Bosworth, Barry P., and Gur Ofer. *Reforming Planned Economics in an Integrating World Economy*. Washington, DC: Brookings Institution, 1995.

Bray, Francesca. *Technology and Gender: Fabrics of Power in Late Imperial China*. Berkeley: University of California Press, 1997.

Bridges, Brian. *Japan and Korea in the 1990s*. Hants, UK: Edward Elgar, 1993.

Bumiller, Elizabeth. *The Secrets of Mariko*. New York: Times Books, 1995.

Cannon, Terry, and Alan Jenkins. *The Geography of Contemporary China: The Impact of Deng Xiaoping's Decade*. London and New York: Routledge, 1990.

Central Intelligence Agency. *CIA Fact Sheet on China*. Washington, DC: CIA, 1995.

Central Intelligence Agency. *Brief on Selected PRC Cities*. Washington DC: Library of Congress, 1975.

Chai, Joseph C.H. Divergent Development and Regional Income in China. *Journal of Contemporary Asia 26*, no. 1 (1996): 46–58.

Chan, Anita, Richard Madsen, and Jonathan Unger. *Chen Village: The Recent History of a Peasant Community in Mao's China*. Berkeley: University of California Press, 1984.

Chang, Pang-Mei Natasha. *Bound Feet and Western Dress: A Memoir*. New York: Anchor Books/Doubleday, 1996.

Chen, Kathy. Boom-Town Bound: A Teenager's Journey Mirrors Inner Migration That's Changing China. *The Wall Street Journal*, October 29, 1996, pp. 1, A6.

Chen, Kathy. Life Lessons: A Year on Her Own, Chinese Teen Learns Limits to Ambition. *The Wall Street Journal*, July 9, 1997, pp. 1, A7.

China: Land of Charm and Beauty. The People's Republic of China, 1976.

China Intercontinental Communication Center. Available at: http://www.chinanews.org/cicc.

China's Economic and Technological Development Zones. Available at: http://www.sezo.gov.cn/eindex.htm.

China's Special Economic Zones. Available at: http://www.chinanews.org/cicc/15th/english/8.html.

Ching, Julia. *Probing China's Soul: Religion, Politics, and Protest in the People's Republic*. San Francisco: Harper & Row, 1990.

Cohen, Paul A., and Merle Goldman, eds. *Ideas Across Cultures: Essays on Chinese Thought in Honor of Benjamin I. Schwartz*. Cambridge, MA: Council on East Asia Studies, Harvard University Press, 1990.

Collingwood, Dean W. *Japan and the Pacific Rim*, 3rd ed. Guilford, CT: Dushkin Publishing Group/Brown & Benchmark, 1995.

Collins Publishers. *A Day in the Life of China Photographed by 90 of the World's Leading Photojournalists on One Day, April 15, 1989*. San Francisco: Collins, 1989.

Cooper, Michael, Arimichi Ebisawa, Fernando G. Guiterrez, and Diego Pacheco. *The Southern Barbarians: The First Europeans in Japan*. Tokyo: Kodansha International, 1971.

Croll, Elisabeth. *Changing Identities of Chinese Women: Rhetoric, Experience and Self-Perception in Twentieth-Century China*. London and New York: Hong Kong University Press and Zed Books, 1995.

Custers, Peter. *Capital Accumulation and Women's Labour in Asian Economies*. London and New York: Zed Books, 1997.

D'Aluisio, Faith, and Peter Menzel. *Women in the Material World*. San Francisco: Sierra Club Books, 1996.

Dathorne, O. R. *Asian Voyages: Two Thousand Years of Constructing the Other*. Westport, CT: Bergin & Garvey, 1996.

Davidson, Cathy N. *36 Views of Mount Fuji*. New York: Dutton, 1993.

Desai, Uday, ed. *Ecological Policy and Politics in Developing Countries: Economic Growth, Democracy, and Environment*. Albany: State University of New York Press, 1998.

Dolan, Ronald E., and Robert L. Worden, eds. *Japan: A Country Study*. Washington, DC: U.S. Government Printing Office, 1991.

Dolgormaa, B., S. Zmambaga, and L. Ojungerel. *Status of Women: Mongolia*. Bangkok: UNESCO Principal Regional Office for Asia and the Pacific, 1990.

Duara, Prasenjit. *Rescuing History from the Nation: Questioning Narratives of Modern China*. Chicago: University of Chicago Press, 1995.

Ebrey, Patricia Buckley. *Confucianism and Family Rituals in Imperial China: A Social History of Writing About Rites.* Princeton, NJ: Princeton University Press, 1991.

Economist Intelligence Unit. *China, North Korea Country Profile 1992–1993.* London: Economist Intelligence Unit, 1992–1993.

Edwards, Mike. The Lash of the Dragon. Pp. 127–179, in *Journey into China.* Washington, DC: National Geographic Society, 1982.

Einhorn, Barbara, and Eileen Janes Yeo, eds. *Women and Market Societies: Crisis and Opportunity.* Aldershot, UK, and Brookfield, CT: Edward Elgar, 1995.

Evers, Hans-Dieter, and Heiko Schrader, eds. *The Moral Economy of Trade: Ethnicity and Developing Markets.* London and New York: Routledge, 1994.

Fairbank, John King. *The United States and China,* 3rd ed. Cambridge, MA: Harvard University Press, 1972 (1948).

Fairbank, John King. *China: A New History.* Cambridge, MA: Belknap Press of Harvard University Press, 1992.

Fan, C. Cindy. Economic Opportunities and Internal Migration: A Case Study of Guangdong Province, China. *The Professional Geographer 48,* no. 1 (1996): 28–45.

Field, Graham. *Economic Growth and Political Change in Asia.* New York: St. Martin's Press, 1995.

Finnane, Antonia. What Should Chinese Women Wear? *Modern China 22,* no. 2 (1996): 99–131.

Fujimura-Fanselow, Kamiko, and Atsuko Kameda, eds. *Japanese Women: New Feminist Perspectives on the Past, Present, and Future.* New York: Feminist Press at the City University of New York, 1995.

Gelb, Joyce, and Marian Lief Palley, eds. *Women of Japan and Korea: Continuity and Change.* Philadelphia: Temple University Press, 1994.

Gernet, Jacques. *Daily Life in China on the Eve of the Mongol Invasion 1250–1276* (translated by H. M. Wright). New York: Macmillan, 1962.

Gilmartin, Christina K., Gail Hershatter, Lisa Rofel, and Tyrene White. *Women, Culture, and the State.* Cambridge, MA: Harvard University Press, 1994.

Go, Lisa. An Unbroken History of Japan's Sex Slaves. *ASA-News,* April 1994.

Goldstein, Melvyn C., and Cynthia M. Beall. *Nomads of Western Tibet: The Survival of a Way of Life.* Berkeley: University of California Press, 1990.

Goldstein, Melvyn C., and Cynthia M. Beall. *The Changing World of Mongolia's Nomads.* Berkeley: University of California Press, 1994.

Graves, William. The Torrent of Life: Pp. 263–307, in *Journey into China.* Washington, DC: National Geographic Society, 1982.

Griffin, Keith, ed. *Poverty and the Transition to a Market Economy in Mongolia.* New York: St. Martin's Press, 1995.

Haigh, M., and D. Elsom. An Environmental Snapshot of South China. *China Now 122* (1987): 24–26.

Halloran, Richard. The Rising East. *Foreign Policy* (Spring 1996): 3–21.

Hane, Mikiso. *Premodern Japan: A Historical Survey.* Boulder, CO: Westview Press, 1991.

Hannan, Kate, ed. *China, Modernization and the Goal of Prosperity: Government Administration and Economic Policy in the Late 1980s.* Cambridge, UK: Cambridge University Press, 1995.

Harrell, Stevan, and Huang Chun-chieh, eds. *Cultural Change in Postwar Taiwan.* Boulder, CO: Westview Press, 1994.

Hassan Ihab. *Between the Eagle and the Sun: Traces of Japan.* Tuscaloosa: University of Alabama Press, 1996.

Hendry, Joy. *Wrapping Culture: Politeness Presentation and Power in Japan and Other Societies.* Oxford, UK: Clarendon Press, 1993.

Herrmann, Albert. *An Historical Atlas of China.* Chicago: Aldine, 1966.

Heyser, Noeleen, James V. Riker, and Antonio B. Quizon, eds. *Government-NGO Relations in Asia: Prospects and Challenges for People-Centered Development.* Kuala Lumpur: Asian and Pacific Development Center, 1995.

Hilger, M. Inez, with the assistance of Chiye Sano and Midori Yamaha. *Together with the Ainu: A Vanishing People.* Norman: University of Oklahoma Press, 1971.

Honig, Emily, and Gail Hershatter. *Personal Voices: Chinese Women in the 1980's.* Stanford, CA: Stanford University Press, 1988.

Hopper, Helen M. *A New Woman of Japan: A Political Biography of Kato Shidzue.* Boulder, CO: Westview Press, 1996.

Howard, Michael C., ed. *Asia's Environmental Crisis.* Boulder, CO: Westview Press, 1993.

Hsieh, Chiao-min. *Atlas of China.* New York: McGraw-Hill, 1973.

Hu, Jason C., ed. *Quiet Revolutions on Taiwan, Republic of China.* Taipei: Kwang Hwa, 1994.

Hunter, Jane. *The Gospel of Gentility: American Women Missionaries in Turn-of-the-Century China.* New Haven, CT: Yale University Press, 1984.

Ikegami, Eiko. *The Taming of the Samurai: Honorific Individualism and the Making of Modern Japan.* Cambridge, MA: Harvard University Press, 1995.

Isaacs, Harold R. *Scratches on Our Minds: American Images of China and India.* Armonk, NY: M. E. Sharpe, 1980 (1958).

Islam, Iyanatul, and Anis Chowdhury. *Asia-Pacific Economies: A Survey.* London and New York: Routledge, 1997.

Itoh, Fumio, ed. *China in the Twenty-first Century: Politics, Economy, and Society.* Tokyo: United Nations University Press, 1997.

Iwao, Sumiko. *The Japanese Woman: Traditional Image and Changing Reality.* New York: Free Press, 1993.

Jacka, Tamara. *Women's Work in Rural China: Change and Continuity in an Era of Reform.* Cambridge, UK: Cambridge University Press, 1997.

Jaschok, Maria, and Suzanne Miers. *Women and Chinese Patriarchy.* London: Zed Books, 1994.

Judd, Ellen R. *Gender and Power in Rural North China.* Stanford, CA: Stanford University Press, 1994.

Kato, Shuichi (translated and adapted from Japanese by Junko Abe and Leza Lowitz). *Japan Spirit and Form.* Rutland, VT: Charles E. Tuttle, 1994.

Katz, Donald R. Caravans of Profit, Cargoes of Ideas. Pp. 181–219, in *Journey into China.* Washington, DC: National Geographic Society, 1982.

Kim, Elaine H., and Chungmoo Choi, eds. *Dangerous Women: Gender and Korean Nationalism.* New York and London: Routledge, 1998.

Kirdar, Uner, ed. *Cities Fit for People*. New York: United Nations, 1997.

Kristof, Nicholas D., and Sheryl Wudunn. *China Wakes: The Struggle for the Soul of a Rising Power*. New York: Time Books/Random House, 1994.

Kubota, Hiroji. *China*. New York: W. W. Norton, 1985.

Kulp, Daniel Harrison II. *Country Life in South China: The Sociology of Familism*, Vol. 1. *Phenix Village, Kwantung, China*. Taipei, Taiwan: Ch'eng-Wen, 1966.

Kuno, Akiko (translated by Kirsten McIvor). *Unexpected Destinations: The Poignant Story of Japan's First Vassar Graduate*. Tokyo: Kodansha International, 1993.

Lai, David Chuenyan. *Land of Genghis Khan: The Rise and Fall of Nation-States in China's Northern Frontiers*, Western Geographical Series, Vol. 30. Victoria, BC: University of Victoria, 1995.

Lawrence, Anthony. *The Love of China*. London: Crescent/Octopus Books, 1979.

Lee, James Z., and Cameron D. Campbell. *Fate and Fortune in Rural China: Social Organization and Population Behavior in Liaoning 1774–1873*. Cambridge, UK: Cambridge University Press, 1997.

Leeming, Frank. *The Changing Geography of China*. Oxford, UK: Blackwell, 1993.

Leipziger, Danny M., ed. *Lessons from East Asia*. Ann Arbor: University of Michigan Press, 1997.

Li Jianchang. *Woguo ziyuan yu huanjing (China's Resources and Environments)*. Beijing: Xinhua Books, 1988.

Lieberthal, Kenneth G., Shuen-fu Lin, and Ernest P. Young, eds. *Constructing China: The Interaction of Culture and Economics*. Ann Arbor: Center for Chinese Studies, University of Michigan, 1997.

Lily, Xiao Hong Lee. *The Virtue of Yin: Studies on Chinese Women*. Broadway, Australia: Wild Peony, 1994.

Liou, Kuotsai Tom. *Managing Economic Reforms in Post-Mao China*. Westport, CT: Praeger, 1998.

Long, Simon. *Taiwan: China's Last Frontier*. Houndmills, Basingstoke, Hampshire, UK: Macmillan, 1991.

Lu, Wende. Zhiyin hunshi hefa be heli (Just because our wedding conformed to law but not to custom). *ZQB (Zhongguo qingnian bao)*, April 17, 1985.

Mackerras, Colin. *China's Minorities: Integration and Modernization in the Twentieth Century*. Oxford, UK, and New York: Oxford University Press, 1994.

Mackerras, Colin, and Amanda Yorke. *The Cambridge Handbook of Contemporary China*. Cambridge, UK: Cambridge University Press, 1991.

Maitland, Derek, ed. *China, the Land, the Cities, the People, the Culture, the Present*. New York: Exeter Books, 1982.

Mandelbaum, Michael. Westernizing Russia and China. *Foreign Affairs* (May/June 1997): 80–95.

Masumi Junnosuke (translated by Lonny E. Carlile). *Contemporary Politics in Japan*. Berkeley: University of California Press, 1995.

Mattielli, Sandra, ed. *Virtues in Conflict: Tradition and the Korean Woman Today*. Seoul: for the Royal Asiatic Society Korean Branch by Samhwa, 1977.

Mendl, Wolf. *Japan's Asia Policy: Regional Security and Global Interests*. London: Routledge, 1995.

Momsen, Janet Henshall. *Women and Development in the Third World*. London: Routledge, 1991.

Mote, Frederick W. *Intellectual Foundations of China*. New York: Knopf, 1971.

Nakano Makiko (translated with introduction and notes by Kazuko Smith). *Makiko's Diary: A Merchant Wife in 1910 Kyoto*. Stanford, CA: Stanford University Press, 1995.

The National Economic Atlas of China. Hong Kong: Oxford University Press, 1994.

National Geographic Society. *Journey into China*. Washington, DC: National Geographic Society, 1982.

Naughton, Barry. *Growing Out of the Plan: Chinese Economic Reform, 1978–1993*. Cambridge, UK: Cambridge University Press, 1995.

Nelson, Barbara J., and Najma Chowdhury, eds. *Women and Politics Worldwide*. New Haven, CT, and London: Yale University Press, 1994.

Nelson, Sarah Milledge. *The Archaeology of Korea*. Cambridge, UK: Cambridge University Press, 1993.

Noland, Marcus. North Korea's International Economic Relations. *Social Science, Japan*, no. 7, August (1996).

Nussbaum, Martha C., and Glover Jonathan, eds. *Women, Culture, and Development: A Study in Human Capabilities*. Oxford, UK: Clarendon Press, 1995.

Ogden, Suzanne. *Global Studies China*, 7th ed. Guilford, CT: Dushkin/McGraw-Hill, 1997.

Oliver, Robert T. *A History of the Korean People in Modern Times: 1800 to the Present*. Newark: University of Delaware Press, 1993.

Overmyer, Daniel L. *Religions of China: The World as a Living System*. San Francisco: Harper & Row, 1986.

Pannell, Clifton W., and Jeffrey S. Torguson. Interpreting Spatial Patterns from the 1990 China Census. *The Geographical Review 81* (1991): 304–315.

Pearson, Veronica, and Benjamin K. P. Leung, eds. *Women in Hong Kong*. Oxford, UK, and New York: Oxford University Press, 1995.

Pope, Geoffrey G. Ancient Asia's Cutting Edge. *Natural History 102*, no. 5 (1993): 54–59.

Potter, David M. *Japan's Foreign Aid to Thailand and the Philippines*. New York: St. Martin's Press, 1996.

Rai, Shirin, Hilary Pilkington, and Annie Phizacklea, eds. *Women in the Face of Change: The Soviet Union, Eastern Europe and China*. London: Routledge, 1992.

Reingold, Edwin M. *Chrysanthemums and Thorns: The Untold Story of Modern Japan*. New York: St. Martin's Press, 1992.

Reza (photos). Pilgrimage to China's Buddhist Caves. *National Geographic 189*, no. 4 (1996): 52–63.

Robinson, David, Catherine Cross, Wang Jianmin, and Amanda Lyerly. *The China Health and Nutrition Survey*. Chapel Hill, NC: Carolina Population Center, University of North Carolina, 1996.

Robison, Richard, and David S. G. Goodman, eds. *The New Rich in Asia: Mobile Phones, McDonald's and Middle-Class Revolution*. New York and London: Routledge, 1996.

Rumley, Dennis, Tatsuya Chiba, Akihiko Takagi, and Yoriko Fukushima, eds. *Global Geopolitical Change and the Asia-Pacific: A Regional Perspective*. Aldershot, UK: Avebury, 1996.

Savada, Andrea Matles, ed. *North Korea: A Country Study*. Washington, DC: U.S. Government Printing Office, 1994.

Savada, Andrea Matles, and William Shaw, eds. *South Korea: A Country Study*. Washington, DC: U.S. Government Printing Office, 1992.

Schell, Orville. *To Get Rich Is Glorious: China in the Eighties*. New York: Pantheon, 1984.

Shigeru, Kayano (translated by Kyoko Selden and Lili Selden). *Our Land Was a Forest: An Ainu Memoir*. Boulder, CO: Westview Press, 1994 (1980).

Simons, Geoff. *Korea: The Search for Sovereignty*. Hampshire, UK: Macmillan, 1995.

Simoons, Frederick J. *Food in China: A Cultural and Historical Inquiry*. Boca Raton, FL: CRC Press, 1991.

Sinkule, Barbara J., and Leonard Ortolano. *Implementing Environmental Policy in China*: Westport, CT: Praeger, 1995.

Sivin, Nathan. *The Contemporary Atlas of China*. Boston: Houghton Mifflin, 1988.

Smith, Christopher J. *China: People and Places in the Land of One Billion*. Boulder, CO: Westview Press, 1991.

Solomon, Charmaine. *The Complete Asian Cookbook*. New York: McGraw-Hill, 1976.

Songqiao, Zhao. *Physical Geography of China*. Beijing and New York: Science Press and Wiley, 1986.

Stafford, Charles. *The Roads of Chinese Childhood: Learning and Identification in Angang [Taiwan]*. Cambridge, UK: Cambridge University Press, 1995.

Steele, Philip. *China: World in View*. Austin, TX: Steck-Vaughn Library, 1989.

Stokes, Edward. *Hong Kong's Wild Places: An Environmental Exploration*. Hong Kong and Oxford, UK: Oxford University Press, 1995.

Strassberg, Richard E., translator. *Inscribed Landscapes: Travel Writing from Imperial China*. Berkeley: University of California Press, 1994.

Tamanoi, Mariko Asano. *Under the Shadow of Nationalism: Politics and Poetics of Rural Japanese Women*. Honolulu: University of Hawaii Press, 1998.

Teikoku-shoin Co. *Teikoku's Complete Atlas of Japan*. Tokyo: Teikoku-shoin, 1977.

Thakur, Ravni. *Rewriting Gender: Reading Contemporary Chinese Women*. London and New York: Zed Books, 1997.

Theroux, Paul. *Riding the Iron Rooster: By Train Through China*. New York: Putnam, 1988.

Tian, Gang. The Emergence of Shanghai's Role as Entrepot Center Since the Mid-1980s. *Journal of Contemporary China* 7 (1994): 3–27.

Tregear, T. R. *A Geography of China*. Chicago: Aldine, 1965.

Tsurumi, Shunsuke. *A Cultural History of Postwar Japan 1945–1980*. London: KPI, 1987 (1984).

Tuchman, Barbara W. *Notes from China*. New York: Collier, 1972.

Tyler, Patrick E. China's Endless Task to Stem Centuries of Floods. *The New York Times*, September 15, 1996, pp. 1, 6.

Tyson, James, and Ann Tyson. *Chinese Awakenings: Life Stories from the Unofficial China*. Boulder, CO: Westview Press, 1995.

UNESCO. *Women's Participation in Higher Education: China, Nepal and the Philippines*. Bangkok: UNESCO Principal Regional Office for Asia and the Pacific, 1990.

U.S. Census Bureau. *Statistical Indicators on Women: An Asian Perspective*, Statistical Brief. Washington, DC: U.S. Census Bureau, November 1993.

Verschuur-Basse, Denyse. *Chinese Women Speak*. Westport, CT: Praeger, 1996.

Wallace, Bret. *Losing Asia: Modernization and the Culture of Development*. Baltimore, MD: Johns Hopkins University Press, 1996.

Wells, Kenneth M., ed. *South Korea's Minjung Movement: The Culture and Politics of Dissidence*. Honolulu: University of Hawaii Press, 1995.

Wolf, Margery. *Women and the Family in Rural Taiwan*. Stanford, CA: Stanford University Press, 1972

Wong, How Man, and Adel A. Dajani. *Islamic Frontiers of China: Silk Road Images*. London: Scorpion, 1990.

Wong, Jan. *Red China Blues*. New York: Doubleday/Anchor Books, 1997.

Worden, Robert L., and Andrea Matles Savada, eds. *Mongolia: A Country Study*. Washington, DC: U.S. Government Printing Office, 1991.

Woronoff, Jon. *The Japanese Social Crisis*. New York: St. Martin's Press, 1997.

Yang, Minchuan. Reshaping Peasant Culture and Community: Rural Industrialization in a Chinese Village. *Modern China 20*, no. 2 (1994): 157–179.

Young Jeh Kim, ed. *The New Pacific Community in the 1990s*. Armonk, NY: M. E. Sharpe, 1996.

Young-ha, Chu. Origin and Change in Kimch'I Culture. *Korea Journal* (Summer 1995): 18–33.

Yuan-li Wu. *China: A Handbook*. New York: Praeger, 1973.

Yung-Chung Kim, ed. and translator. *Women of Korea: A History from Ancient Times to 1945. An Abridged and Translated Edition of Han'guk Yosong-sa*. Seoul: Ewha Womans University Press, 1979.

Zich, Arthur. The Other China Changes Course: Taiwan. *National Geographic*, November 1993, pp. 2–33.

Zich, Arthur. China's Three Gorges: Before the Flood. *National Geographic*, September 1997, pp. 2–33.

Chapter 10 Southeast Asia

Ahmad, Asmah. Gender and the Quality of Life of Households in Raft-Houses, Temerloh, Pahand, Peninsular Malaysia. Pp. 183–196, in *Different Places, Different Voices: Gender and Development in Africa, Asia and Latin America* (Janet H. Momsen and Vivian Kinnaird, eds.). London and New York: Routledge, 1993.

Anderson, Benedict. *Imagined Communities: Reflections on the Origin and Spread of Nationalism*. London and New York: Verso, 1991.

AsiaWeek NewsMap. Available at: http://www.pathfinder.com/asiaweek/97/1226/newsmap/myanmar.html.

Atkinson, Jane Monnig, and Shelly Errington, eds. *Power and Difference: Gender in Island Southeast Asia*. Stanford, CA: Stanford University Press, 1990.

Bacani, Cesar. Surviving the Slump. *Asiaweek*, November 28, 1997. Available at: http://www.pathfinder.com/asiaweek/97/1128/cs1.html.

Barfield, Claude E., ed. *Expanding U.S.-Asian Trade and Investment—New Challenges and Policy Options*. Washington, DC: AEI Press (American Enterprise Institute), 1997.

Barry, Kathleen, ed. *Vietnam's Women in Transition*. Hampshire, UK: Macmillan, 1996.

Barth, Fredrik. *Balinese Worlds.* Chicago: University of Chicago Press, 1993.

Bercuson, Kenneth, with Robert G. Carling, Aasim M. Husain, Thomas Rumbaugh, and Rachel van Elkan. *Singapore: A Case Study in Rapid Development.* Washington, DC: International Monetary Fund, 1995.

Berger, Mark T., and Douglas A. Borer, eds. *The Rise of East Asia: Critical Visions of the Pacific Century.* New York and London: Routledge, 1997.

Bernard, Stephane, and Rodolphe De Koninck. The Retreat of the Forest in Southeast Asia: A Cartographic Assessment. *Singapore Journal of Tropical Geography 17,* no. 1 (1996): 1–14.

Bourdet, Yves. Laos in 1996—Please Don't Rush. *Asian Survey 37,* no. 1 (January 1997): 72–77.

Brauchil, Marcus W., Darren McDermott, and David Wessel. Southeast Asia Seems Still on Track to Grow Despite Currency Slide. *The Wall Street Journal,* August 5, 1997, p. 1.

Brookfield, Harold, ed., with Loene Doube and Barbara Banks. *Transformation with Industrialization in Peninsular Malaysia.* Kuala Lumpur: Oxford University Press, 1994.

Burma: The Longest War. London: J. M. Dent, 1984.

Carroll, James. Annals of Vietnam: A Friendship That Ended the War. *The New Yorker,* October 21 and 28, 1998, pp. 131–156.

Carsten, Janet. *The Heat of the Hearth: The Process of Kinship in a Malay Fishing Community.* Oxford, UK: Clarendon Press, 1997.

Cartographic Division of National Geographic. The Peoples of Mainland Southeast Asia. Map insert, *National Geographic,* March 1971.

Cartographic Division of National Geographic. Indonesia. Map insert, *National Geographic,* February 1996.

Case, William. Brunei Darussalam in 1996: Business as Usual in the "Abode of Peace." *Asian Survey 37,* no. 2 (February 1997): 194–198.

Chant, Sylvia, ed. *Gender and Migration in Developing Countries.* London and New York: Belhaven Press, 1992.

Chin, James. Malaysia in 1996: Mahathir-Anwar Bouts, UMNO Election, and Sarawak Surprise. *Asian Survey 37,* no. 2 (February 1997): 181–187.

Christie, Clive J. *A Modern History of Southeast Asia: Decolonization, Nationalism and Separatism.* London: I. B. Tauris, 1996.

Cleary, Mark, and Shuang Yann Wong. *Oil, Economic Development and Diversification in Brunei Darussalam.* New York: St. Martin's Press, 1994.

Collingwood, Dean W. *Japan and the Pacific Rim.* Guilford, CT: Dushkin Publishing Group, 1991.

Collingwood, Dean W. *Japan and the Pacific Rim.* 3rd ed. Guilford, CT: Dushkin Publishing Group/Brown & Benchmark, 1995.

Cribb, Robert, and Colin Brown. *Modern Indonesia: A History Since 1945.* London: Longman, 1995.

Crossette, Barbara. How the War Goes On (and On) in Cambodia. *The New York Times,* June 22, 1997, p. E1.

Crossette, Barbara. Cambodians Seek Monitoring of New Election. *The New York Times,* September 28, 1997, p. 4.

Dahlby, Tracy, and Karen Kasmauski (photos). The New Saigon. *National Geographic 187,* no. 4 (April 1995): 60–88.

D'Aluisio, Faith, and Peter Menzel. *Women in the Material World.* San Francisco: Sierra Club Books, 1996.

De Koninck, Rodolphe. *Malay Peasants Coping with the World: Breaking the Community Circle?* Singapore: Institute of Southeast Asian Studies, 1992.

Dreifus, Claudia. The Passion of Suu Kyi. *The New York Times:* Magazine section, January 7, 1997, pp. 30–37.

Dumarcay, Jacques, and Michael Smithies. *Cultural Sites of Burma, Thailand, and Cambodia.* Kuala Lumpur: Oxford University Press, 1995.

Dwyer, Daisy, and Judith Bruce, eds. *A Home Divided: Women and Income in the Third World.* Stanford, CA: Stanford University Press, 1988.

Economic and Social Commission for Asia and the Pacific. *Economic and Social Survey of Asia and the Pacific 1995.* New York: United Nations, 1995.

The Economist:

   Wealth in Its Grasp: A Survey of Indonesia. April 17, 1993, special insert

   A Survey of Asia: A Billion Consumers. October 30, 1993, special insert.

   Asia: Fings Ain't Wot They Used to Be. May 28, 1994, pp. 31–32.

   A Survey of Asian Finance: Insatiable. November 12, 1994, special insert.

   A Survey of Vietnam: The Road to Capitalism. July 8, 1995, special insert

   Doublethink in Myanmar. October 5, 1996, p. 37.

   Southeast Asia Loses Its Grip. July 19, 1997, p. 15.

   The Tigers' Fearful Symmetry. July 19, 1997, p. 35.

   South-East Asian Currencies Unpegged. July 19, 1997, p. 36.

   Myanmar and ASEAN: Cook's Orders. September 6, 1997, pp. 40–41.

   More Repression in Myanmar. October 5, 1997, p. 17.

Fagan, Brian M. *World Prehistory: A Brief Introduction.* Boston: Little, Brown, 1979.

Farley, Jennifer. Work Hard, Play Hard in Singapore. *Sky,* October 1995, pp. 85–91.

Fforde, Adam, and Stefan de Vylder. *From Plan to Market: The Economic Transition in Vietnam.* Boulder, CO: Westview Press, 1996.

Field, Graham. *Economic Growth and Political Change in Asia.* New York: St. Martin's Press, 1995.

Frederick, William H., and Robert L. Worden, eds. *Indonesia: A Country Study.* Washington, DC: U.S. Government Printing Office, 1993.

Gamburd, Michele Ruth. Sri Lanka's "Army of Housemaids": Control of Remittances and Gender Transformations. *Anthropologica 37* (1995): 49–88.

Gargan, Edward A. Last Laugh for the Philippines. *The New York Times,* December 11, 1997, pp. B1, 10.

Geisel, Amy. Levi Closes 2 Plants in Knox; 2,221 Laid Off. *The Knoxville News-Sentinel,* November 4, 1997, pp. 1, 3.

Gelb, Joyce, and Marian Lief Palley, eds. *Women of Japan and Korea: Continuity and Change.* Philadelphia: Temple University Press, 1994.

Ghosh, Amitav. A Reporter at Large: Burma. *The New Yorker*, August 12, 1996, pp. 39–54.

Glassman, Jim, and Abdi Ismail Samatar. Development Geography and the Third-World State. *Progress in Human Geography 21*, no. 2 (1997): 164–198.

Grant, Richard, and Jan Nijman. Historical Changes in U.S. and Japanese Foreign Aid to the Asia-Pacific Region. *Annals of the American Association of Geographers 87*, no. 1 (1997): 32–51.

Grove, Noel, and Jodi Cobb (photos). The Many Faces of Thailand. *National Geographic*, February 1996, pp. 82–105.

Guiness, Patrick. *On the Margin of Capitalism: People and Development in Mukim Plentong, Johor, Malaysia.* Singapore: Oxford University Press, 1992.

Gullick, J. M. *Old Kuala Lumpur.* Oxford, UK: Oxford University Press, 1994.

Guyot, James F. Burma in 1996: One Economy, Two Polities. *Asian Survey 37*, no. 2 (February 1997): 188–193.

Hammes, Sara. An Insider's Guide to Seven Cities. Fortune Guide. *Fortune*, 1990, pp. 69–77.

Herbert, Bob. Brutality in Vietnam. *The New York Times*, March 28, 1997, p. A29.

Hobart, Angela, Urs Ramseyer, and Albert Leemann. *The Peoples of Bali.* Oxford, UK: Blackwell, 1996.

Hodgson, Bryan, and James L. Stanfield (photos). Time and Again in Burma. *National Geographic*, July 1984, pp. 90–122.

Hoskins, Janet, ed. *Headhunting and the Social Imagination in Southeast Asia.* Stanford, CA: Stanford University Press, 1996.

Howard, Michael C., ed. *Asia's Environmental Crisis.* Boulder, CO: Westview Press, 1993.

Hoyt, Sarina Hayes. *Old Malacca.* Oxford, UK: Oxford University Press, 1993.

Indonesia: Food: Tasty Bites. *Journey of a Lifetime.* 1997. Available at: http://web3.asia1.com.sg/tnp/journey/travel/indonesia/food.html.

Indonesia Today, 1997. Understanding East Timor; Quick Facts & Economic Trends; Business News; Tropical Forests. http://www.indonesiatoday.com/a4/a4_main.html. Site has been shut down.

Indonesian Central Bureau of Statistics. *Population Statistics,* Statistical Tables, 1997. Available at: wysiwyg://content.34/http://www.bps.go.id/statbysector/population/table.html.

Islam, Iyanatul, and Anis Chowdhury. *Asia-Pacific Economies: A Survey.* London and New York: Routledge, 1997.

Karim, Wazir Jahan. *"Male and Female" in Developing Southeast Asia.* Oxford, UK, and Washington, DC: Berg, 1995.

King, Daniel E. Thailand in 1996: Economic Slowdown Clouds Year. *Asian Survey 37*, no. 2 (February 1997): 160–166.

King, Victor T. *The Peoples of Borneo.* Oxford, UK: Blackwell, 1993.

Kirch, Patrick Vinton. *Feathered Gods and Fishhooks: An Introduction to Hawaiian Archaeology and Prehistory.* Honolulu: University of Hawaii Press, 1985.

Kirch, Patrick Vinton. *The Evolution of the Polynesian Chiefdoms.* Cambridge, UK: Cambridge University Press, 1989.

Leipziger, Danny M., ed. *Lessons from East Asia.* Ann Arbor: University of Michigan Press, 1997.

Liddle, R. William, and Rizal Mallarangeng. Indonesia in 1996—Pressures from Above and Below. *Asian Survey 37*, no. 2 (February 1997): 167–174.

Lintner, Bertil. *Burma in Revolt: Opium and Insurgency Since 1948.* Boulder, CO: Westview Press, 1994.

Lizee, Pierre P. Cambodia in 1996: Of Tigers, Crocodiles, and Doves. *Asian Survey 37*, no. 1 (January 1997): 65–71.

Logan, James. As cited in Angela Hobart, Urs Ramseyer, and Albert Leemann, *The Peoples of Bali.* Oxford, UK: Blackwell, 1996, pp. 1–5.

Marchant, Garry. River of Kings. *World Traveler,* December 1995, pp. 42–50, 100–102.

McDonald's Corporation. The Golden Arches Represent a Unique Passport That Opens Gateways Around the Globe. *The McDonald's Corporation 1996 Annual Report,* 1997, pp. 28–29.

Ministry of Information and the Arts. *Singapore Facts and Pictures 1995.* Singapore: Ministry of Information and the Arts, 1995.

Momsen, Janet Henshall. *Women and Development in the Third World.* London: Routledge, 1991.

Murphy, Denis. As cited in Jeremy Seabrook. In *Cities of the South: Scenes from a Developing World.* London and New York: Verso, 1996, pp. 199–201.

Murray, Alison J. *No Money, No Honey: A Study of Street Traders and Prostitutes in Jakarta.* Singapore: Oxford University Press, 1991.

Mydans, Seth. *The New York Times:*

Gas Pipeline Project Angers Critics of Burmese Rights Abuses. December 8, 1996, p. 12.

In Thai Camps, Fear of Burmese Troops Grows. March 3, 1997.

Nomads of Laos: Last Leftovers of Vietnam War. International section, March 12, 1997.

Seeing Suharto in His Friend's Deals. March 23, 1997, p. 10.

Burmese Officials Return Fugitive in U.S. Heroin Case to Thailand. May 18, 1997, p. 9.

Burmese Regime Wins Role in Southeast Asian Bloc. June 1, 1997, p. 6.

Fear Drives Business from Cambodia. July 23, 1997, p. A6.

Myers, Steven Lee. Trade vs. Rights: A U.S. Debate with a Burmese Focus. *The New York Times.* March 5, 1997.

Nair, Shanti. *Islam in Malaysian Foreign Policy.* London and New York: Routledge, 1997.

Newhall, Christopher G., and Raymundo S. Punongbayan, eds. *Fire and Mud: Eruptions and Lahars of Mount Pinatubo, Philippines.* Seattle: University of Washington Press, 1996.

New York Times Magazine. See Myanmar's Virgins! June 29, 1997.

Niessen, Sandra A. *Batak Cloth and Clothing: A Dynamic Indonesian Tradition.* Kuala Lumpur: Oxford University Press, 1993.

Odzer, Cleo. *Patpong Sisters: An American Woman's View of the Bangkok Sex World.* New York: Arcade, 1994.

O'Neill, Thomas. Irian Jaya: Indonesia's Wild Side. *National Geographic,* February 1996, pp. 2–33.

O'Neill, Thomas, and Michael S. Yamashita (photos). The Mekong. *National Geographic,* February 1993, pp. 2–36.

Papnek, Hanna, and Larel Schwede. Women Are Good with Money: Earning and Managing in an Indonesian City. Pp. 71–98, in *A Home Divided: Women and Income in the Third World* (Daisy Dwyer and Judith Bruce, eds.). Stanford, CA: Stanford University Press, 1988.

Parker, Karen. Republik Maluku: The Case for Self-Determination—A Briefing Paper of Humanitarian Law Project International Educational Development and Association of Humanitarian Lawyers. Paper presented to the United Nations Commission on Human Rights, 1996 Session, March, Geneva. Available at: http://www.webcom.com/hrin/parker/m.html.

Parnwell, Michael J. G., ed. *Uneven Development in Thailand.* Aldershot, UK: Avebury, 1996.

Parnwell, Michael J. G., and Raymond L. Bryant, eds. *Environmental Change in South-East Asia: People, Politics, and Sustainable Development.* London and New York: Routledge, 1996.

Passell, Peter. Asia's Path to More Equality and More Money for All. *The New York Times,* August 25, 1996, p. E5.

Paterniti, Michael. The Laptop Colonialists. *The New York Times:* Magazine section, January 12, 1997, pp. 22–28.

Peebles, Gavin, and Peter Wilson. *The Singapore Economy.* Cheltenham, UK: Edward Elgar, 1996.

Peletz, Michael G. *Reason and Passion: Representations of Gender in a Malay Society.* Berkeley: University of California Press, 1996.

Pinches, Michael. The Philippines' New Rich: Capitalist Transformation Amidst Economic Gloom. Pp. 105–133, *The New Rich in Asia* (Richard Robison and David S. G. Goodman, eds.). London: Routledge, 1996.

Pinto, Constancio, and Matthew Jardine. *East Timor's Unfinished Struggle: Inside the Timorese Resistance.* Boston: South End Press, 1997.

Potter, David M. *Japan's Foreign Aid to Thailand and the Philippines.* New York: St. Martin's Press, 1996.

Potter, Sulamith Heins. *Family Life in a Northern Thai Village.* Berkeley: University of California Press, 1977.

Rajakru, Dang. The State, Family and Industrial Development: The Singapore Case. *Journal of Contemporary Asia* 26, no.1 (1996): 3–27.

Ramage, Douglas E. *Politics in Indonesia: Democracy, Islam and the Ideology of Tolerance.* London and New York: Routledge, 1995.

Reid, T. R., and Stuart Franklin (photos). Malaysia: Rising Star. *National Geographic,* August 1997, pp. 100–121.

Rigg, Jonathan. *Southeast Asia: The Human Landscape of Modernizations and Development.* New York and London: Routledge, 1997.

Robison, Richard, and David S. G. Goodman, eds. *The New Rich in Asia: Mobile Phones, McDonald's and Middle-Class Revolution.* New York and London: Routledge, 1996.

Rodan, Garry. Singapore in 1996: Extended Election Fever. *Asian Survey 37,* no. 2 (February 1997): 176–180.

Rumley, Dennis, Tatsuya Chiba, Akihiko Takagi, and Yoriko Fukushima, eds. *Global Geopolitical Change and the Asia-Pacific: A Regional Perspective.* Aldershot, UK: Avebury, 1996.

Sanger, David E. *The New York Times:*
Hanoi Agrees to Pay Saigon's Debts to U.S. March 11, 1997, international section.
Maybe a Bankrupt Nation Isn't the Worst Thing in the World. October 12 1997, WK 6.
Indonesian Faceoff: Drawing Blood Without Bombs. March 8, 1998, WK1, 18.

SarDesai, D. R. *Southeast Asia Past and Present*, 4th ed. Boulder, CO: Westview Press, 1997.

Saunders, Graham. *A History of Brunei.* Kuala Lumpur: Oxford University Press, 1994.

Seabrook, Jeremy. *In the Cities of the South: Scenes from a Developing World.* London and New York: Verso, 1996.

Sears, Laurie J., ed. *Fantasizing the Feminine in Indonesia.* Durham, NC, and London: Duke University Press, 1996.

Sellato, Bernard. *Nomads of the Borneo Rainforest: The Economics, Politics and Ideology of Settling Down.* Honolulu: University of Hawaii Press, 1994.

Shenon, Philip. AIDS Epidemic, Late to Arrive, Now Explodes in Populous Asia. *The New York Times,* January 21, 1996, pp. 1, 8.

Shenon, Philip. For Asian Nation's First Family, Financial Empire Is in Peril. *The New York Times,* November 5, 1997, pp. A1, D5.

Shepherd, Catherine, and Julian Gearing. Rallying for Change: Thailand's Poor Take to the Streets. *Asiaweek,* November 28, 1997. Available at: http://www.pathfinder.com/asiaweek/97/1128/cs4.html.

Singh, Ajay. Credit Where It's Due: Giving the Poor a New Start. *Asiaweek,* November 1997. Available at: http://pathfinder.com/@@bo3bXAQAPLtCRrf*/Asiaweek/current/issue/cs6.html. Page is no longer available.

Solomon, Charmaine. *The Complete Asian Cookbook.* New York: McGraw-Hill, 1976.

Stremlau, John. Dateline Bangalore: Third World Technopolis. *Foreign Policy* (Spring 1996): 152–168.

Sunindyo, Saraswati. Murder, Gender and the Media. Pp. 120–139, in *Fantasizing the Feminine in Indonesia* (Laurie Sears, ed.). Durham, NC: Duke University Press, 1996.

Suryakusuma, Julia I. The State and Sexuality in New Order Indonesia. Pp. 92–119, in *Fantasizing the Feminine in Indonesia* (Laurie Sears, ed.). Durham, NC: Duke University Press, 1996.

Tesoro, Jose Manuel, and Dominic Faulder. Changing of the Guard: SLORC Fixes Its Name and Purges Some Faces. *Asiaweek,* November 28, 1997. Available at: http://www.pathfinder.com/asiaweek/97/1128/nat4.html.

Thorbecke, Erik, and Theodore van der Pluijm. *Rural Indonesia: Socio-Economic Development in a Changing Environment.* New York: New York University Press, 1993.

UNESCO. *Women's Participation in Higher Education: China, Nepal and the Philippines.* Bangkok: UNESCO Principal Regional Office for Asia and the Pacific, 1990.

Unocal. *Unocal in Myanmar.* 1997. Available at: http://www.unocal.com/myanmar..

U.S. Census Bureau. *Statistical Indicators on Women: An Asian Perspective. Statistical Brief.* Washington, DC: U.S. Census Bureau, November 1993.

U.S. Department of State. *Burma Report on Human Rights Practices for 1996.* Washington, DC: Bureau of Democracy, Human Rights, and Labor, 1997. Available at: gopher://dosfan.lib.uic.edu:70/00ftp%3ADOSFan%

3AGopher%3A03%20Publications%20−%20Major%20Reports%3AHuman%20Rights%20Country%20Practices%3A1997%20HRC%20Report%3A04%20East%20Asia%20and%20Pacific%3ABurma.

Usher, Ann Danaiya. The Race for Power in Laos: The Nordic Connections. Pp. 123−144, in *Environmental Change in Southeast Asia* (Michael J. G. Parnwell and Raymond L. Bryant, eds.). London and New York: Routledge, 1996.

Waldman, Peter. Dam Proposed for Laos Is of Immense Meaning to an Array of Interests. *The Wall Street Journal*, August 12, 1997, p. 1.

Waldman, Peter, and Richard Borsuk. Running Amuk: Indonesia's Riots Put Focus on the Iron Rule and Future of Suharto. *The Wall Street Journal*, May 27, 1997, p. 1.

Waldman, Peter, and Paul M. Sherer. The Go-Go Years in Bangkok Keep Going—and Going. *The Wall Street Journal*, September 26, 1997, p. 1.

Wallenechinsky, David. "A Noble Voice for Freedom": An Interview with Aung San Suu Kyi. *The Knoxville News-Sentinel, Parade Magazine*, January 19, 1997, pp. 4−6.

White, Peter T., and David Alan Harvey (photos). Vietnam: Hard Road to Peace. *National Geographic*, November 1989, pp. 561−621.

White, Peter T., and Seny Norasingh (photos). Laos. *National Geographic*, June 1987, pp. 772−795.

Williams, Louise. Megawati's Boycott Is One Among Millions. *The Sidney Morning Herald*, May 29, 1997. Available at: http://www.smh.com.au/daily/content/970529/world/world2.html. Site and article currently available only for a fee.

Williams, Walter. *Javanese Lives*. Piscataway, NJ: Rutgers University Press, 1991.

Winichakul, Thongchai. *Siam Mapped: A History of the Geo-Body of a Nation*. Honolulu: University of Hawaii Press, 1994.

Winzeler, Robert L. *Latah in Southeast Asia: The History and Ethnography of a Culture-Bound Syndrome*. Cambridge, UK: Cambridge University Press, 1995.

Wolf, Diane Lauren. *Factory Daughters: Gender, Household Dynamics, and Rural Industrialization in Java*. Berkeley: University of California Press, 1992.

Womack, Brantly. Vietnam in 1996: Reform Immobilism. *Asian Survey 37*, no. 1 (January 1997): 79−87.

Wren, Christopher S. Where Opium Reigned, Burmese Claim Inroads. *The New York Times*, April 19, 1998, p. 8.

WuDunn, Sheryl. Asian Economies, Once a Miracle, Now Muddled. *The New York Times*, August 31, 1997, p. 1.

Wurfel, David, and Bruce Burton, eds. *Southeast Asia in the New World Order: The Political Economy of a Dynamic Region*. Hampshire, UK: Macmillan, 1996.

Wysock, Bernard, Jr. Malaysia Is Gambling on a Costly Plunge into a Cyber Future. *The Wall Street Journal*, June 10, 1997, p. 1.

Wysock, Bernard, Jr. In Developing Nations, Many Youths Splurge Mainly on U.S. Goods. *The Wall Street Journal*, June 26, 1997, p. 1.

Yahuda, Michael. *The International Politics of the Asia-Pacific, 1945–1995*. London and New York: Routledge, 1996.

Young Jeh Kim, ed. *The New Pacific Community in the 1990s*. Armonk, NY: M. E. Sharpe, 1996.

Zich, Arthur, and Charles O'Rear (photos). Two Worlds, Time Apart: Indonesia. *National Geographic*, January 1989, pp. 96−128.

Chapter 11 Oceania: Australia, New Zealand, and the Pacific

Anderson, Kay, and Fay Gale, eds. *Inventing Places: Studies in Cultural Geography*. Melbourne: Longman Chesire, 1992.

Aoude, Ibrahim G., ed. *The Political Economy of Hawaii*. Vol. 35. *Social Process in Hawaii Series*. Honolulu: University of Hawaii at Manoa, 1994.

Associated Press. New Zealand Settles Biggest Maori Claim Yet. *The Seattle Times*, October 5, 1996. Available at: http://archives.seattletimes.com/cgi-bin/texis.mummy/web/vortex/display?storyID=36d4e70b3f&query=New+Zealand+settles+biggest+Maori+claim+yet.

AUS Bureau of Statistics. *Population, Australia's States and Territories—1905–2045(a)*. 1997. Available at: http://www.abs.gov.au/websitedbs/c311215.nsf/20564c23f3183fdaca25672100813ef1/8960e14686ce9fdbca2567220072e924?OpenDocument.

The Australian and New Zealand Wine Industry Journal. Varietal Report—Export Chardonnay—Merlot. 1996. Available at: http://www.winetitles.com.au/varietals/chardonnay.html.

Australian Getaways. *Australian Getaways* (various cities), 1997. Available at: http://www.australiangetaways.com.au.<cityname.html>

Australia's Northern Territory. 1999. Available at: http://www.nt.gov.au/sitemap.shtml.

Barfield, Claude E., ed. *Expanding U.S.-Asian Trade and Investment—New Challenges and Policy Options*. Washington, DC: AEI Press (American Enterprise Institute), 1997.

Bora, Bijit, and Christopher Findlay, eds. *Regional Integration and the Asia-Pacific*. Oxford: Oxford University Press, 1996.

Bowman, Sally-Jo. The New Ancient Mariners. *Aloha*, October 1993, pp. 16−21, 54−58.

Brewis, Alexandra. *Lives on the Line: Women and Ecology on a Pacific Atoll*. Fort Worth, TX: Harcourt Brace, 1996.

Buck, Elizabeth. *Paradise Remade: The Politics of Culture and History in Hawaii*. Philadelphia: Temple University Press, 1993.

Burbank, Victoria Katherine. *Fighting Women: Anger and Aggression in Aboriginal Australia*. Berkeley: University of California Press, 1994.

Butler, Joel. *The Wines and Wineries of Australia*, brochure. Burlingame, CA: Australian Wine Importers Association, 1995.

Cameron, Marina. Stop the Jabiluka Mine! *Green Left Weekly*, search back issues, no. 289. September 10, 1997. Available at: http://www.peg.apc.org/~greenleft.

Cayetano, Benjamin J., Governor. Restoring Hawaii's Economic Momentum. 1996. At: http://planet-hawaii.com/~gov/econ/summary.html. No longer available on Web site.

Cockerton, Camilla "Women." Pp. 305−314, in Moshe Rapaport (ed). *The Pacific Islands: Environment and Society*. Honolulu: Bess Press, 1999.

Colbert, Evelyn. *The Pacific Islands: Paths to the Present*. Boulder, CO: Westview Press, 1997.

Collingwood, Dean W. *Japan and the Pacific Rim.* Guilford, CT: Dushkin Publishing Group, 1991.

Collingwood, Dean W. *Japan and the Pacific Rim,* 3rd ed. Guilford, CT: Dushkin Publishing Group/Brown & Benchmark, 1995.

Connah, Graham. *The Archaeology of Australia's History.* Cambridge, UK: Cambridge University Press, 1988.

Cook, Captain James. Quoted in Marshall Sahlins, *Islands of History.* University of Chicago Press, Chicago, 1985, p. 6 fn.

Cook, Len (Government Statistician, New Zealand). *New Zealand's Current and Future Population Dynamics.* Paper presented at the Population Conference, Wellington, November 12–14, 1997. Available at: http://www.stats.govt.nz/statsweb.nsf.

Corliss, Richard. *Toxic Love,* a film review, in *Time of Once Were Warriors.* 1995. Available at: http://www.pathfinder.com/@@261SpkG9BgEAQOc/1995/950306/950306.cinema.warriors.html.

Costello, Katrina. *The Torres Strait: Our Last Frontier.* 1996. Available at: http://www.worldworks.net/qttc/ti.html.

Crocombe, Ron. Geopolitical Change in the Pacific Islands. Pp. 282–300, in *Global Geopolitical Change and the Asia-Pacific: A Regional Perspective* (Rumely et al., eds.). Hampshire, UK: Avebury, 1996.

Das, Dilip K. The Changing Morphology of the Asia-Pacific Region. Pp. 1–44, in *The Changing Business Environment in the Asia-Pacific Region* (Henri-Claude de Bettignies, ed.). London: International Thompson Business Press, 1997.

Dathorne, O. R. *Asian Voyages: Two Thousand Years of Constructing the Other.* Westport, CT: Bergin & Garvey, 1996.

Davis, Gavan. *Shoal of Time: A History of the Hawaiian Islands.* Honolulu: University of Hawaii Press, 1968.

de Coppet, Daniel, and Andre Iteanu, eds. *Cosmos and Society in Oceania.* Oxford, UK: Berg, 1995.

Department of Transportation. *National Rail and Australia's Railways.* 1999. Available at: http://www.dot.gov.au/programs/workwedo.htm#rail.

Economic and Social Commission for Asia and the Pacific. *Economic and Social Survey of Asia and the Pacific 1995.* New York: United Nations, 1995.

The Economist (staff writers). Papua New Guinea: Executive Incomers. March 1, 1997, pp. 39–40.

Eisenstein, Hester. *Inside Agitators: Australian Femocrats and the State.* Philadelphia: Temple University Press, 1996.

Ellis, Joan. *Once Were Warriors, A Nebbadoon Review.* 1995. Available at: http://ellis.nebbadoon.com/docs/joined_reviewfiles/ONCE_WERE_WARRIORS.html.

Environment Australia Online. Available at: http://www.erin.gov.au/portfolio/.

Farnsworth, Clyde H. Where the Sacred Serpent Rests, a Mine Intrudes. *The New York Times:* International section, Friday, July 18, 1997.

Farrell, Don A. *The Americanization 1898–1918. The Pictorial History of Guam Series.* Guam: Micronesian Productions, 1986.

Feher, Joseph. *Hawaii: A Pictorial History.* Honolulu: Bishop Museum Press, 1969.

Feinberg, Richard, ed. *Seafaring in the Contemporary Pacific Islands: Studies in Continuity and Change.* DeKalb: Northern Illinois Press, 1995.

Flanagan, Tom. Traditional Owners Fight Jabiluka Mine. *Green Left Weekly,* Search back issues no. 278, June 18, 1997. Available at: http://www.peg.apc.org/~greenleft.

Government of Guam. Important Details About Guam. 1996. Available at: http://ns.gov.gu/details.html.

Greene, Gervase. Uranium Mine Set to Receive Go-Ahead. *The Age,* Melbourne online: August 28, 1997. http://www.theage.com.au/daily/970825/news/news9.html. Archive currently not available online.

Hawaii Visitors Bureau. Miscellaneous tables on visitors/tourists. 1999. Available at: http://www.hawaii.gov/tourism.

Hayashida, Roanald Hideo. Papua New Guinea in 1996: Problems in the Homestretch. *Asian Survey 37,* no. 2 (February 1997): 199–203.

Henningham, Stephen. *The Pacific Island States: Security and Sovereignty in the Post–Cold War World.* New York: St. Martin's Press, 1995.

Hiatt, L. R. *Arguments About Aborigines: Australia and the Evolution of Social Anthropology.* Cambridge, UK: Cambridge University Press, 1996.

Holmes, Sandra Le Brun. *The Goddess and the Moon Man: The Sacred Art of the Tiwi Aborigines.* Australia: Craftsman House/GB Arts, 1995.

Howard, Michael. *Gauguin.* London: Dorling Kindersley, 1992.

Hviding, Edvard. *Guardians of Marovo Lagoon: Practice, Place and Politics in Maritime Melanesia.* Honolulu: University of Hawaii, 1996.

Ii, John Papa. *Fragments of Hawaiian History.* Honolulu: Bishop Museum Press, 1983.

Islam, Iyanatul, and Anis Chowdhury. *Asia-Pacific Economies: A Survey.* London and New York: Routledge, 1997.

Jolly, Margaret. *Women of the Place: Kastom, Colonialism and Gender in Vanuatu.* Chur, Switzerland: Harwood Academic Publishers, 1994.

Jolly, Margaret, and Martha Macintyre, eds. *Family and Gender in the Pacific: Domestic Contradictions and the Colonial Impact.* Cambridge, UK: Cambridge University Press, 1989.

Juillerat, Bernard. *Children of the Blood: Society, Reproduction and Cosmology in New Guinea.* Oxford, UK: Berg, 1996.

Kamakau, Samuel M. *Ka po'e kahiko: The People of Old.* Honolulu: Bishop Museum Press, 1964.

Kapferer, Judith. *Being All Equal: Identity, Difference and Australian Cultural Practice.* Oxford, UK: Berg, 1996.

Kirch, Patrick Vinton. *Feathered Gods and Fishhooks: An Introduction to Hawaiian Archaeology and Prehistory.* Honolulu: University of Hawaii Press, 1985.

Kirch, Patrick Vinton. *The Evolution of the Polynesian Chiefdoms.* Cambridge, UK: Cambridge University Press, 1989.

KiWi Klan Inc. *Lisamaree. The Story of the Mountains.* 1997. Available at: http://carbon.chem.unsw.edu.au/~kiwi/legend.html.

Kluge, P. F. *The Edge of Paradise: America in Micronesia.* Honolulu: University of Hawaii Press, 1991.

Koroa, M. Carolyn Drew. 'O Bulavinaka': Space and Well-Being in Rural Fiji. Unpublished master's thesis, Department of Geography, University of Tennessee, Knoxville, 1997.

Kuykendall, Ralph S. *The Hawaiian Kingdom,* Vol. I. Honolulu: University of Hawaii Press, 1967.

Lal, Brij V. *Broken Waves: A History of the Fiji Islands in the Twentieth Century.* Honolulu: University of Hawaii Press, 1992.

Lebra, Joyce Chapman. *Women's Voices in Hawaii.* Niwot: University Press of Colorado, 1991.

Linnekin, Jocelyn. *Sacred Queens and Women of Consequence: Rank, Gender, and Colonialism in the Hawaiian Islands.* Ann Arbor: University of Michigan Press, 1990.

Lipin, Steven. On Islands of Palau, Justice Is a Breeze for Larry Miller. *The Wall Street Journal,* August 1, 1997, p. A11.

Lockhart, Douglas G., David Drakakis-Smith, and John Schembri, eds. *The Development Process in Small Island States.* London: Routledge, 1993.

Mack, Louise. Cited in Ros Pesman, *Duty Free—Australian Women Abroad.* Melbourne: Oxford University Press, 1996, p. 5.

Malinowsky, Bronislaw. *Argonauts of the Western Pacific.* New York: Dutton, 1961.

McKnight, Tom L. *Oceania: The Geography of Australia, New Zealand, and the Pacific Islands.* Englewood Cliffs, NJ: Prentice Hall, 1995.

Mead, Margaret. *Coming of Age in Samoa.* New York: American Museum of Natural History, 1973.

Melville, Herman. *Typee: A Peep at Polynesian Life.* Viking/ Penguin, 1995

Mitchell, Andrew. *The Fragile South Pacific: An Ecological Odyssey.* Austin: University of Texas Press, 1990.

Mitchell, Ben. Fischer Says Government Will Approve Jabiluka. *The Age,* Melbourne online, Monday, June 16, 1997. http://www.theage.com.au/daily/970616/news/news4. html. Archive currently not available on online.

Morton, Helen. *Becoming Tongan: An Ethnography of Childhood.* Honolulu: University of Hawaii Press, 1996.

Murcoch, Lindsay. *Chan Quits: 'I Hear the Call.'* Asia OnLine, the Age Network. March 27, 1997. Available at: http:// www.theage.com.au/special/asiaonline/png_xv.htm.

Nile, Richard, and Christian Clerk. *Cultural Atlas of Australia, New Zealand and the South Pacific.* New York: Facts on File, 1996.

North Limited. *The Jabiluka Project Executive Summary,* July 24, 1997. Available at: http://www.north.com.au/era/project. html.

Noyes, Martha H. Aloha, Hawaii. *Honolulu Magazine,* November 1992, pp. 58–63.

Papua New Guinea Online. PNG Online Profile. 1996. Available at: http://www.niugini.com/profile1.htm#4.

Parfit, Michael. New Zealand: Hard Cases and Room for Hope. *Islands: A Treasury of Contemporary Travel Writing.* Santa Barbara, CA: Capra Press, 1992.

Pawson, Eric. Pp. 15–36, in *Inventing Places—Studies in Cultural Geography.* Kay Anderson and Fay Gale (eds). Melbourne: Longman Chesire, 1992.

Pesman, Ros. *Duty Free: Australian Women Abroad.* Melbourne: Oxford University Press, 1996.

Polk, Susan. *Once Were Warriors,* film review. 1995. Available at: http://technoculture.mira.net.au/sponce.htm

Premdas, Ralph R. *Ethnic Conflict and Development: The Case of Fiji.* Aldershot, UK: Avebury, 1995.

Ralston, Caroline. *Grass Huts and Warehouses: Pacific Beach Communities of the Nineteenth Century.* Honolulu: University Press of Hawaii, 1978.

Roberts, Stephen H. Cited in John Pilger, *A Secret Country: The Hidden Australia.* New York: Knopf, 1991, p. 23.

Robillard, Albert B., ed. *Social Change in the Pacific Islands.* London and New York: Kegan Paul International, 1992.

Rumley, Dennis, Tatsuya Chiba, Akihiko Takagi, and Yoriko Fukushima, eds. *Global Geopolitical Change and the Asia-Pacific: A Regional Perspective.* Aldershot, UK: Avebury, 1996.

Sahlins, Marshall. *Islands of History.* Chicago: University of Chicago Press, 1985.

Skehan, Carig. A Tough Future for a PM with a Tough Past. *The Age,* Melbourne Online. 1997. http://www.theage. com.au/daily/971206/news/news25.html Archive currently not available on online.

Smith, Michael French. *Hard Times of Kairiru Island: Poverty, Development, and Morality in a Papua New Guinea Village.* Honolulu: University of Hawaii Press, 1994.

Spriggs, Matthew. *The Island Melanesians.* Oxford, UK: Blackwell, 1997.

State Department of Business, Economic Development, and Tourism. *Economic Trends and Outlook,* January 1999. Available at: http://www.hawaii.gov/dbedt/outlook

State Department of Business, Economic Development, and Tourism. *Statistical and Economic Reports,* Last update, April 14, 1999. Available at: http://www.hawaii.gov/dbedt.

Swarns, Rachel L. Hawaii Bucks the Trench on Welfare Reform. *The New York Times,* September 28, 1997, WK3.

Tasmania, Population and Other Information. Available at: http://www.tased.edu.au/tasfaq/people/PeoplePop.html.

Theroux, Paul. *The Happy Isles of Oceania: Paddling the Pacific.* New York: Putnam, 1992.

Waltzing Matilda. See http://www.crafti.com.au/~wolf/ matildapage.htm; http://www.crafti.com.au/~wolf/ banjopage.htm; http://waltzingmatilda.com/wwwords.html; and http://aaa.com.au/waltzing.com.

Welch, David; Conrad "Mac" Goodwin, and Judy McNeill. *The Development of Agana, Guam, 1500–1991.* Paper presented at the Society for Historical Archaeology 1992 Conference on Historical and Underwater Archaeology, Kingston, Jamaica, January 10, 1992.

White, Geoffrey M., and Lamont Lindstrom, eds. *Chiefs Today: Traditional Pacific Leadership and the Post Colonial State.* Stanford, CA: Stanford University Press, 1997.

Winchester, Hilary. The Construction and Deconstruction of Women's Roles in the Urban Landscape. Pp. 139–156, in *Inventing Places: Studies in Cultural Geography* (Kay Anderson and Fay Gale, eds.). Melbourne: Longman Cheshire, 1992.

Wine Makers Federation of Australia. *Into the Next Century, the Five-Year Plan 1997–2001.* Australian Wine Industry. 1997. Available at: http://www.winetitles.com.au/auswine/ industry/fiveyearplan.html.

World Travel and Tourism Council. *Travel and Tourism and Hawaii's Economy: Impact and Perspective Millennium Vision* (1997). Available at: http://www.hawaii.gov/tourism/ 1997wttc.pdf.

Wright, Tony. Bougainville Warms to Idea of Peace. *The Age,* Melbourne Online. 1997. http://www.theage.com.au/ daily/971216/news/news14.html. Not currently available online.

Young Jeh Kim, ed. *The New Pacific Community in the 1990s.* Armonk, NY: M. E. Sharpe, 1996.

GENERAL SOURCES

Abler, Ronald F., Melvin G. Marcus, and Judy M. Olson, eds. *Geography's Inner Worlds: Pervasive Themes in Contemporary American Geography*. New Brunswick, NJ: Rutgers University Press, 1992.

Allen, John L. *Student Atlas of Economic Development*. Guilford, CT: Dushkin/McGraw-Hill, 1997.

American Foreign Policy 95/96. Annual Editions. Guilford, CT: Dushkin Publishing Group, 1995.

Anderson, Kay, and Fay Gale, eds. *Inventing Places: Studies in Cultural Geography*. Melbourne: Longman Chesire, 1992.

Annals of the Association of American Geographers. All issues, 1989–April 1999

Annual Editions. Geography 93/94. Guilford, CT: Dushkin Publishing Group, 1993.

Annual Editions. Guilford, CT: Dushkin Publishing Group/ Brown & Benchmark.
Developing World 97/98, 1997.
Global Issues 93/94, 1993.
Global Issues 95/96, 1995.
Global Issues 96/97, 1996.
World Politics 95/96, 1995.

Askwith, Michael. *Human Development Under Transition: Europe and CIS*. New York: Regional Bureau for Europe and CIS, United Nations Development Programme, 1997.

Atlas of the World. New York: Oxford University Press, 1996.

Balick, Michael J., and Paul Alan Cox. *Plants, People, and Culture: The Science of Ethnobotany*. New York: Scientific American Library, 1996.

Basu, Amrita, ed. *The Challenge of Local Feminisms: Women's Movements in Global Perspective*. Boulder, CO: Westview Press, 1995.

Belenky, Mary Field, Blythe McVicker Clinchy, Nancy Rule Goldberger, and Jill Mattuck Tarule. *Women's Ways of Knowing—The Development of Self, Voice, and Mind*. New York: Basic Books, 1986.

Bergman, Edward F. *Human Geography: Cultures, Connections, and Landscapes*. Upper Saddle River, NJ: Prentice Hall, 1995.

Bergman, Edward F., and William H. Renwick. *Introduction to Geography: People, Places, and Environment*. Upper Saddle River, NJ: Prentice Hall, 1999.

Blaut, J. M. *The Colonizer's Model of the World*. New York: Guilford Press, 1993.

Blunt, Alison, and Gillian Rose, eds. *Writing Women and Space: Colonial and Postcolonial Geographies*. New York: Guilford Press, 1994.

Boon-Thong, Lee, and Tengku Shamsul Bahrin, eds. *Vanishing Borders: The New International Order of the 21st Century*. Aldershot, UK: Ashgate, 1998.

Boyd, Andrew. *An Atlas of World Affairs*, 10th ed. London and New York: Routledge, 1998.

Bradshaw, Michael. *A World Regional Geography: The New Global Order*. Madison, WI: Brown & Benchmark, 1997.

Burton, Ian, Robert W. Kates, and Gilbert F. White. *The Environment as Hazard*, 2nd ed. New York: Guilford Press, 1993.

Castells, Manuel. *The Information Age: Economy, Society and Culture*. Vol. 3. *End of Millennium*. Malden, MA: Blackwell, 1998.

Central Intelligence Agency. *The World Fact Book 1998*. Washington, DC: CIA, 1998. Available at: http://www.odci.gov/cia/publications/factbook/index.html.

Charlton, Sue Ellen M. *Women in Third World Development*. Boulder, CO: Westview Press, 1984.

Cole, John. *Geography of the World's Major Regions*. London and New York: Routledge, 1996.

Crain, William. *Theories of Development: Concepts and Applications*, 3rd ed. Englewood Cliffs, NJ: Prentice Hall, 1992.

D'Aluisio, Faith, and Peter Menzel. *Women in the Material World*. San Francisco: Sierra Club Books, 1996.

de Blij, H. J. *Human Geography: Culture, Society, and Space*, 5th ed. New York: Wiley, 1996.

de Blij, H. J., and Peter O. Muller. *Physical Geography of the Global Environment*, 2nd ed. New York: Wiley, 1996.

de Blij, H. J., and Peter O. Muller. *Geography: Realms, Regions and Concepts*, 8th ed. New York: Wiley, 1997.

Drucker, Peter F. *Post-Capitalist Society*. New York: HarperCollins, 1993.

Duley, Margot I., and Mary I. Edwards, eds. *The Cross-Cultural Study of Women*. New York: Feminist Press, 1986.

The Economist. Weekly issues. June 1996–April 1999.

The Economist Atlas. New York: Henry Holt, 1992.

The Economist Group. *The World in 1998*. London: The Economist Group, 1997.

Fellmann, Jerome, Arthur Getis, and Judith Getis. *Human Geography*. Dubuque, IA: Brown & Benchmark, 1997.

Fisher, James S., ed. *Geography and Development: A World Regional Approach*, 3rd ed. Columbus, OH: Merrill, 1989.

Geography for Life: National Geography Standards 1994. Washington, DC: National Geographic Research & Exploration, 1994.

Getis, Arthur, Judith Getis, and Jerome D. Fellmann. *Introduction to Geography*, 5th ed. Dubuque, IA: Wm. C. Brown, 1996.

Gregory, Derek, Ron Martin, and Graham Smith, eds. *Human Geography: Society, Space, and Social Science*. Minneapolis: University of Minnesota Press, 1994.

Hammond. *Hammond Times Concise Atlas of World History*. Maplewood, NJ: Hammond, 1994.

Hammond. *Hammond Citation World Atlas*. Maplewood, NJ: Hammond, 1996.

Hammond. *The New Comparative World Atlas*. Maplewood, NJ: Hammond, 1997.

Hepner, George F., and Jesse O. McKee. *World Regional Geography: A Global Approach*. St. Paul, MN: West, 1992.

International Data Base, U.S. Census Bureau. Available at: http://www.census.gov/cgi-bin/ipc/idbpyrs.pl.

International Monetary Fund. *World Economic Outlook, May 1993*. Washington, DC: International Monetary Fund, 1993.

Jackson, Richard H., and Lloyd E. Hudman. *World Regional Geography: Issues for Today*. New York: Wiley, 1990.

Johnston, R. J., Peter J. Taylor, and Michael J. Watts. *Geographies of Global Change: Remapping the World in the Late Twentieth Century*. Oxford, UK: Blackwell, 1995.

Jordan, Terry G., and Lester Rowntree. *The Human Mosaic: A Thematic Introduction to Cultural Geography*, 5th ed. Grand Rapids, MI: Harper & Row, 1990.

Kaplan, Robert D. Travels into America's Future. *The Atlantic Monthly*, August 1998, pp. 37–61.

Katz, Cindi, and Janice Monk, eds. *Full Circles: Geographies of Women over the Life Course*. London and New York: Routledge, 1993.

Kuby, Michael, John Harner, and Patricia Gober. *Human Geography in Action*. New York: Wiley, 1998.

Lewin, Roger. *The Origin of Modern Humans*. New York: Scientific American Library, 1993.

Maidment, Fred, ed. *Annual Editions International Business 96/97*. Guilford, CT: Dushkin Publishing Group/Brown & Benchmark, 1996.

Marsh, William M., and John M. Grossa, Jr. *Environmental Geography: Science, Land Use, and Earth Systems*. New York: Wiley, 1996.

Masters, C. D., D. H. Root, and R.M. Turner. *World of Petroleum*, February 1999. Available at: http://energy.er.usgs.gov/products/papers/World_oil/source/index.htm.

McKnight, Tom L. *Physical Geography: A Landscape Appreciation*, 5th ed. Upper Saddle River, NJ: Prentice Hall, 1996.

McKnight, Tom L. *Physical Geography: A Landscape Appreciation*, 6th ed. Upper Saddle River, NJ: Prentice Hall, 1998.

Momsen, Janet H., and Vivian Kinnaird, eds. *Different Places, Different Voices: Gender and Development in Africa, Asia and Latin America*. London and New York: Routledge, 1993.

Morning Edition and *All Things Considered*. National Public Radio.

Morrison, Philip, and Kosta Tsipis. *Reason Enough to Hope: America and the World of the 21st Century*. Cambridge, MA: MIT Press, 1998.

Morrissey, Mike, advisor. *Atlas for Caribbean Examinations*, 2nd ed. Essex, UK: Addison-Wesley Longman, 1998.

National Geographic. All issues between January 1989 and April 1999.

National Research Council. *Rediscovering Geography: New Relevance for Science and Society*. Washington, DC: National Academy Press, 1997.

Nelson, Ronald E., Robert E. Gabler, and James W. Vining. *Human Geography: People, Cultures, and Landscapes*. Fort Worth, TX: Saunders, 1995.

New Yorker. June 1996–April 1999.

Oxford Atlas of the World. New York: Oxford University Press, 1996.

Population Data Sheet. 1994–1998

Population Today. Monthly Newsletter of Population Reference Bureau. January 1998–March 1999.

Professional Geographer. All issues, 1989–April 1999.

Rand McNally. *Historical Atlas of the World*. Chicago: Rand McNally, 1965.

Rand McNally. *Atlas of World Geography*. New York: Rand McNally, 1997.

Reader's Digest/Bartholomew. *Illustrated Atlas of the World*, 3rd rev. ed. Pleasantville, NY: Reader's Digest, 1997.

Riley, Nancy E. *Gender, Power, and Population Change. Population Bulletin 52*, no. 1 (May 1997).

Rockett, Ian R. H. *Injury and Violence: A Public Health Perspective, Population Bulletin*, December 1998. Washington, DC: Population Reference Bureau, 1998.

Rogers, Alisdair. *Peoples and Cultures*. Oxford, UK: Oxford University Press, 1992.

Rubenstein, James M. *An Introduction to Human Geography*. Upper Saddle River, NJ: Prentice Hall, 1999.

Russett, Bruce, and Harvey Starr. *World Politics: The Menu for Choice*, 5th ed. New York: W. H. Freeman, 1996.

Scientific American. May 1996.

Seager, Joni. *The State of Women in the World Atlas*. New York: Penguin, 1997.

Shelly, Fred M., and Audrey E. Clarke. *Human and Cultural Geography: A Global Perspective*. Dubuque, IA: Wm. C. Brown, 1994.

Simmons, J. G. *Interpreting Nature: Cultural Constructions of the Environment*. London and New York: Routledge, 1996 (1993).

Smith, Bruce D. *The Emergence of Agriculture*. New York: Scientific American Library, 1995.

Southern African Development Community. Available at: http://www.sadc-usa.net.

The Sunday New York Times. Weekly issues. June 1996–April 1999

Thomas, Alan, with Ben Crow, Paul Frenz, Tom Hewitt, Sabrina Kassam, and Steven Treagust. *Third World Atlas*, 2nd ed. Washington, DC: Taylor & Francis, 1994.

Transitions. Monthly issues. November 1997–March 1999

Tuan, Yi-Fu. *Escapism*. Baltimore, MD: The Johns Hopkins University Press, 1998.

United Nations Development Programme:

  Background Papers: Human Development Report 1995. 1996.

  Human Development Report 1996: Economic Growth and Human Development. Available at: http://www.undp.org/hdro/96.htm.

  Human Development Report 1997: Poverty from a Human Development Perspective. Available at: http://www.undp.org/hdro/97.htm.

  Human Development Report 1998: Consumption Patterns and Their Implications for Human Development. Available at: http://www.undp.org/hdro/98.htm.

United Nations Population Fund. *The State of World Population 1997: The Right to Choose: Reproductive Rights and Reproductive Health*. New York: United Nations Population Fund, 1997.

U.S. Census Bureau. International Population Pyramids. *International Data Base*. Available at: http://www.census.gov/ipc/www/idbnew.html.

U.S. Census Bureau. *The World at a Glance: 1994*, Statistical Brief. Washington, DC: U.S. Census Bureau, 1994.

Walter, E. V. *Placeways: A Theory of the Human Environment*. Chapel Hill: University of North Carolina Press, 1988.

Wheeler, Jesse H., Jr., and J. Trenton Kostbade. *Essentials of World Regional Geography*. Fort Worth, TX: Saunders, 1993, 1995.

The World Almanac and Book of Facts. Mahwah, NJ: World Almanac Books, 1997.

World Bank. *Social Indicators of Development 1991–1992*. Baltimore, MD, and London: Johns Hopkins University Press, 1992.

World Bank. *World Resources 1994–95: People and the Environment*. New York: Oxford University Press, 1994.

World Bank. *World Development Report 1995: Workers in an Integrating World*. New York: Oxford University Press, 1995.

World Bank. *World Resources 1996–97: The Urban Environment.* New York: Oxford University Press, 1996.

World Bank. *World Resources 1998–99: Environmental Change and Human Health.* New York: Oxford University Press, 1998.

World Bank:

Advancing Sustainable Development: The World Bank and Agenda 21. 1997.

Expanding the Measure of Wealth: Indicators of Environmentally Sustainable Development. 1997.

The World Book Atlas. Chicago: World Book, 1996.

World Sat. *The Cartographic Satellite Atlas of the World.* Toronto: Warwick, 1997.

Worldwatch Institute. *State of the World 1999: A Worldwatch Institute Report on Progress Toward a Sustainable Society.* New York: W. W. Norton, 1999.

The World's Women 1995: Trends and Statistics. New York: United Nations, 1995.

INDEX

Key
boldface indicates a glossary entry.
italics indicate a subregion name or a foreign word.
Caps and small caps indicate a region name.
i = image caption; *t* = table.

Abiola, Mashood, 349
Aborigines. *See also* Native Americans.
  in East Asia, 434, 452, 458
  in Oceania, 524, 526, 528–531, 530*i*
  in South Asia, 378, 380–381
  in Southeast Asia, 476, 482, 484–485,
    509–510
abortion. *See* birth control; population.
acculturation, 123, 184
acid rain, 63*i*, 79–80, 217, 436, 498. *See
  also* pollution.
acquired immune deficiency syndrome
  (AIDS), 325–327, 326*i*, 327*i*,
  480–481
Aden, 301
Afghanistan and Pakistan [South Asia],
  371, 392–394, 393*i*
Africa. *See* **North Africa and
  Southwest Asia; Sub-Saharan
  Africa.**
African Americans, 57*i*, 68, 69. *See also*
  race.
age of exploration, 175. *See also*
  colonialism.
age structures, 36, 36*i*. *See also*
  population pyramids.
agriculture
  corporate vs. family, 72–73
  cultivation techniques, 445–446, 489
  in East Asia, 419, 425–426, 425*i*,
    445–446, 460, 464
  emergence of and problems with,
    10–12, 11*i*, 271, 272*i*
  in Europe, 191–192, 203–204,
    215–217
  and global crop and animal exchange,
    106, 115, 116*t*, 417–418
  and irrigation, 159, 290–293, 370
  and loess, 54
  in Middle and South America,
    160–161, 163
  mixed, 353–354
  in North Africa and Southwest Asia,
    271, 272*i*, 286, 290–293, 301
  in North America, 72–73, 73*i*
  in Oceania, 541
  plantation, 57, 128

and resistance movements, 133–134
  in Russia and the Eurasian Republics,
    253
  in South Asia, 384–385, 384*i*, 398
  in Southeast Asia, 488–490
  in Sub-Saharan Africa, 330, 336–337,
    353–354, 356–357
  sustainable, 27, 27*i*, 159, 489
  and water shortages, 58, 80, 207,
    249–251, 286
Ahmadabad, 403
AIDS. *See* acquired immune deficiency
  syndrome.
Ainu people, 435, 458
air pollution. *See* pollution.
air pressure, 23, 24*i*
Albania, 220–221
alcoholism, 59, 232, 246
algal blooms, 196
Algeria, 288, 294–297
Allende, Salvador, 136
alluvium, 447
Alps Mountains, 171
altiplano, 158
altruism, 20
Amazon Basin, 108–110, 138–140,
  138*i*, 158
America, 53. *See also* **Middle and South
  America; North America.**
American South (Southeast) [North
  America], 90–93, 91*i*
Amsterdam, 203
Amu Darya River, 249–250
Andes Mountains, 108
Angola, 357–359
animal husbandry. *See also* nomads.
  in East Asia, 417, 451, 464–465
  emergence of, 10–12, 11*i*
  in North America, 94
animism, 378, 480, 485–486, 499. *See
  also* religions.
Annan, Kofi, 315
apartheid, 321, 358, 381. *See also* **racism;**
  segregation.
Appalachians, 54
Arabian Peninsula [North Africa and
  Southwest Asia], 299–302, 299*i*

Arafat, Yasir, 303
Aral Sea, 249–251
archipelago, 473
arctic and high-altitude climates, 29,
  29*i*
Argentina, 159–161
arid climates, 28, 29*i*
Aristide, Jean-Bertrand, 147
Armenia, 259–260
Arunachal Pradesh, 395–396
Aryans, 368
ASEAN. *See* **Association of Southeast
  Asian Nations.**
Asia. *See* **East Asia; North Africa and
  Southwest Asia; Russia and the
  Eurasian Republics; South
  Asia; Southeast Asia.**
Assam, 401
assimilation, 123, 184, 433–434, 482,
  485
**Association of Southeast Asian
  Nations (ASEAN),** 490–491
Aswan High Dam, 298. *See also* dams.
Atacama Desert, 110
Atlantic Provinces [North America],
  84–85, 84*i*
Atlas Mountains, 294
atolls, 519, 519*i*
Auckland, 531
Australia, 519–542
Australo-Melanesians, 476, 484
Austria, 34–36, 36*i*, 38
Austronesians, 476, 484, 524
average population density, 33–34,
  34*i*–35*i*
Azerbaijan, 259–260
Aztecs, 113, 115*i*

baby boom, 70, 180
Bahrain, 300
Balaguer, Joaquín, 136
Balkans, 171, 219–221, 220*i*
Baltic Sea, 196–197, 210, 211*i*, 213, 255
Baltic states, 210–211, 213–214
Bandar Express, 308
Bangalore, 405
Bangkok, 498, 501

Bangladesh, 371, 381, 401–402
Barbados, 147
Basques, 208
Batista, Fulgencio, 136
Bedouins, 272
Beijing, 436–437, 445
Belarus, 254–255
Belgian Congo. *See* Zaire/Congo.
Belgium, 200–202
belief systems, indigenous, 328, 378,
    395. *See also* **animism; religions.**
Belize, 154–155
Benares, 392, 396
Benelux, 200–203
Benin, 348
Berlin Wall, 204
Bhutan, 371, 394–395
Bihar, 400–401
biogeography, 6*t*
biological weapons, 309
bipedalism, 9–10
birth control. *See also* gender roles;
    population.
    in East Asia, 430–431
    in Middle and South America, 120
    in North Africa and Southwest Asia,
        276
    in Russia and the Eurasian Republics,
        223–224
    in South Asia, 373–375, 386
    in Southeast Asia, 479
    in Sub-Saharan Africa, 323–324
Bismarck, Otto von, 319
black market. *See* **informal economy.**
Black Sea, 237, 253, 259, 260
Bodhgaya, 400
Boer War, 321
Bolivia, 157–159
Bolsheviks, 230
Bombay, 403–404
Bosnia, 219–221
Botswana, 334–335, 357–359
boundaries
    between nations, 46–47
    permeable, 100–101
    between regions, 5, 7*i*
boys. *See* men.
Brahmaputra River, 366, 369*i*, 399,
    401
Brahmin caste, 368, 379
brain drain, 123
Brasília, 164
Brazil [Middle and South America],
    161–165, 162*i*
bribery, 387
bride burning, 383
bride price, 383, 431
Britain. *See* United Kingdom.
Brunei, 506
Brussels, 200
Budapest, 217–218
Buddhism, 378, 400, 451–452, 462,
    480, 485–486. *See also* religions.
buffer zones, 478
Bukhara, 261
Bulgaria, 217
Burkina Faso, 348

Burma, 478, 499–503
Burundi, 355–356

Cairo, 298–299
Calcutta, 372, 400–401
Cali, 157
Cambodia, 478–479, 503–504
Cameroon, 350–351
Canada, 53
    compared with the United States, 61*i*,
        62–64
Canadian Shield, 86, 95
Canton. *See* Guangzhou.
capital, 42–43
capitalism
    crony, 491
    in East Asia, 422–423, 429–430, 461,
        466
    in Europe, 194
    in Puerto Rico, 146
    in Russia and the Eurasian Republics,
        235
    in Southeast Asia, 491, 507–508
capitalist free market economy,
    235–236
Caracas, 156
carbon dioxide emissions, 31–32, 32*i*,
    247
Cardoso, Fernando, 163
Caribbean [Middle and South America],
    144–147, 145*i*
carrying capacity, 322–323, 356
cartography, 5, 6*t*
Caspian Sea, 227, 247, 253, 259, 260
caste system, 368, 379–380
Castro, Fidel, 146
Catalonia, 208
Catholicism. *See* Christianity.
Caucasia [Russia and the Eurasian
    Republics], 259–260, 259*i*
Caucasus Mountains, 229
Central Africa [Sub-Saharan Africa],
    350–353, 351*i*
Central African Republic, 350–351
Central America [Middle and South
    America], 107, 151–155, 151*i*
Central Andes [Middle and South
    America], 157–159, 158*i*
Central Asian Republics [Russia and the
    Eurasian Republics], 260–263,
    261*i*
Central China [East Asia], 445–449, 446*i*
Central India [South Asia], 402–404,
    403*i*
Ceylon. *See* Sri Lanka.
CFCs. *See* chlorofluorocarbons.
Chad, 350
chadors, 283, 307, 394
chaebol, 464
Chamorro, Violetta, 154
Chang Jiang (Yangtze River), 414,
    437–439, 445–447, 446*i*
Chao Phraya River, 498–499
Charleston, 82–83
Chechnya, 255, 260
chemical weapons, 287, 309
Chengdu, 446

Chernobyl, 217, 254
Cherokee, 59
Chiang Kai-shek, 419, 454
children
    in East Asia, 467
    in Middle and South America,
        125–126, 161
    in North Africa and Southwest Asia,
        284
    in North America, 70
    in South Asia, 374–375
    in Sub-Saharan Africa, 323–324,
        337–338
Chile, 159–161
China, 432–433. *See also* **East Asia;**
    Overseas Chinese.
China's Northeast [East Asia], 441–445,
    443*i*
China's Northwest [East Asia], 449–452,
    449*i*
chlorofluorocarbons (CFCs), 543. *See
    also* **global warming.**
chocolate industry, 180, 200–202
Choctaw people, 60
Chongqing, 446
Christianity
    in Europe, 175, 205
    in Middle and South America, 119,
        126–127
    in North America, 67–68
    in Russia, 244
    in South Asia, 378
    in Southeast Asia, 477–478, 480,
        485–486
    in Sub-Saharan Africa, 328–329
"City of New Orleans," 52.
civil rights movement, 381
clear-cutting. *See* deforestation.
climate change, 10, 270*i*, 544*i*. *See also*
    global warming; greenhouse
    gases.
climate classification system, Koppen,
    25–26
climate regions, 25–26, 28–29, 29*i*
climatology, 6*t*, 20, 23–26. *See also*
    under specific region.
cocaine, 136–137, 137*i*, 157
coffin art, 328*i*
cold war, 46
    and alliances in Oceania, 527
    and Chinese economic policies, 424
    and collapse of the Soviet Union, 231
    and Japanese economic recovery,
        459
    origins of in postwar Europe, 177,
        178*i*
    in postcolonial Africa, 339–340, 352
    and the Vietnam War, 478
Colombia, 156–157
colonialism, 42. *See also* empires.
    and disease, 56, 113
    in East Asia, 458
    and European expansion, 174–175,
        176*i*, 205
    in Middle and South America, 107,
        115, 117*i*, 161
    in Oceania, 524–526, 538

colonialism *(cont.)*
   and religion, 14–15
   in Russia and the Eurasian Republics, 230
   in South Asia, 369–371
   in Southeast Asia, 477–479, 477*i*, 503
   in Sub-Saharan Africa, 314, 319–321, 320*i*, 352, 357–358
   and underdevelopment, 117–118, 287, 370
colonies, 42, 117*i*
Columbus, Christopher, 57, 106, 113, 175
command economies, 235–237. *See also* communism.
commercial farming, 490
communal conflict, 379
communes, agricultural, 423–424
communism
   in China, 419–420, 422–424
   in Cuba, 146–147
   in Mongolia, 422–424, 464–466
   in North Korea, 422–424, 461
   in Russia, 230–231
   in Vietnam, 505–506
communist welfare, 187
Comoros, 356
comparative advantages, 218
computer industry, 74, 404–405, 490, 507
Confucianism, 417, 421–422, 452, 462–463, 485–486
Confucius, 417
conglomerate companies, 42
Congo, Republic of, 320, 350–351
Congo (physical region), 320, 350
conservative welfare, 187
contested space, 140, 509, 512
continental drift. *See* **plate tectonics.**
Continental Interior [North America], 94–97, 96*i*
contraception. *See* birth control; population.
cool humid climates, 28–29, 29*i*
cooperation, international, 47–48
Copenhagen, 210–211
Copts, 297. *See also* Christianity; religions.
corn, domestication of, 56
Corridor Five, 190, 218
corruption
   in East Asia, 423, 426, 430, 456, 460, 464
   in Middle and South America, 136
   in Russia and the Eurasian Republics, 246–247
   in South Asia, 387, 394
   in Southeast Asia, 491
Cortez, Hernando, 113–114, 147
Costa Rica, 154–155
Côte d'Ivoire, 34–36, 36*i*, 38, 335, 347–348
Creole, 107
crime
   in Europe, 181, 210, 217
   in Middle and South America, 161
   in North America, 90–91, 92*i*
   organized, 210, 217, 238, 247, 388

in Russia and the Eurasian Republics, 238, 246–247
   in South Asia, 388
Croatia, 219–221
crony capitalism, 491
Cuba, 146–147
cultivation. *See* agriculture.
cultural complexity, 484
cultural diversity, 13–14
   in East Asia, 432–435, 433*i*, 460
   in Europe, 182–184, 183*i*
   in Middle and South America, 123–124, 161
   in North Africa and Southwest Asia, 284–285
   in North America, 56, 58, 60, 65–67, 68, 69
   in Oceania, 529–532, 529*i*
   in Russia and the Eurasian Republics, 243
   in South Asia, 405
   in Southeast Asia, 476, 484–485, 491–493, 506, 510–511
   in Sub-Saharan Africa, 339*i*, 354
cultural ecology, 6*t*
cultural geography. *See* sociocultural geography.
cultural hearth (of North America), 84
cultural markers, 16
culturally defined differences (between the sexes), 18
culture, 12
culture groups, 12–16, 315, 332–333, 432–435
Curitiba, 164–165
currency, common European, 189–190
currency devaluation, 336
Cuzco, 159
czars, 230
Czech Republic, 214, 217

Dalai Lama, 434, 451
Dalit caste, 379
dams. *See also* irrigation.
   on the Chang Jiang, 439, 446–447
   on the Danube, 197
   on the Euphrates, 292–293
   on the Nile, 298
   on the Paraná, 140
   in the Tennessee Valley, 78, 292
Danube, 172, 197
debt crisis, 131–132, 336. *See also* **structural adjustment programs.**
Deccan Plateau, 365
deforestation
   in East Asia, 438, 440
   in Middle and South America, 137–140
   in North America, 99
   in Oceania, 542
   in Russia and the Eurasian Republics, 247–248
   in South Asia, 390–391
   in Southeast Asia, 475, 483, 490, 495–496, 509–511
   in Sub-Saharan Africa, 317, 336–337

Delhi, 398–399
deltas, 22, 399
democracy. *See also* political geography.
   in Europe, 177
   in Middle and South America, 136–137.
   in North Africa and Southwest Asia, 288
   in North America, 78
   in Russia, 239–241
   in South Asia, 386, 389
   in Southeast Asia, 493–494
   in Sub-Saharan Africa, 339–341
Democratic Republic of Congo. *See* Zaire/Congo.
demographic transitions, 38, 38*i*, 120, 323, 476
demography, 32–39
   of East Asia, 420
   of Europe, 178–181, 179*i*
   of Middle and South America, 118–123
   of North Africa and Southwest Asia, 275–280, 275*i*
   of North America, 60–62, 61*i*
   of Oceania, 527
   of Russia and the Eurasian Republics, 231–235
   of South Asia, 372–375
   of Southeast Asia, 479–493
   of Sub-Saharan Africa, 321–327
Denmark, 210–212
deposition, 22
desertification, 293, 344–345, 345*i*
deserts, 28, 29*i*. *See also* Atacama Desert; Gobi Desert; Kalahari Desert; Sahara Desert; Thar (Great Indian) Desert.
detritus, 475
development. *See also* economic geography; industrialization.
   economic, 26, 44, 472
   and environmental protection, 440, 544–545
   grassroots rural, 338
   self-reliant, 338, 424
   socialist reformist, 129–131
   sustainable, 26–31
Dineh people, 60
diversity. *See* **cultural diversity.**
Djibouti, 352
doi moi, 505
domestic spaces, 281
double day, 180, 185–186, 330
dowry, 383
Dravidians, 405, 407
drug trade
   in Middle and South America, 136–137, 137*i*, 155, 157
   in Oceania, 512
   in Russia and the Eurasian Republics, 262
   in South Asia, 394
   in Southeast Asia, 499
dry forests, 345–346
Duvalier, François "Papa Doc," 136, 147

earthquakes, 21, 440, 441*i*, 456, 519
East Africa [Sub-Saharan Africa],
354–356, 355*i*
East and Central Europe [Europe], 171,
214–221, 215*i*
EAST ASIA, 410–469
environmental geography of, 435–440
air quality, 435–437
water issues, 437–440
human history of, 416–420
Confucianism, 417
demography, 420
early Chinese civilization, 416–417
and European influence, 417–418
and revolution, 419–420
human well-being in, 435, 436*t*
physical geography of, 413–415
climate, 414–415, 415*i*
landforms, 413–414
political and economic geography of,
421–429
development and market reforms,
424–429
economic rise of Japan, 458–460
government bureaucracies,
421–422
sociocultural geography in, 429–435
and capitalism, 429–430
cultural diversity, 432–435
family structure and gender roles,
417, 430–431
gender roles and work, 431–432
subregions of, 440–467, 442*i*
Central China, 445–449, 446*i*
China's Northeast, 441–445, 443*i*
China's Northwest, 449–452, 449*i*
Japan, 456–461, 457*i*
Korea, North and South, 461–464,
462*i*
Mongolia, 464–467, 465*i*
Southern China, 452–454, 452*i*
Taiwan, 454–456, 454*i*
Eastern Europe, 171
Eastern Mediterranean [North Africa
and Southwest Asia], 302–305,
302*i*
ecology, 6*t*. *See also* environmental
geography; pollution.
**Economic and Technical
Development Zones (ETDZs),**
427–428, 427*i*
Economic Community of West African
States (ECOWAS), 338, 348
Economic Core [North America], 86–90,
87*i*
economic core (of North America), 58
economic development, 26
economic diversification, 286–287
economic geography, 6*t*, 39–46
in East Asia, 422–424, 458–460
in Europe, 188–195, 217
in Middle and South America,
127–137
in North Africa and Southwest Asia,
285–288
in North America, 71–78
in Oceania, 534–538, 535*i*

in Russia and the Eurasian Republics,
235–239, 244–247, 245*t*
in South Asia, 383–386
in Southeast Asia, 488–494
in Sub-Saharan Africa, 333–341
economic integration (of Europe), 178
economy, 41–42. *See also* capitalism;
communism.
capitalist free-market, 235–236
command, 235–237
and demographic transition, 38
ecotourism
in Middle and South America, 137,
139–140, 145, 154–155
ECOWAS. *See* Economic Community
of West African States.
Ecuador, 157–159
education, and fertility rates, 375, 376*i*,
479, 481*i*
Egypt, 297–299
El Niño, 112, 474, 497, 522, 522*i*
El Salvador, 153–154
empires. *See also* colonialism.
British, 175–176, 205, 478, 526
Chinese, 416–417, 418*i*, 476
Dutch, 175
Ghanaian, 318
Incan, 114
Japanese, 419, 458, 459*i*
Mongol, 466
Portuguese, 175
Spanish, 175
enclaves, 251, 255, 321, 418, 454
endemic species, 522
energy consumption, 141*i*, 435–436
energy production. *See* dams;
hydroelectric power.
entertainment. *See* music.
environmental geography, 26–32
and development, 440, 544–545
in East Asia, 435–440
in Europe, 195–198
and fragile environments, 345
and international cooperation, 48
and international investment, 43, 44*i*,
140–141
in Middle and South America,
137–141, 164–165
in North Africa and Southwest Asia,
290–294
in North America, 78–80, 99
in Oceania, 540–545
in Russia and the Eurasian Republics,
247–251
in South Asia, 390–392, 402
in Southeast Asia, 495–498
in Sub-Saharan Africa, 344–347, 358
Equatorial Guinea, 350
Eritrea, 352, 354*i*
erosion, 22, 443–444
Estonia, 210, 213–214
ETDZs. *See* Economic and Technical
Development Zones.
Ethiopia, 319, 352–354
ethnic cleansing, 47*i*, 219–221. *See also*
genocide; Jews; **racism.**
ethnic groups. *See* **culture groups.**

ethnicity. *See* **culture groups.**
ethnocentrism, 315
EU. *See* **European Union.**
Euphrates River, 271, 292–293
EUROPE, 168–223
environmental geography of, 195–198
air, 197–198
rivers, 197
seas, 196–197
human history of, 173–181
demography, 178–181, 179*i*
growth and expansion of, 174–175
postwar, 177–178
revolutions in, 175–177
settlement of, 174
human well-being in, 198–200, 199*t*
physical geography of, 171–173
climate, 172–173, 173*i*
landforms, 171–172
political and economic geography of,
188–195
agricultural economy, 191–193,
215–217
European Union, 188–190
industrial economy, 191
other political challenges, 193–195
tourism, 193, 194*i*, 207–208, 218
sociocultural geography in, 182–188
gender roles and family structure,
184–186
immigration, 182–184, 183*i*
social welfare, 186–188
subregions of, 200–221
East and Central Europe, 171,
214–221, 215*i*
North Europe, 170–171, 210–214,
211*i*
South Europe, 171, 206–210, 207*i*
West Europe, 171, 200–206, 201*i*
European Union (EU), 170, 178, 181,
188–190, 189*i*
evangelical Protestantism, 127,
328–329. *See also* Christianity;
religions.
evolution, 8–10, 9*i*
exchange, 41
exclaves, 214, 255
extended families, 124. *See also* family
structures.
in East Asia, 430
in Europe, 207–208
in Middle and South America, 124
in Oceania, 536
in Southeast Asia, 487–488
in Sub-Saharan Africa, 331
external landscape processes, 22
extraction, 41. *See also* **resources.**
in Middle and South America, 118,
127–129
in Southeast Asia, 496–497, 505
in Sub-Saharan Africa, 334, 357
extractive sector (of the economy), 42
extraregional migration, 483

fall line, 75
family planning. *See* birth control;
population.

family structures. *See also* **extended families;** gender roles; **nuclear families.**
  in East Asia, 420, 464
  in Europe, 184–186, 208
  in Middle and South America, 124–125
  in North Africa and Southwest Asia, 271, 277, 281–284
  in North America, 69–70
  in Oceania, 532–534
  in Russia and the Eurasian Republics, 235
  in South Asia, 380–383
  in Southeast Asia, 487–488
  in Sub-Saharan Africa, 324–325
farms
  collective, 193, 216, 230, 253
  family, 72–73
Faroe Islands, 210–211
fatwas, 382
favelas, 163. *See also* shantytowns.
female genital mutilation, 332
females. *See* women.
Fertile Crescent, 272*i*
fertility rates
  and education, 375, 376*i*, 479, 481*i*
feudalism, 174–175, 416, 419, 458, 465
Fiji, 535
Finland, 210, 212
fjords, 171
floating population, 429
flood control. *See* dams.
floodplains, 21*i*, 22
folkhem, 212
food. *See also* agriculture.
  customs of, 380, 505
  distribution of, 27
  production of, 30*i*, 425
food stability, 425
forests. *See* deforestation; rain forests.
formal economy, 41
  and GNP, 44
Formosa. *See* Taiwan.
fragile environments, 345
France, 177, 203–204
Franco, Francisco, 208
free market economy. *See* **capitalism; capitalist free market economy.**
free market reformist development, 131–132, 424–429
free trade, 43
free trade zones, 479, 490–491. *See also*
  Association of Southeast Asian Nations; Economic and Technical Development Zones; European Union; North American Free Trade Agreement; **Special Economic Zones.**
French Guiana, 155–156
French Revolution, 177
frontal precipitation, 25, 26*i*

Gabon, 350–351
Gambia, 347–348
Gandhi, Indira, 388
Gandhi, Mohandas, 378, 380–381, 407

Gandhi, Rajiv, 382
Ganges River, 366, 391, 398–400
GEM. *See* **Gender Empowerment Measure.**
gender. *See also* gender roles.
  and evolution, 10
Gender Empowerment Measure (GEM), 45, 45*t. See also* gender roles; men; women.
  in East Asia, 435, 436*t*
  in Europe, 184–186, 198–200, 199*t*, 212–213
  in Middle and South America, 142*t*–143*t*, 144
  in North Africa and Southwest Asia, 289*t*, 290
  in North America, 69, 70, 82*t*
  in Oceania, 539–540, 539*t*–540*t*
  in Russia and the Eurasian Republics, 241–242, 242*t*
  in South Asia, 390, 390*t*
  in Southeast Asia, 494*t*, 495
  in Sub-Saharan Africa, 327, 342–344, 342*t*–343*t*
gender geography, 6*t*
gender roles, 17–19, 17*i. See also*
  Confucianism; family structures, **Gender Empowerment Measure; Islamism;** patriarchy.
  in East Asia, 412, 430–432, 451–452, 455, 460–461, 463, 466–467
  in Europe, 184–186, 185*t*, 217–218
  in Middle and South America, 124–125
  in North Africa and Southwest Asia, 271, 277, 281–284
  in North America, 69–70, 70*i*
  in Oceania, 525–526, 532–534
  in Russia and the Eurasian Republics, 239, 244–245, 245*t*, 262
  in South Asia, 380–383, 386, 405, 406
  in Southeast Asia, 487–488
  in Sub-Saharan Africa, 323–324, 329–332
gender structures, 36–37, 36*i*–37*i. See also* population pyramids.
Genghis Khan, 230
genocide, 170, 184, 323, 339. *See also* ethnic cleansing; **racism.**
geographic information systems (GIS), 6*t*
geography, 5
  introduction to, 2–49
  subdisciplines of, 6*t*
geomorphology, 6*t*, 20–22
geopolitics, 46, 340–341
Georgia, 259–260
Germany, 177, 188, 204–205
gers, 262, 262*i*, 450, 465–466
Ghana, 318, 328*i*, 335, 347–348
girls. *See* women.
GIS. *See* geographic information systems.
glaciation, 54, 84, 171, 254
global economy, 39–44. *See also* **globalization.**
global region, 7
global warming, 31–32, 32*i*, 542–543, 544*i*

and deforestation, 139
and fossil-fuel burning, 438
and industrialization, 317
globalization
  defined, 8, 77
  and economic crises, 491
  and environmental protection, 544
  political, 47–48
GNP. *See* **gross national product.**
Gold Coast, 319
Gobi Desert, 465
Gorbachev, Mikhail, 231, 245
gospel of success, 127, 328–329. *See also* Christianity; religions.
Gosplan, 235
Grameen Bank, 386, 402, 408
grassroots rural economic development, 338
Great Barrier Reef, 519
Great Basin, 54, 95
Great Britain. *See* United Kingdom.
Great Lakes, 54
Great Leap Forward, 424, 431
Great Plains, 55
Great Plains Breadbasket [North America], 93–95, 93*i*
Great Wall, 449
Greece, 206
  ancient, 174, 206
Green movement, 195–196, 438
green revolution, 385, 490
greenhouse gases
  and deforestation, 139
  and global warming, 31–32, 32*i*, 542–543
  and industrialization, 317
Greenland, 210–211
gross national product (GNP) per capita, 44–45, 45*t*
  in East Asia, 435, 436*t*
  in Europe, 188, 198, 199*t*
  in Middle and South America, 141, 142*t*–143*t*
  in North Africa and Southwest Asia, 288, 289*t*
  in North America, 81–82, 82*t*
  in Oceania, 538, 539*t*–540*t*
  in Russia and the Eurasian Republics, 241, 242*t*
  in South Asia, 389, 390*t*
  in Southeast Asia, 494–495, 494*t*
  in Sub-Saharan Africa, 334, 342*t*–343*t*, 344
growth poles, 164, 428
Guangzhou (Canton), 453–454
guarantors, 429–430
Guatemala, 153–154
Guayaquil, 157
guerrillas. *See* resistance movements.
guest workers, 182, 276*i*, 277, 301. *See also* **in-migration.**
Guinea, 348
Guinea-Bissau, 314
Gujarat, 402–403
Gulf Stream, 56, 172
Gulf War, 287, 308
Guyana, 155–156

haciendas, 128
Haiti, 147
hajj, 272, 281, 300
Han people, 432–434, 443–444
Hanoi, 505*i*
Harijan caste, 379
Hawaii, 519, 535–536
hazardous waste, 79, 217, 249, 543
HDI. *See* **Human Development Index, human well-being.**
health care systems. *See* public health; **welfare states.**
Helsinki, 211
herders. *See* animal husbandry.
hierarchical societies, 417, 463, 525
high islands, 519
hijab, 283
Himalayan Country [South Asia], 394–396, 395*i*
Himalaya Mountains, 365–366, 392, 413, 473
Hindu Kush, 365, 392–393
Hindus, 378, 398, 480, 485–486
hinterlands, 30
Hispanics, 53, 99
historical geography, 6*t*
history, human, 8–12
    in East Asia, 416–420
    in Europe, 173–181
    in Middle and South America, 113–123
    in North Africa and Southwest Asia, 271–280
    in North America, 56–62
    in Oceania, 524–527, 525*i*
    in Russia and the Eurasian Republics, 229–235
    in South Asia, 366–376
    in Southeast Asia, 475–483
    in Sub-Saharan Africa, 317–327
Hitler, Adolf, 173
HIV. *See* human immunodeficiency virus.
Ho Chi Minh City (Saigon), 472
Honduras, 153–154
Hong Kong (Xianggang), 428, 453–454
Honolulu, 535–536
Honshu, 456
Horn of Africa [Sub-Saharan Africa], 352–354, 353*i*
hot spots, 519, 520*i*
housing, 16, 180, 254, 283*i*, 450
Huang He (Yellow River), 414, 437–438, 441, 444, 444*i*
Hui people, 433–434, 443
Human Development Index (HDI), 45, 45*t*
    in East Asia, 435, 436*t*, 463*t*
    in Europe, 198, 199*t*
    in Middle and South America, 141, 142*t*–143*t*
    in North Africa and Southwest Asia, 288–290, 289*t*
    in North America, 81–82, 82*i*
    in Oceania, 538, 539*t*–540*t*
    in Russia and the Eurasian Republics, 241, 242*t*
    in South Asia, 389–390, 390*t*

in Southeast Asia, 494*t*, 495
    in Sub-Saharan Africa, 334, 342*t*–343*t*, 344
human ecology, 6*t*
human history. *See* history, human.
human immunodeficiency virus (HIV), 325–327, 326*i*, 332, 480, 483
human rights, 14, 332, 502
human well-being, 45–46, 45*t*
    in East Asia, 435, 436*t*
    in Europe, 198–200, 199*t*
    in Middle and South America, 141–144, 142*t*–143*t*
    in North Africa and Southwest Asia, 288–290, 289*t*
    in North America, 80–82, 82*t*
    in Oceania, 538–540, 539*t*–540*t*
    in Russia and the Eurasian Republics, 241–242, 242*t*
    in South Asia, 389–390, 390*t*
    in Southeast Asia, 494–495, 494*t*
    in Sub-Saharan Africa, 334, 342*t*–343*t*, 344
Hungary, 214, 217–218
Hussein, Saddam, 308
hydroelectric power
    in East Asia, 439, 464
    in Europe, 197
    in Middle and South America, 140
    in North Africa and Southwest Asia, 292–293, 305–306
    in North America, 85–86
    in Russia and the Eurasian Republics, 247
    in South Asia, 392
    in Southeast Asia, 490, 497–498, 504
hyperinflation, 163

Iberian Peninsula, 208*i*
ice ages. *See* glaciation.
Iceland, 210–212
illegal aliens, 101–102
immigration. *See also* **migration.**
    to Europe, 182–184, 183*i*
    to Middle and South America, 123–124, 150–151, 161
    to North America, 64–67, 64*i*
    to Oceania, 523, 529
import quotas, 43
import substitution industrialization, 129–131, 161, 385, 386
Incas, 114–115, 157, 159
income disparity. *See also under* wealth.
    in Middle and South America, 127, 131
    in Southeast Asia, 502, 511, 514*t*
India, 370, 385, 386, 396–406
indigenous groups. *See* Aborigines; Maoris; Native Americans.
Indochina, 473, 503
Indonesia [Southeast Asia], 285, 477, 482, 491–493, 508–511, 508*i*
Indore, 403
Indus River, 366, 394
industrial revolution, 175–177, 176*i*, 191
industrial sector (of the economy), 42
    in North America, 86–90, 88*i*

industrialization. *See also* **development.**
    and development, 26
    in East Asia, 424, 435, 445, 456, 458–459, 464
    in Europe, 175–177, 191, 192*i*
    by import substitution, 129, 161
    in Middle and South America, 131–134, 156, 161
    in North Africa and Southwest Asia, 285–288
    in North America, 58, 73–77, 86–90
    in Oceania, 534–538
    in Russia and the Eurasian Republics, 230–231, 236–237, 236*i*
    in South Asia, 369–371, 385, 404–406
    in Southeast Asia, 488, 490, 492, 498, 501, 510
    in Sub-Saharan Africa, 337
infanticide, female, 37, 374, 383, 431
informal economy, 41–42, 44, 135
    in East Asia, 467
    in Europe, 207
    in Middle and South America, 123, 134–136, 164–165
    in North Africa and Southwest Asia, 279–280, 309
    in Oceania, 533
    in Russia and the Eurasian Republics, 237–239
    in South Asia, 389
    in Southeast Asia, 498
    in Sub-Saharan Africa, 337–338
infrastructure, 75
    in East Asia, 419, 424, 445, 462
    in Europe, 190, 190*i*, 218
    in Middle and South America, 131, 140
    in North Africa and Southwest Asia, 308
    in North America, 74
    in Oceania, 537
    in Russia and the Eurasian Republics, 237
    in South Asia, 370
    in Southeast Asia, 501–502
    in Sub-Saharan Africa, 325, 337–338, 355
in-migration, 277–279. *See also* **guest workers.**
Inner Mongolia, 449–450
institutions, 12
internal landscape processes, 21–22
international cooperation, 47–48
International Monetary Fund (IMF), 47–48. *See also* World Bank.
    in Middle and South America, 131–132, 161
    in North Africa and Southwest Asia, 287, 298
    in Southeast Asia, 491
    in Sub-Saharan Africa, 336–337
interstate highway system, 74
intertropical convergence zone (ITCZ), 316, 317*i*, 366, 367*i*, 474
intifada, 304
Iran, 306–307
Iran-Iraq War, 307–309

Iraq, 307–309
Ireland, 205–206
Irian Jaya, 496, 509
iron curtain, 177
irredentism, 262
irrigation. *See also* agriculture; dams.
  in East Asia, 445, 450
  in Europe, 207
  in Middle and South America, 159
  in North Africa and Southwest Asia, 286, 290–293, 298
  in North America, 58, 80, 96–97
  in Oceania, 541
  in Russia and the Eurasian Republics, 249–251
  in South Asia, 370
  in Southeast Asia, 498
  in Sub-Saharan Africa, 347
Islam
  in East Asia, 433–434
  in Europe, 174, 209
  history and intellectual development of, 272–275
  in North Africa and Southwest Asia, 268, 272–273
  in Russia and the Eurasian Republics, 260–262
  in South Asia, 368–369, 378, 381–383
  in Southeast Asia, 476–477, 480, 485–486, 506–507
  in Sub-Saharan Africa, 328–329
  tenets of, 280–281
Islamic fundamentalists, 269, 274–275, 280, 296–297
Islamism, 288
Islamists, 269, 275, 280, 381–382
Island and Peninsula [Southeast Asia], 506–508, 506*i*
Israel, 302–305
Israeli-Palestinian conflict, 287, 302–305
Istanbul, 305–307
Italy, 206, 209–210
ITCZ. *See* **intertropical convergence zone.**
Ivory Coast. *See* Côte d'Ivoire.

J curves, 33, 33*i*
Jakarta, 477, 479, 498, 510–511
Japan [East Asia], 419, 422–423, 434–435, 456–461, 457*i*
Java, 509
Jerusalem, 272, 304–305
Jews. *See also* Judaism, **Zionists.**
  in Europe, 184, 218–219, 303
  in Russia, 244, 255
Jordan, 302–304, 309
Judaism, 302–305

Kabila, Laurence, 353
Kalahari Desert, 357
Kaliningrad, 214, 254–255, 255*i*
Kalipeni, Ezekiel, 323
karst, 453
Kashgar, 433, 434*i*
Kashmir, 387–388, 389*i*, 396

Kazakhstan, 260–263
Kenya, 335, 355–356
Kerala, 374, 405–406
Khatami, Mohammad, 307
Khmer Rouge, 478
Khomeini, Ayatollah, 307
Kirghizstan, 260–263
KMT. *See* Kuomintang.
knowledge systems, 13–14
Kobe, 456
Kootenai people, 60
Koppen climate classification system, 25–26
Koran. *See* **Qur'an.**
Korea, North and South [East Asia], 461–464, 462*i*
Kosovo, 220
Kuala Lumpur, 507
Kuomintang (KMT), 419, 454
Kurds, 305–306
Kuwait, 300

La Paz, 159*i*
labor. *See also* **development.**
  by children, 375
  and unions, 503
ladinos, 151–152
Lake Chad, 345
land reclamation, 202–203
landforms, 20–23. *See also under specific region;* **geomorphology; physical geography.**
landraces, 354
languages, 15–16, 15*i*
  in East Asia, 433
  in Nigeria, 349*i*
  in North Africa and Southwest Asia, 284–285, 284*i*
  in Oceania, 531
  in South Asia, 370, 377*i*, 404
  in Sub-Saharan Africa, 333, 333*i*
Laos, 478–479, 503–504
laterite, 138, 317
Latin America, 107. *See also* **Middle and South America.**
Latino, 53
Latvia, 210, 213–214
leaching, 317
Lebanon, 302–303
Lenin, Vladimir, 230
Lesotho, 357–358
liberation theology, 126–127, 512
Liberia, 319, 348
Libya, 294–295
Lima, 157
lingua franca, 16, 205, 333
literacy, 278*t*, 382*i*
Lithuania, 210, 213–214
Loango, 318
loess, 54, 441–444, 442*i*
Loess Plateau, 414, 438, 441–444
logging
  in the Amazon Basin, 138–140
  in Indonesia, 509–510
  in North America, 58, 99
London, 206
longis, 364

long-lot system, 85
Los Angeles, 101
Low Countries, 200–203
Lumumba, Patrice, 352
Luxembourg, 200

Macedonia, 219
machismo, 125
Madagascar, 356
Madrid, 208
Mafia, 210. *See also* crime.
Magellan, Ferdinand, 524
Maghreb [North Africa and Southwest Asia], 294–297, 295*i*
magma, 21
"maid trade," 483, 483*i*
Mainland: Thailand and Burma [Southeast Asia], 499–503, 500*i*
Mainland: Vietnam, Laos, and Cambodia [Southeast Asia], 503–506, 504*i*
Malawi, 357–358
Malaysia, 478, 506–507
males. *See* men.
Mali, 347–348, 350
Manchuria, 445
Mandela, Nelson, 321, 357–358
Manila, 479, 511, 513
manufacturing sector (of the economy). *See* **industrial sector.**
Mao Zedong, 419
Maoris, 521, 526, 528–531, 542
maquiladoras, 100, 131–132, 148–150, 149*i*, 149*t*
Marcos, Ferdinand, 511–513
marianismo, 125–126
marine west coast temperate climates, 28, 29*i*
market economy. *See* capitalism.
marriage customs, 486. *See also* **bride price; dowry.**
Marshall Islands, 527
marsupials, 522–523
Marx, Karl, 230
mass wasting, 22
material culture, 12, 16, 282
Mauritania, 347–348
Mauritius, 356
meat packing, 96
Mecca, 272, 281, 300, 301*i*
Medellín, 157
Medina, 300
Mediterranean Sea, 196–197
Mediterranean temperate climates, 28, 29*i*
Megalopolis, 75, 456–457
Meiji Restoration, 422
Mekong River, 473, 499, 503–505
Melanesia, 524, 528
melting pot, 485
men. *See also* gender roles.
  gender roles and status of, 17–19, 17*i*
  preferences for male babies, 37, 37*i*, 431
Menchu, Rigoberta, 153
menopause, 10, 488, 533
Mercosur, 132, 133*i*, 161

mestizos, 123
métis, 59
Mexico City, 147
Mexico [Middle and South America], 147–151, 148*i*
microcredit, 386, 402, 407–408, 513
Micronesia, 524–526
MIDDLE AND SOUTH AMERICA, 104–167
  environmental geography of, 137–141
  human history of, 113–123
    demography, 118–123
    and European conquest, 113–115, 114*i*, 115*i*
    and Native Americans, 113
    and underdevelopment, 117–118
  human well-being in, 141–144, 142*t*–143*t*
  physical geography of
    climate, 110–113, 111*i*
    landforms, 107–108, 109*i*
    rivers, 108–110
  political and economic geography of, 127–137
    economic development, 127–134, 129*i*, 130*i*
  sociocultural geography in, 123–127
    children in poverty, 125–126
    cultural diversity, 123–124
    gender roles and family roles, 122, 124–125
    race, 124
    religion, 126–127, 128*i*
  subregions of, 144–165
    Brazil, 161–165, 162*i*
    Caribbean, 144–147, 145*i*
    Central America, 151–155, 151*i*
    Central Andes, 157–159, 158*i*
    Mexico, 147–151, 148*i*
    Northern Andes and Caribbean Coast, 155–157, 156*i*
    Southern Cone, 159–161, 160*i*
Middle East, 269
midlatitude temperate climates, 28, 29*i*
migrant workers, 101
migration. *See also* immigration.
  in East Asia, 426–428
  in Middle and South America, 120–123, 150–151
  in North Africa and Southwest Asia, 277–279
  in North America, 64, 67
  in Russia and the Eurasian Republics, 234–235, 258, 259
  in South Asia, 398
  in Southeast Asia, 481–483, 509
Milan, 210
minifundios, 152*i*
mining, 158, 163, 496–497, 497*i*. *See also* **resources.**
missionaries, 328–329
mixed agriculture, 353–354
Mobuto Sese Seko, 339, 352, 358
modest welfare, 187
Moguls, 369
Mohawk people, 60

Mongolia, 449–450
Mongolia [East Asia], 464–467, 465*i*
Mongols, 230, 273
monotremes, 523
monsoons, 23
  in East Asia, 414–415, 461
  in Oceania, 522
  in South Asia, 366, 367*i*
  in Southeast Asia, 476
Montenegro, 219
Montréal, 85
Montserrat, 108
Moors, 174, 209
Morocco, 294–295
Moscow, 230, 249, 254
Mount Fuji, 414
Mount Pinatubo, 21, 511, 513
Mozambique, 340, 357–358
Muhammad, 272, 281, 283, 300, 304
mujahedeen, 381, 394
multinational corporations, 42, 502. *See also* economic geography.
Mumbai. *See* Bombay.
music.
  "City of New Orleans," 52
  jazz, 260
  rai, 296
  throat singing, 256
  thumb pianos, 359
  "Waltzing Matilda," 534
Muslims. *See* Islam.
mutilation, female genital, 332
Myanmar. *See* Burma.

NAFTA. *See* North American Free Trade Agreement.
Namibia, 358–359
Naples, 210
Napoleon Bonaparte, 173
nation-states, 46, 177
National Front, 193–194, 204
nationalism, 177, 184, 387
nations, 46, 177
Native Americans. *See also* Aborigines.
  and European settlement, 59–60, 59*i*
  in Middle and South America, 110, 153
  peopling of North America, 56
NATO. *See* North Atlantic Treaty Organization
natural resources. *See* **resources.**
Nauru, 527
Nazis, 184, 194, 219, 303
negative rate of natural increase, 180. *See also* **rate of natural increase.**
Nehru, Jawaharlal, 378
neocolonialism, 314, 479. *See also* colonialism.
Nepal, 394–396
Netherlands, 200, 202–203, 202*i*
New England [North America], 84–85, 84*i*
New World, 107. *See also* **Middle and South America; North America.**
New Zealand, 520–542
Nicaragua, 154
Niger, 347–348, 350
Niger River, 347, 350
Nigeria, 285, 339, 348–350

Nile: Egypt and Sudan [North Africa and Southwest Asia], 297–299, 297*i*
Nile River, 271, 297–298
nomadic pastoralism, 465
nomads, 229, 229*i*, 259–263, 417, 464–465. *See also* animal husbandry.
nonviolence, 381
Norilsk, 246
NORTH AFRICA AND SOUTHWEST ASIA, 266–311
  environmental geography of, 290–294
    sustainable development, 293–294
    water and irrigation, 290–293
  human history of, 271–280
    demography, 275–280, 275*i*
    and origins of agriculture, 271, 272*i*
    spread of Islam, 272–273
    and Western domination, 273–275
  human well-being in, 288–290, 289*t*
  physical geography of, 269–271
    climate, 269–270, 269*i*
    landforms, 270–271
  political and economic geography of, 285–288
    agriculture in, 286
    and economic diversity, 286–287
    and hostilities, 287–288
    and Islamism, 288
    oil economy, 285–286, 285*i*
  sociocultural geography in, 280–285
    children, 284
    gender roles and family structure, 271, 277, 281–284
    languages, 284–285
    religion, 280–281
  subregions of, 294–309
    Arabian Peninsula, 299–302, 299*i*
    Eastern Mediterranean, 302–305, 302*i*
    Maghreb (Northwest Africa), 294–297, 295*i*
    Nile, 297–299, 297*i*
    Northeast, 305–309, 306*i*
NORTH AMERICA, 50–103
  environmental geography of, 78–80
    loss of environmental quality, 79–80
    loss of habitat, 80
    loss of resources, 80
  human history of, 56–62
    and African-Americans, 57, 57*i*, 68–69
    demography, 60–62, 62*i*
    European settlement, 56–60
    and Native Americans, 56, 59–60, 59*i*
  human well-being in, 80–82, 82*t*
  physical geography of, 53–56
    climate, 54–56, 55*i*
    landforms, 54
  political and economic geography of, 71–78
    agricultural economy, 72–74, 73*i*
    government and globalization, 77–78
    industrial economy, 74–77

NORTH AMERICA *(cont.)*
  sociocultural geography in, 64–71
    aging, 70–71
    gender roles and family structure,
      69–70, 70*i*
    immigration, 64–67, 64*i*
    race, 68–69
    religion, 67–68
  subregions of, 82–102, 83*i*
    American South (Southeast),
      90–93, 91*i*
    Continental Interior, 94–97, 95*i*
    Economic Core, 86–90, 87*i*
    Great Plains Breadbasket, 93–95,
      93*i*
    New England and the Atlantic
      Provinces, 84–85, 84*i*
    Pacific Northwest, 97–99, 98*i*
    Québec, 85–86, 86*i*
    Southwest, 99–102, 100*i*
North American Free Trade Agreement
    (NAFTA), 77, 99, 102, 132, 134,
    150
North Atlantic Drift, 172
North Atlantic Treaty Organization
    (NATO)
  and European Union, 189, 221
  and Russia, 241
  and Turkey, 305
North China Plain, 415, 444–445
North Europe [Europe], 170–171,
    210–214, 211*i*
North European Plain, 171–172, 227
North Korea, 461–464
North Sea, 172, 210–213
Northeast: Turkey, Iran, and Iraq [North
    Africa and Southwest Asia],
    305–309, 306*i*
Northeastern South Asia [South Asia],
    399–402, 399*i*
Northern Andes and Caribbean Coast
    [Middle and South America],
    155–157, 156*i*
Northwest India [South Asia], 396–399,
    397*i*
Norway, 210–213
Novosibirsk, 257–258
nuclear families, 69, 488. *See also* family
    structures.
nuclear waste. *See* **hazardous waste.**
nuclear weapons
  arsenals of, 241
  testing of, 388–389, 394, 540, 543
  use of, 458

OCEANIA, 516–546
  environmental geography of, 540–545
    aridity in Australia, 541–542
    deforestation in New Zealand, 542
    global warming in the Pacific
      Islands, 543–545
  human history of, 524–527
    demography, 527
    European settlement and
      colonization, 524–526
    peopling, 524
    ties to Asia, 526–527

  human well-being in, 538–540,
    539*t*–540*t*
  physical geography of, 518–523
    climate, 520–522, 521*i*
    flora and fauna, 522–523
    landforms, 519
  political and economic geography of,
    534–538
    export economies, 534–535, 535*i*
    influence of Asia and Europe,
      535–538
    tourism, 535–536, 544
  sociocultural geography in, 527–534
    cultural diversity, 531–532
    cultural roots, 528–531, 529*i*
    gender roles, 532–534
Ogallala aquifer, 80, 81*i*
oil industry, 156, 158, 163
  in North Africa and Southwest Asia,
    285–286, 306
Old World, 107. *See also* **East Asia;**
    Europe; North Africa and
    Southwest Asia; Oceania;
    Russia and the Eurasian
    Republics; South Asia;
    Southeast Asia; Sub-Saharan
    Africa.
old-growth forests, 496
Oman, 300
OPEC. *See* **Organization of**
    Petroleum Exporting
    Countries.
organic matter, 317
Organization of Petroleum Exporting
    Countries (OPEC), 285, 300
Orinoco River, 108
orographic rainfall, 24, 25*i*, 97, 108*i*,
    270, 275
Osaka, 458
Ottoman Empire, 273, 305–306
overpopulation, 39, 460. *See also*
    population.
Overseas Chinese, 485, 486*i*, 491–493
ozone hole, 543

Pacific Northwest [North America],
    97–99, 98*i*
Pacific Rim, 62
Pacific Way, 518, 531, 545
paddy cultivation, 445–446, 489
Pahlavi, Reza, 307
Pakistan, 370, 394
Palestine, 302–305
pampas, 160
Panama, 155
Panama Canal, 155
Pancasila, 493, 498, 508, 510, 532
Pangaea hypothesis, 21, 22*i*. *See also*
    plate tectonics.
  and Africa, 315
  and North America, 54
  and Oceania, 519, 522
Pannonian Plain, 172*i*
Papua New Guinea, 519, 522–524, 531,
    543
Paraguay, 159–161
Paraná River, 108

Paris, 203–204
parliamentary system, 78
Patagonia, 160
patriarchy, 417, 430, 452, 463, 487
patron–client relationships, 387
Peking. *See* Beijing.
People's Republic of China, 419–420.
    See also China; **East Asia.**
perestroika, 505
permeable national borders, 100–101
Perón, Juan, 129
Persian Gulf, 285–286, 300
Peru, 157–159
Philippines [Southeast Asia], 477, 496,
    511–513, 512*i*
physical geography, 20–26
  of East Asia, 413–415
  of Europe, 171–172
  of Middle and South America,
    107–113, 109*i*
  of North Africa and Southwest Asia,
    269–271
  of North America, 53–56
  of Oceania, 518–523
  of Russia and the Eurasian Republics,
    227–229
  of South Asia, 365–366, 367*i*, 368*i*
  of Southeast Asia, 473–475
  of Sub-Saharan Africa, 315–317
pidgins, 531. *See also* languages.
Pillars of Islamic Practice, 280–281,
    300
Pinochet, Augusto, 136, 161
Pizarro, Francisco, 115
planned economy. *See* communism.
plantations, 57, 128, 145, 147, 151,
    336
plate tectonics, 21
  in East Asia, 413–414, 440
  in Europe, 171
  in Middle and South America,
    107–108
  in North Africa and Southwest Asia,
    270–271
  in North America, 54
  in Oceania, 519
  in South Asia, 365, 392
  in Southeast Asia, 473
  in Sub-Saharan Africa, 315
pluralistic states, 46–47
Po River, 209
pogroms, 303. *See also* **racism.**
Poland, 214, 218
political geography, 6*t*, 46–48
  of East Asia, 421–429
  in Europe, 188–195
  in Middle and South America,
    127–137
  in North Africa and Southwest Asia,
    285–288
  in North America, 71–78
  in Oceania, 534–538
  in Russia and the Eurasian Republics,
    239–241
  in South Asia, 386–389
  of Southeast Asia, 488–494
  of Sub-Saharan Africa, 333–341

pollution
   in East Asia, 426, 435–440, 437*t*, 446,
      455*i*, 460
   in Europe, 196–198, 196*i*, 217
   and globalization, 77
   in Middle and South America, 140, 141
   in Oceania, 541–543
   in Russia and the Eurasian Republics,
      232–233, 248–249, 248*i*
   in South Asia, 391–392, 398
   in Southeast Asia, 475, 497, 497*i*
Polo, Marco, 417
polygyny, 331, 331*i*
Polynesia, 524–526, 528
population. *See also* **demography.**
   of cities, 122*t*
   control of, 420, 430–431, 479
   growth of, 33–36, 33*i*, 39, 323–325,
      356, 370–374
   sustainable, 31
population density, average, 33–34,
      34*i*–35*i*
   in East Asia, 420, 421*i*, 440
   in Europe, 179–180, 179*i*
   in Middle and South America, 119*i*,
      153*t*
   in North Africa and Southwest Asia,
      275–276, 275*i*
   in North America, 61*i*
   in Oceania, 528*i*
   in Russia and the Eurasian Republics,
      231, 232*i*
   in South Asia, 372*i*
   in Southeast Asia, 479, 480*i*
   in Sub-Saharan Africa, 321–324, 322*i*
population pyramids, 36*i*. *See also* **age
      structures; gender structures.**
   in East Asia, 431, 432*i*
   in Europe, 180–181, 181*i*
   in North Africa and Southwest Asia,
      276*i*
   in North America, 70–71, 71*i*
   in Russia and the Eurasian Republics,
      234*i*, 235
   in South Asia, 373–374, 374*i*
Portugal, 175, 206
power, hierarchies in, 10. *See also*
      development; gender roles.
prairies, 93
precipitation, 23–26, 25*i*
Preferential Trade Area (PTA), 338
prehistory, 8–12
primary sector (of the economy), 42
primate cities, 121, 325, 481, 501
prostitution. *See* sex workers.
protest movements. *See* resistance
      movements.
Protestant Reformation, 175. *See also*
      Christianity.
public health. *See also* **welfare states.**
   in North America, 76–77, 77*t*
   in Sub-Saharan Africa, 325–327
public spaces, 281
Puerto Rico, 146–147
pull factors for migration, 120, 481
Punjab, 387–388, 398
purdah, 364, 378, 381–382

push factors for migration, 120, 481
pyroclastic flow, 108

qanats, 450
Qatar, 300
Qin dynasty, 416–417
Qinghai Plateau, 413, 450–452
quaternary sector (of the economy), 42
Québec [North America], 85–86, 86*i*
Québecois, 53
Quetzalcoatl, 114
Qur'an, 272, 280, 283–284, 290

race, 19–20
   in Europe, 184
   in Middle and South America, 124
   in North America, 68–69
   in Oceania, 529
racism, 20, 174, 339, 358, 435. *See also*
      apartheid; ethnic cleansing;
      genocide; pogroms; segregation.
rai, 296
rain, 23–26, 25*i*
rain forests
   in Middle and South America,
      108–110, 137–140
   in Oceania, 542
   in Southeast Asia, 475, 476*i*, 489,
      495–496, 509–510
   in Sub-Saharan Africa, 345–346, 350
rain shadows, 24, 110–111, 260
Rajasthan, 397–398
ranches, 128
rate of natural increase, 34–36. *See
      also under* population.
   in Europe, 180–181
   in Middle and South America, 118,
      120*i*, 144
   in North America, 62
raw materials. *See* **resources.**
reefs, 519
refugees, 279–280, 323, 354–355, 483,
      484*i*
regional conflicts, 387
regional geography, 5
regional self-sufficiency, 424
regions, 5–7, 8*i*. *See also specific region.*
   East Asia, 410–469
   Europe, 168–223
   Middle and South America, 104–167
   North Africa and Southwest Asia,
      266–311
   North America, 50–103
   Oceania, 516–546
   Russia and the Eurasian Republics,
      224–265
   South Asia, 362–409
   Southeast Asia, 470–515
   Sub-Saharan Africa, 312–361
   world, 7
religions. *See also* **animism;** belief
      systems, indigenous; **Buddhism;**
      Christianity; Islam; Judaism.
   in East Asia, 433–434
   in Europe, 175, 205
   in Middle and South America, 119,
      126–127, 163

   in North Africa and Southwest Asia,
      272–273, 280–281, 302–305
   in North America, 67–68, 68*i*
   in Russia and the Eurasian Republics,
      243–244, 260–262
   in South Asia, 370, 377–379, 378*i*
   in Southeast Asia, 476, 480, 485–487,
      487*i*
   in Sub-Saharan Africa, 328–329, 330*i*
   as value systems, 14–15, 14*i*
religious fundamentalism, 127, 328, 329.
      See also **evangelical
      Protestantism;** gospel of success;
      Islamic fundamentalists.
religious nationalism, 387–388
religious pluralism, 485–487
remittances, 412, 481–482
remote sensing, 6*t*
Renaissance, 175
resettlement schemes, 482
resistance movements
   in Middle and South America,
      133–134, 153
   in North America, 68–69
   in South Asia, 381
   in Sub-Saharan Africa, 321, 357
resource base, 179–180
resources, 41. *See also* **development.**
   and development, 26–32
   in East Asia, 419–420, 445, 458, 464
   in Europe, 175, 179–180, 191, 192*i*
   in Middle and South America,
      129–130
   in North Africa and Southwest Asia,
      268, 285–286, 285*i*
   in North America, 80, 86
   in Oceania, 534–535, 537*i*
   in Russia and the Eurasian Republics,
      240, 247, 248*i*
   in South Asia, 401
   in Southeast Asia, 495–499, 504–505
   in Sub-Saharan Africa, 319, 322–323,
      334–336, 335*i*, 344–347, 352
responsibility systems, 424
Rhine, 172
Rhodesia. *See* Zimbabwe.
rice. *See* agriculture; **wet rice cultivation.**
Rift Valley, 353, 355
Riga, 213*i*
Ring of Fire, 21
   in the Americas, 519
   in East Asia, 414, 440
   in Southeast Asia, 473, 511
Rio de Janeiro, 163–164
Rocky Mountains, 54, 95
Romania, 218
Rome, ancient, 174, 206, 209
rudimentary welfare, 187–188
rug making, 262*i*
rural to urban migration, 481–483,
      501
Rushdie, Salman, 206
Russia
   European (Western), 251–254
   Far East, 258–259
   internal republics of, 255, 256*i*
   Siberia, 227–228, 237, 248, 255–258

RUSSIA AND THE EURASIAN REPUBLICS, 224–265
  environmental geography of, 247–251
    irrigation, 249–251
    pollution, 232–233, 248–249, 248i
  human history of, 229–235
    demography, 231–235
    growth of the Russian Empire, 229–230
    Soviet Russia, 230–231
  human well-being in, 241–242, 242t
  physical geography of, 227–229
    climate, 227–229
    landforms, 228i, 229
  political and economic geography of, 235–241
    command economy, 235–237
    economic reform, 237–239
    political reform, 239–241
  sociocultural geography in, 242–247
    crime and corruption, 246–247
    cultural diversity, 243
    gender roles and economic opportunity, 244–245, 245t, 262
    religion, 243–244, 260–262
    unemployment, 245–246
  subregions of
    Caucasia, 259–260, 259i
    Central Asian Republics, 260–263, 261i
    Russian Federation and Belarus, 251–259, 252i
Russian Federation and Belarus [Russia and the Eurasian Republics], 251–259, 252i
Rwanda, 355–356

Sahara Desert, 269–270, 347, 350
Sahel, 316, 344–345, 350
Saigon (Ho Chi Minh City), 472
salinization, 286, 291, 345–346
Salish people, 60
Samarkand, 261
Samper, Ernesto, 136, 157
samurai, 458
San Francisco, 99
Sandinistas, 154
São Tomé and Príncipe, 350–351
SAPs. *See* **structural adjustment programs.**
Sarajevo, 221
Saro-Wiwa, Ken, 315, 340, 349
Saudi Arabia, 299–301
savanna, 347
Scandinavia, 210–213
seclusion of women, 282–285, 282i, 307, 394, 486
secondary forests, 496
secondary sector (of the economy), 42
secular states, 281
secularism, 15
segregation, 90. *See also* apartheid; **racism.**
self-reliant development, 338
semiarid climates, 28, 29i
Sen, Amartya, 341
Senegal, 347–348

Serbia, 219–221
sericulture, 447, 453
service sector (of the economy), 42
sex workers, 18, 326, 352, 472, 483, 512
Seychelles, 356
SEZs. *See* **Special Economic Zones.**
Shabak, Ammon, 305
Shanghai, 427–428, 447–449
shantytowns
  in Middle and South America, 121–122, 122i, 134i, 163–165
  in North Africa and Southwest Asia, 287
  in South Asia, 372, 398, 400, 403
  in Southeast Asia, 507, 510i, 511, 513
  in Sub-Saharan Africa, 325i
shari'a, 280, 394
sheiks, 300
Shenzhen, 428
Shevardnadze, Edvard, 247, 260
shifting cultivation, 489. *See also* agriculture, cultivation techniques.
Shi'ites, 280, 308
Siberia, 227–228, 237, 248, 255–258
Siberian Plain, 227–228
Sichuan Basin, 445–446
Sierra Leone, 348
Sierra Madre, 54, 108, 147
Sikhism, 378, 387–388
Silk Road
  in East Asia, 433–434, 441, 447, 450, 451i
  in North Africa and Southwest Asia, 308
  in Russia and the Eurasian Republics, 230, 243, 261–263
Singapore, 490, 506–508
slash-and-burn cultivation, 489
slavery, 57, 69, 113, 123
  and slave trade, 317–319, 356
Slavs, 230
Slovakia, 217
Slovenia, 214, 218–220
slums. *See* shantytowns.
smog, 101, 497
snow. *See* precipitation.
social democratic welfare, 187
social differentiation, 379. *See also* **caste system.**
social geography. *See* sociocultural geography.
social structures, 123
socialist reformist development, 129–131
sociocultural geography, 6t, 12–20
  in East Asia, 429–435
  in Europe, 182–188
  in Middle and South America, 123–127
  in North Africa and Southwest Asia, 280–285
  in North America, 62–70
  in Oceania, 527–534
  in Russia and the Eurasian Republics, 242–247
  in South Asia, 374, 376–383

in Southeast Asia, 484–488
in Sub-Saharan Africa, 327–333
Sofia, 217
soil degradation, 27, 30i
  in East Asia, 443–444
  in Middle and South America, 137–140
  in Oceania, 541–542
  in Southeast Asia, 483, 490
Solomon Islands, 538
Somalia, 352–354
Somoza, Anastasio, 136, 154
sottogoverno, 210
South Africa, 321, 335, 356–358
South America, 107. *See also* **Middle and South America.**
SOUTH ASIA, 362–409
  environmental geography of, 390–392
    deforestation, 390–391, 402
    water rights, 391–392
  human history of, 366–376
    demography, 372–375
    and invasions, 368–369
    postcolonial, 371
    and Western colonialism, 369–371
  physical geography of, 365–366
    climate, 365–366, 367i, 368i
    landforms, 365
  political and economic geography of, 383–389
    agriculture in, 384–385, 384i
    and economic reform, 386
    industrialization, 369–371, 385
    and patron–client relationships, 387
    regional conflicts, 387–389
    and religious nationalism, 387–388
  sociocultural geography in, 374, 376–383
    caste system, 368, 379–380
    female status, 380–383
    language and culture, 376–377
    religion, 377–379
  subregions of, 392–407
    Afghanistan and Pakistan, 392–394, 393i
    Central India, 402–404, 403i
    Himalayan Country, 394–396, 395i
    Northeastern South Asia, 399–402, 399i
    Northwest India, 396–399, 397i
    Southern South Asia, 404–407, 404i
South Europe [Europe], 171, 206–210, 207i
South Korea, 422–423, 461–464
SOUTHEAST ASIA, 470–515
  environmental geography of, 495–498
    deforestation, 495–496
    energy production, 497–498
    mining, 496–497
    pollution, 497
    urbanization, 498
  human history of, 475–483
    demography, 479–483
    early foreign influence, 476–477
    European colonization, 477–478
    political independence, 478–479
    settlement of, 476

Southeast Asia (*cont.*)
 human well-being in, 494–495, 494*t*
 physical geography of, 473–475
  climate, 474–475, 475*i*
  landforms, 473, 474*i*
 political and economic geography of, 488–494
  agriculture, 488–490, 489*i*
  and democracy, 493–494
  economic crises, 491
  free trade zones, 490–491
  industrialization, 490
  resentment of Overseas Chinese, 491–493
 sociocultural geography in, 484–488
  cultural diversity, 484–485
  gender roles at work and in the family, 487–488
  religious diversity, 485–487
 subregions of, 499–513
  Indonesia, 508–511, 508*i*
  Island and Peninsula, 506–508, 506*i*
  Mainland East, 503–506, 504*i*
  Mainland West, 499–503, 500*i*
  Philippines, 511–513, 512*i*
Southern Africa [Sub-Saharan Africa], 356–358, 357*i*
Southern African Development Community (SADC), 338
Southern China [East Asia], 452–454, 452*i*
Southern Cone [Middle and South America], 159–161, 160*i*
Southern South Asia [South Asia], 404–407, 404*i*
Southwest [North America], 99–102, 100*i*
Soviet Union (USSR), 177, 181, 230–231. *See also* Russia.
 and Eastern European agriculture, 215–217
Spain, 175, 206, 208–209
spatial analysis, 5
spatial development, 121
spatial freedom, 284
Special Economic Zones (SEZs), 427–428, 427*i*, 453, 455
sports, 532
squatters. *See* shantytowns.
Sri Lanka, 371, 405–406
Stalin, Joseph, 198, 230–231, 253
steppes, 28, 29*i*, 227, 270–271
street vending, 135
structural adjustment programs (SAPs), 131. *See also* **debt crisis.**
 in Middle and South America, 131–132, 158–159
 in North Africa and Southwest Asia, 287, 298
 in South Asia, 386
 in Southeast Asia, 491
 in Sub-Saharan Africa, 336–337
subduction, 108
subregions. *See also under specific region.*
 defined, 7

Sub-Saharan Africa, 312–361
 environmental geography of, 344–347
  desertification, 344–345
  forest resources, 345–346
  tropical diseases, 346
  water and irrigation, 346–347
 geopolitics, 340–341
 human history of, 317–327
  demography, 321–327
  European colonization of, 319–321, 320*i*
  peopling of, 318–319
  postcolonial, 321
 human well-being in, 342–344, 342*t*–343*t*
 physical geography of, 315–317
  climate, 315–317, 316*i*
  landforms, 315
 political and economic geography of, 333–341
  agriculture, 336–337
  and economic crises, 335–336
  and economic development, 338
  industry, 337
  informal economy, 337–338
  postcolonial economics and politics, 335, 339–341
 sociocultural geography in, 327–333
  female genital mutilation, 332
  gender roles and family structure, 329–332
  languages, 332–333
  religion, 328–329, 330*i*
 subregions of, 347–359
  Central Africa, 350–352, 351*i*
  East Africa, 354–356, 355*i*
  Horn of Africa, 352–354, 353*i*
  Southern Africa, 356–358, 357*i*
  West Africa, 347–350, 347*i*
subsidies, 74
subsistence affluence, 538
subtropical temperate climates, 28, 29*i*
suburbs, 53*i*, 74
Sudan, 297–298
Sudra caste, 379
Suharto, 491–494
"suitcase" industries, 146–147
Sukarno, 493
Sumatra, 509
summer monsoons, 366, 367*i*, 414–415, 437. *See also* **monsoons.**
Sundaland, 473, 474*i*
Sunnis, 280, 308, 354
Suriname, 155–156
sustainable development, 26–31, 293–294, 347
Swaziland, 357–358
sweatshops, 131. *See also **maquiladoras.***
Sweden, 210, 212
syncretism, 328
Syr Darya River, 249–250
Syria, 302–303, 309

Taipei, 440, 455
Taiwan [East Asia], 422–423, 434, 454–456, 454*i*

Tajikistan, 260–263
Taliban, 381, 394
Tamils, 407
Tanzania, 335, 355–356
tariffs, 43, 287, 491, 537. *See also* free trade zones.
 and NAFTA, 77
tea, 400–401
Tel Aviv, 305
temperate climates, 28, 29*i*
temperature, 23
temperature-altitude zones, 110, 112*i*
Tennessee Valley Authority (TVA), 78, 292. *See also* dams.
Tenochtitlán, 114, 147
terrorism, 288, 296–297, 307, 407
tertiary sector (of the economy), 42
Thailand, 472, 478, 493, 499–503
Thar (Great Indian) Desert, 398
theocratic states, 280, 307
thermal inversions, 101
thermal pollution, 247
Three Gorges Dam, 439. *See also* dams.
thumb pianos, 359. *See also* music.
Tianjin, 445
Tibet. *See* Xizang.
Tibetan Plateau, 365
tierra caliente, 110
tierra fria, 110
tierra helada, 110
tierra templada, 110
tigers, economic, 488, 501
Tigris River, 271
Tobolsk, 257
Togo, 348
Tokyo, 456, 460
Toronto, 66, 82
tourism
 in Europe, 193, 194*i*, 207–209, 218
 in Middle and South America, 137, 139–140, 145, 154–155
 in Oceania, 535–536, 544
 in Southeast Asia, 472, 505
 in Sub-Saharan Africa, 356
town charters, 175
toxic waste. *See* **hazardous waste.**
trade blocs, 43–44. *See also* specific organization.
Trans-Siberian Railroad, 237, 248, 257
tropical diseases, 346
tropical humid climates, 28, 29*i*
tropical monsoon climates, 28, 29*i*
tropical wet climates, 28, 29*i*
tsunamis, 440, 456
Tunisia, 294–296
Turin, 210
Turkey, 305–307
Turkmenistan, 260–263
Tutu, Desmond, 315
Tuva, 256
Tuvalu, 527
TVA. *See* Tennessee Valley Authority.

Uganda, 355
Ukraine, 216–218

Ulaanbaatar, 466*i*, 467
Umbanda, 163, 164*i*
Union of Soviet Socialist Republics. *See* Soviet Union.
United Arab Emirates, 300
United Kingdom, 175, 188, 205–206
   as colonial power, 205, 369–371, 418
United Nations, 47–48
United States, 53
   compared with Canada, 62–64, 63*i*
Untouchable caste, 379
Ural Mountains, 171, 228
urban geography, 6*t*
urban sprawl, 89
urbanization, 10
   in East Asia, 429
   in Europe, 180
   and Megalopolis, 75
   in Middle and South America, 120–123, 121*i*, 163–164
   in North Africa and Southwest Asia, 277–279, 279*i*
   in Oceania, 542, 542*i*
   in South Asia, 398, 400–401, 403–404
   in Southeast Asia, 498–499
   in Sub-Saharan Africa, 325–326
   sustainable, 27, 30–31
Uruguay, 159–161
USSR. *See* Soviet Union.
Uzbekistan, 260–263

Vaishya caste, 379
value systems, 13–15
Vanuatu, 531
Varanasi, 392, 396
veils, 283–285, 283*i*
Venezuela, 156–157, 285
Venice, 209
Vietnam, 478–479, 503–506
Vietnam War, 478–479, 505
vilas rural, 165
villages
   in South Asia, 387, 389
   in Sub-Saharan Africa, 324–325
volcanoes, 21
   in East Asia, 21, 414, 440
   in Europe, 210
   in Middle and South America, 108

   in Oceania, 519, 520*i*
   in Southeast Asia, 473, 511
Volga River, 227–228

wadi, 270*i*
Wallacea, 473, 474*i*
"Waltzing Matilda," 534.
wars. *See also* **cold war.**
   Boer War, 321
   Gulf War, 287, 307–308
   Iran-Iraq War, 307–308
   Vietnam War, 478–479, 505
   World War II, 177, 458
wastewater, 30–31
water pollution. *See* pollution.
water resources. *See also* pollution.
   in East Asia, 437–440, 450
   in Europe, 197
   in North Africa and Southwest Asia, 286, 290–293, 305–306
   in North America, 58, 80, 96–97
   in Oceania, 541–542
   provision of, 30, 31*i*
   in Russia and the Eurasian Republics, 249–251
   in South Asia, 391–392
   in Southeast Asia, 496–498, 503–504
   in Sub-Saharan Africa, 322, 346–347, 350
wealth. *See also* income disparity.
   disparities in, 10, 426*i*, 511
   and population growth rates, 38
weapons
   biological, 309
   chemical, 287, 309
   nuclear, 241
weather, 23. *See also* **climatology.**
weathering, 22
welfare states, 177, 537
   in Europe, 186–188, 186*i*, 194, 212
well-being, measures of. *See* **human well-being.**
Wellington, 521
West Africa [Sub-Saharan Africa], 347–350, 347*i*
West Bengal, 400–401
West Europe [Europe], 171, 200–206, 201*i*
Western Europe, 171
wet/dry tropical climates, 28, 29*i*

wet rice cultivation, 445–446, 489
winter monsoons, 366, 367*i*, 414–415. *See also* **monsoons.**
women. *See also* gender roles.
   in East Asian politics, 467
   in European politics, 195, 195*i*, 212–213
   gender roles and status of, 17–19, 17*i*, 184–186, 217–218
   missing, 37, 37*i*, 431
   in North American politics, 78
   in Oceanian politics, 539–540
   in Russian politics, 239
   in South Asia, 364, 380–383, 386
   in Sub-Saharan African politics, 341, 344
   in Yemeni politics, 301–302
workers. *See also* labor.
   in the global economy, 39–41
World Bank, 47–48, 197, 337. *See also* International Money Fund; **structural adjustment programs.**
world region, 7. *See also under* **regions;** *specific region.*
World War II, 177, 458

xerophytic plants, 28
Xi Jiang, 414, 440
Xian, 441, 443
Xianggang. *See* Hong Kong.
Xinjiang, 450
xinyong, 430
Xizang (Tibet), 434, 450–452

Yangtze River. *See* Chang Jiang.
Yellow River. *See* Huang He.
Yeltsin, Boris, 237
Yemen, 300–302
Yokohama, 456
Yugoslavia, 215, 219, 221
Yunnan-Guizhou Plateau, 452–453
yurts, 262, 262*i*, 450, 466*i*. *See also* **gers.**

Zaire, 320
Zaire/Congo, 320, 351–352
Zambia, 357–358
Zimbabwe, 318–319, 325–326, 357–359
Zionists, 303